Defining Federal Crimes

ASPEN CASEBOOK SERIES

Defining Federal Crimes

SECOND EDITION

Daniel C. Richman
Paul J. Kellner Professor of Law
Columbia Law School

Kate Stith
Lafayette S. Foster Professor of Law
Yale Law School

William J. Stuntz
Late of Harvard University

Wolters Kluwer

Published by Wolters Kluwer in New York.

Wolters Kluwer Legal & Regulatory U.S. serves customers worldwide with CCH, Aspen Publishers, and Kluwer Law International products. (www.WKLegaledu.com)

To contact Customer Service, e-mail customer.service@wolterskluwer.com, call 1-800-234-1660, fax 1-800-901-9075, or mail correspondence to:

Wolters Kluwer
Attn: Order Department
PO Box 990
Frederick, MD 21705

Printed in the United States of America.

1 2 3 4 5 6 7 8 9 0

ISBN 978-1-5438-0432-4

Library of Congress Cataloging-in-Publication Data

Names: Richman, Daniel C., author. | Stith, Kate, author. | Stuntz, William J., author.
Title: Defining federal crimes / Daniel C. Richman, Paul J. Kellner Professor of Law, Columbia Law School; Kate Stith, Lafayette S. Foster Professor of Law, Yale Law School; William J. Stuntz, Late of Harvard University.
Description: Second edition. | New York: Wolters Kluwer, [2019] | Series: Aspen casebook series | Includes bibliographical references and index.
Identifiers: LCCN 2018033481 | ISBN 9781543804324
Subjects: LCSH: Criminal law—United States. | Federal government—United States. | LCGFT: Casebooks (Law)
Classification: LCC KF9219.R53 2019 | DDC 345.73—dc23
LC record available at https://lccn.loc.gov/2018033481

About Wolters Kluwer Legal & Regulatory U.S.

Wolters Kluwer Legal & Regulatory U.S. delivers expert content and solutions in the areas of law, corporate compliance, health compliance, reimbursement, and legal education. Its practical solutions help customers successfully navigate the demands of a changing environment to drive their daily activities, enhance decision quality and inspire confident outcomes.

Serving customers worldwide, its legal and regulatory portfolio includes products under the Aspen Publishers, CCH Incorporated, Kluwer Law International, ftwilliam.com and MediRegs names. They are regarded as exceptional and trusted resources for general legal and practice-specific knowledge, compliance and risk management, dynamic workflow solutions, and expert commentary.

To Bill

Summary of Contents

Contents

3 | The Separation of Powers: Interpreting Federal Criminal Statutes   79

4 | Mail and Wire Fraud   181

5 | Extortion   265

10 | Sentencing   **729**

12 Delegating Criminal Lawmaking   867

Preface to the First Edition

In a world where "to make a federal case" out of something is simply to treat it seriously, writing a Federal Criminal Law casebook is asking for trouble. In a pathetic attempt to deflect criticism, we begin by admitting that this book reflects a great many contestable decisions about coverage and focus. Our goal is less to create a canon of federal criminal cases and statutes than to frame federal criminal law in the United States as a distinctive (albeit multifaceted) project created and shaped by the interplay among the three branches of the federal government (Congress, the courts, and the executive) and by institutional dynamics within the branches—between lower courts and the Supreme Court, and within the historically (but variably) decentralized Department of Justice.

In so framing our project, we have given short shrift to certain parts of the federal criminal docket (however large) that reflect policies (or policy incoherence) transcending criminal enforcement decision making; there is little here about offenses relating to immigration, securities, and income taxation. We have largely ceded these territories to other courses not because they are unimportant, but because they are too important to be dealt with in a drive-by fashion. At the same time, we have chosen not to restrict our focus to quintessentially "white collar" crimes that play an outsized role in perceptions of the federal "brand." Any such focus, we believe, risks missing the connections between white collar crimes and other crimes—violent crime, terrorism, civil rights offenses, narcotics trafficking—in the federal criminal docket. Judges, prosecutors, defense lawyers, and Congress think across all these categories when shaping federal criminal law, and so should students.

This is not a comprehensive treatise but the extension of a conversation about Federal Criminal Law we have been having for many years among ourselves and with our students. And we are truly grateful to the many students at Columbia, Yale, and Harvard who, since 2007, have used and commented on earlier drafts. While we have had many research assistants over the years, special thanks are due to Columbia students David Abramowicz, Matt Jasili, Adam Carlis, Elizabeth Moulton, Michael Barnett, Maren Messing, Jeffrey

Izant, Jay Fiddleman, Jack Starcher, Anne Silver, Jack Mizerak, and Garrett Schuman, and to Yale students Angela Cai, Sarah Caruna, Heather Cherry, Jordana Confino, Nathan Gadd, Kory DeClark, Julie Duncan, Halley Epstein, Brendan Groves, Abigail Hinchcliff, Erica Newland, Robert Quigley, Lise Radhert, Yishai Schwartz, Matthew Specht, and Devorah Toren. We appreciate the assistance of Yale Law School librarians Michael VanderHeijden and Sarah Kraus.

We also thank colleagues Mitchell Berman, Brandon Garrett, Jerry Lynch, Trevor Morrison, and Peter Strauss for their criticisms and help.

Our greatest debt is to our co-author at Harvard, Bill Stuntz, who died in 2011. We miss Bill desperately. But we hope the creative and incisive sweep of Bill's mind, as well as his sense of humor and his appreciation of irony, still permeate this book. To lose any part of Bill's voice would only add to the tragedy of his untimely death.

Thanks to Alexandra Bowie for putting up with Danny's whining about this project, and to José Cabranes for his persistent question: "Do you have a publication date yet?" We are also grateful to Ruth Stuntz for all her support.

Daniel C. Richman

Kate Stith

March 2014

Preface to the Second Edition

Critical themes of our first edition were the historically contingent nature of federal enforcement institutional interactions and the constant evolution of federal criminal law itself—courtesy of courts, prosecutors, and sometimes even Congress. It therefore seems like we waited a long time—a whole four years—to write a second edition of this casebook, and not surprising that we've made some significant changes. Among the more significant of those changes are the following:

- In Chapter 2, some reorganization of the domestic Commerce Clause section, and exploration of the Supreme Court's aborted engagement with the Treaty Power, in Bond v. United States, 134 S. Ct. 2077 (2014).
- In Chapter 3, inclusion of the Court's most recent deployment of the "rule of lenity," in Yates v. United States, 135 S. Ct. 1074, 1078 (2015) (the "tangible" fish case), and reorganization of the *mens rea* section, with an assist from Elonis v. United States, 135 S. Ct. 2001 (2015).
- In Chapter 4, revisions to highlight the growing tension between the cases precluding mail fraud liability for deceit that "merely" causes the victim to enter into a transaction and those permitting liability an intangible property "right to control" theory.
- In Chapter 6, considerable revision to the "under color of official right" extortion sections to accommodate McDonnell v. United States, 136 S. Ct. 2355 (2016), and lower court efforts to apply it. We also found Ocasio v. United States, 136 S. Ct. 1423 (2016), a useful vehicle for exploring the interaction between "under color of official right" complicity and victim status in "fear of economic loss" extortion. And even though it is still pending on appeal in the Third Circuit, United States v. Baroni (D.N.J. 2017) (the "Bridgegate Case"), offers an interesting use of the "misapplication" prong of section 666.

- In Chapter 7, the "Bridgegate Case" returns as a civil rights prosecution. And we cover some of the cases finally emerging from the Matthew Shepard and James Byrd, Jr., Hate Crimes Prevention Act of 2009 (18 U.S.C. § 249), including the prosecution of Dylan Roof, and United States v. Miller, 767 F.3d 585 (6th Cir. 2014).

- In Chapter 8, the Aiding and Abetting discussion now includes Rosemond v. United States, 134 S. Ct. 1246 (2014). We also added a section on Accessory after the Fact and Misprision of Felony liability, with an interesting case out of the Ninth Circuit, United States v. Olson, 856 F.3d 1216 (9th Cir. 2017). The Material Support of Terrorism section has been substantially changed, with new cases and analysis.

- Chapter 9 required quite a few significant changes. We cover the Opioid Crisis and enforcement responses to it. We explore the Court's analysis of analogue prosecutions in McFadden v. United States, 135 S. Ct. 2298 (2015), and added substantial matter on "marijuana prosecutions in changing times." Extensive attention is given to Congress's use of its appropriations power to limit the federal prosecution of medicinal marijuana cases in states that allow such use (even as Congress has refused to change the sweeping federal marijuana prohibition), and to United States v. Kleinman, 880 F.3d 1020 (9th Cir. 2017), interpreting that provision. We've also added United States v. Campbell, 743 F.3d 802 (11th Cir. 2014), a case about the Maritime Drug Law Enforcement Act, which is an increasing source of business for federal courts. In the narcotics sentencing section, we added a unit on prior felony informations and their use for plea bargaining leverage, as discussed in United States v. Kupa, 976 F. Supp. 417 (E.D.N.Y. 2013). And we added discussions of the charging policies of Attorneys General Holder and Sessions, and of disparate judicial analyses of the purposes behind narcotics mandatory minimums.

- Chapter 10 extends our exploration of the post-*Booker* world to 2018.

- Chapter 11 extends our discussion of corporate liability to include the most recent judicial efforts to oversee deferred prosecution agreements, and the Justice Department's newly asserted interest in prosecuting individuals rather than firms.

- Chapter 12 has been reorganized, with more attention given to the emerging clash between *Chevron* deference and the rule of lenity—a clash in which a growing number of Justices have taken considerable interest, and which may be in play next Term.

But the biggest change is that this casebook is free for those who download it as an e-book. We are grateful to Joe Terry, the Legal Education

Publisher at Wolters Kluwer Legal & Regulatory U.S., for not just allowing us to do this but for his enthusiastic support of the project. We are grateful to Wolters Kluwer as well, for an act of pure service to law students, law teachers, and those in the broader legal community. Indeed, we are quite looking forward to seeing how our efforts to make sense of federal criminal law get used in the world where it effectively gets made.

Thanks to our students, and to our research assistants Leslie Arffa and Ben Levander, Yale Law School 2018; Rachel Rothberg and Jessie Garland, Yale Law School 2019; and Kelsey Stimson, Yale Law School 2020. Special thanks to the intense research assistance of Nina Cohen (Yale Law School 2018) and Kathleen Ann Marini (Columbia Law School 2017).

Daniel C. Richman
Kate Stith

August 2018

Acknowledgments

The authors wish to thank the following for granting permission to reprint excerpts of their work:

Stephen Breyer, "The Federal Sentencing Guidelines and the Key Compromises Upon Which They Rest," 17 Hofstra L. Rev. 1, 8-12 (1988). Copyright © 1988 by Hofstra Law Review. Reprinted by permission. All rights reserved.

Robert M. Chesney, "Beyond Conspiracy? Anticipatory Prosecution and the Challenge of Unaffiliated Terrorism," 80 S. Cal. L. Rev. 479-480 (2007). Copyright © 2007 by Southern California Law Review. Reprinted by permission. All rights reserved.

Edward B. Diskant, "Note, Comparative Corporate Criminal Liability: Exploring the Uniquely American Doctrine Through Comparative Criminal Procedure," 118 Yale L.J. 126, 134-38 (2008). Copyright © 2008 by the Yale Law Journal Company. Reprinted by permission. All rights reserved.

Nancy Gertner, "Gall, Kimbrough and Me," OSJCL Amici: Views from the Field 1-6 (2008). Copyright © 2008 by Ohio State Journal of Criminal Law. Reprinted by permission. All rights reserved.

Dan M. Kahan, "Is Chevron Relevant to Federal Criminal Law?" 110 Harv. L. Rev. 469 (1996). Copyright © 1996 by Harvard Law Review. Reprinted by permission. All rights reserved.

Gerard E. Lynch, "Letting Guidelines Be Guidelines (and Judges Be Judges)," OSJCL Amici: Views from the Field 1-8 (2008). Copyright © 2008 by Ohio State Journal of Criminal Law. Reprinted by permission. All rights reserved.

Gerard E. Lynch, "Sentencing Eddie," 91 J. Crim. L. & Criminology 547 (2001). Copyright © 2001 by Northwestern University, School of Law. Reprinted by permission. All rights reserved.

Defining Federal Crimes

1 | Institutional Design

A. CHANGING BOUNDARIES

The federal criminal justice system is defined by its borders—by the lines that divide federal law enforcement from local law enforcement, federal law from state law. Those borders are not fixed; rather, they are constantly evolving. Accordingly, the institutional design of federal criminal justice is not so much a design as a story. The following material—adapted and updated from Daniel Richman, The Changing Boundaries Between Federal and Local Enforcement, in 2 Boundary Changes in Criminal Justice Organizations (National Institute of Justice, NCJ 182409, July 2000)—seeks to tell that story:

At the beginning of the twentieth century, a knowledgeable observer could have sketched out some clear boundaries between the federal law enforcement system and the administration of criminal justice by state and local authorities: Federal enforcement agencies, such as they were, protected the basic interests of the federal government. The Secret Service fought counterfeiters and, after the assassination of President McKinley, protected the President. Post Office agents guarded the mails and targeted those who would misuse them. United States Marshals protected court officials and performed sundry other tasks at the behest of the relatively new Department of Justice (established in 1870) and local United States Attorneys' Offices. Other agencies looked to federal revenue collection interests and patrolled federally controlled territory. And—save for occasional emergencies—that was about it. Everything else, ranging from street crime to large-scale financial frauds, fell within the province of state and local authorities. It was an exclusive province.

Flash forward to the beginning of the twenty-first century. The federal enforcement bureaucracy is still quite small, at least as a relative matter. As of 2008 (the most recent official tally), there were only 120,000 federal officers, against 765,000 full-time state and local officers (36,023 in New York City alone). And that federal number included over 36,800 officers in Customs and Border Protection, over 12,400 in Immigration and Customs Enforcement, and over 16,800 Bureau of Prisons officers. The Federal

Bureau of Investigation—the only agency with a general enforcement mandate, and the closest thing to a federal police force—had only 12,760 officers (many of whom had intelligence duties); the Drug Enforcement Administration, 4,308; the Postal Inspection Service, 2,288; and the Bureau of Alcohol, Tobacco, Firearms and Explosives, 2,541. As of 2010, about 79 percent of the over 6,000 Assistant United States Attorneys (AUSAs) in the 94 U.S. Attorneys' Offices worked on criminal cases—which makes about 4,740 prosecutors. See Executive Office for U.S. Attorneys Annual Statistical Report for Fiscal Year 2010. This compares to more than 500 assistant district attorneys in Manhattan alone and approximately 25,000 nationwide.

Moreover, the federal justice system continues to handle only a fraction of the criminal enforcement work in the country. Local police and prosecutors are responsible for roughly two million felony prosecutions each year (that lead to one million felony convictions), plus three to four million misdemeanor cases. Federal prosecutors handle roughly 70,000 criminal cases per year, all but a couple thousand of them felonies. A large proportion of these cases begin with arrests by local police, not federal agents. The numbers of cases per police officer and local prosecutor far exceed the analogous ratios for FBI agents and AUSAs. And in 2015, over 1.33 million prisoners were in state custody, as opposed to about 196,455 prisoners in federal custody.

Yet for the twenty-first-century observer, explaining the boundary that separates federal enforcement concerns from those at the state and local levels is a daunting task indeed. The more one knows, the harder it gets. Federal agents still seek out counterfeiters, but now, they also target violent gangs and gun-toting felons of all sorts, work drug cases against street-sellers as well as international smugglers, investigate corruption and abuse of authority at every level of government, prosecute insider trading, and pursue terrorists.

If there is a boundary clearly separating federal from state and local criminal enforcement concerns in 2018, it is one not amenable to any categorical description. That does not mean, however, that there is no such boundary—or, to be more precise, *boundaries*, since patterns of enforcement differ across the country. What changed most during the twentieth century was not the existence *vel non* of a distinction between federal and state criminal justice concerns but the process by which such lines are defined—a shift from legislative initiative to executive discretion and negotiated *modi vivendi*.

1. The Growth of Federal Criminal Jurisdiction

The story of the changing boundary between federal criminal enforcement and state and local enforcement during the past century is in part one of substantive law. The pace at which Congress has declared various activities already illegal under state law to be federal crimes has increased at a spectacular rate since 1900, particularly since 1970. The conceptual roots of this legislative frenzy, however, might be found in early-twentieth-century developments.

Mindful of the Constitution's failure to give the federal government general police powers, early Congresses limited themselves to targeting activity that injured or interfered with the federal government itself, its property, or its programs. After the Civil War, Congress began to look beyond direct federal interests toward the general welfare of at least some citizens, criminalizing the willful violations of ex-slaves' civil rights as part of Reconstruction (which briefly made the welfare of Freedmen a special federal project) and prohibiting the use of the United States' mails to promote illegal lotteries. The lottery law was the precursor of a more sweeping mail fraud statute in 1872, which targeted any "scheme or artifice to defraud" effected through the use of the mails.

Although the potential scope of the mail fraud statute was enormous (allowing it to become one of the most flexible tools in the modern federal prosecutorial arsenal), the provision did not necessarily mark a huge departure from the limited notions of federal power that prevailed in the nineteenth century. The postal establishment, after all, was a federal instrumentality by virtue of an explicit constitutional grant, and one might naturally expect that the federal government bore some responsibility for misuses of this interstate network for fraudulent purposes. Even when the desire to prevent obstruction of the mails was asserted as an excuse for federal intervention in the turn-of-the-century labor wars, at least the fiction of a limited federal role was maintained. By the end of the nineteenth century, however, Congress began to focus not just on inappropriate uses of an interstate federal instrumentality, but also on abuses of channels of interstate commerce more generally. And provisions like the Sherman Act, enacted in 1890, promised deployment of criminal sanctions to regulate commerce itself. Moreover, Congress recognized the challenge that Americans' increasing mobility presented to state enforcement efforts, which were limited by the territorial basis of each state's jurisdiction and the limited nature of state enforcement assets, and responded with federal criminal statutes that targeted the crossing of state lines for particular illegal purposes. Some of these statutes, like the 1919 Dyer Act, which prohibited the transportation of a stolen motor vehicle across state lines, were straightforwardly economic in their concerns. But many had a decidedly moral focus, like the 1910 White Slave Traffic Act (also known as the "Mann Act"), which prohibited the transportation of a woman over state lines "for the purpose of prostitution or debauchery, or for any other immoral purpose"; the 1913 provision making it a federal offense to bring liquor into a dry state; and the 1914 Harrison Narcotic Drug Act, which established a

comprehensive regulatory scheme for narcotic drugs, backed with criminal
sanctions.

The passage of these statutes marked an important transitional phase
in the evolution of federal criminal law. Congress was no longer concerned
simply with the protection and misuse of federal assets. Instead, federal
legislators showed that they were just as committed as their state brethren
to placing government power at the service of the moral crusades of the
day, and just as susceptible to the political rewards of moral condemnation
through criminalization. Indeed, these new statutes were ostensibly quite
limited in form, showing no general desire to encroach into areas of traditional state concern. If local enforcers could not pursue malefactors over
state lines, and evil could not be contained within such lines, what could
be more natural than giving the federal government, with its constitutional
authority to regulate interstate commerce, a gap-filling role? This was precisely the Supreme Court's reasoning, as it found these statutes consistent
with Congress's constitutional exercise of powers under the Commerce
Clause. See, e.g., Champion v. Ames, 188 U.S. 321 (1903), which is discussed
in Chapter 2.

One story captures the combination of contingency and force of will
that pervades the history of federal criminal enforcement during this period.
During the last few decades of the 1800s, federal prosecutors would regularly borrow Secret Service agents from the Treasury Department to investigate frauds against the government. But at the turn of the century, when
an important series of land fraud investigations targeted several congressmen and other political heavyweights, Congress struck back and prohibited
this arrangement. In response, President Theodore Roosevelt's Attorney
General, Charles Bonaparte (great-nephew of the emperor), reached into
departmental funds and hired a few agents of his own. This was the origin
of what is now the Federal Bureau of Investigation.

Congress's readiness to enlist federal criminal statutes in the service of
national moral crusades reached an early high point in 1919, with the ratification of the Eighteenth Amendment (to take effect a year later) and its
implementation with passage of the Volstead Act. However, while Prohibition
put federal enforcement agents on the front lines, attacking bootleggers
and moonshiners where local police could not—or simply would not—go,
outside the Prohibition context, the overlap between state penal laws and
federal criminal law remained quite limited, a function of comparatively
well-circumscribed legislative initiatives. This would soon change.

Between the 1920s and the late 1960s, a number of developments
occurred that vastly changed prevailing understandings about the proper
sphere of federal authority. Some of these changes were driven by concern
over criminal activity that seemed beyond the capabilities of local enforcers.
White slavers, highway gangsters, big-city racketeers—the menace varied
over time. But each galvanized the media, citizen groups, and ultimately

legislators to call for federal action. Not only did each new threat have interstate dimensions immunizing it from state processes, but there were also fears that local enforcers were not as keen to proceed even where they could. Speculation that immigrants were playing a disproportionate role in some of these criminal threats made federal intervention seem particularly natural, given the federal government's plenary power over immigration.

There were more specific outrages as well, like the kidnapping of Charles Lindbergh's son in March 1932. The aviator's prominence (and the fact that this was not the first celebrity abduction of the era) immediately made the crime a matter of national concern. One paper called it "a challenge to the whole order of the nation." President Hoover responded tepidly. He asked the director of the Justice Department's small "Bureau of Investigation," J. Edgar Hoover, to coordinate federal assistance, but his Administration stressed that "it was not in favor of using the case as an excuse for extending federal authority in the area of law enforcement." "Organized crime," the Attorney General believed, was primarily a local problem. Congress thought differently. Only a federal kidnapping statute, one congressman argued, would avoid the problem of "brave officers stopped at State lines because of red tape [or] professional jealousy." A statute was passed in May, a week after the body of the baby was found.

Public perceptions of national crime problems and congressional receptivity to ameliorative measures occurred against a broader backdrop of expanding political views of the federal government's role in our constitutional system, as well as of expanding doctrinal understandings of how far Congress's Commerce Clause powers could go. Indeed, the distinction between what was local and what was of federal concern often seemed to collapse under pressure from New Deal programs, with the nascent Roosevelt Administration using federal crime-fighting as a potent symbol of the national government's new engagement.

The combination of the political demand for federal criminal intervention and the erosion of constitutional limitations on such enactments led to a steady progression of statutes targeting criminal behavior that had long been the exclusive province of state and local enforcers. In January 1934, President Roosevelt put crime high on his Administration's legislative agenda. See Kenneth O'Reilly, A New Deal for the FBI: The Roosevelt Administration, Crime Control, and National Security, 69 J. Am. Hist. 638 (1982). Between January and June of 1934, 105 bills were introduced in Congress that were "designed to close the gaps in existing federal laws and render more difficult the activities of predatory criminal gangs of the ['Machine Gun'] Kelly and Dillinger types." Many of these bills were passed in 1934, including: the National Stolen Property Act (barring the transportation of stolen property in interstate commerce); the National Firearms Act (taxing and requiring registration of machine guns, sawed-off shotguns, and similar weapons); the Fugitive Felon Act (prohibiting interstate flight to avoid prosecution for enumerated violent felonies); and provisions making it a federal crime to rob a national bank. That same year, Congress also passed the Anti-Racketeering Act of 1934, which allowed for federal prosecutions of the urban gangsters thought to have a stranglehold on various industries.

Once legislators began to think of federal criminal jurisdiction not as protecting certain discrete areas of particular federal concern but as supplementing local enforcement efforts—supporting local exertions and compensating for local inadequacies or corruption—Congress found more and more occasions for federal intervention. One hallmark of this legislative intervention was a series of broadly drafted statutes that laid the groundwork for the elimination of all conceptual boundaries between federal and state criminal law. For instance, the 1946 Hobbs Act, intended to cure certain perceived deficiencies in the Anti-Racketeering Act of 1934, broadly targeted all efforts to "obstruct[], delay[], or affect[] commerce . . . by robbery or extortion," with "extortion" defined as "the obtaining of property by another, with his consent, induced by wrongful use of actual or threatened force, violence or fear, or under color of official right." This provision allowed for federal prosecution of the extortionate rings preying on urban businessmen. Yet its open language—and judicial deference to the plain meaning of such language—has also enabled its use against corrupt federal, state, and local officials, and even robbers of grocery stores and restaurants.

The federal enforcement establishment remained small. While the number of FBI agents more than doubled, from 388 in 1932 to 713 in 1939, the Bureau's "war against the underworld" was quite limited, and indeed was intended to be so: The idea was to go after only those roving gangsters who had proved too big for local enforcement, particularly those whose apprehension made (or could be turned into) headlines. Thereafter, in the 1940s and 1950s, FBI criminal resources were diverted to internal security and counterintelligence matters. During this time, federal enforcement activity was relatively stable. While it jumped from just over 13,000 inmates in 1930 (when the Federal Bureau of Prisons was created) to 24,360 inmates in 1940, the federal prison population did not change appreciably between 1940 and 1980.

Even so, Congress continued to chip away at jurisdictional boundaries. A new wave of legislation came in the 1960s and early 1970s, in response to fears that state and local authorities were not up to the task of fighting organized crime, whose violent and corrupt tentacles had become a favorite topic of congressional inquiries. The Travel Act and the Racketeer Influenced and Corrupt Organizations Act of 1970 (RICO) were critical parts of the legislative response during this period.

The criminal statutes on the books by the mid-1970s thus went far in the direction of eliminating the conceptual distinction between federal and state crimes. This trend has continued, with the last quarter-century marked by an increase in congressional interest in this area. Spurred by the need to look "tough" on crime, and secure in the knowledge that federal prosecutors, not members of Congress, take the political heat for inappropriate prosecutions, Congress has engaged in an orgy of criminal lawmaking whose primary purpose often seems largely symbolic.

By one estimate, there are more than 4,000 federal criminal offenses in the U.S. Code; see John S. Baker, Jr. & Dale E. Bennett, Measuring the Explosive Growth of Federal Crime Legislation 3 (2004); see also ABA Task Force on the Federalization of Criminal Law, The Federalization of Criminal Law 7 (1998) ("More than 40% of the federal criminal provisions enacted since the Civil War have been enacted since 1970."). Note, however, that these numbers can mislead. Federal prosecutions as a percentage of all prosecutions in the United States have continued to hover around 5 percent for decades. Both state and federal prosecutions have increased in recent decades, but neither increase corresponds to the passage of new criminal statutes, which often address activities already illegal under previous laws. See generally Susan R. Klein & Ingrid B. Grobey, Debunking Claims of Over-federalization of Criminal Law, 62 Emory L.J. 1 (2012). One would like to have a reference point, perhaps a "federal crime rate," but of course there isn't one. Still, the recent focus on evils like hate crimes and domestic violence has indeed moved federal criminal law far into the last bastion of exclusive state jurisdiction—non-economically motivated violent crime. There remains some criminal activity that is hard to reach under federal law—and some effort to preserve the "distinction between what is truly national and what is truly local," as Chief Justice Rehnquist put it in United States v. Lopez, 514 U.S. 549, 567-68 (1995). Yet the Supreme Court's occasional interventions to preserve this distinction have not, as yet, amounted to more than speed bumps.

Responsibility for the effective elimination of the boundary between federal and state substantive law does not, of course, rest only with the legislative and judicial branches. The statutes discussed here would not have become law absent presidential signature, and the involvement of executive branch officials has generally been far greater than that. Indeed, Justice Department prosecutors have at times been spectacularly creative in devising legal theories to extend the range of congressional enactments. The legislators who enacted the federal mail fraud statute, for example, probably did not imagine that the provision would be used to prosecute a limitless variety of breaches of fiduciary duty, including official corruption (charged as defrauding the public of the "intangible right" to good government) and insider securities trading (charged as the misappropriation of confidential information).

Moreover, some of the most dramatic increases in federal intervention have relied on substantive laws already on the books without much change, except perhaps on the sentencing side. The jump in federal drug defendants from 9,906 in 1982 to 25,094 in 1990 had less to do with changes in federal narcotics law than with the commitment of the political leadership (executive and legislative) to the War on Drugs. Similarly, the jump in federal weapons prosecutions from 1,970 in 1982 to 12,128 in 1990 reflected a commitment to deploying existing provisions against street crime.

Whatever the causes, this much is clear: Since the last decades of the twentieth century, the difference between the *substantive reach* of federal criminal law and that of state criminal law has virtually disappeared, with the exception of immigration offenses. Federal criminal statutes may look a little different from state penal law. There will be mailing or wire elements, or demands that some interstate nexus be demonstrated. But if a federal prosecutor would like to bring federal charges against someone who has violated a state penal law, odds are that there will be a federal statute she can use. And if a federal agency wants to investigate some apparently antisocial conduct, it will probably be able to cite a potential federal violation as a basis for its inquiry. Although Congress regularly influences federal criminal enforcement priorities, using mechanisms like institutional design and procedural regulation, see Daniel C. Richman, Federal Criminal Law, Congressional Delegation, and Enforcement Discretion, 46 UCLA L. Rev. 757 (1999) (discussing these mechanisms), it has not chosen to limit the supply of substantive criminal law.

2. NEGOTIATED BOUNDARIES

Yet an account based solely on substantive law would be quite misleading. Although the statutory and constitutional constraints on federal "intrusions" may be slight, the political and institutional limitations on the exercise of federal authority are very real and quite powerful. And we see a variety of federal and state actors negotiate the boundaries between state and federal criminal law that can vary greatly across jurisdictions and over time.

The principal constraint on the federal enforcement bureaucracy is its size relative to both the network of state and local agencies and to the number of crimes committed that could potentially be charged federally. This resource disparity ought not to be viewed as some species of unfunded mandate. Rather, it reflects Congress's belief that, whatever the potential scope of enforcement activity authorized by its substantive lawmaking, primary responsibility for fighting crime still remains with the states. It also appears to reflect Congress's belief that the precise boundaries of federal and state responsibility should be set not through substantive federal legislation but through explicit or tacit negotiation among enforcement agencies.

This is not to say that Congress's role in this negotiation process is limited to setting it in motion by creating a gap between federal jurisdiction and federal resources. Bound to state officials by common constituencies, and often by political party, federal legislators can do much to promote coordination between federal enforcers and their state and local counterparts. Sometimes legislators will intervene directly to prevent federal enforcers from intruding into territory that state authorities have claimed. And even as they have assiduously expanded federal enforcement authority in the last half-century, legislators have frequently used budget and oversight hearings to prod federal agencies into cooperating with local authorities.

Legislators can also influence the negotiation of federal-state boundaries by exercising substantial control over who the federal negotiators will be. Here is where the traditionally decentralized nature of authority in the Department of Justice plays a critical role. As a formal matter, all federal prosecutors report to the Attorney General of the United States. Nevertheless, the overwhelming majority of federal criminal cases are brought not by the litigating units of the Justice Department—like the Criminal, Antitrust, and Civil Rights Divisions, which are under the direct control of assistant attorneys general in Washington, D.C.—but by the 94 U.S. Attorneys' Offices, each headed by a presidential appointee responsible only to the Attorney General and the Deputy Attorney General. Although the freedom of the U.S. Attorneys' Offices is far from absolute, and there are many mechanisms through which "Main Justice" (as the Washington bureaucracy is often called) can assert authority over a recalcitrant office, U.S. Attorneys have a long tradition of independence from Washington. While this independence is in part rooted in history (since the U.S. Attorneys' Offices were prosecuting cases before the Justice Department was even created in 1870), it also reflects a desire by the Department, and perhaps even more, by Congress, that prosecutorial discretion—even with respect to nationally applicable laws—be exercised by those most attuned to the needs and values of the diverse communities they serve. The flap in Congress over the firing of several U.S. Attorneys in late 2006 can be seen as much as a reassertion of traditional congressional interest in relative district autonomy as a power play by the new Democratic majority.

Although, as a formal matter, the U.S. Attorneys are appointed by the President and subordinate to the Attorney General, one or more members of a district's congressional delegation (or some other local politico of the President's party) generally play a substantial role in the selection process. Appointees, usually drawn from the local power structure, will likely be quite responsive to local concerns, and to the interests of local enforcement authorities. While U.S. Attorneys do not have hierarchical control over the federal agencies that usually initiate criminal investigations, their offices do have gatekeeping power. Their control over access to federal court—and to certain investigative measures like wiretaps and grand jury subpoena—gives them a powerful voice in the setting of federal enforcement priorities.

For all of these institutional arrangements, however, perhaps the main reason why federal enforcers either stay out of the core state and local enforcement areas like violent crime, or venture into them only with the acquiescence or approval of state and local authorities, is that they generally lack the informational resources to pursue offenses in these areas without state assistance. When going after organized criminal groups, like Mafia families or drug-trafficking networks, federal enforcers can develop their own informants and work their way up. Federal agents can similarly develop information sources in certain areas of special federal concern, like the securities markets, diplomatic communities, or federal contracting communities — areas in which citizens are prone to bring their complaints to federal authorities. In contrast, when agents seek to investigate "more episodic criminal activity," like murders, rapes, and street robberies, they generally must rely on help from local police departments, the only entities who can reach every street corner. Federal carjacking legislation may offend some traditional notions of the federal-state boundary, but the FBI probably will not pursue a particular carjacker, or target carjacking generally, without help from the cops who know the local bad guys and the community. Even somewhat more organized targets like street gangs are generally too loose-knit to be taken down by the Bureau without extensive local cooperation. Although agencies vary in their readiness to "play well with others," the success of a field office's leadership will often turn on its ability to share (or more likely "swap") information with the local police and other state and local agencies.

What, then, does this "negotiated" boundary, which cannot be found in statute books, look like, and how can one estimate its location? In some respects, the line still reflects the traditional notions of federal jurisdiction that Congress often seems to ignore in its substantive lawmaking. Federal enforcers still take primary responsibility for federal program fraud, egregious federal regulatory violations, counterfeiting, international drug smuggling, national security offenses, and other such crimes. Informants and complainants know to go to federal agencies first in these cases, and federal agencies know that they may be held politically responsible for failing to pursue such matters vigorously. Beyond this sphere, in those areas traditionally policed by the states, the line between what goes federally and what is left "stateside" is generally a function of several factors.

The Administration's agenda is one determining factor. While federal enforcers in the field will not necessarily notice the creation of a new criminal offense, they will respond to an Administration's national enforcement initiatives. In recent years, many of these initiatives have reflected the public's (and Congress's) concern with violent crime. Intensive federal interest in this area dates back to the late 1980s, but it continues today. Even after many of the FBI agents working violent crime cases were shifted to counterterrorism programs in the wake of the 9/11 attacks, other federal agents—such as those with the Bureau of Alcohol, Tobacco, Firearms and Explosives (ATF)—picked up some of the slack, usually working in task forces with local personnel. Since the 2008 credit crises, financial and mortgage fraud have become priorities for the FBI and other agencies. And in sheer numbers, if not investigative or prosecutorial resources, the federal criminal docket has recently been dominated by immigration cases, as you can see from the statistics presented in Section C of this chapter.

Pressure for federal involvement in particular cases or classes of cases traditionally handled locally also comes from the local authorities themselves. State enforcers are well aware that their federal counterparts can often devote more resources to a case—e.g., buy money (traceable money used to buy contraband), electronic surveillance, witness protection programs, and prosecutorial support for investigations—and that federal prosecutions generally result in higher sentences, particularly in violent crime cases. Without the political obligations of state authorities to maintain order within a territorial jurisdiction and prosecute every provable serious offense, federal agencies are largely free to invest strategically in the cases they do take (with terrorism and immigration cases being critical exceptions to this rule), and local officials often seek to tap this strategic reserve.

It may seem somewhat anomalous to describe the product of all these forces as a "boundary." Yet in every jurisdiction, enforcers of all stripes have a pretty good idea of what kind of cases should go federally, and what should go stateside—a division of labor that can vary over time. Bank robberies, for example, were once the quintessential federal case, high priorities for the FBI's war on crime in the mid-1930s. By the early 1980s, however, state and local police were handling a large proportion of bank robberies without any FBI involvement, and many more with FBI collaboration. The extent of federal involvement in these matters has been reduced even further since the 9/11 attacks.

The story of the relationships between federal agencies and state and local authorities has of course not been one of consistent harmony and collaboration. There is friction from time to time—the turf wars that make for such great news stories. Given the degree of statutory overlap between the state and federal systems, and the absence of any formal division of authority, what is remarkable is not the occurrence of such disputes but their relative infrequency. Indeed, the bitterness usually reflects one or both sides' belief that some *modus vivendi* has been violated. Outsiders may not always know what this arrangement is, as it appears in no statutory code or manual, but it exists just the same.

There is an important caveat to all this talk of optional federal jurisdiction and negotiated boundaries: Some boundaries are quite clear geographically and do indeed create indefeasible federal responsibilities. All too little attention will be given here to immigration offenses, to federal policing obligations on military bases, national parks, and other federal enclaves, and to the federal criminal justice role in Indian Country, see Kevin K. Washburn, American Indians, Crime, and the Law, 104 Mich. L. Rev. 709 (2006). Suffice it to say that federal responsibilities in these geographically massive areas are significant and complicated.

3. THE COSTS OF NEGOTIATED BOUNDARIES

What, then, could be wrong with this arrangement? Why have so many respected people decried the "over-federalization" of criminal law? Is it out of an attachment to nineteenth-century notions of federalism or to a doctrinal belief that Commerce Clause power has some limits? Have they failed to appreciate that boundaries, however diverse and negotiated, still divide state and federal spheres? These theories have some explanatory power. Yet, even someone with no *a priori* vision of what is "really" a federal crime could fairly be dissatisfied with the current scheme for a number of reasons.

That a state's enforcers are largely satisfied with the allocation of federal and state authority in the criminal area does not necessarily mean that the interests of that state's citizens have been advanced. Sometimes, it is hard to tell. When, for example, a local police force, instead of using state forfeiture procedures that benefit the state's general treasury, turns seized assets over to federal authorities because federal "equitable sharing" provisions reward the police force directly, should we rejoice in this interagency cooperation or question the motives behind the circumvention of state law? And what are we to make of cases that state enforcers refer for federal prosecution because the Federal Rules of Evidence allow the admission of evidence that some state rule would exclude? Why should state officials be free to nullify state legislators' decision to establish supra-constitutional barriers to conviction?

If, given the choice, a state's citizenry would adopt the federal rule over the state law, then the ability of state enforcement authorities to freely circumvent the state rule inappropriately permits state legislators to avoid facing the political costs of their enactments (or inertia). If, on the other hand, the state rules actually reflect the citizenry's preferences, then state enforcement officials ought not have the freedom to nullify them by ceding a case to federal enforcers. Either way, a system of low-visibility negotiated boundaries diminishes the accountability of the system's actors. Similarly, although responsibility for street crime and most other traditionally local offenses has not wholly shifted to the relatively small federal enforcement bureaucracy (and never will), the possibility of federal intervention will often allow state enforcers to evade accountability for failing to prosecute a particular case or class of cases. The pressure on state governments to develop capabilities for ferreting out and prosecuting instances of local corruption, for example, has probably been substantially diminished by the readiness of federal enforcers to pursue these cases.

These questions become even harder once one recognizes that there may not even be unanimity of interest within a state's enforcement community. The local police department that brings a high-profile murder or kidnapping case to the U.S. Attorney's Office in order to take advantage of more lenient evidentiary rules may have much to gain and little to lose. Federal prosecutors, welcoming such cases, will take pains to ensure that the police, and perhaps the mayor, receive full credit for their investigative success. But the local district attorney's office, which otherwise would have gotten the case, may feel quite aggrieved. Even if a local prosecutor is brought in to take part in the proceedings as a "Special Assistant U.S. Attorney," the federal venue will generally ensure that the federal prosecutors receive top billing. As a rule, then, local police agencies are probably going to be keener on federal intervention than local prosecutors. And their readiness to go "federal" will give the police new leverage in their dealings with the local prosecutor, changing the terms of what traditionally was a bilateral monopoly. The possibility of federal intervention may therefore reduce the degree to which local prosecutors—who generally are elected officials—can constrain appointed police officials. Those officials will still be politically accountable, generally through the mayor that appointed them. But a degree of accountability will have been lost, particularly if the mayor's mandate does not significantly rest on his or her criminal justice policies.

Another problem with a system in which effective boundaries are negotiated by enforcers, instead of set by statute, is that enforcers are less apt to internalize the costs that their arrangements impose on the federal court system. The freedom of enforcers to decide, as part of a broader program or on an ad hoc basis, when a case that ordinarily gets prosecuted in state court should go federal has also led to significant horizontal inequities among defendants. Additional fairness questions have arisen when overlapping jurisdiction (coupled with the "dual sovereignty" double jeopardy doctrine) has allowed federal enforcers to bring charges against a defendant previously acquitted (or convicted) in a state case of charges arising out of the same conduct.

4. TOWARD NEW BOUNDARIES?

Realistically, it is inevitable that federal enforcers will exercise enormous discretion. Legislative specificity has high opportunity costs in the criminal area, and, as an affirmative matter, there is broad support for giving enforcers the flexibility to respond to regional diversity and the myriad forms of criminal conduct. Yet some sort of balance between delegation and accountability needs to be struck, and, in recent years, all too little thought has been given to accountability. When federal-state boundary issues are negotiated by enforcers from the involved jurisdictions, the resulting arrangements are not only of far lower visibility than legislative enactments; they are also prone to self-dealing by the enforcers. State agencies are well positioned to check federal initiatives that they deem inappropriately intrusive. But if state enforcers' approval or acquiescence stems from a desire to circumvent state limits on their authority, or to avoid responsibilities imposed on them by state law, the negotiation process becomes a kind of political shell game.

Federal negotiators may have their own self-serving motives as well, some of which are personal. Prosecutors with local political ambitions may seek to enhance their name recognition by going after the grisly murders that seem to dominate tabloid coverage of the criminal justice system. Those seeking mere financial gain may look for the best vehicles for displaying their talents to potential future clients in the private sector. Finally, prosecutors may simply feel the visceral allure of violent cases, to break the monotony of a white-collar diet.

It may well be that the particular equilibrium between federal and state criminal authority that now exists is exactly the right one from the perspective of citizens as well as enforcers. This conclusion, however, should be arrived at openly and with public input. The challenge for Congress in the twenty-first century, therefore, is to move the process of boundary setting back into the substantive lawmaking sphere. In that sphere, citizens might perhaps hear more about the deficiencies and needs of their local police forces, prosecutors, and legislators. At the very least, efforts to educate the public on the limits of federal enforcement resources, and the responsibilities of state and local enforcers, will help reduce the actual or perceived political gains that legislators obtain by proposing and passing new criminal statutes.

To the extent that the public fails to appreciate the limits of federal resources, legislators may also find themselves under increasing pressure from federal enforcement agencies. The more legislators seek political gain through substantive criminal lawmaking, the greater the risk that their constituents will expect prosecutions to be brought under the new statutes. So far, these expectations appear quite limited. When a carjacking occurs, when a prior felon uses a gun, or when there is an incident of domestic violence with some interstate nexus, there generally won't be an immediate outcry for federal involvement. Assumptions that state and local enforcers bear primary responsibility for street crimes are quite robust and do not seem likely to change over time. Public perceptions of what is appropriately "federal" can evolve, however. One has only to look at the frequency, since the Rodney King beating trial, with which abuse-of-force allegations against local police officers have been accompanied by calls for federal intervention. Or demands by political and community leaders that federal agents and prosecutors make recent homicide spikes in a number of cities—most conspicuously Chicago—their top priority. Federal enforcement agencies, as a general matter, are more insulated from political pressure than their state and local counterparts. But they are not immune. And the more federal criminal statutes are perceived as imposing responsibility, instead of merely conferring authority, the harder federal enforcers will strive to ensure that such responsibilities are more narrowly tailored to their capabilities and preferences. Their interest in doing so may become particularly great if the current commitment of scarce federal resources to counterterrorism programs becomes institutionalized. Under this admittedly sanguine analysis, the recent legislative trend might, over time, be self-correcting.

B.   THE UNITED STATES DEPARTMENT OF JUSTICE

The chart below shows the organizational structure of the Department of Justice as of 2015. It should be noted that the Criminal Division is part

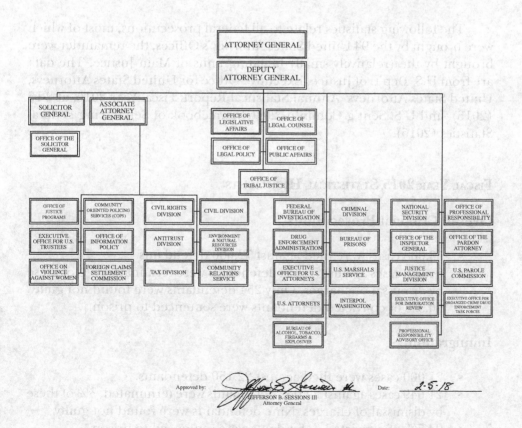

of a very large organization, which has many functions other than criminal prosecution. Moreover, the chart only represents "Main Justice"—the central offices of the Department in Washington, D.C. The 94 United States Attorneys are barely represented in this chart (see the penultimate box at the bottom of the chart for "U.S. Attorneys" and that above it for the "Executive Office for U.S. Attorneys," which primarily provides administrative support). As noted above, U.S. Attorneys, like top officials at Main Justice, are appointed by the President and subject to Senate confirmation. While there are federal criminal prosecutors who work out of Main Justice (for instance, in the Civil Rights Division, the Antitrust Division, and some sections of the Criminal Division), most federal prosecutors are Assistant U.S. Attorneys, working in a U.S. Attorney's Office. With some important exceptions (which we note in this volume), federal prosecutors do not need Main Justice approval before beginning an investigation or seeking an indictment.

C.   FEDERAL CRIMINAL LITIGATION: A SNAPSHOT

The following statistics relate to all federal prosecutions, most of which were brought by the 94 United States Attorney's Offices; the remainder were brought by the (relatively small) litigating units of Main Justice. The data are from U.S. Dep't. of Justice, Executive Office for United States Attorneys, United States Attorneys' Annual Statistical Report: Fiscal Year 2016, at 2-16 (2016), and U.S. Sent'g Comm'n, 2016 Sourcebook of Sentencing Federal Statistics (2016).

FISCAL YEAR 2015 STATISTICAL HIGHLIGHTS

Overall Criminal Prosecutions

- 53,908 cases were filed against 72,006 defendants.
- 54,270 cases against 71,838 defendants were terminated, 5% of these by dismissal of charges. Only 254 defendants were found not guilty.
- 90.3% of convicted defendants were sentenced to prison.

Immigration

- 21,000 cases were filed against 22,150 defendants.
- 21,049 cases against 22,062 defendants were terminated, 3% of these by dismissal of charges. Nine defendants were found not guilty.
- 94.7% of convicted defendants were sentenced to prison.

Narcotics Overall

- 12,582 cases were filed against 24,550 defendants.
- 12,640 cases against 24,296 defendants were terminated, 6% of these by dismissal of charges. Sixty-four defendants were found not guilty.
- 96% of drug trafficking defendants were sentenced to prison.

Civil Rights Prosecutions

- 154 cases filed were against 263 defendants.
- 161 cases against 269 defendants were terminated, 12% of these by dismissal of charges. Fifteen defendants were found not guilty.
- 58.1% of convicted defendants were sentenced to prison.

Violent Crime

- 12,994 cases were filed against 16,327 defendants.
- 12,917 cases against 15,673 defendants were terminated, 5% of these by dismissal of charges. Eighty-four defendants were found not guilty.
- 93.5% of convicted defendants were sentenced to prison.

Terrorism/National Security

- 171 cases were filed against 355 defendants.
- 194 cases against 270 defendants were terminated, 19% of these by dismissal of charges. Two defendants were found not guilty.
- ~87% of convicted defendants were sentenced to prison.

Official Corruption

- 461 cases were filed against 693 defendants.
- 499 cases against 695 defendants were terminated, 6% of these by dismissal of charges. Thirteen defendants were found not guilty.
- ~62% of convicted defendant were sentenced to prison.

White-Collar Crime

- 5431 cases were filed against 8081 defendants.
- 5570 cases against 8605 defendants were terminated, 6% of these by dismissal of charges. Fifty-six defendants were found not guilty.
- ~70% of convicted defendants were sentenced to prison.

INTRODUCTION TO FEDERAL CRIMINAL PRACTICE

When reading the cases in this book, it is useful to keep in mind the following features of federal criminal practice:

1. Federal indictments frequently track the statutory offense language, giving little detail about the nature of the charges. Because discovery is quite limited—compared to federal civil practice, or even to criminal practice in many state systems—a defendant will generally be unable to challenge the government's charging theory in advance of trial. Challenges to the government's legal theory will generally come up for the first time mid-trial, during disputes over how the judge should charge the jury. Should the defendant be convicted, such challenges can be pursued post-trial and on appeal.

2. Should a defendant successfully raise a pre-trial legal challenge to the indictment that results in the dismissal of one or more counts of the indictment, the government often has the option of pursuing an interlocutory appeal to the circuit court, and might even, if the defendant prevails on appeal, seek further review in the Supreme Court, via a petition of certiorari. (Any effort by a U.S. Attorney's Office to seek appellate review requires authorization from the Solicitor General's Office in Washington.) A defendant whose pre-trial legal challenge fails will generally have to wait until conviction to pursue appellate review (since, unlike the government, he can appeal an adverse verdict).

3. A defendant has a statutory right to appeal his criminal conviction. Should the conviction be after trial, he can challenge the sufficiency of the evidence as well as the government's legal theory (and perhaps evidentiary rulings by the trial court). The appellate court's review of the evidence will be highly deferential to the jury's (or the judge's, if it was a bench trial) resolution of the factual issues. Reversal for evidentiary insufficiency is appropriate only if no reasonable jury could have arrived at the guilty verdict. This is an extremely hard standard to satisfy, but such reversals do occur. A U.S. Attorney's Office need not (although it can) consult with Washington about the positions it takes when defending a conviction. When a defendant obtains a reversal on appeal for evidentiary insufficiency, the Double Jeopardy Clause bars his retrial. But he generally can be retried if his conviction was reversed for some other reason, such as a violation of some procedural rule or improper jury instructions.

4. Because of the Fifth Amendment's Double Jeopardy Clause and the consequent absence of statutory authorization, the government cannot appeal an acquittal. Under the "dual sovereignty" doctrine, however, double jeopardy protection is sovereign specific. That means that there generally is no federal constitutional bar to the bringing of federal charges after a defendant has been convicted or acquitted on state charges for the same conduct, or to the bringing of state charges after a federal criminal proceeding (whatever its result).

5. A defendant will generally not be able to attack his indictment or conviction on grounds of "selective prosecution." He can prevail only if he can show not merely that similarly situated individuals have not been prosecuted, but that he was intentionally selected out on some unconstitutional basis (race, religion, etc.).

6. Trials have become increasingly rare. Of the 75,344 defendants "disposed of" by federal district judges in felony and certain misdemeanor cases in Fiscal Year 2016, 68,802 defendants were convicted, with 67,722 of them having pled guilty. Only 1,846 defendants were disposed of after trial verdicts. Of these, a grand total of 196 were acquitted by a jury, and 70 by a judge (in a bench trial). U.S. Sent'g Comm'n, Federal Judicial Caseload Statistics 2016 tbl. D-4.

7. Federal felony trials are held before juries of 12, and unanimity is required for the return of a verdict. Defendants who plead guilty can challenge their sentence on appeal (unless they have specifically waived their right to do so), but are precluded from raising most other challenges to their conviction. Appellate review of the government's charging theory is thus highly unlikely in the vast majority of federal prosecutions.

8. Federal sentences are generally considered stiff. The average length of imprisonment for drug offenses in 2016 was 65 months. For "economic offenses," the average was 33 months. For immigration offenses, the average was 15 months. U.S. Sent'g Comm'n, 2016 Sourcebook of Sentencing Statistics, Figure E.

D. CONSTITUTIONAL STRUCTURE

While the boundaries discussed above have proved shifting and often flexible, one must bear in mind that the reach of the federal criminal law is ultimately rooted in the Constitution.

CONSTITUTION OF THE UNITED STATES
(SELECTED PROVISIONS)

Article I
   Section 8. The Congress shall have Power To lay and collect Taxes, Duties, Imposts and Excises, to pay the Debts and provide for the common Defence and general Welfare of the United States; but all Duties, Imposts and Excises shall be uniform throughout the United States;

   To borrow Money on the credit of the United States;

   To regulate Commerce with foreign Nations, and among the several States, and with the Indian Tribes;

   To establish a uniform Rule of Naturalization, and uniform Laws on the subject of Bankruptcies throughout the United States;

To coin Money, regulate the Value thereof, and of foreign Coin, and fix the Standard of Weights and Measures;

To provide for the Punishment of counterfeiting the Securities and current Coin of the United States;

To establish Post Offices and post Roads;

To promote the Progress of Science and useful Arts, by securing for limited Times to Authors and Inventors the exclusive Right to their respective Writings and Discoveries;

To constitute Tribunals inferior to the supreme Court;

To define and punish Piracies and Felonies committed on the high Seas, and Offences against the Law of Nations;

To declare War, grant Letters of Marque and Reprisal, and make Rules concerning Captures on Land and Water;

To raise and support Armies, but no Appropriation of Money to that Use shall be for a longer Term than two Years;

To provide and maintain a Navy;

To make Rules for the Government and Regulation of the land and naval Forces;

To provide for calling forth the Militia to execute the Laws of the Union, suppress Insurrections and repel Invasions;

To provide for organizing, arming, and disciplining, the Militia, and for governing such Part of them as may be employed in the Service of the United States, reserving to the States respectively, the Appointment of the Officers, and the Authority of training the Militia according to the discipline prescribed by Congress;

To exercise exclusive Legislation in all Cases whatsoever, over such District . . . as may . . . become the Seat of the Government of the United States, and to exercise like Authority over all Places purchased by the Consent of the Legislature of the State in which the Same shall be, for the Erection of Forts, Magazines, Arsenals, dock-Yards, and other needful Buildings;—And

To make all Laws which shall be necessary and proper for carrying into Execution the foregoing Powers, and all other Powers vested by this Constitution in the Government of the United States, or in any Department or Office thereof.

Section 9. . . . The privilege of the Writ of Habeas Corpus shall not be suspended, unless when in Cases of Rebellion or Invasion the public Safety may require it.

No bill of attainder or ex post facto Law shall be passed. . . .

Article II

Section 3. [The President] shall take Care that the Laws be faithfully executed, and shall Commission all the Officers of the United States.

Section 4. The President, Vice President and all civil Officers of the United States, shall be removed from Office on Impeachment for, and Conviction of, Treason, Bribery, or other high Crimes and Misdemeanors.

Article III

Section 2. The judicial Power shall extend to all Cases, in Law and Equity, arising under this Constitution, the Laws of the United States, and Treaties made, or which shall be made, under their Authority; to all Cases affecting Ambassadors, other public Ministers and Consuls; to all Cases of admiralty and maritime Jurisdiction; to Controversies to which the United States shall be a Party. . . .

The Trial of all Crimes, except in Cases of Impeachment, shall be by Jury; and such Trial shall be held in the State where the said Crimes shall have been committed; but when not committed within any State, the Trial shall be at such Place or Places as the Congress may by Law have directed.

Section 3. Treason against the United States shall consist only in levying War against them, or in adhering to their Enemies, giving them Aid and Comfort. No Person shall be convicted of Treason unless on the Testimony of two Witnesses to the same overt Act, or on Confession in open Court.

The Congress shall have Power to declare the Punishment of Treason, but no Attainder of Treason shall work Corruption of Blood, or Forfeiture except during the Life of the Person attainted.

Article IV

Section 3, clause 2. The Congress shall have Power to dispose of and make all needful Rules and Regulations respecting the Territory, or other Property belonging to the United States. . . .

Section 4. The United States shall guarantee to every state in this Union a Republican Form of Government, and shall protect each of them against Invasion; and on Application of the Legislature, or of the Executive (when the Legislature cannot be convened) against domestic Violence.

Amendment XIII

Section 1. Neither slavery nor involuntary servitude, except as a punishment for crime whereof the party shall have been duly convicted, shall exist within the United States, or any place subject to their jurisdiction.

Section 2. Congress shall have power to enforce this article by appropriate legislation.

Amendment XIV

Section 1. All persons born or naturalized in the United States, and subject to the jurisdiction thereof, are citizens of the United States and of the State wherein they reside. No State shall make or enforce any law which shall abridge the privileges or immunities of citizens of the United States; nor shall any State deprive any person of life, liberty, or property, without due process of law; nor deny to any person within its jurisdiction the equal protection of the laws.

Section 5. The Congress shall have power to enforce, by appropriate legislation, the provisions of this article.

Amendment XVIII

Section 1. After one year from the ratification of this article the manufacture, sale, or transportation of intoxicating liquors within, the importation thereof into, or the exportation thereof from the United States and all territory subject to the jurisdiction thereof for beverage purposes is hereby prohibited.

Section 2. The Congress and the several States shall have concurrent power to enforce this article by appropriate legislation.

Amendment XXI

Section 1. The eighteenth article of amendment to the Constitution of the United States is hereby repealed.

Section 2. The transportation or importation into any State, Territory, or possession of the United States for delivery or use therein of intoxicating liquors, in violation of the laws thereof, is hereby prohibited.

THE CONSTITUTION AND FEDERAL CRIMINAL LAW

The provisions quoted above fall into several categories. First comes Article I, Section 8: the section of the original Constitution specifying the subjects about which Congress could legislate. The quoted portions of Articles II and III define executive and judicial power, respectively. The remaining provisions are additional sources of constitutional text that have, or might have, shaped federal criminal law and law enforcement.

Note how few of the listed powers in Article I, Section 8 relate to criminal justice. Judging by the relative space devoted to different subjects, the key focus of the Constitution's drafters was the military and its regulation. The only bodies of criminal law that Article I, Section 8 appears to contemplate are laws against counterfeiting, piracy, "offences against the law of nations," crimes that occur within the military, and crimes that occur within the District of Columbia. Of course, other criminal prohibitions might be deemed "necessary and proper for carrying into Execution the foregoing Powers"—but the Framers likely did not expect that category to be large. Notice that a specific provision authorizing punishment of counterfeiters follows the provision authorizing Congress to print money. The Counterfeiting Clause is necessary only on the assumption that this power is not already implied by the "coin money" clause, which suggests that the scope of implied power to criminally punish was thought to be limited.

Indeed, federal criminal law *was* limited in the decades following independence. The document the Framers produced made no effort to give the federal government general police powers of the sort that states exercised. The only circumstance the Constitution explicitly envisioned as justifying federal measures against "domestic violence" (i.e., riots and rebellions) was when a state certified that federal help was needed. U.S. Const. art. IV, §4. Otherwise, the federal government's only criminal justice interests were those relating to the powers specifically delegated by Article I. While the Bill of Rights gave considerable attention to the procedural safeguards that would apply in federal prosecutions, the range of prosecutions envisioned was thus quite small, and few were brought.

The Thirteenth and Fourteenth Amendments seemed poised to make federal criminal law much larger, and to give it a new role: protecting the rights of citizens against abusive state and local officials. That was a logical role for federal officials to play; had the system followed that path, the Reconstruction Amendments and Article IV's guarantee of "a republican form of government" might be the primary sources of federal criminal jurisdiction. For a time, that scenario looked likely, but the Supreme Court's decision in United States v. Cruikshank, 92 U.S. 542 (1876), placed severe limits on the enterprise of protecting ex-slaves' civil rights through criminal law enforcement. Chapter 7 explores the consequences.

Roughly 40 years later, the Eighteenth Amendment again promised a new role for the federal justice system. The Amendment was passed on January 16, 1919, when Nebraska became the thirty-sixth state (of the then 48 states) to ratify, and became effective on January 17, 1920. While Prohibition lasted, alcohol cases dominated the federal system, and federal criminal cases constituted a larger fraction of total criminal litigation than ever before or since: More than 20 percent of all prison inmates in the United States were incarcerated on federal charges during the 1920s, compared to 11 percent today and less than 10 percent for most of American history. But, as with Reconstruction, Prohibition didn't last: The Twenty-First Amendment undid the Eighteenth in 1933, leaving federal criminal law once more in search of a role.

It still has not found a role: rather, it has found several, and the list continues to grow. Numerous topics, including white-collar crime and official corruption, various forms of gun crime and violence, extortion and racketeering, and, above all, drug crimes, have spawned important (both practically and conceptually) bodies of federal law in the years since Prohibition passed from the scene. These different crimes rely on a variety of jurisdictional grants, including some surprising ones: The postal power has played a large role in the law of white-collar crime — thanks to the mail fraud statute, which remains (in tandem with the wire fraud statute) one of the most commonly used weapons in white-collar law enforcement. But the most important source of constitutional power to define crimes has been Congress's power to regulate "Commerce with foreign Nations, and among the several States." The ebb and flow of the commerce power, which has played such a large part in defining the boundaries of federal criminal justice, is described in Chapter 2.

The story sketched in the last few paragraphs has not been the consequence of some general plan of action or centralized direction. More than most areas of law, federal criminal law just happened—a series of discrete political and legal choices that shaped a field in ways that decision makers did not expect and may not have wished. The balance of this book surveys that field. It may be helpful to keep in mind several of the field's features that flow from its strange constitutional origins. Following are five of the most important ones:

1. Federal criminal law is *optional*. State criminal codes and state justice systems existed before it, would exist without it, and continue to exist alongside it. Those state codes and systems handle the vast majority of crimes for which voters demand punishment. Congress is free to use federal criminal law in different ways, to accomplish different objects.

2. Federal criminal law is *jurisdictionally limited*. Federal criminal statutes must be tied to some express constitutional grant of lawmaking power. State legislatures likewise must stay within constitutional limits—but those limits usually have to do with individual rights: State criminal laws may neither forbid political speech or religious practice, nor invade the sphere of sexual and reproductive privacy that the Supreme Court has defined over the course of the last generation. The constitutional limits that Congress faces are different in character: Congress must tie federal criminal prohibitions to some federal interest, and the federal interest must in turn be tied to some piece of constitutional text. Those limits no longer restrict the subject matter of federal criminal law in any substantial way—as noted above, the federal criminal code covers most of the same subject matter as state criminal codes. But the required link to a constitutionally granted lawmaking power *does* affect—powerfully—the manner in which federal crimes are defined.

3. Thanks to characteristics (1) and (2), federal criminal law is *creative*. Because the field is almost entirely optional, Congress is free to use criminal law in innovative ways. Because criminal statutes must be tied to one or another of the jurisdictional grants in Article I—most of which were designed without criminal law in mind—Congress must innovate: It must find ways to connect the conduct it wishes to prohibit to the relevant constitutional grant of authority. (Often, that means the legal equivalent of jamming a square peg into a round hole.) Many state crimes bear more than a passing resemblance to the analogous offenses defined in Volume 4 of Blackstone's Commentaries. In contrast, Title 18 of the U.S. Code looks nothing like Blackstone or any other historical list of crimes (except for those statutes written to provide basic criminal justice in federal enclaves). In other words, while state criminal law is mostly the product of history and necessity, federal criminal law is, to a much larger degree, the product of creative choices by members of Congress, federal prosecutors, and federal

judges. Of course, Congress *could* rewrite, update, and rationalize its diverse provisions into a real Criminal Code. But, having once tried that and given up, in the early 1970s, it seems to lack interest.

4. Because of characteristics (1), (2), and (3), federal criminal enforcement is frequently an exercise in *indirection*: Prosecutors prove one crime in order to punish another. The criminal statutes that local prosecutors enforce, most of them anyway, define the conduct that the government seeks to punish reasonably accurately. In comparison, the criminal conduct defined by the Travel Act, 18 U.S.C. §1952, is crossing a state line (the crossing must be done with the intent to commit one of a list of offenses); and the conduct term of the mail fraud statute, 18 U.S.C. §1341, is mailing a letter (the letter must be mailed in furtherance of a scheme to defraud). Felon-in-possession statutes are used to lock up violent criminals. Perjury, false statements, and obstruction of justice charges are used against regulatory offenders when the regulatory offense cannot easily be detected or proved. Clearly, indirection is the rule, transparency the exception.

5. Authority over federal criminal law is *shared between politically accountable officials and politically insulated officials.* Most states elect their judges, including the appellate judges who have the most power to define legal doctrine. Nearly all counties elect the district attorneys who prosecute criminal cases. And, of course, all states elect the legislators who write criminal statutes. At the state level, therefore, power over criminal law and law enforcement is not divided among politicians, judges, and bureaucrats; it's more accurate to say that power is shared by different types of politicians. The federal justice system is radically different. Not only are federal judges appointed rather than elected, but they also have life tenure. Federal prosecutors are more closely tied to the world of politics and politicians (though, like judges, they are appointed rather than elected). But they have a large measure of independence from their nominal political masters in Washington; politicians' efforts to manage federal prosecutors have a tendency to backfire. FBI agents (or at least the Director and others atop the Bureau's hierarchy) have traditionally had even more independence, though President Trump's firing of Director James Comey has put that norm in jeopardy. In short, power over federal criminal law and law enforcement is divided among politicians, career law enforcers, and life-tenured federal judges. Disputes about the federal separation of powers quickly become battles between democracy and bureaucracy—or between democracy and law.

2 | Jurisdiction: Federal Criminal Law and the Commerce Power

The Framers of the Constitution did not envision that the federal government would play much of a role in criminal enforcement. To the extent that they contemplated substantive federal criminal law at all, their discussions centered on piracy, crimes against the law of nations, treason, and counterfeiting. The document they produced made no effort to give the federal government general police powers of the sort that states exercised. By one count, only 426 criminal cases were brought in federal courts between 1789 and 1801, a large fraction of which related to the Whiskey Rebellion. See Dwight F. Henderson, Congress, Courts, and Criminals: The Development of Federal Criminal Law, 1801-1829, 13 (1985). In the absence of relevant federal statutes, Federalist judges simply invoked federal common law and looked to state law to try and punish the rebels. See Gordon S. Wood, Empire of Liberty: A History of the Early Republic, 1789-1815, 417-18 (2009).

Congress was not eager to address crime even in areas where it clearly had constitutional jurisdiction to do so. In 1818, the Supreme Court threw out the conviction in a case where a marine had murdered a cook's mate on board the U.S.S. Independence while it was anchored in Boston Harbor. United States v. Bevans, 16 U.S. (3 Wheat.) 336 (1818). Writing for the Court, Chief Justice John Marshall explained that while Congress could have passed a murder statute covering federal warships, it had not, and the matter was thus left to Massachusetts's exclusive jurisdiction. Indeed, exclusive state jurisdiction over criminal matters was very much the rule during most of the nineteenth century. When Congress did pass penal legislation, it generally targeted activities that injured or interfered with federal property (see Art. IV, §3, cl. 2) or interfered with the function of the federal government itself, particularly its ability to collect taxes.

In the last quarter of the nineteenth century, federal criminal law began to take on a new role. No longer was it primarily a means of self-protection. Rather, it became part of a more general (albeit fitful) state-building effort. For a classic account of this general turn, see Stephen Skowronek, Building a New American State: The Expansion of National Administrative Capacities, 1877-1920 (1982). Congress could have relied—and in time did rely—on any number of constitutional jurisdictional grants to spin its thickening web of federal criminal law. In Chapter 4, we will see how the postal power supported an ever-growing body of mail fraud law. Chapter 6 will show the spending power to be a potent weapon against state and local corruption, and Chapter 7 will consider the increasing recourse to the Reconstruction Amendments as a basis for right-deprivation prosecutions. Yet it is the Commerce Clause that has provided the basis for the vast majority of federal criminal laws enacted by Congress since the post-Reconstruction period. We therefore begin with this fountainhead of federal criminal jurisdiction. Section A explores that part of Commerce Clause jurisdiction on which Congress has chiefly relied: the power to regulate "commerce . . . among the several states." Section B considers the part to which Congress has given increasing attention in recent years: the related power to regulate "commerce with foreign nations."

A. "COMMERCE . . . AMONG THE SEVERAL STATES"

There is no evidence that any of the Constitution's Framers thought about criminal law when drafting the Commerce Clause. The commerce power later became a useful source of criminal jurisdiction not because commerce and crime were so obviously connected, but because there was so much commerce. In the late nineteenth and early twentieth centuries—the period of the first great upsurge in federal criminal law—the United States had the fastest growing and, soon, the largest economy in the world. Both immigrant labor and investment dollars flowed into the country in massive amounts. The United States also had, by a large margin, the most railroads serving the most people across the largest distances of any country in the world. Movement of goods and people across state borders was exploding. As a result of this explosion in interstate interaction, questions regarding the meanings of "regulate," "commerce," and "among the several states"—that is, of the contours of Congress's power under the Commerce Clause—became increasingly pressing as the nineteenth century progressed. Of particular interest to Congress during this period was immoral commerce. For this was a period not just of national economic growth but of national crusades against vice—gambling, prostitution, drugs, and liquor.

The following propositions set patterns for federal criminal law—at least as a formal matter, see Gonzales v. Raich, *infra*—that still hold today. First, the federal government had power only over *interstate* commerce, and thus could not forbid all markets relating to the vices in question. When, for example, Prohibitionists sought a nationwide ban of the manufacture and sale of alcoholic beverages, they assumed that they needed a constitutional amendment to enact it. The second proposition followed from the first: The federal criminal law of vice would have to coexist with and overlap state law.

Federal criminal law would cover territory that states covered as well, rather than dealing only with offenses that the states could not touch.

One more proposition—an intensely practical one—is crucial to understanding the historical evolution of the commerce power and its effect on federal criminal justice. Throughout the nineteenth century, the federal law enforcement bureaucracy remained very small. Agents of the postal service protected the mails; U.S. Marshals protected judges and performed sundry other duties; treasury personnel fought smuggling; and, after its creation in 1865, the Secret Service targeted counterfeiting. There were, however, very few agents and prosecutors available to enforce the broad federal crimes of which Congress soon grew fond. Though the office of the Attorney General dates back to the Founding, there was no Justice Department prior to 1870. Until then, the U.S. Attorneys brought prosecutions in their respective federal districts, but with little national coordination and with little control over how the federal law enforcement personnel were deployed. Even after its creation, the Justice Department had scant resources, and initially had to rely on the Treasury's Secret Service agents or Pinkerton Detective Agency operatives for investigative support. The justice system that *enforced* the law grew much more slowly than the *laws* that required enforcing.

There are "three categories of activity that Congress may regulate under its commerce power: (1) 'the use of the channels of interstate commerce'; (2) 'the instrumentalities of interstate commerce, or persons or things in interstate commerce, even though the threat may come only from intrastate activities'; and (3) 'those activities having a substantial relation to interstate commerce, . . . i.e., those activities that substantially affect interstate commerce.'" Taylor v. United States, 136 S. Ct. 2074, 2079 (2016) (citing United States v. Lopez, 514 U.S. 549, 558-59 (1995)). Channels of commerce encompass navigable conduits of interstate commerce, such as water, air, and roadways. Instrumentalities of interstate commerce are the means used to transport goods and persons in interstate commerce including railroad cars, buses, trucks, airplanes, and boats.

When Congress regulates pursuant to (1) or (2) and sometimes (3), it generally makes the interstate nature of the crime an element of the offense (which must be proven beyond a reasonable doubt). We first examine this approach to commerce clause jurisdiction and then turn to jurisdiction based on the categorical proposition that an entire class of criminalized activity has a "substantial effect" on interstate commerce. (The "elemental" vs. "categorical" distinction is of our own devising, but we find it extremely useful.)

1. ELEMENTAL JURISDICTION

When, in the late nineteenth century, Congress sought to lend a national cast to the vice crusades that had hitherto been local matters, the real and perceived limitations on its Commerce Clause authority shaped the nature of its responses. The jurisdictional justification for federal vice laws, regulating the interstate movement of goods and people, had little to do with the *substantive* justification for those laws—that is, the desire to ban the relevant vice. And the jurisdictional "hooks" for the wave of federal vice statutes passed beginning in the 1880s were just that—hooks, not reasons for the criminal prohibitions. See Louis B. Schwartz, Federal Criminal Jurisdiction and Prosecutors' Discretion, 13 Law & Contemp. Probs. 64, 79-80 (1948) (discussing how courts tend to focus on jurisdictional problems at the expense of focusing on substantive issues of criminality).

The following case marks a critical stage in the growth of federal Commerce Clause authority. By the end of the nineteenth century, it was clear that Congress could use its plenary authority to exclude things it did not like—e.g., pornography, lottery tickets, and contraceptive devices—from the U.S. mails. See, e.g., Ex parte Jackson, 96 U.S. 727 (1877) (upholding conviction for mailing of lottery circular); Donna Dennis, Licentious Gotham: Erotic Publishing and Its Prosecution in Nineteenth-Century New York, 258-63 (2009). But canny traffickers in such items turned to private express services; could Congress use the Commerce Clause to reach these transactions as well? In Champion v. Ames, a 5-4 decision, the Supreme Court held that lottery tickets were subject to congressional regulation. Consider how the Court attempts to define the "instrumentalities of commerce" over which Congress has power. How might the logic in this case apply well or poorly to other vices that Congress might wish to police? We will see that this decision did not resolve debates about the extent of Congress's commerce power; many of Chief Justice Fuller's concerns appear in subsequent Supreme Court opinions (though usually, as in *Ames*, in dissent).

Champion v. Ames (The Lottery Case)
188 U.S. 321 (1903)

Mr. Justice HARLAN delivered the opinion of the Court: . . .

The appellant insists that the carrying of lottery tickets from one state to another state by an express company engaged in carrying freight and packages from state to state . . . does not constitute, and cannot by any act of Congress be legally made to constitute, commerce among the States within the meaning of the clause of the Constitution of the United States providing that Congress shall have power "to regulate commerce with foreign nations, and among the several States, and with the Indian tribes"; consequently, that Congress cannot make it an offence to cause such tickets to be carried from one state to another.

The government insists that express companies . . . engaged . . . in the business of transportation from one state to another are instrumentalities of commerce among the states; that the carrying of lottery tickets from one state to another is commerce which Congress may regulate; and that as a means of executing the power to regulate interstate commerce Congress may make it an offence against the United States to cause lottery tickets to be carried from one state to another. . . .

What is the import of the word "commerce" as used in the Constitution? It is not defined by that instrument. Undoubtedly, the carrying from one state to another by independent carriers of things or commodities that are ordinary subjects of traffic, and which have in themselves a recognized value in money, constitutes interstate commerce. But does not commerce among the several states include something more? Does not the carrying from one state to another . . . of lottery tickets that entitle the holder to the payment of a certain amount of money . . . also constitute commerce among the States? . . .

It was said in argument that lottery tickets are not of any real or substantial value in themselves, and therefore are not subjects of commerce. If that were conceded to be the only legal test as to what are to be deemed subjects of the commerce that may be regulated by Congress, we cannot accept as accurate the broad statement that such tickets are of no value. Upon their face they showed that the lottery company offered a large capital prize, to be paid to the holder of the ticket winning the prize at the drawing advertised to be held at Asuncion, Paraguay. Money was placed on deposit in different banks in the United States to be applied by the agents representing the lottery company to the prompt payment of prizes. These tickets were the subject of traffic; they could have been sold; and the holder was assured that the company would pay to him the amount of the prize drawn. . . . Even if a holder did not draw a prize, the tickets, before the drawing, had a money value in the market among those who chose to sell or buy lottery tickets. . . .

We are of opinion that lottery tickets are subjects of traffic, and therefore are subjects of commerce, and the regulation of the carriage of such tickets from state to state, at least by independent carriers, is a regulation of commerce among the several states.

But it is said that the statute in question does not regulate the carrying of lottery tickets from state to state, but by punishing those who cause them to be so carried Congress in effect prohibits such carrying; that in respect of the carrying from one state to another of articles or things that are . . . the subjects of commerce, the authority given Congress was not to *prohibit*, but only to *regulate*. . . .

[T]he Constitution does not define what is to be deemed a legitimate regulation of interstate commerce. In Gibbons v. Ogden, [9 Wheat. 1 (1824)], it was said that the power to regulate such commerce is the power to prescribe the rule by which it is to be governed. But this general observation leaves it to be determined, when the question comes before the court, whether Congress in prescribing a particular rule has exceeded its power under the Constitution. While our Government must be acknowledged by all to be one of enumerated powers, McCulloch

v. Maryland, 4 Wheat. 316, 405, 407 (1819), the Constitution does not attempt to set forth all the means by which such powers may be carried into execution. It leaves to Congress a large discretion as to the means that may be employed in executing a given power. . . .

We have said that the carrying from state to state of lottery tickets constitutes interstate commerce, and that the regulation of such commerce is within the power of Congress under the Constitution. Are we prepared to say that a provision which is, in effect, a *prohibition* of the carriage of such articles from state to state is not a fit or appropriate mode for the regulation of that particular kind of commerce? If lottery traffic, carried on through interstate commerce, is a matter of which Congress may take cognizance and over which its power may be exerted, can it be possible that it must tolerate the traffic, and simply regulate the manner in which it may be carried on? Or may not Congress, for the protection of the people of all the states, and under the power to regulate interstate commerce, devise such means . . . as will drive that traffic out of commerce among the States? . . .

In Phalen v. Virginia, 8 How. 163, 168 (1850), after observing that the suppression of nuisances injurious to public health or morality is among the most important duties of Government, this court said: "Experience has shown that the common forms of gambling are comparatively innocuous when placed in contrast with the widespread pestilence of lotteries. The former are confined to a few persons and places, but the latter infests the whole community; it enters every dwelling; it reaches every class; it preys upon the hard earnings of the poor; it plunders the ignorant and simple." In other cases we have adjudged that authority given by legislative enactment to carry on a lottery, although based upon a consideration in money, was not protected by the contract clause of the Constitution; this, for the reason that no state may bargain away its power to protect the public morals. . . .

If a state, when considering legislation for the suppression of lotteries within its own limits, may properly take into view the evils that inhere in the raising of money, in that mode, why may not Congress, invested with the power to regulate commerce among the several states, provide that such commerce shall not be polluted by the carrying of lottery tickets from one state to another? In this connection it must not be forgotten that the power of Congress to regulate commerce among the states . . . is subject to no limitations except such as may be found in the Constitution. . . .

As a state may, for the purpose of guarding the morals of its own people, forbid all sales of lottery tickets within its limits, so Congress, for the purpose of guarding the people of the United States against the "widespread pestilence of lotteries" and to protect the commerce which concerns all the states, may prohibit the carrying of lottery tickets from one state to another. . . . We should hesitate long before adjudging that an evil of such appalling character, carried on through interstate commerce, cannot be met and crushed by the only power competent to that end. . . .

The whole subject is too important, and the questions suggested by its consideration are too difficult of solution, to justify any attempt to lay down a rule for determining in advance the validity of every statute that may be enacted under the commerce clause. We decide nothing more in the present case than that lottery tickets are subjects of traffic among those who choose to sell or buy them; that the carriage of such tickets by independent carriers from one state to another is therefore interstate commerce; that under its power to regulate commerce among the several states Congress . . . has plenary authority over such commerce, and may prohibit the carriage of such tickets from state to state; and that legislation to that end . . . is not inconsistent with any . . . restriction imposed upon the exercise of the powers granted to Congress. . . .

Mr. Chief Justice FULLER, with whom concur Mr. Justice BREWER, Mr. Justice SHIRAS and Mr. Justice PECKHAM, dissenting:

Although the first section of the Act of March 2, 1895, 28 Stat. 963, c. 191, is inartfully drawn, I accept the contention of the Government that it makes it an offence (1) to bring lottery matter from abroad into the United States; (2) to cause such matter to be deposited in or carried by the mails of the United States; (3) to cause such matter to be carried from one state to another in the United States; and further, to cause any advertisement of a lottery or similar enterprise to be brought into the United States, or be deposited or carried by the mails, or transferred from one state to another. . . .

The power of the state to impose restraints and burdens on persons and property in conservation and promotion of the public health, good order and prosperity is a power originally and always belonging to the states, not surrendered by them to the general government, nor directly restrained by the Constitution of the United States, and essentially exclusive, and the suppression of lotteries as a harmful business falls within this power. . . .

It is urged, however, that because Congress is empowered to regulate commerce between the several states, it, therefore, may suppress lotteries by prohibiting the carriage of lottery matter. Congress may indeed make all laws necessary and proper for carrying the powers granted to it into execution, and doubtless an act prohibiting the carriage of lottery matter would be necessary and proper to the execution of a power to suppress lotteries; but that power belongs to the states and not to Congress. To hold that Congress has general police power would be to hold that it may accomplish objects not entrusted to the general government, and to defeat the operation of the 10th Amendment. . . .

[A]part from the question of bona fides, this act cannot be brought within the power to regulate commerce among the several states, unless lottery tickets are articles of commerce, and, therefore, when carried across state lines, of interstate commerce; or unless the power to regulate interstate commerce includes the absolute and exclusive power to prohibit the transportation of anything or anybody from one state to another. . . .

Is the carriage of lottery tickets from one State to another commercial intercourse?

The lottery ticket purports to create contractual relations and to furnish the means of enforcing a contract right.

This is true of insurance policies, and both are contingent in their nature. Yet this court has held that the issuing of fire, marine, and life insurance policies, in one state, and sending them to another, to be there delivered to the insured on payment of premium, is not interstate commerce. Paul v. Virginia, 8 Wall. 168 (1869); Hooper v. California, 155 U.S. 648 (1895). . . .

If a lottery ticket is not an article of commerce, how can it become so when placed in an envelope or box or other covering, and transported by an express company? To say that the mere carrying of an article which is not an article of commerce in and of itself nevertheless becomes such the moment it is to be transported from one state to another, is to transform a non-commercial article into a commercial one simply because it is transported. I cannot conceive that any such result can properly follow.

It would be to say that everything is an article of commerce the moment it is taken to be transported from place to place, and of interstate commerce if from state to state.

An invitation to dine, or to take a drive, or a note of introduction, all become articles of commerce under the ruling in this case, by being deposited with an express company for transportation. This in effect breaks down all the differences between that which is, and that which is not, an article of commerce, and the necessary consequence is to take from the states all jurisdiction over the subject so far as interstate communication is concerned. It is a long step in the direction of wiping out all traces of state lines, and the creation of a centralized government.

Does the grant to Congress of the power to regulate interstate commerce impart the absolute power to prohibit it?

It was said in Gibbons v. Ogden, [22 U.S. 1 (1824)], that the right of intercourse between state and state was derived from "those laws whose authority is acknowledged by civilized man throughout the world;" but under the Articles of Confederation the states might have interdicted interstate trade, yet when they surrendered the power to deal with commerce as between themselves to the general government it was undoubtedly in order to form a more perfect union by freeing such commerce from state discrimination, and not to transfer the power of restriction. . . .

It will not do to say . . . that state laws have been found to be ineffective for the suppression of lotteries, and therefore Congress should interfere. The scope of the [C]ommerce [C]lause of the Constitution cannot be enlarged because of present views of public interest. . . .

"To what purpose are powers limited, and to what purpose is that limitation committed to writing, if these limits may, at any time, be passed by those intended to be restrained?" asked Marshall, in Marbury v. Madison, [1 Cranch, 137, 176 (1803)]. . . .

NOTES AND QUESTIONS

1. In Hoke v. United States, 227 U.S. 308 (1913), the Supreme Court upheld the 1910 Mann Act, ch. 395, 36 Stat. 825 (1910), also known as the "White Slavery Act," against a Commerce Clause challenge. The Act provided:

That any person who shall knowingly transport or cause to be transported, or aid or assist in obtaining transportation for, or in transporting, in interstate or foreign commerce, or in any Territory or in the District of Columbia, any woman or girl for the purpose of prostitution or debauchery, or for any other immoral purpose, or with the intent and purpose to induce, entice, or compel such woman or girl to become a prostitute or to give herself up to debauchery, or to engage in any other immoral practice; or who shall knowingly procure or obtain . . . any ticket or tickets, or any form of transportation or evidence of the right thereto, to be used by any woman or girl in interstate or foreign commerce . . . in going to any place for the purpose of prostitution or debauchery, or for any other immoral purpose, or with the intent or purpose on the part of such person to induce, entice, or compel her to give herself up to the practice of prostitution, or to give herself up to debauchery, or any other immoral practice, whereby such woman or girl shall be transported in interstate or foreign commerce . . . shall be deemed guilty of a felony, and upon conviction thereof shall be punished by a fine not exceeding five thousand dollars, or by imprisonment of not more than five years, or by both such fine and imprisonment, in the discretion of the court.

Writing for the Court, Justice McKenna noted:

Our dual form of government has its perplexities, state and nation having different spheres of jurisdiction, as we have said, but it must be kept in mind that we are one people; and the powers reserved to the states and those conferred on the nation are adapted to be exercised, whether independently or concurrently, to promote the general welfare, material and moral. This is the effect of the decisions, and surely if the facility of interstate transportation can be taken away from the demoralization of lotteries, the debasement of obscene literature, the contagion of diseased cattle or persons, the impurity of food and drugs, the like facility can be taken away from the systematic enticement to and the enslavement in prostitution and debauchery of women, and, more insistently, of girls.

227 U.S. at 322.

2. Decisions like *Ames* and *Hoke* certainly left Congress free to flex its Commerce Clause muscles with statutes like the National Motor Vehicle Theft Act of 1919 (also known as the Dyer Act), Pub. L. No. 66-70, ch. 89, 41 Stat. 324, which made it a federal offense to transport a stolen motor vehicle across state lines. Once interstate travel became simply the occasion for federal intervention, not the justification, occasions started to abound. Yet Congress often relied on other constitutional provisions. For instance, Congress drew on its taxation authority in 1914 when it passed the Harrison Narcotic Drug Act, ch. 1, 38 Stat. 785, establishing a comprehensive regulatory scheme for narcotic drugs, backed with criminal sanctions. See United States v. Doremus, 249 U.S. 86 (1919) (upholding the Act over the dissent of four Justices who thought it was "a mere attempt by Congress to exert a power not delegated, that is, the reserved police power of the States"). And the ratification of the Eighteenth Amendment, along with the passage of the Volstead Act (National Prohibition Act), ch. 85, 41 Stat. 305 (1919), soon sent federal agents against bootleggers and moonshiners.

A snapshot of federal enforcement in 1930 is instructive. Of the 87,305 total federal prosecutions in 1930, very few resulted from Congress's exercise of its Commerce Clause powers. About 57,000 were for prohibition violations; 8,000 were District of Columbia cases; 7,000 were immigration cases; and 3,500 were drug cases. Of the 4,345 convictions obtained in cases investigated by the 400 agents of the Bureau of Investigation in 1930, 2,452 were for violations of the National Motor Theft Act, and 516 were for Mann Act prosecutions. Daniel Richman, The Past, Present and Future of Violent Crime Federalism, 34 Crime & Just. 377, 385 (2006). Do these statistics support or oppose Chief Justice Fuller's concern in *Ames* that the Commerce Clause would give the federal government too much opportunity to prosecute conduct traditionally handled by the states? Consider this question as you observe how both Commerce Clause doctrine and federal criminal statutes have evolved.

3. Like the statutes in *Ames* and *Hoke*, many important federal criminal statutes—e.g., most federal gun regulations, Hobbs Act robbery and extortion, wire fraud—are "elemental" commerce crimes. By this we mean that part of the government's burden of proof is to show some nexus to commerce, for that is an explicit element of the offense. That said, these jurisdictional elements are, in general, easily proven. For many elemental statutes, a showing of a *de minimis* impact on interstate commerce is sufficient. Moreover, where an activity involves "the use of the channels of interstate commerce [or] the instrumentalities of interstate commerce, or persons or things in interstate commerce," Congress may regulate the

activity "even though the threat may come only from intrastate activities." Taylor v. United States, 136 S. Ct. 2074, 2079 (2016) (citing United States v. Lopez, 514 U.S. 549, 558-59 (1995)).

4. One important elemental statute, the Hobbs Act, illustrates these points well. The Hobbs Act criminalizes robbery or extortion that "*in any way or degree* obstructs, delays, or affects commerce or the movement of any article or commodity in commerce." 18 U.S.C. §1951 (emphasis added). And "[g]iven the statute's broad sweep, even a *de minimis* effect will suffice to meet the commerce element." United States v. Jimenez-Torres, 435 F.3d 3, 7 (1st Cir. 2006). Courts have thus accepted counterfactual arguments about indirect effects on interstate commerce as sufficient for jurisdiction—for example, where a defendant has obtained a victim's property through robbery or extortion, thereby decreasing the victim's ability to engage in interstate commerce. Nonetheless, courts must apply the "*de minimis* standard with some caution, lest every robbery (which by definition has some economic component) become a federal crime." *Jimenez-Torres*, 425 F.3d at 8. When you read Chapter 5, which examines the Hobbs Act at length, you will see that courts have found it difficult in practice to find limiting principles that uphold the distinction between robberies and burglaries that have an interstate nexus and those that are more appropriately addressed in state court.

What do you make of this case-by-case inquiry (required by the Hobbs Act and many other statutes) into whether a particular home burglary, bank robbery, or murder had affected interstate commerce? Do you think this inquiry can be answered in a principled way, with a reasonable and predictable distinction between behavior that does and does not affect commerce? Is this a superior approach to asking, when a statute does not require proof of a specific effect on commerce, whether a particular crime in aggregate has the potential to affect commerce, irrespective of whether it does in any specific instance? Inasmuch as any robbery that leads to murder takes a person out of commerce, does this mean that any such murder can be prosecuted under the Hobbs Act? Should we worry that when the feds want to decline prosecution they can always cite federalism concerns, but when interested they doubtless will find some jurisdictional basis?

5. Consider these questions as you read about the Court's treatment of another important elemental statute, 18 U.S.C. §922(g). Called the "felon-in-possession" statute, §922(g) prohibits individuals previously convicted of a crime "punishable by imprisonment for a term exceeding one year . . . to ship or transport in interstate or foreign commerce, or possess in or affecting commerce, any firearm or ammunition; or to receive any firearm or ammunition which has been shipped or transported in interstate or foreign commerce."

a. Challenges to the commerce scope of elemental statutes—which demand *some* sort of commerce showing in each case—are generally matters of statutory interpretation, rather than constitutional law. Statutory interpretation in this area, however, is frequently done in the shadow of purported limits on Commerce Clause authority. For example, United States v. Bass, 404 U.S. 336 (1971), posed the question of whether the felon-in-possession statute's phrase "in commerce or affecting commerce" applies to "possesses" and "receives," as well as to "transports." The Court determined that it does, because absent proof of interstate commerce in each case, the statute would "dramatically intrude[] upon traditional state jurisdiction." The Court thus held that the government has the burden of proving a commerce nexus in every felon-in-possession case, explaining that without a clear statement of intent to the contrary "[the Court should] not be quick to assume that Congress has meant to effect a significant change in the sensitive relation between federal and state criminal jurisdiction." Id. at 349. Although *Bass* was a statutory, not constitutional, decision, the Court seemed to implicitly assume that the inclusion of a commerce element ensured that the felon-in-possession statute was within Congress's Commerce Clause authority.

A few years later, however, in Scarborough v. United States, 431 U.S. 563 (1977), the Court ensured that the bow *Bass* required to Interstate Commerce could be just a nod. In the course of executing a search warrant on Scarborough's home, police seized four firearms from the defendant's bedroom. As Scarborough had a previous felony conviction for possession of a narcotic with intent to distribute, he was charged with both receipt and possession of the four firearms. The issue before the Court was what proof would satisfy the statute's jurisdictional element. Scarborough argued that "at the time of the offense the possessor must be engaging in commerce or must be carrying the gun at an interstate facility." The Court disagreed, holding instead that the government need only prove that "the firearm possessed by the convicted felon traveled at some time in interstate commerce." In light of the evidence that the guns in Scarborough's possession had been shipped from multiple states, the Court found that his conduct bore a sufficient nexus with interstate conduct to satisfy the statute's elemental requirement.

b. The Growth in Firearm Prosecutions: Given that virtually every firearm has traveled in commerce at some point, the "commerce" element has generally become a mere formality in most federal firearms trials. The extent of federal enforcement activity in this area, licensed by cases like *Scarborough* and championed to various degrees by every Administration since the late 1980s, is detailed in a section from an April 2000 report for the Administrative Office of the U.S. Courts by Patrick Walker and Pragati Patrick, Trends in Firearms Cases from Fiscal Year 1989 Through 1998, and the Workload Implications for the U.S. District Courts (March 2000) (unpublished manuscript) (on file with the Statistics Division of the Administrative Office of the United States Courts). Walker and Patrick note that "[f]rom 1989 to 1998, the number of firearms cases filed in the U.S. district courts increased 61 percent from 2,256 to 3,641," and that during this period, many "defendants who previously would have been prosecuted at the state or local level were prosecuted in federal court to ensure that violent offenders received the maximum sentences available." Moreover, "[i]n comparison to 1989, a firearms case filed in 1998 was more likely to involve multiple defendants, more likely to take longer between filing and disposition of the case, more likely than other types of crimes to result in a jury trial, and more likely to result in a longer prison sentence for the defendant(s)."

By 2016, the number of federal firearms cases had risen to 7,305, about double the number in 1998. Over half of these cases involved a convicted felon who illegally possessed a firearm. U.S. Sent'g Commn., Overview of Federal Criminal Cases: Fiscal Year 2016, at 8-9 (2012). Would it trouble you if a prior felon were charged under §922(g) for possessing a firearm sold to him by undercover federal agents who purposely selected a "prop gun" that satisfied the statute's interstate commerce element? See United States v. Sarraj, 665 F.3d 916 (7th Cir. 2012) (untroubled).

Although the next case, United States v. Lopez, is often (and quite properly) seen as marking the rise of a more restrictive understanding of federal authority, it also ought to be read against the backdrop of the federal firearms enforcement activity just described. By the mid-1990s, a federal firearm case might have been the result of an arrest by local police officers (as in *Lopez*), and the prosecution itself might be handled by local prosecutors deputized to act as Special Assistant U.S. Attorneys. Yet the judges were always federal district judges, many of whom looked askance at the transformation of their courts into "local police courts."

2. CATEGORICAL JURISDICTION

With *Lopez*, we meet a different kind of federal Commerce Clause criminal statute. Instead of taking the retail approach of "elemental" statutes, requiring proof in each case of the nexus between the charged criminal activity and interstate commerce, "categorical" statutes take a wholesale approach to an entire class of conduct. However, while a defendant charged under a categorical statute has no right to demand that the government prove that her *specific* conduct affected interstate commerce, she can challenge Congress's determination that the activity, as a class, substantially affects interstate commerce. That is what happened in the following case.

United States v. Lopez
514 U.S. 549 (1995)

Chief Justice REHNQUIST delivered the opinion of the Court.

In the Gun-Free School Zones Act of 1990, Congress made it a federal offense "for any individual knowingly to possess a firearm at a place that the individual knows, or has reasonable cause to believe, is a school zone." 18 U.S.C. §922(q)(1)(A). The Act neither regulates a commercial activity nor contains a requirement that the possession be connected in any way to interstate commerce. We hold that the Act exceeds the authority of Congress "to regulate Commerce . . . among the several States. . . ." U.S. Const. art. I, §8, cl. 3.

On March 10, 1992, respondent, who was then a 12th-grade student, arrived at Edison High School in San Antonio, Texas, carrying a concealed .38 caliber handgun and five bullets. Acting upon an anonymous tip, school authorities confronted respondent, who admitted that he was carrying the weapon. He was arrested and charged under Texas law with firearm possession on school premises. The next day, the state charges were dismissed after federal agents charged respondent by complaint with violating the Gun-Free School Zones Act of 1990. 18 U.S.C. §922(q)(1)(A).[1]

A federal grand jury indicted respondent on one count of knowing possession of a firearm at a school zone, in violation of §922(q). . . . The District Court conducted a bench trial, found him guilty of violating §922(q), and sentenced him to six months' imprisonment and two years' supervised release.

On appeal, respondent challenged his conviction based on his claim that §922(q) exceeded Congress' power to legislate under the Commerce Clause. The Court of Appeals for the Fifth Circuit agreed and reversed respondent's conviction. It held that, in light of what it characterized as insufficient congressional findings and legislative history, "section 922(q), in the full reach of its terms, is invalid as beyond the power of Congress under the Commerce Clause." Because of the importance of the issue, we granted certiorari, and we now affirm. . . .

Jones & Laughlin Steel, [301 U.S. 1 (1937)], *Darby,* [312 U.S. 100 (1941)], and *Wickard,* [317 U.S. 111 (1942)] ushered in an era of Commerce Clause jurisprudence that greatly expanded the previously defined authority of Congress under that Clause. In part, this was a recognition of the great changes that had occurred in the way business was carried on in this country. Enterprises that had once been local or at

---

1. The term "school zone" is defined as "in, or on the grounds of, a public, parochial or private school" or "within a distance of 1,000 feet from the grounds of a public, parochial or private school." §921(a)(25).

most regional in nature had become national in scope. But the doctrinal change also reflected a view that earlier Commerce Clause cases artificially had constrained the authority of Congress to regulate interstate commerce.

But even these modern-era precedents which have expanded congressional power under the Commerce Clause confirm that this power is subject to outer limits. . . . Since that time, the Court has heeded that warning and undertaken to decide whether a rational basis existed for concluding that a regulated activity sufficiently affected interstate commerce.

Consistent with this structure, we have identified three broad categories of activity that Congress may regulate under its commerce power. . . . First, Congress may regulate the use of the channels of interstate commerce. Second, Congress is empowered to regulate and protect the instrumentalities of interstate commerce, or persons or things in interstate commerce, even though the threat may come only from intrastate activities. Finally, Congress' commerce authority includes the power to regulate those activities having a substantial relation to interstate commerce, i.e., those activities that substantially affect interstate commerce.

Within this final category, admittedly, our case law has not been clear whether an activity must "affect" or "substantially affect" interstate commerce in order to be within Congress' power to regulate it under the Commerce Clause. We conclude, consistent with the great weight of our case law, that the proper test requires an analysis of whether the regulated activity "substantially affects" interstate commerce.

We now turn to consider the power of Congress, in the light of this framework, to enact §922(q). The first two categories of authority may be quickly disposed of: §922(q) is not a regulation of the use of the channels of interstate commerce, nor is it an attempt to prohibit the interstate transportation of a commodity through the channels of commerce; nor can §922(q) be justified as a regulation by which Congress has sought to protect an instrumentality of interstate commerce or a thing in interstate commerce. Thus, if §922(q) is to be sustained, it must be under the third category as a regulation of an activity that substantially affects interstate commerce. . . .

Section 922(q) is a criminal statute that by its terms has nothing to do with "commerce" or any sort of economic enterprise, however broadly one might define those terms.[3] Section 922(q) is not an essential part of a larger regulation of economic activity, in which the regulatory scheme

---

3. Under our federal system, the "States possess primary authority for defining and enforcing the criminal law." Brecht v. Abrahamson, 507 U.S. 619, 635 (1993); see also Screws v. United States, 325 U.S. 91, 109 (1945) (plurality opinion) ("Our national government is one of delegated powers alone. Under our federal system the administration of criminal justice rests with the States except as Congress, acting within the scope of those delegated powers, has created offenses against the United States"). When Congress criminalizes conduct already denounced as criminal by the States, it effects a "change in the sensitive relation between federal and state criminal jurisdiction." United States v. Enmons, 410 U.S. 396, 411-12 (1973). The Government acknowledges that §922(q)

could be undercut unless the intrastate activity were regulated. It cannot, therefore, be sustained under our cases upholding regulations of activities that arise out of or are connected with a commercial transaction, which viewed in the aggregate, substantially affects interstate commerce.

Second, §922(q) contains no jurisdictional element which would ensure, through case-by-case inquiry, that the firearm possession in question affects interstate commerce. . . .

Although as part of our independent evaluation of constitutionality under the Commerce Clause we of course consider legislative findings, . . . the Government concedes that "[n]either the statute nor its legislative history contain[s] express congressional findings regarding the effects upon interstate commerce of gun possession in a school zone." We agree with the Government that Congress normally is not required to make formal findings as to the substantial burdens that an activity has on interstate commerce. But to the extent that congressional findings would enable us to evaluate the legislative judgment that the activity in question substantially affected interstate commerce, even though no such substantial effect was visible to the naked eye, they are lacking here. . . .

The Government argues that possession of a firearm in a school zone may result in violent crime and that violent crime can be expected to affect the functioning of the national economy in two ways. First, the costs of violent crime are substantial, and, through the mechanism of insurance, those costs are spread throughout the population. Second, violent crime reduces the willingness of individuals to travel to areas within the country that are perceived to be unsafe. The Government also argues that the presence of guns in schools poses a substantial threat to the educational process by threatening the learning environment. A handicapped educational process, in turn, will result in a less productive citizenry. That, in turn, would have an adverse effect on the Nation's economic well-being. As a result, the Government argues that Congress could rationally have concluded that §922(q) substantially affects interstate commerce.

We pause to consider the implications of the Government's arguments. The Government admits, under its "costs of crime" reasoning, that Congress could regulate not only all violent crime, but all activities that might lead to violent crime, regardless of how tenuously they relate to interstate commerce. Similarly, under the Government's "national productivity" reasoning, Congress could regulate any activity that it found was related to the economic productivity of individual citizens: family law (including marriage, divorce, and child custody), for example. Under the theories that the Government presents in support of §922(q), it is difficult to perceive any limitation on federal power, even in areas such as criminal law enforcement or education where States historically have

"displace[s] state policy choices in . . . that its prohibitions apply even in States that have chosen not to outlaw the conduct in question." Brief for United States 29, n.18. . . .

been sovereign. Thus, if we were to accept the Government's arguments, we are hard pressed to posit any activity by an individual that Congress is without power to regulate. . . .

For instance, if Congress can, pursuant to its Commerce Clause power, regulate activities that adversely affect the learning environment, then, a fortiori, it also can regulate the educational process directly. Congress could determine that a school's curriculum has a "significant" effect on the extent of classroom learning. As a result, Congress could mandate a federal curriculum for local elementary and secondary schools because what is taught in local schools has a significant "effect on classroom learning," and that, in turn, has a substantial effect on interstate commerce. . . .

The possession of a gun in a local school zone is in no sense an economic activity that might, through repetition elsewhere, substantially affect any sort of interstate commerce. Respondent was a local student at a local school; there is no indication that he had recently moved in interstate commerce, and there is no requirement that his possession of the firearm have any concrete tie to interstate commerce.

To uphold the Government's contentions here, we would have to pile inference upon inference in a manner that would bid fair to convert congressional authority under the Commerce Clause to a general police power of the sort retained by the States. Admittedly, some of our prior cases have taken long steps down that road, giving great deference to congressional action. The broad language in these opinions has suggested the possibility of additional expansion, but we decline here to proceed any further. To do so would require us to conclude that the Constitution's enumeration of powers does not presuppose something not enumerated, and that there never will be a distinction between what is truly national and what is truly local. This we are unwilling to do. . . .

[Justice KENNEDY'S concurring opinion, which Justice O'CONNOR joined, and Justice THOMAS'S concurring opinion are omitted, as are dissenting opinions by Justices SOUTER and STEVENS.]

Justice BREYER, with whom Justice STEVENS, Justice SOUTER, and Justice GINSBURG join, dissenting.

The issue in this case is whether the Commerce Clause authorizes Congress to enact a statute that makes it a crime to possess a gun in, or near, a school. 18 U.S.C. §922(q)(1)(A). In my view, the statute falls well within the scope of the commerce power as this Court has understood that power over the last half century. . . .

[T]he Constitution requires us to judge the connection between a regulated activity and interstate commerce, not directly, but at one remove. Courts must give Congress a degree of leeway in determining the existence of a significant factual connection between the regulated activity and interstate commerce both because the Constitution delegates the commerce power directly to Congress and because the determination requires an empirical judgment of a kind that a legislature is more likely than a court to make with accuracy. The traditional words "rational basis" capture this leeway. . . .

Applying these principles to the case at hand, we must ask whether Congress could have had a *rational basis* for finding a significant (or substantial) connection between gun-related school violence and interstate commerce. . . . [T]he answer to this question must be yes. Numerous reports and studies—generated both inside and outside government—make clear that Congress could reasonably have found the empirical connection that its law, implicitly or explicitly, asserts.

For one thing, reports, hearings, and other readily available literature make clear that the problem of guns in and around schools is widespread and extremely serious. These materials report, for example, that four percent of American high school students (and six percent of inner-city high school students) carry a gun to school at least occasionally, that 12 percent of urban high school students have had guns fired at them, that 20 percent of those students have been threatened with guns, and that, in any 6-month period, several hundred thousand schoolchildren are victims of violent crimes in or near their schools. And, they report that this widespread violence in schools throughout the Nation significantly interferes with the quality of education in those schools. . . . Congress could therefore have found a substantial educational problem—teachers unable to teach, students unable to learn—and concluded that guns near schools contribute substantially to the size and scope of that problem.

Having found that guns in schools significantly undermine the quality of education in our Nation's classrooms, Congress could also have found, given the effect of education upon interstate and foreign commerce, that gun-related violence in and around schools is a commercial, as well as a human, problem. Education, although far more than a matter of economics, has long been inextricably intertwined with the Nation's economy. . . . Scholars on the subject report that technological changes and innovations in management techniques have altered the nature of the workplace so that more jobs now demand greater educational skills. . . .

Increasing global competition also has made primary and secondary education economically more important. . . . [M]ore than 70 percent of American-made goods now compete with imports. Yet, lagging worker productivity has contributed to negative trade balances and to real hourly compensation that has fallen below wages in 10 other industrialized nations. At least some significant part of this serious productivity problem is attributable to students who emerge from classrooms without the reading or mathematical skills necessary to compete with their European or Asian counterparts. . . .

Finally, there is evidence that, today more than ever, many firms base their location decisions upon the presence, or absence, of a work force with a basic education. . . .

The economic links I have just sketched seem fairly obvious. Why then is it not equally obvious, in light of those links, that a widespread, serious, and substantial physical threat to teaching and learning *also* substantially threatens the commerce to which that teaching and learning is inextricably tied? . . . [G]uns in the hands of six percent of inner-city high school students and gun-related violence throughout a city's schools must threaten the trade and commerce that those schools support. The only question, then, is whether the latter threat is (to use the majority's terminology) "substantial." The evidence of (1) the *extent* of the gun-related violence problem, (2) the *extent* of the resulting negative effect on classroom learning, (3) the *extent* of the consequent negative commercial effects, when taken together, indicate a threat to trade and commerce that is "substantial." . . .

In sum, to find this legislation within the scope of the Commerce Clause would permit "Congress . . . to act in terms of economic . . . realities." . . . Upholding this legislation would do no more than simply recognize that Congress had a "rational basis" for finding a significant connection between guns in or near schools and (through their effect on education) the interstate and foreign commerce they threaten. For these reasons, I would reverse the judgment of the Court of Appeals. Respectfully, I dissent.

NOTES AND QUESTIONS

1. Justice Breyer cites "increasing global competition" as a reason that preventing firearms in schools could be seen as sufficiently affecting commerce under Commerce Clause jurisprudence. What is the limiting principle that protects state control of criminal justice if education's ties to global competition are deemed to sufficiently "affect commerce"? Does Congress recognize such limits, at least when it comes to primary and secondary education? Note that when Congress legislates regarding these policy issues in the educational context, it uses its "spending power"—see, for example, the No Child Left Behind Act of 2001, 20 U.S.C. §§6301-7941.

2. Congress responded quickly to *Lopez* by revising 18 U.S.C. §922(q). As you consider this provision, compare the operative language in (2)(A) below with the previous language, which is quoted in *Lopez*. Ask yourself why this legislation is so much more detailed (and contains more exemptions) than the legislation struck down in *Lopez*.

Gun-Free Schools Act of 1995, 18 U.S.C. §992(Q)

(2)(A) It shall be unlawful for any individual knowingly to possess a firearm that has moved in or that otherwise affects interstate or foreign commerce at a place that the individual knows, or has reasonable cause to believe, is a school zone.

(2)(B) Subparagraph (A) does not apply to the possession of a firearm—

(i) on private property not part of school grounds;

(ii) if the individual possessing the firearm is licensed to do so by the State in which the school zone is located or a political subdivision of the State, and the law of the State or political subdivision requires that, before an individual obtains such a license, the law enforcement authorities of the State or political subdivision verify that the individual is qualified under law to receive the license;

(iii) that is—

    (I) not loaded; and

    (II) in a locked container or a locked firearms rack that is on a motor vehicle;

(iv) by an individual for use in a program approved by a school in the school zone;

(v) by an individual in accordance with a contract entered into between a school in the school zone and the individual or an employer of the individual;

(vi) by a law enforcement officer acting in his or her official capacity; or

(vii) that is unloaded and is possessed by an individual while traversing school premises for the purpose of gaining access to public or private lands open to hunting, if the entry on school premises is authorized by school authorities. . . .

In United States v. Dorsey, 418 F.3d 1038, 1046 (9th Cir. 2005), the Ninth Circuit noted: "This new version of §922(q) resolves the shortcomings that the *Lopez* Court found in the prior version of this statute because it incorporates a 'jurisdictional element which would ensure, through case-by-case inquiry, that the firearm possession in question affects interstate commerce.' This jurisdictional element saves §922(q) from the infirmity that defeated it in *Lopez*." Do you agree with the Ninth Circuit on this score?

3. In United States v. Morrison, 529 U.S. 598 (2000), the Supreme Court, in another 5-4 decision, extended the *Lopez* analysis to strike down a provision of the Violence Against Women Act of 1994 that created a federal civil right of action for victims of gender-motivated violence. Writing for the Court, Chief Justice Rehnquist noted:

If accepted, [defenders of the statute's] reasoning would allow Congress to regulate any crime as long as the nationwide, aggregated impact of that crime has substantial effects on employment, production, transit, or consumption. Indeed, if Congress may regulate gender-motivated violence, it would be able to regulate murder or any other type of violence since gender-motivated violence, as a subset of all violent crime, is certain to have lesser economic impacts than the larger class of which it is a part.

Id. at 615.

Morrison took pains not to question the constitutionality of the criminal provision of the Violence Against Women Act, which (in contrast to the civil provision) had an explicit Commerce Clause jurisdictional element. See 18 U.S.C. §2261(a)(1) ("A person who travels across a State line or enters or leaves Indian country with the intent to injure, harass, or intimidate that person's spouse or intimate partner, and who, in the course of or as a result of such travel, intentionally commits a crime of violence and thereby causes bodily injury to such spouse or intimate partner, shall be punished as provided in subsection (b)."). The Court noted with apparent approval: "The Courts of Appeals have uniformly upheld this criminal sanction as an appropriate exercise of Congress' Commerce Clause authority, reasoning that the provision properly falls within the first of *Lopez*'s categories as it regulates the use of channels of interstate commerce—i.e., 'the use of the interstate transportation routes through which persons and goods move.' United States v. Lankford, 196 F.3d 563, 571-72 (5th Cir. 1999) (collecting cases)." 529 U.S. at 613 n.5; see also United States v. Larsen, 615 F.3d 780, 784-86 (7th Cir. 2010).

The precedential status of *Lopez* and *Morrison* turns to a large extent on how one reads Gonzales v. Raich—a 6-3 decision from 2005 upholding Congress's constitutional authority to criminalize personal possession of marijuana for medicinal purposes in the face of a California law that allowed such marijuana use.

Gonzales v. Raich
545 U.S. 1 (2005)

Justice STEVENS delivered the opinion of the Court.

California is one of at least nine States that authorize the use of marijuana for medicinal purposes. The question presented in this case is whether the power vested in Congress by Article I, §8, of the Constitution "[t]o make all Laws which shall be necessary and proper for carrying into Execution" its authority to "regulate Commerce with foreign Nations, and among the several States" includes the power to prohibit the local cultivation and use of marijuana in compliance with California law.

I

California has been a pioneer in the regulation of marijuana. In 1913, California was one of the first States to prohibit the sale and possession of marijuana, and at the end of the century, California became the first State to authorize limited use of the drug for medicinal purposes. In 1996, California voters passed Proposition 215, now codified as the Compassionate Use Act of 1996. The proposition was designed to ensure that "seriously ill" residents of the State have access to marijuana for medical purposes, and to encourage Federal and State Governments to take steps towards ensuring the safe and affordable distribution of the drug to patients in need. The Act creates an exemption from criminal prosecution for physicians, as well as for patients and primary caregivers who possess or cultivate marijuana for medicinal purposes with the recommendation or approval of a physician. A "primary caregiver" is a person who has consistently assumed responsibility for the housing, health, or safety of the patient.

Respondents Angel Raich and Diane Monson are California residents who suffer from a variety of serious medical conditions and have sought to avail themselves of medical marijuana pursuant to the terms of the Compassionate Use Act. They are being treated by licensed, board-certified family practitioners, who have concluded, after prescribing a host of conventional medicines to treat respondents' conditions and to alleviate their associated symptoms, that marijuana is the only drug available that provides effective treatment. Both women have been using marijuana as a medication for several years pursuant to their doctors' recommendation, and both rely heavily on cannabis to function on a daily basis. Indeed, Raich's physician believes that forgoing cannabis treatments would certainly cause Raich excruciating pain and could very well prove fatal.

Respondent Monson cultivates her own marijuana, and ingests the drug in a variety of ways including smoking and using a vaporizer. Respondent Raich, by contrast, is unable to cultivate her own, and thus relies on two caregivers, litigating as "John Does," to provide her with locally grown marijuana at no charge. These caregivers also process the cannabis into hashish or keif, and Raich herself processes some of the marijuana into oils, balms, and foods for consumption.

On August 15, 2002, county deputy sheriffs and agents from the federal Drug Enforcement Administration (DEA) came to Monson's home. After a thorough investigation, the county officials concluded that her use of marijuana was entirely lawful as a matter of California law. Nevertheless, after a 3-hour standoff, the federal agents seized and destroyed all six of her cannabis plants.

Respondents thereafter brought this action against the Attorney General of the United States and the head of the DEA seeking injunctive and declaratory relief prohibiting the enforcement of the federal Controlled Substances Act (CSA), 84 Stat. 1242, 21 U.S.C. §801 et seq., to the extent it prevents them from possessing, obtaining, or manufacturing cannabis for their personal medical use. . . . Respondents claimed that enforcing the CSA against them would violate the Commerce Clause, the Due Process Clause of the Fifth Amendment, the Ninth and Tenth Amendments of the Constitution, and the doctrine of medical necessity.

The District Court denied respondents' motion for a preliminary injunction. . . . A divided panel of the Court of Appeals for the Ninth Circuit reversed and ordered the District Court to enter a preliminary injunction. Raich v. Ashcroft, 352 F.3d 1222 (2003). The court found that respondents had "demonstrated a strong likelihood of success on their claim that, as applied to them, the CSA is an unconstitutional exercise of Congress' Commerce Clause authority." Id. at 1227. The Court of Appeals distinguished prior Circuit cases upholding the CSA in the face of Commerce Clause challenges by focusing on what it deemed to be the "*separate and distinct class of activities*" at issue in this case: "the intrastate, noncommercial cultivation and possession of cannabis for personal medical purposes as recommended by a patient's physician pursuant to valid California state law." Id. at 1228. . . .

The majority placed heavy reliance on our decisions in United States v. Lopez, 514 U.S. 549 (1995), and United States v. Morrison, 529 U.S. 598 (2000), as interpreted by recent Circuit precedent, to hold that this separate class of purely local activities was beyond the reach of federal power. . . .

The obvious importance of the case prompted our grant of certiorari. The case is made difficult by respondents' strong arguments that they will suffer irreparable harm because, despite a congressional finding to the contrary, marijuana does have valid therapeutic purposes. The question before us, however, is not whether it is wise to enforce the statute in these circumstances; rather, it is whether Congress' power to regulate interstate markets for medicinal substances encompasses the portions of those markets that are supplied with drugs produced and consumed locally. Well-settled law controls our answer. The CSA is a valid exercise of federal power, even as applied to the troubling facts of this case. We accordingly vacate the judgment of the Court of Appeals. . . .

II

[A]s early as 1906 Congress enacted federal legislation imposing labeling regulations on medications and prohibiting the manufacture or shipment of any adulterated or misbranded drug traveling in interstate commerce. Aside from these labeling restrictions, most domestic drug regulations prior to 1970 generally came in the guise of revenue laws, with the Department of the Treasury serving as the Federal Government's primary enforcer. . . .

Then in 1970, after declaration of the national "war on drugs," federal drug policy underwent a significant transformation. . . . [P]rompted by a perceived need to consolidate the growing number of piecemeal drug laws and to enhance federal drug enforcement powers, Congress enacted the Comprehensive Drug Abuse Prevention and Control Act.

Title II of that Act, the CSA, repealed most of the earlier antidrug laws in favor of a comprehensive regime to combat the international and interstate traffic in illicit drugs. The main objectives of the CSA were to conquer drug abuse and to control the legitimate and illegitimate traffic in controlled substances.

Congress was particularly concerned with the need to prevent the diversion of drugs from legitimate to illicit channels.

To effectuate these goals, Congress devised a closed regulatory system making it unlawful to manufacture, distribute, dispense, or possess any controlled substance except in a manner authorized by the CSA. The CSA categorizes all controlled substances into five schedules. §812. The drugs are grouped together based on their accepted medical uses, the potential for abuse, and their psychological and physical effects on the body. §§811, 812. Each schedule is associated with a distinct set of controls regarding the manufacture, distribution, and use of the substances listed therein. The CSA and its implementing regulations set forth strict requirements regarding registration, labeling and packaging, production quotas, drug security, and recordkeeping.

In enacting the CSA, Congress classified marijuana as a Schedule I drug. 21 U.S.C. §812(c). This preliminary classification was based, in part, on the recommendation of the Assistant Secretary of HEW "that marihuana [sic] be retained within schedule I at least until the completion of certain studies now underway." Schedule I drugs are categorized as such because of their high potential for abuse, lack of any accepted medical use, and absence of any accepted safety for use in medically supervised treatment. §812(b)(1). These three factors, in varying gradations, are also used to categorize drugs in the other four schedules. For example, Schedule II substances also have a high potential for abuse which may lead to severe psychological or physical dependence, but unlike Schedule I drugs, they have a currently accepted medical use. §812(b)(2). By classifying marijuana as a Schedule I drug, as opposed to listing it on a lesser schedule, the manufacture, distribution, or possession of marijuana became a criminal offense, with the sole exception being use of the drug as part of a Food and Drug Administration pre-approved research study. §§823(f), 841(a)(1), 844(a); see also United States v. Oakland Cannabis Buyers Cooperative, 532 U.S. 483, 490 (2001).

The CSA provides for the periodic updating of schedules and delegates authority to the Attorney General, after consultation with the Secretary of Health and Human Services, to add, remove, or transfer substances to, from, or between schedules. §811. Despite considerable efforts to reschedule marijuana, it remains a Schedule I drug.

III . . .

Our case law firmly establishes Congress' power to regulate purely local activities that are part of an economic "class of activities" that have a substantial effect on interstate commerce. See, e.g., *Perez*, 402 U.S. at 151; *Wickard v. Filburn*, 317 U.S. 111, 128-29 (1942). As we stated in *Wickard*, "even if appellee's activity be local and though it may not be regarded as commerce, it may still, whatever its nature, be reached by Congress if it exerts a substantial economic effect on interstate commerce." Id. at 125. We have never required Congress to legislate with scientific exactitude. When Congress decides that the "total incidence" of a practice poses a threat to a national market, it may regulate the entire class. See *Perez*, 402 U.S. at 154-55. In this vein, we have reiterated that when "a general regulatory statute bears a substantial relation to commerce, the *de minimis* character of individual instances arising under that statute is of no consequence." E.g., *Lopez*, 514 U.S. at 558 (emphasis deleted).

Our decision in *Wickard*, 317 U.S. 111, is of particular relevance. In *Wickard*, we upheld the application of regulations promulgated under the Agricultural Adjustment Act of 1938, 52 Stat. 31, which were designed to control the volume of wheat moving in interstate and foreign commerce in order to avoid surpluses and consequent abnormally low prices. . . . *Wickard* . . . establishes that Congress can regulate purely intrastate activity that is not itself "commercial," in that it is not produced for sale, if it concludes that failure to regulate that class of activity would undercut the regulation of the interstate market in that commodity.

The similarities between this case and *Wickard* are striking. Like the farmer in *Wickard*, respondents are cultivating, for home consumption, a fungible commodity for which there is an established, albeit illegal, interstate market. Just as the Agricultural Adjustment Act was designed "to control the volume [of wheat] moving in interstate and foreign commerce in order to avoid surpluses . . ." and consequently control the market price, id. at 115, a primary purpose of the CSA is to control the supply and demand of controlled substances in both lawful and unlawful drug markets. In *Wickard*, we had no difficulty concluding that Congress had a rational basis for believing that, when viewed in the aggregate, leaving home-consumed wheat outside the regulatory scheme would have a substantial influence on price and market conditions. Here too, Congress had a rational basis for concluding that leaving home-consumed marijuana outside federal control would similarly affect price and market conditions. . . .

While the diversion of homegrown wheat tended to frustrate the federal interest in stabilizing prices by regulating the volume of commercial transactions in the interstate market, the diversion of homegrown marijuana tends to frustrate the federal interest in eliminating commercial transactions in the interstate market in their entirety. In both cases, the regulation is squarely within Congress' commerce power because production of the commodity meant for home consumption, be it wheat or marijuana, has a substantial effect on supply and demand in the national market for that commodity. . . .

In assessing the scope of Congress' authority under the Commerce Clause, we stress that the task before us is a modest one. We need not determine whether respondents' activities, taken in the aggregate, substantially affect interstate commerce in fact, but only whether a "rational basis" exists for so concluding. . . . Given the enforcement difficulties that attend distinguishing between marijuana cultivated locally and marijuana grown elsewhere, 21 U.S.C. §801(5), and concerns about diversion into illicit channels, we have no difficulty concluding that Congress had a rational basis for believing that failure to regulate the intrastate manufacture and possession of marijuana would leave a gaping hole in the CSA. Thus, as in *Wickard*, when it enacted comprehensive legislation to regulate the interstate market in a fungible commodity, Congress was acting well within its authority to "make all Laws which shall be necessary and proper" to "regulate Commerce . . . among the several States." U.S. Const. art. I, §8. That the regulation ensnares some purely intrastate activity is of no moment. . . .

IV . . .

At issue in *Lopez*, 514 U.S. 549, was the validity of the Gun-Free School Zones Act of 1990, which was a brief, single-subject statute making it a crime for an individual to possess a gun in a school zone. 104 Stat. 4844-45, 18 U.S.C. §922(q)(1)(A). The Act did not regulate any economic activity and did not contain any requirement that the possession of a gun have any connection to past interstate activity or a predictable impact on future commercial activity. . . .

Unlike those at issue in *Lopez* and *Morrison*, the activities regulated by the CSA are quintessentially economic. . . . The CSA . . . regulates the production, distribution, and consumption of commodities for which there is an established, and lucrative, interstate market. Prohibiting the intrastate possession or manufacture of an article of commerce is a rational (and commonly utilized) means of regulating commerce in that product. Such prohibitions include specific decisions requiring that a drug be withdrawn from the market as a result of the failure to comply with regulatory requirements as well as decisions excluding Schedule I drugs entirely from the market. Because the CSA is a statute that directly regulates economic, commercial activity, our opinion in *Morrison* casts no doubt on its constitutionality. . . .

The exemption for cultivation by patients and caregivers can only increase the supply of marijuana in the California market. The likelihood that all such production will promptly terminate when patients recover or will precisely match the patients' medical needs during their convalescence seems remote; whereas the danger that excesses will satisfy some of the admittedly enormous demand for recreational use seems obvious. . . . Taking into account the fact that California is only one of at least nine States to have authorized the medical use of marijuana, . . . Congress could have rationally concluded that the aggregate impact on the national market of all the transactions exempted from federal supervision is unquestionably substantial. . . .

Justice SCALIA, concurring in the judgment. . . .

Since Perez v. United States, 402 U.S. 146 (1971), our cases have mechanically recited that the Commerce Clause permits congressional regulation of three categories: (1) the channels of interstate commerce; (2) the instrumentalities of interstate commerce, and persons or things in interstate commerce; and (3) activities that "substantially affect" interstate commerce. The first two categories are self-evident, since they are the ingredients of interstate commerce itself. The third category, however, is different in kind, and its recitation without explanation is misleading and incomplete.

It is *misleading* because, unlike the channels, instrumentalities, and agents of interstate commerce, activities that substantially affect interstate commerce are not themselves part of interstate commerce, and thus the power to regulate them cannot come from the Commerce Clause alone. Rather, as this Court has acknowledged since at least United States v. Coombs, 37 U.S. 72 (1838), Congress' regulatory authority over intrastate activities that are not themselves part of interstate commerce (including activities that have a substantial effect on interstate commerce) derives from the Necessary and Proper Clause. And the category of "activities that substantially affect interstate commerce," [*Lopez*, 514 U.S. at 559], is *incomplete* because the authority to enact laws necessary and proper for the regulation of interstate commerce is not limited to laws governing intrastate activities that substantially affect interstate commerce. Where necessary to make a regulation of interstate commerce effective, Congress may regulate even those intrastate activities that do not themselves substantially affect interstate commerce. . . . [T]he commerce power permits Congress not only to devise rules for the governance of commerce between States but also to facilitate interstate commerce by eliminating potential obstructions, and to restrict it by eliminating potential stimulants. That is why the Court has repeatedly sustained congressional legislation on the ground that the regulated activities had a substantial effect on interstate commerce. . . .

And there are other restraints upon the Necessary and Proper Clause authority. As Chief Justice Marshall wrote in McCulloch v. Maryland, [17 U.S. 316 (1819)], even when the end is constitutional and legitimate, the means must be "appropriate" and "plainly adapted" to that end.

Moreover, they may not be otherwise "prohibited" and must be "consistent with the letter and spirit of the constitution." These phrases are not merely hortatory. . . .

The application of these principles to the case before us is straightforward. In the CSA, Congress has undertaken to extinguish the interstate market in Schedule I controlled substances, including marijuana. The Commerce Clause unquestionably permits this. . . . To effectuate its objective, Congress has prohibited almost all intrastate activities related to Schedule I substances—both economic activities (manufacture, distribution, possession with the intent to distribute) and noneconomic activities (simple possession). . . . As the Court explains, marijuana that is grown at home and possessed for personal use is never more than an instant from the interstate market—and this is so whether or not the possession is for medicinal use or lawful use under the laws of a particular State. Congress need not accept on faith that state law will be effective in maintaining a strict division between a lawful market for "medical" marijuana and the more general marijuana market. . . .

Justice O'CONNOR, with whom THE CHIEF JUSTICE and Justice THOMAS join as to all but [the final two paragraphs], dissenting.

We enforce the "outer limits" of Congress' Commerce Clause authority not for their own sake, but to protect historic spheres of state sovereignty from excessive federal encroachment and thereby to maintain the distribution of power fundamental to our federalist system of government. One of federalism's chief virtues, of course, is that it promotes innovation by allowing for the possibility that "a single courageous State may, if its citizens choose, serve as a laboratory; and try novel social and economic experiments without risk to the rest of the country." New State Ice Co. v. Liebmann, 285 U.S. 262, 311 (1932) (Brandeis, J., dissenting).

This case exemplifies the role of States as laboratories. The States' core police powers have always included authority to define criminal law and to protect the health, safety, and welfare of their citizens. Exercising those powers, California (by ballot initiative and then by legislative codification) has come to its own conclusion about the difficult and sensitive question of whether marijuana should be available to relieve severe pain and suffering. Today the Court sanctions an application of the federal Controlled Substances Act that extinguishes that experiment, without any proof that the personal cultivation, possession, and use of marijuana for medicinal purposes, if economic activity in the first place, has a substantial effect on interstate commerce and is therefore an appropriate subject of federal regulation. . . .

What is the relevant conduct subject to Commerce Clause analysis in this case. . . .

I agree with the Court that we must look beyond respondents' own activities. Otherwise, individual litigants could always exempt themselves from Commerce Clause regulation merely by pointing to the obvious—that their personal activities do not have a substantial effect on interstate commerce. The task is to identify a mode of analysis that allows Congress to regulate more than nothing (by declining to reduce each case to its litigants) and less than everything (by declining to let Congress set the terms of analysis). The analysis may not be the same in every case, for it depends on the regulatory scheme at issue and the federalism concerns implicated. . . .

Respondents challenge only the application of the CSA to medicinal use of marijuana. Moreover, because fundamental structural concerns about dual sovereignty animate our Commerce Clause cases, it is relevant that this case involves the interplay of federal and state regulation in areas of criminal law and social policy, where "States lay claim by right of history and expertise." *Lopez, supra,* at 583 (Kennedy, J., concurring). California, like other States, has drawn on its reserved powers to distinguish the regulation of medicinal marijuana. . . .

Even assuming that economic activity is at issue in this case, the Government has made no showing in fact that the possession and use of homegrown marijuana for medical purposes, in California or elsewhere, has a substantial effect on interstate commerce. Similarly, the Government has not shown that regulating such activity is necessary to an interstate regulatory scheme. . . .

Relying on Congress' abstract assertions, the Court has endorsed making it a federal crime to grow small amounts of marijuana in one's own home for one's own medicinal use. This overreaching stifles an express choice by some States, concerned for the lives and liberties of their people, to regulate medical marijuana differently. If I were a California citizen, I would not have voted for the medical marijuana ballot initiative; if I were a California legislator I would not have supported the Compassionate Use Act. But whatever the wisdom of California's experiment with medical marijuana, the federalism principles that have driven our Commerce Clause cases require that room for experiment be protected in this case. For these reasons I dissent.

Justice THOMAS, dissenting.

Respondents Diane Monson and Angel Raich use marijuana that has never been bought or sold, that has never crossed state lines, and that has had no demonstrable effect on the national market for marijuana. If Congress can regulate this under the Commerce Clause, then it can regulate virtually anything—and the Federal Government is no longer one of limited and enumerated powers. . . .

On its face, a ban on the intrastate cultivation, possession and distribution of marijuana may be plainly adapted to stopping the interstate flow of marijuana. Unregulated local growers and users could swell both the supply and the demand sides of the interstate marijuana market, making the market more difficult to regulate. But respondents do not challenge the CSA on its face. Instead, they challenge it as applied to their conduct. The question is thus whether the intrastate ban is "necessary and proper" as applied to medical marijuana users like respondents. . . .

The Court of Appeals found that respondents' "limited use is distinct from the broader illicit drug market," because "th[eir] medicinal marijuana . . . is not intended for, nor does it enter, the stream of commerce." If that is generally true of individuals who grow and use marijuana for medical purposes under state law, then even assuming Congress has "obvious" and "plain" reasons why regulating intrastate cultivation and possession is necessary to regulating the interstate drug trade, none of those reasons applies to medical marijuana patients like Monson and Raich. . . .

Here, Congress has encroached on States' traditional police powers to define the criminal law and to protect the health, safety, and welfare of their citizens.[5] Further, the Government's rationale—that it may regulate the production or possession of any commodity for which there is an interstate market—threatens to remove the remaining vestiges of States' traditional police powers. This would convert the Necessary and Proper Clause into precisely what Chief Justice Marshall did not envision, a "pretext . . . for the accomplishment of objects not intrusted to the government." *McCulloch, supra*, at 423. . . .

The majority prevents States like California from devising drug policies that they have concluded provide much-needed respite to the seriously ill. It does so without any serious inquiry into the necessity for federal regulation or the propriety of "displac[ing] state regulation in areas of traditional state concern." The majority's rush to embrace federal power "is especially unfortunate given the importance of showing respect for the sovereign States that comprise our Federal Union." United States v. Oakland Cannabis Buyers' Cooperative, 532 U.S. 483, 502 (2001) (Stevens, J., concurring in judgment). Our federalist system, properly understood, allows California and a growing number of other States to decide for themselves how to safeguard the health and welfare of their citizens. I would affirm the judgment of the Court of Appeals. I respectfully dissent.

---

5. In fact, the Anti-Federalists objected that the Necessary and Proper Clause would allow Congress, inter alia, to "*constitute new Crimes*, . . . and extend [its] Power as far as [it] shall think proper; so that the State Legislatures have no Security for the Powers now presumed to remain to them; or the People for their Rights." Mason, Objections to the Constitution Formed by the Convention (1787), in 2 The Complete Anti-Federalist 11, 12-13 (H. Storing, ed. 1981) (emphasis added). Hamilton responded that these objections were gross "misrepresentation[s]." The Federalist No. 33, at 204. He termed the Clause "perfectly harmless," for it merely confirmed Congress' implied authority to enact laws in exercising its enumerated powers. Id. at 205. According to Hamilton, the Clause was needed only "to guard against cavilling refinements" by those seeking to cripple federal power. The Federalist No. 33, at 205; id. No. 44, at 303-304 (J. Madison).

NOTES AND QUESTIONS

1. Do you think that a distinction between medical and recreational marijuana users could be maintained as a matter of law enforcement policy? Would such a distinction be constitutionally sound? Have the "facts on the ground"—the burgeoning "medical marijuana" industries in Colorado, California, and elsewhere—made such a distinction both legally and practically implausible? See Sam Kamin, Medical Marijuana in Colorado and the Future of Marijuana Regulation in the United States, 43 McGeorge L. Rev. 147 (2012). To what extent does *Raich* limit further state legal experimentation? See Robert A. Mikos, On the Limits of Supremacy: Medical Marijuana and the States' Overlooked Power to Legalize Federal Crime, 62 Vand. L. Rev. 1421 (2009).

2. Lower courts have relied on *Raich* when rejecting Commerce Clause challenges to child pornography statutes. Under the Child Protection and Obscenity Enforcement Act of 1988, 18 U.S.C. §2251(a):

> Any person who employs, uses, persuades, induces, entices, or coerces any minor to engage in, or who has a minor assist any other person to engage in, or who transports any minor in interstate or foreign commerce, or in any Territory or Possession of the United States, with the intent that such minor engage in, any sexually explicit conduct for the purpose of producing any visual depiction of such conduct, shall be punished as provided under subsection (e), if such person knows or has reason to know that such visual depiction will be transported in interstate or foreign commerce or mailed, if that visual depiction was produced using materials that have been mailed, shipped, or transported in interstate or foreign commerce by any means, including by computer, or if such visual depiction has actually been transported in interstate or foreign commerce or mailed.

In United States v. Blum, 534 F.3d 608 (7th Cir. 2008), the Seventh Circuit rejected the Commerce Clause challenge of a defendant who manufactured child pornography "at his home in Wisconsin, for his private viewing and possession." Id. at 609. The court noted: "The only movement in interstate commerce that is alleged is that the mini-DV tapes were manufactured outside the state of Wisconsin." Id. at 609. In upholding the statute, the court observed:

> As was the case in *Raich*, the high demand for child pornography in the interstate market presented the real danger that purely-intrastate child pornography would find its way to that market. Similarly, the same difficulty in distinguishing between locally-produced marijuana and interstate marijuana for enforcement purposes is problematic with respect to child pornography as well. Given those substantial concerns, and additionally considering the Congressional determination that the manufacture and possession of any child

pornography itself feeds the market and increases demand for it, we hold that Congress rationally could conclude that Blum's actions, taken in aggregation with others engaged in similar activities, substantially affects interstate commerce. We therefore join our sister circuits in rejecting the Commerce Clause challenge to the application of the statute to intrastate child pornography.

Id. at 611-12.

3. In United States v. Stewart, 451 F.3d 1071 (9th Cir. 2006), the possessor of a homemade machine gun raised a Commerce Clause challenge to his prosecution under a statute that broadly makes it "unlawful for any person to transfer or possess a machine gun." 18 U.S.C. §922(o)(1). Initially, he prevailed, but then *Raich* came down and the Ninth Circuit reversed course in an opinion by Judge Kozinski:

In our earlier opinion, we concluded that section 922(o) was quite similar to the statute at issue in *Lopez*. But *Raich* forces us to reconsider. Like the possession regulation in the Controlled Substances Act, the machine gun possession ban fits within a larger scheme for the regulation of interstate commerce in firearms. Guns, like drugs, are regulated by a detailed and comprehensive statutory regime designed to protect individual firearm ownership while supporting "Federal, State and local law enforcement officials in their fight against crime and violence." Gun Control Act of 1968, Pub. L. No. 90-618, §101, 82 Stat. 1213, 1213. Just as the CSA classifies substances in five different categories, placing different controls on each class based on a combination of its legitimate uses, potential for abuse and effects on the body, the federal firearms statutory regime classifies weapons for differential treatment as well: Some firearms are freely transferrable, others must be registered and, still others (like machine guns) are largely banned.

Nevertheless, there is one major difference between the possession ban in the CSA and section 922(o): The machinegun ban was enacted almost twenty years after the statute establishing the current federal firearms regulatory regime. See Firearms Owners' Protection Act, Pub. L. No. 99-308, §102(9), 100 Stat. 449, 452-53 (1986) (codified at 18 U.S.C. § 922(o)). Nevertheless, we don't read *Raich* as requiring us to consider section 922(o) as standalone legislation like that in *Morrison* and *Lopez*. *Raich* stands for the proposition that Congress can ban possession of an object where it has a rational basis for concluding that object might bleed into the interstate market and affect supply and demand, especially in an area where Congress regulates comprehensively. . . . That Congress took a wait-and-see approach when it created the regime doesn't matter. The Commerce Clause does not prevent Congress from correcting deficiencies in its regulatory scheme in piecemeal fashion. To conclude otherwise would eliminate Congress' ability to regulate with a light touch in the first instance and tinker at the margins in light of experience. *Raich*'s deferential review of comprehensive federal regulatory schemes ensures that Congress retains as much discretion to adjust the details of its regulatory scheme as it had when it created the regime. Therefore, the fact that section 922(o) was passed long after the Gun Control Act is not of constitutional significance. . . .

It doesn't matter, as the amici would have us believe, that the machineguns Stewart manufactured were unique. One of the amici argues that "[b]ecause Mr. Stewart's gun is unique, homemade, and hand-tooled, it does not 'overhang' the market, and threaten to enter the market, and affect prices and demand in the same way as wheat or marijuana." But at some level, everything is unique; fungibility is a matter of degree. One of the motivating concerns underlying the blanket prohibition on possession of marijuana under the CSA is that those in a state of drug-induced euphoria care not a whit whether their marijuana has ever crossed state borders. Similarly, those seeking machineguns care only whether the guns work effectively—whether they discharge large amounts of ammunition with a single trigger pull. To the extent that homemade machineguns function like commercial machineguns, it doesn't matter whether they do so in a unique way; as economic substitutes, they are interchangeable.

451 F.3d at 1076-78.

4. Stewart also raised a Second Amendment claim, which the Ninth Circuit summarily rejected, id. at 1078. In District of Columbia v. Heller, 554 U.S. 570 (2008), the Supreme Court held that a D.C. law banning usable handguns in homes violated the Second Amendment to the Constitution. Justice Scalia wrote in the majority 5-4 opinion, id. at 628-29:

[T]he inherent right of self-defense has been central to the Second Amendment right. The handgun ban amounts to a prohibition of an entire class of "arms" that is overwhelmingly chosen by American society for that lawful purpose. The prohibition extends, moreover, to the home, where the need for defense of self, family, and property is most acute. Under any of the standards of scrutiny that we have applied to enumerated constitutional rights, banning from the home "the most preferred firearm in the nation to 'keep' and use for protection of one's home and family," would fail constitutional muster.

The *Heller* majority could not accept the interest-balancing test proposed in Justice Breyer's dissent because "[t]he very enumeration of the right takes out of the hands of government—even the Third Branch of Government—the power to decide on a case-by-case basis whether the right is really worth insisting upon. A constitutional guarantee subject to future judges' assessments of its usefulness is no constitutional guarantee at all." Id. at 634.

Is *Stewart* still good law after *Heller*, considering that "the enshrinement of constitutional rights necessarily" removes from the table "the absolute prohibition on handguns held and used for self-defense in the home"? Id. at 636. Stewart, after all, possessed his handmade machinegun in his home.

It would, however, seem that *Stewart* is still good law because *Heller* looked to how a "traditional militia" would arm itself: "[T]he Second Amendment does not protect those weapons not typically possessed by law-abiding citizens for lawful purposes, such as short-barreled shotguns. That accords with the historical understanding of the scope of the right." Id. at 625. Moreover, the Court qualified its opinion by saying, "nothing in our opinion should be taken to cast doubt on longstanding prohibitions on the possession of firearms by felons and the mentally ill, or laws forbidding the carrying of firearms in sensitive places such as schools and government buildings, or laws imposing conditions and qualifications on the commercial sale of arms." Id. at 626-27.

Not surprisingly, *Heller* has thus not affected many of the gun laws at issue in Commerce Clause jurisprudence. Laws banning firearm possession by felons, drug addicts, and illegal aliens have all been upheld, as have laws prohibiting certain types of weapons and trafficking by unlicensed firearms dealers. See, e.g., United States v. Hosford, 843 F.3d 16 (4th Cir. 2016) (rejecting Second Amendment challenge to provision targeting unlicensed dealing in firearms); United States v. Moore, 666 F.3d 313 (4th Cir. 2012) (upholding felon prohibition against Second Amendment challenge); United States v. Seay, 620 F.3d 919 (8th Cir. 2010) (upholding prohibition with respect to drug addicts); United States v. Skoien, 614 F.3d 638 (7th Cir. 2010) (en banc) (rejecting constitutional challenge to 18 U.S.C. §922(g)(9), which prohibits possession of a firearm by a person convicted of a misdemeanor crime of domestic violence), cert. denied, 562 U.S. 1303 (2011). While the Supreme Court has not addressed the constitutionality of the misdemeanor domestic violation provision, it has addressed its statutory scope. See Voisine v. United States, 136 S. Ct. 2272 (2016); United States v. Castleman, 134 S. Ct. 1405 (2014).

5. Where a statute requires proof of a commerce nexus, need the offense have been part of a larger statutory scheme, as in *Raich*, or will proof of the legislatively specified nexus, however minimal, be sufficient? Put differently, is *Scarborough* still good law? The Ninth Circuit thinks so. In United States v. Alderman, 565 F.3d 641 (9th Cir. 2009), a panel of that court upheld a federal law prohibiting possession by a felon of body armor that has been "sold or offered for sale in interstate commerce," 18 U.S.C. §§931, 921(a)(35). Judge McKeown said that the constitutional question before the court was "whether the sale of body armor in interstate commerce creates a sufficient nexus between possession of the body armor and commerce to allow for federal regulation under Congress's Commerce Clause authority." The court first explained how came to be prosecuted for violating this federal law:

Cedrick Alderman was arrested in 2005 during a sting operation involving an attempted controlled purchase of cocaine. Officers were aware that

> Alderman had been previously convicted of felony robbery. The arresting officer discovered that Alderman was wearing a bulletproof vest. Alderman was booked for possession of the vest and for violating the conditions of his supervision.
>
> Because Washington state law does not criminalize felon possession of body armor, the matter was referred to the federal authorities. Alderman was indicted under 18 U.S.C. §931(a), which makes it unlawful for a person convicted of a felony involving a "crime of violence" to possess body armor. See James Guelff and Chris McCurley Body Armor Act of 2002, §11009(e)(2)(A), 18 U.S.C. §931 (criminalizing the possession of body armor by felons as of Nov. 2, 2002). . . .
>
> Alderman entered a conditional guilty plea. Under the plea agreement, Alderman preserved for appeal the disputed constitutionality of §931. As part of the factual basis for the plea, the plea agreement included Alderman's admission that the vest had crossed state lines. Specifically, the vest was sold by the manufacturer in California to a distributor in Washington state. The distributor then sold the vest to the Washington State Department of Corrections. Nothing in the record reveals how the vest left the Department of Corrections, but it is undisputed that the vest subsequently came into Alderman's possession. The stipulation and factual recitation were designed to ensure that the jurisdictional element of the statute was met. See 18 U.S.C. §921(a)(35) (limiting the applicability of §931 to vests that have been "sold or offered for sale, in interstate or foreign commerce").

565 F.3d at 643-44. The court found *Raich* and *Morrison* inapplicable because here Congress was invoking its power to regulate instrumentalities of interstate commerce; conviction required proof of the jurisdictional element that the body armor possessed by the felon defendant had crossed state lines. The court noted that in previous post-*Raich* cases, the Ninth Circuit and other circuits had upheld similar felon-in-possession statutes, recognizing "the continuing vitality of *Scarborough*." Judge Paez dissented, objecting that:

> The majority's approach . . . effectively renders the Supreme Court's three-part Commerce Clause analysis superfluous and permits Congress, through the use of a jurisdictional element of any stripe, to "convert congressional authority under the Commerce Clause to a general police power of the sort retained by the States." Lopez, 514 U.S. at 567. . . .

565 F.3d at 648 (Paez, J., dissenting).

6. The Ninth Circuit's request for Supreme Court guidance has so far fallen on deaf ears. Dissenting from the denial of certiorari in *Alderman*, Justice Thomas (joined by Justice Scalia) complained:

> [T]he lower courts' reading of *Scarborough*, by trumping the *Lopez* framework, could very well remove any limit on the commerce power. The Ninth Circuit's

interpretation of *Scarborough* seems to permit Congress to regulate or ban possession of any item that has ever been offered for sale or crossed state lines. Congress arguably could outlaw "the theft of a Hershey kiss from a corner store in Youngstown, Ohio, by a neighborhood juvenile on the basis that the candy once traveled . . . to the store from Hershey, Pennsylvania." United States v. Bishop, 66 F.3d 569, 596 (3d Cir. 1995) (Becker, J., concurring in part and dissenting in part). The Government actually conceded at oral argument in the Ninth Circuit that Congress could ban possession of French fries that have been offered for sale in interstate commerce.

Alderman v. United States, 562 U.S. 1163 (2011) (Thomas, J., dissenting).

How important is Justice Thomas's concern? Does the inclusion of a commerce element requiring that some object relevant to the commission of the offense have, at some point, moved in interstate commerce automatically put a statute within Congress's Commerce Clause power? If this is indeed true, or even substantially true, consider the irony: When a statute has an explicit commerce element, the only judicial review of whether federal enforcement has been properly extended will come from a jury and then an appellate court, using a standard highly deferential to the jury's verdict. (And that's assuming the defendant doesn't plead out.) Moreover, the jury is not likely to care much about this element. You don't want to be the defense lawyer arguing, "maybe my client did the charged conduct, but the gun/computer/etc. never moved 'in commerce.'" The defendant won't likely be able to raise a constitutional challenge either pretrial or later. In sum, this is retail review by a body unlikely to care much. When, on the other hand, a statute takes a categorical approach, a jury will never consider the commerce nexus, but a constitutional challenge might well be available (even if, in narcotics cases, it will quickly lose).

7. The extent to which the Commerce Clause authorizes Congress to regulate and criminalize what private individuals do (or refuse to do) remains a matter of hot contestation. Just read the Supreme Court's recent decision on the constitutionality of the Affordable Care Act of 2010 (ACA), National Federal of Independent Business v. Sebelius, 567 U.S. 519 (2012). In that case, the Court held that Congress had the power to enact the individual healthcare mandate under its taxing authority; five Justices, however, concluded that the mandate could *not* be sustained under the Commerce Clause. The concern of those who worry about cases like *Alderman* is that the constitutional scrutiny courts give to wholesale extensions of federal authority over classes of activities—as occurred in *Lopez*, *Raich*, and the ACA case—gets relaxed, indeed virtually disappears, where the extension of Commerce Clause authority is accomplished by prosecutors at the retail level, with juries asked to consider the interstate commerce nexus on a case-by-case basis. Firearms defendants have not been successful in arguing that the ACA decision casts doubt on the constitutionality of federal laws

banning machine guns—see, e.g., United States v. Henry, 688 F.3d 637, 641 n.4 (9th Cir. 2012)—and banning felons from possessing weapons—see, e.g., United States v. Roszkowski, 700 F.3d 50 (1st Cir. 2012).

Does this concern have a factual basis? Note that criminal statutes in particular make case-by-case, retail power extensions a useful legislative strategy because unlike the ACA, for instance, criminal statutes are necessarily implemented one person (one defendant) at a time. Should we embrace or regret the discretionary ability that such statutes give enforcers to "make a federal case" out of conduct that is not intrinsically of federal concern?

8. Can the government satisfy an *elemental* statute's commerce nexus by showing that the conduct in a particular case implicates an area over which Congress has asserted *categorical* jurisdiction? Put differently, can proof of "categorical" jurisdiction obviate the need to show an effect on interstate commerce even though the statute of conviction is an elemental statute? A majority of the Supreme Court said "yes" in Taylor v. United States, 136 S. Ct. 2074 (2016).

The issue in *Taylor* was "what the Government must prove to satisfy the Hobbs Act's commerce element when a defendant commits a robbery that targets a marijuana dealer's drugs or drug proceeds." The defendant was that rare guy ready to mount a Commerce Clause defense, which may be summarized as: "Sure, weed may have been a target of the alleged robberies. But it was locally grown, and the government should have to prove it wasn't."

Writing for the Court (with only Justice Thomas dissenting), Justice Alito backhanded the claim:

> The case now before us requires no more than that we graft our holding in *Raich* onto the commerce element of the Hobbs Act. The Hobbs Act criminalizes robberies affecting "commerce over which the United States has jurisdiction." §1951(b)(3). Under *Raich*, the market for marijuana, including its intrastate aspects, is "commerce over which the United States has jurisdiction." It therefore follows as a simple matter of logic that a robber who affects or attempts to affect even the intrastate sale of marijuana grown within the State affects or attempts to affect commerce over which the United States has jurisdiction.

Id. at 2080. He went on to note:

> This conclusion does not make the commerce provision of the Hobbs Act superfluous. That statute, unlike the criminal provisions of the CSA, applies to forms of conduct that, even in the aggregate, may not substantially affect commerce. The Act's commerce element ensures that applications of the Act do not exceed Congress's authority. But in a case like this one, where the target of a robbery is a drug dealer, proof that the defendant's conduct in and of itself affected or threatened commerce is not needed. All that is needed is

proof that the defendant's conduct fell within a category of conduct that, in the aggregate, had the requisite effect.

Id. at 2018.

B. "COMMERCE WITH FOREIGN NATIONS"

While a great deal of ink has been spilled concerning how to apply the reach of Congress's commerce power within the boundaries of the United States, far less time has been spent considering Congress's power over foreign commerce and, in particular, on the limits Congress faces when criminalizing behavior that takes place outside the territorial limits of the United States, as in the following case. Note that the complex federalism issues that arise in the domestic context are not present in the foreign context, but that issues of both foreign policy and international law may be implicated.

United States v. Clark
435 F.3d 1100 (9th Cir. 2006)

McKEOWN, Circuit Judge:

In this appeal we are confronted with a question of first impression regarding the scope of Congress's power under the Foreign Commerce Clause. At issue is whether Congress exceeded its authority "to regulate Commerce with foreign Nations," U.S. Const. art. I, §8, cl. 3, in enacting a statute that makes it a felony for any U.S. citizen who travels in "foreign commerce," i.e. to a foreign country, to then engage in an illegal commercial sex act with a minor. 18 U.S.C. §2423(c). We hold that Congress acted within the bounds of its constitutional authority. . . .

BACKGROUND

Michael Lewis Clark, a seventy-one year old U.S. citizen and military veteran, primarily resided in Cambodia from 1998 until his extradition in 2003. He typically took annual trips back to the United States and he also maintained real estate, bank accounts, investment accounts, a driver's license, and a mailing address in this country. Following a family visit in May 2003, Clark left Seattle and flew to Cambodia via Japan, Thailand, and Malaysia. He was traveling on a business visa that he renewed on an annual basis.

Cambodian police arrested Clark after discovering him in a Phnom Penh guesthouse engaging in sex acts with two boys who were approximately ten and thirteen years old. He was charged with debauchery. The United States government received permission from the Cambodian government to take jurisdiction over Clark.

[Clark was convicted of violating 18 U.S.C. §2423(c)] of the newly-enacted Prosecutorial Remedies and Other Tools to End the Exploitation of Children Today Act of 2003 ("PROTECT Act"), Pub. L. No. 108-21, 117 Stat. 650 (2003). . . . On appeal, Clark's challenge centers on the constitutionality of [this provision, which] provides as follows:

> (c) Engaging in illicit sexual conduct in foreign places. Any United States citizen or alien admitted for permanent residence who travels in foreign commerce, and engages in any illicit sexual conduct with another person shall be fined under this title or imprisoned not more than 30 years, or both.

Before the PROTECT Act became law in 2003, §2423(b) required the government to prove that the defendant "travel[ed] in foreign commerce, or conspire[d] to do so, for the *purpose of engaging in*" specified sexual conduct with a person under eighteen years of age. The PROTECT Act replaced this single section with new subsections (b) through (g), with the new subsection (b) remaining substantively the same as the former subsection (b). Subsection (c) is an entirely new section which deletes the "for the purpose of" language. The conference report accompanying the PROTECT Act explains that Congress removed the intent requirement from §2423(c) so that "the government would only have to prove that the defendant engaged in illicit sexual conduct with a minor while in a foreign country." Consequently, for §2423(c) to apply, the two key determinations are whether the defendant "travel[ed] in foreign commerce" and "engages in any illicit sexual conduct. . . ."

ANALYSIS

Clark does not dispute that he traveled in "foreign commerce," nor does he dispute that he engaged in illicit commercial sexual conduct. The challenge he raises is to congressional authority to regulate this conduct. In addition to his Commerce Clause challenge, Clark attacks his conviction on international law, statutory construction, and Due Process grounds. In recognition of the principle that courts have a "strong duty to avoid constitutional issues that need not be resolved in order to determine the rights of the parties to the case under consideration," we begin our analysis with Clark's non-constitutional claims.

[The court first determined that the extraterritorial application of §2423(c) comported with principles of international law, because of Clark's U.S. citizenship.] . . .

III. NO DUE PROCESS VIOLATION

The next question is whether extraterritorial application of §2423(c) violates the Due Process Clause of the Fifth Amendment because there is an insufficient nexus between Clark's conduct and the United States. We hold that, based on Clark's U.S. citizenship, application of §2423(c) to his extraterritorial conduct is neither "arbitrary [n]or fundamentally unfair." Davis v. United States, 905 F.2d 245, 249 (9th Cir. 1990).

Clark is correct that to comply with the Due Process Clause of the Fifth Amendment, extraterritorial application of federal criminal statutes requires the government to demonstrate a sufficient nexus between the defendant and the United States "so that such application would not be arbitrary or fundamentally unfair." Davis, 905 F.2d at 248-49. Indeed, "even resort to the Commerce Clause can[not] defy the standards of due process." Sec'y of Agriculture v. Central Roig Refining Co., 338 U.S. 604, 616 (1950).

In Blackmer v. United States, 284 U.S. 421 (1932), the Supreme Court explained that the extraterritorial application of U.S. law to its citizens abroad did not violate the Fifth Amendment. . . . By virtue of the obligations of citizenship, the United States retained its authority over him, and he was bound by its laws made applicable to him in a foreign country. Id. at 436. This longstanding principle that citizenship alone is sufficient to satisfy Due Process concerns still has force. . . .

IV. CONGRESS'S FOREIGN COMMERCE CLAUSE POWER EXTENDS TO REGULATING COMMERCIAL SEX ACTS ABROAD

In considering whether Congress exceeded its power under the Foreign Commerce Clause in enacting §2423(c), we ground our analysis in the fundamental principle that "[i]t is an essential attribute of [Congress's power over foreign commerce] that it is exclusive and plenary." Bd. of Trustees of Univ. of Ill. v. United States, 289 U.S. 48 (1933). We are further mindful of the Supreme Court's caution that "[d]ue respect for the decisions of a coordinate branch of Government demands that we invalidate a congressional enactment only upon a plain showing that Congress has exceeded its constitutional bounds." United States v. Morrison, 529 U.S. 598, 607 (2000). No plain showing has been made here. In light of Congress's sweeping powers over foreign commerce, we conclude that Congress acted within its constitutional bounds in criminalizing commercial sex acts committed by U.S. citizens who travel abroad in foreign commerce.

At the outset, we highlight that §2423(c) contemplates two types of "illicit sexual conduct": non-commercial and commercial. Clark's conduct falls squarely under the second prong of the definition, which criminalizes "any commercial sex act . . . with a person under 18 years of age." 18 U.S.C. §2423(f)(2). In view of this factual posture, we abide by the rule that courts have a "strong duty to avoid constitutional issues that need not be resolved in order to determine the rights of the parties to the case under consideration," and limit our holding to §2423(c)'s regulation of commercial sex acts.

A. *The Commerce Clause: Structure and History*

Chief Justice Marshall observed long ago that "[t]he objects, to which the power of regulating commerce might be directed, are divided into three distinct classes—foreign nations, the several states, and Indian Tribes. When forming this article, the convention considered them as entirely distinct." Cherokee Nation v. Georgia, 30 U.S. 1, 18 (1831). Looking to the text, the single clause indeed embodies three subclauses for which distinct prepositional language is used: "To regulate Commerce with foreign Nations, and among the several States, and with the Indian Tribes." U.S. Const. art. I, §8, cl. 3.

Among legal scholars there has been considerable debate over the intrasentence unity—or disunity, as the case may be—of the three sub-clauses, considering that they share the common language "[t]o regulate Commerce." Some commentators take the view that Congress's powers over commerce with foreign nations and Indian tribes are broader than over interstate commerce.

Other scholars maintain that Congress has coextensive powers under the Commerce Clause's subdivisions. Despite the long-running lively debate among scholars, no definitive view emerges regarding the relationship among the three subclauses. Nonetheless, Supreme Court precedent points to the conclusion that the Foreign Commerce Clause *is* different than the Interstate Commerce Clause.

Regardless of how separate the three subclauses may be in theory, the reality is that they have been subject to markedly divergent treatment by the courts. This approach is not surprising given the considerably differ-ent interests at stake when Congress regulates in the various arenas. Most notably, regardless of whether the subject matter is drugs, gender-moti-vated violence, or gun possession, a prominent theme runs throughout the interstate commerce cases: concern for state sovereignty and federal-ism. On the other hand, "[t]he principle of duality in our system of gov-ernment does not touch the authority of the Congress in the regulation of foreign commerce." This distinction provides a crucial touchstone in applying the Foreign Commerce Clause, for which Congress's authority to regulate has not been defined with the precision set forth by *Lopez* and *Morrison* in the interstate context. . . .

As with the Indian Commerce Clause, the Foreign Commerce Clause has followed its own distinct evolutionary path. Born largely from a desire for uniform rules governing commercial relations with foreign countries, the Supreme Court has read the Foreign Commerce Clause as granting Congress sweeping powers. This view was laid down nearly two centuries ago when Chief Justice Marshall stated that "[i]t has, we believe, been universally admitted, that [the words of the Commerce Clause] comprehend every species of commercial intercourse between the United States and foreign nations." Gibbons v. Ogden, 22 U.S. (9 Wheat) 1, 193 (1824).

The Court has been unwavering in reading Congress's power over foreign commerce broadly. There is no counterpart to *Lopez* or *Morrison* in the foreign commerce realm that would signal a retreat from the Court's expansive reading of the Foreign Commerce Clause. In fact, the Supreme Court has never struck down an act of Congress as exceeding its powers to regulate foreign commerce.

Federalism and state sovereignty concerns do not restrict Congress's power over foreign commerce, and the need for federal uniformity "is no less paramount" in assessing the so-called "dormant" implications of congressional power under the Foreign Commerce Clause. By contrast, under the dormant Interstate Commerce Clause, "reconciliation of the conflicting claims of state and national power is to be attained only by some appraisal and accommodation of the competing demands of the state and national interests involved."

Clark's case illustrates the predominance of national interests and the absence of state sovereignty concerns in Foreign Commerce Clause jurisprudence. No state has voiced an interest in the proceedings nor is there an indication of any state interest at stake in determining the constitutionality of §2423(c). Because this case is divorced from the common federal/state interplay seen in the Interstate Commerce Clause cases, we find ourselves in sparsely charted waters. We thus look to the text of §2423(c) to discern whether it has a constitutionally tenable nexus with foreign commerce.

B. Section 2423(c)'s Regulation of Commercial Sex Acts Is a Valid Exercise of Congress's Foreign Commerce Clause Powers

Taking a page from *Raich*, we review the statute under the traditional rational basis standard. The question we pose is whether the statute bears a rational relationship to Congress's authority under the Foreign Commerce Clause.

Although it is important to view the statute as a whole, parsing its elements illustrates why the statute fairly relates to foreign commerce. The elements that the government must prove under §2423(c)'s commercial sex acts prong are straightforward. First, the defendant must "travel[]" in foreign commerce." 18 U.S.C. §2423(c). Second, the defendant must "engage[] in any illicit sexual conduct with another person," id., which in this case contemplates "any commercial sex act . . . with a person under 18 years of age." 18 U.S.C. §2423(f)(2). We hold that §2423(c)'s combination of requiring travel in foreign commerce, coupled with engagement in a commercial transaction while abroad, implicates foreign commerce to a constitutionally adequate degree.

Beginning with the first element, the phrase "travels in foreign commerce" unequivocally establishes that Congress specifically invoked the Foreign Commerce Clause. The defendant must therefore have moved in foreign commerce at some point to trigger the statute. In Clark's case, he traveled from the United States to Cambodia.

"Foreign commerce" has been defined broadly for purposes of Title 18 of the U.S. Code, with the statutory definition reading, in full: "The term 'foreign commerce,' as used in this title, includes commerce with a foreign country." 18 U.S.C. §10. Admittedly, this definition is not particularly helpful given its rearrangement of the words being defined in the definition itself. Courts have understandably taken the broad wording to have an expansive reach. We likewise see no basis on which to impose a constrained reading of "foreign commerce" under §2423(c). Clark got on a plane in the United States and journeyed to Cambodia. This act is sufficient to satisfy the "travels in foreign commerce" element of §2423(c).

Once in Cambodia, the second element of §2423(c) was also met, namely, "engage[ment] in any illicit sexual conduct with another person," 18 U.S.C. §2423(c), which in this case was commercial sex under §2423(f)(2). As the Supreme Court recognized centuries ago, the Commerce Clause "comprehend[s] every species of commercial intercourse between the United States and foreign nations." Gibbons, 22 U.S. at 193. Section 2423(c) regulates a pernicious "species of commercial intercourse": commercial sex acts with minors.

The statute expressly includes an economic component by defining "illicit sexual conduct," in pertinent part, as "any commercial sex act . . . with a person under 18 years of age." 18 U.S.C. §2423(f)(2). "Commercial sex act" is defined as "any sex act, on account of which anything of value is given to or received by any person." 18 U.S.C. §1591(c)(1). Thus, in the most sterile terms, the statute covers the situation where a U.S. citizen engages in a commercial transaction through which money is exchanged for sex acts.

The essential economic character of the commercial sex acts regulated by §2423(c) stands in contrast to the non-economic activities regulated by the statutes at issue in Lopez and Morrison. . . . Like the statute regulating illicit drugs at issue in Raich, the activity regulated by the commercial sex prong of §2423(c) is "quintessentially economic,"[17] 545 U.S. at 26, and thus falls within foreign trade and commerce.[18]

As in *Raich*, the fact that §2423(c) has a criminal as well as an economic component does not put it beyond Congress's reach under the Foreign Commerce Clause. Indeed, §2423(c) is far from unique in using the Foreign Commerce Clause to regulate crimes with an economic facet. See, e.g., United States v. Kay, 359 F.3d 738, 741 (5th Cir. 2004) (describing "particular instrumentalities of interstate and foreign commerce that defendants used or caused to be used in carrying out the purported bribery" in violation of the Foreign Corrupt Practices Act); United States v. Hsu, 155 F.3d 189, 195-96 (3d Cir. 1998) (discussing statute enacted as part of the Economic Espionage Act of 1996 that criminalizes the theft of trade secrets related to products "produced for or placed in interstate or foreign commerce"); United States v. Gertz, 249 F.2d 662, 666-67 (9th Cir. 1957) (explaining that statute criminalizing the forging or counterfeiting of foreign currency is based on the Foreign Commerce Clause).

The combination of Clark's travel in foreign commerce and his conduct of an illicit commercial sex act in Cambodia shortly thereafter puts the statute squarely within Congress's Foreign Commerce Clause authority. In reaching this conclusion, we view the Foreign Commerce Clause independently from its domestic brethren. . . .

At times, forcing foreign commerce cases into the domestic commerce rubric is a bit like one of the stepsisters trying to don Cinderella's glass slipper; nonetheless, there is a good argument that, as found by the district court, §2423(c) can also be viewed as a valid regulation of the "channels of commerce." Our previous decisions have recognized that Congress legitimately exercises its authority to regulate the channels of commerce where a crime committed on foreign soil is necessarily tied to travel in foreign commerce, even where the actual use of the channels has ceased. . . .

In sum, Clark has failed to demonstrate "a plain showing that Congress . . . exceeded its constitutional bounds," *Morrison*, 529 U.S. at 607, in enacting §§2423(c) and (f)(2). Traveling to a foreign country and paying a child to engage in sex acts are indispensable ingredients of the crime to which Clark pled guilty. The fact that §§2423(c) and (f)(2) meld these economic and criminal components into a single statute does not

---

17. The evolving definition of "economics" presents a slight quirk to the analysis. Although the definition in the 1966 Webster's Third New International Dictionary cited by the Supreme Court in *Raich* only refers to "the production, distribution, and consumption of commodities," more recent versions of Webster's have added "services" to the definition. See, e.g., Merriam Webster's Collegiate Dictionary 364 (10th ed. 1993) (defining "economics" as the social science concerned with "the production, distribution, and consumption of goods and services"); Merriam-Webster Online Dictionary, www.m-w.com (same).

18. It is now universally acknowledged that foreign trade or commerce includes both goods and services. (Citations omitted).

put the conduct beyond Congress's reach under the Foreign Commerce Clause. The rational nexus requirement is met to a constitutionally sufficient degree. Congress did not exceed its power "to regulate Commerce with foreign Nations," U.S. Const. art. I, §8, cl. 3, in criminalizing commercial sex acts with minors committed by U.S. citizens abroad.

FERGUSON, Circuit Judge, dissenting:

The Constitution cannot be interpreted according to the principle that the end justifies the means. The sexual abuse of children abroad is despicable, but we should not, and need not, refashion our Constitution to address it. . . .

The Constitution authorizes Congress "[t]o regulate Commerce with foreign Nations." [U.S. Const.] art. I, §8, cl. 3. The activity regulated by 18 U.S.C. §2423(c), illicit sexual conduct, does not in any sense of the phrase relate to commerce *with foreign nations*. Rather, §2423(c) is a criminal statute that punishes private conduct fundamentally divorced from foreign commerce. Article I, section 8, clause 3, while giving Congress broad authority over our commercial relations with other nations, is not a grant of international police power. I respectfully dissent from the majority's assertion that the Commerce Clause authorizes Congress to regulate an activity with a bare economic component, as long as that activity occurs subsequent to some form of international travel. I also note that the conduct in this case will not go unpunished, as the reasonable course of action remains of recognizing Cambodia's authority to prosecute Clark under its own criminal laws. . . .

EXTRATERRITORIAL JURISDICTION: CONSTITUTIONAL SOURCES & LIMITATIONS

1. In part because of new prosecutorial priorities, the Foreign Commerce Clause is fast emerging as a new focal point for judicial inquiries into the breadth of federal criminal enforcement authority. For two plausible but very different interpretations of the Clause, see Anthony J. Colangelo, The Foreign Commerce Clause, 96 Va. L. Rev. 949 (2010); Scott Sullivan, The Future of the Foreign Commerce Clause, 83 Fordham L. Rev. 1955 (2015). In spite of this trend, however, the Supreme Court has not yet felt the need to weigh in on the outer bounds of the Foreign Commerce Clause. Consider Justice Thomas's admonishment in a recent dissent from denial of certiorari that the Court should have taken the case to "reaffirm that our Federal Government is one of limited and enumerated powers, not the world's lawgiver." United States v. Baston, 818 F.3d 651 (11th Cir. 2016), cert. denied, 137 S. Ct. 850 (2017).

A Jamaican citizen, Baston was convicted in a Florida district court of violating a federal anti-sex trafficking statute and ordered to pay restitution to his victim. His conviction arose out of conduct in which he engaged on a previous trip to Australia, during which he coerced his Australian victim into prostitution. He challenged his restitution order on the theory that the statute pursuant to which it was levied exceeds Congress's jurisdiction under the FCC. The Eleventh Circuit affirmed the order. In his dissent from denial of certiorari, Justice Thomas warned:

> Taken to the limits of its logic, the consequences of the Court of Appeals' reasoning are startling. The Foreign Commerce Clause would permit Congress to regulate any economic activity anywhere in the world, so long as Congress had a rational basis to conclude that the activity has a substantial effect on commerce between this Nation and any other. Congress would be able not only to criminalize prostitution in Australia, but also to regulate working conditions in factories in China, pollution from power-plants in India, or agricultural methods on farms in France. I am confident that whatever the correct interpretation of the foreign commerce power may be, it does not confer upon Congress a virtually plenary power over global economic activity.

What do you think? Are there institutional constraints that should make us more worried about increasing federal legislative and enforcement forays in this transnational context? Less worried?

2. What if a defendant is charged with committing a *non*-commercial sex act with a minor in Cambodia under the statute at issue in *Clark*? *Clark* did not resolve whether the Foreign Commerce Clause justifies the non-commercial acts prong of §2423(c), although presumably a non-commercial act would have a weaker connection to "commerce." The non-commercial nature of illicit sexual conduct has not, however, proven a barrier to prosecutions under 18 U.S.C. §2423(c).

One way courts have dealt with this issue is to invoke elemental jurisdiction. For example, in United States v. Pendleton, 658 F.3d 299 (3d Cir. 2011), the defendant—who previously had served prison time in New Jersey and Latvia for sex crimes against children—flew from New York to Hamburg, Germany, where, six months later, he sexually molested a 15-year-old. Arrested by German authorities, he served 19 months in a German prison and was arrested by federal authorities on his return to the United States. Upholding his conviction, the Third Circuit declined to adopt the Ninth Circuit's reasoning in *Clark*, but found §2423(c) to pass muster under more restrictive *Lopez/Morrison* analysis, since its "jurisdictional element has an 'express connection' to the channels of foreign commerce." Id. at 311 (citing *Morrison*, 529 U.S. at 612). Referring to precedents upholding provisions of the Sex Offender Registration and Notification Act (SORNA) that make it illegal for a sex offender to fail to register after traveling in interstate commerce, the Third Circuit reasoned:

Congress enacted §2423(c) to regulate persons who use the channels of commerce to circumvent local laws that criminalize child abuse and molestation. And just as Congress may cast a wide net to stop sex offenders from traveling in interstate commerce to evade state registration requirements, so too may it attempt to prevent sex tourists from using the channels of foreign commerce to abuse children.

658 F.3d at 311.

Look for more opinions along these lines as the Justice Department intensifies its focus on foreign sex tourism. See, e.g., United States v. Flath, 845 F. Supp. 2d 951 (E.D. Wis. 2012) (following *Pendleton*). Moreover, stopping for a while doesn't necessarily end someone's "travel in foreign commerce." See United States v. Schmidt, 845 F.3d 153 (4th Cir. 2017) (upholding conviction, based on Cambodian conduct, of defendant who fled the United States for the Philippines to avoid arrest for sexual misconduct with a minor, then, eighteen months later, after his arrest by Philippine authorities for molesting children, fled to Cambodia, where he continued molesting young boys).

3. The Foreign Commerce Clause is not the only source of legislative authority to criminalize conduct abroad. Recall, for example, that even as the Ninth Circuit upheld the commercial sex prong of §2423(c) as a valid exercise of congressional power under the Foreign Commerce Clause, it "acknowledge[d] that Congress's plenary authority over foreign affairs may also provide a sufficient basis for §2423(c)." *Clark*, 435 F.3d at 1109 n.14. Another way courts go is the Treaty Power route. In United States v. Frank, 486 F. Supp. 2d 1353 (S.D. Fla. 2007), which also involved an American citizen charged with improper commercial sex acts with minors in Cambodia, the district court went in the opposite direction to reach the same result. Asserting that "Congress had the authority to enact §2423(c) under the Necessary and Proper Clause to implement a treaty which the Senate had ratified," the district court in *Frank* declined to rule on whether the statute is also valid under the Foreign Commerce Clause. 486 F. Supp. 2d at 1355.

a. A court relying on the Necessary and Proper Clause, or any constitutional provision related to the Treaty Power, would not need to change its analysis based on whether a sex act was commercial. And once conduct—however local—becomes a fit subject for an international treaty, restraints on federal criminal jurisdiction largely seem to melt away. For one, there are few, if any, subject matter limitations on the political branches' concurrent treaty powers. Judge Walker's opinion in United States v. Lue, 134 F.3d 79 (2d Cir. 1997), illustrates this point well. *Lue* involved a prosecution under the Hostage Taking Act, passed to effectuate the International Convention Against the Taking of Hostages, Dec. 18, 1979, T.I.A.S. No. 11,081. One issue in the case was whether the executive could properly enter into the Treaty. Noting the scant limitations on that authority, Judge Walker determined it could:

In Asakura [v. City of Seattle, 265 U.S. 332 (1924)], the Court held that the executive's treaty power "extend[s] to all *proper subjects* of negotiation between our government and other nations." *Asakura*, 265 U.S. at 341. Invoking this standard simply begs the question: What is a "proper subject" of negotiation between governments? Admittedly, there must be certain outer limits, as yet undefined, beyond which the executive's treaty power is constitutionally invalid. See, e.g., Laurence H. Tribe, Taking Text and Structure Seriously: Reflections on Free-Form Method in Constitutional Interpretation, 108 Harv. L. Rev. 1221, 1261 n.133 (1995) (noting that the Treaty Power is subject to certain structural limitations and offering as an example of such limitations: "The President and the Senate could not . . . create a fully operating national health care system in the United States by treaty with Canada. . . ."); Louis Henkin, Foreign Affairs and the United States Constitution, 184-85, 196-98 (2d ed. 1996). But within such generous limits, it is not the province of the judiciary to impinge upon the Executive's prerogative in matters pertaining to foreign affairs.

134 F.3d at 83.

    b. This is not to say, however, that centering an extraterritorial criminal jurisdiction statute on the Treaty Power immunizes such legislation from invalidation. For one, in order to be a valid exercise of Congress's power under the Necessary and Proper Clause, legislation must be rationally related to the treaty it was enacted to implement. Furthermore, as the Supreme Court held in Bond v. United States, 564 U.S. 211 (2011), a criminal defendant has standing to complain that a treaty-based enactment is an unconstitutional intrusion into state affairs. Carol Anne Bond was charged under 18 U.S.C. §229, a statute that criminalizes chemical weapon use pursuant to the "Convention on the Prohibition of the Development, Production, Stockpiling and Use of Chemical Weapons and on Their Destruction," after she spread caustic substances all around the home of her husband's lover "causing. . . a minor thumb burn readily treated by rinsing with water." Bond v. United States, 134 S. Ct. 2077, 2083 (2014) (hereafter *Bond II*). In Bond's first trip to the Supreme Court, the Court determined that the defendant had standing to complain that the implementing statute violated the Tenth Amendment. Bond v. United States, 564 U.S. 211 (2011) (*Bond I*).

    The case made a second appearance before the Supreme Court, addressing the merits of her claim. That time, Chief Justice Roberts framed the question before the Court as whether the application of a chemical weapons statute to "an amateur attempt by a jilted wife to injure her husband's lover" impermissibly intruded on the States' Tenth Amendment right to regulate local criminal conduct and thus was in excess of Congress's power under the Necessary and Proper Clause. The case seemed to pose fundamental constitutional questions that have kicked about for some time: What if any limits does Congress face when it legislates to implement an international treaty? Given the lack of clear subject matter constraints on international agreements, can Congress boldly plunge into areas into which it lacks explicit enumerated power simply because licensed by a Treaty?

Writing for the Court, however, Chief Justice Roberts bracketed these larger issues and instead focused not on the scope of the Convention, but on the scope of §229, which he reasoned "must be read consistent with principles of federalism inherent in our constitutional structure." *Bond II*, 134 S. Ct. at 2088. For the statute did indeed have an extraordinarily expansive definition of what constituted the use of a "chemical weapon." Invoking cases like *Bass* (discussed above), Chief Justice Roberts explained:

> Because our constitutional structure leaves local criminal activity primarily to the States, we have generally declined to read federal law as intruding on that responsibility, unless Congress has clearly indicated that the law should have such reach. The Chemical Weapons Convention Implementation Act contains no such clear indication, and we accordingly conclude that it does not cover the unremarkable local offense at issue here.

Id. at 2083.

He concluded: "The global need to prevent chemical warfare does not require the Federal Government to reach into the kitchen cupboard, or to treat a local assault with a chemical irritant as the deployment of a chemical ✳ weapon. There is no reason to suppose that Congress—in implementing the Convention on Chemical Weapons—thought otherwise." Id. at 2093.

Bond II is a quiet reminder of how positions that a U.S. Attorney's Office takes in trial court—usually without consultation with the Solicitor General's Office—can limit the arguments that the Solicitor General's Office makes to defend a conviction in the Supreme Court. In the district court, the *Bond* prosecutors "expressly disclaimed the Commerce Clause as a basis for Congress's power to approve the Act." 681 F.3d 149, 151 n.1 (2012)—a move that led both the Third Circuit and the Supreme Court to focus only on the Necessary and Proper and Treaty Power justifications for the Chemical Weapons statute. Did the Government make a mistake when it disclaimed reliance on the Commerce Clause?

c. While the Court held that allowing Bond's prosecution under the Chemical Weapon statute would "mark a dramatic departure from that constitutional structure and a serious reallocation of criminal law enforcement authority between the Federal Government and the States," 134 S. Ct. at 2091, it found no need to clarify which uses of the capacious statute would be consistent with congressional intent. Lower courts have had to do that, however. In United States v. Fries, 781 F.3d 1137 (9th Cir. 2015), the Ninth Circuit went out on a limb and held that the defendant's "use of a chlorine bomb produced a dense chlorine gas cloud estimated to have been '1,000 feet long, 100 feet high, and roughly 200 feet deep' that injured several people including first responders, and required the evacuation of an entire neighborhood and implementation of HAZMAT procedures" was easily distinguished from "the purely local crime at issue in *Bond*."

Finding the conduct covered by the statute required the Appeals Court to confront the constitutional question of whether §229 was a valid exercise of Congress's powers under the Necessary and Proper Clause and Treaty Power. Following the analysis of the lower court in *Bond*, the court found that it indeed was. See also United States v. Levenderis, 806 F.3d 390 (6th Cir. 2015) (holding that where defendant manufactured ricin and intended to use it "as part of an elaborate suicide plot in which he would light his house on fire and hang bottles of ricin from the entrances to his home to prevent firefighters from entering to put out the fire," *Bond II* was distinguishable and prosecuting under a treaty-implementing biological toxin statute was proper). To what extent are concerns about the sweep of congressional treaty-implementing authority answered by this case-by-case approach?

4. Criminal defendants sometimes challenge Congress's exercise of its extraterritorial jurisdiction on Fifth Amendment Due Process grounds. Stating the question as whether jurisdiction would be "arbitrary or fundamentally unfair," the *Clark* court, for example, upheld Clark's prosecution, finding that as a United States citizen Clark should have been aware that he is subject to U.S. law.

In what situations would jurisdiction over a *foreign national* who has never set foot in the United States be justified under this standard? Note that §2423(a), unlike §2423(c), is not limited to "United States citizen[s] or alien[s] admitted for permanent residence"; without any stated limitation as to the citizenship status of those bound by the prohibition, §2423(a) prohibits transporting a minor in interstate or foreign commerce for the purpose of prostitution.

Conversely, could Congress enact the domestic equivalent of §2423(c), making it a crime to travel in interstate commerce and engage in sex with a minor? Note that the statute as written only applies to international travel. Given the lack of any *mens rea* requirement, the domestic equivalent would essentially make it a federal crime to engage in sex with a minor if one has ever crossed a state line! Should the absurd implications of this hypothetical domestic analogue call into question the integrity of §2423(c) itself? Note that the older provision, §2423(b), for all its breadth, is functionally equivalent to the Mann Act (discussed above), which criminalizes transporting persons across state lines with intent to engage in prostitution.

In United States v. Weingarten, 632 F.3d 60 (2d Cir. 2011), the Second Circuit explicitly limited the territorial reach of §2423(b). The court's reasoning apparently applies not only to the other sections of §2423, but also to the extraterritorial application of other "transportation" crimes. In *Weingarten*, one of the counts of conviction was based on the defendant's travel from Belgium to Israel, where he engaged in sexual abuse of a minor. In reversing this conviction, the court explained that "[a]lthough we hold that §2423(b) is applicable to conduct occurring outside the United States," jurisdiction under the statute "does not extend to travel occurring wholly between foreign nations and without any territorial nexus to the United States." This holding, the court noted, "appropriately avoids the necessity of addressing whether such an exercise of congressional power would comport with the Constitution." Id. at 70-71.

5. Defendants also invoke international law to challenge Congress's extraterritorial jurisdiction. Recall, for example, that in addition to the previously discussed constitutional claims, the *Clark* court considered whether jurisdiction was consistent with international law. The court said yes, holding that because Clark was a U.S. citizen, jurisdiction was proper under the "nationality principle." Similarly, in United States v. Frank, 599 F.3d 1221 (11th Cir. 2010), the court of appeals held that the extraterritorial application of 18 U.S.C. §2251A(b) (prohibiting taking custody of a minor knowing that "the minor will be portrayed in a visual depiction engaging in . . . sexually explicit conduct") was proper under this principle of international law because Frank was a U.S. citizen.

Suppose, however, that the court in any of these cases had come to a different conclusion—that jurisdiction was not proper under international law. What would the remedy be? Typically, it is understood that international law does not bind Congress or the courts. Although courts will often consider whether applying jurisdiction comports with international law, and will avoid interpretations of statutes that violate international law, Murray v. The Schooner Charming Betsy, 6 U.S. 64 (1804), they ultimately must give effect to a statute even if it violates international law. See United States v. Yousef, 327 F.3d 56, 86 (2d Cir. 2003); see also United States v. Davis, 905 F.2d 245, 248 n.1 (9th Cir. 1990) ("International law principles, standing on their own, do not create substantive rights or affirmative defenses for litigants in United States courts"). In any event, as several of these cases note, it is unlikely that a prosecution that violated international law would pass muster under the Due Process Clause.

In Chapter 9, we will return to the constitutional basis for extraterritorial jurisdiction (and related questions involving due process and international law) in the context of the Maritime Drug Law Enforcement Act of 1980, which provides for extraterritorial criminal jurisdiction over narcotics trafficking aboard vessels in international waters—even when the vessel and its owners are foreign and the trafficking occurs between two foreign countries. The Act arguably pushes extraterritorial jurisdiction to the limits of constitutional and international law. Here, as elsewhere throughout this book, you will see that such constitutional and international law concerns can affect the terms of federal criminal statutes, the interpretation of those statutes by prosecutors and courts, and federal law enforcement strategies.

3 | The Separation of Powers: Interpreting Federal Criminal Statutes

American criminal law, state and federal, is a statutory field. There are no common-law crimes in the United States; judges lack the authority to create or recognize new offenses at the suggestion of enterprising prosecutors. To be sure, judges must construe the statutes they apply, thereby making law interstitially. But that power operates around the edges; the key actors in defining crime are, and have long been, legislators.

The foregoing is the conventional wisdom, but it isn't quite right. The truth is both more complex and more interesting. Begin with state law. Early state criminal codes were more like Restatements than codes—nineteenth-century state legislators codified the common law of crimes, often using language straight out of Book 4 of Blackstone's Commentaries. Long after codification, judges in many states continued to treat criminal law much the way they treated other common-law fields, and consequently enjoyed significant leeway in interpreting and applying criminal statutes. As a practical matter, judges—not state legislators—defined state crimes. Over the course of the twentieth century (especially the century's latter half), statutes became much more prominent in state cases, probably because core state-law crimes have been the subject of repeated legislation. Today, crimes like rape, robbery, and burglary are not defined in three or four cursory lines, as in Blackstone. Instead, the norm is a long list of multiple overlapping offenses, with detailed definitions of contested terms. Judges have less room to make law; on a host of subjects, legislators have beaten them to the punch. While state criminal law began as a species of common law and remained so for much longer than is commonly believed, legislation now dominates the field.

Federal criminal law followed the opposite path: It began with legislation and then became more common-law-like over time. Thanks to United States v. Hudson & Goodwin, 11 U.S. 32 (1812), and its less famous but equally important successor, United States v. Bevans, 16 U.S. 336 (1818), the common law of crimes never applied in federal court. So federal criminal statutes did not codify preexisting common-law crimes; instead, federal statutes established *new* crimes. Congress, not courts, defined the field's subject matter.

Often, though, federal criminal legislation left large gaps—gaps that federal judges felt compelled, or at least permitted, to fill. The filling (or not) of those gaps is the subject of this chapter. There are two key sets of questions: First, under what circumstances may federal judges make common law today? That is, how closely must judges stick to the text of federal criminal statutes? Second, what is the status of existing common-law doctrines—for example, the doctrines that define most federal defenses? On what basis do federal judges—who enjoy lifetime appointments—get to devise doctrines that limit the reach of the federal criminal offenses defined by the elected legislature? The separation of powers is a small factor in state criminal law. Yet, in federal criminal law, it looms large.

The remainder of the chapter is divided into four sections. The first is brief. It deals with the longstanding ban on federal common-law crimes; *Hudson & Goodwin*, in which the Supreme Court held that federal courts have no inherent authority to define new crimes, is the only excerpted case. Section B addresses the definition of criminal conduct; the main case is *Brogan*, a 1998 decision rejecting a judicially developed exception to federal liability for false statements. Section C looks at the definition of criminal defenses; the main case is a 2006 decision in which the Justices accepted common-law defenses to federal crimes, but could not agree why they did so. Section D examines an area of law in which federal judges have been especially open to common lawmaking: the definition of criminal intent. In the late twentieth century, federal judges crafted—in the teeth of congressional resistance—a remarkably broad excuse for legal ignorance that was founded on neither common-law precedent nor clear statutory direction. The boundaries of that excuse have since been narrowed, but it remains one of the most doctrinally distinctive characteristics of federal criminal law.

As you read these cases, keep the following questions in mind: What is a judge's proper role in deciding issues of this sort? How closely should judges stick to the text of federal criminal statutes? What limits, if any, should be read into laws that on their face sweep in a variety of common behaviors? Where are the sources of federal criminal law?

A.   THE BAN ON COMMON-LAW CRIMES

United States v. Hudson & Goodwin
11 U.S. 32 (1812)

[Editors' Note: Barzillai Hudson and George Goodwin were Federalist newspaper editors who had accused then-President Thomas Jefferson of bribing Napoleon's government to arrange a favorable treaty with Spain (which, at the time, was ruled by a puppet government under Napoleon's control). Urged on by a federal judge who was a member of Jefferson's Republican party, a federal grand jury in Connecticut indicted Hudson and Goodwin for seditious libel: meaning, basically, unfair criticism of government officials. In large measure, the prosecution was political payback. Connecticut had been under Federalist control for most of the nation's history to this point, and the state's Federalists had prosecuted a number of Republican newspapermen and pamphleteers for seditious libel for criticizing Federalist officials. When the Republicans attained power, they were eager to return the favor.

Since the Sedition Act of 1798 had been repealed, seditious libel prosecutions in federal court had only one possible legal basis: the common law of crimes. Federalist judges had regularly held that the common law applied in federal court as in state court; Presidents Jefferson and Madison, along with the Republican party they led, viewed those decisions as illegitimate. By the time *Hudson & Goodwin* reached the Supreme Court, the Court had a Republican majority, which delivered a decidedly Republican opinion on the limits of federal judicial power.]

[T]he following opinion was delivered . . . by JOHNSON, J.

The only question which this case presents is, whether the Circuit Courts* of the United States can exercise a common law jurisdiction in criminal cases. . . .

Although this question is brought up now for the first time to be decided by this Court, we consider it as having been long since settled in public opinion. In no other case for many years has this jurisdiction been asserted; and the general acquiescence of legal men shews the prevalence of opinion in favor of the negative of the proposition.

The course of reasoning which leads to this conclusion is simple, obvious, and admits of but little illustration. The powers of the general Government are made up of concessions from the several states—whatever is not expressly given to the former, the latter expressly reserve. The judicial power of the United States is a constituent part of those concessions—that power is to be exercised by Courts organized for the purpose, and brought into existence by an effort of the legislative power of the Union. Of all Courts which the United States may, under their general powers, constitute, one only, the Supreme Court, possesses jurisdiction derived immediately from the constitution, and of which the legislative power cannot deprive it. All other Courts created by the general Government possess no jurisdiction but what is given them by the power that creates them, and can be vested with none but what the power ceded to the general Government will authorize them to confer.

---

* [Editors' Note: Federal trial courts at this time were called Circuit Courts.]

It is not necessary to inquire whether the general Government, in any and what extent, possesses the power of conferring on its Courts a jurisdiction in cases similar to the present; it is enough that such jurisdiction has not been conferred by any legislative act. . . .

The only ground on which it has ever been contended that this jurisdiction could be maintained is, that, upon the formation of any political body, an implied power to preserve its own existence and promote the end and object of its creation, necessarily results to it. But, without examining how far this consideration is applicable to the peculiar character of our constitution, it may be remarked that it is a principle by no means peculiar to the common law. It is coeval, probably, with the first formation of a limited Government; belongs to a system of universal law, and may as well support the assumption of many other powers as those more peculiarly acknowledged by the common law of England.

But if admitted as applicable to the state of things in this country, the consequence would not result from it which is here contended for. If it may communicate certain implied powers to the general Government, it would not follow that the Courts of that Government are vested with jurisdiction over any particular act done by an individual in supposed violation of the peace and dignity of the sovereign power. The legislative authority of the Union must first make an act a crime, affix a punishment to it, and declare the Court that shall have jurisdiction of the offence.

Certain implied powers must necessarily result to our Courts of justice from the nature of their institution. But jurisdiction of crimes against the state is not among those powers. To fine for contempt—imprison for contumacy—inforce the observance of order, &c. are powers which cannot be dispensed with in a Court, because they are necessary to the exercise of all others: and so far our Courts no doubt possess powers not immediately derived from statute; but all exercise of criminal jurisdiction in common law cases we are of opinion is not within their implied powers.

NOTES AND QUESTIONS

1. Bruce Ackerman portrays John Marshall as being heartbroken by *Hudson & Goodwin*—the bitterest pill Marshall had to swallow in his 34-year reign as Chief Justice. See Bruce Ackerman, The Failure of the Founding Fathers: Jefferson, Marshall, and the Rise of Presidential Democracy 233-40 (2005). Marshall would surely have dissented, Ackerman writes, save for his desire to preserve the appearance of judicial consensus.

Perhaps so. But if the pill was bitter, it went down better than might be expected, judging from the unanimous decision in United States v. Bevans, 16 U.S. (3 Wheat.) 336 (1818), which was authored by none other than Chief Justice Marshall. *Bevans* arose when a marine murdered a cook's mate while on board the U.S.S. Independence, which was then anchored in Boston Harbor. Bevans was indicted for murder in federal court. Article I, Section 8 of the Constitution expressly gives Congress the power "[t]o define and punish Piracies and Felonies committed on the high Seas," and "[t]o establish and maintain a Navy." Article III gives federal courts the power to hear "all Cases of admiralty or maritime Jurisdiction." *Hudson & Goodwin* was potentially distinguishable: No clause of the Constitution gives Congress or the federal judiciary power to hear sedition cases; on the contrary, the First Amendment appears to have taken that (arguably non-existent) power off the table. Marshall nevertheless held that, because no federal statute expressly authorized the charge, federal courts lacked power to hear the case.

Marshall invoked *Bevans* a few year later, when barring the prosecution of the American master of an American merchant ship who killed an American seaman upriver in China. United States v. Wiltberger, 18 U.S. (5 Wheat.) 76, 89 (1820) ("[T]he judicial authority is of no avail, unless there be a corresponding power in Congress; that as the judicial authority is unavailing without a legislative act, it is to the act of Congress alone we must look for the extent of the jurisdiction."). Responding to the Government's invocation of congressional intent, Marshall replied with a classic articulation of the "rule of lenity" (see *infra*):

> The rule that penal laws are to be construed strictly, is perhaps not much less old than construction itself. It is founded on the tenderness of the law for the rights of individuals; and on the plain principle that the power of punishment is vested in the legislative, not in the judicial department. It is the legislature, not the Court, which is to define a crime, and ordain its punishment.

Id. at 95.

2. When we turn to specific statutory areas, like mail fraud and extortion, you will wonder how much bite *Hudson & Goodwin* has. But the bar on federal criminal common lawmaking has consequences. Consider the law on attempts. Noting the absence of a general federal "attempt" statute, the Ninth Circuit recently highlighted the rule across Circuits:

> We have long recognized that "[t]here is no general federal 'attempt' statute. A defendant therefore can only be found guilty of an attempt to commit a federal offense if the statute defining the offense also expressly proscribes an attempt." United States v. Hopkins, 703 F.2d 1102, 1104 (9th Cir. 1983); see also United States v. Joe, 452 F.2d 653, 654 (10th Cir. 1972) ("[I]t is well settled that the only attempts to commit crimes which are made Federal crimes are those specifically so proscribed by Federal law."); United States v. Padilla, 374 F.2d 782, 787 n.7 (2d Cir. 1967) ("[U]nlike many state criminal codes, federal criminal statutes contain no general attempt provision. An attempt to commit

a federal crime is punishable only where the section defining the crime specifically includes an attempt within its proscription."

United States v. Chi Tong Kuok, 671 F.3d 931, 941 (9th Cir. 2012) (vacating conviction for attempting to cause an export of defense articles without a license).

3. Taken together, *Hudson & Goodwin* and *Bevans* ensured that federal
criminal law would look very different from its state-law counterparts. These
cases held that the ordinary crimes that were (and are) the staples of state-
court criminal dockets were not federal crimes even when committed by
or against federal officials or federal property. At least not unless Congress
says so—and for a long time, Congress *didn't* say so. When John F. Kennedy
was assassinated in 1963, the Dallas police ran the initial investigation
because, incredibly, no federal crime had been committed; the murder of
the President of the United States was a state-law offense. By the time John
Hinckley shot Ronald Reagan, it was a different story. See 18 U.S.C. §1751.

So instead of murder, rape, robbery, and burglary, federal prosecution focused on different kinds of crimes: criminal violations of ex-slaves'
civil rights, interstate transportation of lottery tickets, Mann Act violations,
Prohibition cases, mail fraud cases, and so on. These crimes often had no
clear counterparts at common law; where they did, the law was still developing, still in flux. While state judges construed state criminal statutes according to the principles expounded by Blackstone, Coke, and Hale, federal
judges had to craft different principles. This often led to even more extensive
judicial lawmaking than in state cases. Call it *Hudson & Goodwin*'s revenge:
Federal courts wound up exercising more power than if the field had been
a part of the common law from the beginning, as John Marshall—the great
defender of federal judicial power—allegedly wanted.

4. For one famous example of this dynamic in action, see Durland v.
United States, 161 U.S. 306 (1896) (*Durland* is considered again in Section A
of Chapter 4). The defendants in *Durland* were late-nineteenth-century con
artists who used the mails to advertise "bonds" that would return profits of
50 percent in six months, with no intention of paying even the principal,
much less any interest. To twenty-first-century readers, it may seem surprising
that the common law of fraud did not cover such conduct. The common-law
offense of "false pretenses" (the most nearly analogous common-law offense)
required proof of false statements of material fact; false promises of future
performance—such as Durland's promise to pay interest on the bonds in
question—did not suffice. The government nevertheless prosecuted Durland
and his colleagues for mail fraud, and the Supreme Court concluded that the
mail fraud statute extended further than the common law:

> [B]eyond the letter of the statute is the evil sought to be remedied,
> which is always significant in determining the meaning. It is common knowl-
> edge that nothing is more alluring than the expectation of receiving large
> returns on small investments. Eagerness to take the chances of large gains lies

at the foundation of all lottery schemes, and, even when the matter of chance is eliminated, any scheme or plan which holds out the prospect of receiving more than is parted with appeals to the cupidity of all.

In the light of this the statute must be read, and, so read, it includes everything designed to defraud by representations as to the past or present, or suggestions and promises as to the future. The significant fact is the intent and purpose. . . .

161 U.S. at 313. *Hudson & Goodwin* and *Bevans* rejected the notion that common law could be a basis for extending federal criminal law to cover what legislation had not. But common law—common judicial understandings that often extend across jurisdictions—can also put a brake on criminal-law expansion. *Durland* shows that the common law, by providing definitions through which to interpret statutory provisions, might also serve as a limit on federal power—a means of placing boundaries on otherwise unbounded criminal offenses. Perhaps the absence of those common-law boundaries helps explain the breadth of the federal criminal code.

5. Though *Durland* remains good law, present-day federal courts are quicker to rely on the common law when construing criminal statutes—at least when those statutes use common-law terminology. The defendant in Neder v. United States, 527 U.S. 1 (1999), was charged with mail, wire, and bank fraud; the issue in the case was whether his various falsehoods had to be "material" (meaning, roughly, significant or important to the relevant transactions) in order to violate those statutes. The word "material" did not appear in the statutes at issue, but materiality was an element of common-law fraud. *Durland* suggested that common-law definitions don't matter, at least when fraud is the term being defined. *Neder* suggests otherwise:

> [T]he Government is correct that the fraud statutes did not incorporate *all* the elements of common-law fraud. The common-law requirements of "justifiable reliance" and "damages," for example, plainly have no place in the federal fraud statutes. By prohibiting the "scheme to defraud," rather than the completed fraud, the elements of reliance and damage would clearly be inconsistent with the statutes Congress enacted. But while the language of the fraud statutes is incompatible with these requirements, the Government has failed to show that this language is inconsistent with a materiality requirement.
>
> Accordingly, we hold that materiality of falsehood is an element of the federal mail fraud, wire fraud, and bank fraud statutes. . . .

527 U.S. at 24-25. It is hard to square *Durland* and *Neder*. The bottom line seems to be that common-law definitions are sometimes controlling, and sometimes not.

6. What about common-law methods? Often, the issue is not whether to apply some common-law definition or doctrine, but whether judges should make legal doctrine in order to deal with some problem that the text of the relevant criminal statute doesn't address. Consider the next case.

B.   THE DEFINITION OF CRIMINAL CONDUCT

Brogan v. United States
522 U.S. 398 (1998)

Justice SCALIA delivered the opinion of the Court.

This case presents the question of whether there is an exception to criminal liability under 18 U.S.C. §1001 for a false statement that consists of the mere denial of wrongdoing, the so-called "exculpatory no."

I

While acting as a union officer during 1987 and 1988, petitioner James Brogan accepted cash payments from JRD Management Corporation, a real estate company whose employees were represented by the union. On October 4, 1993, federal agents from the Department of Labor and the Internal Revenue Service visited petitioner at his home. The agents identified themselves and explained that they were seeking petitioner's cooperation in an investigation of JRD and various individuals. They told petitioner that if he wished to cooperate, he should have an attorney contact the U.S. Attorney's Office, and that if he could not afford an attorney, one could be appointed for him.

The agents then asked petitioner if he would answer some questions, and he agreed. One question was whether he had received any cash or gifts from JRD when he was a union officer. Petitioner's response was "no." At that point, the agents disclosed that a search of JRD headquarters had produced company records showing the contrary. They also told petitioner that lying to federal agents in the course of an investigation was a crime. Petitioner did not modify his answers, and the interview ended shortly thereafter.

Petitioner was indicted for accepting unlawful cash payments from an employer in violation of 29 U.S.C. §§186(b)(1), (a)(2) and (d)(2), and making a false statement within the jurisdiction of a federal agency in violation of 18 U.S.C. §1001. He was tried, along with several co-defendants, before a jury in the United States District Court for the Southern District of New York, and was found guilty. The United States Court of Appeals for the Second Circuit affirmed the convictions. . . .

II

At the time petitioner falsely replied "no" to the Government investigators' question, 18 U.S.C. §1001 (1988 ed.) provided:

"Whoever, in any matter within the jurisdiction of any department or agency of the United States knowingly and willfully falsifies, conceals or covers up by any trick, scheme, or device a material fact, or makes any false, fictitious or fraudulent statements or representations, or makes or uses any false writing or document knowing the same to contain any false, fictitious or fraudulent statement or entry, shall be fined not more than $10,000 or imprisoned not more than five years, or both."

By its terms, 18 U.S.C. §1001 covers "any" false statement. . . . The word "no" in response to a question assuredly makes a "statement," and petitioner does not contest that his utterance was false or that it was made "knowingly and willfully." In fact, petitioner concedes that under a "literal reading" of the statute he loses. Brief for Petitioner 5.

Petitioner asks us, however, to depart from the literal text that Congress has enacted, and to approve the doctrine adopted by many Circuits which excludes from the scope of §1001 the "exculpatory no." The central feature of this doctrine is that a simple denial of guilt does not come within the statute. There is considerable variation among the Circuits concerning, among other things, what degree of elaborated tale-telling carries a statement beyond simple denial. In the present case, however, the Second Circuit agreed with petitioner that his statement would constitute a "true 'exculpatory no' as recognized in other circuits," [United States v. Wiener, 96 F.3d 35, 37 (2d Cir. 1996)], but aligned itself with the Fifth Circuit in categorically rejecting the doctrine.

Petitioner's argument in support of the "exculpatory no" doctrine proceeds from the major premise that §1001 criminalizes only those statements to Government investigators that "pervert governmental functions"; to the minor premise that simple denials of guilt to government investigators do not pervert governmental functions; to the conclusion that §1001 does not criminalize simple denials of guilt to Government investigators. Both premises seem to us mistaken. As to the minor: We cannot imagine how it could be true that falsely denying guilt in a Government investigation does not pervert a governmental function. Certainly the investigation of wrongdoing is a proper governmental function; and since it is the very *purpose* of an investigation to uncover the truth, any falsehood relating to the subject of the investigation perverts that function. It could be argued, perhaps, that a *disbelieved* falsehood does not pervert an investigation. But making the existence of this crime turn upon the credulousness of the federal investigator (or the persuasiveness of the liar) would be exceedingly strange; such a defense to the analogous crime of perjury is certainly unheard of. Moreover, as we shall see, the only support for the "perversion of governmental functions" limitation is a statement of this Court referring to the *possibility* (as opposed to the certainty) of perversion of function—a possibility that exists whenever investigators are told a falsehood relevant to their task.

In any event, we find no basis for the major premise that only those falsehoods that pervert governmental functions are covered by §1001. Petitioner derives this premise from a comment we made in United States v. Gilliland, 312 U.S. 86 (1941), a case involving the predecessor to §1001. That earlier version of the statute subjected to criminal liability

> whoever shall knowingly and willfully . . . make or cause to be made any false or fraudulent statements or representations, or make or use or cause to be made or used any false bill, receipt, voucher, roll, account, claim, certificate, affidavit, or deposition, knowing the same to contain any fraudulent or fictitious statement or entry, in any matter within the jurisdiction of any department or agency of the United States. . . .

The defendant in *Gilliland* . . . argued that the statute should be read to apply only to matters in which the Government has a financial or proprietary interest. In rejecting that argument, we noted that Congress had specifically amended the statute to cover "any matter within the jurisdiction of any department or agency of the United States," thereby indicating "the congressional intent to protect the authorized functions of governmental departments and agencies from the perversion which might result from the deceptive practices described." Id. at 93. Petitioner would elevate this statement to a holding that §1001 does not apply where a perversion of governmental functions does not exist. But it is not, and cannot be, our practice to restrict the unqualified language of a statute to the particular evil that Congress was trying to remedy—even assuming that it is possible to identify that evil from something other than the text of the statute itself. . . .

Petitioner repeats the argument made by many supporters of the "exculpatory no," that the doctrine is necessary to eliminate the grave risk that §1001 will become an instrument of prosecutorial abuse. The supposed danger is that overzealous prosecutors will use this provision as a means of "piling on" offenses—sometimes punishing the denial of wrongdoing more severely than the wrongdoing itself. The objectors' principal grievance on this score, however, lies not with the hypothetical prosecutors but with Congress itself, which has decreed the obstruction of a legitimate investigation to be a separate offense, and a serious one. It is not for us to revise that judgment. . . . [F]inally, if there is a problem of supposed "overreaching" it is hard to see how the doctrine of the "exculpatory no" could solve it. It is easy enough for an interrogator to press the liar from the initial simple denial to a more detailed fabrication that would not qualify for the exemption.

III

A brief word in response to the dissent's assertion that the Court may interpret a criminal statute more narrowly than it is written: Some of the cases it cites for that proposition represent instances in which the Court . . . applied what it thought to be a background interpretive principle of general application. Staples v. United States, 511 U.S. 600, 619 (1994) (construing statute to contain common-law requirement of *mens rea*); Sorrells v. United States, 287 U.S. 435, 446 (1932) (construing statute not to cover violations produced by entrapment); United States v. Palmer, 16 U.S. (3 Wheat.) 610, 631 (1818) (construing statute not to apply extraterritorially to noncitizens). Also into this last category falls the dissent's correct assertion that the present statute does not "mak[e] it a crime for an undercover narcotics agent to make a false statement to a drug peddler." Criminal prohibitions do not generally apply to reasonable enforcement actions by officers of the law. See, e.g., 2 P. Robinson, Criminal Law Defenses §142(a), at 121 (1984) ("Every American jurisdiction recognizes some form of law enforcement authority justification").

It is one thing to acknowledge and accept such well defined (or even newly enunciated), generally applicable, background principles of assumed legislative intent. It is quite another to espouse the broad proposition that criminal statutes do not have to be read as broadly as they are written, but are subject to case-by-case exceptions. The problem with adopting such an expansive, user-friendly judicial rule is that there is no way of knowing when, or how, the rule is to be invoked. As to the when: The only reason Justice Stevens adduces for invoking it here is that a felony conviction for this offense seems to him harsh. Which it may well be. But the instances in which courts may ignore harsh penalties are set forth in the Constitution, see Art. 1, §9; Art. III, §3; Amdt. 8; Amdt. 14, §1; and to go beyond them will surely leave us at sea. And as to the how: There is no reason in principle why the dissent chooses to mitigate the harshness by saying that §1001 does not embrace the "exculpatory no," rather than by saying that §1001 has no application unless the defendant has been warned of the consequences of lying, or indeed unless the defendant has been put under oath. We are again at sea. . . .

In sum, we find nothing to support the "exculpatory no" doctrine except the many Court of Appeals decisions that have embraced it. . . . Courts may not create their own limitations on legislation, no matter how alluring the policy arguments for doing so, and no matter how widely the blame may be spread. Because the plain language of §1001 admits of no exception for an "exculpatory no," we affirm the judgment of the Court of Appeals.

Justice SOUTER, concurring in part and concurring in the judgment.

I join the opinion of the Court except for its response to petitioner's argument premised on the potential for prosecutorial abuse of 18 U.S.C. §1001 as now written. On that point I have joined Justice Ginsburg's opinion espousing congressional attention to the risks inherent in the statute's current breadth.

Justice GINSBURG, with whom Justice SOUTER joins, concurring in the judgment.

Because a false denial fits the unqualified language of 18 U.S.C. §1001, I concur in the affirmance of Brogan's conviction. I write separately, however, to call attention to the extraordinary authority Congress, perhaps unwittingly, has conferred on prosecutors to manufacture crimes. . . .

I

At the time of Brogan's offense, §1001 made it a felony "knowingly and willfully" to make "any false, fictitious or fraudulent statements or representations" in "any matter within the jurisdiction of any department or agency of the United States." That encompassing formulation arms Government agents with authority not simply to apprehend lawbreakers, but to generate felonies, crimes of a kind that only a Government officer could prompt.

This case is illustrative. Two federal investigators paid an unannounced visit one evening to James Brogan's home. The investigators already possessed records indicating that Brogan, a union officer, had received cash from a company that employed members of the union Brogan served. (The agents gave no advance warning, one later testified, because they wanted to retain the element of surprise.) When the agents asked Brogan whether he had received any money or gifts from the company, Brogan responded "No." The agents asked no further questions. *After* Brogan just said "No," however, the agents told him: (1) the Government had in hand the records indicating that his answer was false; and (2) lying to federal agents in the course of an investigation is a crime. Had counsel appeared on the spot, Brogan likely would have received and followed advice to amend his answer, to say immediately: "Strike that; I plead not guilty." But no counsel attended the unannounced interview, and Brogan divulged nothing more. Thus, when the interview ended, a federal offense had been completed—even though, for all we can tell, Brogan's unadorned denial misled no one.

A further illustration. In United States v. Tabor, 788 F.2d 714 (11th Cir. 1986), an Internal Revenue Service agent discovered that Tabor, a notary public, had violated Florida law by notarizing a deed even though two signatories had not personally appeared before her (one had died five weeks before the document was signed). With this knowledge in hand, and without "warn[ing] Tabor of the possible consequences of her statements," the agent went to her home with a deputy sheriff and questioned her about the transaction. When Tabor, regrettably but humanly, denied wrongdoing, the Government prosecuted her under §1001. An IRS agent thus turned a violation of state law into a federal felony by eliciting a lie that misled no one. (The Eleventh Circuit reversed the §1001 conviction, relying on the "exculpatory no" doctrine.)

As these not altogether uncommon episodes show,[2] §1001 may apply to encounters between agents and their targets "under extremely informal circumstances which do not sufficiently alert the person interviewed to the danger that false statements may lead to a felony conviction." United States v. Ehrlichman, 379 F. Supp. 291, 292 (D.D.C. 1974). . . . Unlike proceedings in which a false statement can be prosecuted as perjury, there may be no oath, no pause to concentrate the speaker's mind on the importance of his or her answers. As in Brogan's case, the target may not be informed that a false "No" is a criminal offense until *after* he speaks.

At oral argument, the Solicitor General forthrightly observed that §1001 could even be used to "escalate completely innocent conduct into a felony." . . . If the statute of limitations has run on an offense—as it had on four of the five payments Brogan was accused of accepting—the prosecutor can endeavor to revive the case by instructing an investigator to elicit a fresh denial of guilt. Prosecution in these circumstances is not an instance of Government "punishing the denial of wrongdoing more severely than the wrongdoing itself"; it is, instead, Government generation of a crime when the underlying suspected wrongdoing is or has become nonpunishable. . . .

Thus, the prospect remains that an overzealous prosecutor or investigator—aware that a person has committed some suspicious acts, but unable to make a criminal case—will create a crime by surprising the suspect, asking about those acts, and receiving a false denial. Congress alone can provide the appropriate instruction.

Congress has been alert to our decisions in this area. . . . [A]fter today's decision, Congress may advert to the "exculpatory no" doctrine and the problem that prompted its formulation. . . .

Justice STEVENS, with whom Justice BREYER joins, dissenting. . . .

The mere fact that a false denial fits within the unqualified language of 18 U.S.C. §1001 is not, in my opinion, a sufficient reason for rejecting a well-settled interpretation of that statute. It is not at all unusual for this Court to conclude that the literal text of a criminal statute is broader than the coverage intended by Congress. See, e.g., Staples v. United States, 511

---

2. See, e.g., United States v. Stoffey, 279 F.2d 924, 927 (CA7 1960) (defendant prosecuted for falsely denying, while effectively detained by agents, that he participated in illegal gambling; court concluded that "purpose of the agents was not to investigate or to obtain information, but to obtain admissions," and that "they were not thereafter diverted from their course by alleged false statements of defendant"); United States v. Dempsey, 740 F. Supp. 1299, 1306 (N.D. Ill. 1990) (after determining what charges would be brought against defendants, agents visited them "with the purpose of obtaining incriminating statements"; when the agents "received denials from certain defendants rather than admissions," Government brought §1001 charges); see also United States v. Goldfine, 538 F.2d 815, 820 (CA9 1976) (agents asked defendant had he made any out-of-state purchases, investigators already knew he had, he stated he had not; . . . defendant was prosecuted for violating §1001).

U.S. 600, 605, 619 (1994); Williams v. United States, 458 U.S. 279, 286 (1982) (holding that statute prohibiting the making of false statements to a bank was inapplicable to depositing of a "bad check" because "the Government's interpretation . . . would make a surprisingly broad range of unremarkable conduct a violation of federal law"); Sorrells v. United States, 287 U.S. 435, 448 (1932) ("We are unable to conclude that it was the intention of the Congress in enacting [a Prohibition Act] statute that its processes of detection and enforcement should be abused by the instigation by government officials of an act on the part of persons otherwise innocent in order to lure them to its commission and to punish them"); United States v. Palmer, 16 U.S. 610, 3 Wheat. 610, 631 (1818) (opinion of Marshall, C.J.) (holding that although "words 'any person or persons,' [in maritime robbery statute] are broad enough to comprehend every human being[,] . . . general words must not only be limited to cases within the jurisdiction of the state, but also to those objects to which the legislature intended to apply them"). Although the text of §1001, read literally, makes it a crime for an undercover narcotics agent to make a false statement to a drug peddler, I am confident that Congress did not intend any such result. . . .

Accordingly, I respectfully dissent.

NOTES AND QUESTIONS

1. Perhaps the central issue in contemporary American law and legal theory is the degree to which judges—especially federal judges—should apply "the literal text" of statutes and constitutional provisions, even when there is a strong argument for a common-law doctrine like the one that, before *Brogan* (in most Circuits), exempted an "exculpatory no" from the coverage of the federal false statements statute. Justice Scalia, author of the *Brogan* majority opinion, was the leading judicial proponent of the textualist side of that debate. See Antonin Scalia, A Matter of Interpretation: Federal Courts and the Law (1998). Justice Stevens, author of the *Brogan* dissent, has been among the leading proponents of a looser style of statutory and constitutional texts; in recent years, Justice Breyer has taken up that role. See Stephen G. Breyer, Active Liberty: Interpreting Our Democratic Constitution (2006).

Which position seems more persuasive in *Brogan*? On the one hand, the "exculpatory no" doctrine seems more a rewriting of the false statements statute than an interpretation of it. If judges have the authority to rewrite statutes (and, even more so, constitutional provisions), judicial power will be broad indeed. On the other hand, if a simple "no" that misled no one constitutes a federal felony, federal criminal liability will be broad indeed. Which danger is greater? Which one(s) should judges worry about?

2. Justice Ginsburg's opinion seems, at first blush, an attractive way to split the difference between the majority and the dissent: Ginsburg accepts the majority's textualist analysis but seeks to persuade Congress to adopt some form of "exculpatory no" doctrine by statute. In fact, Congress did no such thing, and *Brogan* remains good law today. This may indicate that the Congress of the late 1990s agreed with the result in *Brogan*. Why do you suppose Congress has never adopted the "exculpatory no" doctrine? When answering, bear in mind that §1001—which covers all false statements made to federal agents, and does not require that they have been made under oath—is a workhorse of federal prosecutors, regularly charged and even more frequently threatened.

3. The argument in *Brogan* is played out again and again, with curiously inconsistent results. Take, for example, two cases handed down by the Supreme Court on the same day: Small v. United States, 544 U.S. 385 (2005), and Pasquantino v. United States, 544 U.S. 349 (2005).

a. Here are the facts in *Small*:

> In December 1992, Small shipped a 19-gallon electric water heater from the United States to Okinawa, Japan, ostensibly as a present for someone in Okinawa. Small had sent two other water heaters to Japan that same year. Thinking it unusual for a person to ship a water tank from overseas as a present, Japanese customs officials searched the heater and discovered 2 rifles, 8 semiautomatic pistols, and 410 rounds of ammunition.
>
> The Japanese Government indicted Small on multiple counts of violating Japan's weapons-control and customs laws. [He was convicted on all counts in 1994, sentenced to prison in Japan, and paroled in November 1996.] A week after completing parole for his Japanese convictions, on June 2, 1998, Small purchased a 9-millimeter SWD Cobray pistol from a firearms dealer in Pennsylvania. Some time later, a search of his residence, business premises, and automobile revealed a .380 caliber Browning pistol and more than 300 rounds of ammunition. . . .

544 U.S. at 395-96 (Thomas, J., dissenting). Small was prosecuted under the felon-in-possession statute, 18 U.S.C. §922(g)(1), which makes it "unlawful for any person . . . who has been convicted in any court of[] a crime punishable by imprisonment for a term exceeding one year . . . to . . . possess . . . any firearm." The question was whether Small's conviction in Japan counts as a "convict[ion]" under that statute.

Based on *Brogan*, one might reasonably conclude that "any" means what it says, that the Japanese conviction therefore counts, and that Small loses. Justice Thomas's dissent, which was joined by Justices Kennedy and Scalia, took that position. Justice Breyer and four of his colleagues came to a different conclusion, based on some un-*Brogan*-like reasoning:

> The question before us is whether the statutory reference "convicted in *any* court" includes a conviction entered in a *foreign* court. The word "any"

considered alone cannot answer this question. In ordinary life, a speaker who says, "I'll see any film," may or may not mean to include films shown in another city. In law, a legislature that uses the statutory phrase "'any person'" may or may not mean to include "'persons'" outside "the jurisdiction of the state." See, e.g., United States v. Palmer, [16 U.S. 610, 631] (1818) (Marshall, C.J.). . . .

In determining the scope of the statutory phrase we find help in the "commonsense notion that Congress generally legislates with domestic concerns in mind." Smith v. United States, 507 U.S. 197, 204, n.5 (1993). This notion has led the Court to adopt the legal presumption that Congress ordinarily intends its statutes to have domestic, not extraterritorial, application. . . . [A]lthough the presumption against extraterritorial application does not apply directly to this case, we believe a similar assumption is appropriate when [considering] the scope of the phrase "convicted in any court" here. . . .

[C]onsidered as a group, foreign convictions differ from domestic convictions in important ways. Past foreign convictions for crimes punishable by more than one year's imprisonment may include a conviction for conduct that domestic laws would permit, for example, for engaging in economic conduct that our society might encourage. See, e.g., Art. 153 of the Criminal Code of the Russian Soviet Federated Socialist Republic, in Soviet Criminal Law and Procedure 171 (H. Berman & J. Spindler transls. 2d ed. 1972) (criminalizing "Private Entrepreneurial Activity"); cf. e.g., Gaceta Oficial de la Republica de Cuba, ch. II, Art. 103, p. 68 (Dec. 30, 1987) (forbidding propaganda that incites against the social order, international solidarity, or the Communist State). They would include a conviction from a legal system that is inconsistent with an American understanding of fairness. And they would include a conviction for conduct that domestic law punishes far less severely. See, e.g., Singapore Vandalism Act, ch. 108, §§2, 3, III Statutes of Republic of Singapore, pp. 257-258 (imprisonment for up to three years for an act of vandalism). Thus, the key statutory phrase "convicted in any court of[] a crime punishable by imprisonment for a term exceeding one year" somewhat less reliably identifies dangerous individuals for the purposes of U.S. law where foreign convictions, rather than domestic convictions, are at issue. . . .

We consequently assume a congressional intent that the phrase "convicted in any court" applies domestically, not extraterritorially. . . .

544 U.S. at 388-91.

Note that in the last excerpted sentence the Court said "assume" a congressional intent, not "find" one. Justice Breyer went on to explain that the government had prosecuted no more than a dozen cases in which a foreign conviction served as the predicate for a felon-in-possession case. From that fact, Breyer inferred that "Congress . . . paid no attention to the matter," id. at 394, and it was thus up to the Court to decide.

b. The Court decided differently in *Pasquantino*, where three defendants smuggled a large quantity of liquor into Canada without paying that nation's customs duties. This scheme to defraud Canada's tax collectors was planned, in part, over American phone lines, leading to a federal wire fraud prosecution. The defendants argued that American fraud laws should not be used to enforce Canadian tax laws. In light of the Court's decision in *Small*, it seems a strong argument. The *Pasquantino* majority—authored by Justice Thomas, who wrote the dissent in *Small*—thought otherwise. This time, the opinion *did* read like *Brogan*:

> The statute prohibits using interstate wires to effect "any scheme or artifice to defraud, or for obtaining money or property by means of false or fraudulent pretenses, representations, or promises." 18 U.S.C. §1343. Two elements of this crime, and the only two that petitioners dispute here, are that the defendant engage in a "scheme or artifice to defraud," and that the "object of the fraud . . . be '[money or] property' in the victim's hands," Cleveland v. United States, 531 U.S. 12, 26 (2000). Petitioners' smuggling operation satisfies both elements.
>
> Taking the latter element first, Canada's right to uncollected excise taxes on the liquor petitioners imported into Canada is "property" in its hands. This right is an entitlement to collect money from petitioners, the possession of which is "something of value" to the Government of Canada. McNally v. United States, 483 U.S. 350, 358 (1987). Valuable entitlements like these are "property" as that term ordinarily is employed. . . .
>
> Turning to the second element at issue here, petitioners' plot was a "scheme or artifice to defraud" Canada of its valuable entitlement to tax revenue. The evidence showed that petitioners routinely concealed imported liquor from Canadian officials and failed to declare those goods on customs forms. By this conduct, they represented to Canadian customs officials that their drivers had no goods to declare. This, then, was a scheme "designed to defraud by representations," Durland v. United States, 161 U.S. 306, 313 (1896), and therefore a "scheme or artifice to defraud" Canada of taxes due on the smuggled goods.

544 U.S. at 355-57. Justice Thomas went on to explain that the longstanding common-law revenue rule, which held that American law does not enforce another country's tax laws, was consistent with the *Pasquantino* prosecution because the defendants were being prosecuted for fraud, not for Canadian tax violations, and such a prosecution was not, according to Justice Thomas, inconsistent with cases that had applied the common-law revenue rule. The argument was largely formal.

Justice Ginsburg wrote the dissent; she was joined by Justices Scalia, Souter, and Breyer—an unusual combination, but unusual combinations seem common in this field. Justices Ginsburg and Breyer argued for function over form, asserting that the presumption against extraterritoriality should govern, just as it governed in *Small*. See id. at 375-81 (Ginsburg, J., dissenting). All four dissenters argued that the fraud charge was, in function, a means of enforcing Canadian tax law, which was both bad policy and in conflict with the revenue rule. Id. at 381-83.

Which side was right in *Small?* In *Pasquantino?* Are the two cases distinguishable? Are they consistent with *Brogan?* Note that Justice Scalia, the author of the *Brogan* majority opinion, dissented in both *Small* and *Pasquantino.*

c. One of the defense arguments in *Pasquantino* rested on the federal anti-smuggling statute, 18 U.S.C. §546. According to the defendants, the existence of a statute specifically targeting smuggling from the United States into foreign countries suggested that Congress did not mean to cover such conduct with the general language of the wire fraud statute. In most regulatory fields, that argument would carry the day. But Justice Thomas quickly dismissed this interpretive argument in *Pasquantino* in a footnote, noting that "[t]he Federal Criminal Code is replete with provisions that criminalize overlapping conduct," and concluding that "[t]he mere fact that two federal criminal statutes criminalize similar conduct says little about the scope of either." 544 U.S. at 358 n.4.

That might sound surprising, but it is the conventional approach to interpreting federal criminal statutes, as United States v. Wells, 519 U.S. 482 (1997), illustrates. The defendant in *Wells* was charged with lying on a loan application. The question before the Supreme Court was whether the relevant federal statute required proof that the defendant's misrepresentation was material. The statute did not include the word "material," so the Court held that proof of materiality was not required; the majority opinion reads a good deal like Justice Scalia's majority opinion in *Brogan*. As in *Brogan*, Justice Stevens dissented in *Wells*. The heart of Justice Stevens's dissent was a passage in which he listed 96 fraud and misrepresentation statutes — some of which contained the word "material," and others of which did not:

> [A]t least 100 federal false statement statutes may be found in the United States Code. About 42 of them contain an express materiality requirement; approximately 54 do not. The kinds of false statements found in the first category[9] are, to my eyes at least, indistinguishable from those in the second category.[10] Nor is there any obvious distinction between the range of punishments

---

9. See [United States v. Gaudin, 28 F.3d 943, 959 n.3 (9th Cir. 1994) (Kozinski, J.)] (". . . 18 U.S.C. §1919 (maximum one-year prison term for false statement of material fact knowingly made to obtain unemployment compensation for federal service); . . . 20 U.S.C. §1097(b) (maximum one-year prison term for knowingly and willfully concealing material information in connection with assignment of federally insured student loan); . . . 42 U.S.C. §1383a(a)(1) (maximum one-year prison term for knowingly and willfully making false statement of material fact in application for Supplemental Security Income benefits); . . . 46 U.S.C. App. §839 (maximum five-year prison term for knowingly making false statement of material fact to secure required approval of Secretary of Transportation). . . .").

10. See [*Gaudin*, 28 F.3d] at 960, n.4 (". . . 18 U.S.C. §287 (penalizing false claims against U.S. government); . . . 18 U.S.C. §1014 (penalizing false statement to influence federal loan or credit agency); . . . 18 U.S.C. §1920 (penalizing false statement to obtain Federal employees' compensation); . . . 42 U.S.C. §408 (penalizing false statement to obtain

authorized by the two different groups of statutes. . . . It seems farfetched
that Congress made a deliberate decision to include or to omit a materiality
requirement every time it created a false statement offense. Far more likely, in
my view, Congress simply assumed . . . that the materiality requirement would
be implied wherever it was not explicit.

519 U.S. at 505-09 & nn.9-10 (Stevens, J., dissenting).

As the statutes cited in Justice Stevens's *Wells* dissent demonstrate,
members of Congress write criminal statutes one by one, often failing to
consider the relationships among them. The consequence is that title 18
of the U.S. Code contains many doctrinal lines that do not conform to any
rational theory. What, if anything, should federal judges do about this? One
thing they cannot do is try to harmonize overlapping criminal statutes by
liberally asserting "repeal by implication." See Morton v. Mancari, 417 U.S.
535, 550 (1974) ("In the absence of some affirmative showing of an intention to repeal, the only permissible justification for a repeal by implication
is when the earlier and later statutes are irreconcilable."). Should they still
strive to make the definition of criminal conduct more rational? More fair?
Or should judges just stick to statutory texts and let Congress worry about
whether these texts make sense?

4. In criminal law, as elsewhere, inertia is the single strongest force in
the legislative process. The response to *Lopez* was the exception, not the rule.
Because passing legislation is difficult, whatever interpretation the courts
adopt tends to remain in place, whether or not a congressional majority
agrees with it. Moreover, when Congress does act, it is more likely to do so
in response to judicial decisions that favor defendants (as it did post-*Lopez*).
Between 1978 and 1984, the Supreme Court decided 34 cases interpreting
statutes unfavorably to criminal defendants. Congress overturned just one
of those 34 decisions. During the same six years, Congress overturned five
of 24 statutory interpretation decisions that were unfavorable to the federal government. See William N. Eskridge, Jr., Overriding Supreme Court
Statutory Interpretation Decisions, 101 Yale L.J. 331, 348 tbl. 7, 351 tbl. 9
(1991). What conclusion do you draw from those data?

THE SO-CALLED RULE OF LENITY

1. The rule of lenity—which Chief Justice Marshall invoked *supra* in
United States v. Wiltberger, 18 U.S. (5 Wheat.) 76, 89 (1820)—holds that

---

social security benefits); . . . 45 U.S.C. §359(a) (penalizing knowing false statement to
obtain unemployment insurance); . . . 49 U.S.C. App. §2216 (penalizing U.S. officials who
knowingly make false statement regarding projects submitted for approval of Secretary of
Transportation)").

ambiguities in criminal statutes should be resolved in the defendant's favor. This principle would seem to resolve cases like *Brogan, Pasquantino, Wells,* and *Small,* in which Supreme Court Justices disagreed about the meaning of the relevant criminal statute (a fair indication that those statutes are ambiguous, or so one might think). But three of those four cases were decided in the government's favor, and in the fourth—*Small*—the Court ignored the rule. That is no surprise; the Court often ignores the rule of lenity. So do lower federal courts. Increasingly, federal judges put the word "rule" in quotes, or label the doctrine the "so-called rule of lenity." For representative uses of the latter phrase, see, for example, Moskal v. United States, 498 U.S. 103, 131 (1990) (Scalia, J., dissenting); United States v. Balint, 201 F.3d 928, 934 (7th Cir. 2000); United States v. Workinger, 90 F.3d 1409, 1419 (9th Cir. 1996) (Kozinski, J., concurring); and United States v. Garrett, 984 F.2d 1402, 1411 (5th Cir. 1993). What is the rationale for this alleged rule, and why is it an "alleged" rule?

2. United States v. Bass, 404 U.S. 336, 347-48 (1971), contains the best statement of the rule and its rationale:

> [A]s we have recently reaffirmed, "ambiguity concerning the ambit of criminal statutes should be resolved in favor of lenity." Rewis v. United States, 401 U.S. 808, 812 (1971). In various ways over the years, we have stated that "when choice has to be made between two readings of what conduct Congress has made a crime, it is appropriate, before we choose the harsher alternative, to require that Congress should have spoken in language that is clear and definite." United States v. Universal C.I.T. Credit Corp., 344 U.S. 218, 221-222 (1952). This principle is founded on two policies that have long been part of our tradition. First, "a fair warning should be given to the world in language that the common world will understand, of what the law intends to do if a certain line is passed. To make the warning fair, so far as possible the line should be clear." McBoyle v. United States, 283 U.S. 25, 27 (1931) (Holmes. J.). Second, because of the seriousness of criminal penalties, and because criminal punishment usually represents the moral condemnation of the community, legislatures and not courts should define criminal activity. This policy embodies "the instinctive distastes against men languishing in prison unless the lawmaker has clearly said they should." H. Friendly, Mr. Justice Frankfurter and the Reading of Statutes, in Benchmarks 196, 209 (1967). Thus, where there is ambiguity in a criminal statute, doubts are resolved in favor of the defendant.

Noble words, and persuasive ones.

3. Then why is the rule only "so-called"? The doctrinal answer is that the rule applies only when the statutory ambiguity cannot be resolved one way or the other. Consider Muscarello v. United States, 524 U.S. 125 (1998). The defendants in *Muscarello* were charged under a federal statute that applies to anyone who "uses or carries a firearm" "during and in relation

to" a "drug trafficking crime." 18 U.S.C. §924(c)(1). The defendants drove their respective vehicles to the site of the relevant drug transactions, where they were arrested and searched. One defendant had a handgun in the locked glove compartment of his pickup truck. Two other defendants had a bag filled with guns in the trunk of their car. The question was whether these three defendants were "carr[ying]" the guns at the time of the drug sales. The Court split 5-4 on the meaning of "carries": The majority held that one "carries" a weapon when it is reasonably accessible in a nearby vehicle; the dissenters argued that one "carries" only the items on one's person. Both Justice Breyer's majority opinion and Justice Ginsburg's dissent cited dictionaries, usage guides, and the Bible for their preferred interpretations—powerful evidence that the issue was a close one, since the conventional sources offered such divided counsel. Even so, the *Muscarello* majority did not find it a close call:

> Finally, petitioners and the dissent invoke the "rule of lenity." The simple existence of some statutory ambiguity, however, is not sufficient to warrant application of that rule, for most statutes are ambiguous to some degree. "'The rule of lenity applies only if, "after seizing everything from which aid can be derived," . . . we can make "no more than a guess as to what Congress intended."'" United States v. Wells, 519 U.S. 482, 499 (1997). To invoke the rule, we must conclude that there is a ""'grievous ambiguity or uncertainty"' in the statute." Staples v. United States, 511 U.S. 600, 619, n.17 (1994).
>
> Certainly, our decision today is based on much more than "a guess as to what Congress intended," and there is no "grievous ambiguity" here. The problem of statutory interpretation in these cases is indeed no different from that in many of the criminal cases that confront us. Yet, this Court has never held that the rule of lenity automatically permits a defendant to win.

524 U.S. at 138-39. Few cases show the "grievous ambiguity" required to trigger the rule.

4. There is also a psychological answer to the question of why this alleged rule rarely does much work in practice. The answer begins with this fact: The rule of lenity is irrelevant in cases in which the court decides the defendant has the better statutory argument—even without it, the defendant wins such cases. The rule matters only when judges conclude *both* (1) that all things considered, the government's interpretation is at least as good as the defendant's, *and* (2) that the case is close enough to trigger the rule. Those conclusions sit uncomfortably together. Most people find it awkward to conclude that their conclusions are suspect, and federal judges are probably less self-critical than most people (though perhaps more self-critical than law professors). So, with rare exceptions, the rule of lenity is a throwaway argument—sometimes cited when statutory ambiguities are resolved in defendants' favor, and ignored when they aren't. It isn't clear whether this "so-called rule" actually changes any case outcomes. Should it? Should

courts give criminal defendants the benefit of the doubt when evaluating statutory interpretation arguments? Did Brogan deserve the benefit of the doubt?

5. Perhaps the rule of lenity will be invoked more frequently in the wake of a recent case, Yates v. United States, 135 S. Ct. 1074, 1078 (2015). Yates, a commercial fisherman, was approached at sea by an officer of the Florida Fish and Wildlife Conservation Commission. Pursuant to his authorization to enforce federal fisheries law, the officer boarded the vessel and noticed that the catch included red grouper that fell short of the minimum 20 inches required by federal law. He then issued a citation and informed Yates that the fish would be confiscated upon arrival at port. Contrary to the officer's instructions, Yates directed his crew to throw the undersize fish back in the sea in order "[t]o prevent federal authorities from confirming that he had harvested . . . the suspect catch." *Yates*, 135 S. Ct. at 1074.

For this conduct, Yates was convicted of destruction and falsification of evidence, in violation of the Sarbanes-Oxley Act of 2002's obstruction of justice provision, which prohibits destroying, concealing, or making a false entry "in any record, document, or tangible object" with intent to obstruct a federal investigation. 18 U.S.C. §1519. The issue before the Supreme Court was whether a fish is a "tangible object" for the purpose of §1519.

Justice Ginsburg, joined by Chief Justice Roberts, Justice Breyer, and Justice Sotomayor, thought not:

> Section 1519 was enacted . . . to protect investors and restore trust in financial markets following the collapse of Enron Corporation. A fish is no doubt an object that is tangible; fish can be seen, caught, and handled, and a catch, as this case illustrates, is vulnerable to destruction. But it would cut §1519 loose from its financial-fraud mooring to hold that it encompasses any and all objects, whatever their size or significance, destroyed with obstructive intent. Mindful that in Sarbanes-Oxley, Congress trained its attention on corporate and accounting deception and cover-ups, we conclude that a matching construction of §1519 is in order: A tangible object captured by §1519, we hold, must be one used to record or preserve information.

Id. at 1079. One of the canons of statutory construction that Justice Ginsburg relied on was the "rule of lenity."* Id. at 1088.

Writing in dissent, Justice Kagan, along with Scalia, Kennedy, and Thomas, argued that "tangible object" should be given its ordinary meaning:

> This case raises the question whether the term "tangible object" means the same thing in §1519 as it means in everyday language—any object capable

---

* [Editors' Note: Justice Alito provided the fifth vote to reverse the conviction; his reasoning largely followed that of Justice Ginsburg but without reference to the rule of lenity. Id. at 1078-80 (Alito, J., concurring).]

of being touched. The answer should be easy: Yes. The term "tangible object" is broad, but clear. . . . All the words surrounding "tangible object" show that Congress meant the term to have a wide range. That fits with Congress's evident purpose in enacting §1519: to punish those who alter or destroy physical evidence — *any* physical evidence — with the intent of thwarting federal law enforcement. . . . A fish is, of course, a discrete thing that possesses physical form. See generally Dr. Seuss, One Fish Two Fish Red Fish Blue Fish (1960). So the ordinary meaning of the term "tangible object" in §1519, as no one here disputes, covers fish (including too-small red grouper).

Id. at 1090-91. Despite referring to the majority's methods of statutory interpretation as a "fishing expedition," Justice Kagan wrote "§1519 is a bad law — too broad and undifferentiated, with too-high maximum penalties, which give prosecutors too much leverage and sentencers too much discretion. And I'd go further: In those ways, §1519 is unfortunately not an outlier, but an emblem of a deeper pathology in the federal criminal code." Id. at 1101. "But," she wrote, "whatever the wisdom or folly of §1519, this Court does not get to rewrite the law." Id.

Do you agree that there is something fishy, as it were, about applying an obstruction of justice statute with a 20-year maximum sentence when there is another statute (which Yates was also convicted of violating) that specifically prohibits removal of property to prevent its lawful seizure by the government — a statute with a maximum sentence of five years? See 18 U.S.C. §2232(a). Or did the Court unnecessarily refuse to give full effect to the law that Congress enacted? Yates, by the way, was sentenced to 30 days in prison.

Overlaps and inconsistencies abound in federal criminal law, but they may be especially striking in a densely legislated area like obstruction of justice. See Julie R. O'Sullivan, The Federal Criminal "Code" is a Disgrace: Obstruction Statutes as Case Study, 96 J. Crim. L. & Criminology 643 (2006). As Justice Kagan noted in her *Yates* dissent, prosecutorial discretion becomes especially important in these circumstances.

6. Should judges interpreting statutes consider how prosecutors will exercise discretion? Should courts endeavor to explicitly preclude de minimis or silly cases or should they just trust such cases won't be brought? In Marinello v. United States, the issue was how broadly to read the "Omnibus Clause" of the Internal Revenue Code, 26 U.S.C. §7212(a), which forbids "corruptly or by force or threats of force . . . obstruct[ing] or imped[ing], or endeavor[ing] to obstruct or impede, the due administration of [the Internal Revenue Code]." Justice Breyer explained the Court's interpretation of the Clause:

Does it cover virtually all governmental efforts to collect taxes? Or does it have a narrower scope? In our view, "due administration of [the Tax Code]" does not cover routine administrative procedures that are near-universally applied to all taxpayers, such as the ordinary processing of income tax returns. Rather, the clause as a whole refers to specific interference with targeted governmental tax-related proceedings, such as a particular investigation or audit.

138 S. Ct. 1101, 1104 (2018). He went on to note how the Trump Administration's guidance to prosecutors cut against trusting prosecutors not to charge in routine tax processing situations:

> Neither can we rely upon prosecutorial discretion to narrow the statute's scope. True, the Government used the Omnibus Clause only sparingly during the first few decades after its enactment. But it used the clause more often after the early 1990's. Brief for Petitioner 9. And, at oral argument the Government told us that, where more punitive and less punitive criminal provisions both apply to a defendant's conduct, the Government will charge a violation of the more punitive provision as long as it can readily prove that violation at trial. Tr. of Oral Arg. 46-47, 55-57; see Office of the Attorney General, Department Charging and Sentencing Policy (May 10, 2017).
>
> Regardless, to rely upon prosecutorial discretion to narrow the otherwise wide-ranging scope of a criminal statute's highly abstract general statutory language places great power in the hands of the prosecutor. Doing so risks allowing "policemen, prosecutors, and juries to pursue their personal predilections," Smith v. Goguen, 415 U.S. 566, 575 (1974), which could result in the nonuniform execution of that power across time and geographic location. And insofar as the public fears arbitrary prosecution, it risks undermining necessary confidence in the criminal justice system. That is one reason why we have said that we "cannot construe a criminal statute on the assumption that the Government will 'use it responsibly.'" McDonnell v. United States, 136 S. Ct. 2355, 2372-2373 (2016) (quoting United States v. Stevens, 559 U.S. 460, 480 (2010)).

Id. at 1108-09.

C.   CRIMINAL DEFENSES

Defenses to federal crimes are almost all non-statutory. How can this be, given *Hudson & Goodwin*? What is the status in federal court of common-law defenses to crime? In the case below, the Court discusses which side bears the burden of proving or disproving duress when this defense is invoked by the defendant. As you read this case, ask yourself: What is the role of common-law principles in interpreting recently enacted statutes? To what degree should courts expect Congress to be cognizant of principles of common law when enacting legislation? How should courts interpret congressional silence on important legal issues? What is the relationship between *mens rea* elements and defenses?

Dixon v. United States
548 U.S. 1 (2006)

Justice STEVENS delivered the opinion of the Court.

In January 2003, petitioner Keshia Dixon purchased multiple fire-arms at two gun shows, during the course of which she provided an incorrect address and falsely stated that she was not under indictment for a felony. As a result of these illegal acts, petitioner was indicted and convicted on one count of receiving a firearm while under indictment in violation of 18 U.S.C. §922(n) and eight counts of making false statements in connection with the acquisition of a firearm in violation of §922(a)(6). At trial, petitioner admitted that she knew she was under indictment when she made the purchases and that she knew doing so was a crime; her defense was that she acted under duress because her boyfriend threatened to kill her or hurt her daughters if she did not buy the guns for him.

Petitioner contends that the trial judge's instructions to the jury erroneously required her to prove duress by a preponderance of the evidence instead of requiring the Government to prove beyond a reasonable doubt that she did not act under duress. The Court of Appeals rejected petitioner's contention, 413 F.3d 520 (C.A.5 2005); given contrary treatment of the issue by other federal courts,[1] we granted certiorari.

I

At trial, in her request for jury instructions on her defense of duress, petitioner contended that she "should have the burden of production, and then that the Government should be required to disprove beyond a reasonable doubt the duress." . . . [T]he judge's instructions to the jury defined the elements of the duress defense[2] and stated that petitioner has

---

1. Cf., e.g., United States v. Talbott, 78 F.3d 1183, 1186 (C.A.7 1996) (per curiam); United States v. Riffe, 28 F.3d 565, 568, n.2 (6th Cir. 1994); United States v. Simpson, 979 F.2d 1282, 1287 (8th Cir. 1992).

2. There is no federal statute defining the elements of the duress defense. We have not specified the elements of the defense, see, e.g., United States v. Bailey, 444 U.S. 394, 409-410 (1980), and need not do so today. Instead, we presume the accuracy of the District Court's description of these elements: (1) The defendant was under an unlawful and imminent threat of such a nature as to induce a well-grounded apprehension of death or serious bodily injury; (2) the defendant had not recklessly or negligently placed herself in a situation in which it was probable that she would be forced to perform the criminal conduct; (3) the defendant had no reasonable, legal alternative to violating the law, that is, a chance both to refuse to perform the criminal act and also to avoid the threatened harm; and (4) that a direct causal relationship may be reasonably anticipated between the criminal act and the avoidance of the threatened harm.

"the burden of proof to establish the defense of duress by a preponderance of the evidence."

Petitioner argues here, as she did in the District Court and the Court of Appeals, that federal law requires the Government to bear the burden of disproving her defense beyond a reasonable doubt and that the trial court's erroneous instruction on this point entitles her to a new trial. . . .

II

The crimes for which petitioner was convicted require that she have acted "knowingly" or "willfully." As we have explained, "unless the text of the statute dictates a different result, the term 'knowingly' merely requires proof of knowledge of the facts that constitute the offense." Bryan v. United States, 524 U.S. 184, 193 (1998). And the term "willfully" in §924(a)(1)(D) requires a defendant to have "acted with knowledge that his conduct was unlawful." Ibid. In this case, then, the Government bore the burden of proving beyond a reasonable doubt that petitioner knew she was making false statements in connection with the acquisition of firearms and that she knew she was breaking the law when she acquired a firearm while under indictment. See In re Winship, 397 U.S. 358, 364 (1970). . . . [T]he Government . . . clearly met its burden when petitioner testified that she knowingly committed certain acts—she put a false address on the forms she completed to purchase the firearms, falsely claimed that she was the actual buyer of the firearms, and falsely stated that she was not under indictment at the time of the purchase—and when she testified that she knew she was breaking the law when, as an individual under indictment at the time, she purchased a firearm.

Petitioner contends, however, that she cannot have formed the necessary *mens rea* for these crimes because she did not freely choose to commit the acts in question. But even if we assume that petitioner's will was overborne by the threats made against her and her daughters, she still *knew* that she was making false statements and *knew* that she was breaking the law by buying a firearm. The duress defense, like the defense of necessity that we considered in United States v. Bailey, 444 U.S. 394, 409-410 (1980), may excuse conduct that would otherwise be punishable, but the existence of duress normally does not controvert any of the elements of the offense itself.[4]

---

4. As the Government recognized at oral argument, there may be crimes where the nature of the *mens rea* would require the Government to disprove the existence of duress beyond a reasonable doubt. See Tr. of Oral Arg. 26-27; see also, e.g., 1 W. LaFave, Substantive Criminal Law §5.1, p. 333 (2d ed. 2003) explaining that some common-law crimes require that the crime be done "maliciously'"); Black's Law Dictionary 968 (7th ed. 1999) (defining malice as "[t]he intent, without justification or excuse, to commit a wrongful act").

As we explained in *Bailey*, "[c]riminal liability is normally based upon the concurrence of two factors, 'an evil-meaning mind [and] an evil-doing hand [sic]. . . .'" Id. at 402. Like the defense of necessity, the defense of duress does not negate a defendant's criminal state of mind when the applicable offense requires a defendant to have acted knowingly or willfully; instead, it allows the defendant to "avoid liability . . . because coercive conditions or necessity negates a conclusion of guilt even though the necessary *mens rea* was present." [Ibid.] . . .

Congress defined the crimes at issue to punish defendants who act "knowingly," §922(a)(6), or "willfully," §924(a)(1)(D). It is these specific mental states, rather than some vague "evil mind" or "'criminal' intent" that the Government is required to prove beyond a reasonable doubt. The jury instructions in this case were consistent with this requirement and, as such, did not run afoul of the Due Process Clause when they placed the burden on petitioner to establish the existence of duress by a preponderance of the evidence.

III . . .

[U]ntil the end of the 19th century, common-law courts generally adhered to the rule that "the proponent of an issue bears the burden of persuasion on the factual premises for applying the rule." Fletcher, Two Kinds of Legal Rules: A Comparative Study of Burden-of-Persuasion Practices in Criminal Cases, 77 Yale L.J. 880, 898 (1967-1968). In petitioner's view, however, two important developments have established a contrary common-law rule that now prevails in federal courts: this Court's decision in Davis v. United States, 160 U.S. 469 (1895), which placed the burden on the Government to prove a defendant's sanity, and the publication of the Model Penal Code in 1962. . . .

Davis [] interpreted a defendant's sanity to controvert the necessary *mens rea* for the crime of murder committed "feloniously, wilfully, and of his malice aforethought," id. at 474, as "[o]ne who takes human life cannot be said to be actuated by malice aforethought, or to have deliberately intended to take life, or to have 'a wicked, depraved, and malignant heart,' . . . unless at the time he had sufficient mind to comprehend the criminality or the right and wrong of such an act," id. at 485. . . . [T]his reasoning . . . does not help petitioner: The evidence of duress she adduced at trial does not contradict or tend to disprove any element of the statutory offenses that she committed. . . .

[P]etitioner's reliance on *Davis* ignores the fact that federal crimes "are solely creatures of statute," [Liparota v. United States, 471 U.S. 419, 424 (1985)], and therefore that we are required to effectuate the duress defense as Congress "may have contemplated" it in the context of these specific offenses, *United States v. Oakland Cannabis Buyers' Cooperative*, 532 U.S. 483, 491, n.3 (2001). The offenses at issue in this case were created by statute in 1968, when Congress enacted the Omnibus Crime Control and Safe Streets Act. See 82 Stat. 197. There is no evidence in the Act's structure or history that Congress actually considered the question of how the duress defense should work in this context. . . . Assuming that a defense of duress is available to the statutory crimes at issue, then, we must determine what that defense would look like as Congress "may have contemplated" it.

As discussed above, the common law long required the defendant to bear the burden of proving the existence of duress. Similarly, even where Congress has enacted an affirmative defense in the proviso of a statute, the "settled rule . . . [is] that it is incumbent on one who relies on such an exception to set it up and establish it." *McKelvey v. United States*, 260 U.S. 353, 357 (1922). Even though the Safe Streets Act does not mention the defense of duress, we can safely assume that the 1968 Congress was familiar with both the long-established common-law rule and the rule applied in *McKelvey* and that it would have expected federal courts to apply a similar approach to any affirmative defense that might be asserted as a justification or excuse for violating the new law. . . .

[F]or us [to accept petitioner's argument], we would need to find an overwhelming consensus among federal courts that it is the Government's burden to disprove the existence of duress beyond a reasonable doubt. The existence today of disagreement among the Federal Courts of Appeals on this issue . . . demonstrates that no such consensus has ever existed. Also undermining petitioner's argument is the fact that, in 1970, the National Commission on Reform of Federal Criminal Laws proposed that a defendant prove the existence of duress by a preponderance of the evidence. See [National Commission on Reform of Federal Criminal Laws,] 1 Working Papers 278 [(1970)]. . . .

It is for a similar reason that we give no weight to the publication of the Model Penal Code in 1962. As petitioner notes, the Code would place the burden on the government to disprove the existence of duress beyond a reasonable doubt. See ALI, Model Penal Code §1.12 (stating that each element of an offense must be proved beyond a reasonable doubt); §1.13(9)(c) (defining as an element anything that negatives an excuse for the conduct at issue); §2.09 (establishing affirmative defense of duress). . . . [E]ven if we assume Congress' familiarity with the Code and the rule it would establish, there is no evidence that Congress endorsed the Code's views or incorporated them into the Safe Streets Act.

In fact, the Act itself provides evidence to the contrary. Despite the Code's careful delineation of mental states, see Model Penal Code §2.02, the Safe Streets Act attached no explicit *mens rea* requirement to the crime of receiving a firearm while under indictment, §924(a), 82 Stat. 233 ("Whoever violates any provision of this chapter . . . shall be fined not more than $5,000 or imprisoned not more than five years, or both"). And when Congress amended the Act to impose a *mens rea* requirement, it punished people who "willfully" violate the statute, see 100 Stat. 456, a mental state that has not been embraced by the Code. . . .

IV

Congress can, if it chooses, enact a duress defense that places the burden on the Government to disprove duress beyond a reasonable doubt. In light of Congress' silence on the issue, however, it is up to the federal courts to effectuate the affirmative defense of duress as Congress "may have contemplated" it in an offense-specific context. In the context of the firearms offenses at issue—as will usually be the case, given the long-established common-law rule—we presume that Congress intended the petitioner to bear the burden of proving the defense of duress by a preponderance of the evidence. Accordingly, the judgment of the Court of Appeals is affirmed.

Justice KENNEDY, concurring. . . .

When issues of congressional intent with respect to the nature, extent, and definition of federal crimes arise, we assume Congress acted against certain background understandings set forth in judicial decisions in the Anglo-American legal tradition. Those decisions, in turn, consult sources such as legal treatises and the American Legal Institute's Model Penal Code. All of these sources rely upon the insight gained over time. . . . Absent some contrary indication in the statute, we can assume that Congress would not want to foreclose the courts from consulting these newer sources and considering innovative arguments in resolving issues not confronted in the statute and not within the likely purview of Congress. . . .

While the Court looks to the state of the law at the time the statute was enacted, the better reading of the Court's opinion is that isolated authorities or writings do not control unless they were indicative of guiding principles upon which Congress likely would have relied. Otherwise, it seems altogether a fiction to attribute to Congress any intent one way or the other in assigning the burden of proof. It seems unlikely, moreover, that Congress would have wanted the burden of proof for duress to vary from statute to statute depending upon the date of enactment. Consistent with these propositions, the Court looks not only to our precedents and common-law traditions, but also to the treatment of the insanity defense in a 1984 statute and a proposal of the National Commission on Reform of Federal Criminal Laws, even though they both postdated the passage of the [Omnibus Crime Control and Safe Streets Act].

As there is no reason to suppose that Congress wanted to depart from the traditional principles for allocating the burden of proof, the proper approach is simply to apply these principles to the context of duress. The facts needed to prove or disprove the defense "lie peculiarly in the knowledge of" the defendant. 2 K. Broun, McCormick on Evidence §337, p. 475 (6th ed. 2006). The claim of duress in most instances depends upon conduct that takes place before the criminal act; and, as the person who allegedly coerced the defendant is often unwilling to come forward and testify, the prosecution may be without any practical means of disproving the defendant's allegations. There is good reason, then, to maintain the usual rule of placing the burden of production and persuasion together on the party raising the issue. The analysis may come to a different result, of course, for other defenses.

With these observations, I join the Court's opinion.

Justice ALITO, with whom Justice SCALIA joins, concurring.

I join the opinion of the Court with the understanding that it does not hold that the allocation of the burden of persuasion on the defense of duress may vary from one federal criminal statute to another.

Duress was an established defense at common law. See 4 W. Blackstone, Commentaries on the Laws of England 30 (1769). When Congress began to enact federal criminal statutes, it presumptively intended for those offenses to be subject to this defense. Moreover, Congress presumptively intended for the burdens of production and persuasion to be placed, as they were at common law, on the defendant. Although Congress is certainly free to alter this pattern and place one or both burdens on the prosecution, either for all or selected federal crimes, Congress has not done so but instead has continued to revise the federal criminal laws and to create new federal crimes without addressing the issue of duress. Under these circumstances, I believe that the burdens remain where they were when Congress began enacting federal criminal statutes.

I do not assume that Congress makes a new, implicit judgment about the allocation of these burdens whenever it creates a new federal crime or, for that matter, whenever it substantially revises an existing criminal statute. It is unrealistic to assume that on every such occasion Congress surveys the allocation of the burdens of proof on duress under the existing federal case law and under the law of the States and tacitly adopts whatever the predominant position happens to be at the time. . . . If the allocation differed for different offenses, there might be federal criminal cases in which the trial judge would be forced to instruct the jury that the defendant bears the burden of persuasion on this defense for some of the offenses charged in the indictment and that the prosecution bears the burden on others.

I would also not assume, as Justice Breyer does, that Congress has implicitly delegated to the federal courts the task of deciding in the manner of a common-law court where the burden of persuasion should be allocated. The allocation of this burden is a debatable policy question with an important empirical component. In the absence of specific direction from Congress, I would not assume that Congress has conferred this authority on the Judiciary.

Justice BREYER, with whom Justice SOUTER joins, dissenting.

Courts have long recognized that "duress" constitutes a defense to a criminal charge. Historically, that defense "excuse[d] criminal conduct" if (1) a "threat of imminent death or serious bodily injury" led the defendant to commit the crime, (2) the defendant had no reasonable, legal alternative to breaking the law, and (3) the defendant was not responsible for creating the threat. United States v. Bailey, 444 U.S. 394, 409-410 (1980); see also 2 W. LaFave, Substantive Criminal Law §9.7(b), pp. 74-82 (2003). The Court decides today in respect to *federal* crimes that the defense must bear the burden of both producing evidence of duress and persuading the jury. I agree with the majority that the burden of production lies on the defendant, that here the burden of persuasion issue is not constitutional, and that Congress may allocate that burden as it sees fit. But I also believe that, in the absence of any indication of a different congressional intent, the burden of persuading the jury beyond a reasonable doubt should lie where such burdens normally lie in criminal cases, upon the prosecution.

I

My disagreement with the majority in part reflects my different view about how we should determine the relevant congressional intent. Where Congress speaks about burdens of proof, we must, of course, follow what it says. But suppose, as is normally the case, that the relevant federal statute is silent. The majority proceeds on the assumption that Congress wished courts to fill the gap by examining judicial practice *at the time that Congress enacted the particular criminal statute in question*. I would not follow that approach.

To believe Congress intended the placement of such burdens to vary from statute to statute and time to time is both unrealistic and risks unnecessary complexity, jury confusion, and unfairness. It is unrealistic because the silence could well mean only that Congress did not specifically consider the "burden of persuasion" in respect to a duress defense. . . . Had it done so, would Congress have wanted courts to freeze current practice statute by statute? Would it have wanted to impose different burden-of-proof requirements where claims of duress are identical, where statutes are similar, where the *only* relevant difference is the time of enactment? Why? Indeed, individual instances of criminal conduct often violate several statutes. In a trial for those violations, is the judge to instruct the jury to apply different standards of proof to a duress defense depending upon when Congress enacted the particular statute in question? . . .

I would assume instead that Congress' silence typically means that Congress expected the courts to develop [burden of proof] rules governing affirmative defenses as they have done in the past, by beginning with the common law and taking full account of the subsequent need for that law to evolve through judicial practice informed by reason and experience. That approach would produce uniform federal practice across different affirmative defenses, as well as across statutes passed at different points in time.

II

My approach leads me to conclude that in federal criminal cases, the prosecution should bear the duress defense burden of persuasion. The issue is a close one. In Blackstone's time the accused bore the burden of proof for all affirmative defenses. See 4 W. Blackstone, Commentaries *201. And 20th-century experts have taken different positions on the matter. The Model Penal Code, for example, recommends placing the burden of persuasion on the prosecution. The Brown Commission recommends placing it upon the defendant. 1 National Commission on Reform of Federal Criminal Laws, 1 Working Papers 278 (1970). And the proposed revision of the federal criminal code, agnostically, would have turned the matter over to the courts for decision. S. 1722, 96th Cong., 1st Sess., §501 (1979). Moreover, there is a practical argument that favors the Government's position here, namely that defendants should bear the burden of persuasion because defendants often have superior access to the relevant proof.

Nonetheless, several factors favor placing the burden on the prosecution. For one thing, in certain respects the question of duress resembles that of *mens rea*, an issue that is always for the prosecution to prove beyond a reasonable doubt. . . .

[W]here a defendant acts under duress, she lacks any semblance of a meaningful choice . . . . As Blackstone wrote, the criminal law punishes "abuse[s] of th[e] free will"; hence "it is highly just and equitable that a man should be excused for those acts, which are done through unavoidable force and compulsion." 4 Commentaries *27. And it is in this "force and compulsion," acting upon the will, that the resemblance to lack of *mens rea* lies. Davis v. United States, [160 U.S. 469 (1895)], allocated the federal insanity defense burden to the Government partly for these reasons. That case, read in light of Leland v. Oregon, 343 U.S. 790, 797 (1952), suggests that, even if insanity does not always show the absence of *mens rea*, it does show the absence of a "'*vicious* will.'" *Davis*, 160 U.S. at 484 (citing Blackstone; emphasis added).

For another thing, federal courts . . . have imposed the federal-crime burden of persuasion upon the prosecution in respect to self-defense, insanity, and entrapment, which resemble the duress defense in certain relevant ways. In respect to both duress and self-defense, for example, the defendant's illegal act is voluntary . . . but the circumstances deprive the defendant of any meaningful ability or opportunity to act otherwise, depriving the defendant of a choice that is free. Insanity . . . may involve circumstances that resemble, but are not identical to, a lack of *mens rea*. And entrapment requires the prosecution to prove that the defendant was "predisposed" to commit the crime—a matter sometimes best known to the defendant. . . .

In a word, I cannot evaluate the claim of practicality without somewhat more systematic evidence of the existence of a problem, say, in those Circuits that for many years have imposed the burden on the prosecutor. And, of course, if I am wrong about the Government's practical need (and were my views to prevail), the Government would remain free to ask Congress to reallocate the burden.

Finally, there is a virtue in uniformity, in treating the federal statutory burden of persuasion similarly in respect to *actus reus*, *mens rea*, mistake, self-defense, entrapment, and duress. The Second Circuit, when imposing the burden of persuasion for duress on the prosecution, wrote that differences in this respect create "a grave possibility of juror confusion." United States v. Mitchell, 725 F.2d 832, 836 (1983) (Newman, J., joined by Feinberg, C.J., and Friendly, J.). They risk unfairness as well.

For these reasons I believe that, in the absence of an indication of congressional intent to the contrary, federal criminal law should place the burden of persuasion in respect to the duress defense upon the prosecution, which, as is now common in respect to many affirmative defenses, it must prove beyond a reasonable doubt. With respect, I dissent.

NOTES AND QUESTIONS

1. The narrow issue in *Dixon* concerns the burden of persuasion with respect to duress claims in federal cases. But our chief concern is the broader issue: the legal status of the federal common law of defenses.

2. None of the Justices in *Dixon* doubted the existence of a duress defense, even though it has never been codified by Congress. Nevertheless, in *Dixon*, there are three distinct interpretive positions, none of which appears to have the allegiance of a majority of the Court. First, Justice Stevens and at least some of his colleagues take the view that the existence of such a defense, and its appropriate contours, is to be determined statute by statute. Second, Justices Kennedy, Breyer, and Souter employ common-law reasoning to define the bounds of duress and other criminal defenses that they maintain apply to the entirety of federal criminal law. Justices Alito and Scalia take a third approach: They accept the existence of the duress defense not because state legislatures and state and federal judges adopt

and apply it *now*, but because it existed at common law "[w]hen Congress began to enact federal criminal statutes."

Which of these positions seems most consistent with congressional intent? Which represents the wisest exercise of judicial power? Are your answers the same?

3. Two issues divide the Justices in *Dixon*. The first concerns the scope of judicial power over federal criminal law. The second is less obvious, but no less important: The Justices disagree about which doctrines are appropriately seen as *trans-substantive*—i.e., which doctrines should apply across the board to all federal crimes, or at least to all save for a small number of exceptions. Historically, the law of defenses, including the burden of proof that applies to duress claims, has been trans-substantive. Should it be? Different intent standards apply to different crimes—why not make different defenses available for different criminal charges? In effect, that is what the "exculpatory no" doctrine did: It established a limited defense for federal misrepresentation cases.

4. Congress has by statute defined one trans-substantive defense—the insanity defense. Congress acted to narrow this common-law federal defense in the wake of John Hinckley's acquittal for shooting then-President Reagan. Post-*Hinckley*, federal criminal defendants claiming insanity must prove the defense by clear and convincing evidence. 18 U.S.C. §17. The same federal statute also removed the portion of the insanity defense based on irresistible impulses, and added a required showing that the defendant's "mental disease or defect" is "severe." Id. Do these legislative moves affect your view of *Dixon*?

5. Congress has not exactly been loath to define new federal crimes. Why has it been so slow to define defenses?

6. The definition of duress used in footnote 2 of Justice Stevens's opinion in *Dixon* is widely cited by lower federal courts. It appears to be the dominant formula not only for duress, but also for self-defense and necessity. These three doctrines are often lumped together in judicial opinions as aspects of a general federal defense of justification. Judging by the reported opinions, claims of duress (and of the related defense of "necessity") are fairly common—though almost never successful. In an opinion (written before *Dixon*) rejecting one such claim, Richard Posner explained why:

> Perez's felony, conviction of which deprived him of the right to possess a gun, was for drug offenses, and he was suspected of having resumed the drug trade after his release from prison. The DEA decided to conduct a surveillance of Perez. Three agents, in two unmarked cars, watched his apartment from various vantage points in the street and alley next to the apartment building. Perez saw them from the window of his apartment one afternoon and he contends . . . that he thought they were crooks planning to rob him. As it happened, he wanted to go to the bank that afternoon and deposit $600

in cash and checks. Fearful of being robbed when he left the apartment and got into his car, Perez took his girlfriend's pistol from the bedroom dresser of the apartment (which they shared) and slipped it into his waistband before leaving. The agents had just learned that there was an outstanding warrant for Perez's arrest, so when they saw him get into his Cadillac and start to drive off they arrested him. . . .

Even crediting fully Perez's assertion that he genuinely believed the men in the cars would try to rob him when he left the apartment, he has not come close to satisfying the elements of the defense of necessity. If ex-felons who feel endangered can carry guns, felon-in-possession laws will be dead letters. Upon release from prison most felons return to their accustomed haunts. . . . Many of them will not go straight, but will return to dangerous activities such as the drug trade. Every drug dealer has a well-grounded fear of being robbed or assaulted, so that if Perez's defense were accepted felon-in-possession laws would as a practical matter not apply to drug dealers.

The defense of necessity will rarely lie in a felon-in-possession case. . . . Rarely does not mean never; for a pertinent illustration, see United States v. Panter, 688 F.2d 268, 271-272 (5th Cir. 1982). But only in the most extraordinary circumstances, illustrated by United States v. Gomez, [92 F.3d 770] (9th Cir. 1996), where the defendant had sought protection from the authorities without success, will the defense entitle the ex-felon to arm himself in advance of the crisis merely because he fears, however sincerely and reasonably, that he is in serious danger of deadly harm. More often than not the basis of his fear will be his own involvement in illegal activities; and when the danger that gives rise to the fear results from engaging in such activities—from "looking for trouble"—the defense is barred.

United States v. Perez, 86 F.3d 735, 736-37 (7th Cir. 1996). For two more recent decisions taking that tack, see United States v. Butler, 485 F.3d 569 (10th Cir. 2007); United States v. Leahy, 473 F.3d 401 (1st Cir. 2007). Both *Butler* and *Leahy* were felon-in-possession cases in which the defendants claimed they needed the weapons for self-defense.

7. The two cases Judge Posner cited in the opinion above have fairly extreme facts; if they are representative of the cases in which defendants have valid justification defenses, such cases will be very rare indeed. In *Panter*, the defendant shot an assailant who had already stabbed him, though the government claimed he possessed the weapon before that threat materialized. In *Gomez*, the defendant had volunteered to serve as a government informant in an attempted murder-for-hire case. After the government disclosed his identity (with no warning), the man on whom Gomez informed put a contract on his life. Gomez asked to be placed in protective custody but the government refused, whereupon he obtained a shotgun. Two days later, he was arrested for violating his parole and was subsequently charged under the federal felon-in-possession statute (he had been previously convicted of a state felony).

Gomez claimed he acted out of necessity and in self-defense; the government contended that those defenses did not apply to the felon-in-possession statute, and the district court appears to have bought the government's argument. The Ninth Circuit reversed and held that these defenses are available in felon-in-possession cases.

8. *Perez* and *Gomez* assumed that common-law defenses to federal crimes exist; the question at issue in those cases was whether the defenses were applicable under the relevant circumstances. United States v. Oakland Cannabis Buyers' Cooperative, 532 U.S. 483 (2001), suggested that common-law defenses, or at least the defense of necessity, may not exist. The Cooperative was a non-profit organization, staffed by doctors and nurses, that provided marijuana to cancer patients. Federal officials sought and obtained an injunction ordering the Cooperative to cease its activities. The Cooperative violated the injunction, was charged with contempt, and asserted a defense of "medical necessity." The district court denied the defense; the Ninth Circuit reversed, and the Supreme Court—as is its recent pattern—reversed the Ninth Circuit, unanimously. Justice Thomas wrote the majority opinion:

> As an initial matter, we note that it is an open question whether federal courts ever have authority to recognize a necessity defense not provided by statute. A necessity defense "traditionally covered the situation where physical forces beyond the actor's control rendered illegal conduct the lesser of two evils." United States v. Bailey, 444 U.S. 394, 410 (1980). Even at common law, the defense of necessity was somewhat controversial. See, e.g., Queen v. Dudley & Stephens, 14 Q.B. 273 (1884). And under our constitutional system, in which federal crimes are defined by statute rather than by common law, see United States v. Hudson, 11 U.S. (7 Cranch) 32 (1812), it is especially so. As we have stated: "Whether, as a policy matter, an exemption should be created is a question for legislative judgment, not judicial inference." United States v. Rutherford, 442 U.S. 544, 559 (1979). Nonetheless, we recognize that this Court has discussed the possibility of a necessity defense without altogether rejecting it. See, e.g., *Bailey*, 444 U.S. at 415.[3]

---

3. The Cooperative is incorrect to suggest that *Bailey* has settled the question whether federal courts have authority to recognize a necessity defense not provided by statute. There, the Court rejected the necessity defense of a prisoner who contended that adverse prison conditions justified his prison escape. The Court held that the necessity defense is unavailable to prisoners, like Bailey, who fail to present evidence of a bona fide effort to surrender as soon as the claimed necessity had lost its coercive force. 444 U.S. at 415. It was not argued, and so there was no occasion to consider, whether the statute might be unable to bear any necessity defense at all. And although the Court noted that Congress "legislates against a background of Anglo-Saxon common law" and thus "may" have contemplated a necessity defense, the Court refused to "balanc[e] [the] harms," explaining that "we are construing an Act of Congress, not drafting it." Id. at 415, n.11.

We need not decide, however, whether necessity can ever be a defense when the federal statute does not expressly provide for it. In this case, to resolve the question presented, we need only recognize that a medical necessity exception for marijuana is at odds with the terms of the Controlled Substances Act. The statute, to be sure, does not explicitly abrogate the defense.[4] But its provisions leave no doubt that the defense is unavailable. . . .

[The Controlled Substances Act] divides drugs into five schedules, depending in part on whether the particular drug has a currently accepted medical use. The Act then imposes restrictions on the manufacture and distribution of the substance according to the schedule in which it has been placed. Schedule I is the most restrictive schedule. The Attorney General can include a drug in schedule I only if the drug "has no currently accepted medical use in treatment in the United States," "has a high potential for abuse," and has "a lack of accepted safety for use . . . under medical supervision." §§812(b)(1)(A)-(C). . . .

The Cooperative points out, however, that the Attorney General did not place marijuana into schedule I. Congress put it there, and Congress was not required to find that a drug lacks an accepted medical use before including the drug in schedule I. We are not persuaded that this distinction has any significance. . . . Under the Cooperative's logic, drugs that Congress places in schedule I could be distributed when medically necessary whereas drugs that the Attorney General places in schedule I could not. Nothing in the statute, however, suggests that there are two tiers of schedule I narcotics, with drugs in one tier more readily available than drugs in the other. On the contrary, the statute consistently treats all schedule I drugs alike. . . .

The Cooperative further argues that use of schedule I drugs generally—whether placed in schedule I by Congress or the Attorney General—can be medically necessary, notwithstanding that they have "no currently accepted medical use." According to the Cooperative, a drug may not yet have achieved general acceptance as a medical treatment but may nonetheless have medical benefits to a particular patient or class of patients. We decline to parse the statute in this manner. . . .

For these reasons, we hold that medical necessity is not a defense to manufacturing and distributing marijuana.[7]. . .

532 U.S. at 490-94.

---

4. We reject the Cooperative's intimation that elimination of the defense requires an "explici[t]" statement. Brief for Respondents 21. Considering that we have never held necessity to be a viable justification for violating a federal statute, and that such a defense would entail a social balancing that is better left to Congress, we decline to set the bar so high.

7. Lest there be any confusion, we clarify that nothing in our analysis, or the statute, suggests that a distinction should be drawn between the prohibitions on manufacturing and distributing and the other prohibitions in the Controlled Substances Act. Furthermore, the very point of our holding is that there is no medical necessity exception to the prohibitions at issue, even when the patient is "seriously ill" and lacks alternative avenues for relief. . . .

Justice Stevens joined the judgment in *Oakland Cannabis Buyers*, but objected to the language casting doubt on the common-law defenses of necessity in federal cases:

> [T]he Court takes two unwarranted and unfortunate excursions that prevent me from joining its opinion. First, the Court reaches beyond its holding, and beyond the facts of the case, by suggesting that the defense of necessity is unavailable for anyone under the Controlled Substances Act. Because necessity was raised in this case as a defense to distribution, the Court need not venture an opinion on whether the defense is available to anyone other than distributors. Most notably, whether the defense might be available to a seriously ill patient for whom there is no alternative means of avoiding starvation or extraordinary suffering is a difficult issue that is not presented here.
>
> Second, the Court gratuitously casts doubt on "whether necessity can ever be a defense" to *any* federal statute that does not explicitly provide for it, calling [the existence of] such a defense . . . an "open question." By contrast, our precedent has expressed no doubt about the viability of the common-law defense. . . . See, e.g., United States v. Bailey, 444 U.S. 394, 415 (1980) ("We therefore hold that, where a criminal defendant is charged with escape and claims that he is entitled to an instruction on the theory of duress or necessity, he must proffer evidence of a bona fide effort to surrender or return to custody as soon as the claimed duress or necessity had lost its coercive force"); id. at 416, n.11 ("Our principal difference with the dissent, therefore, is not as to the *existence* of such a defense but as to the importance of surrender as an element of it" (emphasis added)).

532 U.S. at 500-01 (Stevens, J., concurring in the judgment). Justices Ginsburg and Souter agreed with Justice Stevens; Justice Breyer took no part in the case.

Oakland Cannabis Buyers may not be squarely at odds with *Dixon*, but the two cases are surely in tension. Has *Dixon* answered the questions raised by Justice Thomas in the earlier case? Or might the common-law defense of necessity have a less secure legal status in federal court than that of duress? Would, in the odd event that such a case were brought, Justice Thomas preclude a shipwrecked sailor who, having been cast up starving on an island with an uninhabited federal lighthouse, broke into the premises to take food from raising a necessity defense against the charge of theft of government property? (Note how judicial rigidity on this score puts the onus on prosecutors.) Or, to use a more realistic example, when the general federal assault statute explicitly includes "without just cause or excuse" in its "assault with a dangerous weapon" subsection but makes no such reference in other subsections, does that mean that common-law justification and excuse defenses are not available for the other assault offenses? The Third Circuit said "maybe," in a federal prison assault case. United States v. Taylor, 686 F.3d 182, 194 (3d Cir. 2012). Thereafter, a provision (§906) in the "Safety for Indian Women" title (IX) of the Violence Against Women Reauthorization Act of 2013, Pub. L. No. 113-4, struck this language from the "dangerous weapon" subsection. Does this mean that the common-law defenses of "just cause" (necessity) and "excuse" are unavailable in all federal assault defenses? For more on the current state of these defenses, see Monu Bedi, Excusing Behavior: Reclassifying the Federal Common Law Defenses of Duress and Necessity Relying on the Victim's Role, 101 J. Crim. L. & Criminology 575 (2011).

For an example of the common law license federal courts appear to exercise when recognizing and shaping the contour of defenses, consider United States v. Waldman, 835 F.3d 751 (7th Cir. 2016). There, in the prosecution of a federal inmate for assault, under §111, for head-butting a corrections officer during an argument about a pat-down search, the Court considered whether the inmate needed to have feared "serious bodily harm or death" before he could assert self-defense at trial:

> While 18 U.S.C. §111 does not explicitly address self-defense, when a statute is silent on the question of affirmative defenses, we are to effectuate the defense as "Congress may have contemplated it," looking to the common law as a guide. See United States v. Dixon, 548 U.S. 1, 13-14 (2006). At common law, self-defense is the use of force necessary to defend against the imminent use of unlawful force. But what is unlawful force in a prison setting? Obviously correctional officers will sometimes need to use force to maintain order inside prison walls. The government urges that we adopt the definition of unlawful force used by the Fourth Circuit, and hold that an inmate is only permitted to use force in self-defense against a correctional officer if the inmate faces an "unlawful and present threat of serious bodily injury or death." United States v. Gore, 592 F.3d 489, 494 (4th Cir. 2010). But unlike the defenses of duress or necessity, fearing death or serious bodily harm is not required to make out a claim of self-defense. While using lethal force to defend oneself may require such a serious threat, under our own Pattern Instructions, non-lethal force (like head-butting, for example) does not contain such a requirement. See Pattern Criminal Jury Instructions of the Seventh Circuit 6.01 at 85 (2012).
>
> Rather than fashioning our own definition of unlawful force in a prison setting, we look to the Eighth Amendment, which already sets the legal limits on prison officials' acts towards inmates. Sometimes, it is within the bounds of the Eighth Amendment for correctional officers to use force that would be unlawful outside of prison walls. That is because "lawful incarceration brings about the necessary withdrawal or limitation of many privileges or rights, a retraction justified by the considerations of our penal system." Bell v. Wolfish, 441 U.S. 520, 545-46 (1979). And corrections officers face the difficult task of balancing the need to maintain or restore discipline through force against the risk of injury to inmates. So whether a prison security measure violates the Eighth Amendment turns on whether "force was applied in a good faith effort to maintain or restore discipline or maliciously and sadistically for the

very purpose of causing harm." Whitley v. Albers, 475 U.S. 312, 320-21 (1986). We think this test is as useful in determining if an inmate is justified in using self-defense as it is in determining if a prisoner has an Eighth Amendment claim against his jailers.

The government argues that if self-defense is not contingent upon fearing serious bodily injury or death, inmates will be allowed to use force against guards any time they believe the officer might be using slightly more force than necessary against them. But such a danger is overblown. Prisoners will still need to prove their fear was reasonable, meaning that there was an objective reason to believe that officers intended to cause sadistic and malicious harm. That is not an easy burden. A prisoner cannot prevail under the Eighth Amendment because he "reasonably believed his handcuffs were too tight causing momentary interruption of his circulation." *Gore*, 592 F.3d at 495. Indeed, under the Eighth Amendment, "not every push or shove by a prison guard violates a prisoner's constitutional rights." DeWalt v. Carter, 224 F.3d 607, 620 (7th Cir. 2000). Similarly, the fear that "guards would second-guess every use of force to ascertain whether the force used exceeded, even by a bit, what was necessary" is no different than the fear that guards already have that they will be sued for using excessive force. *Gore*, 592 F.3d at 495. So we hold that an inmate may act in self-defense if he reasonably fears imminent use of sadistic and malicious force by a prison official for the very purpose of causing him harm.

The opposite holding would prevent inmates from protecting themselves from sadistic and malicious acts which do not cause serious bodily harm, but which everyone can agree are egregious violations of the Eighth Amendment. For example, what about cases of sexual abuse of inmates? We have previously held that forcing a prisoner to perform sexually provocative acts in front of spectators is a viable Eighth Amendment claim. Calhoun v. DeTella, 319 F.3d 936, 940 (7th Cir. 2003). Prisoners should not endure such abuse when they could easily act to stop it because they would risk being convicted of assaulting an officer. Under the federal definition of "serious bodily harm," without a substantial risk of death, extreme physical pain, protracted and obvious disfigurement, or protracted loss of the function of a bodily member, organ or mental faculty, inmates would risk further incarceration if they tried to resist such abuse. See 18 U.S.C. §1365(h)(3) (defining "serious bodily harm"). In the midst of enduring abuse by officials, prisoners should not be expected to calculate whether the requisite disfigurement or loss of bodily function will come to pass before acting to protect themselves. Such a result is not consistent with the Eighth Amendment, and would "give prison officials free reign to maliciously and sadistically inflict psychological torture on prisoners, so long as they take care not to inflict any physical injury in the process." *Calhoun*, 319 F.3d at 940. Under common law principles, requiring the threat of serious bodily injury or death certainly might be appropriate for use of lethal force in self-defense, see, e.g., United States v. White Feather, 768 F.3d 735, 740 (7th Cir. 2013). But in a case where a prisoner is simply acting to stop abuse completely untethered to official discipline, which can only be interpreted as sadistic, malicious, and intended to cause harm, she is entitled to act in

self-defense. And while Congress clearly intended to protect correctional officers from harm in passing 18 U.S.C. §111, that purpose must be harmonized
with Eighth Amendment protections, not supersede them.

835 F.3d at 754-56.

9. The defense of entrapment finds its origins not in federal common
law but rather in a muscular species of statutory interpretation. In Sorrells v.
United States, 287 U.S. 435 (1932), where a Prohibition agent had badgered
the defendant into selling him some whiskey, the Court overturned the conviction, explaining: "We are unable to conclude that it was the intention
of the Congress in enacting this statute that its processes of detection and
enforcement should be abused by the instigation by government officials of
an act on the part of persons otherwise innocent in order to lure them to its
commission and to punish them." Id. at 448. Later courts have continued to
read a similar lack of congressional intent into every criminal statute they
have encountered. See, e.g., Jacobson v. United States, 503 U.S. 540, 553-
54 (1992); see generally Jessica A. Roth, The Anomaly of Entrapment, 91
Wash. U. L. Rev. 979 (2014). Is the fact that the Court presents entrapment
as a matter of statutory interpretation, not common law, just a historical
accident?

Professor Roth explains the current contours of the entrapment
defense:

> [A] defendant asserting entrapment must show that he or she was induced
> to commit the offense by an (undercover) government agent. If induce-
> ment has been shown, the burden shifts to the government to show that the
> defendant nevertheless was "predisposed" to commit the offense. In other
> words, if the government can establish that the defendant was predisposed
> to commit similar offenses before being induced by a government agent to
> commit the offense charged in the particular case, the entrapment defense
> fails.

Id. at 983.

The defense of entrapment—which must be presented to the
jury—should not be confused with the "defense" of "outrageous government conduct," which invokes a court's supervisory powers or the Due
Process Clause and is a matter for the court. The Circuits are divided on
whether the latter remains a valid avenue for relief, but even courts that recognize that avenue seldom quash prosecutions on this ground, see United
States v. Augustin, 661 F.3d 1105, 1122 (11th Cir. 2011); United States v.
Lakhani, 480 F.3d 171, 180-82 (3d Cir. 2007); United States v. Cromitie, 727
F.3d 194, 217-26 (2d Cir. 2013). One recurring source of (usually unsuccessful) claims of "outrageous government conduct" have been "reverse sting"
operations of the following sort:

For several decades, the Bureau of Alcohol, Tobacco, and Firearms ("ATF") has conducted reverse sting operations in order to identify and apprehend people who can be enticed into robbing fictitious drug "stash houses" (houses in which drugs are "stashed"). In these "stash house stings," an undercover agent poses as a disgruntled drug courier with knowledge about a stash house protected by armed guards and containing a large amount of cocaine. The agent suggests to targets of the reverse sting that they join forces, rob the house, and split the proceeds. Once the targets have taken steps to rob the fictional house, they are arrested and charged with conspiracy to violate federal narcotics laws.

United States v. Pedrin, 797 F.3d 792, 794 (9th Cir. 2015) (rejecting defense); see also United States v. Hare, 820 F.3d 93, 104 (4th Cir. 2016) (noting that no court of appeals has sustained the defense in a stash house case). But see United States v. Kindle, 698 F.3d 401, 414-15 (7th Cir. 2012) (Posner, J., dissenting) (explaining that stash house stings are "a disreputable tactic" in part because "the police can convince a suspect that the stash house robbery would be a shockingly simple and easy crime to commit").

D.   CRIMINAL INTENT

If the law of defenses has been shaped by common-law doctrines, the same is true of the law of criminal intent in federal cases. Congress often fails to mention the defendant's state of mind in criminal statutes—and when *mens rea* is mentioned, it is often "defined" only by a single vague term, leaving courts to flesh out the term's meaning. Unless federal criminal law is to consist of strict liability crimes and crimes as to which *mens rea* is basically undefined—see subsection 1, below—common-law *mens rea* terms appear to be the only viable options.

On the other hand, many federal offenses do have statutory *mens rea* terms, so the law of criminal intent is bound to be more statutory—more of a mix between common law and statutory text—than the law of defenses. What will the mix look like? How is the balance between judicial and legislative power to be struck? The three parts below tell the tale, in rough outline. Subsection 1 deals with a great debate in mid-twentieth-century federal criminal law between judicial supporters of strict liability and judicial proponents of the proposition that the government must prove some kind of wrongful intent, at least in cases not involving the prosecution of large businesses. The latter side of that debate ultimately prevailed—a fact that shapes the law discussed in subsections 2 and 3. Subsection 2 concerns the kind and amount of factual knowledge that the government must prove in order to convict. Subsection 3 explores a more hotly contested issue: the kind and amount of *legal* knowledge that the government must prove in order to convict.

1.   THE HISTORICAL DEBATE

United States v. Dotterweich
320 U.S. 277 (1943)

Mr. Justice FRANKFURTER delivered the opinion of the Court.

This was a prosecution begun by two informations, consolidated for trial, charging Buffalo Pharmacal Company, Inc., and Dotterweich, its president and general manager, with violations of the Act of Congress of June 25, 1938, 52 Stat. 1040, 21 U.S.C. §§301-392, known as the Federal Food, Drug, and Cosmetic Act. The Company, a jobber in drugs, purchased them from their manufacturers and shipped them, repacked under its own label, in interstate commerce. . . . The informations were based on §301 of that Act, 21 U.S.C. §331, paragraph (a) of which prohibits "The introduction or delivery for introduction into interstate commerce of any . . . drug . . . that is adulterated or misbranded." "Any person" violating this provision is, by paragraph (a) of §303, 21 U.S.C. §333, made "guilty of a misdemeanor." Three counts went to the jury—two, for shipping misbranded drugs in interstate commerce, and a third, for so shipping an adulterated drug. The jury disagreed as to the corporation and found Dotterweich guilty on all three counts. . . .*

The Circuit Court of Appeals . . . reversed the conviction on the ground that only the corporation was the "person" subject to prosecution. . . .

The Food and Drugs Act of 1906 was an exertion by Congress of its power to keep impure and adulterated food and drugs out of the channels of commerce. By the Act of 1938, Congress extended the range of its control over illicit and noxious articles and stiffened the penalties for disobedience. The purposes of this legislation thus touch phases of the lives and health of people which, in the circumstances of modern industrialism, are largely beyond self-protection. Regard for these purposes should infuse construction of the legislation if it is to be treated as a working instrument of government. . . . The prosecution to which Dotterweich was subjected is based on a now familiar type of legislation whereby penalties serve as effective means of regulation. Such legislation dispenses with the conventional requirement for criminal conduct—awareness of some wrongdoing. In the interest of the larger good it puts the burden of acting at hazard upon a person otherwise innocent but standing in responsible relation to a public danger. United States v. Balint, 258 U.S. 250. And so it is clear that shipments like those now in issue are "punished by the statute if the article is misbranded [or adulterated], and that the

---

* [Editors' Note: Dotterweich was fined $500 on each count, with payment suspended on two counts, and sentenced to 60 days probation on each count, to run concurrently. United States v. Dotterweich, 131 F.2d 500, 501 (2d Cir. 1942).]

article may be misbranded [or adulterated] without any conscious fraud at all. It was natural enough to throw this risk on shippers with regard to the identity of their wares. . . ." United States v. Johnson, 221 U.S. 488, 497-498. . . .

Hardship there doubtless may be under a statute which thus penalizes the transaction though consciousness of wrongdoing be totally wanting. Balancing relative hardships, Congress has preferred to place it upon those who have at least the opportunity of informing themselves of the existence of conditions imposed for the protection of consumers before sharing in illicit commerce, rather than to throw the hazard on the innocent public who are wholly helpless.

It would be too treacherous to define or even to indicate by way of illustration the class of employees which stands in such a responsible relation. To attempt a formula embracing the variety of conduct whereby persons may responsibly contribute in furthering a transaction forbidden by an Act of Congress, to wit, to send illicit goods across state lines, would be mischievous futility. In such matters the good sense of prosecutors, the wise guidance of trial judges, and the ultimate judgment of juries must be trusted. Our system of criminal justice necessarily depends on "conscience and circumspection in prosecuting officers," Nash v. United States, 229 U.S. 373, 378, even when the consequences are far more drastic than they are under the provision of law before us. See United States v. Balint, 258 U.S. 250 (involving a maximum sentence of five years). For present purpose it suffices to say that . . . the District Court properly left the question of the responsibility of Dotterweich for the shipment to the jury, and there was sufficient evidence to support its verdict. . . .

Mr. Justice MURPHY, dissenting. . . .

There is no evidence in this case of any personal guilt on the part of the respondent. There is no proof or claim that he ever knew of the introduction into commerce of the adulterated drugs in question, much less that he actively participated in their introduction. Guilt is imputed to the respondent solely on the basis of his authority and responsibility as president and general manager of the corporation.

It is a fundamental principle of Anglo-Saxon jurisprudence that guilt is personal and that it ought not lightly to be imputed to a citizen who, like the respondent, has no evil intention or consciousness of wrongdoing. It may be proper to charge him with responsibility to the corporation and the stockholders for negligence and mismanagement. But in the absence of clear statutory authorization it is inconsistent with established canons of criminal law to rest liability on an act in which the accused did not participate and of which he had no personal knowledge. Before we place the stigma of a criminal conviction upon any such citizen the legislative mandate must be clear and unambiguous. . . .

To erect standards of responsibility is a difficult legislative task and the opinion of this Court admits that it is "too treacherous" and a "mischievous futility" for us to engage in such pursuits. But the only alternative is a blind resort to "the good sense of prosecutors, the wise guidance of trial judges, and the ultimate judgment of juries." Yet that situation is precisely what our constitutional system sought to avoid. . . . The legislative power to restrain the liberty and to imperil the good reputation of citizens must not rest upon the variable attitudes and opinions of those charged with the duties of interpreting and enforcing the mandates of the law. I therefore cannot approve the decision of the Court in this case.

Mr. Justice ROBERTS, Mr. Justice REED, and Mr. Justice RUTLEDGE join in this dissent.

NOTES AND QUESTIONS

1. Had the law required the government to prove that Dotterweich knew the drugs were adulterated, Dotterweich and a host of similarly regulated actors would not have been convictable. If the law *didn't* require proof of knowledge, criminal punishment would have been imposed even in cases with "no evidence . . . of any personal guilt." Both results seem problematic: The government has a strong interest in requiring that drugs be safe, but individual defendants have a strong interest in avoiding prison sentences for conduct that is at worst civilly negligent. Is there a way out of this box? Of course there is. The law can regulate the conduct of people like Dotterweich without criminally punishing them. Civil regulations that impose strict liability and hefty fines for violators—including, perhaps, individual violators like Dotterweich—can ensure reasonably high levels of safety without the need for criminal prosecutions. Criminal law can require substantial proof of criminal intent, as the four dissenting Justices contended, without disabling the regulatory state.

2. That proposition seems obvious today—but to many in the New Deal generation, it was anything but. Today, criminal punishment is seen as a special form of government power, limited in special ways. That understanding was less common in 1943. Most of the New Deal's core statutes included provisions criminalizing violations. The most committed New Dealers (like Felix Frankfurter, author of the majority opinion in *Dotterweich*) feared that if the law restricted criminal prosecution too much, the regulatory state would be unable to regulate effectively. For their part, anti–New Deal politicians and judges often embraced restrictions on criminal prosecution and punishment because they sought to limit government power generally—and hoped to limit the authority of the many government agencies that FDR and his followers created.

3. Though *Dotterweich* was the product of New Deal–era debates, it is more than a historical curiosity. Thirty years later, the Supreme Court reaffirmed that "responsible corporate officers" (RCO) could be held liable for regulatory violations of the FDCA. See United States v. Park, 421 U.S. 658 (1975) (upholding conviction of the president of a supermarket chain who had the power to prevent, but did not personally participate in or know of, the food adulteration offense that occurred). The RCO doctrine has been applied to other statutes as well. In Chapter 11 we consider the scope and arguable rationales for the judge-made rule that corporate officers may be held criminally responsible for certain offenses occurring within the corporate entity.

4. *Dotterweich* raises the broader question of when, if ever, it is appropriate to punish defendants who lack culpable intent. That question is at the heart of the next case.

Morissette v. United States
342 U.S. 246 (1952)

Mr. Justice JACKSON delivered the opinion of the Court.

This would have remained a profoundly insignificant case to all except its immediate parties had it not been so tried and submitted to the jury as to raise questions both fundamental and far-reaching in federal criminal law, for which reason we granted certiorari.

On a large tract of uninhabited and untilled land in a wooded and sparsely populated area of Michigan, the Government established a practice bombing range over which the Air Force dropped simulated bombs at ground targets. These bombs consisted of a metal cylinder about forty inches long and eight inches across, filled with sand and enough black powder to cause a smoke puff by which the strike could be located. At various places about the range signs read "Danger—Keep Out—Bombing Range." Nevertheless, the range was known as good deer country and was extensively hunted.

Spent bomb casings were cleared from the targets and thrown into piles "so that they will be out of the way." They were not stacked or piled in any order but were dumped in heaps, some of which had been accumulating for four years or upwards, were exposed to the weather and rusting away.

Morissette, in December of 1948, went hunting in this area but did not get a deer. He thought to meet expenses of the trip by salvaging some of these casings. He loaded three tons of them on his truck and took them to a nearby farm, where they were flattened by driving a tractor over them. After expending this labor and trucking them to market in Flint, he realized $84.

Morissette, by occupation, is a fruit stand operator in summer and a trucker and scrap iron collector in winter. An honorably discharged veteran of World War II, he enjoys a good name among his neighbors and has had no blemish on his record more disreputable than a conviction for reckless driving.

The loading, crushing and transporting of these casings were all in broad daylight, in full view of passers-by, without the slightest effort at concealment. When an investigation was started, Morissette voluntarily, promptly and candidly told the whole story to the authorities, saying that he had no intention of stealing but thought the property was abandoned, unwanted and considered of no value to the Government. He was indicted, however, on the charge that he "did unlawfully, wilfully and knowingly steal and convert" property of the United States of the value of $84, in violation of 18 U.S.C. §641, which provides that "whoever embezzles, steals, purloins, or knowingly converts" government property is punishable by fine and imprisonment.[2]

Morissette was convicted and sentenced to imprisonment for two months or to pay a fine of $200. The Court of Appeals affirmed. . . .

On his trial, Morissette, as he had at all times told investigating officers, testified that from appearances he believed the casings were cast-off and abandoned, that he did not intend to steal the property, and took it with no wrongful or criminal intent. The trial court, however, was unimpressed, and ruled: "[H]e took it because he thought it was abandoned and he knew he was on government property. . . . That is no defense. . . . I don't think anybody can have the defense they thought the property was abandoned on another man's piece of property." The court stated: "I will not permit you to show this man thought it was abandoned. . . . I hold in this case that there is no question of abandoned property." The court refused to submit or to allow counsel to argue to the jury whether Morissette acted with innocent intention. It charged: "And I instruct you that if you believe the testimony of the government in this case, he intended to take it. . . . He had no right to take this property. . . . [A]nd it is no defense to claim that it was abandoned, because it was on private property. . . . And I instruct you to this effect: That if this young man took this property (and he says he did), without any permission (he says he did), that was on the property of the United States Government (he says it was), that it was of the value of one cent or more (and evidently

_____

2. 18 U.S.C. §641, so far as pertinent, reads:

   Whoever embezzles, steals, purloins, or knowingly converts to his use or the use of another, or without authority, sells, conveys or disposes of any record, voucher, money, or thing of value of the United States or of any department or agency thereof, or any property made or being made under contract for the United States or any department or agency thereof; . . . shall be fined not more than $10,000 or imprisoned not more than ten years, or both; but if the value of such property does not exceed the sum of $100, he shall be fined not more than $1,000 or imprisoned not more than one year, or both.

it was), that he is guilty of the offense charged here. If you believe the government, he is guilty. . . . The question on intent is whether or not he intended to take the property. He says he did. Therefore, if you believe either side, he is guilty." Petitioner's counsel contended, "But the taking must have been with a felonious intent." The court ruled, however: "That is presumed by his own act."

The Court of Appeals [affirmed]. . . . This conclusion was thought to be required by . . . this Court's decisions in United States v. Behrman, 258 U.S. 280 [1922], and United States v. Balint, 258 U.S. 250 [1922].

I

In those cases this Court did construe mere omission from a criminal enactment of any mention of criminal intent as dispensing with it. If they be deemed precedents for principles of construction generally applicable to federal penal statutes, they authorize this conviction. Indeed, such adoption of the literal reasoning announced in those cases would do this and more—it would sweep out of all federal crimes, except when expressly preserved, the ancient requirement of a culpable state of mind. We think a résumé of their historical background is convincing that an effect has been ascribed to them more comprehensive than was contemplated and one inconsistent with our philosophy of criminal law.

The contention that an injury can amount to a crime only when inflicted by intention is no provincial or transient notion. It is as universal and persistent in mature systems of law as belief in freedom of the human will and a consequent ability and duty of the normal individual to choose between good and evil. A relation between some mental element and punishment for a harmful act is almost as instinctive as the child's familiar exculpatory "But I didn't mean to," and has afforded the rational basis for a tardy and unfinished substitution of deterrence and reformation in place of retaliation and vengeance as the motivation for public prosecution.[5] Unqualified acceptance of this doctrine by English common law in the Eighteenth Century was indicated by Blackstone's sweeping statement that to constitute any crime there must first be a "vicious will." Common-law commentators of the Nineteenth Century early pronounced the same principle. . . .

---

5. In Williams v. People of State of New York, 337 U.S. 241, 248 [1949], we observed that "Retribution is no longer the dominant objective of the criminal law. Reformation and rehabilitation of offenders have become important goals of criminal jurisprudence." We also there referred to ". . . a prevalent modern philosophy of penology that the punishment should fit the offender and not merely the crime." Id. at 247. Such ends would seem illusory if there were no mental element in crime.

Crime, as a compound concept, generally constituted only from concurrence of an evil-meaning mind with an evil-doing hand, was congenial to an intense individualism and took deep and early root in American soil. As the states codified the common law of crimes, even if their enactments were silent on the subject, their courts assumed that the omission did not signify disapproval of the principle but merely recognized that intent was so inherent in the idea of the offense that it required no statutory affirmation. Courts, with little hesitation or division, found an implication of the requirement as to offenses that were taken over from the common law. The unanimity with which they have adhered to the central thought that wrongdoing must be conscious to be criminal is emphasized by the variety, disparity and confusion of their definitions of the requisite but elusive mental element. However, courts of various jurisdictions, and for the purposes of different offenses, have devised working formulae, if not scientific ones, for the instruction of juries around such terms as "felonious intent," "criminal intent," "malice aforethought," "guilty knowledge," "fraudulent intent," "wilfulness," "*scienter*," to denote guilty knowledge, or "*mens rea*," to signify an evil purpose or mental culpability. By use or combination of these various tokens, they have sought to protect those who were not blameworthy in mind from conviction of infamous common-law crimes.

However, the *Balint* and *Behrman* offenses belong to a category of another character, with very different antecedents and origins. The crimes there involved depend on no mental element but consist only of forbidden acts or omissions. This, while not expressed by the Court, is made clear from examination of a century-old but accelerating tendency, discernible both here and in England, to call into existence new duties and crimes which disregard any ingredient of intent. The industrial revolution multiplied the number of workmen exposed to injury from increasingly powerful and complex mechanisms, driven by freshly discovered sources of energy, requiring higher precautions by employers. . . . Congestion of cities and crowding of quarters called for health and welfare regulations undreamed of in simpler times. Wide distribution of goods became an instrument of wide distribution of harm when those who dispersed food, drink, drugs, and even securities, did not comply with reasonable standards of quality, integrity, disclosure and care. Such dangers have engendered increasingly numerous and detailed regulations which heighten the duties of those in control of particular industries, trades, properties or activities that affect public health, safety or welfare.

While many of these duties are sanctioned by a more strict civil liability, lawmakers, whether wisely or not, have sought to make such regulations more effective by invoking criminal sanctions. . . . This has confronted the courts with a multitude of prosecutions . . . for what have been aptly called "public welfare offenses." These cases do not fit neatly into any of such accepted classifications of common-law offenses, such as those against the state, the person, property, or public morals. Many of these offenses are not in the nature of positive aggressions or invasions, with which the common law so often dealt, but are in the nature of neglect where the law requires care, or inaction where it imposes a duty. Many violations of such regulations result in no direct or immediate injury to person or property but merely create the danger or probability of it which the law seeks to minimize. While such offenses do not threaten the security of the state in the manner of treason, they may be regarded as offenses against its authority, for their occurrence impairs the efficiency of controls deemed essential to the social order. . . . Hence, legislation applicable to such offenses, as a matter of policy, does not specify intent as a necessary element. The accused, if he does not will the violation, usually is in a position to prevent it with no more care than society might reasonably expect. . . . Also, penalties commonly are relatively small, and conviction does no grave damage to an offender's reputation. Under such considerations, courts have turned to construing statutes and regulations which make no mention of intent as dispensing with it. . . .

In overruling a contention that there can be no conviction on an indictment which makes no charge of criminal intent but alleges only making of a sale of a narcotic forbidden by law, Chief Justice Taft, wrote: "While the general rule at common law was that the *scienter* was a necessary element in the indictment and proof of every crime, and this was followed in regard to statutory crimes even where the statutory definition did not in terms include it . . . , there has been a modification of this view in respect to prosecutions under statutes the purpose of which would be obstructed by such a requirement. It is a question of legislative intent to be construed by the court. . . ." United States v. Balint, 258 U.S. at 251-52.

He referred, however, to "regulatory measures in the exercise of what is called the police power where the emphasis of the statute is evidently upon achievement of some social betterment rather than the punishment of the crimes as in cases of *mala in se*," and drew his citation of supporting authority chiefly from state court cases dealing with regulatory offenses. Id. at 252.

On the same day, the Court determined that an offense under the Narcotic Drug Act does not require intent, saying, "If the offense be a statutory one, and intent or knowledge is not made an element of it, the indictment need not charge such knowledge or intent." United States v. Behrman, 258 U.S. at 288.

Of course, the purpose of every statute would be "obstructed" by requiring a finding of intent, if we assume that it had a purpose to convict without it. . . . And since no federal crime can exist except by force of statute, the reasoning of the *Behrman* opinion, if read literally, would work far-reaching changes in the composition of all federal crimes. . . .

It was not until recently that the Court took occasion more explicitly to relate abandonment of the ingredient of intent . . . with the peculiar nature and quality of the offense. We referred to ". . . a now familiar type of legislation whereby penalties serve as effective means of regulation," and continued, "such legislation dispenses with the conventional requirement for criminal conduct—awareness of some wrongdoing. In the interest of the larger good it puts the burden of acting at hazard upon a person otherwise innocent but standing in responsible relation to a public danger." But we warned: "Hardship there doubtless may be under a statute which thus penalizes the transaction though consciousness of wrongdoing be totally wanting." United States v. Dotterweich, 320 U.S. 277, 280-81, 284.

Neither this Court nor, so far as we are aware, any other has undertaken to delineate a precise line or set forth comprehensive criteria for distinguishing between crimes that require a mental element and crimes that do not. We attempt no closed definition, for the law on the subject is neither settled nor static. The conclusion reached in the *Balint* and *Behrman* cases has our approval and adherence for the circumstances to which it was there applied. A quite different question [] is whether we will expand the doctrine of crimes without intent to include those charged here.

Stealing, larceny, and its variants and equivalents, were among the earliest offenses known to the law that existed before legislation; they are invasions of rights of property which stir a sense of insecurity in the whole community and arouse public demand for retribution, the penalty is high and, when a sufficient amount is involved, the infamy is that of a felony, which, says Maitland, is ". . .as bad a word as you can give to man or thing." State courts of last resort, on whom fall the heaviest burden of interpreting criminal law in this country, have consistently retained the requirement of intent in larceny-type offenses. . . .

Congress, therefore, omitted any express prescription of criminal intent from the enactment before us in the light of an unbroken course of judicial decision in all constituent states of the Union holding intent inherent in this class of offense, even when not expressed in a statute. Congressional silence as to mental elements in an Act merely adopting into federal statutory law a concept of crime already so well defined in common law and statutory interpretation by the states may warrant quite contrary inferences than the same silence in creating an offense new to general law, for whose definition the courts have no guidance except the Act. Because the offenses before this Court in the *Balint* and *Behrman* cases were of this latter class, we cannot accept them as authority for eliminating intent from offenses incorporated from the common law. . . .

The spirit of the doctrine which denies to the federal judiciary power to create crimes forthrightly[22] admonishes that we should not enlarge the reach of enacted crimes by constituting them from anything less than the incriminating components contemplated by the words used in the statute. And where Congress borrows terms of art in which are accumulated the

---

22. United States v. Hudson and Goodwin, 7 Cranch 32.

legal tradition and meaning of centuries of practice, it presumably knows and adopts the cluster of ideas that were attached to each borrowed word in the body of learning from which it was taken. . . . In such case, absence of contrary direction may be taken as satisfaction with widely accepted definitions, not as a departure from them. . . .

We hold that mere omission from §641 of any mention of intent will not be construed as eliminating that element from the crimes denounced.

II

It is suggested, however, that the history and purposes of §641 imply . . . elimination of intent from at least one of the offenses charged under it in this case. The argument does not contest that criminal intent is retained in the offenses of embezzlement, stealing and purloining, as incorporated into this section. But it is urged that Congress joined with those, as a new, separate and distinct offense, knowingly to convert government property, under circumstances which imply that it is an offense in which the mental element of intent is not necessary. . . .

Congress, by the language of this section, has been at pains to incriminate only "knowing" conversions. . . .

Had the statute applied to conversions without qualification, it would have made crimes of all unwitting, inadvertent and unintended conversions. Knowledge, of course, is not identical with intent and may not have been the most apt words of limitation. But knowing conversion requires more than knowledge that defendant was taking the property into his possession. He must have had knowledge of the facts, though not necessarily the law, that made the taking a conversion. In the case before us, whether the mental element that Congress required be spoken of as knowledge or as intent, would not seem to alter its bearing on guilt. For it is not apparent how Morissette could have knowingly or intentionally converted property that he did not know could be converted, as would be the case if it was in fact abandoned or if he truly believed it to be abandoned and unwanted property.

It is said, and at first blush the claim has plausibility, that, if we construe the statute to require a mental element as part of criminal conversion, it becomes a meaningless duplication of the offense of stealing, and that conversion can be given meaning only by interpreting it to disregard intention. But here again a broader view of the evolution of these crimes throws a different light on the legislation.

It is not surprising if there is considerable overlapping in the embezzlement, stealing, purloining and knowing conversion grouped in this statute. What has concerned codifiers of the larceny-type offense is that gaps or crevices have separated particular crimes of this general class and guilty men have escaped through the breaches. The books contain a surfeit of cases drawing fine distinctions between slightly different circumstances under which one may obtain wrongful advantages from another's property. The codifiers wanted to reach all such instances. Probably every stealing is a conversion, but certainly not every knowing conversion is a stealing. "To steal means to *takeaway from one* in lawful possession without right with the *intention to keep wrongfully*." Irving Trust Co. v. Leff, 253 N.Y. 359, 364, 171 N.E. 569, 571. Conversion, however, may be consummated without any intent to keep and without any wrongful taking, where the initial possession by the converter was entirely lawful. Conversion may include misuse or abuse of property. . . . Money rightfully taken into one's custody may be converted without any intent to keep or embezzle it merely by commingling it with the custodian's own, if he was under a duty to keep it separate and intact. . . . Knowing conversion adds significantly to the range of protection of government property without interpreting it to punish unwitting conversions. . . .

We find no grounds for inferring any affirmative instruction from Congress to eliminate intent from any offense with which this defendant was charged.

III

As we read the record, this case was tried on the theory that even if criminal intent were essential its presence (a) should be decided by the court (b) as a presumption of law, apparently conclusive, (c) predicated upon the isolated act of taking rather than upon all of the circumstances. In each of these respects we believe the trial court was in error. . . .

The court thought the only question was, "Did he intend to take the property?" That the removal of them was a conscious and intentional act was admitted. But that isolated fact is not an adequate basis on which the jury should find [] criminal intent . . . wrongfully to deprive another of possession of property. Whether that intent existed, the jury must determine, not only from the act of taking, but from that together with defendant's testimony and all of the surrounding circumstances.

Of course, the jury, considering Morissette's awareness that these casings were on government property, his failure to seek any permission for their removal and his self-interest as a witness, might have disbelieved his profession of innocent intent and concluded that his assertion of a belief that the casings were abandoned was an afterthought. Had the jury convicted on proper instructions it would be the end of the matter. But juries are not bound by what seems inescapable logic to judges. They might have concluded that the heaps of spent casings left in the hinterland to rust away presented an appearance of unwanted and abandoned junk, and that lack of any conscious deprivation of property or intentional injury was indicated by Morissette's good character, the openness of the taking, crushing and transporting of the casings, and the candor with which it was all admitted. They might have refused to brand Morissette as a thief. Had they done so, that too would have been the end of the matter. . . .

Mr. Justice DOUGLAS concurs in the result.

NOTES AND QUESTIONS

1. Exactly what mental state must the prosecution prove to convict Morissette? The question is hard to answer precisely. Justice Jackson's opinion says that a properly instructed jury might have found that Morissette was not guilty of "any conscious deprivation of property or intentional injury," 342 U.S. at 276, and thus was not guilty of stealing government property. But Jackson also says that the jury "might have refused to brand Morissette as a thief," id. —without specifying the conditions that would support such a refusal. Why so much imprecision? Recall Justice Frankfurter's majority opinion in *Dotterweich*, which held that the food and drug legislation at issue in that case "dispenses with the conventional requirement for criminal conduct—awareness of some wrongdoing." Apparently, *Morissette* applies that allegedly "conventional requirement" to the case at hand. Why the difference between the two decisions?

2. In fact, proof of "awareness of some wrongdoing" is *not* part of conventional *mens rea* doctrine in the United States—at least not when state law is at issue. State-law crimes ordinarily require proof of either general intent or specific intent. A defendant acted with general intent if he intended to engage in the conduct that constituted the crime. A defendant acted with specific intent if he additionally intended to bring about some legally forbidden result. Morissette may well have been guilty under either standard. (For what it's worth, most theft offenses require proof of specific intent.) But, had the trial judge not virtually issued a directed verdict against Morissette, the jury might well have found that he acted without "awareness of some wrongdoing." Is that a sufficient reason to exempt him from criminal liability? Why might federal and state law deal differently with defendants like Morissette—Dotterweich too, for that matter?

3. Before the Harrison Narcotics Act (the legislation at issue in *Balint* and *Behrman*—cases cited and discussed in *Morissette*), the use of various opium products was both legal and common in many parts of the United States. Doctors often prescribed such drugs. Unsurprisingly, the use and sale of these drugs did not immediately cease when the Act took effect. It takes time for ordinary people to understand that the rules have changed and that previously acceptable conduct is now impermissible. Also unsurprisingly, the government tried to speed that process along, by prosecuting both doctors who prescribed such drugs and otherwise legitimate businesses that sold

them without the requisite permission. How should such cases be resolved? Defendants claim, justifiably, that they cannot be expected to know about every legal change that might govern their conduct. Prosecutors contend, also justifiably, that if defendants can excuse their violations by claiming ignorance of the law, new legal rules will be unenforceable and federal criminal law will be unable to change and adapt to new circumstances. Is there a way out of this dilemma? If not, which side should prevail? Or do you think that most of those prosecuted for failing to abide by the registration and taxation requirements of the Harrison Narcotics Act in fact knew they were violating the law, and the Supreme Court in *Balint* and *Behrman* refused to recognize the defense of ignorance of the law for the usual reasons that the common law (and other systems of law) rejected the defense; among other matters, it would be difficult in many cases to prove knowledge of the law?

4. Recently, in Elonis v. United States, 135 S. Ct. 2001 (2015), the Court cited *Morissette* for the proposition that "mere omission from a criminal enactment of any mention of criminal intent' should not be read 'as dispensing with it.'" *Elonis* also approvingly quoted *Morissette*'s "rule of construction reflect[ing] the basic principle that 'wrongdoing must be conscious to be criminal'" and *Morissette*'s "central thought [] that a defendant must be 'blameworthy in mind' before he can be found guilty." Id. at 2009 (quoting 342 U.S. at 252). This chapter ends with further consideration of *Elonis*, which contains the Court's latest pronouncements on federal *mens rea* standards. But you must first understand important developments in the interim—after *Morissette* and before *Elonis*. As you read these cases, consider whether the bright-line distinction (recognized in both *Dotterweich* and *Morissette*) between traditional common-law crimes and public-welfare offenses is adequate to separate those who are and are not "blameworthy."

2. DISTINGUISHING CULPABLE FROM INNOCENT CONDUCT

In *Morissette*, the question before the Court may seem, on first reading, to be only whether the defendant had to "know" the *facts* that made his conduct criminal. In the case of traditional common-law crimes, the answer was "yes"; for newer, regulatory crimes, the answer was "no." But close beneath the surface, *Morissette* arguably addressed an additional question—whether the defendant knew his conduct was unlawful (or at least likely to be unlawful). See 342 U.S. at 270-71 ("But knowing conversion requires more than knowledge that defendant was taking the property into his possession. He must have had knowledge of the facts, though not necessarily the [property] law, that made the taking a conversion.").

The cases below deal with two related questions highlighted in that passage from *Morissette*. First, what *facts* must the defendant know in order to be properly convicted under a given statute? Second, when, if ever, must a defendant also know that his actions were (or likely were) in violation of the *criminal law?* Several decades after *Morissette,* the Court addressed the latter question in a case involving unauthorized distribution of food stamps. On a simple, layperson level, unauthorized trading in food stamps does not appear altogether different from taking spent bombshell casings that the military has apparently abandoned. Whether or not you agree with us that one way of reading *Morissette* is that the jury needed to find that the defendant knew that what he did was (likely) criminal, you will see that the next case, decided more than 30 years after *Morissette,* took that idea and ran with it.

Liparota v. United States
471 U.S. 419 (1985)

Justice BRENNAN delivered the opinion of the Court.

The federal statute governing food stamp fraud provides that "whoever knowingly uses, transfers, acquires, alters, or possesses coupons or authorization cards in any manner not authorized by [the statute] or the regulations" is subject to a fine and imprisonment. 78 Stat. 708, as amended, 7 U.S.C. §2024(b)(1). The question presented is whether in a prosecution under this provision the Government must prove that the defendant knew that he was acting in a manner not authorized by statute or regulations.

I

Petitioner Frank Liparota was the co-owner with his brother of Moon's Sandwich Shop in Chicago, Illinois. He was indicted for acquiring and possessing food stamps in violation of §2024(b)(1). The Department of Agriculture had not authorized petitioner's restaurant to accept food stamps.[2] At trial, the Government proved that petitioner on three occasions purchased food stamps from an undercover Department of Agriculture agent for substantially less than their face value. On the first occasion, the agent informed petitioner that she had $195 worth of food stamps to sell. The agent then accepted petitioner's offer of $150 and consummated the transaction in a back room of the restaurant with petitioner's brother. A similar transaction occurred one week later, in which the agent sold $500

---

2. Food stamps are provided by the Government to those who meet certain need-related criteria. See 7 U.S.C. §§2014(a), 2014(c). They generally may be used only to purchase food in retail food stores. 7 U.S.C. §2016(b). If a restaurant receives proper authorization from the Department of Agriculture, it may receive food stamps as payment for meals under certain special circumstances not relevant here.

worth of coupons for $350. Approximately one month later, petitioner bought $500 worth of food stamps from the agent for $300.

In submitting the case to the jury, the District Court rejected petitioner's proposed "specific intent" instruction, which would have instructed the jury that the Government must prove that "the defendant knowingly did an act which the law forbids, purposely intending to violate the law." Concluding that "[t]his is not a specific intent crime" but rather a "knowledge case," the District Court instead instructed the jury as follows:

> When the word "knowingly" is used in these instructions, it means that the Defendant realized what he was doing, and was aware of the nature of his conduct, and did not act through ignorance, mistake, or accident. Knowledge may be proved by defendant's conduct and by all of the facts and circumstances surrounding the case.

The District Court also instructed that the Government had to prove that "the Defendant acquired and possessed food stamp coupons for cash in a manner not authorized by federal statute or regulations" and that "the Defendant knowingly and wilfully acquired the food stamps." Petitioner objected that this instruction required the jury to find merely that he knew that he was acquiring or possessing food stamps; he argued that the statute should be construed instead to reach only "people who knew that they were acting unlawfully." The judge did not alter or supplement his instructions, and the jury returned a verdict of guilty.

Petitioner appealed his conviction to the Court of Appeals for the Seventh Circuit, arguing that the District Court erred in refusing to instruct the jury that "specific intent" is required in a prosecution under 7 U.S.C. §2024(b)(1). The Court of Appeals rejected petitioner's arguments. 735 F.2d 1044 (1984). Because this decision conflicted with recent decisions of three other Courts of Appeals, we granted certiorari. . . . We reverse.

II

The controversy between the parties concerns the mental state, if any, that the Government must show in proving that petitioner acted "in any manner not authorized by [the statute] or the regulations." The Government argues that petitioner violated the statute if he knew that he acquired or possessed food stamps and if in fact that acquisition or possession was in a manner not authorized by statute or regulations. According to the Government, no *mens rea*, or "evil-meaning mind," Morissette v. United States, 342 U.S. 246, 251 (1952), is necessary for conviction. Petitioner claims that the Government's interpretation, by dispensing with *mens rea*, dispenses with the only morally blameworthy element in the definition of the crime. To avoid this allegedly untoward result, he claims that an individual violates the statute if he knows that he has acquired or possessed food stamps *and* if he also knows that he has done so in an unauthorized manner. Our task is to determine which meaning Congress intended.

The definition of the elements of a criminal offense is entrusted to the legislature, particularly in the case of federal crimes, which are solely creatures of statute. United States v. Hudson, 7 Cranch 32 (1812). With respect to the element at issue in this case, however, Congress has not explicitly spelled out the mental state required. Although Congress certainly intended by use of the word "knowingly" to require *some* mental state with respect to *some* element of the crime defined in §2024(b)(1), the interpretations proffered by both parties accord with congressional intent to this extent. Beyond this, the words themselves provide little guidance. Either interpretation would accord with ordinary usage. The legislative history of the statute contains nothing that would clarify the congressional purpose on this point.

Absent indication of contrary purpose in the language or legislative history of the statute, we believe that §2024(b)(1) requires a showing that the defendant knew his conduct to be unauthorized by statute or regulations. "The contention that an injury can amount to a crime only when inflicted by intention is no provincial or transient notion. It is as universal and persistent in mature systems of law as belief in freedom of the human will and a consequent ability and duty of the normal individual to choose between good and evil." Morissette v. United States, 342 U.S. 246, 250 (1952). . . . [T]he failure of Congress explicitly and unambiguously to indicate whether *mens rea* is required does not signal a departure from this background assumption of our criminal law.

This construction is particularly appropriate where, as here, to interpret the statute otherwise would be to criminalize a broad range of apparently innocent conduct. For instance, §2024(b)(1) declares it criminal to use, transfer, acquire, alter, or possess food stamps in any manner not authorized by statute or regulations. The statute provides further that "[c]oupons issued to eligible households shall be used by them only to purchase food in retail food stores which have been approved for participation in the food stamp program *at prices prevailing in such stores.*" 7 U.S.C. §2016(b) (emphasis added). This seems to be the *only* authorized use. A strict reading of the statute with no knowledge-of-illegality requirement would thus render criminal a food stamp recipient who, for example, used stamps to purchase food from a store that, unknown to him, charged higher than normal prices to food stamp program participants. Such a reading would also render criminal a nonrecipient of food stamps who "possessed" stamps because he was mistakenly sent them through the mail due to administrative error, "altered" them by tearing them up, and "transferred" them by throwing them away. Of course, Congress *could* have intended that this broad range of conduct be made illegal, perhaps with the understanding that prosecutors would exercise their discretion to avoid such harsh results. However, given the paucity of material suggesting that Congress did so intend, we are reluctant to adopt such a sweeping interpretation. . . .

The Government argues, however, that a comparison between §2024(b)(1) and its companion, §2024(c), demonstrates a congressional purpose not to require proof of the defendant's knowledge of illegality in a §2024(b)(1) prosecution. Section 2024(c) is directed primarily at stores authorized to accept food stamps from program participants. It provides that "[w]hoever presents, or causes to be presented, coupons for payment or redemption . . . *knowing* the same to have been received, transferred, or used in any manner in violation of [the statute] or the regulations" is subject to fine and imprisonment (emphasis added). The Government contrasts this language with that of §2024(b)(1), in which the word "knowingly" is placed differently: "whoever *knowingly* uses, transfers . . ." (emphasis added). Since §2024(c) undeniably requires a knowledge of illegality, the suggested inference is that the difference in wording and structure between the two sections indicates that §2024(b)(1) does not.

The Government urges that this distinction between the mental state required for a §2024(c) violation and that required for a §2024(b)(1) violation is a sensible one. Absent a requirement of *mens rea,* a grocer presenting food stamps for payment might be criminally liable under §2024(c) even if his customer or employees have illegally procured or transferred the stamps without the grocer's knowledge. Requiring knowledge of illegality in a §2024(c) prosecution is allegedly necessary to avoid this kind of vicarious, and non-fault-based, criminal liability. Since the offense defined in §2024(b)(1) — using, transferring, acquiring, altering, or possessing food stamps in an unauthorized manner — does not involve this possibility of vicarious liability, argues the Government, Congress had no reason to impose a similar knowledge of illegality requirement in that section.

We do not find this argument persuasive. The difference in wording between §2024(b)(1) and §2024(c) is too slender a reed to support the attempted distinction, for if the Government's argument were accepted, it would lead to the demise of the very distinction that Congress is said to have desired. . . . If only §2024(c) — and not §2024(b)(1) — required the Government to prove knowledge of illegality, the result would be that the Government could *always* avoid proving knowledge of illegality in food stamp fraud cases, simply by bringing its prosecutions under §2024(b)(1). If Congress wanted to require the Government to prove knowledge of illegality in some, but not all, food stamp fraud cases, it thus chose a peculiar way to do so. . . .

The Government advances two additional arguments in support of its reading of the statute. First, the Government contends that this Court's decision last Term in United States v. Yermian, 468 U.S. 63 (1984), supports its interpretation. *Yermian* involved a prosecution for violation of the federal false statement statute, 18 U.S.C. §1001. All parties agreed that the statute required proof at least that the defendant "knowingly and willfully" made a false statement. Thus, unlike the instant case, all parties in *Yermian* agreed that the Government had to prove the defendant's *mens rea*. The controversy in *Yermian* centered on whether the Government also had to prove that the defendant knew that the false statement was made in a matter within the jurisdiction of a federal agency. With respect to this element, although the Court held that the Government did not have to prove actual knowledge of federal agency jurisdiction, the Court explicitly reserved the question whether *some* culpability was necessary with respect even to the jurisdictional element. 468 U.S. at 75, n.14. In contrast, the Government in the instant case argues that *no mens rea* is required with respect to any element of the crime. Finally, *Yermian* found that the statutory language was unambiguous and that the legislative history supported its interpretation. The statute at issue in this case differs in both respects.

Second, the Government contends that the §2024(b)(1) offense is a "public welfare" offense, which the Court defined in *Morissette*, 342 U.S. at 252-253, to "depend on no mental element but consist only of forbidden acts or omissions." Yet the offense at issue here differs substantially from those "public welfare offenses" we have previously recognized. In most previous instances, Congress has rendered criminal a type of conduct that a reasonable person should know is subject to stringent public regulation and may seriously threaten the community's health or safety. Thus, in United States v. Freed, 401 U.S. 601 (1971), we examined the federal statute making it illegal to receive or possess an unregistered firearm. In holding that the Government did not have to prove that the recipient of unregistered hand grenades knew that they were unregistered, we noted that "one would hardly be surprised to learn that possession of hand grenades is not an innocent act." Id. at 609. Similarly, in United States v. Dotterweich, 320 U.S. 277, 284 (1943), the Court held that a corporate officer could violate the Food, Drug, and Cosmetic Act when his firm shipped adulterated and misbranded drugs, even "though consciousness of wrongdoing be totally wanting." See also United States v. Balint, 258 U.S. 250 (1922). The distinctions between these cases and the instant case are clear. A food stamp can hardly be compared to a hand grenade, see *Freed*, nor can the unauthorized acquisition or possession of food stamps be compared to the selling of adulterated drugs, as in *Dotterweich*.

III

We hold that in a prosecution for violation of §2024(b)(1), the Government must prove that the defendant knew that his acquisition or possession of food stamps was in a manner unauthorized by statute or regulations. This holding does not put an unduly heavy burden on the Government in prosecuting violators of §2024(b)(1). To prove that petitioner knew that his acquisition or possession of food stamps was unauthorized, for example, the Government need not show that he had knowledge of specific regulations governing food stamp acquisition or possession. Nor must the Government introduce any extraordinary evidence that would conclusively demonstrate petitioner's state of mind. Rather, as in any other criminal prosecution requiring *mens rea*, the Government may prove by reference to facts and circumstances surrounding the case that petitioner knew that his conduct was unauthorized or illegal.[17] . . .

Justice POWELL, took no part in the consideration or decision of this case.

Justice WHITE, with whom the CHIEF JUSTICE joins, dissenting.
Forsaking reliance on either the language or the history of §2024(b)(1), the majority bases its result on the absence of an explicit rejection of the general principle that criminal liability requires not only an *actus reus*, but a *mens rea*. . . .

In relying on the "background assumption of our criminal law" that *mens rea* is required, the Court ignores the equally well founded assumption that ignorance of the law is no excuse. . . .

NOTES AND QUESTIONS

1. Re-read footnote 17. How much of a victory did Liparota win?
2. In its explanation of why the unauthorized use of food stamps is not a "public welfare offense," *Liparota* contrasts the food stamp crime with the more inherently dangerous conduct at issue in *Dotterweich* and in United States v. Freed, 401 U.S. 601 (1971). See 471 U.S. at 433 ("A food stamp can hardly be compared to a hand grenade, see *Freed*, nor can the unauthorized acquisition or possession of food stamps be compared to the selling of adulterated drugs, as in *Dotterweich*."). Indeed, the Court often cites *Freed* in *mens rea* cases as a paradigmatic example of prohibited conduct that is so obviously dangerous that courts can dispense with the scienter term for a key element of the crime.

---

17. In this case, for instance, the Government introduced evidence that petitioner bought food stamps at a substantial discount from face value and that he conducted part of the transaction in a back room of his restaurant to avoid the presence of the other patrons. Moreover, the Government asserts that food stamps themselves are stamped "nontransferable." A jury could have inferred from this evidence that petitioner knew that his acquisition and possession of the stamps were unauthorized.

Freed involved an indictment under the federal statute that prohibited the possession or receipt of an unregistered firearm. The district court had granted the defendants' motions to dismiss their indictment for possession of and conspiracy to possess unregistered hand grenades on the grounds that, *inter alia*, the indictment failed to allege scienter. The defendants knew the items in their possession were grenades, so the question presented was whether the statute additionally required that the defendants know the grenades were unregistered. The Court, hearing the case on direct appeal, reversed the dismissal, explaining:

> The present case is . . . closer to *Dotterweich* [than to *Morissette*]. This is a regulatory measure in the interest of the public safety, which may well be premised on the theory that one would hardly be surprised to learn that possession of hand grenades is not an innocent act. They are highly dangerous offensive weapons, no less dangerous than the narcotics involved in United States v. Balint, 258 U.S. 250, 254, where a defendant was convicted of sale of narcotics against his claim that he did not know the drugs were covered by a federal act. We say with Chief Justice Taft in that case:
>
>> "'It is very evident . . . that the emphasis of the section is in securing a close supervision of the business of dealing in these dangerous drugs by the taxing officers of the Government and that it merely uses a criminal penalty to secure recorded evidence of the disposition of such drugs as a means of taxing and restraining the traffic. Its manifest purpose is to require every person dealing in drugs to ascertain at his peril whether that which he sells comes within the inhibition of the statute, and if he sells the inhibited drug in ignorance of its character, to penalize him. Congress weighed the possible injustice of subjecting an innocent seller to a penalty against the evil of exposing innocent purchasers to danger from the drug, and concluded that the latter was the result preferably to be avoided." Id. at 253-54.

Freed, 401 U.S. at 609-10 (1971). Was *Freed* rightly decided? We will see in Chapter 9 that the Court recently held that, under the Drug Control Act of 1970 (the successor to the Harrison Narcotics Act), the government must prove *either* that the defendant knew the identity of the drug (e.g., heroin), whether or not he knew it was illegal under federal law, *or* that he knew that the drug was illegal under federal law, whether or not he knew the drug's identity. See McFadden v. United States, 135 S. Ct. 2298 (2015), discussed in detail in Chapter 9. Bottom line: Balint would not have fared any better today.

The following case involved conduct that the Court said was not as dangerous to the public as that in *Freed* or *Dotterweich*. But the conduct was also not as innocuous or potentially common as the food stamp offense in *Liparota.* The conduct: possession of an unregistered firearm (the same offense as in *Freed*), here an automatic weapon. How would you come out on the question whether the defendant had to know the weapon was "automatic" as opposed to "semi-automatic"?

Staples v. United States
511 U.S. 600 (1994)

Justice THOMAS delivered the opinion of the Court.

The National Firearms Act makes it unlawful for any person to possess a machinegun that is not properly registered with the Federal Government. Petitioner contends that, to convict him under the Act, the Government should have been required to prove beyond a reasonable doubt that he knew the weapon he possessed had the characteristics that brought it within the statutory definition of a machinegun. We agree and accordingly reverse the judgment of the Court of Appeals.

I

The National Firearms Act (Act), 26 U.S.C. §§5801-5872, imposes strict registration requirements on statutorily defined "firearms." The Act includes within the term "firearm" a machinegun, §5845(a)(6), and further defines a machinegun as "any weapon which shoots, . . . or can be readily restored to shoot, automatically more than one shot, without manual reloading, by a single function of the trigger," §5845(b). Thus, any fully automatic weapon is a "firearm" within the meaning of the Act. Under the Act, all firearms must be registered in the National Firearms Registration and Transfer Record maintained by the Secretary of the Treasury. §5841. Section 5861(d) makes it a crime, punishable by up to 10 years in prison, see §5871, for any person to possess a firearm that is not properly registered.

Upon executing a search warrant at petitioner's home, local police and agents of the Bureau of Alcohol, Tobacco and Firearms (BATF) recovered, among other things, an AR-15 rifle. The AR-15 is the civilian version of the military's M-16 rifle, and is, unless modified, a semiautomatic weapon. The M-16, in contrast, is a selective fire rifle that allows the operator, by rotating a selector switch, to choose semiautomatic or automatic fire. Many M-16 parts are interchangeable with those in the AR-15 and can be used to convert the AR-15 into an automatic weapon. No doubt to inhibit such conversions, the AR-15 is manufactured with a metal stop on its receiver that will prevent an M-16 selector switch, if installed, from rotating to the fully automatic position. The metal stop on petitioner's rifle, however, had been filed away, and the rifle had been assembled with an M-16 selector switch and several other M-16 internal parts, including a hammer, disconnector, and trigger. Suspecting that the AR-15 had been modified to be capable of fully automatic fire, BATF agents seized the weapon. Petitioner subsequently was indicted for unlawful possession of an unregistered machinegun in violation of §5861(d).

At trial, BATF agents testified that when the AR-15 was tested, it fired more than one shot with a single pull of the trigger. It was undisputed that the weapon was not registered as required by §5861(d). Petitioner testified that the rifle had never fired automatically when it was in his possession. He insisted that the AR-15 had operated only semiautomatically, and even then imperfectly, often requiring manual ejection of the spent casing and chambering of the next round. According to petitioner, his alleged ignorance of any automatic firing capability should have shielded him from criminal liability for his failure to register the weapon. He requested the District Court to instruct the jury that, to establish a violation of §5861(d), the Government must prove beyond a reasonable doubt that the defendant "knew that the gun would fire fully automatically."

The District Court rejected petitioner's proposed instruction and instead charged the jury as follows:

> "The Government need not prove the defendant knows he's dealing with a weapon possessing every last characteristic [which subjects it] to the regulation. It would be enough to prove he knows that he is dealing with a dangerous device of a type as would alert one to the likelihood of regulation." Tr. 465.

Petitioner was convicted and sentenced to five years' probation and a $5,000 fine.

The Court of Appeals affirmed. . . .

II

Whether or not §5861(d) requires proof that a defendant knew of the characteristics of his weapon that made it a "firearm" under the Act is a question of statutory construction. As we observed in Liparota v. United States, 471 U.S. 419 (1985), "[t]he definition of the elements of a criminal offense is entrusted to the legislature, particularly in the case of federal crimes, which are solely creatures of statute." Id. at 424. . . . [D]etermining the mental state required for commission of a federal crime requires "construction of the statute and . . . inference of the intent of Congress." United States v. Balint, 258 U.S. 250, 253 (1922).

The language of the statute, the starting place in our inquiry, provides little explicit guidance in this case. Section 5861(d) is silent concerning the *mens rea* required for a violation. It states simply that "[i]t shall be unlawful for any person . . . to receive or possess a firearm which is not registered to him in the National Firearms Registration and Transfer Record." 26 U.S.C. §5861(d). Nevertheless, silence on this point by itself does not necessarily suggest that Congress intended to dispense with a conventional *mens rea* element, which would require that the defendant know the facts that make his conduct illegal. See *Balint*, 258 U.S. at 251 (stating that traditionally, "*scienter*" was a necessary element in every crime). On the contrary, we must construe the statute in light of the background rules of the common law, in which the requirement of some *mens rea* . . . is firmly embedded. . . .

According to the Government, however, the nature and purpose of the Act suggest that the presumption favoring *mens rea* does not apply to this case. The Government argues that Congress intended the Act to regulate and restrict the circulation of dangerous weapons. Consequently, in the Government's view, this case fits in a line of precedent concerning what we have termed "public welfare" or "regulatory" offenses, in which we have understood Congress to impose a form of strict criminal liability. . . .

For example, in *Balint*, we concluded that the Narcotic Act of 1914, which was intended in part to minimize the spread of addictive drugs by criminalizing undocumented sales of certain narcotics, required proof only that the defendant knew that he was selling drugs, not that he knew the specific items he had sold were "narcotics" within the ambit of the statute. See *Balint*, 258 U.S. at 254. Cf. United States v. Dotterweich, 320 U.S. 277, 281 (1943) (stating in dicta that a statute criminalizing the shipment of adulterated or misbranded drugs did not require knowledge that the items were misbranded or adulterated). As we explained in *Dotterweich*, *Balint* dealt with "a now familiar type of legislation whereby penalties serve as effective means of regulation. Such legislation dispenses with the conventional requirement for criminal conduct—awareness of some wrongdoing." 320 U.S. at 280-281. . . .

Typically, our cases recognizing such offenses involve statutes that regulate potentially harmful or injurious items. In such situations, we have reasoned that as long as a defendant knows that he is dealing with a dangerous device of a character that places him "in responsible relation to a public danger," *Dotterweich*, 320 U.S. at 281, he should be alerted to the probability of strict regulation. . . .

The Government argues that §5861(d) defines precisely the sort of regulatory offense described in *Balint*. In this view, all guns, whether or not they are statutory "firearms," are dangerous devices that put gun owners on notice that they must determine . . . whether their weapons come within the scope of the Act. On this understanding, the District Court's instruction in this case was correct, because a conviction can rest simply on proof that a defendant knew he possessed a "firearm" in the ordinary sense of the term.

The Government seeks support for its position from our decision in United States v. Freed, 401 U.S. 601 (1971), which involved a prosecution for possession of unregistered grenades under §5861(d). The defendant knew that the items in his possession were grenades, and we concluded that §5861(d) did not require the Government to prove the defendant also knew that the grenades were unregistered. Id. at 609. To be sure, in deciding that *mens rea* was not required with respect to that element of the offense, we suggested that the Act "is a regulatory measure in the interest of the public safety, which may well be premised on the theory that . . . possession of hand grenades is not an innocent act." Ibid. Grenades, we explained, "are highly dangerous offensive weapons, no less dangerous than the narcotics involved in United States v. Balint." Ibid. But that reasoning provides little support for dispensing with *mens rea* in this case.

As the Government concedes, *Freed* did not address the issue presented here. In *Freed*, we decided only that §5861(d) does not require proof of knowledge that a firearm is *unregistered*. The question presented by a defendant who possesses a weapon that is a "firearm" for purposes of the Act, but who knows only that he has a "firearm" in the general sense of the term, was not raised or considered. . . . Moreover, our analysis in *Freed* likening the Act to the public welfare statute in *Balint* rested entirely on the assumption that the defendant knew that he was dealing with hand grenades—that is, that he knew he possessed a particularly dangerous type of weapon (one within the statutory definition of a "firearm"), possession of which was not entirely "innocent" in and of itself. 401 U.S. at 609. . . .

Notwithstanding these distinctions, the Government urges that *Freed*'s logic applies because guns, no less than grenades, are highly dangerous devices that should alert their owners to the probability of regulation. But the gap between *Freed* and this case is too wide to bridge. In glossing over the distinction between grenades and guns, the Government ignores the particular care we have taken to avoid construing a statute to dispense with *mens rea* where doing so would "criminalize a broad range of apparently innocent conduct." *Liparota*, 471 U.S. at 426. In *Liparota*, we considered a statute that made unlawful the unauthorized acquisition or possession of food stamps. We determined that the statute required proof that the defendant knew his possession of food stamps was unauthorized. . . . Our conclusion that the statute should not be treated as defining a public welfare offense rested on the commonsense distinction that a "food stamp can hardly be compared to a hand grenade." Id. at 433.

Neither, in our view, can all guns be compared to hand grenades. . . . [T]here is a long tradition of widespread lawful gun ownership by private individuals in this country. Such a tradition did not apply to the possession of hand grenades in *Freed* or to the selling of dangerous drugs that we considered in *Balint*. . . . [I]n *Freed* we construed §5861(d) under the assumption that "one would hardly be surprised to learn that possession of hand grenades is not an innocent act." *Freed*, 401 U.S. at 609. Here, the Government essentially suggests that we should interpret the section under the altogether different assumption that "one would hardly be surprised to learn that owning a gun is not an innocent act." That proposition is simply not supported by common experience. Guns in general are not "deleterious devices or products or obnoxious waste materials," [United States v. International Minerals and Chemical Corp., 402 U.S. 558, 565 (1971)], that put their owners on notice that they stand "in responsible relation to a public danger," *Dotterweich*, 320 U.S. at 281.

The Government protests that guns, unlike food stamps, but like grenades and narcotics, are potentially harmful devices. . . . But that an item is "dangerous" in some general sense does not necessarily suggest, as the Government seems to assume, that it is not also entirely innocent. Even dangerous items can, in some cases, be so commonplace and generally available that we would not consider them to alert individuals to the likelihood of strict regulation. . . . [D]espite their potential for harm, guns generally can be owned in perfect innocence. Of course, we might surely classify certain categories of guns—no doubt including the machine-guns, sawed-off shotguns, and artillery pieces that Congress has subjected to regulation—as items the ownership of which would have the same quasi-suspect character we attributed to owning hand grenades in *Freed*. But precisely because guns falling outside those categories traditionally have been widely accepted as lawful possessions, their destructive potential . . . [does not] put gun owners sufficiently on notice of the likelihood of regulation to justify interpreting §5861(d) as not requiring proof of knowledge of a weapon's characteristics.

On a slightly different tack, the Government suggests that guns are subject to an array of regulations at the federal, state, and local levels that put gun owners on notice that they must determine the characteristics of their weapons and comply with all legal requirements. But regulation in itself is not sufficient to place gun ownership in the category of the sale of narcotics in *Balint*. The food stamps at issue in *Liparota* were subject to comprehensive regulations, yet we did not understand the statute there to dispense with a *mens rea* requirement. Moreover, . . . we question whether regulations on guns are sufficiently intrusive that they impinge upon the common experience that owning a gun is usually licit and blameless conduct. Roughly 50 percent of American homes contain at least one firearm of some sort, and in the vast majority of States, buying a shotgun or rifle is a simple transaction that would not alert a person to regulation any more than would buying a car.

If we were to accept as a general rule the Government's suggestion . . . , we would undoubtedly reach some untoward results. Automobiles, for example, might also be termed "dangerous" devices and are highly regulated at both the state and federal levels. Congress might see fit to criminalize the violation of certain regulations concerning automobiles, and thus might make it a crime to operate a vehicle without a properly functioning emission control system. . . . [W]e [] would hesitate to conclude . . . that Congress intended a prison term to apply to a car owner whose vehicle's emissions levels, wholly unbeknownst to him, began to exceed legal limits between regular inspection dates.

Here, there can be little doubt that, as in *Liparota*, the Government's construction of the statute potentially would impose criminal sanctions on a class of persons whose mental state—ignorance of the characteristics of weapons in their possession—makes their actions entirely innocent. The Government does not dispute the contention that virtually any semiautomatic weapon may be converted, either by internal modification or, in some cases, simply by wear and tear, into a machinegun. . . . Such a gun may give no externally visible indication that it is fully automatic. But in the government's view, any person who has purchased what he believes to be a semiautomatic rifle or handgun, or who simply has inherited a gun from a relative and left it untouched in an attic or basement, can be subject to imprisonment, despite absolute ignorance of the gun's firing capabilities, if the gun turns out to be an automatic. . . .

The potentially harsh penalty attached to violation of §5861(d)—up to 10 years' imprisonment—confirms our reading of the Act. Historically, the penalty imposed under a statute has been a significant consideration in determining whether the statute should be construed as dispensing with *mens rea*. Certainly, the cases that first defined the concept of the public welfare offense almost uniformly involved statutes that provided for only light penalties such as fines or short jail sentences, not imprisonment in the state penitentiary. . . .

[The label "public welfare offense"] hardly seems apt, however, for a crime that is a felony, as is violation of §5861(d). After all, "felony" is, as we noted in distinguishing certain common-law crimes from public welfare offenses, "'as bad a word as you can give to man or thing.'" Id. at 260 (quoting 2 F. Pollock & F. Maitland, History of English Law 465 (2d ed. 1899)). Close adherence to the early cases described above might suggest that punishing a violation as a felony is simply incompatible with the theory of the public welfare offense. In this view, absent a clear statement from Congress that *mens rea* is not required, we should not apply the public welfare offense rationale to interpret any statute defining a felony offense as dispensing with *mens rea*.

We need not adopt such a definitive rule of construction to decide this case, however. Instead, we note only that where, as here, dispensing with *mens rea* would require the defendant to have knowledge only of traditionally lawful conduct, a severe penalty . . . [tends] to suggest that Congress did not intend to eliminate a *mens rea* requirement. In such a case, the usual presumption that a defendant must know the facts that make his conduct illegal should apply. . . .

We emphasize that our holding is a narrow one. As in our prior cases, our reasoning depends upon a commonsense evaluation of the nature of the particular device or substance Congress has subjected to regulation and the expectations that individuals may legitimately have in dealing with the regulated items. In addition, we think that the penalty attached to §5861(d) suggests that Congress did not intend to eliminate a *mens rea* requirement for violation of the section. . . . [I]f Congress had intended to make outlaws of gun owners who were wholly ignorant of the offending characteristics of their weapons, and to subject them to lengthy prison terms, it would have spoken more clearly to that effect. . . .

Justice GINSBURG, with whom Justice O'CONNOR joins, concurring in the judgment.

The statute petitioner Harold E. Staples is charged with violating . . . makes it a crime for any person to "receive or possess a firearm which is not registered to him." Although the word "knowingly" does not appear in the statute's text, courts generally assume that Congress, absent a contrary indication, means to retain a *mens rea* requirement. See Liparota v. United States, 471 U.S. 419, 426 (1985). Thus, our holding in United States v. Freed, 401 U.S. 601 (1971), that §5861(d) does not require proof of knowledge that the firearm is unregistered, rested on the premise that the defendant indeed knew the items he possessed were hand grenades. Id. at 607; id. at 612 (Brennan, J., concurring in judgment) ("The Government and the Court agree that the prosecutor must prove knowing possession of the items and also knowledge that the items possessed were hand grenades.").

Conviction under §5861(d), the Government accordingly concedes, requires proof that Staples "knowingly" possessed the machinegun. Brief for United States 23. The question before us is not *whether* knowledge of possession is required, but what level of knowledge suffices: (1) knowledge simply of possession of the object; (2) knowledge, in addition, that the object is a dangerous weapon; (3) knowledge, beyond dangerousness, of the characteristics that render the object subject to regulation, for example, awareness that the weapon is a machinegun.

Recognizing that the first reading effectively dispenses with *mens rea*, the Government adopts the second, contending that it avoids criminalizing "apparently innocent conduct," *Liparota*, 471 U.S. at 426, because under the second reading, "a defendant who possessed what he thought was a toy or a violin case, but which in fact was a machinegun, could not be convicted." Brief for United States 23. The Government, however, does not take adequate account of the "widespread lawful gun ownership" Congress and the States have allowed to persist in this country. See United States v. Harris, 959 F.2d 246, 261 (D.C. Cir. 1992) (*per curiam*). . . .

The Nation's legislators chose to place under a registration requirement only a very limited class of firearms, those they considered especially dangerous. The generally "dangerous" character of all guns, the Court therefore observes, did not suffice to give individuals in Staples' situation cause to inquire about the need for registration. Only the third reading, then, suits the purpose of the *mens rea* requirement—to shield people against punishment for apparently innocent activity.

The indictment in Staples' case charges that he "knowingly received and possessed firearms." "Firearms" has a circumscribed statutory definition. See 26 U.S.C. §5845(a). The "firear[m]" the Government contends Staples possessed in violation of §5861(d) is a machinegun. See §5845(a)(6). The indictment thus effectively charged that Staples *knowingly possessed a machinegun*. "Knowingly possessed" logically means "possessed and knew that he possessed." The Government can reconcile the jury instruction with the indictment only on the implausible assumption that the term "firear[m]" has two different meanings when used once in the same charge—simply "gun" when referring to what petitioner knew, and "machinegun" when referring to what he possessed.

For these reasons, I conclude that conviction under §5861(d) requires proof that the defendant knew he possessed not simply a gun, but a machinegun. The indictment in this case, but not the jury instruction, properly described this knowledge requirement. I therefore concur in the Court's judgment.

Justice STEVENS, with whom Justice BLACKMUN joins, dissenting.

To avoid a slight possibility of injustice to unsophisticated owners of machineguns and sawed-off shotguns, the Court has substituted its views of sound policy for the judgment Congress made when it enacted the National Firearms Act. . . .

The relevant section of the Act makes it "unlawful for any person . . . to receive or possess a firearm which is not registered to him in the National Firearms Registration and Transfer Record." 26 U.S.C. §5861(d). Significantly, the section contains no knowledge requirement, nor does it describe a common-law crime.

The common law generally did not condemn acts as criminal unless the actor had "an evil purpose or mental culpability," Morissette v. United States, 342 U.S. 246, 252 (1952), and was aware of all the facts that made the conduct unlawful, United States v. Balint, 258 U.S. 250, 251-252 (1922). In interpreting statutes that codified traditional common-law offenses, courts usually followed this rule, even when the text of the statute contained no such requirement. Because the offense involved in this case is entirely a creature of statute, however, . . . different rules of construction apply. . . .

Although the lack of an express knowledge requirement in §5861(d) is not dispositive, its absence suggests that Congress did not intend to require proof that the defendant knew all of the facts that made his conduct illegal. . . .

The provision's place in the overall statutory scheme confirms this intention. In 1934, when Congress originally enacted the statute, it limited the coverage of the 1934 Act to a relatively narrow category of weapons such as submachineguns and sawed-off shotguns—weapons characteristically used only by professional gangsters like Al Capone, Pretty Boy Floyd, and their henchmen. At the time, the Act would have had little application to guns used by hunters or guns kept at home as protection against unwelcome intruders. Congress therefore could reasonably presume that a person found in possession of an unregistered machinegun or sawed-off shotgun intended to use it for criminal purposes. . . .

An examination of §5861(d) in light of our precedent dictates that the crime of possession of an unregistered machinegun is in a category of offenses described as "public welfare" crimes. Our decisions interpreting such offenses clearly require affirmance of petitioner's conviction. [The Court cited United States v. Balint, United States v. Dotterweich, and United States v. International Minerals & Chemical Corp., 402 U.S. 558 (1971).] . . .

The National Firearms Act unquestionably is a public welfare statute. United States v. Freed, 401 U.S. 601, 609 (1971) (holding that this statute "is a regulatory measure in the interest of the public safety"). Congress fashioned a legislative scheme to regulate the commerce and possession of certain types of dangerous devices, including specific kinds of weapons, to protect the health and welfare of the citizenry. To enforce this scheme, Congress created criminal penalties for certain acts and omissions. The text of some of these offenses—including the one at issue here—contains no knowledge requirement. . . .

Both the Court and Justice Ginsburg erroneously rely upon the "tradition[al]" innocence of gun ownership to find that Congress must have intended the Government to prove knowledge of all the characteristics that make a weapon a statutory "firearm." We held in *Freed*, however, that a §5861(d) offense may be committed by one with no awareness of either wrongdoing or of all the facts that constitute the offense. 401 U.S. at 607-610. Nevertheless, the Court, asserting that the Government "gloss[es] over the distinction between grenades and guns," determines that "the gap between *Freed* and this case is too wide to bridge." As such, the Court instead reaches the rather surprising conclusion that guns are more analogous to food stamps than to hand grenades. Even if one accepts that dubious proposition, the Court founds it upon a faulty premise: its mischaracterization of the Government's submission as one contending that "*all guns* . . . are dangerous devices that put gun owners on notice. . . ." (emphasis added). Accurately identified, the Government's position presents the question whether guns such as the one possessed by petitioner "'are highly dangerous offensive weapons, no less dangerous than the narcotics'" in *Balint* or the hand grenades in *Freed* (quoting *Freed*, 401 U.S. at 609).

Thus, even assuming that the Court is correct that the mere possession of an ordinary rifle or pistol does not entail sufficient danger to alert one to the possibility of regulation, that conclusion does not resolve this case. Petitioner knowingly possessed a semiautomatic weapon that was readily convertible into a machinegun. The "'character and nature'" of such a weapon is sufficiently hazardous to place the possessor on notice of the possibility of regulation. No significant difference exists between imposing upon the possessor a duty to determine whether such a weapon is registered, *Freed*, 401 U.S. at 607-610, and imposing a duty to determine whether that weapon has been converted into a machinegun. . . .

I would affirm the judgment of the Court of Appeals.

NOTES AND QUESTIONS

1. Justice Thomas overstates the matter in contending that "conventional *mens rea*" under the common law would "require that the defendant know [all] the facts that make his conduct illegal." But it is true that the common law did, at least as a general matter, require enough proof of intent to ensure that only culpable defendants were criminally punished. That is evidently Justice Thomas's goal in *Staples*. Why not say so —and admit that the Court is crafting a new intent doctrine adapted to the particular circumstances of federal criminal statutes, which often have no *mens rea* language at all?

2. In a portion of his dissenting opinion that is not excerpted above, Justice Stevens states that "only about 15 percent of all the guns in the United States are semiautomatic." Which side in *Staples* does that statistic support?

3. The National Firearms Act of 1934 was a New Deal–era regulatory statute. But the regulated actors were very different from those in many of the regulatory regimes initiated in that era, such as the Securities Act of 1933, the Securities and Exchange Act of 1934, and the Food, Drug, and Cosmetic Act of 1938. The regulated actors that Congress sought to punish under the National Firearms Act were, as Justice Stevens put it in *Staples*, "professional gangsters like Al Capone, Pretty Boy Floyd, and their henchmen." Notice two things about the Firearms Act. First, the Act targeted criminals, not crimes. Second, the criminals in question were traditionally the responsibility of local police and local prosecutors, not FBI agents and U.S. Attorneys. The New Dealers didn't try to displace those local officials or the state laws they enforced, but instead sought to supplement them —and, along the way, to grab some political credit for fighting crime. Is that a legitimate goal? Is it fair to criminalize easily provable misconduct in order to punish harder-to-prove crimes indirectly? Do these goals bear on the *mens rea* issue in *Staples*? Note that just months after *Staples* was decided, Congress enacted more robust control legislation, including an "assault weapons ban"

on most semiautomatics; see Violent Crime Control and Law Enforcement Act, Pub. L. No. 103-322 (1994). That statute expired a decade later, in 2004, and thus far Congress has taken no further action. For now, then, only "machine guns," not semi-automatic weapons, are illegal under federal law.

4. In the same Term that it decided *Staples*, the Court had to interpret the *mens rea* requirement of another federal criminal law, this one touching on First Amendment values. The defendant in United States v. X-Citement Video, Inc., 513 U.S. 64 (1994), shipped pornographic videos showing an underage actress (Traci Lords) to a federal undercover agent. The defendant was charged under the Protection of Children Against Sexual Exploitation Act of 1977; the relevant provision read as follows:

> (a) Any person who—
> (1) knowingly transports or ships in interstate or foreign commerce by any means including by computer or mails, any visual depiction, if—(A) the producing of such visual depiction involves the use of a minor engaging in sexually explicit conduct; and (B) such visual depiction is of such conduct;
> (2) knowingly receives, or distributes, any visual depiction . . . that has been mailed, or has been shipped or transported in . . . interstate or foreign commerce, or which contains materials which have been mailed or so shipped or transported, by any means including by computer, or knowingly reproduces any visual depiction for distribution . . . in interstate or foreign commerce. . .or through the mails, if—(A) the producing of such visual depiction involves the use of a minor engaging in sexually explicit conduct; and (B) such visual depiction is of such conduct; . . . shall be punished as provided in subsection (b) of this section.

18 U.S.C. §2252(a). In a decision issued a few months after *Staples*, the Supreme Court held that, in order to convict under this statute, the government must prove knowledge that at least one of the actors in the video was a minor:

> The critical determination . . . is whether the term "knowingly" in subsections (1) and (2) modifies the phrase "the use of a minor" in subsections (1)(A) and (2)(A). The most natural grammatical reading, adopted by the Ninth Circuit, suggests that the term "knowingly" modifies only the surrounding verbs: transports, ships, receives, distributes, or reproduces. . . . But we do not think this is the end of the matter. . . .
> If we were to conclude that "knowingly" only modifies the relevant verbs in §2252, we would sweep within the ambit of the statute actors who had no idea that they were even dealing with sexually explicit material. For instance, a retail druggist who returns an uninspected roll of developed film to a customer "knowingly distributes" a visual depiction and would be criminally liable if it were later discovered that the visual depiction contained images of children engaged in sexually explicit conduct. Or, a new resident of an apartment

might receive mail for the prior resident and store the mail unopened. If the prior tenant had requested delivery of materials covered by §2252, his residential successor could be prosecuted for "knowing receipt" of such materials. Similarly, a Federal Express courier who delivers a box in which the shipper has declared the contents to be "film" "knowingly transports" such film. We do not assume that Congress . . . intended such results. . . .

Our reluctance to simply follow the most grammatical reading of the statute is heightened by our cases interpreting criminal statutes to include broadly applicable scienter requirements, even where the statute by its terms does not contain them. . . .

Liparota v. United States, 471 U.S. 419 (1985), posed a challenge to a federal statute prohibiting certain actions with respect to food stamps. The statute's use of "knowingly" could be read only to modify "uses, transfers, acquires, alters, or possesses" or it could be read also to modify "in any manner not authorized by [the statute].". . . . [T]he Court was concerned with the broader reading which would "criminalize a broad range of apparently innocent conduct." 471 U.S. at 426. . . .

The same analysis drove the recent conclusion in Staples v. United States, 511 U.S. 600 (1994), that to be criminally liable a defendant must know that his weapon possessed automatic firing capability so as to make it a machine-gun as defined by the National Firearms Act. Congress had not expressly imposed any *mens rea* requirement in the provision criminalizing the possession of a firearm in the absence of proper registration. 26 U.S.C. §5861(d). The Court first rejected the argument that the statute described a public welfare offense, traditionally excepted from the background principle favoring scienter. The Court then expressed concern with a statutory reading that would criminalize behavior that a defendant believed fell within "a long tradition of widespread lawful gun ownership by private individuals." *Staples*, 511 U.S. at 610. The Court also emphasized the harsh penalties attaching to violations of the statute as a "significant consideration in determining whether the statute should be construed as dispensing with *mens rea*." Id. at 616.

Applying these principles, we think the Ninth Circuit's plain language reading of §2252 is not so plain. First, §2252 is not a public welfare offense. Persons do not harbor settled expectations that the contents of magazines and film are generally subject to stringent public regulation. In fact, First Amendment constraints presuppose the opposite view. Rather, the statute is more akin to the common-law offenses against the "state, the person, property, or public morals," [Morissette v. United States, 342 U.S. 246, 255 (1952)] that presume a scienter requirement in the absence of express contrary intent. Second, *Staples*' concern with harsh penalties looms equally large respecting §2252: Violations are punishable by up to 10 years in prison as well as substantial fines and forfeiture. . . .

513 U.S. at 68-72.

Just as *Staples* was not a Second Amendment case, *X-Citement Video* was not a First Amendment case. Still, do they read like they're protecting constitutional norms?

5. Compare *X-Citement Video* with <u>United States v. Jones,</u> 471 F.3d 535 (4th Cir. 2006). Jones was convicted of transporting an underage girl across state lines "to act as a prostitute at a truck stop." The relevant federal statute applies to:

> [Any] person who knowingly transports an individual who has not attained the age of 18 years in interstate or foreign commerce, or in any common-wealth, territory or possession of the United States, with intent that the indi-vidual engage in prostitution, or in any sexual activity for which any person can be charged with a criminal offense. . . .

18 U.S.C. §2423(a). Writing for a unanimous panel, Judge Wilkinson decided that "knowingly" modifies only "transports":

> Adverbs generally modify verbs, and the thought that they would typi-cally modify the infinite hereafters of statutory sentences would cause gram-marians to recoil. We see nothing on the face of this statute to suggest that the modifying force of "knowingly" extends beyond the verb to other components of the offense. . . .
> The defendant's interpretation, meanwhile, would strip the statute of its clear purpose: the protection of minors. If the prosecution were required to prove knowledge with regard to the victim's age, it would be the rare defen-dant who would not claim to have mistaken the victim for an adult. Imposing such a *mens rea* requirement would be tantamount to permitting adults to prey upon minors so long as they cultivate ignorance of their victims' age. But "the statute is intended to protect young persons who are transported for illicit purposes, and not transporters who remain ignorant of the age of those whom they transport." [United States v. Taylor, 239 F.3d 994, 996 (9th Cir. 2001)]. It would be nonsensical to require proof of knowledge of the victim's age when the statute exists to provide special protection for all minors, including, if not especially, those who could too easily be mistaken for adults. . . .

471 F.3d at 539-40. So far, *Jones* sounds squarely at odds with *Staples* and *X-Citement Video*. But Judge Wilkinson found those cases easily distinguishable:

> In this case, the reasoning of *X-Citement Video* and *Staples* is inapposite. . . . [Those cases were] "directed at awareness of the elements that define cir-cumstances upon which criminality turns." But in §2423(a), the minority of the victim is hardly a factor that distinguishes the defendant's actions from "innocent conduct." *X-Citement Video*, 513 U.S. at 72. To the contrary, "the transportation of *any* individual for purposes of prostitution or other criminal sexual activity is already unlawful under federal law." . . .

471 F.3d at 541. The grammar rule invoked in *Jones* (an adverb modifies only verbs) is different from the rule enunciated in *X-Citement Video* (a *mens rea* adverb modifies all subsequent statutory elements). But at a higher level of

generality, *Jones* is consistent with both *Staples* and *X-Citement Video*. All three decisions explicitly seek to specify a required *mens rea* that would distinguish wrongful from innocent conduct, the blameworthy from the non-blame-worthy. When should federal judges pay attention to statutory grammar and plain language, and when should they focus on arguments about *mens rea* policy?

6. The Court has become seemingly enamored of the grammar rule enunciated in *X-Citement Video*. In Flores-Figueroa v. United States, 556 U.S. 646 (2009), the defendant was charged with aggravated identity theft. Justice Breyer's majority opinion described the relevant statute as follows:

> The statutory provision in question references a set of predicate crimes, including, for example, theft of government property, fraud, or engaging in various unlawful activities related to passports, visas, and immigration. [18 U.S.C.] §1028A(c)]. It then provides that if any person who commits any of those other crimes (in doing so) "knowingly transfers, possesses, or uses, without lawful authority, a means of identification of another person," the judge must add two years' imprisonment to the offender's underlying sentence. §1028A(a)(1). All parties agree that the provision applies only where the offender knows that he is transferring, possessing, or using *something*. And the Government reluctantly concedes that the offender likely must know that he is transferring, possessing, or using that *something* without lawful authority. But they do not agree whether the provision requires that a defendant also know that the *something* he has unlawfully transferred is, for example, a real ID belonging to another person rather than, say, a fake ID (i.e., a group of numbers that does not correspond to any real Social Security number).

556 U.S. at 648. In an opinion that emphasized grammar and "ordinary" speech patterns, the Court concluded that the adverb "knowingly," when it appears in federal criminal statutes, ordinarily modifies *all* elements of those statutes:

> As a matter of ordinary English grammar, it seems natural to read the statute's word "knowingly" as applying to all the subsequently listed elements of the crime. The Government cannot easily claim that the word "knowingly" applies only to the statute's first four words, or even its first seven. It makes little sense to read the provision's language as heavily penalizing a person who "transfers, possesses, or uses, without lawful authority" a *something*, but does not know, at the very least, that the "something" (perhaps inside a box) is a "means of identification." Would we apply a statute that makes it unlawful "*knowingly* to possess drugs" to a person who steals a passenger's bag without knowing that the bag has drugs inside?

Id. at 650. That bottom line, the Court reasoned, was consistent with *X-Citement Video*. In that case,

[W]e had to interpret a statute that penalizes "[a]ny person who — (1) knowingly transports or ships using any means or facility of interstate or foreign commerce by any means including by computer or mails, any visual depiction, if — (A) the producing of such visual depiction involves the use of a minor engaging in sexually explicit conduct." 18 U.S.C. §2252(a)(1)(A); *X-Citement Video, supra.* In issue was whether the term "knowingly" in paragraph (1) modified the phrase "the use of a minor" in subparagraph (A). Id. at 69. The language in issue in *X-Citement Video* . . . was more ambiguous than the language here not only because the phrase "the use of a minor" was not the direct object of the verbs modified by "knowingly," but also because it appeared in a different subsection. 513 U.S. at 68-69. Moreover, the fact that many sex crimes involving minors do not ordinarily require that a perpetrator know that his victim is a minor supported the Government's position. Nonetheless, we again found that the intent element applied to "the use of a minor." Id. at 72.

556 U.S. at 652-53. Notice the similarity between the holdings in *Flores-Figueroa* and *Staples*—even though the identity theft statute contained the term "knowingly" and the gun law at issue in *Staples* contained no intent term. How much does statutory language matter in this area?

7. Justice Breyer's majority opinion in *Flores-Figueroa* spoke in broad terms about "ordinary English grammar" and suggested that it was providing a rule of construction that could be applied throughout federal criminal law. Justice Alito wrote separately "because I am concerned that the Court's opinion may be read by some as adopting an overly rigid rule of statutory construction." *Flores-Figueroa,* 556 U.S. at 659 (Alito, J., concurring). After criticizing the majority's grammatical analysis as "overstated," Justice Alito explained:

> In interpreting a criminal statute such as the one before us, I think it is fair to begin with a general presumption that the specified *mens rea* applies to all the elements of an offense, but it must be recognized that there are instances in which context may well rebut that presumption. For example, 18 U.S.C. §2423(a) makes it unlawful to "knowingly transpor[t] an individual who has not attained the age of 18 years in interstate or foreign commerce . . . with intent that the individual engage in prostitution, or in any sexual activity for which any person can be charged with a criminal offense." The Courts of Appeals have uniformly held that a defendant need not know the victim's age to be guilty under this statute. See, e.g., United States v. Griffith, 284 F.3d 338, 350-351 (C.A.2 2002); United States v. Taylor, 239 F.3d 994, 997 (C.A.9 2001); cf. United States v. Chin, 981 F.2d 1275, 1280 (C.A.D.C. 1992) (R. Ginsburg, J.) (holding that 21 U.S.C. §861(a)(1), which makes it unlawful to "knowingly and intentionally . . . employ, hire, use, persuade, induce, entice, or coerce, a person under eighteen years of age to violate" drug laws, does not require the defendant to have knowledge of the minor's age). Similarly, 8 U.S.C. §1327 makes it unlawful to "knowingly ai[d] or assis[t] any alien inadmissible under

section 1182(a)(2) (insofar as an alien inadmissible under such section has been convicted of an aggravated felony) . . . to enter the United States." The Courts of Appeals have held that the term "knowingly" in this context does not require the defendant to know that the alien had been convicted of an aggravated felony. See, e.g., United States v. Flores-Garcia, 198 F.3d 1119, 1121-1123 (C.A.9 2000); United States v. Figueroa, 165 F.3d 111, 118-119 (C.A.2 1998).

In the present case, however, the Government has not pointed to contextual features that warrant interpreting 18 U.S.C. §1028A(a)(1) in a similar way. Indeed, the Government's interpretation leads to exceedingly odd results. Under that interpretation, if a defendant uses a made-up Social Security number without having any reason to know whether it belongs to a real person, the defendant's liability under §1028A(a)(1) depends on chance: If it turns out that the number belongs to a real person, two years will be added to the defendant's sentence, but if the defendant is lucky and the number does not belong to another person, the statute is not violated.

I therefore concur in the judgment and join the opinion of the Court except insofar as it may be read to adopt an inflexible rule of construction that can rarely be overcome by contextual features pointing to a contrary reading.

Flores-Figueroa, 556 U.S. at 660-61 (Alito, J., concurring). The Courts of Appeals have picked up on Justice Alito's concurrence and have repeatedly cited it in their refusals to adopt an inflexible rule of construction. For example, in United States v. Washington, 743 F.3d 938 (4th Cir. 2014), the question whether *Flores-Figueroa* had abrogated *Jones* was squarely before the Fourth Circuit. The Fourth Circuit analyzed the effect of the *Flores-Figueroa* case and joined its sister circuits in agreeing with Justice Alito's concurrence:

> Washington contends that *Flores-Figueroa* undermines our analysis in *Jones*. We disagree. . .
>
> [In *Flores-Figueroa*,] the Court did not purport to establish a bright-line rule that a specified mens rea always applies to every element of the offense. Instead, it approvingly cited Justice Alito's concurrence for the proposition that "the inquiry into a sentence's meaning is a contextual one." Id. at 652, 129 S. Ct. 1886. The majority noted that some statutes may "involve special contexts or themselves provide a more detailed explanation of background circumstances" that call for a different result, but it did not find a "special context" in the case before it. Id.
>
> Justice Alito wrote separately out of a "concern[] that the Court's opinion may be read by some as adopting an overly rigid rule of statutory construction." Id. at 659, 129 S. Ct. 1886 (Alito, J., concurring). He agreed with the general presumption that the specified mens rea applies to all of the offense's elements but emphasized that context may rebut that presumption. Id. at 660, 129 S. Ct. 1886. As an example, he referenced §2423(a) — the statute at issue here — and noted that the courts of appeals have uniformly held that knowledge of the victim's age is not required. Id.

Several circuits have addressed the effect of *Flores-Figueroa* on §2423(a) and have universally concluded that the knowledge requirement does *not* apply to the victim's age. See United States v. Tavares, 705 F.3d 4, 19-20 (1st Cir.); United States v. Daniels, 653 F.3d 399, 410 (6th Cir. 2011); *Cox*, 577 F.3d at 838; cf. United States v. Daniels, 685 F.3d 1237, 1248 (11th Cir. 2012) denied (adopting the reasoning of circuits that have considered the issue under §2423(a), and "find[ing] that §2422(b) likewise does not require that the government prove that a defendant knew his victim was under the age of eighteen in order to convict"). [See *Tavares*, 705 F.3d at 19 ("These circuits agree that the context of §2423(a) compels a reading of the statute that does *not* require 'knowingly' to be applied to the victim's age.").]

We agree with our sister circuits and join them today. *Flores-Figueroa* does not undermine our decision in *Jones*. To the contrary, the "special context" of §2423(a) supports our previous interpretation of the statute. *See Flores-Figueroa*, 556 U.S at 660, 129 S. Ct. 1886 (Alito, J., concurring) (listing §2423(a) as an example of a potential special context).

We previously identified this "special context" in *Jones*, although we did not use that phrase. . . .

This special context is sufficient to rebut the general presumption that a specified *mens rea* applies to all elements of the offense. *Flores-Figueroa* thus does not compel a different result from the one we reached in *Jones*. Accordingly, the district court correctly instructed the jury that under §2423(a), the government was not required to prove that Washington knew that R.C. was a minor.

Washington, 743 F.3d 942-43. Although the Fourth Circuit focused on the "special context" of §2423(a) in refusing to overturn *Jones*, other Courts of Appeals have cited Justice Alito's concurrence outside the context of underage victims. See, e.g., United States v. Stone, 706 F.3d 1145, 1147 (9th Cir. 2013) (rejecting the argument that *Flores-Figueroa* requires that the knowledge requirement of 18 U.S.C. §§922(g)(1) and 924(a)(2) extend to the interstate commerce element).

8. Consider United States v. Yermian, 468 U.S. 63 (1984). Esmail Yermian lied on a security questionnaire, which he filled out when applying for a job with a defense contractor. He failed to disclose a prior fraud conviction in response to one question, and, in response to another, stated that he previously held two jobs that in fact he had never held. Yermian was charged with three counts of violating the federal false statements statute, 18 U.S.C. §1001. That statute applied (at the time, and with minor changes still applies) to anyone who, "in any matter within the jurisdiction of any department or agency of the United States, knowingly and willfully . . . makes any false . . . statements or representations." Yermian argued that although he may have known his statements were false, he *didn't* know that he made them on a matter within the jurisdiction of a government agency. The Court said it didn't matter for two reasons. First, Congress had placed the jurisdictional clause before "knowingly and willfully":

Respondent argues that absent proof of actual knowledge of federal agency jurisdiction, §1001 becomes a "trap for the unwary," imposing criminal sanctions on "wholly innocent conduct." Whether or not respondent fairly may characterize the intentional and deliberate lies prohibited by the statute . . . as "wholly innocent conduct," this argument is not sufficient to overcome the express statutory language of §1001. Respondent does not argue that Congress lacks the power to impose criminal sanctions for deliberately false statements submitted to a federal agency, regardless of whether the person who made such statements actually knew that they were being submitted to the Federal Government. That is precisely what Congress has done here. In the unlikely event that §1001 could be the basis for imposing an unduly harsh result on those who intentionally make false statements to the Federal Government, it is for Congress and not this Court to amend the criminal statute. . . .

468 U.S. at 74-75. The Court added in a footnote that "[i]n the context of this case, respondent's argument that §1001 is a 'trap for the unwary' is particularly misplaced. It is worth noting that the jury was instructed, without objection from the prosecution, that the Government must prove that respondent 'knew or should have known' that his false statements were made within the jurisdiction of a federal agency." Id. at 75 n.14.

Second, and at least as important, the Court had previously differentiated the *mens rea* required for jurisdictional elements from that required for other elements of a crime:

Jurisdictional language need not contain the same culpability requirement as other elements of the offense. Indeed, we have held that "the existence of the fact that confers federal jurisdiction need not be one in the mind of the actor at the time he perpetrates the act made criminal by the federal statute." United States v. Feola, 420 U.S. 671, 676-77, n.9 (1975).

Yermian, 468 U.S. at 68-69. In *Feola*, the Court had addressed the scienter required for conviction under the federal statute making it illegal to assault federal officers in the performance of their official duties. *Feola* held that the statute required only a proof of intent to assault, not proof of knowledge that the victims were federal officers, because the identity of the victim was just a jurisdictional element meant to provide a federal forum in which to try alleged offenders. In doing so, the Court applied, without explicitly acknowledging it was doing so, the Model Penal Code's differentiation between the *mens rea* required for jurisdiction elements and that required for the "material elements" of a crime. ALI, Model Penal Code §§1.13(10) and 2.02(4).

Is *Yermian* better understood as a case about grammar and congressional intent, or as a case about the special role of jurisdictional elements in the judicial interpretation of *mens rea*? What level of intent should the government have to prove with respect to the jurisdictional fact in *Yermian*?

Does *Feola* necessarily support *Yermian*? An assault is an assault, and whether the victim is a federal officer or not makes little difference in culpability. But is a lie a lie?

9. In Chapter 8, you will see that the "knowledge" required by a statute can usually be satisfied by evidence that the defendant "consciously avoided" having such knowledge. As you might expect, this doctrine can considerably lighten the prosecution's burden of proof.

10. *Legal Knowledge.* As Justice White noted in his dissent in *Liparota*, 471 U.S. at 441 (White, J., dissenting), one of the most familiar criminal law doctrines stems from the adage "ignorance of the law is no excuse." In other words, the fact that a defendant did not realize his conduct was criminal is ordinarily no defense to a criminal charge. Yet, we've seen that some form of this defense is indeed available under certain circumstances, including in *Liparota*, where knowledge-of-illegality was required in order to avoid criminalizing a broad range of relatively benign food stamp misuse.

Even historically there were classic examples of exceptions to the traditional rule that ignorance of the law is no excuse. But those exceptions all involved mistakes of *non-criminal law* that are more accurately conceived of as mistakes of fact. For example, the question whether the defendant in a prosecution for bigamy knew that he was not actually divorced is technically a legal question. But it is a legal question about state *family law*, not the criminal law of bigamy. However, in cases like *Liparota*, and other cases in the Notes below, the Supreme Court has gone a step further and held that the defendant actually had to know the federal criminal law — that what he did was a crime.

Along with creating true exceptions to the famous common-law maxim about ignorance of the law, the modern Supreme Court has also blurred the traditional divide between "factual knowledge" and "legal knowledge." At the beginning of this subsection, we noted that these cases deal with two related questions. First, what *facts* must the defendant "know" in order to be properly convicted under a given statute? Second, when, if ever, must a defendant "know" that his actions violated federal criminal *law*? These questions often have been viewed separately from one another in the study of criminal law (including, perhaps, in the basic Criminal Law course that you took). Yet, federal criminal law no longer lends itself to such a clear distinction between factual knowledge cases and legal knowledge cases. Indeed, we have seen that the Court cites and relies on "legal knowledge" decisions — such as *Liparota* — in "factual knowledge" cases, such as *Staples* and *X-Citement Video*! (Likewise, the Court relies on "factual knowledge" cases in "legal knowledge" cases such as *Ratzlaf*, below.) In the federal courts, the doctrines relating to knowledge of "facts" and of "law" (that is, criminal law) have become so intertwined that they cannot be considered independently of one another. Or so we clearly believe, which is why we do not treat them in separate subsections of this chapter.

11. Perhaps, then, the better way of considering these issues is to recognize that both "legal knowledge" issues and "factual knowledge" issues are subparts of a broader issue: ensuring that criminal prohibitions (whether traditional, common-law crimes or newer regulatory prohibitions) do not become a trap for those who are not blameworthy. We posit that the rare instances in which the Court requires knowledge of illegality are a natural outgrowth of the general requirement that a defendant have knowledge of the facts that make his conduct unlawful. The Court interprets federal criminal statutes as requiring knowledge of illegality when, but only when, allowing conviction based on proof of factual knowledge alone would "criminalize a broad range of apparently innocent conduct." *Liparota*, 471 U.S. at 426. Indeed, that line from *Liparota*—quoted in the key "factual knowledge" cases (see *Staples*, 511 U.S. at 610; *X-Citement Video*, 513 U.S. at 71; and *Elonis*, 135 S. Ct. at 2009)—gets at the fundamental question the Court seeks to answer in *all* of these cases: What is the mental state required to separate innocent from guilty conduct?

The Court said as much in its most recent *mens rea* outing: "When interpreting federal criminal statutes that are silent on the required mental state, we read into the statute only that *mens rea* which is necessary to separate wrongful conduct from otherwise innocent conduct." *Elonis*, 135 S. Ct. at 2010. As you read the remaining cases in this chapter, ask yourself whether you believe the Court has succeeded in reading in a level of knowledge—either legal or factual—that accomplishes this essential task at the heart of both doctrines.

12. Before we consider *Elonis* in depth, we look at three other cases decided after *Liparota* in which the Court explored additional circumstances in which ignorance of the law could be a defense to a criminal charge.

In Cheek v. United States, 498 U.S. 192 (1991), the Court addressed *mens rea* in the context of violations of the Internal Revenue Code—a labyrinthine set of provisions. The basic prohibition of tax evasion requires a "willful" violation. See 26 U.S.C. §7201 ("Any person who willfully attempts in any manner to evade or defeat any tax imposed by this title . . . shall . . . . be guilty of a felony and, upon conviction thereof, shall be fined not more than $100,000 . . . or imprisoned not more than 5 years, or both . . . ."). John Cheek was a tax protester who regularly failed to file income tax returns. When charged with willfully failing to pay his taxes, Cheek claimed, among other things, that his non-payment was not "willful" because he honestly believed (1) that ordinary wages were not taxable "income," and (2) that the tax laws were unconstitutional. See *Cheek*, 498 U.S. at 195. At Cheek's trial, the district judge told jurors that negligent misunderstandings of the law amounted to willfulness. The Supreme Court, in an opinion by Justice White (who had dissented in *Liparota*), disagreed:

The proliferation of statutes and regulations has sometimes made it difficult for the average citizen to . . . comprehend the extent of the duties and obligations imposed by the tax laws. Congress has accordingly softened the impact of the common-law presumption [that every person knows the law] by making specific intent to violate the law an element of certain federal criminal tax offenses. . . .

In United States v. Bishop, 412 U.S. 346, 360 (1973), we described the term "willfully" [as used in federal criminal tax statutes] as connoting "a voluntary, intentional violation of a known legal duty". . . .

Willfulness, as construed by our prior decisions in criminal tax cases, [thus] requires the Government to prove that the law imposed a duty on the defendant, that the defendant knew of this duty, and that he voluntarily and intentionally violated that duty. . . .

In this case, if Cheek asserted that he truly believed that the Internal Revenue Code did not purport to treat wages as income, and the jury believed him, the Government would not have carried its burden to prove willfulness, however unreasonable a court might deem such a belief. . . .

498 U.S. at 200-02. With respect to Cheek's constitutional misunderstandings, the Court was less generous:

Claims that some of the provisions of the tax code are unconstitutional are submissions of a different order. They do not arise from innocent mistakes caused by the complexity of the Internal Revenue Code. Rather, they reveal full knowledge of the provisions at issue and a studied conclusion, however wrong, that those provisions are invalid. . . . [I]n this case, Cheek paid his taxes for years, but after attending various seminars and based on his own study, he concluded that the income tax laws could not constitutionally require him to pay a tax.

We do not believe that Congress contemplated that such a taxpayer, without risking criminal prosecution, could ignore the duties imposed upon him by the Internal Revenue Code. . . . Cheek . . . was free to pay the tax that the law purported to require, file for a refund and, if denied, present his claims of [constitutional] invalidity . . . to the courts. See 26 U.S.C. §7422. Also, without paying the tax, he could have challenged claims of tax deficiencies in the Tax Court, §6213, with the right to appeal to a higher court if unsuccessful. §7482(a)(1). Cheek took neither course in some years, and when he did was unwilling to accept the outcome. As we see it, he is in no position to claim that his good-faith belief about the validity of the Internal Revenue Code negates willfulness or provides a defense to criminal prosecution under §§7201 and 7203. Of course, Cheek was free in this very case to present his claims of invalidity and have them adjudicated, but like defendants in criminal cases in other contexts, who "willfully" refuse to comply with the duties placed upon them by the law, he must take the risk of being wrong.

Id. at 205-06. Justice Scalia concurred in the judgment in *Cheek*; he agreed with the Court that even negligent errors about the meaning of "income" negated willfulness — but he went further, arguing that Cheek's claim that the tax code is unconstitutional likewise negates *mens rea.* Does the Court's distinction between statutory and constitutional misunderstandings make sense?

13. *Cheek* is generally seen as binding only in tax cases. The same cannot be said of Ratzlaf v. United States, 510 U.S. 135 (1994):

> On the evening of October 20, 1988, defendant-petitioner Waldemar Ratzlaf ran up a debt of $160,000 playing blackjack at the High Sierra Casino in Reno, Nevada. The casino gave him one week to pay. On the due date, Ratzlaf returned to the casino with cash of $100,000 in hand. A casino official informed Ratzlaf that all transactions involving more than $10,000 in cash had to be reported to state and federal authorities. The official added that the casino could accept a cashier's check for the full amount due without triggering any reporting requirement. The casino helpfully placed a limousine at Ratzlaf's disposal, and assigned an employee to accompany him to banks in the vicinity. Informed that banks, too, are required to report cash transactions in excess of $10,000, Ratzlaf purchased cashier's checks, each for less than $10,000 and each from a different bank. He delivered these checks to the High Sierra Casino.
>
> Based on this endeavor, Ratzlaf was charged with "structuring transactions" to evade the banks' obligation to report cash transactions exceeding $10,000; this conduct, the indictment alleged, violated 31 U.S.C. §§5322(a) and 5324(3). The trial judge instructed the jury that the Government had to prove defendant's knowledge of the banks' reporting obligation and his attempt to evade that obligation, but did not have to prove defendant knew the structuring was unlawful. Ratzlaf was convicted, fined, and sentenced to prison.
>
> Ratzlaf maintained on appeal that he could not be convicted of "willfully violating" the antistructuring law solely on the basis of his knowledge that a financial institution must report currency transactions in excess of $10,000 and his intention to avoid such reporting. To gain a conviction for "willful" conduct, he asserted, the Government must prove he was aware of the illegality of the "structuring" in which he engaged. . . .

510 U.S. at 137-38. Ratzlaf's argument depended on three federal statutes. 31 U.S.C. §5313 and associated federal regulations establish the $10,000 reporting requirement about which the casino advised Ratzlaf. The second provision, 31 U.S.C. §5324, read at the time of *Ratzlaf:*

> No person shall for the purpose of evading the reporting requirements of section 5313(a) with respect to such transaction — . . .

> (3) structure or assist in structuring, or attempt to structure or assist in structuring, any transaction with one or more domestic financial institutions.

Finally, 31 U.S.C. §5322(a) stated that "[a] person willfully violating this subchapter, or a regulation prescribed under this subchapter . . . shall be fined not more than $250,000 or [imprisoned for] not more than five years, or both."

By a 5-4 vote, the Supreme Court bought Ratzlaf's argument. The key passage in Justice Ginsburg's majority opinion reads as follows:

> Section 5324 forbids structuring transactions with a "purpose of evading the reporting requirements of section 5313(a)." Ratzlaf admits that he structured cash transactions, and that he did so with knowledge of, and a purpose to avoid, the banks' duty to report currency transactions in excess of $10,000. The statutory formulation (§5322) under which Ratzlaf was prosecuted, however, calls for proof of "willful[ness]" on the actor's part. The trial judge in Ratzlaf's case, with the Ninth Circuit's approbation, treated §5322(a)'s "willfulness" requirement essentially as surplusage—as words of no consequence. Judges should hesitate so to treat statutory terms in any setting, and resistance should be heightened when the words describe an element of a criminal offense. . . .
>
> The United States urges, however, that §5324 violators, by their very conduct, exhibit a purpose to do wrong, which suffices to show "willfulness". . . .
>
> Undoubtedly there are bad men who attempt to elude official reporting requirements in order to hide from Government inspectors such criminal activity as laundering drug money or tax evasion. *But currency structuring is not inevitably nefarious.* Consider, for example, the small business operator who knows that reports filed under 31 U.S.C. §5313(a) are available to the Internal Revenue Service. To reduce the risk of an IRS audit, she brings $9,500 in cash to the bank twice each week, in lieu of transporting over $10,000 once each week. That person, if the United States is right, has committed a criminal offense, because she structured cash transactions "for the specific purpose of depriving the Government of the information that Section 5313(a) is designed to obtain." Brief for United States 28-29. Nor is a person who structures a currency transaction invariably motivated by a desire to keep the Government in the dark. But under the Government's construction an individual would commit a felony against the United States by making cash deposits in small doses, fearful that the bank's reports would increase the likelihood of burglary, or in an endeavor to keep a former spouse unaware of his wealth. . . .
>
> In light of these examples, we are unpersuaded by the argument that structuring is so obviously "evil" or inherently "bad" that the "willfulness" requirement is satisfied irrespective of the defendant's knowledge of the illegality of structuring. . . .

510 U.S. at 140-46 (emphasis added).

Justice Blackmun, joined by Chief Justice Rehnquist and Justices O'Connor and Thomas, closed his *Ratzlaf* dissent with these words: "Now Congress must try again to fill a hole it rightly felt it had filled before." These words proved to be prophetic: Within a few months of the Court's decision, Congress revised the anti-structuring statute and eliminated the willfulness term. Thus, *Ratzlaf* is no longer good law for crimes like those of the defendant in that case.

Consider this discussion of *Ratzlaf*, penned shortly after the decision was issued:

> Justice Ginsburg's opinion for the Court maintained that if this alternative interpretation were accepted, the enforcement provision's "willfulness" requirement would be superfluous. . . . But the Court is frequently willing to read a statute in a way that renders some language . . . superfluous if the superfluity is an apparent drafting oversight. It seems likely that Congress . . . was simply inattentive to possible superfluities. In dropping the anti-structuring provision into the Act by its 1986 amendment, Congress focused only on filling a regulatory gap, and was apparently unaware that the new anti-structuring provision was the only one in the revised statutory scheme that had a separate scienter requirement.

William N. Eskridge, Jr. & Philip Frickey, Foreword: Law as Equilibrium, 108 Harv. L. Rev. 26, 59 (1994). Recall Justice Stevens's dissent in United States v. Wells, 519 U.S. 482 (1997), discussed in Section B of this chapter. As that dissent noted, approximately 42 federal misrepresentation statutes include the term "material," while roughly 54 do not. Justice Stevens contended that courts should read a materiality term into the latter category of statutes. If Professors Eskridge and Frickey are right, perhaps courts should read the term *out of* the statutes that include it. Should courts decide which terms in statutes are and are not superfluous? If so, how should they make these decisions?

14. Was *Ratzlaf* rightly decided? Justice Ginsburg's majority opinion bases its ultimate holding that the defendant must have knowledge of illegality on the belief that "currency structuring is not inevitably nefarious." 510 U.S. at 144. Under this view, legal knowledge should be required because factual knowledge of the *actus reus* is not enough to distinguish innocent from nefarious conduct under the statute as it was written at the time. But do you agree with the underlying factual assumption that currency structuring may include a broad range of innocent conduct? Should someone who structures transactions to avoid the $10,000 reporting rule be considered an "ensnared innocent"?

15. A third (and especially unsatisfying) case to consider is Bryan v. United States, 524 U.S. 184 (1998). There the Court discussed *mens rea* in the context of federal gun registration regulations, and the majority intimated that the reasoning of *Cheek* and *Ratzlaf* would only apply in a very limited set of circumstances. The evidence produced by the government at trial in *Bryan* proved:

that petitioner did not have a federal license to deal in firearms; that he used so-called "straw purchasers" in Ohio to acquire pistols that he could not have purchased himself; that the straw purchasers made false statements when purchasing the guns; that petitioner assured the straw purchasers that he would file the serial numbers off the guns; and that he resold the guns on Brooklyn street corners known for drug dealing. The evidence was unquestionably adequate to prove that petitioner was dealing in firearms, and that he knew that his conduct was unlawful. There was, however, no evidence that he was aware of the federal law that prohibits dealing in firearms without a federal license.

Bryan, 524 U.S. at 189. The question presented was whether the statute of conviction, 18 U.S.C. §924(a)(1)(D) — which provides that whoever "willfully violates any other provision of this chapter" shall be fined, imprisoned for up to 5 years, or both — required "proof that the defendant knew that his conduct was unlawful, or whether it also require[d] proof that he knew of the federal licensing requirement." 524 U.S. at 186.

In the key passage of the majority opinion, Justice Stevens distinguished *Cheek* and *Ratzlaf* as involving "highly technical statutes that presented the danger of ensnaring individuals engaged in apparently innocent conduct":

> Petitioner . . . argues that we must read §924(a)(1)(D) to require knowledge of the law because of our interpretation of "willfully" in two other contexts. In certain cases involving willful violations of the tax laws, we have concluded that the jury must find that the defendant was aware of the specific provision of the tax code that he was charged with violating. See, e.g., Cheek v. United States, 498 U.S. 192, 201 (1991). Similarly, in order to satisfy a willful violation in *Ratzlaf*, we concluded that the jury had to find that the defendant knew that his structuring of cash transactions to avoid a reporting requirement was unlawful. See 510 U.S. at 138, 149. Those cases, however, are readily distinguishable. Both the tax cases and *Ratzlaf* involved highly technical statutes that presented the danger of ensnaring individuals engaged in apparently innocent conduct. As a result, we held that these statutes "carv[e] out an exception to the traditional rule" that ignorance of the law is no excuse and require that the defendant have knowledge of the law. The danger of convicting individuals engaged in apparently innocent activity that motivated our decisions in the tax cases and *Ratzlaf* is not present here because the jury found that this petitioner knew that his conduct was unlawful.
>
> Thus, the willfulness requirement of §924(a)(1)(D) does not carve out an exception to the traditional rule that ignorance of the law is no excuse; knowledge that the conduct is unlawful is all that is required. . . .

Bryan, 524 U.S. at 193-96. Justice Scalia, joined by Chief Justice Rehnquist and Justice Ginsburg, dissented. The dissent argued that by requiring only general knowledge of illegality, as opposed to knowledge of the federal licensing requirement, the majority had "accept[ed] a *mens rea* so 'general' that it is entirely divorced from the *actus reus* this statute was enacted to punish." Id. at 202 (Scalia, J., dissenting). According to the dissent, under the Court's decision:

> Bryan would be guilty of "willfully" dealing in firearms without a federal license even if, for example, he had never heard of the licensing requirement but was aware that he had violated the law by using straw purchasers or filing the serial numbers off the pistols. The Court does not even limit (for there is no rational basis to limit) the universe of relevant laws to federal *firearms* statutes. Bryan would also be "act[ing] with an evil-meaning mind," and hence presumably be guilty of "willfully" dealing in firearms without a license, if he knew that his street-corner transactions violated New York City's business licensing or sales tax ordinances. (For that matter, it ought to suffice if Bryan knew that the car out of which he sold the guns was illegally double-parked, or if, in order to meet the appointed time for the sale, he intentionally violated Pennsylvania's speed limit on the drive back from the gun purchase in Ohio.) Once we stop focusing on the conduct the defendant is actually charged with (i.e., selling guns without a license), I see no principled way to determine what law the defendant must be conscious of violating.

Id. at 202-03 (Scalia, J., dissenting).

To what cases does *Bryan* apply? The defendant in United States v. George, 386 F.3d 383 (2d Cir. 2004), was convicted of "willfully and knowingly" making a false statement in a passport application, in violation of 18 U.S.C. §1542. The court, in an opinion by then-Judge Sotomayor, held that §1542 "requires that a defendant provide in a passport application information he or she knows to be false and does not mandate that the defendant act with a specific purpose to make false statements or to violate the law, either generally or §1542 specifically." 386 F.3d at 389. The court explained that this result was required because "[t]he approach undertaken by the Supreme Court and the Second Circuit in interpreting the criminal statutory *mens rea* term 'willful' to require only the minimum *mens rea* necessary to separate innocent from wrongful conduct governs our present reading of §1542." Id. at 394. Is *George* consistent with *Bryan*? With *Ratzlaf*?

16. During the course of Carlton Wilson's divorce proceedings, an Illinois judge issued a protective order barring Wilson from contacting his soon-to-be-ex-wife. While subject to that order, Wilson was arrested for another offense—a search incident to arrest turned up a shotgun. Wilson was then charged and convicted of violating 18 U.S.C. §922(g)(8), which bars possession of firearms by persons subject to protective orders. Pursuant to §924(a)(2), the government had to prove that Wilson "knowingly" violated §922(g)(8). Wilson conceded that he knew he possessed the gun, but claimed he did *not* know that doing so was a crime, and so lacked the intent necessary for conviction. In an opinion issued shortly after *Bryan* was decided, a Seventh Circuit panel rejected the argument:

To the extent that Wilson is arguing that he was unaware of the law and that his conviction therefore cannot stand, he is also incorrect. The traditional rule in American jurisprudence is that ignorance of the law is no defense to a criminal prosecution. Cheek v. United States, 498 U.S. 192, 199 (1991); Lambert v. People of the State of California, 355 U.S. 225, 228 (1957) (rule that "ignorance of the law will not excuse" is deeply rooted in American law). Wilson has not shown that the present statute falls into an exception to this general rule, see [Bryan v. United States, 524 U.S. 184, 194 (1998)] (noting exception for "highly technical statutes that present [] the danger of ensnaring individuals engaged in apparently innocent conduct"), and *Lambert*, 355 U.S. at 228 (notice required when penalty may be exacted for failing to act), and the fact that he was unaware of the existence of §922(g)(8) does not render his conviction erroneous.

United States v. Wilson, 159 F.3d 280, 288-89 (7th Cir. 1998). Judge Posner authored a vigorous dissent:

Congress created, and the Department of Justice sprang, a trap on Carlton Wilson as a result of which he will serve more than three years in federal prison for an act (actually an omission to act) that he could not have suspected was a crime. . . . We can release him from the trap by interpreting the statute under which he was convicted to require the government to prove that the violator knew that he was committing a crime. This is the standard device by which the courts avoid having to explore the outer boundaries of the constitutional requirement of fair notice of potential criminal liability. See, e.g., Ratzlaf v. United States, 510 U.S. 135 (1994). . . .

[Section 922(g)(8)] was enacted in 1994 and the number of prosecutions for violating it has been minuscule (perhaps fewer than 10, though I have not been able to discover the exact number, which is not a reported statistic) in relation to the probable number of violations. I estimate that every year the law has been in effect almost one hundred *thousand* restraining orders against domestic violence have been issued (estimated from Patricia Tjaden & Nancy Thoenes, Stalking in America: Findings From the National Violence Against Women Survey 3, 6, 12 (1998)). Since 40 percent of U.S. households own guns, there can be very little doubt that a large percentage of those orders were issued against gun owners.

How many of these gun owners, when they got notice of the restraining order, dispossessed themselves of their guns? I doubt that any did. The law is *malum prohibitum*, not *malum in se*; that is, it is not the kind of law that a lay person would intuit existed because the conduct it forbade was contrary to the moral code of his society. Compare United States v. Robinson, 137 F.3d 652, 654 (1st Cir. 1998) ("child pornography offends the moral sensibility of the community at large"), with United States v. Grigsby, 111 F.3d 806, 816-821 (11th Cir. 1997) (importation of ivory in violation of the African Elephant Conservation Act not criminal without knowledge of the Act). Yet the Department of Justice took no steps to publicize the existence of the law until long after Wilson violated it. . . .

The federal criminal code contains thousands of separate prohibitions, many ridiculously obscure, such as the one against using the coat of arms of Switzerland in advertising, 18 U.S.C. §708, or using "Johnny Horizon" as a trade name without the authorization of the Department of the Interior. 18 U.S.C. §714. The prohibition in section 922(g)(8) is one of the most obscure. A person owns a hunting rifle. He knows or should know that if he is convicted of a felony he will have to get rid of the gun; if he doesn't know, the judge or the probation service will tell him. But should he be made subject to a restraining order telling him to keep away from his ex-wife, whom he has *not* ever threatened with his hunting rifle . . . , it will not occur to him that he must give up the gun unless the judge issuing the order tells him. The judge didn't tell Wilson; so far as appears, the judge was unaware of the law. . . . No one told him. And there is no reason that he should have guessed, for while he had beaten his wife and threatened to kill her, there is no indication that guns played any part in the beating or the threats. . . .

When a defendant is morally culpable for failing to know or guess that he is violating *some* law . . . , we rely on conscience to provide all the notice that is required. Sometimes the existence of the law is common knowledge, as in the case of laws forbidding people to own hand grenades (see United States v. Freed, 401 U.S. 601, 609 (1971)), forbidding convicted felons to own any firearms, and requiring a license to carry a handgun. And sometimes, though the law is obscure to the population at large and nonintuitive, the defendant had a reasonable opportunity to learn about it, as in the case of persons engaged in the shipment of pharmaceuticals who run afoul of the criminal prohibitions in the federal food and drug laws. See United States v. Dotterweich, 320 U.S. 277 (1943). . . . If none of the conditions that make it reasonable to dispense with proof of knowledge of the law is present, then to intone "ignorance of the law is no defense" is to condone a violation of fundamental principles for the sake of a modest economy in the administration of criminal justice. . . .

We thus have an example of those "highly technical statutes that present . . . the danger of ensnaring individuals engaged in apparently innocent conduct" of which the Supreme Court spoke in Bryan v. United States, 524 U.S. 184, 194 (1998). This case differs from *Bryan* because the statute here is easy to understand; but it is hard to discover, and that comes to the same thing, as we know from Lambert v. California, 355 U.S. 225 (1957). The law challenged in that case required a felon to register with the police. Lambert, a felon, failed to do so. She "had no actual knowledge of the requirement"; there was no showing of "the probability of such knowledge"; "violation of [the law's] provisions [was] unaccompanied by any activity whatever"; and "circumstances which might move one to inquire as to the necessity of registration [were] completely lacking." Id. at 227-29. The Court voided Lambert's conviction. We should do the same for Wilson's conviction.

159 F.3d at 293-96 (Posner, C.J., dissenting). Is Judge Posner right? Note the tossed-off reference to the fact that Wilson "had beaten his wife and threatened to kill her." Does that change your view of *Wilson*? Does it make Wilson's subsequent gun possession culpable? For a recent Supreme Court case addressing some of these issues, see Voisine v. United States, 136 S. Ct. 2272 (2016).

17. Perhaps *Wilson* is best seen as a federal prosecution for a state-law crime: in that case, domestic violence. Federal gun laws are often used to subject violent felons guilty of crimes like armed robbery to tougher federal sentencing rules. That was the idea behind Project Exile, a joint federal-local task force that aimed to reduce criminal violence in Richmond, Virginia; the approach has been widely copied and has spawned a large literature. See, e.g., Daniel C. Richman, "Project Exile" and the Allocation of Federal Law Enforcement Authority, 43 Ariz. L. Rev. 369 (2001). Is that an appropriate use of federal criminal law? How does it bear on the *mens rea* issue presented in *Bryan* and *Wilson*?

Liparota, Cheek, Ratzlaf, and *Bryan* are all written as statutory interpretation decisions. But their reasoning depends on the proposition that the intent standards applied in those cases were necessary in order to ensure that the law punishes only those defendants who had fair notice that their conduct might get them in trouble. Fair notice is a constitutional value, not just a statutory one—the vagueness doctrine rests on it, as does Lambert v. California, 355 U.S. 225 (1957), the due process case discussed in *Wilson.* For an argument that at least some of the decisions excerpted above represent an emerging law of "constitutional innocence," see Alan C. Michaels, Constitutional Innocence, 112 Harv. L. Rev. 828 (1999). Is Michaels right? Is *Morissette* best seen as a piece of constitutional law or as a part of the federal law of theft? What about *Bryan*?

The final case we consider, *Elonis v. United States,* has these same constitutional undertones relating to fair notice, and in some ways is a nice, threaded-together summary of this section of Chapter 3. But *Elonis* also has another important constitutional inflexion point: the First Amendment's protection of free speech. The Court was called upon to decide what *mens rea* is required for conviction under 18 U.S.C. §875(c), which criminalizes transmitting in interstate commerce "any threat to injure the person of another." The provision contained no scienter term. You will examine another subsection of §875, (d), in Chapter 5—a prohibition on threats to injure another's reputation with "intent to extort" money from the other person; the majority references this provision in *Elonis.*

Elonis v. United States
135 S. Ct. 2001 (2015)

Chief Justice ROBERTS delivered the opinion of the Court.

Federal law makes it a crime to transmit in interstate commerce "any communication containing any threat . . . to injure the person of another." 18 U.S.C. §875(c). Petitioner was convicted of violating this provision under instructions that required the jury to find that he communicated what a reasonable person would regard as a threat. The question is whether the statute also requires that the defendant be aware of the threatening nature of the communication, and—if not—whether the First Amendment requires such a showing.

I

A . . .

Anthony Douglas Elonis was an active user of the social networking Web site Facebook. Users of that Web site may post items on their Facebook page that are accessible to other users, including Facebook "friends" who are notified when new content is posted. In May 2010, Elonis's wife of nearly seven years left him, taking with her their two young children. Elonis began "listening to more violent music" and posting self-styled "rap" lyrics inspired by the music. Eventually, Elonis changed the user name on his Facebook page from his actual name to a rap-style nom de plume, "Tone Dougie," to distinguish himself from his "on-line persona." The lyrics Elonis posted as "Tone Dougie" included graphically violent language and imagery. This material was often interspersed with disclaimers that the lyrics were "fictitious," with no intentional "resemblance to real persons." Elonis posted an explanation to another Facebook user that "I'm doing this for me. My writing is therapeutic.". . .

Elonis's co-workers and friends viewed the posts in a different light. . . . [The Court described in detail the posts that formed the basis of the five counts of making threats for which Elonis was indicted.]

B

A grand jury indicted Elonis for making threats to injure patrons and employees of the park, his estranged wife, police officers, a kindergarten class, and an FBI agent, all in violation of 18 U.S.C. §875(c). In the District Court, Elonis moved to dismiss the indictment for failing to allege that he had intended to threaten anyone. The District Court denied the motion, holding that Third Circuit precedent required only that Elonis "intentionally made the communication, not that he intended to make a threat." At trial, Elonis testified that his posts emulated the rap lyrics of the well-known performer Eminem, some of which involve fantasies about killing his ex-wife. In Elonis's view, he had posted "nothing . . . that hasn't been said already." The Government presented as witnesses Elonis's wife and co-workers, all of whom said they felt afraid and viewed Elonis's posts as serious threats.

Elonis requested a jury instruction that "the government must prove that he intended to communicate a true threat." The District Court denied that request. The jury instructions instead informed the jury that

"A statement is a true threat when a defendant intentionally makes a statement in a context or under such circumstances wherein a reasonable person would foresee that the statement would be interpreted by those to whom the maker communicates the statement as a serious expression of an intention to inflict bodily injury or take the life of an individual."

The Government's closing argument emphasized that it was irrelevant whether Elonis intended the postings to be threats—"it doesn't matter what he thinks." A jury convicted Elonis on four of the five counts against him, acquitting only on the charge of threatening park patrons and employees. Elonis was sentenced to three years, eight months' imprisonment and three years' supervised release.

Elonis renewed his challenge to the jury instructions in the Court of Appeals, contending that the jury should have been required to find that he intended his posts to be threats. The Court of Appeals disagreed, holding that the intent required by Section 875(c) is only the intent to communicate words that the defendant understands, and that a reasonable person would view as a threat. . . .

II

A . . .

18 U.S.C. §875(c). . . . does not indicate whether the defendant must intend that his communication contain a threat.

Elonis argues that the word "threat" itself in Section 875(c) imposes such a requirement. According to Elonis, every definition of "threat" or "threaten" conveys the notion of an intent to inflict harm. . . . E.g., 11 Oxford English Dictionary 353 (1933) ("to declare (usually conditionally) one's intention of inflicting injury upon"); Webster's New International Dictionary 2633 (2d ed. 1954) ("*Law,* specif., an expression of an intention to inflict loss or harm on another by illegal means"); Black's Law Dictionary 1519 (8th ed. 2004) ("A communicated intent to inflict harm or loss on another").

These definitions, however, speak to what the statement conveys—not to the mental state of the author. For example, an anonymous letter that says "I'm going to kill you" is "an expression of an intention to inflict loss or harm" regardless of the author's intent. A victim who receives that letter in the mail has received a threat, even if the author believes (wrongly) that his message will be taken as a joke.

For its part, the Government argues that Section 875(c) should be read in light of its neighboring provisions, Sections 875(b) and 875(d). Those provisions also prohibit certain types of threats, but expressly include a mental state requirement of an "intent to extort." See 18 U.S.C. §875(b) (proscribing threats to injure or kidnap made "with intent to extort"); §875(d) (proscribing threats to property or reputation made "with intent to extort"). According to the Government, the express "intent to extort" requirements in Sections 875(b) and (d) should preclude courts from implying an unexpressed "intent to threaten" requirement in Section 875(c). . . .

The Government takes this *expressio unius est exclusio alterius* canon too far. The fact that Congress excluded the requirement of an "intent to extort" from Section 875(c) is strong evidence that Congress did not mean to confine Section 875(c) to crimes of extortion. But that does not suggest that Congress, at the same time, also meant to exclude a requirement that a defendant act with a certain mental state in communicating a threat. The most we can conclude from the language of Section 875(c) and its neighboring provisions is that Congress meant to proscribe a broad class of threats in Section 875(c), but did not identify what mental state, if any, a defendant must have to be convicted.

In sum, neither Elonis nor the Government has identified any indication of a particular mental state requirement in the text of Section 875(c).

B

The fact that the statute does not specify any required mental state, however, does not mean that none exists. We have repeatedly held that "mere omission from a criminal enactment of any mention of criminal intent" should not be read "as dispensing with it." Morissette v. United States, 342 U.S. 246, 250 (1952). This rule of construction reflects the basic principle that "wrongdoing must be conscious to be criminal." Id. at 252. As Justice Jackson explained, this principle is "as universal and persistent in mature systems of law as belief in freedom of the human will and a consequent ability and duty of the normal individual to choose between good and evil." Id. at 250. The "central thought" is that a defendant must be "blameworthy in mind" before he can be found guilty, a concept courts have expressed over time through various terms such as *mens rea*, scienter, malice aforethought, guilty knowledge, and the like. Id. at 252. . . . Although there are exceptions, the "general rule" is that a guilty mind is "a necessary element in the indictment and proof of every crime." United States v. Balint, 258 U.S. 250, 251 (1922). We therefore generally "interpret [] criminal statutes to include broadly applicable scienter requirements, even where the statute by its terms does not contain them." United States v. X-Citement Video, Inc., 513 U.S. 64, 70 (1994).

This is not to say that a defendant must know that his conduct is illegal before he may be found guilty. The familiar maxim "ignorance of the law is no excuse" typically holds true. Instead, our cases have explained that a defendant generally must "know the facts that make his conduct fit the definition of the offense," Staples v. United States, 511 U.S. 600, 608, n.3 (1994), even if he does not know that those facts give rise to a crime.

Morissette, for example, involved an individual who had taken spent shell casings from a Government bombing range, believing them to have been abandoned. During his trial for "knowingly convert[ing]" property of the United States, the judge instructed the jury that the only question was whether the defendant had knowingly taken the property without authorization. 342 U.S. at 248-249. This Court reversed the defendant's conviction, ruling that he had to know not only that he was taking the casings, but also that someone else still had property rights in them. He could not be found liable "if he truly believed [the casings] to be abandoned." Id. at 271. . . .

By the same token, in Liparota v. United States, we considered a statute making it a crime to knowingly possess or use food stamps in an unauthorized manner. 471 U.S. 419, 420 (1985). The Government's argument, similar to its position in this case, was that a defendant's conviction could be upheld if he knowingly possessed or used the food stamps, and in fact his possession or use was unauthorized. Id. at 423. But this Court rejected that interpretation of the statute, because it would have criminalized "a broad range of apparently innocent conduct" and swept in individuals who had no knowledge of the facts that made their conduct blameworthy. Id. at 426. For example, the statute made it illegal to use food stamps at a store that charged higher prices to food stamp customers. Without a mental state requirement in the statute, an individual who unwittingly paid higher prices would be guilty under the Government's interpretation. The Court noted that Congress *could* have intended to cover such a "broad range of conduct," but declined "to adopt such a sweeping interpretation" in the absence of a clear indication that Congress intended that result. Id. at 427. The Court instead construed the statute to require knowledge of the facts that made the use of the food stamps unauthorized. Id. at 425. . . .

And again, in *X-Citement Video*, we considered a statute criminalizing the distribution of visual depictions of minors engaged in sexually explicit conduct. 513 U.S. at 68. We rejected a reading of the statute which would have required only that a defendant knowingly send the prohibited materials, regardless of whether he knew the age of the performers. Id. at 68-69. We held instead that a defendant must also know that those depicted were minors, because that was "the crucial element separating legal innocence from wrongful conduct." Id. at 73. . . .

When interpreting federal criminal statutes that are silent on the required mental state, we read into the statute "only that *mens rea* which is necessary to separate wrongful conduct from 'otherwise innocent conduct.'" Carter v. United States, 530 U.S. 255, 269 (2000) (quoting *X-Citement Video*, 513 U.S. at 72). In some cases, a general requirement that a defendant *act* knowingly is itself an adequate safeguard. For example, in *Carter*, we considered whether a conviction under 18 U.S.C. §2113(a), for taking "by force and violence" items of value belonging to or in the care of a bank, requires that a defendant have the intent to steal. 530 U.S. at 261. We held that once the Government proves the defendant forcibly took the money, "the concerns underlying the presumption in favor of scienter are fully satisfied, for a forceful taking—even by a defendant who takes under a good-faith claim of right—falls outside the realm of . . . 'otherwise innocent' " conduct. Id. at 269-270. In other instances, however, requiring only that the defendant act knowingly "would fail to protect the innocent actor." Id. at 269. A statute similar to Section 2113(a) that did not require a forcible taking or the intent to steal "would run the risk of punishing seemingly innocent conduct in the case of a defendant who peaceably takes money believing it to be his." Ibid. In such a case, the Court explained, the statute "would need to be read to require . . . that the defendant take the money with 'intent to steal or purloin.'" Ibid.

C

Section 875(c), as noted, requires proof that a communication was transmitted and that it contained a threat. The "presumption in favor of a scienter requirement should apply to *each* of the statutory elements that criminalize otherwise innocent conduct." *X-Citement Video*, 513 U.S. at 72 (emphasis added). The parties agree that a defendant under Section 875(c) must know that he is transmitting a communication. But communicating *something* is not what makes the conduct "wrongful." Here "the crucial element separating legal innocence from wrongful conduct" is the threatening nature of the communication. Id. at 73. The mental state requirement must therefore apply to the fact that the communication contains a threat.

Elonis's conviction, however, was premised solely on how his posts would be understood by a reasonable person. Such a "reasonable person" standard is a familiar feature of civil liability in tort law, but is inconsistent with "the conventional requirement for criminal conduct—*awareness* of some wrongdoing." *Staples*, 511 U.S. at 606-607. . . . Having liability turn on whether a "reasonable person" regards the communication as a threat—regardless of what the defendant thinks—"reduces culpability on the all-important element of the crime to negligence," *Jeffries*, 692 F.3d at 484 (Sutton, J., *dubitante*), and we "have long been reluctant to infer that a negligence standard was intended in criminal statutes". . . . Under these principles, "what [Elonis] thinks" does matter.

The Government is at pains to characterize its position as something other than a negligence standard, emphasizing that its approach would require proof that a defendant "comprehended [the] contents and context" of the communication. The Government gives two examples of individuals who, in its view, would lack this necessary mental state—a "foreigner, ignorant of the English language," who would not know the meaning of the words at issue, or an individual mailing a sealed envelope without knowing its contents. But the fact that the Government would require a defendant to actually know the words of and circumstances surrounding a communication does not amount to a rejection of negligence. Criminal negligence standards often incorporate "the circumstances known" to a defendant. ALI, Model Penal Code §2.02(2)(d) (1985). . . . Courts then ask, however, whether a reasonable person equipped with that knowledge, not the actual defendant, would have recognized the harmfulness of his conduct. That is precisely the Government's position here: Elonis can be convicted, the Government contends, if he himself knew the contents and context of his posts, and a reasonable person would have recognized that the posts would be read as genuine threats. That is a negligence standard. . . .

* * *

In light of the foregoing, Elonis's conviction cannot stand. The jury was instructed that the Government need prove only that a reasonable person would regard Elonis's communications as threats, and that was error. Federal criminal liability generally does not turn solely on the results of an act without considering the defendant's mental state. That understanding "took deep and early root in American soil" and Congress left it intact here: Under Section 875(c), "wrongdoing must be conscious to be criminal." *Morissette*, 342 U.S. at 252.

There is no dispute that the mental state requirement in Section 875(c) is satisfied if the defendant transmits a communication for the purpose of issuing a threat, or with knowledge that the communication will be viewed as a threat. In response to a question at oral argument, Elonis stated that a finding of recklessness would not be sufficient. Neither Elonis nor the Government has briefed or argued that point, and we accordingly decline to address it. . . .

Both Justice Alito and Justice Thomas complain about our not deciding whether recklessness suffices for liability under Section 875(c). . . . Justice Alito contends that each party "argued" this issue, but they did not address it at all until oral argument, and even then only briefly.

Justice Alito also suggests that we have not clarified confusion in the lower courts. That is wrong. Our holding makes clear that negligence is not sufficient to support a conviction under Section 875(c), contrary to the view of nine Courts of Appeals. There was and is no circuit conflict over the question Justice Alito and Justice Thomas would have us decide—whether recklessness suffices for liability under Section 875(c). No Court of Appeals has even addressed that question. We think that is more than sufficient "justification" for us to decline to be the first appellate tribunal to do so. . . .

We may be "capable of deciding the recklessness issue" but following our usual practice of awaiting a decision below and hearing from the parties would help ensure that we decide it correctly. . . .

Justice ALITO, concurring in part and dissenting in part.

In Marbury v. Madison, the Court famously proclaimed: "It is emphatically the province and duty of the judicial department to say what the law is." Today, the Court announces: It is emphatically the prerogative of this Court to say only what the law is not.

The Court's disposition of this case is certain to cause confusion and serious problems. Attorneys and judges need to know which mental state is required for conviction under 18 U.S.C. §875(c), an important criminal statute. This case squarely presents that issue, but the Court provides only a partial answer. The Court holds that the jury instructions in this case were defective because they required only negligence in conveying a threat. But the Court refuses to explain what type of intent was necessary. Did the jury need to find that Elonis had the *purpose* of conveying a true threat? Was it enough if he *knew* that his words conveyed such a threat? Would *recklessness* suffice? The Court declines to say. Attorneys and judges are left to guess. . . .

There is no justification for the Court's refusal to provide an answer. . . . If the Court thinks that we cannot decide the recklessness question without additional help from the parties, we can order further briefing and argument. In my view, however, we are capable of deciding the recklessness issue, and we should resolve that question now. . . .

At issue in this case is the *mens rea* required with respect to the second element—that the thing transmitted was a threat to injure the person of another. . . . In my view, . . . it must be shown that the defendant was at least reckless as to whether the transmission met that requirement.

Why is recklessness enough? My analysis of the *mens rea* issue follows the same track as the Court's, as far as it goes. I agree with the Court that we should presume that criminal statutes require some sort of *mens rea* for conviction . . . [and] that we should presume that an offense like that created by §875(c) requires more than negligence with respect to a critical element like the one at issue here. . . . Whether negligence is morally culpable is an interesting philosophical question, but the answer is at least sufficiently debatable to justify the presumption that a serious offense against the person that lacks any clear common-law counterpart should be presumed to require more.

Once we have passed negligence, however, no further presumptions are defensible. In the hierarchy of mental states that may be required as a condition for criminal liability, the *mens rea* just above negligence is reck-lessness. Negligence requires only that the defendant "should [have] be [en] aware of a substantial and unjustifiable risk," ALI, Model Penal Code §2.02(2)(d), p. 226 (1985), while recklessness exists "when a person dis-regards a risk of harm of which he is aware," Model Penal Code §2.02(2)(c). And when Congress does not specify a *mens rea* in a criminal statute, we have no justification for inferring that anything more than recklessness is needed. It is quite unusual for us to interpret a statute to contain a requirement that is nowhere set out in the text. Once we have reached recklessness, we have gone as far as we can without stepping over the line that separates interpretation from amendment.

There can be no real dispute that recklessness regarding a risk of serious harm is wrongful conduct. . . . Someone who acts recklessly with respect to conveying a threat necessarily grasps that he is not engaged in innocent conduct. He is not merely careless. He is aware that others could regard his statements as a threat, but he delivers them anyway.

Accordingly, I would hold that a defendant may be convicted under §875(c) if he or she consciously disregards the risk that the communi-cation transmitted will be interpreted as a true threat. Nothing in the Court's non-committal opinion prevents lower courts from adopting that standard. . . .

III

[B]ecause the jury instructions in this case did not require proof of recklessness, I would vacate the judgment below and remand for the Court of Appeals to decide in the first instance whether Elonis's convic-tion could be upheld under a recklessness standard.

[Justice THOMAS dissented.]

NOTES AND QUESTIONS

1. Do you agree with Justice Alito's view that recklessness with regard to how the communication will be interpreted is sufficient for a conviction? The Model Penal Code, cited by both the majority and by Justice Alito, has a hierarchy of scienter terms: "purpose" being the highest, followed by "knowledge," then "recklessness," and, finally, "negligence." The MPC defines no crimes with no scienter (i.e., strict liability, as in *Dotterweich*) and strongly urges against a serious prohibition based on mere negligence. But it also provides as a default rule that when no scienter term is expressly provided for, "recklessness" (and by definition "knowledge" or "purpose")

suffices. Is Justice Alito proposing this approach just for the special context of §875(c), or for the whole federal criminal code?

2. Chief Justice Roberts, writing for the majority, argues that the Court should avoid deciding whether recklessness is sufficient until the issue has been addressed by lower courts and briefed by parties before the Supreme Court. Justice Alito suggests that in the context of a criminal statute—under which innocents might be convicted or guilty defendants might go free while the recklessness question percolates in lower courts—such judicial restraint is no virtue. Who do you think has the better argument here?

3. On remand, the Third Circuit once again affirmed Elonis's conviction, holding that the erroneous jury instruction was harmless error. United States v. Elonis, 841 F.3d 589 (3d Cir. 2016). The Third Circuit explained:

> We believe Section 875(c) contains both a subjective and objective component, and the Government must satisfy both in order to convict a defendant under the statute. The Supreme Court focused on the subjective component. It held that to satisfy the subjective component of Section 875(c), the Government must demonstrate beyond a reasonable doubt that the defendant transmitted a communication for the purpose of issuing a threat or with knowledge that the communication would be viewed as a threat.
>
> The Government must also satisfy the objective component, which requires it to prove beyond a reasonable doubt that the defendant transmitted a communication that a reasonable person would view as a threat. The objective component of Section 875(c) shields individuals from culpability for communications that are not threatening to a reasonable person, distinguishing true threats from hyperbole, satire, or humor. See Watts v. United States, 394 U.S. 705, 708 (1969). It requires the jury to consider the context and circumstances in which a communication was made to determine whether a reasonable person would consider the communication to be a serious expression of an intent to inflict bodily injury on an individual. . . .
>
> While it is clear that a defendant can be convicted under Section 875(c) for transmitting an objectively threatening communication "with knowledge that the communication will be viewed as a threat," Elonis and the Government disagree on the application of that standard. Elonis contends the Government must show the defendant "acted with knowledge of *a reasonable person's* interpretation of the speech as threatening," reasoning that "knowledge that particular persons would consider the communications threatening is not necessarily equivalent to knowledge of how a reasonable person would understand them." Were this not the standard, Elonis argues, a defendant could violate Section 875(c) merely by "post[ing] photos of his pit bull on Facebook . . . knowing that some members of the Facebook community unreasonably found photos of such dogs threatening. . . ."
>
> Elonis's concerns are unfounded. The objective component of Section 875(c) ensures that a defendant can only be convicted for transmitting communications that are objectively threatening. Moreover, his approach would render the objective component meaningless. Instead of asking the jury

whether the defendant's communication was objectively threatening, Elonis would ask only whether the defendant believed his communication was objectively threatening. But it is not for the defendant to determine whether a communication is objectively threatening—that is the jury's role. If a defendant transmits a communication for the purpose of issuing a threat or with knowledge that the recipient will view it as a threat, and a jury determines that communication is objectively threatening, then the defendant has violated Section 875(c) whether or not he agrees the communication was objectively threatening.

841 F.3d at 596-97. Applying this standard, the Third Circuit held that "[t]he record contains overwhelming evidence demonstrating beyond a reasonable doubt that Elonis knew the threatening nature of his communications, and therefore would have been convicted absent the error." Id. at 598. Due to its disposition of the case on the issue of harmless error, the court of appeals found "no occasion to determine whether a finding of recklessness would be sufficient to satisfy the mental state requirement of Section 875(c)." Id. at 601.

Did the Third Circuit properly interpret the Supreme Court's decision? In the wake of the Third Circuit's decision on remand, Elonis again filed a petition for certiorari, which may present the Court with another opportunity to address the role, if any, of recklessness in this statute.

In this chapter, we have considered some of the doctrines, constitutional and statutory, that govern the interpretation of federal criminal statutes. Several points deserve mentioning. First, the interpretive doctrines explored in this chapter are inconsistently applied. In Section A, you learned that only Congress may define crimes. It is not enough that Congress could legislate—i.e., that it has jurisdiction pursuant to its enumerated powers under Article I, Section 8 of the Constitution—the political branches must have in fact crafted a law that defines the prohibited conduct. But the lesson of the rest of the chapter is that the "ban on common-law crimes" still leaves a lot of room for courts to exercise their interpretive authority in ways that narrow or broaden the reach of a statutory prohibition. We saw that dynamic at play in three specific contexts: *actus reas* (Section B); federal defenses (Section C); and *mens rea* (Section D). That last section, for example, demonstrated that federal statutes often fail to define *mens rea*. Sometimes the Court interprets Congress's silence as dispensing with any proof of *mens rea*, as in *Dotterweich*, but more often it purports to find legislative intent to require some level of scienter, as in *Staples* and *Elonis*. While those decisions are presented as interpretations of particular statutes, the last several decades have seen a recommitment to the principal of *Morissette*: that the federal criminal law should not be a "trap for the unwary."

Second, what's at stake in these interpretive doctrines is a debate about the proper role of the federal courts—especially the Supreme Court—in interpreting duly enacted federal criminal laws. The material in this chapter is trans-substantive: Institutional concerns about the proper role of the courts apply, at least in theory, to all federal prohibitions. The next four chapters, however, deal with particular prohibitions—against fraud, extortion, bribery, and civil rights violations. As you read those materials, consider the extent to which the federal courts are more or less faithful to the general contours of proper criminal law "interpretation" set forth in Chapter 3. You will see that the tug of war in most of these areas involves not only Congress and the federal courts, but, critically, also federal prosecutors and the great discretion that *they* have, as an initial matter at least, in interpreting broadly worded federal prohibitions.

4 | Mail and Wire Fraud

Although there is no general federal fraud statute, the mail fraud statute, 18 U.S.C. §1341, and the wire fraud statute, 18 U.S.C. §1343, are among the most flexible weapons in the federal prosecutorial arsenal.

---

§1341. Frauds and swindles

Whoever, having devised or intending to devise any scheme or artifice to defraud, or for obtaining money or property by means of false or fraudulent pretenses, representations, or promises, or to sell, dispose of, loan, exchange, alter, give away, distribute, supply, or furnish or procure for unlawful use any counterfeit or spurious coin, obligation, security, or other article, or anything represented to be or intimated or held out to be such counterfeit or spurious article, for the purpose of executing such scheme or artifice or attempting so to do, places in any post office or authorized depository for mail matter, any matter or thing whatever to be sent or delivered by the Postal Service, or deposits or causes to be deposited any matter or thing whatever to be sent or delivered by any private or commercial interstate carrier, or takes or receives therefrom, any such matter or thing, or knowingly causes to be delivered by mail or such carrier according to the direction thereon, or at the place at which it is directed to be delivered by the person to whom it is addressed, any such matter or thing, shall be fined under this title or imprisoned not more than 20 years, or both. If the violation affects a financial institution, such person shall be fined not more than $1,000,000 or imprisoned not more than 30 years, or both.

Note that the current version of the statute reflects the extension of the "mailing" element to include "any private or commercial interstate carrier."

---

§1343. Fraud by wire, radio, or television

Whoever, having devised or intending to devise any scheme or artifice to defraud, or for obtaining money or property by means of false or fraudulent pretenses, representations, or promises, transmits or causes to be transmitted by means of wire, radio, or television communication in interstate or foreign commerce, any writings, signs, signals, pictures, or sounds for the purpose of executing such scheme or artifice, shall be fined under this title or imprisoned not more than 20 years, or both. If the violation affects a financial institution, such person shall be fined not more than $1,000,000 or imprisoned not more than 30 years, or both.

Until recently, the maximum penalty for violation of §§1341 or 1343 was five years' imprisonment. The current 20-year maximum penalties for these offenses are the product of the Sarbanes-Oxley Act of 2002, Pub. L. No. 107-204, which also added a separate conspiracy provision, codified at 18 U.S.C. §1349, making fraud conspiracies punishable by 20 years, instead of the usual five years set by the general conspiracy provision, 18 U.S.C. §371.

Most prosecutions under the mail and wire fraud statutes are not particularly controversial—or particularly interesting. A typical case might involve an advertisement, through the mails or on the Internet, for "gold bars" that the buyer learns, after payment that cannot be retrieved, are only gold-plated. Here, the elements of a mail or wire fraud offense will easily be found: (1) the use of either mail or wire communications in the foreseeable furtherance (2) of a scheme to defraud (3) involving a material deception (4) with the intent to deprive another of (5) property. See Charles Doyle, Congressional Research Service, Mail and Wire Fraud: A Brief Overview of Federal Criminal Law (July 21, 2011).

These kinds of cases, which occupy the heartland of criminal fraud, are not the focus of this chapter. Rather, our focus is on the reach of the mail and wire fraud statutes; you will see that federal prosecutors have used these laws to attack a wide variety of forms of dishonesty in both commercial and governmental settings. In Section A of this chapter, we consider an important early case that endorsed a broad interpretation of the mail fraud statute and then consider more generally what constitutes "fraud" under §§1341 and 1343 (cases addressing the meaning of "fraud" rely on the two provisions interchangeably). The deprivations in Section A, however, are simply of money. Next we consider how fraud doctrine has come to encompass a variety of non-monetary deprivations. The deprivations considered in Section B are of intangible forms of property—an area of increasing growth as prosecutors and courts explore the various "bundles of sticks" that constitute property rights. Section C looks at an area of even greater doctrinal growth, then contraction, then growth, and now maybe contraction: prosecutions of "honest services fraud," which have been the subject of considerable attention from Congress and the Supreme Court in recent years. In Section D, we will consider the degree to which the "postal" or "wire" nexus required by these provisions limits federal fraud prosecutions. Finally, after having visited the special modified common-law world of mail fraud, Section E includes a critique, by Professor Dan Kahan, of this and similar projects.

A.   SCHEME TO DEFRAUD

In the early days of the mail fraud statute, some courts were wary of its potential reach and sought to confine its scope to frauds necessarily dependent on the mails. See, e.g., United States v. Owens, 17 F. 72 (E.D. Mo. 1883) (quashing the mail fraud indictment of a defendant who mailed 50 cents to a business creditor but claimed in the accompanying letter to be enclosing his entire debt of $162.50). Over time, however, courts, including the Supreme Court, interpreted the statute far more expansively. Recall the facts of Durland v. United States, 161 U.S. 306 (1896), discussed briefly in Chapter 3. Durland and his co-defendants were con artists who used the mails to advertise "bonds" that would return profits of 50 percent in six months—but they had no intention of paying the principal, much less any interest. The government prosecuted Durland under the mail fraud statute originally enacted in 1872, which prohibited using or causing the use of the mails in attempted execution of any "scheme or artifice to defraud." Strangely enough, however, the common-law crime of fraud did not cover their conduct. As we noted in Chapter 2, the most closely analogous common-law offense, "false pretenses," required proof of false statements of material fact; it did not cover—as Durland argued in challenging his indictment—"the mere intention not to carry out a contract in the future." Id. at 313. Nevertheless, the Supreme Court upheld Durland's conviction, concluding that the statute extended further than the common law.

Durland v. United States
161 U.S. 306 (1896)

Mr. Justice BREWER, after stating the case, delivered the opinion of the Court.

Inasmuch as the testimony has not been preserved, we must assume that it was sufficient to substantiate the charges in the indictments; that this was a scheme and artifice to defraud, and that the defendant did not intend that the bonds should mature, or that although money was received, any should be returned, but that it should be appropriated to his own use. In other words, he was trying to entrap the unwary, and to secure money from them on the faith of a scheme glittering and attractive in form, yet unreal and deceptive in fact, and known to him to be such. So far as the moral element is concerned it must be taken that the defendant's guilt was established.

But the contention on his part is that the statute reaches only such cases as, at common law, would come within the definition of "false pretences," in order to make out which there must be a misrepresentation as to some existing fact and not a mere promise as to the future. It is urged that there was no misrepresentation as to the existence or solvency of the corporation, the Provident Bond and Investment Company, or as to its modes of doing business, no suggestion that it failed to issue its bonds to any and every one advancing the required dues, or that its promise of payment according to the conditions named in the bond was not a valid and binding promise. . . .

The statute is broader than is claimed. Its letter shows this: "Any scheme or artifice to defraud." Some schemes may be promoted through mere representations and promises as to the future, yet are none the less schemes and artifices to defraud. Punishment because of the fraudulent purpose is no new thing. As said by Mr. Justice Brown, in Evans v. United States, 153 U.S. 584, 592 [1894], "if a person buy goods on credit in good faith, knowing that he is unable to pay for them at the time, but believing that he will be able to pay for them at the maturity of the bill, he is guilty of no offence even if he be disappointed in making such payment. But if he purchases them, knowing that he will not be able to pay for them, and with an intent to cheat the vendor, this is a plain fraud, and made punishable as such by statutes in many of the States."

But beyond the letter of the statute is the evil sought to be remedied, which is always significant in determining the meaning. It is common knowledge that nothing is more alluring than the expectation of receiving large returns on small investments. Eagerness to take the chances of large gains lies at the foundation of all lottery schemes, and, even when the matter of chance is eliminated, any scheme or plan which holds out the prospect of receiving more than is parted with appeals to the cupidity of all.

In the light of this the statute must be read, and so read it includes everything designed to defraud by representations as to the past or present, or suggestions and promises as to the future. The significant fact is the intent and purpose. . . . If the testimony had shown that this Provident company, and the defendant, as its president, had entered in good faith upon that business, believing that out of the moneys received they could by investment or otherwise make enough to justify the promised returns, no conviction could be sustained, no matter how visionary might seem the scheme. The charge is that in putting forth this scheme it was not the intent of the defendant to make an honest effort for its success, but that he resorted to this form and pretence of a bond without a thought that he or the company would ever make good its promises. It was with the purpose of protecting the public against all such intentional efforts to despoil, and to prevent the post office from being used to carry them into effect, that this statute was passed; and it would strip it of value to confine it to such cases as disclose an actual misrepresentation as to some existing fact, and exclude those in which is only the allurement of a specious and glittering promise. . . .

NOTES AND QUESTIONS

1. When Congress recodified much of criminal law in 1909, it incorporated the judicial gloss *Durland* put on the mail fraud statute, expanding it to reach schemes "for obtaining money or property by means of false or fraudulent pretenses, representations, or promises." For an insightful

history of the mail fraud statute from its origins in 1872 through Durland v. United States, and the 1909 amendments to the statute, see Jed S. Rakoff, The Federal Mail Fraud Statute (Part I), 18 Duq. L. Rev. 771 (1980).

Thereafter, the mail fraud statute has had a full and active life, with frequent use against garden variety frauds involving money and property—that is, against defendants like Durland. See generally Daniel P. Carpenter, The Forging of Bureaucratic Autonomy: Reputations, Networks, and Policy Innovation in Executive Agencies, 1862-1928 (2001). The extent of enforcement zeal in this era and decades thereafter reflected private as well as public interest. Particularly in the 1920s, private anti-fraud groups, funded by established commercial enterprises, would hire ex-prosecutors and postal inspectors to develop cases and present them to state and federal prosecutors. As inevitably happens when interest groups provide such assistance, some voiced concerns about skewed enforcement priorities: the anti-fraud units, it was alleged, were tools of the elite, targeting peripheral economic players, particularly immigrants, and were blind to the seamier practices of the financial institutions on which the units relied for support. See Edward Balleisen, Private Cops on the Fraud Beat: The Limits of American Business Self-Regulation, 1895-1932, 83 Business Hist. Rev. 113 (2009).

2. Fraudulent schemes like Durland's have existed as long as commerce and finance have existed. See Edward J. Balleisen, Fraud: An American History from Barnum to Madoff (2017). If markets function more efficiently when cheating is discouraged, then a broad criminal law of fraud should pose a more effective deterrent. For arguments favoring broad statutory coverage in this area, see two articles by Samuel W. Buell, Novel Criminal Fraud, 81 N.Y.U. L. Rev. 1971 (2006), and The Upside of Overbreadth, 83 N.Y.U. L. Rev. 1491 (2008). Yet the common law in this area was extraordinarily narrow. Why?

One possible answer goes like this: The line between cheats like Durland and simple breaches of contract is often unclear. Extravagant promises that go unfulfilled could signal either fraud or foolish business practices, with the latter better handled by the civil justice system than by criminal prosecution. An important point follows: Criminal prohibitions broad enough to catch all instances of core dishonesty and fraud may also cover a wide range of marginal misconduct. We have seen this phenomenon previously in some of the statutes at issue in Chapter 3 (remember, for instance, Brogan v. United States, 522 U.S. 398 (1998)). Even more than other areas of criminal law, the law of fraud faces a choice between criminalizing too little and criminalizing too much. As you read this section, consider not only what actions are being criminalized, but also which decision makers shape the doctrine.

3. The common law of crimes—the body of law that didn't cover Durland—was created as an adjunct to the law of tort. Crime victims often prosecuted criminal cases, but no centralized gatekeeper controlled access to criminal litigation as government prosecutors do now. It seems more than

coincidental that the law of white-collar fraud expanded *after* the rise of professional prosecutors with the discretion not to pursue cases they deemed mere commercial disputes.

4. By 1980, the Fifth Circuit could broadly declare regarding the mail fraud statute:

> The statute does not forbid merely the use of the mails to perpetrate an act made criminal by state or federal law; it reaches any plan, consummated by the use of the mails, in which artifice or deceit is employed to obtain something of value with the intention of depriving the owner of his property. The scheme is to be measured by a non-technical standard; the measure of fraud is its departure from moral uprightness, fundamental honesty, fair play and candid dealings in the general life of members of society. However, the statute does not reject all business practices that do not fulfill expectations, nor does it taint every breach of a business contract. Its condemnation of a "scheme or artifice to defraud" implicates only plans calculated to deceive. The government must prove not only that there was fraudulent activity but also that the defendant had a "conscious knowing intent to defraud." United States v. Kyle, 257 F.2d 559, 564 (2d Cir. 1958).

United States v. Kreimer, 609 F.2d 126, 128 (5th Cir. 1980).

Even while acknowledging the breadth of the statute, however, courts have worked hard to identify limiting principles. They have held that although a defendant's victims need not have actually been injured, the defendant must have contemplated actual harm to them.

And deceit itself may not be enough. The Second Circuit explained:

> Our cases have drawn a fine line between schemes that do no more than cause their victims to enter into transactions they would otherwise avoid — which do not violate the mail or wire fraud statutes — and schemes that depend for their completion on a misrepresentation of an essential element of the bargain[,] which do violate the mail and wire fraud statutes.

United States v. Shellef, 507 F.3d 82, 108 (2d Cir. 2007). In one such case, the Circuit overturned the conviction of stationery sellers who had told their sales personnel to misrepresent their identities in order to sign up customers. Lies like false claims about referrals were, the court found, "not directed to the quality, adequacy or price of goods to be sold, or otherwise to the nature of the bargain." United States v. Regent Office Supply Co., 421 F.2d 1174, 1179 (2d Cir. 1970). More recently, the Eleventh Circuit drew on this line of cases to explain why the "scheme to defraud" targeted by the statute "refers only to those schemes in which a defendant lies about the nature of the bargain itself." United States v. Takhalov, 827 F.3d 1307, 1313 (11th Cir. 2016). The court explained (in a hypothetical inspired by the case):

[A] young woman asks a rich businessman to buy her a drink at Bob's Bar. The businessman buys the drink, and afterwards the young woman decides to leave. Did the man get what he bargained for? Yes. He received his drink, and he had the opportunity to buy a young woman a drink. Does it change things if the woman is Bob's sister and he paid her to recruit customers? No; regardless of Bob's relationship with the woman, the businessman got exactly what he bargained for. If, on the other hand, Bob promised to pour the man a glass of Pappy Van Winkle [very rare and expensive] but gave him a slug of Old Crow [less so] instead, well, that would be fraud. Why? Because the misrepresentation goes to the value of the bargain.

Id. (That the opinion was written by a visiting judge from Kentucky helps explain its deep knowledge of matters bourbon.)

A focus on the "materiality" of a misrepresentation will usually allow courts to sort misrepresentations about collateral matters from those going to the nature of the bargain. A statement is material if the "misrepresentation or omission would naturally tend to lead or is capable of leading a reasonable person to change his conduct." United States v. Weaver, 2017 WL 2661596 (2d Cir. 2017); see also United States v. Weimert, 819 F.3d 351, 357 (7th Cir. 2016) (explaining that while some deceptions in commercial negotiations can support a fraud prosecution, deception about a party's negotiating positions, "such as a party's bottom-line reserve price or how important a particular non-price term is" cannot).

Actual reliance (a focus in civil suits for damages) has no place in the criminal fraud analysis, however, nor does actual injury, since the statute requires only that the government show that defendants merely contemplated some actual harm or injury to their victims. Note that the "materiality" requirement comes from common law. In Neder v. United States, 527 U.S. 1 (1999), the Court explained its general approach—squaring this importation with *Durland*: Consider the common law to inform Congress's intent unless the statute itself gives reason to think otherwise. Id. at 24-25. The Second Circuit recently followed just this approach when it relied on the common law "contemporaneous fraudulent intent" principle to hold that absent "proof of fraudulent intent not to perform the promise at the time of contract execution," a subsequent breach of that promise—even where willful and intentional—cannot in itself transform the promise into a fraud." United States ex rel. O'Donnell v. Countrywide Home Loans, 822 F.3d 650, 662 (2d Cir. 2016).

Need there be "convergence" between the intended victim of a fraud and the party that defendant has deceived? No, say those Circuits that have resolved the issue. Thus, in United States v. Greenberg, 835 F.3d 295 (2d Cir. 2016), a defendant who made misrepresentations to banks as part of a scheme to put fraudulent credit card charges on the bills of former customers got nowhere by arguing that he hadn't deceived the customers.

5. The statute covers certain omissions as well as affirmative misrepresentations. Yet defining the precise range of covered omissions has been a challenge. As the First Circuit noted in the context of a civil RICO suit:

> A defendant's failure to disclose information, without more, cannot make out a violation of the mail and wire fraud statutes. The authorities are less uniform on what "more" must be shown to transform a non-actionable nondisclosure into fraud in this context. Some courts have required a duty to disclose, triggered by an independent statutory scheme, the relationship between the parties, or the defendant's "partial or ambiguous statements that require further disclosure in order to avoid being misleading," while others have held that withholding information with the intent to deceive is enough.
>
> We considered the issue in Bonilla v. Volvo Car Corp., 150 F.3d 62 (1st Cir. 1998). There, we took the view that, without "a legal, professional or contractual duty" to disclose, the failure to do so generally cannot support a mail or wire fraud claim, though we acknowledged the existence of a "shadowy area" where nondisclosures in the absence of such a duty, if deliberate, could arguably "be treated as artifices to defraud under the federal statutes." Id. at 70. We nevertheless observed that "[i]t would be a truly revolutionary change to make a criminal out of every salesman (assuming the use of the mails or telephone) who did not take the initiative to reveal negative information about the product and who—a jury might find—secretly harbored in his heart the hope that the buyer would never ask." Id.

Sanchez v. Triple-S Management Corp., 492 F.3d 1, 10 (1st Cir. 2007); see United States v. Colton, 231 F.3d 890, 898-904 (4th Cir. 2000) (noting difference between nondisclosure and concealment, and explaining that the latter is actionable as fraud even without an independent statutory or fiduciary duty to disclose).

6. In United States v. Svete, the Eleventh Circuit considered whether the mail fraud statute "requires proof that the scheme be capable of deceiving a reasonably prudent person or whether schemes aimed at the gullible or improvident are also prohibited." 556 F.3d 1157 (11th Cir. 2009) (en banc). Defendants sold "financial interests in viatical settlements, which are financial products based on agreements with persons (known as viators) who have terminal illnesses and sell their life insurance policies to third parties for less than the mature value of the policies to benefit from the proceeds while alive." Id. at 1160. Charged with misleading investors about the life expectancies of viators—who were not terminally ill—and the risks associated with the investments, defendants pointed to the place in the contracts where investors acknowledged that they had not relied on any representations outside the contract. "The contracts also contained acknowledgments that the investors were sophisticated in financial matters and had sought or had access to professional advice and that the projected demise dates were only estimates." Id.

Overruling its own (outlier) precedent in the process, the Eleventh Circuit made short work of defendants' claim that these contractual provisions vitiated any allegation of fraud:

> Although the common law crime of cheat applied only to frauds that would deceive a person of ordinary prudence, by the time Congress enacted the prohibition of mail fraud, statutes that prohibited false pretenses had remedied this deficiency in the common law. 2 Francis Wharton, A Treatise on the Criminal Law of the United States §§2056, 2128 at 514, 560 (7th ed., Philadelphia, Kay & Brother, 1874). As a commentator explained, "It was in part to meet this difficulty that the statute of false pretenses was passed, and under this statute it has been repeatedly held that it matters not how patent the falsity of a pretense may be, if it succeeds in defrauding." Id. §2128, at 560. The trend of case law in the 1870s and 1880s was that statutes against false pretenses protected both the gullible and the savvy. . . .
>
> Congress has never used any language that would limit the coverage of the mail fraud statute to schemes that would deceive only prudent persons. To the contrary, the sponsor of the original statute explained that its purpose was "'to prevent the frauds which are mostly gotten up in the large cities . . . by thieves, forgers, and rapscallions generally, for the purpose of deceiving and fleecing the innocent people in the country.'" McNally [v. United States, 483 U.S. 350, 356 (1987)] (quoting Cong. Globe, 41 Cong., 3d Sess. 35 (1870) (remarks of Rep. Farnsworth during debate in previous Congress)). When the statute was amended in 1889 to prohibit schemes to sell counterfeit money, the Senate report reiterated a concern for the ignorant and naive:
>
> > A certain class of persons . . . send out circulars through the United States mails which appeal to the cupidity of the ignorant and hold out to the unfortunate the temptation to try to better their fortunes. . . . Farmers and country merchants and country postmasters are constantly plied with these circulars, . . . and plain as the fraud is upon its face, these men reap a golden harvest. The city papers frequently contain notices of the ignorant victims who venture to the cities and are relieved of their money; but there is no notice of the many smaller dupes who send their money through the mails in answer to these advertisements and pocket their losses. . . . This bill . . . will, if properly enforced, put an end to this infamous business.
>
> S. Rep. No. 50-2566, at 2 (1889). When the statute was amended in 1909 to "codify the holding of *Durland,*" *McNally,* 483 U.S. at 357, by adding the words "or for obtaining money or property by means of false or fraudulent pretenses, representations, or promises" after the phrase "any scheme or artifice to defraud," a wealth of case law explained that the crime of false pretenses did not have a reasonable victim requirement and that a contrary rule was against "the great weight of authority." State v. Phelps, 41 Wash. 470, 84 P. 24, 26 (Wash. 1906). . . .

Because the focus of the mail fraud statute, like any criminal statute, is on the violator, the purpose of the element of materiality is to ensure that a defendant actually intended to create a scheme to defraud. Proof that a defendant created a scheme to deceive reasonable people is sufficient evidence that the defendant intended to deceive, but a defendant who intends to deceive the ignorant or gullible by preying on their infirmities is no less guilty. Either way, the defendant has criminal intent.

Neder [v. United States, 527 U.S. 1 (1999)], instructs us to reject the elements of the common law that "would clearly be inconsistent with the statutes Congress enacted," 527 U.S. at 25, and whatever role, if any, a victim's negligence plays as a bar to civil recovery, it makes little sense as a defense under a criminal statute that embraces "*any* scheme or artifice to defraud." 18 U.S.C. §1341 (emphasis added). A perpetrator of fraud is no less guilty of fraud because his victim is also guilty of negligence. See Keeton et al., §108, at 751. . . .

Despite the plain text of the statute and longstanding precedents of the Supreme Court, in [United States v. Brown, 79 F.3d 1550 (11th Cir. 1996)], we held that mail fraud requires proof of a scheme to defraud that is objectively reliable unless the defendant is a fiduciary of the intended victim. We reversed convictions of defendants who had "approved and promoted lies about the investment potential" of real estate in Florida because the prospective investors in those homes could have discovered the truth from "readily available external sources." Id. at 1558-1560. We held that "federal criminal fraud requires proof that a person of ordinary prudence would rely on a representation or a deception[,]" id. at 1558, and concluded that a person of ordinary prudence would have investigated the value of Florida real estate instead of relying on the misrepresentations by the defendants, id. at 1561. . . .

Because *Brown* is inconsistent with both the broadly worded text of the mail fraud statute, 18 U.S.C. §1341, and the interpretation of that statute by the Supreme Court, *Neder*, 527 U.S. at 25; *Durland*, 161 U.S. at 313, we overrule our holding in *Brown* that the offense of mail fraud requires proof of a scheme calculated to deceive a person of ordinary prudence. . . .

Svete, 556 F.3d at 1162-66.

B.   PROSECUTORIAL INNOVATIONS AND JUDICIAL CONSTRAINTS IN MAIL AND WIRE FRAUD

Notwithstanding the broad definition of "fraudulent scheme" in *Durland*, the mail fraud statute was not clearly suited for the two new jobs that federal prosecutors in the early 1970s began to give it: as a tool for prosecuting (1) public sector corruption cases and (2) private sector kickbacks and bribes. Suppose a sum of money passes from a regulated business to a government official, who then grants some regulatory favor or lucrative government contract in exchange.

The party from whom the official obtains money was not defrauded. The parties who *were* defrauded—the voters (or is it the taxpayers, or the "public" more generally?)—may not have lost any money (or the loss may be difficult to prove), depending on the nature of the regulation or contract. Until the passage of the federal program bribery statute (18 U.S.C. §666, which bars the gift or receipt of bribes by anyone administering a program that receives $10,000 or more in federal aid and which we examine in Chapter 6) in 1984, no federal statute plainly criminalized corruption by state and local officials. Nor was it obvious that the mail fraud statute covered the payment of kickbacks to private employees.

In the early 1970s, prosecutors began deploying the mail fraud statute in both of these situations, alleging that the corrupt official had deprived the citizenry (or the corrupt employee had deprived his employer) of "the intangible right of honest services." See United States v. States, 488 F.2d 761, 766 (8th Cir. 1973) (upholding a conviction for election fraud under the mail fraud statute despite the absence of allegations that the defendant intended to deprive election authorities or anyone else of money or property). In time, through some combination of prosecutorial selection and judicial accommodation, a considerable body of law had developed in the lower courts, see Charles F.C. Ruff, Federal Prosecution of Local Corruption: A Case Study in the Making of Law Enforcement Policy, 65 Geo. L.J. 1171 (1977), with only the occasional judge rejecting the proposition that local corruption could be prosecuted as mail fraud, see United States v. Margiotta, 588 F.2d 108, 139 (2d Cir. 1982) (Winter, J., concurring in part and dissenting in part). Then, to federal prosecutors' chagrin, the Supreme Court put an end to this cottage industry in McNally v. United States. As you read *McNally*, consider the basis, or lack thereof, for the lower court decisions. Also consider why the Supreme Court might have come down so hard on a theory that lower federal courts found so easy to accept. Is this the kind of case the federal government should be prosecuting? In the scheme for which McNally and his co-defendant were prosecuted, whom (if anyone) did they intend to deprive of what item of value?

McNally v. United States
483 U.S. 350 (1987)

Justice WHITE delivered the opinion of the Court.

This action involves the prosecution of petitioner Gray, a former public official of the Commonwealth of Kentucky, and petitioner McNally, a private individual, for alleged violation of the federal mail fraud statute, 18 U.S.C. §1341. The prosecution's principal theory of the case, which was accepted by the courts below, was that petitioners' participation in a self-dealing patronage scheme defrauded the citizens and government of Kentucky of certain "intangible rights," such as the right to have the

Commonwealth's affairs conducted honestly. We must consider whether the jury charge permitted a conviction for conduct not within the scope of the mail fraud statute.

We accept for the sake of argument the Government's view of the evidence, as follows. Petitioners and a third individual, Howard P. "Sonny" Hunt, were politically active in the Democratic Party in the Commonwealth of Kentucky during the 1970s. After Democrat Julian Carroll was elected Governor of Kentucky in 1974, Hunt was made chairman of the state Democratic Party and given *de facto* control over selecting the insurance agencies from which the Commonwealth would purchase its policies. In 1975, the Wombwell Insurance Company of Lexington, Kentucky (Wombwell), which since 1971 had acted as the Commonwealth's agent for securing a workmen's compensation policy, agreed with Hunt that in exchange for a continued agency relationship it would share any resulting commissions in excess of $50,000 a year with other insurance agencies specified by him. The commissions in question were paid to Wombwell by the large insurance companies from which it secured coverage for the Commonwealth.

From 1975 to 1979, Wombwell funneled $851,000 in commissions to 21 separate insurance agencies designated by Hunt. Among the recipients of these payments was Seton Investments, Inc. (Seton), a company controlled by Hunt and petitioner Gray and nominally owned and operated by petitioner McNally.

Gray served as Secretary of Public Protection and Regulation from 1976 to 1978 and also as Secretary of the Governor's Cabinet from 1977 to 1979. Prior to his 1976 appointment, he and Hunt established Seton for the sole purpose of sharing in the commissions distributed by Wombwell. Wombwell paid some $200,000 to Seton between 1975 and 1979, and the money was used to benefit Gray and Hunt. Pursuant to Hunt's direction, Wombwell also made excess commission payments to the Snodgrass Insurance Agency, which in turn gave the money to McNally.

On account of the foregoing activities, Hunt was charged with and pleaded guilty to mail and tax fraud and was sentenced to three years' imprisonment. Petitioners were charged with one count of conspiracy and seven counts of mail fraud, six of which were dismissed before trial. The remaining mail fraud count was based on the mailing of a commission check to Wombwell by the insurance company from which it had secured coverage for the State. This count alleged that petitioners had devised a scheme (1) to defraud the citizens and government of Kentucky of their right to have the Commonwealth's affairs conducted honestly, and (2) to obtain, directly and indirectly, money and other things of value by means of false pretenses and the concealment of material facts. The conspiracy count alleged that petitioners had (1) conspired to violate the mail fraud statute through the scheme just described and (2) conspired to defraud the United States by obstructing the collection of federal taxes[, each conspiracy in violation of 18 U.S.C. §371]. . . .

The jury convicted petitioners on both the mail fraud and conspiracy counts, and the Court of Appeals affirmed the convictions. . . .

We granted certiorari, and now reverse.

The mail fraud statute clearly protects property rights, but does not refer to the intangible right of the citizenry to good government. As first enacted in 1872, as part of a recodification of the postal laws, the statute contained a general proscription against using the mails to initiate correspondence in furtherance of "any scheme or artifice to defraud." The sponsor of the recodification stated, in apparent reference to the anti-fraud provision, that measures were needed "to prevent the frauds which are mostly gotten up in the large cities . . . by thieves, forgers, and rapscallions generally, for the purpose of deceiving and fleecing the innocent people in the country." Insofar as the sparse legislative history reveals anything, it indicates that the original impetus behind the mail fraud statute was to protect the people from schemes to deprive them of their money or property.

Durland v. United States, 161 U.S. 306 (1896), the first case in which this Court construed the meaning of the phrase "any scheme or artifice to defraud," held that the phrase is to be interpreted broadly insofar as property rights are concerned, but did not indicate that the statute had a more extensive reach. . . .

Congress codified the holding of *Durland* in 1909, and in doing so gave further indication that the statute's purpose is protecting property rights. The amendment added the words "or for obtaining money or property by means of false or fraudulent pretenses, representations, or promises" after the original phrase "any scheme or artifice to defraud." Act of Mar. 4, 1909, ch. 321, §215, 35 Stat. 1130. The new language is based on the statement in *Durland* that the statute reaches "everything designed to defraud by representations as to the past or present, or suggestions and promises as to the future." However, instead of the phrase "everything designed to defraud" Congress used the words "[any scheme or artifice] for obtaining money or property."

After 1909, therefore, the mail fraud statute criminalized schemes or artifices "to defraud" or "for obtaining money or property by means of false or fraudulent pretenses, representation, or promises. . . ." Because the two phrases identifying the proscribed schemes appear in the disjunctive, it is arguable that they are to be construed independently and that the money-or-property requirement of the latter phrase does not limit schemes to defraud to those aimed at causing deprivation of money or property. This is the approach that has been taken by each of the Courts of Appeals that has addressed the issue: schemes to defraud include those designed to deprive individuals, the people, or the government of intangible rights, such as the right to have public officials perform their duties honestly.

As the Court long ago stated, however, the words "to defraud" commonly refer "to wronging one in his property rights by dishonest methods or schemes," and "usually signify the deprivation of something of value by trick, deceit, chicane or overreaching." Hammerschmidt v. United States, 265 U.S. 182, 188 (1924).[8]

The codification of the holding in *Durland* in 1909 does not indicate that Congress was departing from this common understanding. As we see it, adding the second phrase simply made it unmistakable that the statute reached false promises and misrepresentations as to the future as well as other frauds involving money or property.

We believe that Congress' intent in passing the mail fraud statute was to prevent the use of the mails in furtherance of such schemes. The Court has often stated that when there are two rational readings of a criminal statute, one harsher than the other, we are to choose the harsher only when Congress has spoken in clear and definite language. As the Court said in a mail fraud case years ago: "There are no constructive offenses; and before one can be punished, it must be shown that his case is plainly within the statute." Fasulo v. United States, 272 U.S. 620, 629 (1926). Rather than construe the statute in a manner that leaves its outer boundaries ambiguous and involves the Federal Government in setting standards of disclosure and good government for local and state officials, we read §1341 as limited in scope to the protection of property rights. If Congress desires to go further, it must speak more clearly than it has.

For purposes of this action, we assume that Hunt, as well as Gray, was a state officer. The issue is thus whether a state officer violates the mail fraud statute if he chooses an insurance agent to provide insurance for the State but specifies that the agent must share its commissions with other named insurance agencies, in one of which the officer has an ownership interest and hence profits when his agency receives part of the commissions. We note that as the action comes to us, there was no charge and the jury was not required to find that the Commonwealth itself was defrauded of any

---

8. *Hammerschmidt* concerned the scope of the predecessor of 18 U.S.C. §371, which makes criminal any conspiracy "to defraud the United States, or any agency thereof in any manner or for any purpose." *Hammerschmidt* indicates, in regard to that statute, that while "to conspire to defraud the United States means primarily to cheat the Government out of property or money, . . . it also means to interfere with or obstruct one of its lawful governmental functions by deceit, craft or trickery, or at least by means that are dishonest." 265 U.S. at 188. Other cases have held that §371 reaches conspiracies other than those directed at property interests. See, e.g., Haas v. Henkel, 216 U.S. 462 (1910) (predecessor of §371 reaches conspiracy to defraud the Government by bribing a Government official to make an advance disclosure of a cotton crop report); Glasser v. United States, 315 U.S. 60 (1942) (predecessor of §371 reaches conspiracy to defraud the United States by bribing a United States attorney). However, we believe that this broad construction of §371 is based on a consideration not applicable to the mail fraud statute. . . .

Section 371 is a statute aimed at protecting the Federal Government alone; however, the mail fraud statute, as we have indicated, had its origin in the desire to protect individual property rights, and any benefit which the Government derives from the statute must be limited to the Government's interests as property holder.

money or property. It was not charged that in the absence of the alleged scheme the Commonwealth would have paid a lower premium or secured better insurance. Hunt and Gray received part of the commissions but those commissions were not the Commonwealth's money. Nor was the jury charged that to convict it must find that the Commonwealth was deprived of control over how its money was spent. Indeed, the premium for insurance would have been paid to some agency, and what Hunt and Gray did was to assert control that the Commonwealth might not otherwise have made over the commissions paid by the insurance company to its agent.[9] Although the Government now relies in part on the assertion that petitioners obtained property by means of false representations to Wombwell, there was nothing in the jury charge that required such a finding. We hold, therefore, that the jury instruction on the substantive mail fraud count permitted a conviction for conduct not within the reach of §1341. . . .

The judgment of the Court of Appeals is reversed, and the case is remanded for proceedings consistent with this opinion.

It is so ordered.

Justice STEVENS, with whom Justice O'CONNOR joins as to Parts I, II, and III, dissenting.

Congress has broadly prohibited the use of the United States mails to carry out "any scheme or artifice to defraud." 18 U.S.C. §1341. The question presented is whether that prohibition is restricted to fraudulent schemes to deprive others of money or property, or whether it also includes fraudulent schemes to deprive individuals of other rights to which they are entitled. Specifically, we must decide whether the statute's prohibition embraces a secret agreement by state officials to place the State's workmen's compensation insurance with a particular agency in exchange for that company's agreement to share a major portion of its commissions with a list of agents provided by the officials, including sham agencies under the control of the officials themselves.

The same question of statutory construction has arisen in a variety of contexts over the past few decades. In the public sector, judges, State

---

9. Justice Stevens would affirm the convictions even though it was not charged that requiring the Wombwell agency to share commissions violated state law. We should assume that it did not. For the same reason we should assume that it was not illegal under state law for Hunt and Gray to own one of the agencies sharing in the commissions and hence to profit from the arrangement, whether or not they disclosed it to others in the state government. It is worth observing as well that it was not alleged that the mail fraud statute would have been violated had Hunt and Gray reported to state officials the fact of their financial gain. The violation asserted is the failure to disclose their financial interest, even if state law did not require it, to other persons in the state government whose actions could have been affected by the disclosure. It was in this way that the indictment charged that the people of Kentucky had been deprived of their right to have the Commonwealth's affairs conducted honestly. . . .

Governors, chairmen of state political parties, state cabinet officers, city aldermen, Congressmen and many other state and federal officials have been convicted of defrauding citizens of their right to the honest services of their governmental officials. In most of these cases, the officials have secretly made governmental decisions with the objective of benefiting themselves or promoting their own interests, instead of fulfilling their legal commitment to provide the citizens of the State or local government with their loyal service and honest government. Similarly, many elected officials and their campaign workers have been convicted of mail fraud when they have used the mails to falsify votes, thus defrauding the citizenry of its right to an honest election. In the private sector, purchasing agents, brokers, union leaders, and others with clear fiduciary duties to their employers or unions have been found guilty of defrauding their employers or unions by accepting kickbacks or selling confidential information. In other cases, defendants have been found guilty of using the mails to defraud individuals of their rights to privacy and other nonmonetary rights. All of these cases have something in common — they involved what the Court now refers to as "intangible rights." They also share something else in common. The many federal courts that have confronted the question whether these sorts of schemes constitute a "scheme or artifice to defraud" have uniformly and consistently read the statute in the same, sensible way. . . .

II

The cases discussed above demonstrate that the construction the courts have consistently given the statute is consistent with the common understanding of the term "fraud," and Congress' intent in enacting the statute. It is also consistent with the manner in which the term has been interpreted in an analogous federal statute; the way the term was interpreted at the time of this statute's enactment; and the statute's scant legislative history. There is no reason, therefore, to upset the settled, sensible construction that the federal courts have consistently endorsed.

The term "defraud" is not unique to §1341. Another federal statute, 18 U.S.C. §371, uses the identical term in prohibiting conspiracies to "defraud the United States," and the construction we have given to that statute should be virtually dispositive here. [Cases interpreting §371 make] clear that a conspiracy to defraud the United States does not require any evidence that the Government has suffered any property or pecuniary loss.

There is no basis for concluding that the term "defraud" means something different in §1341 (first enacted in 1872) than what it means in §371 (first enacted in 1867). . . .

The Court nonetheless suggests that interpreting the two statutes differently can be justified because §371 applies exclusively to frauds against the United States, while §1341 benefits private individuals. This argument is wide of the mark. The purpose of §1341 is to protect the integrity of the United States Postal Service, and, as I have explained, it is ludicrous to think that a Congress intent on preserving the integrity of the Postal Service would have used the term "defraud" in a narrow sense so as to allow mailings whose purpose was merely to defraud citizens of rights other than money or property. . . .

The general definition of the term "defraud" does not support, much less compel, today's decision.

Even if there were historical evidence of a limited definition of "fraud," the Court's holding would reflect a strange interpretation of legislation enacted by the Congress in the 19th century. Statutes like the Sherman Act, the civil rights legislation, and the mail fraud statute were written in broad general language on the understanding that the courts would have wide latitude in construing them to achieve the remedial purposes that Congress had identified. The wide open spaces in statutes such as these are most appropriately interpreted as implicit delegations of authority to the courts to fill in the gaps in the common-law tradition of case-by-case adjudication. The notion that the meaning of the words "any scheme or artifice to defraud" was frozen by a special conception of the term recognized by Congress in 1872 is manifestly untenable. . . .

Finally, there is nothing in the legislative history of the mail fraud statute that suggests that Congress intended the word "fraud" to have a narrower meaning in that statute than its common meaning and the meaning that it has in §371. . . .

III

To support its crabbed construction of the Act, the Court makes a straightforward but unpersuasive argument. Since there is no explicit, unambiguous evidence that Congress actually contemplated "intangible rights" when it enacted the mail fraud statute in 1872, the Court explains, any ambiguity in the meaning of the criminal statute should be resolved in favor of lenity. The doctrine of lenity is, of course, sound, for the citizen is entitled to fair notice of what sort of conduct may give rise to punishment. But the Court's reliance on that doctrine in this case is misplaced for several reasons.

To begin with, "although criminal statutes are to be construed strictly . . . this does not mean that every criminal statute must be given the narrowest possible meaning in complete disregard of the purpose of the legislature." McElroy v. United States, 455 U.S. 642, 658 (1982). Especially in light of the statutory purpose, I believe that §1341 unambiguously prohibits all schemes to defraud that use the United States mails—whether or not they involve money or property.

In any event, this asserted ambiguity in the meaning of the word "defraud," if it ever existed, was removed by judicial construction long ago. . . .

NOTES AND QUESTIONS

1. Note the striking difference between the ways that Justice White and Justice Stevens articulate the role of the Supreme Court (or federal courts more generally) in construing federal statutes. Justice White and the majority are not prepared to interpret the statute in a way that "involves the Federal Government in setting standards of disclosure and good government for local and state officials." But for Justice Stevens, Article III courts must be open to novel prosecutions under broadly worded statutes ("Statutes like . . . the mail fraud statute were written in broad general language on the understanding that the courts would have wide latitude in construing them to achieve the remedial purposes that Congress had identified."). The majority challenged Congress, if it wanted a broader statute, to "speak more clearly than it has." Congress accepted the challenge. After *McNally*, Congress amended the mail and wire fraud statutes as follows:

---

§1346. Definition of "scheme or artifice to defraud"

For the purposes of this chapter, the term "scheme or artifice to defraud" includes a scheme or artifice to deprive another of the intangible right of honest services.

This provision, part of the Anti-Drug Abuse Act of 1988, Pub. L. No. 100-690, left lower courts to figure out what it means to "deprive another" of such a right. We consider cases under §1346 in Sections C and D of this chapter. However, before we tackle the issue of "honest services" fraud, we first explore deprivations of "intangible property."

2. In *McNally*, the Court briefly (see Note 1) put an end to attempts by prosecutors and lower courts to use §§1341 and 1343 to reach certain types of intangible deprivations. Until Congress responded, this closed off one potential avenue for the prosecution of corrupt public officials or dishonest employees. A question that remained, however, was the extent to which the Court's analysis precluded mail fraud theories based on the deprivation of intangible *property* (as opposed to intangible non-property *rights*).

The answer came six months later, in *Carpenter v. United States*, when the Court (in an opinion by the author of *McNally*) approved a different but equally creative use of the mail and wire fraud statutes. Before returning to the fate of "honest services" fraud, we will look at *Carpenter* and other cases involving new property theories that suddenly became more attractive to prosecutors in the wake of *McNally*.

Carpenter v. United States
484 U.S. 19 (1987)

Justice White delivered the opinion of the Court.

Petitioners Kenneth Felis and R. Foster Winans were convicted of violating §10(b) of the Securities Exchange Act of 1934, 15 U.S.C. §78j(b), and Rule 10b-5. They were also found guilty of violating the federal mail and wire fraud statutes, 18 U.S.C. §§1341, 1343, and were convicted for conspiracy under U.S.C. §371. Petitioner David Carpenter, Winans' roommate, was convicted for aiding and abetting. . . .

I

In 1981, Winans became a reporter for the *Wall Street Journal* (the *Journal*) and in the summer of 1982 became one of the two writers of a daily column, "Heard on the Street." That column discussed selected stocks or groups of stocks, giving positive and negative information about those stocks and taking "a point of view with respect to investment in the stocks that it reviews." Winans regularly interviewed corporate executives to put together interesting perspectives on the stocks that would be highlighted in upcoming columns, but, at least for the columns at issue here, none contained corporate inside information or any "hold for release" information. Because of the "Heard" column's perceived quality and integrity, it had the potential of affecting the price of the stocks which it examined. The District Court concluded on the basis of testimony presented at trial that the "Heard" column "does have an impact on the market, difficult though it may be to quantify in any particular case.". . .

The official policy and practice at the Journal was that prior to publication, the contents of the column were the Journal's confidential information. Despite the rule, with which Winans was familiar, he entered into a scheme in October 1983 with Peter Brant and petitioner Felis, both connected with the Kidder Peabody brokerage firm in New York City, to give them advance information as to the timing and contents of the "Heard" column. This permitted Brant and Felis and another conspirator, David Clark, a client of Brant, to buy or sell based on the probable impact of the column on the market. Profits were to be shared. The conspirators agreed that the scheme would not affect the journalistic purity of the

"Heard" column, and the District Court did not find that the contents of any of the articles were altered to further the profit potential of petitioners' stock-trading scheme. Over a 4-month period, the brokers made prepublication trades on the basis of information given them by Winans about the contents of some 27 "Heard" columns. The net profits from these trades were about $690,000.

In November 1983, correlations between the "Heard" articles and trading in the Clark and Felis accounts were noted at Kidder Peabody and inquiries began. Brant and Felis denied knowing anyone at the Journal and took steps to conceal the trades. Later, the Securities and Exchange Commission began an investigation. Questions were met by denials both by the brokers at Kidder Peabody and by Winans at the Journal. As the investigation progressed, the conspirators quarreled, and on March 29, 1984, Winans and Carpenter went to the SEC and revealed the entire scheme. This indictment and a bench trial followed. Brant, who had pleaded guilty under a plea agreement, was a witness for the Government. . . .

The Court is evenly divided with respect to the convictions under the securities laws and for that reason affirms the judgment below on those counts. For the reasons that follow, we also affirm the judgment with respect to the mail and wire fraud convictions.

II

Petitioners assert that their activities were not a scheme to defraud the Journal within the meaning of the mail and wire fraud statutes; and that in any event, they did not obtain any "money or property" from the Journal, which is a necessary element of the crime under our decision last Term in McNally v. United States, 483 U.S. 350 (1987). We are unpersuaded by either submission and address the latter first.

We held in McNally that the mail fraud statute does not reach "schemes to defraud citizens of their intangible rights to honest and impartial government," id. at 355, and that the statute is "limited in scope to the protection of property rights." Id. at 360. Petitioners argue that the Journal's interest in prepublication confidentiality for the "Heard" columns is no more than an intangible consideration outside the reach of §1341; nor does that law, it is urged, protect against mere injury to reputation. This is not a case like McNally, however. The Journal, as Winans' employer, was defrauded of much more than its contractual right to his honest and faithful service, an interest too ethereal in itself to fall within the protection of the mail fraud statute, which "had its origin in the desire to protect individual property rights." McNally, supra, at 359 n.8. Here, the object of the scheme was to take the Journal's confidential business information — the publication schedule and contents of the "Heard" column — and its intangible nature does not make it any less "property" protected by the mail and wire fraud statutes. *McNally* did not limit the scope of §1341 to tangible as distinguished from intangible property rights. . . .

Confidential business information has long been recognized as property. "Confidential information acquired or compiled by a corporation in the course and conduct of its business is a species of property to which the corporation has the exclusive right and benefit, and which a court of equity will protect through the injunctive process or other appropriate remedy." 3 W. Fletcher, Cyclopedia of Law of Private Corporations §857.1, at 260 (rev. ed. 1986). The Journal had a property right in keeping confidential and making exclusive use, prior to publication, of the schedule and contents of the "Heard" column. As the Court has observed before:

> "[N]ews matter, however little susceptible of ownership or dominion in the absolute sense, is stock in trade, to be gathered at the cost of enterprise, organization, skill, labor, and money, and to be distributed and sold to those who will pay money for it, as for any other merchandise." International News Service v. Associated Press, 248 U.S. 215, 236 (1918).

Petitioners' arguments that they did not interfere with the Journal's use of the information or did not publicize it and deprive the Journal of the first public use of it miss the point. The confidential information was generated from the business, and the business had a right to decide how to use it prior to disclosing it to the public. Petitioners cannot successfully contend based on *Associated Press* that a scheme to defraud requires a monetary loss, such as giving the information to a competitor; it is sufficient that the Journal has been deprived of its right to exclusive use of the information, for exclusivity is an important aspect of confidential business information and most private property for that matter.

We cannot accept petitioners' further argument that Winans' conduct in revealing prepublication information was no more than a violation of workplace rules and did not amount to fraudulent activity that is proscribed by the mail fraud statute. Sections 1341 and 1343 reach any scheme to deprive another of money or property by means of false or fraudulent pretenses, representations, or promises. . . . The concept of "fraud" includes the act of embezzlement, which is "the fraudulent appropriation to one's own use of the money or goods entrusted to one's care by another." Grin v. Shine, 187 U.S. 181, 189 (1902).

The District Court found that Winans' undertaking at the Journal was not to reveal prepublication information about his column, a promise that became a sham when in violation of his duty he passed along to his co-conspirators confidential information belonging to the Journal, pursuant to an ongoing scheme to share profits from trading in anticipation of the "Heard" column's impact on the stock market. In Snepp v. United States, 444 U.S. 507, 515, n.11 (1980) . . . we noted the similar prohibitions of the common law, that "even in the absence of a written contract, an employee has a fiduciary obligation to protect confidential information obtained during the course of his employment." As the New York courts have recognized: "It is well established, as a general proposition, that a person who acquires special knowledge or information by virtue of a confidential or fiduciary relationship with another is not free to exploit that knowledge or information for his own personal benefit but must account to his principal for any profits derived therefrom." Diamond v. Oreamuno, 24 N.Y.2d 494, 497 (1969); see also Restatement (Second) of Agency §§388, Comment c, 396(c) (1958). . . .

Lastly, we reject the submission that using the wires and the mail to print and send the Journal to its customers did not satisfy the requirement that those mediums be used to execute the scheme at issue. The courts below were quite right in observing that circulation of the "Heard" column was not only anticipated but an essential part of the scheme. Had the column not been made available to Journal customers, there would have been no effect on stock prices and no likelihood of profiting from the information leaked by Winans.

The judgment below is *Affirmed.*

NOTES AND QUESTIONS

1. *Carpenter* unanimously affirmed the mail and wire fraud convictions, holding that confidential business information constitutes "property" for the purposes of the mail and wire fraud statutes, and that misappropriation of that property for private gain constitutes a scheme to defraud. At the same time, the Court split, 4-4, on whether the charged insider trading also violated §10(b) of the Securities Exchange Act (Justice Lewis Powell had retired in June 1987, and just a few weeks before *Carpenter* came down, the Senate voted not to confirm Robert Bork, President Reagan's initial nominee to replace Powell). The insider trading issue that would not be resolved until United States v. O'Hagan, 521 U.S. 642 (1997) (holding that criminal liability under §10(b) of the Securities Exchange Act may be predicated on misappropriation of confidential information). We take up *O'Hagan* in Chapter 12. Defendants will regularly find themselves charged with both securities fraud and mail/wire fraud. See United States v. Ragensberg, 604 F. Supp. 2d 625 (S.D.N.Y. 2009) (rejecting multiplicity argument).

2. What is the difference between an intangible property right, like the one protected in *Carpenter*, and an intangible right to "honest services," like the one left unprotected after *McNally*? The Court says that "honest services" are more "ethereal," and further from the traditional center of the mail fraud statute—protecting tangible property. Is this persuasive? Can prosecutors get around *McNally* by alleging, in what would otherwise be an "honest services" case, a deprivation of intangible property? We take up this question later in the chapter.

3. One issue that arose after *Carpenter* was whether the mail fraud statute reached fraudulent efforts to obtain licenses from a government licensing authority. In Cleveland v. United States, 531 U.S. 12 (2000), the Supreme Court resolved the issue by holding that state and municipal licenses did not rank as property for purposes of §1341.

The following case explores both the holding in *Cleveland* and, more generally, what intangible interests can be protected through mail fraud prosecutions.

United States v. Al Hedaithy
392 F.3d 580 (3d Cir. 2004)

STAPLETON, Circuit Judge: . . .

Al-Aiban and Al Hedaithy (collectively, "Defendants") are two of approximately sixty foreign nationals of Arab and/or Middle Eastern descent who were charged in the United States District Court for the District of New Jersey for allegedly participating in a scheme by which imposters were paid to sit for the Test of English as a Foreign Language ("TOEFL"), a standardized test administered by the Educational Testing Service ("ETS"). The purpose of the scheme was allegedly to create the false appearance that Defendants, among others, had taken and achieved an acceptable score on the TOEFL exam so that they could remain eligible to live in the United States under a student visa. . . .

I . . .

ETS is in the business of designing and administering certain standardized tests. One of those tests, TOEFL, is commonly used by educational institutions in the United States when considering a student for admission to its academic program. Certain schools require foreign students, as a condition of admission, to achieve a minimum score on the TOEFL exam in order to demonstrate proficiency in the English language. Full-time enrollment at a federally approved school, college, or university is, in turn, a requirement for foreign nationals to obtain a student visa and thus reside legally in the United States.

According to the Government, ETS possesses, and attempts to maintain, goodwill that it has accumulated based upon the integrity of its TOEFL product. ETS has also endeavored to keep its TOEFL exam exclusive, secure, and confidential. It owns registered trademarks in the terms "Educational Testing Service," "ETS," and "TOEFL." It uses these trademarks on its TOEFL examinations and the score reports that it generates for each applicant who takes TOEFL. ETS also owns copyrights in the TOEFL examination itself and in the questions used on each exam. Furthermore, the company restricts access to, and use of, its copyrighted TOEFL exam and questions, its trademarked score reports, and its test administration and scoring services. . . .

In 1999, the Government became aware of a scheme in which Defendants, both Saudi Arabian nationals, and numerous other foreign nationals of Arab and/or Middle Eastern descent, paid an imposter to take and pass the TOEFL exam for them. The purpose of the scheme was to create the false appearance that Defendants themselves had taken and achieved an acceptable score on the TOEFL exam. In furtherance of this scheme, each Defendant applied to take the exam, and then paid money to an imposter to appear at the designated test center and falsely identify himself as the respective Defendant. The imposter then signed the confidentiality statement, had his photograph taken, sat for the TOEFL exam using the respective Defendant's name, and directed that his exam results be mailed to a California address under the control of one Mahmoud Firas. ETS then processed the exam, and the results were mailed to the pre-designated location in California. There, Firas or one of his associates substituted each Defendant's photograph in place of the imposter's photograph. This doctored score report was then sent to legitimate educational institutions in a phony envelope bearing ETS's trademark. . . .

A

"To prove mail or wire fraud, the evidence must establish beyond a reasonable doubt (1) the defendant's knowing and willful participation in a scheme or artifice to defraud, (2) with the specific intent to defraud, and (3) the use of the mails or interstate wire communications in furtherance of the scheme." United States v. Antico, 275 F.3d 245, 261 (3d Cir. 2001). . . . Additionally, the object of the alleged scheme or artifice to defraud must be a traditionally recognized property right. . . . This rule is embodied in a trilogy of Supreme Court cases that, each party agrees, governs the outcome of this appeal: McNally v. United States, 483 U.S. 350 (1987), Carpenter v. United States, 484 U.S. 19 (1988), and, most recently, Cleveland v. United States, 531 U.S. 12 (2000). We agree that these three decisions must frame our analysis, and we review each in turn. . . .

[In *McNally*,] the Supreme Court decided that §1341 must be read "as limited in scope to the protection of property rights." [483 U.S.] at 360. As such, the Court held that a scheme to deprive the Commonwealth of Kentucky of "honest services" was not within the scope of §1341 and therefore reversed the defendants' convictions. Id. at 361. . . .

The Supreme Court next addressed the mail fraud statute in *Carpenter*, in which the defendant was alleged to have violated that statute by defrauding the Wall Street Journal (the "Journal") of "confidential business information.". . .

Finally, in *Cleveland*, the defendant was charged and convicted of violating the mail fraud statute by making false statements in applying to the Louisiana State Police for a license to operate video poker machines. The question addressed by the Supreme Court was whether the Louisiana video poker license qualified as "property" within the scope of §1341. In deciding this issue, the Court held that "it does not suffice . . . that the object of the fraud may become property in the recipient's hands; for purposes of the mail fraud statute, the thing obtained must be property in the hands of the victim." [531 U.S.] at 15. Accordingly, the Supreme Court went on to consider "whether a government regulator parts with 'property' when it issues a license." Id. at 20. In analyzing this issue, the Court first noted that Louisiana's "core concern" in issuing licenses was regulatory, and, as such, Louisiana law established a typical regulatory program for issuing video poker licenses. Id. at 20-21. The function of this regulatory scheme, according to the Court, resembled other licensing schemes that have long been characterized as the exercise of state police powers.

The Court rejected the assertion that Louisiana had a property interest in its licenses merely because of the substantial sums of money it receives in exchange for each license. The Court acknowledged that Louisiana had a substantial economic stake in the video poker industry, but also noted that the lion's share of fees received by the state with respect to the licenses is received only after the license is issued; not pre-issuance. Moreover, the Court reasoned that: "[w]ere an entitlement of this order sufficient to establish a state property right, one could scarcely avoid the conclusion that States have property rights in any license or permit requiring an upfront fee, including drivers' licenses, medical licenses, and fishing and hunting licenses." Id. at 22.

The Court also rejected the assertion that the licenses were property because of the state's significant control over the issuance, renewal, suspension, and revocation of the licenses. According to the Court, "Louisiana's right to choose the persons to whom it issues video poker licenses" was not an interest long recognized as property. Rather, such "intangible rights of allocation, exclusion, and control amount to no more and no less than Louisiana's sovereign power to regulate. . . . Even when tied to an expected stream of revenue, the State's right of control does not create a property interest any more than a law licensing liquor sales in a State that levies a sales tax on liquor. Such regulations are paradigmatic exercises of the States' traditional police powers." Id. at 23.

The Court further rejected the Government's assertion that Louisiana's licensing power was no different than a franchisor's right to select its franchisees. The crucial difference between these two rights, the Court stated, is that "a franchisor's right to select its franchisees typically derives from its ownership of a trademark, brand name, business strategy, or other product that it may trade or sell in the open market." Louisiana's authority, on the other hand, rested not upon any such asset but upon the state's "sovereign right to exclude applicants deemed unsuitable to run video poker operations." Id. at 24.

Because the Court concluded that the video poker license at issue was not property in the hands of the State of Louisiana, it held that the defendant's conduct did not fall within the scope of the mail fraud statute, and therefore reversed the defendant's conviction.

B

According to the Government, . . . the superseding indictments properly allege that ETS was defrauded of at least two traditionally recognized property interests: (1) its confidential business information, and (2) its tangible score reports. We address each of these theories below.

As noted above, the superseding indictments alleged that ETS possesses a property interest in the materials bearing its trademarks and its copyrighted materials, "such as the TOEFL exam and its questions." The superseding indictments sufficiently alleged, according to the Government, that the TOEFL exam and its questions constituted the confidential business information of ETS. The Government contends that this case is like *Carpenter* inasmuch as the superseding indictments allege that the Defendants' scheme required the hired test-takers to make a misrepresentation to ETS in order to gain access to, and sit for, the TOEFL exam. We agree with the Government's analysis.

"'Confidential information acquired or compiled by a corporation in the course and conduct of its business is a species of property to which the corporation has the exclusive right and benefit.'" *Carpenter*, 484 U.S. at 26 (quoting 3 W. Fletcher, Cyclopedia of Law of Private Corporations, §857.1, at 260) (rev. ed. 1986)). Such information includes trade secrets, which are defined as "any formula, pattern, device or compilation of information which is used in one's business, and which gives him an opportunity to obtain an advantage over competitors who do not know or use it." Ruckelshaus [v. Monsanto Co., 467 U.S. 986], 1001 [(1984)]. In our case, ETS's TOEFL exam satisfies this definition. According to the indictments, ETS is in the business of preparing and administering the TOEFL exam. The examination provided ETS with a competitive advantage over others in the business of test administration insofar as performance on the exam, according to the indictments, was the yardstick by which educational institutions measured English proficiency in their admissions processes. The indictments also indicate that ETS therefore goes to great lengths to protect the confidentiality and exclusivity of its exam. No person is permitted access to sit for the TOEFL exam unless he pays a fee, promises to preserve the confidentiality of the exam, and represents to ETS that he is the person whose name and address were used in applying to sit for the exam. The facts alleged in the superseding indictment are therefore sufficient to conclude that the TOEFL exam and its questions were confidential business information. The only question remaining with respect to this theory of mail fraud liability is whether Defendants engaged in a scheme "to defraud" ETS of such property. . . .

Carpenter dictates that ETS "had a property right in keeping confidential and making exclusive use" of its confidential business information. 484 U.S. at 26. *Carpenter* further instructs that the Government need not allege that ETS suffered a monetary loss. Rather, for purposes of showing a mail fraud violation, it is sufficient to allege that ETS "has been deprived of its right to exclusive use of the [confidential business] information." Id. at 26-27. Such deprivation was clearly set forth in the superseding indictments.

According to the indictments, ETS assiduously protected the exclusivity of its TOEFL exam, allowing access only to those persons who agreed to keep the exam confidential and who provided a representation as to their identity. Defendants' alleged scheme, however, required hired test-takers to gain access to ETS's TOEFL exam on terms other than those prescribed by ETS. The indictments allege that ETS would not have allowed the hired test-takers to sit for the exam had it known that they were not actually the Defendants, and had it known that they did not actually agree to preserve the exam's confidentiality. Accordingly, it was sufficiently alleged that ETS was deprived of a recognized property interest: the "right to decide how to use" its confidential business information, i.e., the TOEFL exam.

Finally, the scheme alleged in the superseding indictments required hired test-takers to falsely identify themselves as each Defendant, thereby misrepresenting to ETS their true identities. The scheme further required the hired test-takers to sign ETS's confidentiality statement in the name of each Defendant, giving ETS the false impression that the signatories had agreed to preserve the confidentiality of the TOEFL exam. We therefore have little trouble concluding that the superseding indictments sufficiently alleged that the deprivation of ETS's property right was accomplished through deceit, trickery, chicanery, or other fraudulent means. . . .

The Government also contends that the superseding indictments clearly alleged that ETS was defrauded of tangible property. As we noted above, the indictments alleged that ETS possesses a property interest in the "materials bearing its trademarks, such as the TOEFL . . . score report." The same misrepresentations that the hired test-takers made in order to gain access to the TOEFL exam, the Government claims, were also used to fraudulently obtain tangible documents from ETS. In accordance with the alleged scheme, these documents bore the name of each Defendant, but in fact reflected both the photograph of, and the exam score achieved by, the hired test-taker. Defendants do not dispute that the scheme alleged in the indictments involved obtaining the TOEFL score reports through misrepresentations. Rather, they contend that these documents cannot be considered property cognizable under the mail fraud statute. While Defendants' argument merits some discussion, we conclude that it is ultimately unavailing.

As Defendants suggest, *Cleveland* dictates that, in order to be cognizable under the mail fraud statute, the score reports must be considered property in the hands of ETS. Defendants insist, however, that a score report does not exist except to be given to the test-taker, that ETS cannot use it for any other purpose, and that ETS cannot sell one person's score report to any other person. Rather, according to Defendants, it is nothing more than the embodiment of the services that ETS provides, and that the paper and ink used to create a score report does not make it property. Defendants also argue that, because *Cleveland* clearly holds that such a score report would not be property if it was issued by a governmental entity, to hold that ETS's score report is property in the hands of ETS would create a serious anomaly whereby the Defendants' alleged scheme would not be considered mail fraud if it related to a state licensing examination, such as a bar exam or a medical licensing exam, but would be considered mail fraud with respect to the TOEFL exam, the Scholastic Aptitude Test, the Law School Admissions Test, or any other privately administered standardized test.

As to Defendants' first contention—that the score reports are not property in the hands of ETS—we disagree. ETS is alleged to be in the business of administering the TOEFL exam and issuing score reports. While it is true that the score reports represent the end result of the services provided by ETS, they are nonetheless tangible items produced by ETS, and ETS reserves the right to convey these items only to those individuals who meet its prescribed conditions. We do not think it credible for Defendants to contend that tangible items, held in the physical possession of a private entity, are not property. To the extent that Defendants pursue this argument, we construe it as a contention that the mail fraud statute does not apply to property with *de minimis* value.

In support of a *de minimis* exception to the mail fraud statute, Defendants cite United States v. Schwartz, 924 F.2d 410, 417-418 (2d Cir. 1991), and United States v. Granberry, 908 F.2d 278, 280 (8th Cir. 1990). Both *Schwartz* and *Granberry* addressed the question of whether unissued licenses were property in the hands of a governmental entity for purposes of the federal fraud statutes. Correctly foretelling the outcome in *Cleveland*, both Courts held that such unissued licenses were not property. *Schwartz* and *Granberry* also addressed the Government's argument that the licenses were nonetheless property by virtue of the paper they were printed on. In rejecting this argument, the Second Circuit stated:

This proposition is patently absurd. In the present instance, the [governmental entity] was not in the paper and ink business, it is a regulatory agency with the power to grant or withhold a license. The paper licenses given appellants were merely the expression of its regulatory imprimatur, and they had no other effect as "property" beyond their role as representatives of this regulatory grant. . . . Further, the value of the paper, ink and seal at issue is plainly inconsequential and—as *McNally* held that "to defraud" meant depriving individuals or the government of something of value—must be deemed *de minimis* as a matter of law. . . .

Even if we read *Schwartz* and *Granberry* in the manner suggested by Defendants, however, we must reject their arguments because our recognition of a generally applicable *de minimis* exception would conflict with a prior decision of this Court [United States v. Martinez, 905 F.2d 709 (3d Cir. 1990)]. . . .

The D.C. Circuit Court of Appeals' decision in United States v. DeFries, 43 F.3d 707, 707-708 (D.C. Cir. 1995), is also persuasive on this issue. In *DeFries*, several union officials were charged with mail fraud for the alleged theft, alteration, and destruction of ballots in a 1988 union merger referendum. The District Court dismissed the indictment on the ground that the theft of ballots did not constitute significant enough deprivations and thus, under *McNally*, were not cognizable under §1341. In defending that dismissal on appeal, the defendants conceded that the ballots were the tangible property of the union, but argued that they were of such *de minimis* value—worth no more than the paper or ink used in their printing—that they failed to meet some threshold standard of significance implicit in the mail fraud statute. . . . [T]he D.C. Circuit . . . expressed significant doubts regarding the *de minimis* exception recognized in *Schwartz* and *Granberry*. Nonetheless, the Court concluded that it need not decide the issue because the ballots in question had more than *de minimis* value . . .

We are confronted with circumstances nearly identical to *DeFries*, and we find the D.C. Circuit's analysis persuasive. Here, even assuming the existence of a *de minimis* exception under the mail fraud statute, the superseding indictments sufficiently allege that the score reports obtained under Defendants' scheme were valuable. Like the ballots in *DeFries*, ETS's score reports are the sole physical embodiment of substantial and valuable services that ETS provides. Moreover, even though the Defendants' scheme allegedly defrauded ETS of only approximately sixty score reports, the fraud allegedly perpetrated on ETS (like the theft of union ballots in *DeFries*) undermined its credibility, "and thus the value of [its] entire investment in the process." Id. Insofar as the superseding indictments allege that ETS has developed substantial goodwill due to the integrity of its TOEFL testing process, we conclude that such goodwill makes ETS's score reports valuable, exceeding any potential *de minimis* threshold that may be required by the mail fraud statute.

As to Defendants' second contention—that finding ETS's score report to constitute property would lead to a result inconsistent with
Cleveland—such an argument misunderstands the fundamental basis of the
Supreme Court's reasoning in that case. As we explained above, the result
in *Cleveland* was based upon the conclusion that the issuance of government
licenses is an exercise of a state's police powers to regulate. Because the
issuance of such a license is a component of the state's regulatory scheme,
the license was held not to be "property" in the hands of the regulator. Such
reasoning is wholly inapplicable in this case. Here, ETS is a private business
that provides a service and reports test results in pursuit of a profit-seeking
endeavor. Unlike a state, ETS has no sovereign power to regulate. . . .

In accordance with the foregoing, we hold that the superseding
indictments sufficiently alleged that Defendants engaged in a scheme to
defraud ETS of traditionally recognized property interests in its confidential business information and TOEFL score reports. . . .

NOTES AND QUESTIONS

1. In addition to challenging the government's legal theory, the two
defendants in *Al Hedaithy*, who were among the approximately 60 Middle
Eastern males arrested in May 2002 for this cheating scheme, also raised
a selective prosecution claim. The Third Circuit, however, found that they
had not met the demanding standard of United States v. Armstrong, 517
U.S. 456 (1996), for discovery on their claim. (Under *Armstrong*, before a
defendant is entitled to discover government materials that might support
a selective prosecution claim, he must make a threshold showing that similarly situated defendants of other races could have been prosecuted but
were not.) Both defendants in the case became ineligible to remain in the
United States as a result of their convictions.

2. Consider the discussion of *de minimis* cases in *Al Hedaithy*. When
should courts consider barring such cases as a matter of law, as opposed to
trusting in prosecutorial discretion? For better or worse, federal fraud statutes are regularly violated under circumstances in which most reasonable
people would deem a federal felony prosecution inappropriate. Should
judges be crafting doctrines to capture any such consensus? How should
Congress's inaction on this issue be viewed by courts? By prosecutors?

3. Can the government get around *Cleveland* by, say, reframing a fraudulent scheme to obtain medical licenses from the state as a property fraud on
the unsuspecting healthcare consumers treated by the doctors? In United
States v. Berroa, 856 F.3d 141 (1st Cir. 2017), the First Circuit rejected this
argument. Relying on the analysis in Loughlin v. United States, 134 S. Ct.
2384 (2014), of the constraining effects of "by means of" language in the
bank fraud statute, the Circuit reasoned that "the defendants' alleged

fraud in obtaining their medical licenses cannot be said to have 'naturally induc[ed]' healthcare consumers to part with their money years later." 856 F.3d at 149-50 (quoting 134 S. Ct. at 2393).

4. *Al Hedaithy* highlights—and finds *Cleveland* but a slight impediment to—the richness of the mail fraud "property" deprivation law that developed parallel (and in response) to the twists and turns in "intangible rights" deprivation doctrine—twists and turns that we address in the next section of this chapter. As the Second Circuit has noted: "While the interests protected by the mail and wire fraud statutes do not generally extend to intangible rights (except as modified by 18 U.S.C. §1346), they do extend to all kinds of property interests, both tangible and intangible." United States v. Carlo, 507 F.3d 799, 801-02 (2d Cir. 2007) (citing Carpenter v. United States, 484 U.S. 19, 25 (1987)). Thus, prosecutors have charged and lower courts have sustained mail fraud charges where the "property" the defendant fraudulently obtained was the victim's "right to control its assets," Carlo, 507 F.3d at 802; the victim's "right to control the disposition of its assets," United States v. Gray, 405 F.3d 227, 234 (4th Cir. 2005); and the victim's "right to control its risk of loss," United States v. Catalfo, 64 F.3d 1070, 1077 (7th Cir. 1995). See also United States v. Welch, 327 F.3d 1081 (10th Cir. 2003), which upheld property deprivation charges against executives of the Salt Lake City Bid Committee ("SLBC") for the 2002 Winter Olympics for allegedly making unauthorized payments of SLBC funds to members of the International Olympic Committee. In reinstating the indictment, which the district court had dismissed, the Tenth Circuit noted:

> Just as a borrower still commits bank fraud if he knowingly provides or withholds from a bank materially false information to induce a loan and then repays it, . . . one still may commit mail or wire fraud if he knowingly provides or withholds materially false information which imposes a substantial risk of loss on another (in this case for example, the SLBC's possible loss of donors, tax-exempt status, or even the Games) even if the risk does not materialize.

Id. at 1108.

Note that this line of cases requires courts to sort between situations that "merely" involve deceit that does not go to the nature of the transaction and those that deprive the victim of a valuable right of control. As Judge Gerard Lynch explained in United States v. Binday, 804 F.2d 558 (2d Cir. 2015), after noting that a cognizable property deprivation can be found "where the defendant's scheme "den[ies] the victim the right to control its assets by depriving it of information necessary to make discretionary economic decisions,"

> It is not sufficient, however, to show merely that the victim would not have entered into a discretionary economic transaction but for the defendant's misrepresentations. The "right to control one's assets" does not render

every transaction induced by deceit actionable under the mail and wire fraud statutes. Rather, the deceit must deprive the victim "of potentially valuable economic information." "Our cases have drawn a fine line between schemes that do no more than cause their victims to enter into transactions they would otherwise avoid—which do not violate the mail or wire fraud statutes—and schemes that depend for their completion on a misrepresentation of an essential element of the bargain—which do violate the mail and wire fraud statutes."

Thus, we have repeatedly rejected application of the mail and wire fraud statutes where the purported victim received the full economic benefit of its bargain. But we have upheld convictions for mail and wire fraud where the deceit affected the victim's economic calculus or the benefits and burdens of the agreement. The requisite harm is also shown where defendants' misrepresentations pertained to the quality of services bargained for, such as where defendant attorneys "consistently misrepresented to their clients the nature and quality of the legal services they were providing . . . for a hefty fee." Lastly, we have repeatedly upheld convictions where defendants' misrepresentations in a loan or insurance application or claim exposed the lender or insurer to unexpected economic risk.

Id. at 570-71; see also United States v. Finazzo, 850 F.3d 94, 111 (2d Cir. 2017) ("[M]isrepresentations or non-disclosure of information cannot support a conviction under the 'right to control' theory unless those misrepresentations or non–disclosures can or do result in tangible economic harm. This economic harm can be manifested directly—such as by increasing the price the victim paid for a good—or indirectly—such as by providing the victim with lower–quality goods than it otherwise could have received.").

Is the line between "mere deceit" and deprivation of "tangible economic benefit" clear? Or is it some sort of a prosecutorial IQ test? Let's go back to the planted bar denizens in *Takhalov*, discussed *supra*. Would the analysis change from "mere deceit" to cognizable economic deprivation if the government alleged and proved that a victim really wanted supposed "tourists" he bought drinks for "to like him for who he was" rather than be shills trying to increase bar revenue? Is the main evidentiary problem that many individual human concerns are not normally monetized? Compare United States v. Schwartz, 924 F.2d 410, 420-21 (2d Cir. 1991) (affirming wire fraud convictions for misrepresentations to seller that night-vision goggles would not be used illegally, even though the seller suffered no direct pecuniary harm, in part because the use of the night-vision goggles to violate arms export laws cost the seller "good will").

Note that some Circuits are particularly hostile to expansive uses of this theory. In United States v. Sadler, 750 F.3d 585 (6th Cir. 2014), where the defendant lied to pharmaceutical distributors when she ordered massive quantities of hydrocodone for her pain-management clinic, the court noted:

All that the evidence shows is that [defendant] paid full price for all the drugs she purchased and did so on time. How, then, did [defendant] deprive the distributors of property?

The government's opening bid offers this answer: [Defendant] deprived the distributors of their pills. Well, yes, in one sense: The pills were gone after the transaction. But paying the going rate for a product does not square with the conventional understanding of "deprive." Cleveland, 531 U.S. at 19; Webster's Third New International Dictionary 606 (2002). Stealing the pills would be one thing; paying full price for them is another. Case law reinforces that the conventional meaning of "deprive" applies in the fraud context. . . . [Defendant] may have had many unflattering motives in mind in buying the pills, but unfairly depriving the distributors of their property was not one of them. As to the wire-fraud count, she ordered pills and paid the distributors' asking price, nothing more.

As an alternative, the government offers another potential deprivation: [Defendant]'s lies convinced the distributors to sell controlled substances that they would not have sold had they known the truth. [Defendant] in other words deprived the companies of what might be called a right to accurate information before selling the pills. To support this theory, the government points to the testimony of one distributor's representative, who said she would have been "concern[ed]" had she known more about [defendant]'s operation. But the statute is "limited in scope to the protection of *property rights*," and the ethereal right to accurate information doesn't fit that description. McNally, 483 U.S. at 360 (emphasis added). Nor can it plausibly be said that the right to accurate information amounts to an interest that "has long been recognized as property." Cleveland, 531 U.S. at 23.

750 F.3d at 590-91. It's worth noting that even as the Circuit reversed the wire fraud conviction on this basis, it affirmed defendant's drug-related convictions.

5. Do government units also have a "property right" to control how their money is spent? Several Circuits have upheld the convictions of contractors charged with depriving government entities of "property" by falsely claiming to have complied with the entities' requirement that some work be performed by socially and economically disadvantaged companies. See United States v. Harris, 821 F.3d 589 (5th Cir. 2016); United States v. Maxwell, 579 F.3d 1282 (11th Cir. 2009); United States v. Leahy, 464 F.3d 773 (7th Cir. 2005); United States v. Tulio, 263 F. App'x. 258 (3d Cir. 2008) (unpublished); United States v. Brothers Construction Co., 219 F.3d 300 (4th Cir. 2000). These cases can be distinguished from *Cleveland* because they involve the state seeking to further a stated public interest in the course of paying money. Does this distinction between simply regulating and regulating while spending make sense?

———————————————

Distinctions between public and private expenditures also play a critical role in the following case.

United States v. Ratcliff
488 F.3d 639 (5th Cir. 2007)

KING, Circuit Judge:

Defendant-appellee-cross-appellant Barney Dewey Ratcliff, Jr. was charged by indictment with fourteen counts of mail fraud, in violation of 18 U.S.C. §1341, based on alleged activities involving election fraud in Louisiana. The district court granted Ratcliff's motion to dismiss the counts, concluding that the indictment did not allege a scheme to defraud anyone of money or property, thereby failing to state the offense of mail fraud under §1341. The United States now appeals, arguing that a scheme to obtain the salary and employment benefits of elected office through election fraud satisfies the requirements of the mail fraud statute. We AFFIRM.

I.   FACTUAL AND PROCEDURAL BACKGROUND

Livingston Parish, Louisiana, operates under a home rule charter providing that its citizens elect a parish president for a four-year term. In 1999, Ratcliff was the incumbent Livingston Parish president and a candidate for reelection.

Candidates for public office in Louisiana must abide by the provisions of Louisiana's Campaign Finance Disclosure Act ("CFDA"), [which] prohibits any candidate for parishwide elective office, including the parish presidency, from receiving contributions, loans, or loan guarantees in excess of $2500 from any individual [and requires candidates to] file campaign finance disclosure reports with the Louisiana Board of Ethics (the "Board" or "Board of Ethics")....

According to the indictment, Ratcliff obtained several loans violative of the CFDA from September to November 1999. On September 23, 1999, Ratcliff obtained a $50,000 bank loan for the purpose of financing his reelection campaign. Ratcliff had insufficient income and assets to qualify for the loan, and a local businessman with sufficient assets served as cosigner. One week later, on October 7, Ratcliff obtained another $50,000 loan with the same businessman as cosigner. The cosigner also assigned a $50,000 certificate of deposit as collateral.

On October 12, Ratcliff filed with the Board of Ethics a campaign finance disclosure report in which he disclosed the first loan and the businessman's guarantee of that loan. On October 19, a staff member of the Board advised Ratcliff that the businessman's guarantee possibly violated the CFDA. In response, Ratcliff informed the Board that he had instructed the bank to prepare new loan documents for his signature alone.

On October 22, Ratcliff obtained two new loans to pay off the loans that had been improperly guaranteed by the businessman. The indictment charges that the new loans were secured by a pledge of $99,000 in cash, supplied by one of Ratcliff's wealthy supporters who had a financial interest in the transfer of a permit for operation of a landfill in Livingston Parish to Waste Management, Inc. ("Waste Management"). The transfer, which was allegedly supported by Ratcliff, was a major election issue. Ratcliff obtained another $50,000 loan on November 3, allegedly secured by a pledge of $55,000 in cash supplied by the same wealthy supporter. The indictment asserts that Ratcliff knew that his receipt of the cash for all three loans violated the $2500 individual loan limitation and that he did not report it in his campaign finance disclosure reports.

Ratcliff was reelected as parish president on November 20. During the course of the campaign, Ratcliff had contracted with a political consultant to help with his reelection bid, and by the time of the election, Ratcliff owed the consultant over $57,000. On November 22, a Waste Management lobbyist allegedly gave Ratcliff approximately $44,000 in cash for Ratcliff's political consultant to hold as collateral until Ratcliff paid the consultant the money owed. The indictment alleges that Ratcliff knew that his use of the cash to secure a campaign debt violated the $2500 statutory limitation and that Ratcliff did not disclose the illegal loan in his campaign finance disclosure reports.

In addition to Ratcliff's failure to report the amount and source of certain cash and loans he received, he allegedly misled the Board of Ethics during its investigation of his activities. Specifically, the indictment alleges that Ratcliff falsely represented that he had the creditworthiness to obtain the original loans on September 23 and October 7, 1999, without a cosigner and that the replacement loans were obtained on the basis of his independent creditworthiness. . . .

After Ratcliff's reelection as parish president, Ratcliff served in office from January 10, 2000, to January 12, 2004. During this term, Ratcliff allegedly received over $300,000 in salary and employment benefits from the parish.

On November 3, 2004, Ratcliff was charged by indictment with fourteen counts of mail fraud and one count of making a false statement to a financial institution. With regard to the mail fraud counts, the Government alleged that Ratcliff used the mails in a scheme to defraud Livingston Parish of the salary and employment benefits of elected office through misrepresentations he made to the Board of Ethics concerning the financing of his campaign. According to the Government, Ratcliff secured his reelection as parish president by obtaining the illegal funding and concealing his violations from the Board of Ethics. . . .

II.   DISCUSSION

The Government contends that Ratcliff's indictment sufficiently charged the offense of mail fraud because the salary and employment benefits of elected office constitute "money or property" under the mail fraud statute and because fraudulent job procurement can constitute mail fraud in the election context just as it can in the typical hiring context. Ratcliff counters that any misrepresentations he allegedly made to the Board of Ethics, which is a state entity, were unrelated to the salary and benefits paid as a matter of course by Livingston Parish, which is a distinct, local entity. . . .

We do not dispute the Government's contention that a salary and other financial employment benefits can constitute "money or property" under the statute; as the Eighth Circuit put it when discussing a scheme to defraud an employer of wages, "[m]oney is money, and 'money' is specifically mentioned in the statutory words." United States v. Granberry, 908 F.2d 278, 280 (8th Cir. 1990); see also Pasquantino v. United States, 544 U.S. 349, 356-357 (2005) (recognizing that money in the public treasury is the government's "money" for purposes of the mail fraud statute). But the real question before us is whether the indictment alleges a scheme to defraud the alleged victim—Livingston Parish—of that money. As the Supreme Court has explained, "the words 'to defraud' commonly refer 'to wronging one in his property rights by dishonest methods or schemes,' and 'usually signify the deprivation of something of value by trick, deceit, chicane, or overreaching.'" McNally v. United States, 483 U.S. 350, 359 (1987). Accordingly, in determining whether the indictment alleges a scheme to defraud Livingston Parish of money or property, we must look to whether the alleged scheme is one to deprive the parish of money or property through misrepresentations, thereby wronging the parish's property rights. . . .

Applying these principles, it is evident that Ratcliff's indictment does not allege a scheme to defraud Livingston Parish of any money or property. According to the indictment, Ratcliff devised a scheme (1) to conceal campaign finance violations from the Board of Ethics, which would (2) deceive the voting public about the campaign contributions he received, which would (3) secure his reelection to office, which would (4) cause Livingston Parish to pay him the salary and other financial benefits budgeted for the parish president. Although the charged scheme involves Ratcliff ultimately receiving money from the parish, it cannot be said that the parish would be deprived of this money by means of Ratcliff's misrepresentations, as the financial benefits budgeted for the parish president go to the winning candidate regardless of who that person is. Nor would the parish be deprived of its control over the money by means of Ratcliff's fraud, as the parish has no such control other than ensuring that the benefits are paid to the duly elected candidate. There are no allegations, for example, that the parish was deceived into paying the parish president's salary to someone who did not win the election or to someone who failed to meet the parish's minimum requirements for office. Indeed, there are no allegations that the parish would be deceived, either directly or indirectly, into taking any action at all; rather, the indictment alleges a scheme to deceive the Board of Ethics and the voters. Though the misrepresentations in a mail fraud scheme need not be made directly to the scheme's victim, the alleged scheme must nevertheless be one to defraud the victim. Ratcliff's indictment provides no basis to find a scheme to defraud Livingston Parish through misrepresentations made to the Board of Ethics. The misrepresentations simply did not implicate the parish's property rights.

The Sixth Circuit recently reached a similar result in United States v. Turner, 465 F.3d 667 (6th Cir. 2006). In that case, Turner was indicted on charges that, *inter alia*, he engaged in a scheme to violate state campaign finance laws and to mail false campaign finance reports to the state in order to cover up the violations, thereby assisting the election of two state officials who received salaries from the state while in office. . . . Looking to the merits of the theory, the court determined that in the election fraud context, "the government and citizens have not been deprived of any money or property because the relevant salary would be paid to someone regardless of the fraud. In such a case, the citizens have simply lost the intangible right to elect the official who will receive the salary." Id. at 680. The court further decided that the allegedly defrauded state had "no control over the appropriation of the salary beyond ensuring payment to the duly elected official," and that "[a]lthough the salary comes from the public fisc, there is no discretion regarding either whether or to whom it is paid." Id. at 682. Accordingly, the court concluded that "there is no resulting property deprivation" from the alleged scheme. Id.

The Government makes several arguments seeking to avoid this conclusion here. First, the Government contends that several courts in other circuits have embraced the so-called "salary theory," under which a mail fraud charge can be supported by a scheme to use deceit to obtain a job and the salary that comes with it. Yet even if the salary theory were to be accepted in this circuit, the cases discussing and accepting the theory involve situations in which a job applicant falsely represented his qualifications or skills in order to obtain a job, deceiving the employer into hiring or promoting someone that he would not have otherwise hired or promoted. In United States v. Granberry, for example, the defendant obtained the job of school-bus driver by concealing a murder conviction, which would have prevented his hiring if known to the school district. The Eighth Circuit reversed the district court's dismissal of the indictment, holding that the defendant's alleged scheme deprived the school district of money because the district did not get what it paid for—a school-bus driver who had not been convicted of a felony. The court also concluded that the scheme deprived the school district of the property right to choose the person to whom it transferred money. Similarly, the defendants in United States v. Doherty were Boston policemen who schemed to steal copies of civil service examinations and sell them to other policemen so that they could cheat and obtain promotions. 867 F.2d 47, 51 (1st Cir. 1989). The First Circuit held that such a scheme fell within the prohibition of the mail fraud statute because it deprived the employer "of control over how its money was spent." Id. at 60 (quoting *McNally*, 483 U.S. at 360). Unlike these situations, Ratcliff's charged conduct posed no harm to any of Livingston Parish's property rights: the parish does not bargain for elected officials of a particular quality such that Ratcliff's fraud could have denied it the value for which it paid, and the parish does not have control over the recipient of the parish president's salary such that Ratcliff's misrepresentations deprived it of that control. As the Sixth Circuit summarized when distinguishing these cases, "these examples, which address the government's role as employer, where job qualifications can be economically quantified, are not analogous to an election fraud case, where the government's role is purely administrative and the public's role is a political one." *Turner*, 465 F.3d at 682.

Responding to these distinctions, the Government contends that if a job procurement theory can successfully support a charge of mail fraud when a government employer is making the hiring decision itself, the result should not change merely because the parish has effectively delegated its hiring decision to the electorate. We disagree, however, with the notion that the electoral process constitutes an effective delegation of hiring authority from the parish government to the voters. The power to select the parish president does not originate from the parish government, but rather is vested in the electorate under the Louisiana Constitution and Livingston Parish's Home Rule Charter. Although the parish government is obligated to pay whichever candidate the voters elect, it has no discretion in the matter; its role is purely administrative, "implicat[ing] the [g]overnment's role as sovereign, not as property holder." *Cleveland*, 531 U.S. at 23-24. There is thus no basis to view the electorate as an agent of the government such that false statements influencing the voters could be viewed as a fraud on the parish.

Finally, the Government contends that the scheme alleged in this case is no different than fraudulent contract procurement schemes, in that courts have allowed mail fraud charges to be brought in such situations without any actual financial loss to the victim. But the cases cited by the Government do not address the scope of the mail fraud statute, instead discussing whether fraudulently procured contracts can cause a financial loss to the victim for sentencing purposes if the contracts were properly performed by the perpetrator of the fraud. . . . We have not suggested that a mail fraud scheme must actually cause a financial loss to the victim; merely that a scheme to defraud a victim of money or property, if successful, must wrong the victim's property rights in some way. Unlike fraudulent contract procurement schemes in which the employer is deprived of value for which it contracted or control over its money, the scheme alleged in the indictment implicates none of Livingston Parish's property rights.

Our analysis in this appeal also takes into account federalism concerns, and on this front we are informed by the Supreme Court's decision in Cleveland v. United States, 531 U.S. 12 (2000). . . .

Like the poker licensing system at issue in *Cleveland*, Louisiana law establishes a comprehensive regulatory system governing campaign contributions and finance disclosures for state and local elections, with state civil and criminal penalties in place for making misrepresentations on campaign finance disclosure reports. And like the Court in *Cleveland*, "[w]e resist the Government's reading of §1341 . . . because it invites us to approve a sweeping expansion of federal criminal jurisdiction in the absence of a clear statement by Congress." 531 U.S. at 24. Finding a scheme to defraud a governmental entity of the salary of elected office based on misrepresentations made during a campaign would "subject to federal mail fraud prosecution a wide range of conduct traditionally regulated by state and local authorities." Id. In practice, the Government's theory in this case would extend far beyond the context of campaign finance disclosures to any misrepresentations that seek to influence the voters in order to gain office, bringing state election fraud fully within the province of the federal fraud statutes. The mail fraud statute does not evince any clear statement conveying such a purpose, and the terms of the statute, as interpreted by Supreme Court precedent, simply do not proscribe the conduct for which Ratcliff was indicted. See *Turner*, 465 F.3d at 683. . . .

NOTES AND QUESTIONS

1. Would the Fifth Circuit have sustained the indictment if it had alleged that the defendant schemed to defraud the voters (or the taxpayers) of Livingston Parish, rather than the parish itself? If not, why not? If so, why wasn't the scheme charged this way?

2. The appeals court reasoned that "the parish does not bargain for elected officials of a particular quality such that Ratcliff's fraud could have denied it the value for which it paid." 488 F.3d at 647. Do you agree? Didn't the parish "bargain" for an elected official who followed Louisiana's Campaign Finance Disclosure Act? Explain in your own words why the salary that a private employee obtains after misrepresenting his qualifications can qualify as a "property" deprivation but the salary that an elected official obtained cannot, or at least did not in this case. Might the court's real concern be with transforming a civil violation of local election law into a federal felony? That said, it would be a mistake to read *Ratcliff* as making local elections a mail-fraud-free zone. See United States v. Reed, 2016 WL 6946983 at *9 (E.D. La. 2016) (upholding conviction of district attorney and son for using campaign funds for personal purposes, and noting that *Ratcliff* "does not establish a blanket prohibition against federal prosecution of fraud committed under the auspices of a campaign for state office").

3. As you read the next section, ask yourself why Ratcliff wasn't charged with honest services fraud. Is the answer that a candidate for office, as opposed to an elected official, does not owe anyone his or her honest services?

C.   HONEST SERVICES FRAUD

As noted earlier in Section B, Congress overturned the Supreme Court's decision in McNally v. United States less than a year later by enacting 18 U.S.C. §1346, which provides that "the term 'scheme or artifice to defraud' includes a scheme or artifice to deprive another of the intangible right of honest services." *McNally* had tried to end several decades of what it held to be misbegotten lawmaking by lower courts. Congress's legislative response was to demand that courts return to the fray. Yet the statutory language it chose would turn out to be of limited help, and the legislative history was virtually non-existent. Section 1346 makes it clear enough that there needs to be some legal relationship between the defendant and the victim that creates a "right" to honesty. After all, Kant's imperative is not the law, and ordinary citizens do not owe each other a duty of candor. But precisely *when* does such a right arise? And what does it take to violate such a right? Between 1988 and 2010, when the Supreme Court intervened in Skilling v. United States, 561 U.S. 358 (2010), the lower courts developed two interacting lines of cases—with inevitable variation across Circuits—one for public sector deprivations, one for private.

INTERPRETIVE STRATEGIES BETWEEN MCNALLY *AND* SKILLING

1. Shortly before *Skilling*, the Third Circuit canvassed some of the case law that had developed since the passage of §1346, giving a sense both of the facts on which prosecutors had deployed that provision and of the doctrinal moves that courts had used to limit its ostensible breadth:

> In our three principal honest services fraud cases decided after *McNally*—United States v. Antico, 275 F.3d 245 (3d Cir. 2001); United States v. Panarella, 277 F.3d 678 (3d Cir. 2002); and United States v. Murphy, 323 F.3d 102 (3d Cir. 2003)—the "honest services" at issue were allegedly owed not by private individuals but by either a public official or, in the case of *Murphy*, a county political party chairman alleged to have attained the status of a de facto public official by his participation in the county's political system.
>   The defendant in *Antico* was an official in Philadelphia's Department of Licenses and Inspections who failed to disclose a variety of improper financial arrangements, including one in which he regularly referred individuals who

were willing to pay for assistance in completing licensing and permit applications to the mother of his child as a means to avoid his obligation to make
direct child support payments. We concluded that Antico's obligation to disclose his personal interest in the official business he was handling arose by
virtue of both state and local laws. . . . [Antico violated not just these statutory
conflict of interest provisions but also] "the fiduciary relationship between a
public servant charged with disinterested decision-making and the public he
serves." [274 F.3d] at 264. This fiduciary relationship, we explained, imposed
upon the official a duty "to disclose material information affecting an official's impartial decision-making and to recuse himself . . . regardless of a state
or local law." Id. Because Antico's intentional concealment of his conflict of
interest violated both state and local law, as well as his fiduciary duty to the
public, we concluded that there was sufficient evidence to uphold Antico's
conviction for honest services fraud under §§1341, 1343, and 1346.

In *Panarella*, [where a state senator was alleged to have concealed a financial interest in a tax collection business contrary to Pennsylvania's disclosure
statute, the Circuit Court held] that "where a public official takes discretionary
action that the official knows will directly benefit a financial interest that the official has concealed in violation of a state criminal law, that official has deprived
the public of his honest services under 18 U.S.C. §1346." [277 F.3d] at 691.

In rejecting Panarella's argument, we reasoned that the determination
of whether a public official had misused his office for personal gain was an
ambiguous standard. Id. at 692-93. The violation of Pennsylvania's disclosure
statute served as a "better limiting principle for purposes of determining
when an official's failure to disclose a conflict of interest amounts to honest
services fraud." Id. The state statute at issue in *Panarella* provided clear notice
for purposes of the rule of lenity that nondisclosure of the official's conflict of
interest was criminal. Id. at 693. In addition, "the intrusion into state autonomy is significantly muted, since the conduct that amounts to honest services
fraud is conduct that the state itself has chosen to criminalize." Id. at 694. . . .

In contrast to the status of the actors in *Antico* and *Panarella*, the defendant in *Murphy* . . . served as the chairman of a county political party. 323 F.3d
at 104. We reversed Murphy's conviction for honest services fraud because the
Government failed to identify "any clearly established fiduciary relationship
or legal duty in either federal or state law between Murphy and Passaic County
or its citizens." Id. at 117. . . .

United States v. McGeehan, 584 F.3d 560, 566-67 (3d Cir. 2009). The
McGeehan court then noted that *Antico* and *Panarella* had similarly used collateral state laws to limit the scope of honest services fraud. As *McGeehan*
explained, these cases required "the anchor of a fiduciary relationship
established by state or federal law." Id. at 567.

The trilogy of cases discussed in *McGeehan* illustrates the difficulties
courts face in identifying the source and scope of a "right" to honest services. *Antico* and *Panarella* both dealt with the duties of public officials;
Murphy discussed the duties of a political party official who the government

argued should be treated as a de facto public official. The theory of honest services fraud as applied to public officials

> holds that a public official stands in a fiduciary relationship with the public, and can commit honest services fraud by breaching fiduciary duties in the course of that relationship, such as by theft, accepting a bribe, or concealing a financial conflict of interest. In close cases we have not been unmindful of the potential for overreaching when prosecutors pursue this theory. Most prominently, in *Murphy* we deployed a "limiting principle" to guard against that potential in the public official context: we "endorse[d] . . . the decisions of other Courts of Appeals that have interpreted §1346 more stringently and required a state law limiting principle," 323 F.3d at 116, namely "that state law must provide the specific honest services owed by the defendant in a fiduciary relationship," id. at 116 n.5 (citing United States v. Brumley, 116 F.3d 728, 734 (5th Cir. 1997)). . . .

McGeehan, 584 F.3d at 568. The Third Circuit then explained why all of this interpretive maneuvering was necessary. The next paragraph highlights the court's key concern: federalism, and, in particular, the ways that federalism complicates notice. As the court noted:

> One purpose of the limiting principle we identified is to avoid placing federal prosecutors and courts in the role of regulating state and local politics, which might risk subverting the delicate relationship between state and federal governance. But there is another reason to require a limiting principle or principles: the exercise of interpreting a malleable term in a criminal statute which applies to a wide variety of activity may generate nebulous standards that are not discernable to people of ordinary intelligence. The latter problem is not confined to cases involving public officials. Defining the scope of the statute in its application to business relationships, like those at issue here, is also important. The federalization under the criminal law of the law of contracts and other business transactions—quintessential matters for state regulation—is a real concern. All of these considerations give pause to an expansive judicial interpretation of §1346.

Id. at 569. The court then discussed honest services fraud in the private sector. None of the court's prior §1346 cases dealt with purely private actors, and, as noted by the court,

> "The classic application of the intangible right to honest services doctrine has been to a corrupt public servant who has deprived the public of his honest services." United States v. Frost, 125 F.3d 346, 365 (6th Cir. 1997). As one of our sister circuits has opined, "[t]he right of the public to the honest services of its officials derives at least in part from the concept that corruption and denigration of the common good violates 'the essence of the political contract.'" Id. (quoting United States v. Jain, 93 F.3d 436, 442 (8th Cir. 1996)).

Although "the literal language of §1346 extends to private sector schemes," *Jain*, 93 F.3d at 441, "[e]nforcement of an intangible right to honest services in the private sector" arguably has a "weaker justification because relationships in the private sector generally rest upon concerns and expectations less ethereal and more economic than the abstract satisfaction of receiving 'honest services' for their own sake." *Frost*, 125 F.3d at 365.

Nonetheless, caselaw supports the conclusion that private actors can owe "honest services" under §1346. As we have noted, because "commentary and judicial reflection indicate that [§1346] was enacted to overturn *McNally* and restore the evolution of mail and wire fraud to its pre-*McNally* status," *Antico*, 275 F.3d at 262, in construing §1346 we look to "pre-*McNally* cases interpreting §1341 and §1343 for guidance." *Panarella*, 277 F.3d at 690 []. As these cases show, honest services fraud has been found to encompass "purchasing agents, brokers, union leaders, and others with clear fiduciary duties to their employers or unions [who defrauded] their employers or unions by accepting kickbacks or selling confidential information," as well as private actors who have "us[ed] the mails to defraud individuals of their rights to privacy and other nonmonetary rights." *McNally*, 483 U.S. at 363 & nn.3 & 4 (Stevens, J., dissenting) (listing cases). . . .

McGeehan, 584 F.3d at 568-70.

2. While, in *McGeehan*, the Third Circuit found that no clear fiduciary duty had been alleged or proved, the Sixth Circuit, in United States v. Frost, 125 F.3d 346 (6th Cir. 1997), found the "axiomatic" duty of an employee to protect the property of his employer at the core of the honest services deprivation committed by two professors, Frost and Turner. In *Frost*, the court found that the two professors had defrauded the University of Tennessee Space Institute by allowing certain students to pass off material written by others as their own theses or dissertations, and then concealed from the other members of the oral examination committees that the thesis or dissertation under review was not the student's own work. (The students were government employees who could steer contracts to the professors' consulting firm.) The court explained:

> Ultimately, a university is a business: in return for tuition money and scholarly effort, it agrees to provide an education and a degree. The number of degrees which a university may award is finite, and the decision to award a degree is in part a business decision. Awarding degrees to inept students, or to students who have not earned them, will decrease the value of degrees in general. More specifically, it will hurt the reputation of the school and thereby impair its ability to attract other students willing to pay tuition, as well as its ability to raise money. The University of Tennessee therefore has a property right in its unissued degrees, and Frost and Turner had a fiduciary duty to the University when exerting their considerable influence over whether the school would give a degree to a student.

Id. at 367. Under this analysis, would a professor who secretly violated a university's non-fraternization policy by dating a student also be guilty of honest services mail fraud? Which negative reputation would hurt a school more: one for degrees obtainable via plagiarism or one for sexually predatory faculty members?

3. Prosecutors were deeply attracted to a theory that allowed conviction for an undisclosed conflict of interest, even without evidence of actual bribery. No one doubted that the Supreme Court would eventually have to step in. The harder question is why the Court waited so long to address the Circuit variations in honest services doctrine that were so widely noted and decried. To what should we attribute this passivity?

Finally, in October Term 2009, the Court took under consideration three cases in which defendants challenged their honest services fraud convictions on the grounds that the statute was unconstitutionally vague. While the Court rejected that claim, it did narrow the scope of what constitutes deprivation of honest services. Interestingly, the Court did not use any of the interpretive strategies used by the Courts of Appeals. Justice Ginsburg's opinion for the Court does reference these strategies (see footnote 36 in the next case), but the Court found a way to reverse the convictions before it on yet another theory.

Skilling v. United States
561 U.S. 358 (2010)

Justice GINSBURG delivered the opinion of the Court.

In 2001, Enron Corporation, then the seventh highest-revenue-grossing company in America, crashed into bankruptcy. We consider in this opinion two questions arising from the prosecution of Jeffrey Skilling, a longtime Enron executive, for crimes committed before the corporation's collapse. First, did pretrial publicity and community prejudice prevent Skilling from obtaining a fair trial? Second, did the jury improperly convict Skilling of conspiracy to commit "honest-services" wire fraud, 18 U.S.C. §§371, 1343, 1346?

Answering no to both questions, the Fifth Circuit affirmed Skilling's convictions. We conclude, in common with the Court of Appeals, that Skilling's fair-trial argument fails. . . . But we disagree with the Fifth Circuit's honest-services ruling. In proscribing fraudulent deprivations of "the intangible right of honest services," §1346, Congress intended at least to reach schemes to defraud involving bribes and kickbacks. Construing the honest-services statute to extend beyond that core meaning, we conclude, would encounter a vagueness shoal. We therefore hold that §1346 covers only bribery and kickback schemes. Because Skilling's alleged misconduct entailed no bribe or kickback, it does not fall within §1346's proscription. We therefore affirm in part and vacate in part.

I

Founded in 1985, Enron Corporation grew from its headquarters in Houston, Texas, into one of the world's leading energy companies. Skilling launched his career there in 1990 when Kenneth Lay, the company's founder, hired him to head an Enron subsidiary. Skilling steadily rose through the corporation's ranks, serving as president and chief operating officer, and then, beginning in February 2001, as chief executive officer. Six months later, on August 14, 2001, Skilling resigned from Enron.

Less than four months after Skilling's departure, Enron spiraled into bankruptcy. The company's stock, which had traded at $90 per share in August 2000, plummeted to pennies per share in late 2001. Attempting to comprehend what caused the corporation's collapse, the U.S. Department of Justice formed an Enron Task Force, comprising prosecutors and FBI agents from around the Nation. The Government's investigation uncovered an elaborate conspiracy to prop up Enron's short-run stock prices by overstating the company's financial well-being. In the years following Enron's bankruptcy, the Government prosecuted dozens of Enron employees who participated in the scheme. In time, the Government worked its way up the corporation's chain of command: On July 7, 2004, a grand jury indicted Skilling, Lay, and Richard Causey, Enron's former chief accounting officer.

These three defendants, the indictment alleged,

"engaged in a wide-ranging scheme to deceive the investing public, including Enron's shareholders, . . . about the true performance of Enron's businesses by: (a) manipulating Enron's publicly reported financial results; and (b) making public statements and representations about Enron's financial performance and results that were false and misleading."

Skilling and his co-conspirators, the indictment continued, "enriched themselves as a result of the scheme through salary, bonuses, grants of stock and stock options, other profits, and prestige."

Count 1 of the indictment charged Skilling with conspiracy to commit securities and wire fraud; in particular, it alleged that Skilling had sought to "depriv[e] Enron and its shareholders of the intangible right of [his] honest services." The indictment further charged Skilling with more than 25 substantive counts of securities fraud, wire fraud, making false representations to Enron's auditors, and insider trading. . . .

Following a 4-month trial and nearly five days of deliberation, the jury found Skilling guilty of 19 counts, including the honest-services-fraud conspiracy charge, and not guilty of 9 insider-trading counts. The District Court sentenced Skilling to 292 months' imprisonment, 3 years' supervised release, and $45 million in restitution. . . .

[On appeal, the Fifth Circuit] rejected Skilling's claim that his conduct did not indicate any conspiracy to commit honest-services fraud. "[T]he jury was entitled to convict Skilling," the court stated, "on these elements": "(1) a material breach of a fiduciary duty . . . (2) that results in a detriment to the employer," including one occasioned by an employee's decision to "withhold material information, i.e., information that he had reason to believe would lead a reasonable employer to change its conduct." [554 F.3d 529, 547 (5th Cir. 2009)]. The Fifth Circuit did not address Skilling's argument that the honest-services statute, if not interpreted to exclude his actions, should be invalidated as unconstitutionally vague. . . .

[We omit the portion of the Court's opinion rejecting Skilling's argument that the publicity that attended Enron's collapse and the subsequent prosecutions prevented him from receiving a fair trial by an impartial jury.] . . .

III

We next consider whether Skilling's conspiracy conviction was premised on an improper theory of honest-services wire fraud. The honest-services statute, §1346, Skilling maintains, is unconstitutionally vague. Alternatively, he contends that his conduct does not fall within the statute's compass.

A

Enacted in 1872, the original mail-fraud provision, the predecessor of the modern-day mail- and wire-fraud laws, proscribed, without further elaboration, use of the mails to advance "any scheme or artifice to defraud." See McNally v. United States, 483 U.S. 350, 356 (1987). In 1909, Congress amended the statute to prohibit, as it does today, "any scheme or artifice to defraud, *or for obtaining money or property by means of false or fraudulent pretenses, representations, or promises.*" §1341 (emphasis added). Emphasizing Congress' disjunctive phrasing, the Courts of Appeals, one after the other, interpreted the term "scheme or artifice to defraud" to include deprivations not only of money or property, but also of intangible rights.

In an opinion credited with first presenting the intangible-rights theory, Shushan v. United States, 117 F.2d 110 (1941), the Fifth Circuit reviewed the mail-fraud prosecution of a public official who allegedly accepted bribes from entrepreneurs in exchange for urging city action beneficial to the bribe payers. "It is not true that because the [city] was to make and did make a saving by the operations there could not have been an intent to defraud," the Court of Appeals maintained. Id. at 119. "A scheme to get a public contract on more favorable terms than would likely be got otherwise by bribing a public official," the court observed, "would not only be a plan to commit the crime of bribery, but would also be a scheme to defraud the public." Id. at 115.

The Fifth Circuit's opinion in *Shushan* stimulated the development of an "honest-services" doctrine. Unlike fraud in which the victim's loss of money or property supplied the defendant's gain, with one the mirror image of the other, the honest-services theory targeted corruption that lacked similar symmetry. While the offender profited, the betrayed party suffered no deprivation of money or property; instead, a third party, who had not been deceived, provided the enrichment. For example, if a city mayor (the offender) accepted a bribe from a third party in exchange for awarding that party a city contract, yet the contract terms were the same as any that could have been negotiated at arm's length, the city (the betrayed party) would suffer no tangible loss. Even if the scheme occasioned a money or property *gain* for the betrayed party, courts reasoned, actionable harm lay in the denial of that party's right to the offender's "honest services." See, e.g., United States v. Dixon, 536 F.2d 1388, 1400 (C.A. 2 1976).

"Most often these cases . . . involved bribery of public officials," United States v. Bohonus, 628 F.2d 1167, 1171 (9th Cir. 1980), but courts also recognized private-sector honest-services fraud. In perhaps the earliest application of the theory to private actors, a District Court, reviewing a bribery scheme, explained:

"When one tampers with [the employer-employee] relationship for the purpose of causing the employee to breach his duty [to his employer], he in effect is defrauding the employer of a lawful right. The actual deception that is practised is in the continued representation of the employee to the employer that he is honest and loyal to the employer's interests." United States v. Procter & Gamble Co., 47 F. Supp. 676, 678 (Mass. 1942).

Over time, "[a]n increasing number of courts" recognized that "a recreant employee" — public or private — "c[ould] be prosecuted under [the mail-fraud statute] if he breache[d] his allegiance to his employer by accepting bribes or kickbacks in the course of his employment," United States v. McNeive, 536 F.2d 1245, 1249 (8th Cir. 1976); by 1982, all Courts of Appeals had embraced the honest-services theory of fraud.

In 1987, this Court, in McNally v. United States, stopped the development of the intangible-rights doctrine in its tracks. *McNally* involved a state officer who, in selecting Kentucky's insurance agent, arranged to procure a share of the agent's commissions via kickbacks paid to companies the official partially controlled. 483 U.S. at 360. The prosecutor did not charge that, "in the absence of the alleged scheme[,] the Commonwealth would have paid a lower premium or secured better insurance." Ibid. Instead, the prosecutor maintained that the kickback scheme "defraud[ed] the citizens and government of Kentucky of their right to have the Commonwealth's affairs conducted honestly." Id. at 353.

We held that the scheme did not qualify as mail fraud. "Rather than constru[ing] the statute in a manner that leaves its outer boundaries ambiguous and involves the Federal Government in setting standards of disclosure and good government for local and state officials," we read the statute "as limited in scope to the protection of property rights." Id. at 360. "If Congress desires to go further," we stated, "it must speak more clearly." Ibid.

Congress responded swiftly. The following year, it enacted a new statute "specifically to cover . . . "the intangible right of honest services.'" Cleveland v. United States, 531 U.S. 12, 19-20 (2000). In full, the honest-services statute stated:

> "For the purposes of th[e] chapter [of the United States Code that prohibits, *inter alia*, mail fraud, §1341, and wire fraud, §1343], the term 'scheme or artifice to defraud' includes a scheme or artifice to deprive another of the intangible right of honest services." §1346.

B

Congress, Skilling charges, reacted quickly but not clearly: He asserts that §1346 is unconstitutionally vague. To satisfy due process, "a penal statute [must] define the criminal offense [1] with sufficient definiteness that ordinary people can understand what conduct is prohibited and [2] in a manner that does not encourage arbitrary and discriminatory enforcement." Kolender v. Lawson, 461 U.S. 352, 357 (1983). . . .

According to Skilling, §1346 meets neither of the two due process essentials. First, the phrase "the intangible right of honest services," he contends, does not adequately define what behavior it bars. Brief for Petitioner 38-39. Second, he alleges, §1346's "standardless sweep allows policemen, prosecutors, and juries to pursue their personal predilections," thereby "facilitat[ing] opportunistic and arbitrary prosecutions." Id. at 44 (quoting *Kolender*, 461 U.S. at 358).

In urging invalidation of §1346, Skilling swims against our case law's current, which requires us, if we can, to construe, not condemn, Congress' enactments. See also United States v. National Dairy Products Corp., 372 U.S. 29, 32 (1963) (stressing, in response to a vagueness challenge, "[t]he strong presumptive validity that attaches to an Act of Congress"). Alert to §1346's potential breadth, the Courts of Appeals have divided on how best to interpret the statute.[36] Uniformly, however, they have declined to throw out the statute as irremediably vague.

We agree that §1346 should be construed rather than invalidated. First, we look to the doctrine developed in pre-*McNally* cases in an endeavor to ascertain the meaning of the phrase "the intangible right of honest services." Second, to preserve what Congress certainly intended the statute to cover, we pare that body of precedent down to its core: In the main, the pre-*McNally* cases involved fraudulent schemes to deprive another of honest services through bribes or kickbacks supplied by a third party who had not been deceived. Confined to these paramount applications, §1346 presents no vagueness problem.

1

There is no doubt that Congress intended §1346 to refer to and incorporate the honest-services doctrine recognized in Court of Appeals' decisions before *McNally* derailed the intangible-rights theory of fraud. . . . Congress enacted §1346 on the heels of *McNally* and drafted the statute using that decision's terminology. See 483 U.S. at 355 ("intangible righ[t]"); id. at 362 (Stevens, J., dissenting) ("right to . . . honest services"). As the Second Circuit observed in its leading analysis of §1346:

> "The definite article 'the' suggests that 'intangible right of honest services' had a specific meaning to Congress when it enacted the statute —Congress was recriminalizing mail- and wire-fraud schemes to deprive others of *that* 'intangible right of honest services,' which had been protected before *McNally*, not *all* intangible rights of honest services whatever they might be thought to be." United States v. Rybicki, 354 F.3d 124, 137-138 (2003) (en banc).

2

Satisfied that Congress, by enacting §1346, "meant to reinstate the body of pre-*McNally* honest-services law" (opinion of Scalia, J.), we have surveyed that case law. In parsing the Courts of Appeals decisions, we acknowledge that Skilling's vagueness challenge has force, for honest-services decisions

---

36. Courts have disagreed about whether §1346 prosecutions must be based on a violation of state law; compare, e.g., United States v. Brumley, 116 F.3d 728, 734-735 (C.A. 5 1997) (en banc), with, e.g., United States v. Weyhrauch, 548 F.3d 1237, 1245-1246 (C.A.9 2008), vacated and remanded [today]; whether a defendant must contemplate that the victim suffer economic harm, compare, e.g., United States v. Sun-Diamond Growers of Cal., 138 F.3d 961, 973 (C.A.D.C. 1998), with, e.g., United States v. Black, 530 F.3d 596, 600-602 (C.A. 7 2008), vacated and remanded [today]; and whether the defendant must act in pursuit of private gain, compare, e.g., United States v. Bloom, 149 F.3d 649, 655 (C.A. 7 1998), with, e.g., United States v. Panarella, 277 F.3d 678, 692 (C.A. 3 2002).

preceding *McNally* were not models of clarity or consistency. While the honest-services cases preceding *McNally* dominantly and consistently applied the fraud statute to bribery and kickback schemes—schemes that were the basis of most honest-services prosecutions—there was considerable disarray over the statute's application to conduct outside that core category. In light of this disarray, Skilling urges us, as he urged the Fifth Circuit, to invalidate the statute *in toto* [as "unconstitutionally vague"].

It has long been our practice, however, before striking a federal statute as impermissibly vague, to consider whether the prescription is amenable to a limiting construction. See, e.g., Hooper v. California, 155 U.S. 648, 657 (1895) ("The elementary rule is that *every reasonable construction* must be resorted to, in order to save a statute from unconstitutionality." (emphasis added)). We have accordingly instructed "the federal courts . . . to avoid constitutional difficulties by [adopting a limiting interpretation] if such a construction is fairly possible." [Boos v. Barry, 485 U.S. 312, 331 (1988)]. . . .

Although some applications of the pre-*McNally* honest-services doctrine occasioned disagreement among the Courts of Appeals, these cases do not cloud the doctrine's solid core: The "vast majority" of the honest-services cases involved offenders who, in violation of a fiduciary duty, participated in bribery or kickback schemes. United States v. Runnels, 833 F.2d 1183, 1187 (6th Cir. 1987); see Brief for United States 42, and n.4 (citing dozens of examples). Indeed, the *McNally* case itself, which spurred Congress to enact §1346, presented a paradigmatic kickback fact pattern. Congress' reversal of *McNally* and reinstatement of the honest-services doctrine, we conclude, can and should be salvaged by confining its scope to the core pre-*McNally* applications. . . .

In view of this history, there is no doubt that Congress intended §1346 to reach *at least* bribes and kickbacks. Reading the statute to proscribe a wider range of offensive conduct, we acknowledge, would raise the due process concerns underlying the vagueness doctrine. To preserve the statute without transgressing constitutional limitations, we now hold that §1346 criminalizes *only* the bribe-and-kickback core of the pre-*McNally* case law.

3

The Government urges us to go further by locating within §1346's compass another category of proscribed conduct: "undisclosed self-dealing by a public official or private employee—i.e., the taking of official action by the employee that furthers his own undisclosed financial interests while purporting to act in the interests of those to whom he owes a fiduciary duty." [Brief for the United States] at 43-44. "[T]he theory of liability in *McNally* itself was nondisclosure of a conflicting financial interest," the Government observes, and "Congress clearly intended to revive th[at] nondisclosure theory." Id. at 44. Moreover, "[a]lthough not as numerous as the bribery and kickback cases," the Government asserts, "the pre-*McNally* cases involving undisclosed self-dealing were abundant." Ibid.

Neither of these contentions withstands close inspection. *McNally*, as we have already observed, involved a classic kickback scheme: A public official, in exchange for routing Kentucky's insurance business through a middleman company, arranged for that company to share its commissions with entities in which the official held an interest. This was no mere failure to disclose a conflict of interest; rather, the official conspired with a third party so that both would profit from wealth generated by public contracts. Reading §1346 to proscribe bribes and kickbacks—and nothing more—satisfies Congress' undoubted aim to reverse *McNally* on its facts.

Nor are we persuaded that the pre-*McNally* conflict-of-interest cases constitute core applications of the honest-services doctrine. Although the Courts of Appeals upheld honest-services convictions for "some schemes of non-disclosure and concealment of material information," *Mandel*, 591 F.2d 1347, 1361, they reached no consensus on which schemes qualified. In light of the relative infrequency of conflict-of-interest prosecutions in comparison to bribery and kickback charges, and the inter-circuit inconsistencies they produced, we conclude that a reasonable limiting construction of §1346 must exclude this amorphous category of cases. . . .

In sum, our construction of §1346 "establish[es] a uniform national standard, define[s] honest services with clarity, reach[es] only seriously culpable conduct, and accomplish[es] Congress's goal of 'overruling' *McNally*." Brief for Albert W. Alschuler as *Amicus Curiae* in Weyhrauch v. United States, O.T. 2009, No. 08-1196, pp. 28-29. "If Congress desires to go further," we reiterate, "it must speak more clearly than it has." *McNally*, 483 U.S. at 360.[44]

4

Interpreted to encompass only bribery and kickback schemes, §1346 is not unconstitutionally vague. Recall that the void-for-vagueness doctrine addresses concerns about (1) fair notice and (2) arbitrary and

---

44. If Congress were to take up the enterprise of criminalizing "undisclosed self-dealing by a public official or private employee," Brief for United States 43, it would have to employ standards of sufficient definiteness and specificity to overcome due process concerns. The Government proposes a standard that prohibits the "taking of official action by the employee that furthers his own undisclosed financial interests while purporting to act in the interests of those to whom he owes a fiduciary duty," so long as the employee acts with a specific intent to deceive and the undisclosed conduct could influence the victim to change its behavior. Id. at 43-44. See also id. at 40-41. That formulation, however, leaves many questions unanswered. How direct or significant does the conflicting financial interest have to be? To what extent does the official action have to further that interest in order to amount to fraud? To whom should the disclosure be made and what information should it convey? These questions and others call for particular care in attempting to formulate an adequate criminal prohibition in this context.

discriminatory prosecutions. See *Kolender*, 461 U.S. at 357. A prohibition on fraudulently depriving another of one's honest services by accepting bribes or kickbacks does not present a problem on either score.

As to fair notice, "whatever the school of thought concerning the scope and meaning of" §1346, it has always been "as plain as a pikestaff that" bribes and kickbacks constitute honest-services fraud, Williams v. United States, 341 U.S. 97, 101 (1951), and the statute's *mens rea* requirement further blunts any notice concern. . . .

As to arbitrary prosecutions, we perceive no significant risk that the honest-services statute, as we interpret it today, will be stretched out of shape. Its prohibition on bribes and kickbacks draws content not only from the pre-*McNally* case law, but also from federal statutes proscribing—and defining—similar crimes. See, e.g., 18 U.S.C. §§201(b), 666(a)(2); 41 U.S.C. §52(2) ("The term 'kickback' means any money, fee, commission, credit, gift, gratuity, thing of value, or compensation of any kind which is provided, directly or indirectly, to [enumerated persons] for the purpose of improperly obtaining or rewarding favorable treatment in connection with [enumerated circumstances]."). See also United States v. Ganim, 510 F.3d 134, 147-149 (2d Cir. 2007) (Sotomayor, J.) (reviewing honest-services conviction involving bribery in light of elements of bribery under other federal statutes). A criminal defendant who participated in a bribery or kickback scheme, in short, cannot tenably complain about prosecution under §1346 on vagueness grounds.

C

It remains to determine whether Skilling's conduct violated §1346. Skilling's honest-services prosecution, the Government concedes, was not "prototypical." Brief for United States 49. The Government charged Skilling with conspiring to defraud Enron's shareholders by misrepresenting the company's fiscal health, thereby artificially inflating its stock price. It was the Government's theory at trial that Skilling "profited from the fraudulent scheme . . . through the receipt of salary and bonuses, . . . and through the sale of approximately $200 million in Enron stock, which netted him $89 million." Id. at 51.

The Government did not, at any time, allege that Skilling solicited or accepted side payments from a third party in exchange for making these misrepresentations. It is therefore clear that, as we read §1346, Skilling did not commit honest-services fraud. . . .

Justice SCALIA, with whom Justice THOMAS joins [as does Justice KENNEDY as to the parts here], concurring in part and concurring in the judgment.

I agree with the Court . . . that the decision upholding Skilling's conviction for so-called "honest-services fraud" must be reversed, but for a

different reason. In my view, the specification in 18 U.S.C. §1346 that
"scheme or artifice to defraud" in the mail-fraud and wire-fraud statutes,
§§1341 and 1343, includes "a scheme or artifice to deprive another of the
intangible right of honest services," is vague, and therefore violates the
Due Process Clause of the Fifth Amendment. The Court strikes a pose of
judicial humility in proclaiming that our task is "not to destroy the Act . . .
but to construe it[.]" But in transforming the prohibition of "honest-services fraud" into a prohibition of "bribery and kick-backs" it is wielding a
power we long ago abjured: the power to define new federal crimes. See
United States v. Hudson, 7 Cranch 32, 34 (1812).

I

A criminal statute must clearly define the conduct it proscribes; see
Grayned v. City of Rockford, 408 U.S. 104, 108 (1972). . . . Our cases
have described vague statutes as failing "to provide a person of ordinary
intelligence fair notice of what is prohibited, or [as being] so standardless
that [they] authoriz[e] or encourag[e] seriously discriminatory enforcement." United States v. Williams, 553 U.S. 285, 304 (2008). Here, Skilling
argues that §1346 fails to provide fair notice and encourages arbitrary
enforcement because it provides no definition of the right of honest services whose deprivation it prohibits. In my view Skilling is correct.

The Court maintains that "the intangible right of honest services"
means the right not to have one's fiduciaries accept "bribes or kickbacks."
Its first step in reaching that conclusion is the assertion that the phrase
refers to "the doctrine developed" in cases decided by lower federal courts
prior to our decision in McNally v. United States, 483 U.S. 350 (1987). . . .
I agree that Congress used the novel phrase to adopt the lower-court case
law that had been disapproved by McNally. . . . The problem is that that
doctrine provides no "ascertainable standard of guilt," United States v. L.
Cohen Grocery Co., 255 U.S. 81, 89 (1921), and certainly is not limited to
"bribes or kickbacks."

Investigation into the meaning of "the pre-McNally honest-services
doctrine" might logically begin with McNally itself, which rejected it. That
case repudiated the many Court of Appeals holdings that had expanded
the meaning of "fraud" in the mail-fraud and wire-fraud statutes beyond
deceptive schemes to obtain property. 483 U.S. at 360. If the repudiated
cases stood for a prohibition of "bribery and kickbacks," one would have
expected those words to appear in the opinion's description of the cases.
In fact, they do not. Not at all. Nor did McNally even provide a consistent definition of the pre-existing theory of fraud it rejected. It referred
variously to a right of citizens "to have the [State]'s affairs conducted
honestly," id. at 353, to "honest and impartial government," id. at 355, to
"good government," id. at 356, and "to have public officials perform their

duties honestly," id. at 358. It described prior case law as holding that "a public official owes a fiduciary duty to the public, and misuse of his office for private gain is a fraud," id. at 355.

But the pre-*McNally* Court of Appeals opinions were not limited to fraud by public officials. Some courts had held that those fiduciaries subject to the "honest services" obligation included private individuals who merely participated in public decisions, see, e.g., United States v. Gray, 790 F.2d 1290, 1295-1296 (6th Cir. 1986) (citing United States v. Margiotta, 688 F.2d 108, 122 (2d Cir. 1982)), and even private employees who had no role in public decisions, see, e.g., United States v. Lemire, 720 F.2d 1327, 1335-1336 (D.C. Cir. 1983); United States v. Von Barta, 635 F.2d 999, 1007 (2d Cir. 1980). Moreover, "to say that a man is a fiduciary only begins [the] analysis; it gives direction to further inquiry. . . . What obligations does he owe as a fiduciary?" SEC v. Chenery Corp., 318 U.S. 80, 85-86 (1943). None of the "honest services" cases, neither those pertaining to public officials nor those pertaining to private employees, defined the nature and content of the fiduciary duty central to the "fraud" offense.

There was not even universal agreement concerning the *source* of the fiduciary obligation—whether it must be positive state or federal law, see, e.g., United States v. Rabbitt, 583 F.2d 1014, 1026 (8th Cir. 1978), or merely general principles, such as the "obligations of loyalty and fidelity" that inhere in the "employment relationship," *Lemire, supra*, at 1336. The decision *McNally* reversed had grounded the duty in general (not jurisdiction-specific) trust law, see *Gray, supra*, at 1294. . . . Another pre-*McNally* case referred to the general law of agency, United States v. Ballard, 663 F.2d 534, 543, n.22 (5th Cir. 1981), modified on other grounds by 680 F.2d 352 (1982), which imposes duties quite different from those of a trustee.[1] See Restatement (Second) of Agency §§377-398 (1957). . . .

The indefiniteness of the fiduciary duty is not all. Many courts held that some *je-ne-sais-quoi* beyond a mere breach of fiduciary duty was needed to establish honest services fraud. See, e.g., *Von Barta, supra*, at 1006 (collecting cases). [Justice Scalia then noted that there were disagreements about whether there was some additional requirement, such as actual harm, and how any such requirement might be applied differently in public, rather than private, settings.] . . .

---

1. The Court is untroubled by these divisions because "these debates were rare in bribe and kickback cases," in which "[t]he existence of a fiduciary relationship, under any definition of that term, was usually beyond dispute," ante at n.41. This misses the point. The Courts of Appeals may have consistently found unlawful the acceptance of a bribe or kickback by one or another sort of fiduciary, but they have not consistently described (as the statute does not) any test for who is a fiduciary.

In short, . . . [t]he pre-*McNally* cases provide no clear indication of what constitutes a denial of the right of honest services. The possibilities range from any action that is contrary to public policy or otherwise immoral, to only the disloyalty of a public official or employee to his principal, to only the secret use of a perpetrator's position of trust in order to harm whomever he is beholden to. The duty probably did not have to be rooted in state law, but maybe it did. It might have been more demanding in the case of public officials, but perhaps not. At the time §1346 was enacted there was no settled criterion for choosing among these options, for conclusively settling what was in and what was out.[2]

II

The Court is aware of all this. It knows that adopting by reference "the pre-*McNally* honest-services doctrine" is adopting by reference nothing more precise than the referring term itself ("the intangible right of honest services"). Hence the *deus ex machina*: "[W]e pare that body of precedent down to its core[.]" Since the honest-services doctrine "had its genesis" in bribery prosecutions, and since several cases and counsel for Skilling referred to bribery and kickback schemes as "core" or "paradigm" or "typical" examples, or "[t]he most obvious form," of honest services fraud . . . THEREFORE it must be the case that they are *all* Congress meant by its reference to the honest-services doctrine.

Even if that conclusion followed from its premises, it would not suffice to eliminate the vagueness of the statute. It would solve (perhaps) the indeterminacy of what acts constitute a breach of the "honest services" obligation under the pre-*McNally* law. But it would not solve the most fundamental indeterminacy: the character of the "fiduciary capacity" to which the bribery and kickback restriction applies. Does it apply only to public officials? Or in addition to private individuals who contract with the public? Or to everyone, including the corporate officer here? The pre-*McNally* case law does not provide an answer. Thus, even with the bribery and kickback limitation the statute does not answer the question "What is the criterion of guilt?"

But that is perhaps beside the point, because it is obvious that mere prohibition of bribery and kickbacks was not the intent of the statute. To

---

2. Courts since §1346's enactment have fared no better, reproducing some of the same disputes that predated *McNally*. See, e.g., Sorich v. United States, 555 U.S. 1204 (2009) (Scalia, J., dissenting from denial of certiorari) (slip op., at 3-4) (collecting cases). We have previously found important to our vagueness analysis "the conflicting results which have arisen from the painstaking attempts of enlightened judges in seeking to carry out [a] statute in cases brought before them." United States v. L. Cohen Grocery Co., 255 U.S. 81, 89 (1921). I am at a loss to explain why the Court barely mentions those conflicts today.

say that bribery and kickbacks represented "the core" of the doctrine, or that most cases applying the doctrine involved those offenses, is not to say that they *are* the doctrine. All it proves is that the multifarious versions of the doctrine *overlap* with regard to those offenses. But the doctrine itself is much more. Among all the pre-*McNally* smorgasbord-offerings of varieties of honest services fraud, *not one* is limited to bribery and kickbacks. That is a dish the Court has cooked up all on its own.

Thus, the Court's claim to "respec[t] the legislature," ante at n.44 (emphasis deleted), is false. It is entirely clear (as the Court and I agree) that Congress meant to reinstate the body of pre-*McNally* honest-services law; and entirely clear that that prohibited much more (though precisely what more is uncertain) than bribery and kickbacks. Perhaps it is true that "Congress intended §1346 to reach *at least* bribes and kickbacks[.]" That simply does not mean, as the Court now holds, that "§1346 criminalizes *only*" bribery and kickbacks, ibid.

Arriving at that conclusion requires not interpretation but invention. The Court replaces a vague criminal standard that Congress adopted with a more narrow one (included within the vague one) that can pass constitutional muster. I know of no precedent for such "paring down," and it seems to me clearly beyond judicial power. This is not . . . simply a matter of adopting a limiting construction in the face of potential unconstitutionality. To do that, our cases have been careful to note, the narrowing construction must be "fairly possible," Boos v. Barry, 485 U.S. 312, 331 (1988), "reasonable," Hooper v. California, 155 U.S. 648, 657 (1895), or not "plainly contrary to the intent of Congress," Edward J. DeBartolo Corp. v. Florida Gulf Coast Building & Constr. Trades Council, 485 U.S. 568, 575 (1988). As we have seen (and the Court does not contest), *no court* before *McNally* concluded that the "deprivation of honest services" meant *only* the acceptance of bribes or kickbacks. If it were a "fairly possible" or "reasonable" construction, not "contrary to the intent of Congress," one would think that *some* court would have adopted it. The Court does not even point to a post-*McNally* case that reads §1346 to cover only bribery and kickbacks, and I am aware of none. . . .

I certainly agree with the Court that we must, "if we can," uphold, rather than "condemn," Congress's enactments. But I do not believe we have the power, in order to uphold an enactment, to rewrite it. Congress enacted the entirety of the pre-*McNally* honest-services law, the content of which is (to put it mildly) unclear. . . . I would . . . reverse Skilling's conviction on the basis that §1346 provides no "ascertainable standard" for the conduct it condemns, *L. Cohen*, 255 U.S. at 89. Instead, the Court today adds to our functions the prescription of criminal law. . . .

[Justice Alito's opinion concurring in part and in the judgment, and Justice Sotomayor's opinion concurring in part and dissenting in part, joined by Justices Breyer and Stevens, are omitted. Each of these Justices subscribed fully to the Court's analysis on the honest-services issue.]

NOTES AND QUESTIONS

1. Consider the statutory interpretation dynamic in this area. When the Supreme Court interpreted the mail fraud statute expansively in *Durland*, Congress thereafter ratified the decision by amending the statute. When, in *McNally*, the Court rejected expansive lower court interpretations of the statute, Congress legislatively overturned its decision. What effect(s) do you think this peculiar inter-branch conversation has had on the Supreme Court, or any court, when it considers mail fraud cases? See William N. Eskridge, Jr., Overriding Supreme Court Statutory Interpretation Decisions, 101 Yale L.J. 331 (1991). Now comes *Skilling*. Did the Court read *McNally* and its legislative response fairly? Should we expect Congress to respond? Certainly, the *Skilling* Court envisioned that possibility and seemed to be addressing Congress in footnote 44.

2. Note the enforcement issue: The main reason prosecutors and lower courts were open to conflict of interest theories was that proving the actual giving or taking of bribes can be difficult. The Third Circuit noted in United States v. Panarella, 277 F.3d 678 (2002):

> Were it easy to detect and prosecute public officials for bribery, the need for public officials to disclose conflicts of interest would be greatly reduced. As long as a public official does not act on a conflict of interest, the conflict of interest by itself poses little threat to the public. One reason why federal and state law mandates disclosure of conflicts of interest, however, is that it is often difficult or impossible to know for sure whether a public official has acted on a conflict of interest. . . . The only difference between a public official who accepts a bribe and a public official who receives payments while taking discretionary action that benefits that payor . . . is the existence of a *quid pro quo* whereby the public official and the payor agree that the discretionary action taken by the public official is in exchange for payment. Recognizing the practical difficulties in proving the existence of such a *quid pro quo*, disclosure laws permit the public to judge for itself whether an official has acted on a conflict of interest.
>
> To sum up, we reject [the] argument that an allegation of bribery or other misuse of office is necessary to sustain a conviction for honest services wire fraud. Rather, for the reasons discussed above, we hold that if a public official fails to disclose a financial interest in violation of state criminal law and takes discretionary action that the official knows will directly benefit that interest, then that public official has committed honest services fraud.

Id. at 697. As the Ninth Circuit similarly noted: "[I]mposing a *quid pro quo* requirement on all §1346 cases"—i.e., requiring that the government specifically show an official act and the improper benefit that the official obtained in exchange for it—"risks being under-inclusive, because some honest services fraud, such as the failure to disclose a conflict of interest

where required, may not confer a direct or easily demonstrated benefit."
United States v. Kincaid-Chauncey, 556 F.3d 923, 940-41 (9th Cir. 2009).

After *Skilling*, the government did drop several honest services prosecutions. Still, a study of 600 published decisions under the honest-services
statute "reveals that the overwhelming majority of such cases involved [ ]
allegations of a bribe or kickback, or conduct that was, or could have been,
charged as a traditional wire/mail fraud or under other federal statutes
such as those prohibiting securities fraud, extortion, and bribery." Mark J.
Stein & Joshua A. Levine, *Skilling*: Is It Really a Game-Changer for Mail and
Wire Fraud Cases?, 1831 Corp. L. & Practice Course Handbook 933, 938-39
(2010). And a number of pre-*Skilling* convictions by juries that had been
instructed that a guilty verdict could be based on the very sort of conflict
of interest theory that the *Skilling* Court thereafter rejected were thereafter
upheld on a "harmless error" analysis. See United States v. Post, 950 F. Supp.
2d 519, 534-42 (S.D.N.Y. 2013) (reviewing cases); see also United States v.
Bruno, 661 F.3d 733 (2d Cir. 2011) (allowing retrial of state senator who was
tried and convicted pre-*Skilling* on undisclosed payments theory because
government had presented sufficient evidence for a jury to have found a
quid pro quo); United States v. Urciuoli, 613 F.3d 11, 18 (1st Cir. 2010)
(after convictions were overturned because of *Skilling*, defendants were
retried and convicted by a properly instructed jury).

If the effect of *Skilling* is simply to have the government prosecute the
same cases with the same evidence but to ask the jury to infer that undisclosed payments were "really" a "bribe" or "kickback," how much will have
Skilling accomplished? Perhaps the point is that undisclosed conflicts of
interests usually are undisclosed precisely because they are accompanied by
bribes or kickbacks. But see also McDonnell v. United States, 136 S. Ct. 2355
(2016) (narrowing official actions that qualify in quid pro quo bribery). We
consider *McDonnell* in depth in Chapter 6.

3. So what is a "kickback" anyway? In United States v. DeMizio, 741 F.3d
373 (2d Cir. 2014), the court of appeals explained:

> A kickback scheme typically involves an employee's steering business
> of his employer to a third party in exchange for a share of the third party's
> profits on that business. See, e.g., Black's Law Dictionary 948 (9th ed. 2009)
> (defining "kickback" as the "return of a portion of a monetary sum received,
> esp. as a result of coercion or a secret agreement"). We reject at the outset
> DeMizio's suggestion that, in determining whether the evidence against him
> was sufficient under §1346, we should ignore cases involving public officials
> (see DeMizio brief on appeal at 32). The *Skilling* Court noted that although
> honest-services cases most often involved bribery of public officials, private
> sector honest-services fraud had been recognized at least as early as 1942.
> The Court analyzed cases involving public officials as well as cases involving
> employees in the private sector in deciding the appeal brought by *Skilling*

himself, a private-sector employee; and it noted that while the principal federal bribery statute, 18 U.S.C. §201, "generally applies only to federal public officials, . . . §1346's application to . . . private-sector fraud reaches misconduct that might otherwise go unpunished." 561 U.S. at 413 n.45.

[The Court also rejected defendant's] argument that kickbacks (a) do not include payments made to entities other than the employee who steers his employer's business to a third party in exchange for those payments, and (b) do not include payments of large sums of money to those recipients so long as they perform some minimal amount of work. Although the kickback amount frequently is paid directly to the employee who steered the contract, the scheme is no less a kickback scheme when the employee directs the third party to share its profits with an entity designated by the employee in which the employee has an interest. . . .

In this vein, payoff schemes have been viewed as involving kickbacks when the defendant has directed that the contracting party's profit be shared with family, friends, or others loyal to the defendant.

741 F.3d at 381-82.

4. When it comes to defining what counts as a "bribe" within the meaning of *Skilling*, lower courts followed *Skilling*'s suggestion and turned to case law involving other corruption statutes for guidance. And we will see in Chapter 6, those statutes generally require a *quid pro quo*—a trade of public decision-making for private gain. Jacob Eisler, *McDonnell* and Anti-Corruption's Last Stand, 50 U.C. Davis L. Rev. 1619, 1631 (2017). Thus, in United States v. Ring, 706 F.3d 460 (D.C. Cir. 2013), the D.C. Circuit looked to the Hobbs Act to decide that, at least outside the campaign contribution context, the *quid pro quo* arrangement need not be explicit. And it looked to the federal bribery statute to decide that the mere offer of something of value with the intent to influence an official act is enough for honest services fraud; the official does not have "to agree to actually complete a corrupt exchange." Id. at 467. As we will see in Chapter 6, the Hobbs Act cases try to screen out "normal" transactions, like an elected official's appointment of a big campaign contributor to official office (so long as there wasn't an "abnormal" explicit buy-sell arrangement). Should mail fraud law strive to do the same? The Second Circuit, too, found its Hobbs Act cases helpful in deciding that the "official act" envisioned by honest service fraud need not have been pre-specified and might simply entail the exercise of influence "as opportunities arise." United States v. Rosen, 716 F.3d 691 (2d Cir. 2013). Yet, as we will also see in Chapter 6, the Court's idiosyncratic and possibly provisional use of other statutory frameworks in McDonnell v. United States, 136 S. Ct. 2355 (2016), to inform the honest services law has required reconsideration of some of this lower court case law.

The questions that were kicking around in the Circuits before *Skilling* remain. To what extent should state law drive the analysis of the duty owed by a public official, particularly when, like a great many state and local officials, she is part-time? The Eleventh Circuit has reasoned that "[p]ublic officials inherently owe a fiduciary duty to the public to make governmental decisions in the public's best interest," United States v. Nelson, 712 F.3d 498, 509 (11th Cir. 2013) — an approach not necessarily tethered to state law. Other courts seem to disagree. See United States v. Grace, 568 F. App'x. 344, 348-49 (5th Cir. 2014) ("In order to convict for the federal crime of honest services fraud under §1346, the government must prove that the conduct of a state official breached a duty respecting the provision of services owed to that official's employer under state law.") Which approach makes more sense?

Expect more judicial and, perhaps, legislative reactions to *Skilling* and *McDonnell.* But regardless, there is no question that undisclosed conflicts of interests, no matter how potentially detrimental to a principal's interest, cannot by themselves support a federal fraud prosecution anymore. Is that good or bad?

5. Prosecutors may respond to *Skilling* the way they responded to *McNally*: by trying to reframe targeted schemes as depriving a victim of "property" rather than honest services. Consider the facts in United States v. Henry, 29 F.3d 112 (3d Cir. 1994):

> Between 1986 and 1988, Thomas Henry was the Comptroller of the Delaware River Joint Toll Bridge Commission (the "Commission"). The Commission, a bi-state agency, operates and maintains twenty-one bridges spanning the Delaware River between New Jersey and Pennsylvania. Among these bridges are seven toll bridges that generate more than ten million dollars in revenue annually.

> The Commission is governed by ten Commissioners, five of whom are appointed by the Governor of New Jersey and confirmed by the New Jersey Senate and five of whom represent Pennsylvania's Governor, Treasurer, Auditor General and Transportation Secretary. Mowry Mike, Pennsylvania's Executive Deputy Auditor General, served as Auditor General Donald Bailey's representative on the Commission between 1986 and 1988. Mike also was a political operative and campaign fund-raiser for Bailey during his unsuccessful runs in 1986 for the Democratic nomination for the United States Senate and in 1988 for re-election as Auditor General.

> The charges in the indictment were based on Henry's and Mike's alleged corruption of the process by which banks were chosen to be the depositories of the Commission's toll bridge revenues. The Commission invested the money in short-term certificates of deposit at banks selected through competitive bidding. As the Commission's Comptroller, Henry was responsible for this process and, according to the indictment, had "a fiduciary obligation to deal with Commission funds and other public money in a forthright and honest fashion." He would notify interested banks that the Commission had money it wished to deposit and that they could submit confidential bids to him in writing or by telephone by a certain deadline. After the deadline passed, the funds would be deposited with the bank meeting the Commission's financial requirements that offered the highest interest rate on the certificates of deposit.

According to the indictment, on ten occasions Henry disclosed bid information to Mike and another individual in the Auditor General's office, who in turn disclosed it to a representative of one bank, Bank A. Bank A was thus allegedly able to narrowly outbid the other banks by offering a slightly higher rate of interest and, as a result, received deposits of $34,278,000 in Commission funds. In return, representatives of Bank A allegedly afforded Mike expedited handling on a $50,000 car loan and contributed more than $10,000 to various political campaigns, including Auditor General Bailey's Senate campaign, in which Mike was involved.

Id. at 112-13.

In the wake of *McNally*, and because the conduct predated the passage of §1346, the government could not charge Henry and Mike with depriving the public of honest services. Were the same scenario to happen now, after *Skilling*, could the government charge them under §1346? In the actual case, the government argued that the defendants had defrauded the banks that competed with Bank A of their property interest in a "fair bidding opportunity." The Third Circuit rejected this theory, finding that although "each bidding bank's chance of receiving property—the deposits if its bid were accepted—was, at least in part, dependent on the condition that the bidding process would be fair," this condition was "not a traditionally recognized, enforceable property right." 29 F.3d at 115. Because it had not been charged in the indictment, the Circuit rejected the government's argument that "Henry's and Mike's scheme also defrauded the Commission of its confidential business information and the right to control how its money was invested." Id. at 114. Had that theory been charged, would it have been proper then, or now?

See also United States v. Post, 950 F. Supp. 2d 519, 539 (S.D.N.Y. 2013) ("suggesting that, had government charged it, intangible property loss could have been [the city]'s right to control its assets on the basis of fair and disinterested information"). If prosecutors and lower courts are free to respond along these lines to Supreme Court limitations on mail fraud doctrine, can that Court ever do more than simply channel doctrinal development? For the recent state of play, see Brette M. Tannenbaum, Note, Framing the Right: Using Theories of Intangible Property to Target Honest Services After *Skilling*, 112 Colum. L. Rev. 359 (2012).

D.   JURISDICTION—MAILINGS AND WIRE COMMUNICATIONS

We have come a long way from the early days of the mail fraud statute, when courts often restricted chargeable frauds to those necessarily dependent on the mails. But the need to prove a mailing or wire element in the offense remains. The following cases illustrate the limited constraint this factor continues to exert, proving how far we have moved toward a general "federal fraud" statute. If appellate courts are not closely supervising the nexus between a fraud and a mailing or telephone call, we should not expect a jury to give the matter much attention in its fact-finding. A defense lawyer will not likely get far with the jury by arguing: "OK, perhaps the evidence against my client does suggest a scheme to defraud. But the important thing, I submit, is that none of the charged mailings has the connection to the scheme that the law requires."

Schmuck v. United States
489 U.S. 705 (1988)

Justice BLACKMUN delivered the opinion of the Court.

I

In August 1983, petitioner Wayne T. Schmuck, a used-car distributor, was indicted in the United States District Court for the Western District of Wisconsin on 12 counts of mail fraud, in violation of 18 U.S.C. §§1341 and 1342.

The alleged fraud was a common and straightforward one. Schmuck purchased used cars, rolled back their odometers, and then sold the automobiles to Wisconsin retail dealers for prices artificially inflated because of the low-mileage readings. These unwitting car dealers, relying on the altered odometer figures, then resold the cars to customers, who in turn paid prices reflecting Schmuck's fraud. To complete the resale of each automobile, the dealer who purchased it from Schmuck would submit a title-application form to the Wisconsin Department of Transportation on behalf of his retail customer. The receipt of a Wisconsin title was a prerequisite for completing the resale; without it, the dealer could not transfer title to the customer and the customer could not obtain Wisconsin tags. The submission of the title-application form supplied the mailing element of each of the alleged mail frauds.

Before trial, Schmuck moved to dismiss the indictment on the ground that the mailings at issue—the submissions of the title-application forms by the automobile dealers—were not in furtherance of the fraudulent scheme and, thus, did not satisfy the mailing element of the crime of mail fraud. . . .

II

"The federal mail fraud statute does not purport to reach all frauds, but only those limited instances in which the use of the mails is a part of the execution of the fraud, leaving all other cases to be dealt with by appropriate state law." Kann v. United States, 323 U.S. 88, 95 (1944). To be part of the execution of the fraud, however, the use of the mails need not be an essential element of the scheme. Pereira v. United States, 347 U.S. 1, 8 (1954). It is sufficient for the mailing to be "incident to an essential part of the scheme," or "a step in [the] plot." Badders v. United States, 240 U.S. 391, 394 (1916).

Schmuck, relying principally on this Court's decisions in *Kann, supra,* Parr v. United States, 363 U.S. 370 (1960), and United States v. Maze, 414 U.S. 395 (1974), argues that mail fraud can be predicated only on a mailing that affirmatively assists the perpetrator in carrying out his fraudulent scheme. The mailing element of the offense, he contends, cannot be satisfied by a mailing, such as those at issue here, that is routine and innocent in and of itself, and that, far from furthering the execution of the fraud, occurs after the fraud has come to fruition, is merely tangentially related to the fraud, and is counterproductive in that it creates a "paper trail" from which the fraud may be discovered. We disagree both with this characterization of the mailings in the present case and with this description of the applicable law.

We begin by considering the scope of Schmuck's fraudulent scheme. Schmuck was charged with devising and executing a scheme to defraud Wisconsin retail automobile customers who based their decisions to purchase certain automobiles at least in part on the low-mileage readings provided by the tampered odometers. This was a fairly large-scale operation. Evidence at trial indicated that Schmuck had employed a man known only as "Fred" to turn back the odometers on about 150 different cars. Schmuck then marketed these cars to a number of dealers, several of whom he dealt with on a consistent basis over a period of about 15 years. Indeed, of the 12 automobiles that are the subject of the counts of the indictment, 5 were sold to "P and A Sales," and 4 to "Southside Auto." Thus, Schmuck's was not a "one-shot" operation in which he sold a single car to an isolated dealer. His was an ongoing fraudulent venture. A rational jury could have concluded that the success of Schmuck's venture depended upon his continued harmonious relations with, and good reputation among, retail dealers, which in turn required the smooth flow of cars from the dealers to their Wisconsin customers.

Under these circumstances, we believe that a rational jury could have found that the title-registration mailings were part of the execution of the fraudulent scheme, a scheme which did not reach fruition until the retail dealers resold the cars and effected transfers of title. Schmuck's scheme would have come to an abrupt halt if the dealers either had lost faith in Schmuck or had not been able to resell the cars obtained from him. These resales and Schmuck's relationships with the retail dealers naturally depended on the successful passage of title among the various parties. Thus, although the registration-form mailings may not have contributed directly to the duping of either the retail dealers or the customers, they were necessary to the passage of title, which in turn was essential to the perpetuation of Schmuck's scheme. As noted earlier, a mailing that is "incident to an essential part of the scheme," satisfies the mailing element of the mail fraud offense. The mailings here fit this description. . . .

Once the full flavor of Schmuck's scheme is appreciated, the critical distinctions between this case and the three cases in which this Court has delimited the reach of the mail fraud statute — *Kann, Parr,* and *Maze* — are readily apparent. The defendants in *Kann* were corporate officers and directors accused of setting up a dummy corporation through which to divert profits into their own pockets. As part of this fraudulent scheme, the defendants caused the corporation to issue two checks payable to them. The defendants cashed these checks at local banks, which then mailed the checks to the drawee banks for collection. This Court held that the mailing of the cashed checks to the drawee banks could not supply the mailing element of the mail fraud charges. The defendants' fraudulent scheme had reached fruition. "It was immaterial to them, or to any consummation of the scheme, how the bank which paid or credited the check would collect from the drawee bank." 323 U.S. at 94.

In *Parr,* several defendants were charged, *inter alia,* with having fraudulently obtained gasoline and a variety of other products and services through the unauthorized use of a credit card issued to the school district which employed them. The mailing element of the mail fraud charges in *Parr* was purportedly satisfied when the oil company which issued the credit card mailed invoices to the school district for payment, and when the district mailed payment in the form of a check. Relying on *Kann,* this Court held that these mailings were not in execution of the scheme as required by the statute because it was immaterial to the defendants how the oil company went about collecting its payment. 363 U.S. at 393.

Later, in *Maze,* the defendant allegedly stole his roommate's credit card, headed south on a winter jaunt, and obtained food and lodging at motels along the route by placing the charges on the stolen card. The mailing element of the mail fraud charge was supplied by the fact that the defendant knew that each motel proprietor would mail an invoice to the bank that had issued the credit card, which in turn would mail a bill to the card owner for payment. The Court found that these mailings could not support mail fraud charges because the defendant's scheme had reached fruition when he checked out of each motel. The success of his scheme in no way depended on the mailings; they merely determined which of his victims would ultimately bear the loss.

The title-registration mailings at issue here served a function different from the mailings in *Kann, Parr,* and *Maze.* The intrabank mailings in *Kann* and the credit card invoice mailings in *Parr* and *Maze* involved little more than post-fraud accounting among the potential victims of the various schemes, and the long-term success of the fraud did not turn on which of the potential victims bore the ultimate loss. Here, in contrast, a jury rationally could have found that Schmuck by no means was indifferent to the fact of who bore the loss. The mailing of the title-registration forms was an essential step in the successful passage of title to the retail purchasers. Moreover, a failure of this passage of title would have jeopardized Schmuck's relationship of trust and goodwill with the retail dealers upon whose unwitting cooperation his scheme depended. Schmuck's reliance on our prior cases limiting the reach of the mail fraud statute is simply misplaced.

To the extent that Schmuck would draw from these previous cases a general rule that routine mailings that are innocent in themselves cannot supply the mailing element of the mail fraud offense, he misapprehends this Court's precedents. . . .

We also reject Schmuck's contention that mailings that someday may contribute to the uncovering of a fraudulent scheme cannot supply the mailing element of the mail fraud offense. The relevant question at all times is whether the mailing is part of the execution of the scheme as conceived by the perpetrator at the time, regardless of whether the mailing later, through hindsight, may prove to have been counterproductive and return to haunt the perpetrator of the fraud. The mail fraud statute includes no guarantee that the use of the mails for the purpose of executing a fraudulent scheme will be risk free. Those who use the mails to defraud proceed at their peril.

For these reasons, we agree with the Court of Appeals that the mailings in this case satisfy the mailing element of the mail fraud offenses. . . .

Justice SCALIA, with whom Justice BRENNAN, Justice MARSHALL, and Justice O'CONNOR join, dissenting. . . .

The purpose of the mail fraud statute is "to prevent the post office from being used to carry [fraudulent schemes] into effect." Durland v. United States, 161 U.S. 306, 314 (1896); Parr v. United States, 363 U.S. 370, 389 (1960). The law does not establish a general federal remedy against fraudulent conduct, with use of the mails as the jurisdictional hook, but reaches only "those limited instances in which the use of the mails is *a part of the execution of the fraud*, leaving all other cases to be dealt with by appropriate state law." Kann v. United States, 323 U.S. 88, 95 (1944) (emphasis added). In other words, it is mail fraud, not mail and fraud, that incurs liability. This federal statute is not violated by a fraudulent scheme in which, at some point, a mailing happens to occur—nor even by one in which a mailing predictably and necessarily occurs. The mailing must be in furtherance of the fraud. . . .

Nor can the force of our cases be avoided by combining all of the individual transactions into a single scheme, and saying, as the Court does, that if the dealers' mailings obtaining title for each retail purchaser had not occurred then the dealers would have stopped trusting petitioner for future transactions. (That conclusion seems to me a non sequitur, but I accept it for the sake of argument.) This establishes, at most, that the scheme could not technically have been consummated if the mechanical step of the mailings to obtain conveyance of title had not occurred. But we have held that the indispensability of such mechanical mailings, not strictly in furtherance of the fraud, is not enough to invoke the statute. . . .

NOTES AND QUESTIONS

1. In *Schmuck*, the Court focused on the scope of the defendant's operation. And it distinguished *Maze*—its prior foray into the mailing nexus—by framing the horrible roommate's conduct in the earlier case as a series of discrete schemes, each of which ended when he checked out of each motel. What would the result be were facts like those in *Maze* to arise in a case after *Schmuck* and were the government to frame the conduct as a single comprehensive scheme to fraudulently stay at motels for free? Would the mailings in this new case still be considered "post-fraud"? Indeed, was the allegation of the scope of the fraud in *Schmuck* simply a purely formalistic way around the holding in *Maze*?

2. *Schmuck* also adopts a subjective standard whereby whether the mailing is in furtherance of the fraud depends on the defendant's expectation regarding events in the future. To what extent does a subjective standard allow the government to pitch to the jury what otherwise might seem a one-shot discrete fraud that involved a post-fraud mailing as actually the beginning of a long-term scheme? To what extent does this approach allow the government to charge a fraud that would otherwise be time-barred, by claiming that the scheme encompassed mailings that would occur after the primary goal of the fraud had been completed? See, e.g., United States v. Boisture, 563 F.3d 295 (7th Cir. 2009).

3. A sustained fraud might offer prosecutors a large selection of qualifying mailings from which to choose—each of which can form the basis of a mail fraud count and perhaps provide venue. In United States v. Hebshie, 549 F.3d 30 (1st Cir. 2008), for example, the First Circuit explained how each letter among the "'criss-cross of mailings that would reasonably be expected when false claims are submitted to insurance companies, are processed, and are ultimately paid'" could satisfy the statutory mailing requirement. Id. at 36 (quoting United States v. Morrow, 39 F.3d 1228, 1237 (1st Cir. 1994)). For a sense of how a fraud that involves a geographically broad range of mailings or wire communications creates venue in a broad range of districts, see United States v. Lange, 834 F.3d 58 (2d Cir. 2016); see also Jack E. Robinson, The Federal Mail and Wire Fraud Statutes: Correct Standards for Determining Jurisdiction and Venue, 44 Willamette L. Rev. 479, 480 (2008) ("My review of virtually all of the reported Supreme Court and courts of

appeals mail and wire fraud decisions spanning the past 60 years leads to the inescapable conclusion that the federal judiciary allows federal prosecutors far too much leeway when it comes to determining whether a mail or wire fraud prosecution even belongs in federal court to begin with or, for that matter, whether it belongs in a particular district (often chosen by federal prosecutors because it is more convenient for the prosecution team and less convenient—and much more costly—for the defendant).").

4. Although *Schmuck* has led federal courts to be more flexible as to the nature of the nexus between the fraud and a mailing or wire transmission—see United States v. Cacho-Bonilla, 404 F.3d 84, 91 (1st Cir. 2005) ("The courts have generously construed the 'furtherance' requirement.")—there are still reversals, including at least one in a recent high-profile case. See Greg Burns, "Kansas Enron" Case Stirs Wrath; In Topeka Class Warfare Simmers Just Below the Surface as Former Utility Executives Go on Trial, Chi. Trib., June 19, 2005, at C1. In United States v. Lake, 472 F.3d 1247 (10th Cir. 2007), the government claimed that two executives from Kansas's largest public utility, Westar Energy, "had conducted a far-reaching scheme to milk the company for all they could through a pattern of fraud and deceit." Id. at 1249. The Court of Appeals overturned the convictions because the charged mailings (reports to the SEC) were both required by law and accurate. In the course of its opinion, the court in *Lake* discussed an early decision by the Supreme Court, Parr v. United States, 363 U.S. 370 (1960), on the necessary relationship between the fraud and the mailing.

> The scheme in [*Parr*] was the misappropriation of school-district funds for the personal benefit of the defendants. The mailings, including "letters, tax statements, checks and receipts," were all "legally compelled mailings" related to the assessment and collection of taxes by the school district. Id. at 389. The taxes collected, of course, were the source of the funds that were then misappropriated. There could be no doubt that the collection of tax money was necessary to accomplish the defendants' scheme; after all, if no taxes were collected, there would be no money to misappropriate. Nevertheless, in setting aside the convictions the Court wrote:
>
> > [W]e think it cannot be said that mailings made or caused to be made under the imperative command of duty imposed by state law are criminal under the federal mail fraud statute, even though some of those who are so required to do the mailing for the District plan to steal, when or after received, some indefinite part of its moneys.

Mail req. by law

United States v. Lake, 472 F.3d at 1256 (quoting *Parr*, 363 U.S. at 391-92).[*] Is there anything in the text or history of the mail fraud statute that justifies

---

[*] [Editors' Note: For the backstory to *Parr*, and the role of then-Senator Lyndon Johnson in getting reversal of his political ally's conviction, see Robert A. Caro, The Years of Lyndon Johnson: The Passage of Power 55-56 (2012).]

the seemingly outcome-determinative role given to the fact that the mailings in question were required by law to be sent?

5. Before *Skilling*, at least one court suggested that scrutiny of the mailing or wire element may also be a way to rein in "honest services" mail fraud prosecutions. In United States v. Turner, 551 F.3d 657 (7th Cir. 2008), an Illinois state official (Turner) responsible for supervising a maintenance staff assisted a group of janitors in their fraudulent scheme to get paid for hours they did not work. The charged wire transmission was the direct deposit of two of the janitors' inflated paychecks. Turner argued "that this use of the interstate wires was a regular part of the janitors' employment, unrelated to, and therefore not 'in furtherance of,' their fraudulent scheme." Id. at 667. The Court of Appeals rejected the argument, with a caveat:

> Turner argues that if the direct deposit of a paycheck can satisfy the use of the wires element of wire fraud, then every employee who commits an act of malfeasance on the job and is paid by direct deposit will be guilty of wire fraud, and the reach of the statute will be unlimited. If the conduct at issue involved an honest services fraud alone —not a money or property fraud—we might share this concern. That is, if a fiduciary breach (or other act of employee dishonesty) plus a paycheck directly deposited (or mailed, for that matter) were enough for liability under §1346's alternative definition of "scheme to defraud," then the federal mail and wire-fraud statutes would potentially reach a vast array of fiduciary and employee misconduct otherwise governed only by state law.
>
> In contrast, here, as we have noted, the evidence established not a deprivation of honest services only but a theft by fraud of money or property. The whole point of the janitors' scheme—the "money or property" object of their scheme to defraud—was to obtain falsely inflated salaries. Turner provided the supervisory cover for this money-for-nothing scheme. That some of the fraudulently obtained wages were paid by way of direct deposit supplies the "use of the wires" element necessary to make this a federal wire fraud.

551 F.3d at 667-68.

Stricter scrutiny of the nexus between a mailing or wire communication and a fraudulent scheme would obviously provide a way to limit the government's strategic use of mailings to create venue, multiply the number of counts in an indictment, and perhaps extend the statute of limitations. To what extent ought such scrutiny be used as a means of limiting the government's ability to pursue certain kinds of frauds, i.e., those in which the charged deprivation is of "honest services"? See United States v. Tavares, 844 F.3d 46, 61 (1st Cir. 2016) (in alleged scheme of agency officials to appoint job candidates favored by state legislators in exchange for legislative action favoring the agency, rejection letters sent to unsuccessful applicants were not "in furtherance" because they "furthered neither the perpetration nor the perpetuation of the scheme").

6. Can honest services fraud go global? In United States v. Giffen, 326 F. Supp. 2d 497 (S.D.N.Y. 2004), the defendant was alleged to have made more than $80 million in payments to senior officials of the Republic of Kazakhstan and was indicted for violation of the Foreign Corrupt Practices Act (FCPA), mail and wire fraud, money laundering, and tax evasion. While allowing the FCPA counts to go forward, the district court dismissed the fraud counts. It explained:

> The concept of the Kazakh people's intangible right to honest services by their government officials requires definition. See United States v. Brumley, 116 F.3d 728, 734 (5th Cir. 1997) (noting that, under Section 1346, a court must first decide the duty owed by a defendant). The indictment does not allege any facts or law regarding the meaning of honest services by Kazakh officials to the Kazakh people. The Government's argument that "the notion that government officials owe a duty to provide honest services to the public is not so idiosyncratically American as to have no application at all to Kazakhstan" is inapposite and begs the question. In a jarring disconnect, the Government acknowledges that "Kazakhstan has sought to derail the investigation and eventual prosecution of this matter by numerous appeals to officials . . . in the executive branch including . . . [the] Departments of State and Justice." Implicit in the Government's observation is the suggestion that Kazakhstan itself is unable to define "honest services" within its own polity.
>
> In effect, the Government urges that American notions of honesty in public service developed over two centuries be engrafted on Kazakh jurisprudence. "While admittedly some . . . countries do not take their [anti-corruption] responsibilities seriously, the correct answer to such a situation is not the extraterritorial application of United States law but rather cooperation between [the appropriate] home and host country . . . authorities." Rose Hall, Ltd. v. Chase Manhattan Overseas Banking Corp., 576 F. Supp. 107, 164 (D. Del. 1983). "An argument in favor of the export of United States law represents not only a form of legal imperialism but also embodies the essence of sanctimonious chauvinism." [Id. at] 163. While well intentioned, the Government's suggestion that American legal standards be exported to Kazakhstan is simply a bridge too far.

326 F. Supp. 2d at 507.

To the extent you agree with the court's reasoning, would you change your position if the Kazakh government had supported the prosecution? What if the case involved bribes paid to officials of a different foreign country? Note that the analysis can be different when the fraud is on the United Nations. See United States v. Bahel, 662 F.3d 610, 632 (2d Cir. 2011) ("*Giffen* does not dictate the outcome of this case, not only because this Court has not itself so construed Section 1346, but also because, unlike in *Giffen*, the conduct at issue in this case took place within the territorial United States, and the victim was—not a foreign government's citizens—but the United Nations, an organization headquartered in the United States, entitled to defendant's honest services in the United States, and receiving its largest financial contributions from the United States").

INTER- VERSUS INTRA-STATE COMMUNICATIONS

In United States v. Photogrammetric Data Services, 259 F.3d 229 (4th Cir. 2001), the Fourth Circuit explained how, in the wake of 1994 legislation, the mail fraud statute covers, in addition to mailings through the U.S. Postal Service, use of private interstate delivery services, regardless of whether the items are delivered out of state:

> Prior to 1994, the mail fraud statute criminalized the use of the United States Postal Service to execute a fraudulent scheme, but had no application to private or commercial interstate carriers. Then, as now, the statute made no distinction between intrastate and interstate mailings, and it had been extended to both as a proper exercise of the Postal Power.
>
> In 1994, however, Congress broadened the application of the mail fraud statute to also criminalize "depositing or causing to be deposited any matter or thing whatever to be sent or delivered by any *private or commercial interstate carrier*" for the purpose of carrying out a scheme or artifice to defraud. Violent Crime Control and Law Enforcement Act of 1994, Pub. L. No. 103-322, §250006, 108 Stat. 1796, 2087 (1994). Although the amendment was added pursuant to the Commerce Clause power, and was obviously intended to extend the mail fraud statute to reach those defendants who use commercial interstate carriers such as UPS and Federal Express in lieu of the United States Postal Service, Congress added no distinction which would serve to exempt from the statute's intended reach intrastate mailings handled by such private or commercial interstate carriers.
>
> We believe that the unambiguous language of current §1341 criminalizes all mailings in furtherance of a fraudulent scheme if the mailings are placed with either the United States Postal Service or with other private or commercial mail delivery services which operate interstate, regardless of whether any particular mailing actually crosses state lines. Had Congress intended to criminalize only interstate deliveries by such interstate private or commercial carriers, and thereby create a different jurisdictional requirement when such carriers are used in lieu of the United States Postal Service, it could easily have done so. For example, the drafters need only have inserted the words "interstate" or "across state lines" immediately after the phrase "sent or delivered." Instead, Congress elected to use virtually identical language as that dealing with the use of the United States mail. . . . Consequently, we find no indication that Congress, in amending a statute which criminalizes depositing things with the United States Postal Service for delivery, interstate or intrastate, intended to limit the extension to private and commercial interstate carriers for only interstate deliveries. On the contrary, we think it obvious that

Congress intended to prohibit the use of private and commercial interstate carriers to further fraudulent activity in the same way such use of the United States mail had long been prohibited.

259 F.3d at 247-48. Do you think that this expansion of the mail fraud statute is within Congress's powers, presumably its Commerce Clause authority?

The analysis appears to be different for wire communications, as the following case explains.

United States v. Phillips
376 F. Supp. 2d 6 (D. Mass. 2005)

PONSOR, District Judge . . .

At trial, the government took the position that, in order to satisfy the elements of this offense, it was *not* necessary to present evidence that the pertinent wire communications themselves actually crossed state lines, as long as the communications (whether interstate or intrastate) traveled via an "instrument of an integrated system of interstate commerce," such as the interstate phone system. . . .

Having now had time to consider the matter further, the court has concluded that the defendants' view of the matter presents the more accurate picture of the law. . . .

In reaching this conclusion, the court has relied primarily on three considerations.

First, the plain words of the wire fraud statute, 18 U.S.C. §1343, extend only to situations where the defendant "transmits or causes to be transmitted by means of wire, radio or television communication in interstate or foreign commerce, any writings, signs, signals, pictures, or sounds" for the purpose of executing an artifice or scheme to defraud. No reference is made in the text to mere "use" of the mechanisms of interstate commerce, as is the case with other statutes. The transmission itself must be "in interstate or foreign commerce."

Second, Congress on two occasions has considered but declined to enact amendments to 18 U.S.C. §1343 extending the law to cover simple use of an interstate instrumentality. The Crime Prevention Act of 1989, S. 327, 101st Cong. §4 (1989) and the Crime Prevention Act of 1995, S. 1495, 104th Cong. §1102 (1995), both contained amendments that would have changed the language of the statute to include the use of a facility of interstate commerce. Specifically, the bills each would have amended 18 U.S.C. §1343 by:

striking "transmits or causes to be transmitted by means of wire, radio, or television communication in interstate or foreign commerce, any writings, signs, signals, pictures, or sounds" and inserting "uses or causes to be used any facility of interstate or foreign commerce."

The bills would also have changed the heading of §1343 from "Fraud by wire, radio, or television" to "Fraud by use of facility of interstate commerce." Although of course the precise inference to be drawn from Congress' inaction is not clear, this history seems to suggest that Congress was unwilling to take the step that the government would have the court take in this case.

Third, in United States v. Darby, 37 F.3d 1059 (4th Cir. 1994), the Court of Appeals held that a prosecution under 18 U.S.C. §875(c), for transmitting a threatening communication, requires that the communication actually cross state lines. The court held that under that statute "the Government was required to prove that Darby's phone call crossed a state line" to meet the "jurisdictional peg on which to hang the federal prosecution." Id. at 1067. The language of §875(c) requires that the defendant "transmit in interstate or foreign commerce" a communication containing a threat. The text, lacking any reference to "instrumentality" or other similar language, is substantively identical to that of 18 U.S.C. §1343.

In reaching its conclusion, the court is mindful of the First Circuit's ruling in United States v. Gilbert, 181 F.3d 152 (1st Cir. 1999), relied upon by the government, which held that an intrastate communication sent via an interstate instrumentality was sufficient to support a conviction under 18 U.S.C. §844 (e). That statute, however — unlike both §875 (c) and §1343 — makes explicit use of "instrumentality" language, stating: "Whoever, through the use of the mail, telephone, telegraph or other *instrument* of interstate or foreign commerce . . . willfully makes any threat" is guilty of a crime. 18 U.S.C. §844(e) (emphasis supplied). The contrast in this language to the wire fraud statute underlines the weakness of the government's position here. . . .

It is obvious that Congress has, at times, chosen to make criminal the mere improper use of an instrumentality of interstate commerce; at other times, it has acted more narrowly, making criminal only actual transmissions that themselves occur in interstate or foreign commerce. Although the issue is not crystal clear, the better view is that, in crafting §1343, Congress opted for a narrower criminal footprint. As such, the government was required to prove beyond a reasonable doubt that the pertinent wire transmissions actually crossed state lines. . . .

WIRE-FRAUD JURISDICTION

One can't help but wonder whether Congress will continue to permit this technical detail to derail wire fraud prosecutions. The issue itself has come up in other contexts, drawing congressional response. For example, under an early version of 18 U.S.C. §2252A, which criminalizes receiving child pornography that has been mailed or transported "in interstate commerce," most Courts of Appeals presumed that pictures transported over the Internet had crossed state lines. Nevertheless, in United States v. Schaefer, 501 F.3d 1197 (10th Cir. 2007), the Tenth Circuit rejected that presumption and concluded that the prosecution must prove that the particular image crossed state lines. Congress quickly reacted, amending the statute so that "such an assumption will be tenable in future cases." United States v. Swenson, 335 F. App'x. 751, 753 (10th Cir. 2009) (Gorsuch, J.).

E.   AN ALTERNATIVE VISION OF LAW DEVELOPMENT

We have seen several actors playing critical roles in the development of mail and wire fraud law: Congress, which first enacted the statutes and then responded to decisions by the Supreme Court; the Supreme Court, which responded to legislative enactments, and to some extent to lower court decisions; and, of course, the prosecutors who picked the cases and decided to deploy innovative theories. For the last 40 years, the rough outline of the game has been: prosecutorial innovation, lower court acceptance, Supreme Court intervention, congressional overturning of the Court's decision. Whether *Skilling* sparks a new cycle remains to be seen. Is there anything wrong with this? The following excerpt from an article by Dan Kahan considers federal criminal law generally; yet it seems particularly pertinent to the peculiar legislative dynamic explored in this chapter.

Dan M. Kahan, Is *Chevron** Relevant to Federal Criminal Law?
110 Harv. L. Rev. 469 (1996)

I.   THE REAL BASELINE: FEDERAL COMMON LAW CRIMES

Who makes federal criminal law? The standard answer is Congress. . . .

---

* [Editors' Note: *Chevron* is one of the most influential administrative law cases decided by the Supreme Court. The case involved the Environmental Protection Agency's interpretation of regulations under the Clean Air Act. In the opinion, the Court outlined a two-part analysis to review an agency's construction of a statute it was delegated to administer. "First, always, is the question whether Congress has directly spoken to the precise question at issue. If the intent of Congress is clear, that is the end of the matter; for the court, as well as the agency, must give effect to the unambiguously expressed intent of Congress. If, however, the court determines Congress has not directly addressed the precise question at issue, the court does not simply impose its own construction on the statute, as would be

But the proposition that federal crimes are "solely creatures of statute" is a truth so partial that it is nearly a lie. To be sure, Congress must speak before a person can be convicted of a federal crime, but it needn't say much of anything when it does. Most federal crimes—including RICO, mail fraud, and theft—derive from exceedingly open-textured statutes. These statutes are brought into contact with the real world only through the mediation of intricate judge-made doctrines that specify what these laws actually prohibit. . . .

A.   FEDERAL CRIMINAL LAW AS A COMMON LAW-MAKING SYSTEM . . .

Delegation—whether express or implied, whether to agencies or courts—is a strategy for maximizing Congress's policymaking influence in the face of constraints on its power to make law. The most dramatic of these constraints is political. The difficulty of generating consensus on politically charged issues can easily stifle legislation, particularly criminal legislation. In such circumstances, members of Congress are likely to avail themselves of the "virtues of vagueness," drafting statutes in terms sufficiently general that legislators on both sides of a disputed issue can "tell [their] constituents that [they] obtained language to protect them" while leaving it to courts "to devise an interpretation of what 'congressional intent' was."

Other constraints on Congress's lawmaking are more mundane but equally powerful. They include the limited time that members of Congress have to satisfy the demands of important constituents before they must stand for re-election. Criminal law-making, in this respect, confronts members of Congress with high opportunity costs: time spent enacting criminal legislation necessarily comes at the expense of time that could be spent enacting legislation sought by small, highly organized interest groups, which are more likely than the public at large to reward legislators for benefits conferred and to punish them for disabilities imposed. Again, one solution is highly general (even purely symbolic) criminal legislation, which takes little time to enact and which is likely to be sufficient to satisfy the public's demand for criminal law.

Whenever Congress resorts to general statutory language to reduce the institutional cost of resolving particular issues itself, it necessarily transfers lawmaking responsibility to courts (or prosecutors). The result is a rich tapestry of federal common law, including federal common law crimes. . . .

---

necessary in the absence of an administrative interpretation. Rather, if the statute is silent or ambiguous with respect to the specific issue, the question for the court is whether the agency's answer is based on a permissible construction of the statute." Chevron U.S.A., Inc. v. Natural Resources Defense Council, Inc., 467 U.S. 837, 842-843 (1984).]

By incorporating "fraud" (or its cognates) into a host of important federal criminal statutes—including those defining conspiracy to defraud the United States and mail and wire fraud—Congress did not make law as much as create a void in the law that courts would be obliged to fill.

They have, and with enthusiasm. Early in the life of these statutes (and regularly thereafter), the Supreme Court rejected the suggestion that fraud should be confined to its "common law" meaning (as expansive as that was), to forms of misconduct actionable under state law, or to any particular schedule of wrongs that may have prompted Congress to enact them. Instead, courts were to determine the proper scope of the federal criminal fraud statutes by reference only to the general "evil sought to be remedied.". . .

B.   ONLY COURTS?

The claim that federal criminal law is a system of delegated common law-making is subject to one important qualification. It's true that Congress routinely uses incomplete specification to reduce the practical and political costs of legislating, and it's true that the inevitable consequence of doing so is the diminution of Congress's own role in defining operative rules of criminal law. But it isn't necessarily the case that *all* of the power that Congress gives away ends up being exercised by *courts.* . . . [F]ederal prosecutors, too, end up with a significant share of delegated lawmaking authority. . . .

[P]rosecutors enjoy the *power of initiative.* Federal courts can exercise delegated lawmaking power only incident to their authority to adjudicate actual cases and controversies. . . . [B]ecause individual prosecutors enjoy the power of initiative, it is much more likely that the rules they do urge on courts will be adopted. By paying close attention to the facts of the cases they select as vehicles for novel statutory readings, federal prosecutors can highlight the benefits and suppress the costs of the interpretations that they favor. . . .

Ironically, when courts pay homage to separation of powers by piously denying their own criminal lawmaking power, narrow statutory readings exist only at the mutable sufferance of individual U.S. Attorneys.

C.   AN ASSESSMENT . . .

1. Theoretical Benefits. —The primary advantage of criminal common law-making is its efficiency. Delegated criminal law costs less than legislatively specified criminal law and is more effective to boot. Furthermore, delegated criminal law-making, if properly conducted, poses no threat to the values that strict separation of powers is supposed to promote.

A system of common law crimes is cheaper than a system of legislatively specified crimes because of the generative character of open-textured statutory norms. When treated as delegations of lawmaking authority, RICO, the criminal fraud statutes, and like offenses spawn scores of distinct prohibitions. To achieve the same result without delegation, Congress would have to bear the high practical and political costs of specifying each of these prohibitions itself. Higher cost means reduced output—either of criminal law, or of the other types of legislation that Congress must forgo in order to devote more resources to producing criminal statutes. These are real social costs.

Delegated common law-making also promotes the efficient updating of the criminal code. As markets and technologies change, so do the forms of criminality that feed on them. Keeping up with the advent of new crimes would severely tax Congress's lawmaking resources, and no doubt often exceed them, were Congress itself obliged to specify all operative rules of criminal law. It is much easier for courts to keep the criminal law up to date by simply adapting incompletely specified statutes to new crimes. . . .

A related efficiency associated with delegated common law-making is its power to avoid loopholes. . . .

Delegated common law-making not only reduces the cost of federal criminal law, but also improves its quality. Congress necessarily makes rules in anticipation of future cases. As a result, it lacks full information about how these rules will operate in the real world. Courts, in contrast, perform their delegated lawmaking function in the course of deciding actual cases. Consequently, they see more completely how statutes interact with real world circumstances and with each other, and can use this information to fashion rules of law that fully implement legislative goals and that avoid unforeseen conflicts with other values and policies. Had Congress attempted, for example, to define "property" for the purposes of federal criminal law—either statute-by-statute or generally—it seems unlikely that Congress would have crafted a set of distinctions as context-sensitive, and thus generally sensible, as the ones courts have developed.

Orthodox criminal law theory defends separation of powers not because it is efficient, but primarily because it is thought to be essential to the rule of law and democratic accountability. How does delegated common law-making affect these values? The answer is minimally, at least so long as delegated common law-making is carried out with a modest dose of good sense.

Consider the core rule of law value: "fair warning" or notice. Notice is most important when law is used to mark the boundary between socially desirable and socially undesirable conduct; in negotiating the technical requirements of the tax code or securities laws, for example, actors predictably and legitimately look to law to guide their conduct. But notice is much less important when the law is regulating clearly undesirable conduct; potential offenders don't need the law to tell them that theft or organized criminality is wrong, because ordinary morality suffices.

Indeed, persons who self-consciously search out gaps between common morality and law are engaged in a culpable form of loop-holing, which ambiguity can justly be used to discourage. . . .

Nor is there any necessary tension between delegated common law-making and democracy. To begin, the suggestion that democracy requires confining criminal lawmaking authority to Congress rests on a false premise—namely, that Congress is perfectly able to satisfy the electorate's demand for criminal law. It isn't, because of the practical and political constraints on its lawmaking capacities. The law is likely to be closer in quantity and quality to what the public demands when courts, at the behest of Congress, accept responsibility for updating the law, closing loopholes, and infusing the law with the practical insights of experience.

Even more importantly, the suggestion that it is undemocratic for courts to participate in defining the elements of criminal statutes overlooks the role of federal prosecutors. Through the power of initiative, individual prosecutors have a vital say in determining the content of incompletely specified statutes. Because federal prosecutors are appointed by the President and are accountable to the Attorney General, their participation in constructing a system of federal common law crimes assures that its content will be responsive to public sensibilities—at least in theory.

2. Practical Costs.—But of course, reality is more complicated. Federal criminal law is beset by three distinct pathologies that counteract some of the advantages associated with delegated common law-making.

The first is the limited expertise of federal judges. Although the judiciary's contact with real world facts gives it a lawmaking advantage relative to Congress, the experience of individual judges (particularly at the appellate level) with criminal law remains limited and sporadic. . . .

The costs of limited expertise are highest in the elaboration of statutes that mark the boundary line between socially desirable and socially undesirable behavior. The securities fraud provisions are the best example. Full legislative (or even judicial) specification of these statutes would be infeasible; the wrongful acts that they seek to prohibit are too heterogeneous. At the same time, analysts, arbitrageurs, corporate executives, and market participants must consult the law to guide legitimate economic activity. The track record of courts in resolving this tension has been poor. Misled, in part, by the sensational facts of the cases selected for prosecution, courts have fashioned a body of formless doctrines that create unacceptably high risks of overdeterrence and unfair surprise when applied generally.

The second pathology is judicial dissensus. . . . Differences of opinion on what open-textured criminal statutes *ought* to mean are inevitable in a system comprised of 649 district court judges, who handle over 45,000 criminal cases annually and who are subject to review by twelve distinct courts of appeals. Such conflicts must ultimately be resolved either by the Supreme Court, which then must divert itself from other cases, or by Congress, which then loses the legislative economies associated with implied delegation. Moreover, in the time it takes to straighten matters out, participants in the legal system and society generally must endure the costs that accompany uncertainty over the scope of the law.

The third and final pathology is prosecutorial overreaching. U.S. Attorneys are extraordinarily ambitious and frequently enter electoral politics after leaving office. For this reason, they have strong incentives to use their power while in office to cater to—or to circumvent—local political establishments. The acquiescence of the Department of Justice in such behavior does not demonstrate that the interests of politically ambitious U.S. Attorneys coincide with those of the national electorate. Although nominally subordinate to the Attorney General, U.S. Attorneys enjoy a strong history and culture of independence; for many, disregard of the *United States Attorneys' Manual*—a detailed set of guidelines issued by the Justice Department to guide interpretation of criminal statutes—is a source of pride. The Department, for its part, lacks the adequate political incentives to check individual U.S. Attorneys, especially once they have initiated sensational prosecutions. The result can be an unhealthy distortion in the prosecutor's contribution to delegated criminal law-making. . . .

Individual U.S. Attorneys internalize the political benefits and externalize the practical and human costs of adventurous readings of federal criminal law. The Department of Justice, which should internalize these costs through the President's electoral accountability, lacks the political and organizational wherewithal to combat this form of overreaching. Courts have the power to counteract it through the wise exercise of their common lawmaking power. But they don't, partly because they are weakened by lack of expertise and consensus, and partly because they cede too much of their lawmaking power to individual prosecutors. As a result, federal criminal law is broader and looser than it would be were it aligned with the interests of the national electorate. This agency cost is the most subtle but also the most serious threat to the benefits generated by Congress's delegation of criminal lawmaking power.

3. Overall.—On the whole, the pluses of criminal common law-making probably outweigh the minuses. As draining as the pathologies of this regime are, it seems unlikely that they completely vitiate the immense, systemic advantages of delegation. If we must choose between a system of federal common law crimes and a system of legislatively specified ones, then it probably makes sense to embrace the former.

But are these really the only two alternatives? Is there any way to retool the machinery of federal criminal law-making so as to conserve the positive effects of delegation while eliminating or reducing the negative ones? There is—by *Chevron*izing it.

II.   THE ALTERNATIVE: A FEDERAL ADMINISTRATIVE LAW OF CRIMES

The core of my argument can be stated succinctly. Applying the *Chevron* doctrine would improve the content of federal criminal law by shifting to the Justice Department the delegated lawmaking powers now exercised jointly by courts and individual prosecutors. This transfer of authority would preserve essentially all the benefits associated with delegation and, at the same time, effectively treat all of the pathologies that afflict it. The Justice Department has greater lawmaking expertise than do courts because it comes into contact with all manner of crimes at all stages of the justice system. Its readings are more likely to be uniform than those of courts because it is a single, integrated agency. Finally, the Department is less likely to overreach than are individual U.S. Attorneys because it has less incentive to pander to local interests and is more likely to internalize the costs of unduly broad statutory readings. This Part develops these claims in greater detail. . . .

B.   AN ASSESSMENT . . .

The Justice Department . . . is in fact better situated than courts are to exercise the lawmaking power that Congress implicitly delegates when it enacts incompletely specified criminal statutes. Federal criminal law will be better in content, more legitimate in its origins, and more consistent with the rule of law if it is treated as an administrative lawmaking system rather than as a common law-making one.

1. Chevron and the Efficiency of Delegation. —For starters, *Chevron*izing federal criminal law would conserve essentially all of the benefits associated with implied delegation. Congress enjoys the institutional economies of incomplete specification regardless of whether it's the judiciary or the Justice Department that finishes the task. In addition, the Justice Department, like courts, can update the law more quickly than Congress can, and can use its contact with actual cases to tailor the law to circumstances unforeseen by Congress. . . .

2. Chevron and the Pathologies of Criminal Common Law-Making. — . . . *Chevron*izing federal criminal law would counteract all three [pathologies associated with criminal common law-making].

(a) Expertise. —Transferring delegated lawmaking authority from courts to the Department of Justice would likely avert many of the miscues associated with the judiciary's limited expertise in criminal law. The instrumentalities of the Justice Department handle many times the number of cases that district courts handle. Moreover, the Justice Department has close contact with cases at all stages of development; district courts see only the unusual ones that don't end in plea bargains, and circuit courts only

the even more unusual ones that generate appeals. Because its involvement in criminal law is so much more extensive than that of any court, the Justice Department is more likely to appreciate all the policy implications of a disputed statutory issue. The policymaking insights stemming from such day-to-day regulatory responsibilities provide one of the primary rationales for requiring courts to give agency readings *Chevron* deference.

(b) Uniformity. —The *Chevron*ization of federal criminal law would also solve the problem of inconsistent judicial interpretations. Frequent disagreements are inevitable when 649 district judges, reviewed by twelve separate courts of appeals, are all independently empowered to identify the best readings of ambiguous criminal statutes. The Department of Justice, in contrast, is a single, integrated agency; for *Chevron* purposes, it would speak with a single voice in declaring what incompletely specified statutes mean. Courts would still review these readings under *Chevron*, but courts are much more likely to agree about whether the Justice Department's reading of an ambiguous statute is within the range of permissible interpretations than they are about which particular reading within that range is best. . . .

(c) Prosecutorial Overreaching. —Perhaps the strongest objection to *Chevron*izing federal criminal law is that it would involve institutional self-dealing. How can it be fair to permit the law-enforcer to say what the law is? The whole point of separation of powers, according to this objection, is to exclude the natural biases of prosecutors from law-making and law-interpreting. This anxiety, however, is misplaced: far from making criminal law-making more partisan, *Chevron* would moderate it substantially. . . .

*Chevron*izing federal criminal law would not only transfer lawmaking authority from the judiciary to the executive, but also reallocate it within the executive branch itself. At present, the executive branch influences the formation of federal common law crimes almost entirely through the uncoordinated actions of individual U.S. Attorneys. But under *Chevron*, prosecutorial readings would be entitled to deference only if endorsed and defended in advance by the Justice Department itself. As a result, officials within the Department, and not U.S. Attorneys, would have the final word on how the executive's interpretive lawmaking powers should be exercised.

This shift in responsibility would help counteract prosecutorial overreaching. Distant and largely invisible bureaucrats within the Justice Department lack the incentives that individual U.S. Attorneys have to bend the law to serve purely local interests. In addition, the Department is more likely than are U.S. Attorneys to internalize the social costs of bad readings. Because the Department, through the President, is accountable to the national electorate, it is more likely to be responsive to interests hurt by adventurous readings, particularly readings that discourage socially desirable market activities. The Department also has much more reason to care about the impact of such interpretations on the public fisc.

Accordingly, *Chevron* should make the executive's interpretations of criminal statutes both milder and more consistent with nationwide interests than they are now.

Shifting authority from individual U.S. Attorneys to the Justice Department should reduce the influence of interest groups for the same reasons that shifting power from independent agencies to the President does. The reason that the President is better at resisting interest-group domination than are independent agencies is not that the President typically has better motives than do agency heads; rather, the explanation is Madison's axiom that the influence of factions diminishes as their numbers grow. Because he or she is responsive to a large collection of unruly national constituencies, the President is less likely to be captured by any one of them than is an agency, which typically oversees only a single industry, the members of which are well positioned to influence the relevant congressional oversight committee. . . . Likewise, we should expect the Justice Department to behave more moderately than individual U.S. Attorneys do in construing federal criminal statutes—not because the Department is less subject to interest group pressures, but because it is subject to many more such pressures emanating from a greater variety of sources. . . .

3. Post Hoc Rationalizations. — . . . Permitting courts to approve only those statutory readings defended by the Justice Department in advance of prosecution would prevent courts from siphoning away the executive branch's delegated criminal lawmaking powers. Even more importantly, such an approach would be essential to securing the benefits associated with reallocating power within the executive branch. Without the rule against post hoc rationalizations, courts would be obliged to defer to the litigating positions of individual U.S. Attorneys, who are much more likely than is the Justice Department itself to advance unduly broad readings for short-term political gain.

But there remains an ambiguity about how the rule against post hoc rationalizations should be adapted to federal criminal law. Courts could read it to bar deference only to those interpretations articulated by U.S. Attorneys in the course of prosecutions. Under this weak conception of the rule, the Justice Department proper would retain the power to issue interpretations that would be immediately effective, even in pending cases—an outcome tantamount to retroactive application of those interpretations. But under a stronger view, the rule would treat as post hoc rationalizations all readings issued after the conduct for which the defendant is being prosecuted and would thus make the Justice Department's interpretive law-making purely prospective. . . .

The principal advantage of the weak conception is that it would enhance deterrence. Giving the Justice Department the authority to announce retroactively binding interpretations would discourage offenders from seeking out loopholes in ambiguous criminal statutes.

The advantage of the strong conception is that it would promote rule of law values. Courts necessarily give content to underspecified statutes in the course of applying them. This approach risks denying citizens fair warning, at least when the law is being used to regulate conduct that produces licit utility. The strong conception of the rule against post hoc rationalizations would increase notice because it would give Justice Department readings purely prospective effect.

The strong conception would also reinforce prosecutorial evenhandedness. Although it is less likely to be captured by parochial interests than are individual U.S. Attorneys, the Justice Department would still be too likely to err on the side of excess if allowed to specify rules with retroactive effect. That power would create too strong a temptation to fashion broad readings for the sake of winning particular cases or satisfying transient public demands for retribution. Giving Justice Department readings only prospective deference would immunize the Department's interpretive lawmaking from these distorting influences.

On balance, the stronger conception seems superior. The deterrence gains associated with the weak approach are real but small; indeed, even if the Justice Department is limited to prospective interpretive law-making, criminal administrative law-making is likely to deter just as effectively as criminal common law-making, given the greater speed with which the Justice Department can announce clear statutory interpretations. The rule of law losses associated with the weak conception, in contrast, are substantial and unavoidable. These losses are at the heart of the pathologies that now afflict the federal common law of crimes. The strong conception is preferable, then, because it would allow an administrative law of crimes to combine the legality of full legislative specification with most or all the efficiency of judicial common law-making. . . .

III.   GETTING THERE FROM HERE . . .

Courts can effectively simulate the *Chevron*ization of federal criminal law, consistent with existing precedent, simply by alternating their application of two established canons of statutory interpretation: the *Skidmore* doctrine [based on Skidmore v. Swift & Co., 323 U.S. 134 (1944)], which courts should use to uphold statutory constructions formally defended by the Department of Justice in advance of prosecution; and the rule of lenity, which courts should use to compel narrow interpretations in all other cases. . . .

Now consider the rule of lenity. Lenity is the canon of construction that directs courts to select narrow rather than broad interpretations of ambiguous criminal statutes. The rule is notoriously underenforced. Indeed, its abrogation is a necessary condition of criminal common law-making. Defaulting to the narrowest reasonable reading would render incompletely specified statutes generatively inert, thereby forcing Congress itself to specify all operative rules of criminal law. In effect, the rule of lenity, conventionally understood, is an anti-delegation doctrine. Given the high cost and futility of complete legislative specification of criminal offenses, it's a good thing that courts have traditionally ignored this rule.

But lenity can play a much more salutary role as part of an administrative law of crimes. In such a regime, the court would adopt the narrowest reasonable reading of a criminal statute only when the Department of Justice has failed to give a reasoned justification for a broad reading in advance of prosecution; otherwise, the court would defer to the Department's reading under *Skidmore*. This approach would create appropriate institutional incentives for the Justice Department to engage in reasoned elaboration of criminal statutes. Moreover, lenity in such a regime wouldn't prevent Congress from ceding its lawmaking power through incomplete specification; it would merely assure that the power that Congress gives away is exercised by the executive branch rather than by the judiciary. When combined with *Skidmore*, lenity (like *Chevron*) functions not as an anti-delegation doctrine but as a useful delegation-tracking device. . . .

C. WHAT: REASONED DECISION MAKING, EXPOSED TO PUBLIC VIEW

The value of formality would be high in an administrative law of crimes. Making the Justice Department's interpretations of incompletely specified statutes publicly accessible would promote both deterrence and fair notice. Even more importantly, public exposure of agency reasoning is essential to counteract the political dynamics that lead to prosecutorial overreaching. *Chevron* has the potential to moderate criminal law by shifting lawmaking responsibility from individual U.S. Attorneys, who frequently advance bad statutory readings for political gain, to the Justice Department, which gets much less benefit from such readings and which is much more likely to internalize the costs of them. This effect is accentuated when the Justice Department must justify its broad interpretations in public, for then it knows that it cannot escape being held accountable by interests who oppose such readings.

NOTES AND QUESTIONS

1. In another part of his article, Kahan writes that he would not allow the Justice Department to have interpretive lawmaking power when certain federalism values are at stake—in order to limit the Department's ability

"to substitute federal for local criminal law." How broadly does this caveat sweep when it comes to the application of his proposal to mail fraud law? To the extent his proposal does apply to mail fraud law, is it indeed more attractive than the common-law case development we've explored?

2. Do you agree with Kahan's diagnosis of the judicial lawmaking problem? To what extent does Kahan's proposal reflect normative views about the balance between federal enforcement zeal and restraint? He seems to assume that Main Justice will better internalize the costs of federal prosecutions. Is that necessarily true? To the extent it is true, is that a good thing? For a critique, see Daniel C. Richman, Federal Criminal Law, Congressional Delegation, and Enforcement Discretion, 46 UCLA L. Rev. 757, 803-05 (1999).

3. Another—and quite different—approach would be to use Main Justice to set limits on novel or questionable criminal prosecutions by requiring internal (Main Justice) approval of certain categories of prosecutions that may be especially susceptible to what Kahan calls "adventurous" legal theories. For instance, by internal regulation, Main Justice already must approve criminal civil rights prosecutions (discussed in Chapter 7) and RICO prosecutions (discussed in Chapter 8), and Main Justice originates all antitrust and many tax prosecutions. See Richman, Federal Criminal Law, *supra*, at 804-06 (discussing relative infrequency with which Main Justice approval is required). Perhaps there is an argument to be made that Main Justice should approve all "honest services" fraud prosecutions. But Kahan's proposal is quite different: He would have the Department spell out in advance what theories it would (and hence would not) use in prosecutions under various broad federal laws. Which route do you think is more likely to result in effective restraint on federal prosecutors: (1) requiring internal, private, Main Justice approval before a particular prosecution can go forward, or (2) a public declaration by Main Justice of non-statutory limitations on future prosecutions? With respect to the latter (Kahan's) approach, do you think that the Department of Justice is likely to bind its own hands in any significant way?

5 | Extortion

Extortion is a curious hybrid. Like robbery, it involves wrongful threats to extract money from victims. But unlike robbery, there is a greater degree of consent involved—enough so that care must be taken to ensure that the offense does not cover simple commercial transactions that the "victim" wishes had been on more favorable terms. In federal law, this care must be exercised in a variety of settings, for Congress, while not clearly defining extortion, has fired considerable statutory ammunition at it. The Hobbs Act, 18 U.S.C. §1951, reaches anyone who "obstructs, delays or affects commerce or the movement of any article or commodity in commerce" by extortion; the Travel Act, 18 U.S.C. §1952, reaches anyone who "travels in interstate . . . commerce or uses the mail or any facility in interstate or foreign commerce, with intent to," among other things, promote extortion "in violation of the laws of the State in which committed or of the United States"; and 18 U.S.C. §875(d)—just one of the many extortion provisions in chapter 41 of Title 18—reaches anyone who, "with intent to extort from any person . . . any money or thing of value, transmits in interstate or foreign commerce any communication containing any threat to injure the property or reputation of the addressee or of another . . . or any threat to accuse the addressee or any other person of a crime."

Extortion is defined in the Hobbs Act as follows: "'[E]xtortion' means the obtaining of property from another, with his consent, induced by wrongful use of actual or threatened force, violence, or fear, or under color of official right." §1951(b)(2). The last clause of that definition—extortion "under color of official right"—is covered in the next chapter, which deals with bribes and gratuities. In this chapter, we consider other contexts in which extortion may occur.

As we will see, the range of threats that the Hobbs Act reaches is broad indeed, and it is limited more by determined (and sometimes contestable) judicial line-drawing than by congressional fiat. Notwithstanding the statute's broad coverage and the judiciary's willingness to amalgamate seemingly distinct offenses, some distinctions between robbery, traditional informational blackmail, and extortion carried out through threats of violence have been implemented at the sentencing level. For example, under the Federal Sentencing Guidelines robbery and extortion by force or threat of injury carry heavier penalties than extortion through blackmail. As a result, a first-time offender convicted of informational blackmail under the Hobbs Act faces a recommended sentence of four to ten months, while a first-time offender convicted of forcible extortion faces 27-33 months, and a first-time offender convicted of robbery faces 30-41 months. (Chapter 10 addresses the Sentencing Guidelines and their role in determining the severity of punishment for federal crimes.)

Section A deals with the requirement that the defendant obtain money or property "with [the] consent" of the victim. It covers three different kinds of coercion that can wrongfully induce such "consent": threats of violence, economic harm, and injury to victims' reputations—each of which has generated its own body of law. These three types of threats cover a lot of ground, as do the main cases in Section A. The first case arose from a robbery by an urban gang; the second, from political opposition to a real estate development; and the third, out of a failed extortion attempt by a woman claiming to be Bill Cosby's illegitimate daughter. Notice that the last of these cases (and perhaps the last two cases) describes what we often think of as "blackmail," but which is treated as a form of extortion in federal law.

Section B then turns to "the obtaining of property" and the application of that phrase to intangible property interests. As we saw in Chapter 4, prosecutors have used, and courts have tolerated, a wide array of intangible property theories in the mail and wire fraud context. The degree to which "property" protected under the fraud statutes can be "obtained" within the meaning of the Hobbs Act has been the subject of considerable and varied judicial attention in recent years. To give you a sense of the current state of doctrinal play, Section B presents, first, a 2006 Second Circuit decision arising out of the prosecution of Peter Gotti and a number of his associates in the Gambino family. While Mafia shakedowns have a long history in extortion law, the goals of these particular shakedowns required the court to work through the ramifications of a set of Supreme Court decisions involving protests at abortion clinics. We will consider how much of the *Gotti* analysis is good law in light of the Supreme Court's 2013 decision in Sekhar v. United States, 133 S. Ct. 2720 (2013).

As you read the following case, which deals with threats of violence, think about the consent requirement and the line between extortion and robbery.

A.   COERCION AND CONSENT

Hobbs Act, 18 U.S.C. §1951. Interference with commerce by threats or violence

(a) Whoever in any way or degree obstructs, delays, or affects commerce or the movement of any article or commodity in commerce, by robbery or extortion or attempts or conspires so to do, or commits or threatens physical violence to any person or property in furtherance of a plan or purpose to do anything in violation of this section shall be fined under this title or imprisoned not more than twenty years, or both.

(b) As used in this section —

(1) The term "robbery" means the unlawful taking or obtaining of personal property from the person or in the presence of another, against his will, by means of actual or threatened force, or violence, or fear of injury, immediate or future, to his person or property, or property in his custody or possession, or the person or property of a relative or member of his family or of anyone in his company at the time of the taking or obtaining.

(2) The term "extortion" means the obtaining of property from another, with his consent, induced by wrongful use of actual or threatened force, violence, or fear, or under color of official right. . . .

1. VIOLENCE

United States v. Zhou
428 F.3d 361 (2d Cir. 2005)

MINER, Circuit Judge.

Defendants-appellants . . . appeal from judgments of conviction entered in the United States District Court for the Southern District of New York, following a jury trial, convicting each of the Appellants . . . of one count of conspiracy to commit extortion, in violation of 18 U.S.C. §1951; one count of extortion, in violation of 18 U.S.C. §§2 and 1951 . . . ; and four counts of using, carrying, and possessing a firearm during and in relation to participation in the charged extortion . . . in violation of 18 U.S.C. §924(c)(1)(A)(ii). . . .

BACKGROUND . . .

The charges in the Indictment have their genesis in a series of robberies and related incidents that occurred in Manhattan's "Chinatown" during a six-month period between the summer of 2001 and the early months of 2002. The first such incident occurred in or around July 2001 at 75 Eldridge Street — an illegal gambling parlor located behind a clothing store. On or about July 23, 2001, at approximately 6:00 P.M., an unknown caller telephoned Chen Tin Hua ("Hua"), a "shareholder" in the gambling operation, and identified himself as being associated with "Vietnamese Boy" — presumably, co-defendant/cooperating witness Xiao Qin Zhou ("Xiao"). The caller stated that Vietnamese Boy would come to the gambling parlor later that day to pick up $10,000, which the caller instructed Hua to place in a red envelope. Hua told the caller that he had no money and hung up.

Later that evening, while in the parlor, Hua was summoned outside by a group of men demanding to speak with him. Awaiting Hua were Appellants—Chen and Lin—along with Xiao and co-defendant Li Wei. All four pointed guns at Hua, and Xiao demanded that he give them $10,000. Hua told the group that he had no money. Xiao struck Hua on the head, and Li Wei, using his gun, struck Hua in the stomach. Xiao then ripped a necklace from around Hua's neck, and the group fled the scene in a vehicle. . . .

[The evidence before the district court demonstrated that soon after this incident Chen, Lin, and Xiao, along with other members of their "gang," "began to terrorize the neighborhood systematically" through a series of robberies and attempted robberies targeting other gambling parlors.]

DISCUSSION . . .

Appellants contend that the evidence adduced at trial was insufficient to sustain the convictions of Appellants on the extortion-related crimes charged in Counts One and Two. . . .

Here, the object of the alleged conspiracy was to commit extortion, which, in the context of federal crimes, in relevant part, "means the obtaining of property from another, *with his consent*, induced by wrongful of actual or threatened force, violence, or fear." 18 U.S.C. §1951(b)(2) (emphasis added). Extortion is frequently exemplified by "revenue-producing measures . . . utilized by organized crime to generate income"—measures "such as shakedown rackets and loan-sharking." United States v. Nardello, 393 U.S. 286, 295 (1969). . . .

Choice on the part of the victim is a common theme in all extortion cases. "[T]he Hobbs Act definition of coercion speaks of obtaining property from another 'with his consent.'" United States v. Arena, 180 F.3d 380, 394 (2d Cir. 1999). [The Hobbs Act's proponents] "understood extortion to encompass situations in which a victim is given the option of relinquishing some property immediately or risking unlawful violence resulting in other losses, and he simply *chooses* what he perceives to be the lesser harm." Id. at 395 (emphasis added). "In order to foreclose any argument by an extortionist that the relinquishment of property in such circumstances was [truly] voluntary, [however,] the Hobbs Act definition of extortion simply prohibits the extortionist from forcing the victim to make such a choice." Id.

At bottom, undeniably, the victim of an extortion acts from fear. . . . But both the language of the statute and the relevant precedents make clear that he or she always retains some degree of choice in whether to comply with the extortionate threat, however much of a Hobson's choice that may be. Indeed, this element of consent is the razor's edge that distinguishes extortion from robbery, which, in contrast, is defined in pertinent part as the unlawful taking or obtaining of personal property from the person or in the presence of another, *against his will*, by means of actual or threatened force, or violence, or fear of injury, immediate or future, to his person or property, or property in his custody or possession, or the person or property of a relative or member of his family or of anyone in his company at the time of the taking or obtaining.

18 U.S.C. §1951(b)(1) (emphasis added).

Among the essential elements of the federal crime of extortion, then, are (i) the defendant's "use of actual or threatened force, violence, or fear," and (ii) the victim's consent—however forced—to the transfer of the property. 18 U.S.C. §1951(b)(2). And concordantly, essential to a determination of conspiracy to commit extortion are (i) an agreement to use actual or threatened force to obtain property with the consent of the victim and (ii) actions taken in affirmative furtherance of that agreement.

Here, the Government's theory is that Appellants conspired to extort—and in fact committed extortion, and not robbery—when they "informed Hua by telephone that [Xiao] was coming to the gambling parlor to collect $10,000 from him," instructing him to leave the money for Xiao's pick-up in a red envelope, and, later, when they "summoned Hua outside the parlor and attempted to collect the money that had been demanded in the extortionate telephone call." The Government contends that "this call clearly represented a request, albeit under duress, for the money, rather than a forcible taking." "After all," the Government observes, "robbers typically do not telephone in their requests to victims ahead of time." In making this distinction between robbery and extortion, however, the Government fails to identify any element of "duress," either express or implied, in the telephone call, thus calling into question whether the Government has proved each and every element of the extortion-related crimes charged in the Indictment. . . .

Hua, the victim of the 75 Eldridge Street crime, testified as follows regarding the above-noted telephone call that he received on July 23, 2001: . . .

> Q. Did [the caller] identify himself by name?
> A. He did. He identified himself as Vietnamese [B]oy, and he demanded money from me. . . .
> Q. And what specifically did he say to you?
> A. He said Vietnamese [B]oy, he will come over to me to pick up money and I should give him $10,000. . . .
> Q. Did he say anything about how Vietnamese [B]oy [would] pick up that money?
> A. He said that I should put it in the red envelope, $10,000 worth, inside the red envelope.
> Q. What, if anything, did you say to the caller?

A. I said I have no money.
Q. Did the caller say anything back to you at that point?
A. No. I h[u]ng up the phone.

Hua further testified that four individuals came to 75 Eldridge Street at approximately 8:00 P.M. on July 23, 2001. These individuals asked another employee of the gambling parlor to summon Hua outside. When Hua went outside, four individuals were waiting, pointing guns at him. Thereafter, Xiao, aka "Vietnamese Boy," asked Hua for $10,000. When Hua said that he had no money, one of the other men poked Hua in the side with his gun, and Xiao hit Hua on his head. Xiao then ripped the necklace from Hua's neck, after which all four of the men got into a car and drove off. . . .

[A]bsent from the Record is any indication that Appellants thought, or sought, to obtain property from Hua, or anyone else at 75 Eldridge Street, by means of a forced consent. Rather, the Record supports an agreement among, and an actual effort by, Appellants and others to get a person at that location to open a door so that Appellants and others could enter the establishment and rob it. Indeed, this very method of robbery was discussed. But the only evidence that even arguably can be identified as indicating extortion came from Hua, who testified that he was gambling at the 75 Eldridge Street parlor when he received a phone call, either from Xiao or someone on Xiao's behalf. . . .

Absent from Hua's testimony is any suggestion that either Appellant was even involved in the alleged extortionate phone call. Hua's testimony was inconsistent as to the identity of the caller, and he never identified either of the Appellants as the caller. . . .

The Government contends, however, that the fact of the phone call *combined* with the facts surrounding the gang's visit to 75 Eldridge reasonably supports the inference that the purpose of the call was to extort, since the demand for $10,000, which was initially made by telephone, was then repeated by the gang in person before they resorted to violence and took the chain. Thus, concludes the Government, the phone call was both an attempted extortion and an act in furtherance of an extortion conspiracy. But again, there was no testimony that the call itself was threatening in any way. Nor was there any testimony from Xiao, or any other witness, to fill this gap and place the call in a threatening and thus extortionate context.

The caller recited no consequences—deleterious or otherwise—of a failure to tender the $10,000, and no evidence was put before the jury suggesting that any such consequences were implied by the caller or understood implicitly by Hua. Moreover, there was nothing in Hua's testimony from which one could reasonably infer that he was placed in a subjective state of fear, or felt threatened in any way, by the call. Hua testified that Xiao "was somewhat familiar" to him; that he had seen Xiao "once or twice in Chinatown"; and that he knew Xiao by the name "Vietnamese

[B]oy." But Hua said nothing from which a juror could reasonably infer that Xiao was feared in the neighborhood or known to be involved in criminal activities; nor was there anything else in the Record to support such an inference. . . . If the name "Vietnamese Boy" was intended to strike fear in the heart of Hua, there is simply no evidence that it in fact did so. Indeed, that Hua hung up the phone after stating simply that he had no money suggests that he saw no negative consequences in refusing to consent to the demand or, for that matter, in ignoring the call altogether. . . .

A robbery plus a cryptic and ambiguous phone call does not equal extortion—at least, not on the facts presented to us in this case. . . .

In light of the foregoing, we conclude that the evidence put forward by the Government to prove the charged extortion and conspiracy to extort, even viewed in the light most favorable to the prosecution, was insufficient as a matter of law to prove the crimes charged in Counts One and Two of the Indictment. At best, the evidence proves an uncharged conspiracy to rob, and the robbery of, an individual at 75 Eldridge Street. Accordingly, we reverse the convictions of Appellants under Counts One and Two, for the crimes of conspiracy to extort and extortion, respectively.

EXTORTION AND THREATS OF VIOLENCE

1. Hobbs Act Jurisdictional Requirement: Federal jurisdiction under the Hobbs Act rests on the Commerce Clause. While the burden is on the government to show that the accused's conduct affected interstate commerce, the government can satisfy this requirement by showing that the charged conduct had a *de minimis* effect. See, e.g., United States v. Baylor, 517 F.3d 899, 902 (6th Cir. 2008) (holding that the *de minimis* standard remains applicable even after Gonzales v. Raich, 545 U.S. 1 (2005)). Where there is no actual effect on interstate commerce, showing a "realistic probability" of a *de minimis* effect will suffice. United States v. Watkins, 509 F.3d 277, 281 (6th Cir. 2007). The Supreme Court has read the statute expansively to reach the full extent of Congress's Commerce Clause power. See Stirone v. United States, 361 U.S. 212, 215 (1960) (finding that the Hobbs Act manifests Congress's intent to "use all the constitutional power [it] has to punish interference with interstate commerce by extortion, robbery or physical violence."). As a result, the Hobbs Act turns nearly all extortionate acts into federal crimes.

a. In *Zhou*, there are a number of ways that the prosecution could have satisfied the jurisdictional element. It could have elicited testimony that the gambling parlor attracted out-of-state customers, see United States v. Rodriguez, 218 F.3d 1243, 1245 (11th Cir. 2000); that, in order to gain access to the $10,000, Hua would have had to liquidate stocks or mutual funds, see United States v. McCormack, 371 F.3d 22, 28 (1st Cir. 2004); or even that the gambling parlor itself sold goods that had travelled in interstate commerce. Indeed, when the alleged crime has any economic effect, courts seem willing to find the interstate effect required by the Hobbs Act. In United States v. Jiménez-Torres, 435 F.3d 3 (1st Cir. 2006), the defendant's Hobbs Act conviction arose out of his participation in a home invasion, robbery, and murder of Flores, a gas station owner in Puerto Rico. Rejecting the claim that there was "insufficient evidence that the robbery of Flores' home affected interstate commerce—a prerequisite to conviction under the Hobbs Act," the court noted:

> For the government to successfully prove a violation of the Hobbs Act, it must demonstrate that the robbery had an effect on interstate commerce. . . . Given the statute's broad sweep, even a de minimis effect will suffice to meet the commerce element. Where, as in this case, the crime concerns the robbery of a home rather than of a business, we approach the task of applying the de minimis standard with some caution, lest every robbery (which by definition has some economic component) become a federal crime.
>
> The government offered two ways in which the robbery of Flores' home affected interstate commerce. First, Flores' murder led to the closing of the gas station, a business which had been engaged in interstate commerce. Second, the robbery depleted the assets available to the gas station to participate in interstate commerce. . . . [The court found that the government had presented sufficient evidence to support both theories]. In sum, whether the government's theories are considered individually or in tandem, there was sufficient proof that the robbery affected interstate commerce.

✳ 435 F.3d at 7-10. Judge Torruella wrote a separate concurrence:

> I write separately, because although both the majority and I are required to affirm Jiménez's conviction by reason of binding circuit precedent, I believe that this precedent is based on an interpretation of the Hobbs Act, 18 U.S.C. §1951(a), that extends Congress' power to regulate interstate commerce beyond what is authorized by the Constitution. . . .We are not faced here with the robbery of decedent's local gas station. . . . Nor is this a case of Jiménez waylaying the decedent on his way to the bank with the proceeds of interstate sales. It is not even a case of the robbers intercepting decedent and forcibly depriving him of the local gas station's receipts while he was on the way home. Although all of these scenarios would cause me to hesitate as to the impact of such criminal activity on interstate commerce, certainly those examples would be closer to providing the required constitutional jurisdictional nexus [than] the present case. Here, all criminal activity took place in decedent's home, the stolen funds had come to rest in decedent's kitchen, and there is no evidence that Jiménez or his cohorts even knew of their existence before decedent's home was fortuitously picked to be burglarized. There was in fact no connection between the perpetrators of the robbery and decedent's business. . . .

[P]erhaps the day will come when the federal government will see fit to prosecute the robbery of a child's roadside lemonade stand because the lemons came from California, the sugar was refined in Philadelphia, and the paper cups were manufactured in China. I cannot agree that the federal government has the constitutional power to prosecute Jiménez for a violation of the Hobbs Act given the facts proven in this case. However, because precedent binds me until such time as the Supreme Court puts an end to the fictions that allow the apparently limitless aggrandizement of federal power into areas reserved to the states by the Constitution, I have no choice but to concur in the affirmance of Jiménez's conviction.

435 F.3d at 13-15 (Torruella, J., concurring). What do you make of this case-by-case inquiry (required by the Hobbs Act) into whether a particular home burglary, bank robbery, or murder had affected interstate commerce? Do you think this inquiry can be answered in a principled way, with a reasonable and predictable distinction between behavior that does and does not affect commerce? Is this approach, (which, in Chapter 2, we refer to as "elemental jurisdiction"), superior to asking, when a statute does not require proof of a specific effect on commerce, whether a particular crime in aggregate has the potential to affect commerce irrespective of whether it does in any specific instance ("categorical jurisdiction")? Inasmuch as any robbery that leads to murder takes a person out of commerce, does this mean that any such murder can be prosecuted under the Hobbs Act? Should we worry that when the feds want to decline prosecution they can always cite federalism concerns, but when interested they doubtless will find some jurisdictional basis?

b. What if the defendants in *Zhou* had robbed Hua of drugs rather than a necklace? In a recent case, the Supreme Court held 7-1 that "a Hobbs Act robbery case satisfies the Act's commerce element if it shows that the defendant robbed or attempted to rob a drug dealer of drugs or drug proceeds." Taylor v. United States, 136 S. Ct. 2074, 2076 (2016) (which we briefly noted in Chapter 2). Justice Alito explained:

The case now before us requires no more than that we graft our holding in *Raich* onto the commerce element of the Hobbs Act. The Hobbs Act criminalizes robberies affecting "commerce over which the United States has jurisdiction." §1951(b)(3). Under *Raich*, the market for marijuana, including its intrastate aspects, is "commerce over which the United States has jurisdiction." It therefore follows as a simple matter of logic that a robber who affects or attempts to affect even the intrastate sale of marijuana grown within the State affects or attempts to affect commerce over which the United States has jurisdiction. . . .

This conclusion does not make the commerce provision of the Hobbs Act superfluous. That statute, unlike the criminal provisions of the CSA, applies to forms of conduct that, even in the aggregate, may not substantially affect commerce. The Act's commerce element ensures that applications of the Act do not exceed Congress's authority. But in a case like this one, where the target of a robbery is a drug dealer, proof that the defendant's conduct in and of itself affected or threatened commerce is not needed. All that is needed is proof that the defendant's conduct fell within a category of conduct that, in the aggregate, had the requisite effect.

Id. 2080-81.

2. What makes the incident in *Zhou* robbery rather than extortion? Is it the fact that the victim had no choice? In *Zhou* itself, that distinction works: The robbers "ripped a necklace from around Hua's neck, and the group fled the scene. . . ." But in many robbery cases, the victim hands the money over in order to avoid being shot or stabbed. *Those* victims also have a choice—they can refuse to cooperate and face the consequences. Yet courts continue to call such cases robberies. Why? If victim "consent" is not what distinguishes extortion from robbery, what is?

Stuart Green argues that the defining feature of extortion (including the form that might also be called blackmail) is not the presence of consent, but its absence: Green calls extortion "theft by coercion"—which appears to be the *Zhou* court's definition of robbery. See Stuart P. Green, Lying, Cheating, and Stealing: A Moral Theory of White Collar Crime 212-24 (2006); Stuart P. Green, Theft by Coercion: Extortion, Blackmail, and Hard Bargaining, 44 Washburn L.J. 553 (2005). Green's theory plainly finds support in the Hobbs Act, which bars "the obtaining of property" through "force, violence, or fear." §1951(b)(2). Yet the Act also requires that property be obtained "with [the victim's] consent." Id. How can a taking be both coerced and consensual?

3. The ability to distinguish coercion from consent, and by extension, robbery from extortion, may be affected by the differing temporal characteristics of the two crimes. In a robbery case, the threat, the point at which the threatened act will occur, and the consent all happen around the same time: The robber says "your money or your life," and the victim, fearing immediate harm, hands over his wallet. The consent—in the face of an imminent threat—is obviously fictive. Extortion, by contrast, is less easily identifiable. In extortion cases, the *threat* happens at one time and place, the threatened *harm* will occur at some future point, and the *money* will change hands later (possibly weeks or months later). And when a threat, a threatened action, and an exchange of property happen at different times, such a transfer may look—at least outwardly—entirely legitimate. This captures the essence of the extortion offense: It is the functional equivalent of robbery, but is generally designed to look like an ordinary legal exchange of money for goods or services. Put another way, extortion is robbery that the uninformed observer will not recognize as such. In *Zhou*, the prosecution was counting on

the threatening phone call to prove that, viewed in context, the defendants attempted to extort the victim. Apparently, the victim's testimony about the phone call was insufficient. What testimony would have been adequate to uphold an extortion conviction? Would Hua have had to testify that he was aware of "Vietnamese Boy's" reputation for violence and feared for his physical safety? Would it have been enough for Hua to merely claim that he feared violent reprisal if the money was not handed over? What about testimony indicating no more than that Hua knew "Vietnamese Boy" was the caller? As we will see in United States v. Gotti, discussed in Section B, extortion-by-fear need not always involve explicit threats of violence, and the identity of the extortionist may be a key factor in the commission of the offense.

Given the tenuous footing on which the extortion charge rested, why weren't the defendants also charged with attempted robbery for pointing the gun at Hua and demanding money? When the facts could go either way at trial, is it proper for the prosecutor to charge both extortion and robbery under the Hobbs Act, and let the jury sort out which crime was committed? Do you think the fact that the *Zhou* panel also upheld defendants' convictions on numerous other robbery and gun counts, which guaranteed a massive sentence even after reversal of the extortion counts, helps explain the court's fine line-drawing?

4. At common law, extortion was a close relative not of robbery but of bribery. Blackstone defined extortion as "an abuse of public justice, which consists in an officer's unlawfully taking, by colour of his office, from any man, any money or thing of value, that is not due to him, or more than is due, or before it is due." 4 William Blackstone, Commentaries *141. This public-sector branch of extortion doctrine still survives and is covered in Chapter 6. Notice that violence seems to play no part in Blackstone's definition. As you will see below, many contemporary extortion cases likewise do not involve violence; threats of economic or reputational harm may supply the necessary element of coercion.

Even so, violence lies at the heart of the history of the *federal* law of extortion. <u>Labor violence</u> was of particular concern to both those who drafted and supported the relevant criminal statutes and those who worried about the statutes' broad scope. The story begins with a piece of New Deal legislation called the Anti-Racketeering Act of 1934, one of 11 bills passed during the early months of 1934 to "render more difficult the activities of predatory criminal gangs of the Kelly and Dillinger types." S. Rep. No. 1440, 73d Cong., §2 (1934). Section 2 of the Act reads as follows:

> Any person who, in connection with or in relation to any act in any way or in any degree affecting trade or commerce or any article or commodity moving or about to move in trade or commerce—
>
>   (a) Obtains or attempts to obtain, by the use of or attempt to use or threat to use force, violence, or coercion, the payment of money or other valuable

considerations, or the purchase or rental of property or protective services, not including, however, the payment of wages of a bona-fide employer to a bona-fide employee; or

(b) Obtains the property of another, with his consent, induced by wrongful use of force or fear, or under color of official right; or

(c) Commits or threatens to commit an act of physical violence or physical injury to a person or property in furtherance of a plan or purpose to violate sections (a) or (b); or

(d) Conspires or acts concertedly with any other person or persons to commit any of the foregoing acts; shall, upon conviction thereof, be guilty of a felony and shall be punished by imprisonment from one to ten years or by a fine of $10,000, or both.

"Labor racketeering," as understood at the time, did not necessarily spring from the avarice of labor. Sometimes it was the means by which an employer trade association enforced an anticompetitive scheme. See Note, Legal Implications of Labor Racketeering, 37 Colum. L. Rev. 993, 994-95 (1937). Sometimes it was the means through which mobsters extracted profits from both employers and employees. See James B. Jacobs, Mobsters, Unions, and Feds: The Mafia and the American Labor Movement 23-35 (2006). But most of the labor violence of that era—which frequently arose from the friction that accompanied picket lines and the use of "scabs" by anti-union employers—had nothing to do with cartels or mobsters.

Congress tried to draw a line: Racketeers with illegitimate goals who used threats of violence to extract money from either unions or employers were covered by the Act; workers involved in sometimes-violent strikes for higher wages were not. The line was drawn in two ways. First, excepted from §2(a) were "attempts to obtain . . . the payment of wages of a bona-fide employer to a bona-fide employee." This precluded the prosecution of striking workers who used violence to obtain a better contract. Second, §6 explicitly protected "the rights of bona-fide labor organizations in lawfully carrying out the legitimate objects thereof." This provision appeared to distinguish "so-called 'unions'—that is, organizations for levying tribute upon employees by threatening to prevent them from working by the use of violence" from "legitimate trade-unions." S. Rep. No. 1189 (1934). The former category included rackets designed to enrich "unscrupulous foremen" skimming wages off the top and "gangsters" offering "protection" in exchange for payments. Id. To ensure this boundary was appropriately policed, Congress initially required prosecutions under the Act to "be commenced only upon the express direction of the Attorney General of the United States." Act of June 18, 1934, ch. 569, 48 Stat. 979, 980.

5. The line between racketeers and legitimate labor activists soon collapsed. The key case was United States v. Local 807, International Brotherhood of Teamsters, 315 U.S. 521 (1942). The defendants in *Local*

807 were teamsters accused of violating the Anti-Racketeering Act of 1934. The Court laid out the facts as follows:

> Local 807 includes in its membership nearly all the motor truck drivers and helpers in the city of New York. . . . Large quantities of the merchandise which goes into the city from neighboring states is transported in "over-the-road" trucks which are usually manned by drivers and helpers who reside in the localities from which the shipments are made and who are consequently not members of Local 807. . . .
>
> [D]efendants conspired to use and did use violence and threats to obtain from the owners of these "over-the-road" trucks $9.42 for each large truck and $8.41 for each small truck entering the city. These amounts were the regular union rates for a day's work of driving and unloading. There was proof that in some cases the out-of-state driver was compelled to drive the truck to a point close to the city limits and there to turn it over to one or more of the defendants. These defendants would then drive the truck to its destination, do the unloading, pick up the merchandise for the return trip and surrender the truck to the out-of-state driver at the point where they had taken it over. In other cases . . . the money was demanded and obtained, but the owners or drivers rejected the offers of the defendants to do or help with the driving or unloading. And in several cases the jury could have found that the defendants either failed to offer to work, or refused to work for the money when asked to do so. Eventually many of the owners signed contracts with Local 807 under whose terms the defendants were to do the driving and unloading within the city and to receive regular union rates for the work.

Id. at 525-26. In effect, the defendants barred non-union truckers from entering New York unless they first paid union wages to union members—even though many of these union members were not performing the work for which they demanded payment.

● By 1942, most members of Congress probably assumed that the defendants in *Local 807* were guilty of racketeering. Surprisingly, the Supreme Court held otherwise. According to Justice Byrnes, the money paid to the defendants constituted "the payment of wages of a bona-fide employer to a bona-fide employee" under §2(a) of the Anti-Racketeering Act because the defendants were willing to (and occasionally did) unload the trucks. The Court reasoned:

> Congress intended to leave unaffected the ordinary activities of labor unions. The proviso in §6 safeguarding "the rights of bona-fide labor organizations in lawfully carrying out the legitimate objects thereof," although obscure indeed, strengthens us somewhat in that opinion. The test must therefore be whether the particular activity was among or is akin to labor union activities with which Congress must be taken to have been familiar when this measure was enacted. Accepting payments even where services are refused is such an activity. The Circuit Court has referred to the "stand-by" orchestra device, by

which a union local requires that its members be substituted for visiting musicians, or, if the producer or conductor insists upon using his own musicians, that the members of the local be paid the sums which they would have earned had they performed. . . . There can be no question that he demands the payment of money regardless of the management's willingness to accept his labor. If, as it is agreed, the musician would escape punishment under this Act even though he obtained his "stand-by job" by force or threats, it is certainly difficult to see how a teamster could be punished for engaging in the same practice. It is not our province either to approve or disapprove such tactics. But we do believe that they are not "the activities of predatory criminal gangs of the Kelly and Dillinger types" at which the Act was aimed. . . .

As we have said, the jury was bound to acquit the defendants if it found that their objective and purpose was to obtain by the use or threat of violence the chance to work for the money but to accept the money even if the employers refused to permit them to work.

Id. at 535-38. The result in *Local 807* seemed to leave the Anti-Racketeering Act a dead letter, at least with respect to labor-related activities.

6. Labor-related violence soon became a hot political issue. In response, the Hobbs Act was passed in 1946. The Act's sponsors, who included Alabama Representative Samuel Hobbs, sought to preserve the core of the Anti-Racketeering Act while overturning the result in *Local 807*. President Truman initially vetoed the bill and called for Congress to make "clear in express terms that [the amendments do] not make it a felony to strike and picket peacefully, and to take other legitimate and peaceful concerted action." 92 Cong. Rec. 6676 (1946). Congress did not back down and quickly re-passed the bill without any mention of an exception for organized labor. Truman now signed, noting that the Attorney General had advised him that the bill did "not in any way interfere with the rights of unions in carrying out their legitimate objectives." Special Message to Congress Upon Approving the Hobbs Bill, No. 157, Public Papers Harry S. Truman (July 3, 1946). The Act's text reads as follows:

(a) Whoever in any way or degree obstructs, delays, or affects commerce or the movement of any article or commodity in commerce, by robbery or extortion or attempts or conspires so to do, or commits or threatens physical violence to any person or property in furtherance of a plan or purpose to do anything in violation of this section shall be fined under this title or imprisoned not more than twenty years, or both.

(b) As used in this section—

(1) The term "robbery" means the unlawful taking or obtaining of personal property from the person or in the presence of another, against his will, by means of actual or threatened force, or violence, or fear of injury, immediate or future, to his person or property, or property in his custody or possession, or the person or property of a relative or member of his family or of anyone in his company at the time of the taking or obtaining.

(2) The term "extortion" means the obtaining of property from another, with his consent, induced by wrongful use of actual or threatened force, violence, or fear, or under color of official right.

18 U.S.C. §1951. The definition of "extortion" was taken, almost verbatim, from New York's 1909 anti-racketeering law. Although the Hobbs Act is not the only federal extortion statute, it lies at the foundation of federal extortion law, and (believe it or not) contains the most detailed definition of "extortion" in the federal code.

7. The legal status of labor violence under the Hobbs Act remained contested for some time after the Act was passed. The issue was finally settled by United States v. Enmons, 410 U.S. 396 (1973). *Enmons* arose out of a successful strike against a utility company. The extortion charges were based on several acts of violence that occurred during the course of that strike: Union members allegedly fired high-powered rifles at three transformers, drained the oil from one transformer, and blew up one transformer substation. The government claimed that those acts of violence helped the union win the strike, and that the wage gains in the post-strike contract were therefore "property" that was "obtained" by extortion.

The Court rejected this theory on the ground that, while the defendants' violent *means* were unlawful, their *end*—higher wages for striking workers—was not "wrongful," and hence did not fit the Hobbs Act's definition of extortion. The Court reasoned that "'wrongful' has meaning in the Act only if it limits the statute's coverage to those instances where the obtaining of the property would itself be 'wrongful' because the alleged extortionist has no lawful claim to that property." Id. at 400. It differentiated "instances where union officials threatened force or violence against an employer in order to obtain personal payoffs" from those where violence was used to obtain "higher wages in return for genuine services which the employer seeks." Id.

The *Enmons* Court rested its opinion on a narrow interpretation of Congress's disapproval of the *Local 807* decision. It concluded, based on the Hobbs Act's legislative history, that the Act was designed to have only the "limited effect" of preventing union members from using "their protected status to exact payments from employers for imposed, unwanted, and superfluous services." Id. at 402. *Local 807* was distinguishable, the Court held, because the defendants in that case sought money for services that either they were unwilling to perform or for which the victim had no need. Id. at 408. The *Enmons* defendants, by contrast, sought higher wages for work they actually performed. The Court concluded that "it would require statutory language much more explicit than that before us here to lead to the conclusion that Congress intended to put the Federal Government in the business of policing the orderly conduct of strikes." Id. at 411. As a result, *Enmons* left violence by striking union members outside the scope of the Hobbs Act, where it remains today.

Does it make sense that the *Enmons* line of cases is limited almost entirely to threats or use of force by labor unions to secure a better contract during collective bargaining? See, e.g., United States v. Jones, 766 F.2d 994, 1002 (6th Cir. 1985) ("Subsequent decisions of various courts of appeals have refrained from extending the rationale of *Enmons* beyond the facts of that case."); see also United States v. Markle, 628 F.3d 58, 63 (2d Cir. 2010) (holding that inter-union violence relating to work allocation did not have a legitimate collective-bargaining objective and was therefore not exempt from Hobbs Act liability). Should the exception extend to law students who engage in violence against their school in order to increase the wages paid to student researchers? If not, is there a principled distinction between that hypothetical and the facts in *Enmons*?

Many times during this course, you may well bemoan Congress's failure to legislate clearly—certainly you will read many judicial opinions expressing that view. On the other hand, some decisions demonstrate a passive-aggressive style of statutory interpretation that the Supreme Court (and sometimes a lower court) periodically deploys when it wants to limit the authority of prosecutors in a particularly sensitive policy space. In which category does *Enmons* fall? Is the Court's interpretation of the word "wrongful" a reasonable one, or was it merely an attempt to preserve what it viewed as the proper role of federal criminal law with regard to labor disputes? Should it matter that Representative Hobbs declared that the "bill does not cover strikes or any question relating to strikes"? 410 U.S. at 405. If you were counsel to a Member of Congress seeking to legislatively overturn *Enmons*, what statutory language would you recommend? Does your answer suggest that the *Enmons* Court erred in interpreting the Hobbs Act?

8. Although the outcome in *Enmons* matters chiefly in labor cases, the reasoning could have far-reaching implications. While the scope of "actual or threatened force, violence, or fear" in the extortion context is remarkably wide, only the "wrongful use" of these things is forbidden. Does the holding in *Enmons* have the seeds of a broader argument allowing threatened force, violence, or fear whenever there is a claim of right? Courts have held the line. See United States v. Castor, 937 F.3d 293, 299 (7th Cir. 1991) ("Whatever the contours of [the claim of right] defense may be, they do not reach extortions based on threats of physical violence outside the labor context. [Y]ou cannot beat someone up to collect a debt, even if you believe he owes it to you"); see also United States v. Villalobos, 748 F.3d 953, 956 (9th Cir. 2014) ("Outside the labor context, there are some attempts to obtain property that are so inherently wrongful that whether the defendant had a lawful claim to the property demanded is not relevant in determining whether extortion or attempted extortion has been proven.").

Whose perspective, the threat maker or the victim's, should determine whether a threat is really of violence? In Elonis v. United States, 135 S. Ct. 2001

(2015), the Supreme Court held that threats of violence, for the purposes of 18 U.S.C. §875(c)—which broadly targets threats to injure—are covered only when the maker intends to convey a threat or understands that it will be viewed as a threat. Id. at 2011-12. This analysis, however, has limited relevance when a threat of violence is made to extort. As the Fourth Circuit noted, in the context of §875(b), which targets threats of injury made to extort:

> [I]t would be passing strange, indeed impossible, for a defendant to intend to obtain something by communicating such a threat without also intending, understanding, or, possibly, recklessly disregarding that the communication would be perceived as threatening, as *Elonis* requires. The reason is straight-forward: Extortion only works if the recipient of the communication fears that not paying will invite an unsavory result. Thus, to intend to extort one must necessarily intend to instill fear of harm (for purposes of §875(b), in the form of kidnapping or physical injury). . . . In other words, the intent to carry out an unlawful act by use of a threat necessarily subsumes the intent to threaten.

United States v. White, 810 F.3d 212, 223 (4th Cir. 2016).

One quiet theme of federal criminal law statutory interpretation is the way federal courts limit broadly-worded criminal prohibitions' interference with activities that may be socially beneficial and that are subject to complex regulatory regimes. Here, those activities involve union actions. As you read the rest of this chapter, be on the lookout for other judicial "carve-outs" to the Hobbs Act and related extortion statutes. And think of others not pursued but normatively appealing.

2.   ECONOMIC THREATS

The threat of physical violence can easily induce fear, and cases involving the use of such threats to obtain money are so clearly within the purview of the Hobbs Act that, while of great interest to prosecutors, they attract little judicial or academic attention (unless federal jurisdiction or protest activity is at issue).

Efforts to obtain money though threat of *economic harm* get far more scrutiny in the case law, and with good reason. As Robert L. Hale, a seminal Legal Realist, noted, "nearly all incomes are the product of private coercion, some with the help of the state, some without it." Robert L. Hale, Coercion and Distribution in a Supposedly Non-Coercive State, 38 Pol. Sci. Q. 470, 474 (1923); see also Robert L. Hale, Bargaining, Duress, and Economic Liberty, 43 Colum. L. Rev. 603 (1943). Threats to inflict economic loss can range from "give me money or I will burn down your house" (a threat to do something illegal, which theorists would call "extortion"); to "give me money or

I will sell my life story, in which you're a co-star, to the tabloids" (a threat to do something that is not inherently criminal, which might amount to what theorists call "blackmail"); to "give me money or I won't give you the goods and services you so desperately need" (a normal trip to the shopping mall).

How does one draw the line between entrepreneurship and illegal extortion? The question has long challenged philosophers and legal scholars. See, e.g., Robert Nozick, Socratic Puzzles 15 (1997) (analysis of "coercion"); Stuart Green, Lying, Cheating, and Stealing, *supra*, at 93-97; Kent Greenawalt, Speech, Crime, and the Uses of Language (1992); Mitchell N. Berman, The Normative Functions of Coercion Claims, 8 Legal Theory 45 (2002). Certainly, the text of the Hobbs Act provides little guidance on which threats of economic harm should be federal offenses. Nor does it specify when it is illegal to conditionally threaten something that would, if simply done, be perfectly legal. How and how well have the federal courts filled this gaping doctrinal hole?

One useful approach is to first consider the nature of the threat. As the Ninth Circuit has explained: "[W]here a nonviolent threat to obtain property is [employed] . . . a court must first consider whether the threat, as actually used in the case at issue (the 'means'), is wrongful, without regard to the property demanded by the defendant (the 'ends'). If a nonviolent threat is wrongful under the circumstances, then it is sufficient to sustain a conviction for extortion or attempted extortion. In such situations, a court need not consider whether the defendant has a lawful claim to the property demanded." United States v. Villalobos, 748 F.3d 953, 956-57 (9th Cir. 2014).

The issue of "wrongfulness" may be bound up in the determination of whether a proffered arrangement even involves a threat. United States v. Capo, 817 F.2d 947 (2d Cir. 1987) (en banc), established what has become the standard test for determining what constitutes a threat of economic harm in extortion cases. *Capo* holds that such threats are extortionate when "the defendant purports to have the power to hurt the victim in economic terms and fear is induced." 817 F.2d at 954. The *Capo* defendants sold jobs at a Kodak plant near Rochester, New York. Interested applicants would give one of the defendants a few hundred dollars and would get a factory job in return. Here is the court's description of one such transaction involving defendant Walter Snacki:

> [Walter's friend Paul] Kelso wanted to separate from his wife, Marjorie Ann, but with two children and his wife unemployed, it was not then economically feasible. Although Marjorie Ann previously had applied to Kodak on her own, she had not been successful. Walter informed Kelso that he could get a job for Marjorie Ann for $500. When Kelso balked at having to pay, Walter responded: "You want her to get a job, don't you?" Once Kelso agreed to pay, Marjorie Ann was hired.

817 F.2d at 950. The court held that this scheme did not amount to extortion, because it was not sufficiently coercive:

> The absence or presence of fear of economic loss must be considered from the perspective of the victim, not the extortionist; the proof need establish that the victim *reasonably* believed: first, that the defendant had the power to harm the victim, and second, that the defendant would exploit that power to the victim's detriment. See [United States v. Rastelli, 551 F.2d 902, 905 (2d Cir. 1977)]. Here, although there is at least a serious question whether it would have been reasonable for the "victims" to believe defendants had the power to harm them, there is no evidence at all to suggest that it would have been reasonable for the "victims" to believe that if they did not pay, the defendants would exploit any such power to diminish their employment opportunities.
>
> This circuit's case law on extortion by wrongful use of fear of economic loss is comprised of cases in which the evidence was plain that nonpayment would result in preclusion from or diminished opportunity for some existing or potential economic benefit. For instance, in [United States v. Brecht, 540 F.2d 45 (2d Cir. 1976)], the evidence established that the defendant was the manager of Westinghouse's technical publications group, which position afforded him discretion to award outside subcontracts for the production of Westinghouse's technical manuals. At a meeting with a subcontractor's representative, the defendant "*demanded* a $1,000 kickback *as a condition for the award* of the contract to [the subcontractor]." 540 F.2d at 47 (emphasis added). We affirmed defendant's conviction for extortion by wrongful use of fear of economic loss "since the evidence showed that he obtained the $1,000 by the use of fear, attempting to convince the victim that he *would be denied any chance* to obtain a contract *unless he paid.*" Id. at 52 (emphasis added). . . .
>
> [We] hold that the evidence of fear of economic loss was insufficient here as a matter of law. First, there was no evidence that any defendant did, in fact, negatively influence any hiring decision or even attempt to do so. When defendants did intervene in Kodak's hiring it was only to assist these "victims."
>
> Furthermore, review of the trial transcript reveals that not one witness testified to any fear that nonpayment would result in one of the defendants adversely affecting his or her chances for a job at Kodak; indeed, most of the "victims" testified that they had no such fear, while the others simply were not asked. Instead, the evidence establishes that these "victims" were willing participants seeking to improve their chances. . . . Thus, the second part of the *Rastelli* test—that the victim reasonably believed that the defendant would exploit his power to the victim's detriment—is not satisfied here. . . .
>
> Perhaps the best example . . . of the absence of any fear of economic loss on the part of these "victims" is the story of Brian Gauthier. After Bernard Gauthier, Brian's father, paid $800 to Bob Capo and was hired at Kodak, he approached Capo about a job for Brian. Bernard gave Capo another $800 along with Brian's completed application; however, shortly thereafter, Brian got an interview through an application he had earlier filed at Kodak on his own. Bernard then called Capo and told him not to put through Brian's

paid-for application in order to give Brian an opportunity to be hired through the normal hiring process. Capo agreed and did not process that application until Brian learned that he had not been hired. Given the go-ahead, Capo then submitted Brian's application, which was soon granted. Certainly, if Capo were threatening to impair hiring prospects, or even implying that he would impair the prospects of applicants who did not pay, he would not have acted as he did. Conversely, if either of the Gauthiers in any way feared a reprisal by Capo they would not likely have felt comfortable asking him to hold Brian's application; indeed, most probably they would not even have told Capo about it.

817 F.2d at 951-53.

Did the court apply its own test accurately? What inferences would you draw from Brian Gauthier's story? The court seems to assume that the job applicants who did not pay Capo, relying instead on "the normal hiring process," had the same employment prospects they would have had if the job-selling scheme had never existed. Does that sound right? Would the case be different had a government witness reported or opined that only a limited number of jobs were available in the Kodak plant in Rochester?

Indeed, in a part of its opinion not excerpted, the court says that Kodak had a sudden need to hire 2,300 people "to commence production of the company's new 'disc camera,'" that "the standard application system . . . collapsed under [this] dramatic demand," and that "[i]t was in this hectic setting . . . that the instant job-selling scheme took hold." Id. at 949. Were the two dissenting judges in *Capo* right to suggest that the majority failed to defer to the jury's evident conclusion that the payments were made out of "fear that defendants could or would impede the victims' being hired at Kodak"? 817 F.2d at 956 (Kearse, J., dissenting). Why do you think the court was determined to substitute its judgment?

Zhou focuses on the line between extortion and robbery. *Capo* and the next principal case, United States v. Albertson, deal with the line between extortion and bribery. According to *Zhou*, robberies are not extortionate because robbers do not obtain their victims' consent. According to *Capo* and cases like it, commercial bribery is not extortionate when bribe-takers do not threaten their victims with economic harm. The essence of bribery is voluntariness; the essence of extortion is duress. Robbery is purely coercive; bribery is purely consensual. Extortion mixes coercion and consent. How exactly does one draw the lines required by *Capo*? Consider one court's efforts.

United States v. Albertson
971 F. Supp. 837 (D. Del. 1997), aff'd without opinion, 156 F.3d 1225 (3d Cir. 1998)

MURRAY M. SCHWARTZ, Senior District Judge.

I. INTRODUCTION

Kirk Albertson ("Albertson") was charged in a single-count indictment with attempted extortion in violation of the Hobbs Act, 18 U.S.C. §1951. A jury returned a verdict of guilty after a four-day trial. . . .

The core issue presented here is a narrow one: whether one who organizes and leads legitimate legal and political opposition that impedes a developer's efforts to utilize land commits a Hobbs Act violation when he requests $20,000 in return for dropping his opposition. Stated differently with regard to the facts adduced at trial and related below, the question is whether Albertson's unsolicited offer to drop his opposition to a proposed land development known as Applewood Farms in exchange for a $20,000 sponsorship for the Dover Destroyers, his semi-pro football team, constituted the "wrongful" use of economic fear within the ambit of the Hobbs Act. . . .

For the reasons that follow, the Court holds Albertson's conduct does not constitute a violation of the Hobbs Act. Albertson's motion for judgment of acquittal will be granted, rendering moot his motion for a new trial.

II. FACTUAL BACKGROUND

This tale began innocently enough with an attempt by Joseph Corrado and his business partners to develop approximately eighty acres of land in Camden, Delaware. Corrado wanted to construct a manufactured home community to be rustically dubbed "Applewood Farms." To that end, Corrado applied to the Camden Town Council in October of 1995 for conditional use approvals and to rezone the eighty acres from partly industrial and partly preservation to residential. According to his administrative assistant, Corrado sank nearly $650,000 into the property all told, including the purchase price.

In a December 5, 1995 public hearing, the Camden Town Council approved the rezoning and conditional use over the vocal opposition of many Camden residents and Albertson, a resident of nearby Wyoming, Delaware. Despite the approval, opposition to the Applewood Farms project continued, mainly through the efforts of a newly formed group called the "Concerned Citizens of Camden" ("CCC"). While Albertson was not an officer of CCC, he spearheaded their resistance to the Applewood Farms project.

The labors of CCC, and particularly Albertson, proved not to be in vain. For example, in the February 1996 Camden Town Council elections, two antidevelopment candidates—recruited and aided by CCC and Albertson—supplanted the mayor and a councilman, both of whom had supported Corrado's application. In addition, Albertson and the wife of the newly elected antidevelopment mayor petitioned the Delaware Attorney General's Office to invalidate the rezoning of Corrado's eighty acres. . . .

Throughout this period, moreover, both Corrado and antidevelopment forces engaged in a vitriolic campaign to sway local public opinion in favor of their respective viewpoints. Both sides distributed flyers accusing the other of distorting the truth, and Albertson wrote several opinion pieces in the Delaware State News, a local newspaper, attacking the Applewood Farms project. The pitched public-relations battle spilled into the courtroom when Corrado filed suit on August 8, 1996 in Delaware Chancery Court against the Town of Camden, the mayor's wife, and Albertson. Corrado sought an injunction against another public hearing, a declaration the rezoning was lawful, and attorney's fees.

This was essentially how matters stood until October 30, 1996, when Albertson telephoned Corrado at work with a surprising proposition: sponsor Albertson's newly acquired semi-pro football team, the Dover Destroyers, in the form of a $20,000 donation, and Albertson would drop his opposition to the Applewood Farms development. . . .

Corrado's next move was to hire Lewis W. Hyden III, a recently retired Federal Bureau of Investigation Agent for advice on how to handle Albertson's "proposition." Under Hyden's tutelage, Corrado initiated and recorded a telephone conversation with Albertson on November 20, 1996. During that conversation, Albertson informed Corrado he was "serious about the cause," but had "another thing that has risen up [i.e., his football team]." Albertson told Corrado he was "pretty excited" about the semi-pro football team, and advised Corrado a $20,000 donation would "show possibly good intentions on your side in the community." Curious about what he would receive in return, Corrado prodded Albertson further by stating, "Um, you know, you said you could fix things and take away all the opposition."

"I remove myself from the puzzle," Albertson responded. He elaborated by analogizing, "If you cut the head off the dragon, the dragon can't operate."

When Corrado asked if Albertson could "make the Mayor go away or what[,]" Albertson laughed and said "you've got that to do yet. . . . [T]he Mayor is your neighbor." In fact, Albertson confirmed he could not state he had any "influence" with the Mayor. Later in the conversation, Albertson emphasized he "can't control the whole situation, . . . but you'll have removed a large portion of your splinter." When further pressed by Corrado whether he would "go away" for $20,000, Albertson replied, "For a twenty thousand dollar sponsorship, I would be more than grateful that you've helped my team out." The two men then planned to meet at a local restaurant. Before Corrado left to meet Albertson, Hyden contacted his former colleagues at the Wilmington FBI.

The remainder of the Government's case was principally composed of four ensuing conversations between Albertson and Corrado. At the restaurant on November 20th, Albertson explained his position to Corrado:

> I controlled all the meetings. I put all the people in, in, I didn't personally put them in, the people voted them in, but I gave the people something to vote for. . . . I've got 800 more fliers sitting out there ready to go to town. Cause you've got these elections coming up, you've got four people on the council that are opposed to you, your chances start getting slimmer all the way down the line. You know, like I said, I don't think it's a good idea. You've got your own reasons. You'll make some money from it, I mean that's your reasons for coming into Camden and doing something there. You've got land, you've got two pieces of land, you know those are all your reasons. I'm truly 100% against it. But, if you do what you're going to do and sponsor my football team, I'll not stand in your way anymore, and I will show you after your check clears the bank or whatever, how to let me walk out of this whole thing where neither one of us are put up on a pedestal that makes both of us look bad.

While he conceded his absence from the opposition would not guarantee the success of Applewood Farms, Albertson suggested he could subtly influence the mayor to drop opposition to the project. . . .

Corrado called Albertson on December 5, 1996, and the two met again at a local diner. Once more, Albertson detailed what Corrado would be getting for a $20,000 sponsorship of the Dover Destroyers. Again, Albertson emphasized Corrado was primarily purchasing Albertson's inaction; that is, Corrado would not "see flyers on the street, paper interviews or anything like that." During the meeting, Albertson told Corrado he would contact his attorney in the Chancery Court action and inform him he would no longer oppose the Applewood Farms project. Corrado gave Albertson a check for $5,000, offering to pay the balance after Albertson showed him "something positive." Albertson signed a stipulation of dismissal from the lawsuit in Chancery Court on December 18, 1996.

On December 23, Albertson went one last time to a local diner to meet Corrado, who was to pay Albertson the remaining $15,000. At the diner, Albertson met the FBI, who arrested him for the attempted extortion of Joseph Corrado.

III. DISCUSSION . . .

[T]he dispute between the parties can be characterized as a result of two different views of the Hobbs Act. The Government views the law under the Hobbs Act as simple and well-settled: if the defendant has no lawful claim to the property involved, he is guilty under the Hobbs Act. Albertson, on the other hand, advocates a different perspective: if the payor receives something of value in exchange for his property, there can be no Hobbs Act violation. . . .

After extended debate and thorough deliberation, the Court crafted its own instruction, which was read and given to the jury. This instruction provided:

> The Government must prove beyond a reasonable doubt that the defendant attempted to obtain the money or property of another by the "wrongful" use of actual or threatened fear of economic loss.
>
> The use of fear of economic loss is not always "wrongful." For our purposes, the use of fear of economic loss is wrongful if the defendant had no claim of right to the property he attempted to obtain, and the defendant attempted to obtain the property by exploiting Mr. Corrado's fear of economic loss.
>
> Please keep in mind, however, that the defendant did not act wrongfully merely by requesting and receiving money in exchange for settling litigation and/or merely by seeking contribution or sponsorship for his football team, despite the fact that he did not have a claim of right to that contribution or sponsorship. Also, keep in mind Mr. Corrado had no right to be free from opposition to its development project. Therefore, the defendant also did not act wrongfully by actively opposing Mr. Corrado's project—all of us have the right to participate in the political process and oppose real estate projects of developers. *The defendant only acted wrongfully if, for the purpose of exploiting Mr. Corrado's fear of economic loss, he threatened to continue opposition to Mr. Corrado's project so that the defendant might gain sponsorship and/or contribution for his football team.* [emphasis in original]

By returning a verdict of guilty, then, the jury found Albertson exploited Corrado's fear of economic loss by threatening to continue his opposition to Applewood Farms, a position he truly believed in, but sacrificed on the mantle of greed. The remainder of this opinion is premised on that finding. . . .

D.   WRONGFUL USE OF FEAR

The debate over the propriety of the jury instructions is a reflection of a wrinkle in Hobbs Act jurisprudence: not all economic threats are outlawed by federal law and the Hobbs Act intercedes in private dealings only when economic threats are used for a wrongful purpose. The Hobbs Act does not define "wrongful"; instead, courts have been left to determine on a case-by-case basis whether the Hobbs Act extends to the conduct at issue. As will be demonstrated, the line separating the legitimate economic threat from the wrongful (and hence extortionate) demand can be a fine one indeed. At one end of the Hobbs Act spectrum there is what the First Circuit Court of Appeals has described as the "straightforward example of a lawful economic threat": when one party threatens litigation in an effort to persuade another party to honor a contract which the first party believes has been breached. United States v. Kattar, 840 F.2d 118, 123 (1st Cir. 1988). At the other end there is the instance when one party threatens to retain and use property that belongs to another party unless the first party receives payment. See United States v. Inigo, 925 F.2d 641, 649-50 (3d Cir. 1991). But other threats, such as the ones made by Albertson, fall somewhere between those two extremes. Thus, at bottom, the question to which the parties' efforts are addressed is whether the Hobbs Act criminalizes Albertson's conduct. . . .

[T]he Government proposed a jury instruction that described any attempt to obtain money to which one has no lawful claim by a threat of economic injury as "wrongful" under the Hobbs Act. This definition is legally correct, at least in the union violence context, see United States v. Enmons, 410 U.S. 396, 400 (1973), and accordingly, the Government views this case as a simple one: Albertson had no lawful claim to a $20,000 sponsorship and therefore must be found guilty of extortion. This argument assumes a broad reading of the Hobbs Act, however—that Albertson had no "lawful claim" to the $20,000 sponsorship and that the Hobbs Act should be interpreted to encompass the type of conduct admittedly engaged in by Albertson.

Pointing to cases elucidating the difference between "hard-bargaining" and extortion, Albertson attacks this assumption and the Government's view regarding the breadth of the Hobbs Act. In Viacom Int'l, Inc. v. Icahn, a "greenmail"[10] case, the Southern District of New York described the difference between "hard bargaining" and extortion as follows:

> In a "hard bargaining" scenario the alleged victim has no pre-existing right to pursue his business interests free of the fear he is quelling by receiving value in return for transferring property to the defendant, but in an extortion scenario the alleged victim has a pre-existing entitlement to pursue his business interests free of the fear he is quelling by receiving value in return for transferring property to the defendant. If a victim is entitled by law to be free from the fear he is quelling by giving property to the defendant, then the "something of value" the victim receives is, as a matter of law, as "imposed, unwanted, superfluous and fictitious" as the hiring of a second worker to do the job that another worker is already doing.

747 F. Supp. 205, 213 (S.D.N.Y. 1990) (emphasis added). Seizing upon this language, Albertson sees [sic] a judicially crafted limitation on the broad language of the Hobbs Act. Thus, argues Albertson, if the victim receives

---

10. Greenmail is defined as causing a "target company to buy the shares already obtained by the hostile would-be acquirer at a substantial premium over the latter's cost, with the understanding that he, she, or it will stop the takeover attempt." Robert C. Clark, Corporate Law 574 (1986). See also Tracy Greer, Note, The Hobbs Act and RICO: A Remedy for Greenmail?, 66 Tex L. Rev. 647, 649-651 (1988) (examining greenmail phenomenon).

something *of value*—in other words, something to which he is not already legally entitled and hence not "imposed, unwanted, superfluous and fictitious"—then a transaction cannot be extortionate. Analogizing to this case, Albertson notes it is undisputed that in exchange for $20,000, Corrado received a covenant from Albertson that he would not continue his political and legal opposition to Applewood Farms—this covenant was of considerable value to Corrado and was far from "imposed, unwanted, superfluous, and fictitious." Since Corrado, as a land developer, had no right to pursue his business interests in Camden without political opposition, Albertson concludes he cannot be found guilty of extortion as a matter of law.

The Government responds to the distinction in *Viacom* by arguing two related points. First, the Government asserts the *Viacom* court, in excusing "hard-bargaining" from the prohibitions of the Hobbs Act, drew a distinction that runs counter to precedent from the Third Circuit Court of Appeals, as well as from the First and Seventh Circuit Courts of Appeal. Under these authorities, argues the Government, the proper perspective in defining "wrongful" is focussed not on what the victim is receiving or giving up, but on what the alleged extortionist has obtained in return and whether he has a claim of right to that property. Accordingly, the Government presses, because Albertson had no legal right to charge Corrado for ceasing his otherwise lawful activities, Albertson's attempt to obtain $20,000 was extortionate; it is irrelevant that Corrado might have received something of value in return.

The Government's second argument is Albertson committed attempted extortion because, unlike that of the corporate raider in *Viacom*, Albertson's conduct was secretive, not overt, and aimed at personal enrichment, not for the public benefit. Because of these distinctions, the Government urges, Albertson's conduct is forbidden under the Hobbs Act. The Court will address each of these arguments in turn.

1. The Government's First Argument: The "Hard Bargaining"/Extortion Distinction Drawn in Viacom Is Incorrect

[The court began by rejecting the Government's attempt to equate this case with United States v. Cerilli, 603 F.2d 415 (3d Cir. 1979), in which "public officials conditioned an award of public contracts upon the payment of a political contribution." *Cerilli* had rejected the defendants' argument that they were "insulated" from the Hobbs Act because their conduct was "inextricably linked to protected political activity," id. at 421.] Unlike the officials in *Cerilli*, who had the sole power to award contracts, Albertson was in no position to remove *all* opposition to Applewood Farms. Nor was he able to grant Corrado the necessary permits to complete the Applewood Farms project. As Albertson acknowledged, the most he could do was remove his personal (albeit considerable) opposition and perhaps render advice and influence on how to obtain ultimate approval for the project. In short, *Cerilli* is different in that it represents a clear instance of "pay to play." The public officials in *Cerilli* required payments in exchange for an opportunity to compete for a state contract. In contrast, even had Corrado decided not to provide a sponsorship, he would not lose his opportunity to compete—to wit, he could still operate through legal and political means to obtain clearance for Applewood Farms.

A recent decision from the Sixth Circuit Court of Appeals, United States v. Collins, 78 F.3d 1021, 1030 (6th Cir. 1996), is instructive in clarifying this distinction. In *Collins*, the husband of the Kentucky Governor solicited contributions for the Governor's political party in exchange for the right to contend for state contracts. In upholding the Hobbs Act conviction of the spouse, the Sixth Circuit Court of Appeals reasoned "the evidence in this case was sufficient to establish that [the payors] acted out of fear that without the payments they could lose the opportunity to compete for government contracts on a level playing field, an opportunity to which they were legally entitled." Id. at 1030. The *Collins* court elaborated:

> [The payors] all faced the threat that if they did not contribute to the party . . . , they would not be considered for state contracts. They would not be able to get in the door. They received the clear message that in order to compete for bond business in Kentucky, they would have to pay the gate keeper, [the defendant].

Id.

While couched in slightly different terms, both *Viacom* and *Collins* are striking at the same principle: [A] payor must be deprived of a "level playing field" to be the victim of a Hobbs Act violation. In other words, if the payor is paying the defendant for the opportunity to compete like everybody else, then the payor is a "victim" under the Hobbs Act; while he has received something for his money, it was something to which he was otherwise entitled—a level playing field—and therefore what was received was "imposed, unwanted, or superfluous." On the other hand, if a payor willingly transfers property to the defendant in an effort to gain an advantage and will not suffer more than anybody else for not making the payment, then there is no Hobbs Act violation. What Albertson offered Corrado was the opportunity to make considerable headway on an already level playing field, an opportunity from which Corrado was free to walk away with impunity. . . .

2.   The Government's Second Argument: Albertson Committed Extortion Because His Behavior Was Covert and Aimed at Personal Enrichment—Viacom Distinguished

[The court found no distinction between overt agreements, as in *Viacom*, and clandestine agreements, as in *Albertson*. It then proceeded to reject the Government's contention that there is a distinction between "economic threats designed for public benefit and those designed for personal enrichment" on the ground that neither the language of the Hobbs Act nor binding precedent justifies such a distinction.]

E. CONCLUSION . . .

In this area of federal law, the legality and illegality of conduct turns on the peculiar facts of each case. . . .

Tying the law to the facts of each case necessitates judicial line-drawing. All can agree the Hobbs Act has been expanded to cover conduct beyond that contemplated by Congress in drafting the statute. The question then becomes: what is a principled basis for drawing the line between legality and illegality? Further, is not a criminal defendant entitled to fair warning his conduct will transgress that line? Consider the following series of hypotheticals, and whether the conduct is violative of the Hobbs Act.

(1) Assume a land developer and civic association have become embroiled in sundry political and legal disputes over a proposed development project. It is not uncommon (indeed, it has become the norm) for developers to meet with civic associations and their leaders to ascertain what the developer must provide in order to assuage resistance so as to obtain the necessary permits more easily. Thus, if a civic association (through its leaders, of course) demands that certain lands be devoted to public purposes in exchange for dropping opposition to a development project, are the leaders guilty of a Hobbs Act violation? I think not. If a civic association successfully defeats a developer's proposal, and then approaches a developer and requests lands for public use in exchange for supporting reapplication, is that a Hobbs Act violation? Again, I think not. The line is clear. But consider the following variations:

(2) The same civic association, having flexed its political muscle and quashed the efforts of the developer, now publicly insists upon land to be used for any purpose determined by the association—not necessarily for the public good. The association couples this demand with a condition the developer provide a sum of money (say, $100,000), again to be used by the civic association for its own purposes.

(3) Same facts as above, but the negotiations are conducted secretly.

(4) Same facts as above, but this time the leaders of the civic association secretly offer (a) to drop their personal political and legal opposition to the development projects, with the knowledge the association's resistance will flounder and perhaps fold without their involvement, and (b) move behind the scenes to promote the development project, in exchange for $100,000.

(5) Same facts as above, but the leaders retain an attorney, who meets with the attorneys for the developer. After a stylized negotiation dance, the parties reach the same agreement as above.

It is apparent hypotheticals (2) through (4), and perhaps (5), inch progressively closer to, and some would argue cross, the line separating lawful bargaining from extortion. As noted earlier, the Government suggests there are two principled bases for distinguishing between lawful bargaining and extortion: (1) lawful bargaining is generally not conducted secretly, but publicly; and (2) the aim of lawful bargaining is the public good, not private purse strings. But as explained earlier, secrecy and public benefit are nowhere to be found in the Hobbs Act or the jurisprudence interpreting the Hobbs Act. Nor is the Court prepared to state these are principled bases for distinction in construing the Hobbs Act.

In sum, Albertson's "proposition" was disgraceful, offensive, and ethically repugnant. But the Hobbs Act does not police all disgraceful, offensive, and ethically repugnant behavior; it only prohibits the "wrongful" use of economic fear. Because Corrado stood to receive something "of value" in return for his $20,000 sponsorship, Albertson's economic threats were not wrongful and not violative of the Hobbs Act. Accordingly, an appropriate order will follow, granting Albertson's motion for judgment of acquittal as a matter of law.

NOTES AND QUESTIONS

1. To determine whether a defendant committed or sought to commit extortion, it might be helpful to ask three questions: (1) Did a threat by the defendant induce consent by the victim? (2) Was the threat that the victim would lose something to which she was entitled? (3) Did the defendant make the threat in order to obtain something to which she was not entitled? Generally, in order to qualify as extortion, the answer to all three questions must be yes. (We will see an exception to this rule when we discuss informational blackmail later in this section.)

In *Capo*, for example, the Second Circuit held that Walter Snacki's scheme to get payors jobs at Kodak was not extortion, primarily because there was insufficient evidence that Snacki had implicitly threatened to keep the victims from obtaining jobs unless they paid him (the answer to both (1) and (2) is no). On the other hand, although Albertson *did* threaten Corrado and induce his consent to pay $20,000, Corrado did not lose anything to which he was entitled: He had no right to be free from political opposition to his housing development. It may be morally repugnant, but if Corrado was willing to pay $20,000 to get Albertson to drop his opposition, Albertson was "entitled" to that money. This means that the answer to both (2) and (3) was no; hence Albertson was not guilty of extortion.

It is also important to note that for extortion under the Hobbs Act, the defendant must have sought to obtain and to exercise the property right that the victim lost. In other words, the defendant or his preferred recipient must gain what the victim loses. See Scheidler v. National Org. for Women, Inc., 537 U.S. 393 (2003), discussed in Section B of this chapter.

2. What if Albertson had, from the beginning, concocted his opposition to the development in order to later cash it out? Or, what if he had initially been a good faith opponent but at some point decided to keep protesting only in order to be bought off? Mitchell Berman has argued that motives matter very much, see The Normative Functions of Coercion Claims, 8 Legal Theory (2002); Meta-Blackmail and the Evidentiary Theory: Still Taking Motives Seriously, 94 Geo. L.J. 787 (2006); The Evidentiary Theory of Blackmail, 65 U. Chi. L. Rev. 795 (1998), and the judge in *Albertson* seems to agree. But if the case turns on whether Albertson — had he been rebuffed — would have continued his vocal opposition to the development, shouldn't we just defer to the jury's guilty verdict? On the other hand, there is a real risk that a fact-finder's hindsight bias — based on the fact that at some point a person was willing to settle or remain quiet for money — would end up chilling expressive conduct.

It is tempting to look to whether the "victim" of alleged extortion had a legal entitlement to what he had to pay to obtain. Certainly, the developer in *Albertson* was not "legally entitled" to build Applewood Farms without public opposition. Still, there is something unsatisfying about this reasoning. Remember Judge Kearse's dissent in *Capo*. She argued that the government had shown (and the jury found) that the circumstances of employment in and around the Kodak factory were such that Capo was able to significantly alter the likelihood that any particular applicant could obtain a job. As a result, failure to pay Capo for assistance substantially diminished an applicant's chances of obtaining employment. Judge Kearse concluded — and, but for different views about what inferences the evidence supported, the rest of the en banc court would have likely agreed — that diminished opportunity to obtain a job was a sufficient threat to sustain a Hobbs Act prosecution. To use the *Albertson* court's own terminology, the existence of the job-selling scheme denied non-payors "a level playing field" (or, put another way, the playing field for non-payors dropped to below sea level).

3. But if diminished opportunity is enough of a threat to constitute extortion, what distinguishes Capo from a well-connected headhunter in an otherwise tight labor market? Is the difference that the headhunter operates openly and is an honest agent of her principal? Recall the discussion in *Albertson* about covert versus open bargaining, and about the possible relevance of "public benefit." But where do these considerations come from? Can they be formulated in a way that is helpful doctrine to guide future prosecutors and judges?

4. Article 223.4 of the Model Penal Code, which defines "Theft by Extortion," states: "A person is guilty of theft if he purposely obtains property of another by threatening to . . . bring about or continue a strike, boycott or other collective unofficial action, if the property is not demanded or

received for the benefit of the group in whose interest the actor purports to act."

While *Albertson* focused on whether the defendant had offered something of value in return for the developer's money, the Model Penal Code would distinguish extortion from hard bargaining based on whether the defendant had shared any benefit she received from the exchange. Should it matter whether Albertson kept the $20,000 for himself or shared it with his fellow anti-sprawl campaigners? Which rule does a better job of separating out "wrongful use of actual or threatened force, violence, or fear" from non-wrongful offers? Which rule is more in keeping with the statutory text? Why do you think that no federal court of appeals has extended the Hobbs Act to include the Model Penal Code's "Theft by Extortion"?

5. Lurking in the background of analysis in *Albertson* may have been a concern about the intrusion of criminal law into activities that involve political expression. Some courts have brought this concern to the foreground. In United States v. Pendergraft, 297 F.3d 1198 (11th Cir. 2002), the defendants "threatened to amend an existing lawsuit . . . backed by fabricated evidence," id. at 1206. The Eleventh Circuit explained why "[a] threat to litigate, by itself, is not necessarily 'wrongful' within the meaning of the Hobbs Act":

> After all, under our system, parties are encouraged to resort to courts for the redress of wrongs and the enforcement of rights. For this reason, litigants may be sanctioned for only the most frivolous of actions. These sanctions include tort actions for malicious prosecution and abuse of process, and in some cases recovery of attorney's fees, but even these remedies are heavily disfavored because they discourage the resort to courts.
>
> History has taught us that, if people take the law into their own hands, an endless cycle of violence can erupt, and we therefore encourage people to take their problems to court. We trust the courts, and their time-tested procedures, to produce reliable results, separating validity from invalidity, honesty from dishonesty. While our process is sometimes expensive, and occasionally inaccurate, we have confidence in it. When a citizen avails himself of this process, his doing so is not inherently "wrongful."
>
> Moreover, in this case, we are not dealing with a typical threat to litigate. Instead, we are dealing with a threat to litigate against a county government. The right of citizens to petition their government for the redress of grievances is fundamental to our constitutional structure. See U.S. Const. amend. I. A threat to file suit against a government, then, cannot be "wrongful" in itself.
>
> But, in this case, we have an allegation that [defendants] fabricated evidence to support their suit. The fabrication of evidence is certainly not "rightful." The question is whether the fabrication of evidence makes a threat to sue a government "wrongful."
>
> We recognize that the fabrication of evidence is criminalized by the perjury statute. While the same conduct can violate several statutes, we do not think that [defendants'] conduct does. The law jealously guards witnesses

who participate in judicial proceedings; witnesses should be "unafraid to testify fully and openly." See Charles v. Wade, 665 F.2d 661, 667 (5th Cir. 1982). Because the rigors of cross-examination and the penalty of perjury sufficiently protect the reliability of witnesses, courts have been unwilling to expand the scope of witness liability, since, by doing so, "'the risk of self-censorship becomes too great.'"

Criminalizing false testimony via the Hobbs Act would expand the scope of witness liability. Witnesses might decline to provide affidavits in questionable lawsuits against a government, fearing that they could be charged with conspiracy to commit extortion if the lawsuit fails. Such a possibility is unsettling, and we do not believe that Congress intended to expand the scope of witness liability in this way. The fabrication of evidence, then, does not make a threat to sue a government "wrongful" within the meaning of the Hobbs Act.

While the case before us involves a threat to sue a government, we are troubled by *any* use of this federal criminal statute to punish civil litigants. Sanctions for filing lawsuits, such as malicious prosecution, lead to collateral disputes and "a piling of litigation on litigation without end." Allowing litigants to be charged with extortion would open yet another collateral way for litigants to attack one another. The reality is that litigating parties often accuse each other of bad faith. The prospect of such civil cases ending as criminal prosecutions gives us pause.

Moreover, this addition to the federal criminal arsenal would have other disconcerting implications in the civil arena. As we have noted, the cases rejecting extortion for threats to litigate arise in the civil RICO context when parties attempt to graft a RICO claim on their claims for malicious prosecution. In those cases, the courts express concern about transforming a state common-law action into a federal crime. We share this concern.

Pendergraft, 297 F.3d at 1206-08.

Are you convinced that nuisance suits and "strike suits" are not a form of extortion? Or perhaps the court is saying something different: that because the policing of good and bad lawsuits is not a proper function of federal prosecutors in enforcing the Hobbs Act, the Act should simply be understood not to encompass such suits. Recall the earlier suggestion that the one reason the Supreme Court might have twice exempted some labor actions from the reach of racketeering laws is that the delicate political balance between unions and employers is primarily accomplished through complex labor statutes and regulatory decisions. If litigation is a favored social activity (as it certainly appears to be in the United States) and has its own self-limiting mechanisms, perhaps the federal courts understandably want to minimize interference by prosecutors. Likewise, as suggested above, *Albertson* may be understood as an effort to limit the reach of the broadly worded Hobbs Act in the arena of democratic politics, an especially favored social activity.

6. The way in which extortion is distinguished from robbery and bribery has two important implications. The first has to do with the legal status of victims. The victim is guilty of nothing in *Zhou*, regardless of whether the

defendants' conduct is labeled robbery or extortion. Whether an offense is prosecuted as bribery or extortion, however, has important consequences for the victim, who can be prosecuted for violating bribery laws but cannot be charged, even as an accomplice or co-conspirator, if the offense is charged as extortion—at least under the "fear" prong of the Hobbs Act. As we will see in Chapter 6, the analysis will be different for the "under color of official right" prong, which is akin to bribery. (Recall that in bribery cases brought under the federal mail and wire fraud statutes, payors and payees alike can be charged with conspiracy to deprive others of their "intangible right of honest services.") The second implication has to do with the relationship between the relevant crimes. Extortion and robbery are mutually exclusive; in *Zhou*, the defendants could be guilty of one of these two crimes, but not both. In contrast, extortion and bribery are *not* mutually exclusive; defendants can be guilty of both. The same is true of extortion and "intangible rights" fraud, which is a chief means by which federal prosecutors prosecute both political and commercial bribery cases.

Now consider the combined effect of those two implications. Suppose the defendants' conduct in *Capo* had been sufficiently threatening to satisfy the Second Circuit. Suppose further that, following the defendants' extortion convictions, federal prosecutors had charged the extortion "victims"—the applicants who paid bribes to get their factory jobs—with aiding and abetting mail or wire fraud, on the theory that they helped Capo and Snacki deprive Kodak of the honest services of its employees. What result would be reached? The job applicants would likely argue that they were coerced. But the level of coercion required for a Hobbs Act conviction falls far short of the level of coercion required for a duress defense. (Recall from your basic course in criminal law that common-law duress is limited to situations in which the actor fears immediate serious bodily injury or the equivalent.) Thus, the extortion victims could be charged with and convicted of mail or wire fraud involving bribery. Does that seem fair? If not, what could be done to remedy this problem? We return to this issue in Chapter 6.

3. INFORMATIONAL BLACKMAIL AND CLAIMS OF RIGHT

Neither the *Capo* nor the *Albertson* court was presented with a defendant's claim that he had some preexisting "right" to the money he sought. What is the analysis when a defendant makes such a claim? What about the former associate who is willing to give up the exposé he was planning to self-publish or the putative litigant who offers to settle his "valuable" claim? These questions can arise in cases involving what theorists would call "blackmail" but that federal law makes a subspecies of "extortion."

Mitchell Berman explains that while extortion is the conditional threat to do something that it would be unlawful to do ("If you don't do X, I will commit a wrong against you"), blackmail is a wrongful conditional threat to do something (i.e., disclose damaging information) that would otherwise be permissible to do. See Mitchell N. Berman, Blackmail, The Oxford Handbook on the Philosophy of the Criminal Law (2009). Despite its relatively prominent role in popular culture, there is a massive academic literature debating whether blackmail should even constitute a crime. The "so-called paradox of blackmail" that Berman describes is as follows: "I am legally free to reveal embarrassing information about you. Generally speaking, I am also free to negotiate payment to refrain from exercising a legal right. But if I combine the two—offering to remain silent for a fee—I am guilty of a felony: blackmail. Why?" Mitchell N. Berman, The Evidentiary Theory of Blackmail, 65 U. Chi. L. Rev. 795, 795 (1998); see also Leo Katz, Blackmail and Other Forms of Arm-Twisting, 141 U. Pa. L. Rev. 1567 (1993); George N. Fletcher, Blackmail: The Paradigmatic Crime, 141 U. Pa. L. Rev. 1617 (1993); Douglas H. Ginsburg & Paul Shechtman, Blackmail: An Economic Analysis of the Law, 141 U. Pa. L. Rev. 1849 (1993); James Lindgren, Unraveling the Paradox of Blackmail, 84 Colum. L. Rev. 670, 670-71 (1984); Richard Epstein, Blackmail, Inc., 50 U. Chi. L. Rev. 553 (1983).

The following case offers some guidance on how to separate legitimate offers from "wrongful" ones. And, in an interesting twist, it does so in a prosecution based on a statute that does not even use the term "wrongful." As you read this case, think about the three requirements we suggested in Note 1 above to help determine whether the defendant committed extortion. In informational blackmail cases, have courts dispensed with the second requirement—that the victim be threatened with the loss of something to which he is entitled?

United States v. Jackson
180 F.3d 55 (2d Cir. 1999)

KEARSE, Circuit Judge:
Defendants Autumn Jackson, Jose Medina, and Boris Sabas appeal from judgments of conviction entered in the United States District Court for the Southern District of New York following a jury trial. . . .

I. BACKGROUND

The present prosecution arises out of defendants' attempts to obtain up to $40 million from William H. ("Bill") Cosby, Jr., a well-known actor and entertainer, by threatening to cause tabloid newspapers to publish Jackson's claim to be Cosby's daughter out-of-wedlock. . . . Taken in the light most favorable to the government, the evidence showed the following.

A. JACKSON'S RELATIONSHIP WITH COSBY

In the early 1970s, Cosby had a brief extramarital affair with Jackson's mother, Shawn Thompson. After Jackson was born in 1974, Thompson told Cosby that he was the father. Cosby disputed that assertion, and according to Jackson's birth certificate, her father was one Gerald Jackson. Jackson's grandmother testified, however, that she and Thompson told Jackson, as Jackson was growing up, that Cosby was her biological father. The grandmother told Jackson that Cosby had said that, so long as they "didn't tell anyone about it, that he would take care of her mother and her, and take care of his responsibility."

For more than 20 years after Jackson's birth, Cosby provided Thompson with substantial sums of money, provided her with a car, and paid for her admission to substance-abuse treatment programs. . . . In addition, Cosby, who had funded college educations for some 300 persons outside of his own immediate family, . . . had offered to pay for the education of Jackson and of Thompson's other two children. In about 1990, after a telephone conversation with Jackson's grandmother, Cosby became concerned that Jackson's education was being hampered by conditions at her California home, and he arranged to have Jackson finish high school at a preparatory school in Florida associated with a Florida college. Cosby thereafter also created a trust to pay for Jackson's college tuition and for certain personal expenses such as food, rent, utilities, and medical costs while Jackson was attending college. This trust was administered by Schmitt's law partner Susan F. Bloom. Jackson subsequently enrolled in a community college in Florida. While Jackson was in school, Cosby spoke with her by telephone approximately 15 times to encourage her to pursue her education, telling her that although he was not her father, he "loved her very, very much" and would be a "father figure" for her. . . .

In April 1995, Bloom learned that Jackson had dropped out of college, and Bloom therefore ceased making payments to Jackson from the college education trust. . . .

B. THE EVENTS OF DECEMBER 1996 AND EARLY
JANUARY 1997

In the fall of 1996, Jackson and her then-fiancé Antonay Williams were living in California and working for a production company in Burbank, California, headed by Medina. Medina's company, which operated out of his hotel suite, was attempting to produce a children's television show. Jackson, Williams, and Sabas had acting roles in the show; along with cooperating witness Placido Macaraeg, they also had administrative positions. Jackson worked without pay, but she expected to receive a commission when the television show was sold.

In December 1996, Jackson reinitiated contact with Cosby. Within a four-day period, she telephoned him seven times and left urgent messages asking him to return her calls. In one instance, Jackson identified herself as "Autumn Cosby," a message that Cosby perceived as "some sort of threat." When he returned Jackson's call, he reproached her for using his name. Jackson described the project on which she was working, told Cosby that she was homeless, and asked him to lend her $2100. Cosby initially refused and suggested that she instead get an advance from the person for whom she was working. After further reflection, Cosby called Jackson back and agreed to send her the $2100 she had requested, plus an additional $900; he urged her to return to school, and he renewed his offer to pay for her education. Cosby directed his attorneys to tell Jackson that he would pay for her education and related expenses if she returned to school, maintained a B average, and got a part-time job [and they did so]. . . .

[O]n January 6, Jackson left a voice-mail message for Peter Lund, president and chief executive officer of CBS, whose television network currently carried Cosby's prime-time program. Stating that her name was Autumn Jackson, Jackson said:

> I am the daughter of Doctor William Cosby, Jr. I need to speak with you . . . regarding this relationship [] that he and I have, and how this will affect CBS if I go to any tabloids. . . .

[O]n January 7, Jackson telephoned Schmitt and asked if there was any chance that Cosby "would send her money to live on." When Schmitt responded in the negative, Jackson said that if she did not receive money from Cosby, she would have to go to the news media. Schmitt testified that he replied that if Jackson meant that "she was planning to go to the news media with what she believed was damaging information and would refrain from doing so only if Mr. Cosby paid her money, that that was extortion, that was both illegal and disgraceful." . . . Jackson stated that she had "checked [it] out and she knew what she was doing."

During the week of January 6, Jackson and Medina discussed ways to intensify the pressure on Cosby and his corporate sponsors. . . . [Those] discussions resulted in . . . the mailing on January 10 and 11 of company solicitation letters that . . . included a paragraph referring to Jackson as the daughter of a "CBS megastar" who was "CBS's most prized property," and stating that, contrary to the star's public image as an advocate of parenting, the star had left Jackson "cold, penniless, and homeless." Letters containing this paragraph were sent to the President and Vice President of the United States, the Governor of California, the Mayor of New York City, CBS, Eastman Kodak, Philip Morris Company, which was another Cosby sponsor, two publishing companies that had published Cosby's books, and many other companies. . . .

C.   THE EVENTS OF JANUARY 15-18, 1997

On January 15, 1997, after the telephone calls and letters of the week before had failed to produce the desired results, Medina and Jackson contacted Christopher Doherty, a reporter for The Globe tabloid newspaper. Medina and Jackson told Doherty that Cosby was Jackson's father and asked what her story would be worth. To support the story, Medina described for Doherty an affidavit in which Jackson had stated (falsely) that Cosby admitted his paternity. Medina faxed Doherty a copy of Bloom's December 13, 1996 letter to Jackson setting out the terms under which Cosby offered to pay Jackson's tuition. After some negotiation of terms, Doherty agreed that The Globe would purchase the rights to Jackson's story of her relationship to Cosby for $25,000. . . .

That evening, Doherty brought to Medina's hotel a "source agreement," for the signatures of both Jackson and Medina, setting forth the terms under which The Globe would buy the rights to Jackson's story. . . .

The agreement with The Globe was never signed. Instead, on the following morning, January 16, Jackson faxed a copy of the agreement, after obliterating the $25,000 price, to Schmitt. In addition, Jackson faxed Schmitt a letter stating, "I need monies and I need monies now." Jackson's letter . . . concluded:

> If I don't hear from you by today for a discussion about my father and my affairs, then I will have to have someone else in CBS to contact my father for me. I want to talk to my father because I need money and I don't want to do anything to harm my father in any way, if at all possible to avoid.
>
> Enclosed you will find a copy of a contract that someone is offering monies for my story, which is the only property I have to sell in order to survive.

The fax cover letter directed Schmitt to "R.S.V.P." to Jackson in Medina's hotel suite.

Schmitt called Jackson [the next] morning. Medina, Jackson, Williams, Sabas, and Macaraeg were present. . . . With Medina mouthing words and passing notes to Jackson, Jackson and Schmitt had the following conversation: . . .

> SCHMITT: [Clears throat] How, how much money are you asking for, Autumn?
> JACKSON: I'm wanting to settle, once and finally.
> SCHMITT: What, what are you asking for?
> JACKSON: I'm asking for 40 million, to settle it completely.
> SCHMITT: And if our answer to that is no?
> JACKSON: Well, like I said, I have offers, and I will go through with those offers.
> SCHMITT: And those offers are to sell your story to the Globe? [Pause]. Autumn, are you there?

> JACKSON: Yes I am.
> SCHMITT: Is that what you're referring to, the contract that you sent me, that, for sale to the Globe of your story?
> JACKSON: Them, as well as any others. [Pause].
> SCHMITT: Well, I'm, I'm sure you know the answer to that is no, Autumn. Thank you very much.

Jackson asked to have her "father" call her; Schmitt responded that Jackson's father was "Mr. Jackson," and that she should "not expect a call from Mr. Cosby." Macaraeg testified that when the conversation ended, Jackson looked frustrated and told the group that Schmitt "doesn't understand the meaning of the term settlement," and Medina said, "if [Cosby] doesn't want this to get out, he's going to have to pay a lot of money.". . .

Some hours later, Jackson and Medina faxed a letter to CBS president Lund. They attached a copy of the unsigned source agreement with The Globe, again with the price redacted. In the letter, which was signed "Autumn J. Jackson-Cosby" and bore the heading "ATTENTION: PLEASE FORWARD THIS LETTER TO MY FATHER, WILLIAM H. COSBY, JR.," Jackson said that Cosby's failure to acknowledge her as his daughter had left her mentally anguished and financially impoverished. . . . Jackson's letter to Lund concluded:

> I am willing to decline this offer and all others upon a fair settlement. . . . [Cosby's] show and his private life just happens [*sic*] to be one of your best properties and this disclosure . . . could undoubtedly effect [*sic*] your ratings negatively. . . .

When Schmitt informed Cosby of Jackson's demand for $40 million dollars, Cosby responded that he would not pay. . . . That afternoon, Cosby instructed Schmitt to report Jackson's threats to the Federal Bureau of Investigation.

At the direction of the FBI agents, Schmitt telephoned Jackson for the purpose of allowing the agents to hear and record her demands. In that conversation, Schmitt told Jackson that Cosby had changed his mind and now wanted to come to an arrangement with her. Schmitt asked Jackson how much money she needed, saying her $40 million demand was unreasonable. Schmitt and Jackson negotiated and eventually arrived at the figure of $24 million. Schmitt told Jackson that she and Medina would have to come to New York to pick up a check. Jackson said that Medina was to receive 25 percent of the money and asked Schmitt to make out one check for $18 million and the other for $6 million. Schmitt . . . asked Jackson to meet him in his office [in New York] the next morning to execute a written agreement and pick up the checks. . . .

On the morning of January 18, 1997, Jackson and Medina met Schmitt at the offices of his law firm in Manhattan. Jackson and Medina reviewed a draft agreement, prepared by Schmitt under the direction of the FBI, which provided that, in consideration for $24 million, Jackson and Medina would "refrain from providing any information whatsoever about Mr. Cosby to any third party," would "terminate any and all discussion with . . . The Globe," and would "not initiate any further discussions with The Globe or any other media outlet, with respect to Ms. Jackson's story that she is the daughter of Mr. Cosby." When Jackson and Medina had signed, Schmitt left the room on the pretense of getting the checks, and FBI agents entered and arrested Jackson and Medina. . . .

E. THE PRESENT PROSECUTION . . .

The [] indictment alleged three counts against each defendant: (1) conspiracy to violate 18 U.S.C. §875(d) and the Travel Act, 18 U.S.C. §1952(a)(3), in violation of 18 U.S.C. §371; (2) interstate transmission of threats to injure another person's reputation with the intent to extort money, in violation of 18 U.S.C. §§875(d) and 2; and (3) interstate travel in order to promote extortion, as prohibited by §875(d) and the New York State extortion statute, N.Y. Penal Law §155.05(2)(e)(v), in violation of the Travel Act, 18 U.S.C. §1952(a)(3). Following a jury trial, Jackson and Medina were convicted on all three counts. Sabas was convicted of conspiracy and violating the Travel Act but was acquitted on the §875(d) extortion count.

II. DISCUSSION

A. EXTORTION IN VIOLATION OF 18 U.S.C. §875(D)

Section 875(d), the extortion statute under which Jackson and Medina were convicted, provides as follows:

(d) Whoever, with intent to extort from any person . . . any money or other thing of value, transmits in interstate or foreign commerce any communication containing any threat to injure the property or reputation of the addressee or of another . . . shall be fined under this title or imprisoned not more than two years, or both.

18 U.S.C. §875(d). This statute does not define the terms "extort" or "intent to extort." At trial, Jackson asked the court [to instruct the jury] that

[T]he government must prove beyond a reasonable doubt, *first*, that the defendant had no lawful claim or right to the money or property he or she sought or attempted to obtain, and, *second*, that the defendant knew that he or she had no lawful claim or right to the money or property he or she sought or attempted to obtain. . . .

The court informed the parties that it would not give these requested instructions, stating its view that "threatening someone's reputation for money or a thing of value is inherently wrongful." Consistent with that view, . . . the court described the "intent to extort" element as follows, without mentioning any ingredient of wrongfulness: . . .

The final element that the government must prove beyond a reasonable doubt is that the defendant you are considering acted with the intent to extort money or a thing of value from Bill Cosby. You should use your common sense to determine whether the defendant you are considering had the requisite intent to extort. In this connection, *to extort means to obtain money or a thing of value from another by use of threats to reputation. . . .*

[I]t is not a defense that the alleged threats to another's reputation are based on true facts. In other words, it is irrelevant whether Bill Cosby in fact is the father of Autumn Jackson. Rather, you must determine whether the defendant you are considering communicated a threat to injure Bill Cosby's reputation, and whether that defendant did so with intent to extort money from Bill Cosby.

In addition, if you find that the government has proved beyond a reasonable doubt a particular defendant threatened to injure Bill Cosby's reputation in order to obtain money from him, *it makes no difference whether the defendant was actually owed any money by Bill Cosby or thought he or she was.* That is because *the law does not permit someone to obtain money or a thing of value by threatening to injure another person's reputation. . . .*

The government contends that §875(d) contains no "wrongfulness" requirement, and that even if such a requirement is inferred, threats to injure another person's reputation are inherently wrongful. These arguments are not without . . . support. The subsection itself contains no explicit wrongfulness requirement, and it parallels a subsection that prohibits, with intent to extort, a "threat to kidnap" a person, 18 U.S.C. §875(b), and a "threat to injure the person of another," id. Given the inherent wrongfulness of kidnaping [sic] and assault, the parallelism of subsection (b)'s prohibitions with §875(d)'s prohibition against threats to injure reputation or property may support an inference that Congress considered threats to injure reputation to be inherently wrongful methods of obtaining money. Such an inference would be consistent with the established principle that, when a threat is made to injure the reputation of another, the truth of the damaging allegations underlying the threat is not a defense to a charge of extortion under §875(d). Cf. United States v. Pascucci, 943 F.2d 1032, 1033-1034, 1036-1037 (9th Cir. 1991) (§875(d) conviction upheld where defendant threatened to send genuine tape of extramarital sexual encounter to victim's employer). . . .

[Still,] we are troubled that §875(d) should be interpreted to contain no element of wrongfulness, for plainly not all threats to engage in speech that will [harm] another person's reputation, even if a forbearance from speaking is conditioned on the payment of money, are wrongful. For example, the purchaser of an allegedly defective product may threaten to complain to a consumer protection agency or to bring suit in a public forum if the manufacturer does not make good on its warranty. . . . Or a private club may threaten to post a list of the club members who have not yet paid their dues. We doubt that Congress intended §875(d) to criminalize acts such as these. . . .

The Hobbs Act prohibits, *inter alia*, obstructing, delaying, or affecting commerce "by robbery or extortion," id. §1951(a), and it defines extortion as follows . . . :

> the obtaining of property from another, with his consent, induced by *wrongful* use of actual or threatened force, violence, or fear, or under color of official right,

Id. §1951(b)(2) (emphasis added). The Travel Act refers to "extortion" without defining it. That Act has nonetheless been interpreted as using the term in its "generic" sense, a sense that inherently signifies wrongfulness. Thus, in determining whether the term "extortion" as used in [18 U.S.C.] §1952 was meant to encompass acts that at common law were classified as blackmail but not as extortion (because not committed by a public official), the Supreme Court accepted the

> Government['s] . . . suggest[ion] that Congress intended that extortion should refer to those acts prohibited by state law which would be *generically* classified as extortionate, i.e., obtaining something of value from another with his consent induced by the *wrongful* use of force, fear, or threats.

United States v. Nardello, 393 U.S. 286, 290 (1969).

In sum, in sections of the Criminal Code other than §875(d), the words "extort," "extortionate," and "extortion" either are defined to have a wrongfulness component or implicitly contain such a component. If Congress had meant the word "extort" in §875(d) to have a different connotation, we doubt that it would have chosen to convey that intention by means of silence. . . .

Under the Hobbs Act definition of extortion, which includes obtaining property from another through a wrongful threat of force or fear, the use of a threat can be wrongful because it causes the victim to fear a harm that is itself wrongful, such as physical injury, or because the means is wrongful, such as violence. However, the Hobbs Act may also be violated by a threat that causes the victim to fear only an economic loss. Yet as we discussed in United States v. Clemente, 640 F.2d 1069, 1077 (2d Cir. 1981), a threat to cause economic loss is not inherently wrongful; it becomes wrongful only when it is used to obtain property to which the threatener is not entitled.

In *Clemente*, we considered challenges to Hobbs Act convictions on the ground that the trial court's instructions permitted the jury to "convict [Clemente] solely upon finding that he used fear of economic loss to obtain money," and that as a matter of law "the use of fear of economic loss is not inherently wrongful." 640 F.2d at 1077. We rejected the challenge because Clemente's factual premise was erroneous. The trial court had in fact informed the jury . . . that "extortion" means obtaining property from another, with his consent, induced by the "wrongful" use of actual or threatened force or fear, id. at 1076, and had instructed that "[w]rongful" meant that the defendant in question had instilled in his victim the fear of economic loss of property to which the defendant "had no lawful right," id. at 1077. . . .

We are persuaded that a similar interpretation of §875(d) is appropriate. Given Congress's contemporaneous consideration of the predecessors of §875(d) and the Hobbs Act, both of which focused on extortion, we infer that Congress's concept of extortion was the same with respect to both statutes. . . . And since, like threats of economic harm, not every threat to make a disclosure that would harm another person's reputation is wrongful, we adopt an interpretation of §875(d) similar to *Clemente*'s interpretation of the Hobbs Act. We conclude that not all threats to reputation are within the scope of §875(d), that the objective of the party employing fear of economic loss or damage to reputation will have a bearing on the lawfulness of its use, and that it is material whether the defendant had a claim of right to the money demanded.

We do, however, view as inherently wrongful the type of threat to reputation that has no nexus to a claim of right. There are significant differences between, on the one hand, threatened disclosures of such matters as consumer complaints and nonpayment of dues, as to which the threatener has a plausible claim of right, and, on the other hand, threatened disclosures of such matters as sexual indiscretions that have no nexus with any plausible claim of right. In the former category of threats, the disclosures themselves—not only the threats—have the potential for causing payment of the money demanded; in the latter category, it is only the threat that has that potential, and actual disclosure would frustrate the prospect of payment. Thus, if the club posts a list of members with unpaid dues and its list is accurate, the dues generally will be paid; if the consumer lodges her complaint and is right, she is likely to receive her refund; and both matters are thereby concluded. In contrast, if a threatener having no claim of right discloses the victim's secret, regardless of whether her information is correct she normally gets nothing from the target of her threats. And if the victim makes the demanded payment, thereby avoiding disclosure, there is nothing to prevent the threatener from repeatedly demanding money even after prior demands have been fully met. . . .

Within this framework, we conclude that the district court's instruction to the jury on the meaning of "extort" as that term is used in §875(d) was erroneous. The court instructed simply that "to extort means to obtain money or a thing of value from another by use of threats to reputation." The court gave no other explanation of the term "extort" and did not limit the scope of that term to the obtaining of property to which the defendant had no actual, or reasonable belief of, entitlement. . . .

The evidence at trial was plainly sufficient to support verdicts of guilty had the jury been properly instructed. Even if Jackson were Cosby's child, a rational jury could find that her demand, given her age (22) and the amount ($40 million), did not reflect a plausible claim for support. The evidence supported an inference that Jackson had no right to demand money from Cosby pursuant to a contract or promise and no right to insist that she be included in his will. The jury thus could have found that her threat to disclose was the only leverage she had to extract money from him; that if she sold her story to The Globe, she would lose that leverage; and that if Cosby had capitulated and paid her in order to prevent disclosure, there was no logical guarantee that there would not be a similar threat and demand in the future. . . .

We conclude, however, that the court's failure to inform the jury of the proper scope of the intent-to-extort element of §875(d) erroneously allowed the jury to find defendants guilty of violating that section on the premise that any and every threat to reputation in order to obtain money is inherently wrongful. Accordingly, Jackson and Medina are entitled to a new trial on the §875(d) count. [The court went on to reverse the other counts on the ground that the jury instructions were faulty, and remanded for a new trial on all counts.]

NOTES AND QUESTIONS

1. As we suggested above, extortion under the Hobbs Act appears to require *both* that the defendant was seeking something to which he was not entitled *and* that the victim was threatened with the loss of something to which he was entitled. The Second Circuit proceeded on the assumption that informational blackmail under 18 U.S.C. §875(d) is parallel to extortion under the Hobbs Act. Yet the court held that the trial court's error was in failing to instruct the jury that Jackson had to be seeking money to which she had no plausible claim; apparently, it was irrelevant whether Cosby could be said to have a "right" not to have embarrassing but true information revealed. Why might courts treat informational blackmail differently from economic extortion? Could it be that there is generally no social value in revealing embarrassing information about an individual, even an eminent entertainer?

2. On rehearing, the *Jackson* panel—presented with the Supreme Court's intervening expansion of the harmless error doctrine in Neder v. United States, 527 U.S. 1 (1999)—reinstated the defendants' convictions. It was "persuaded beyond a reasonable doubt that a properly instructed jury would nonetheless have found [them] guilty, rejecting the proposition that [Jackson] had any plausible claim of right to $40 million." 196 F.3d 383, 388 (2d Cir. 1999). Other courts have similarly looked to whether the defendant "knew he was not entitled to" the money he sought. See, e.g., United States v. Greer, 640 F.3d 1011 (9th Cir. 2011) (trucker who, in a recycling delivery, found scads of documents with client information from Las Vegas casinos convicted after trying to sell the information back to the casinos).

3. *Jackson* held that not every threat to make a disclosure that would harm another person's reputation is "wrongful." Assuming that Autumn Jackson is Bill Cosby's biological daughter, what made her threat "wrongful"? Was it the amount demanded (first $40 million and then $25 million)? If so, would a more gently worded request for $1 million be permissible? How about $100,000? Does it matter that Jackson demanded millions from Cosby even though the tabloids had offered her only $25,000? Do your answers depend on whether Jackson has any viable state-law claims for support from Cosby? If so, how viable must those claims be?

4. Does "wrongful" necessarily mean "unlawful"? In United States v. Coss, 677 F.3d 278 (6th Cir. 2012), where defendants were convicted under §875(d) of trying to use "bad" photographs to extort $680,000 from the actor John Stamos, the Sixth Circuit drew on *Jackson*'s analysis and noted:

> At least some "wrongful" threats under the Second Circuit's "claim of right" definition would also be unlawful in a criminal or civil sense—such threats could implicate defamation or fraud. Moreover, identification of a "claim of right" requires reference to preexisting legal standards and thereby utilizes these standards in distinguishing lawful from unlawful conduct. Nevertheless, the two standards implicate an important difference. To require that a threat be unlawful would be to require that the prosecution demonstrate beyond a reasonable doubt that the threat in question was independently illegal in either the criminal or civil sense. We see no reason, nor any historical or statutory basis, for reading such a requirement into 18 U.S.C. §875(d).

Id. at 286-87.

5. Suppose, as often happens, a tabloid owns some embarrassing pictures of a celebrity. The tabloid expects to make $50,000 in extra sales and advertising revenue by publishing these pictures. The publisher of the tabloid, in what he claims is an act of kindness, contacts the celebrity and offers to destroy the pictures in exchange for $75,000 to be paid to the company that owns the tabloid. (Perhaps the tabloid imposes a surcharge because it does not want to get a reputation for leniency toward celebrities.) Is the offer extortionate? Does the answer depend on the nature of the pictures?

6. Recall Neder v. United States, 527 U.S. 1 (1999), and United States v. Wells, 519 U.S. 482 (1997). (*Neder* and *Wells* are discussed in Section B of Chapter 3.) In *Neder*, the Supreme Court held that several federal fraud statutes require proof that the defendant's misrepresentations were material. At common law, the definition of "fraud" included materiality. According to Chief Justice Rehnquist's majority opinion, Congress incorporated the materiality element of the common-law definition when it used the term in criminal statutes. *Wells* was a prosecution under a federal statute banning misrepresentation in loan applications. As in *Neder*, the question in *Wells* was whether the statute included an implied materiality requirement. The Court held that there was no such requirement—the statute did not use any common-law terms, so it did not include any common-law definitions.

Do *Neder* and *Wells* bear on the issue in *Jackson*? Wrongfulness is not an explicit element of the common-law definition of extortion; its source is the Hobbs Act, not the common law. Hence *Neder* does not appear to support the *Jackson* court's decision. Nor does the Hobbs Act. In general, federal courts do not read terms from one criminal statute into another, as *Wells* illustrates. In his dissent in that case, Justice Stevens pointed to dozens of federal misrepresentation statutes that include materiality terms and argued that materiality should be seen as an implied term in statutes that do not explicitly require materiality. *Jackson* seems more consistent with Justice Stevens's dissent than with the *Wells* majority opinion. Why should the Hobbs Act's definition govern extortion cases brought under federal statutes other than the Hobbs Act?

B.   OBTAINING PROPERTY

Recall that under the statutory definition of extortion—found in the Hobbs Act—the defendant must obtain property, and must do so by coercing the victim into consenting to his victimization. Having discussed the consent requirement and the different kinds of coercion that may induce it, we now turn to the "obtaining of property" and the application of that phrase to intangible property interests. We will use *Gotti* to give you at least one Circuit's view of the law before the Supreme Court's important 2013 decision in *Sekhar*. Then we will consider *Sekhar* and its ramifications.

United States v. Gotti
459 F.3d 296 (2d Cir. 2006)

KATZMANN, Circuit Judge.
This case raises an issue of first impression for this Court: the scope of the Supreme Court's holding in Scheidler v. National Org. for Women, Inc.,

537 U.S. 393 (2003) ("*Scheidler II*"),[1] in which the Supreme Court tightened the requirements for finding that a defendant has committed extortion under the Hobbs Act, 18 U.S.C. §1951. On appeal, the defendants-appellants—Peter Gotti, Richard G. Gotti, Anthony ("Sonny") Ciccone, and Richard Bondi—argue that *Scheidler II* invalidates all of the Hobbs Act counts in this case that were premised on the extortion of intangible property rights. We hold, however, that *Scheidler II* did not invalidate the challenged extortion counts at issue in this case, because *Scheidler II*—far from holding that a Hobbs Act extortion could not be premised on the extortion of intangible property rights—simply clarified that for Hobbs Act liability to attach, there must be a showing that the defendant did not merely seek to deprive the victim of the property right in question, but also sought to obtain that right for himself. That standard, which can be satisfied regardless of whether the property right at issue is tangible or intangible, has been met by each of the Hobbs Act counts at issue here. . . .

I.   BACKGROUND: THE INDICTMENT, TRIAL, VERDICTS, AND SENTENCES

A.   THE INDICTMENT

The 68-count indictment in this case centered on the corrupt influence of the Gambino Family over certain labor unions, businesses, and individuals operating at the piers in Brooklyn and Staten Island. The indictment was brought against seventeen Gambino Family members and associates, including the four defendants-appellants here: (1) Peter Gotti, described in the indictment as the acting boss of the Gambino Family; (2) Ciccone, described as a Gambino Family captain; (3) Richard G. Gotti, described as a "made member" of the Gambino Family, and (4) Bondi, described as a Gambino Family associate.

[Defendants were ultimately convicted of numerous counts of extortion. For ease of review, the court separated them into 14 categories, five of which—(1) the International Longshoremen's Association, AFL-CIO ("ILA") Counts, (2) the Management-International Longshoremen's Association Managed Health Care Trust Fund ("MILA") Counts, (3) the Tommy Ragucci ("Ragucci") Counts, (4) the Eduard Alayev ("Alayev")

---

1. This decision is frequently abbreviated as "*Scheidler II*," because it represented the case's second journey up to the Supreme Court. The case's first visit to the Supreme Court—National Organization for Women, Inc. v. Scheidler, 510 U.S. 249 (1994)—is generally referred to as "*Scheidler I*." A recent ruling by the Supreme Court on yet another issue in the case, Scheidler v. National Organization for Women, Inc., 126 S. Ct. 1264 (2006), is known as "*Scheidler III*." For purposes of clarity, we employ these abbreviations in this opinion.

Counts, and (5) the Steven Seagal ("Seagal") Counts—are discussed below.]

B.   THE TRIAL

1.   The ILA Counts

The gravamen of the ILA Counts was that certain members and associates of the Gambino Family, including defendant-appellant Ciccone, had exercised control over the affairs of the union, first by using force to determine "who filled various International Executive Officer and other ILA positions" in order to "ensure that organized crime associates would be placed in these positions," and then by directing the activities of those office-holders. These activities gave rise to counts of both extortion and fraud.

With regard to extortion, the indictment alleged that the defendants had wrongfully obtained the following property of ILA union members: "(1) ILA labor union positions, money paid as wages and employee benefits, and other economic benefits that such ILA union members would have obtained but for the defendants' corrupt influence over such union; (2) the right of ILA union members to free speech and democratic participation in the affairs of their labor organization as guaranteed by [§§411 and 481 of the Labor-Management Reporting Disclosure Act (LMRDA), 29 U.S.C. §§401 et seq.]; and (3) the right of ILA union members to have the officers, agents, delegates, employees and other representatives of their labor organization manage the money, property and financial affairs of the organization in accordance with [§501(a) of the LMRDA]." . . .

At trial, the government adduced substantial evidence in support of the ILA charges. George Barone—a member of the [Genovese Family]—testified that there had been a long-held understanding between the Gambino Family and the Genovese Family concerning the ILA's activities, whereby the Gambino Family "would take care of Staten Island and Brooklyn" and the Genovese Family "would take care of New York and New Jersey." Barone stated that in the late 1970s, Ciccone became the Gambino representative in charge of the waterfront for Staten Island and Brooklyn, and served as a vice president of the ILA, with the local ILA union officials essentially under his control. . . .

Additionally, Frank Scollo—former president of Local 1814, an ILA Chapter in Brooklyn—testified that "Mr. Ciccone would tell me on many occasions what to do, what not to do." Scollo explained that he feared losing his job as president if he contradicted Ciccone's orders. He stated his predecessor, Frank Lonardo, had similarly taken instructions from Ciccone. Scollo further testified that he kept his relationship with Ciccone secret from all of the other union members.

Scollo also specifically testified that prior to the July 2000 ILA convention in Lake Tahoe . . . , Ciccone gave him instructions as to which individuals should be elected to various ILA leadership positions. . . .

2.   *The MILA Counts*

The MILA Counts related to a scheme of the Gambino and Genovese Families to use their control over MILA (the ILA's national health plan) to ensure that a particular company called GPP/VIP—which was partially owned by Gambino Family associate Vincent Nasso, and which paid substantial kickbacks—was awarded MILA's lucrative pharmaceutical services contract. Ciccone was the only defendant-appellant named in these counts. . . .

[At trial, t]he government [] adduced evidence that helped to explain why certain ILA trustees had been such strong supporters of GPP/VIP, notwithstanding its higher rates: Ciccone had so ordered. . . .

8.   *The Tommy Ragucci Counts*

These counts alleged that certain defendants, including defendant-appellant Ciccone, had conspired and unsuccessfully attempted to extort Tommy Ragucci (referred to in the indictment as "John Doe 1"), an employee at Howland Hook (and the brother of Carmine Ragucci), by ordering him to resign from his position there so that it could be filled by Bobby Anastasia, who was related to a Gambino Family member.

In support of these charges, the government introduced testimony from Scollo, who stated that in the summer of 2001, Ciccone . . . ordered him to tell Tommy Ragucci to leave his position. Scollo explained that Ciccone wanted to remove Tommy Ragucci from the position so that Bobby Anastasia could be placed there. Scollo further testified that he carried out these orders, but that Tommy Ragucci said that he would not resign.

Tommy Ragucci, in turn, testified that in approximately August of 2001, Scollo approached him and stated "that his boss wanted me to step down." He asked Scollo who his boss was; Scollo responded, "Sonny." Tommy understood that this meant "Sonny Ciccone." He stated that upon receiving this order, "I felt very—I would say I felt intimidated.". . .

The government also presented . . . a July 26, 2001 wiretapped conversation, in which Scollo reported to Ciccone: "I grabbed Tommy yesterday and I told him, listen to me." Ciccone responded, "Tell him I don't want him there. Tell him I don't want him there. . . . That's it. Now you're out." Scollo replied, "I told him as soon as possible." Ciccone reiterated, "And not the end of the summer. As soon as possible, maybe within the next thirty days.". . .

Evidently, however, the matter was ultimately dropped, because as of the trial, Tommy Ragucci was still working at the Howland Hook terminal. . . .

11. The Alayev Counts

These counts alleged that certain defendants—including defendants-appellants Ciccone and Bondi—had conspired to extort, and had extorted, the following property interests from Eduard Alayev, the owner of a cafe in Brooklyn: (1) money; (2) the right to refuse to keep illegal gambling machines at a business; and (3) the right to sell a business free from outside pressure.

At trial, Alayev testified that he and his business partner (his brother) had purchased the cafe—called Cafe Roma—in October of 1999 from someone named Rocco Ritorto. He further testified that about two months after purchasing Cafe Roma, Cassarino and Bondi . . . came together to tell him that they wanted to install gambling machines at the cafe. Alayev refused, but Cassarino "responded by saying, 'Whether you want it or not, I'm going to install the gambling machines.'" Cassarino stated that if Alayev would not let him install the machines, Alayev would have to pay him $1,000 each month, adding that "the neighborhood [was] all his territory." Id. Alayev wanted to call the authorities, but was "very afraid for [his] family," and thus did not do so.

Alayev stated that three gambling machines were subsequently installed in the back room of his restaurant while he was out shopping. Alayev told Cassarino that he was afraid that if the gambling machines were found, Cafe Roma would lose its liquor license, to which Cassarino responded, "[Y]ou are not going to be responsible for anything, if any tickets [] come, we'd pay your ticket." Alayev added that Bondi began coming to Cafe Roma to collect money from the machines, and would typically give him a portion of the proceeds.

The police subsequently appeared at Cafe Roma, broke all of the gambling machines, and arrested Alayev. Alayev moved the broken machines down to the basement and told Cassarino that the machines "are not going to be here anymore." Someone nonetheless subsequently came to Cafe Roma to install one or two new gambling machines. . . .

In December of 2000, Alayev decided that he wanted to sell Cafe Roma. Cassarino ultimately became closely involved in the details of this sale, telling Alayev that he wanted Cafe Roma to be sold to someone named Lenny Kogan, and that Alayev "should not sell it to anybody but Lenny." He told Alayev that Kogan would pay $40,000 for Cafe Roma. Cassarino ended up taking a portion of that money for himself. . . .

12. The Seagal Counts

These counts alleged that certain defendants . . . conspired and attempted to extort the film actor Steven Seagal, by trying to obtain money from him and attempting to get him to do business with them.

At trial, Steven Seagal testified that he became good friends with Jules Nasso (the brother of Vincent Nasso of GPP/VIP) in the late 1980s. At Jules Nasso's request, Seagal brought him into the movie business, and the two men formed a production company called Seagal-Nasso. [Later,] Seagal . . . decided that he did not want to work with Jules Nasso any longer and severed the business relationship in the late 1990s. According to Seagal, Jules Nasso was unhappy about the end of the relationship, and told Seagal that Seagal owed him approximately one million dollars. Seagal's accountants and attorneys, however, disagreed, telling Seagal that Jules Nasso owed him money, rather than vice versa. . . .

Seagal testified that he later met with Ciccone in New York, after having received many calls from Vincent Nasso telling him that Ciccone "wanted to see me." When Seagal arrived at the Nassos' mother's house for the meeting, he was informed that the meeting had been moved somewhere else, which made Seagal feel "increasingly uncomfortable." Seagal then got into a car (accompanied by his assistant) and was taken to a restaurant, where Ciccone, Cassarino, Jules Nasso, and Vincent Nasso were sitting at an upstairs table. Ciccone began talking to Seagal about "monies that I owed Jules . . . he then went into the fact that he wanted me to work with Jules and that was important to him and I again told him that I'm trying." . . . Ciccone then said: "Look, we're proud people and you work with Jules . . . Jules is going to get a little and the pot will be split up. . . . We'll take a little." The meeting ended with Seagal stating that he "would try to work with Jules." Seagal testified that as he walked out of the restaurant, Jules started walking with him and said "something to the effect of 'You know, it's a good thing you said this and didn't say that because if you would have said the wrong thing, they were going to kill you.'"

Seagal further testified that on the morning of the March 2001 premiere of "Exit Wounds," Ciccone—accompanied by Jules and Vincent Nasso, Cassarino, and another man—showed up at his home, at which point Ciccone claimed that Seagal owed them $3 million, stating "I told you what I want and I don't think you are getting it." Ultimately, Seagal paid Jules Nasso between $500,000 and $700,000, which he testified at trial arose from a previous "stock issue where he had put some of his own money up to buy stock with me." . . . Jules subsequently filed a $60 million civil lawsuit against Seagal.

The government also introduced a wiretapped conversation in which Ciccone and Jules Nasso discussed their interactions with Steven Seagal, and in which Ciccone stated, "We were gonna tell [Seagal] that every movie he makes . . . we want a hundred and fifty thousand," and told Jules, ". . . Don't treat him with kid gloves." . . .

II.   CHALLENGES BY THE DEFENDANTS TO THEIR CONVICTIONS

A.   THE DEFENDANTS' CHALLENGE UNDER SCHEIDLER v. NATIONAL ORGANIZATION FOR WOMEN, INC., 537 U.S. 393 (2003) (SCHEIDLER II)

The defendants-appellants [] argue that numerous extortion counts in the indictment became invalid upon the issuance of *Scheidler II*, which was decided by the Supreme Court on February 26, 2003, just as the trial in this case was concluding. . . .

1.   The Scheidler II *Decision* . . .

The Hobbs Act [] defines "extortion" as

> *the obtaining of property from another*, with his consent, induced by wrongful use of actual or threatened force, violence, or fear, or under color of official right.

18 U.S.C. §1951(b)(2) (emphasis added).

Before *Scheidler II*, this Circuit (and others) had interpreted the phrase "the obtaining of property from another" quite broadly, in two key respects: (1) "property" had been held to encompass intangible as well as tangible property rights; and (2) "obtaining" had been held to encompass cases where the defendant caused a loss of or interference to the victim's property rights, even though the defendant had not actually sought to exercise those property rights for himself or herself. Clear examples of these two propositions can be found in our precedents.

old definition

As to the first proposition—namely, the expansive interpretation of "property"—our Circuit's decision in United States v. Tropiano, 418 F.2d 1069 (2d Cir. 1969), stands as an early landmark case. The *Tropiano* defendants were partners in a garbage collection company who were displeased when a new competitor, Caron Refuse Removal, Inc. ("Caron"), started soliciting business in their vicinity and taking away some of their customers. They then used threats of violence to force Caron to stop recruiting their customers and to agree not to solicit any business in the area. On appeal, this Court upheld the *Tropiano* defendants' Hobbs Act extortion convictions, rejecting their argument that "nothing more than 'the right to do business' in the Milford area was surrendered by Caron and that such a right was not 'property' 'obtained' by the appellants." We explained:

property = any valuable right

> The concept of property under the Hobbs Act . . . is not limited to physical or tangible property or things but includes, in a broad sense, any valuable right . . . and does not depend upon a direct benefit being conferred on the person who obtains the property.

Obviously, Caron had a right to solicit business from anyone in any area without any territorial restrictions by the appellants and only by the exercise of such a right could Caron obtain customers whose accounts were admittedly valuable. Some indication of the value of the right to solicit customers appears from the fact that when the [*Tropiano* defendants' company's] accounts were sold for $53,135, [the] agreement [obtained from Caron] not to solicit those customers was valued at an additional $15,000. . . . . Caron's right to solicit accounts in Milford, Connecticut constituted property within the Hobbs Act definition.

Id. at 1075-1076. More recently, this Circuit similarly held that "[t]he right of the members of a union to democratic participation in a union election is property; that the right is intangible does not divest it of protection under the Hobbs Act," and on that basis, crime families who sought to replace control of the union could be found guilty of conspiracy to commit extortion. United States v. Bellomo, 176 F.3d 580, 592-593 (2d Cir. 1999). . . .

Th[e] second proposition was [at issue] . . . in *Scheidler II*. . . . In *Scheidler II*, the defendants were anti-abortion protestors who had attempted to shut down abortion clinics. The plaintiffs argued that these defendants—"by using or threatening to use force, violence, or fear to cause respondents 'to give up' property rights, namely, 'a woman's right to seek medical service from a clinic, the right of the doctors, nurses, or other clinic staff to perform their jobs, and the right of the clinics to provide medical services free from wrongful threats, violence, coercion, and fear'"—had committed extortion under the Hobbs Act. The Seventh Circuit agreed. . . .

The Supreme Court reversed. Initially, the Court noted that on appeal, the respondents "had shifted the thrust of their theory" with regard to precisely which property rights had been extorted from them. It stated that although the respondents had argued below that the extorted property rights were those of the women and the clinics to receive and perform medical services, they

now assert that petitioners violated the Hobbs Act by "seeking to get control of the use and disposition of respondents' property." They argue that because the right to control the use and disposition of an asset is property, petitioners, who interfered with, and in some instances completely disrupted, the ability of the clinics to function, obtained or attempted to obtain respondents' property.

The United States offers a view similar to that of respondents, asserting that "where the property at issue is a business's *intangible* right to exercise exclusive control over the use of its assets, [a] defendant obtained that property by obtaining control over the use of those assets."

Id. (alteration and emphasis in original).

The Court then concluded that even this revised construction was inconsistent with the Hobbs Act's explicit reference to "obtaining of property from another." It stated that

> [w]e need not now trace what are the boundaries of extortion liability under the Hobbs Act, so that liability might be based on obtaining something as intangible as another's right to exercise exclusive control over the use of a party's business assets. . . . Whatever the outer boundaries may be, the effort to characterize petitioners' actions here as an "obtaining of property from" respondents is well beyond them.

Id. at 402. The Court went on to state that the anti-abortion protesters had neither pursued nor received something of value from respondents that they could exercise, transfer, or sell. To conclude that such actions constituted extortion would effectively discard the statutory requirement that property must be obtained from another, replacing it instead with the notion that merely interfering with or depriving someone of property is sufficient to constitute extortion. Id. at 405.

The Court also explained that such a construction would eliminate the distinction between "extortion and the separate [state-law] crime of coercion. . . . The crime of coercion, which more accurately describes the nature of petitioners' actions, involves the use of force or threat of force to restrict another's freedom of action." Id. The Court found it telling that in drafting the Hobbs Act, Congress had specifically included extortion as a Hobbs Act violation, while not including coercion. Id. at 406-407. The Court concluded that "[b]ecause . . . [the anti-abortion protestors] did not obtain or attempt to obtain property from respondents, . . . there was no basis upon which to find that they committed extortion under the Hobbs Act." Id. at 409.

Justice Stevens, the lone dissenter, protested that the *Scheidler II* majority's "murky opinion seems to hold that this phrase ['the obtaining of property from another'] covers nothing more than the acquisition of tangible property," and that "[n]o other federal court has ever construed this statute so narrowly." Id. at 412 (Stevens, J., dissenting). In other words, Justice Stevens argued that *Scheidler II* had struck down not only the second proposition (the expansive definition of "obtaining") but also the first proposition (the expansive definition of "property"). Id. at 412-416.

The majority opinion, however, expressly disclaimed the notion that it swept so broadly. Indeed, in addition to stating that it "need not now trace what are the outer boundaries of extortion liability under the Hobbs Act," such as whether "liability might be based on obtaining something as intangible as another's right to exercise exclusive control over the use of a party's business assets," the majority explicitly stated that "the dissent is mistaken to suggest that our decision reaches, much less rejects, lower court decisions such as . . . *Tropiano* . . . , in which the Second Circuit concluded that the intangible right to solicit refuse collection accounts constituted property within the Hobbs Act definition." Id. at 402 & n.6. . . .

[W]e believe that the appropriate interpretation of *Scheidler II* must be one that co-exists with *Tropiano*, both as to the "property" and "obtaining" prongs. Thus, as an initial matter, we easily conclude that *Scheidler II* did not overturn *Tropiano*'s broad interpretation of the Hobbs Act's reference to "property," nor [did it] suggest that only tangible property rights can be extorted under the Hobbs Act. . . .

The more complex question is precisely what, pursuant to *Scheidler II*, it means to "obtain" a property right. The *Scheidler II* Court framed this question as a two-part inquiry that requires both a deprivation and an acquisition of property, explaining that while the anti-abortion protestors in that case "may have deprived or sought to deprive respondents of their alleged property right of exclusive control of their business assets, . . . they did not acquire any such property." Id. at 404-405. . . . [E]xplaining why the anti-abortion protestors could not be viewed as having acquired such property, the Court stated that they had "neither pursued nor received something of value from respondents that they could *exercise, transfer, or sell.*" Id. at 405 (emphasis added).

This explanation, in our view, provides the key to understanding what it means, pursuant to *Scheidler II*, to acquire property and thus to obtain it. We read the Court's emphasis on the possibility of exercising, transferring, or selling the property as a concern with the extortionist's *intent* with respect to the property at issue. The "ultimate goal" of the anti-abortion protestors in *Scheidler II* was merely "'shutting down' a clinic that performed abortions." Id. at 405. This did not constitute acquisition in the eyes of the *Scheidler II* Court, we believe, because there was no further intended activity on the part of the protestors. . . . [H]ad the protestors sought to take further action after having deprived the clinics of their right to conduct their business as they wished — by, for example, forcing the clinic staff to provide different types of services, forcing the clinic to turn its operations over to the protestors, or selling the clinic or its property to a third party — we believe [] they would have satisfied the *Scheidler II* Court's definition of "obtaining."

Against this backdrop, it becomes clear why the Supreme Court indicated that *Tropiano* remains good law. . . . The *Scheidler II* Court characterized the right at issue in *Tropiano* as "the intangible right to solicit refuse collection accounts." Id. at 402 n.6. Had the *Tropiano* defendants sought merely to get Caron to stop soliciting collection accounts because they believed that the Milford area should be entirely free from any solicitation, *Tropiano* could not stand; like the anti-abortion protestors, the *Tropiano* defendants would have been seeking simply to deprive someone of a right without doing anything affirmative with that right themselves. But unlike the anti-abortion protestors, the *Tropiano* defendants *did* seek to take action with respect to Caron's solicitation rights; they sought to

transfer those rights to themselves so that they could continue their own
solicitation unimpeded by competition, and thus in a sense broaden their
own solicitation rights. In other words, the *Tropiano* defendants essentially
forced Caron to give them—at no cost—a non-competition agreement,
which, according to the *Tropiano* Court, was valued at about $15,000, and
they used that non-competition agreement to further their own business
activities. *Tropiano*, 418 F.2d at 1076. Their goal was ultimately to enrich
themselves . . . [by] appropriating to themselves the economic value of
Caron's property rights. These actions, unlike those in *Scheidler II*, constituted extortion under the Hobbs Act.

Thus, we hold that in evaluating an extortion count's conformity
with *Scheidler II* . . . the key inquiry is whether the defendant is (1) alleged
to have carried out (or . . . attempted to carry out) the deprivation of a
property right from another, with (2) the intent to exercise, sell, transfer,
or take some other analogous action with respect to that right. A motive
ultimately to profit by cashing out the value of the property right will generally serve as powerful evidence that the defendant's goal was to obtain
the right for himself, rather than merely to deprive the victim of that
right. . . .

2. The Challenged Extortion Counts

A.   THE INDICTMENT

i.   The ILA . . . Counts

On . . . the ILA-related . . . extortion counts, the indictment alleged
that the defendants sought to obtain, and did obtain, the union members' LMRDA rights to free speech and democratic participation in union
affairs as well as their LMRDA rights to loyal representation by their officers, agents, and other representatives. It further stated that the defendants
sought to exercise those rights themselves, by telling various delegates
whom to vote for in certain leadership positions, and by controlling various elected officials' performance of their union duties. We believe that
these allegations satisfy our interpretation of *Scheidler II*, because the government charges not only that the defendants caused the relinquishment
of the union members' LMRDA rights, but also that the defendants did
so in order to exercise those rights for themselves—indeed, in a way that
would profit them financially. . . .

[T]he defendants-appellants have also argued that these counts must
fail because they could not *legally* exercise the union members' LMRDA
rights, and therefore cannot be said to have obtained them. . . .

We [believe] . . . that intangible property can qualify as extortable
property under the Hobbs Act regardless of whether its exercise, transfer,
or sale would be legal. . . . [A]s the government points out, [the alternative

approach, which holds that intangible property rights can qualify as extortable property under the Hobbs Act only if they can be *lawfully* exercised, transferred, or sold] . . . gives rise to the untenable implication that one can never "extort" . . . illegal property (such as narcotics) because such property cannot be legally used, sold, or transferred. . . . [We see no] basis for imposing a "legality" requirement on the extortion of both tangible and intangible property. Accordingly, we hold that the ILA-related and Local 1-related Hobbs Act extortion counts all survived *Scheidler II*.

ii.   The MILA Counts

Similarly, as to the MILA-related extortion counts, the indictment alleges that the defendants sought to obtain, and did obtain, the MILA participants' and beneficiaries' rights to have the MILA trustees contract with the service provider of prescription drugs of the trustees' choice, and to have MILA trustees and fiduciaries discharge their duties in MILA's best interest. The indictment further asserts that the defendants sought to exercise these rights for themselves by telling the MILA trustees which service provider to support, and thereby ensuring the selection of a Gambino-associated enterprise (GPP/VIP) that would pay kickbacks. Here, too, the allegation is that the defendants exercised the rights in question in order to profit themselves. Thus, the MILA-related Hobbs Act extortion counts satisfy the dictates of *Scheidler II*.

iii.   The Tommy Ragucci Counts

As to the Tommy Ragucci counts, the relevant portion of the indictment alleges that the defendants attempted to obtain "money and the right of John Doe 1 [Tommy Ragucci] to be an employee of Howland Hook Container Terminal." In its brief, the government similarly characterizes the extorted property from Tommy Ragucci as his "salary and right to be employed at Howland Hook." . . . [W]hile Tommy Ragucci was presumably an at-will employee with no guaranteed right to continued employment at Howland Hook, he surely had the right to [work] there for as long as he sought the job and his employer would have him. The defendants unquestionably sought to deprive him of that right, and of its attendant salary, when they ordered him to quit. The defendants also sought to take affirmative steps with respect to those rights of employment and salary, insofar as their ultimate goal was to transfer those rights to their own preferred candidate. Thus, for the same reason that we believe *Tropiano* survives *Scheidler II*, we conclude that the Tommy Ragucci counts similarly survive: in both cases, the defendants tried to force their victim to relinquish a property right so that they could transfer that right either to themselves (as in *Tropiano*) or to a third party of their choice (as in the Tommy Ragucci counts).

iv.   The Alayev Counts

The Alayev counts also state a claim for Hobbs Act extortion under our interpretation of *Scheidler II*. Here, in relevant part, the indictment alleges that the defendants obtained Alayev's intangible property rights to make various business decisions (such as whether to keep illegal gambling machines on the premises) free from outside pressure. As the government aptly states in its brief, "[t]he defendants did not seek merely to 'shut down' Alayev's business but essentially made themselves his silent partners and exercised his rights to their own advantage." Because here the allegation is that the defendants sought to exercise for themselves Alayev's rights in a manner that would profit them, the Alayev counts survive *Scheidler II*.

v.   The Seagal Counts

Finally, the Seagal Counts also satisfy the *Scheidler II* standard. Here, it is alleged that the defendants sought to exercise for themselves Seagal's right to make his own business decisions, by threatening him with possible violence unless he worked with Jules Nasso again. Thus, here the defendants sought to exercise for themselves Seagal's intangible right to decide with whom to work, in order to secure profit for themselves. This constitutes Hobbs Act extortion under *Scheidler II*. . . .

NOTES AND QUESTIONS

1. You may be wondering why a case called *Scheidler v. National Organization for Women* receives so much attention in a casebook on federal criminal law. As the case name suggests, *Scheidler* was a civil suit, brought by abortion clinics and various organizations supporting them against Operation Rescue and various individuals affiliated with it. Operation Rescue was a pro-life organization that employed violent means to shut down abortion clinics. The suit was brought under the Racketeer Influenced and Corrupt Organizations Act (RICO), a federal statute that bans the operation of criminal enterprises through "a pattern of racketeering activity." See 18 U.S.C. §1962(c), which we examine thoroughly in Chapter 8. The RICO statute defines "racketeering activity" to include a long list of federal and state crimes, including violations of the Hobbs Act. Id. §1961(1). In addition to stiff criminal penalties and forfeiture provisions, RICO includes a feature rarely seen in criminal statutes: a provision establishing civil damages liability for violations—treble damages, in fact. Id. §1964(c).

So, in a nutshell, the *Scheidler* plaintiffs could (in theory) obtain a great deal of money from the defendants if they could prove multiple instances—under RICO, two acts of racketeering activity can constitute a "pattern"—of Hobbs Act extortion. The plaintiffs produced plenty of evidence of violent and threatening conduct by the defendants. This conduct, however, was clearly motivated by a desire to stop the clinics from performing abortions, not by a desire to make money or to take over the operation of the clinics. The basic issue throughout the *Scheidler* litigation was whether violence gives rise to liability under RICO and the Hobbs Act when it is not motivated by, and does not achieve, financial gain for the defendants.

2. All three of the Supreme Court's *Scheidler* decisions addressed that issue. In *Scheidler I*, 510 U.S. 249 (1994), the question was whether RICO liability required an economic motive. In a decision handed down only a year after the first World Trade Center bombing, the Court held that no such motive was required. As a result, *Scheidler I* preserved the option of using RICO against terrorist organizations (though the government has rarely exercised that option since). In *Scheidler II*, 537 U.S. 393 (2003), the defendants made a similar argument under the Hobbs Act—that they did not "obtain" any of the plaintiffs' property. The defendants argued that they sought to destroy—not profit from or otherwise exercise—the relevant property interests. This time the defendants won, as the Second Circuit explains in *Gotti*. After *Scheidler II*, the plaintiffs tried a new theory. They argued that in addition to robbery and extortion, the Hobbs Act bars violent conduct that interferes with interstate commerce but does *not* involve the "obtaining" of "property." A Seventh Circuit panel bought the argument. In *Scheidler III*, 547 U.S. 9 (2006), the Supreme Court reversed.

After *Scheidler*, it remains an open question of what it means to "obtain" the property of another. It is clear that mere deprivation is not enough, and that defendants must be capable of exercising, transferring, selling, or otherwise utilizing the property right in question. Still, the boundary between a Hobbs Act violation and a mere illegal deprivation is not clear. Let's take the Alayev counts in *Gotti* as an example. The defendants forced gambling machines into the building. In what way was this "obtaining property" as required by *Scheidler*? The Second Circuit found, among other things, a deprivation of the "right to refuse to keep illegal gambling machines at a business." *Gotti*, 459 F.3d at 328. Moreover, the court said, the defendants "exercised" this right by stripping the decision-making power from the victim, and deciding for themselves whether or not the property interest in question would be exercised. *Scheidler II*, at least according to the Second Circuit, is not contrary to this ruling.

But couldn't the same reasoning apply to the facts in *Scheidler*? Couldn't it be said that Operation Rescue sought to obtain the clinic's right to control its operations, including setting the working hours of their employees? Certainly, the defendants were at least indirectly seeking to control the clinic's operations, by forcing it to shut down and thereby forcing the employees out of work. In the corporate context, "control" is a valuable asset (which often can be purchased at a premium price), separate from the enterprise's other assets. Why does seeking to obtain, indirectly or not, control of all operations not constitute deprivation of a property right plus exercise of that right? The answer cannot be that the right of control (or its components, including the right to set working hours) is an "intangible" one; *Scheidler II* expressly disavowed such a distinction. 537 U.S. at 402 n.6 (stating that the decision doesn't "reach[], much less reject[], lower court decisions such as *United States v. Tropiano*, in which the Second Circuit concluded that the intangible right to solicit refuse collection accounts 'constituted property within the Hobbs Act definition'"). Is *Gotti* simply wrong on this point? Or perhaps the question of whether property is "obtained" depends on the level of abstraction through which the property interest is viewed. The *Scheidler II* Court described the property interest in question, not as the right to set working hours, but rather as the right to "exclusive control of their business assets." Id. at 405. Obviously, Operation Rescue never sought to exercise such a far-reaching right, for it was not seeking *all* business assets. Could the plaintiffs in *Scheidler* file another suit using the Second Circuit's *Gotti* theory?

3. Reread the summary of Steven Seagal's conversation with Sonny Ciccone, and imagine that the subsequent conversation with Jules Nasso (in which Nasso told Seagal that if he were less cooperative, he would have been killed) had not taken place. Could the government still have made out an extortion case? Judging by the Second Circuit's decision—particularly the court's discussion of the Tommy Ragucci counts—the answer is yes. Ciccone did not threaten Seagal because he did not have to. The real threat stems from Ciccone's reputation. This is a man who gets what he wants; people who cross him live Hobbesian lives—nasty, brutish, and short. Once such a reputation is acquired, the threats need never be uttered.

Yet the government can convict anyway. This is the beauty of extortion charges from the government's point of view. Recall *Zhou*, which established that extortion differs from robbery in how openly the threat of force and violence is displayed—the threatened use of force is out in the open in robbery cases, but subtle and implicit in extortion cases. Threats that defendants do not intend and lack the power to carry out may suffice, as long as they have the desired effect on the extorted victim. (And possibly even if they do *not* have the desired effect on the victim, as is suggested by the *Gotti* court's discussion of the Tommy Ragucci counts.) Mafia-style criminal organizations make money by leveraging a reputation for violence. The Hobbs Act seems to criminalize precisely that style of leverage.

What must the government prove in order to convict? Not the utterance of an explicit threat, and not the existence of a genuine threat. Ragucci kept his job and was unharmed; it was far from obvious that Nasso was telling Seagal the truth about the harm he would incur if he rejected Ciccone's overtures. Hints and implications—*possible* threats—appear to be sufficient. It is up to the jury to decide what the defendants' conduct and words imply. Do you think the courts have fairly constrained the scope of the Hobbs Act? They appear to be proceeding under the assumption that the range of conduct Congress intended to criminalize in the Hobbs Act cannot be precisely specified.

4. For another take on what exactly counts as "property" that can be obtained within the meaning of the Hobbs Act—one that arises not just in "threat" cases (the subject of this chapter), but also in "under color of official right" cases (explored in the next chapter)—consider United States v. McFall, 558 F.3d 951 (9th Cir. 2009). The defendant, who was a lobbyist and former local elected official, had a consulting contract with Sunlaw, a power company that sought the right to build a plant in the Port of Stockton. To ensure that Sunlaw got the contract, McFall sought to force Calpine, a competing power company, to withdraw by threatening Calpine that if it did not drop its bid for the Port of Stockton site, he would use his political influence to create a "public outcry" over Calpine's plans to build another plant in Alameda County. Id. at 954.

Relying on *Scheidler II*, the Ninth Circuit reversed McFall's conviction. It noted:

> McFall argues that the government did not prove—or even allege—that he attempted to obtain Calpine's property within the meaning of the Hobbs Act. The indictment charged McFall and his collaborators with "attempt[ing] to obtain from Calpine Corporation a financial benefit not due any of them, that is, its right to solicit business in San Joaquin County, to bid on the construction of a power plant and to construct a power plant at the Port of Stockton." In essence, McFall argues, the government charged him with employing coercion to derail Calpine's bid to build a power plant at the Port of Stockton, thereby *increasing* the probability, at least theoretically, that Sunlaw would secure the right to build the plant at the contested site.
>
> We agree that decreasing a competitor's chance of winning a contract, standing alone, does not amount to *obtaining* a transferable asset for oneself (or one's client). Neither Calpine nor Sunlaw had a vested right to build at the contested site, and there was no guarantee that either company would secure such a right. The district court concluded that McFall's "improper attempt to secure a business advantage" satisfied the Hobbs Act's obtaining element, but this formulation fails to account for *Scheidler*'s principal point: To violate the Hobbs Act, an alleged extortionist must actually appropriate (or attempt to appropriate) the victim's property such that it can be exercised, transferred or sold. It is not enough to gain some speculative benefit by hindering a competitor.
>
> Moreover, *Scheidler* made clear that the rule of lenity applies to ambiguous applications of the Hobbs Act. Thus, even if a coherent argument could be made that attempting to thwart Calpine's bid to build a plant at the Port of Stockton amounted to an attempt to "obtain" an increased probability of winning a right to build for Sunlaw, we must resolve the ambiguity in favor of McFall.

The government stresses that *Scheidler* expressly left intact a lower court decision assigning an expansive definition to the term "property" as used in the act. See 537 U.S. at 402 n.6 (explaining that the holding does not disturb the Second Circuit's decision in United States v. Tropiano, 418 F.2d 1069, 1076 (2d Cir. 1969), where the court "concluded that the intangible right to solicit refuse collection accounts constituted property within the Hobbs Act definition") (internal quotation marks omitted). *Tropiano*, however, does not help the government to satisfy the Hobbs Act's obtaining element. Even assuming that the intangible right to bid on a power plant site constitutes property for Hobbs Act purposes, the government must establish that McFall attempted to acquire that property right such that he alone could sell, transfer, or exercise it. Cf. United States v. Gotti, 459 F.3d 296, 323 (2d Cir. 2006) (holding that *Scheidler* effected a general tightening of the Hobbs Act's obtaining requirement, but did not undermine Second Circuit precedent holding that intangible property rights can qualify as "extortable property"). Even assuming that the right to submit a bid is property within the meaning of the Hobbs Act, McFall did not, and indeed could not, attempt to exercise Calpine's right to submit a bid. Instead, according to the evidence introduced at trial, he sought to increase Sunlaw's odds of prevailing on its own bid by restricting the activities of a competitor—conduct that cannot amount to obtaining under *Scheidler*.

Because the evidence did not establish, nor did the indictment allege, that McFall obtained or attempted to obtain any property or intangible right from Calpine, we conclude that the evidence is insufficient to sustain a conviction . . . on those counts.

McFall, 558 F.3d at 956-58.

In 2013, the Supreme Court sought to clarify the doctrine—or at least one would like to think that was its intent.

Sekhar v. United States
133 S. Ct. 2720 (2013)

Justice SCALIA delivered the opinion of the Court.

We consider whether attempting to compel a person to recommend that his employer approve an investment constitutes "the obtaining of property from another" under 18 U.S.C. §1951(b)(2). New York's Common Retirement Fund is an employee pension fund for the State of New York and its local governments. As sole trustee of the Fund, the State Comptroller chooses Fund investments. When the Comptroller decides to approve an investment he issues a "Commitment." A Commitment, however, does not actually bind the Fund. For that to happen, the Fund and the recipient of the investment must enter into a limited partnership agreement.

Petitioner Giridhar Sekhar was a managing partner of FA Technology Ventures. In October 2009, the Comptroller's office was considering whether to invest in a fund managed by that firm. The office's general counsel made a written recommendation to the Comptroller not to invest in the fund, after learning that the Office of the New York Attorney General was investigating another fund managed by the firm. The Comptroller decided not to issue a Commitment and notified a partner of FA Technology Ventures. That partner had previously heard rumors that the general counsel was having an extramarital affair.

The general counsel then received a series of anonymous e-mails demanding that he recommend moving forward with the investment and threatening, if he did not, to disclose information about his alleged affair to his wife, government officials, and the media. . . . The general counsel contacted law enforcement, which traced some of the e-mails to petitioner's home computer and other e-mails to offices of FA Technology Ventures.

Petitioner was indicted for, and a jury convicted him of, attempted extortion, in violation of the Hobbs Act, 18 U.S.C. §1951(a). . . . On the verdict form, the jury was asked to specify the property that petitioner attempted to extort: (1) "the Commitment"; (2) "the Comptroller's approval of the Commitment"; or (3) "the General Counsel's recommendation to approve the Commitment." The jury chose only the third option.

The Court of Appeals for the Second Circuit affirmed the conviction. The court held that the general counsel "had a property right in rendering sound legal advice to the Comptroller and, specifically, to recommend—free from threats—whether the Comptroller should issue a Commitment for [the funds]." The court concluded that petitioner not only attempted to deprive the general counsel of his "property right," but that petitioner also "attempted to exercise that right by forcing the General Counsel to make a recommendation determined by [petitioner].". . .

II

A

Whether viewed from the standpoint of the common law, the text and genesis of the statute at issue here, or the jurisprudence of this Court's prior cases, what was charged in this case was not extortion.

It is a settled principle of interpretation that, absent other indication, "Congress intends to incorporate the well-settled meaning of the common-law terms it uses." Neder v. United States, 527 U.S. 1, 23 (1999). . . .

The Hobbs Act punishes "extortion," one of the oldest crimes in our legal tradition, see E. Coke, The Third Part of the Institutes of the Laws of England 148-150 (1648) (reprint 2008). The crime originally applied only to extortionate action by public officials, but was later extended by statute to private extortion. See 4 C. Torcia, Wharton's Criminal Law §§695, 699 (14th ed. 1981). As far as is known, no case predating the Hobbs Act—English, federal, or state—ever identified conduct such as that charged here as extortionate. Extortion required the obtaining of items of value, typically cash, from the victim. It did not cover mere coercion to act, or to refrain from acting.

The text of the statute at issue confirms that the alleged property here cannot be extorted. Enacted in 1946, the Hobbs Act defines its crime of "extortion" as "the *obtaining of property from another*, with his consent, induced by wrongful use of actual or threatened force, violence, or fear, or under color of official right." 18 U.S.C. §1951(b)(2) (emphasis added). Obtaining property requires "not only the deprivation but also the acquisition of property." Scheidler v. National Organization for Women, Inc., 537 U.S. 393, 404 (2003). That is, it requires that the victim "part with" his property, R. Perkins & R. Boyce, Criminal Law 451 (3d ed. 1982), and that the extortionist "gain possession" of it, *Scheidler*, supra, at 403, n.8. The property extorted must therefore be *transferable*—that is, capable of passing from one person to another. The alleged property here lacks that defining feature.[2]

The genesis of the Hobbs Act reinforces that conclusion. The Act was modeled after §850 of the New York Penal Law (1909), which was derived from the famous Field Code, a 19th-century model penal code, see 4 Commissioners of the Code, Penal Code of the State of New York §613, p. 220 (1865) (reprint 1998). Congress borrowed, nearly verbatim, the New York statute's definition of extortion. See *Scheidler*, 537 U.S. at 403. The New York statute contained, in addition to the felony crime of extortion, a new (that is to say, nonexistent at common law) misdemeanor crime of coercion. Whereas the former required, as we have said, "'the criminal acquisition of . . . property,'" ibid., the latter required merely the use of threats "to compel another person to do or to abstain from doing an act which such other such person has a legal right to do or to abstain from doing." N.Y. Penal Law §530 (1909), earlier codified in N.Y. Penal Code §653 (1881). Congress did not copy the coercion provision. The omission must have been deliberate, since it was perfectly clear that extortion did not include coercion. At the time of the borrowing (1946), New York courts had consistently held that the sort of *interference* with

---

2. It may well be proper under the Hobbs Act for the Government to charge a person who obtains money by threatening a third party, who obtains funds belonging to a corporate or governmental entity by threatening the entity's agent, or who obtains "goodwill and customer revenues" by threatening a market competitor, see, e.g., United States v. Zemek, 634 F.2d 1159, 1173 (CA9 1980). Each of these might be considered "obtaining property from another." We need not consider those situations, however, because the Government did not charge any of them here.

rights that occurred here was coercion. See, e.g., People v. Ginsberg, 262 N.Y. 556 (1933) (*per curiam*) (compelling store owner to become a member of a trade association and to remove advertisements); People v. Scotti, 266 N.Y. 480 (App. Div. 1934) (compelling victim to enter into agreement with union); People v. Kaplan, 240 App. Div. 72, 74-75, aff'd, 264 N.Y. 675 (1934) (compelling union members to drop lawsuits against union leadership). And finally, this Court's own precedent similarly demands reversal of petitioner's convictions. In *Scheidler*, we held that protesters did not commit extortion under the Hobbs Act, even though they "interfered with, disrupted, and in some instances completely deprived" abortion clinics of their ability to run their business. 537 U.S. at 404-405. We reasoned that the protesters may have deprived the clinics of an "alleged property right," but they did not pursue or receive "'something of value from'" the clinics that they could then "exercise, transfer, or sell" themselves. . . .

This case is easier than *Scheidler*, where one might at least have said that physical occupation of property amounted to obtaining that property. The deprivation alleged here is far more abstract. *Scheidler* rested its decision, as we do, on the term "obtaining." Id. at 402, n.6. The principle announced there—that a defendant must pursue something of value from the victim that can be exercised, transferred, or sold—applies with equal force here.[4] Whether one considers the personal right at issue to be "property" in a broad sense or not, it certainly was not *obtainable property* under the Hobbs Act.[5]

---

4. The Government's attempt to distinguish *Scheidler* is unconvincing. In its view, had the protesters sought to force the clinics to provide services other than abortion, extortion would have been a proper charge. Petitioner committed extortion here, the Government says, because he did not merely attempt to prevent the general counsel from giving a recommendation but tried instead to force him to issue one. That distinction is, not to put too fine a point on it, nonsensical. It is coercion, not extortion, when a person is forced to do something and when he is forced to do nothing. See, e.g., N.Y. Penal Law §530 (1909) (it is a misdemeanor to coerce a "person to do or to abstain from doing an act"). Congress's enactment of the Hobbs Act did not, through the phrase "obtaining of property from another," suddenly transform every act that coerces affirmative conduct into a crime punishable for up to 20 years, while leaving those who "merely" coerce inaction immune from federal punishment.

5. The concurrence contends that the "right to make [a] recommendation" is not property. *Post*, at 4 (Alito, J., concurring in judgment). We are not sure of that. If one defines property to include anything of value, surely some rights to make recommendations would qualify—for example, a member of the Pulitzer Prize Committee's right to recommend the recipient of the prize. We suppose that a prominent journalist would not give up that right (he cannot, of course, transfer it) for a significant sum of money—so it must be valuable. But the point relevant to the present case is that *it cannot be transferred*, so it cannot be the object of extortion under the statute.

B

The Government's shifting and imprecise characterization of the alleged property at issue betrays the weakness of its case. According to the jury's verdict form, the "property" that petitioner attempted to extort was "the General Counsel's recommendation to approve the Commitment." App. 142. But the Government expends minuscule effort in defending that theory of conviction. And for good reason—to wit, our decision in Cleveland v. United States, 531 U.S. 12 (2000), which reversed a business owner's mail-fraud conviction for "obtaining money or property" through misrepresentations made in an application for a video-poker license issued by the State. We held that a "license" is not "property" while in the State's hands and so cannot be "obtained" from the State. Even less so can an employee's yet-to-be-issued recommendation be called obtainable property, and less so still a yet-to-be-issued recommendation that would merely approve (but not effect) a particular investment.

Hence the Government's reliance on an alternative, more sophisticated (and sophistic) description of the property. Instead of defending the jury's description, the Government hinges its case on the general counsel's "intangible property right to give his disinterested legal opinion to his client free of improper outside interference." Brief for United States 39. But *what*, exactly, would the petitioner have obtained for himself? A right to give *his own* disinterested legal opinion to *his own* client free of improper interference? Or perhaps, a right to give *the general counsel's* disinterested legal opinion to *the general counsel's* client?

Either formulation sounds absurd, because it is. Clearly, petitioner's goal was not to acquire the general counsel's "intangible property right to give disinterested legal advice." It was to force the general counsel to offer advice that accorded with petitioner's wishes. But again, that is coercion, not extortion. No fluent speaker of English would say that "petitioner *obtained and exercised* the general counsel's right to make a recommendation," any more than he would say that a person "*obtained and exercised* another's right to free speech." He would say that "petitioner *forced* the general counsel to make a particular recommendation," just as he would say that a person "*forced* another to make a statement." Adopting the Government's theory here would not only make nonsense of words; it would collapse the longstanding distinction between extortion and coercion and ignore Congress's choice to penalize one but not the other. See *Scheidler*, supra, at 409. That we cannot do.

The judgment of the Court of Appeals for the Second Circuit is reversed.

Justice ALITO, with whom Justice KENNEDY and Justice SOTOMAYOR join, concurring in the judgment.

Concurrence:

Issue

The question that we must decide in this case is whether "the General Counsel's recommendation to approve the Commitment," App. 142—or his right to make that recommendation—is property that is capable of being extorted under the Hobbs Act, 18 U.S.C. §1951. In my view, they are not.

I

The jury in this case returned a special verdict form and stated that the property that petitioner attempted to extort was "the General Counsel's recommendation to approve the Commitment." What the jury obviously meant by this was the general counsel's internal suggestion to his superior that the state government issue a nonbinding commitment to invest in a fund managed by FA Technology Ventures. We must therefore decide whether this nonbinding internal recommendation by a salaried state employee constitutes "property" within the meaning of the Hobbs Act, which defines "extortion" as "the obtaining of property from another, with his consent, induced by wrongful use of actual or threatened force, violence, or fear, or under color of official right." §1951(b)(2).

The Hobbs Act does not define the term "property, but even at common law the offense of extortion was understood to include the obtaining of any thing of value. 2 E. Coke, The First Part of the Institutes of the Laws of England 368b (18th English ed. 1823) ("Extortion . . . is a great misprison, by wresting or unlawfully taking by any officer, by colour of his office, any money or valuable thing of or from any man"); 4 W. Blackstone, Commentaries *141 (extortion is "an abuse of public, justice which consists in any officer's unlawfully taking, by colour of his office, from any man, any money or thing of value"). See also 2 J. Bishop, Criminal Law §401, pp. 331-332 (9th ed. 1923) ("In most cases, the thing obtained is money. . . . But probably anything of value will suffice"); 3 F. Wharton, A Treatise on Criminal Law §1898, p. 2095 (11th ed. 1912) ("[I]t is enough if any valuable thing is received").

At the time Congress enacted the Hobbs Act, the contemporary edition of Black's Law Dictionary included an expansive definition of the term. See Black's Law Dictionary 1446 (3d ed. 1933). It stated that "[t]he term is said to extend to every species of valuable right and interest. . . . The word is also commonly used to denote everything which is the subject of ownership, corporeal or incorporeal, tangible or intangible, visible or invisible, real or personal; everything that has an exchangeable value or which goes to make up wealth or estate." Id. at 1446-1447. And the lower courts have long given the term a similarly expansive construction. See, e.g., United States v. Tropiano, 418 F.2d 1069, 1075 (CA2 1969) ("The concept of property under the Hobbs Act . . . includes, in a broad sense, any valuable right considered as a source or element of wealth").

Despite the breadth of some of these formulations, however, the term "property" plainly does not reach everything that a person may hold dear; nor does it extend to everything that might in some indirect way portend the possibility of future economic gain. I do not suggest that the current lower court case law is necessarily correct, but it seems clear that the case now before us is an outlier and that the jury's verdict stretches the concept of property beyond the breaking point.

It is not customary to refer to an internal recommendation to make a government decision as a form of property. It would seem strange to say that the government or its employees have a property interest in their internal recommendations regarding such things as the issuance of a building permit, the content of an environmental impact statement, the approval of a new drug, or the indictment of an individual or a corporation. And it would be even stranger to say that a private party who might be affected by the government's decision can obtain a property interest in a recommendation to make the decision. See, e.g., Doyle v. University of Alabama, 680 F.2d 1323, 1326 (CA11 1982) ("Doyle had no protected property interest in the mere recommendation for a raise; thus she was not entitled to due process safeguards when the recommended raise was disapproved by the University").

Our decision in Cleveland v. United States, 531 U.S. 12 (2000), supports the conclusion that internal recommendations regarding government decisions are not property. In *Cleveland*, we vacated a business owner's conviction under the federal mail fraud statute, 18 U.S.C. §1341, for "obtaining money or property" through misrepresentations made in an application for a video poker license issued by the State. We held that a video poker license is not property in the hands of the State. I do not suggest that the concepts of property under the mail fraud statute and the Hobbs Act are necessarily the same. But surely a video poker license has a stronger claim to be classified as property than a mere internal recommendation that a state government take an initial step that might lead eventually to an investment that would be beneficial to private parties. . . .

. . . If an internal recommendation regarding a government decision does not constitute property, then surely a government employee's right to make such a recommendation is not property either (nor could it be deemed a *property* right).

II

The Government argues that the recommendation was the general counsel's *personal* property because it was inextricably related to his right to pursue his profession as an attorney. See id. at 34-35. But that argument is clearly wrong: If the general counsel had left the State's employ before submitting the recommendation, he could not have taken the recommendation with him, and he certainly could not have given it or sold it to someone else. Therefore, it is obvious that the recommendation (and the right to make it) were inextricably related to the general counsel's position with the government, and not to his broader personal right to pursue the practice of law.

The general counsel's job surely had economic value to him, as did his labor as a lawyer, his law license, and his reputation as an attorney. But the indictment did not allege, and the jury did not find, that petitioner attempted to obtain those things. Nor would such a theory make sense in the context of this case. Petitioner did not, for example, seek the general counsel's legal advice or demand that the general counsel represent him in a legal proceeding. Cf. United States v. Thompson, 647 F.3d 180, 186-187 (CA5 2011) (a person's labor is property capable of being extorted). Nor did petitioner attempt to enhance his own ability to compete with the general counsel for legal work by threatening to do something that would, say, tarnish the general counsel's reputation or cause his law license to be revoked. Cf. Tropiano, 418 F.2d at 1071-1072, 1075-1077 (threats to competitor in order to obtain customers constitute extortion); United States v. Zemek, 634 F.2d 1159, 1173-1174 (CA9 1980) (same); United States v. Coffey, 361 F. Supp. 2d 102, 108-109 (E.D.N.Y. 2005) (the right to pursue a lawful business is extortable property under the Hobbs Act).

The Court holds that petitioner's conduct does not amount to attempted extortion, but for a different reason: According to the Court, the alleged property that petitioner pursued was not transferable and therefore is not capable of being "obtained." Ante, at 4-5, 7-8. Because I do not believe that the item in question constitutes property, it is unnecessary for me to determine whether or not petitioner sought to obtain it. . . .

QUESTIONS

1. To what extent is *Sekhar* the distinguishable product of an adventurous charging theory and an interesting special verdict? How easily could one (with 20-20 hindsight) charge extortion here without running afoul of the Court's analysis? A district court recently observed that

several post-*Sekhar* extortion cases have held that "property" within the meaning of the Hobbs Act extends to, inter alia, a warehouse tenancy; confidential business information; information from a client list; union members' voting rights; and the right to solicit restaurant patrons and good will from those patrons. See Re v. United States, 736 F.3d 1121, 1123 (7th Cir. 2013); United

States v. Silver, 117 F. Supp. 3d 461, 467 n.8 (S.D.N.Y. 2015); United States v. Colvard, No. 13-CR-109, 2015 WL 5123893, at *6 (M.D. Pa. Sept. 1, 2015); United States v. Perry, 37 F. Supp. 3d 546, 554 (D. Mass. 2014); United States v. D'Anna, No. 13-20119, 2015 WL 5737165, at *2 (E.D. Mich. Oct. 1, 2015); cf. United States v. Larson, No. 07-CR-304S, 2013 WL 5573046, at *6 (W.D.N.Y. Oct. 9, 2013) ("jobs and pay" remain obtainable property under the Hobbs Act, whereas the right to make business decisions free from interference do not). All of these courts found that the sorts of intangible property at issue could effectively be acquired to further defendants' own interests and benefit.

United States v. Soha, 2017 WL 2222244, at *5 (W.D.N.Y. 2017).

2. Do the foregoing cases have it right? Is *Gotti* good law? In particular, does Justice Scalia's point in footnote 5 about a Pulitzer Prize vote's lack of transferability mean that the Hobbs Act cannot reach extortions of intangible property rights that can practically but not legally be exercised by others? The First Circuit has expressed doubts that, in the wake of *Sekhar*, "LMRDA rights constitute property under the Hobbs Act." United States v. Burhoe, 871 F.3d 1, 25 (1st Cir. 2017). Was that case merely a pleading failure or should *Sekhar* put an end to cases like *Gotti*?

6 | Official Corruption

We have already seen some of the federal statutes used to prosecute political corruption. Chapter 4 discussed how a public official's acceptance of a bribe can be charged as "honest services" mail or wire fraud. Chapter 5 discussed how a threatened exercise of official authority that wrongfully induces a fear of economic loss can amount to "extortion." In all of these cases, however, the abuse of trust or authority has ready private sector analogues. At the heart of each offense is the notion that public office is just another sort of agency relationship. This chapter will consider offenses specifically concerned with official power and public trust: extortion "under color of official right" and bribery and gratuity provisions.

That the offenses considered in this chapter specifically target public officers—and in the case of certain offenses, only federal officials (or those exercising federal responsibilities)—makes for a peculiar statutory interpretation dynamic. Even where Congress has acted with specificity quite absent from, say, the mail fraud statute, the courts have often done considerable fine-tuning.

There are a number of reasons why Congress might legislate more precisely when it comes to federal bribery statutes, and why the courts, when faced with relatively detailed statutes, might continue to tinker with their scope. First of all, federal legislators and judges not only take a special interest in the integrity of federal governance, but are themselves potential statutory targets. Enforcement pressure is surely another cause. Federal agencies—not just the FBI, but all the departmental inspectors general—have a special duty to look out for ethical violations. The press also takes an interest from time to time. If such violations come to light, the public will often demand action. At that point, the choices are stark: federal prosecution, administrative discipline, or nothing. Unlike other areas, the matter cannot simply be left to the state to handle (or not). And with the disciplinary route seeming like a "slap on the wrist" to some—and perhaps also being unduly cumbersome, the allure of the quick and forceful criminal process is considerable. (The lure of a forceful criminal response may be even greater when "independent" or "special" counsels are assigned to look into a matter.)

The statutory drafting and interpretation challenges are themselves considerable in this area. Even in the mail fraud context, we saw some courts, pre-*Skilling*, attempt to distinguish between bribes and "mere" gratuities. Those distinctions were based on state law. See, e.g., United States v. Brumley, 116 F.3d 729, 735 (5th Cir. 1997) (en banc), which is mentioned in Section C of Chapter 4. What is the difference between these two kinds of improper payments under federal law? Does it make any difference whether an official demands money or just accepts it?

Other questions arise as well: To what extent should federal criminal law be co-extensive with lobbying and campaign finance regulations? What precisely separates the legislator who takes money or the guarantee of a lobbyist position in the future from the legislator who steers appropriations to his district in order to get reelected (thereby increasing the personal benefits he will enjoy as a legislator and thereafter as a lobbyist for a highly regulated industry)? Is the difference just one of risk aversion? Of timing? Given that the mail/wire fraud statute and the Hobbs Act can be used against corrupt state and local officials, what—if any—value is there to legislation specifically targeting corruption within governmental units that receive federal funds (especially since virtually all do)?

A.   EXTORTION UNDER COLOR OF OFFICIAL RIGHT

Where an official (federal, state, or local) threatens economic harm in order to extract a payoff, he can be charged under the Hobbs Act with obtaining money through the "wrongful use" of "fear." See Chapter 5. The Hobbs Act offers an alternative charging theory, however, that looks not to the use of fear but to whether the official obtained the money "under color of official right." The range of possible interpretations of this phrase—and the possible scope of Hobbs Act liability—emerges (all too dimly) in a pair of Supreme Court cases, McCormick v. United States and Evans v. United States, excerpted below. Note how the Court initially bracketed the question of whether the official had to have "induced" the payment, and went right to the question that hangs over all "under color" cases: How does one square a statute targeting open-palmed officials with a political system in which elected officials are regularly (perhaps constantly) raising money for the next (or the last) campaign?

McCormick v. United States
500 U.S. 257 (1991)

Justice WHITE delivered the opinion of the Court.

This case requires us to consider whether the Court of Appeals properly affirmed the conviction of petitioner, an elected public official, for extorting property under color of official right in violation of the Hobbs Act, 18 U.S.C. §1951. . . .

I

Petitioner Robert L. McCormick was a member of the West Virginia House of Delegates in 1984. He represented a district that had long suffered from a shortage of medical doctors. For several years, West Virginia had allowed foreign medical school graduates to practice under temporary permits while studying for the state licensing exams. Under this program, some doctors were allowed to practice under temporary permits for years even though they repeatedly failed the state exams. McCormick was a leading advocate and supporter of this program.

In the early 1980s, following a move in the House of Delegates to end the temporary permit program, several of the temporarily licensed doctors formed an organization to press their interests in Charleston. The organization hired a lobbyist, John Vandergrift, who in 1984 worked for legislation that would extend the expiration date of the temporary permit program. McCormick sponsored the House version of the proposed legislation, and a bill was passed extending the program for another year. Shortly thereafter, Vandergrift and McCormick discussed the possibility of introducing legislation during the 1985 session that would grant the doctors a permanent medical license by virtue of their years of experience. McCormick agreed to sponsor such legislation.

During his 1984 reelection campaign, McCormick informed Vandergrift that his campaign was expensive, that he had paid considerable sums out of his own pocket, and that he had not heard anything from the foreign doctors. Vandergrift told McCormick that he would contact the doctors and see what he could do. Vandergrift contacted one of the foreign doctors and later received from the doctors $1,200 in cash. Vandergrift delivered an envelope containing nine $100 bills to McCormick. Later the same day, a second delivery of $2,000 in cash was made to McCormick. During the fall of 1984, McCormick received two more cash payments from the doctors. McCormick did not list any of these payments as campaign contributions,[1] nor did he report the money as income on his 1984 federal income tax return. And although the doctors' organization kept detailed books of its expenditures, the cash payments were not listed as campaign contributions. Rather, the entries for the payments were

---

1. West Virginia law prohibits cash campaign contributions in excess of $50 per person. W. Va. Code §3-8-5d (1990).

accompanied only by initials or other codes signifying that the money was for McCormick.

In the spring of 1985, McCormick sponsored legislation permitting experienced doctors to be permanently licensed without passing the state licensing exams. McCormick spoke at length in favor of the bill during floor debate, and the bill ultimately was enacted into law. Two weeks after the legislation was enacted, McCormick received another cash payment from the foreign doctors.

Following an investigation, a federal grand jury returned an indictment charging McCormick with five counts of violating the Hobbs Act by extorting payments under color of official right. . . . At the close of a 6-day trial, the jury was instructed that to establish a Hobbs Act violation the Government had to prove that McCormick induced a cash payment and that he did so knowingly and willfully by extortion. . . .

The next day the jury informed the court that it "would like to hear the instructions again with particular emphasis on the definition of extortion under the color of official right. . . ." The court then reread most of the extortion instructions to the jury, but reordered some of the paragraphs and made the following significant addition:

"Extortion under color of official right means the obtaining of money by a public official when the money obtained was not lawfully due and owing to him or to his office. Of course, extortion does not occur where one who is a public official receives a legitimate gift or a voluntary political contribution even though the political contribution may have been made in cash in violation of local law. Voluntary is that which is freely given without expectation of benefit.". . .

The jury convicted McCormick of the first Hobbs Act count (charging him with receiving the initial $900 cash payment) . . . but could not reach verdicts on the remaining four Hobbs Act counts. The District Court declared a mistrial on those four counts.

The Court of Appeals affirmed, observing that nonelected officials may be convicted under the Hobbs Act without proof that they have granted or agreed to grant some benefit or advantage in exchange for money paid to them[,] and that elected officials should be held to the same standard when they receive money other than "legitimate" campaign contributions. 896 F.2d 61 (CA4 1990). After stating that McCormick could not be prosecuted under the Hobbs Act for receiving voluntary campaign contributions, id. at 65, the court rejected McCormick's contention that conviction of an elected official under the Act requires, under all circumstances, proof of a *quid pro quo*, i.e., a promise of official action or inaction in exchange for any payment or property received, id. at 66. Rather, the court interpreted the statute as not requiring such a showing where the parties never intended the payments to be "legitimate" campaign contributions. . . .

Because of disagreement in the Courts of Appeals regarding the meaning of the phrase "under color of official right" as it is used in the Hobbs Act,[5] we granted certiorari. We reverse and remand for further proceedings.'

II

McCormick's challenge to the judgment below affirming his conviction is limited to the Court of Appeals' rejection of his claim that the payments made to him by or on behalf of the doctors were campaign contributions, the receipt of which did not violate the Hobbs Act. . . . [W]e agree with McCormick that the Court of Appeals erred. . . .

---

5. Until the early 1970s, extortion prosecutions under the Hobbs Act rested on allegations that the consent of the transferor of property had been "induced by wrongful use of actual or threatened force, violence, or fear"; public officials had not been prosecuted under the "color of official right" phrase standing alone. Beginning with the conviction involved in United States v. Kenny, 462 F.2d 1205 (CA3 1972), however, the federal courts accepted the Government's submission that because of the disjunctive language of §1951(b)(2), allegations of force, violence, or fear were not necessary. Only proof of the obtaining of property under claims of official right was necessary. Furthermore, every Court of Appeals to have construed the phrase held that it did not require a showing that the public official "induced" the payor's consent by some affirmative act such as a demand or solicitation. Although there was some difference in the language of these holdings, the "color of official right" element required no more than proof of the payee's acceptance knowing that the payment was made for the purpose of influencing his official actions. In 1984, however, the Court of Appeals for the Second Circuit, en banc, held that some affirmative act of inducement by the official had to be shown to prove the Government's case. United States v. O'Grady, 742 F.2d 682 (1984). In 1988, the Ninth Circuit, en banc, agreed with the Second Circuit, overruling a prior decision expressing the majority rule. United States v. Aguon, 851 F.2d 1158 (1988). Other courts have been unimpressed with the view expressed in O'Grady and Aguon. See, e.g., United States v. Evans, 910 F.2d 790, 796-797 (CA11 1990), cert. pending, No. 90-6105; United States v. Spitler, 800 F.2d 1267, 1274 (CA4 1986); United States v. Paschall, 772 F.2d 68, 71 (CA4 1985).

The conflict on this issue is clear, but this case is not the occasion to resolve it. The trial court instructed that proof of inducement was essential to the Government's case, but stated that the requirement could be satisfied by showing the receipt of money by McCormick knowing that it was proffered with the expectation of benefit and on account of his office, proof that would be inadequate under the O'Grady view of inducement. McCormick did not challenge this instruction in the trial court or the Court of Appeals, nor does he here. . . .

Justice Stevens in dissent makes the bald assertion that "[i]t is perfectly clear . . . that the evidence presented to the jury was adequate to prove beyond a reasonable doubt that petitioner knowingly used his public office to make or imply promises or threats to his constituents for purposes of pressuring them to make payments that were not lawfully due him." 500 U.S. at 1820. Contrary to Justice Stevens' apparent suggestion, the main issue throughout this case has been whether under proper instructions the evidence established a Hobbs Act violation and, as our opinion indicates, it is far from "perfectly clear" that the Government has met its burden in this regard.

[I]n a case like this it is proper to inquire whether payments made to an elected official are in fact campaign contributions, and we agree that the intention of the parties is a relevant consideration in pursuing this inquiry. But we cannot accept the Court of Appeals' approach to distinguishing between legal and illegal campaign contributions. The Court of Appeals stated that payments to elected officials could violate the Hobbs Act without proof of an explicit *quid pro quo* by proving that the payments "were never intended to be *legitimate* campaign contributions." 896 F.2d at 66 (emphasis added). This issue, as we read the Court of Appeals' opinion, actually involved two inquiries; for after applying the factors the Court of Appeals considered relevant, it arrived at two conclusions: first, that McCormick was extorting money for his continued support of the 1985 legislation and "[f]urther," id. at 67, that the money was never intended by the parties to be a campaign contribution at all. The first conclusion, especially when considered in light of the second, asserts that the campaign contributions were illegitimate, extortionate payments. . . .

Serving constituents and supporting legislation that will benefit the district and individuals and groups therein is the everyday business of a legislator. It is also true that campaigns must be run and financed. Money is constantly being solicited on behalf of candidates, who run on platforms and who claim support on the basis of their views and what they intend to do or have done. Whatever ethical considerations and appearances may indicate, to hold that legislators commit the federal crime of extortion when they act for the benefit of constituents or support legislation furthering the interests of some of their constituents, shortly before or after campaign contributions are solicited and received from those beneficiaries, is an unrealistic assessment of what Congress could have meant by making it a crime to obtain property from another, with his consent, "under color of official right." To hold otherwise would open to prosecution not only conduct that has long been thought to be well within the law but also conduct that in a very real sense is unavoidable so long as election campaigns are financed by private contributions or expenditures, as they have been from the beginning of the Nation. It would require statutory language more explicit than the Hobbs Act contains to justify a contrary conclusion. Cf. United States v. Enmons, 410 U.S. 396, 411 (1973).

This is not to say that it is impossible for an elected official to commit extortion in the course of financing an election campaign. Political contributions are of course vulnerable if induced by the use of force, violence, or fear. The receipt of such contributions is also vulnerable under the Act as having been taken under color of official right, but only if the payments are made in return for an explicit promise or undertaking by the official to perform or not to perform an official act. In such situations the official asserts that his official conduct will be controlled by the terms of the promise or undertaking. This is the receipt of money by an elected official under color of official right within the meaning of the Hobbs Act.

This formulation defines the forbidden zone of conduct with sufficient clarity. As the Court of Appeals for the Fifth Circuit observed in United States v. Dozier, 672 F.2d 531, 537 (1982):

"A moment's reflection should enable one to distinguish, at least in the abstract, a legitimate solicitation from the exaction of a fee for a benefit conferred or an injury withheld. Whether described familiarly as a payoff or with the Latinate precision of *quid pro quo*, the prohibited exchange is the same: a public official may not demand payment as inducement for the promise to perform (or not to perform) an official act."

The United States agrees that if the payments to McCormick were campaign contributions, proof of a *quid pro quo* would be essential for an extortion conviction, and quotes the instruction given on this subject in 9 Department of Justice Manual §9-85A.306, at 9-1938.134 (Supp. 1988-2): "[C]ampaign contributions will not be authorized as the subject of a Hobbs Act prosecution unless they can be proven to have been given in return for the performance of or abstaining from an official act; otherwise any campaign contribution might constitute a violation."

We thus disagree with the Court of Appeals' holding in this case that a *quid pro quo* is not necessary for conviction under the Hobbs Act when an official receives a campaign contribution.[10] By the same token, we hold, as McCormick urges, that the District Court's instruction to the same effect was error.[11]

[handwritten margin note: proof of the agreement is needed.]

III

The Government nevertheless insists that a properly instructed jury in this case found that the payment at issue was not a campaign contribution at all and that the evidence amply supports this finding. . . . [I]t is true that the trial court instructed that the receipt of voluntary campaign contributions did not violate the Hobbs Act. But under the instructions a contribution was not "voluntary" if given with *any* expectation of benefit; and as we read the instructions, taken as a whole, the jury was told that it could find McCormick guilty of extortion if any of the payments,

---

10. . . . McCormick's sole contention in this case is that the payments made to him were campaign contributions. Therefore, we do not decide whether a *quid pro quo* requirement exists in other contexts, such as when an elected official receives gifts, meals, travel expenses, or other items of value.

11. In so holding, we do not resolve the conflict mentioned in n.5, *supra*, with respect to the necessity of proving inducement.

even though a campaign contribution, was made by the doctors with the expectation that McCormick's official action would be influenced for their benefit and if McCormick knew that the payment was made with that expectation. It may be that the jury found that none of the payments was a campaign contribution, but it is mere speculation that the jury convicted on this basis rather than on the impermissible basis that even though the first payment was such a contribution, McCormick's receipt of it was a violation of the Hobbs Act. . . .

V

holding

Accordingly, we reverse the judgment of the Court of Appeals and remand the case for further proceedings consistent with this opinion.

Justice SCALIA, concurring.

I agree with the Court's conclusion and, given the assumption on which this case was briefed and argued, with the reasons the Court assigns. If the prohibition of the Hobbs Act, 18 U.S.C. §1951, against receipt of money "under color of official right" includes receipt of money from a private source for the performance of official duties, that ambiguously described crime assuredly need not, and for the reasons the Court discusses should not, be interpreted to cover campaign contributions with anticipation of favorable future action, as opposed to campaign contributions in exchange for an explicit promise of favorable future action.

I find it unusual and unsettling, however, to make such a distinction without any hint of a justification in the statutory text: §1951 contains not even a colorable allusion to campaign contributions or *quid pro quo*s. I find it doubly unsettling because there is another interpretation of §1951, contrary to the one that has been the assumption of argument here, that would render the distinction unnecessary. While I do not feel justified in adopting that interpretation without briefing and argument, neither do I feel comfortable giving tacit approval to the assumption that contradicts it. I write, therefore, a few words concerning the text of this statute and the history that has produced the unexamined assumption underlying our opinion.

Section 1951(a) provides: "Whoever in any way or degree obstructs, delays, or affects commerce or the movement of any article or commodity in commerce, by robbery or extortion . . . shall be fined not more than $10,000 or imprisoned not more than twenty years, or both." Section 1951(b)(2) defines "extortion" as "the obtaining of property from another, with his consent, induced by wrongful use of actual or threatened force, violence, or fear, or under color of official right." The relevant provisions were enacted as part of the Anti-Racketeering Act of 1934, 48 Stat. 979, and were carried forward without change in the Hobbs Act of 1948. For

"circuit split on what "under color of official right" means

more than 30 years after enactment, there is no indication that they were applied to the sort of conduct alleged here.

When . . . it first occurred to federal prosecutors to use the Hobbs Act to reach what was essentially the soliciting of bribes by state officials, courts were unimpressed with the notion. They thought that public officials were not guilty of extortion when they accepted, or even when they requested, *voluntary* payments designed to influence or procure their official action. United States v. Hyde, 448 F.2d 815, 833 (CA5 1971) ("The distinction from bribery is therefore . . . the fear and lack of voluntariness on the part of the victim"); United States v. Addonizio, 451 F.2d 49, 72 (CA3 1971) ("[W]hile the essence of bribery is voluntariness, the essence of extortion is duress"). Not until 1972 did any court apply the Hobbs Act to bribery. See United States v. Kenny, 462 F.2d 1205, 1229 (CA3 1972) ("kickbacks" by construction contractors to public officials established extortion "under color of official right," despite absence of "threat, fear, or duress"). That holding was soon followed by the Seventh Circuit in United States v. Braasch, 505 F.2d 139, 151 (1974), which said that "[s]o long as the motivation for the payment focuses on the recipient's office, the conduct falls within the ambit of 18 U.S.C. §1951." While *Kenny, Braasch,* and subsequent cases were debated in academic writing, compare Ruff, Federal Prosecution of Local Corruption: A Case Study in the Making of Law Enforcement Policy, 65 Geo. L.J. 1171 (1977) (criticizing *Kenny*), with Lindgren, The Elusive Distinction between Bribery and Extortion: From the Common Law to the Hobbs Act, 35 UCLA L. Rev. 815 (1988) (defending *Kenny*), the Courts of Appeals accepted the expansion with little disagreement, and this Court has never had occasion to consider the matter.

It is acceptance of the assumption that "under color of official right" means "on account of one's office" that brings bribery cases within the statute's reach, and that creates the necessity for the reasonable but textually inexplicable distinction the Court makes today. That assumption is questionable. "The obtaining of property . . . under color of official *right*" more naturally connotes some false assertion of official *entitlement* to the property. This interpretation might have the effect of making the §1951 definition of extortion comport with the definition of "extortion" at common law. One treatise writer, describing "extortion by a public officer," states: "At common law it was essential that the money or property be obtained under color of office, that is, under the pretense that the officer was entitled thereto by virtue of his office. The money or thing received must have been claimed or accepted in right of office, and the person paying must have yielded to official authority." 3 R. Anderson, Wharton's Criminal Law and Procedure 790-791 (1957).

It also appears to be the case that under New York law, which has long contained identical "under color of official right" language and upon which the Hobbs Act is said to have been based—see Ruff, *supra*, at

1183—bribery and extortion were separate offenses. An official charged with extortion could defend on the ground that the payment was voluntary and thus he was guilty only of bribery. People v. Feld, 28 N.Y.S.2d 796, 797 (Sup. Ct. 1941). I am aware of only one pre-Hobbs Act New York prosecution involving extortion "under color of official right," and there the defendant, a justice of the peace, had extracted a payment from a litigant on the false ground that it was due him as a court fee. People v. Whaley, 6 Cow. 661, 661-663 (N.Y. 1827).

Finally, where the United States Code explicitly criminalizes conduct such as that alleged in the present case, it calls the crime bribery, not extortion—and like all bribery laws I am aware of (but unlike §1951 and all other extortion laws I am aware of) it punishes not only the person receiving the payment but the person making it. See 18 U.S.C. §201(b) (criminalizing bribery of and by federal officials). Cf. 18 U.S.C. §872 (criminalizing extortion by federal officials, making no provision for punishment of person extorted). McCormick, though not a federal official, is subject to federal prosecution for bribery under the Travel Act, 18 U.S.C. §1952, which criminalizes the use of interstate commerce for purposes of bribery—and reaches, of course, both the person giving and the person receiving the bribe.

I mean only to raise this argument, not to decide it, for it has not been advanced and there may be persuasive responses. See, e.g., Lindgren, *supra*, at 837-889 (arguing that under early common law bribery and extortion were not separate offenses and that extortion did not require proof of a coerced payment). But unexamined assumptions have a way of becoming, by force of usage, unsound law. Before we are asked to go further down the road of making reasonable but textually unapparent distinctions in a federal "payment for official action" statute—as we unquestionably will be asked—I think it well to bear in mind that the statute may not exist.

Justice STEVENS, with whom Justice BLACKMUN and Justice O'CONNOR join, dissenting. . . .

Petitioner's crime was committed in two stages. Toward the end of May 1984, petitioner held an "unfriendly" conversation with Vandergrift, the representative of the unlicensed doctors, which the jury could have interpreted as an implied threat to take no action on the licensing legislation unless he received a cash payment as well as an implicit promise to support the legislation if an appropriate cash payment was made. . . . [T]hat inducement was comparable to a known thug's offer to protect a storekeeper against the risk of severe property damage in exchange for a cash consideration. Neither the legislator nor the thug needs to make an explicit threat or an explicit promise to get his message across.

The extortion was completed on June 1, 1984, when Vandergrift personally delivered an envelope containing nine $100 bills to petitioner.

The fact that the payment was not reported as a campaign contribution, as required by West Virginia law, or as taxable income, as required by federal law, together with other circumstantial evidence, adequately supports the conclusion that the money was intended as a payment to petitioner personally to induce him to act favorably on the licensing legislation. . . .

As I understand its opinion, the Court would agree that these facts would constitute a violation of the Hobbs Act if the understanding that the money was a personal payment rather than a campaign contribution had been explicit . . . and if the understanding that, in response to the payment, petitioner would endeavor to provide the payers with the specific benefit they sought had also been explicit. . . . In my opinion . . . [s]ubtle extortion is just as wrongful—and probably much more common—than the kind of express understanding that the Court's opinion seems to require.

[Justice Stevens goes on to say that there still must be a "mutual understanding" between the parties that the payment was motivated by the "payer's desire to avoid a specific threatened harm or to obtain a promised benefit."] . . .

When petitioner took the money, he was either guilty or not guilty. For that reason, proof of a subsequent *quid pro quo*—his actual support of the legislation—was not necessary for the Government's case. And conversely, evidence that petitioner would have supported the legislation anyway is not a defense to the already completed crime. The thug who extorts protection money cannot defend on the ground that his threat was only a bluff because he would not have smashed the shopkeeper's windows even if the extortion had been unsuccessful. . . .

This Court's criticism of the District Court's instructions focuses on this single sentence: "Voluntary is that which is freely given without expectation of benefit." The Court treats this sentence as though it authorized the jury to find that a legitimate campaign contribution is involuntary and constitutes extortion whenever the contributor expects to benefit from the candidate's election. In my opinion this is a gross misreading of that sentence in the context of the entire set of instructions.

In context, the sentence in question advised the jury that a payment is voluntary if it is made without the expectation of a benefit that is specifically contingent upon the payment. An expectation that the donor will benefit from the election of a candidate who, once in office, would support particular legislation regardless of whether or not the contribution is made, would not make the payment contingent or involuntary in that sense; such a payment would be "voluntary" under a fair reading of the instructions, and the candidate's solicitation of such contributions from donors who would benefit from his or her election is perfectly legitimate. If, however, the donor and candidate know that the candidate's support of the proposed legislation is contingent upon the payment, the contribution may be found by a jury to have been involuntary or extorted.

NOTES AND QUESTIONS

1. It should not have been surprising that the *McCormick* Court rejected the lower court's reasoning and required proof of a *quid pro quo*. The Justice Department's own United States Attorneys' Manual (USAM) demanded as much, as had many Circuit Courts of Appeals. See, e.g., United States v. Bibby, 752 F.2d 1116, 1127 n.1 (6th Cir. 1985) ("What the Hobbs Act proscribes is the taking of money by a public official in exchange for *specific* promises to do or refrain from doing *specific* things. . . . In other words, there must be a *quid pro quo*."); United States v. Dozier, 672 F.2d 531, 537 (5th Cir. 1982) ("Whether described familiarly as a payoff or with the Latinate precision of *quid pro quo*, the prohibited exchange is the same: a public official may not demand payment as inducement for the promise to perform (or not to perform) an official act.") In fact, the Solicitor General conceded the point before the Court.

Perhaps both the Justice Department's Manual and the Solicitor General's ability to shift the grounds on which a prosecution is defended once the case goes before the Supreme Court—as happened in *McCormick*—are soft versions of the centralized control over doctrinal development advocated by Dan Kahan, excerpted in Section E of Chapter 4. Both can be seen as efforts by Washington to manage the doctrinal development of the criminal law, and thereby limit the influence of individual prosecutors on criminal common lawmaking.

2. As the Court noted in *McCormick*, a substantial hurdle to prosecuting legislators for accepting campaign contributions related to their support of legislation is the fact that virtually all campaigns are financed by private constituents who are beneficiaries of the actions of legislators. Yet the Court also makes clear that this does not mean it is "impossible for an elected official to commit extortion in the course of financing an election campaign." 500 U.S. at 273. Certainly, elected officials can be found guilty of accepting bribes, even if those bribes are in the form of campaign contributions. But the campaign contribution must be accepted "for or because" of a specific official act—there must be a *quid pro quo*. This requirement is consistent with the elements needed to prove the crime of bribery of federal officials, 18 U.S.C. §201. See *infra* Section B. See also United States v. Myers, 692 F.2d 823, 842 (2d Cir. 1982) ("In some circumstances a prosecution of a Congressman for bribery can present a close question as to whether money was received as an illegal bribe or a lawful campaign contribution. In such cases the jury must be carefully instructed as the distinction and must show 'specific knowledge of a definitive official act for which payment is made.'") (quoting United States v. Brewster, 50 F.2d 62, 81 (D.C. Cir. 1974)).

3. What precisely would constitute proof of a *quid pro quo*? In *McCormick*, the Court noted in footnote 5 that a petition for review was pending in United States v. Evans, a case raising that precise issue.

The Court granted the petition in *Evans* and discussed the *quid pro quo* requirement in an opinion by Justice Stevens, who had dissented in *McCormick*.

Evans v. United States
504 U.S. 255 (1992)

Justice STEVENS delivered the opinion of the Court.

We granted certiorari to resolve a conflict in the Circuits over the question whether an affirmative act of inducement by a public official, such as a demand, is an element of the offense of extortion "under color of official right" prohibited by the Hobbs Act, 18 U.S.C. §1951. We agree with the Court of Appeals for the Eleventh Circuit that it is not, and therefore affirm the judgment of the court below.

I

Petitioner was an elected member of the Board of Commissioners of DeKalb County, Georgia. . . . [B]etween March 1985 and October 1986, . . . an FBI agent posing as a real estate developer . . . sought petitioner's assistance in an effort to rezone a 25-acre tract of land for high-density residential use. On July 25, 1986, the agent handed petitioner cash totaling $7,000 and a check, payable to petitioner's campaign, for $1,000. Petitioner reported the check, but not the cash, on his state campaign-financing disclosure form; he also did not report the $7,000 on his 1986 federal income tax return. . . . Viewing the evidence in the light most favorable to the Government, . . . we assume that the jury found that petitioner accepted the cash knowing that it was intended to ensure that he would vote in favor of the rezoning application and that he would try to persuade his fellow commissioners to do likewise. Thus, although petitioner did not initiate the transaction, his acceptance of the bribe constituted an implicit promise to use his official position to serve the interests of the bribegiver.

In a two-count indictment, petitioner was charged with extortion in violation of 18 U.S.C. §1951 and with failure to report income in violation of 26 U.S.C. §7206(1). He was convicted by a jury on both counts. With respect to the extortion count, the trial judge gave the following instruction:

> "The defendant contends that the $8,000 he received from agent Cormany was a campaign contribution. The solicitation of campaign contributions from any person is a necessary and permissible form of political

activity on the part of persons who seek political office and persons who have been elected to political office. Thus, the acceptance by an elected official of a campaign contribution does not, in itself, constitute a violation of the Hobbs Act even though the donor has business pending before the official.

However, if a public official demands or accepts money in exchange for [a] specific requested exercise of his or her official power, such a demand or acceptance does constitute a violation of the Hobbs Act regardless of whether the payment is made in the form of a campaign contribution."

proc. hist.

In affirming petitioner's conviction, the . . . Court of Appeals held [] that "passive acceptance of a benefit by a public official is sufficient to form the basis of a Hobbs Act violation if the official knows that he is being offered the payment in exchange for a specific requested exercise of his official power. . . ." [910 F.2d 790, 796 (CA11 1990).]

circuit split

This statement of the law by the Court of Appeals for the Eleventh Circuit is consistent with holdings in eight other Circuits. Two Circuits, however, have held that an affirmative act of inducement by the public official is required to support a conviction of extortion under color of official right. United States v. O'Grady, 742 F.2d 682, 687 (CA2 1984) (en banc) ("Although receipt of benefits by a public official is a necessary element of the crime, there must also be proof that the public official did something, under color of his public office, to cause the giving of benefits."); United States v. Aguon, 851 F.2d 1158, 1166 (CA9 1988) (en banc) ("We find ourselves in accord with the Second Circuit's conclusion that inducement is an element required for conviction under the Hobbs Act."). Because the majority view is consistent with the common-law definition of extortion, which we believe Congress intended to adopt, we endorse that position.

holding

II

It is a familiar "maxim that a statutory term is generally presumed to have its common-law meaning." Taylor v. United States, 495 U.S. 575, 592 (1990). As we have explained: "[W]here Congress borrows terms of art in which are accumulated the legal tradition and meaning of centuries of practice, it presumably knows and adopts the cluster of ideas that were attached to each borrowed word in the body of learning from which it was taken. . . . In such case, absence of contrary direction may be taken as satisfaction with widely accepted definitions, not as a departure from them." Morissette v. United States, 342 U.S. 246, 263 (1952). At common law, extortion was an offense committed by a public official who took "by colour of his office"[4] money that was not due to him for

---

4. Blackstone described extortion as "an abuse of public justice, which consists in an officer's unlawfully taking, *by colour of his office*, from any man, any money or thing of

the performance of his official duties. A demand, or request, by the public official was not an element of the offense. Extortion by the public official was the rough equivalent of what we would now describe as "taking a bribe." It is clear that petitioner committed that offense. The question is whether the federal statute, insofar as it applies to official extortion, has narrowed the common-law definition.

Congress has unquestionably *expanded* the common-law definition of extortion to include acts by private individuals pursuant to which property is obtained by means of force, fear, or threats. It did so by implication in the Travel Act, 18 U.S.C. §1952, see United States v. Nardello, 393 U.S. 286, 289-296 (1969), and expressly in the Hobbs Act. . . .

Although the present statutory text is much broader than the common-law definition of extortion because it encompasses conduct by a private individual as well as conduct by a public official, the portion of the statute that refers to official misconduct continues to mirror the common-law definition. There is nothing in either the statutory text or the legislative history that could fairly be described as a "contrary direction," Morissette v. United States, 342 U.S. at 263, from Congress to narrow the scope of the offense. . . .

The two courts that have disagreed with the decision to apply the common-law definition have interpreted the word "induced" as requiring a wrongful use of official power that "begins with the public official, not with the gratuitous actions of another." United States v. O'Grady, 742 F.2d at 691; see United States v. Aguon, 851 F.2d at 1166 ("'inducement' can be in the overt form of a 'demand,' or in a more subtle form such as 'custom' or 'expectation'"). If we had no common-law history to guide our interpretation of the statutory text, that reading would be plausible. For two reasons, however, we are convinced that it is incorrect.

First, we think the word "induced" is a part of the definition of the offense by the private individual, but not the offense by the public official. In the case of the private individual, the victim's consent must be "induced by wrongful use of actual or threatened force, violence or fear." In the case of the public official, however, there is no such requirement. The statute merely requires of the public official that he obtain "property from another, with his consent, . . . under color of official right." The

---

value, that is not due to him, or more than is due, or before it is due." 4 W. Blackstone, Commentaries *141 (emphasis added). He used the phrase "by colour of his office," rather than the phrase "under color of official right," which appears in the Hobbs Act. Petitioner does not argue that there is any difference in the phrases. Hawkins' definition of extortion is probably the source for the official right language used in the Hobbs Act. See Lindgren, The Elusive Distinction Between Bribery and Extortion: From the Common Law to the Hobbs Act, 35 UCLA L. Rev. 815, 864 (1988). Hawkins defined extortion as follows: "[I]t is said, That extortion in a large sense signifies any oppression under colour of right; but that in a strict sense, it signifies the taking of money by any officer, by colour of his office, either where none at all is due, or not so much is due, or where it is not yet due." 1 W. Hawkins, Pleas of the Crown 316 (6th ed. 1787).

use of the word "or" before "under color of official right" supports this reading.

② Second, even if the statute were parsed so that the word "induced" applied to the public officeholder, we do not believe the word "induced" necessarily indicates that the transaction must be *initiated* by the recipient of the bribe. Many of the cases applying the majority rule have concluded that the wrongful acceptance of a bribe establishes all the inducement that the statute requires. They conclude that the coercive element is provided by the public office itself. And even the two courts that have adopted an inducement requirement for extortion under color of official right do not require proof that the inducement took the form of a threat or demand. See United States v. O'Grady, 742 F.2d at 687; United States v. Aguon, 851 F.2d at 1166.[17]

Petitioner argues that the jury charge with respect to extortion allowed the jury to convict him on the basis of the "passive acceptance of a contribution." Brief for Petitioner 24.[18]

He contends that the instruction did not require the jury to find "an element of duress such as a demand," id. at 22, and it did not properly describe the *quid pro quo* requirement for conviction if the jury found that the payment was a campaign contribution. *def. Argument*

We reject petitioner's criticism of the instruction, and conclude that it satisfies the *quid pro quo* requirement of McCormick v. United States, 500 U.S. 257 (1991). . . . We also reject petitioner's contention that an

---

17. Moreover, we note that while the statute does not require that affirmative inducement be proven as a distinct element of the Hobbs Act, there is evidence in the record establishing that petitioner received the money with the understanding that he would use his office to aid the bribegiver. Petitioner and the agent had several exchanges in which they tried to clarify their understanding with each other. For example, petitioner said to the agent: "I understand both of us are groping . . . for what we need to say to each other. . . . I'm gonna work. Let me tell you I'm gonna work, if you didn't give me but three [thousand dollars], on this, I've promised to help you. I'm gonna work to do that. You understand what I mean. . . . If you gave me six, I'll do exactly what I said I was gonna do for you. If you gave me one, I'll do exactly what I said I was gonna do for you. I wanna make sure you're clear on that part. So it doesn't really matter. If I promised to help, that's what I'm gonna do.". . .

18. Petitioner also makes the point that "[t]he evidence at trial against [petitioner] is more conducive to a charge of bribery than one of extortion." Brief for Petitioner 40. Although the evidence in this case may have supported a charge of bribery, it is not a defense to a charge of extortion under color of official right that the defendant could also have been convicted of bribery. . . .

[One] commentator has argued that bribery and extortion were overlapping crimes, see Lindgren, [35 UCLA L. Rev. at 905,] 908, and has located an early New York case in which the defendant was convicted of both bribery and extortion under color of official right, see People v. Hansen, 241 N.Y. 532, (1925). He also makes the point that the cases usually cited for the proposition that extortion and bribery are mutually exclusive crimes are cases involving extortion by fear and bribery. . . . We agree with the Seventh Circuit in United States v. Braasch, 505 F.2d 139, 151, n.7 (1974), that "the modern trend of the federal courts is to hold that bribery and extortion as used in the Hobbs Ac[t] are not mutually exclusive."

affirmative step is an element of the offense of extortion "under color of official right" and need be included in the instruction. . . . We hold today that the Government need only show that a public official has obtained ~Rule~ a payment to which he was not entitled, knowing that the payment was — made in return for official acts. . . .

III

An argument not raised by petitioner is now advanced by the dissent. It contends that common-law extortion was *limited* to wrongful takings under a false pretense of official right. It is perfectly clear, however, that although extortion accomplished by fraud was a well-recognized type of extortion, there were other types as well. As the court explained in Commonwealth v. Wilson, 30 Pa. Super. 26 (1906), an extortion case involving a payment by a would-be brothel owner to a police captain to ensure the opening of her house:

"The form of extortion most commonly dealt with in the decisions is the corrupt taking by a person in office of a fee for services which should be rendered gratuitously; . . . but this is not a complete definition of the offense, by which I mean that it does not include every form of common-law extortion." Id. at 30.

See also Commonwealth v. Brown, 23 Pa. Super. 470, 488-489 (1903) (defendants charged with and convicted of conspiracy to extort because they accepted pay for obtaining and procuring the election of certain persons to the position of schoolteachers); State v. Barts, 38 A.2d 838, 841, 844 (N.J. 1944) (police officer, who received $1,000 for not arresting someone who had stolen money, was properly convicted of extortion because "generically extortion is an abuse of public justice and a misuse by oppression of the power with which the law clothes a public officer"). . . .

[The cases the dissent cites] merely support the proposition that the services for which the fee is paid must be official and that the official must not be entitled to the fee that he collected — both elements of the offense that are clearly satisfied in this case. . . .

The judgment is affirmed.

[The opinions of Justices O'Connor and Kennedy, concurring in part and in the judgment, are omitted.]

Justice THOMAS, with whom THE CHIEF JUSTICE and Justice SCALIA join, dissenting. . . .

Extortion is one of the oldest crimes in Anglo-American jurisprudence. Hawkins provides the classic common-law definition: "[I]t is said, that Extortion in a large Sense signifies any Oppression *under Colour of Right*; but that in a strict Sense it signifies the Taking of Money by any

Officer, *by Colour of his Office*, either where none at all is due, or not so much is due, or where it is not yet due." 1 W. Hawkins, Pleas of the Crown 170 (2d ed. 1724) (emphasis added). Blackstone echoed that definition: "Extortion is an abuse of public justice, which consists in any officer's unlawfully taking, *by colour of his office*, from any man, any money or thing of value, that is not due to him, or more than is due, or before it is due." 4 W. Blackstone, Commentaries 141 (1769) (emphasis added).

These definitions pose, but do not answer, the critical question: What does it mean for an official to take money "by colour of his office"? The Court fails to address this question, simply assuming that common-law extortion encompassed *any* taking by a public official of something of value that he was not "due."

The "under color of office" element of extortion, however, had a definite and well-established meaning at common law. "At common law it was essential that the money or property be obtained under color of office, *that is, under the pretense that the officer was entitled thereto by virtue of his office.* The money or thing received must have been claimed or accepted in right of office, and the person paying must have yielded to official authority." 3 R. Anderson, Wharton's Criminal Law and Procedure §1393, at 790-791 (1957) (emphasis added). . . .

A survey of 19th- and early 20th-century cases construing state extortion statutes in light of the common law makes plain that the offense was understood to involve not merely a wrongful taking by a public official, but a wrongful taking *under a false pretense of official right.* . . .

Because the Court misapprehends the "color of office" requirement, the crime it describes today is not the common-law crime that Congress presumably incorporated into the Hobbs Act. The explanation for this error is clear. The Court's historical foray has the single-minded purpose of proving that common-law extortion did *not* include an element of "inducement"; in its haste to reach that conclusion, the Court fails to consider the elements that common-law extortion *did* include. Even if the Court were correct that an official *could* commit extortion at common law simply by receiving (but not "inducing") an unlawful payment, it does not follow either historically or logically that an official *automatically* committed extortion whenever he received such a payment.

The Court, therefore, errs in asserting that common-law extortion is the "rough equivalent of what we would now describe as 'taking a bribe.'" . . . [B]ribery and extortion are different crimes. An official who solicits or takes a bribe does not do so "under color of office"; i.e., under any pretense of official entitlement. . . . Where extortion is at issue, the public official is the sole wrongdoer; because he acts "under color of office," the law regards the payor as an innocent victim and not an accomplice. With bribery, in contrast, the payor *knows* the recipient official is not entitled to the payment; he, as well as the official, may be punished for the offense. Congress is well aware of the distinction between the crimes; it has always treated them separately. Compare 18 U.S.C. §872 ("extortion by officers or employees of the United States," which criminalizes extortion by federal officials, and makes no provision for punishment of the payor), with 18 U.S.C. §201 ("bribery of public officials and witnesses," which criminalizes [both payor and payee]). By stretching the bounds of extortion to make it encompass bribery, the Court today blurs the traditional distinction between the crimes. . . .

Perhaps because the common-law crime—as the Court defines it—is so expansive, the Court, at the very end of its opinion, appends a qualification: "We hold today that the Government need only show that a public official has obtained a payment to which he was not entitled, *knowing that the payment was made in return for official acts.*" (Emphasis added.) This *quid pro quo* requirement is simply made up. The Court does not suggest that it has any basis in the common law or the language of the Hobbs Act, and I have found no treatise or dictionary that refers to any such requirement in defining "extortion."

Its only conceivable source, in fact, is our opinion last Term in McCormick v. United States, 500 U.S. 257 (1991). Quite sensibly, we insisted in that case that, unless the Government established the existence of a *quid pro quo*, a public official could not be convicted of extortion under the Hobbs Act for accepting a campaign contribution. We did not purport to discern that requirement in the common law or statutory text, but imposed it to prevent the Hobbs Act from effecting a radical (and absurd) change in American political life. . . . We expressly limited our holding to campaign contributions. Id. at 274, n.10 ("We do not decide whether a *quid pro quo* requirement exists in other contexts, such as when an elected official receives gifts, meals, travel expenses, or other items of value").

Because the common-law history of extortion was neither properly briefed nor argued in *McCormick*, the *quid pro quo* limitation imposed there represented a reasonable first step in the right direction. Now that we squarely consider that history, however, it is apparent that that limitation was in fact overly modest: at common law, McCormick was innocent of extortion not because he failed to offer a *quid pro quo* in return for campaign contributions, but because he did not take the contributions under color of official right. . . .

The Court's construction of the Hobbs Act is [also] repugnant . . . to basic tenets of federalism. Over the past 20 years, the Hobbs Act has served as the engine for a stunning expansion of federal criminal jurisdiction into a field traditionally policed by state and local laws—acts of public corruption by state and local officials. That expansion was born of a single sentence in a Third Circuit opinion: "[The 'under color of official right' language in the Hobbs Act] repeats the common law definition of extortion, a crime which could only be committed by a public official, and which did not require proof of threat, fear, or duress." United States v. Kenny, 462 F.2d 1205, 1229 (1972). . . . By overlooking the traditional meaning of "under color of official right," *Kenny* obliterated the distinction between extortion and bribery, essentially creating a new crime encompassing both. . . .

After *Kenny*, federal prosecutors came to view the Hobbs Act as a license for ferreting out all wrongdoing at the state and local level. . . . In short order, most other Circuits followed *Kenny*'s lead and upheld, based on a bribery rationale, the Hobbs Act extortion convictions of an astonishing variety of state and local officials, from a State Governor, see United States v. Hall, 536 F.2d 313, 320-321 (CA10 1976), down to a local policeman, see United States v. Braasch, 505 F.2d 139, 151 (CA7 1974). . . .

It is clear, of course, that the Hobbs Act's proscription of extortion "under color of official right" applies to all public officials, including those at the state and local level. As our cases emphasize, however, even when Congress has clearly decided to [regulate] state governmental officials, concerns of federalism play a vital role in evaluating the *scope* of the regulation. The Court today mocks this jurisprudence by reading two significant limitations (the textual requirement of "inducement" and the common-law requirement of "under color of office") out of the Hobbs Act's definition of official extortion. . . .

Petitioner Evans was elected to the Board of Commissioners of DeKalb County, Georgia, in 1982. He was no local tyrant—just one of five part-time commissioners earning an annual salary of approximately $16,000. The board's activities were entirely local, including the quintessentially local activity of zoning property. The United States does not suggest that there were any allegations of corruption or malfeasance against Evans.

In early 1985, as part of an investigation into "allegations of public corruption in the Atlanta area," a Federal Bureau of Investigation agent, Clifford Cormany, Jr., set up a bogus firm, "WDH Developers," and pretended to be a land developer. Cormany sought and obtained a meeting with Evans. From March 1985 until October 1987, a period of some *two and a half years*, Cormany or one of his associates held 33 conversations with Evans. Every one of these contacts was initiated by the agents. During these conversations, the agents repeatedly requested Evans' assistance in securing a favorable zoning decision, and repeatedly brought up the subject of campaign contributions. Agent Cormany eventually contributed $8,000 to Evans' reelection campaign, and Evans accepted the money. There is no suggestion that he claimed an official entitlement to the payment. . . .

The Court is surely correct that there is sufficient evidence to support the jury's verdict that Evans committed "extortion" under the Court's expansive interpretation of the crime. But that interpretation has no basis in the statute that Congress passed in 1946. If the Court makes up this version of the crime today, who is to say what version it will make up tomorrow when confronted with the next perceived rascal? Until now, the Justice Department, with good reason, has been . . . cautious in advancing the theory that official extortion contains no inducement requirement. "*Until the Supreme Court decides upon the validity of this type of conviction*, prosecutorial discretion should be used to insure that any case which might reach that level of review is worthy of federal prosecution. Such restraint would require that only significant amounts of money and reasonably high levels of office should be involved." See U.S. Dept. of Justice, United States Attorneys' Manual §9-131.180 (1984) (emphasis added). Having detected no "[s]uch restraint" in this case, I certainly have no reason to expect it in the future.

Our criminal justice system runs on the premise that prosecutors will respect, and courts will enforce, the boundaries on criminal conduct set by the legislature. Where, as here, those boundaries are breached, it becomes impossible to tell where prosecutorial discretion ends and prosecutorial abuse . . . begins . . . .

"COLOR OF RIGHT" EXTORTION

1. *McCormick*, while noting a Circuit conflict on the issue of "inducement," focused only on whether an explicit *quid pro quo* was needed in cases involving campaign contributions. It did not get to the "inducement" question until *Evans*. What effect does case-by-case adjudication have on the articulation of the criminal law? Justice Stevens (a *McCormick* dissenter) asserts that the *quid pro quo* inquiry in *Evans* is simply the one set out in *McCormick*. Do you agree? If so, what exactly caused Stevens to dissent in *McCormick*? Moreover, the question of whether a payment had been made in the campaign context—so important in *McCormick*—seems to play little part in the *Evans* analysis. How can one explain this silence? Based on the Court's reasoning, should *Evans* apply outside of the campaign context as well?

2. The Hobbs Act defines extortion as "the obtaining of property from another, with his consent, induced by wrongful use of actual or threatened force, violence, or fear, or under color of official right." 18 U.S.C. §1951(b)(2). In interpreting this statute, the *Evans* majority found that the inducement requirement applied to extortion "by wrongful use of force, violence, or fear," but not to extortion committed "under color of official right." For Justice Thomas, a "more natural" construction would apply the verb "induced" to "*both* types of extortion described in the statute." *Evans*, 504 U.S. at 288 (Thomas, J., dissenting). Do you agree with his reading of the statute? Even if you do not, is Justice Thomas correct in his assertion that, since "the Court's expansive interpretation of the statute is not the only plausible one, the rule of lenity compels adoption of the narrower interpretation"?

3. Reread Justice Thomas's account of the police investigation that led to the charges in *Evans*. Should the government be required to prove more

in cases that begin with a government "sting" than in cases that do not? To what extent should the Court consider the means by which the government gained information about the alleged extortion? Should evidence based on a sting be more heavily scrutinized? Is it enough that stings will likely provide a level of evidentiary certainty (e.g., taped conversations) unavailable when a party to the illegal transactions gives retrospective testimony (as occurred in *McCormick* when lobbyist Vandergrift testified, see Brief for the United States. Between McCormick and Evans, who is more deserving of punishment?

4. Justice Scalia's concurrence in *McCormick* and Justice Thomas's dissent in *Evans* do a good job of surveying the history of "color of right" extortion. The chief dispute in the literature is the one addressed in *Evans*: whether older extortion cases covered conduct that we would call bribery. The leading academic authority on the side of the *Evans* majority is Jim Lindgren, whose article on the subject is cited in both *McCormick* and *Evans*. See James Lindgren, The Elusive Distinction Between Bribery and Extortion: From the Common Law to the Hobbs Act, 35 UCLA L. Rev. 815 (1988). But see John T. Noonan, Bribes: The Intellectual History of a Moral Idea 584-91 (1984); Joseph Maurice Harary, Note, Misapplication of the Hobbs Act to Bribery, 85 Colum. L. Rev. 1340 (1985).

5. Based on Lindgren's (and Justice Stevens's) description, there seems to be little connection between "color of right" extortion (the only "extortion" recognized under common law) and the "force, violence, or fear" extortion cases covered in Chapter 5. While the Chapter 5 cases involve coercive threats—of violence, reputational harm, or economic injury—the "extortion" envisioned by Justice Stevens in *Evans* covers consensual transactions in which both the payor of the bribe and the recipient are pleased to make the exchange. If Stevens is right about the common law on this score, it seems odd that twentieth-century legislators targeting racketeers (like Sonny Ciccone in *Gotti*, see Chapter 5) would use extortion as their statutory vehicle. By contrast, if Justice Thomas is right in *Evans*, the legislative extension seems more natural: There was an element of coercion even in common law, arising out of the power of the state. A common-law extorter leveraged the government's authority for his personal profit, just as defendants like Sonny Ciccone leverage their reputation for violence for *their* personal profit. Is public power inherently coercive? Or are you as troubled as Justice Thomas is in his dissent that "[n]ow, apparently, we assume that all public officials exude an aura of coercion at *all* places and at *all* times"? To what extent did the majority decision overstate the coercive power of our public officials?

6. The application of "under color of right" extortion to forms of public corruption traditionally associated with bribery did not come from Congress, nor did the idea come from the courts. Rather, it was a federal prosecutor's creative argument, which federal judges found persuasive. This

is the "power of initiative" that Dan Kahan's piece discussed in Chapter 4. Notice the timing of the legal development: The early 1970s were the age of Watergate, when political corruption and official misconduct suddenly became major forces in American public life, and—thanks to United States v. Kenny, discussed at length in Justice Thomas's dissent in *Evans*, and the intangible rights cases—in federal criminal law. Indeed, in 1973, the U.S. Attorney in Maryland had prepared an indictment of the Vice President of the United States, Spiro Agnew, in which Agnew would have been charged with both "color of right" extortion and economic extortion under the Hobbs Act for kickbacks he received as Baltimore County Executive and as Governor of Maryland from contractors doing business with the State. (In the end, Agnew was allowed to plead *nolo contendere* to a single charge of failing to report income subject to federal taxation in return for resigning the Office of Vice President; according to the extensive statement submitted for the record by prosecutors in the case, Agnew had also received several cash payments while serving as Vice President.) Is the doctrinal creativity shown in those cases, placing a new emphasis on public corruption, appropriate? Federal judges in the 1970s thought so. For obvious reasons, Congress was slow to criminalize political misconduct; also for obvious reasons, state and local officials were unlikely to uncover and prosecute well-connected local power brokers paying for influence. Is reticence of state and federal officials, or post-Watergate concern about corruption, sufficient justification for what amounts to common-law crime creation?

In *McNally*, the Supreme Court, invoking federalism concerns, tried to curtail lower courts' use of the mail fraud statute. See Chapter 4. Yet no such federalism-based curtailment is evident in the Court's Hobbs Act "under color" cases. Do you think Congress's quick legislative reversal of *McNally* figured into the Court's calculus? Should it have?

7. *McCormick* and *Evans* left the scope of "color of right" extortion more than a little uncertain. Specifically, it remained unclear whether there was a higher *quid pro quo* standard for a public official's receipt of campaign contributions (as in *McCormick*) than for receipt of non-campaign contributions (such as some of the payments at issue in *Evans*). In United States v. Giles, 246 F.3d 966 (7th Cir. 2001), the Appeals Court surveyed the landscape:

> Although not all courts of appeals that have considered the issue have found the *Evans* holding entirely clear, see United States v. Blandford, 33 F.3d 685 (6th Cir. 1994), several have determined that the *quid pro quo* requirement does, in fact, apply to all Hobbs Act extortion prosecutions. See, e.g., United States v. Collins, 78 F.3d 1021 (6th Cir. 1996); United States v. Hairston, 46 F.3d 361 (4th Cir. 1995); United States v. Martinez, 14 F.3d 543 (11th Cir. 1994); United States v. Garcia, 992 F.2d 409 (2d Cir. 1993). . . .
>
> We are not convinced that *Evans* clearly settles the question. And we recognize a policy concern which might justify distinguishing campaign

contributions from other payments. After all, campaign contributions often are made with the hope that the recipient, if elected, will further interests with which the contributor agrees; there is nothing illegal about such contributions. To distinguish legal from illegal campaign contributions, it makes sense to require the government to prove that a particular contribution was made in exchange for an explicit promise or undertaking by the official. Other payments to officials are not clothed with the same degree of respectability as ordinary campaign contributions. For that reason, perhaps it should be easier to prove that those payments are in violation of the law.

However, it is our view that this policy concern is outweighed by language in *Evans*, which, although not entirely clear, can easily be read to lend support to an inference that the *quid pro quo* requirement applies in all ["color of right"] extortion prosecutions under the Hobbs Act. . . . We therefore join the circuits that require a *quid pro quo* showing in all cases. That said, we also agree with the Ninth Circuit in *Tucker* that the government need not show an explicit agreement, but only that the payment was made in return for official acts — that the public official understood that as a result of the payment he was expected to exercise particular kinds of influence on behalf of the payor. . . .

246 F.3d at 971-72.

8. Should campaign contribution cases and other "color of right" extortion cases be treated the same? Should the answer depend on whether the public official is appointed and therefore has no need for election campaign contributions? What is the right answer as a matter of policy? *Giles* suggests there should be a *quid pro quo* requirement across the board, and other circuits have agreed, see, e.g., United States v. Kincaid-Chauncey, 556 F.3d 923, 937 (9th Cir. 2009). Is it doctrinally stable to require a *quid pro quo* regardless of the context, but to note that "not all *quid pro quo*s are made of the same stuff"? See United States v. Abbey, 560 F.3d 513, 517-18 (6th Cir. 2009) (noting also that, "outside the campaign context . . . merely knowing that the payment was made in return for official acts is enough"). Consider how judicial pronouncements about the informality of possible *quid pro quo*s in the non-campaign contribution context (in contrast to the formal exchanges required for prosecutions involving campaign contributions) can effectively raise the evidentiary barriers to prosecuting campaign cases. Is that an unintended consequence of these cases, or is it a motivating fact in the judicial interpretation?

9. Although the "color of official right" extortion doctrine and the mail/ wire fraud prosecutions based on the deprivation of honest services (considered in Chapter 4) arose at roughly the same time, the underlying theories are somewhat different. For one, as discussed in Section B of Chapter 5, the Hobbs Act requires that property be "obtained." When the Speaker of the New York State Assembly, Sheldon Silver, was charged with "color of official right" extortion for disbursing state funds to a research center in exchange

for referrals of potential clients for the Speaker and his law firm by a doctor associated with the center, he argued that the scheme

> is analogous to the charged conduct in *Sekhar*, because what Silver obtained in exchange for his allegedly extortionate conduct was a mere recommendation, conveyed by Doctor-1 to his patients. Silver claims that Doctor-1's decision to refer his patients to [the Speaker's firm] was not transferable property; even if such a recommendation could be "intangible property," it was clearly not "transferred" to Silver or to [the firm].

United States v. Silver, 117 F. Supp. 3d 461, 466 (S.D.N.Y. 2015).

Refusing to dismiss the charges, the district court noted:

> Silver's argument addresses only one of the three ways that the events at issue could be described. If Silver's conduct led only to Doctor-1's recommending [Silver's firm] to his patients, such a scenario would not constitute extortion, as Doctor-1's recommendation is not "transferrable" as defined by Sekhar.
>
> If, however, Silver's conduct caused Doctor-1 to provide Silver with confidential, transferable information, that intangible property is transferrable and thus can form the basis of a Hobbs Act extortion charge. . . .
>
> The Superseding Indictment also alleges facts consistent with a theory of third-party extortion—to wit, that Doctor-1 caused his patients to provide a stake in their "valuable legal claims" to [Silver's firm]. Id. Silver argues that he "cannot have obtained the claims from Doctor-1, as the claims belonged to Doctor-1's patients, not Doctor-1." But under a third-party extortion theory, the Government could prove that Silver obtained the patients' claims from the patients by extorting Doctor-1. Although Silver points out that Doctor-1's patients were presumably unaware of Silver's "color of official right" or any other coercive behavior, "Section 1951(b)(2) speaks of obtaining property 'from another'; it does not say that the 'another' must be the threat's recipient,"
>
> Finally, Silver's argument that the [] patients did not "transfer" their legal claims to [his firm] lacks merit. Legal claims have value, and their value may be assigned or split pursuant to a contingent-fee agreement. After agreeing to transfer her claim, a patient would no longer possess 100 percent of the claim that she previously possessed; such a transfer would be sufficient to trigger Hobbs Act liability.

117 F. Supp. 3d at 466-68 (citations omitted). Even though the Second Circuit later reversed Silver's conviction because the jury instructions were prejudicially inconsistent with McDonnell v. United States (excerpted *infra*), it held the evidence of a Hobbs Act violation sufficient because the Government had indeed shown a property deprivation. The patient leads that Silver obtained, the panel reasoned, "were valuable and transferable property (albeit intangible property)." 864 F.3d 102 (2d Cir. 2017).

10. After *Evans* (as widely interpreted) and *Skilling*, proof of some sort of *quid pro quo* would be required in both "color of right" extortion and honest services prosecutions. But what sort of *quid pro quo*? How specific did the understanding between payor and payee have to be? Certainly, given the differences in statutory language and underlying theories, one could image different legal requirements for the *quid pro quo* required for each statute. The most recent guidance from the Supreme Court, however, has raised more questions than it has answered.

McDonnell v. United States
136 S. Ct. 2355 (2016)

Chief Justice Roberts delivered the opinion of the Court.

In 2014, the Federal Government indicted former Virginia Governor Robert McDonnell and his wife, Maureen McDonnell, on bribery charges. The charges related to the acceptance by the McDonnells of $175,000 in loans, gifts, and other benefits from Virginia businessman Jonnie Williams, while Governor McDonnell was in office. Williams was the chief executive officer of Star Scientific, a Virginia-based company that had developed a nutritional supplement made from anatabine, a compound found in tobacco. Star Scientific hoped that Virginia's public universities would perform research studies on anatabine, and Williams wanted Governor McDonnell's assistance in obtaining those studies.

To convict the McDonnells of bribery, the Government was required to show that Governor McDonnell committed (or agreed to commit) an "official act" in exchange for the loans and gifts. The parties did not agree, however, on what counts as an "official act." The Government alleged in the indictment, and maintains on appeal, that Governor McDonnell committed at least five "official acts." Those acts included "arranging meetings" for Williams with other Virginia officials to discuss Star Scientific's product, "hosting" events for Star Scientific at the Governor's Mansion, and "contacting other government officials" concerning studies of anatabine. The Government also argued more broadly that these activities constituted "official action" because they related to Virginia business development, a priority of Governor McDonnell's administration. Governor McDonnell contends that merely setting up a meeting, hosting an event, or contacting an official—without more—does not count as an "official act."

At trial, the District Court instructed the jury according to the Government's broad understanding of what constitutes an "official act," and the jury convicted both Governor and Mrs. McDonnell on the bribery charges. The Fourth Circuit affirmed Governor McDonnell's conviction, and we granted review to clarify the meaning of "official act."

I

A

On November 3, 2009, petitioner Robert McDonnell was elected the 71st Governor of Virginia. His campaign slogan was "Bob's for Jobs," and his focus in office was on promoting business in Virginia. As Governor, McDonnell spoke about economic development in Virginia "on a daily basis" and attended numerous "events, ribbon cuttings," and "plant facility openings." He also referred thousands of constituents to meetings with members of his staff and other government officials. According to long-time staffers, Governor McDonnell likely had more events at the Virginia Governor's Mansion to promote Virginia business than had occurred in "any other administration."

This case concerns Governor McDonnell's interactions with one of his constituents, Virginia businessman Jonnie Williams. Williams was the CEO of Star Scientific, a Virginia-based company that developed and marketed Anatabloc, a nutritional supplement made from anatabine, a compound found in tobacco. Star Scientific hoped to obtain Food and Drug Administration approval of Anatabloc as an anti-inflammatory drug. An important step in securing that approval was initiating independent research studies on the health benefits of anatabine. Star Scientific hoped Virginia's public universities would undertake such studies, pursuant to a grant from Virginia's Tobacco Commission.

Governor McDonnell first met Williams in 2009, when Williams offered McDonnell transportation on his private airplane to assist with McDonnell's election campaign. Shortly after the election, Williams had dinner with Governor and Mrs. McDonnell at a restaurant in New York. The conversation turned to Mrs. McDonnell's search for a dress for the inauguration, which led Williams to offer to purchase a gown for her. Governor McDonnell's counsel later instructed Williams not to buy the dress, and Mrs. McDonnell told Williams that she would take a rain check.

In October 2010, Governor McDonnell and Williams met again on Williams's plane. During the flight, Williams told Governor McDonnell that he "needed his help" moving forward on the research studies at Virginia's public universities, and he asked to be introduced to the person that he "needed to talk to." Governor McDonnell agreed to introduce Williams to Dr. William Hazel, Virginia's Secretary of Health and Human Resources. Williams met with Dr. Hazel the following month, but the meeting was unfruitful; Dr. Hazel was skeptical of the science behind Anatabloc and did not assist Williams in obtaining the studies.

Six months later, Governor McDonnell's wife, Maureen McDonnell, offered to seat Williams next to the Governor at a political rally. Shortly before the event, Williams took Mrs. McDonnell on a shopping trip and bought her $20,000 worth of designer clothing. The McDonnells later had Williams over for dinner at the Governor's Mansion, where they discussed research studies on Anatabloc.

Two days after that dinner, Williams had an article about Star Scientific's research e-mailed to Mrs. McDonnell, which she forwarded to her husband. Less than an hour later, Governor McDonnell texted his sister to discuss the financial situation of certain rental properties they owned in Virginia Beach. Governor McDonnell also e-mailed his daughter to ask about expenses for her upcoming wedding.

The next day, Williams returned to the Governor's Mansion for a meeting with Mrs. McDonnell. At the meeting, Mrs. McDonnell described the family's financial problems, including their struggling rental properties in Virginia Beach and their daughter's wedding expenses. Mrs. McDonnell, who had experience selling nutritional supplements, told Williams that she had a background in the area and could help him with Anatabloc. According to Williams, she explained that the "Governor says it's okay for me to help you and—but I need you to help me. I need you to help me with this financial situation." Mrs. McDonnell then asked Williams for a $50,000 loan, in addition to a $15,000 gift to help pay for her daughter's wedding, and Williams agreed.

Williams testified that he called Governor McDonnell after the meeting and said, "I understand the financial problems and I'm willing to help. I just wanted to make sure that you knew about this." According to Williams, Governor McDonnell thanked him for his help. Governor McDonnell testified, in contrast, that he did not know about the loan at the time, and that when he learned of it he was upset that Mrs. McDonnell had requested the loan from Williams. Three days after the meeting between Williams and Mrs. McDonnell, Governor McDonnell directed his assistant to forward the article on Star Scientific to Dr. Hazel.

In June 2011, Williams sent Mrs. McDonnell's chief of staff a letter containing a proposed research protocol for the Anatabloc studies. The letter was addressed to Governor McDonnell, and it suggested that the Governor "use the attached protocol to initiate the 'Virginia Study' of Anatabloc at the Medical College of Virginia and the University of Virginia School of Medicine." Governor McDonnell gave the letter to Dr. Hazel. Williams testified at trial that he did not "recall any response" to the letter.

In July 2011, the McDonnell family visited Williams's vacation home for the weekend, and Governor McDonnell borrowed Williams's Ferrari while there. Shortly thereafter, Governor McDonnell asked Dr. Hazel to send an aide to a meeting with Williams and Mrs. McDonnell to discuss research studies on Anatabloc. The aide later testified that she did not feel pressured by Governor or Mrs. McDonnell to do "anything other than have the meeting," and that Williams did not ask anything of her at the meeting. Id. at 3075. After the meeting, the aide sent Williams a "polite blow-off" e-mail.

At a subsequent meeting at the Governor's Mansion, Mrs. McDonnell admired Williams's Rolex and mentioned that she wanted to get one for Governor McDonnell. Williams asked if Mrs. McDonnell wanted him to purchase a Rolex for the Governor, and Mrs. McDonnell responded, "Yes, that would be nice." Williams did so, and Mrs. McDonnell later gave the Rolex to Governor McDonnell as a Christmas present.

In August 2011, the McDonnells hosted a lunch event for Star Scientific at the Governor's Mansion. According to Williams, the purpose of the event was to launch Anatabloc. According to Governor McDonnell's gubernatorial counsel, however, it was just lunch.

The guest list for the event included researchers at the University of Virginia and Virginia Commonwealth University. During the event, Star Scientific distributed free samples of Anatabloc, in addition to eight $25,000 checks that researchers could use in preparing grant proposals for studying Anatabloc. Governor McDonnell asked researchers at the event whether they thought "there was some scientific validity" to Anatabloc and "whether or not there was any reason to explore this further." He also asked whether this could "be something good for the Commonwealth, particularly as it relates to economy or job creation." When Williams asked Governor McDonnell whether he would support funding for the research studies, Governor McDonnell "very politely" replied, "I have limited decision-making power in this area."

In January 2012, Mrs. McDonnell asked Williams for an additional loan for the Virginia Beach rental properties, and Williams agreed. On February 3, Governor McDonnell followed up on that conversation by calling Williams to discuss a $50,000 loan.

Several days later, Williams complained to Mrs. McDonnell that the Virginia universities were not returning Star Scientific's calls. She passed Williams's complaint on to the Governor. While Mrs. McDonnell was driving with Governor McDonnell, she also e-mailed Governor McDonnell's counsel, stating that the Governor "wants to know why nothing has developed" with the research studies after Williams had provided the eight $25,000 checks for preparing grant proposals, and that the Governor "wants to get this going" at the universities. According to Governor McDonnell, however, Mrs. McDonnell acted without his knowledge or permission, and he never made the statements she attributed to him.

On February 16, Governor McDonnell e-mailed Williams to check on the status of documents related to the $50,000 loan. A few minutes later, Governor McDonnell e-mailed his counsel stating, "Please see me about Anatabloc issues at VCU and UVA. Thanks." Governor McDonnell's counsel replied, "Will do. We need to be careful with this issue." The next day, Governor McDonnell's counsel called Star Scientific's lobbyist in order to "change the expectations" of Star Scientific regarding the involvement of the Governor's Office in the studies.

At the end of February, Governor McDonnell hosted a healthcare industry reception at the Governor's Mansion, which Williams attended. Mrs. McDonnell also invited a number of guests recommended by Williams, including researchers at the Virginia universities. Governor McDonnell was present, but did not mention Star Scientific, Williams, or Anatabloc during the event. That same day, Governor McDonnell and Williams spoke about the $50,000 loan, and Williams loaned the money to the McDonnells shortly thereafter.

In March 2012, Governor McDonnell met with Lisa Hicks-Thomas, the Virginia Secretary of Administration, and Sara Wilson, the Director of the Virginia Department of Human Resource Management. The purpose of the meeting was to discuss Virginia's health plan for state employees. At that time, Governor McDonnell was taking Anatabloc several times a day. He took a pill during the meeting, and told Hicks-Thomas and Wilson that the pills "were working well for him" and "would be good for" state employees. Hicks-Thomas recalled Governor McDonnell asking them to meet with a representative from Star Scientific; Wilson had no such recollection. After the discussion with Governor McDonnell, Hicks-Thomas and Wilson looked up Anatabloc on the Internet, but they did not set up a meeting with Star Scientific or conduct any other follow-up. It is undisputed that Virginia's health plan for state employees does not cover nutritional supplements such as Anatabloc.

In May 2012, Governor McDonnell requested an additional $20,000 loan, which Williams provided. Throughout this period, Williams also paid for several rounds of golf for Governor McDonnell and his children, took the McDonnells on a weekend trip, and gave $10,000 as a wedding gift to one of the McDonnells' daughters. In total, Williams gave the McDonnells over $175,000 in gifts and loans.

B

In January 2014, Governor McDonnell was indicted for accepting payments, loans, gifts, and other things of value from Williams and Star Scientific in exchange for "performing official actions on an as-needed basis, as opportunities arose, to legitimize, promote, and obtain research studies for Star Scientific's products." The charges against him comprised one count of conspiracy to commit honest services fraud, three counts of honest services fraud, one count of conspiracy to commit Hobbs Act extortion, six counts of Hobbs Act extortion, and two counts of making a false statement. See 18 U.S.C. §§1343, 1349 (honest services fraud); §1951(a) (Hobbs Act extortion); §1014 (false statement). Mrs. McDonnell was indicted on similar charges, plus obstructing official proceedings, based on her alleged involvement in the scheme. See §1512(c)(2) (obstruction).

The theory underlying both the honest services fraud and Hobbs Act extortion charges was that Governor McDonnell had accepted bribes from Williams. See Skilling v. United States, 561 U.S. 358, 404 (2010) (construing honest services fraud to forbid "fraudulent schemes to deprive another of honest services through bribes or kickbacks"); Evans v. United States, 504 U.S. 255, 260, 269 (1992) (construing Hobbs Act extortion to include " 'taking a bribe' ").

The parties agreed that they would define honest services fraud with reference to the federal bribery statute, 18 U.S.C. §201. That statute makes it a crime for "a public official or person selected to be a public official, directly or indirectly, corruptly" to demand, seek, receive, accept, or agree "to receive or accept anything of value" in return for being "influenced in the performance of any official act." §201(b)(2). An "official act" is defined as "any decision or action on any question, matter, cause, suit, proceeding or controversy, which may at any time be pending, or which may by law be brought before any public official, in such official's official capacity, or in such official's place of trust or profit." §201(a)(3).

The parties also agreed that obtaining a "thing of value . . . knowing that the thing of value was given in return for official action" was an element of Hobbs Act extortion, and that they would use the definition of "official act" found in the federal bribery statute to define "official action" under the Hobbs Act. 792 F.3d 478, 505 (C.A.4 2015).

As a result of all this, the Government was required to prove that Governor McDonnell committed or agreed to commit an "official act" in exchange for the loans and gifts from Williams. See Evans, 504 U.S. at 268 ("the offense is completed at the time when the public official receives a payment in return for his agreement to perform specific official acts; fulfillment of the quid pro quo is not an element of the offense").

The Government alleged that Governor McDonnell had committed *Gov argument* at least five "official acts":

(1) "arranging meetings for [Williams] with Virginia government officials, who were subordinates of the Governor, to discuss and promote Anatabloc";
(2) "hosting, and . . . attending, events at the Governor's Mansion designed to encourage Virginia university researchers to initiate studies of anatabine and to promote Star Scientific's products to doctors for referral to their patients";
(3) "contacting other government officials in the [Governor's Office] as part of an effort to encourage Virginia state research universities to initiate studies of anatabine";
(4) "promoting Star Scientific's products and facilitating its relationships with Virginia government officials by allowing [Williams] to invite individuals important to Star Scientific's business to exclusive events at the Governor's Mansion"; and
(5) "recommending that senior government officials in the [Governor's Office] meet with Star Scientific executives to discuss ways that the company's products could lower healthcare costs."

The case proceeded to a jury trial, which lasted five weeks. Pursuant to an immunity agreement, Williams testified that he had given the gifts and loans to the McDonnells to obtain the Governor's "help with the testing" of Anatabloc at Virginia's medical schools. Governor McDonnell acknowledged that he had requested loans and accepted gifts from Williams. He testified, however, that setting up meetings with government officials was something he did "literally thousands of times" as Governor, and that he did not expect his staff "to do anything other than to meet" with Williams.

Several state officials testified that they had discussed Anatabloc with Williams or Governor McDonnell, but had not taken any action to further the research studies. A UVA employee in the university research office, who had never spoken with the Governor about Anatabloc, testified that she wrote a pro/con list concerning research studies on Anatabloc. The first "pro" was the "[p]erception to Governor that UVA would like to work with local companies," and the first "con" was the "[p]olitical pressure from Governor and impact on future UVA requests from the Governor."

Following closing arguments, the District Court instructed the jury that to convict Governor McDonnell it must find that he agreed "to accept a thing of value in exchange for official action." The court described the five alleged "official acts" set forth in the indictment, which involved arranging meetings, hosting events, and contacting other government officials. The court then quoted the statutory definition of "official act," and—as the Government had requested—advised the jury that the term encompassed "acts that a public official customarily performs," including acts "in furtherance of longer-term goals" or "in a series of steps to exercise influence or achieve an end."

Governor McDonnell had requested the court to further instruct the jury that the "fact that an activity is a routine activity, or a 'settled practice,' of an office-holder does not alone make it an 'official act,'" and that "merely arranging a meeting, attending an event, hosting a reception, or making a speech are not, standing alone, 'official acts,' even if they are settled practices of the official," because they "are not decisions on matters pending before the government." He also asked the court to explain to the jury that an "official act" must intend to or "in fact influence a specific official decision the government actually makes—such as awarding a contract, hiring a government employee, issuing a license, passing a law, or implementing a regulation." The District Court declined to give Governor McDonnell's proposed instruction to the jury.

The jury convicted Governor McDonnell on the honest services fraud and Hobbs Act extortion charges, but acquitted him on the false statement charges. Mrs. McDonnell was also convicted on most of the charges against her. Although the Government requested a sentence of at least ten years for Governor McDonnell, the District Court sentenced him to two years in prison. Mrs. McDonnell received a one-year sentence.

Governor McDonnell appealed his convictions to the Fourth Circuit, challenging the definition of "official action" in the jury instructions on the ground that it deemed "virtually all of a public servant's activities 'official,' no matter how minor or innocuous. He also reiterated his challenges to the sufficiency of the evidence and the constitutionality of the statutes under which he was convicted.

The Fourth Circuit affirmed, and we granted certiorari. Mrs. McDonnell's separate appeal remains pending before the Court of Appeals.

II

The issue in this case is the proper interpretation of the term "official act." Section 201(a)(3) defines an "official act" as "any decision or action on any question, matter, cause, suit, proceeding or controversy, which may at any time be pending, or which may by law be brought before any public official, in such official's official capacity, or in such official's place of trust or profit."

According to the Government, "Congress used intentionally broad language" in §201(a)(3) to embrace "any decision or action, on any question or matter, that may at any time be pending, or which may by law be brought before any public official, in such official's official capacity." The Government concludes that the term "official act" therefore encompasses nearly any activity by a public official. In the Government's view, "official act" specifically includes arranging a meeting, contacting another public official, or hosting an event—without more—concerning any subject, including a broad policy issue such as Virginia economic development.

Gov Arg.

Governor McDonnell, in contrast, contends that statutory context compels a more circumscribed reading, limiting "official acts" to those acts that "direct [] a particular resolution of a specific governmental decision," or that pressure another official to do so. He also claims that "vague corruption laws" such as §201 implicate serious constitutional concerns, militating "in favor of a narrow, cautious reading of these criminal statutes."

Taking into account the text of the statute, the precedent of this Court, and the constitutional concerns raised by Governor McDonnell, we reject the Government's reading of §201(a)(3) and adopt a more bounded interpretation of "official act." Under that interpretation, setting up a meeting, calling another public official, or hosting an event does not, standing alone, qualify as an "official act."

A

The text of §201(a)(3) sets forth two requirements for an "official act": First, the Government must identify a "question, matter, cause, suit, proceeding or controversy" that "may at any time be pending" or "may by law be brought" before a public official. Second, the Government must prove that the public official made a decision or took an action "on" that question, matter, cause, suit, proceeding, or controversy, or agreed to do so. The issue here is whether arranging a meeting, contacting another official, or hosting an event—without more—can be a "question, matter, cause, suit, proceeding or controversy," and if not, whether it can be a decision or action on a "question, matter, cause, suit, proceeding or controversy."

The first inquiry is whether a typical meeting, call, or event is itself a "question, matter, cause, suit, proceeding or controversy." The Government argues that nearly any activity by a public official qualifies as a question or matter—from workaday functions, such as the typical call, meeting, or event, to the broadest issues the government confronts, such as fostering economic development. We conclude, however, that the terms "question, matter, cause, suit, proceeding or controversy" do not sweep so broadly.

The last four words in that list—"cause," "suit," "proceeding," and "controversy"—connote a formal exercise of governmental power, such as a lawsuit, hearing, or administrative determination. See, e.g., Crimes Act of 1790, §21, 1 Stat. 117 (using "cause," "suit," and "controversy" in a related statutory context to refer to judicial proceedings); Black's Law Dictionary 278-279, 400, 1602-1603 (4th ed. 1951) (defining "cause," "suit," and "controversy" as judicial proceedings); 18 U.S.C. §201(b)(3) (using "proceeding" to refer to trials, hearings, or the like "before any court, any committee of either House or both Houses of Congress, or any agency, commission, or officer"). Although it may be difficult to define the precise reach of those terms, it seems clear that a typical meeting, telephone call, or event arranged by a public official does not qualify as a "cause, suit, proceeding or controversy."

But what about a "question" or "matter"? A "question" could mean any "subject or aspect that is in dispute, open for discussion, or to be inquired into," and a "matter" any "subject" of "interest or relevance." Webster's Third New International Dictionary 1394, 1863 (1961). If those meanings were adopted, a typical meeting, call, or event would qualify as a "question" or "matter." A "question" may also be interpreted more narrowly, however, as "a subject or point of debate or a proposition being or to be voted on in a meeting," such as a question "before the senate." Similarly, a "matter" may be limited to "a topic under active and usually serious or practical consideration," such as a matter that "will come before the committee."

To choose between those competing definitions, we look to the context in which the words appear. Under the familiar interpretive canon *noscitur a sociis,* "a word is known by the company it keeps." Jarecki v. G.D. Searle & Co., 367 U.S. 303, 307 (1961). While "not an inescapable rule," this canon "is often wisely applied where a word is capable of many meanings in order to avoid the giving of unintended breadth to the Acts of Congress." Ibid.

Applying that same approach here, we conclude that a "question" or "matter" must be similar in nature to a "cause, suit, proceeding or controversy." Because a typical meeting, call, or event arranged by a public official is not of the same stripe as a lawsuit before a court, a determination before an agency, or a hearing before a committee, it does not qualify as a "question" or "matter" under §201(a)(3).

That more limited reading also comports with the presumption "that statutory language is not superfluous." If "question" and "matter" were as unlimited in scope as the Government argues, the terms "cause, suit, proceeding or controversy" would serve no role in the statute—every "cause, suit, proceeding or controversy" would also be a "question" or "matter." Under a more confined interpretation, however, "question" and "matter" may be understood to refer to a formal exercise of governmental power that is similar in nature to a "cause, suit, proceeding or controversy," but that does not necessarily fall into one of those prescribed categories.

Because a typical meeting, call, or event is not itself a question or matter, the next step is to determine whether arranging a meeting, contacting another official, or hosting an event may qualify as a "decision or action" on a different question or matter. That requires us to first establish what counts as a question or matter in this case.

In addition to the requirements we have described, §201(a)(3) states that the question or matter must be "pending" or "may by law be brought" before "any public official." "Pending" and "may by law be brought" suggest something that is relatively circumscribed—the kind of thing that can be put on an agenda, tracked for progress, and then checked off as complete. In particular, "may by law be brought" conveys something within the specific duties of an official's position—the function conferred by the authority of his office. The word "any" conveys that the matter may be pending either before the public official who is performing the official act, or before another public official.

The District Court, however, determined that the relevant matter in this case could be considered at a much higher level of generality as "Virginia business and economic development," or—as it was often put to the jury—"Bob's for Jobs." Economic development is not naturally described as a matter "pending" before a public official—or something that may be brought "by law" before him—any more than "justice" is pending or may be brought by law before a judge, or "national security" is pending or may be brought by law before an officer of the Armed Forces. Under §201(a)(3), the pertinent "question, matter, cause, suit, proceeding or controversy" must be more focused and concrete.

For its part, the Fourth Circuit found at least three questions or matters at issue in this case: (1) "whether researchers at any of Virginia's state universities would initiate a study of Anatabloc"; (2) "whether the state-created Tobacco Indemnification and Community Revitalization

Commission" would "allocate grant money for the study of anatabine"; and (3) "whether the health insurance plan for state employees in Virginia would include Anatabloc as a covered drug." We agree that those qualify as questions or matters under §201(a)(3). Each is focused and concrete, and each involves a formal exercise of governmental power that is similar in nature to a lawsuit, administrative determination, or hearing.

second inquiry

The question remains whether—as the Government argues—merely setting up a meeting, hosting an event, or calling another official qualifies as a decision or action on any of those three questions or matters. Although the word "decision," and especially the word "action," could be read expansively to support the Government's view, our opinion in United States v. Sun-Diamond Growers of Cal., 526 U.S. 398 (1999), rejects that interpretation.

In *Sun-Diamond*, the Court stated that it was not an "official act" under §201 for the President to host a championship sports team at the White House, the Secretary of Education to visit a high school, or the Secretary of Agriculture to deliver a speech to "farmers concerning various matters of USDA policy." Id. at 407. We recognized that "the Secretary of Agriculture always has before him or in prospect matters that affect farmers, just as the President always has before him or in prospect matters that affect college and professional sports, and the Secretary of Education matters that affect high schools." Ibid. But we concluded that the existence of such pending matters was not enough to find that any action related to them constituted an "official act." Ibid. It was possible to avoid the "absurdities" of convicting individuals on corruption charges for engaging in such conduct, we explained, "through the definition of that term," i.e., by adopting a more limited definition of "official acts." Id. at 408.

It is apparent from *Sun-Diamond* that hosting an event, meeting with other officials, or speaking with interested parties is not, standing alone, a "decision or action" within the meaning of §201(a)(3), even if the event, meeting, or speech is related to a pending question or matter. Instead, something more is required: §201(a)(3) specifies that the public official must make a decision or take an action on that question or matter, or agree to do so.

examples of official Acts

For example, a decision or action to initiate a research study—or a decision or action on a qualifying step, such as narrowing down the list of potential research topics—would qualify as an "official act." A public official may also make a decision or take an action on a "question, matter, cause, suit, proceeding or controversy" by using his official position to exert pressure on another official to perform an "official act." In addition, if a public official uses his official position to provide advice to another official, knowing or intending that such advice will form the basis for an "official act" by another official, that too can qualify as a decision or action for purposes of §201(a)(3). See United States v. Birdsall, 233 U.S. 223, 234 (1914) (finding "official action" on the part of subordinates where their superiors "would necessarily rely largely upon the reports and advice of subordinates . . . who were more directly acquainted with" the "facts and circumstances of particular cases").

Under this Court's precedents, a public official is not required to actually make a decision or take an action on a "question, matter, cause, suit, proceeding or controversy"; it is enough that the official agree to do so. See Evans, 504 U.S. at 268. . . .

Setting up a meeting, hosting an event, or calling an official (or agreeing to do so) merely to talk about a research study or to gather additional information, however, does not qualify as a decision or action on the pending question of whether to initiate the study. Simply expressing support for the research study at a meeting, event, or call—or sending a subordinate to such a meeting, event, or call—similarly does not qualify as a decision or action on the study, as long as the public official does not intend to exert pressure on another official or provide advice, knowing or intending such advice to form the basis for an "official act." Otherwise, if every action somehow related to the research study were an "official act," the requirement that the public official make a decision or take an action on that study, or agree to do so, would be meaningless.

Of course, this is not to say that setting up a meeting, hosting an event, or making a phone call is always an innocent act, or is irrelevant, in cases like this one. If an official sets up a meeting, hosts an event, or makes a phone call on a question or matter that is or could be pending before another official, that could serve as evidence of an agreement to take an official act. A jury could conclude, for example, that the official was attempting to pressure or advise another official on a pending matter. And if the official agreed to exert that pressure or give that advice in exchange for a thing of value, that would be illegal.

The Government relies on this Court's decision in *Birdsall* to support a more expansive interpretation of "official act," but *Birdsall* is fully consistent with our reading of §201(a)(3). We held in *Birdsall* that "official action" could be established by custom rather than "by statute" or "a written rule or regulation," and need not be a formal part of an official's decisionmaking process. 233 U.S. at 230-231. That does not mean, however, that every decision or action customarily performed by a public official—such as the myriad decisions to refer a constituent to another official—counts as an "official act." The "official action" at issue in *Birdsall* was "advis[ing] the Commissioner of Indian Affairs, contrary to the truth," that the facts of the case warranted granting leniency to certain defendants convicted of "unlawfully selling liquor to Indians." Id. at 227-230. That "decision or action" fits neatly within our understanding of §201(a) (3): It reflected a decision or action to advise another official on the pending question whether to grant leniency.

In sum, an "official act" is a decision or action on a "question, matter, cause, suit, proceeding or controversy." The "question, matter, cause, suit, proceeding or controversy" must involve a formal exercise of governmental power that is similar in nature to a lawsuit before a court, a determination before an agency, or a hearing before a committee. It must also be something specific and focused that is "pending" or "may by law be brought" before a public official. To qualify as an "official act," the public official must make a decision or take an action on that "question, matter, cause, suit, proceeding or controversy," or agree to do so. That decision or action may include using his official position to exert pressure on another official to perform an "official act," or to advise another official, knowing or intending that such advice will form the basis for an "official act" by another official. Setting up a meeting, talking to another official, or organizing an event (or agreeing to do so)—without more—does not fit that definition of "official act."

B

In addition to being inconsistent with both text and precedent, the Government's expansive interpretation of "official act" would raise significant constitutional concerns. Section 201 prohibits quid pro quo corruption—the exchange of a thing of value for an "official act." In the Government's view, nearly anything a public official accepts—from a campaign contribution to lunch—counts as a quid; and nearly anything a public official does—from arranging a meeting to inviting a guest to an event—counts as a quo.

But conscientious public officials arrange meetings for constituents, contact other officials on their behalf, and include them in events all the time. The basic compact underlying representative government assumes that public officials will hear from their constituents and act appropriately on their concerns—whether it is the union official worried about a plant closing or the homeowners who wonder why it took five days to restore power to their neighborhood after a storm. The Government's position could cast a pall of potential prosecution over these relationships if the union had given a campaign contribution in the past or the homeowners invited the official to join them on their annual outing to the ballgame. Officials might wonder whether they could respond to even the most commonplace requests for assistance, and citizens with legitimate concerns might shrink from participating in democratic discourse.

This concern is substantial. White House counsel who worked in every administration from that of President Reagan to President Obama warn that the Government's "breathtaking expansion of public-corruption law would likely chill federal officials' interactions with the people they serve and thus damage their ability effectively to perform their duties." Six former Virginia attorneys general—four Democrats and two Republicans—also filed an amicus brief in this Court echoing those concerns, as did 77 former state attorneys general from States other than Virginia—41 Democrats, 35 Republicans, and 1 independent.

None of this, of course, is to suggest that the facts of this case typify normal political interaction between public officials and their constituents. Far from it. But the Government's legal interpretation is not confined to cases involving extravagant gifts or large sums of money, and we cannot construe a criminal statute on the assumption that the Government will "use it responsibly." The Court in *Sun-Diamond* declined to rely on "the Government's discretion" to protect against overzealous prosecutions under §201, concluding instead that "a statute in this field that can linguistically be interpreted to be either a meat axe or a scalpel should reasonably be taken to be the latter." 526 U.S. at 408.

A related concern is that, under the Government's interpretation, the term "official act" is not defined "with sufficient definiteness that ordinary people can understand what conduct is prohibited," or "in a manner that does not encourage arbitrary and discriminatory enforcement." *Skilling*, 561 U.S. at 402-403. Under the " 'standardless sweep' " of the Government's reading, Kolender v. Lawson, 461 U.S. 352, 35 (1983), public officials could be subject to prosecution, without fair notice, for the most prosaic interactions. "Invoking so shapeless a provision to condemn someone to prison" for up to 15 years raises the serious concern that the provision "does not comport with the Constitution's guarantee of due process." Our more constrained interpretation of §201(a)(3) avoids this "vagueness shoal." *Skilling*, 561 U.S. at 368.

The Government's position also raises significant federalism concerns. A State defines itself as a sovereign through "the structure of its government, and the character of those who exercise government authority." Gregory v. Ashcroft, 501 U.S. 452, 460 (1991). That includes the prerogative to regulate the permissible scope of interactions between state officials and their constituents. Here, where a more limited interpretation of "official act" is supported by both text and precedent, we decline to "construe the statute in a manner that leaves its outer boundaries ambiguous and involves the Federal Government in setting standards" of "good government for local and state officials." McNally v. United States, 483 U.S. 350, 360 (1987); see also United States v. Enmons, 410 U.S. 396, 410-411 (1973) (rejecting a "broad concept of extortion" that would lead to "an unprecedented incursion into the criminal jurisdiction of the States").

III

A

Governor McDonnell argues that his convictions must be vacated because the jury was improperly instructed on the meaning of "official act" under §201(a)(3) of the federal bribery statute. According to Governor McDonnell, the District Court "refused to convey any meaningful limits on 'official act,' giving an instruction that allowed the jury to convict [him] for lawful conduct." We agree.

The jury instructions included the statutory definition of "official action," and further defined the term to include "actions that have been clearly established by settled practice as part of a public official's position, even if the action was not taken pursuant to responsibilities explicitly assigned by law." The instructions also stated that "official actions may include acts that a public official customarily performs," including acts "in furtherance of longer-term goals" or "in a series of steps to exercise influence or achieve an end." In light of our interpretation of the term "official acts," those instructions lacked important qualifications, rendering them significantly overinclusive.

First, the instructions did not adequately explain to the jury how to identify the "question, matter, cause, suit, proceeding or controversy." As noted, the Fourth Circuit held that "the Government presented evidence of three questions or matters": (1) "whether researchers at any of Virginia's state universities would initiate a study of Anatabloc"; (2) "whether the state-created Tobacco Indemnification and Community Revitalization Commission" would "allocate grant money for the study of anatabine"; and (3) "whether the health insurance plan for state employees in Virginia would include Anatabloc as a covered drug."

The problem with the District Court's instructions is that they provided no assurance that the jury reached its verdict after finding those questions or matters. The testimony at trial described how Governor McDonnell set up meetings, contacted other officials, and hosted events. It is possible the jury thought that a typical meeting, call, or event was itself a "question, matter, cause, suit, proceeding or controversy." If so, the jury could have convicted Governor McDonnell without finding that he committed or agreed to commit an "official act," as properly defined. To prevent this problem, the District Court should have instructed the jury that it must identify a "question, matter, cause, suit, proceeding or controversy" involving the formal exercise of governmental power.

Second, the instructions did not inform the jury that the "question, matter, cause, suit, proceeding or controversy" must be more specific and focused than a broad policy objective. The Government told the jury in its closing argument that "[w]hatever it was" Governor McDonnell had done, "it's all official action." Based on that remark, and the repeated references to "Bob's for Jobs" at trial, the jury could have thought that the relevant "question, matter, cause, suit, proceeding or controversy" was something as nebulous as "Virginia business and economic development," as the District Court itself concluded. To avoid that misconception, the District Court should have instructed the jury that the pertinent "question, matter, cause, suit, proceeding or controversy" must be something specific and focused that is "pending" or "may by law be brought before any public official," such as the question whether to initiate the research studies.

Third, the District Court did not instruct the jury that to convict Governor McDonnell, it had to find that he made a decision or took an action—or agreed to do so—on the identified "question, matter, cause, suit, proceeding or controversy," as we have construed that requirement. At trial, several of Governor McDonnell's subordinates testified that he asked them to attend a meeting, not that he expected them to do anything other than that. If that testimony reflects what Governor McDonnell agreed to do at the time he accepted the loans and gifts from Williams, then he did not agree to make a decision or take an action on any of the three questions or matters described by the Fourth Circuit.

The jury may have disbelieved that testimony or found other evidence that Governor McDonnell agreed to exert pressure on those officials to initiate the research studies or add Anatabloc to the state health plan, but it is also possible that the jury convicted Governor McDonnell without finding that he agreed to make a decision or take an action on a properly defined "question, matter, cause, suit, proceeding or controversy." To forestall that possibility, the District Court should have instructed the jury that merely arranging a meeting or hosting an event to discuss a matter does not count as a decision or action on that matter.

Because the jury was not correctly instructed on the meaning of "official act," it may have convicted Governor McDonnell for conduct that is not unlawful. For that reason, we cannot conclude that the errors in the jury instructions were "harmless beyond a reasonable doubt." We accordingly vacate Governor McDonnell's convictions.

holding

B

Governor McDonnell raises two additional claims. First, he argues that the charges against him must be dismissed because the honest services statute and the Hobbs Act are unconstitutionally vague. We reject that claim. For purposes of this case, the parties defined honest services fraud and Hobbs Act extortion with reference to §201 of the federal bribery statute. Because we have interpreted the term "official act" in §201(a)(3) in a way that avoids the vagueness concerns raised by Governor McDonnell, we decline to invalidate those statutes under the facts here.

Second, Governor McDonnell argues that the charges must be dismissed because there is insufficient evidence that he committed an "official act," or that he agreed to do so. Because the parties have not had an opportunity to address that question in light of the interpretation of §201(a)(3) adopted by this Court, we leave it for the Court of Appeals to resolve in the first instance. If the court below determines that there is sufficient evidence for a jury to convict Governor McDonnell of committing or agreeing to commit an "official act," his case may be set for a new trial. If the court instead determines that the evidence is insufficient, the charges against him must be dismissed. We express no view on that question.

* * *

There is no doubt that this case is distasteful; it may be worse than that. But our concern is not with tawdry tales of Ferraris, Rolexes, and ball gowns. It is instead with the broader legal implications of the Government's boundless interpretation of the federal bribery statute. A more limited interpretation of the term "official act" leaves ample room for prosecuting corruption, while comporting with the text of the statute and the precedent of this Court.

The judgment of the Court of Appeals is vacated, and the case is remanded for further proceedings consistent with this opinion.

NOTES AND QUESTIONS

1. Sounds like it's good to be the Governor of Virginia. People seem to just give stuff to you and your family. (On the other hand, people don't always do what you ask.) Having followed the Court's doctrinal moves in this area, you may not be surprised by a decision that "tribute" (as a Roman might have called it) from a highly interested party does not necessarily fall within extortion "under color of official right." But, as a policy matter, are you comfortable with where the Court ended up? The Court made much of a State's "prerogative to regulate the permissible scope of interactions between state officials and their constituents." If Virginia's legislature or the officials charged with enforcing Virginia law decide that a regime of "cash for official favors that fall short of 'official acts'" is just fine, should the federal interest be at an end?

2. The Government chose not to retry McDonnell after the reversal of his convictions. Based on the Court's analysis, might the facts have legally supported such a prosecution? On what theory or theories? The Court seemed concerned about officials being prosecuted for "mere" meetings or phone calls made on behest of constituents who are often contributors. Yet it observed:

If an official sets up a meeting, hosts an event, or makes a phone call on a question or matter that is or could be pending before another official, that could serve as evidence of an agreement to take an official act. A jury could conclude, for example, that the official was attempting to pressure or advise

another official on a pending matter. And if the official agreed to exert that
pressure or give that advice in exchange for a thing of value, that would be
illegal.

136 S. Ct. at 2371. And the Court soon reiterated that an "official act"
can include a defendant's "using his official position to exert pressure on
another official to perform an 'official act,' or to advise another official,
knowing or intending that such advice will form the basis for an 'official
act' by another official." Id. at 2372. If the necessary "official act" can come
from the subordinate whom a Governor calls or the regulatory official that a
legislator contacts, will *McDonnell* have done much to protect "conscientious
public officials"? Was the real problem in *McDonnell* that prosecutors did not
focus on the formal decision making of those the Governor called on behalf
of Williams and Anatabloc?

   3. To what extent did the Court's entire analysis rest on the stipulation
of the parties that the §201 "official act" analysis should drive the interpretation of the Hobbs Act and honest services fraud? Was this an appropriate
way for the Court to proceed? Did the Court mean to suggest that the elements of honest services fraud and the elements of "color of right" extor-
tion/bribery are exactly the same as the elements of §201 bribery? We think
it did not intend to do so (though the Court did not do anyone a favor by
failing to make this clear). After all, while *Skilling* cited §201 as an example
of "bribery" constituting honest services fraud, see *supra* Chapter 4, it didn't
say that *only* §201 bribery is covered by 18 U.S.C. §1346. Nor did Justice
Steven's assertion in *Evans* that color-of-right extortion is "the rough equivalent of what we would now describe as 'taking a bribe'" go on to specify the
elements of "bribery" charged as Hobbs Act extortion. Do you think that
prosecutors, seeking to be freed from *McDonnell*'s narrowing definition of
"official act," will soon be arguing that both color-of-right extortion schemes
and honest services fraud in the form of bribery are broader than the bribery prohibition in §201? (Does the sun rise in the east?)

   4. Unless and until a lower court departs from the lawmaking-by-
stipulation in *McDonnell*, the focus will be—in addition to determining
whether a *quid pro quo* occurred—on sorting qualifying "official acts" from
non-qualifying actions. What about a powerful state legislator's letter to a
not-for-profit organization that receives state funds recommending that the
not-for-profit hire the son of someone from whom the legislator has received
something of value (perhaps a donation, but not necessarily)? How about
when the same legislator has a staff member call a state judge to ask him to
hire the same person's daughter as an unpaid intern? Will it always be an
"official act" when a legislator proposes a proclamation honoring someone?
Would your answer to the last question change if you learned, as the court
in United States v. Silver, 864 F.3d 102 (2d Cir. 2017) (the source of all this
paragraph's examples) noted, that such resolutions were routine measures

that, among other things, honored newly designated Eagle Scouts and high
school sports teams? See id. at 121 (while suggesting they might indeed be
"official acts," noting that a jury might find "that, though certainly 'official,'
the prolific and perfunctory nature of these resolutions make them *de minimis quos* unworthy of a *quid.*").

5. Before *McDonnell*, some lower courts were comfortable with an "as
opportunities arise" theory of "color of right" extortion. As the Second
Circuit explained (in an opinion by then-Judge Sotomayor):

> [S]o long as the jury finds that an official accepted gifts in exchange for a
> promise to perform official acts for the giver, it need not find that the specific
> act to be performed was identified at the time of the promise, nor need it link
> each specific benefit to a single official act. To require otherwise could sub-
> vert the ends of justice in cases—such as the one before us—involving ongo-
> ing schemes. In our view, a scheme involving payments at regular intervals in
> exchange for specific official acts as the opportunities to commit those acts
> arise does not dilute the requisite criminal intent or make the scheme any less
> "extortionate." Indeed, a reading of the statute that excluded such schemes
> would legalize some of the most pervasive and entrenched corruption, and
> cannot be what Congress intended.

United States v. Ganim, 510 F.3d 134, 146-47 (2d Cir. 2007) (upholding
conviction of the former mayor of Bridgeport, Connecticut[*]). Affirming the
conviction of former Louisiana Congressman William Jefferson, the Fourth
Circuit followed *Ganim* and noted:

> There was, in this case, an ongoing course of illicit and repugnant conduct by
> Jefferson—conduct for which he was compensated considerably by those on
> whose behalf he was acting. An absurd result would occur if we were to deem
> Jefferson's illicit actions as outside the purview of the bribery statute, sim-
> ply because he was rewarded by periodic payments to his family's businesses.
> Given the choice between a "meat axe or a scalpel" when interpreting a stat-
> ute, we, like the Supreme Court, favor the scalpel. See *Sun-Diamond*, 526 U.S.
> at 412. We will not, however, carve from the bribery statute a criterion that
> depends on the public official's preferred method of payment.

United States v. Jefferson, 674 F.3d 332, 359 (4th Cir. 2012). Are these cases
good law after *McDonnell?* The Second Circuit appears to think so. See
United States v. Skelos, No. 16-1618-CR, 2017 WL 4250021, at *3 (2d Cir.
Sept. 26, 2017) (nonprecedental summary order).

6. Soon we will see whether *McDonnell*'s constrained reading of federal
bribery provisions leads federal prosecutors to turn to state law. The Travel

---

* [Editors' Note: After serving seven years in federal prison, Ganim returned to
Bridgeport, and was re-elected to the mayoralty in 2015. He is now running for Governor.]

Act prohibits the use of interstate travel, mail, or facilities with the intent to carry out any "unlawful act," 18 U.S.C. §1952(a)(3). The definition of "unlawful activity," includes "bribery . . . in violation of the laws of the State in which committed." §1952(b)(2). In United States v. Ferriero, 866 F.3d 107 (3d Cir. 2017), a New Jersey party official was convicted under the Travel Act (and RICO) with violating New Jersey's prohibition against "[b]ribery in official and political matters." N.J. Stat. Ann. §2C:27-2. According to that provision, "[a] person is guilty of bribery if he directly or indirectly offers, confers or agrees to confer upon another, or solicits, accepts or agrees to accept . . . [a]ny benefit as consideration for a decision, opinion, recommendation, vote or exercise of discretion of a public servant, party official or voter on any public issue or in any public election." Id. Rejecting defendant's effort to invoke *McDonnell*, the Circuit noted: "Although the statutes in *McDonnell* and here both involve bribery, we see no reason for transplanting the conclusions in *McDonnell* that stem solely from the Court's application of general statutory-construction principles to the particular statute at issue in that case." 866 F.3d at 128. And it went on to observe

> this case lacks the federalism concerns present in *McDonnell*. *McDonnell* involved a congressionally written standard that governed the conduct of state officials. Though this case applies a federal statute to a nonfederal, local party official, it applies a standard from a New Jersey statute written by New Jersey legislators. It simply does not "'involve [] the Federal Government in setting standards' of 'good government for local and state officials.'" *McDonnell*, 136 S. Ct. at 2373 (quoting *McNally*, 483 U.S. at 360).

866 F.3d at 128. Should federalism considerations drop out when federal prosecutors deploy state law in this manner?

7. When an official-payee is charged with "extortion," does that preclude charging the payor? If "color of right" extortion includes cases of bribery, and bribe payors can be charged as accessories to and co-conspirators of mail/wire fraud, why can't bribe payors be charged as co-conspirators and accessories to (rather than treated as victims of) extortion? In the following case, the Court took a stab at answering:

Ocasio v. United States
136 S. Ct. 1423 (2016)

Justice ALITO delivered the opinion of the Court.

Petitioner Samuel Ocasio, a former officer in the Baltimore Police Department, participated in a kickback scheme with the owners of a local auto repair shop. When petitioner and other Baltimore officers reported to the scene of an auto accident, they persuaded the owners of damaged cars to have their vehicles towed to the repair shop, and in exchange for this service the officers received payments from the shopowners. Petitioner was convicted of obtaining money from the shopowners under color of official right, in violation of the Hobbs Act, 18 U.S.C. §1951, and of conspiring to violate the Hobbs Act, in violation of 18 U.S.C. §371. He now challenges his conspiracy conviction, contending that, as a matter of law, he cannot be convicted of conspiring with the shopowners to obtain money from them under color of official right. We reject this argument because it is contrary to age-old principles of conspiracy law.

I

Hernan Alexis Moreno Mejia (known as Moreno) and Edwin Javier Mejia (known as Mejia) are brothers who co-owned and operated the Majestic Auto Repair Shop (Majestic). In 2008, Majestic was struggling to attract customers, so Moreno and Mejia made a deal with a Baltimore police officer, Jhonn Corona. In exchange for kickbacks, Officer Corona would refer motorists whose cars were damaged in accidents to Majestic for towing and repairs. Officer Corona then spread the word to other members of the force, and eventually as many as 60 other officers sent damaged cars to Majestic in exchange for payments of $150 to $300 per referral.

Petitioner began to participate in this scheme in 2009. On several occasions from 2009 to 2011, he convinced accident victims to have their cars towed to Majestic. Often, before sending a car to Majestic, petitioner called Moreno from the scene of an accident to ensure that the make and model of the car, the extent of the damage, and the car's insurance coverage would allow the shopowners to turn a profit on the repairs. After directing a vehicle to Majestic, petitioner would call Moreno and request his payment.

Because police are often among the first to arrive at the scene of an accident, the Baltimore officers were well positioned to route damaged vehicles to Majestic. As a result, the kickback scheme was highly successful: It substantially increased Majestic's volume of business and profits, and by early 2011 it provided Majestic with at least 90% of its customers.

Moreno, Mejia, petitioner, and nine other Baltimore officers were indicted in 2011. The shopowners and most of the other officers eventually pleaded guilty pursuant to plea deals, but petitioner did not.

In a superseding indictment, petitioner was charged with three counts of violating the Hobbs Act, 18 U.S.C. §1951, by extorting money from Moreno with his consent and under color of official right. As all parties agree, the type of extortion for which petitioner was convicted—obtaining property from another with his consent and under color of official right—is the "rough equivalent of what we would now describe as 'taking a bribe.'" *Evans v. United States,* 504 U.S. 255, 260 (1992). To prove this offense, the Government "need only show that a public official has obtained a payment to which he was not entitled, knowing that the payment was made in return for official acts." Id. at 268.

II

B

[The] basic principles of conspiracy law resolve this case. In order to establish the existence of a conspiracy to violate the Hobbs Act, the Government has no obligation to demonstrate that each conspirator agreed personally to commit—or was even capable of committing—the substantive offense of Hobbs Act extortion. It is sufficient to prove that the conspirators agreed that the underlying crime *be committed* by a member of the conspiracy who was capable of committing it. In other words, each conspirator must have specifically intended that *some conspirator* commit each element of the substantive offense.

That is exactly what happened here: Petitioner, Moreno, and Mejia "share[d] a common purpose," namely, that *petitioner* and other police officers would commit every element of the substantive extortion offense. Petitioner and other officers would obtain property "under color of official right," something that Moreno and Mejia were incapable of doing because they were not public officials. And petitioner and other officers would obtain that money from "another," i.e., from Moreno, Mejia, or Majestic. Although Moreno and Mejia were incapable of committing the underlying substantive offense as principals,[9] they could . . . conspire to commit Hobbs Act extortion by agreeing to help petitioner and other officers commit the substantive offense. . . . For these reasons, it is clear that petitioner could be convicted of conspiring to obtain property from the shopowners with their consent and under color of official right.

C

In an effort to escape this conclusion, petitioner argues that the usual rules do not apply to the type of Hobbs Act conspiracy charged in this case. His basic argument, as ultimately clarified, is as follows. All members of a conspiracy must share the same criminal objective. The objective of the conspiracy charged in this case was to obtain money "from another,

---

9. The Government argues that the lower courts have long held that a private person may be guilty of this type of Hobbs Act extortion as an aider and abettor. See Brief for United States 36-37. We have no occasion to reach that question here.

with his consent . . . under color of official right." But Moreno and Mejia did not have the objective of obtaining money "from another" because the money in question was their own. Accordingly, they were incapable of being members of the conspiracy charged in this case. And since there is insufficient evidence in the record to show that petitioner conspired with anyone other than Moreno and Mejia, he must be acquitted.

This argument fails for a very simple reason: Contrary to petitioner's claim, he and the shopowners *did* have a common criminal objective. The objective was not that each conspirator, including Moreno and Mejia, would obtain money from "another" but rather that petitioner and other Baltimore officers would do so. Petitioner does not dispute that he was properly convicted for three substantive Hobbs Act violations based on proof that he obtained money "from another." The criminal objective on which petitioner, Moreno, and Mejia agreed was that *petitioner and other Baltimore officers* would commit substantive violations of this nature. Thus, under well-established rules of conspiracy law, petitioner was properly charged with and convicted of conspiring with the shopowners. Nothing in the text of the Hobbs Act even remotely undermines this conclusion, and petitioner's invocation of the rule of lenity and principles of federalism is unavailing.

1

Petitioner argues that our interpretation makes the Hobbs Act sweep too broadly, creating a national antibribery law and displacing a carefully crafted network of state and federal statutes. He contends that a charge of conspiring to obtain money from a conspirator with his consent and under color of official right is tantamount to a charge of soliciting or accepting a bribe and that allowing such a charge undermines 18 U.S.C. §666 (a federal bribery statute applicable to state and local officials) and state bribery laws. He also argues that extortion conspiracies of this sort were not known prior to the enactment of the Hobbs Act and that there is no evidence that Congress meant for that Act to plow this new ground.

The subtext of these arguments is that it seems unnatural to prosecute bribery on the basis of a statute prohibiting "extortion," but this Court held in *Evans* that Hobbs Act extortion "under color of official right" includes the "rough equivalent of what we would now describe as 'taking a bribe.'" 504 U.S. at 260. Petitioner does not ask us to overturn *Evans*, and we have no occasion to do so. Having already held that §1951 prohibits the "rough equivalent" of bribery, we have no principled basis for precluding the prosecution of conspiracies to commit that same offense.

Petitioner also exaggerates the reach of our decision. It does not, as he claims, dissolve the distinction between extortion and conspiracy to commit extortion. Because every act of extortion under the Hobbs Act requires property to be obtained with "consent," petitioner argues, proof of that consent will always or nearly always establish the existence of a conspiratorial agreement and thus allow the Government to turn virtually every such extortion case into a conspiracy case. But there are plenty of instances in which the "consent" required under the Hobbs Act will not be enough to constitute the sort of agreement needed under the law of conspiracy.

As used in the Hobbs Act, the phrase "with his consent" is designed to distinguish extortion ("obtaining of property from another, *with his consent*," 18 U.S.C. §1951(b)(2) (emphasis added)) from robbery ("obtaining of personal property from the person or in the presence of another, *against his will*," §1951(b)(1) (emphasis added)). Thus, "consent" simply signifies the taking of property under circumstances falling short of robbery, and such "consent" is quite different from the *mens rea* necessary for a conspiracy.

This conclusion is clear from the language of §1951 prohibiting the obtaining of property "from another, with his consent, *induced by wrongful use of actual or threatened force, violence, or fear.*" §1951(b)(2) (emphasis added). This language applies when, for example, a store owner makes periodic protection payments to gang members out of fear that they will otherwise trash the store. While these payments are obtained with the store owner's grudging consent, the store owner, simply by making the demanded payments, does not enter into a conspiratorial agreement with the gang members conducting the shakedown. . . . [T[he minimal "consent" required to trigger §1951 is insufficient to form a conspiratorial agreement. Our interpretation thus does not turn virtually every act of extortion into a conspiracy.

Nor does our reading transform every bribe of a public official into a conspiracy to commit extortion. The "consent" required to pay a bribe does not necessarily create a conspiratorial agreement. In cases where the bribe payor is merely complying with an official demand, the payor lacks the *mens rea* necessary for a conspiracy. . . . For example, imagine that a health inspector demands a bribe from a restaurant owner, threatening to close down the restaurant if the owner does not pay. If the owner reluctantly pays the bribe in order to keep the business open, the owner has "consented" to the inspector's demand, but this mere acquiescence in the demand does not form a conspiracy.

2

While petitioner exaggerates the impact of our decision, his argument would create serious practical problems. The validity of a charge of Hobbs Act conspiracy would often depend on difficult property-law questions having little to do with criminal culpability. In this case, for example, ownership of the money obtained by petitioner is far from clear. It appears that the funds came from Majestic's account, and there is evidence that during the period of petitioner's membership in the conspiracy, Majestic was converted from a limited liability company to a regular business corporation. After that transformation, the money obtained by petitioner may have come from corporate funds. A corporation is an entity distinct from its shareholders, and therefore, even under petitioner's interpretation of the applicable law, Moreno and Mejia would have agreed that petitioner would obtain money "from another," not from them.

Suppose that Moreno or Mejia had made the payments by taking money from a personal bank account. Would that dictate a different outcome? Or suppose that Majestic was a partnership and the payments came from a company account. Would that mean that Moreno agreed that officers would obtain money "from another" insofar as they would obtain Mejia's share of the partnership funds and that Mejia similarly agreed that officers would obtain money "from another" insofar as they would obtain the share belonging to Moreno?

Or consider this example. Suppose that the owner and manager of a nightclub reach an agreement with a public official under which the owner will bribe the official to approve the club's liquor license application. Under petitioner's approach, the public official and the club manager may be guilty of conspiring to commit extortion, because they agreed that the official would obtain property "from another"—that is, the owner. But as "the 'another' from whom the property is obtained," Reply Brief 10, the owner could not be prosecuted. There is no apparent reason, however, why the manager but not the owner should be culpable in this situation.

III

A defendant may be convicted of conspiring to violate the Hobbs Act based on proof that he reached an agreement with the owner of the property in question to obtain that property under color of official right. Because petitioner joined such an agreement, his conspiracy conviction must stand.

Justice BREYER, concurring.

I agree with the sentiment expressed in the dissenting opinion of Justice THOMAS that *Evans v. United States,* 504 U.S. 255 (1992), may well have been wrongly decided. I think it is an exceptionally difficult question whether "extortion" within the meaning of the Hobbs Act is really "the rough equivalent of . . . taking a bribe," *Evans,* 504 U.S. at 260—especially when we admittedly decided that question in that case without the benefit of full briefing on extortion's common-law history.

The present case underscores some of the problems that *Evans* raises. For example, as in the scenario presented by today's Court, where the public health inspector asks for money from a restaurant owner in exchange for favorable reports, courts (and juries) will have to draw the difficult distinction between the somewhat involuntary behavior of the bribe payor and the voluntary behavior of the same bribe payor, which may determine whether there is or is not a conspiracy.

Nonetheless, we must in this case take *Evans* as good law. That being so, I join the majority's opinion in full.

Justice THOMAS, dissenting.

Today the Court holds that an extortionist can conspire to commit extortion with the person whom he is extorting. See *ante,* at 1436. This holding further exposes the flaw in this Court's understanding of extortion. In my view, the Court started down the wrong path in Evans v. United States, 504 U.S. 255 (1992), which wrongly equated extortion with bribery. In so holding, *Evans* made it seem plausible that an extortionist could conspire with his victim. Rather than embrace that view, I would not extend *Evans'* errors further. Accordingly, I respectfully dissent.

I . . .

Given the established meaning of under-color-of-official-right extortion adopted in the Hobbs Act, the Court in *Evans* erred in equating common-law extortion with taking a bribe. Id. at 283. Bribery and extortion are different crimes. Ibid. With extortion, "the public official is the sole wrongdoer." *Ibid.* Because the official "acts 'under color of office,' the law regards the payor as an innocent victim and not an accomplice." Ibid. An official who solicits or takes a bribe, by contrast, does not do so "under color of office"—that is, "under [a] pretense of official entitlement." Ibid. With bribery, "the payor knows the recipient official is not entitled to the payment," and "he, as well as the official, may be punished for the offense." Ibid. (emphasis deleted).

II

Relying on *Evans'* definition of Hobbs Act extortion, the Court holds that an extortionist can conspire to commit extortion with the person whom he is extorting. That holding is irreconcilable with a correct understanding of Hobbs Act extortion and needlessly extends *Evans'* error to the conspiracy context. . . .

To be sure, the Court's conclusion is plausible under *Evans'* redefinition of extortion. But that is a reason not to extend *Evans'* error. Only by blurring the distinction between bribery and extortion could *Evans* make it seem plausible that an extortionist and a victim can conspire to extort the victim. The Court today takes another step away from the common-law understanding of extortion that the Hobbs Act adopted.

III

The Court's decision is unfortunate because it expands federal criminal liability in a way that conflicts with principles of federalism. Even when *Evans* was decided nearly 25 years ago, the Hobbs Act had already "served as the engine for a stunning expansion of federal criminal jurisdiction into a field traditionally policed by state and local laws—acts of public corruption by state and local officials." 504 U.S. at 290 (Thomas, J., dissenting). By disregarding the distinction between extortion and bribery, *Evans* expanded the Hobbs Act to allow federal prosecutors to reach more conduct by state and local government officials. . . .

Today the Court again broadens the Hobbs Act's reach to enable federal prosecutors to punish for conspiracy all participants in a public-official bribery scheme. The invasion of state sovereign functions is again substantial. The Federal Government can now more expansively charge state and local officials. And it can now more easily obtain pleas or convictions from these officials: Because the Government can prosecute bribe-payors with sweeping conspiracy charges, it will be easier to induce those payors to plead out and testify against state and local officials. The Court thus further wrenches from States the presumptive control that they should have over their own officials' wrongdoing. . . .

Consistent with the Hobbs Act's text, I would hold that an extortionist cannot conspire to commit extortion with the person whom he is extorting. Accordingly, I would reverse the Court of Appeals' judgment upholding Ocasio's conspiracy conviction. . . .

Justice SOTOMAYOR, with whom THE CHIEF JUSTICE joins, dissenting.

If a group of conspirators sets out to extort "another" person, we ordinarily think that they are proposing to extort money or property from a victim outside their group, not one of themselves. Their group is the conspiratorial entity and the victim is "another" person.

But in upholding the conspiracy conviction here, the Court interprets the phrase extorting property "from another" in the Hobbs Act contrary to that natural understanding. It holds that a group of conspirators can agree to obtain property "from another" in violation of the Act even if they agree only to transfer property among themselves.

That is not a natural or logical way to interpret the phrase "from another." I respectfully dissent.

II

The Hobbs Act criminalizes extortion where a public official obtains property "from another." §1951(b)(2). The question here is how to define "another" in the context of a conspiracy to commit extortion. "Another" is a relational word. It describes how one entity is connected to a different entity. In particular, it describes an entity "different or distinct from the one first considered." Merriam-Webster's Collegiate Dictionary 51 (11th ed. 2003). . . .

The most natural reading of "conspiring" to obtain property "from another," then, is a collective agreement to obtain property from an entity different or distinct from the conspiracy. But Ocasio, Moreno, and Mejia did not agree that Ocasio would obtain property from a person different or distinct from the conspirators as a group. They agreed only that Ocasio would take property from Moreno and Mejia—people who are *part of* rather than *distinct from* the conspiracy. "These three people did not agree, and could not have agreed, to obtain property from 'another' when no other person was involved." United States v. Brock, 501 F.3d 762, 767 (6th Cir. 2007).

This understanding of "another"—that it refers to someone outside the conspiracy—is consistent not only with the plain meaning of the Hobbs Act, but also with this Court's precedent explaining that the purpose of conspiracy law is to target the conduct of group crimes. . . .

[W]hether a criminal conspiracy exists depends on what the conspirators agreed to do as a group. This principle confirms that "from another" is best understood as relating the conspiratorial enterprise to another person outside the conspiracy. A conspiracy to obtain property "from another," then, is the group agreement that at least one member of the group will obtain property from someone who is not a part of their endeavor.

Departing from this natural reading of the text, the Court holds that Ocasio can be punished for conspiracy because Ocasio obtained property "from another" (Moreno and Mejia) and Ocasio, Moreno, and Mejia agreed that Ocasio would engage in that conduct. In order to reach this conclusion, the Court implicitly assumes that the Hobbs Act's use of "from another" takes as its reference point only a single member of the conspiracy, here, Ocasio, rather than the group of conspirators as a whole.

But what is the basis for that assumption? The Court never explains. It is not based on the plain language of the Hobbs Act. A natural reading of the text seems to foreclose it—Moreno and Mejia are not "distinct or different from" the group that formed the "collective criminal agreement." And the Court's assumption does not follow from prior precedent or any first principles of conspiracy law. See Part III, *infra*.

Both the plain meaning of the statute and general principles of conspiracy law lead to the same conclusion: A conspiracy to commit extortion by obtaining property "from another" in violation of the Hobbs Act should exist only when the conspirators agree to obtain property from someone outside the conspiracy.

III . . .

[T]he Court argues that its interpretation is correct because Mejia and Moreno can be held liable for conspiring to commit extortion even though they were incapable of committing the substantive crime themselves. (Because they are not public officials, Mejia and Moreno cannot obtain property "under color of official right." *Ante,* at 1429-1430.) True enough. But this principle does not lead to the conclusion that "from another" takes the perspective of Ocasio as its reference point, as opposed to the conspiratorial group.

For example, suppose a politician and a lobbyist conspire to have the lobbyist tell his clients to pay the politician bribes in exchange for official acts. The lobbyist cannot obtain those bribes under color of official right and so could not be charged with a substantive Hobbs Act extortion violation. But the conspiracy would still violate the Hobbs Act, see *Evans,* 504 U.S. at 268, because the conspiratorial group obtained property "from another," i.e., from the clients who are outside the conspiracy that exists between the lobbyist and the politician. Now suppose the lobbyist instead agrees to pay the bribe himself. We would be back to the question at the heart of this case.

The Court's incapable-of-committing-the-substantive-offense principle therefore cannot do the work the Court thinks it does. It is entirely consistent to say obtaining property "from another" in violation of the Hobbs Act requires the conspirators to agree to obtain property from someone outside the conspiracy, and to say that every conspirator who enters into that agreement need not be capable of committing the substantive offense himself.

Finally, the Court raises policy concerns: It mentions that it would be odd to immunize the ostensible victims of a conspiracy to commit extortion—here, Mejia and Moreno—if they play just as active a role in the conspiracy as other members.

While perhaps odd, that concern does not warrant the Court's contortion of conspiracy law where there are other criminal statutes—like federal antibribery laws and state laws—that reach similar conduct. See, e.g., 18 U.S.C. §666 (criminalizing bribery of state, local, or tribal officials in specified circumstances); Md. Crim. Law Code Ann. §9–201 (2012) (criminalizing bribery of public employee). Of course, the Government could have attempted to convict Ocasio for conspiracy on these facts without relying on the Court's odd theory—for example, by proving that Ocasio conspired with other Baltimore police officers to extort property from the brothers. . . .

Here, without any textual hook in the Hobbs Act, the Court rests on no more than intuitions drawn from basic examples. If a restaurant owner threatened with closure by a health official reluctantly pays a bribe, the Court says that the owner is not guilty of conspiracy. *Ante,* at 1435-1436. According to the Court, he "consented" to extortion, but his mere acquiescence to an "official demand" did not create a conspiratorial agreement. Ibid. By contrast, the Court says, if a nightclub owner pursues a liquor license by asking his manager to bribe a public official, he is clearly guilty of conspiracy. He agreed with the public official that the official would obtain property "from another," i.e., from him, in exchange for a license.

These examples raise more questions than answers. When does mere "consent" tip over into conspiracy? Does it depend on whose idea it was? Whether the bribe was floated as an "official demand" or a suggestion? How happy the citizen is to pay off the public official? How much money is involved? Whether the citizen gained a benefit (a liquor license) or avoided a loss (closing the restaurant)? How many times the citizen paid the bribes? Whether he ever resisted paying or called the police? The Court does not say. It leaves it for federal prosecutors to answer those questions in the first instance, raising the specter of potentially charging everybody with conspiracy and seeing what sticks and who flips. . . .

When three people agree to obtain property "from another," the everyday understanding of their agreement is that they intend to obtain property from someone outside of their conspiracy. The Court reaches the opposite conclusion, based entirely on an assumption that the Hobbs Act's use of "from another" takes as its reference point the vantage of Ocasio alone, rather than the group endeavor that constitutes conspiracy. The Court offers no explanation—grounded in either the text of the statute or so-called "age-old principles of conspiracy law"—for why that assumption is correct. . . .

NOTES AND QUESTIONS

1. Why is it that we could, but won't, string-cite federal corruption cases involving the police and towing operations? Suppose that in the course of investigating a scheme by health inspectors to extract money illegally from restaurant owners, the Government learns of one particular owner who simply paid an inspector the "going rate" and received a passing grade. The prosecutor is not keen to charge the owner with bribery and would rather turn him into a cooperating witness whom she could present to the jury as a victim. Fearing that other inspectors might retaliate were he to help the Government, the owner refuses to speak. Can he assert a sufficient "fear of prosecution" to support invocation of a Fifth Amendment right against self-incrimination? Assuming that he does so, and that the Government seeks to play hard-ball by charging him with conspiring to commit "under color" extortion, what must he show to avoid conviction?

Even as it embraces the overlap between the two offenses, the *Ocasio* Court assures us that its analysis does not "transform every bribe of a public official into a conspiracy to commit extortion." In our case (unlike the hypo in *Ocasio*), the inspector did not actually threaten to close the place down if the owner does not pay. And let's complicate matters further by adding that, in this city, a passing grade comes with a benefit—freedom from normal inspections for the next four years. Does our owner have an economic duress defense? Does he have to be a victim within the meaning of the "fear of economic loss" prong of the Hobbs Act (see Chapter 5) in order to escape liability under the "under color" prong of the Hobbs Act? Would such line-drawing make sense as a matter of law or policy?

Long ago, the Seventh Circuit noted, in a case involving a corrupt state judge:

> It could be argued . . . that every person who knuckles under to an extortionate demand does so intending to influence the extortionist not to carry out his threat, and that this should be enough to prove bribery. Yet there is some authority that one can be a victim of extortion but not a briber, . . . and that would surely be right in a case where the victim had paid the extortionist at the point of a gun, though the present case is far removed from this, and perhaps in every case of extortion under color of right the extortionist is also a bribe-taker.

United States v. Holzer, 840 F.2d 1343, 1351-52 (7th Cir. 1988) (Posner, J.). This analysis seems to look to physical duress for line drawing. Courts have considered economic coercion defense to bribery, but only grudgingly. See United States v. West, 746 F. Supp. 2d 932, 940 (N.D. Ill. 2010) (canvassing cases in Seventh Circuit and beyond and noting: "If a valid economic duress defense at all exists in this circuit, it would at least require that Defendants act under the threat of losing something to which they felt legally entitled."). Where does *Ocasio* move the line? We consider the implications of *Ocasio* with respect to the federal law of conspiracy (and perhaps the federal law of complicity) in Chapter 8.

2. What happens when a mere *candidate* for office accepts bribes when he lacks any official position? Does the answer depend on whether the candidate wins the election? Certainly, if economic coercion is involved, he can be charged under the prong of the Hobbs Act discussed in Chapter 5. But to what extent can he be charged (regardless of coercion) under the official-corruption prong? In United States v. Manzo, the Third Circuit, explicitly finding no need to invoke the "rule of lenity," held:

> In accordance with the legislative history, the congressional purpose underlying the Hobbs Act and centuries of interpretation of the phrase "under color of official right," we conclude that the Manzos [an unsuccessful candidate for mayor of Jersey City and his campaign-manager brother] were not acting "under color of official right," as defined in the Hobbs Act.

636 F.3d 56, 65 (3d Cir. 2011). The court also rejected prosecution arguments that the non-officials could be charged on conspiracy or attempt theories:

> A Hobbs Act inchoate offense prohibits a person acting "under color of official right" from attempting or conspiring to use his or her public office in exchange for payments. It does not prohibit a private person who is a candidate from attempting or conspiring to use a future public office to extort money at a future date.

Id. at 68-69. Does this reasoning make sense?

It is worth noting that 18 U.S.C. §599 provides: "Whoever, being a candidate, directly or indirectly promises or pledges the appointment, or the use of his influence or support for the appointment of any person to any public of private position or employment, for the purpose of procuring support in his candidacy shall be fined under this title or imprisoned not more than one year, or both; and if the violation was willful, shall be fined under this title or imprisoned not more than two years, or both." The important things to note about this statute is that (1) it covers only a narrow range of candidate promises, i.e. those relating to appointments; (2) it is a misdemeanor; and (3) it is never used, see United States v. Manzo, 851 F. Supp. 2d 797 (D.N.J. 2012) (reporting only three citations to provision, none involving prosecutions under it). See also United States v. Blagojevich, 794 F.3d 729, 737 (7th Cir. 2015) (wondering whether statute is "compatible with the First Amendment" and noting that it would cover some historians' account of how Earl Warren came to be Chief Justice of the United States).

Is the under-coverage of candidate promises by criminal statues as actually enforced a "bug" or a "feature" of our great democracy?

B.   BRIBES AND GRATUITIES

In keeping with some common-law understandings of "bribery," the first federal bribery statute focused only on judicial bribery. See Act of Apr. 15, 1790, ch. 9, §21, 1 Stat. 117; see also James Lindgren, The Elusive Distinction Between Bribery and Extortion: From the Common Law to the Hobbs Act, 35 UCLA L. Rev. 815, 865 (1988) (noting that "[a]s bribery expanded beyond the sphere of judicial decision-making [its overlap with extortion] became more pronounced"). Still, Article II, §4 of the Constitution singled out "bribery" as an impeachable offense for "the President, Vice President and all civil Officers of the United States." And by 1853, Congress had extended the federal criminal provision to include "any officer of the United States, or person holding any place of trust or profit, or discharging any official function under, or in connection with, any department of the Government of the United States." Act of Feb. 26, 1853, ch. 81, §6, 10 Stat. 171. These are the origins of 18 U.S.C. §201—which you just met, perhaps unexpectedly, as the driver of a Hobbs Act and honest services analysis in *McDonnell*—which criminalizes the bribery of, and the giving of gratuities to, federal officials.

---

18 U.S.C. §201. Bribery of public officials and witnesses

(a) For the purpose of this section—

(1) the term "public official" means Member of Congress, Delegate, or Resident Commissioner, either before or after such official has qualified, or an officer or employee or person acting for or on behalf of the United States, or any department, agency or branch of Government thereof. . . .

(3) the term "official act" means any decision or action on any question, matter, cause, suit, proceeding or controversy, which may at any time be pending, or which may by law be brought before any public official, in such official's official capacity, or in such official's place of trust or profit.

(b) Whoever—

(1) directly or indirectly, corruptly gives, offers or promises anything of value to any public official or person who has been selected to be a public official, or offers or promises any public official or any person who has been selected to be a public official to give anything of value to any other person or entity, with intent—

(A) to influence any official act; or

(B) to influence such . . . official to commit or aid in committing, or collude in, or allow, any fraud, or make opportunity for the commission of any fraud, on the United States; or

(C) to induce such . . . official to do or omit to do any act in violation of the lawful duty of such official or person;

(2) being a public official or person selected to be a public official, directly or indirectly, corruptly demands, seeks, receives, accepts, or agrees to receive or accept anything of value personally or for any other person or entity, in return for:

(A) being influenced in his performance of any official act;

(B) being influenced to commit or aid in committing, or to collude in, or allow, any fraud, or make opportunity for the commission of any fraud, on the United States; or

(C) being induced to do or omit to do any act in violation of the official duty of such official or person; . . . shall be fined under this title or not more than three times the monetary equivalent of the thing of value, whichever is greater, or imprisoned for not more than fifteen years, or both, and may be disqualified from holding any office of honor, trust, or profit under the United States.

(c) Whoever—

(1) otherwise than as provided by law for the proper discharge of official duty—

(A) directly or indirectly gives, offers, or promises anything of value to any public official, former public official, or person selected to be a public official, for or because of any official act performed or to be performed by such . . . official; or

(B) being a public official, former public official, or person selected to be a public official, . . . directly or indirectly demands, seeks, receives, accepts, or agrees to receive or accept anything of value personally for or because of any official act performed or to be performed by such official or person; . . . shall be fined under this title or imprisoned for not more than two years, or both. . . .

(e) The offenses and penalties prescribed in this section are separate from and in addition to those prescribed in sections 1503, 1504, and 1505 [18 U.S.C. §§1503, 1504, and 1505] of this title.

NOTES AND QUESTIONS

1. The discussions of "bribery" under this provision almost invariably contrast it with the lesser "gratuity" offense. As the Second Circuit explained in United States v. Alfisi, 308 F.3d 144, 149 (2d Cir. 2002):

> The bribery provision, 18 U.S.C. §201(b)(1)(A), renders it unlawful for any person to "directly or indirectly, corruptly give[], offer[] or promise[] anything of value to any public official . . . with intent . . . to influence any official act." The payment of an unlawful gratuity involves an act where a person "directly or indirectly gives, offers, or promises anything of value to any public official . . . for or because of any official act performed or to be performed." 18 U.S.C. §201(c)(1)(A). Bribery therefore requires that the payor intend "to influence" an official act "corruptly" while the payment of an unlawful gratuity requires only that the payment be "for or because of" an official act. See United States v. Sun-Diamond Growers of California, 526 U.S. 398, 404 (1999).
>
> The "corrupt" intent necessary to a bribery conviction is in the nature of a *quid pro quo* requirement; that is, there must be "a specific intent to give . . . something of value in exchange for an official act." *Sun-Diamond Growers*, 526 U.S. at 404-405. Putting it only slightly differently, bribery involves the giving of value to procure a specific official action from a public official. See United States v. Myers, 692 F.2d 823, 841 (2d Cir. 1982). The element of a *quid pro quo* or a direct exchange is absent from the offense of paying an unlawful gratuity. To commit that offense, it is enough that the payment be a reward for a past official act. . . .

2. What made *Alfisi* interesting was the defendant's claim that his payments to U.S. Agriculture Department produce inspectors had been solely to get them to do their jobs, not to obtain false inspection results. Indeed, the defendant was allowed to raise an economic duress defense, claiming

that he had been the victim of an extortion scheme. After the jury rejected that defense and convicted him, he argued on appeal that, because he had given the money simply to get the officials to do their duty, his intent was not "corrupt." The Second Circuit gave two reasons for its rejection of this interpretation of the bribery statute: First, the reading "does not rest comfortably within the statutory language. Subsection (b)(1)(A) . . . outlaws payments made with a corrupt intent—to procure a *quid pro quo* agreement—'to influence any official act.'" 138 F.3d at 150. Second,

> there is no lack of sound legislative purpose in defining bribery to include payments in exchange for an act to which the payor is legally entitled. On the one hand, there is of course a danger of over-inclusion in a broad definition, in particular, the risk here that marginally culpable conduct by those facing insistent extortionists will be criminalized. That danger is eliminated or at least minimalized, however, by the existence of the economic coercion defense, which the jury rejected in the present case.
>
> On the other hand, a danger of underinclusion inheres in the narrow definition suggested by *Alfisi*. This is particularly so in cases where the official duties require the exercise of some judgment or discretion. In such cases, if the government must prove beyond a reasonable doubt actual or intended violations of official duties, many highly culpable payments would go underpunished as unlawful gratuities, or unpunished altogether.
>
> For example, if a party to litigation were to pay a judge money in exchange for a favorable decision, that conduct would—and should—constitute bribery, even if a trier of fact might conclude ex post that the judgment was, on the merits, legally proper. This principle was at stake and upheld in a decision arising from the most lamentable episode in this court's history. See United States v. Manton, 107 F.2d 834, 845-46 (2d Cir. 1939) (rejecting Chief Circuit Judge's defense that payments in exchange for particular decisions were not obstruction of justice where decisions rendered were legally correct). In such a case, the key element of the offense is the intent of the payor to purchase a particular decision "without regard to the merits," id. at 846, as opposed to an impartial judgment. The legal merits, or lack thereof, of the judgment rendered is not an element of the offense.

Id. at 151-52.

3. Does a federal official violate §201(b)(2) if he seeks money but has no intention of doing anything in return? Sure, he might be guilty of extortion or fraud, but doesn't the federal bribery statute require that he actually be "influenced" or "induced"? Looking to the legislative history of §201 to resolve what it admitted to be an ambiguity, the Fifth Circuit found that Congress "intended the statute to be violated when an official took the bribe, knowing that it was given for the purpose of inducing him to violate his official duty, whether or not he actually intended to follow through with the violation." United States v. Valle, 538 F.3d 341, 346 (5th Cir. 2008).

Citing *Skilling*'s reliance on §201 to inform honest services law, the Fifth Circuit has extended this analysis to honest services prosecutions. United States v. Nagin, 810 F.3d 348, 351 (5th Cir. 2015).

4. How do the bribery and gratuity provisions of §201 differ? One important distinction is in their temporal focus: Bribery offenses are always future-oriented, while gratuity offenses may be past-, present-, or future-oriented. That is, one gives or promises a bribe in return only for future action by a public official, but one can provide a gratuity to reward past, present, *or* future action that is favorable.

In the following case, the Supreme Court explained other distinctions between the two criminal offenses.

United States v. Sun-Diamond Growers of California
526 U.S. 398 (1999)

Justice SCALIA delivered the opinion of the Court.

Talmudic sages believed that judges who accepted bribes would be punished by . . . losing all knowledge of the divine law. The Federal Government, dealing with many public officials who are not judges, and with at least some judges for whom this sanction holds no terror, has constructed a framework of human laws and regulations defining various sorts of impermissible gifts, and punishing those who give or receive them with administrative sanctions, fines, and incarceration. One element of that framework is 18 U.S.C. §201(c)(1)(A), the "illegal gratuity statute," which prohibits giving "anything of value" to a present, past, or future public official "for or because of any official act performed or to be performed by such public official." In this case, we consider whether conviction under the illegal gratuity statute requires any showing beyond the fact that a gratuity was given because of the recipient's official position.

I

Respondent is a trade association that engaged in marketing and lobbying activities on behalf of its member cooperatives, which were owned by approximately 5,000 individual growers of raisins, figs, walnuts, prunes, and hazelnuts. Petitioner United States is represented by Independent Counsel Donald Smaltz, who, as a consequence of his investigation of former Secretary of Agriculture Michael Espy, charged respondent with . . .

making illegal gifts to Espy in violation of §201(c)(1)(A). That statute provides, in relevant part, that anyone who

"otherwise than as provided by law for the proper discharge of official duty . . . directly or indirectly gives, offers, or promises anything of value to any public official, former public official, or person selected to be a public official, for or because of any official act performed or to be performed by such public official, former public official, or person selected to be a public official . . . shall be fined under this title or imprisoned for not more than two years, or both."

Count One of the indictment charged Sun-Diamond with giving Espy approximately $5,900 in illegal gratuities: tickets to the 1993 U.S. Open Tennis Tournament (worth $2,295), luggage ($2,427), meals ($665), and a framed print and crystal bowl ($524). The indictment alluded to two matters in which respondent had an interest in favorable treatment from the Secretary at the time it bestowed the gratuities. First, respondent's member cooperatives participated in the Market Promotion Plan (MPP), a grant program administered by the Department of Agriculture to promote the sale of U.S. farm commodities in foreign countries. The cooperatives belonged to trade organizations, such as the California Prune Board and the Raisin Administrative Committee, which submitted overseas marketing plans for their respective commodities. If their plans were approved by the Secretary of Agriculture, the trade organizations received funds to be used in defraying the foreign marketing expenses of their constituents. Each of respondent's member cooperatives was the largest member of its respective trade organization, and each received significant MPP funding. Respondent was understandably concerned, then, when Congress in 1993 instructed the Secretary to promulgate regulations giving small-sized entities preference in obtaining MPP funds. Omnibus Budget Reconciliation Act of 1993, Pub. L. 103-166, §1302(b)(2)(A), 107 Stat. 330-331. If the Secretary did not deem respondent's member cooperatives to be small-sized entities, there was a good chance they would no longer receive MPP grants. Thus, respondent had an interest in persuading the Secretary to adopt a regulatory definition of "small-sized entity" that would include its member cooperatives.

Second, respondent had an interest in the Federal Government's regulation of methyl bromide, a low-cost pesticide used by many individual growers in respondent's member cooperatives. In 1992, the Environmental Protection Agency announced plans to promulgate a rule to phase out the use of methyl bromide in the United States. The indictment alleged that respondent sought the Department of Agriculture's assistance in persuading EPA to abandon its proposed rule altogether, or at least to mitigate its impact. . . .

Although describing these two matters before the Secretary in which respondent had an interest, the indictment did not allege a specific connection between either of them—or between any other action of the Secretary—and the gratuities conferred. The District Court denied respondent's motion to dismiss Count One because of this omission. 941 F. Supp. 1262 (D.D.C. 1996). The court stated:

> "[T]o sustain a charge under the gratuity statute, it is not necessary for the indictment to allege a direct nexus between the value conferred to Secretary Espy by Sun-Diamond and an official act performed or to be performed by Secretary Espy. It is sufficient for the indictment to allege that Sun-Diamond provided things of value to Secretary Espy because of his position." Id. at 1265.

At trial, the District Court instructed the jury along these same lines. It read §201(c)(1)(A) to the jury twice (along with the definition of "official act" from §201(a)(3)), but then placed an expansive gloss on that statutory language, saying, among other things, that "[i]t is sufficient if Sun-Diamond provided Espy with unauthorized compensation simply because he held public office," and that "[t]he government need not prove that the alleged gratuity was linked to a specific or identifiable official act or any act at all." The jury convicted respondent on . . . Count One (the only subject of this appeal), and the District Court sentenced respondent on this count to pay a fine of $400,000.

The Court of Appeals reversed the conviction on Count One and remanded for a new trial. . . . 138 F.3d 961 (CADC 1998). In rejecting respondent's attack on the indictment, however, the court stated that the Government need not show that a gratuity was given "for or because of" any *particular* act or acts: "That an official has an abundance of relevant matters on his plate should not insulate him or his benefactors from the gratuity statute—as long as the jury is required to find the requisite intent to reward past favorable acts or to make future ones more likely." Id. at 969. . . .

II

Initially, it will be helpful to place §201(c)(1)(A) within the context of the statutory scheme. Subsection (a) of §201 sets forth definitions applicable to the section—including a definition of "official act," §201(a)(3). Subsections (b) and (c) then set forth, respectively, two separate crimes—or two pairs of crimes, if one counts the giving and receiving of unlawful gifts as separate crimes—with two different sets of elements and authorized punishments. The first crime, described in §201(b)(1) as to the giver, and §201(b)(2) as to the recipient, is bribery, which requires a showing that something of value was corruptly given, offered, or promised to a public official (as to the giver) or corruptly demanded, sought, received, accepted, or agreed to be received or accepted by a public official (as to the recipient) with intent . . . "to influence any official act" (giver) or in return for "being influenced in the performance of any official act" (recipient). The second crime, defined in §201(c)(1)(A) as to the giver, and §201(c)(1)(B) as to the recipient, is illegal gratuity, which requires a showing that something of value was given, offered, or promised to a public official (as to the giver), or demanded, sought, received, accepted, or agreed to be received or accepted by a public official (as to the recipient), "for or because of any official act performed or to be performed by such public official."

The distinguishing feature of each crime is its intent element. Bribery requires intent "to influence" an official act or "to be influenced" in an official act, while illegal gratuity requires only that the gratuity be given or accepted "for or because of" an official act. In other words, for bribery there must be a *quid pro quo*—a specific intent to give or receive something of value *in exchange* for an official act. An illegal gratuity, on the other hand, may constitute merely a reward for some future act that the public official will take (and may already have determined to take), or for a past act that he has already taken. The punishments prescribed for the two offenses reflect their relative seriousness: Bribery may be punished by up to 15 years' imprisonment, a fine of $250,000 ($500,000 for organizations) or triple the value of the bribe, whichever is greater, and disqualification from holding government office. See 18 U.S.C. §§201(b) and 3571. Violation of the illegal gratuity statute, on the other hand, may be punished by up to two years' imprisonment and a fine of $250,000 ($500,000 for organizations). See §§201(c) and 3571.

The District Court's instructions in this case, in differentiating between a bribe and an illegal gratuity, correctly noted that only a bribe requires proof of a *quid pro quo*. The point in controversy here is that the instructions went on to suggest that §201(c)(1)(A), unlike the bribery statute, did not require any connection between respondent's intent and a specific official act. It would be satisfied, according to the instructions, merely by a showing that respondent gave Secretary Espy a gratuity because of his official position—perhaps, for example, to build a reservoir of goodwill that might ultimately affect one or more of a multitude of unspecified acts, now and in the future. The United States . . . [contends] that this instruction was correct. The Independent Counsel asserts that "section 201(c)(1)(A) reaches any effort to buy favor or generalized goodwill from an official who either has been, is, or may at some unknown, unspecified later time, be *in a position to act* favorably to the giver's interests." Brief for United States 22 (emphasis added). The Solicitor General contends that §201(c)(1)(A) requires only a showing that a "gift was motivated, at least in part, by the recipient's *capacity to exercise governmental power or influence* in the donor's favor" without necessarily showing that it was connected to a particular official act. Brief for the United States Dept. of Justice as Amicus Curiae 17 (emphasis added).

In our view, this interpretation does not fit comfortably with the statutory text, which prohibits only gratuities given or received "for or because of *any official act* performed or to be performed" (emphasis added). It seems to us that this means "for or because of some particular official act of whatever identity"—just as the question "Do you like any composer?" normally means "Do you like some particular composer?" It is linguistically possible, of course, for the phrase to mean "for or because of official acts in general, without specification as to which one"—just as the question "Do you like any composer?" could mean "Do you like all composers, no matter what their names or music?" But the former seems to us the more natural meaning, especially given the complex structure of the provision before us here. Why go through the trouble of requiring that the gift be made "for or because of any official act performed or to be performed by such public official," and then defining "official act" (in §201(a)(3)) to mean "any decision or action on any question, matter, cause, suit, proceeding or controversy, which may at any time be pending, or which may by law be brought before any public official, in such official's official capacity," when, if the Government's interpretation were correct, it would have sufficed to say "for or because of such official's ability to favor the donor in executing the functions of his office"? The insistence upon an "official act," carefully defined, seems pregnant with the requirement that some particular official act be identified and proved.

Besides thinking that this is the more natural meaning of §201(c)(1)(A), we are inclined to believe it correct because of the peculiar results that the Government's alternative reading would produce. It would criminalize, for example, token gifts to the President based on his official position and not linked to any identifiable act—such as the replica jerseys given by championship sports teams each year during ceremonial White House visits. Similarly, it would criminalize a high school principal's gift of a school baseball cap to the Secretary of Education, by reason of his office, on the occasion of the latter's visit to the school. That these examples are not fanciful is demonstrated by the fact that counsel for the United States maintained at oral argument that a group of farmers would violate §201(c)(1)(A) by providing a complimentary lunch for the Secretary of Agriculture in conjunction with his speech to the farmers concerning various matters of USDA policy—so long as the Secretary had before him, or had in prospect, matters affecting the farmers. Of course the Secretary of Agriculture *always* has before him or in prospect matters that affect farmers, just as the President always has before him or in prospect matters that affect college and professional sports, and the Secretary of Education matters that affect high schools.

It might be said in reply . . . that the more narrow interpretation of the statute can also produce some peculiar results. In fact, in the above-given examples, the gifts could easily be regarded as having been conferred, not only because of the official's position as President or Secretary, but also (and perhaps principally) "for or because of" the official acts of receiving the sports teams at the White House, visiting the high school, and speaking to the farmers about USDA policy, respectively. The answer to this objection is that those actions—while they are assuredly "official acts" in some sense—are not "official acts" within the meaning of the statute, which, as we have noted, defines "official act" to mean "any decision or action on any question, matter, cause, suit, proceeding or controversy, which may at any time be pending, or which may by law be brought before any public official, in such official's official capacity, or in such official's place of trust or profit." 18 U.S.C. §201(a)(3). Thus, when the violation is linked to a particular "official act," it is possible to eliminate the absurdities *through the definition of that term.* When, however, no particular "official act" need be identified, and the giving of gifts by reason of the recipient's mere tenure in office constitutes a violation, nothing but the Government's discretion prevents the foregoing examples from being prosecuted. . . .

Our refusal to read §201(c)(1)(A) as a prohibition of gifts given by reason of the donee's office is supported by the fact that when Congress has wanted to adopt such a broadly prophylactic criminal prohibition upon gift giving, it has done so in a more precise and more administrable fashion. For example, another provision of Chapter 11 of Title 18, the chapter entitled "Bribery, Graft, and Conflicts of Interest," criminalizes the giving or receiving of any "supplementation" of an Executive official's salary, without regard to the purpose of the payment. See 18 U.S.C. §209(a). Other provisions of the same chapter make it a crime for a bank employee to give a bank examiner, and for a bank examiner to receive from a bank employee, "any loan or gratuity," again without regard to the purpose for which it is given. See §§212-213. A provision of the Labor Management Relations Act makes it a felony for an employer to give to a union representative, and for a union representative to receive from an employer, anything of value. 29 U.S.C. §186. With clearly framed and easily administrable provisions such as these on the books imposing gift-giving and gift-receiving prohibitions specifically based upon the holding of office, it seems to us most implausible that Congress intended the language of the gratuity statute—"for or because of any official act performed or to be performed"—to pertain to the office rather than (as the language more naturally suggests) to *particular* official acts.

Finally, a narrow, rather than a sweeping, prohibition is more compatible with the fact that §201(c)(1)(A) is merely one strand of an intricate web of regulations, both administrative and criminal, governing the acceptance of gifts and other self-enriching actions by public officials. For example, the provisions following §201 in Chapter 11 of Title 18 make it a crime to give any compensation to a federal employee, or for the employee to receive compensation, in consideration of his representational assistance to anyone involved in a proceeding in which the United

States has a direct and substantial interest, §203; for a federal employee to act as "agent or attorney" for anyone prosecuting a claim against the United States, §205(a)(1); for a federal employee to act as "agent or attorney" for anyone appearing before virtually any Government tribunal in connection with a matter in which the United States has a direct and substantial interest, §205(a)(2); for various types of federal employees to engage in various activities after completion of their federal service, §207; for an Executive employee to participate in any decision or proceeding relating to a matter in which he has a financial interest, §208; for an employee of the Executive Branch or an independent agency to receive "any contribution to or supplementation of salary . . . from any source other than the Government of the United States," §209; and for a federal employee to accept a gift in connection with the "compromise, adjustment, or cancellation of any farm indebtedness," §217. A provision of the Internal Revenue Code makes it criminal for a federal employee to accept a gift for the "compromise, adjustment, or settlement of any charge or complaint" for violation of the revenue laws. 26 U.S.C. §7214(a)(9).

And the criminal statutes are merely the tip of the regulatory iceberg. In 5 U.S.C. §7353, which announces broadly that no "employee of the executive, legislative, or judicial branch shall solicit or accept anything of value from a person . . . whose interests may be substantially affected by the performance or nonperformance of the individual's official duties," §7353(a)(2), Congress has authorized the promulgation of ethical rules for each branch of the Federal Government, §7353(b)(1). Pursuant to that provision, each branch of Government regulates its employees' acceptance of gratuities in some fashion. . . .

All of the regulations, and some of the statutes, described above contain exceptions for various kinds of gratuities given by various donors for various purposes. Many of those exceptions would be snares for the unwary, given that there are no exceptions to the broad prohibition that the Government claims is imposed by §201(c)(1). . . .

[T]he numerous . . . regulations and statutes littering this [field] demonstrate that this is an area where precisely targeted prohibitions are commonplace, and where more general prohibitions have been qualified by numerous exceptions. Given that reality, a statute in this field that can linguistically be interpreted to be either a meat axe or a scalpel should reasonably be taken to be the latter. Absent a text that clearly requires it, we ought not expand this one piece of the regulatory puzzle so dramatically as to make many other pieces misfits. As discussed earlier, not only does the text here not require that result; its more natural reading forbids it. . . .

We hold that, in order to establish a violation of 18 U.S.C. §201(c)(1)(A), the Government must prove a link between a thing of value conferred upon a public official and a specific "official act" for or because of which it was given. We affirm the judgment of the Court of Appeals, which remanded the case to the District Court for a new trial on Count

One. Our decision today casts doubt upon the lower courts' resolution of respondent's challenge to the sufficiency of the indictment on Count One—an issue on which certiorari was neither sought nor granted. We leave it to the District Court to determine whether that issue should be reopened on remand.

NOTES AND QUESTIONS

1. *Sun-Diamond* quotes two slightly different versions of the position of the United States, one attributed to the Independent Counsel's "Brief for United States," and the other to the Solicitor General's "Brief for the United States Dep't of Justice as Amicus Curiae." This curious division of responsibilities occurred because the case was prosecuted by an "Independent Counsel," appointed by a special court under provisions of the Ethics in Government Act, in force from 1978 to 1992 and again from 1994 to 1999. Congress enacted the Independent Counsel law to avoid the reality and appearance of political conflict of interest if the Department of Justice (headed by an Attorney General who could be removed by the President) were in charge of investigating allegations of criminal wrongdoing by a variety of high executive branch officials. The law provided that a special three-judge court would appoint a lawyer to investigate and, where indictment was forthcoming, to prosecute the accused official. The appointed counsel was authorized to act independent of the Justice Department and could not be removed by the Attorney General or even the President. (The Act responded to the firing of Archibald Cox, the first Watergate Special Prosecutor, at the behest of Richard Nixon in 1972.) Notable Independent Counsel cases included the Iran/Contra investigation headed by Lawrence Walsh, which resulted in the prosecution of, among others, Oliver North, and the Whitewater investigation headed by Kenneth Starr, which led to the exposure of President Clinton's affair with Monica Lewinsky and ultimately to the impeachment of the President—but there were many other, less celebrated cases entrusted to Independent Counsels, including the Sun-Diamond investigation and prosecution.

What differences in the exercise of prosecutorial discretion and in the interpretation of criminal statutes might you expect between regular prosecutors and special counsel assigned to investigate and if necessary prosecute a single politically sensitive case, operating in the glare of press attention, with an unlimited budget and a mandate not only to bring criminal cases but to write a definitive report on their findings at the conclusion of their work? See H. Geoffrey Moulton, Jr. & Daniel C. Richman, Of Prosecutors and Special Prosecutors: An Organizational Perspective, 5 Widener L. Symp. J. 79 (2000). After the Independent Counsel law expired for a second time in 1999, virtually no one, at least in Washington, wanted to reauthorize it—though that may change.

2. In its unanimous decision, the Court in *Sun-Diamond* required a nexus between a particular official act and the offer or receipt of something of value. In our Note before *Sun-Diamond*, we observed that one important difference between the bribery and gratuity provisions in §201 is their temporal focus. *Sun-Diamond* adds another distinction: the intent element. Whereas bribery requires both that payors have the intent to influence an official act and that payees know of this expectation, gratuities merely require that the payment be given (or accepted) "for or because of" an official act. Prior to *Sun-Diamond*, many thought that there was a third distinction: that only bribery required a nexus with a particular official act. In an unexpected move, the *Sun-Diamond* Court held that in prosecutions involving gratuities, as in those involving bribes, the government must show a nexus to a specific act by the payee.

3. Why are we not supposed to be troubled by "token gifts to the President based on his official position . . . such as the replica jerseys given by championship sports teams each year during ceremonial White House visits . . . [or] a high school principal's gift of a school baseball cap to the Secretary of Education, by reason of his office"? What is the best way to draw lines between serious corruption and trivial gifts? One way is to focus on the relationship between the gifts and the relevant official's conduct. That is the path followed in *McCormick*, with its *quid pro quo* requirement; in *McDonnell*, with its "official act" analysis; and in *Sun-Diamond*, with its interpretation of the "for or because of" language in §201. Is that the best approach? Why not focus instead on the size of the gifts? One answer is that the relevant statutory language does not distinguish between large and small gifts. Another answer is that the significance of the gift depends on its context. A gift that might seem trivial when the recipient is the Secretary of Agriculture might seem a good deal more substantial if given to a low-level bureaucrat in the Agriculture Department. For a cogent argument that *Sun-Diamond* has created an enforcement gap that requires legislative attention, see Sarah N. Welling, Reviving the Federal Crime of Gratuities, 55 Ariz. L. Rev. 417 (2013). Yet *Sun-Diamond* is easily explained by the general rule that if the prosecution theory covers conduct that the judge herself does and doesn't feel guilty about—like accepting school swag when judging a moot court—the government will lose.

4. The scope of the federal corruption statutes is certainly worthy of judicial and congressional attention. But consider the critical enforcement issues that even the most painstaking substantive legislation will not address: Should special attention be given to investigations into the conduct of federal officials over and above that given to conduct involving private persons and state and local officials? What institutional design would promote or impede your policy preferences? To what extent, for example, should such investigations be handled by the Public Integrity Section in Main Justice? That Section used to have a reputation for what some might call prudence,

others insufficient zeal. An effort by the Bush (II) Administration to shake things up resulted, according to one report, in the overly aggressive pursuit of minor cases. See Charles Savage, Elite Unit's Problems Pose Test for Attorney General, N.Y. Times, May 8, 2009, at A20. To what extent are Main Justice prosecuting offices more prone to cycling of this sort than are the U.S. Attorneys' Offices?

Regardless of whether the Public Integrity Section or a U.S. Attorney's Office handles a case, what consideration should be given to the timing of indictments or arrests? (Indeed, this question arises in cases against state and local as well as federal elected officials.) Senator Ted Stevens, for example, was indicted 28 days before the Alaska primary and 98 days before the general election. Just one week before the general election, Stevens was convicted of seven counts of making false statements; he then lost the election by 3,724 votes. Three months later, however, Stevens's conviction was thrown out on grounds of prosecutorial misconduct unrelated to the timing of the indictment. Though Stevens's conviction was wiped from the books, his seat in the Senate was gone for good.

Should a prosecutor deprive voters of relevant but damning information by waiting until the election is over? Should she risk crippling the candidacy of an official who could not be vindicated until after the election? (Let us put aside the sleazy and illegal middle course of waiting but leaking.) A standard prosecutorial response to this dilemma is the mantra that cases are brought "when they're ready." See Jennifer Yachnin & Shira Toeplitz, Stevens Gets Trial Date in September, Roll Call, Aug. 1, 2008 ("Although not explicit policy, generally the government will bring the case when it's ready to be brought. However, they normally try not to bring a case on the eve of an election for fear that their timing in and of itself is influencing the electoral process."). Yet the readiness of cases will itself be affected by staffing decisions and the speed with which approvals are sought and given.

Prosecutors rarely announce they have concluded an investigation without charges and their former targets are regularly left twisting in the wind. But these announcements, while still quite rare, are increasing in corruption cases where the fact of investigation is publicly known. Is that a good thing? The investigation of Hillary Clinton's misuse of her private email server was not a corruption case, but the July 2016 announcement by then-FBI Director James Comey that he was recommending against charges (after a high-profile investigation) raised these and other issues (as did his later October announcement, shortly before the November presidential election, that the Bureau had re-opened the inquiry and sought a search warrant after discovering a new trove of emails.) See Matt Apuzzo, Michael Schmidt et al., Comey Tried to Shield the F.B.I. from Politics. Then He Shaped an Election, N.Y. Times, Apr. 22, 2017, at A1.

The extent to which federal legislators effectively have immunity from prosecution because of the Speech and Debate Clause—"[A]nd for any

Speech or Debate in either House, [the Senators and Representatives] shall not be questioned in any other Place." U.S. Const. art. I, §6, cl. 1—is currently the subject of conflicting lower court decisions. Compare United States v. Renzi, 651 F.3d 1012 (9th Cir. 2011) (broadly rejecting a former congressman's claim that the Speech and Debate Clause barred his prosecution for taking bribes for future legislative acts), with United States v. Rayburn House Office Bldg., 497 F.3d 654 (D.C. Cir. 2007) (taking a more expansive view than the Ninth Circuit of legislative immunity); see also United States v. Menendez, 831 F.3d 155 (3d Cir. 2016).

C. PROGRAM BRIBERY

Section 201 reaches only federal officials or those "acting for or on behalf of the United States." In Dixson v. United States, 465 U.S. 482 (1984)—where the defendants were employed by a non-profit that administered part of the federal block grant to the city of Peoria—the Court broadly read this definition to include anyone occupying "a position of public trust with official federal responsibilities." Before *Dixson* was even decided, Congress moved to address corruption that, while not involving federal officials, related to the receipt of federal funds. The result was the enactment of a general federal program theft and bribery statute in 1984. For more on the history of this measure, see George D. Brown, Stealth Statute—Corruption, the Spending Power, and the Rise of 18 U.S.C. §666, 73 Notre Dame L. Rev. 247, 272-81 (1998).

---

18 U.S.C. §666. Theft or bribery concerning programs receiving Federal funds

(a) Whoever, if the circumstance described in subsection (b) of this section exists—

(1) being an agent of an organization, or of a State, local, or Indian tribal government, or any agency thereof—

(A) embezzles, steals, obtains by fraud, or otherwise without authority knowingly converts to the use of any person other than the rightful owner or intentionally misapplies, property that—

(i) is valued at $5,000 or more, and

(ii) is owned by, or is under the care, custody, or control of such organization, government, or agency; or

(B) corruptly solicits or demands for the benefit of any person, or accepts or agrees to accept, anything of value from any person, intending to be influenced or rewarded in connection with any business, transaction, or series of transactions of such organization, government, or agency involving any thing of value of $5,000 or more; or

(2) corruptly gives, offers, or agrees to give anything of value to any person, with intent to influence or reward an agent of an organization or of a State, local or Indian tribal government, or any agency thereof, in connection with any business, transaction, or series of transactions of such organization, government, or agency involving anything of value of $5,000 or more;

shall be fined under this title, imprisoned not more than 10 years, or both.

(b) The circumstance referred to in subsection (a) of this section is that the organization, government, or agency receives, in any one-year period, benefits in excess of $10,000 under a Federal program involving a grant, contract, subsidy, loan, guarantee, insurance, or other form of Federal assistance.

(c) This section does not apply to bona fide salary, wages, fees, or other compensation paid, or expenses paid or reimbursed, in the usual course of business.

(d) As used in this section —

(1) the term "agent" means a person authorized to act on behalf of another person or a government and, in the case of an organization or government, includes a servant or employee, and a partner, director, officer, manager, and representative;

(2) the term "government agency" means a subdivision of the executive, legislative, judicial, or other branch of government, including a department, independent establishment, commission, administration, authority, board, and bureau, and a corporation or other legal entity established, and subject to control, by a government or governments for the execution of a governmental or intergovernmental program;

(3) the term "local" means of or pertaining to a political subdivision within a State;

(4) the term "State" includes a State of the United States, the District of Columbia, and any commonwealth, territory, or possession of the United States; and

(5) the term "in any one-year period" means a continuous period that commences no earlier than twelve months before the commission of the offense or that ends no later than twelve months after the commission of the offense. Such period may include time both before and after the commission of the offense.

Notice that the statute allows for federal prosecution of state, local, and tribal officials, as well as "agent[s] of an organization"—even a nongovernmental organization. So long as a state or local government, an agency, or a private organization receives "in any one-year period, benefits in excess of $10,000 under a Federal program involving a grant, contract, subsidy, loan, guarantee, insurance, or other form of Federal assistance," its officials or agents may be prosecuted federally for violation of 18 U.S.C. §666. See, e.g., Fischer v. United States, 529 U.S. 667 (2000) (affirming defendant's conviction under §666 for defrauding a hospital that received more than

$10,000 in Medicare funds). Is this a constitutional use of Congress's power under the Spending Clause?

———

The following case entertains a facial constitutional challenge to the federal program bribery statute. In it, the Supreme Court upholds criminal prosecution of bribery at the state and local level as a reasonable way to protect the money the federal government distributes through its programs.

Sabri v. United States
541 U.S. 600 (2004)

Justice SOUTER delivered the opinion of the Court.

The question is whether 18 U.S.C. §666(a)(2), proscribing bribery of state, local, and tribal officials of entities that receive at least $10,000 in federal funds, is a valid exercise of congressional authority under Article I of the Constitution. We hold that it is.

Petitioner Basim Omar Sabri is a real estate developer who proposed to build a hotel and retail structure in the city of Minneapolis. Sabri lacked confidence, however, in his ability to adapt to the lawful administration of licensing and zoning laws, and offered three separate bribes to a city councilman, Brian Herron, according to the grand jury indictment that gave rise to this case. At the time the bribes were allegedly offered (between July 2, 2001, and July 17, 2001), Herron served as a member of the Board of Commissioners of the Minneapolis Community Development Agency (MCDA), a public body created by the city council to fund housing and economic development within the city.

Count 1 of the indictment charged Sabri with offering a $5,000 kickback for obtaining various regulatory approvals, and according to Count 2, Sabri offered Herron a $10,000 bribe to set up and attend a meeting with owners of land near the site Sabri had in mind, at which Herron would threaten to use the city's eminent domain authority to seize their property if they were troublesome to Sabri. Count 3 alleged that Sabri offered Herron a commission of 10% on some $800,000 in community economic development grants that Sabri sought from the city, the MCDA, and other sources.

The charges were brought under 18 U.S.C. §666(a)(2).... In 2001, the City Council of Minneapolis administered about $29 million in federal funds paid to the city, and in the same period, the MCDA received some $23 million of federal money.

Before trial, Sabri moved to dismiss the indictment on the ground that §666(a)(2) is unconstitutional on its face for failure to require proof of a connection between the federal funds and the alleged bribe, as an element of liability. The Government responded that "even if an additional nexus between the bribery conduct and the federal funds is required, the evidence in this case will easily meet such a standard" because Sabri's alleged actions related to federal dollars. Although Sabri did not contradict this factual claim, the District Court agreed with him that the law was facially invalid. A divided panel of the Eighth Circuit reversed, holding that there was nothing fatal in the absence of an express requirement to prove some connection between a given bribe and federally pedigreed dollars, and that the statute was constitutional under the Necessary and Proper Clause in serving the objects of the congressional spending power. 326 F.3d 937 (2003). . . .

We granted certiorari to resolve a split among the Courts of Appeals over the need to require connection between forbidden conduct and federal funds. We now affirm.

Sabri raises what he calls a facial challenge to §666(a)(2): the law can never be applied constitutionally because it fails to require proof of any connection between a bribe or kickback and some federal money. . . . Sabri claims his attack meets the demanding standard set out in United States v. Salerno, 481 U.S. 739, 745 (1987), since he says no prosecution can satisfy the Constitution under this statute, owing to its failure to require proof that its particular application falls within Congress's jurisdiction to legislate.

We can readily dispose of this position that, to qualify as a valid exercise of Article I power, the statute must require proof of connection with federal money as an element of the offense. We simply do not presume the unconstitutionality of federal criminal statutes lacking explicit provision of a jurisdictional hook, and there is no occasion even to consider the need for such a requirement where there is no reason to suspect that enforcement of a criminal statute would extend beyond a legitimate interest cognizable under Article I, §8.

Congress has authority under the Spending Clause to appropriate federal monies to promote the general welfare, Art. I, §8, cl. 1, and it has corresponding authority under the Necessary and Proper Clause, Art. I, §8, cl. 18, to see to it that taxpayer dollars appropriated under that power are in fact spent for the general welfare, and not frittered away in graft or on projects undermined when funds are siphoned off or corrupt public officers are derelict about demanding value for dollars. See generally McCulloch v. Maryland, 17 U.S. 316 (1819) (establishing review for means-ends rationality under the Necessary and Proper Clause). Congress does not have to sit by and accept the risk of operations thwarted by local and state improbity. See, e.g., *McCulloch, supra* at 417 (power to "establish post-offices and post-roads" entails authority to punish those who steal letters). Section 666(a)(2) addresses the problem at the sources of bribes, by rational means, to safeguard the integrity of the state, local, and tribal recipients of federal dollars.

It is true, just as Sabri says, that not every bribe or kickback offered or paid to agents of governments covered by §666(b) will be traceably skimmed from specific federal payments, or show up in the guise of a *quid pro quo* for some dereliction in spending a federal grant. But . . . [m]oney is fungible, bribed officials are untrustworthy stewards of federal funds, and corrupt contractors do not deliver dollar-for-dollar value. Liquidity is not a financial term for nothing; money can be drained off here because a federal grant is pouring in there. And officials are not any the less threatening to the objects behind federal spending just because they may accept general retainers. It is . . . enough that the statutes condition the offense on a threshold amount of federal dollars defining the federal interest, such as that provided here. . . .

[Distinguishing United States v. Lopez, 514 U.S. 549 (1995), and United States v. Morrison, 529 U.S. 598 (2000), the Court noted:] No piling [of inferences] is needed here to show that Congress was within its prerogative to protect spending objects from the menace of local administrators on the take. The power to keep a watchful eye on expenditures and on the reliability of those who use public money is bound up with congressional authority to spend in the first place, and Sabri would be hard pressed to claim, in the words of the *Lopez* Court, that §666(a)(2) "has nothing to do with" the congressional spending power. . . .

[The concurring opinion of Justice Kennedy, with whom Justice Scalia joins, is omitted.]

Justice THOMAS, concurring in the judgment.

Title 18 U.S.C. §666(a)(2) is a valid exercise of Congress' power to regulate commerce, at least under this Court's precedent. Cf. Perez v. United States, 402 U.S. 146, 154 (1971). I continue to doubt that we have correctly interpreted the Commerce Clause. See United States v. Morrison, 529 U.S. 598, 627 (2000) (Thomas, J., concurring); United States v. Lopez, 514 U.S. 549, 584-585 (1995) (Thomas, J., concurring). But until this Court reconsiders its precedents, and because neither party requests us to do so here, our prior case law controls the outcome of this case. . . .

The Court does a not-wholly-unconvincing job of tying the broad scope of §666(a)(2) to a federal interest in federal funds and programs. But simply noting that "[m]oney is fungible" . . . does not explain how there could be any federal interest in "prosecut[ing] a bribe paid to a city's meat inspector in connection with a substantial transaction just because the city's parks department had received a federal grant of $10,000," United States v. Santopietro, 166 F.3d 88, 93 (2d Cir. 1999). It would be difficult to describe the chain of inferences and assumptions in which the Court would have to indulge to connect such a bribe to a federal interest in any federal funds or programs as being "plainly adapted" to their protection. . . . [Y]et the bribe is covered by the expansive language of §666(a)(2). . . .

Because I would decide this case on the Court's Commerce Clause jurisprudence, I do not ultimately decide whether Congress' power to spend combined with the Necessary and Proper Clause could authorize the enactment of §666(a)(2). But regardless of the particular outcome of this case under the correct test, the Court's approach seems to greatly and improperly expand the reach of Congress' power under the Necessary and Proper Clause. Accordingly, I concur in the judgment.

NOTES AND QUESTIONS

1. Since *Sabri*, courts have flatly "declined to require any connection between federal funds and the activity that constitutes a violation of §666." United States v. Hines, 541 F.3d 833, 836 (8th Cir. 2008); see also United States v. Thomas, 847 F.3d 193 (5th Cir. 2017) (upholding embezzlement prosecution of municipal court contractor based on municipalities receipt of federal funds). The statute is broad in other respects as well. See United States v. [Bravo] Fernandez, 722 F.3d 1 (1st Cir. 2013) (noting that every member of Puerto Rico legislature is an "agent" of the Commonwealth, and could be prosecuted under §666 even though legislature had no control over federal funds received by territory) (excerpted *infra*); United States v. Willis, 844 F.3d 155 (3d Cir. 2016) (same analysis for member of Virgin Islands Legislature). In the current world of massive and ubiquitous federal spending, how far should prosecutors push the authority they've been given under the Spending Clause?

2. Consider a source of federal jurisdiction not mentioned in *Sabri*: Article IV, Section 4 of the Constitution states that "[t]he United States shall guarantee to every State in this Union a Republican Form of Government." Bribery puts government up for sale—when officials take bribes, dollars trump votes. That seems contrary to the "republican form of government" that the federal government is supposed to "guarantee." Why isn't jurisdiction over local corruption cases justified under that clause? The short answer is that Congress has never rested its authority on the "republican form of government" clause of Article IV. Why not, particularly given that it seems to provide a more pertinent basis for federal authority than the spending power? See Adam H. Kurland, The Guarantee Clause as a Basis for Federal Prosecutions of State and Local Officials, 62 S. Cal. L. Rev. 367 (1989).

Another aspect of the breadth of §666 is that it reaches not just thefts and bribery but "misapplications" as well. Consider the following misapplication analysis.

United States v. Thompson
484 F.3d 877 (7th Cir. 2007)

EASTERBROOK, Chief Judge.
In 2005 Wisconsin selected Adelman Travel Group as its travel agent for about 40% of its annual travel budget of $75 million. The selection

came after an elaborate process presided over by Georgia Thompson, a section chief in the state's Bureau of Procurement. Statutes and regulations require procurement decisions to be made on the basis of cost and service rather than politics. Wis. Stat. §§16.70-16.78; Wis. Admin. Code §10.08. Thompson steered the contract to Adelman Travel, the low bidder, even though other members of the selection group rated its rivals more highly. A jury convicted Thompson of violating 18 U.S.C. §666 and §1341. The prosecution's theory was that any politically motivated departure from state administrative rules is a federal crime, when either the mails or federal funds are involved. Thompson was sentenced to 18 months' imprisonment and compelled to begin serving that term while her appeal was pending. After concluding that Thompson is innocent, we reversed her conviction so that she could be released. This opinion is the explanation that our order of April 5 promised.

Adelman Travel was the low bidder, but a low price for lousy service is no bargain. Wisconsin's rules give price only a 25% weight (300 of 1200 points) in the selection process. About 58% (700 points) goes to service, which a working group evaluates subjectively based on written presentations. Adelman had the second-best score for service; Omega World Travel came in third. The combined price-and-service rating had Adelman in the lead. (Fox World Travel received the best service score but had a noncompetitive price.) The final 17% of the score (200 points) depends on the working group's assessment of oral presentations. These presentations (often dubbed "beauty contests" or "dog-and-pony shows" that may reward the flashiest PowerPoint slides) need not be related to either price or the pitchman's probable quality of service; why the state gives them any weight, independent of price or quality, is a mystery, but not one we need unravel. Adelman Travel must have made a bad presentation, for six of the seven members of the working group gave it poor marks (from a low of 120 points to a high of 165), while awarding Omega scores between 155 and 200. Thompson alone gave Adelman a higher score (185 for Adelman, 160 for Omega). Adelman Travel's disastrous oral presentation left Omega World Travel with the highest total score.

The prosecution's theory is that Omega should have received the contract on the spot but that for political reasons Thompson ordered a delay. Thompson told her colleagues that a decision for Omega, which is based on the East Coast, would not go over well with her boss, Pat Farley. A jury also could conclude that Thompson said something to the effect that for "political reasons" Adelman Travel had to get this contract. . . .

Thompson tried to engage in logrolling, offering to change her scores for bidders on other travel contracts if members of the working group would change their scores on this contract. Horse-trading proved to be unacceptable to the selection group, but a member other than Thompson suggested that the contract be rebid on a best-and-final basis, as state law permitted. Wis. Stat. §16.72(2)(e), (g). Adelman Travel reduced its price, which—keeping all other elements of the score constant—left Adelman and Omega with 1027 points apiece. The tie depended on rounding to the nearest whole number. Adelman Travel's score was 1026.6, while Omega World Travel's score was 1027.3. After Thompson (with her supervisors' consent) deemed the contest a draw — sensibly, as the difference was trivial compared to the amount of subjectivity and variance in the committee members' evaluations — Thompson employed a tie-breaking procedure, specified by state law, that gave weight to items not previously figured into the price comparison and declared Adelman Travel to be the winner.

The prosecutor contends that this episode played a role in the Bureau of Procurement's decision three months later to give Thompson a $1,000 raise in her annual salary. *Post hoc ergo propter hoc* is the name of a logical error, not a reason to infer causation. But Thompson does not contend that the evidence was insufficient to allow the jury to find that the raise was related to the travel contract, so we shall assume that this link has been established. The jury also learned that Craig Adelman, one of the principal owners and managers of Adelman Travel, supported Wisconsin's Governor and made contributions to his campaign both before and after Adelman Travel was selected for this contract. The prosecution does not contend, however, that any of these contributions was unlawful — they were properly disclosed, and no *quid pro quo* was entailed. There is not so much as a whiff of a kickback or any similar impropriety. Nor does the prosecution contend that Thompson knew or cared about these contributions.

What, then, were the "political" considerations to which Thompson referred? We may assume that Thompson learned that her boss preferred Adelman Travel to Omega World Travel, and Thompson knew that Farley held a political rather than a civil-service appointment. But *why* was Adelman Travel the favored bidder?

One possibility is that Farley knew about, and sought to reward, Craig Adelman's past and potential financial support of the Governor. If that was Farley's motive, then the selection was open to question under O'Hare Truck Service, Inc. v. Northlake, 518 U.S. 712 (1996), and Board of County Commissioners v. Umbehr, 518 U.S. 668 (1996), which hold that the First Amendment limits the extent to which political support of office holders may justify the withholding of public contracts. But these decisions do not say that the Constitution forbids all politically motivated contracting practices — and they certainly do not hold that any error in implementing the Supreme Court's multi-factor-balancing approach is a crime.

Perhaps, however, Farley favored Adelman Travel because it was cheaper. This would be a political position in the best sense of that term. Many a person runs for office on a platform of cutting the cost of government. . . . Low prices may advance the public interest even if they discomfit public employees, and recognition that driving down the cost of government is good politics for incumbents does not transgress any federal statute of which we are aware. Still another possibility is that Farley (and thus

Thompson) sought to favor a local firm over one from another state. The Supreme Court has held that states, as market participants, may buy preferentially from their own citizens. See, e.g., White v. Massachusetts Council of Construction Employers, Inc., 460 U.S. 204 (1983). A preference for in-state suppliers who can vote, over competitors who can't, may be smart politics. Again no federal statute regulates such behavior, let alone declares it to be a felony. Wisconsin law specifies a preference for domestic bidders, though only when the out-of-state bidder hales [sic] from a jurisdiction that favors its own citizens in procurement decisions. Wis. Stat. §16.75(1)(a) §2.

The evidence of record would not permit a jury to find beyond a reasonable doubt which of these three "political" reasons was Farley's, let alone whether Farley's reason also was Thompson's—for Thompson may have been trying to be a faithful subordinate without questioning her boss's *bona fides*. Nor was the jury asked to determine Thompson's motive. The United States maintains that Thompson's objective is irrelevant. It is enough, the prosecutor insists, that Thompson deflected the decision from the one that should have been made under the administrative process. When coupled with a personal benefit (the raise), such a deflection is criminal under federal law, the United States insists. In other words, the prosecutor's argument is that any public employee's knowing deviation from state procurement rules is a federal felony, no matter why the employee chose to bend the rules, as long as the employee gains in the process. (In stating the argument this way, we are assuming that the jury could and did find beyond a reasonable doubt that Thompson knew that the state's procurement rules entitled Omega World Travel to the contract, given her fellow employees' favorable view of Omega's oral presentation.)

Thompson was convicted of violating . . . §666. . . . The prosecution's theory is that she "intentionally misapplie[d]" more than $5,000 by diverting it from Omega World Travel to Adelman Travel. This assumes, however, that a *mistake* is the same thing as a *misapplication*, and the statute does not say this. (It isn't even clear that Thompson made a mistake: She had authority to order the best-and-final procedure, a statistical tie ensued, and the tiebreakers were carried out accurately.) Approving a payment for goods or services not supplied would be a misapplication, but hiring the low bidder does not sound like "misapplication" of funds. The federal government saved money because of Thompson's decisions.

Section 666 is captioned "Theft or bribery concerning programs receiving Federal funds," and the Supreme Court refers to it as an anti-bribery rule. See Sabri v. United States, 541 U.S. 600 (2004). Neither Thompson nor anyone else in state government was accused of taking a bribe or receiving a kickback. A statute's caption does not override its text, but the word "misapplies" is not a defined term. We could read that word broadly, so that it means any disbursement that would not have occurred had all state laws been enforced without any political considerations. Or we could read it narrowly, so that it means a disbursement in exchange for services not rendered (as with ghost workers), or to suppliers that would not have received any contract but for bribes, or for services that were overpriced (to cover the cost of baksheesh), or for shoddy goods at the price prevailing for high-quality goods. All of these conditions were satisfied in cases such as United States v. Spano, 421 F.3d 599 (7th Cir. 2005), and United States v. Martin, 195 F.3d 961 (7th Cir. 1999). None is satisfied here.

Faced with a choice between a broad reading that turns all . . . state-law errors or political considerations in state procurement into federal crimes, and a narrow reading that limits §666 to theft, extortion, bribery, and similarly corrupt acts, a court properly uses the statute's caption for guidance. . . .

Imagine how the prosecutor's reading of §666 would apply to a state official charged with implementing the Medicaid program. Someone applies for payment of medical expenses; a state employee approves; later it comes to light that the applicant made just a little too much money to be eligible, so the decision was erroneous. A violation of regulations and perhaps of some statutes has occurred, but is the error a crime? As we read §666, the answer is no unless the public employee is on the take or the applicant is a relative (for indirect benefits are another form of payoff). An error—even a deliberate one, in which the employee winks at the rules in order to help out someone he believes deserving but barely over the eligibility threshold—is a civil rather than a criminal transgression. Likewise the sin is civil (if it is any wrong at all) when a public employee manipulates the rules, as Thompson did, to save the state money or favor a home-state producer that supports elected officials.

Public employees often implement rules with which they disagree, and they are tempted to bend these rules to achieve what they deem better outcomes. As long as the state gets what it contracts for, at the market price, no funds have been misapplied, even if the state's rules should have led it to buy something more expensive. . . . Evidence showing that Thompson believed that Adelman Travel provided less value for money than its competitors might support an inference that funds had been misapplied, but this record does not imply that Thompson's deeds were at variance with her thoughts. . . .

NOTES AND QUESTIONS

1. Despite the Seventh Circuit's indignation, isn't there an argument that Thompson's actions *did* fit within the terms of §666? The court acknowledges that she "manipulate[d] the rules" in order to redirect more than $5,000 from Omega World to Adelman—"a home-state producer that support[ed]" her boss. She even offered "to change her scores for bidders on

other travel contracts if members of the working group would change their scores on this contract." So didn't she do something wrong? Is the real problem here that Thompson's actions hardly constitute political corruption worth a federal prosecution, and hence the court felt compelled to read a de minimis exception into a statute that had no such exception on its face?

2. Can §666's "misapplication" provision be used where government funds, including a salary, are paid under circumstances that violate applicable conflict of interest rules? Perhaps so, the Eleventh Circuit has said—citing a First Circuit case—but more than "evidence of an undisclosed conflict of interest" is needed. United States v. Jimenez, 705 F.3d 1305, 1310-11 (11th Cir. 2013) (citing United States v. Cornier-Ortiz, 361 F.3d 29 (1st Cir. 2004)). Why do courts seem so careful about "misapplication" theories?

3. Consider this one: Several defendants close to New Jersey Governor Chris Christie (including Deputy Director of the Port Authority Bill Baroni but not Christie himself) were prosecuted for concocting a sham traffic study that closed lanes to the George Washington Bridge in order to punish the Mayor of Fort Lee for the sin of not endorsing Christie for re-election. In addition to civil rights charges (to be discussed in Chapter 7), the indictment charged a violation of §666(a)(1)(A). After the jury convicted, the district court upheld the verdict:

> Defendants seek judgments of acquittal on Counts One and Two, arguing 1) that Section 666(a)(1)(A) is void for vagueness as applied, 2) the government failed to present sufficient evidence that Defendants "agreed to or did obtain property by fraud, act without authority, or intentionally misapply property of the Port Authority," and 3) the government failed to present sufficient evidence that the property in question had a value of at least $5,000.
>
> *1. Void for Vagueness. . . .*
>
> Defendants take the position that Section 666 is void for vagueness as applied to them because the "misapplication" provision, §666(a)(1)(A), fails to provide sufficient guidance to "ordinary people" or law enforcement to "understand what conduct is prohibited." (BB at 18-24.) Baroni specifically asserts that the "misapplication" provision "effectively criminalizes making any decision to expend Port Authority resources with political considerations in mind." (BB at 20.)
>
> As this Court noted previously, "[t]he statutory language of §666(a)(1)(A) is broad, but not unclear." *Baroni*, 2016 WL 3388302 at *3 n.3; see also Salinas v. United States, 522 U.S. 52, 52, 57 (1997) (describing the statute as having "plain and unambiguous meaning" and "expansive, unqualified language"). Moreover, courts have specifically held that "[t]he term 'intentionally misapply,' as it is used in §666, is not unconstitutionally vague." United States v. Urlacher, 979 F.2d 935, 939 (2d Cir. 1992). . . .
>
> Defendants' argument that the statute improperly criminalizes political activities is not persuasive. That argument conflates motive (political considerations) with *mens reas* and conduct (intentional misapplication). . . . [T]

he former is merely the reason a defendant may engage in activities that violate Section 666, while the latter is what triggers prosecution under the statute. This Court is satisfied that both the plain text of the statute, as well as court decisions, put Defendants on notice that intentional misapplication of Port Authority resources was criminal and gave appropriate guidance to law enforcement as to what conduct would violate the statute.

Further, as applied to Defendants, the evidence introduced at trial was sufficient for a reasonable jury to conclude that Defendants understood that what they were doing was wrong. Specifically, the Government produced evidence that Defendants concealed the real reason for the lane closures from Port Authority personnel, Fort Lee officials, the New Jersey Legislature and the media both during and after the closures occurred. Viewing the evidence in the light most favorable to the prosecution, this Court finds that a reasonable jury could have inferred an intent to misapply Port Authority funds in violation of Section 666 from Defendants' efforts to conceal their activities. See, e.g., United States v. Dubón-Otero, 292 F.3d 1, 11-12 (1st Cir. 2002) (citing evidence of concealment introduced at trial as a basis upon which "a jury could find that defendants 'without valid authority' embezzled, stole or obtained by fraud money or property"). Accordingly, Defendants' void-for-vagueness challenge as to their convictions is unavailing.

2. Sufficiency of the Evidence

Defendants also argue that the Government failed to introduce sufficient evidence to warrant a conviction under Section 666, because 1) property is limited to tangible property, 2) neither defendant personally benefitted from the lane closures, 3) Baroni had the authority "to undertake every action alleged in the Indictment," and 4) the value of the property at issue was under the $5,000 statutory minimum.

First, Section 666 does not limit the definition of property to tangible goods. *Baroni*, 2016 WL 3388302, at *6 (discussing the definition of property under the statute); see also United States v. Lawson, No. Crim. 3:08-21-DCR, 2009 WL 1324157, at *2 (E.D. Ky. May 11, 2009) (finding that "employee time is property within the meaning of this term in §666(a)(1)(A) because this term includes both tangible and intangible property" and holding that "engineer estimates constitute 'property'" for the purposes of §666(a)(1)(A)). Accordingly, "'compensation paid to [Port Authority] personnel in connection with the lane realignment,' losses incurred from repeating a spoiled traffic study, and the value of the access lanes and toll booths" are permissible under Section 666.

Second, as this Court has ruled previously, a person may violate Section 666 even if he or she does not realize a personal gain. See id. at *6 (finding that "[m]isapplication can refer to any improper use of property, whether or not for personal gain, and can even encompass situations in which an organization benefits from the misuse"); see also United States v. Frazier, 53 F.3d 1105 (10th Cir. 1995) (finding misappropriation of property under §666(a)(1)(A) where an employee falsely certified that federal funds were used for training purposes, but instead used those funds to purchase computers for the organization); 3d Cir. Model Crim. Jury Instr. §6.18.666A1A-3 (stating that misapplication "includes the wrongful use of the money or property for an unauthorized purpose, even if such use benefitted the organization").

Third, although Baroni had substantial authority as the Deputy Director of the Port Authority, the Executive Director, Pat Foye, testified at trial that Baroni violated Port Authority policies regarding lane closures. Additional testimony indicated that the lane reductions were not in line with routine Port Authority procedures and departed significantly from prior practices. Tellingly, witnesses testified that traffic studies are ordinarily conducted without any lane closures or disruptions to traffic. The trial testimony also indicates that the failure of Port Authority personnel to respond to Mayor Sokolich's requests for information or assistance ran counter to the Port Authority's typical efforts to communicate with local officials. Accordingly, the jury could have reasonably found that Baroni did not have the authority to close or realign the lanes as he did.

Finally, in order "to avoid prosecutions for minor kickbacks and limit violations to cases of outright corruption," charges under Section 666 may only be brought if the property in question is worth at least $5,000. Defendants argue that the Government "failed to prove that the salary and wages paid to Port Authority employees were not bona fide salary or wages under §666(c)" and "failed to prove that a significant amount of the expenses incurred by the Port Authority [were] reasonably foreseeable." This Court finds no support, nor do Defendants provide any, for their proximate cause argument. Defendants' "knowledge of jurisdictional fact[s] is irrelevant." United States v. Crutchley, 502 F.2d 1195, 1201 (3d Cir. 1974). The determination of whether wages are "bona fide" and subject to the provision's protection is a question of fact for the jury. See, e.g., United States v. Williams, 507 F.3d 905, 909 (5th Cir. 2007) (noting that "[w]hether wages are bona fide and earned in the usual course of business is a question of fact for the jury to decide"). As this Court previously held, "although §666(c)'s safe harbor provision protects bona fide compensation paid in the 'usual course of business,' it does not apply where employee services have been diverted to work that is not part of an organization's usual course of business." See *Baroni*, 2016 WL 3388302 at *6 (citing cases). Here, the Government introduced evidence that Defendants diverted Port Authority personnel to do work that was not part of the agency's "usual course of business" when reconfiguring the access lanes. The jury could reasonably find that the value of compensation paid to Port Authority personnel, losses from a ruined traffic study, and the value of the lanes and toll booths were not bona fide and satisfied the $5,000.00 threshold.

United States v. Baroni, 2017 WL 787122, at *3-*6 (D.N.J. 2017). The case is now up on appeal. We consider the civil rights charges in *Baroni* in Chapter 7.

4. When "bribery" is charged under §666, need the jury find a *quid pro quo*? Courts have noted the absence of an "official act" requirement like the one that the *McDonnell* Court found in §201 and arguably read into honest services fraud and "under color" extortion cases (see Chapter 5). See United

States v. Boyland, 862 F.3d 279, 291 (2d Cir. 2017) (noting that under §201, "official act[s]" are limited to acts on pending 'question[s], matter[s], cause [s], suit[s], proceeding[s], or controver[ies]'"; while §"666 . . . is more expansive [in prohibiting] individuals from 'solicit[ing] . . . anything of value from any person, *intending to be influenced* or rewarded *in connection* with any business, transaction, or series of transactions of [an] organization, government, or agency.'") (emphases in original).

Writing before *McDonnell*, a Tenth Circuit judge observed "some uncertainty in the law as to what type of *quid pro quo*, if any, is necessary to satisfy the statutory requirement that the bribe be solicited with the bribee 'intending to be influenced or rewarded in connection with' official business." However, he found that §666 "does demand a quid-pro-quo showing, but only in the sense of a loose exchange of payment for official action, not in the sense that the bribee must bestow a precise favor that was identified at the time of the bribe. United States v. Morgan, 635 F. App'x. 423, 452-54 (10th Cir. 2015) (Holmes, J., concurring). What sort of *quid pro quo*, if any, should §666 be read to require after *McDonnell*? Given the suggestion of the *McDonnell* Court that its "official act" analysis was driven by concerns about unconstitutional vagueness, might the absence of such a requirement mean that §666 is void for vagueness?

5. Because §666 explicitly speaks of a payment to "reward," can it be used to prosecute what would be a "mere" gratuity under 18 U.S.C. §201?

United States v. [Bravo] Fernandez
722 F.3d 1 (1st Cir. 2013)

[In a case involving a Puerto Rico legislator and a Commonwealth businessman who were charged, inter alia, with unlawfully exchanging a trip to Las Vegas to attend a prize fight for favorable action on legislation, the First Circuit (Lipez, J.), having found that the jury instruction permitted a §666 conviction based on a gratuity theory, went on to determine whether the statute indeed covers gratuities.] . . .

One of the most conspicuous differences between the texts of §666 and §201 concerns the intent element: while §666 prohibits one from corruptly offering a thing of value with intent to "influence *or reward*" an agent, and prohibits an agent from corruptly soliciting or demanding a thing of value with intent to be "influenced *or rewarded*," the bribery provision applicable to federal officials, §201(b), does not include the alternative "reward": it prohibits one from corruptly offering a thing of value with intent to "influence" an act, and prohibits an official from corruptly soliciting a thing of value with an intent to be "influenced." The word "reward" in §666 is open to (at least) two different interpretations.

Under the first interpretation, when a payor intends to *influence* an official's future actions, the payment constitutes a bribe; when a payor intends to *reward* the official's past conduct (or future conduct the official is already committed to taking), the payment constitutes a gratuity. United States v. Anderson, 517 F.3d 953, 961 (7th Cir. 2008). Several circuits have adopted this reading of the language. Id.; United States v. Ganim, 510 F.3d 134, 150 (2d Cir. 2007) ("[A] payment made to 'influence' connotes bribery, whereas a payment made to 'reward' connotes an illegal gratuity."); United States v. Zimmerman, 509 F.3d 920, 927 (8th Cir. 2007) (citing §666(a)(1)(B)'s "influenced or rewarded" language in support of finding that "Section 666(a)(1)(B) prohibits both the acceptance of bribes and the acceptance of gratuities intended to be a bonus for taking official action"); United States v. Agostino, 132 F.3d 1183, 1195 (7th Cir. 1997).

Under the second interpretation, the word "reward" does not create a separate gratuity offense in §666, but rather serves a more modest purpose: it merely clarifies "that a bribe can be promised before, but paid after, the official's action on the payor's behalf." United States v. Jennings, 160 F.3d 1006, 1015 n.3 (4th Cir. 1998). "This definition accords with the traditional meaning of the term 'reward' as something offered to induce another to act favorably on one's behalf (for example, a bounty offered for the capture of a fugitive)." Id. Under this reading, the terms "influence" and "reward" each retain independent meaning. "Influence" would be used in situations in which, for instance, a payment was made to a local government commissioner in order to induce him to vote in a certain way on a particular matter. "Reward" would be used if a *promise* of payment was made, contingent upon that commissioner's vote; once the commissioner voted in the way the payor requested, a "reward" would follow. Both of these situations involve a *quid pro quo*, and both therefore constitute bribes. What matters, of course, is that the *offer* of payment precedes the official act.

Moreover, a reading consistent with the second interpretation would help to explain the presence of the "corruptly" language in §666(a)(1)(B) and (a)(2). As discussed *supra*, §201 uses the word corruptly *only* in its bribery provision, §201(b), not in the gratuity provision, §201(c). The Fourth Circuit puzzled over this issue in United States v. Jennings, "namely, why §666(a)(2)'s language prohibiting 'rewards' given 'corruptly' should be interpreted to cover gratuities, when under §201 *any* payment made 'corruptly' is a bribe, not an illegal gratuity." Id. (emphasis added). If the inclusion of the word "reward" in §666 does no more than clarify that the *payment* of a bribe can occur after the act that is the subject of the bribe is completed (so long as the *agreement* to pay the bribe for the act or acts is made before the act or acts takes place), the statute still applies only to bribery, and the use of the word "corruptly" in §666 would comport with the use of the same word in §201(b): any payment made "corruptly" is a bribe. Cf. *Anderson*, 517 F.3d at 961 ("Unlike a gratuity, a bribe is a payment made with 'a corrupt purpose, such as inducing a public official to participate in a fraud or to influence his official action.'" (quoting [the United States Sentencing Guideline on bribery]).

Another critical difference between §666 and §201 is the maximum penalty authorized under the statutes. One who violates §201(b), the bribery provision, may be fined, "or *imprisoned for not more than fifteen years*, or both." 18 U.S.C. §201(b) (emphasis added). For a violation—*any* violation—of §666, the statute provides a punishment of a fine, a term of imprisonment of "*not more than 10 years*," or both. Id. §666(a) (emphasis added). An even more striking difference in penalties, however, exists between §666 and §201's gratuity subsection, the latter of which calls for a term of imprisonment of "*not more than two years*," id. §201(c) (emphasis added)—meaning that §666 authorizes a term of imprisonment *five times* longer than that allowed by §201's gratuities provision.

This dramatic discrepancy in maximum penalties between §666 and §201(c) makes it difficult to accept that the statutes target the same type of crime—illegal gratuities. The difference in sentences contemplated by §201(b) and §666 is both less dramatic and more understandable: §201(b) targets (primarily) federal officials, while §666 targets non-federal officials who happen to have a connection to federal funds. It is reasonable to assume that the federal government viewed corrupt federal officials involved in the receipt of bribes as more culpable.[14]

The distinct penalties for bribes and gratuities contained in §201 highlights an obvious yet important structural difference between §§666 and 201: §666 does not have separate bribery and gratuity subsections. For those circuits that have found that §666 criminalizes gratuities, two subsections of §666 do the same work as four subsections of §201. We think it unlikely that Congress would condense two distinct offenses into the same subsection in §666 when the statute upon which it is based has separate subsections for each offense. See George D. Brown, Stealth Statute—Corruption, the Spending Power, and the Rise of 18 U.S.C. §666, 73 Notre Dame L. Rev. 247, 310 (1998) ("Congress did not . . . enact a mirror image of §201 for nonfederal officials. Section 201 contains separate subsections to deal with bribery and gratuities. Section 666 does not. It is a mistake to attempt to read the two statutes as equal in reach."). Furthermore, if Congress did choose to condense bribes and gratuities into a single provision in §666, it would be odd to do so by merely plugging slightly modified language from §201(b), its bribery provision, into the statute. Surely the word "gratuity"—which is, of course, mentioned nowhere in the text or legislative history of §666—was not foreign to Congress in 1986.

---

14. The legislative history of §666 sheds no light on the reason for these differences in penalties.

Although §666 was enacted to supplement §201, we can easily hypoth-esize at least two reasons why Congress may have chosen to supplement only §201's prohibition of bribery. First, bribes are simply worse than ille-gal gratuities. See *Sun-Diamond*, 526 U.S. at 405 (noting the difference in the maximum sentences allowed under §201(b) and (c) and stating that "[t]he punishments prescribed for the two offenses reflect their relative seriousness"); Charles N. Whitaker, Note, Federal Prosecution of State and Local Bribery: Inappropriate Tools and the Need for a Structured Approach, 78 Va. L. Rev. 1617, 1622 (1992) ("The typical one- to two-year penalty under gratuities statutes evidences the lesser degree of culpabil-ity in accepting a gratuity as opposed to a bribe."). Under this theory, Congress may have viewed bribery as far more of a threat to the proper functioning of federally funded programs than gratuities. Because the application of §666 to gratuities offenses would "take[] the statute deeply into a range of government ethics issues that may be better handled at the state level," Congress may have intended to cabin §666 "to the hard-core area of bribery[,] where any federal interest in government integrity will be stronger." Brown, *supra*, at 310.

A second (and related) reason why Congress may have limited §666 to bribery is to avoid what has been characterized as federal overcrim-inalization. See Alex Kozinski & Misha Tseyltin, You're (Probably) a Federal Criminal, *in* In the Name of Justice 43-56 (Timothy Lynch ed., 2009); Sanford H. Kadish, Comment: The Folly of Overfederalization, 46 Hastings L.J. 1247, 1249-50 (1995). In other words, Congress may have been wary of venturing too far into the thickets of state and local corrup-tion, which often implicate the political processes of the state. See Brown, *supra*, at 310.

In *Sun-Diamond*, a case addressing the scope of §201's gratuity provi-sion, the Supreme Court noted that,

> when Congress has wanted to adopt . . . a broadly prophylactic criminal prohibition upon gift giving, it has done so in a more precise and more administrable fashion. . . . [Because] this is an area where precisely targeted prohibitions are commonplace, and where more general prohibitions have been qualified by numerous exceptions . . . a statute in this field that can linguistically be interpreted to be either a meat axe or a scalpel should rea-sonably be taken to be the latter.

526 U.S. at 408, 412. Here, too, we feel obligated to choose the scalpel. Other than the ambiguous use of the word "rewarded," the text of §666, as well as its legislative history and purpose, do not support the argu-ment that Congress intended the statute to reach gratuities. The statute was amended in a way that brought its language closer to §201's bribery provision, and further from §201's gratuity provision, suggesting the true targets of §666 are bribes, not gratuities. Critically, accepting that §666

criminalizes gratuities would expose defendants convicted of gratuities violations under §666 to penalties far greater than those faced by individuals convicted of gratuities violations under §201 — a strange outcome that we doubt Congress intended. We therefore hold that gratuities are not criminalized under §666.[15] . . .

NOTES AND QUESTIONS

1. Which parts of the First Circuit's analysis did you find most persuasive? Least? In United States v. Bahel, 662 F.3d 610 (2d Cir. 2011), the Second Circuit came to a different conclusion as to whether §666 prohibits gratuities.

In United States v. Rooney, 37 F.3d 847 (2d Cir. 1994), we considered the meaning of the term "corrupt" as used in Section 666, concluding that "a fundamental component of a 'corrupt' act is a breach of some official duty owed to the government or the public at large." Id. at 852. We concluded that "[i]t is an obvious violation of duty and public trust for a public official or some other person responsible for parceling out government benefits to accept or demand a personal benefit intending to be improperly influenced in one's official duties." Id. at 853 (collecting cases). Although *Rooney* involved bribery, our analysis of Section 666 in that case, coupled with the plain language and what we referred to as the "conspicuous breadth" of that section, id. at 852, makes clear that, in the case of a gratuity, the corrupt intent required under Section 666 refers to an individual's state of mind at the time the payment is received — Section 666 makes it illegal, inter alia, "to corruptly . . . accept, anything of value from any person, intending to be . . . rewarded in connection

---

15. We . . . acknowledge . . . that the Federal Sentencing Guidelines Manual applies separate guidelines for bribes and gratuities under §201, and it states that *both* of these guidelines are applicable to §666. U.S. Sentencing Guidelines Manual app. A (2011). Some have suggested that this determination on the part of the Sentencing Commission "weighs in favour of a conclusion that §666 encompasses bribes and gratuities." See, e.g., Marks S. Gaioni, Note, Federal Anticorruption Law in the State and Local Context: Defining the Scope of 18 U.S.C. §666.46 Colum. J.L. & Soc. Probs. 207, 239-241 (2012). We disagree. The Sentencing Commission is in the business of "establish[ing] sentencing policies and practices for the Federal criminal justice system" and "develop[ing] means of measuring the degree to which the sentencing, penal, and correctional practices are effective," 28 U.S.C. §991(b); it is not in the business of determining what type of conduct a statute does and does not criminalize. See, e.g., United States v. Morales, 590 F.3d 1049, 1052 (9th Cir.2010) ("Of course, the Commission can't tell Federal courts how to interpet statutes."). The Commission's choice to apply the gratuities guideline to §666 therefore carries no weight in our analysis. Cf. *DePierre v. United States*, 564 U.S. 70, 87 ("We have never held that, when interpreting a criminal statute, deference is warranted to the Sentencing Commission's definition of the same term in the Guidelines."). . . . [Editors' note: The Sentencing Guidelines are examined in Chapter 10.]

with any business, transaction, or series of transactions of such organization." 18 U.S.C. §666(a)(1)(B) (emphasis added). Accordingly, we find no error in the district court's instructions to the jury insofar as they provided that the jury could convict Bahel under Section 666 based on an illegal gratuity theory, and because we conclude that Section 666 covers illegal gratuities, we also find no error in charges in the indictment relating to Section 666 insofar as they were premised on a gratuity theory of liability.

Id. at 638.

You'd think the Supreme Court would want to weigh in on this Circuit split. And it certainly is aware of it, as it noted when *Fernandez* went up on an unrelated double jeopardy issue. 137 S. Ct. 352, 361 n.4 (2016). How do you explain the Court's tolerance of the divided authority? Might it be that true gratuities rarely get prosecuted, since they so often involve repeat players who aren't simply being rewarded but rather expect such payments to continue into the future and affect official behavior? To be sure, *McDonnell* may constrain the use of bribery theories here, but this remains to be seen.

2. Unlike §201, §666 sets a monetary threshold requiring proof that a bribe has been paid in connection with a transaction "involving anything of value of $5000 or more." Courts have allowed the government to aggregate transactions to meet this jurisdictional minimum. See United States v. Newell, 658 F.3d 1, 24 (1st Cir. 2011). But how does this work for intangible benefits? In United States v. Townsend, 630 F.3d 1003 (11th Cir. 2011), a corrections officer, in exchange for bribes, gave a drug dealer indicted on state charges more freedom than was permitted by the terms of his supervised release. Quoting Kris Kristofferson, the Eleventh Circuit mused:

> How should we value freedom and increments of it in monetary terms? There is lyrical authority for the proposition that, "Freedom's just another word for nothin' left to lose / And nothin' ain't worth nothin', but it's free." Rejecting that view in this case, we adopt instead a non-lyrical, free-market approach that pegs the value of freedom and other intangible benefits to the price settled upon by the bribe-giver and the bribe-taker. Under that approach the value in bribes paid by the defendant on pretrial release to his supervising corrections officer in exchange for greater freedom while on release and freedom from jail does satisfy §666(a)(1)(B)'s monetary requirement.

630 F.3d at 1006. Does the court's prosaic approach—which the Seventh Circuit has also used, see United States v. Robinson, 663 F.3d 265 (7th Cir. 2011) (value of diverting police attention from drug trafficking operation)—undercut the statutory threshold? And how does one value government action for which less than $5,000 was paid? See United States v. Owen, 697 F.3d 657 (7th Cir. 2012) (reversing conviction of zoning inspector

who accepted two $600 bribes in exchange for issuing certificates of occupancy for four new homes).

D.   THE FOREIGN CORRUPT PRACTICES ACT

Federal criminal law also reaches bribery of *foreign* public officials in order to "obtain[] or retain[] business." The Foreign Corrupt Practices Act was first enacted in 1977, in the wake of disclosures about widespread bribery of foreign officials by American firms. After considerable legislative negotiation, the Act targeted only those payments designed to induce a foreign official to act corruptly. While the legislative history indicates an effort to exempt "grease payments" intended to induce simply ministerial actions (like the approval of a shipment or the placement of a telephone call), no such exception was written into the statute. American business interests soon pushed for an explicit clarification of the Act, and in 1988, the Act was amended to expressly exempt payments made in order to "expedite or to secure the performance of a routine governmental action. . . ." Ten years later, the Act was amended again, this time in an effort to implement the Organization of Economic Cooperation and Development's Convention of Combating Bribery of Foreign Public Officials in International Business Transactions (OECD Convention). The Act currently prohibits payments to foreign officials (excepting grease payments) for purposes of:

> (i) influencing any act or decision of such foreign official in his official capacity, (ii) inducing such foreign official to do or omit to do any act in violation of the lawful duty of such official, or (iii) securing any improper advantage . . . in order to assist [the firm making the payment] in obtaining or retaining business for or with, or directing business to, any person.

15 U.S.C. §78dd-1(a)(1); see United States v. Kay, 359 F.3d 738, 746-55 (5th Cir. 2004) (recounting the Act's legislative history); Steven R. Salbu, Bribery in the Global Market: A Critical Analysis of the Foreign Corrupt Practices Act, 54 Wash. & Lee L. Rev. 229 (1997); see also Elizabeth Spahn, International Bribery: The Moral Imperialism Critiques, 18 Minn. J. Int'l L. 155 (2009). The Act applies both to corporate entities and to individuals. See United States v. Jefferson, 674 F.3d 332 (4th Cir. 2012) (affirming conviction of congressman under FCPA, among other statutes).

NOTES AND QUESTIONS

1. For decades there were few criminal prosecutions under the FCPA, but the Department of Justice has recently taken renewed interest in

it. The Act is also enforced civilly by both the SEC and the DOJ. In the shadow of these enforcers, an enormous corporate compliance industry has developed. See Rachel Brewster & Samuel W. Buell, The Market for Global Anticorruption Enforcement, 80 L. & Contemp. Probs. 193 (2017); Brandon Garrett, Globalized Corporate Prosecutions, 97 Va. L. Rev. 1775 (2011).

The FCPA statute and its enforcement regime have a number of traits rarely seen in other areas of federal criminal law:

- Congress has explicitly excepted grease payments from the Act, instead of trusting prosecutorial discretion. Why don't we see similar *de minimis* or economic-necessity exceptions in other federal criminal statutes? For an argument favoring elimination of the exception, see Alexandros Zervos, Amending the Foreign Corrupt Practices Act: Repealing the Exemption for Routine Government Action Payments, 25 Penn. St. Int'l L. Rev. 251 (2006).
- FCPA cases are the subject of extraordinary control by Main Justice: Express authorization from Washington is required before an investigation or prosecution can take place. See U.S. Attorneys' Manual, 9-47.110. Consider why no such central approval is required for federal prosecutions of state and local officials.

The risk of criminal liability from a broadly sweeping statute—and the extraordinary scope of corporate liability itself, see Chapter 11—are somewhat ameliorated by the Department of Justice's issuance of advisory opinions. Opinion procedures are catalogued at https://www.justice.gov/sites /default/files/criminal-fraud/legacy/2012/11/14/frgncrpt.pdf; the opinions themselves are available at https://www.justice.gov/criminal-fraud /opinion-procedure-releases. This process enables corporations and individuals doing business abroad to obtain the DOJ's opinion on whether a particular practice violates the FCPA without actually having to partake in that practice. Not only does this let the requesting entity know what behavior the DOJ considers a violation of the FCPA (remember, they sign off on every prosecution), but it also creates a body of advisory opinions that other entities can use to guide their actions. In addition, in late 2012, the Criminal Division of the Department of Justice and the Enforcement Division of the SEC jointly published a detailed "Resource Guide" to the FCPA, including many hypothetical questions and answers. As would be expected, the Guide generally interprets the FCPA to prohibit every payment within the literal terms of the broad statutory language. The Guide is available at https:// www.justice.gov/sites/default/files/criminal-fraud/legacy/2015/01/16 /guide.pdf.

FCPA Blog is devoted to the statute. For more on global anti-corruption efforts, see the website of Transparency International, www.transparency. org.

2. Why do you think Congress acquiesced to industry demands for a *de minimis* exception to the FCPA? Surely, the tight control Main Justice has over FCPA prosecutions would make frivolous prosecutions unlikely. In other instances where criminal prosecution requires Main Justice approval (such as criminal violations of constitutional rights under 18 U.S.C. §241, see Chapter 7), centralized control was deemed sufficient, and no *de minimis* exception was written into law. Similarly, in other bribery statutes—notably the Hobbs Act and §201—there is neither centralized control nor a *de minimis* exception. Even the *de minimis* exception to prosecutions under §666—likely in place as a concession to federalism—is not accompanied by centralized control. So why have both protections in this context?

As we have seen throughout this chapter, gifts to United States officials—whether they are bribes, gratuities, or extorted payments—can form the basis of a successful corruption prosecution, regardless of their size. Is there something that makes similar payments to foreign officials less wrongful? Should it matter whether the payments are made in violation of the law of the foreign nation? The small number of FCPA cases that go to trial make predictions hard. But several recent setbacks in FCPA prosecutions suggest that enforcement efforts will be scrutinized with particular care by judges and juries. See Mike Koehler, What Percentage of DOJ FCPA Losses Is Acceptable?, 90 Crim. L. Rptr. 823 (2012).

3. The FCPA targets bribe payors, not the foreign officials who receive them. The Act itself does not cover the officials, and relying on United States v. Gerbardi, 287 U.S. 112 (1932)—which we discuss in Chapter 8—courts have also barred FCPA conspiracy prosecutions of such officials. See United States v. Castle, 925 F.2d 831 (5th Cir. 1991). Is *Castle* still good law? Or, could a court applying the [allegedly] "age-old principles of conspiracy law" set forth in *Ocasio, supra*, 136 S. Ct. at 1427, find that a bribe-taking foreign official can conspire to bribe him or herself? See Michael F. Dearington, Ocasio v. United States: The Supreme Court's Sudden Expansion of Conspiracy Liability (and Why Bribe-Taking Foreign Officials Should Take Note) (Feb. 27, 2017) (un-published manuscript) (on file with author) (arguing that Ocasio supports this inference); accord Kate Stith, No Entrenchment: Thomas on the Hobbs Act, the Ocasio Mess, and the Vagueness Doctrine, 127 Yale L.J.F. 233 (2017), ("[*Ocasio*] may foretell reconsideration of what constitutes a criminal conspiracy, at least as regards the Hobbs Act. . . . There may also be, waiting in the wings, reconsideration of whether foreign officials may be prosecuted for conspiracy to receive bribes the giving of which was in contravention of the Foreign Corrupt Practices Act."). Can a non-resident foreign national corporate employee be charged as an aider and abettor in connection with a bribe paid to a foreign office? One

court has said "no," United States v. Hoskins, 123 F. Supp. 3d 316 (D. Conn. 2015), and an appeal by the government to the Second Circuit is pending. See Shu-en Wee & Daniel Richman, Bribery Conspiracies, Foreign and Domestic: Ocasio v. United States and Its Implications for FCPA Complicity Theories (with Compliance & Enforcement Blog) (2016).

Can the government prosecute a foreign official who takes a bribe while in the United States for Hobbs Act extortion? In United States v. Mikerin, 8:14-cr-00529 (D. Md. 2016), the court found the FCPA's statutory scheme no bar to a "fear of economic loss" Hobbs Act indictment of a Russian official. (He later pled guilty to another charge.) Might an "under color of law" theory be used against a foreign official visiting the United States who takes a bribe from a United States business seeking, not a level playing field, but a valuable benefit?

7 | Criminal Violations of Constitutional Rights

We have already seen the tension (to put it mildly) between the repeated insistence that there are no federal common-law crimes and the common-law style of interpretation through which federal courts, usually at the behest of federal prosecutors, flesh out such terms as "fraud" and "extortion." An even starker challenge to rule-of-law concerns is presented by the two basic criminal civil rights statutes, 18 U.S.C. §241 and 18 U.S.C. §242. Sections 241 and 242 reach any "conspiracy between two or more people" (§241) or effort "under color of law" (§242) to deprive another of rights secured by the federal Constitution or laws of the United States. The contours of federal constitutional rights change over time through judicial decisions, and can change radically. It is fair to conclude that Americans live under a common-law constitution. See David A. Strauss, The Irrelevance of Constitutional Amendments, 114 Harv. L. Rev. 1457 (2001); David A. Strauss, Common Law Constitutional Interpretation, 63 U. Chi. L. Rev. 877 (1996). Most of the constitutional common lawmaking that sets conduct rules for individuals occurs not in criminal civil rights prosecutions, but in civil lawsuits brought under Bivens v. Six Unknown Named Agents of the Federal Bureau of Narcotics, 403 U.S. 388 (1971) (which creates a civil cause of action for constitutional violations by federal officials), and under 42 U.S.C. §1983 (which provides a civil cause of action for constitutional violations by state and local officials). For this reason, the norm barring common-law crime creation is not relevant to most constitutional litigation. Still, concerns about common lawmaking routinely surface in federal *criminal* litigation under §§241 and 242.*

---

* [Editors' Note: It should be noted that decisions reached in criminal cases often influence later decisions in the civil context. For example, in Monroe v. Pape, 365 U.S. 167 (1961), the Court determined the meaning of "under color of" law in 42 U.S.C. §1983. In so doing, it relied heavily on the definition first applied in United States v. Classic, 313 U.S. 299 (1941); *Classic*, a §242 case, is discussed later in this section.]

---

18 U.S.C. §241. Conspiracy against rights

If two or more persons conspire to injure, oppress, threaten, or intimidate any person . . . in the free exercise or enjoyment of any right or privilege secured to him by the Constitution or laws of the United States, or because of his having so exercised the same; or

If two or more persons go in disguise on the highway, or on the premises of another, with intent to prevent or hinder his free exercise or enjoyment of any right or privilege so secured—

They shall be fined under this title or imprisoned not more than ten years, or both; and if death results from the acts committed in violation of this section or if such acts include kidnapping or an attempt to kidnap, aggravated sexual abuse or an attempt to commit aggravated sexual abuse, or an attempt to kill, they shall be fined under this title or imprisoned for any term of years or for life, or both, or may be sentenced to death.

---

18 U.S.C. §242. Deprivation of rights under color of law

Whoever, under color of any law, statute, ordinance, regulation, or custom, willfully subjects any person . . . to the deprivation of any rights, privileges, or immunities secured or protected by the Constitution or laws of the United States, or to different punishments, pains, or penalties, on account of such person being an alien, or by reason of his color, or race, than are prescribed for the punishment of citizens, shall be fined under this title or imprisoned not more than one year, or both; and if bodily injury results from the acts committed in violation of this section or if such acts include the use, attempted use, or threatened use of a dangerous weapon, explosives, or fire, shall be fined under this title or imprisoned not more than ten years, or both; and if death results from the acts committed in violation of this section or if such acts include kidnapping or an attempt to kidnap, aggravated sexual abuse, or an attempt to commit aggravated sexual abuse, or an attempt to kill, shall be fined under this title, or imprisoned for any term of years or for life, or both, or may be sentenced to death.

THE HISTORY OF CRIMINAL ENFORCEMENT OF CIVIL RIGHTS

1. Congress enacted the precursors to the two federal criminal civil rights statutes excerpted above in the years immediately following the Civil War. Section 242 has its roots in the Civil Rights Act of 1866, which, among other things, targeted civil rights violations committed under color of law. Section 241 has its roots in the Enforcement Act of 1870, which extended criminal enforcement to private (as well as "under color of law") interference with the "free exercise" of a constitutional right. See Frederick M. Lawrence, Civil Rights and Criminal Wrongs: The Mens Rea of Federal Civil Rights Crimes, 67 Tul. L. Rev. 2113, 2138 (1993).

2. The texts of these criminal statutes (and others, like the Ku Klux Klan Act of 1871) seemed to promise a broad federal commitment to protecting the rights of newly freed slaves, and potentially all other Americans as well. Yet, enforcing these broad protections turned out to be harder than the statutes' drafters expected—in part because of resistance by the federal judiciary, which seemed to balk at "legal theories that affirmed the primacy of national authority to enforce and protect fundamental rights." Robert J. Kaczorowski, The Politics of Judicial Interpretation: The Federal Courts, Department of Justice and Civil Rights, 1866-1876 xxiii-xxiv (1985). In short order, federal judges—especially Supreme Court Justices—would considerably narrow the broad crimes defined by Congress.

The Slaughter-House Cases, 83 U.S. (16 Wall.) 36 (1873), articulated a very limited notion of the rights protected by federal constitutional law. The Privileges and Immunities Clause of the Fourteenth Amendment, the Court held, simply protected interests that were already protected by other federal provisions, and did not give the federal government plenary power to enforce unenumerated fundamental rights. The implications of this decision soon became clear in United States v. Cruikshank, 92 U.S. 542 (1876), "the first Supreme Court case to review a conviction for a civil rights crime." Lawrence, *supra*, at 2151.

In April 1873, after supporters of the Republican claimants to local office sealed off the village of Colfax, Louisiana, in an election dispute, a group of white Democrats attacked them with rifles and a small cannon. As many as 150 Black people may have been killed in what came to be known as "the Colfax massacre." Within days, President Grant's Attorney General, George H. Williams, directed the U.S. Attorney for Louisiana, James R. Beckwith, to investigate and seek indictments against those responsible for the massacre. Many of the perpetrators escaped apprehension, and of the 97 defendants indicted under the Enforcement Act of 1870, only nine went to trial. They were charged with conspiring to deprive two victims—"citizens of the United States, of African descent and persons of color," Cruikshank, 92 U.S. at 548—of the rights to assemble peacefully, to bear arms, to vote, and not to be deprived of life, liberty, or property without due process of law. Six were acquitted, and three convicted, but Supreme Court Justice Joseph P. Bradley, presiding over the trial as Circuit Justice, granted defendants' motion to overturn the verdicts. See United States v. Cruikshank, 25 F. Cas. 707 (C.C.D. La. 1874). Bradley, applying the *Slaughterhouse* decision from which he had dissented, found that the Fourteenth Amendment did not confer any rights by itself, and authorized federal enforcement action only where a state had violated an existing federal right. He also concluded that the Fifteenth Amendment merely conferred a right not to be excluded from voting by reason of race or color—not a right to vote. Further, although the Thirteenth Amendment did give the federal government authority over crimes committed with racial animus, Bradley held that most of the counts in the indictment in the case failed to allege racial motivation. Because the Court, in the *Slaughterhouse Cases*, had "affirmed the primacy of state authority over the butchers' fundamental rights, it could not easily assert the primacy of national authority over the fundamental rights of the freedmen." Kaczorowski, *supra*, at 184. And neither the politics of the late 1800s, nor the accepted legal theories of that time, compelled the Court to look hard for a distinction. Id. at 184-85.

Thereafter, the Supreme Court adopted Justice Bradley's restrictive view of the Fourteenth Amendment in an opinion by Chief Justice Waite. United States v. Cruikshank, 92 U.S. 542 (1876); see also McDonald v. City of Chicago, 130 S. Ct. 3020, 3030 (2010); id. at 3060 (Thomas, J., concurring) (discussing *Cruikshank*). Bradley's restrictive view of the Fifteenth Amendment was adopted in another case, handed down the same day as *Cruikshank*, United States v. Reese, 92 U.S. 214 (1876). And shortly thereafter, in the Civil Rights Cases, 109 U.S. 3 (1883), Bradley abandoned his view that the Thirteenth Amendment can be a source of federal jurisdiction over racially motivated crimes. See Lawrence, *supra*, at 2152-63.

3. The executive branch's commitment to enforcing civil rights also waned. In 1873, only two years after the passage of the Klan Act, and seven years after the Civil Rights Act of 1866, President Grant "ordered the Department of Justice to stop bringing prosecutions against Southern lawbreakers, and he pardoned those who earlier had been convicted and incarcerated by the federal courts." Kaczorowski, *supra*, at xxiv. The enforcement void resulted in a surge of violence throughout the South. Yet, in 1874, when the Attorney General "ordered a resumption of federal prosecution of civil rights violators," he discovered that the *Slaughterhouse Cases, Cruikshank*, and their progeny meant that "the federal courts no longer recognized federal jurisdiction over the administration of criminal justice." Id. As a result, civil rights enforcement in the South was left to local law and local law enforcement agencies—institutions either "unable or unwilling to redress civil rights violations." Id. See also Jack Balkin, The Reconstruction Power, 85 N.Y.U. L. Rev. 1801, 1845 (2010) ("*Cruikshank*'s crabbed, unsympathetic reading of the Constitution and Congress's 1870 Enforcement Act made it quite difficult for blacks to protect their constitutional rights in the face of a systematic campaign of terror and violence in the South.").

The Reconstruction rights-enforcement project was also quickly deprived of enforcement personnel. Federal marshals—responsible for enforcing the civil rights statutes—could not have done their work in the South without support from the Army. Opposition to this military assistance, and particularly to the role federal troops played in supervising elections, led to the Posse Comitatus Act of 1878, which outlaws the use of military units to enforce federal law absent express congressional or constitutional authorization. See Charles Doyle & Jennifer K. Elsea, The Posse Comitatus Act and Related Matters: The Use of the Military to Execute Civilian Law (2012) (CRS Report); Andrew Buttaro, The Posse Comitatus Act of 1878 and the End of Reconstruction, 47 St. Mary's L.J. 135 (2015); see also Richard White, The Republic For Which It Stands 336 (2017) ("After 1877 federal troops would for the rest of the nineteenth century never be deployed to protect the constitutional rights of black citizens.")

4. After *Cruikshank*, §§241 and 242 were largely ignored. The Court, motivated by an "overriding concern [for] the preservation of state police powers from what they perceived as a potential usurpation by the national government," Kaczorowski, *supra*, at 149, had all but eliminated the power of the federal government to enforce its view of civil rights. Frederick Lawrence reports: "No aggressive federal criminal civil rights enforcement occurred from the mid-1870's until the mid-1930's. Congress passed no civil rights crimes legislation, the enforcement policies of the Department of Justice were modest at best, and the courts generally were unsympathetic to those prosecutions that were brought." Lawrence, *supra*, at 2166; see also Jeffery A. Jenkins, Justin Peck & Vesla Weaver, Between Reconstructions: Congressional Action on Civil Rights, 1891-1940, 24 Stud. in Am. Pol. Dev. 57 (2010) (recounting failed anti-lynching initiatives in Congress).

5. A new era of criminal civil rights enforcement came with the election of Franklin Roosevelt and the creation by his Attorney General, Frank Murphy, of the Civil Rights Section of the Department of Justice. "Establishment of the Unit was solely an act of administrative discretion. Congress did not create it by law; Congress was asked for no new legislation giving it additional authority beyond that already existing." Robert K. Carr, Federal Protection of Civil Rights: Quest for a Sword 29 (1947); see generally Brian K. Landsberg, Enforcing Civil Rights: Race Discrimination and the Department of Justice (1997).

In keeping with this effort to work with existing legislative frameworks, the "conceptual core" of the new Section's prosecutions initially involved violations of the Thirteenth Amendment—the anti-slavery provision that incontestably targeted private as well as state action. Risa L. Goluboff, The Lost Promise of Civil Rights 142 (2007). The Peonage Act of 1867 proved to be a potent tool for attacking not just cases of involuntary servitude accomplished through debt, violence, and legal coercion, but also "extreme forms of economic coercion." Id. at 143. (Forced labor prosecutions are still being brought. See United States v. Murra, 879 F.3d 669 (5th Cir. 2018); United States v. Sabhnani, 599 F.3d 215 (2d Cir. 2010)).

The Civil Rights Section's first major Supreme Court case, United States v. Classic, 313 U.S. 299 (1941), similarly reflected the Section's commitment to incremental doctrinal expansion. *Classic* arose out of the prosecution of members of a "reform" movement that was challenging the remnants of the Huey Long machine in a state primary election in Louisiana; the defendants were charged (under precursors of §§241 and 242) with depriving voters of their right to have their votes properly counted. Carr, *supra*, at 85. The voters so victimized were White; but since the whole idea of excluding African Americans from ostensibly "private" primaries was being challenged at around that time in litigation brought by the NAACP, "most contemporaries," including (soon to be) Chief Justice Stone, "assumed" that the case had racial implications. See Michael J. Klarman, From Jim Crow to Civil Rights: The Supreme Court and the Struggle for Racial Equality 198 (2004). Few were surprised, then, when three years after *Classic*, the Supreme Court declared white primaries unconstitutional in Smith v. Allwright, 321 U.S. 649 (1944), see Klarman, *supra*, at 198-99.

In *Classic*, the Court held that the right of qualified voters to have their votes counted in a primary election was a right "secured by the Constitution," and that conspiracies to infringe upon that right could properly be prosecuted under the general federal criminal civil rights provisions codified in §§241 and 242. Justice William O. Douglas dissented. "It is one thing," he noted, "to allow wide and generous scope to the express and implied powers of Congress; it is distinctly another to read into the vague and general language of an act of Congress specifications of crimes." 313 U.S. at 331 (Douglas, J., dissenting). This concern with the breadth and vagueness of constitutionally based criminal offenses would lie at the heart of the Court's subsequent efforts to define each element of these crimes. In the following case, Justice Douglas—despite his dissent in *Classic*—wrote for the Court in upholding the broad language of 18 U.S.C. §242, while reading in a heightened *mens rea* requirement.

A. DEPRIVATION OF RIGHTS UNDER COLOR OF LAW

1. "WILLFULLY"

Screws v. United States
325 U.S. 91 (1945)

Mr. Justice DOUGLAS announced the judgment of the Court and delivered the following opinion, in which THE CHIEF JUSTICE, Mr. Justice BLACK and Mr. Justice REED, concur.

This case involves a shocking and revolting episode in law enforcement. Petitioner Screws was sheriff of Baker County, Georgia. He enlisted the assistance of petitioner Jones, a policeman, and petitioner Kelley, a special deputy, in arresting Robert Hall, a citizen of the United States and of Georgia. The arrest was made late at night at Hall's home on a warrant charging Hall with theft of a tire. Hall, a young negro about thirty years of age, was handcuffed and taken by car to the court house. As Hall alighted from the car at the courthouse square, the three petitioners began beating him with their fists and with a solid-bar blackjack about eight inches long and weighing two pounds. They claimed Hall had reached for a gun and had used insulting language as he alighted from the car. But after Hall, still handcuffed, had been knocked to the ground they continued to beat him from fifteen to thirty minutes until he was unconscious. Hall was then dragged feet first through the court house yard into the jail and thrown upon the floor dying. An ambulance was called and Hall was removed to a hospital where he died within the hour and without regaining consciousness. There was evidence that Screws held a grudge against Hall and had threatened to "get" him.

An indictment was returned against petitioners — one count charging a violation of §20 of the Criminal Code, 18 U.S.C. §52 [now 18 U.S.C. §242], and another charging a conspiracy to violate §20 contrary to §37 of the Criminal Code, 18 U.S.C. §88 [now 18 U.S.C. §371]. Sec. 20 provides:

> Whoever, under color of any law, statute, ordinance, regulation, or custom, willfully subjects, or causes to be subjected, any inhabitant of any State, Territory, or District to the deprivation of any rights, privileges, or immunities secured or protected by the Constitution and laws of the United States, or to different punishments, pains, or penalties, on account of such inhabitant being an alien, or by reason of his color, or race, than are prescribed for the punishment of citizens, shall be fined not more than $1,000, or imprisoned not more than one year, or both.

The indictment charged that petitioners, acting under color of the laws of Georgia, "willfully" caused Hall to be deprived of "rights, privileges, or immunities secured or protected" to him by the Fourteenth Amendment — the right not to be deprived of life without due process of law; the right to be tried, upon the charge on which he was arrested, by due process of law and if found guilty to be punished in accordance with the laws of Georgia; that is to say that petitioners "unlawfully and wrongfully did assault, strike and beat the said Robert Hall about the head with human fists and a blackjack causing injuries" to Hall "which were the proximate and immediate cause of his death." A like charge was made in the conspiracy count.

The case was tried to a jury. The court charged the jury that due process of law gave one charged with a crime the right to be tried by a jury and sentenced by a court. On the question of intent it charged that

> ... if these defendants, without its being necessary to make the arrest effectual or necessary to their own personal protection, beat this man, assaulted him or killed him while he was under arrest, then they would be acting

> illegally under color of law, as stated by this statute, and would be depriving the prisoner of certain constitutional rights guaranteed to him by the Constitution of the United States and consented to by the State of Georgia.

The jury returned a verdict of guilty and a fine and imprisonment on each count was imposed. The Circuit Court of Appeals affirmed the judgment of conviction, one judge dissenting. 140 F.2d 662. The case is here on a petition for a writ of certiorari which we granted because of the importance in the administration of the criminal laws of the questions presented.

I

We are met at the outset with the claim that §20 is unconstitutional, insofar as it makes criminal acts in violation of the due process clause of the Fourteenth Amendment. The argument runs as follows: It is true that this Act as construed in United States v. Classic, 313 U.S. 299, 328 [(1941)], was upheld in its application to certain ballot box frauds committed by state officials. But in that case the constitutional rights protected were the rights to vote specifically guaranteed by Art. I, §2 and §4 of the Constitution. Here there is no ascertainable standard of guilt. There have been conflicting views in the Court as to the proper construction of the due process clause. The majority have quite consistently construed it in broad general terms. . . . In Snyder v. Massachusetts, 291 U.S. 97, 105 [(1934)], it was said that due process prevents state action which "offends some principle of justice so rooted in the traditions and conscience of our people as to be ranked as fundamental." The same standard was expressed in Palko v. Connecticut, 302 U.S. 319, 325 [(1937)], in terms of a "scheme of ordered liberty." And the same idea was recently phrased as follows:

> The phrase formulates a concept less rigid and more fluid than those envisaged in other specific and particular provisions of the Bill of Rights. Its application is less a matter of rule. Asserted denial is to be tested by an appraisal of the totality of facts in a given case. That which may, in one setting, constitute a denial of fundamental fairness, shocking to the universal sense of justice, may, in other circumstances, and in the light of other considerations, fall short of such denial.

Betts v. Brady, 316 U.S. 455, 462 [(1942)].

It is said that the Act must be read as if it contained those broad and fluid definitions of due process and that if it is so read it provides no ascertainable standard of guilt. . . . In the instant case the decisions of the courts are, to be sure, a source of reference for ascertaining the specific content of the concept of due process. But even so the Act would incorporate by reference a large body of changing and uncertain law. That law is not always reducible to specific rules, is expressible only in general terms, and turns many times on the facts of a particular case. Accordingly, it is argued that such a body of legal principles lacks the basic specificity necessary for criminal statutes under our system of government. Congress did not define what it desired to punish but referred the citizen to a comprehensive law library in order to ascertain what acts were prohibited. To enforce such a statute would be like sanctioning the practice of Caligula who "published the law, but it was written in a very small hand, and posted up in a corner, so that no one could make a copy of it." Suetonius, Lives of the Twelve Caesars, p. 278.

The serious character of that challenge to the constitutionality of the Act is emphasized if the customary standard of guilt for statutory crimes is taken. As we shall see, specific intent is at times required. Holmes, The Common Law, pp. 66 et seq. But the general rule was stated in Ellis v. United States, 206 U.S. 246, 257 [(1907)], as follows: "If a man intentionally adopts certain conduct in certain circumstances known to him, and that conduct is forbidden by the law under those circumstances, he intentionally breaks the law in the only sense in which the law ever considers intent." Under that test a local law enforcement officer violates §20 and commits a federal offense for which he can be sent to the penitentiary if he does an act which some court later holds deprives a person of due process of law. And he is a criminal though his motive was pure and though his purpose was unrelated to the disregard of any constitutional guarantee. The treacherous ground on which state officials—police, prosecutors, legislators, and judges—would walk is indicated by the character and closeness of decisions of this Court interpreting the due process clause of the Fourteenth Amendment. A confession obtained by too long questioning (Ashcraft v. Tennessee, 322 U.S. 143 [(1944)]); the enforcement of an ordinance requiring a license for the distribution of religious literature (Murdock v. Pennsylvania, 319 U.S. 105 [(1943)]); the denial of the assistance of counsel in certain types of cases (Cf. Powell v. Alabama, 287 U.S. 45 [(1932)]); the enforcement of certain types of anti-picketing statutes (Thornhill v. Alabama, 310 U.S. 88 [(1940)]); the enforcement of state price control laws (Olsen v. Nebraska, 313 U.S. 236 [(1941)]); the requirement that public school children salute the flag (Board of Education v. Barnette, 319 U.S. 624 [(1943)])—these are illustrative of the kind of state action which might or might not be caught in the broad reaches of §20 dependent on the prevailing view of the Court as constituted when the case arose. Those who enforced local law today might not know for many months (and meanwhile could not find out) whether what they did deprived some one of due process of law. The enforcement of a criminal statute so construed would indeed cast law enforcement agencies loose at their own risk on a vast uncharted sea.

If such a construction is not necessary, it should be avoided. . . . Sec. 20 was enacted to enforce the Fourteenth Amendment. It derives from

§2 of the Civil Rights Act of April 9, 1866. 14 Stat. 27. Senator Trumbull, chairman of the Senate Judiciary Committee which reported the bill, stated that its purpose was "to protect all persons in the United States in their civil rights, and furnish the means of their vindication." In origin it was an antidiscrimination measure (as its language indicated), framed to protect Negroes in their newly won rights. It was amended by §17 of the Act of May 31, 1870, 16 Stat. 144, and made applicable to "any inhabitant of any State or Territory." The prohibition against the "deprivation of any rights, privileges, or immunities, secured or protected by the Constitution and laws of the United States" was introduced by the revisers in 1874. R. S. §5510. Those words were taken over from §1 of the Act of April 20, 1871, 17 Stat. 13 (the so-called Ku-Klux Act) which provided civil suits for redress of such wrongs. The 1874 revision was applicable to any person who under color of law, etc., "subjects, or causes to be subjected" any inhabitant to the deprivation of any rights, etc. The requirement for a "willful" violation was introduced by the draftsmen of the Criminal Code of 1909. And we are told "willfully" was added to §20 in order to make the section "less severe." 43 Cong. Rec., 60th Cong., 2nd Sess., p. 3599.

We hesitate to say that when Congress sought to enforce the Fourteenth Amendment in this fashion it did a vain thing. We hesitate to conclude that for 80 years this effort of Congress, renewed several times, to protect the important rights of the individual guaranteed by the Fourteenth Amendment has been an idle gesture. . . . Only if no construction can save the Act from this claim of unconstitutionality are we willing to reach that result. We do not reach it, for we are of the view that if §20 is confined more narrowly than the lower courts confined it, it can be preserved as one of the sanctions to the great rights which the Fourteenth Amendment was designed to secure.

II

We recently pointed out that "willful" is a word "of many meanings, its construction often being influenced by its context." Spies v. United States, 317 U.S. 492, 497 [(1943)]. At times, . . . the word denotes an act which is intentional rather than accidental. But "when used in a criminal statute it generally means an act done with a bad purpose." [United States v. Illinois Central R. Co., 303 U.S. 239, 394 (1938)]. In that event something more is required than the doing of the act proscribed by the statute. An evil motive to accomplish that which the statute condemns becomes a constituent element of the crime. And that issue must be submitted to the jury under appropriate instructions. . . .

Once the section is given that construction, we think that the claim that the section lacks an ascertainable standard of guilt must fail. The constitutional requirement that a criminal statute be definite serves a high function. It gives a person acting with reference to the statute fair warning that his conduct is within its prohibition. This requirement is met when a statute prohibits only "willful" acts in the sense we have explained. One who does act with such specific intent is aware that what he does is precisely that which the statute forbids. He is under no necessity of guessing whether the statute applies to him for he either knows or acts in reckless disregard of its prohibition of the deprivation of a defined constitutional or other federal right. Nor is such an act beyond the understanding and comprehension of juries summoned to pass on them. The Act would then not become a trap for law enforcement agencies acting in good faith. "A mind intent upon willful evasion is inconsistent with surprised innocence." United States v. Ragen, [314 U.S. 513, 524 (1942)].

It is said, however, that. . .neither a law enforcement official nor a trial judge can know with sufficient definiteness the range of rights that are constitutional. But that criticism is wide of the mark. For the specific intent required by the Act is an intent to deprive a person of a right which has been made specific either by the express terms of the Constitution or laws of the United States or by decisions interpreting them. Take the case of a local officer who persists in enforcing a type of ordinance which the Court has held invalid as violative of the guarantees of free speech or freedom of worship. Or a local official continues to select juries in a manner which flies in the teeth of decisions of the Court. If those acts are done willfully, how can the officer possibly claim that he had no fair warning that his acts were prohibited by the statute? He violates the statute not merely because he has a bad purpose but because he acts in defiance of announced rules of law. He who defies a decision interpreting the Constitution knows precisely what he is doing. . . . Of course, willful conduct cannot make definite that which is undefined. But willful violators of constitutional requirements, which have been defined, certainly are in no position to say that they had no adequate advance notice that they would be visited with punishment. When they act willfully in the sense in which we use the word, they act in open defiance or in reckless disregard of a constitutional requirement which has been made specific and definite. When they are convicted for so acting, they are not punished for violating an unknowable something. . . .

United States v. Classic, [313 U.S. 299 (1941)], met the test we suggest. In that case we were dealing merely with the validity of an indictment, not with instructions to the jury. The indictment was sufficient since it charged a willful failure and refusal of the defendant election officials to count the votes cast, by their alteration of the ballots and by their false certification of the number of votes cast for the respective candidates. 313 U.S. pp. 308-309. The right so to vote is guaranteed by Art. I, §2 and §4 of the Constitution. Such a charge is adequate since he who alters ballots or without legal justification destroys them would be acting willfully in the sense in which §20 uses the term. The fact that the defendants may not have been thinking in constitutional terms is not material where their aim was not to enforce local law but to deprive a citizen of a right and that right was protected by the Constitution. When they so act they at least act in reckless disregard of constitutional prohibitions or guarantees. Likewise, it is plain that basic to the concept of due process of law in a criminal case is a trial—a trial in a court of law, not a "trial by ordeal." Brown v. Mississippi, 297 U.S. 278, 285 [(1936)]. It could hardly be doubted that they who "under color of any law, statute, ordinance, regulation, or custom" act with that evil motive violate §20. Those who decide to take the law into their own hands and act as prosecutor, jury, judge, and executioner plainly act to deprive a prisoner of the trial which due process of law guarantees him. And such a purpose need not be expressed; it may at times be reasonably inferred from all the circumstances attendant on the act.

The difficulty here is that this question of intent was not submitted to the jury with the proper instructions. The court charged that petitioners acted illegally if they applied more force than was necessary to make the arrest effectual or to protect themselves from the prisoner's alleged assault. But in view of our construction of the word "willfully" the jury should have been further instructed that it was not sufficient that petitioners had a generally bad purpose. To convict it was necessary for them to find that petitioners had the purpose to deprive the prisoner of a constitutional right, e.g. the right to be tried by a court rather than by ordeal. And in determining whether that requisite bad purpose was present the jury would be entitled to consider all the attendant circumstances—the malice of petitioners, the weapons used in the assault, its character and duration, the provocation, if any, and the like.

It is true that no exception was taken to the trial court's charge. Normally we would under those circumstances not take note of the error. But there are exceptions to that rule. And where the error is so fundamental as not to submit to the jury the essential ingredients of the only offense on which the conviction could rest, we think it is necessary to take note of it on our own motion. Even those guilty of the most heinous offenses are entitled to a fair trial. Whatever the degree of guilt, those charged with a federal crime are entitled to be tried by the standards of guilt which Congress has prescribed. . . .

Since there must be a new trial, the judgment below is *Reversed*.

[Justice Rutledge's concurrence in the judgment, Justice Murphy's dissent, and Justice Roberts' dissent, joined by Justices Frankfurter and Jackson, are omitted.]

NOTES AND QUESTIONS

1. What is Justice Douglas worried about? What possible unfairness can there be in punishing Screws for Hall's murder? If the answer is "none," what is the point of the *mens rea* standard that Douglas articulates in *Screws*?

2. *Screws* produced an odd vote. The four Justices in the plurality opinion written by Justice Douglas voted to overturn the conviction on the ground that the *mens rea* standard applied below was insufficiently protective. Justice Murphy (who as Attorney General had created the Civil Rights Section) wrote an impassioned dissent, arguing that Screws' conviction should be affirmed:

> [T]he right not to be deprived of life without due process of law is distinctly and lucidly protected by the Fourteenth Amendment. There is nothing vague or indefinite in these references to this most basic of all human rights. Knowledge of a comprehensive law library is unnecessary for officers of the law to know that the right to murder individuals in the course of their duties is unrecognized in this nation. No appreciable amount of intelligence or conjecture on the part of the lowliest state official is needed for him to realize that fact; nor should it surprise him to find out that the Constitution protects persons from his reckless disregard of human life and that statutes punish him therefor. To subject a state official to punishment under §20 for such acts is not to penalize him without fair and definite warning. Rather it is to uphold elementary standards of decency and to make American principles of law and our constitutional guarantees mean something more than pious rhetoric.

325 U.S. at 136. Justices Roberts, Frankfurter, and Jackson dissented on very different grounds: They argued that only Georgia had the legal authority to punish Screws' heinous conduct—otherwise, §242 would transform "every lawless act of the policeman on the beat or in the station house" into a federal offense. Id. at 144. (You will recall similar federalism concerns in some of the opinions—mostly dissents—in Chapter 2.) Would that be a bad idea? The Roberts dissent also argued that Screws' misconduct did not happen "under color of" state law, as it was "perpetrated by State officers *in flagrant defiance* of State law." Id. at 148 (emphasis added). (This aspect of the *Screws* opinion is considered in Section A.3, *infra*.)

Justice Rutledge cast the decisive vote. On the merits, Rutledge agreed with Murphy; his preference was to affirm the conviction. But a vote to affirm would have left the lower courts in an impossible position, with seven of the nine Justices voting to reverse, six of the nine upholding the lower court's "under color of law" finding, and only four of the nine rejecting the lower court's definition of willfulness. So Rutledge concurred in the judgment—meaning, in effect, he accepted the plurality's bottom line because of the need for a disposition in the case, though he objected to the reasoning that produced it.

Despite the unclear guidance provided by *Screws*, the statute's mere endurance arguably provided a major victory in the history of civil rights litigation. Judge Paul Watford argues that *Screws* paved the way for modern federal criminal prosecution of racially motivated crimes and acts of police brutality.

The most important legacy of *Screws* is that Section 242 survived. And that had importance in terms of both its direct impact on police brutality cases like Screws and its more indirect effect on the broader social changes that occurred in the decades that followed. In terms of its most immediate effect, the survival of Section 242 meant that the federal government would have a role in combating the widespread problem of police brutality toward African Americans and other minorities, particularly in the South. Had the statute instead been struck down, the power of the federal government to prosecute such abuses would have been drastically curtailed. No other statute remained that would have allowed the federal government to prosecute violations of the most basic rights under the Fourteenth Amendment.

Paul J. Watford, Screws v. United States and the Birth of Federal Civil Rights Enforcement, 98 Marq. L. Rev. 465, 483 (2014).

3. The biggest surprise in *Screws* is that the defendant was prosecuted and convicted in the first place—not exactly a common occurrence in the South in the 1940s. For an excellent discussion of the case and its background, see Klarman, *supra*, at 269-71. Baker County, Georgia, where Claude Screws was sheriff, had a population of only 700 or 800 people, and, as Francis Biddle (then Solicitor General and later Attorney General) recalled, every juror "must have personally known the defendants." Francis Biddle, In Brief Authority 157 (1962). The requirement of trial by locally selected juries, together with the then-universal practice of excluding blacks from Southern juries, made criminal prosecution difficult at best in cases like *Screws*. The nature of the relationship between federal and state authorities further hampered effective prosecution: Federal investigations frequently required the cooperation of local police—cooperation that was a good deal harder to obtain if local police forces saw federal officials as potential adversaries.

4. Justice Douglas likely assumed that, given the requisite instructions, a jury would convict again—after all, *Screws* appeared to be a straightforward case on its facts. But Screws was acquitted on retrial. Robert Carr notes that "it would have been little short of a miracle had the federal government persuaded two southern juries, deciding the same case, to vote to convict white men for a crime committed against a Negro." According to one of the prosecutors in the case, part of the reason for the different result in the second trial was the willfulness element: "The jury tended to believe that the personal side of the quarrel between Screws and Hall was extremely important, thus making it more difficult for the government to convince them that Screws had willfully used his authority as sheriff to deprive Hall of his constitutional rights." Robert K. Carr, Federal Protection of Civil Rights: Quest for a Sword 29, 114-15 (1947). Several years after his acquittal, Screws was elected to the Georgia state senate. See Frederick Lawrence, Punishing Hate: Bias Crimes Under American Law 136 (1999).

5. What did Justice Douglas mean in *Screws* when he required that the government prove not just that the defendants had a "generally bad purpose," but that they "had the purpose to deprive the prisoner of a constitutional right"? Must defendants be "thinking in constitutional terms"? Surely not, Douglas says. It is enough that their "aim was not to enforce local law but to deprive a citizen of a right. . . . When they so act they at least act in reckless disregard of constitutional prohibitions or guarantees." 325 U.S. at 106. But what does this actually mean? That mere reckless disregard is enough to satisfy the *mens rea* requirement? If so, that would make police brutality cases far easier to bring and would help to extend the application of the criminal civil rights statutes beyond standard civil rights enforcement. What effect would such a *mens rea* standard have on the vagueness problem that Douglas purported to address? Frederick Lawrence answers:

> This alternative formulation of Justice Douglas' standard, although far more realistic than the constitutionally specific intent standard, fails to solve the vagueness problem. Whereas the defendant who consciously intended to deprive Robert Hall of a constitutional right could not fairly contend that he lacked knowledge of that constitutional right, the same cannot be said of the defendant who neither thought in constitutional terms, nor even consciously disregarded any constitutional rights of his victim. This defendant could complain that, although he had fair warning that his conduct violated state law, he had no similar warning that his conduct violated constitutional rights and thus federal law.

Lawrence, *supra*, 67 Tul. L. Rev. at 2185. Judge Edward Becker later observed:

> As is evident from the text, and has oft been noted, *Screws* is not a model of clarity. Some of the sentences therein, examined in isolation, resist easy explanation and can be reconciled only by way of tortuous logic. Our task, however, is to read these sentences in light of the text of *Screws* in its entirety. The plurality in *Screws* believed its pronouncements to be consistent; we must do the same.

United States v. Johnstone, 107 F.3d 200, 208 (3d Cir. 1997). Judge Becker concluded:

> In simpler terms, "willful[]" in §242 means either particular purpose or reckless disregard. Therefore, it is enough to trigger §242 liability if it can be proved—by circumstantial evidence or otherwise—that a defendant exhibited reckless disregard for a constitutional or federal right. Reckless disregard has different meanings in different contexts. In the context of §242, we have only *Screws* to guide us.

Id. at 208-09. How much guidance does *Screws* actually provide? How should it be applied to less egregious police misconduct? Consider United States v. Bradley, the next excerpted case.

6. Although §242 and §241 survived *Screws*, they have never been commonly employed. What is perhaps most surprising about federal enforcement of §§241 and 242 is not the extent of judicial power, but the infrequency of the cases. In fiscal year 2016, only 137 civil rights prosecutions were brought against 245 defendants, U.S. Attorneys' Annual Statistical Report, FY 2016, at 11 tbl. 3A. In a nation in which police make 13 million arrests each year, and in which constitutional law governs nearly every aspect of arrest, search and seizure, and police interrogation (not to mention the interaction of correction officers with inmates), that number may seem quite small. Why are federal constitutional rights so rarely enforced through criminal prosecution? Should federal prosecutors bring more cases? If so, which kinds? Consider these questions as you read the material that follows.

7. One reason that there are so few cases brought under §§241 and 242 is the relatively strict centralized control asserted by Main Justice. At the outset of an investigation into a violation of either statute, the United States Attorney must "advise the Civil Rights Division in writing." United States Attorneys' Manual, 8-3.120. While prior approval to indict is only required when "the case has been deemed by the Assistant Attorney General as a case of national interest," prior notice of a pending indictment must be given. Id. at 8-3.140. As a result, it is unlikely that a case will move forward absent at least informal approval by Main Justice, particularly because "[t]he Assistant Attorney General of the Civil Rights Division retains the final and on-going authority to determine the staffing of any criminal civil rights matter." Id. at 8-3.120. Lawyers from the Criminal Section of the Civil Rights Division—located in Washington, with no field offices—will generally coordinate with local law enforcement, local FBI agents, and local prosecutors to bring cases across the United States. What effect do you think the centralized, and somewhat removed, nature of the Criminal Section has on the type of civil rights cases brought and how they are prosecuted? If you were charged with creating the organizational design for identifying and prosecuting violations of the federal civil rights laws, what would that scheme look like? Recall Professor Kahan's proposal and the questions posed in Chapter 4.

—————————————

In the next case, we see that ordinary assaults and other crimes when committed by agents of the government, such as police officers, may be prosecuted under §242 even when no racial motivation is apparent.

United States v. Bradley
196 F.3d 762 (7th Cir. 1999)

Bauer, Circuit Judge.

A jury convicted former police officer Adolph Bradley ("Bradley") on one count of willfully depriving a person of constitutional rights under color of law in violation of 18 U.S.C. §242. . . . Bradley now appeals his conviction. . . .

The facts of this case read like something out of a *Dirty Harry* movie. . . . Bradley is a 72-year-old man who has spent more than forty years of his life working as a law enforcement officer in small towns throughout southern Illinois. . . . Up until the events that led to Bradley's criminal prosecution and conviction, Bradley had enjoyed a good reputation as a police officer and had strong ties with members of the communities in which he worked.

On June 30, 1998, Bradley was a police officer with the Brooklyn, Illinois Police Department and began working the 11:00 p.m. to 7:00 a.m. shift with his partner, officer Khalid Ashkar ("Ashkar"). That night, Bradley and Ashkar were patrolling the streets of Brooklyn in an unmarked black Chevrolet Caprice that had police emergency lights on the inside front and rear dashboards of the car, but otherwise resembled a civilian car. . . . Ashkar was driving the unmarked police car. Bradley was armed with a six-inch Smith & Wesson .357 magnum revolver loaded with hollow point bullets.

On the morning of July 1, 1998 at about 5:30 a.m., a 60-year-old resident of southern Illinois named Roosevelt Marshall was driving his 1984 Dodge Aries station wagon from his home in Lovejoy, Illinois to his job at the Cahokia, Illinois School District. While on patrol, Bradley and Ashkar observed Marshall's station wagon roll through a stop sign and decided to stop the station wagon for this traffic violation. Ashkar and Bradley began following the station wagon and activated the red emergency light on the front dashboard of their unmarked car. Marshall continued driving at a speed of about 25 miles per hour and did not stop. Later Marshall said he did not recognize the unmarked vehicle following him as a police car. Neither Bradley nor Ashkar could see who was driving the station wagon they were pursuing.

As Ashkar drove the unmarked police car within twelve feet of the station wagon, Bradley suddenly drew his .357 revolver, leaned out the window of the moving patrol car, and fired one shot. Although Ashkar testified that he could not see in what direction Bradley fired, Bradley claimed that he merely fired a warning shot into the air and did not take aim at the station wagon. Marshall, still driving in what had now become a low-speed chase, heard the gunshot but did not stop. Seconds later, Bradley again leaned out the window with his .357 in hand and this time took aim at the driver of the station wagon. With his second shot, Bradley blasted a hollow point bullet through the rear tailgate of Marshall's station wagon; the bullet then passed through some shoe-shine equipment in the rear of Marshall's car and pierced the cushion and steel plate of the rear passenger seat. The bullet penetrated the padding in the back of the driver's seat where Marshall was seated and became embedded in a steel plate directly in line with Marshall's back. Marshall felt a shock in his back. After hearing the second shot and feeling the blow to his back, Marshall pulled over his car. . . .

Bradley got out of the police car with his .357 drawn and ordered Marshall out of the station wagon by shouting, "get out of this car mother fucker before I blow your God damned brains out!" When Marshall emerged from the vehicle, Bradley and Marshall recognized each other, as they had been boyhood friends. Bradley told Marshall that he had run a stop sign and asked Marshall why he did not stop when he saw the police lights. After a brief exchange, Bradley let Marshall leave and did not issue Marshall a traffic citation. . . .

After the shooting, Marshall went to the FBI office in Fairview Heights, Illinois and reported the incident. An agent from the FBI interviewed Marshall, inspected his station wagon, and recovered the bullet from the steel plate in the driver's seat. The FBI conducted a further investigation by interviewing Ashkar and Bradley. Based on the information collected by the FBI, Bradley was indicted on one count of willfully depriving a person of constitutional rights under color of law in violation of 18 U.S.C. §242. The indictment charged that Bradley intentionally deprived Marshall of his Fourth Amendment right to be free from the use of unreasonable force during an arrest.

After a three-day trial at which Bradley testified in his own defense, the jury found Bradley guilty as charged. . . .

Bradley . . . contends that the evidence did not support the jury's finding that he acted "willfully" because he acted out of fear for his own safety rather than a specific intent to deprive Marshall of his constitutional rights. To show a willful deprivation of a civil right under §242, the government must establish that the defendant acted "in open defiance or in reckless disregard of a constitutional requirement." Screws v. United States, 325 U.S. 91, 105 (1945). A defendant need not "have been thinking in constitutional terms" to willfully violate a constitutional right. Id. at 106. Willfulness may be shown by circumstantial evidence so long as the purpose may "be reasonably inferred from all the circumstances attendant on the act." *Screws*, 325 U.S. at 106.

We find that the evidence supports the jury's conclusion that Bradley acted willfully. Bradley and Ashkar were chasing Marshall with a police emergency light flashing and Marshall refused to stop. In an effort to bring the chase to a halt, Bradley leaned out the window of a moving police car and fired a bullet into Marshall's station wagon. Although Bradley claims that he believed Marshall may have been reaching for a gun, Ashkar contradicted this statement and testified that he observed no furtive gestures from the station wagon's driver. Neither Bradley nor Ashkar ever saw the driver of the station wagon brandish a weapon of any kind or do anything that could be reasonably perceived as life-threatening. Nevertheless, in an attempt to stop the station wagon's flight, Bradley used deadly force by firing a gunshot into the station wagon that would have hit (and possibly killed) Marshall had it not been for the steel plate in the seat of Marshall's car. Bradley's actions in these circumstances were clearly unreasonable and excessive. The jury had ample evidence to reasonably conclude that Bradley willfully violated Marshall's Fourth Amendment right to be free from the use of excessive force during an arrest.

Bradley's final attack on his conviction focuses on the trial court's jury instructions. . . . Bradley's proposed definition of the willfulness element stated:

The word "willfully" as used in the indictment and these instructions means deliberately and intentionally, as distinguished from something which is merely careless, inadvertent or negligent, that is to say the Defendant must have known that his acts would deprive Mr. Marshall of his constitutional rights and must have specifically intended that Mr. Marshall be deprived of such rights.

The trial judge refused to give this proposed instruction, and instead gave the following instructions which commented on the intent requirement of a §242 violation:

The government must prove that the defendant acted with the intent that Roosevelt Marshall be deprived of his right not to be deprived of liberty without due process of law, which includes the right to be secure in his person and free from the use of unreasonable force by one acting under the color of law. The defendant need not have known that these rights were secured by the Constitution or the laws of the United States.

One factor which you may consider in your determination of whether the defendant had the requisite specific intent to deprive the victim of a right is the nature and degree of force used by the defendant. . . . If the force used by defendant was greater than the force that would appear reasonably necessary to an ordinary, reasonable and prudent law enforcement officer, you may consider that excessive force as evidence that the defendant acted with the requisite specific intent, that is, that he specifically intended to do that which the law forbids.

The issue in this case is whether Adolph Bradley willfully violated Mr. Marshall's rights under the United States Constitution. Conduct by a police officer that violates some state law or police department regulation is not necessarily a violation of the federal Constitution or laws of the United States. In order to find Adolph Bradley guilty of the offense charged in the indictment, you must find beyond a reasonable doubt that his actions violated Mr. Marshall's rights under the United States Constitution and that Adolph Bradley intended to violate those constitutional rights.

In order to find the Defendant Adolph Bradley guilty of the offense charged in the indictment, you must find that he acted "willfully" to deprive Mr. Marshall of his constitutional right not to be deprived of liberty without due process of law.

When read as a whole, we cannot say that these jury instructions failed to provide a fair and accurate summary of the willfulness element of a §242 violation or that they could have clouded the jury's comprehension of the issue to such an extent that it prejudiced Bradley. Willfulness under §242 essentially requires that the defendant intend to commit the unconstitutional act without necessarily intending to do that act for the specific purpose of depriving another of a constitutional right. In other words, to act "willfully" in the §242 sense, the defendant must intend to commit an act that results in the deprivation of an established constitutional right as a reasonable person would have understood that right.

Here, the jury instructions fairly and accurately conveyed the intent requirement of §242. Those instructions told the jury that the government had to prove that Bradley "acted with the intent that Roosevelt Marshall be deprived of his right not to be deprived" of a constitutional right. The judge also instructed to find Bradley guilty he must have "acted with the requisite specific intent, that is, that he specifically intended to do that which the law forbids." Finally, Judge Riley informed the jurors that "[i]n order to find Adolph Bradley guilty of the offense charged in the indictment, you must find beyond a reasonable doubt that his actions violated Mr. Marshall's rights under the United States Constitution and that Adolph Bradley intended to violate those constitutional rights." Because these instructions concerning Bradley's intent expressed the essence of §242's willfulness requirement, we find no error in the jury instructions. . . .

NOTES AND QUESTIONS

1. The court in *Bradley* agreed with the trial judge that a finding of specific intent under §242 required only that Bradley have used deadly force with the purpose of depriving Marshall of federally protected interests. Under this formulation, Bradley need not have been aware of the unconstitutionality of his use of force. This decision is not an outlier. See, e.g., United States v. Coté, 544 F.3d 88 (2d Cir. 2008) (reversing judgment of acquittal entered for prison guard; finding evidence of intent in clear excessiveness of force and proof that officer acted in bad faith). Do you think Bradley acted "not to enforce local law but to deprive a citizen of a right" as envisioned by *Screws*? Did Bradley demonstrate "reckless disregard of constitutional prohibitions or guarantees" under *Screws*?

The trial judge might well have had some qualms about the prosecution of Bradley, as he sentenced Bradley to three years' probation and 300 hours of community service. In addition to affirming Bradley's conviction, the Seventh Circuit vacated Bradley's sentence on the government's cross-appeal. 196 F.3d at 771. Before he could be resentenced, however, Bradley's conviction was soon vacated, after evidence emerged that the trial judge had had ex parte communication with the jury (in this and other cases). United States v. Bishawi, 272 F.3d 458 (7th Cir. 2001).

2. The jury was instructed that "[i]f the force used by defendant was greater than the force that would appear *reasonably necessary to an ordinary, reasonable and prudent law enforcement officer*," it could "consider that excessive force as evidence that the defendant acted with the requisite specific intent. . . ." 196 F.3d at 769-70 (emphasis added). Does the Seventh Circuit's approval of the phrases "reasonably necessary" and "reasonable and prudent law enforcement officer" suggest that the *mens rea* required for a conviction under §242 is not "knowledge" or even "reckless disregard," but merely negligence? Compare the instructions in this case with the instructions the Supreme Court rejected in *Screws*. Are they really so different?

3. The vast majority of §242 prosecutions today are brought against state or local law enforcement officers and correctional officials. See Brian R. Johnson & Phillip B. Bridgmon, Depriving Civil Rights: An Exploration of 18 U.S.C. 242 Criminal Prosecutions 2001-2006, 34 Crim. Jus. Rev. 196, 202 (2009).

4. The Second Circuit recently canvassed jury instructions on the *Screws* "willfulness" standard in §242 prosecutions *not* alleging racial motivation. See United States v. Pendergrass, 648 F. App'x. 29 (2d Cir. 2016) (per curiam). The defendant, a probationary captain in the New York City Department of Correction on Rikers Island, was convicted of violating §242 after a jury found that he had been deliberately indifferent to an inmate housed in the mental health unit who had ingested a ball of soap, causing immense physical distress and eventually leading to his death. On the *mens rea* issue, the court explained:

> With respect to willfulness, Pendergrass requested that the jury instruction include language explaining that "willfulness" means that the defendant acted "with a bad purpose or evil intent." In response, the district court amended its instructions to include the phrase "bad purpose," but not the phrase "evil intent." The relevant portion of the instruction read: "[T]o act . . . willfully means to . . . engage in conduct voluntarily and purposely with the intent to do something the law forbids. That is to say with a bad purpose either to disobey or to disregard the law."
>
> Pendergrass contends that the court's omission of the word "evil" essentially lessened the government's burden of proof and "tilt[ed] the litigation from a criminal prosecution toward a medical negligence case." In support of this position, he largely relies on Screws v. United States, 325 U.S. 91(1945), in which the Supreme Court noted that "willful," when used in a criminal statute,

"'generally means an act done with a bad purpose.' . . . An evil motive to accomplish that which the statute condemns becomes a constituent element of the crime." Id. at 101. However, the plain text of Screws does not require judges to instruct juries using both phrases, "bad purpose" and "evil intent," to adequately define the term "willful," and we know of no authority that supports such an interpretation. In fact, a number of other circuit courts have upheld willfulness instructions pursuant to 18 U.S.C. §242 that are substantively identical to the instructions delivered in this case. See, e.g., United States v. Johnstone, 107 F.3d 200, 209-10 (3d Cir. 1997) (approving an instruction that a person acts willfully under 18 U.S.C. §242 where an act "is done voluntarily and intentionally, and with a specific intent to do something the law forbids, that is, as relevant here, with an intent to violate a protected right"); United States v. Garza, 754 F.2d 1202, 1210 (5th Cir. 1985) (approving an instruction that a person acts willfully when "the act was committed voluntarily and purposely with the specific intent to do something the law forbids. That is to say, with a bad purpose either to disobey or to disregard the law."); United States v. Couch, 1995 WL 369318 at *4 (6th Cir. 1995) (unpublished opinion) (noting that "[n]o further instruction that the accused acted with 'bad or evil intent' is necessary" where the instruction read as follows: "[A]n act is done willfully if it is done voluntarily and intentionally, and with the specific intent to do something which the law forbids; that is, with an intent to violate a specific protected right."); cf. United States v. Pomponio, 429 U.S. 10, 12-13 (1976) (expressly rejecting an argument that a jury instruction on willfulness for a crime of fraud or false statements under 26 U.S.C. §7206(1) must include "evil motive" language and upholding a willfulness instruction nearly identical to the instruction used in Pendergrass's case).

Considering the entirety of the willfulness instruction, we conclude that the district court "delivered a correct interpretation of the law." Carr, 880 F.2d at 1555. Accordingly, we decline to reverse Pendergrass's conviction on that ground.

648 F. App'x. at 32-34; see also United States v. Brown, 2016 WL 806552 at *2 (N.D.Ill. 2016) (upholding a §242 jury verdict and noting: "It was perfectly reasonable for the jury to determine that when [defendant Chicago police officer] punched and kicked [victim] when [victim] was not acting aggressively toward him that he intended to commit an act that resulted in the violation of the established constitutional right to be free from unreasonable use of force as a reasonable person would have understand that right.").

Rikers Island, the New York City jail at which Pendergrass was formerly employed, has been the target of vociferous criticism. Officials there have been accused of rampant corruption and fostering an environment of violence and abuse. See A More Just New York City, Independent Commission on New York City Criminal Justice and Incarceration Reform 11 (2016) (concluding that Rikers operates as "an expensive penal colony" and "must be closed"). See also Nick Corasaniti, Rikers Island Commission Unveils Plan to Shut Down Jail Complex, N.Y. Times, April 2, 2017 (reporting that the Independent Commission on New York City Criminal Justice and Incarceration Reform subsequently proposed replacing Rikers with smaller jails near courthouses in the City's five boroughs).

As for the Brooklyn, Illinois Police Department: It was put under the oversight of a state commission in 2012. In 2015, the state police and county sheriff raided it in connection with allegations that, among other things, officers were towing vehicles to generate money for their paychecks. Carolyn P. Smith, Brooklyn Police Chief Quits as Towing Scheme Unfolds, Following Raid, Belleville News-Democrat, Mar. 30, 2015.

2.   DEPRIVATION OF "RIGHTS"

In addition to proving willfulness, the government must prove a violation of a right "protected by the Constitution or laws of the United States" in order to convict under §242. How clearly must such rights be defined? Who does the defining? Is it enough that first a jury, and later an appellate court, finds that what the defendant did violated the victim's right to "due process"? Or must the legal violation have been specified by a court decision before the violation occurred? If so, which court decisions count? The next case addresses these questions, drawing heavily on civil rights cases brought under 42 U.S.C. §1983.

United States v. Lanier
520 U.S. 259 (1997)

Justice SOUTER delivered the opinion of the Court.

Respondent David Lanier was convicted under 18 U.S.C. §242 of criminally violating the constitutional rights of five women by assaulting them sexually while Lanier served as a state judge. The Sixth Circuit reversed his convictions on the ground that the constitutional right in issue had not previously been identified by this Court in a case with fundamentally similar facts. The question is whether this standard of notice is higher than the Constitution requires, and we hold that it is.

I

David Lanier was formerly the sole state Chancery Court judge for two rural counties in western Tennessee. The trial record, read most favorably to the jury's verdict, shows that from 1989 to 1991, while Lanier was in office, he sexually assaulted several women in his judicial chambers. The two most serious assaults were against a woman whose divorce proceedings had come before Lanier and whose daughter's custody remained subject to his jurisdiction. When the woman applied for a secretarial job at Lanier's courthouse, Lanier interviewed her and suggested that he might have to reexamine the daughter's custody. When the woman got up to leave, Lanier grabbed her, sexually assaulted her, and finally committed oral rape. A few weeks later, Lanier inveigled the woman into returning to the courthouse again to get information about another job opportunity, and again sexually assaulted and orally raped her. On five other occasions Lanier sexually assaulted four other women: two of his secretaries, a Youth Services Officer of the juvenile court over which Lanier presided, and a local coordinator for a federal program who was in Lanier's chambers to discuss a matter affecting the same court.

Ultimately, Lanier was charged with 11 violations of §242, each count of the indictment alleging that, acting willfully and under color of Tennessee law, he had deprived the victim of "rights and privileges which are secured and protected by the Constitution and the laws of the United States, namely the right not to be deprived of liberty without due process of law, including the right to be free from willful sexual assault." . . .

The trial judge instructed the jury on the Government's burden to prove as an element of the offense that the defendant deprived the victim of rights secured or protected by the Constitution or laws of the United States:

> Included in the liberty protected by the [Due Process Clause of the] Fourteenth Amendment is the concept of personal bodily integrity and the right to be free of unauthorized and unlawful physical abuse by state intrusion. Thus, this protected right of liberty provides that no person shall be subject to physical or bodily abuse without lawful justification by a state official acting or claiming to act under the color of the laws of any state of the United States when that official's conduct is so demeaning and harmful under all the circumstances as to shock one's conscience. Freedom from such physical abuse includes the right to be free from certain sexually motivated physical assaults and coerced sexual battery. It is not, however, every unjustified touching or grabbing by a state official that constitutes a violation of a person's constitutional rights. The physical abuse must be of a serious substantial nature that involves physical force, mental coercion, bodily injury or emotional damage which is shocking to one's consci[ence].

The jury returned verdicts of guilty on seven counts, and not guilty on three (one count having been dismissed at the close of the Government's evidence). It also found that the two oral rapes resulted in "bodily injury," for which Lanier was subject to 10-year terms of imprisonment on each count, in addition to 1-year terms under the other five counts of conviction, see §242. He was sentenced to consecutive maximum terms totaling 25 years.

A panel of the Court of Appeals for the Sixth Circuit affirmed the convictions and sentence, 33 F.3d 639 (1994), but the full Court vacated that decision and granted rehearing en banc. On rehearing, the Court set aside Lanier's convictions for "lack of any notice to the public that this ambiguous criminal statute [i.e., §242] includes simple or sexual assault crimes within its coverage." 73 F.3d 1380, 1384 (1996). Invoking general canons for interpreting criminal statutes, as well as this Court's plurality opinion in Screws v. United States, 325 U.S. 91 (1945), the Sixth Circuit held that criminal liability may be imposed under §242 only if the constitutional right said to have been violated is first identified in a decision of this Court (not any other federal, or state, court), and only when the right has been held to apply in "a factual situation fundamentally similar to the one at bar." The Court of Appeals regarded these combined requirements as "substantially higher than the "clearly established" standard used to judge qualified immunity" in civil cases under 42 U.S.C. §1983. 73 F.3d, at 1393. Finding no decision of this Court applying a right to be free from unjustified assault or invasions of bodily integrity in a situation "fundamentally similar" to those charged, the Sixth Circuit reversed the judgment of conviction with instructions to dismiss the indictment. . . .

We granted certiorari to review the standard for determining whether particular conduct falls within the range of criminal liability under §242. We now vacate and remand.

II

Section 242 is a Reconstruction Era civil rights statute making it criminal to act (1) "willfully" and (2) under color of law (3) to deprive a person of rights protected by the Constitution or laws of the United States. 18 U.S.C. §242. The en banc decision of the Sixth Circuit dealt only with the last of these elements, and it is with that element alone that we are concerned here.

The general language of §242, referring to "the deprivation of any rights, privileges, or immunities secured or protected by the Constitution or laws of the United States," is matched by the breadth of its companion conspiracy statute, §241, which speaks of conspiracies to prevent "the free exercise or enjoyment of any right or privilege secured to [any person] by the Constitution or laws of the United States." Thus, in lieu of describing the specific conduct it forbids, each statute's general terms incorporate constitutional law by reference, and many of the incorporated constitutional guarantees are, of course, themselves stated with some catholicity of phrasing. The result is that neither the statutes nor a good many of their constitutional referents delineate the range of forbidden conduct with particularity.

The right to due process enforced by §242 and said to have been violated by Lanier presents a case in point, with the irony that a prosecution to enforce one application of its spacious protection of liberty can threaten the accused with deprivation of another: what Justice Holmes spoke of as "fair warning . . . in language that the common world will understand, of what the law intends to do if a certain line is passed. To make the warning fair, so far as possible the line should be clear." McBoyle v. United States, 283 U.S. 25, 27 (1931). "The . . . principle is that no man shall be held criminally responsible for conduct which he could not reasonably understand to be proscribed." Bouie v. City of Columbia, 378 U.S. 347, 351 (1964).[5]

There are three related manifestations of the fair warning requirement. First, the vagueness doctrine bars enforcement of "a statute which either forbids or requires the doing of an act in terms so vague that men of common intelligence must necessarily guess at its meaning and differ as to its application." Connally v. General Constr. Co., 269, 385, 391 (1926). Second, as a sort of "junior version of the vagueness doctrine," H. Packer, The Limits of the Criminal Sanction 95 (1968), the canon of strict construction of criminal statutes, or rule of lenity, ensures fair warning by so resolving ambiguity in a criminal statute as to apply it only to conduct clearly covered. See, e.g., Liparota v. United States, 471 U.S. 419, 427 (1985). Third, although clarity at the requisite level may be supplied by judicial gloss on an otherwise uncertain statute, see J. Jeffries, Legality, Vagueness, and the Construction of Penal Statutes, 71 Va. L. Rev. 189, 207 (1985), due process bars courts from applying a novel construction of a criminal statute to conduct that neither the statute nor any prior judicial decision has fairly disclosed to be within its scope. In each of these guises, the touchstone is whether the statute, either standing alone or as construed, made it reasonably clear at the relevant time that the defendant's conduct was criminal.

We applied this standard in Screws v. United States, 325 U.S. 91 (1945), which recognized that the expansive language of due process that provides a basis for judicial review is, when incorporated by reference into §242, generally ill-suited to the far different task of giving fair warning about the scope of criminal liability. The *Screws* plurality identified the affront to the warning requirement posed by employing §242 to place "the accused . . . on trial for an offense, the nature of which the statute does not define and hence of which it gives no warning." Id. at 101. At the same time, the same Justices recognized that this constitutional difficulty does not arise when the accused is charged with violating a "right which has been made specific either by the express terms of the Constitution or laws of the United States or by decisions interpreting them." Id. at 104. When broad constitutional requirements have been "made specific" by the text or settled interpretations, willful violators "certainly are in no position to say that they had no adequate advance notice that they would be visited with punishment. . . . [T]hey are not punished for violating an unknowable something." Id. at 105. Accordingly, *Screws* limited the

---

5. The fair warning requirement also reflects the deference due to the legislature, which possesses the power to define crimes and their punishment.

statute's coverage to rights fairly warned of, having been "made specific" by the time of the charged conduct.[6]

The Sixth Circuit, in this case, added two glosses to the made-specific standard of fair warning. In its view, a generally phrased constitutional right has been made specific within the meaning of *Screws* only if a prior decision of this Court has declared the right, and then only when this Court has applied its ruling in a case with facts "fundamentally similar" to the case being prosecuted. 73 F.3d at 1393. None of the considerations advanced in this case, however, persuades us that either a decision of this Court or the extreme level of factual specificity envisioned by the Court of Appeals is necessary in every instance to give fair warning. . . .

Nor have our decisions demanded precedents that applied the right at issue to a factual situation that is "fundamentally similar" at the level of specificity meant by the Sixth Circuit in using that phrase. To the contrary, we have upheld convictions under §241 or §242 despite notable factual distinctions between the precedents relied on and the cases then before the Court, so long as the prior decisions gave reasonable warning that the conduct then at issue violated constitutional rights. See United States v. Guest, 383 U.S. 745, 759, n.17 (1966) (prior cases established right of interstate travel, but later case was the first to address the deprivation of this right by private persons); United States v. Saylor, 322 U.S. 385 (1944) (pre-*Screws*; prior cases established right to have legitimate vote counted, whereas later case involved dilution of legitimate votes through casting of fraudulent ballots); United States v. Classic, 313 U.S. 299, 321-324 (1941) (pre-*Screws*; prior cases established right to have vote counted in general election, whereas later case involved primary election).

But even putting these examples aside, we think that the Sixth Circuit's "fundamentally similar" standard would lead trial judges to demand a degree of certainty at once unnecessarily high and likely to beget much wrangling. This danger flows from the Court of Appeals' stated view that due process under §242 demands more than the "clearly established" law required for a public officer to be held civilly liable for a constitutional violation under §1983 or *Bivens*. This, we think, is error.

In the civil sphere, we have explained that qualified immunity seeks to ensure that defendants "reasonably can anticipate when their conduct may give rise to liability," [Davis v. Scherer, 468 U.S. 183, 195 (1984)], by

---

6. This process of "making specific" does not, as the Sixth Circuit believed, qualify *Screws* as "the only Supreme Court case in our legal history in which a majority of the Court seems [to have been] willing to create a common law crime." 73 F.3d 1380, 1391 (1996). Federal crimes are defined by Congress, not the courts, and *Screws* did not "create a common law crime"; it narrowly construed a broadly worded act of Congress, and the policies favoring strict construction of criminal statutes oblige us to carry out congressional intent as far as the Constitution will admit. . . .

attaching liability only if "[t]he contours of the right [violated are] sufficiently clear that a reasonable official would understand that what he is doing violates that right," [Anderson v. Creighton, 483 U.S. 635, 640 (1987)]. So conceived, the object of the "clearly established" immunity standard is not different from that of "fair warning" as it relates to law "made specific" for the purpose of validly applying §242. The fact that one has a civil and the other a criminal law role is of no significance; both serve the same objective, and in effect the qualified immunity test is simply the adaptation of the fair warning standard to give officials (and, ultimately, governments) the same protection from civil liability and its consequences that individuals have traditionally possessed in the face of vague criminal statutes. To require something clearer than "clearly established" would, then, call for something beyond "fair warning."

This is not to say, of course, that the single warning standard points to a single level of specificity sufficient in every instance. In some circumstances, as when an earlier case expressly leaves open whether a general rule applies to the particular type of conduct at issue, a very high degree of prior factual particularity may be necessary. But general statements of the law are not inherently incapable of giving fair and clear warning, and in other instances a general constitutional rule already identified in the decisional law may apply with obvious clarity to the specific conduct in question, even though "the very action in question has [not] previously been held unlawful," *Anderson, supra*, at 640. As Judge Daughtrey noted in her dissenting opinion in this case: "The easiest cases don't even arise. There has never been . . . a section 1983 case accusing welfare officials of selling foster children into slavery; it does not follow that if such a case arose, the officials would be immune from damages [or criminal] liability." 73 F.3d at 1410. In sum, as with civil liability under §1983 or *Bivens*, all that can usefully be said about criminal liability under §242 is that it may be imposed for deprivation of a constitutional right if, but only if, "in the light of pre-existing law the unlawfulness [under the Constitution is] apparent," *Anderson, supra*, at 640. Where it is, the constitutional requirement of fair warning is satisfied.

Because the Court of Appeals used the wrong gauge in deciding whether prior judicial decisions gave fair warning that respondent's actions violated constitutional rights, we vacate the judgment and remand for application of the proper standard.

NOTES AND QUESTIONS

1. You may wonder why Justice Souter didn't refer to the explicit language in §242 about sexual assaults. Lanier sexually assaulted women between 1989 and 1991. At that time, 18 U.S.C. §242 increased penalties only when sexual assault resulted in bodily injury or death; the statute did

not include any language about aggravated sexual assault. In 1994, Congress amended §242 to include enhanced penalties for specific acts including, among others, aggravated sexual abuse. Because the sexual assaults of which he was accused occurred prior to the enactment of the 1994 amendment, Lanier was able to argue that the statute was ambiguous as to whether or not it included sexual assault crimes.

You may also wonder what happened to Lanier. Following the Supreme Court's remand, the Sixth Circuit ordered supplemental briefing and revoked Lanier's bond, ordering him back to jail pending rehearing of his appeal. Lanier, however, failed to surrender. The Sixth Circuit dismissed the appeal under the fugitive disentitlement doctrine. Soon afterward, the U.S. Marshals found Lanier living in Mexico. Lanier's appeals having failed, he is currently serving his original 25-year sentence. When, in response to a §1983 suit by one of his victims, Lanier (appearing pro se) invoked absolute judicial immunity, the Sixth Circuit went out on a limb and held "that stalking and sexually assaulting a person, no matter the circumstances, do not constitute 'judicial acts.'" Archie v. Lanier, 95 F.3d 438, 441 (6th Cir. 1996).

2. Is Lanier any different from an ordinary rapist? Sexual assault is a state-law crime. Why should Lanier's offense be prosecuted in federal court? Recall that three of the four dissenting Justices in *Screws* believed that case opened the door to broad federal jurisdiction over assault and homicide committed by state and local officials. Does *Lanier* open the door further? Should the door be closed?

3. *Lanier* considers the constitutional requirement of fair notice. *Screws* also focused on the meaning of fair notice. But in *Screws*, the Court addressed the notice problems by refining its definition of willfulness. In contrast, the *Lanier* Court addressed such problems by requiring a measure of clarity concerning the underlying constitutional right. Why the difference? Ordinarily, whether the defendant had notice (and hence knowledge) is part of the *mens rea* inquiry—yet *Lanier* is about the definition of the criminal act. It is true that §242 defines the crime by reference to constitutional rights, but is the clarity of a constitutional basis for a particular right an appropriate proxy for notice? While no Supreme Court decision had held that color-of-law sexual assault violates a constitutional right, several lower courts had done so. See, e.g., Dang Vang v. Vang Xiong X. Toyed, 944 F.2d 476, 479 (9th Cir. 1991). Why didn't Justice Souter cite any of these cases?

4. Courts continue to grapple with *Lanier*'s "made specific" standard of fair warning. The Eleventh Circuit recently reviewed a case with a fact pattern similar to that in *Lanier*. In United States v. Cochran, 682 F. App'x 828 (11th Cir. 2017) (per curiam), the defendant was a former state magistrate judge who was convicted on multiple §242 counts of sexual assault and other unsavory behavior including planting methamphetamine in one of his victim's cars and having her arrested. One of the counts on which Cochran was convicted involved his search of his secretary's cell phone without her

consent. Cochran protested that he did not have "fair warning" that such a search violated his secretary's Fourth Amendment rights. Id. at 832. The Court of Appeals found this argument persuasive, noting:

> The Supreme Court has held that defendants must have "fair warning" that their actions violate a constitutional right, which requires that they "reasonably can anticipate when their conduct may give rise to liability, by attaching liability only if the contours of the right violated are sufficiently clear that a reasonable official would understand that what he is doing violates that right." Lanier, 520 U.S. at 270. This Court uses two methods to determine whether a reasonable official would understand that his conduct violates a constitutional right. Under the first, we ask whether "binding opinions from the United States Supreme Court, the Eleventh Circuit Court of Appeals, and the highest court in the state where the action is filed . . . gave [the defendant] fair warning that his [action] was unconstitutional." . . . In the second—the so-called "obvious clarity" inquiry—we ask whether the defendant's "'conduct lies so obviously at the very core of what [federal law] prohibits that the unlawfulness of the conduct was readily apparent . . . notwithstanding the lack of fact-specific case law' on point." . . .
>
> [A]lthough the Fourth Amendment is clearly implicated, we cannot conclude that either the Supreme Court or this Court has clearly established law that would have constituted "fair warning" to Cochran that his actions with respect to S.P.'s cellphone violated the Fourth Amendment. . . .
>
> [T]he decisions of this Court and the Supreme Court have established little more than the following proposition: "[W]here a Fourth Amendment intrusion serves special governmental needs, beyond the normal need for law enforcement, it is necessary to balance the individual's privacy expectations against the Government's interests." Nat'l Treasury Empl'ees Union v. Von Raab, 489 U.S. 656, 665 (1989). However, in the context of a cellphone and the protections it is afforded in the contemporary government workplace, neither the individual's privacy expectation nor the government's interest are clearly established and accordingly we cannot conclude that Cochran had "fair warning." . . .
>
> No decision of the Supreme Court, this Court, or the highest court of Georgia has further clarified the standards by which intrusions into the privacy expectations of governmental employees at work must be judged. And no such decision has addressed a sufficiently similar factual situation so as to provide reasonable warning to Cochran that his conduct violated the constitutional rights of S.P. Accordingly, because we are unable to conclude that Cochran had the required "fair warning" that his actions were in violation of a clearly established constitutional right, his conviction on Count Three must be vacated.

Id. at 838-41.

5. Does the question of whether Lanier's conduct violates due process function as a jurisdictional element? Is this the basis for Congress's power

to enact §242? Recall the normal rule with respect to federal jurisdictional elements: As a general matter, the government need not prove any *mens rea* with respect to such elements—jurisdictional facts go not to the question of whether the defendant deserves punishment, but only to the question of whether federal officials will do the punishing. Yet *Lanier* says the conduct must "clearly" violate the Constitution. Does this suggest that in federal civil rights prosecutions, the existence of a constitutional right is more than simply a "hook" giving Congress a basis for jurisdiction? Because the content of constitutional protections changes over time, clarity may be especially important. Moreover, defendants who willfully and clearly violate the Constitution may, in the view of Congress and/or the public, be especially culpable.

6. Suppose a state university admissions office uses an affirmative action program that is very similar to programs that have been invalidated in courts around the nation. Suppose further that the head of admissions knows about those court rulings, and proceeds to apply the school's customary affirmative action criteria as a matter of principle: She believes that the court decisions are wrong, and that racial and ethnic diversity in college classes is crucial to her school's mission. Plainly, she could be held civilly liable for violating the Equal Protection Clause of the Fourteenth Amendment. Moreover, it appears that her conduct and intent meet the standards articulated in *Screws, Bradley,* and *Lanier.* If prosecuted, should the admissions officer be convicted? If not, why not? Is there something missing from §242's definition of criminal conduct and intent? If so, what is the missing element?

3.   New Horizons in Rights Vindicating Prosecutions

Section 1983 has been applied to vindicate a wide range of constitutional rights. At the same time, the courts have not always accepted prosecutors' novel applications of the mail and wire fraud statutes or the Hobbs Act against egregious official misconduct by state and local officials. Hence one might expect that prosecutors might turn to civil rights prohibitions to go after corruption that lacks the dimension of self-enrichment usually required by the corruption statutes that we examined in Chapter 6. That is exactly what happened in a recent case arising in New Jersey.

The so-called "Bridge-gate" scandal erupted after officials closed the Fort Lee, New Jersey, local access lanes to the George Washington Bridge (GWB), which spans the Hudson River, connecting New Jersey and New York, suddenly and without public warning for several days. The closure precipitated thousands of hours of vehicle delays for long-suffering Fort Lee commuters and others. The closures were allegedly ordered by Bill Baroni, Deputy Executive Director of the Port Authority of New York and

New Jersey, and Bridget Kelly, Deputy Chief of Staff to New Jersey Governor Chris Christie. Port Authority officials at first claimed that the closures had been for the purpose of conducting a "traffic study." But that cover story soon unraveled. The U.S. Attorney's Office for the District of New Jersey alleged in its indictment that Kelly and Baroni had ordered the lanes closed to enact retribution against the Fort Lee Mayor Mark Soklovich (D), for his refusal to endorse Governor Christie (R) for reelection (Christie won anyway).

The defendants sought to dismiss the civil rights charges on the ground that there is no clearly established constitutional right to "localized travel on public roadways." The district court ruled against the defendants in the decision excerpted below.

United States v. Baroni
2016 WL 3388302 (D.N.J. June 13, 2016)

[The indictment contained nine counts against the defendants, including conspiracy to violate and violation of the federal program bribery statute, 18 U.S.C. §666(a)(1)(A), by misapplying funds; conspiracy to commit wire fraud and three counts of wire fraud. In addition, in Counts 8 and 9, the indictment alleged that Baroni and Kelly "knowingly and willfully conspired and agreed with each other and others . . . to injure and oppress the residents of Fort Lee in the free exercise and enjoyment of the rights and privileges secured to them by the Constitution and the laws of the United States, namely the right to localized travel on public roadways free from restrictions unrelated to legitimate government objectives" in violation of 18 U.S.C. §§214, 242. See Indictment, United States v. Baroni, Case No. 2:15-cr-00193-SDW (D.N.J. April 23, 2015). The defendants sought to dismiss the charges on various grounds. The excerpt below responds to their arguments regarding the civil rights counts.] . . .

Defendants argue that Counts Eight and Nine must be dismissed because there is no constitutional right to "localized travel on public roadways," and even if such a right exists, it has not yet been "clearly established."

It is true that the Supreme Court has not yet recognized a constitutional right to localized travel, see, e.g., Bray v. Alexandria Women's Health Clinic, 506 U.S. 263, 275 (1993) (differentiating between interstate, which is constitutionally protected, and intrastate travel) and the federal appellate courts are split on the issue. . . . In 1990, however, the Third Circuit, explicitly recognized the right to intrastate travel in its decision in Lutz v. City of York, 899 F.2d 255 (3d Cir. 1990). In *Lutz*, the Third Circuit held that a right to intrastate travel exists under even the narrowest conception of substantive due process and held that restrictions on that right are only permissible if they are narrowly tailored to meet significant government objectives. Id. at 268, 270 (upholding an anti-cruising ordinance imposed during the city's rush hour in order to eliminate traffic that, among other things, impeded emergency vehicles). In so doing, the Third Circuit concluded "that the right to move freely about one's neighborhood or town, even by automobile, is indeed 'implicit in the concept of ordered liberty' and 'deeply rooted in the Nation's history.'" Id. at 268.

A right is "clearly established," not when every possible factual scenario as to that right is identified, but rather when parties are on notice that their actions would be unconstitutional. See, e.g., . . . United States v. Lanier, 520 U.S. 259, 269 (1997). . . . *Lutz* made it clear that individuals have a right to intrastate travel, and that the right may only be curtailed by a significant government objective, narrowly tailored to achieve that goal. *Lutz,* 776 F.2d at 269. . . . As such, public officials in this Circuit are on notice that they may only restrict the right of citizens to travel within a state for legitimate purposes.

The Government has not exceeded its authority in bringing charges against Defendants for violating that right. Here, the Indictment alleges that Defendants conspired to, and in fact did, disrupt traffic for Fort Lee residents on the GWB, impeding their right to travel inside the state of New Jersey free from arbitrary impediments. Defendants did so, the Indictment charges, not to achieve a legitimate and significant government interest, but rather to achieve an illegitimate political end—i.e. the punishment of Fort Lee's mayor for failing to support Governor Christie's re-election. A reasonable public official should have known that that conduct was "patently violative" of the constitutional right to intrastate travel recognized by the Third Circuit in *Lutz.* Political payback is not a significant government interest.[1] Taking those facts as true, as this Court must on a motion to dismiss the Indictment, this Court finds them sufficient to sustain the charges under 18 U.S.C. §§241, 242 and 2. Defendants' motions to dismiss Counts Eight and Nine, therefore, are denied. . . .

NOTES AND QUESTIONS

1. At the time of this writing, *Baroni* is on appeal to the Third Circuit; oral argument took place on April 24, 2018. Given that prosecutors also

---

1. Defendants argue that the right to intrastate travel articulated in *Lutz* does not create a "constitutional right to be free from improperly created traffic." The right articulated in *Lutz* is freedom to travel within a state, subject to abridgement by a significant government interest narrowly tailored to achieve that goal. Where traffic is a byproduct of a significant government interest imposed in a limited fashion to meet that goal, it may be constitutional. That is not what is alleged here, however.

brought charges under §666 and §1343, why might they still have found civil rights charges particularly useful?

2. Use of the civil rights statutes to prosecute political scandals has been rare, but that sparse history is storied. Indeed, the civil rights statutes were employed in the scandal from which "Bridge-gate" derived its name: Watergate. In 1971, President Richard Nixon's aides authorized a covert operation to break into the office of Lewis Fielding, the psychiatrist of RAND Corporation employee Daniel Ellsberg. Ellsberg had supplied the *New York Times* with a multi-volume classified history of the Vietnam War, excerpts of which the *Times* published as the "Pentagon Papers."

Though the period is now remembered for the failed 1972 break-in at the Democratic National Committee's Watergate office complex, the Fielding break-in constituted one of the first illicit acts by Nixon's team of "plumbers." More significantly for our purposes, the prosecution led to several members of Nixon's administration spending years in federal prison after being convicted of violating §241 (which we consider in the next section of this chapter). Specifically, Nixon Special Assistant John Ehrlichman—along with others whose names are more likely to be unknown to you—was convicted of violating Fielding's "right to be free from unreasonable search and seizure." United States v. Ehrlichman, 546 F.2d 910, 919-29 (D.C. Cir. 1976). Ehrlichman's deputy, Egil Krogh, later pled guilty to the same offense. See Egil Krogh, The Break-in That History Forgot, N.Y. Times, June 30, 2007. For a notable, if partially fictionalized, account of Watergate, see Bob Woodward & Carl Bernstein, All The President's Men (1974).

3. *Baroni* reveals (again) the difficulty of applying *Lanier*'s standard relating to "clearly" established constitutional rights. Indeed, New Jersey residents might be surprised to hear that they have a "clearly established" right to be free of traffic that results from public acts not taken "to achieve a legitimate and significant government interest." They might also be surprised to learn that they had a federal right to "intrastate travel." The Third Circuit case recognizing the latter right concerned the constitutionality of an anti-"cruising" ordinance. See Lutz v. City of York, 899 F.2d 255, 268 (3d Cir. 1990) ("unnecessary repetitive driving" defined in ordinance as "driving a motor vehicle on a street past a traffic control point, as designated by the York City Police Department, more than twice in any two (2) hour period, between the hours of 7:00 P.M. and 3:30 A.M."). Yet, as the District Court noted, the Supreme Court has not recognized such a right and the federal circuit courts remain split on the issue. At what point do you think a constitutionally based right becomes "clearly established"—a decision by the Supreme Court, a circuit court, a state court? What do you think of the prosecutor's use of *Lutz* to charge that politically motivated traffic delays violate 18 U.S.C. §§241 and 242? How do you think the Third Circuit will come down?

4. Should we be wary of broadening the range of rights vindicated through §242 prosecutions (as opposed to specific criminal prohibitions

targeting the unlawful conduct)? Some scholars and jurists have urged that §242 should be used to go after prosecutorial misconduct. See Alexandra White Dunahoe, Revisiting the Cost-Benefit Calculus of the Misbehaving Prosecutor: Deterrence Economics and Transitory Prosecutors, NYU Ann. Survey of Am. Law 83-84 (2005) (arguing that §242 should be used to punish and thereby deter *Brady* violations). The Supreme Court pointed to §242's potential in this area in Imbler v. Pachtman, 424 U.S. 409 (1976):

> We emphasize that the immunity of prosecutors from liability in suits under section 1983 does not leave the public powerless to deter misconduct or to punish that which occurs. . . . Even judges, cloaked with absolute civil immunity for centuries, could be punished criminally for willful deprivations of constitutional rights on the strength of 18 U.S.C. §242, the criminal analog of section 1983.

Id. at 428-29 (1976).

Depending on how the Third Circuit views the creative use of §242 in *Baroni*, the case may pave the way for a broader range of official misconduct prosecutions under the statute. See, e.g., United States v. Love, 2016 WL 2607127 (W.D. Wash. April 13, 2016) (sentencing memorandum of defendant, former Immigrations and Customs Enforcement Officer, who pleaded guilty to violating §242 by forging documents relating to immigration proceedings; Westlaw docket entry of April 20, 2016 shows defendant received a sentence of 30 days' imprisonment, as jointly recommended by the parties). Do you think prosecutors should use §242 more frequently against public corruption that is not quite captured by the statutes in Chapter 6?

4.   "UNDER COLOR OF LAW"

We now return to a different aspect of *Screws* and explore what it means to act "under color of law." Is it enough that a defendant's official status provides him with an opportunity to perpetrate the alleged infringement? Need he actually invoke that status?

Screws v. United States
325 U.S. 91 (1945)

Mr. Justice DOUGLAS announced the judgment of the Court and delivered the following opinion, in which THE CHIEF JUSTICE, Mr. Justice BLACK and Mr. Justice REED, concur.

[The facts and procedural history are set forth in the previous excerpt from *Screws.*]

It is said [] that petitioners did not act "under color of any law" within the meaning of §20 [now 18 U.S.C. §242] of the Criminal Code. We disagree. We are of the view that petitioners acted under "color" of law in making the arrest of Robert Hall and in assaulting him. They were officers of the law who made the arrest. By their own admissions they assaulted Hall in order to protect themselves and to keep their prisoner from escaping. It was their duty under Georgia law to make the arrest effective. Hence, their conduct comes within the statute.

Some of the arguments which have been advanced in support of the contrary conclusion suggest that the question under §20 is whether Congress has made it a federal offense for a state officer to violate the law of his State. But there is no warrant for treating the question in state law terms. The problem is not whether state law has been violated but whether an inhabitant of a State has been deprived of a federal right by one who acts under "color of any law." He who acts under "color" of law may be a federal officer or a state officer. He may act under "color" of federal law or of state law. The statute does not come into play merely because the federal law or the state law under which the officer purports to act is violated. It is applicable when and only when someone is deprived of a federal right by that action. The fact that it is also a violation of state law does not make it any the less a federal offense punishable as such. Nor does its punishment by federal authority encroach on state authority or relieve the state from its responsibility for punishing state offenses.

We agree that when this statute is applied to the action of state officials, it should be construed so as to respect the proper balance between the States and the federal government in law enforcement. . . . The fact that a prisoner is assaulted, injured, or even murdered by state officials does not necessarily mean that he is deprived of any right protected or secured by the Constitution or laws of the United States. The Fourteenth Amendment did not alter the basic relations between the States and the national government. Our national government is one of delegated powers alone. Under our federal system the administration of criminal justice rests with the States except as Congress, acting within the scope of those delegated powers, has created offenses against the United States. As stated in United States v. Cruikshank, 92 U.S. 542, 553-554 [(1876)], "It is no more the duty or within the power of the United States to punish for a conspiracy to falsely imprison or murder within a State, than it would be to punish for false imprisonment or murder itself." It is only state action of a "particular character" that is prohibited by the Fourteenth Amendment and against which the Amendment authorizes Congress to afford relief. *Civil Rights Cases*, 109 U.S. 3, 11, 13[(1883)]. Thus Congress in §20 of the Criminal Code did not undertake to make all torts of state officials federal crimes. It brought within §20 only specified acts done "under color" of law and then only those acts which deprived a person of some right secured by the Constitution or laws of the United States.

This section was before us in United States v. Classic, 313 U.S. 299, 326 [(1941)], where we said: "Misuse of power, possessed by virtue of state law and made possible only because the wrongdoer is clothed with the authority of state law, is action taken "under color of" state law. In that case state election officials were charged with failure to count the votes as cast, alteration of the ballots, and false certification of the number of votes cast for the respective candidates. . . .

We are not dealing here with a case where an officer not authorized to act nevertheless takes action. Here the state officers were authorized to make an arrest and to take such steps as were necessary to make the arrest effective. They acted without authority only in the sense that they used excessive force in making the arrest effective. It is clear that under "color" of law means under "pretense" of law. Thus acts of officers in the ambit of their personal pursuits are plainly excluded. Acts of officers who undertake to perform their official duties are included whether they hew to the line of their authority or overstep it. If, as suggested, the statute was designed to embrace only action which the State in fact authorized, the words "under color of any law" were hardly apt words to express the idea. . . .

Since there must be a new trial, the judgment below is *Reversed*.

UNDER COLOR OF WHOSE LAW?

Justice Rutledge concurred in the judgment. Justice Murphy dissented. Justice Roberts also dissented, joined by Justices Frankfurter and Jackson. Justice Roberts's dissent recognized that the defendants were subject to punishment—but under state, not federal, law. Roberts disagreed with Justice Douglas's opinion that the offense occurred "under color of law" within the meaning of §242:

But assuming unreservedly that conduct such as that now before us, perpetrated by State officers in flagrant defiance of State law, may be attributed to the State under the Fourteenth Amendment, this does not make it action under "color of any law." Section 20 is much narrower than the power of Congress. Even though Congress might have swept within the federal criminal law any action that could be deemed within the vast reach of the Fourteenth Amendment, Congress did not do so. The presuppositions of our federal system, the pronouncements of the statesmen who shaped this legislation, and the normal meaning of language powerfully counsel against attributing to Congress intrusion into the sphere of criminal law traditionally and naturally reserved for the States alone. When due account is taken of the considerations that have heretofore controlled the political and legal relations between the States and the National Government, there is not the slightest warrant in the reason of things for torturing language plainly designed for nullifying a claim of acting under a State law that conflicts with the Constitution so as to apply to situations where State law is in conformity with the

Constitution and local misconduct is in undisputed violation of that State law. In the absence of clear direction by Congress we should leave to the States the enforcement of their criminal law, and not relieve States of the responsibility for vindicating wrongdoing that is essentially local or weaken the habits of local law enforcement by tempting reliance on federal authority for an occasional unpleasant task of local enforcement.

325 U.S. at 148-49. Justice Roberts's concern is that §242's "color of law" language fits awkwardly in situations where the underlying behavior clearly violates state law. This argument is similar to that made, decades later, by Justice Thomas with respect to extortion under "color of official right," see Section A of Chapter 6. But both Justice Roberts's and Justice Thomas's arguments were rejected by a majority of the Court. As a matter of policy, what weight should be given to the fact that a potential §242 defendant violated state as well as local law?

————————————

The next case addresses another "color of law" issue: What constitutes sufficient proof that the defendant's actions, illegal under state law, bear a relation to his official position?

United States v. Giordano
442 F.3d 30 (2d Cir. 2006)

SOTOMAYOR, Circuit Judge.
Defendant-appellant Philip A. Giordano appeals from a June 13, 2003 judgment of conviction and sentence entered after a jury trial before the United States District Court for the District of Connecticut. Giordano, formerly the mayor of Waterbury, Connecticut, was convicted of two counts of civil rights violations under color of law in violation of 18 U.S.C. §242, one count of conspiracy to use a facility of interstate commerce for the purpose of enticing a person under the age of sixteen years to engage in sexual activity in violation of 18 U.S.C. §§371 and 2425, and fourteen substantive counts of such use of a facility of interstate commerce in violation of §2425. All of the convictions stem from Giordano's repeated sexual abuse of the minor daughter and niece of a prostitute. . . .

BACKGROUND

1. GIORDANO'S INVESTIGATION AND ARREST

Giordano's prosecution on the charges that led to this appeal grew out of an unrelated investigation by the FBI and IRS into political corruption in the city of Waterbury. Giordano, then mayor of Waterbury, was a target of this investigation. On February 18, 2001, the government obtained . . . an *ex parte* order authorizing it to intercept phone communications of Giordano and other targets of the investigation pursuant to the federal wiretap statute. . . .

In the course of this surveillance, the government intercepted 151 calls on Giordano's cell phones to or from Guitana Jones, a prostitute with whom Giordano had a long-term sex-for-money relationship. On July 12, 2001, the government reviewed the contents of a brief July 9 call between Jones and Giordano that suggested that Jones was bringing a nine-year-old girl to Giordano for sex. In another, equally brief July 12 call, Giordano asked if Jones would have with her the nine-year-old or another female whose age was not discussed. The government had an undercover police officer call Giordano's cell phone on the afternoon of July 12 and leave an anonymous message telling him, in threatening and profane but vague terms, that the caller knew about the little kids and would tell the media if Giordano did not desist. On July 13, the government intercepted a call between Giordano and Jones in which Giordano told Jones about the message and discussed who might have left it. Giordano asked if the father of the second individual was alive, to which Jones replied: "No, [she] don't say nothin'. . . . [T]hey, them kids haven't said anything. They do not say nothing." Giordano answered, "Well someone said something to someone because this dude knew." Later in the same conversation, Jones said: "Nobody knows about them. Nobody. Nobody knows about them at all "cause they don't even say nothing "cause I got them to the point where they're scared, if they say somethin' they're gonna get in trouble. They don't say anything." . . .

In the early hours of July 21, 2001, state authorities removed Jones' nine-year-old daughter (whom we refer to as "V1") and her eleven-year-old niece ("V2"), from the Jones household. The FBI intercepted a call soon after in which Jones advised Giordano that state authorities had removed the girls. Jones falsely told Giordano that a driver who had taken Jones, V1 and V2 to see Giordano was demanding $200 not to tell the authorities. Giordano placed this sum in an envelope in the mailbox outside his house. The FBI arrested Jones shortly after she retrieved the money.

At the behest of the FBI, Jones then called Giordano and falsely told him the driver was demanding additional payment. Giordano and Jones agreed to meet in a commuter parking lot on July 23, where Giordano would give her $500. On that date, after Giordano had given Jones money at the parking lot, agents approached him and informed him that they had evidence of his sexual misconduct and other corrupt activities not relevant to the instant appeal. Over the next seventy-two hours, Giordano cooperated with the agents in the ongoing investigation of other targets of the original corruption investigation. On July 26, Giordano was arrested.

2.   INDICTMENT AND RELEVANT PRE-TRIAL PROCEEDINGS

A federal grand jury returned [an] indictment against Giordano on September 12, 2001. . . . Before trial, Giordano moved to dismiss the indictment on various grounds. . . . The district court rejected his motion in a published decision, United States v. Giordano, 260 F. Supp. 2d 477 (D. Conn. 2002). . . .

3.   THE TRIAL

Giordano was tried before a jury from March 12 to March 24, 2003. In all, some fifty-three witnesses testified. The heart of the government's case was the testimony of Jones, V1 and V2, and the intercepted phone calls. Jones testified that she met Giordano well before his 1995 election to the mayor's office, when Giordano was a lawyer in private practice. From the time she first met him until the time of her arrest in 2001, she frequently had sex with Giordano in exchange for money, which she used to support her addiction to crack cocaine. She met him as often as two or three times a week, usually at his law office, and sometimes arranged for other women to come with her. Jones testified that in the summer of 2000, while he was mayor of Waterbury, Giordano asked her to bring "young girls" to perform sexual services. In response to this request, Jones brought several girls between the ages of fourteen and sixteen, including a niece, to perform oral sex on Giordano.

Jones testified that in November of 2000, on an occasion when Jones had brought her daughter V1, her niece V2, a nephew and a son with her to Giordano's law office, Giordano asked her elliptically "What about [V1]?", which Jones understood as a request that V1, then eight years old, perform oral sex on him. Jones testified that she said no, but at a subsequent visit [about one week later,] . . . Jones brought both V1 and V2, who [was] then ten years old, to the office, where Jones performed oral sex on Giordano in the girls' presence. During the next visit, V1 performed oral sex on Giordano. At the conclusion of this episode, Jones testified, Giordano warned her, "Make sure she don't say nothing to no-one." Jones was paid for all of these activities.

Jones claimed that similar episodes of oral sex for money began to occur with regularity, usually at Giordano's law office but occasionally at Jones' or Giordano's home or an apartment belonging to a friend of Giordano's. . . . On a school holiday in the winter of 2000-2001, the date of which Jones could not recall, she brought V1 and V2 to the mayor's office at City Hall, entering through the back door. On that occasion, she directed both V1 and V2 to perform oral sex on Giordano. Jones testified that Giordano told her in a "calm voice" at the conclusion of this visit to "make sure the kids don't tell anyone [or] I'll get in trouble, I'll go to jail. . . . So I made sure they never said anything to anybody." He also told the girls directly that they would "get in trouble" and that Jones would go to jail if they told anyone about the abuse. Jones maintained that it was Giordano's consistent practice to warn her and the girls to remain silent:

> Q.   And did he repeat that [warning] at any other time?
> A.   Yeah, every time after it happened. And I made sure the girls never said anything because I was scared. I didn't want to go to jail.

According to Jones, the abuse occurred at City Hall two or three more times. In addition, on two or three other occasions, when the law office was occupied by other people, Jones, Giordano and V1 used Giordano's official city car for V1 to perform oral sex. . . .

The victims also testified that they were hurt by and disliked the abuse but did not tell anyone about it out of fear of what Giordano could do to them. V2, who was twelve at the time of the trial, testified that she learned that Giordano was the mayor from V1 after she first met him. She "thought the Mayor could rule people, like be their boss." She believed Giordano "would have someone hurt my family or that either I would get in trouble," because Jones "would threaten me pretty often". . . . V2 testified that the abuse hurt her physically and that it also "hurt [her] inside" "[be]cause [she] wouldn't think he would make [her] do something like that.". . .

Giordano testified in his own defense. He admitted to paying Jones for sex beginning at some point prior to February of 1993 and to having "occasional" sexual contact with her from that time until his arrest, but denied ever having any sexual contact of any kind with either V1 or V2. . . .

The jury convicted Giordano on every count of the indictment save one of the §2425 counts, on which it returned no verdict. . . . On June 13, 2003, the district court sentenced Giordano principally to 444 months' imprisonment on each of the two §242 counts; 60 months on the conspiracy count; and 60 months on each of the fourteen §2425 counts, all to be served concurrently, for a total of 444 months of imprisonment. . . .

DISCUSSION

Giordano [] challenges his conviction of two counts of violating 18 U.S.C. §242. That statute "mak[es] it criminal to act (1) "willfully" and (2) under color of law (3) to deprive a person of rights protected by the Constitution or laws of the United States." United States v. Lanier, 520 U.S. 259, 264 (1997). The first count of the indictment charged that between November 2000 and July 2001, Giordano, "while acting under color of the laws of the State of Connecticut," deprived V1 of her

Fourteenth Amendment right "to be free from aggravated sexual abuse and sexual abuse. . . ." Count two of the indictment contained the same charges as to V2.

Giordano argues that the evidence was insufficient as to the "under color of law" element of these counts. . . .

"The Supreme Court has broadly interpreted the color of law requirement, concluding that "[m]isuse of power, possessed by virtue of state law and made possible only because the wrongdoer is clothed with the authority of state law, is action taken under color of state law."[16] United States v. Walsh, 194 F.3d 37, 50 (2d Cir. 1999) (quoting United States v. Classic, 313 U.S. 299, 326 (1941)). The fact that someone holds an office or otherwise exercises power under state law does not mean, of course, that any wrong that person commits is "under color of law." "It is clear that under "color" of law means under "pretense" of law. Thus acts of officers in the ambit of their personal pursuits are plainly excluded." Screws v. United States, 325 U.S. 91, 111 (1945). As we have observed, however, "there is no bright line test for distinguishing personal pursuits from actions taken under color of law." Pitchell v. Callan, 13 F.3d 545, 548 (2d Cir. 1994).

Giordano argues that he cannot have acted under color of law because his actions, although they took place during his mayoralty, "were clearly a part of and derived from [his] personal relationship with Jones" [which] was unrelated to and predated his mayoralty. . . . [However,] it is well-established that an official may act under color of law even when he or she encounters the victim outside the conduct of official business and acts for reasons unconnected to his or her office, so long as he or she employs the authority of the state in the commission of the crime. . . .

Moreover, we have found that officials acted under color of law when their misuse of official power made the commission of a constitutional wrong possible, even though the official committed abusive acts for personal reasons far removed from the scope of official duties. [The §1983 complaint in] Monsky v. Moraghan, 127 F.3d 243 (2d Cir. 1997), . . . alleged that a state judge allowed his dog to approach and "aggressively nuzzle" a litigant who was researching records in the court clerk's office. Id. at 244. . . . [W]e concluded that the complaint adequately alleged action under color of law because it charged that the judge "was known to, and deferred to by, personnel of the office" and "was allowed to enter the office with his dog and remain there . . . because he was a judge." Id. at 246. Similarly, in United States v. Tarpley, 945 F.2d 806 (5th Cir. 1991), . . . the Fifth Circuit held that a police officer acted under color of when he lured his wife's lover to the officer's home, beat him, and threatened to kill him if he reported the incident, telling his victim, "I'll kill you. I'm a cop. I can." 945 F.2d at 808. . . . In *Walsh*, we affirmed

[margin handwritten note: Defendant's Argument]

_____

16. The "under color of law" requirement of §242 is identical to the requirement under 42 U.S.C. §1983 that an official act under color of law. United States v. Price, 383 U.S. 787, 794 n.7 (1966). Our discussion therefore draws on cases relating to both statutes.

a conviction under §242 of the defendant prison guard who sadistically assaulted an inmate, Fowlks. . . . In rejecting Walsh's argument that his assault was not undertaken under color of law, we held:

> The fact that the defendant was a corrections officer, in charge of supervising, caring for, and disciplining the victim, provided Walsh with the access and opportunity to *exercise his power over* Fowlks. To say that Fowlks *would have submitted* to any other individual, who did not have the same degree of power over him as the defendant, is a factual assumption we decline to make.

[194 F.3d] at 51 (emphasis added). . . .

Giordano, like the officer in *Tarpley*, threatened his victims by invoking a "special authority" to undertake retaliatory action, and [] like the official in *Walsh* . . . used his authority to cause the victims to submit to repeated abuse, in this case by causing the victims to fear that he would use his power to harm them if they reported the abuse. . . . [Jones] testified that she ensured [V1 and V2] told no-one "because I was scared. I didn't want to go to jail." She further testified that Giordano repeatedly mentioned his presence at crime scenes, and understood from that and his request that she call him at home so he could tell his wife that he was needed on police business, that "he had a lot to do with the police. . . . He had control of what the police does. . . ."

evidence

The evidence here, viewed in the light most favorable to the government, supports the finding that Giordano actively and deliberately used his apparent authority as mayor to ensure that the victims did not resist or report the ongoing abuse. In consequence, there was sufficient evidence [to support the finding] that the abuse was "made possible only because the wrongdoer is clothed with the authority of state law." *Walsh*, 194 F.3d at 51. . . .

We hold, in sum, that Giordano's crime was committed "under color of state law" within the meaning of §242 because Giordano used the victim's fear of the power he wielded as mayor to keep them from reporting the ongoing abuse, and that the victims had a right under the Fourteenth Amendment to be free from sexual abuse by a state actor. . . .

holding

[The opinion of Judge Jacobs, concurring in part and dissenting in part, is omitted.]

NOTES AND QUESTIONS

1. What kind of nexus should be required between the conduct of a government official and his official duties and responsibilities? Holding other factors constant, it would appear that the more outrageous the official's conduct was, the more tangential it was to the officer's public duties and

office. This issue regularly comes up with respect to police officers. See, e.g., United States v. Causey, 185 F.3d 407 (5th Cir. 1999) (holding that a New Orleans police officer acted under color of law when he arranged for the execution-style murder of a woman who had filed a complaint against him with the Internal Affairs Division of the New Orleans Police Department alleging that he engaged in police brutality). In United States v. Christian, 342 F.3d 744, 751-52 (7th Cir. 2003), the court noted:

> We have stated that a police officer may be acting under color of law even though the officer is off-duty at the time of the deprivation of rights. "Deciding whether a police officer acted under color of state law should turn largely on the nature of the specific acts the police officer performed, rather than on merely whether he was actively assigned at the moment to the performance of police duties." An officer can be held to be acting under color of law when he or she is in uniform and displaying a badge. See also United States v. Colbert, 172 F.3d 594, 596 (8th Cir. 1999) (officer acted under color of law even though he was not on duty at the time he attacked a prisoner, his motivation was personal and his anger at the prisoner arose from a personal cause; the events took place in a restricted area of a jail that he was able to access as a police officer, he had keys to the cell and had authority to remove the victim from his cell).

2. Why did Giordano lose—because he used his authority as mayor to enable his awful conduct, or simply because his conduct was awful? Were his crimes inexorably related to his job? Or was the sexual abuse just criminal behavior that happened to be perpetrated by an official? Recall the language in *Screws* (also cited in *Giordano*): "It is clear that under 'color' of law means under 'pretense' of law. Thus acts of officers in the ambit of their personal pursuits are plainly excluded." How close must the connection be? How close should it be?

3. *Giordano* refers to the Supreme Court's holding in *Classic* that "misuse of power possessed by virtue of state law and made possible only because the wrongdoer is clothed with the authority of state law, is action taken 'under color of' state law." 313 U.S. at 229. And in United States v. Price, 383 U.S. 787, 794 n.7 (1966), the Court explained that "'under color' of law means the same thing in §242 that it does in . . . 42 U.S.C. §1983" and that "'under color' of law" in §1983 cases "has consistently been treated as the same thing as the 'state action' required under the Fourteenth Amendment." (Note that *Price* is cited in footnote 16 of Giordano, 442 F.3d at 42 n.16.) The scope of "under color" can thus be quite broad. Can it include action that a police officer takes while off duty?

Consider the following facts:

> Mark White, a police officer with the City of Gary, Indiana, held a part-time job as a security guard at Delilah's Fantasy Dolls Club, a strip club in

downtown Gary. The owner and employees of Delilah's knew that White was a police officer and he often wore his badge and gun while at Delilah's.

Late in the evening of March 15, 2000, Brenda Pryor, a dancer at the club, got into an argument with the bartenders over her pay for the evening. White, who was working security that evening, asked her to leave the club. An argument ensued between White and Pryor, which quickly escalated to violence when Pryor used a racial epithet to describe White. White, who was 6'3" and over 300 pounds, struck Pryor several times and eventually she was thrown to the ground. During the criminal trial, the jury heard testimony that White was wearing his badge and his gun on the night in question. Testimony was also presented that during the altercation Pryor tried to call the police, but White grabbed the cellular phone from her hand and shouted "I am the [expletive] police." Eventually the police were called to the scene by another employee and Pryor was taken to the hospital. She suffered bruises and swelling of her face, a laceration to her lip, and needed stitches on the inside and outside of her mouth due to a hole in her cheek caused by White's blows.

After the club closed for the night, White returned to the police station and prepared an arrest report for Pryor.

In that report, White identified himself as the complainant, the arresting officer, the booking officer, and the reporting officer, either as "Cpl. M. White," "M. White," or "Mark White" with his badge number. The arrest report charged Pryor with "intimidation [,] resisting law enforcement [, and] battery on law enforcement/disorderly conduct." Based in part on White's arrest report, two Gary police officers went to the hospital and placed Pryor under arrest. The charges were eventually dropped after an investigation.

United States v. White, 68 F. App'x. 707 (7th Cir. 2003). Affirming White's §242 conviction, the Seventh Circuit explained:

In prior decisions, we have explained that one important factor that juries may consider in 18 U.S.C. §242 cases involving police officers performing private acts, is whether the officer was "displaying signs of state authority and advertising the presence of a state actor" during the incident. . . . Indeed, we have held that those signs may be enough, on their own, to establish action under color of law. In this case, the jury was presented evidence that when White assaulted Pryor, he was displaying signs of state authority. White made his police affiliation known to others throughout his employment at Delilah's, and testimony was presented that during his assault on Pryor he was wearing both his gun and badge. Furthermore, White declared himself to be a police officer during the assault and prevented Pryor from calling other officers. In addition, the charges that White himself specified in his arrest report reflect action allegedly taken against him as a police officer during the assault. The fact that he filed an official report that resulted in Pryor's arrest underscores his imposition of state authority. White concedes that this "particle" piece of evidence is probative, although not conclusive. However, in combination with all of the aforementioned evidence presented at trial, a rational jury could have determined that White was acting under color of law when he assaulted Pryor.

Id. at 709. What if White had not prepared an arrest report? Same result? Under what circumstances can you imagine that one or more instances of domestic violence against a partner could (at least in theory) permit the prosecution of a police officer under §242?

4. The facts in *Giordano* highlight how pure happenstance can spark at least some of the small number of federal civil rights prosecutions. The FBI was investigating municipal corruption in Waterbury and kickbacks that Mayor Giordano may have been receiving from city contractors, including one with alleged organized crime connections. Six months after wiretaps went up, agents intercepted Giordano's conversations with Jones arranging to have sex with her daughter and niece. "The municipal corruption scandal took a back seat as agents scrambled to secretly arrest Jones, and placed Giordano under 24-hour surveillance. An anonymous call shaking Giordano down for money was devised to keep him away from the children. Jones agreed to cooperate with the FBI, and lured Giordano to a commuter parking lot to pay hush money. Suddenly, he was surrounded by agents and hustled into the back of an unmarked car." Lynne Tuohy, A Payback for Nightmares; Judge Describes Child Victims' Anxiety, Self-Loathing as He Sentences Giordano to 37 Years, Hartford Courant, June 14, 2003, at A1.

B.   CIVIL RIGHTS PROSECUTIONS OF PRIVATE ACTORS

Relatively few prosecutions are brought under either §242 or §241, but in recent years, even fewer under the latter than under the former. However broad and vague §242 is, its targets at least will have acted "under color of law" and thus, arguably, can be fairly held to some higher standard of conduct and knowledge. No such justification is available where private actors are charged under §241, which lacks any "under color" element and can ostensibly be used whenever two or more people conspire to interfere with anyone's "free exercise or enjoyment of any right or privilege secured to him by the Constitution or laws of the United States." Most prosecutions under §241, like those under §242, involve deprivation of rights on account of race. The following case is a typical prosecution under the rarely used §241.

United States v. Magleby
241 F.3d 1306 (10th Cir. 2001)

TACHA, Chief Judge.
Defendant Michael Brad Magleby was convicted of four counts of an indictment stemming from the burning of a cross on the property of an

interracial family. On appeal, Mr. Magleby argues that the evidence of his guilt regarding three of these four counts was insufficient to support his conviction. He also argues that the district court submitted two erroneous instructions to the jury. . . .

I.   BACKGROUND

On the evening of September 6, 1996, the defendant, Michael Brad Magleby, hosted a barbecue at his home. His friends Andy Whitlock, Steve Meguerditchian, Justin Merriam, Mr. Merriam's date Liz Cannon, and fifteen-year-old L.M. were in attendance. . . . On this occasion, as on other occasions, Mr. Magleby joined his friends in expressing prejudicial views of African-Americans. They told racist jokes, used racial slurs, and listened to racist CDs. The group accessed internet sites with racist jokes and other internet hate sites on Mr. Magleby's computer.

At some point during the evening, Mr. Magleby began talking about some Tongans, alleged gang members, who lived in his neighborhood. He later testified that he did not like having the Tongans in his neighborhood. L.M. also testified that the Tongans had previously assaulted Mr. Magleby. During the course of this conversation, Mr. Magleby and L.M. began talking about burning a cross at the Tongans' house. Mr. Merriam taunted Mr. Magleby, telling him that he did not dare burn a cross there. Mr. Merriam told Mr. Magleby that if he were really going to do it, he should stop talking about it and just do it.

At about 1:00 A.M., after several hours of drinking, Mr. Magleby and L.M. gathered wood from Mr. Magleby's garage to build a cross. . . . After the cross was ready, Mr. Magleby and L.M. carried it to Mr. Magleby's jeep and drove off with Mr. Magleby behind the wheel. They stopped at a gas station to fill a beer bottle with gasoline which they planned to pour over the cross to ensure that it would burn. They then set out for the Tongans' house [but decided against burning the cross there because several men were gathered outside the home]. . . .

At that point, Mr. Magleby told L.M. that they still had to burn the cross because their friends would ridicule them if they did not. The parties dispute what happened next. Mr. Magleby argues that L.M. told him that he knew where a "crackhead" lived and that they could burn the cross at his house. The government argues that L.M. told him that he knew where a black man lived and that they could burn the cross there. The parties agree that Mr. Magleby knew nothing about the Henrys prior to that moment. Mr. Magleby and L.M. then drove to the house where Ron and Robyn Henry and their eleven-year-old son lived. The Henrys are an interracial family: Ron is African-American and Robyn is white.

When Mr. Magleby and L.M. arrived at the Henrys' home, Mr. Magleby took the cross out of the jeep, placed it in the Henrys' yard, poured gasoline on it, and then ignited it. The two immediately returned to Mr. Magleby's house. . . .

On December 10, 1999, Mr. Magleby was convicted by a jury of conspiracy against rights in violation of 18 U.S.C. §241 [as well as violations under the Fair Housing Act, 42 U.S.C. §3631(a); 18 U.S.C. §844(h)(1) (using fire or an explosive in the commission of a felony); and 18 U.S.C. §1512(b)(3) (witness tampering)]. . . .

II. DISCUSSION

Mr. Magleby argues that the district court erred by denying his motion for judgment of acquittal because there was insufficient evidence to support his convictions under 18 U.S.C. §241. . . .

Section 241 is violated "[i]f two or more persons conspire to injure, oppress, threaten, or intimidate any person . . . in the free exercise or enjoyment of any right or privilege secured to him by the Constitution or laws of the United States." Section 241 requires that a "specific intent to interfere with the Federal right . . . be proved." United States v. Guest, 383 U.S. 745, 760 (1966). Mr. Magleby does not argue that the Henrys do not have a federally protected right to occupy their home. Rather, Mr. Magleby contends that the evidence was insufficient to prove beyond a reasonable doubt that he intended to "oppress, threaten, or intimidate" the Henrys in their enjoyment of that right. We disagree.

The record contains substantial evidence of Mr. Magleby's intent. Mr. Magleby testified that he decided to burn a cross to "rile people up." He acknowledged that he knew the public found cross-burning highly objectionable. He anticipated that the cross-burning would receive the attention of the news media. He admitted that he understood the message of racial hatred conveyed by a burning cross. Mr. Magleby further admitted that he intended to burn and did burn the cross in the Henrys' yard. Given this evidence of Mr. Magleby's understanding of the meaning of a burning cross to the general public and the placement of the burning cross in the Henrys' yard, we conclude that the jury could reasonably infer that Mr. Magleby intended to oppress, threaten, and intimidate the Henrys in the free exercise of their federal right to occupy property.

Furthermore, the district court properly instructed the jury that they could consider the Henrys' reactions when deciding whether Mr. Magleby's actions were intended to be a threat. Robyn Henry testified that the cross-burning "terrified" her. She testified that she discussed with her husband moving from their neighborhood. She testified that she was "scared, confused, anxious, [and] didn't sleep well at night." She stopped sitting on their porch because she feared for her safety. The Henrys' eleven-year-old son testified that he was scared because he "didn't know if they were still going to try to hurt [him]." He testified that he started carrying a baseball bat with him when he would walk in his neighborhood. He also testified that he started sleeping with this baseball bat under his bed at night "[i]n case somebody came in [his] house." Ron Henry testified that the significance of the cross-burning to him was "move, leave, you're not welcome here, . . . you were in trouble somewhere and they wanted you to leave, leave the community." He testified that he was "afraid for [himself] as well as the members of [his] family." He also testified that he made several modifications to his home to improve security and protect his family. The jury was shown photographs of these modifications. From this evidence, the jury could reasonably infer that a reasonable person would foresee a burning cross in another's yard being interpreted in a like manner.

Having viewed the above evidence in the light most favorable to the government, we find that there was sufficient evidence for a reasonable jury to find beyond a reasonable doubt that Mr. Magleby intended to oppress, threaten, and intimidate the Henrys in the free exercise of their federal right to occupy property. We therefore find that the district court properly denied Mr. Magleby's motion for judgment of acquittal on these counts. . . .

NOTES AND QUESTIONS

1. In addition to his conviction under §241, Magleby was charged with, and convicted of, violating 42 U.S.C. §3631(a) — the provision of the Fair Housing Act of 1968 that criminalizes actions taken with the intent to "injure, intimidate or interfere with . . . any person . . . because of his race, color, religion, sex, . . . or national origin and because he is or has been selling, purchasing, renting, financing, occupying, or contracting or negotiating for the sale, purchase, rental, financing or occupation of any dwelling." Unlike 18 U.S.C. §241, 42 U.S.C. §3631(a) has an explicit racial *mens rea* requirement. In *Magleby*, the jury was properly instructed that they could convict the defendant of violating §3631(a) if they found his actions were taken "for the purpose of intimidating or interfering with Robyn Henry because she was associating with an African-American or with Ron Henry because he is African-American *and because either was occupying a dwelling*," 241 F.3d at 1310 (emphasis added). See also United States v. Piekarsky, 687 F.3d 134, 2012 U.S. App. 12279 (3d Cir. 2012) (holding "that a conviction based on 'mixed motives' falls well within the reach of §3631, so long as the evidence is sufficient to show that the defendant's actions were taken because of the defendant's animus toward a protected class and on account of an intent to intimidate a member of that protected class of individuals from exercising his housing rights under the Act"); Jeannine Bell, Continuing the Mission

to Eliminate Housing Discrimination and Segregation: The Fair Housing Act and Extralegal Terror, 41 Ind. L. Rev. 537 (2008). Does the existence of more targeted criminal civil rights statutes, like 42 U.S.C. §3631(a), make 18 U.S.C. §241 less necessary? Does it change the way you feel about prosecution under this provision where no other federal civil rights crime is charged?

2. Magleby's conviction under 18 U.S.C. §241 did not rest on the deprivation of the Henrys' constitutional rights; it was based on the provision's language prohibiting interference with any "privilege secured . . . by the . . . laws of the United States." Although the court, in describing the basis for the conviction under §241, referred (in a sort of short-hand) to the "federally protected right to occupy [one's] home," we may assume that the jury was properly instructed that in order to find a violation under §241, it had to find beyond a reasonable doubt that the defendant conspired with at least one other person "to injure, oppress, threaten, or intimidate" the Henrys' enjoyment of the particular right guaranteed in 42 U.S.C. §3631 (see previous Note). Still, the possibility of resting a prosecution on the deprivation of a privilege secured by *any* federal law makes the scope of conspiracies reached by §241 quite broad. In addition, there is no overt act requirement written into the statute. Do these factors explain why the approval of Main Justice is required before a §241 prosecution can be brought?

3. As we saw in the Note above about the *Ehrlichman* case, §241, like §242, can be used to prosecute public corruption. In United States v. Robinson, 813 F.3d 251 (6th Cir. 2016), the mayor of Martin, Kentucky and some of her family members were convicted of violating §241 by engaging in a civil rights conspiracy during the mayor's reelection campaign. Their efforts — which included bribery, coercion, and intimidation of voters — fell just short of their goal, as Robinson lost the general election by three votes. Id. at 254. The defendants were convicted of vote buying, which was prohibited by 42 U.S.C. §1973i(c) (now 52 U.S.C. §10307(c)), as well as 18 U.S.C. §241. The latter was charged as a conspiracy to interfere "with the right of voters to have their votes free from dilution by unlawfully procured votes"; the Sixth Circuit affirmed the convictions. See 813 F.3d at 256 (citing Anderson v. United States, 417 U.S. 211, 227 (1974)).

4. Does the potential breadth of §241 also explain why there have been persistent concerns that it may run afoul of the Due Process Clause, the First Amendment, or both? Would a KKK parade in a predominantly minority neighborhood violate this statute? Probably not. See Brandenburg v. Ohio, 395 U.S. 444 (1969). What is the relevant difference between this hypothetical and the facts in *Magleby*? See also United States v. Guest, 383 U.S. 745, 785-86 (1966) (Brennan, J., concurring in part and dissenting in part) (noting that §241's effectiveness is limited by "Congress' failure to define — with any measure of specificity — the rights encompassed" but finding that the

high scienter requirement "saves §241 from condemnation as a criminal statute failing to provide adequate notice of the proscribed conduct").

It was in the face of concerns about §241's breadth and vagueness that Congress in 1968 enacted 42 U.S.C. §3631 (of which Magleby was convicted) and 18 U.S.C. §245—a civil rights statute of much greater specificity. Both statutes supplement, rather than replace, §241. After considering the text of §245, we present a case in which both offenses were charged.

---

18 U.S.C. §245. Federally protected activities

(a)

(1) Nothing in this section shall be construed as indicating an intent on the part of Congress to prevent any State, any possession or Commonwealth of the United States, or the District of Columbia, from exercising jurisdiction over any offense over which it would have jurisdiction in the absence of this section, nor shall anything in this section be construed as depriving State and local law enforcement authorities of responsibility for prosecuting acts that may be violations of this section and that are violations of State and local law. No prosecution of any offense described in this section shall be undertaken by the United States except upon the certification in writing of the Attorney General, the Deputy Attorney General, the Associate Attorney General, or any Assistant Attorney General specially designated by the Attorney General that in his judgment a prosecution by the United States is in the public interest and necessary to secure substantial justice, which function of certification may not be delegated.

(2) Nothing in this subsection shall be construed to limit the authority of Federal officers, or a Federal grand jury, to investigate possible violations of this section.

(b) Whoever, whether or not acting under color of law, by force or threat of force willfully injures, intimidates or interferes with, or attempts to injure, intimidate or interfere with—

(1) any person because he is or has been, or in order to intimidate such person or any other person or any class of persons from—

(A) voting or qualifying to vote, qualifying or campaigning as a candidate for elective office, or qualifying or acting as a poll watcher, or any legally authorized election official, in any primary, special, or general election;

(B) participating in or enjoying any benefit, service, privilege, program, facility, or activity provided or administered by the United States;

(C) applying for or enjoying employment, or any perquisite thereof, by any agency of the United States;

(D) serving, or attending upon any court in connection with possible service, as a grand or petit juror in any court of the United States;

(E) participating in or enjoying the benefits of any program or activity receiving Federal financial assistance; or

(2) any person because of his race, color, religion or national origin and because he is or has been —

(A) enrolling in or attending any public school or public college;

(B) participating in or enjoying any benefit, service, privilege, program, facility or activity provided or administered by any State or subdivision thereof;

(C) applying for or enjoying employment, or any perquisite thereof, by any private employer or any agency of any State or subdivision thereof, or joining or using the services or advantages of any labor organization, hiring hall, or employment agency;

(D) serving, or attending upon any court of any State in connection with possible service, as a grand or petit juror;

(E) traveling in or using any facility of interstate commerce, or using any vehicle, terminal, or facility of any common carrier by motor, rail, water, or air;

(F) enjoying the goods, services, facilities, privileges, advantages, or accommodations of any inn, hotel, motel, or other establishment which provides lodging to transient guests, or of any restaurant, cafeteria, lunchroom, lunch counter, soda fountain, or other facility which serves the public and which is principally engaged in selling food or beverages for consumption on the premises, or of any gasoline station, or of any motion picture house, theater, concert hall, sports arena, stadium, or any other place of exhibition or entertainment which serves the public, or of any other establishment which serves the public and (i) which is located within the premises of any of the aforesaid establishments or within the premises of which is physically located any of the aforesaid establishments, and (ii) which holds itself out as serving patrons of such establishments; or

(3) during or incident to a riot or civil disorder, any person engaged in a business in commerce or affecting commerce, including, but not limited to, any person engaged in a business which sells or offers for sale to interstate travelers a substantial portion of the articles, commodities, or services which it sells or where a substantial portion of the articles or commodities which it sells or offers for sale have moved in commerce; or

(4) any person because he is or has been, or in order to intimidate such person or any other person or any class of persons from —

(A) participating, without discrimination on account of race, color, religion or national origin, in any of the benefits or activities described in subparagraphs (1)(A) through (1)(E) or subparagraphs (2)(A) through (2)(F); or

(B) affording another person or class of persons opportunity or protection to so participate; or

(5) any citizen because he is or has been, or in order to intimidate such citizen or any other citizen from lawfully aiding or encouraging other persons to participate, without discrimination on account of race, color, religion or national origin, in any of the benefits or activities described in

subparagraphs (1)(A) through (1)(E) or subparagraphs (2)(A) through (2)(F), or participating lawfully in speech or peaceful assembly opposing any denial of the opportunity to so participate—

   shall be fined under this title, or imprisoned not more than one year, or both; and if bodily injury results from the acts committed in violation of this section or if such acts include the use, attempted use, or threatened use of a dangerous weapon, explosives, or fire shall be fined under this title, or imprisoned not more than ten years, or both; and if death results from the acts committed in violation of this section or if such acts include kidnapping or an attempt to kidnap, aggravated sexual abuse or an attempt to commit aggravated sexual abuse, or an attempt to kill, shall be fined under this title or imprisoned for any term of years or for life, or both, or may be sentenced to death. . . .

NOTES AND QUESTIONS

1. What are we (and courts) to make of Congress's decision to supplement an extraordinarily broad statute with a far more particularized one, and to statutorily mandate a high degree of centralized control over the particularized statute that is not so mandated in the broad statute? To be sure, the Department of Justice has, through its own guidelines, kept firm and centralized control over §241 prosecutions, and Congress is well aware of that fact. Why not rely on those guidelines for §245 prosecutions as well? If Congress (or perhaps the Civil Rights Division, specifically) is worried about overly aggressive U.S. Attorneys' Offices in one context, why not in the other?

2. Moreover, §245, like §241, is susceptible to another constitutional challenge—the same challenge that proved fatal to the Gun Free School Zone Act (in United States v. Lopez), and to the private right of action in the Violence Against Women Act (in United States v. Morrison), see Chapter 2: On what basis can Congress target non-economic private activity, however hateful or harmful?

3. Courts have found a jurisdictional basis for both §241 and §245 in some combination of the Commerce Clause and the Thirteenth Amendment (which, in contrast to the Fourteenth Amendment, does not have a state action component, see Jones v. Alfred H. Mayer Co., 392 U.S. 409 (1968)). The next case addresses these constitutional questions.

United States v. Allen
341 F.3d 870 (9th Cir. 2003)

   Paez, Circuit Judge.
   At around 10:30 p.m. on July 29, 2000, Spring Ramirez, a Hispanic woman, Jason Clark, an African American man, and Pat Tellez, a Hispanic

man, were socializing at Pioneer Park, a local park in Billings, Montana, when approximately nine white supremacists who were "patrolling" the park for racial minorities and Jews, surrounded them wielding weapons, berated them with racial epithets, and forced them out of the park for no reason other than their race. A federal grand jury indicted the defendants in this case—Sean Allen, Eric Dixon, Ryan Flaherty, Michael Flom, Jason Potter, and Jeremiah Skidmore—with violating 18 U.S.C. §§241 and 245(b)(2)(B), statutes that protect against the interference with federally protected rights on the basis of race and religion. The defendants appeal their convictions and sentences.

The principal issues on appeal are whether Pioneer Park is a place of "public accommodation" such that the defendants properly were convicted under §241 and whether §245(b)(2)(B) was validly enacted pursuant to Congress's Commerce Clause and Thirteenth Amendment powers. . . .

I

The defendants first contend that they were wrongfully convicted under 18 U.S.C. §241 because Pioneer Park was not a place of "public accommodation." . . . Here, the §241 charge against the defendants was premised on a violation of 42 U.S.C. §2000a, which states that:

> All persons shall be entitled to the full and equal enjoyment of the goods, services, facilities, privileges, advantages, and accommodations of any place of public accommodation, as defined in this section, without discrimination or segregation on the ground of race, color, religion, or national origin. . . .

> Each of the following establishments which serves the public is a place of public accommodation within the meaning of this subchapter if its operations affect commerce, or if discrimination or segregation by it is supported by State action: . . . (3) any motion picture house, theater, concert hall, sports arena, stadium or other place of exhibition or entertainment.

42 U.S.C. §§2000a(a) & (b)(3).

The defendants contend that (1) Pioneer Park was not a place of "public accommodation" because it did not provide sources of entertainment that affected interstate commerce and (2) their actions in carrying out the "park patrol" did not affect interstate commerce. We disagree. The question is not whether the "park patrol" affected interstate commerce, but rather, whether Pioneer Park's *operations* affected interstate commerce. See 42 U.S.C. §2000a(b)(3) (stating that an establishment is a place of public accommodation if its "operations affect commerce"). There was ample evidence in the record that they did. Moreover, a "place of exhibition or entertainment" "moves in commerce" if it "customarily presents films, performances, athletic teams, exhibitions, or other sources of entertainment." 42 U.S.C. §2000a(c)(3). There also was ample evidence that Pioneer Park was a place for "performances," "exhibitions," and "other sources of entertainment." For example, (1) playground equipment was purchased from Utah; (2) picnic tables, barbecue grills, and related materials were purchased in Ohio, Iowa, and Utah; (3) out-of-state visitors used the park; (4) national organizations such as the March of Dimes and the American Cancer Society obtained permits to use the park for their events, which attracted out-of-state visitors; (5) Saturday Live, a fundraising event sponsored by the Billings Public School Foundation, which had national sponsors such as Exxon, Pepsi, and the Marriott, was held at the park; (6) the Montana AIDS Vaccine Ride, which used out-of-state coordinators and attracted out-of-state participants, was held at the park; and (7) the Billings Symphony performed at the park and included out-of-state musicians and sound systems. . . .

[A]lthough "most of the discussion in Congress regarding the coverage of Title II focused on places of spectator entertainment rather than recreational areas," it "does not follow that the scope of [§2000a(b)(3)] should be restricted to the primary objects of Congress's concern when a natural reading of its text would call for broader coverage." Daniel v. Paul, 395 U.S. 298, 307 (1969); see also Miller v. Amusement Enters., Inc., 394 F.2d 342, 348, 350 (5th Cir. 1968) (en banc) ("We are unable to agree with those concepts which would prefer, or those which would demand, that the Civil Rights Act be narrowly construed. . . . We find that the phrase "place of entertainment" as used in [§2000a(b)(3)] includes both establishments which present shows, performances and exhibitions to a passive audience and those establishments which provide recreational or other activities for the amusement or enjoyment of its patrons."). "[T]he statutory language "place of entertainment" should be given full effect according to its generally accepted meaning *and applied to recreational areas.*" *Daniel*, 395 U.S. at 308 (emphasis added); see also United States v. Baird, 85 F.3d 450, 453 (9th Cir. 1996) (holding that a 7-11 store that contained two video game machines was a "place of entertainment" because "people play video games in order to amuse themselves and pass the time agreeably"). . . .

We hold that Pioneer Park was a place of "public accommodation" as defined by 42 U.S.C. §2000a and that the defendants therefore were properly convicted for violating §241.

II

Allen, Dixon, Flaherty, Flom, and Potter were convicted of violating 18 U.S.C. §245(b)(2)(B). . . . [T]hey contend that the enactment of §245(b)(2)(B) was an invalid exercise of Congress's power under the

Commerce Clause because the statute regulates noneconomic, intrastate criminal activities that do not affect interstate commerce and that should be regulated by state law. . . .

A. THE CONSTITUTIONALITY OF §245(B)(2)(B)

Whether 18 U.S.C. §245(b)(2)(B) was a valid exercise of Congress's Commerce Clause power is an issue we have not addressed in this circuit. The defendants liken §245(b)(2)(B) to the Gun-Free School Zones Act of 1990, 18 U.S.C. §922(q)(1)(A), and the federal civil remedy provision of the Violence Against Women Act, 42 U.S.C. §13981, which the Supreme Court struck down in United States v. Lopez, 514 U.S. 549 (1995), and United States v. Morrison, 529 U.S. 598 (2000), respectively, as invalid exercises of Congress's power under the Commerce Clause. The defendants maintain that their actions in Pioneer Park on July 29, 2000, as well as other activities and events at Pioneer Park, were purely local and did not affect interstate commerce. In contrast, the government contends that the enactment of §245(b)(2)(B) was a valid exercise of Congress's power under the Commerce Clause, even in light of *Lopez* and *Morrison*, and that, alternatively, it was a valid exercise of Congress's authority under the Thirteenth Amendment.

1. Commerce Clause

As in *Lopez* and *Morrison*, we are concerned with whether the activities that §245(b)(2)(B) regulates "substantially affect" interstate commerce. We conclude that they do. "Due respect for the decisions of a coordinate branch of Government demands that we invalidate a congressional enactment only upon a plain showing that Congress has exceeded its constitutional bounds." *Morrison*, 529 U.S. at 607. Indeed, if Congress had a rational basis for concluding that the activities regulated by §245(b)(2) (B) affected interstate commerce, then we must uphold the statute.

The Supreme Court was concerned in *Morrison* that "Congress might use the Commerce Clause to completely obliterate the Constitution's distinction between national and local authority." *Morrison*, 529 U.S. at 615. The Court emphasized that "[t]he regulation and punishment of intrastate violence that is not directed at the instrumentalities, channels, or goods involved in interstate commerce has always been the province of the States." Id. at 618. Section 245(b)(2)(B) regulates only a specific type of violence; namely, violence that interferes with federal civil rights on the basis of "race, color, religion or national origin." This is not merely intrastate violence, but rather, violence that affects civil rights, which are traditionally of federal concern. See United States v. Nelson, 277 F.3d 164, 191 n.28 (2d Cir. [2002]) ("[P]rivate violence motivated by a discriminatory animus against members of a race or religion, etc., who use public facilities, etc., is anything but intrinsically a matter of purely local concern."). In its congressional findings, Congress recognized the federal nature of the violence that §245(b)(2)(B) prohibits:

> Too often in recent years, racial violence has been used to deny affirmative Federal rights; this action reflects a purpose to flout the clearly expressed will of the Congress. . . . Such lawless acts are distinctly Federal crimes and it is, therefore, appropriate that responsibility for vindication of the rights infringed should be committed to the Federal courts.

S. Rep. No. 90-721, *reprinted in* 1968 U.S.C.C.A.N. at 1840.

Unlike the Gun-Free School Zones Act of 1990 and the VAWA, §245(b)(2)(B) was enacted as "part of a comprehensive federal body of civil rights legislation aimed at eradicating discrimination found to have an adverse impact on interstate commerce." *Furrow*, 125 F. Supp. 2d at 1183. Indeed, the Supreme Court upheld this federal body of civil rights legislation, in particular, Title II of the Civil Rights Act of 1964, as a valid exercise of Congress's Commerce Clause power [citing Heart of Atlanta Motel, Inc. v. United States, 379 U.S. 241, 257, 261 (1964), and Katzenbach v. McClung, 379 U.S. 294, 305 (1964)]. . . . Moreover, the Court upheld Title II even though the legislation regulated local, intrastate activities. See *Katzenbach*, 379 U.S. at 302 (stating that Congress's Commerce Clause power "extends to those activities intrastate which so affect interstate commerce . . . as to make regulation of them appropriate means to the attainment of a legitimate end, the effective execution of the granted power to regulate interstate commerce"). Section 245 is merely the criminal counterpart to Title II and is based on the same findings about the effect of racial discrimination on interstate commerce.

Violence that interferes with the exercise of federal civil rights must be prohibited in order to protect these rights and give them meaning. As Congress noted, "it is all too clear that if racial violence directed against activities closely related to those protected by Federal antidiscrimination legislation is permitted to go unpunished, the exercise of the protected activities will be deterred." 1968 U.S.C.C.A.N. at 1842. . . .

We conclude that §245(b)(2)(B) was a constitutional exercise of Congress's Commerce Clause power. Although the actual "park patrol" occurred at a local park in Billings, the patrol was a racially-motivated hate crime that interfered with the victims' exercise of their federally-recognized and protected civil rights. If civil interference with these federal civil rights affects interstate commerce, then criminal interference with them does so as well.

2. Thirteenth Amendment

We are not the first circuit to consider whether Congress validly enacted §245(b)(2)(B) pursuant to its authority under the Thirteenth Amendment. Indeed, both the Second and Eighth Circuits have addressed this very issue and concluded that §245(b)(2)(B) was a constitutional exercise of Congress's authority under the Thirteenth Amendment. See United States v. Nelson, 277 F.3d 164 (2d Cir. 2002); United States v. Bledsoe, 728 F.2d 1094 (8th Cir. 1984).

In *Nelson,* the court began its thorough analysis of this issue by reviewing the Thirteenth Amendment in general. The Court noted that Section Two of the Thirteenth Amendment "clothed Congress with power to pass *all laws necessary and proper for abolishing all badges and incidents of slavery in the United States.*" 277 F.3d at 183 (citing Jones v. Alfred H. Mayer Co., 392 U.S. 409, 439 (1968)). Indeed, "Congress has the power under the Thirteenth Amendment rationally to determine what are the badges and the incidents of slavery, and the authority to translate that determination into effective legislation." Id. (citing *Jones,* 392 U.S. at 440). The court specifically noted that, unlike the Fourteenth Amendment, the Thirteenth Amendment reaches purely private conduct. Id. at 176.

The court then framed its analysis as follows: "We must . . . ask whether Congress could rationally have determined that the acts of violence covered by §245(b)(2)(B) impose a badge or incident of servitude on their victims." Id. at 185. In answering this question, the court relied on the fact that §245(b)(2)(B) "does not seek to reach most force-based injuries, intimidations, or interferences and by no means attempts to create a general, undifferentiated federal law of criminal assault." Id. Indeed, the statute requires that victims be harmed *because of* their race or religion and *because of* their use of a public facility. Id. at 185-186. In light of these two specific prohibitions, the court concluded that §245(b)(2)(B) "falls comfortably within Congress's "power under the Thirteenth Amendment rationally to determine what are the badges and the incidents of slavery, and [its] authority to translate that determination into effective legislation," id. at 190-191 (citing *Jones,* 392 U.S. at 440), and therefore was a constitutional exercise of Congress's authority under the Thirteenth Amendment, id. at 191. . . .

We agree with the Second and Eighth Circuits . . . that the enactment of §245(b)(2)(B) was a constitutional exercise of Congress's authority under the Thirteenth Amendment. . . .

NOTES AND QUESTIONS

1. The defendants in this case were members of a neo-Nazi gang known as the Montana Front Working Class Skinheads. One of the defendants,

Thomas Edelman, openly admitted to committing various acts of vio-
lence against people of color, including beating a Native American man in
Riverfront Park and using a gun to threaten an African American man in
Pioneer Park, see Tom Howard, Former Skinhead Describes Patrols, Billings
Gazette, Oct. 26, 2001. He testified that these crimes were carried out to
win the approval of his fellow gang members, see Tom Howard, Skinhead
Witness Has No Use for Minorities: Emily Ehersman Doesn't Care Much for
Black People, Native Americans or Jews, Billings Gazette, Nov. 2, 2001. The
plan to "patrol" Pioneer Park was hatched as members of the group gath-
ered for a barbecue at the home of one of the gang's leaders.

2. One can't help but wonder how this case ended up in federal court.
After being chased from the park, Mr. Clark escaped by taking refuge in
a nearby house. From there, he called the local police (not the FBI), who
arrived shortly thereafter and arrested the defendants at the scene. The case
itself was investigated by the Big Sky Safe Streets Task Force, which includes
both local law enforcement officers and FBI agents and has no special focus
on civil rights or hate crimes. This does not appear to be a situation where
state laws were unable to hold defendants accountable. Chasing individuals
with deadly weapons almost certainly constitutes a felony in Montana, and
state law provides a penalty enhancement for crimes committed "because of
the victim's race, creed, religion, color, [or] national origin. . . ." Mont. Code
Ann. §45-5-222 (1989). Furthermore, Mont. Code Ann. §45-5-221, enacted
the same year as §45-5-222, makes it a felony for a person acting with the
intent "to terrify, intimidate, threaten, harass, annoy, or offend" another
because of his race (among other things), to cause "bodily injury," "reasonable apprehension of injury," or damage to property. However, Westlaw, as
of August 2017, reveals no Montana state court opinion applying §45-5-222,
and only three decisions involving a prosecution under §45-5-221. Are we to
conclude that federal prosecutors believed the state was unwilling to mete
out sufficient punishment in this case? That state officials *preferred* that the
feds take the case?

3. As noted above, §245 supplements but does not replace §241.
Prosecutors are free to use the two statutes in tandem when targeting racially
motivated crimes. See, e.g., United States v. Cazares, 788 F.3d 956 (9th Cir.
2015) (affirming convictions for violation of both §245 and §241 where members of a Latin American street gang engaged in a campaign of harassment,
intimidation, and murder of African-American citizens for the purpose of
interfering with their right to occupy a dwelling, in violation of §241, and
for the purpose of deterring their use of "facilities provided and administered by a subdivision of the State, namely the public streets of Los Angeles,"
in violation of §245(b)(2)(B)). Id. at 962.

4. Section 245 targets what are commonly called "hate crimes"—a
subject of considerable scholarly and political attention. Why should an
offender face a special charge or have his punishment enhanced when it

is shown that he acted out of racial (or other such) animus (as opposed to, say, greed, anger, or sadism)? Where does the additional harm lie or the additional culpability? To what extent should we worry about punishing thought, as opposed to the conduct manifested? Additional questions arise when otherwise local "hate crimes" become the subject of federal law. These and related issues are discussed in James B. Jacobs & Kimberly Potter, Hate Crimes: Criminal Law & Identity Politics (1998) (suggesting that the enhancement of punishment for criminal activity through hate-crimes legislation is inherently problematic and ultimately counterproductive); Frederick M. Lawrence, Punishing Hate: Bias Crimes Under American Law (1999) (arguing that bias crimes—particularly those that are racially motivated—warrant enhanced punishment, and that hate-crimes legislation is consistent with the constitutional guarantee of freedom of expression); John S. Baker, Jr., Symposium, United States v. Morrison and Other Arguments Against "Hate Crimes" Legislation, 80 B.U. L. Rev. 1191, 1214-15 (2000) (discussing punishment for the status of being a bigot); Sara Sun Beale, Symposium, Federalizing Hate Crimes: Symbolic Politics, Expressive Law, or Tool for Criminal Enforcement?, 80 B.U. L. Rev. 1227, 1247-54 (2000) (discussing hate-crimes legislation as symbolic politics); Alon Harel & Gideon Parchomovsky, On Hate and Equality, 109 Yale L.J. 507 (1999) (rejecting the "wrongfulness-culpability" justifications for hate-crimes legislation in favor of broader social concerns); Heidi Hurd, Why Liberals Should Hate Hate Crime Legislation, 20 Law & Philosophy 215 (2001) (suggesting that criminalizing hate and bias is alien to traditional criminal law principles and antithetical to liberal political philosophy); Carol S. Steiker, Punishing Hateful Motives: Old Wine in a New Bottle Revives Calls for Prohibition, 97 Mich. L. Rev. 1857 (1999) (reviewing James B. Jacobs & Kimberly Potter, Hate Crimes: Criminal Law and Identity Politics (1998), and discussing punishment of thought).

Despite these concerns, Congress has gone beyond §245 to create a broad hate-crimes offense. Consider the text of the most recent federal hate-crimes statute, enacted in 2009 and now codified at 18 U.S.C. §249. Notice in what ways it differs from §245 above.

---

18 U.S.C. §249. Hate crime acts

(a) In general.—

(1) Offenses involving actual or perceived race, color, religion, or national origin.—Whoever, whether or not acting under color of law, willfully causes bodily injury to any person or, through the use of fire, a firearm, a dangerous weapon, or an explosive or incendiary device, attempts to cause bodily

injury to any person, because of the actual or perceived race, color, religion, or national origin of any person—

    (A) shall be imprisoned not more than 10 years, fined in accordance with this title, or both; and

    (B) shall be imprisoned for any term of years or for life, fined in accordance with this title, or both, if—

        (i) death results from the offense; or

        (ii) the offense includes kidnapping or an attempt to kidnap, aggravated sexual abuse or an attempt to commit aggravated sexual abuse, or an attempt to kill.

(2) Offenses involving actual or perceived religion, national origin, gender, sexual orientation, gender identity, or disability.—

    (A) In general.—Whoever, whether or not acting under color of law, in any circumstance described in subparagraph (B) or paragraph (3), willfully causes bodily injury to any person or, through the use of fire, a firearm, a dangerous weapon, or an explosive or incendiary device, attempts to cause bodily injury to any person, because of the actual or perceived religion, national origin, gender, sexual orientation, gender identity, or disability of any person—

        (i) shall be imprisoned not more than 10 years, fined in accordance with this title, or both; and

        (ii) shall be imprisoned for any term of years or for life, fined in accordance with this title, or both, if—

            (I) death results from the offense; or

            (II) the offense includes kidnapping or an attempt to kidnap, aggravated sexual abuse or an attempt to commit aggravated sexual abuse, or an attempt to kill.

    (B) Circumstances described.—For purposes of subparagraph (A), the circumstances described in this subparagraph are that—

        (i) the conduct described in subparagraph (A) occurs during the course of, or as the result of, the travel of the defendant or the victim—

            (I) across a State line or national border; or

            (II) using a channel, facility, or instrumentality of interstate or foreign commerce;

        (ii) the defendant uses a channel, facility, or instrumentality of interstate or foreign commerce in connection with the conduct described in subparagraph (A);

        (iii) in connection with the conduct described in subparagraph (A), the defendant employs a firearm, dangerous weapon, explosive or incendiary device, or other weapon that has traveled in interstate or foreign commerce; or

        (iv) the conduct described in subparagraph (A)—

            (I) interferes with commercial or other economic activity in which the victim is engaged at the time of the conduct; or

            (II) otherwise affects interstate or foreign commerce. . . .

(4) Guidelines.—All prosecutions conducted by the United States under this section shall be undertaken pursuant to guidelines issued by the Attorney General, or the designee of the Attorney General, to be included

in the United States Attorneys' Manual that shall establish neutral and objective criteria for determining whether a crime was committed because of the actual or perceived status of any person.

(b) Certification requirement.—

(1) In general.—No prosecution of any offense described in this subsection may be undertaken by the United States, except under the certification in writing of the Attorney General, or a designee, that—

(A) the State does not have jurisdiction;

(B) the State has requested that the Federal Government assume jurisdiction;

(C) the verdict or sentence obtained pursuant to State charges left demonstratively unvindicated the Federal interest in eradicating bias-motivated violence; or

(D) a prosecution by the United States is in the public interest and necessary to secure substantial justice.

NOTES AND QUESTIONS

1. The full legislative title of 18 U.S.C. §249 is The Mathew Shepard and James Byrd, Jr., Hate Crimes Prevention Act of 2009. Shepard had been a student at the University of Wyoming when he died from a brutal beating in 1998; witnesses said he had been targeted because he was homosexual. Byrd was an African American who was fatally injured that same year in Jasper, Texas, when he was chained by his ankles to the back of a pick-up truck and dragged for three miles. Shepard's killers were both convicted of first-degree murder in Wyoming and given life sentences. Byrd's murderer was prosecuted in Texas courts and executed in 2011.

The coverage of §249 is narrower in some respects than that of §§241 and 245, but broader in others. Section 249 gets rid of the double intent requirement in §245(b)(2), and also avoids potential First Amendment problems by restricting its reach to violent acts: While it includes attempts, it does not include mere "threats." On the other hand, it covers violent acts committed because of the victim's "gender, disability, sexual orientation, or gender identity." In pressing for the legislation, Attorney General Holder asserted that, previously, such violent hate crimes "fell entirely outside the scope of federal jurisdiction."

2. What is the source of Congress's power to enact this new legislation? Look carefully at the difference in what the government must prove in different types of cases. Where the violence is based on victim attributes mentioned in the previous Note, the government must prove an effect on interstate commerce, see §249(a)(2). As the trial court hearing the first prosecution under this provision for an assault based on sexual orientation noted:

If wholly intrastate non-economic activity can be transformed into conduct that the federal government may punish simply because the defendant used a car or a road to get there, the Interstate Commerce Clause continues to cast a very large shadow, indeed, and very little activity remains in the exclusive province of the police powers of the state. Even so, this is the ultimate outcome of the current prevailing constitutional precedents in this Circuit as applied to these facts.

United States v. Jenkins, 909 F. Supp. 2d 758, 773 (E.D. Ky. 2012) (declining to quash the indictment).

Where the violence is based on the victim's race, ethnicity, national origin, or religion, no such effect must be shown, see §249 (a)(1). Why is this? According to the Civil Rights Division's website, "Section 249(a)(1) was passed pursuant to Congress's Thirteenth Amendment authority to eradicate badges and incidents of slavery. The government need prove no other "'jurisdictional' element to obtain a conviction." Courts have agreed, on the theories we saw invoked, they uphold §256(b)(2)(b). See, e.g., United States v. Maybee, 687 F.3d 1026, 1031 (8th Cir. 2012).

3. The issue of the constitutionality of §249 gained national attention in 2016, during the prosecution of a notorious hate crime defendant. Dylann Roof perpetrated the shootings at the Emmanuel African Methodist Episcopal Church in Charleston, South Carolina. Roof entered the church with a concealed pistol while a bible study group was in session and ultimately drew his weapon and began firing, killing nine people. He was allegedly motivated to commit this mass murder by a desire to resist racial integration and to avenge wrongs committed against white people. A federal grand jury returned a 33-count indictment against Roof, including nine counts of violating §249, specifically due to his commission of "racially motivated hate crimes resulting in death."

After he was indicted, Roof argued that §249 was unconstitutional because it was not authorized by the Thirteenth Amendment, and failed to respect the states' police power. Rejecting his argument, the court reasoned:

> The Hate Crimes Act subjects certain private conduct to federal criminal penalty—it does not regulate state criminal procedures in any way. Further, powers the Constitution grants to Congress necessarily are not powers the Constitution exclusively reserves to the states. United States v. Comstock, 560 U.S. 126, 143-44 (2010). The Thirteenth Amendment grants Congress authority to enact "appropriate legislation" to abolish all "badges and incidents" of slavery. *Jones*, 392 U.S. at 409. Whether appropriate legislation in some way touches on police powers is immaterial.
>
> In enacting §249(a)(1), Congress found that "[s]lavery and involuntary servitude were enforced, both prior to and after the adoption of the 13th amendment . . . through widespread public and private violence directed at persons because of their race, color, or ancestry, or perceived race, color, or

ancestry" and that "eliminating racially motivated violence is an important means of eliminating, to the extent possible, the badges, incidents, and relics of slavery and involuntary servitude." Hate Crimes Act §4702. Defendant has not challenged the identification of racially motivated violence as a badge and incident of slavery, which indeed seems inarguable.

The "badges of slavery" have been construed as "the customs that formed and maintained this institution." See Miller, *supra*, at 1838, 1845-46. Such customs include housing discrimination, educational discrimination, employment discrimination, and racially motivated violence. See, e.g., Runyon v. McCrary, 427 U.S. 160, 173-75 (1976) . . . Such customs also include attacks on African-American churches. Indeed, Defendant was not the first person to attack Mother Emanuel in an effort to promote white supremacy. Mother Emanuel was founded in 1816 in protest to a white congregation's plan to build a garage on a black cemetery. Douglas R. Egerton, The Long, Troubled History of Charleston's Emanuel AME Church, New Republic, June 18, 2015. Charleston authorities repeatedly closed the church—arresting and whipping congregants—because the church taught literacy to African-Americans, a threat to the institution of slavery. Id. In 1822, it was burned for suspected involvement with the Denmark Vesey slave revolt. Emanuel AME Church, Church History, http://www.emanuelamechurch.org/churchhistory.php. In 1834, all black churches in Charleston were outlawed as threats to slavery, and the congregation could only meet in secret. Id.

Another prominent badge of slavery was the ineffectiveness of laws protecting African-Americans even when such laws existed . . .

That evil—failure to punish the violence the law forbids when that violence serves the cause of white supremacy—is exactly what §249(a)(1) remedies. It allows federal prosecution of racially motivated violent crimes when state efforts would not fully vindicate federal interests in eradicating such crimes and in securing substantial justice. See 18 U.S.C. §249(b)(1). The Court therefore holds §249(a)(1) is an attempt to abolish what is rationally identified as a badge or incident of slavery in the United States.

United States v. Roof, 225 F. Supp. 3d 438, 444-47 (D.S.C. 2016).

The Courts of Appeals that have considered the constitutionality of §249 have offered similar reasoning. See United States v. Cannon, 750 F.3d 492 (5th Cir. 2014) (concluding that "we cannot say that Congress was irrational in determining that racially motivated violence is a badge or incident of slavery."); United States v. Hatch, 722 F.3d 1193 (10th Cir. 2013) ("physically attacking a person of a particular race because of animus toward or a desire to assert superiority over that race is a badge or incident of slavery."); United States v. Maybee, 687 F.3d 1026, 1031 (8th Cir. 2012) (noting that while defendant "argues that §249(a)(1) sweeps more broadly than §245(b)(2)(B), he provides no substantial argument as to why the particular scope of §249(a)(1) renders it constitutionally infirm").

The South Carolina jury sentenced Roof to death in January 2017. The death sentence was available not under §249 but under §924(j), for charges relating to the use of a firearm to commit murder during and in relation to a crime of violence. See 225 F. Supp. 3d 413, 417 (D.S.C. 2016).

4. Note the "certification" requirement in §249(b). That this statute stretches to the edges of (if not beyond) Congress's police powers is consistent with this instruction to use it judiciously. In fact, local prosecutors litigate the majority of hate-crimes cases, and this legislation was not intended to alter that state of affairs, see H.R. Rep. 111-86, at 6 (2009). Perhaps this provision can be understood as a proclamation by Congress that violent hate crimes must be prosecuted vigorously—but by state authorities, with the certification requirement an inducement for local officials to act: "If you don't, the feds will, and you won't look good at the press conference announcing certification by DOJ because you failed to vindicate justice in this case."

In the first five years after the passage of §249, the Department of Justice convicted forty-nine defendants of violating it. Benjamin B. Wagner, Celebrating the Fifth Anniversary of the Shepard-Byrd Hate Crime Prevention Act, Dep't of Justice (Apr. 7, 2015). Compare that number of federal prosecutions with the *5,850* hate crime incidents reported by the FBI *in a single year*, 2015. Over half of these were allegedly motivated by racial bias, while around 20 percent were allegedly motivated by sexual-orientation bias. Uniform Crime Report: Hate Crimes Statistics, Fed. Bureau of Investigation (2015), https://ucr.fbi.gov/hate-crime/2015/topic-pages /incidentsandoffenses_final.pdf. The small number of cases brought so far gives each one a symbolic status, which might be subject to political contestation. Indeed, such contestation can occur even when the federal role may be limited to assisting in a state prosecution, as occurred when Attorney General Session dispatched a civil-rights prosecutor to assist in the Iowa trials of two defendants charged with first-degree murder of a gender-fluid teenager. See Monica Davey, Guilty Verdict in the Death of a Gender-Fluid Teenager, N.Y. Times, Nov. 3, 2017.

The certification requirement in §249(b) is not to be sniffed at. It has the potential to develop into a contested locus of judicial review. In United States v. Hill, 182 F. Supp. 3d 546 (E.D. Va. 2016), the court reviewed a certification decision in a case in which the defendant had assaulted his co-worker at an Amazon warehouse, later revealing that he did so because of his victim's sexual orientation. The defendant brought a challenge in the District Court to the AG's certification decision. Not surprisingly, the government responded that §249's certification requirement represents an exercise of prosecutorial discretion not subject to judicial review. The court rejected the government's argument, holding that the statute does allow for judicial review of the certification decision to ensure that the prosecution is "in the public interest and necessary to secure substantial justice." Id. at 550 (quoting §249(b)(1)(D)). The court did caution that such review is "limited" and "deferential" and found that the government had met the certification requirement because Virginia's hate crime statute did not cover crimes based on sexual orientation. Id. at 551-52. *Hill* may not be an outlier. The decision in *Roof,* discussed above, adopted the *Hill* court's reasoning in holding that it had the authority to review the AG's certification decision. United States v. Roof, 225 F. Supp. at 450.

Hill also indicates that the constitutional inquiry may be less deferential to the government in cases involving violence motivated by sexual-orientation bias. The court held that the Hate Crimes Prevention Act as applied to the defendant was an unconstitutional expansion of Congress's authority to pass legislation under the Commerce Clause. 182 F.3d at 553. Applying the *Lopez* framework for assessing whether an activity "substantially effects" interstate commerce, the court concluded that "[p]unching someone who is filling up boxes in a warehouse is not the kind of substantial effect on the economy required by the Constitution." Id. At the same time, *Hill* cast doubt on the facial constitutionality of the Act, noting that "[a]fter *Lopez* and *Morrison,* it is difficult to imagine any set of facts in which the HCPA could qualify as economic legislation." Id.

Prosecutions brought under §249 necessarily entail a tricky inquiry into the motivation of the assailant. The next case demonstrates how one of the only Court of Appeals to thus far address this issue resolved the question of motive attribution.

United States v. Miller
767 F.3d 585 (6th Cir. 2014)

SUTTON, Circuit Judge.
A string of assaults in several Amish communities in Ohio gave rise to this prosecution under Section 2 of The Matthew Shepard and James Byrd, Jr. Hate Crimes Prevention Act of 2009. The assaults were not everyday occurrences, whether one looks at the setting (several normally peaceful Amish communities), the method of attack (cutting the hair and shaving the beards of the victims), the mode of transportation to them (hired drivers), the relationship between the assailants and their victims (two of them involved children attacking their parents), or the alleged motive (religious-based hatred between members of the same faith). A jury found that four of the five attacks amounted to hate crimes under the Act and convicted sixteen members of the Bergholz Amish community for their roles in them.

At stake in this appeal is whether their hate-crime convictions may stand. No one questions that the assaults occurred, and only a few defendants question their participation in them. The central issue at trial was

whether the defendants committed the assaults "because of" the religion
of the victims. 18 U.S.C. §249(a)(2)(A). In instructing the jury on this
point, the district court rejected the defendants' proposed instruction
(that the faith of the victims must be a "but for" cause of the assaults) and
adopted the government's proposed instruction (that the faith of the victims must be a "significant factor" in motivating the assaults). Regrettably
for all concerned, a case decided *after* this trial confirms that the court
should have given a but-for instruction on causation in the context of
this criminal trial. *Burrage v. United States,* 134 S. Ct. 881, 887-89 (2014).
Because this error was not harmless, and indeed went to the central factual debate at trial, we must reverse these convictions.

I

In 1995, Samuel Mullet bought land in Jefferson County, Ohio. That
land became the Bergholz Amish community in 2001, when a sufficient
number of ordained ministers qualified it as a separate Amish church
district. The new community appointed Samuel as its bishop. . . .

In 2006, Samuel excommunicated several church members who
questioned Bergholz community practices and his leadership. Included
in the group were Lavern and Mattie Troyer, whose son Aden was married
to Samuel's daughter Wilma, as well as Melvin and Anna Shrock, whose
son Emanuel was married to Samuel's daughter Linda. The excommunications were not good for relationships between and within the affected
families. In one case, they led to a divorce. Aden left Wilma to join his
parents in a Pennsylvania Amish community after unsuccessfully trying
to convince her to join him. In another case, they led to parent-child ani-
mosity. Emanuel refused to leave Bergholz with his parents despite their
repeated efforts to persuade him to do so.

The Bergholz excommunications also tested church doctrine. Amish
communities as a general rule practice strict shunning, meaning that if one
Old Order Amish community excommunicates a community member, all
other Old Order communities must excommunicate him until he obtains
forgiveness from the community that first shunned him. The Bergholz
excommunications proved to be an exception. After fleeing Bergholz
for another community in Pennsylvania, the Troyers asked not to be subject to the strict-shunning rule. Citing unusual practices in Bergholz, the
Troyers asked their new bishop to admit them to the Pennsylvania church
without requiring them to seek forgiveness from Samuel—the Elmer
Gantry of the Amish community to their mind. Given the number of former Bergholz residents in similar situations, Amish bishops from all over
the country met in September 2006 to address the issue. Three hundred
bishops convened, and they voted unanimously to reverse the Bergholz
excommunications.

At the same time that the ruling allowed the Troyers to settle into their new Pennsylvania community, it also exacerbated a custody battle between Wilma and Aden over their two children. The dispute began when a SWAT team took the children under an emergency temporary custody order issued to Aden. It ended two years, and one trial, later when Aden's temporary custody of the children became permanent in an order declaring that "[a]ll parenting time shall be in Pennsylvania. Under no circumstances shall parenting time take place in Bergholz, Ohio." *Id.* at 152.

Losing Wilma's children brought the Bergholz community to its knees and sparked a change in their faith-based traditions. Typically, Amish men do not trim their beards and Amish women do not cut their hair as a way of symbolizing their piety, demonstrating righteousness and conveying an Amish identity. Believing that the loss of Wilma's children resulted from their lack of faith, several Bergholz residents cut their own hair and trimmed their own beards as a way to atone for their sins. The Bergholz community saw these acts as penance and as a symbol of rededication to their faith.

The Bergholz community did not confine this ritual to their own ranks. They also used it to punish or harm others who were not members of the church district. From September 6 to November 9, 2011, several Bergholz community members committed five separate attacks on nine different individuals, slicing off the men's beards and cutting the women's hair. Religious and personal ties connected the nine victims of these attacks to the Bergholz community. Some were parents of Bergholz residents, some were friends, and some were associated with family members who had left Bergholz for other Amish districts. Also linking the victims was that they participated in overturning the Bergholz excommunications and that, in the eyes of the assailants, they were "Amish hypocrites."

A federal grand jury indicted sixteen members of the Bergholz community for violating, and conspiring to violate, the Hate Crimes Prevention Act. . . .

In responding to the hate-crime charges at trial, none of the Bergholz defendants disputed that the assaults happened, and few disputed that they participated in them. To prove that the defendants' actions amounted to a federal hate crime, though, the prosecution had to show that the defendants assaulted the victims *and* that they assaulted the victims "because of" their religious beliefs. *See* 18 U.S.C. §249(a)(2)(A). That extra burden gave rise to a central issue at trial: Why did the defendants assault these individuals? The defendants argued that a mix of interpersonal issues—parental mistreatment, personality conflicts, harassment, power struggles, and interference with family relationships—motivated the assaults. The prosecution argued that faith—a desire to punish those whom Samuel saw as Amish hypocrites and who did not properly practice their Amish faith—motivated the assaults.

The jury sided with the prosecution on four assaults and with the defense on one of them. All told, it convicted all sixteen defendants of at least one violation of the hate-crime statute. . . .

II

The federal hate-crime statute prohibits "willfully caus[ing] bodily injury to any person . . . because of the actual or perceived . . . religion . . . of [that] person." 18 U.S.C. §249(a)(2)(A). Of note here, the crime contains a motive element, requiring the government to show that the defendant attacked the victim "because of" the victim's "actual or perceived" religion. *Id.* The district court instructed the jury that the motive element could be satisfied by showing that "a person's actual or perceived religion was a *significant motivating factor* for a [d]efendant's action" "even if he or she had other reasons for doing what he or she did as well." In taking issue with this instruction, the defendants argue that the phrase "because of" requires but-for causation—a showing that they would not have acted *but for* the victim's actual or perceived religious beliefs. The defendants have the better of the argument.

In everyday usage, the phrase "because of" indicates a but-for causal link between the action that comes before it and the circumstance that comes afterwards. John carried an umbrella because of the rain. Jane stayed home from school because of her fever. Dictionary definitions of the phrase reflect this common-sense understanding: "Because of" means "by reason of" or "on account of" the explanation that follows. Webster's Second New International Dictionary 242 (1950). . . . Put in the context of this statute, a defendant "causes bodily injury to a [] person . . . because of [that person's] actual or perceived . . . religion," 18 U.S.C. §249(a)(2) (A), when the person's actual or perceived religion was a but-for reason the defendant decided to act.

Consistent with these definitions, the Supreme Court has "insiste[d]" that "statutes using the term 'because of'" require a showing of "but-for causality." *Burrage,* 134 S. Ct. at 889. It has applied this requirement in criminal and civil cases alike. . . . And it maintains this requirement regardless of whether "because of" refers to an easier-to-show prohibited act or a harder-to-prove prohibited motive. . . .

A defendant thus "causes bodily injury to a[] person . . . because of [that person's] actual or perceived . . . religion," 18 U.S.C. §249(a)(2) (A), when the person's actual or perceived religion was "the 'reason'" the defendant decided to act, *Gross,* 557 U.S. at 176—that is, "the straw that broke the camel's back," *Burrage,* 134 S. Ct. at 888. . . .

That conclusion makes good sense in the context of a criminal case implicating the motives of the defendants. The alternative proposed definition of the phrase ("significant motivating factor") does not sufficiently define the prohibited conduct. How should a jury measure whether a specific motive was significant in inspiring a defendant to act? Is a motive significant if it is one of three reasons he acted? One of ten? . . . In point of fact, the members of the Court who do not think "because of" means but-for causation in the setting of a civil statute, Univ. of Texas Southwestern

Med'l Center v. Nassar, 133 S. Ct. 2517, 2546 (Ginsburg, J., dissenting), agree that it requires but-for causation in the setting of a criminal statute in view of the rule of lenity, *see Burrage*, 134 S. Ct. at 892 (Ginsburg, J., concurring in the judgment).

Any standard that requires less than but-for causality, moreover, treads uncomfortably close to the line separating constitutional regulation of conduct and unconstitutional regulation of beliefs. The government may punish "bias-inspired *conduct*" without offending the First Amendment because bigoted conduct "inflict[s] greater individual and societal harm." *Wisconsin v. Mitchell*, 508 U.S. 476, 487-88 (1993) (emphasis added). *But punishment* of a defendant's "abstract beliefs," no matter how "morally reprehensible" they may be, violates the First Amendment. *See Dawson v. Delaware*, 503 U.S. 159, 167 (1992). Requiring a causal connection between a defendant's biased attitudes and his impermissible actions ensures that the criminal law targets conduct, not bigoted beliefs that have little connection to the crime. . . .

What seems clear to us today, we must acknowledge, might not have looked as clear at the time of trial. It was not until 2014, when the Court decided *Burrage*, that several contours of this debate came into focus. In deciding that the phrase "results from" in a criminal statute requires but-for causation, *Burrage* made several points directly applicable here. It noted that, under dictionary definitions, "results from" ordinarily "imposes . . . a requirement of actual causality." 134 S. Ct. at 887. It noted that, under its decisions in *Nassar, Gross* and *Burr,* "results from" and "because of" customarily mean the same thing and that both phrases require but-for causation. *Id.* at 888-89. It cited decisions from other courts that reached the same conclusion, including one similar to this case—an Iowa Supreme Court decision interpreting "because of" in the motive element of Iowa's hate-crime statute to require a showing of but-for causation. *Id.* at 889 (citing *State v. Hennings*, 791 N.W.2d 828, 833-35 (Iowa 2010)). And it relied on the criminal setting of the statute to require but-for causation rather than some lesser causal connection between the defendant's actions and the victim's death. *Id.* at 891-92. Just so here: The "because of" element of a prosecution under the Hate Crimes Act requires the government to establish but-for causation. . . .

III . . .

C

Even if the district court incorrectly instructed the jury on this score, the government adds, any error was harmless. But motive played a starring role at trial, and the defendants presented evidence of other, non-religious motives for the assaults. The error was not harmless.

Motive was *the key issue* the defendants presented to the jury, and they presented enough evidence to support a finding in their favor on this score. . . .

1

The defendants perpetrated the first hair-shearing and beard-cutting attack against Martin and Barbara Miller in September 2011. According to the defendants, this attack was "not about religion" but "about bad parenting."

Evidence backed up their position. The Millers were attacked by their children and their children's spouses, and they had a strained relationship with their children before the assault. . . .

A jury could reasonably have found that the Millers' constant criticism and rejection of their children, not the children's disagreement with their parents' faith, spawned the attacks.

How could this be, the government responds, given the religious nature of the attacks: cutting the hair or beards of the victims? But assaults involving religious symbolism do not invariably stem from religious motives. Imagine that an adult male assaults a child. The father of the child confronts the man. After yelling at the man over what he has done, the father violently grabs a cross pendant hanging from the man's neck, yelling "You hypocrite," and injures the man's neck in the process. The religious nature of the cross is important, to be sure, but it does not necessarily show, as the dissent claims here, that the father assaulted the man "because of" of his faith.

Or, given that this is the Matthew Shepard Act, imagine that a child tells his parents he is gay. As a result of their faith, the parents ask the child to undergo reparative therapy. The child resists, the parents dig in, all three fight verbally about everything from faith to family obligations. At some point, the child snaps. He assaults the parents and does so in a faith-offensive way—by physically forcing them to eat non-kosher food, by tattooing 666 on their arms or by taking some other action that deeply offends their faith. No doubt faith entered the mix from both sides of the assault, but there *is* doubt about whether the parents' faith broke the camel's back in terms of why the child committed the assault. That the means of assault involved religious symbolism confirms only that he knew how best to hurt his parents. It does not seal the deal that his parents' faith, as opposed to their lack of support for him, was a but-for motive of the assault. . . .

[The court went on to assess all of the various attacks perpetrated by the defendants and concluded that there was sufficient evidence of non-religious motives to reverse and remand on all of the §249 convictions]. . . .

6

In an effort to support a contrary outcome, the dissent points to evidence that supports a religious-motive theory of the assaults. No doubt, such evidence exists. Had there not been probable cause to support the government's theory of the case, there never would have been an indictment. But, as we have explained at length, this is not the *only* way to read the evidence; it is merely the *best* way to read the evidence — for the prosecution. That is not how harmless error works. One must consider the evidence in support of the government *and* the evidence in support of the defendants. . . .

Sargus, District Judge, dissenting.

This is the first appellate case involving a religious hate crime under the Hate Crimes Prevention Act of 2009, 18 U.S.C. §249. While I respect the majority's efforts to construe a deceivingly simple, but actually complex, statute, I dissent. In my view, the majority has adopted an unduly restrictive interpretation of the statute. . . .

[A]lthough the majority correctly defines "but-for causality," it ultimately fails to apply this correct definition to the facts of this case. As explained below, the pertinent inquiry is not whether religion was *the sole* but-for cause of the victims' injury, but rather whether it was *a* but-for cause. Here, this requires that "bodily injury" would not have happened but for "the religion of the victim." Overwhelming and uncontested evidence adduced at trial demonstrates that "but for" the victims' Amish religion, their beards and hair would not have been cut. Because the record contains no evidence undermining the conclusion that the victims' Amish religion was a but-for cause of the injury, the trial court's causation-instruction error was harmless. . . .

As the majority acknowledges, *Burrage,* decided after the trial in this case, provides definitive guidance concerning the appropriate construction of the term "because of" that the trial court simply did not have at the time of trial. At issue in *Burrage* was a statutory enhancement provision that calls for increased penalties "on a defendant who unlawfully distributes a Schedule I or II drug, when 'death or serious bodily injury *results from* the use of such substance.'" 134 S. Ct. at 885 (emphasis added) (quoting 21 U.S.C. §841(a)(1), (b)(1)(A)-(C) (2012)). The purchaser of the drug died following a binge consisting of five drugs, including heroin, which the defendant had distributed. *Id. Both of the medical experts testifying at trial opined that the heroin was a contributing factor, but neither could say whether the decedent would have lived had he not taken the heroin. See id.* at 885-86. The parties disputed the appropriate language for the jury instruction regarding causation. *See id.* at 886.

It is within this context that the *Burrage* Court set about defining the phrase "results from." Within its analysis, the Court reviewed both case law and dictionary definitions of the phrase "because of," noting that the definitions of the phrases "because of" and "results from" "resemble" one another, in that each requires but-for causality. *Id.* at 889. The *Burrage* Court concluded that these phrases "require[] proof 'that the harm would not have occurred in the absence of—that is, but for—the defendant's conduct.'" *Id.* at 887-88. . . .

[T]here often exists more than one but-for cause; a number of necessary causes may operate concurrently to produce a given outcome. Such is the case here. . . .

NOTES AND QUESTIONS

1. You may wonder what happened to the rather distinctive group of defendants in *Miller.* While the Sixth Circuit vacated and remanded on the §249 convictions, the court let stand the defendants' convictions on various counts related to their concealing evidence and making false statements to the FBI. On remand, the government declined to re-try the hate crime charges, and the defendants were re-sentenced for the remaining convictions. Of the sixteen defendants, the court resentenced eight defendants to time served and eight to terms ranging from 43 to 129 months. All of the *Miller* defendants except one once again appealed to the Sixth Circuit, but this time the court rejected all of their arguments. See United States v. Mullet, 822 F.3d 842, 846 (6th Cir. 2016). The defendants' allegedly religious motivation may not have sufficed for a conviction under §249, but this claim was not completely irrelevant to their ultimate fates. As you will learn (if you didn't already know) in Chapter 10, the sentencing judge can take account of conduct that is relevant to the crime of conviction even if that conduct was not separately charged, or pertained to a vacated conviction. See id. at 851. In *Mullet,* the defendants' sentences were enhanced because the sentencing judge found that their obstruction of justice hampered a "hate crimes investigation." Chapter 10 explores in detail the nature of federal judges' sentencing discretion.

2. Given the concerns raised in *Hill,* you may also wonder how the government satisfied the jurisdictional element here. The defendants were convicted of violating §249(a)(2)—which is not an exercise of congressional authority under the Thirteenth or Fourteenth Amendment, but instead under the Commerce Clause. The district court found sufficient the prosecution's argument that the shears used by the defendants to forcibly cut their victims' hair and beards had been made in New York and transported to Ohio, thereby satisfying the commerce nexus. United States v. Mullett, 868 F. Supp. 2d 618, 621-23 (N.D. Ohio 2012). Even a community dedicated to rejecting the conveniences of modern technology, it seems, cannot escape participation in contemporary interstate commerce.

3. Who do you think gets the better of the argument between the majority and the dissent regarding the question of "but-for" causality?

Other courts have also struggled with mixed motives analysis when applying the Hate Crimes Prevention Act of 2009. In the first prosecution brought under the statute for violence allegedly based on the victim's sexual orientation, a court in the Eastern District of Kentucky held that the words "because of" in the Act mandate a jury instruction that "the sexual orientation of the victim is a necessary prerequisite to the assault." United States v. Jenkins, 120 F. Supp. 3d 650 (2013). The court in *Jenkins* observed:

> Admittedly, it is a difficult task to choose words that convey the notion that just because a physical assault would not have occurred "but for" someone's sexual orientation does not necessarily mean that sexual orientation was the "sole" reason for that assault. But jury instructions often rest on the imperfect endeavor of describing the human condition. This is particularly true when it comes to trying to guide jurors in the task of ascertaining mental state. That is why we candidly admit that "Ordinarily, there is no way that a defendant's state of mind can be proved directly, because no one can read another person's mind and tell what that person is thinking." Sixth Circuit Pattern Jury Instruction 2.08(2).

Id. at 657.

This discussion of §249 demonstrates the way in which mixed motive analysis in criminal law—where discerning motive can be elusive yet also outcome determinative—remains an area of great debate. For a discussion of federal courts' struggles to engage in "mixed motives" analysis generally, see Andrew Verstein, The Jurisprudence of Mixed Motives, 127 Yale L.J. 1106 (2018).

8 | The Law of Criminal Organizations

Most crime is disorganized, impulsive, ad hoc, and perpetrated by individuals acting alone. Assaults, murders, and thefts are usually committed because would-be offenders get mad and act on their anger, or see what look like opportunities for gain and seize them. The spontaneity of such crimes often makes them easy to solve, since the offenders act with little forethought and assistance from others, and take few precautions to avoid detection. These crimes may also be easy to deter by, for example, concentrating police in high-crime areas to limit opportunistic criminal activity.

This chapter addresses laws designed to deal with a second class of crimes that has very different characteristics: Instead of individuals acting solo, offenders work together as part of a team. Such groups are often well organized, with a clear and rational division of labor. They usually plan their crimes in advance and take precautions against the most obvious risks of detection. The crimes committed by these groups may be connected over time or over space, and often serve some larger plan, or advance some medium- or long-term business goal. Such offenses are what most of us have in mind when we use the phrase "organized crime."

Traditionally, local police forces and district attorneys' offices have handled the overwhelming majority of the first class of criminal offenses. Federal agents and U.S. Attorney's Offices now handle an increasingly large fraction of the second class. Federal criminal law and federal law enforcers are not the sole means of combatting organized crime in the United States, but the federal government has played a disproportionately large role in this enterprise. From the Mafia to money laundering, from drug conspiracies to environmental business crime, federal law has become the chief weapon against crimes committed by organized groups.

The nature of group crimes has changed over time. The phrase "organized crime" conjures images of *The Godfather* and *Goodfellas*, and Mafia cases have indeed played a large role in some of the bodies of law surveyed in this chapter. But today, more loosely organized street gangs are the chief criminal organizations in most American cities. Even as local enforcers go after crimes committed by gang members, federal law enforcement agencies—in many cases, working in conjunction with local authorities—often seek to investigate the gang as an entity, focusing not on a single crime at a time, but on the gamut of crimes committed by group members over time. Business crimes and political corruption constitute additional types of modern organized crime. These offenses generally involve significant organization and planning, as well as the cooperation of multiple criminal actors. Similarly, crimes that take place in markets—consider the distribution of child pornography or narcotics—require organized networks for the relevant markets to function.

The nature of the legal weaponry used against group crime has changed as well. In this chapter, we briefly cover two established legal tools, and then consider at greater length three newer culpability theories. The first tool we discuss is also the first to arise historically: the law of accomplice liability, commonly known as "aiding and abetting." Accomplice liability is the subject of Section A. In Section B, we briefly consider two liability theories—"accessory after the fact" and "misprision of felony"—if only to show their limits. In Section C, we examine another familiar legal weapon: the law of conspiracy. The third theory of liability we address is a recent addition to the prosecutor's arsenal: the federal money-laundering statutes. These statutes, addressed in Section D, attack criminal organizations indirectly by criminalizing the receipt or transfer of the money such organizations make. Fourth, we turn to RICO—the Racketeer Influenced and Corrupt Organizations Act, 18 U.S.C. §§1961-1964. If money laundering is a prime example of an indirect enforcement strategy against criminal groups, then RICO is the paradigm direct approach: It criminalizes participation in the affairs of a "criminal enterprise."* A vast body of law has arisen to define the meaning of this term; Section E explores the key elements. Finally, Section F examines those statutes that criminalize material support for terrorism.

Those who worry that the extension of criminal liability doctrine to peripheral actors risks over-penalizing low-level players are often reassured that issues of comparative liability can be explored at sentencing. As we shall see when we address sentencing in Chapter 10, however, that is not always true. While the truly peripheral actor often gets a lighter sentence (or avoids prosecution altogether by cooperating with the government or by simply not being worth the government's trouble), he cannot always count on that outcome, especially when there are relevant statutory mandatory minimum sentences. It is therefore important to understand the substantive law and the extent to which it constrains prosecutorial and sentencing discretion.

---

* In Chapter 9, we consider another "enterprise" statute, 21 U.S.C. §848, which makes it a crime to commit or conspire to commit a continuing series of drug trafficking offenses in concert with five or more other individuals. Formally titled the Continuing Criminal Enterprise statute, this provision is commonly referred to as the "drug kingpin" statute.

A. ACCOMPLICE LIABILITY

---

18 U.S.C. §2. Principals

(a) Whoever commits an offense against the United States or aids, abets, counsels, commands, induces or procures its commission, is punishable as a principal.

(b) Whoever willfully causes an act to be done which if directly performed by him or another would be an offense against the United States, is punishable as a principal.

It may be helpful to begin by thinking of complicity not as a crime in and of itself, but simply as another way of committing an existing crime. See United States v. Smith, 198 F.3d 377, 383 (2d Cir. 1999) ("[A]iding and abetting does not constitute a discrete criminal offense but only serves as a more particularized way of identifying 'persons involved.'"). An accomplice is liable for assisting another—a principal—in that person's commission of an offense. Two conclusions flow from this understanding. First, accomplice liability is contingent upon the actual occurrence of an offense (which may be only an attempted crime). Second, for purposes of establishing criminal liability, it makes no sense to say that the defendant was "only" an aider and abettor of a particular offense; the jury is instructed to convict the defendant of that offense if the facts support the theory of accomplice liability. Just as digital technology effectively ended the difference between an "original" and a "copy," so too the general accomplice liability statute has made the common-law distinction between "principal" and "accessory" largely anachronistic in federal law. While §2(a) requires the government to prove that someone committed the substantive offense, its failure to convict (or even prosecute) that person does not preclude the conviction of an aider and abettor. Indeed, the government does not have to identify the principal at all, so long as it shows that the underlying crime was committed by someone. See United States v. Litwok, 678 F.2d 208, 214 n.1 (2d Cir. 2012).

1. ACTUS REUS

What type of assistance must an individual provide to be guilty of a crime as an accomplice? In other words, precisely how much facilitation is sufficient to obtain a conviction? Until recently, a minority of courts demanded that the defendant have facilitated every element of the underlying offense. The Supreme Court recently clarified, however:

> [T]he common law [principle that] every little bit helps—and a contribution to some part of a crime aids the whole . . . continues to govern aiding and

abetting law under §2: As almost every court of appeals has held, "[a] defendant can be convicted as an aider and abettor without proof that he participated in each and every element of the offense." United States v. Sigalow, 812 F.2d 783, 785 (C.A.2 1987). In proscribing aiding and abetting, Congress used language that "comprehends all assistance rendered by words, acts, encouragement, support, or presence," Reves v. Ernst & Young, 507 U.S. 170, 178 (1993) — even if that aid relates to only one (or some) of a crime's phases or elements. So, for example, in upholding convictions for abetting a tax evasion scheme, this Court found "irrelevant" the defendants' "non-participation" in filing a false return; we thought they had amply facilitated the illegal scheme by helping a confederate conceal his assets. United States v. Johnson, 319 U.S. 503, 515, 518 (1943). "[A]ll who shared in [the overall crime's] execution," we explained, "have equal responsibility before the law, whatever may have been [their] different roles." Id. at 515. And similarly, we approved a conviction for abetting mail fraud even though the defendant had played no part in mailing the fraudulent documents; it was enough to satisfy the law's conduct requirement that he had in other ways aided the deception. See Pereira v. United States, 347 U.S. 1, 8-11 (1954). The division of labor between two (or more) confederates thus has no significance: A strategy of "you take that element, I'll take this one" would free neither party from liability.

Rosemond v. United States, 134 S. Ct. 1240, 1246-47 (2014).

Before *Rosemond*, courts sometimes engaged in fine-line-drawing where accomplice liability was sought for a particular aspect of a criminal undertaking that carries an additional penalty, the classic example being statutes that separately punish use of a firearm during a felony. In *Rosemond*, however, the Court instructed that the general rule outlined above (that facilitation of just one element of an offense is sufficient for accomplice liability) applies identically to such "compound" crimes.

Rosemond took part in a drug deal in which one of the dealers fired a gun. Because witnesses disagreed about the shooter's identity, the government charged Rosemond with violating 18 U.S.C. §924(c) by using or carrying a gun in connection with a drug trafficking crime, or, in the alternative, aiding and abetting that offense under 18 U.S.C. §2 (in addition to the underlying drug offense). As a result of his conviction under §924(c), a consecutive 10 years of imprisonment was added to his sentence. Rosemond did not dispute that he actively participated in a drug transaction; he alleged, however, that "he took no action with respect to any firearm. He did not buy or borrow a gun to facilitate the narcotics deal; he did not carry a gun to the scene; he did not use a gun during the subsequent events constituting this criminal misadventure." *Rosemond*, 134 S. Ct. at 1246. Applying the general rule that an act in furtherance of one or more elements of a crime is sufficient for accomplice liability, the Court ruled that the §924(c)'s act element was satisfied even if Rosemond had in no way assisted with its firearm component.

2.   *MENS REA*

Mental state, which we consider here, is the biggest factual issue in most aiding and abetting cases. As Judge Boudin has observed, "[O]nce [the mental state of] knowledge on the part of the aider and abettor is established, it does not take much to satisfy the facilitation element." United States v. Bennett, 75 F.3d 40, 45 (1st Cir. 1996). The big issue with respect to mental state, however, is whether "knowledge" of facilitation is sufficient, or whether the heightened *mens rea* of "purpose" is required. For instance, where the crime has a result element (e.g., murder), need an accomplice act with the *purpose* of bringing about a certain result, or need she only *know* that the result will happen? More generally, is it sufficient that the accomplice knows that her actions are aiding the principal's crime? Or must she act with the purpose of aiding that crime?

a.   Traditional Formulation(s?)

The asserted authoritative formulation of *mens rea* for accomplice liability draws on Judge Learned Hand's classic language in United States v. Peoni, 100 F.2d 401 (2d Cir. 1938):

> To establish aiding and abetting liability, the government must prove that the defendant "associate[d] himself with the venture . . . , participate[d] in it as in something he wishe[d] to bring about, and [sought] by his actions to make it succeed."

Id. at 402. See also Nye & Nissen v. United States, 336 U.S. 613, 619 (1949) (adopting Hand's formulation); United States v. Rodriguez Cortes, 949 F.2d 532, 539 (1st Cir. 1991) (same).

1. Consistent application of the *Peoni* standard has proven elusive. Even as all of the courts of appeals purport to adopt the *Peoni* standard, they vary as to what that standard is. Sometimes the same Circuit—and in fact, the same *judge*—has vacillated between a strict *Peoni* and a knowledge standard. For example, in United States v. Ortega, 44 F.3d 505 (7th Cir. 1995), Judge Richard Posner wrote:

> One who, knowing the criminal nature of another's act, deliberately renders what he knows to be active aid in the carrying out of the act is, we think, an aider and abettor even if there is no evidence that he wants the act to succeed. . . . *Peoni*'s formula for aiding and abetting, if read literally, implies that the defendant must to be convicted have some actual desire for his principal to succeed. But in the actual administration of the law it has always been enough that the defendant, knowing what the principal was trying to do,

rendered assistance that he believed would (whether or not he cared that it would) make the principal's success more likely. . . . No more is required to make the defendant guilty of joining the principal's venture and adopting its aims for his own within the meaning of *Peoni* and the cases that follow it.

Id. at 508. Yet Judge Posner has not always followed his own approach. In an oft-quoted decision handed down a decade before *Ortega* (and not referenced therein), Judge Posner attempted to distinguish between levels of culpability based on the severity of the offense, giving two hypothetical crimes:

In the first [case], a shopkeeper sells dresses to a woman whom he knows to be a prostitute. The shopkeeper would not be guilty of aiding and abetting prostitution unless the prosecution could establish the elements of Judge Hand's test. Little would be gained by imposing criminal liability in such a case. Prostitution, anyway a minor crime, would be but trivially deterred, since the prostitute could easily get her clothes from a shopkeeper ignorant of her occupation. In the second case, a man buys a gun from a gun dealer after telling the dealer that he wants it in order to kill his mother-in-law, and he does kill her. The dealer would be guilty of aiding and abetting the murder. This liability would help to deter — and perhaps not trivially given public regulation of the sale of guns — a most serious crime. We hold that aiding and abetting murder is established by proof beyond a reasonable doubt that the supplier of the murder weapon knew the purpose for which it would be used. This interpretation of the federal aider and abettor statute is consistent with though not compelled by precedent. . . .

United States v. Fountain, 768 F.2d 790, 798 (7th Cir. 1985). Judge Posner most recently reaffirmed the views he stated in *Fountain*; see United States v. Colon, 549 F.3d 565, 571 (7th Cir. 2008) (using a similar example, and noting that the dress shopkeeper "probably want[s] the [prostitute's] activity to succeed[,] since if it fails she'll stop buying the dress and [the shopkeeper's] income will be less"). Nor is it clear that Judge Posner's views, whatever they may be, have been clearly adopted by the Seventh Circuit. In another case, that court held, "knowledge alone is not sufficient to convict [the defendant] of aiding and abetting; the government must also show intent to further the crime. . . ." United States v. Woods, 148 F.3d 843, 847 (7th Cir. 1998).

What makes the most sense to you? Should we require knowledge or intent for aiding and abetting liability? Should the standard vary with the severity of the offense in question? And, if you opt for such a sliding scale, would you ground it in legislative intent, or would you simply admit that it is common law?

2. *Foreknowledge?* The Supreme Court has recently introduced another potential wrinkle to *Peoni* — the apparent introduction of an "advance knowledge" or "opportunity to refrain" requirement. Despite rejecting

Rosemond's *actus reus* argument (see *supra* Note 2), the Court found that the trial judge had erroneously instructed the jury as to the *mens rea* the government had to prove for Rosemond to be liable under 18 U.S.C. §924(c) and 18 U.S.C. §2 as an accomplice to the use of gun in furtherance of drug trafficking. The trial judge had instructed the jury "to consider merely whether Rosemond 'knew his cohort used a firearm.'" But "the court did not direct the jury to determine *when* Rosemond obtained the requisite knowledge." 134 S. Ct. at 1251-52. And this, according to Justice Kagan for the majority, was error. Under the *Peoni* standard, she explained, "the intent requirement is satisfied when a person actively participates in a criminal venture with full knowledge of the circumstances constituting the charged offense." Id. at 1248-49. In order to fully know the circumstances constituting a violation of §924(c), however:

> [T]he defendant's knowledge of a firearm must be advance knowledge—or otherwise said, knowledge that enables him to make the relevant legal (and indeed, moral) choice. When an accomplice knows beforehand of a confederate's design to carry a gun, he can attempt to alter that plan or, if unsuccessful, withdraw from the enterprise; it is deciding instead to go ahead with his role in the venture that shows his intent to aid an *armed* offense. But when an accomplice knows nothing of a gun until it appears at the scene, he may already have completed his acts of assistance; or even if not, he may at that late point have no realistic opportunity to quit the crime. And when that is so, the defendant has not shown the requisite intent to assist a crime involving a gun. As even the Government concedes, an unarmed accomplice cannot aid and abet a §924(c) violation unless he has "foreknowledge that his confederate will commit the offense with a firearm. . . ." For the reasons just given, we think that means knowledge at a time the accomplice can do something with it—most notably, opt to walk away.

Id. at 1249-50.

Justice Alito, joined by Justice Thomas, dissented on this point, calling the foreknowledge requirement an "important and unprecedented alteration of the law of aiding and abetting and of the law of intentionality generally." He explained:

> The Court confuses two fundamentally distinct concepts: intent and motive. It seems to assume that, if a defendant's *motive* in aiding a criminal venture is to avoid some greater evil, he does not have the *intent* that the venture succeed. . . . [T]he fact that a defendant carries out a crime because he feels he must do so on pain of terrible consequences [here, that he might be shot] does not mean he does not intend to carry out the crime. When Jean Valjean stole a loaf of bread to feed his starving family, he certainly intended to commit theft; the fact that, had he been living in America today, he may have pleaded necessity as a defense does not change that fact. See V. Hugo, Les Misérables 54 (Fall River Press ed. 2012). . . .

The Court requires the Government to prove that a defendant in Rosemond's situation could have walked away without risking harm greater than he would cause by continuing with the crime—circumstances that traditionally would support a necessity or duress defense. It imposes this requirement on the Government despite the fact that such dangerous circumstances simply do not bear on whether the defendant intends the §924(c) offense to succeed, as (on the Court's reading) is required for aiding and abetting liability. . . . The Court's rule breaks with the common-law tradition and our case law. It also makes no sense.

Id. at 1255-56 (Alito, J., dissenting).

Which side has the better argument? The jury found that Rosemond knew, when he committed the crime of drug trafficking, that his cohort had a firearm. But the Supreme Court said that unless the jury found Rosemond knew this at a time when he could (realistically?) "walk away," such knowledge is insufficient for accomplice liability. Is the Court construing 18 U.S.C. §924(c)? Is it construing 18 U.S.C. §2? Is it postulating a substantive due process limitation on accomplice liability more generally—that one cannot be found guilty of aiding a crime unless one knows in advance (in time to "walk away") all of its elements? Do you think the Court would have used the same analysis if the §924(c) count didn't come with a severe additional punishment (which we examine in the next chapter)?

b.   *Willful Blindness*

Federal law arguably waters down the *mens rea* requirement of knowledge by means of a jury instruction that permits knowledge to be established by "willful blindness" (sometimes called "conscious disregard" or "conscious avoidance"; note also that "willful" is sometimes written with the British spelling, "wilful"). Under the willful blindness doctrine, the prosecution may satisfy a *mens rea* of knowledge by proving that the defendant consciously chose "to avoid learning the truth." United States v. Jewell, 532 F.2d 697, 700-04 (9th Cir. 1976) (en banc). The doctrine may seem strange: "[I]t is hard to see how ignorance . . . can *be* knowledge. A particular explanation of why a defendant remains ignorant might justify treating him as *though* he had knowledge, but it cannot, through some mysterious alchemy, convert ignorance *into* knowledge." Douglas N. Husak & Craig A. Callender, Wilful Ignorance, Knowledge, and the "Equal Culpability" Thesis: A Study of the Deeper Significance of the Principle of Legality, 1994 Wis. L. Rev. 29, 52. Nevertheless, the doctrine of "willful blindness" has been widely used in a variety of settings, including conspiracy cases, see *infra* Section C. The Supreme Court acknowledged the doctrine of willful blindness only in the last decade and, oddly enough, in a civil patent infringement case. In Global-Tech Appliances v. SEB, 563 U.S. 754 (2011), the Court noted:

The doctrine of willful blindness is well established in criminal law. Many criminal statutes require proof that a defendant acted knowingly or willfully, and courts applying the doctrine of willful blindness hold that defendants cannot escape the reach of these statutes by deliberately shielding themselves from clear evidence of critical facts that are strongly suggested by the circumstances. The traditional rationale for this doctrine is that defendants who behave in this manner are just as culpable as those who have actual knowledge. Edwards, The Criminal Degrees of Knowledge, 17 Mod. L. Rev. 294, 302 (1954) (observing on the basis of English authorities that "up to the present day, no real doubt has been cast on the proposition that [willful blindness] is as culpable as actual knowledge"). It is also said that persons who know enough to blind themselves to direct proof of critical facts in effect have actual knowledge of those facts. See United States v. Jewell, 532 F.2d 697, 700 (C.A.9 1976) (en banc).

This Court's opinion more than a century ago in Spurr v. United States, 174 U.S. 728 (1899), while not using the term "willful blindness," endorsed a similar concept. The case involved a criminal statute that prohibited a bank officer from "willfully" certifying a check drawn against insufficient funds. We said that a willful violation would occur "if the [bank] officer purposely keeps himself in ignorance of whether the drawer has money in the bank." Id. at 735. Following our decision in *Spurr*, several federal prosecutions in the first half of the 20th century invoked the doctrine of willful blindness. Later, a 1962 proposed draft of the Model Penal Code, which has since become official, attempted to incorporate the doctrine by defining "knowledge of the existence of a particular fact" to include a situation in which "a person is aware of a high probability of [the fact's] existence, unless he actually believes that it does not exist." ALI, Model Penal Code §2.02(7) (Proposed Official Draft 1962). Our Court has used the Code's definition as a guide in analyzing whether certain statutory presumptions of knowledge comported with due process. See Turner v. United States, 396 U.S. 398, 416-417 (1970); Leary v. United States, 395 U.S. 6, 46-47, and n.93 (1969). And every Court of Appeals—with the possible exception of the District of Columbia Circuit—has fully embraced willful blindness, applying the doctrine to a wide range of criminal statutes.

563 U.S. at 766-68. See also United States v. Jinwright, 683 F.3d 471, 480 (4th Cir. 2012) (a criminal tax prosecution in which the court noted, quoting *Global-Tech*, 563 U.S. at 769-70: "*Global-Tech* synthesized the case law on willful blindness to identify 'two basic requirements': '(1) the defendant must subjectively believe that there is a high probability that a fact exists and (2) the defendant must take deliberate actions to avoid learning of that fact.'"); United States v. Goffer, 721 F.3d 113, 128 (2d Cir. 2013) (finding that *Global-Tech* "simply describes existing case law"). Has the Supreme Court outsourced the development of *mens rea* doctrine in this area to the lower federal courts and the ALI? Should it? What, if any, role should Congress have?

Even if "willful blindness" can count as "knowledge" for *mens rea* purposes, should it be enough for aiding and abetting culpability, given that *Peoni* appears to adopt a "purpose"—not merely a "knowledge"—standard? Yes, some courts have said. See, e.g., United States v. Flood, 327 F. App'x. 356, 359 (3d Cir. 2009) ("Liability for aiding and abetting . . . requires 'the specific intent of facilitating the crime' and we have held that a finding of 'willful blindness' or 'deliberate ignorance' satisfies the intent prong for such a crime."); United States v. Perez-Melendez, 599 F.3d 31, 41 (1st Cir. 2010) (noting that "[w]illful blindness serves as an alternate theory on which the government may prove knowledge," but finding insufficient evidence).

c. *18 U.S.C. §2(b)*

In contrast to §2(a), §2(b) has an explicit "willfulness" requirement for those who cause another person's criminal conduct. Note that Section 2(b)'s requirement refers not to "willful blindness," but to the higher mental state of purpose. In other words, to be guilty under §2(b), a defendant must have the *mens rea* required by the criminal statute that he caused the intermediary to violate, and he must also have *intended* to cause the prohibited *actus reus*. See United States v. Gumbs, 283 F.3d 128, 134 (3d Cir. 2002). As such, an offender may be held liable under §2(b) for causing an innocent intermediary to commit a crime. For example, a tax protestor can be convicted of filing false returns for selling his own special kit (e.g., "How to Avoid Federal Taxes") to customers, even though the actual filers may not have known their returns were false. United States v. Causey, 835 F.2d 1289, 1291-92 (9th Cir. 1987). Similarly, a lawyer can be convicted of making false statements to the government in a lease agreement "even though the person submitting the document (i.e., 'making' the representations) did not know the statements were false." Id. at 1292 (discussing United States v. Vaughn, 797 F.2d 1485, 1490-91 (9th Cir. 1986)).

3. SOME COMPLICATIONS OF ACCOMPLICE LIABILITY

a. When Congress passes a new criminal statute, 18 U.S.C. §2 usually kicks in to expand the scope of liability, making "aiders and abettors" punishable as principals unless there is clear legislative intent to the contrary. See United States v. Wasserson, 418 F.3d 225 (3d Cir. 2005); see also United States v. Ali, 718 F.3d 929 (D.C. Cir. 2013) (upholding prosecution for aiding and abetting piracy on the high seas). Yet there are also some historically and logically grounded exceptions to this rule, as the First Circuit noted in United States v. Southard, 700 F.2d 1 (1st Cir. 1983):

The first exception is that the victim of a crime may not be indicted as an aider or abettor even if his conduct significantly assisted in the commission of the crime. Examples are persons who pay extortion[*] blackmail, or ransom monies. . . .

The next exception embraces criminal statutes enacted to protect a certain group of persons thought to be in need of special protection. Accomplice liability will not be imposed upon the protected group absent an affirmative legislative policy to include them as aiders and abettors. For example, a woman who is transported willingly across state lines for the purpose of engaging in illicit sexual intercourse is not an accomplice to the male transporter's Mann Act violation. Gebardi v. United States, 287 U.S. 112, 119 (1932). . . .

The final exception to accomplice liability . . . occurs when the crime is so defined that participation by another is necessary to its commission. The rationale is that the legislature, by specifying the kind of individual who is to be found guilty when participating in a transaction necessarily involving one or more other persons, must not have intended to include the participation by others in the offense as a crime. This exception applies even though the statute was not intended to protect the other participants. Thus, one having intercourse with a prostitute is not liable for aiding and abetting prostitution, and a purchaser is not an accomplice to an illegal sale. See generally W. LaFave and A. Scott, Criminal Law, §65, at 521-522 (1977). . . .

700 F.2d at 19-20.

Most of the difficult modern cases turn on legislative intent, and the Courts of Appeals have disagreed about whether certain newer statutes permit convictions premised on accomplice liability. Such disagreement is especially pronounced when it appears that Congress has decided to impose severe punishment on a particular and limited class of wrongdoers. Can you think of instances in which it might be desirable to punish the subordinates who "aided and abetted" differently from the principal? Compare United States v. Amen, 831 F.2d 373, 381-82 (2d Cir. 1987) (holding that one cannot be convicted of aiding and abetting a violation of the narcotics "kingpin" statute) with United States v. Pino-Perez, 870 F.2d 1230, 1234 (7th Cir. 1989) (en banc) (holding that one can).

The Supreme Court has resolved a dispute in an analogous setting that involved, not the "aiding and abetting" statute, but a statute that makes it a felony "to use any communication facility in committing or in causing or facilitating" certain drug-related felonies. 21 U.S.C. §843(b). Rejecting the government's effort to bring this charge against someone who had simply used the telephone to arrange two misdemeanor drug purchases, a unanimous Court started with plain meaning and reasoned:

Where a transaction like a sale necessarily presupposes two parties with specific roles, it would be odd to speak of one party as facilitating the conduct of the other. A buyer does not just make a sale easier; he makes the sale possible.

No buyer, no sale; the buyer's part is already implied by the term "sale," and the word "facilitate" adds nothing. We would not say that the borrower facilitates the bank loan.

Abuelhawa v. United States, 556 U.S. 816, 820 (2009). The Court went on to note that any broader reading of "facilitate" would, practically speaking, skew the congressional calibration of respective buyer-seller penalties. The "buyer-seller exception" to aiding and abetting liability is therefore based on legislative intent: Congress intended to treat sellers more harshly than those who only possessed narcotics. (As we will see, courts have used a similar analysis, often referred to as Wharton's Rule, in conspiracy cases).

b. Suppose three thieves decided to break into a warehouse at night and steal some of the more valuable (and portable) merchandise inside. The thief in charge does the actual break-in, a second stands lookout, and the third waits in a getaway car to drive the first two away when the offense is completed. The crime goes off as planned, but all three thieves are caught afterward. Which ones are guilty of burglary? Without the law of accomplice liability, the answer is: only the thief who actually broke into the warehouse. The driver of the getaway car did not enter a closed building, structure, or room with the intent to commit a felony—the usual elements of burglary. The driver had the requisite intent but did not commit the requisite act. The same is true of the lookout. Criminal liability is individual, not collective; but this hypothetical crime was collective, not individual, and consequently, two-thirds of this three-man team would be immune from prosecution. The law of aiding and abetting is designed to address this problem. Not only may the thief who broke into the warehouse be convicted of burglary, but liability also extends to anyone who knowingly helped him—lookouts and drivers of getaway cars included.

What gives rise to the problem that the law of accomplice liability is designed to solve? Even simple criminal organizations operate on principles similar to those that drive legitimate business organizations. One such principle is the division of labor: Different actors perform different tasks and together they accomplish more than each could working alone. But consider a case like United States v. Wasserson, 418 F.3d 225 (3d Cir. 2005), where the defendant was a corporate executive who had directed an employee to dispose of hazardous waste in an improper manner. The boss was the accomplice and the underling who disposed of the waste was the principal. This pattern is also common in organized crime cases: The boss may order the hit, but he does not pull the trigger.

Does it make sense to do as federal law has done and have a general rule making accomplices and principals indistinguishable for purposes of criminal liability? If accomplices are underlings, shouldn't they be punished less severely than principals? And if they are bosses like Wasserson, shouldn't they be punished more severely? In fact, some legal systems do just that. Germany, for example, explicitly recognizes a distinction between two types of accessories: "Any person who intentionally induces another to intentionally commit an unlawful act (abettor)" is liable as a principal, while "[a]ny person who intentionally assists another" in the perpetration of a crime ("aider") receives mitigated punishment. Strafgesetzbuch [StGB] [Penal Code], Nov. 13, 1998, Bundesgesetzblatt [BGBl. I], sec. 26, 27. See also George Fletcher, Rethinking Criminal Law 640 (1978). Why do you suppose American law treats all accessories the same as principals for purposes of criminal liability?

c. "Aiding and abetting" a criminal offense is itself a crime, but it can also produce civil liability. Curiously, accessorial liability is sometimes more limited in civil cases than in criminal cases. In Central Bank of Denver v. First Interstate Bank of Denver, 511 U.S. 164 (1993), in the course of concluding that there is no "aiding and abetting" liability in private securities actions, the Supreme Court noted:

> Aiding and abetting is an ancient criminal law doctrine. See United States v. Peoni, 100 F.2d 401, 402 (CA2 1938); 1 M. Hale, Pleas of the Crown 615 (1736). Though there is no federal common law of crimes, Congress in 1909 enacted what is now 18 U.S.C. §2, a general aiding and abetting statute applicable to all federal criminal offenses. Act of Mar. 4, 1909, §332, 35 Stat. 1152. The statute decrees that those who provide knowing aid to persons committing federal crimes, with the intent to facilitate the crime, are themselves committing a crime. Nye & Nissen v. United States, 336 U.S. 613, 619 (1949).
>
> The Restatement of Torts, under a concert of action principle, accepts a doctrine with rough similarity to criminal aiding and abetting. An actor is liable for harm resulting to a third person from the tortious conduct of another "if he . . . knows that the other's conduct constitutes a breach of duty and gives substantial assistance or encouragement to the other. . . ." Restatement (Second) of Torts §876(b) (1977). The doctrine has been at best uncertain in application, however. As the Court of Appeals for the District of Columbia Circuit noted in a comprehensive opinion on the subject, the leading cases applying this doctrine are statutory securities cases, with the common-law precedents "largely confined to isolated acts of adolescents in rural society." Halberstam v. Welch, 705 F.2d 472, 489 (1983). Indeed, in some States, it is still unclear whether there is aiding and abetting tort liability of the kind set forth in §876(b) of the Restatement.
>
> More to the point, Congress has not enacted a general civil aiding and abetting statute—either for suits by the Government (when the Government sues for civil penalties or injunctive relief) or for suits by private parties. Thus, when Congress enacts a statute under which a person may sue and recover damages from a private defendant for the defendant's violation of some statutory norm, there is no general presumption that the plaintiff may also sue aiders and abettors.

511 U.S. at 181-82. One might suppose that criminal liability is always narrower than civil liability: Civil wrongs are, after all, punished by damages and injunctions, while crimes may lead to incarceration. It makes sense to reserve the worst punishments for the worst wrongs. Why might this seemingly natural order be reversed in the context of accessorial liability? How

much of the justification for the distinction turns on the trust placed in prosecutorial gate-keeping?

B.   ACCESSORY AFTER THE FACT AND MISPRISION OF FELONY LIABILITY

Although we do not want to give undue attention to two statutes that allow the prosecutions of particularly peripheral players—indeed, the most significant aspect of our short exploration is that these charges are rarely brought—we will briefly explore two post-crime liability theories, accessory after the fact (18 U.S.C. §3) and misprision of felony (18 U.S.C. §4). One theme here is how courts strive to constrain theories that sit uncomfortably with the general notion that one citizen is not legally obliged to inform on another in the absence of a specific statutory duty. The disfavored nature of these offenses means that analyses of them frequently appear in cases where they were not charged—as when defendants seek to plead to them in lieu of conspiracy or aiding and abetting charges or to have them go to the jury as lesser included offenses (which they generally aren't). Charges are brought from time to time, however, as we will now see. While §3 and §4 have different elements, their coverage certainly overlaps and a defendant may find himself charged with both. See United States v. Boyd, 640 F.3d 657 (6th Cir. 2011).

1.   ACCESSORY AFTER THE FACT

---

18 U.S.C. §3 Accessory after the fact

Whoever, knowing that an offense against the United States has been committed, receives, relieves, comforts or assists the offender in order to hinder or prevent his apprehension, trial or punishment, is an accessory after the fact.

Except as otherwise expressly provided by any Act of Congress, an accessory after the fact shall be imprisoned not more than one-half the maximum term of imprisonment or (notwithstanding section 3571) fined not more than one-half the maximum fine prescribed for the punishment of the principal, or both; or if the principal is punishable by life imprisonment or death, the accessory shall be imprisoned not more than 15 years.

In United States v. White, 771 F.3d 225 (4th Cir. 2014), the defendant was charged under §3 "when he knowingly made a false and misleading statement to an insurance representative for the purpose of helping [a co-defendant]—and ultimately himself—avoid apprehension" in connection with an arson. The court set out the elements of the offense as:

(1) the commission of an underlying offense against the United States; (2) the defendant's knowledge of that offense; and (3) assistance by the defendant in order to prevent the apprehension, trial, or punishment of the offender.

Id. at 232-33; see also United States v. Bell, 819 F.3d 310, 323 (7th Cir. 2016). The statute — as well as the misprision statute (*infra*) and the harboring statute, 18 U.S.C. §1071 ("Concealing person from arrest") — can raise close questions in the family context. As the Ninth Circuit noted in United States v. Hill, 279 F.3d 731 (9th Cir. 2002):

> The harboring and accessory statutes prohibit, among other things, providing shelter, material support, assistance and comfort to a criminal or fugitive. Providing such to a spouse is the norm in the context of marriage — indeed, it is expected and integral to the relationship. Thus, caring for a spouse in the normal and expected manner could provide a basis for liability under the harboring and accessory statutes. Similarly, the statutes might create an incentive for terminating such normal care and support, in order to avoid liability. Thus, the statutes could conceivably operate directly on an intimate relation of a marriage and exert a maximum destructive impact upon it. In other words, basing a harboring or accessory conviction on normal and expected spousal conduct might well violate Griswold [v. Connecticut, 381 U.S. 479, 485 (1965) (marriage relationship lies "within the zone of privacy created by several fundamental constitutional guarantees")].
>
> However, it does not follow that *Griswold* categorically bars harboring or accessory liability based on conduct between spouses. Unlike the *Griswold* statute, the harboring and accessory statutes do not "sweep unnecessarily broadly." Harboring and accessory liability is limited to conduct *intended* to "prevent [the fugitive's] discovery or arrest," or "to hinder or prevent [the fugitive's] apprehension, trial or judgment." Thus, by their terms, the harboring and accessory statutes reach only conduct that is intended to frustrate law enforcement. This conceptually simple proposition does not readily yield an easily applied rule for deciding cases, however, because intent is generally inferred from conduct. Thus, the core *Griswold* issue in the context of harboring and accessory liability is where lies the line between conduct that is normal spousal support and sharing of resources, and conduct that demonstrates an intent to frustrate law enforcement.

279 F.3d at 736-37.

Courts will also closely parse defendant's *mens rea* with respect to the underlying offense (which drives sentencing exposure under the statute). See United States v. Calderon, 785 F.3d 847 (2d Cir. 2015) (reversing conviction for being accessory-after-the-fact to a homicide where defendant might have known that gang member she drove away from crime scene had shot someone, but evidence was insufficient that she knew victim was dead or dying).

2.   MISPRISION OF FELONY

A close focus on both state of mind and affirmative activity is also found in misprision doctrine.

---

18 U.S.C. §4. Misprision of felony

Whoever, having knowledge of the actual commission of a felony cognizable by a court of the United States, conceals and does not as soon as possible make known the same to some judge or other person in civil or military authority under the United States, shall be fined under this title or imprisoned not more than three years, or both.

In United States v. Brantley, 803 F.3d 1265 (11th Cir. 2015), even while observing that misprision is "an infrequently charged crime," the Eleventh Circuit related:

> The misprision charge brought against Brantley stems from tragic events that occurred on June 29, 2010. Brantley was pulled over in a routine traffic stop. Brantley's boyfriend, convicted felon Dontae Morris, was a passenger in her car. Upon questioning by the police, he emerged from the car and shot and killed two officers. He then fled on foot as Brantley sped away. Within minutes, Brantley spoke with Morris on a cell phone, and thereafter hid the car and exchanged texts with Morris. The traffic stop itself—including the shootings—was recorded by the dashboard video camera in a police car. The video was played for the jury.
>
> At trial, the jury ultimately found that Brantley knew about a federal felony (her convicted-felon boyfriend's possession of the firearm which he used to shoot the officers), did not report that crime to the authorities, and, in the aftermath of the murders, took affirmative steps to conceal Morris's felony from the authorities.

803 F.3d at 1268-69. Affirming Brantley conviction, the court waved off her Fifth Amendment claim, noting:

> [S]he was not prosecuted for her silence. Rather, she was prosecuted because she knowingly participated in affirmative acts of concealment of Morris's crime—i.e., (1) hiding herself and the car and (2) calling and texting Morris in an effort to conceal *his* crime. Given the facts of this case, we need not decide whether the Fifth Amendment would protect Brantley from prosecution if all she did was remain silent. Here, Brantley did not merely remain silent. As the jury determined, she also concealed evidence. And the Fifth Amendment does not shield a defendant from prosecution for her affirmative acts of concealment.

Id. at 1274-75. The following case sets out the elements of §4 and with particular attention to one *mens rea* aspect:

United States v. Olson
856 F.3d 1216 (9th Cir. 2017)

FISHER, Circuit Judge:

Karen Olson appeals her conviction for misprision of felony under 18 U.S.C. §4. She was convicted of concealing and failing to notify authorities of her business partner's submission of false statements to the United States Department of Agriculture Rural Development Program (USDA) in connection with a federal grant application. She challenges her conviction, arguing the government failed to prove she knew the conduct she concealed constituted a felony. . . .

BACKGROUND

The USDA awarded a grant to Robert Wells to open a milk processing facility. The terms of the grant provided that certain equipment was to be purchased wholly or in part with grant funds, and that the USDA would hold a first lien position on any equipment purchased with grant money. Although the grant was in Wells' name, he had an informal "handshake" partnership with Olson, a former Alaska executive director of the USDA Farm Service Agency who wrote Wells' grant application. Wells described her as the "brains" behind the grant, and their informal partnership entitled her to 50 percent of the profits from the milk processing facility.

Around the same time, Kyle Beus received a separate USDA grant to establish an ice cream and cheese manufacturing facility. The paperwork for both Wells' and Beus' grant applications warned that anyone who made false, fictitious or fraudulent statements could be fined or imprisoned for up to five years.

Wells, Beus and Olson agreed to locate their two projects at the same facility. Unbeknownst to Wells and Olson, Beus instructed his contractor, Nether Industries, to inflate the value of certain dairy processing equipment—including a clean-in-place (CIP) system and a glycol chilling system—on papers submitted to the USDA for reimbursement. Beus also submitted invoices to Nether, allegedly for project expenses, so he could personally receive a portion of the grant money the USDA disbursed.

A year into the enterprise, Beus told Wells and Olson he had leased certain "technologically obsolete" pieces of equipment rather than purchase new equipment as agreed in the original grant application, including a "really cheap old glycol unit" and an "incomplete clean-in-place system." As to some of this equipment, Olson informed the USDA there had been a change of plans that called for "leasing instead of outright purchasing some of the original smaller equipment." She did not do so, however, with respect to the CIP system and glycol cooling system. The attached "Proposed Money Grant Expenditure" included a CIP system listed at $35,000 and a glycol cooling system listed at $50,000 when, in fact, those systems had been leased rather than purchased.

After the USDA disbursed the grant funds, Olson filed a final report with the department. It included a "Final List of Expenditures by Category and Completion" that once again falsely listed the purchase of a $35,000 CIP system and a $50,000 glycol cooling system.

Olson later became aware that Beus had been misappropriating grant funds by submitting false invoices to Nether Industries and receiving payments—which Olson described as "kickbacks"—in return. Olson also discovered Beus had improperly used grant funds to make a $71,000 personal investment in a milk jug manufacturer. An entry in her day planner around this time reveals that she knew Beus' actions were improper. She wrote: "Began full-time work on financials/straightening out Kyle's mess. Learning of questionable deals—Nether—Kyle spent $190,000 of our grant on others, so Nether way over budget. Also, Kyle misused our [] advance $ as his own stock purchases—!" Olson told the project's office assistant she "could send [Beus'] ass to jail." She wrote members of her board that "[t]he revelations of the past week have crystallized for me that [Beus' agreement to co-locate the projects] was simply a way to divert our grant money into a grandiose plan that has not worked," and that Beus "has put the entire dairy industry at risk for an ever-widening investigation closing off all loan sources and public goodwill."

Olson was convicted after a jury trial of misprision of felony under 18 U.S.C. §4. Her conviction was based on her knowledge that Beus, the principal, submitted false statements to the USDA in furtherance of his scheme to misappropriate grant funds in violation of 18 U.S.C. §1014—a felony under federal law. Olson appeals. . . .

DISCUSSION

I

The misprision of felony statute states:

> Whoever, *having knowledge of the actual commission of a felony cognizable by a court of the United States,* conceals and does not as soon as possible make known the same to some judge or other person in civil or military authority under the United States, shall be fined under this title or imprisoned not more than three years, or both.

18 U.S.C. §4 (emphasis added).

To establish misprision of felony, the government must prove beyond a reasonable doubt: "(1) that the principal . . . committed and completed the felony alleged; (2) that the defendant had full knowledge of that fact; (3) that he failed to notify the authorities; and (4) that he took affirmative steps to conceal the crime of the principal." Lancey v. United States, 356 F.2d 407, 409 (9th Cir. 1966) (alterations omitted) (quoting Neal v. United States, 102 F.2d 643, 646 (8th Cir. 1939)). Only the second element is at issue here.

To show a defendant has "knowledge of the actual commission of a felony cognizable by a court of the United States," 18 U.S.C. §4, the parties agree the government must prove at least that the defendant knew the principal *engaged in conduct* that satisfies the essential elements of the underlying felony. In other words, the defendant must "know the facts that make [certain] conduct fit the definition of the offense." Elonis v. United States, 135 S. Ct. 2001, 2009 (2015) (quoting Staples v. United States, 511 U.S. 600, 608 n.3 (1994)). The parties disagree as to whether—and to what extent—the government must also prove the defendant knew such conduct *was a felony*. We conclude Olson has the stronger argument.

First, Olson's construction is consistent with the general presumption that a mens rea requirement applies to each element of an offense. "Absent indication of contrary purpose in the language or legislative history of the statute," Liparota v. United States, 471 U.S. 419, 425 (1985), we "ordinarily read a phrase in a criminal statute that introduces the elements of a crime with the word 'knowingly' as applying that word to each element," *Flores-Figueroa*, 556 U.S. at 652. This "presumption in favor of a scienter requirement," *X-Citement Video*, 513 U.S. at 72 "reflects the basic principal that 'wrongdoing must be conscious to be criminal,'" *Elonis*, 135 S. Ct. at 2009 (quoting *Morissette v. United States*, 342 U.S. 246, 252 (1952)). As a general matter, "a defendant must be 'blameworthy in mind' before he can be found guilty." Id. (quoting *Morissette*, 342 U.S. at 252). . . .

[A]s in *Liparota*, the text of the misprision statute alone does not make clear whether the knowledge requirement applies to each element. Compare 18 U.S.C. §4 ("Whoever, having knowledge of the actual commission of a felony cognizable by a court of the United States. . . ."), with 7 U.S.C. §2024(b)(1) (1985) ("[W]hoever knowingly uses, transfers, acquires, alters, or possesses coupons or authorization cards in any manner not authorized by this chapter. . . ."). Putting aside the *Flores-Figueroa* presumption, the mental state in §4 could plausibly be read to modify only "actual commission" or both "actual commission" and "of a felony cognizable by a court of the United States." Under *Flores-Figueroa*, however, we presume Congress intended the knowledge requirement to apply to both phrases, see 556 U.S. at 652, and nothing in the text or legislative history negates the presumption that Congress so intended. The government has not pointed to anything suggesting Congress intended to penalize some-one who did not know she was witnessing the commission of a felony. Accordingly, given the language of §4 and the *Flores-Figueroa* presumption, the statute is best interpreted as requiring proof that, in addition to showing the defendant knew the principal engaged in conduct satisfying the essential elements of the underlying felony, the government must also show the defendant knew such conduct was a felony.

Second, even putting the presumption aside, the history of misprision also supports Olson's construction. In England, before the advent of professional police forces, individual citizens bore the responsibility for combating crime. See Carl Wilson Mullis III, Misprision of Felony: A Reappraisal, 23 Emory L.J. 1095, 1114 (1974). They had "a duty to raise the hue and cry and report felonies to the authorities." Branzburg v. Hayes, 408 U.S. 665, 696 (1972). See Hue and Cry, Black's Law Dictionary (10th ed. 2014) ("The public uproar that, at common law, a citizen was expected to initiate after discovering a crime."). A citizen who breached this duty could be charged with misprision. See Mullis, *supra*, at 1095. In this country, the First Congress enacted the American misprision statute as part of the Crimes Act of 1790, the current version of which is "functionally identical" to its predecessor. United States v. Phillips, 827 F.3d 1171, 1175 (9th Cir. 2016).

This context suggests Congress intended the misprision statute to apply solely to conduct the average person would understand as criminal and serious. As an English court has explained, requiring knowledge of the serious criminal nature of the underlying offense "disposes of many of the supposed absurdities, such as boys stealing apples, which many laymen would rank as a misdemeanour and no one would think he was bound to report to the police. . . . [M]isprision comprehends an offence which is of so serious a character that an ordinary law-abiding citizen would realise he ought to report it to the police." Sykes v. Dir. of Pub. Prosecutions, [1962] A.C. 528 at 563. . . .

In sum, in light of Supreme Court precedent and relevant history, we hold the misprision statute requires knowledge not only that the principal engaged in conduct that satisfies the essential elements of the underlying felony, but also that the underlying offense is a felony.[4]

---

4. Olson asks us to go further by holding the government must show the defendant knew the relevant conduct was a felony under *federal* law, based on the statute's language stating "of a felony *cognizable by a court of the United States.*" 18 U.S.C. §4 (emphasis added). We decline to do so. "The concept of criminal intent does not extend so far as to require that the actor understand not only the nature of his act but also its consequence for the choice of a judicial forum." United States v. Feola, 420 U.S. 671, 685 (1975). The requirement that the felony be cognizable by a court of the United States was included in the statute to state the foundation for federal jurisdiction. See United States v. Howey, 427 F.2d 1017, 1018 (9th Cir. 1970). "A defendant's knowledge of the jurisdictional fact is

II

The question then becomes: What does it mean to know conduct constitutes a felony?

When a term used in a statute is defined by that statute or by "any other relevant statutory provision," Taniguchi v. Kan Pac. Saipan, Ltd., 566 U.S. 560 (2012), we generally presume that definition applies to the statute's use of the term. . . .

This presumption is not absolute, however. If interpreting a term consistently with its statutory definition would, for instance, lead to "obvious incongruities" or would "destroy one of the major [congressional] purposes," the statutory definition may yield to context.

Here, the term "felony" is defined as part of the federal criminal code as a crime punishable by death or a term of imprisonment exceeding one year. See 18 U.S.C. §3559(a); see also Burgess v. United States, 553 U.S. 124, 130 (2008) ("[T]he term 'felony' is commonly defined to mean a crime punishable by imprisonment for more than one year." (citing 18 U.S.C. §3559(a))). Although the misprision offense and the felony definition are in separate sections of the United States Code, they were included in the same statute at least twice. In 1909, Congress passed an act to "codify, revise, and amend the penal laws of the United States." See Criminal Code of 1909, ch. 321, 35 Stat. 1088, 1088 (preamble) (the "1909 Crime Act"). Along with a slightly modified version of the original misprision statute, see id. §146, 35 Stat. at 1114, the 1909 Crime Act included, apparently for the first time, a statutory definition for the term "felony," see id. §335, 35 Stat. at 1152 ("All offenses which may be punished by death, or imprisonment for a term exceeding one year, shall be deemed felonies."). The 1948 Crimes and Criminal Procedure Act (the "1948 Crime Act"), enacted to "revise, codify, and enact into positive law, Title 18 of the United States Code, entitled 'Crimes and Criminal Procedure,' " Crimes and Criminal Procedure Act, Pub. L. No. 80-772, 62 Stat. 683, 683 (1948) (preamble), similarly included versions of both provisions. See id. §§1, 4, 62 Stat. at 684. Indeed, the 1948 Crime Act actually included the felony definition and the misprision offense on the very same page. See id.

This is a case, therefore, in which Congress has adopted a statute using a term — "felony" — and in the same statute adopted a definition that presumptively applies. Moreover, it does not appear the presumption

---

irrelevant," id., as has been held in numerous cases interpreting analogous statutory provisions. See, e.g., United States v. Felix-Gutierrez, 940 F.2d 1200, 1206-07 (9th Cir. 1991) (holding a defendant charged with being an accessory after the fact need not know the principal crime was one against the United States despite the presence of such language in the statute); *Feola*, 420 U.S. at 687 (holding a defendant charged with conspiracy need not know his conduct violated federal law despite the statute's prohibition on conspiring to commit an offense against the United States).

is rebutted by context. Applying the statutory definition, for instance, neither leads to incongruities nor destroys Congress' purposes. See *Lawson*, 336 U.S. at 201. The drafting history of the 1909 and 1948 Crime Acts supports this conclusion. Before 1909, the term "felony" lacked a uniform definition. A Senate Report on the 1909 Crime Act explained that the term "felony" had an "indefinite classification," resulting in its being "indiscriminately applied." S. Rep. No. 60-10, at 12 (1908). The report therefore underscored the need for a uniform definition, which would "characterize the whole system rather than pertain to any particular part of it." Id. Far from "destroy[ing] one of the major [congressional] purposes," see *Lawson*, 336 U.S. at 201, incorporating §3559's definition into the misprision statute furthers Congress' intent to bring a measure of uniformity to the criminal code. . . .

[W]e affirm Olson's conviction.

CONCLUSION

We hold 18 U.S.C. §4 requires the government to prove the defendant knew the principal engaged in conduct that satisfies the essential elements of the underlying felony *and* that the defendant knew such conduct was a felony. To establish the latter, the government must prove the defendant knew the offense was punishable by death or a term of imprisonment exceeding one year. . . .

[Judge Hurwitz's concurring opinion is omitted.]

QUESTION

Do you think the court's analysis reflects a special wariness about post-crime liability for peripheral players?

C.   CONSPIRACY

Federal conspiracy law radically increases the scope of federal criminal liability in two different ways. First, there is the breadth of conspiratorial liability itself. Second, whereas aiding and abetting a crime is one way that a person can be liable for an offense committed by another person, conspiracy is a separate offense in its own right. Indeed, defendants often find themselves charged with both—the "substantive" offense, defined by some other provision (like mail fraud) and the "conspiracy" offense, defined by a conspiracy provision—in the same indictment. The general federal conspiracy statute is 18 U.S.C. §371:

---

18 U.S.C. §371. Conspiracy to commit offense or to defraud United States

If two or more persons conspire either to commit any offense against the United States, or to defraud the United States, or any agency thereof in any manner or for any purpose, and one or more of such persons do any act to effect the object of the conspiracy, each shall be fined under this title or imprisoned not more than five years, or both.

If, however, the offense, the commission of which is the object of the conspiracy, is a misdemeanor only, the punishment for such conspiracy shall not exceed the maximum punishment provided for such misdemeanor.

Note that while §371 is the general conspiracy statute, some federal criminal laws have their own conspiracy provisions. And there are important differences between §371 and these specialized provisions. For one, §371 requires proof of an overt act, while many other conspiracy provisions do not. Moreover, the maximum penalty under 18 U.S.C. §371 is five years of imprisonment. Because this is a relatively low maximum (for a federal felony) and because, as we will see, §371 is not a predicate offense for complex crimes like RICO and money laundering, Congress regularly enacts and prosecutors use more specialized conspiracy statutes, such as 18 U.S.C. §1349 (conspiracy to commit certain fraud offenses) or 21 U.S.C. §846 (the narcotics conspiracy statute), which generally carry higher maximum penalties.

1.   THE FEDERAL LAW OF CONSPIRACY

Conspiracy is usually defined to include two conduct elements. One element is the criminal agreement, and the other is an overt act in furtherance of the agreement. Crucially, the overt act may be committed by any of the conspirators; for the conviction of any individual defendant, the only conduct that the government must prove is the agreement.

a.   Conspiratorial Agreements

1. *Meeting of the Minds.* Agreement has as much to do with a defendant's intent as with his conduct. This is why, in the law of contracts, a precondition for a binding bargain is called a "meeting of the minds." What must the government prove in order to establish that criminal minds have met? The answer comes in two parts. First, the defendant must have knowingly entered into the agreement. Second, he must have "joined in the illegal agreement with the intent of helping it succeed in its criminal purpose." United States

v. Svoboda, 347 F.3d 471, 479 (2d Cir. 2003). Compare this latter require-ment of intentionally aiding the underlying crime with the *mens rea* required for accomplice liability, which as we have seen in Section A of this chapter may be (at least in some formulations) knowledge that one is aiding the crime. The second part of *Svoboda*'s formulation also explains why there is no such thing as a conspiracy to commit manslaughter: Manslaughter is *reckless* killing, and conspiracy requires a *purpose* to bring about the underly-ing crime. Conspiracy to commit murder is possible; conspiracy to commit lesser forms of homicide is not. For the same reason, one cannot conspire with a government agent because the agent does not have true purpose for the crime to succeed.[*]

2. *Wharton's Rule(s)*. Because the essence of conspiracy is the criminal agreement and more than one person is required to make an agreement, conspiracy can be charged only when two or more people agree to commit a crime. Yet, some crimes by definition can only be completed through the coordinated acts of two or more individuals. You may recall Wharton's Rule, an exception to conspiracy, from your introductory criminal law class: If the elements of a substantive crime are such that it can only be committed through the coordinated acts of two or more individuals, traditionally the government is precluded from charging the group with conspiracy to com-mit the substantive offense. The Supreme Court has explained:

> The classic Wharton's Rule offenses—adultery, incest, bigamy, duelling—are crimes that are characterized by the general congruence of the agreement and the completed substantive offense. The parties to the agreement are the only persons who participate in commission of the substantive offense, and the immediate consequences of the crime rest on the parties themselves rather than on society at large.

Iannelli v. United States, 420 U.S. 770, 782-83 (1975).

But determining when a crime is "characterized by the general congru-ence of the agreement and the completed substantive offense"—thereby preventing the collapse of conspiracy into the substantive offense—can be tricky where the putative victims of the conspiracy are also party to the agreement. Consider the somewhat puzzling holding in Ocasio v. United States, 136 S. Ct. 1423, 1436 (2016) (which we first considered in Chapter 6).

---

* [Editors' Note: However, "the presence of a government agent does not destroy a conspiracy in which at least two other private individuals have agreed to engage in an unlawful venture." United States v. Miranda-Ortiz, 926 F.2d 172, 175 (2d Cir. 1991). And the physical location of an informant or agent in a district may provide venue for a conspiracy prosecution to be brought in that district. See United States v. Gonzalez, 683 F.3d 1221 (9th Cir. 2012).]

The Court held that a defendant can be liable for conspiracy to violate the Hobbs Act "based on proof that he reached an agreement with the owner of the property in question to obtain that property under color of official right." In other words, the "victim" of a color-of-right extortion can conspire in his own extortion.

Yet in an apparent effort to avoid a situation in which every color-of-right bribe payor is also a conspirator in her own extortion, Justice Alito distinguished between a conspiratorial agreement, on the one hand, and the "minimal consent" by a victim required to trigger liability under the Hobbs Act: "When [a] person's consent or acquiescence is inherent in the underlying substantive offense, something more than bare consent or acquiescence may be needed to prove that the person was a conspirator." 136 S. Ct. at 1432.

Do you think that Justice Alito's "bare consent" limitation suffices to prevent every act of extortion from also becoming a conspiracy? Or, to the contrary, is the consent required to pay a bribe always sufficient to form a conspiratorial agreement? If you agree with the majority that a bribe paid "begrudgingly" is insufficient to supply *mens rea* for conspiracy and thus conspiracy liability does not follow automatically from extortion, consider the evidentiary challenges of administering this rule. Also consider the dynamics of statutory interpretation that formed the basis of Justice Sotomayor's dissent in *Ocasio*: Does it make sense to interpret the Hobbs Act's language of "obtaining property from another" to encompass the property of individuals who are party to the conspiracy? Finally, to what other crimes, besides Hobbs Act extortion, might the *Ocasio* distinction between "agreement" and "consent" apply?

3. *Circumstantial Evidence and Willful Blindness.* While explicit written agreements are common in the world of legal contracts, criminal bargains are different. First, the bargainers rarely reduce their deal to writing. Second, even if all of the terms *are* made explicit, this usually happens in ways (i.e., private conversations) that cannot easily be proven in court. Absent a covert recording of the conspirators by an informant or with a court-authorized wiretap, how are prosecutors supposed to prove that defendants knowingly entered into an agreement? Often, circumstantial evidence will be available, providing sufficient proof of both the existence of a conspiracy and the defendants' knowledge of it. In addition, just "a single act may be sufficient for an inference of involvement in a criminal enterprise of substantial scope if the act is of a nature justifying an inference of knowledge of the broader conspiracy." United States v. Tramunti, 513 F.2d 1087, 1112 (2d Cir. 1975).

Instead of, or in addition to, using circumstantial evidence to establish that the defendant had knowledge that he was entering into an agreement, the government might argue "willful blindness" (or "conscious avoidance"), as it may argue with respect to accomplice liability, see *supra*. "The conscious avoidance doctrine provides that a defendant's knowledge of a fact required to prove the defendant's guilt may be found when the jury is persuaded that the defendant consciously avoided learning that fact while aware of a high probability of its existence. In such circumstances, a conscious avoidance instruction to the jury permits a finding of knowledge even where there is no evidence that the defendant possessed actual knowledge." United States v. Svoboda, 347 F.3d 471, 477-78 (2d Cir. 2003). In *Svoboda*, defendant Michael Robles was convicted of conspiracy to commit securities fraud. The underlying fraud was insider trading. The district court instructed the jury that "[i]n determining whether the defendant acted knowingly, you may consider whether the defendant deliberately closed his eyes to what would otherwise have been obvious to him." Id. at 476 n.5. On appeal, Robles contended "that a two-person conspiracy requires proof that each alleged co-conspirator possessed actual knowledge of the unlawful objectives of the charged scheme—otherwise . . . there can be no illicit agreement." Id. at 479-80. The Second Circuit disagreed, finding that "[i]n the context of a two-person conspiracy, intent to participate may be shown by a finding that the defendant either knew, or consciously avoided knowing, the unlawful aims of the charged scheme and intended to advance those unlawful ends." Id. at 480. With regard to the jury instructions, the Second Circuit held that "a conscious avoidance instruction 'may only be given if (1) the defendant asserts the lack of some specific aspect of knowledge required for conviction, . . . and (2) the appropriate factual predicate for the charge exists, i.e., the evidence is such that a rational juror may reach [the] conclusion beyond a reasonable doubt . . . that [the defendant] was aware of a high probability [of the fact in dispute] and consciously avoided confirming that fact[.]'" Id. (quoting United States v. Ferrarini, 219 F.3d 145, 154 (2d Cir. 2000)).

The court then explained how the facts of the case supported a conscious avoidance jury instruction:

> First, the source of Svoboda's information was suspicious—Robles knew that Svoboda was a credit officer at Nations Bank and would thus be privy to confidential financial information. Second, the timing of Robles' trades was suspicious—for example, some of Robles' trades occurred as little as a day before a tender offer announcement. Third, the success of the trades was suspicious—Robles realized large returns, up to 400%, on trades based on Svoboda's advice. These facts suggest a high probability that Svoboda's tips were based on inside information and that any lack of actual knowledge on Robles' part was due to a conscious effort to avoid confirming an otherwise obvious fact.

Id. at 480-81. Is it any stranger to use conscious avoidance to satisfy the *mens rea* inquiry in the conspiracy context than in the context of substantive or aiding and abetting liability? How often is a person "willfully blind" as to whether he's entered into an agreement? Do you think that in conspiracy cases, a willful blindness instruction is not likely to get the fact-finder over the proof-beyond-a-reasonable-doubt hurdle unless the defendant's actions are consistent with an agreement having been made?

b.   Overt Act Requirement

When conspiracy is charged under 18 U.S.C. §371, the government must prove an overt act in furtherance of the conspiracy. Not so as to other federal conspiracy provisions. For example, the Supreme Court in United States v. Shabani, 513 U.S. 10 (1994), held that 21 U.S.C. §846 does not require proof of an overt act. Justice O'Connor's majority opinion cited Nash v. United States, 229 U.S. 373 (1913), a Sherman Act case holding that no overt act need be proven in antitrust conspiracy cases. Neither 21 U.S.C. §846 nor the Sherman Act mention overt acts. Like Brogan v. United States, 522 U.S. 398 (1998), and United States v. Wells, 519 U.S. 482 (1997) (both in Chapter 3, Section B), *Shabani* and *Nash* declined to read conduct terms into criminal statutes that did not contain them.

Whether or not an overt act is required is not of much significance in actual investigations and prosecutions. Even when a conspiracy statute clearly requires an overt act, as §371 does, the prosecution is able to meet that burden by proving *any* action in furtherance of the conspiracy by *any* of the conspirators. The act may be entirely insignificant or preliminary. Many actions that suffice as overt acts for a conspiracy prosecution would not come close to sufficing as the "substantial step" required in a prosecution for criminal attempt. See, e.g., United States v. Bertling, 510 F.3d 804, 810 (8th Cir. 2007) (holding that "further discussions of how to achieve the purpose of the agreement can be overt acts in furtherance of the agreement").

c.   Distinguishing Conspiracy and Attempt

The practical insignificance of §371's overt act requirement may sound alarming, and it would in fact be alarming if the law of conspiracy were used as a substitute for the law of criminal attempt. In practice, however, conspiracy law plays a very different role than attempt law. Prosecutors usually prove agreement by tying particular conspirators to completed crimes— something that is not possible if the underlying crimes have not been committed. Occasionally, conspiracy charges are used to stop a scheme before a substantive crime has been committed. Such anticipatory prosecutions are particularly attractive when prosecutors get wind of a plot that poses a grievous threat to life or property.

Thus in most cases, conspiracy law is used less to move criminal liability back in time—the way attempt is used—than it is to further two other objectives. First, it increases the punishment for crimes committed by groups. Second, conspiracy charges are a means by which the government can threaten fringe actors in criminal organizations with severe criminal punishment, thereby inducing them to finger their more culpable colleagues. In most federal prosecutions, then, conspiracy law is functionally akin not to attempt liability, but to accomplice liability: It expands the net of criminal law to include many actors beyond the single principal who directly committed the underlying criminal offense.

d. The Buyer-Seller "Exception"

While the case law discussed so far highlights the broad scope of conspiratorial liability, courts have worked hard to carve out a buyer-seller "exception" to conspiracy law, similar in theory to the long-established exceptions in the common law for accomplice liability for the victim of crimes such as extortion or blackmail, see Section A of Chapter 5. In United States v. Parker, 554 F.3d 230 (2d Cir. 2009), the Second Circuit noted:

> As a literal matter, when a buyer purchases illegal drugs from a seller, two persons have agreed to a concerted effort to achieve the unlawful transfer of the drugs from the seller to the buyer. According to the customary definition, that would constitute a conspiracy with the alleged objective of a transfer of drugs. Our case law, however, has carved out a narrow exception to the general conspiracy rule for such transactions. Under [our case law], notwithstanding that a seller and a buyer agree together that they will cooperate to accomplish an illegal transfer of drugs, the objective to transfer the drugs from the seller to the buyer cannot serve as the basis for a charge of conspiracy to transfer drugs.
>
> This exception from the customary standards of conspiracy preserves important priorities and distinctions of the federal narcotics laws, which would otherwise be obliterated. The federal scheme of prohibition of controlled substances distinguishes importantly between, on the one hand, distribution of a controlled substance, which is heavily punished, and, on the other, possession or acquisition of a controlled substance, which is punished far less severely, if at all. (No doubt, considerations underlying this distinction include a policy judgment that persons who acquire or possess illegal drugs for their own consumption because they are addicted are less reprehensible and should not be punished with the severity directed against those who distribute drugs[)]. . . . At the same time, inchoate offenses, such as conspiracy and attempt are generally punished in the same manner and with the same severity as the completed offense. See 21 U.S.C. §846 ("Any person who attempts or conspires to commit an offense defined in this subchapter shall be subject to the same penalties as those prescribed for the offense"). Therefore, if an addicted purchaser, who acquired drugs for his own use and without

intent to distribute it to others, were deemed to have joined in a conspiracy with his seller for the illegal transfer of the drugs from the seller to himself, the purchaser would be guilty of substantially the same crime, and liable for the same punishment, as the seller. The policy to distinguish between transfer of an illegal drug and the acquisition or possession of the drug would be frustrated. The buyer-seller exception thus protects a buyer or transferee from the severe liabilities intended only for transferors. . . . On the other hand, if we consider a hypothetical seller who is running a profit-motivated business of selling drugs in wholesale amounts, this seller may well realize that his buyers' ability to buy and pay for substantial amounts of drugs, and hence, his profit, will depend on the buyers' ability to resell. The business of selling wholesale quantities depends on the ability of the customers to resell. A seller in such circumstances may well share with the buyer an intention that the buyer succeed in reselling and may be seen as having a stake in the buyer's resale. In such case, the liability of buyer and seller for having conspired together to transfer drugs would depend not on the seller's mere knowledge of the buyer's intent to retransfer, but on a further showing of the seller's interest, shared with the buyer, in the success of the buyer's resale.

554 F.3d at 234-36.

e.   Withdrawal

Withdrawing from a conspiracy may benefit a defendant in two ways, as the Supreme Court explained in Smith v. United States, 568 U.S. 106 (2013): First, while a defendant who withdraws "remains guilty of conspiracy," "[w]ithdrawal terminates the defendant's liability for postwithdrawal acts of his co-conspirators." Id. at 111. Second, withdrawal "also starts the clock running on the time within which the defendant may be prosecuted, and provides a complete defense when the withdrawal occurs beyond the applicable statute-of-limitations period." Id. at 112. But Smith held that the defendant bears the burden of showing withdrawal. Writing for a unanimous Court, Justice Scalia presumed, in the absence of any explicit indication, that Congress had left the "traditional burden of proof undisturbed," and went on to note:

On the matter of withdrawal, the informational asymmetry heavily favors the defendant. Passive nonparticipation in the continuing scheme is not enough to sever the meeting of minds that constitutes the conspiracy. "[T]o avert a continuing criminality" there must be "affirmative action . . . to disavow or defeat the purpose" of the conspiracy. Hyde [v. United States, 225 U.S. 347, 369 (1912)]. The defendant knows what steps, if any, he took to dissociate from his confederates. He can testify to his act of withdrawal or direct the court to other evidence substantiating his claim. It would be nearly impossible for the Government to prove the negative that an act of withdrawal never happened.

568 U.S. at 113. He concluded:

> Having joined forces to achieve collectively more evil than he could accomplish alone, Smith tied his fate to that of the group. His individual change of heart (assuming it occurred) could not put the conspiracy genie back in the bottle. We punish him for the havoc wreaked by the unlawful scheme, whether or not he remained actively involved. It is his withdrawal that must be active, and it was his burden to show that.

Id. at 114.

2. DISTINGUISHING BETWEEN CONSPIRACY AND ACCOMPLICE LIABILITY

In many federal prosecutions, conspiracy serves a function similar to that of accomplice liability: It expands the reach of criminal law beyond the single principal who committed the underlying offense. And in practice in a multi-defendant case, all defendants will have been charged with both the underlying crime(s) and conspiracy to commit the crime(s). This is because the *mens rea* elements of conspiracy and accomplice liability are very similar once a crime has been completed; In other words, the same actions that show the agreement often suffice to satisfy the *Peoni* standard. Thus, "[t]ypically, the same evidence will support both a conspiracy and an aiding and abetting conviction." United States v. Singh, 922 F.2d 1169, 1173 (5th Cir. 1991).

Yet there are important differences between conspiracy and accomplice liability. A person who "aids, abets, counsels, commands, induces, or procures" the commission of a crime is liable as a principal—that is, as though she had committed the offense herself. 18 U.S.C. §2. Conspiracy, on the other hand, punishes only the making of an agreement to commit a crime. Several propositions follow from this distinction:

> First, the substantive offense which may be the object in a . . . conspiracy need not be completed. Second, the emphasis in a §371 conspiracy is on whether one or more overt acts was undertaken. [Where a statute's conspiracy provision does not require an overt act, the emphasis is simply upon whether an agreement was reached.] This language necessarily is couched in passive voice for it matters only that a co-conspirator commit the overt act, not necessarily that the accused herself does so. In an aiding and abetting case, not only must the underlying *substantive offense* actually be completed by someone, but the

accused must take some action, a *substantial step*, toward associating herself with the criminal venture. . . .

United States v. Hernandez-Orellana, 539 F.3d 994, 1006-07 (9th Cir. 2008).

And federal conspiracy law increases the scope of criminal liability in a third way: by making conspirators potentially liable for crimes committed by co-conspirators even if those crimes were not the object of the conspiratorial agreement. In the next case, Pinkerton v. United States, the Supreme Court held that conspirators may be convicted of the substantive offenses committed by their co-conspirators even if they do not meet the *mens rea* requirements of these substantive offenses. As the Fourth Circuit has explained:

> The *Pinkerton* doctrine is distinct from the substantive offense of conspiracy, which makes the very act of conspiring criminal. See 18 U.S.C. §371. Instead, the *Pinkerton* doctrine is a means of apportioning criminal responsibility for the commission of substantive offenses. . . . It provides that a person can commit an offense not only by engaging in the forbidden conduct himself but also by participating in a conspiracy that leads a confederate to engage in that conduct.

United States v. Ashley, 606 F.3d 135, 140 (4th Cir. 2010).

Pinkerton v. United States
328 U.S. 640 (1946)

Mr. Justice DOUGLAS delivered the opinion of the Court.

Walter and Daniel Pinkerton are brothers who live a short distance from each other on Daniel's farm. They were indicted for violations of the Internal Revenue Code. The indictment contained ten substantive counts and one conspiracy count. The jury found Walter guilty on nine of the substantive counts and on the conspiracy count. It found Daniel guilty on six of the substantive counts and on the conspiracy count. Walter was fined $500 and sentenced generally on the substantive counts to imprisonment for thirty months. On the conspiracy count he was given a two-year sentence to run concurrently with the other sentence. Daniel was fined $1,000 and sentenced generally on the substantive counts to imprisonment for thirty months. On the conspiracy count he was fined $500 and given a two-year sentence to run concurrently with the other sentence. . . .

A single conspiracy was charged and proved. Some of the overt acts charged in the conspiracy count were the same acts charged in the substantive counts. Each of the substantive offenses found was committed pursuant to the conspiracy. Petitioners therefore contend that the substantive counts became merged in the conspiracy count, and that only a single sentence not exceeding the maximum two-year penalty provided by the conspiracy statute could be imposed. Or to state the matter differently, they contend that each of the substantive counts became a separate conspiracy count but, since only a single conspiracy was charged and proved, only a single sentence for conspiracy could be imposed. . . .

[We cannot] accept the proposition that the substantive offenses were merged in the conspiracy. There are, of course, instances where a conspiracy charge may not be added to the substantive charge. One is where the agreement of two persons is necessary for the completion of the substantive crime and there is no ingredient in the conspiracy which is not present in the completed crime. See Gebardi v. United States, 287 U.S. 112, 121-122 [(1932)]. Another is where the definition of the substantive offense excludes from punishment for conspiracy one who voluntarily participates in another's crime. [Ibid.] But those exceptions are of a limited character. The common law rule that the substantive offense, if a felony, was merged in the conspiracy, has little vitality in this country. It has been long and consistently recognized by the Court that the commission of the substantive offense and a conspiracy to commit it are separate and distinct offenses. The power of Congress to separate the two and to affix to each a different penalty is well established. A conviction for the conspiracy may be had though the substantive offense was completed. And the plea of double jeopardy is no defense to a conviction for both offenses. Carter v. McClaughry, 183 U.S. 365, 395 [(1902)]. It is only an identity of offenses which is fatal. See Gavieres v. United States, 220 U.S. 338, 342. A conspiracy is a partnership in crime. It has ingredients, as well as implications, distinct from the completion of the unlawful project. As stated in United States v. Rabinowich, 238 U.S. 78, 88 [(1915)]:

> For two or more to confederate and combine together to commit or cause to be committed a breach of the criminal laws, is an offense of the gravest character, sometimes quite outweighing, in injury to the public, the mere commission of the contemplated crime. It involves deliberate plotting to subvert the laws, educating and preparing the conspirators for further and habitual criminal practices. And it is characterized by secrecy, rendering it difficult of detection, requiring more time for its discovery, and adding to the importance of punishing it when discovered.

Moreover, it is not material that overt acts charged in the conspiracy counts were also charged and proved as substantive offenses. As stated in Sneed v. United States, [298 F. 911, 913 (1924)], "If the overt act be the offense which was the object of the conspiracy, and is also punished, there is not a double punishment of it." The agreement to do an unlawful act is even then distinct from the doing of the act. It is contended that there was insufficient evidence to implicate Daniel in the conspiracy. But we think there was enough evidence for submission of the issue to the jury.

There is, however, no evidence to show that Daniel participated directly in the commission of the substantive offenses on which his conviction has been sustained, although there was evidence to show that these substantive offenses were in fact committed by Walter in furtherance of the unlawful agreement or conspiracy existing between the brothers. The question was submitted to the jury on the theory that each petitioner could be found guilty of the substantive offenses, if it was found at the time those offenses were committed petitioners were parties to an unlawful conspiracy and the substantive offenses charged were in fact committed in furtherance of it.

Daniel relies on United States v. Sall, [116 F.2d 745 (1940)]. That case held that participation in the conspiracy was not itself enough to sustain a conviction for the substantive offense even though it was committed in furtherance of the conspiracy. The court held that, in addition to evidence that the offense was in fact committed in furtherance of the conspiracy, evidence of direct participation in the commission of the substantive offense or other evidence from which participation might fairly be inferred was necessary.

We take a different view. We have here a continuous conspiracy. There is here no evidence of the affirmative action on the part of Daniel which is necessary to establish his withdrawal from it. Hyde v. United States, 225 U.S. 347, 369 [(1912)]. As stated in that case, "Having joined in an unlawful scheme, having constituted agents for its performance, scheme and agency to be continuous until full fruition be secured, until he does some act to disavow or defeat the purpose he is in no situation to claim the delay of the law. As the offense has not been terminated or accomplished he is still offending. And we think, consciously offending, offending as certainly, as we have said, as at the first moment of his confederation, and consciously through every moment of its existence." Id., p. 369. And so long as the partnership in crime continues, the partners act for each other in carrying it forward. It is settled that "an overt act of one partner may be the act of all without any new agreement specifically directed to that act." Motive or intent may be proved by the acts or declarations of some of the conspirators in furtherance of the common objective. A scheme to use the mails to defraud, which is joined in by more than one person, is a conspiracy. Yet all members are responsible, though only one did the mailing. The governing principle is the same when the substantive offense is committed by one of the conspirators in furtherance of the unlawful project. The criminal intent to do the act is established by the formation of the conspiracy. Each conspirator instigated the commission of the crime. The unlawful agreement contemplated precisely what was done. It was formed for the purpose. The act done was in execution of the enterprise. The rule which holds responsible one who counsels, procures, or commands another to commit a crime is founded on the same principle. That principle is recognized in the law of conspiracy when the overt act of one partner in crime is attributable to all. An overt act is an essential ingredient of the crime of conspiracy under [what is now 18 U.S.C. §371]. If that can be supplied by the act of one conspirator, we fail to see why the same or other acts in furtherance of the conspiracy are likewise not attributable to the others for the purpose of holding them responsible for the substantive offense.

A different case would arise if the substantive offense committed by one of the conspirators was not in fact done in furtherance of the conspiracy, did not fall within the scope of the unlawful project, or was merely a part of the ramifications of the plan which could not be reasonably foreseen as a necessary or natural consequence of the unlawful agreement. But as we read this record, that is not this case.

Justice RUTLEDGE, dissenting in part.

The judgment concerning Daniel Pinkerton should be reversed. In my opinion it is without precedent here and is a dangerous precedent to establish.

Daniel and Walter, who were brothers living near each other, were charged in several counts with substantive offenses, and then a conspiracy count was added naming those offenses as overt acts. The proof showed that Walter alone committed the substantive crimes. There was none to establish that Daniel participated in them, aided and abetted Walter in committing them, or knew that he had done so. Daniel in fact was in the penitentiary, under sentence for other crimes, when some of Walter's crimes were done.

There was evidence, however, to show that over several years Daniel and Walter had confederated to commit similar crimes concerned with unlawful possession, transportation, and dealing in whiskey, in fraud of the federal revenues. On this evidence both were convicted of conspiracy. Walter also was convicted on the substantive counts on the proof of his committing the crimes charged. Then, on that evidence without more than the proof of Daniel's criminal agreement with Walter and the latter's overt acts, which were also the substantive offenses charged, the court told the jury they could find Daniel guilty of those substantive offenses. They did so.

I think this ruling violates both the letter and the spirit of what Congress did when it separately defined the three classes of crime, namely, (1) completed substantive offenses; (2) aiding, abetting or counseling another to commit them; and (3) conspiracy to commit them. Not only does this ignore the distinctions Congress has prescribed shall be observed. It either convicts one man for another's crime or punishes the man convicted twice for the same offense. . . .

The old doctrine of merger of conspiracy in the substantive crime has not obtained [in this country]. But the dangers for abuse, which in part it sought to avoid, in applying the law of conspiracy have not altogether disappeared. There is some evidence that they may be increasing. The looseness with which the charge may be proved, the almost unlimited scope of vicarious responsibility for others' acts which follows once agreement is shown, the psychological advantages of such trials for securing convictions by attributing to one proof against another, these and other inducements require that the broad limits of discretion allowed to prosecuting officers in relation to such charges and trials be not expanded into new, wider and more dubious areas of choice. If the matter is not generally of constitutional proportions, it is one for the exercise of this Court's supervisory power over the modes of conducting federal criminal prosecutions. . . .

I think that power should be exercised in this case with respect to Daniel's conviction. If it does not violate the letter of constitutional right, it fractures the spirit. . . . Daniel has been held guilty of the substantive crimes committed only by Walter on proof that he did no more than conspire with him to commit offenses of the same general character. There was no evidence that he counseled, advised or had knowledge of those particular acts or offenses. There was, therefore, none that he aided, abetted or took part in them. There was only evidence sufficient to show that he had agreed with Walter at some past time to engage in such transactions generally. As to Daniel this was only evidence of conspiracy, not of substantive crime.

The Court's theory seems to be that Daniel and Walter became general partners in crime by virtue of their agreement and because of that agreement without more on his part Daniel became criminally responsible as a principal for everything Walter did thereafter in the nature of a criminal offense of the general sort the agreement contemplated, so long as there was not clear evidence that Daniel had withdrawn from or revoked the agreement. Whether or not his commitment to the penitentiary had that effect, the result is a vicarious criminal responsibility as broad as, or broader than, the vicarious civil liability of a partner for acts done by a copartner in the course of the firm's business.

Such analogies from private commercial law and the law of torts are dangerous, in my judgment, for transfer to the criminal field. Guilt there with us remains personal, not vicarious, for the more serious offenses. It should be kept so. . . .

NOTES AND QUESTIONS

1. *Pinkerton* is the classic example of the net-widening role of conspiracy law: The aggregate punishment that may be imposed on the two brothers is much greater than it would be if either had committed the same array of crimes on his own. Understand that the increased punishment comes in two forms: First, each brother may be convicted of (and sentenced for) conspiracy in addition to the underlying crimes of bootlegging; second, each brother may be convicted of the underlying crimes committed by the other. The former type of increased liability is characteristic of the conspiracy law

in nearly every jurisdiction in the United States. The latter type of liability (called "*Pinkerton*" liability) is far more controversial and is associated primarily with the federal system. As the Fifth Circuit has noted: "Many state courts have required a greater showing for conspirators to be held liable for substantive offenses committed during the conspiracy, the Model Penal Code rejects *Pinkerton* liability, and the academy's view of the decision is 'overwhelmingly negative.' See Matthew A. Pauley, The Pinkerton Doctrine and Murder, 4 Pierce L. Rev. 1, 4 (2005)." United States v. Gonzales, 841 F.3d 339, 351 n.12 (5th Cir. 2016). How might we explain why the theory persists in federal criminal law and struggles elsewhere?

What is the rationale for "*Pinkerton*" liability? Why should Daniel Pinkerton be punished for his brother's crimes, some of which were committed while Daniel was incarcerated? Is the *Pinkerton* doctrine retributively fair? Is it a useful deterrent? What, exactly, does it deter?

Perhaps those are the wrong questions. They presuppose that the goal of the law of conspiracy, *Pinkerton* included, is to impose the proper level of punishment on deserving defendants. But that may not be the doctrine's actual goal. Instead, the reason for threatening (though not necessarily imposing) increased punishment may be to induce some conspirators to finger others — that is, conspiracy's second role may explain the first. If so, rules like the one in *Pinkerton* may be designed to impose *too much* punishment, not the (retributively) right amount. The law may be unfair by choice, not by accident. Maybe the *Pinkerton* doctrine in particular, and federal conspiracy law in general, are best judged not (or not only) by the usual criteria by which criminal liability rules are judged, but by how much they aid in the dismantling of criminal networks. Cf. John C. Jeffries, Jr. & John Gleeson, The Federalization of Organized Crime: Advantages of Federal Prosecution, 46 Hastings L.J. 1095 (1995) (applying this argument to the federal law of organized crime more generally).

This is not to say that conspiracy law, and *Pinkerton* liability in particular, may not be abused in particular cases. For an exploration of possible constitutional limits on *Pinkerton* liability, see Mark L. Noferi, Towards Attenuation: A "New" Due Process Limit on Pinkerton Conspiracy Liability, 33 Am. J. Crim. L. 91 (2006).

2. It seems a poor defense of a criminal law doctrine to say that it is *supposed to* inflict excessive criminal punishment. Here is another, possibly better defense: Defendants in conspiracy cases do not usually receive the full punishment that the law entitles the government to impose. Rules like *Pinkerton* create incentives to bargain; less culpable conspirators gain considerable advantage by telling prosecutors what they know and receiving favorable charging and sentencing decisions in return. In the law of contract, such rules are called "information-forcing defaults" or, sometimes, "penalty defaults." See, e.g., Ian Ayres & Robert Gertner, Strategic Contractual Inefficiency and the Optimal Choice of Legal Rules, 101 Yale L.J. 729 (1992).

The party with privately held information is penalized in later litigation if he holds onto that information, but is rewarded if he discloses it at the time of the bargain. So too in conspiracy cases. The actual *effect* of the *Pinkerton* doctrine may not be to increase the punishment of fringe conspirators. Rather, it may be to shift the power over that punishment from sentencing judges to the prosecutors, who must bargain for information and testimony and whose charging decisions go some distance toward determining what sentences different conspirators actually receive. More so than most criminal prohibitions, conspiracy law seems to have been designed with plea bargaining and incentives to cooperate in mind. More generally, group crimes are more likely to produce potential cooperating defendants than crimes committed by a single individual. But do these strategic aspects of conspiracy liability make you think better of the legal doctrine, or worse?

3. *Pinkerton* offers an alternative liability basis when the government has charged a member of a conspiracy with aiding and abetting a substantive crime, even murder (when there is a relevant federal murder statute). In United States v. Rosalez, 711 F.3d 1194 (10th Cir. 2013), the defendant who ordered the severe "beat down" of another inmate argued that the government should not have been allowed to support a close case on aiding and abetting murder—since defendant had ordered "merely" the infliction of severe injury—with a *Pinkerton* theory. The Tenth Circuit upheld the conviction. Noting that defendant "was properly held liable for the murder of [victim] because the murder was a foreseeable result of an offense, i.e., assault, that [defendant] knew was the direct object of the conspiracy and that was going to be carried out against [victim]," the court observed "the Supreme Court has held that 'aiding and abetting and *Pinkerton* are alternative theories by which the government may prove joint criminal liability for a substantive offense.'" And it added that "[e]ven in the absence of evidence supporting an aiding and abetting conviction, persons indicted as aiders and abettors may be convicted pursuant to a *Pinkerton* instruction." 711 F.3d 1194 (citations omitted); see also United States v. Gonzales, 841 F.3d 339, 352 (5th Cir. 2016) (upholding murder conviction on *Pinkerton* theory for defendant who participated in drug trafficking organization's armed effort to retrieve stolen drugs, since the murder that ensued was foreseeable result).

D.   MONEY LAUNDERING

In federal criminal law, "follow the money" has traditionally been an investigative strategy used to trace and uncover criminal behavior. Investigating agencies will often find promising leads into the nature and scope of illegal activity by following the "paper trails" created by drug dealers as they attempt to integrate the crumpled $20 bills generated by their

illegal enterprises into the legitimate financial system, or by fraud perpetrators as they try to insert insulating layers between themselves and their
illegal financial transactions. Pulling on the strands connecting the criminal
activity to the legitimate economy can provide evidentiary support for the
prosecution of the underlying crimes. Beginning in the mid-1980s, "follow
the money" took on another meaning. Congress created new offenses that
independently target "money laundering" efforts, reaching even those who
have not actually conspired to commit the underlying crimes. One can see
the money-laundering statute as *prospective*, in that it makes liable those
individuals who facilitate continuing crimes, or *retrospective*, as punishing
accessories after the fact. As we saw in Part B, while 18 U.S.C. §3 has long
criminalized being an accessory after the fact, few offenses are prosecuted
under this statute.

One goal of the new federal money-laundering statutes is to freeze illegal funds out of the legitimate economy. If cash generated through criminal
activity cannot be translated into economic power in legitimate markets, the
value of ill-gotten gains is greatly diminished. The statutes also supply an
extra sanction for those criminals whose work is to hide illegally obtained
funds. At the very least, the risk of criminal liability will encourage financial
intermediaries to charge more for their integration services, thus driving up
the cost of the underlying crimes. See Michael Levi & Peter Reuter, Money
Laundering, 34 Crime & Just. 289, 350 (2006). Financial intermediaries
can find themselves subject to prosecution when the criminal whose loot
they "laundered" is apprehended and cooperates against them in exchange
for leniency, and the threat of prosecution can turn the launderers into
cooperating witnesses against the criminals who obtained the illegal funds.
In effect, the money-laundering statutes thus function as an extension of,
or a supplement to, conspiracy provisions, which also may be strategically
employed to encourage cooperation, see Note 2 immediately above.

1.   18 U.S.C. §1956

a. *Regulatory Background.* Even before Congress made "money laundering" a crime, it began to construct what has become a vast regime for track-
ing currency transactions. See Peter Reuter & Edwin M. Truman, Chasing
Dirty Money: The Fight Against Money Laundering 45-103 (2004). Under
the Bank Secrecy Act of 1970, banks and other financial institutions must file
Currency Transaction Reports (CTRs) for all cash transactions of more than
$10,000. 31 U.S.C. §5313. Congress amended the Bank Secrecy Act in 1986
to impose criminal liability on any person who: (1) causes a financial institution to fail to file a CTR; (2) causes a financial institution to report false
information on a CTR; or (3) structures transactions in an attempt to evade

the CTR reporting requirement. 31 U.S.C. §5324. (Recall Ratzlaf v. United States, 510 U.S. 135 (1994), considered in Chapter 3.) One goal of this legislation was to target "smurfs"—the low-level accomplices who are used to make deposits in multiple banks. See United States v. Phipps, 81 F.3d 1056 (11th Cir. 1996) (explaining the contours of "structuring" offenses); see also Sarah N. Welling, Smurfs, Money Laundering and the Federal Criminal Law: The Crime of Structuring Transactions, 41 Fla. L. Rev. 287 (1989); Courtney J. Linn, Redefining the Bank Secrecy Act: Currency Reporting and the Crime of Structuring, 50 Santa Clara L. Rev. 407 (2010).

Regardless of whether a CTR needs to be filed, a financial institution is also required to file a Suspicious Activity Report (SAR) when it knows, suspects, or has reason to believe that a transaction relates to illicit activity. Title III of the USA PATRIOT Act of 2001 goes even further, requiring certain financial institutions to set up extensive compliance programs to prevent money laundering or terrorist financing. See Pub. L. No. 107-56, §§311, 312, 314, 319, 325. During fiscal year 2011, about 14.8 million Currency Transaction Reports, and 1.4 million Suspicious Activity Reports, were filed. See Dep't of Treasury, Financial Crimes Enforcement Network[FinCEN], Annual Report: Fiscal Year 2011, at 7. Nearly two million SARs were filed in 2016. For reports of how federal investigators have used CTR and SAR filings to gain investigative leads, see Government Accountability Office, Bank Secrecy Act: Increased Use of Exemption Provisions Could Reduce Currency Transaction Reporting While Maintaining Usefulness to Law Enforcement Efforts (Feb. 2008). Indeed, it was the filing of SARs by two financial institutions that is said to have triggered the federal inquiry into former New York Governor Eliot Spitzer's involvement with a prostitution ring. See Richard K. Gordon, Trysts or Terrorists? Financial Institutions and the Search for Bad Guys, 43 Wake Forest L. Rev. 699 (2009).

Over time, Congress has extended this regulatory regime to include entities besides financial institutions. Anyone engaged in a "trade or business" must report cash transactions of over $10,000 to the Internal Revenue Service (using a Form 8300). 26 U.S.C. §6050I. Although there are some exceptions to this rule, 184,305 of these forms were filed in fiscal year 2008. And to move more than $10,000 in cash in or out of the country, one must file a Currency or Monetary Instrument Report. 31 U.S.C. §5316.

b. It was not until 1986 that Congress passed laws criminalizing forms of money laundering to supplement the prophylactic regulatory regime it began to establish in 1970. These money-laundering statutes define a wide range of offenses, only a few of which will be considered here. The goal is to give you a sense of the protean nature of this class of offenses. The statute excerpted below, 18 U.S.C. §1956, defines the offense of money laundering and lists the underlying offenses that constitute "specified unlawful activity" under the statute.

18 U.S.C. §1956. Laundering of monetary instruments

(a) (1) Whoever, knowing that the property involved in a financial transaction represents the proceeds of some form of unlawful activity, conducts or attempts to conduct such a financial transaction which in fact involves the proceeds of specified unlawful activity—

(A)

(i) with the intent to promote the carrying on of specified unlawful activity; or

(ii) with intent to engage in conduct constituting a violation of section 7201 or 7206 of the Internal Revenue Code of 1986 [26 U.S.C. §7201 or 7206]; or

(B) knowing that the transaction is designed in whole or in part—

(i) to conceal or disguise the nature, the location, the source, the ownership, or the control of the proceeds of specified unlawful activity; or

(ii) to avoid a transaction reporting requirement under State or Federal law, shall be sentenced to a fine of not more than $500,000 or twice the value of the property involved in the transaction, whichever is greater, or imprisonment for not more than twenty years, or both. For purposes of this paragraph, a financial transaction shall be considered to be one involving the proceeds of specified unlawful activity if it is part of a set of parallel or dependent transactions, any one of which involves the proceeds of specified unlawful activity, and all of which are part of a single plan or arrangement.

(a) (2) Whoever transports, transmits, or transfers, or attempts to transport, transmit, or transfer a monetary instrument or funds from a place in the United States to or through a place outside the United States or to a place in the United States from or through a place outside the United States—

(A) with the intent to promote the carrying on of specified unlawful activity; or

(B) knowing that the monetary instrument or funds involved in the transportation represent the proceeds of some form of unlawful activity and knowing that such transportation, transmission, or transfer is designed in whole or in part—

(i) to conceal or disguise the nature, the location, the source, the ownership, or the control of the proceeds of specified unlawful activity; or

(ii) to avoid a transaction reporting requirement under State or Federal law, shall be sentenced to a fine of not more than $500,000 or twice the value of the monetary instrument or funds involved in the transportation, transmission, or transfer, whichever is greater, or imprisonment for not more than twenty years, or both. For the purpose of the offense described in subparagraph (B), the defendant's knowledge may be established by proof that a law enforcement officer represented the matter specified in subparagraph (B) as true, and the defendant's subsequent statements or actions indicate that the defendant believed such representations to be true.

(a) (3) Whoever, with the intent—

(A) to promote the carrying on of specified unlawful activity;

(B) to conceal or disguise the nature, location, source, ownership, or control of property believed to be the proceeds of specified unlawful activity; or

(C) to avoid a transaction reporting requirement under State or Federal law, conducts or attempts to conduct a financial transaction involving property represented to be the proceeds of specified unlawful activity, or property used to conduct or facilitate specified unlawful activity, shall be fined under this title or imprisoned for not more than 20 years, or both. For purposes of this paragraph and paragraph (2), the term "represented" means any representation made by a law enforcement officer or by another person at the direction of, or with the approval of, a Federal official authorized to investigate or prosecute violations of this section.

(b) Penalties.—

(1) In general.—Whoever conducts or attempts to conduct a transaction described in subsection (a)(1) or (a)(3), or section 1957 [18 U.S.C. §1957], or a transportation, transmission, or transfer described in subsection (a)(2), is liable to the United States for a civil penalty of not more than the greater of—

(A) the value of the property, funds, or monetary instruments involved in the transaction; or

(B) $10,000. . . .

(c) As used in this section—

(1) the term "knowing that the property involved in a financial transaction represents the proceeds of some form of unlawful activity" means that the person knew the property involved in the transaction represented proceeds from some form, though not necessarily which form, of activity that constitutes a felony under State, Federal, or foreign law, regardless of whether or not such activity is specified in paragraph (7);

(2) the term "conducts" includes initiating, concluding, or participating in initiating, or concluding a transaction;

(3) the term "transaction" includes a purchase, sale, loan, pledge, gift, transfer, delivery, or other disposition, and with respect to a financial institution includes a deposit, withdrawal, transfer between accounts, exchange of currency, loan, extension of credit, purchase or sale of any stock, bond, certificate of deposit, or other monetary instrument, use of a safe deposit box, or any other payment, transfer, or delivery by, through, or to a financial institution, by whatever means effected;

(4) the term "financial transaction" means (A) a transaction which in any way or degree affects interstate or foreign commerce (i) involving the movement of funds by wire or other means or (ii) involving one or more monetary instruments, or (iii) involving the transfer of title to any real property, vehicle, vessel, or aircraft, or (B) a transaction involving the use of a financial institution which is engaged in, or the activities of which affect, interstate or foreign commerce in any way or degree;

(5) the term "monetary instruments" means (i) coin or currency of the United States or of any other country, travelers' checks, personal checks, bank checks, and money orders, or (ii) investment securities or

negotiable instruments, in bearer form or otherwise in such form that title thereto passes upon delivery;

(6) the term "financial institution" includes—

(A) any financial institution, as defined in section 5312(a)(2) of title 31, United States Code, or the regulations promulgated thereunder; and

(B) any foreign bank, as defined in section 1 of the International Banking Act of 1978 (12 U.S.C. 3101);

(7) the term "specified unlawful activity" means—

(A) any act or activity constituting an offense listed in section 1961(1) of this title except an act which is indictable under subchapter II of chapter 53 of title 31 [31 U.S.C. §§5311 et seq. (which involve financial reporting)];

(B) with respect to a financial transaction occurring in whole or in part in the United States, an offense against a foreign nation involving—

(i) the manufacture, importation, sale, or distribution of a controlled substance (as such term is defined for the purposes of the Controlled Substances Act);

(ii) murder, kidnapping, robbery, extortion, destruction of property by means of explosive or fire, or a crime of violence (as defined in section 16 [18 U.S.C. §16]);

(iii) fraud, or any scheme or attempt to defraud, by or against a foreign bank; . . .

(h) Any person who conspires to commit any offense defined in this section or section 1957 [18 U.S.C. §1957] shall be subject to the same penalties as those prescribed for the offense the commission of which was the object of the conspiracy.

2. DISTINGUISHING MONEY LAUNDERING FROM THE UNDERLYING CRIMINAL ACTIVITY

Quite a sprawling statute, but we will focus on the offenses most likely to be charged and that bear on the complicity theme of this chapter. Subsection (a)(1) targets "a financial transaction" that in fact involves the proceeds of some underlying "specified unlawful activity" (SUA) and that is done either (A) to "promote" the carrying on of an SUA, or (B) knowing that the transaction is designed to "conceal or disguise" the nature of those proceeds. Subsection (a)(1) thus has two different charging theories: a reinvestment or "promotion" prong and a classic laundering or "concealment" prong. Subsection (a)(2) creates a different set of offenses, focusing on the international transportation of the proceeds of an SUA. And (a)(3) allows for the prosecution of those who "promote" or "conceal" when the proceeds are not really from a SUA but have been represented as such by a government agent in a "sting" operation. See, e.g., United States v. Cedeno-Perez, 579 F.3d 54 (1st Cir. 2009).

In many cases, it is difficult to distinguish the money-laundering activities under §1956 from the underlying SUA—a challenge that can arise whenever a defendant is charged either with using the proceeds of an illegal activity specified in the statute to promote those activities, or with concealing the proceeds of the illegal activity. In United States v. Esterman, 324 F.3d 565 (7th Cir. 2003), Judge Wood described the level of concealment the government must prove:

> We have struggled in the past to define precisely what amount of concealment must occur before mere use of ill-gotten gains becomes money laundering prohibited by subpart [(a)(1)](B)(i) of the statute. At least two broad principles have emerged. First, we have tried to maintain some separation between the initial transaction from which illegal proceeds were derived and further transactions designed to conceal the source of those proceeds. See United States v. Mankarious, 151 F.3d 694, 705 (7th Cir. 1998) ("[M]oney laundering criminalizes a transaction in proceeds, not the transaction that creates the proceeds"). Second, we have stressed that the mere transfer and spending of funds is not enough to sweep conduct within the money laundering statute; instead, subsequent transactions must be specifically designed "to hide the provenance of the funds involved." United States v. Jackson, 935 F.2d 832, 843 (7th Cir. 1991). . . .
>
> Most fraud victims probably assume that their money has either been spent or placed in an account *of some sort*, even if they do not know the specific destination of the funds. If that were enough to show money laundering at the same time, there would be no distinction left between money laundering and the underlying fraud, and individuals who perpetrate simple fraud by transferring ill-gotten funds into a personal account would always be triable as money launderers. . . .
>
> Many courts have recognized the importance of maintaining a distinction between these grounds of criminal liability. These decisions spell out the point that something more than mere transfer and spending is needed for money laundering, even if that "something more" is hard to articulate. Cases concluding that the line has been crossed into the "money laundering" territory include United States v. Thayer, 204 F.3d 1352, 1354-55 (11th Cir. 2000) (funneling illegal funds through various fictitious business accounts); United States v. Majors, 196 F.3d 1206, 1212-13 (11th Cir. 1999) ("elaborate shell game" involving multiple inter-company transfers with a variety of signatory names); United States v. Willey, 57 F.3d 1374, 1387 (5th Cir. 1995) ("highly unusual" transactions involving cashier's checks, third party deposits, and trust accounts used to disguise source of funds). These cases have in common the existence of more than one transaction, coupled with either direct evidence of intent to conceal or sufficiently complex transactions that such an intent could be inferred. In contrast, the cases in which money laundering charges have not succeeded are typically simple transactions that can be

followed with relative ease, or transactions that involve nothing but the initial crime. In sum, it is important, even if difficult at times, to ensure that the money laundering statute not turn into a "money spending statute."

324 F.3d at 570-74. The need to distinguish between transactions that "promote" an SUA and the SUA itself underlay the Supreme Court's effort to define "proceeds" in United States v. Santos.

United States v. Santos
553 U.S. 507 (2008)

Justice SCALIA announced the judgment of the Court and delivered an opinion, in which Justice SOUTER and Justice GINSBURG join, and in which Justice THOMAS joins as to all but Part IV.

We consider whether the term "proceeds" in the federal money-laundering statute, 18 U.S.C. §1956(a)(1), means "receipts" or "profits."

I

From the 1970s until 1994, respondent Santos operated a lottery in Indiana that was illegal under state law. Santos employed a number of helpers to run the lottery. At bars and restaurants, Santos's runners gathered bets from gamblers, kept a portion of the bets (between 15% and 25%) as their commissions, and delivered the rest to Santos's collectors. Collectors, one of whom was respondent Diaz, then delivered the money to Santos, who used some of it to pay the salaries of collectors (including Diaz) and to pay the winners.

These payments to runners, collectors, and winners formed the basis of a 10-count indictment filed in the United States District Court for the Northern District of Indiana, naming Santos, Diaz, and 11 others. A jury found Santos guilty of one count of conspiracy to run an illegal gambling business (§371), one count of running an illegal gambling business (§1955), one count of conspiracy to launder money (§1956(a)(1)(A)(i) and §1956(h)), and two counts of money laundering (§1956(a)(1)(A)(i)). The court sentenced Santos to 60 months of imprisonment on the two gambling counts and to 210 months of imprisonment on the three money-laundering counts. . . .

Thereafter, respondents filed motions under 28 U.S.C. §2255, collaterally attacking their convictions and sentences. The District Court rejected all of their claims but one, a challenge to their money-laundering convictions based on the Seventh Circuit's subsequent decision in United States v. Scialabba, 282 F.3d 475 (2002), which held that the federal money-laundering statute's prohibition of transactions involving criminal "proceeds" applies only to transactions involving criminal profits, not criminal receipts. Applying that holding to respondents' cases, the District Court found no evidence that the transactions on which the money-laundering convictions were based (Santos's payments to runners, winners, and collectors and Diaz's receipt of payment for his collection services) involved profits, as opposed to receipts, of the illegal lottery, and accordingly vacated the money-laundering convictions. The Court of Appeals affirmed, rejecting the Government's contention that *Scialabba* was wrong and should be overruled. We granted certiorari.

II

The federal money-laundering statute prohibits a number of activities involving criminal "proceeds." Most relevant to this case is 18 U.S.C. §1956(a)(1)(A)(i), which criminalizes transactions to promote criminal activity. This provision uses the term "proceeds" in describing two elements of the offense: the Government must prove that a charged transaction "in fact involve[d] the proceeds of specified unlawful activity" (the proceeds element), and it also must prove that a defendant knew "that the property involved in" the charged transaction "represent[ed] the proceeds of some form of unlawful activity" (the knowledge element). §1956(a)(1).

The federal money-laundering statute does not define "proceeds." When a term is undefined, we give it its ordinary meaning. "Proceeds" can mean either "receipts" or "profits." Both meanings are accepted, and have long been accepted, in ordinary usage. See, e.g., 12 Oxford English Dictionary 544 (2d ed. 1989); Random House Dictionary of the English Language 1542 (2d ed. 1987); Webster's New International Dictionary 1972 (2d ed. 1957).... "Proceeds," moreover, has not acquired a common meaning in the provisions of the Federal Criminal Code.... Congress... sometimes has defined it to mean "receipts" and sometimes "profits"....

The word appears repeatedly throughout the [money-laundering] statute, but all of those appearances leave the ambiguity intact. Section 1956(a)(1) itself, for instance, makes sense under either definition: One can engage in a financial transaction with either receipts or profits of a crime; one can intend to promote the carrying on of a crime with either its receipts or its profits; and one can try to conceal the nature, location, etc., of either receipts or profits. The same is true of all the other provisions of this legislation in which the term "proceeds" is used. They make sense under either definition.

Justice Alito's dissent (the principal dissent) makes much of the fact that 14 States that use *and define* the word "proceeds" in their money-laundering statutes, the Model Money Laundering Act, and an international treaty on the subject, all define the term to include gross receipts. We do not think this evidence shows that the drafters of the federal money-laundering statute used "proceeds" as a term of art for "receipts." Most of the state laws cited by the dissent, the Model Act, and the treaty postdate the 1986 federal money-laundering statute by several years, so Congress was not acting against the backdrop of those definitions when it enacted the federal statute. If anything, they show that "proceeds" is ambiguous and that others who believed that money-laundering statutes ought to include gross receipts sought to clarify the ambiguity that Congress created when it left the term undefined. . . .

Under a long line of our decisions, the tie must go to the defendant. The rule of lenity requires ambiguous criminal laws to be interpreted in favor of the defendants subjected to them. This venerable rule not only vindicates the fundamental principle that no citizen should be held accountable for a violation of a statute whose commands are uncertain, or subjected to punishment that is not clearly prescribed. It also places the weight of inertia upon the party that can best induce Congress to speak more clearly and keeps courts from making criminal law in Congress's stead. Because the "profits" definition of "proceeds" is always more defendant-friendly than the "receipts" definition, the rule of lenity dictates that it should be adopted.

III

Stopping short of calling the "profits" interpretation absurd, the Government contends that the interpretation should nonetheless be rejected because it fails to give the federal money-laundering statute its proper scope and because it hinders effective enforcement of the law. . . .

A

If we accepted the Government's invitation to speculate about congressional purpose, we would also have to confront and explain the strange consequence of the "receipts" interpretation, which respondents have described as a "merger problem." If "proceeds" meant "receipts," nearly every violation of the illegal-lottery statute would also be a violation of the money-laundering statute, because paying a winning bettor is a transaction involving receipts that the defendant intends to promote the carrying on of the lottery. Since few lotteries, if any, will not pay their winners, the statute criminalizing illegal lotteries, 18 U.S.C. §1955, would "merge" with the money-laundering statute. Congress evidently decided that lottery operators ordinarily deserve up to 5 years of imprisonment, §1955(a), but as a result of merger they would face an additional 20 years, §1956(a)(1). Prosecutors, of course, would acquire the discretion to charge the lesser lottery offense, the greater money-laundering offense, or both—which would predictably be used to induce a plea bargain to the lesser charge.

The merger problem is not limited to lottery operators. . . . Generally speaking, any specified unlawful activity, an episode of which includes transactions which are not elements of the offense and in which a participant passes receipts on to someone else, would merge with money laundering. There are more than 250 predicate offenses for the money-laundering statute, see Dept. of Justice, Bureau of Justice Statistics, M. Motivans, Money Laundering Offenders 1994-2001, p. 2 (2003), and many foreseeably entail such transactions, see 18 U.S.C. §1956(c)(7) (establishing as predicate offenses a number of illegal trafficking and selling offenses, the expenses of which might be paid after the illegal transportation or sale).

The Government suggests no explanation for why Congress would have wanted a transaction that is a normal part of a crime it had duly considered and appropriately punished elsewhere in the Criminal Code to radically increase the sentence for that crime. Interpreting "proceeds" to mean "profits" eliminates the merger problem. Transactions that normally occur during the course of running a lottery are not identifiable uses of profits and thus do not violate the money-laundering statute. More generally, a criminal who enters into a transaction paying the expenses of his illegal activity cannot possibly violate the money-laundering statute, because by definition profits consist of what remains after expenses are paid. Defraying an activity's costs with its receipts simply will not be covered. . . .

B

The Government also argues for the "receipts" interpretation because—quite frankly—it is easier to prosecute. Proving the proceeds and knowledge elements of the federal money-laundering offense under the "profits" interpretation will unquestionably require proof that is more difficult to obtain. Essentially, the Government asks us to resolve the statutory ambiguity in light of Congress's presumptive intent to facilitate money-laundering prosecutions. That position turns the rule of lenity upside-down. We interpret ambiguous criminal statutes in favor of defendants, not prosecutors. . . .

[The] Government exaggerates the difficulties. The "proceeds of specified unlawful activity" are the proceeds from the conduct sufficient to prove *one* predicate offense. Thus, to establish the proceeds element under the "profits" interpretation, the prosecution needs to show only that a single instance of specified unlawful activity was profitable and gave rise to the money involved in a charged transaction. And the Government, of course, can select the instances for which the profitability is clearest. Contrary to the principal dissent's view, the factfinder will not need to consider gains, expenses, and losses attributable to other instances of specified unlawful activity, which go to the profitability of some entire criminal enterprise. What counts is whether the receipts from the charged unlawful act exceeded the costs fairly attributable to it. . . .

As for the knowledge element of the money-laundering offense—knowledge that the transaction involves profits of unlawful activity—that will be provable (as knowledge must almost always be proved) by circumstantial evidence. For example, someone accepting receipts from what he knows to be a long-continuing drug-dealing operation can be found to know that they include some profits. And a jury could infer from a long-running launderer-criminal relationship that the launderer knew he was hiding the criminal's profits. Moreover, the Government will be entitled to a willful blindness instruction if the professional money launderer, aware of a high probability that the laundered funds were profits, deliberately avoids learning the truth about them—as might be the case when he knows that the underlying crime is one that is rarely unprofitable.

IV

Concurring in the judgment, Justice Stevens . . . would interpret "proceeds" to mean "profits" for some predicate crimes, "receipts" for others.

Justice Stevens' position is original with him; neither the United States nor any *amicus* suggested it; it has no precedent in our cases. . . .

Our obligation to maintain the consistent meaning of words in statutory text does not disappear when the rule of lenity is involved. . . . If anything, the rule of lenity is an additional reason to remain consistent, lest those subject to the criminal law be misled. And even if, as Justice Stevens contends, statutory ambiguity "effectively" licenses us to write a brand-new law, we cannot accept that power in a criminal case, where the law must be written by Congress. See United States v. Hudson, [11 U.S. 32], 7 Cranch 32, 34 (1812). . . .

V

The money-laundering charges brought against Santos were based on his payments to the lottery winners and his employees, and the money-laundering charge brought against Diaz was based on his receipt of payments as an employee. Neither type of transaction can fairly be characterized as involving the lottery's profits. Indeed, the Government did not try to prove, and respondents have not admitted, that they laundered criminal profits. We accordingly affirm the judgment of the Court of Appeals.

It is so ordered.

[Justice Stevens concurred, suggesting the Court interpret "proceeds" to mean "profits" for certain predicate crimes, and "receipts" for others].

Justice BREYER, dissenting.

I join Justice Alito's dissent while adding the following observations about what has been referred to as the "merger problem." Like the plurality, I doubt that Congress intended the money laundering statute automatically to cover financial transactions that constitute an essential part of a different underlying crime. Operating an illegal gambling business, for example, inevitably involves investment in overhead as well as payments to employees and winning customers; a drug offense normally involves payment for drugs; and bank robbery may well require the distribution of stolen cash to confederates. If the money laundering statute applies to this kind of transaction (i.e., if the transaction is automatically a "financial transaction" that "involves the proceeds of specified unlawful activity" made "with the intent to promote the carrying on of specified unlawful activity"), then the Government can seek a heavier money laundering penalty (say, 20 years), even though the only conduct at issue is conduct that warranted a lighter penalty (say, 5 years for illegal gambling). 18 U.S.C. §1956(a)(1). . . .

Thus, like the plurality, I see a "merger" problem. But, unlike the plurality, I do not believe that we should look to the word "proceeds" for a solution. For one thing, the plurality's interpretation of that word creates the serious logical and practical difficulties that Justice Alito describes. For another thing, there are other, more legally felicitous places to look for a solution. The Tenth Circuit, for example, has simply held that the money laundering offense and the underlying offense that generated the money to be laundered must be distinct in order to be separately punishable. *Edgmon*, [952 F.2d 1206], 1214 [(10th Cir. 1991)]. Alternatively the money laundering statute's phrase "with the intent *to promote* the carrying on of specified unlawful activity" may not apply where, for example, only one instance of that underlying activity is at issue. . . .

Finally, if the "merger" problem is essentially a problem of fairness in sentencing, the Sentencing Commission has adequate authority to address it. . . . My hope is that the Commission's past efforts to tie more closely the offense level for money laundering to the offense level of the underlying crime, suggest a willingness to consider directly this kind of disparity. Such an approach could solve the "merger" problem without resort to creating complex interpretations of the statute's language. And any such solution could be applied retroactively. See 28 U.S.C. §994(u).

In light of these alternative possibilities, I dissent.

Justice ALITO, with whom THE CHIEF JUSTICE, Justice KENNEDY, and Justice BREYER join, dissenting.

Fairly read, the term "proceeds," as used in the principal federal money laundering statute, 18 U.S.C. §1956(a), means "the total amount brought in," the primary dictionary definition. Webster's Third New International Dictionary 1807 (1976) (hereinafter Webster's 3d. . . . Concluding that "proceeds" means "profits," the plurality opinion's interpretation would frustrate Congress's intent and maim a statute that was enacted as an important defense against organized criminal enterprises. . . .

I

A . . .

The federal money laundering statute is not the only money laundering provision that uses the term "proceeds." On the contrary, the term is a staple of money laundering laws. . . . [The dissent goes on to discuss the U.N. Convention Against Transnational Organized Crime, the Model Money Laundering Act, and 14 states' money-laundering statutes, all of which define the term "proceeds" to include gross receipts.]

This pattern of usage is revealing. It strongly suggests that when lawmakers, knowledgeable about the nature and problem of money laundering, use the term "proceeds" in a money laundering provision, they customarily mean for the term to reach all receipts and not just profits.

B

There is a very good reason for this uniform pattern of usage. Money laundering provisions serve two chief ends. First, they provide deterrence by preventing drug traffickers and other criminals who amass large quantities of cash from using these funds "to support a luxurious lifestyle" or otherwise to enjoy the fruits of their crimes. [Citation omitted]. Second, they inhibit the growth of criminal enterprises by preventing the use of dirty money to promote the enterprise's growth.

Both of these objectives are frustrated if a money laundering statute is limited to profits. Dirty money may be used to support "a luxurious lifestyle" and to grow an illegal enterprise whenever the enterprise possesses large amounts of illegally obtained cash. And illegal enterprises may acquire such cash while engaging in unlawful activity that is unprofitable. . . .

[N]arrowing a money laundering statute so that it reaches only profits produces two perverse results that Congress cannot have wanted. First, it immunizes successful criminal enterprises during those periods when they are operating temporarily in the red. Second, and more important, it introduces pointless and difficult problems of proof. Because the dangers presented by money laundering are present whenever criminals have large stores of illegally derived funds on their hands, there is little reason to require proof—which may be harder to assemble than the plurality opinion acknowledges—that the funds represent profits.

C

The implausibility of a net income interpretation is highlighted in cases involving professionals and others who are hired to launder money. Those who are knowledgeable about money laundering stress the importance of prosecuting these hired money launderers. See, e.g., Depts. of Treasury and Justice, The 2001 National Money Laundering Strategy, pp. ix-x, 1-2 (Sept. 2001).

A net income interpretation would risk hamstringing such prosecutions. To violate 18 U.S.C. §1956(a)(1), a defendant must "kno[w] the property involved in a financial transaction represents the proceeds of some form of unlawful activity." A professional money launderer is not likely to know (or perhaps even to care) whether the enterprise is operating in the black when the funds in question were acquired. Therefore, under a net income interpretation, financial specialists and others who are hired to launder funds would generally be beyond the reach of the statute, something that Congress almost certainly did not intend.

It is revealing that the money laundering statute explicitly provides that a money launderer need only know that "the property involved in the transaction represented proceeds from some form, though not necessarily which form, of [specified illegal] activity." §1956(c)(1). Thus, the prosecution is not required to prove that a hired money launderer knew that funds provided for laundering derived from, say, drug sales as opposed to gambling. There is no reason to think that hired money launderers are more likely to know whether funds include profits than they are to know the nature of the illegal activity from which the funds were derived. Consequently, §1956(c) suggests that Congress did not intend to require proof that a hired money launderer knew that funds provided for laundering included profits. . . .

D . . .

Although the plurality opinion begins by touting the "single instance" theory as a cure for the accounting and proof problems that a "profits" interpretation produces, the plurality's application of the "single instance" theory to the case at hand shows that this theory will not work. In this case, the "unlawful activity" that produced the funds at issue in the substantive money laundering counts was the operation of the Santos lottery, and it is hardly apparent what constitutes a "single instance" of running a gambling business. Did each lottery drawing represent a separate "instance"? Each wager? And how long does each gambling "instance" last? A day? A week? A month?

When the plurality opinion addresses these questions, it turns out that "a single instance" means all instances that are charged, i.e., it means that the Government had to show that receipts exceeded costs during the time the defendant allegedly conducted, financed, etc., the gambling operation. . . .

If this is where the "single instance" theory leads, the theory plainly does not solve the accounting and proof problems we have noted. And the plurality's suggestion that the Government had to show that the gambling operation was profitable for this entire period leads to preposterous results. Suppose that the lottery was profitable for the first five years and, at the end of each year, respondents laundered funds derived from the business. Suppose that in the sixth year the business incurred heavy losses—losses so heavy that they wiped out all of the profits from the first five years. According to the plurality, if respondents were found to have operated the lottery during the entire 6-year period, then the financial transactions that occurred at the end of years one, two, three, four, and five would not violate the money laundering statute, even though an accounting done at those times would have come to the conclusion that the funds included profits. That result makes no sense. . . .

For all these reasons, I am convinced that the term "proceeds" in the money laundering statute means gross receipts, not net income. And contrary to the approach taken by Justice Stevens, I do not see how the meaning of the term "proceeds" can vary depending on the nature of the illegal activity that produced the laundered funds.

NOTES AND QUESTIONS

1. For an example of a defendant benefitted by *Santos*, see United States v. Cloud, 680 F.3d 396 (4th Cir. 2012) (overturning promotional money-laundering convictions based on mortgage fraud defendant's "essential expenses" to recruiters and buyers). Given the lack of a majority opinion, what was the Court's holding in *Santos*? In United States v. Brown, 553 F.3d 768, 784 (5th Cir. 2008), the Fifth Circuit noted:

Thus the outcome could be that in a future case in the contraband realm, Justice Stevens would switch his definition to receipts, but one or more *Santos* dissenter would join the majority in holding that "proceeds" means *profits*—not because they have changed their minds about what Congress intended, but because principles of stare decisis and statutory interpretation demand that "proceeds" in this statute be interpreted consistently.

2. In May 2009, President Obama signed the Fraud Enforcement and Recovery Act of 2009, S.386, 111th Congress, 1st Session, which included a provision effectively overturning *Santos*. Section 2(f) of the Act now defines "proceeds" as "any property derived from or obtained or retained, directly or indirectly, through some form of unlawful activity, including the gross receipts of such activity." Backers of the legislation argued that even criminals with high overheads—and therefore no profits—should face money-laundering prosecution.

However, §2(g) adds:

(1) SENSE OF CONGRESS.—It is the sense of the Congress that no prosecution of an offense under section 1956 or 1957 of title 18, United States Code, should be undertaken in combination with the prosecution of any other offense, without prior approval of the Attorney General, the Deputy Attorney General, the Assistant Attorney General in charge of the Criminal Division, a Deputy Assistant Attorney General in the Criminal Division, or the relevant United States Attorney, if the conduct to be charged as "specified unlawful activity" in connection with the offense under section 1956 or 1957 is so closely connected with the conduct to be charged as the other offense that there is no clear delineation between the two offenses.

The "sense of Congress" is essentially the Tenth Circuit rule in the *Edgmon* case mentioned in Justice Breyer's dissent in *Santos*. To what extent do you think this "sense of Congress" will affect prosecutorial decision making? How significant is an approval requirement when any U.S. Attorney can satisfy it? To the extent this one has any bite, would it be desirable to have more of these "soft" legislative restraints in federal criminal law? Fewer?

3. Determining what constitutes an intention to "conceal" within the meaning of §1956 is critical not only when the issue is whether the conduct charged under §1956 "merges" with the underlying SUA, but also when the issue is whether someone who might *not* have been criminally involved in the underlying SUA can be charged with money laundering. When might financial intermediaries be liable under the money-laundering statute?

3. THIRD PARTY INTERMEDIARY LIABILITY

The following two cases focus on the criminal liability of third-party intermediaries who may not have been involved with the underlying criminal activity. Note that these cases may not be representative of §1956 cases as a whole for the simple reason that reported money-laundering cases generally involve defendants who have (or could have) been charged with at least one underlying SUA—a fact that may raise questions about why the money-laundering charges were brought in the two cases excerpted below.

United States v. Corchado-Peralta
318 F.3d 255 (1st Cir. 2003)

BOUDIN, Chief Judge.

Between 1987 and 1996, Ubaldo Rivera Colon ("Colon") smuggled over 150 kilograms of cocaine into Puerto Rico, yielding some $4 million in profits, which he then laundered through a variety of investments and purchases. Colon was indicted on drug, bank fraud, and conspiracy charges and, based on a plea agreement, was sentenced in June 2002 to over 20 years in prison. This case concerns not Colon but three peripheral figures, including his wife.

Colon's wife, Elena Corchado Peralta ("Corchado"), and two associates, Basilio Rivera Rodriguez ("Rivera") and Oscar Trinidad Rodriguez ("Trinidad") were indicted and tried together on one count of conspiring with Colon to launder money. 18 U.S.C. §§1956(a)(1)(B) and (h). Corchado was also indicted on one count of bank fraud. 18 U.S.C. §1344. During their eight-day trial, Colon provided extensive testimony about his money laundering methods, which included a variety of transactions (purchases, investments, and loans) involving the defendants.

All three defendants were convicted on the charges against them. Corchado received a 27-month sentence, Rivera, 57 months, and Trinidad, 63 months. [On appeal, each defendant argued that the evidence was not sufficient to support the jury's verdicts of guilty.] . . .

The money laundering statute, 18 U.S.C. §1956, among other things makes it criminal for anyone, "knowing that the property involved in a financial transaction represents the proceeds of some form of unlawful activity" to "conduct . . . such a financial transaction which in fact involves the proceeds of specified unlawful activity" —

(A) (i) with the intent to promote the carrying on of specified unlawful activity; or . . .

(B) knowing that the transaction is designed in whole or in part—
    (i) to conceal or disguise the nature, the location, the source, the ownership or the control of the proceeds of specified unlawful activity; . . .

Id. §1956(a)(1).

The three defendants in this case were charged under subsection (B)(i), based on knowledge of "design[]," and not under (A)(i), based on an "intent to promote." In each instance, there is no doubt that the defendant did engage in one or more financial transactions involving Colon's drug proceeds. The issue turns, rather, on state of mind elements. Pertinently, as to Corchado, she disputes knowing either that the "property" represented proceeds of drug dealing or that "the transaction" was "designed . . . to conceal or disguise. . . ." The evidence, taken most favorably to the government, showed the following.

Elena Corchado Peralta met Colon sometime in the early 1990s and they were married in 1994. Corchado, then about 25 years old, was a student when they met and later worked part-time in her mother's jewelry store. She has a college degree in business administration and some training in accounting. Colon testified that he held himself out as a successful legitimate businessman throughout their relationship and that his wife knew about neither his drug smuggling nor his own money laundering activities.

Corchado performed many transactions involving Colon's drug proceeds. These transactions fell into two broad categories—expenditures and deposits. On the expenditure side, Colon directed Corchado to write and endorse checks to purchase a cornucopia of expensive cars, boats, real estate, and personal services. Colon maintained that his wife thought that the money was derived from legitimate businesses.

The purchases themselves were extensive and expensive, affording the couple a fancy lifestyle. For example, Corchado purchased a BMW, a Mercedes Benz, and a Porsche for the couple. At another time, she made a single monthly payment to American Express of $18,384 for interior decorating purchases. And on another day, she signed three checks totaling $350,000 that were used to purchase land for one of Colon's businesses. In total, Corchado signed the majority of 253 checks, representing many hundreds of thousands of dollars of purchases.

With respect to deposits, Corchado's main responsibility was to deposit $6,000 checks on a monthly basis into one of Colon's accounts. . . . At trial, the government also presented evidence showing that on one occasion Corchado wired $40,000 to a Florida company at Colon's request.

Tax records signed by Corchado showed that she knew that her husband's reported income from his legitimate businesses was far less than the money she was handling. For example, the joint tax return that Corchado signed for 1995 listed a total amount of claimed income of only $12,390. The government presented evidence showing that the couple's total reported income between 1992 and 1997 was only approximately $150,000. Corchado did not testify at trial.

We begin with the first knowledge requirement—namely, that Corchado was aware, at the time of the transactions she conducted, that the money she was handling, at least much of the time, was derived from drug dealings. Corchado argues, correctly, that there is no direct evidence of her knowledge. . . . Indeed, [Colon] testified repeatedly that she was unaware of his drug business; that in response to a question from her he had denied doing anything unlawful; [and] that he never allowed her to attend meetings involving his drug business. . . .

Needless to say, the jury did not have to accept Colon's exculpatory testimony. It was clearly self-interested since Corchado was his wife and mother of their two children. But here, at least, the jury's disbelief could not count for much in the way of affirmative proof. Rather, whether there was knowledge of drug dealing, or so much awareness that ignorance was willful blindness, turns in this case on the same circumstantial evidence.

What the evidence shows is that Corchado knew that the family expenditures were huge, that reported income was a fraction of what was being spent and that legitimate sources were not so obvious as to banish all thoughts of possible illegal origin—as demonstrated by Colon's testimony that Corchado once raised the issue. Interviewed by an FBI agent, Corchado told him that her husband had been involved in the cattle business and, more recently, in real estate development but that none of the businesses had employees and that Colon had worked mainly out of his house. And, as the government fairly points out, Corchado was herself well educated and involved in the family bookkeeping.

This might seem to some a modest basis for concluding—beyond a reasonable doubt—that Corchado knew that her husband's income was badly tainted. But the issue turns on judgments about relationships within families and about inferences that might be drawn in the community from certain patterns of working and spending. Further, it is enough to know that the proceeds came from "some form, though not necessarily which form," of felony under state or federal law. 18 U.S.C. §1956(c)(1). The jury's judgment on this factual issue cannot be called irrational.

The other knowledge requirement is harder for the government. Here, the statute requires, somewhat confusingly, that Corchado have known that "the transaction" was "designed," at least in part, "to conceal or disguise the nature, the location, the source, the ownership or the control of the proceeds." 18 U.S.C. §1956(a)(1)(B)(i). We will assume that it would be enough if Corchado herself undertook a transaction for her husband, knowing that her husband had such a design to conceal or disguise the proceeds, or if she undertook a transaction on her own having such a design herself. Other variations might exist, but these two seem the foremost possibilities.

It may help to treat separately the purchases on the one hand and the check deposits (and in one case a transfer) on the other. Any purchase of goods or services, whether by cash or by check, has a potential to conceal or disguise proceeds simply because it transforms them from money into objects or dissipates them in the performance of the services. But if this were enough, every expenditure of proceeds known to be tainted would itself be unlawful. Instead, the statute requires that someone—the instigator or spender—must have an intent to disguise or conceal and the spender must share or know of that intent.

Here, the government showed that from their marriage onward Corchado wrote most of the checks used by the couple to purchase expensive items . . . and pay off credit card bills and that some of these payments were very large. . . . And, for reasons already given, it is assumed that the jury permissibly found that Corchado knew that some of the money she was spending was criminally derived. Finally, the government stresses that she must have known that Colon was bringing in and spending far more than he reported on his income tax returns. Is this enough for the jury to infer a specific intent to conceal or disguise and impute the intent itself, or knowledge of it, to Corchado?

In this case, nothing about the purchases, or their manner, points toward concealment or disguise beyond the fact that virtually *all expenditures* transform cash into something else. Here, the purchased assets were not readily concealable (e.g., diamonds) nor peculiarly concealed (e.g., buried in the garden) nor acquired in someone else's name nor spirited away to a foreign repository (e.g., a Swiss bank deposit box). Indicia of this kind have been stressed in cases upholding money laundering charges and their absence noted in cases coming out the other way. See, e.g., United States v. Martinez-Medina, 279 F.3d 105, 115-116 (1st Cir. 2002).

To hold that a jury may convict on this evidence—that Corchado spent her husband's money knowing that the money was tainted—is to make it unlawful wherever a wife spends any of her husband's money, knowing or believing him to be a criminal. That the purchases here were lavish or numerous hardly distinguishes this case from one in which a thief's wife buys a jar of baby food; if anything, Corchado's more flamboyant purchases were less likely than the baby food to disguise or conceal. Perhaps a hard-nosed Congress might be willing to adopt such a statute, [compare 18 U.S.C. §1957], but it did not do so here.

Less need be said about the deposit and transfer side. So far as we can tell, Corchado mostly did no more than make large regular deposits in an account given to her by her husband; there was no inference of concealment or disguise. As for the single transfer she made to another person at her husband's request, nothing suspicious about the circumstances is cited to us, let alone anything that would suggest knowledge on Corchado's part that the transfer was meant to conceal or disguise proceeds—as opposed to merely paying off a debt, making an investment, or conducting some other transaction incident to a business, lawful or otherwise. . . .

[The court went on to affirm Corchado's conviction on the bank fraud count.]

United States v. Rivera-Rodriguez
318 F.3d 268 (1st Cir. 2003)

BOUDIN, Chief Judge.

In this decision, we address the appeals of Basilio Rivera Rodriguez ("Rivera") and Oscar Trinidad Rodriguez ("Trinidad") who were convicted along with Elena Corchado Peralta of conspiring to launder money. 18 U.S.C. §§1956(a)(1)(B) and (h). . . . The Rivera and Trinidad transactions have some resemblance to each other but are quite distinct from those of Corchado, whose appeal is addressed in a separate decision.

At the outset, both Rivera and Trinidad challenge the sufficiency of the evidence. . . . Colon himself was a major drug dealer who earned several million dollars in profits smuggling cocaine into Puerto Rico during the period between 1987 and 1996. Rivera and Trinidad are accused only of participating in transactions to launder the proceeds.

As the indictment was framed, the government had to show that each defendant:

1.   conducted "a financial transaction" involving the proceeds of some form of unlawful activity, "knowing" that the proceeds were thus tainted; and
2.   knew that the transaction was "designed in whole or in part . . . to conceal or disguise the nature, the location, the source, the ownership or the control of the proceeds. . . ."

18 U.S.C. §1956(a)(1). The defendant is not required to know what type of felony spawned the proceeds but only that some felony did so. Id. §1956 (c)(1). And "knowledge" can be established by showing that a defendant was "willfully blind" to facts patently before him. See United States v. Frigerio-Migiano, 254 F.3d 30, 35 (1st Cir. 2001).

Trinidad. We begin with Trinidad. . . . In 1994, Trinidad, who raced speedboats, was introduced to Colon, who was also a speedboat enthusiast. Colon and Trinidad testified that at this meeting Colon held himself out as a legitimate car and cattle businessman. As a result of their meeting, Colon suggested that they purchase an expensive speedboat, *Budweiser,* as a joint venture.

In May 1994, Colon took $100,000 from a hiding place on a cattle farm and gave it to Trinidad. Trinidad then gave two associates $18,000 of the money to purchase two manager's checks apiece from different banks in the amount of $9,000 each. Trinidad himself also purchased manager's checks in approximately the same amount from two different banks. These checks totaling $36,000, along with other funds contributed by Colon totaling $100,000, were deposited in a boat merchant's bank account, and were used to buy *Budweiser.*

The title of the boat eventually was placed in Trinidad's name. Trinidad testified that it was placed in his name because the two of them had a sports partnership. Trinidad, however, put up no money for the purchase of the speedboat, and it was Colon alone who later decided to sell it. However, during a tax investigation, Trinidad falsely told local agents that he had paid for the boat.

Trinidad also aided Colon in similar transactions. On at least one occasion, he carried $200,000 in cash to Florida as part of the purchase of another speedboat for Colon. (Trinidad testified that although he knew he was carrying cash for Colon, he did not know the amount.) Colon also gave Trinidad over $60,000 in cash to pay for boat maintenance and parts. Trinidad also assisted Colon in the latter's unsuccessful attempt to buy a South Florida apartment for cash.

On appeal, Trinidad concedes that the evidence sufficed to show *Def. Arg.* that he knew the transactions he took part in were designed to conceal the source of the funds involved; the size of the cash transactions together with the use of $9,000 deposits, just under the limit for bank reporting, bears this out. However, he disputes whether a reasonable jury could find that he knew that transactions involved illegal proceeds. His primary argument is that he did not know that Colon had been a drug dealer.

Under the statute, it would be enough if a jury could conclude that some felony—drug dealing is merely the most obvious candidate—was so *Analysis* obviously the source that Trinidad had to know it. 18 U.S.C. §1956(c)(1). Indeed, because governing law equates willful blindness with knowledge, *Frigerio-Migiano*, 254 F.3d at 35, it would suffice for the jury to conclude that Trinidad consciously averted his eyes from the obvious explanation for the funds. . . . And the jury was free to draw common-sense inferences from the nature of the transactions and efforts to conceal. . . .

Sometimes one of these red-flag events—cash, concealment, false *holding 1* ownership—can occur even with lawfully derived income (e.g., to foster tax evasion or the concealment of income from a spouse). But taken together, the pattern was surely that of an effort to launder illegally obtained proceeds, or at least a jury could reasonably so conclude. . . .

Rivera. Basilio Rivera-Rodriguez operated a business called BVF Construction. The government's evidence focused on a set of transactions made by Colon and Rivera through that business. In the first of these, which took place in June 1995, Colon gave Rivera upwards of $105,000 *facts* (of which $89,000 was in cash) to deposit in a BVF bank account. Rivera then purchased a manager's check in the amount of $105,000, which was then given to a boat company . . . as payment for a 46-foot racing boat. Colon then took possession of the boat. Later, in November, Rivera wrote checks from the BVF account to Colon for $2,900 in unspecified boat expenses.

In the second set of transactions, Colon in August 1995 wrote a check to BVF Construction for $130,000. On the same day, Colon's father wrote a check for $65,000 to BVF, drawing upon his son's drug money. This money was deposited in a BVF account, where it stayed, untouched, until

November 1995, when Rivera wrote checks to Colon for nearly the full amount deposited—$192,900.

The government argues that Rivera's BVF corporation effectively served as a clearing house for Colon's drug funds. Thus, when Colon decided to purchase the boat, he did it with money channeled through BVF so as to muddy the trail of the purchase. Similarly, by depositing $195,000 in the BVF account and withdrawing it later, the government argues that Colon hoped to give that money a patina of legitimacy.

At trial, inconsistent stories were told as to the purpose of the transactions. Colon testified that he had given funds to BVF to invest in the construction of ATM bank branches, and that he then withdrew some of the funds when he needed to make other purchases. Colon admitted that no bank branches were ever built. Evidence was also given that Rivera—who did not testify at trial—had said in a deposition in a civil case that the payments to Colon were for labor that Colon had performed. But again, Colon testified that he had never performed any labor for Rivera or BVF.

Rivera objects on appeal that there was no evidence that he conspired or that he knew that the transactions were intended to disguise the source of funds or that he knew that the funds were the proceeds of drug dealing or any other unlawful activity. On the contrary, the pattern was a classic example of money laundering. See United States v. Martinez-Medina, 279 F.3d 105, 116 (1st Cir. 2002).

In one case, a huge cash payment into a business, for no demonstrated legitimate reason, was followed by the use of the funds to purchase property for the original depositor. In the other case, an outsider's money was run into the business and then backed out to the depositor, again with no apparent reason except to provide a seemingly legitimate source.

From these facts, a reasonable jury could conclude that the obvious, and only plausible, explanation was that Colon was trying to disguise the origin of his proceeds by making it appear that the money had come to him from a legitimate business; that the obvious explanation for this conduct was that the funds were illegally derived, most likely from drug dealing; and that these facts were necessarily apparent to Rivera. As for "conspiracy," an agreement between Colon and Rivera can plainly be inferred from the fact that the transactions occurred at all, even though the conversations and *quid pro quo* are unknown to us.

Of course, payments by anyone—including a drug dealer—to a business and payments back out may be legitimate in context: Colon could have sent a check to a mutual fund and received dividends in exchange. It is the details—the cash, the near equivalence of dollars in and out, and above all the lack of legitimate motive—that distinguish this case. It is not logically impossible for there to have been some legitimate explanation for the transactions; but one who is caught with a smoking gun and a dead victim can hardly complain if, absent some explanation, the jury draws the natural inferences from the facts. . . .

NOTES AND QUESTIONS

1. As *Rivera-Rodriguez* suggests, money-laundering charges are often used to target major drug dealers and those in their immediate circle. This targeting is hardly surprising. The government may find it hard to connect particular shipments of drugs to the dealers who are doing the shipping; linking high-level dealers to the money they make and spend can be easier. Is this a wise use of money-laundering doctrine? For an argument that a better allocation of resources would use money-laundering laws primarily to target financial institutions and intermediaries rather than drug dealers, see Mariano-Florentino Cuéllar, The Tenuous Relationship Between the Fight Against Money-Laundering and the Disruption of Criminal Finance, 93 J. Crim. L. & Criminology 311 (2003).

Professor (now California Supreme Court Justice) Cuéllar may well be right. Consider: When Mafia families or similar criminal networks take over legitimate businesses, the takeover nearly always *increases* the businesses' costs. The goal is to take as much money out of the enterprise as possible, as quickly as possible. That is why mobbed-up businesses either go under quickly or exist in geographically bounded, cartelized industries. In a genuinely competitive market, such businesses cannot compete; their criminal association makes it harder for the businesses to make money, not easier. Money laundering has the opposite tendency: Financial institutions—big or small—that "move" dirty money are *more* profitable than their competitors, not less so. Corrupt financial institutions thus have a competitive advantage over honest ones; in an unconstrained market, money laundering tends to spread and to take over the market. This makes the effort to stamp out corrupt financial institutions very important indeed.

2. At the same time, it is usually harder—often a great deal harder—to convict officials in banks or other financial institutions than it is to convict drug dealers like Colon. Recall the passage from *Esterman* that is discussed earlier in this section. The government proves concealment by showing that the relevant financial transactions were substantially more complex than the norm; complexity, the government argues, suggests that the defendant was hiding something. Financial transactions involving large sums of money are often complex even when the money is perfectly clean, with person-to-person banking interactions the exception rather than the rule. It follows that proving the requisite concealment can be difficult, even impossible. The kinds of money-laundering prosecutions that seem most socially valuable may be the kinds that are most expensive for the government. On the other hand, banks and other financial institutions are the objects of considerable

regulatory activity, and are regularly sanctioned (with high fines) for failing to have adequate compliance programs or to file SARs when appropriate. For a listing of enforcement actions, see FinCEN, Enforcement Actions, https://www.fincen.gov/news-room/enforcement-actions. In Chapter 11 we will consider the world created by (1) black letter doctrine allowing an enormous financial institution to be held criminally liable for the money laundering activity of a single employee and (2) a strong policy preference for not pursuing that institution if it has sought to obey the law and has cooperated in the government's investigation

3. One might think from the *Corchado-Peralta* decision that the bigger the purchase, the less circumstantial the evidence for money laundering—after all, the court notes that the defendant's purchase of expensive cars was not "readily concealable" in the way that, say, diamonds might be. Be wary of this line of reasoning, because there is no question that one can be liable for laundering money through large purchases of real property. For example, the money-laundering charges in United State v. Tekle arose from defendant's purchase of a house and a grocery store. United States v. Tekle, 329 F.3d 1108, 1113-14 (9th Cir. 2003). Unlike the Corchado-Peralta court, the Ninth Circuit ruled that Tekle's purchase of property was sufficiently covert (not, that is, an "open and notorious" transaction) to support liability. Id. Thus, it is less the *type* of property that one purchases than the *way* in which one purchases it that seems to matter in money-laundering prosecutions. *Tekle* also clarified that the fact that the purchases were not designed to conceal the defendant's identity was irrelevant: "[t]he necessary concealment . . . is that of the source of the funds, not the identity of the money-launderer." Id. at 1114 (citations omitted).

4. *Elements of concealment.* To be convicted for concealment under §1956(a)(1)(B)(1), a defendant needs to know that the transaction involves the "proceeds of some form of illegal activity" and needs to know that the transaction was designed to conceal. And the "proceeds" must in fact have come from an SUA listed in the statute. But need the defendant *know* that the money came from a listed SUA? *Corchado-Peralta* suggests the answer is "no," and other courts agree. See United States v. Flores, 454 F.3d 149 (3d Cir. 2004) ("[B]ecause the monetary transactions that Flores conducted . . . were 'derived from specified unlawful activity,' the only question is whether the Government produced sufficient evidence that Flores *knew* that the monetary transactions represented the proceeds of *criminally derived property.* For the same reasons provided above, the defense's argument—that the Government needed to prove that Flores knew of, or was willfully blind to, the fact that the funds originated in drug trafficking to obtain a money laundering conviction—fails. See 18 U.S.C. §1957(c)").

5. Conspiracies to commit money-laundering offenses are generally charged under the separate conspiracy provision in the primary money-laundering statute, §1956(h), not under §371, the general conspiracy

statute. While §371 carries a five-year maximum penalty, the maximum penalty for a §1956(h) conspiracy is that of the underlying money-laundering offense — 20 years for a §1956 offense and ten years for a §1957 offense. The §1956(h) charge also does not require that the government prove an overt act. In Whitfield v. United States, 543 U.S. 209 (2005), the Court relied on United States v. Shabani, 513 U.S. 10 (1994) (the narcotics conspiracy case discussed in Section B), and held: "Because the text of §1956(h) does not expressly make the commission of an overt act an element of the conspiracy offense, the Government need not prove an overt act to obtain a conviction." 543 U.S. at 214. Does a statute's omission of an overt act requirement make any practical difference? Recall also, from Section C, that proof of an overt act is seldom an obstacle to prosecution.

4.   18 U.S.C. §1957

At the end of the excerpted portion of the first case above, *Corchado-Peralta,* Judge Boudin references another money-laundering statute, 18 U.S.C. §1957, and appears to suggest that §1957 might yield a different outcome with respect to whether Corchado could be convicted based on evidence that she "spent her husband's money knowing that the money was tainted." Title 18, §1957, makes it a crime for a third party to knowingly conduct a "monetary transaction" with property representing the proceeds of illegal activity. Section 1957 provides as follows:

---

18 U.S.C. §1957. Engaging in monetary transactions in property derived from specified unlawful activity

(a) Whoever . . . knowingly engages or attempts to engage in a monetary transaction in criminally derived property that is of a value greater than $10,000 and is derived from specified unlawful activity, shall be punished as provided in subsection (b).

(b)

(1) Except as provided in paragraph (2), the punishment for an offense under this section is a fine under title 18, United States Code, or imprisonment for not more than ten years or both.

(2) The court may impose an alternate fine to that imposable under paragraph (1) of not more than twice the amount of the criminally derived property involved in the transaction.

(c) In a prosecution for an offense under this section, the Government is not required to prove the defendant knew that the offense from which the criminally derived property was derived was specified unlawful activity. . . .

(f) As used in this section —

(1) the term "monetary transaction" means the deposit, withdrawal, transfer, or exchange, in or affecting interstate or foreign commerce, of funds or a monetary instrument (as defined in section 1956(c)(5) of this

title [18 U.S.C. §1956(c)(5)]) by, through, or to a financial institution (as defined in section 1956 of this title [18 U.S.C. §1956]), including any transaction that would be a financial transaction under section 1956(c)(4)(B) of this title [18 U.S.C. §1956(c)(4)(B)], but such term does not include any transaction necessary to preserve a person's right to representation as guaranteed by the sixth amendment to the Constitution;

(2) the term "criminally derived property" means any property constituting, or derived from, proceeds obtained from a criminal offense; and

(3) the terms "specified unlawful activity" and "proceeds" shall have the meaning given those term in section 1956 of this title [18 U.S.C. §1956].

a. How do §1956 and §1957 differ? Reread §1957(a) carefully and notice how the intent requirement differs from §1956. Unlike §1956, §1957 does not require that the defendant have acted with either "the intent to promote the carrying on of specified unlawful activity" nor with the knowledge "that the transaction is designed in whole or part — (i) to conceal or disguise the nature, the location, the source, the ownership, or the control of the proceeds of specified unlawful activity; or (ii) to avoid a transaction reporting requirement. . . ." But §1957 has a $10,000 threshold requirement for criminally derived property. Why might this be? Section 1957 also defines "criminally derived property" as "any property constituting, or derived from, proceeds obtained from a criminal offense." 18 U.S.C. §1957(f)(2) (emphasis added). Section 1956 sets different parameters and refers only to property that "represents the proceeds of some form of unlawful activity." §1956(a)(1).

Does the broader scope of §1957 explain that provision's $10,000 threshold requirement? On the issue of whether this threshold requirement has been met, compare United States v. Rutgard, 108 F.3d 1041, 1063 (9th Cir. 1997) (where SUA proceeds have been deposited in an account that contains other funds, a court should presume, if possible, that a withdrawal consisted primarily of clean funds), with United States v. Haddad, 462 F.3d 783, 792 (7th Cir. 2006) (no such presumption should be made where the "vast majority" of funds in the account came from fraud). See Stefan D. Cassella, The Money Laundering Statutes (18 U.S.C. §§1956 and 1957), 55 U.S. Attorneys' Bull. 21, 29-30 (2007).

b. Section 1957 explicitly exempts "any transaction necessary to preserve a person's right to representation as guaranteed by the sixth amendment to the Constitution." §1957(f)(1). However, as the court noted in United States v. Elso, 422 F.3d 1305, 1309-10 (11th Cir. 2005), "it does not follow that this exemption carries over into §1956." If the defendant "had the requisite knowledge and intent to support a conviction under §1956," the court reasoned, the "issue of whether the money involved in [the] transaction was for an attorney's fee would not [be] relevant" to that charge. Id. at 1310. Does it make any sense to subject lawyers to prosecution under

§1956, but not §1957? The gap between the two statutes may not be very large if §1957 is read narrowly. See United States v. Blair, 661 F.3d 755 (4th Cir. 2011) (rejecting invocation of provision by defense lawyer who used drug money to "bankroll counsel for others").

E. ENTERPRISE CRIME

In 1970, Congress passed the Racketeer Influenced and Corrupt Organizations Act (RICO), codified at 18 U.S.C. §§1961-1964 (2000). The purpose of the Act was to eradicate "organized crime":

> The Congress finds that (1) organized crime in the United States is a highly sophisticated, diversified, and widespread activity that annually drains billions of dollars from America's economy by unlawful conduct and the illegal use of force, fraud, and corruption; (2) organized crime derives a major portion of its power through money obtained from such illegal endeavors as syndicated gambling, loan sharking, the theft and fencing of property, the importation and distribution of narcotics and other dangerous drugs, and other forms of social exploitation; (3) this money and power are increasingly used to infiltrate and corrupt legitimate business and labor unions and to subvert and corrupt our democratic processes; (4) organized crime activities in the United States weaken the stability of the Nation's economic system, harm innocent investors and competing organizations, interfere with free competition, seriously burden interstate and foreign commerce, threaten the domestic security, and undermine the general welfare of the Nation and its citizens; and (5) organized crime continues to grow because of defects in the evidence-gathering process of the law inhibiting the development of the legally admissible evidence necessary to bring criminal and other sanctions or remedies to bear on the unlawful activities of those engaged in organized crime and because the sanctions and remedies available to the Government are unnecessarily limited in scope and impact.

Statement of Findings and Purpose, Pub. L. No. 91-452; 84 Stat. 922. The RICO statute was intended to attack the criminal activities and influence of organizations like the Mafia; it has since been applied to very different organizations and in very different contexts. The portions of the statute excerpted below include RICO's key terms, the elements of a RICO crime, RICO penalties, and RICO civil remedies.

---

18 U.S.C. §§1961-1964 [RICO]

§1961. Definitions

    As used in this chapter—

      (1) "racketeering activity" means (A) any act or threat involving murder, kidnapping, gambling, arson, robbery, bribery, extortion, dealing in obscene

matter, or dealing in a controlled substance or listed chemical (as defined in section 102 of the Controlled Substances Act [21 U.S.C. §802]), which is chargeable under State law and punishable by imprisonment for more than one year; (B) any act which is indictable under any of the following provisions of title 18, United States Code: Section 201 (relating to bribery), section 224 (relating to sports bribery), sections 471, 472, and 473 (relating to counterfeiting), section 659 (relating to theft from interstate shipment) if the act indictable under section 659 is felonious, section 664 (relating to embezzlement from pension and welfare funds), sections 891-894 (relating to extortionate credit transactions), section 1028 (relating to fraud and related activity in connection with identification documents), section 1029 (relating to fraud and related activity in connection with access devices), section 1084 (relating to the transmission of gambling information), section 1341 (relating to mail fraud), section 1343 (relating to wire fraud), section 1344 (relating to financial institution fraud), section 1425 (relating to the procurement of citizenship or nationalization unlawfully), section 1426 (relating to the reproduction of naturalization or citizenship papers), section 1427 (relating to the sale of naturalization or citizenship papers), sections 1461-1465 (relating to obscene matter), section 1503 (relating to obstruction of justice), section 1510 (relating to obstruction of criminal investigations), section 1511 (relating to the obstruction of State or local law enforcement), section 1512 (relating to tampering with a witness, victim, or an informant), section 1513 (relating to retaliating against a witness, victim, or an informant), section 1542 (relating to false statement in application and use of passport), section 1543 (relating to forgery or false use of passport), section 1544 (relating to misuse of passport), section 1546 (relating to fraud and misuse of visas, permits, and other documents), sections 1581-1592 (relating to peonage, slavery, and trafficking in persons), section 1951 (relating to interference with commerce, robbery, or extortion), section 1952 (relating to racketeering), section 1953 (relating to interstate transportation of wagering paraphernalia), section 1954 (relating to unlawful welfare fund payments), section 1955 (relating to the prohibition of illegal gambling businesses), section 1956 (relating to the laundering of monetary instruments), section 1957 (relating to engaging in monetary transactions in property derived from specified unlawful activity), section 1958 (relating to use of interstate commerce facilities in the commission of murder-for-hire), section 1960 (relating to illegal money transmitters), sections 2251, 2251A, 2252, and 2260 (relating to sexual exploitation of children), sections 2312 and 2313 (relating to interstate transportation of stolen motor vehicles), sections 2314 and 2315 (relating to interstate transportation of stolen property), section 2318 (relating to trafficking in counterfeit labels for phonorecords, computer programs or computer program documentation or packaging and copies of motion pictures or other audiovisual works), section 2319 (relating to criminal infringement of a copyright), section 2319A (relating to unauthorized fixation of and trafficking in sound recordings and music videos of live musical performances), section 2320 (relating to trafficking in goods or services bearing counterfeit marks), section 2321 (relating to trafficking in certain motor vehicles or motor vehicle parts), sections 2341-2346 (relating to trafficking in contraband cigarettes), sections 2421-2424 (relating to white slave traffic), sections 175-178 (relating to biological weapons), sections 229-229F (relating to chemical weapons), section 831 (relating to nuclear materials), (C) an act which is indictable under title 29, United States Code, section 186 (dealing with restrictions on payments and loans to labor organizations) or section 501(c) (relating to embezzlement from union funds), (D) any offense involving fraud connected with a case under title 11 (except a case under section 157 of this title), fraud in the sale of securities, or the felonious manufacture, importation, receiving, concealment, buying, selling, or otherwise dealing in a controlled substance or listed chemical (as defined in section 102 of the Controlled Substances Act [21 U.S.C. §802]), punishable under any law of the United States, (E) any act which is indictable under the Currency and Foreign Transactions Reporting Act, (F) any act which is indictable under the Immigration and Nationality Act, section 274 [8 U.S.C. §1324] (relating to bringing in and harboring certain aliens), section 277 [8 U.S.C. §1327] (relating to aiding or assisting certain aliens to enter the United States), or section 278 [8 U.S.C. §1328] (relating to importation of alien for immoral purpose) if the act indictable under such section of such Act was committed for the purpose of financial gain, or (G) any act that is indictable under any provision listed in section 2332b(g)(5)(B) [18 U.S.C. §2332b(g)(5)(B)];

(2) "State" means any State of the United States, the District of Columbia, the Commonwealth of Puerto Rico, any territory or possession of the United States, any political subdivision, or any department, agency, or instrumentality thereof;

(3) "person" includes any individual or entity capable of holding a legal or beneficial interest in property;

(4) "enterprise" includes any individual, partnership, corporation, association, or other legal entity, and any union or group of individuals associated in fact although not a legal entity;

(5) "pattern of racketeering activity" requires at least two acts of racketeering activity, one of which occurred after the effective date of this chapter and the last of which occurred within ten years (excluding any period of imprisonment) after the commission of a prior act of racketeering activity;

(6) "unlawful debt" means a debt (A) incurred or contracted in gambling activity which was in violation of the law of the United States, a State or political subdivision thereof, or which is unenforceable under State or Federal law in whole or in part as to principal or interest because of the laws relating to usury, and (B) which was incurred in connection with the business of gambling in violation of the law of the United States, a State or political subdivision thereof, or the business of lending money or a thing of value at a rate usurious under State or Federal law, where the usurious rate is at least twice the enforceable rate; . . .

§1962. Prohibited activities

(a) It shall be unlawful for any person who has received any income derived, directly or indirectly, from a pattern of racketeering activity or through collection of an unlawful debt in which such person has participated as a principal within the meaning of section 2, title 18, United States Code, to use or invest, directly or indirectly, any part of such income, or the proceeds of such income, in acquisition of any interest in, or the establishment or operation of, any enterprise which is engaged in, or the activities of which affect, interstate or foreign commerce. A purchase of securities on the open market for purposes of investment, and without the intention of controlling or participating in the control of the issuer, or of assisting another to do so, shall not be unlawful under this subsection if the securities of the issuer held by the purchaser, the members of his immediate family, and his or their accomplices in any pattern or racketeering activity or the collection of an unlawful debt after such purchase do not amount in the aggregate to one percent of the outstanding securities of any one class, and do not confer, either in law or in fact, the power to elect one or more directors of the issuer.

(b) It shall be unlawful for any person through a pattern of racketeering activity or through collection of an unlawful debt to acquire or maintain, directly or indirectly, any interest in or control of any enterprise which is engaged in, or the activities of which affect, interstate or foreign commerce.

(c) It shall be unlawful for any person employed by or associated with any enterprise engaged in, or the activities of which affect, interstate or foreign commerce, to conduct or participate, directly or indirectly, in the conduct of such enterprise's affairs through a pattern of racketeering activity or collection of unlawful debt.

(d) It shall be unlawful for any person to conspire to violate any of the provisions of subsection (a), (b), or (c) of this section.

§1963. Criminal penalties

(a) Whoever violates any provision of section 1962 of this chapter [18 U.S.C. §1962] shall be fined under this title or imprisoned not more than 20 years (or for life if the violation is based on a racketeering activity for which the maximum penalty includes life imprisonment), or both, and shall forfeit to the United States, irrespective of any provision of State law—

(1) any interest the person has acquired or maintained in violation of section 1962

(2) any—

(A) interest in;

(B) security of;

(C) claim against; or

(D) property or contractual right of any kind affording a source of influence over any enterprise which the person has established, operated, controlled, conducted, or participated in the conduct of, in violation of section 1962; and

(3) any property constituting, or derived from, any proceeds which the person obtained, directly or indirectly, from racketeering activity or unlawful debt collection in violation of section 1962.

The court, in imposing sentence on such person shall order, in addition to any other sentence imposed pursuant to this section, that the person forfeit to the United States all property described in this subsection. In lieu of a fine otherwise authorized by this section, a defendant who derives profits or other proceeds from an offense may be fined not more than twice the gross profits or other proceeds. . . .

§1964. Civil remedies. . . .

(c) Any person injured in his business or property by reason of a violation of section 1962 of this chapter may sue therefor in any appropriate United States district court and shall recover threefold the damages he sustains and the cost of the suit, including a reasonable attorney's fee, except that no person may rely upon any conduct that would have been actionable as fraud in the purchase or sale of securities to establish a violation of section 1962. The exception contained in the preceding sentence does not apply to an action against any person that is criminally convicted in connection with the fraud, in which case the statute of limitations shall start to run on the date on which the conviction becomes final. . . .

1. This expansive, rambling statute creates three new offenses, specified in 18 U.S.C. §1962(a) through §1962(c), along with a conspiracy offense in subsection (d) that will be discussed later in this section. The paradigmatic subsection (a) case is bad guys as passive investors: Having gained income from racketeering (or from the collection of an unlawful debt), the defendants acquire an interest in a legitimate business. Today this might be a standard money-laundering case (note that the RICO statute predates the money-laundering statute by 16 years). The paradigmatic subsection (b) case is infiltration: Bad guys gain control of an enterprise through either racketeering or the collection of an unlawful debt.

Subsection (c) does not envision a single paradigm. A (c) enterprise could be an otherwise legitimate entity that conducts some of its affairs "through a pattern of racketeering activity or collection of unlawful debt." Or it could be the "mob," a thoroughly illegitimate entity whose principal activities involve racketeering and extortion. Notice that the first two sections appear designed to capture criminals' use of the legitimate economy—either by investing in it (§1962(a)), or by acquiring control over parts of it (§1962(b)). Likewise, the third section (§1962(c)) could encompass persons using criminal means to manage otherwise legitimate enterprises, but it also appears to encompass criminal enterprises themselves.

2. While the sponsors of the RICO statute meant it to be used primarily to combat criminal control of legitimate enterprises, prosecutors have not used it in the intended manner. The only substantive RICO offense that is regularly charged is the offense specified by subsection (c); with rare exceptions, subsection (a) and (b) charges arise only in civil cases. And although the various parts of §1962 speak of a "pattern of racketeering" and "collection of unlawful debt" as alternative ways of committing the relevant offenses, the second of those alternatives is rarely charged. See United

States v. Schiro, 679 F.3d 521, 533 (7th Cir. 2012) (Wood, J., dissenting) (noting inability to "find any cases that address whether pattern of racketeering activity and collection of unlawful debts are separate elements of a RICO violation"). The focus here will be on §1962(c) cases involving "a pattern of racketeering activity"—the most common basis for criminal RICO charges.

3. One reason for the large measure of convergence in prosecutors' use of RICO charges is that the Department of Justice exercises an exceptional degree of centralized control in this area, as the following excerpts from the United States Attorneys' Manual clearly require:

9-110.101 Division Approval

No RICO criminal indictment or information or civil complaint shall be filed, and no civil investigative demand shall be issued, without the prior approval of the Criminal Division. . . .

9-110.200 RICO Guidelines Preface

The decision to institute a federal criminal prosecution involves balancing society's interest in effective law enforcement against the consequences for the accused. Utilization of the RICO statute, more so than most other federal criminal sanctions, requires particularly careful and reasoned application, because, among other things, RICO incorporates certain state crimes. One purpose of these guidelines is to reemphasize the principle that the primary responsibility for enforcing state laws rests with the state concerned. Despite the broad statutory language of RICO and the legislative intent that the statute " . . . shall be liberally construed to effectuate its remedial purpose," it is the policy of the Criminal Division that RICO be selectively and uniformly used. It is the purpose of these guidelines to make it clear that not every proposed RICO charge that meets the technical requirements of a RICO violation will be approved. Further, the Criminal Division will not approve "imaginative" prosecutions under RICO which are far afield from the congressional purpose of the RICO statute. A RICO count which merely duplicates the elements of proof of traditional Hobbs Act, Travel Act, mail fraud, wire fraud, gambling or controlled substances cases, will not be approved unless it serves some special RICO purpose. Only in exceptional circumstances will approval be granted when RICO is sought merely to serve some evidentiary purpose.

See also Paul E. Coffey, The Selection, Analysis, and Approval of Federal RICO Prosecutions, 65 Notre Dame L. Rev. 1035 (1990). In May 2016, DOJ published the sixth edition of its nearly 500 page Manual for Federal Prosecutors devoted entirely to criminal RICO.

4. The Justice Department's extraordinary restraint with respect to criminal charges under the RICO statute stands in stark contrast to the way the statute is used on the civil side, where private plaintiffs can seek treble damages and attorney's fees for RICO violations under §1964(c), the statute's private right of action provision. Not only is there no governmental

gate-keeping with respect to private RICO claims, there is a selection bias away from the organized crime groups that the statute was designed to target. See Gerard E. Lynch, RICO: The Crime of Being a Criminal, Parts I and II, 87 Colum. L. Rev. 661 (1987) (discussing legislative history). After all, few private plaintiffs sue Mafia families, street gangs, or even corrupt politicians.

How does the fact that private plaintiffs regularly, and sometimes abusively, file RICO complaints affect the "power of initiation" that, according to Dan Kahan (see Section E of Chapter 4), federal prosecutors generally exercise over the development of federal criminal law? This is a variant of the dual-track lawmaking problem that courts confront in the civil rights area, where the scope of criminal liability under civil rights statutes 18 U.S.C. §§241 and 242 is subject to expansion in civil suits brought under 42 U.S.C. §1983 and *Bivens*. See United States v. Lanier, 520 U.S. 259 (1997), excerpted in Section A of Chapter 7. To some extent, courts can separate the two tracks by focusing on RICO "standing"—one aspect of a private RICO action that does not mirror the elements of a RICO criminal indictment. See Anza v. Ideal Steel Corp., 547 U.S. 451 (2006). (For another important difference between the scope of civil and criminal RICO, see *infra* note 6.)

Moreover, there are certain statutory interpretation issues that are far more likely to arise in civil RICO cases than in criminal cases, such as the degree of permissible overlap between the RICO "person" (the civil defendant) and the alleged "enterprise." See Cedric Kushner Promotions, Ltd. v. King, 533 U.S. 158 (2001); Fitzgerald v. Chrysler Corp., 116 F.3d 225 (7th Cir. 1997) (refusing to read RICO so broadly as to transform every civil fraud claim into a federal RICO claim). Nevertheless, the challenge of integrating—or segregating—these two bodies of law remains substantial. Below, our focus is on RICO doctrine as it is applied in criminal cases. However, you should keep in mind that civil RICO law may be broader even than criminal RICO law, in large part because civil claims are often brought under §1962(a) and (b), which clearly encompass alleged "racketeering" activity by legitimate businesses.

5. Why does the Justice Department exercise such control over RICO indictments, as opposed to, say, mail fraud indictments? What's the big deal about RICO? One reason for DOJ oversight may be that allegations that one is a "racketeer" can be damaging. Yet this cannot be the whole answer, for private citizens are free to make such allegations without DOJ gate-keeping. See Sedima, S.P.R.L. v. Imrex Co., 473 U.S. 479 (1985). A second concern may be that RICO convictions bring stiff sentences—up to 20 years, or even life, if the violation is based on underlying "activity" for which the maximum penalty is life. Still, by now you realize that 20-year maximums are par for the course in federal criminal law. Federalism concerns may provide a third reason for the DOJ's exercise of control over RICO indictments; RICO charges can be based on racketeering activity covered by state law, and the statute therefore creates the possibility of massive federal intrusion into

areas of traditional state and local enforcement. But so does the Travel Act, 18 U.S.C. §1952, which (to add insult to injury) is one of the "racketeering activities" included in the long list of RICO predicates in §1961(1).

More significantly, RICO indictments allow the government to cast a wide net that drags a large and diverse cast of defendants and a broad variety of acts into the same courtroom, or at least into the same indictment—with all the potential for "spillover prejudice" (as defense lawyers would claim) or "synergistic benefits" (as prosecutors might put it) that inevitably results from liberal joinder. A conspiracy indictment can potentially do the same thing, and often does. But the scope of any one conspiracy is necessarily limited (remember that the essence of a conspiracy is a single agreement by all co-conspirators). By tying criminal liability to an "enterprise" instead of a single agreement, RICO extends much further. And by allowing prosecutors to draw many diverse crimes together in a single case, the RICO statute creates a framework that makes both conviction and substantial punishment more likely. See Gerard E. Lynch, RICO: The Crime of Being a Criminal, Parts III and IV, 87 Colum. L. Rev. 920 (1987).

6. Does RICO apply to conduct that occurs abroad? In a recent opinion, RJR Nabisco, Inc. v. European Community, 136 S. Ct. 2090 (2016), the Supreme Court said "it depends." The European Community and 26 of its member states filed suit under RICO, alleging that RJR Nabisco participated in a global money-laundering scheme in association with various organized crime groups in which drug traffickers smuggled narcotics into Europe and sold them for euros that were used to pay for large shipments of RJR cigarettes into Europe.

RJR argued, first, that RICO does not apply to racketeering activity that occurs outside U.S. territory. To this, the Court responded:

> RICO defines racketeering activity to include a number of predicates that plainly apply to at least some foreign conduct, such as the prohibition[s] against [money laundering], . . . the assassination of Government officials, and . . . hostage taking. Congress has thus given a clear, affirmative indication that §1962 applies to foreign racketeering activity—*but only to the extent that the predicates alleged in a particular case themselves apply extraterritorially.*

Id. at 2094 (emphasis added).

Significantly, the majority distinguished §1962, containing RICO's criminal prohibitions, and §1964(c), providing for a private cause of action. It held that while the former may apply extraterritoriality, the latter provision does not. Interpreting §1964(c)'s text, the Court concluded that respondents could not overcome the presumption of extraterritoriality and "thus a private RICO plaintiff must allege and prove a domestic injury." Id. at 2106, 2011. This was quite a feat, right? The Court at once preserved criminal RICO as a powerful tool for prosecutors to go after international criminal networks (including terrorism), while keeping private efforts to secure money damages or other private relief out of federal court unless there is a domestic nexus charged. The Court effectively cut the Gordian knot that had caused trouble in Scheidler v. National Organization for Women, 510 U.S. 249 (1994) (*Scheidler I*), where in order to preserve the use of RICO in international terrorism prosecutions, it held that the defendants in a civil case against abortion clinic protesters need not have had an economic motive, as we noted in Chapter 5, and which we discuss *infra* in a Note after Boyle v. United States, 556 U.S. 398 (2009).

RJR's second argument was that RICO does not apply to foreign enterprises. The Court was not prepared to accept this categorical statement, either:

> Although we find that RICO imposes no domestic enterprise requirement, this does not mean that every foreign enterprise will qualify. . . . [A] RICO enterprise must engage in, or affect in some significant way, commerce directly involving the United States—e.g., commerce between the United States and a foreign country. Enterprises whose activities lack that anchor to U.S. commerce cannot sustain a RICO violation.

Id. at 2105. Noting that at least two of the charged predicates—money laundering and material support for terrorism—expressly provide for extraterritorial application and that RJR depended on sales conducted through U.S. mails and wires, the Court held that "respondents' allegations that RJR violated §§1962(b) and (c) do not involve an impermissibly extraterritorial application of RICO." Id. at 2106.

7. The elements of the standard RICO prosecution against a "person" (defendant) under §1962(c) are: (1) the existence of an "enterprise"; (2) the person's "association with" or "employment" by the enterprise; (3) the requisite connection between the enterprise and interstate or foreign commerce; and (4) "conduct" or "participation in the conduct" of the enterprise's affairs, (5) through "a pattern of racketeering activity."

Our focus here will be on where the difficult factual and legal issues generally arise: with respect to the "enterprise" element, the "conduct" element, and the "pattern" element (that is, elements (1), (4), and (5)). The interstate commerce nexus rarely presents more than a speed-hump to a RICO prosecution. See, e.g., United States v. Nascimento, 491 F.3d 25, 30 (1st Cir. 2007) (affirming RICO convictions for a gang "engaged in violent, but noneconomic"—that is, not profitable—criminal activity because the enterprise's "cacophony of ongoing mayhem" did have a de minimis effect on interstate commerce). Compare Waucaush v. United States, 380 F.3d 251, 256 (6th Cir. 2004) (requiring more than a de minimis effect on interstate commerce where the RICO enterprise is not engaged in economic activity), with United States v. Cornell, 780 F.3d 616, 622 (4th Cir. 2015) (questioning validity of *Waucaush* in light of Gonzales v. Raich). The Supreme Court in *RJR Nabisco* adopted a rule similar to *Waucaush* for extraterritorial RICO cases. It held that where the alleged conduct occurred abroad, the government must prove that the "RICO enterprise engage[d] in, or affect[ed] in some significant way, commerce directly involving the United States—e.g., commerce between the United States and a foreign country. Enterprises whose activities lack that anchor to U.S. commerce cannot sustain a RICO violation." 136 S. Ct. at 2015.

And the requirement of association with the relevant enterprise tends to be subsumed in the requirement that the defendant participate in the conduct of the enterprise's affairs.

1.   DEFINING THE RICO "ENTERPRISE"

Initially—and curiously, in view of the clear wording of §1962(c)—there was some doubt about whether a RICO "enterprise" could be an illegitimate entity. It was assumed that the statute's primary target was the infiltration and use of *legitimate* businesses by organized crime. Principally, there was concern that the federal/state balance in criminal law enforcement might be upended if federal RICO criminal liability existed even where there was no legitimate business for organized crime to infiltrate. Whether "enterprise" under RICO could include purely criminal organizations was considered in a 1981 conversation between Gennaro J. Angiulo, then Boss of the Boston Cosa Nostra, and one of his lieutenants, Ilario M. A. Zannino—a conversation that, as it happened, was picked up by an FBI bug:

> Mr. Angiulo: "Our arguments is we're illegitimate business."
> Mr. Zannino: "We're a shylock."
> Mr. Angiulo: "We are a bookmaker. We're selling marijuana. We are illegal here, illegal there. Arsonists. We are everything."
> Mr. Zannino: "Pimps."
> Mr. Angiulo: "So what?"
> Mr. Zannino: "Prostitutes."
> Mr. Angiulo: "The law does not cover us, is that right?"
> Mr. Zannino: "That's the argument."
> Mr. Angiulo: "They can stick RICO. . . . I wouldn't be in a legitimate business for all the [expletive] money in the world."

Thomas S. O'Neill, Functions of the RICO Enterprise Concept, 64 Notre Dame L. Rev. 646, 662 n. 64 (1989) (quoting portion of wiretap transcript heard by the jury in United States v. Angiulo, et al., D. Mass., 1:83-CR-00235 (filled Sept. 20, 1983), affirmed, 897 F.2d 1169 (1st Cir. 1990)).

Later that year, in United States v. Turkette, 452 U.S. 576 (1981), the Supreme Court rejected the mobsters' view of the law—which, to be fair, had been successful in their own Circuit. The Court's inquiry began, and ended, with the statutory language:

> Section 1962(c) makes it unlawful "for any person employed by or associated with any enterprise engaged in, or the activities of which affect, interstate or foreign commerce, to conduct or participate, directly or indirectly, in the conduct of such enterprise's affairs through a pattern of racketeering activity or collection of unlawful debt." The term "enterprise" is defined as including "any individual, partnership, corporation, association, or other legal entity, and any union or group of individuals associated in fact although not a legal entity." §1961(4). There is no restriction upon the associations embraced by the definition: an enterprise includes any union or group of individuals associated in fact. On its face, the definition appears to include both legitimate and illegitimate enterprises within its scope; it no more excludes criminal enterprises than it does legitimate ones. Had Congress not intended to reach criminal associations, it could easily have narrowed the sweep of the definition by inserting a single word, "legitimate." But it did nothing to indicate that an enterprise consisting of a group of individuals was not covered by RICO if the purpose of the enterprise was exclusively criminal.

452 U.S. at 580-81. And in concluding, the Court noted:

> [I]t is urged that the interpretation of RICO to include both legitimate and illegitimate enterprises will substantially alter the balance between federal and state enforcement of criminal law. This is particularly true, so the argument goes, since included within the definition of racketeering activity are a significant number of acts made criminal under state law. 18 U.S.C. §1961(1). But even assuming that the more inclusive definition of enterprise will have the effect suggested, the language of the statute and its legislative history indicate that Congress was well aware that it was entering a new domain of federal involvement through the enactment of this measure. Indeed, the very purpose of the Organized Crime Control Act of 1970 was to enable the Federal Government to address a large and seemingly neglected problem. The view was that existing law, state and federal, was not adequate to address the problem, which was of national dimensions. That Congress included within the definition of racketeering activities a number of state crimes strongly indicates that RICO criminalized conduct that was also criminal under state law, at least when the requisite elements of a RICO offense are present.

452 U.S. at 586. *Turkette* made clear that a RICO enterprise could be a criminal gang or organized crime family. But can an "association-in-fact" enterprise under RICO be just any group of people committing crimes together? The Court returned to this issue nearly 30 years after *Turkette*.

Boyle v. United States
556 U.S. 938 (2009)

Justice ALITO delivered the opinion of the Court.

We are asked in this case to decide whether an association-in-fact enterprise under the Racketeer Influenced and Corrupt Organizations Act (RICO), 18 U.S.C. §1961 et seq., must have "an ascertainable structure beyond that inherent in the pattern of racketeering activity in which it engages." We hold that such an enterprise must have a "structure" but that an instruction framed in this precise language is not necessary. The District Court properly instructed the jury in this case. We therefore affirm the judgment of the Court of Appeals.

I

A

The evidence at petitioner's trial was sufficient to prove the following: Petitioner and others participated in a series of bank thefts in New York, New Jersey, Ohio, and Wisconsin during the 1990s. The participants in these crimes included a core group, along with others who were recruited from time to time. Although the participants sometimes attempted bank-vault burglaries and bank robberies, the group usually targeted cash-laden night-deposit boxes, which are often found in banks in retail areas.

Each theft was typically carried out by a group of participants who met beforehand to plan the crime, gather tools (such as crowbars, fishing gaffs, and walkie-talkies), and assign the roles that each participant would play (such as lookout and driver). The participants generally split the proceeds from the thefts. The group was loosely and informally organized. It does not appear to have had a leader or hierarchy; nor does it appear that the participants ever formulated any long-term master plan or agreement.

From 1991 to 1994, the core group was responsible for more than 30 night-deposit-box thefts. By 1994, petitioner had joined the group, and over the next five years, he participated in numerous attempted night-deposit-box thefts and at least two attempted bank-vault burglaries.

In 2003, petitioner was indicted for participation in the conduct of the affairs of an enterprise through a pattern of racketeering activity, in violation of 18 U.S.C. §1962(c); conspiracy to commit that offense, in violation of §1962(d); conspiracy to commit bank burglary, in violation of §371; and nine counts of bank burglary and attempted bank burglary, in violation of §2113(a).

B

In instructing the jury on the meaning of a RICO "enterprise," the District Court relied largely on language in United States v. Turkette, 452 U.S. 576 (1981). The court told the jurors that, in order to establish the existence of such an enterprise, the Government had to prove that: "(1) There [was] an ongoing organization with some sort of framework, formal or informal, for carrying out its objectives; and (2) the various members and associates of the association function[ed] as a continuing unit to achieve a common purpose." Over petitioner's objection, the court also told the jury that it could "find an enterprise where an association of individuals, without structural hierarchy, form[ed] solely for the purpose of carrying out a pattern of racketeering acts" and that "[c]ommon sense suggests that the existence of an association-in-fact is oftentimes more readily proven by what it does, rather than by abstract analysis of its structure."

Petitioner requested an instruction that the Government was required to prove that the enterprise "had an ongoing organization, a core membership that functioned as a continuing unit, and an ascertainable structural hierarchy distinct from the charged predicate acts." The District Court refused to give that instruction. . . . W]e granted certiorari to resolve conflicts among the Courts of Appeals concerning the meaning of a RICO enterprise.

II

A

RICO makes it "unlawful for any person employed by or *associated with any enterprise* engaged in, or the activities of which affect, interstate or foreign commerce, to conduct or participate, directly or indirectly, in the conduct of such enterprise's affairs through a pattern of racketeering activity or collection of unlawful debt." 18 U.S.C. §1962(c) (emphasis added).

The statute does not specifically define the outer boundaries of the "enterprise" concept but states that the term "includes any individual, partnership, corporation, association, or other legal entity, and any union or group of individuals associated in fact although not a legal entity." §1961(4). This enumeration of included enterprises is obviously broad, encompassing "*any* . . . group of individuals associated in fact." Ibid. (emphasis added). The term "any" ensures that the definition has a wide reach, and the very concept of an association in fact is expansive. In addition, the RICO statute provides that its terms are to be "liberally construed to effectuate its remedial purposes." §904(a), 84 Stat. 947, note following 18 U.S.C. §1961; see also, e.g., National Organization for Women, Inc. v. Scheidler, 510 U.S. 249, 257 (1994) ("RICO broadly defines 'enterprise'").

In light of these statutory features, we explained in *Turkette* that "an enterprise includes any union or group of individuals associated in fact" and that RICO reaches "a group of persons associated together for a common purpose of engaging in a course of conduct. " 452 U.S. at 580, 583. Such an enterprise, we said, "is proved by evidence of an ongoing organization, formal or informal, and by evidence that the various associates function as a continuing unit." Id. at 583.

Notwithstanding these precedents, the dissent asserts that the definition of a RICO enterprise is limited to "business-like entities." See *post*, at 2247-2250 (opinion of Stevens, J.). We see no basis to impose such an extratextual requirement.

case law

B

As noted, the specific question on which we granted certiorari is whether an association-in-fact enterprise must have "an ascertainable structure beyond that inherent in the pattern of racketeering activity in which it engages." We will break this question into three parts. First, must an association-in-fact enterprise have a "structure"? Second, must the structure be "ascertainable"? Third, must the "structure" go "beyond that inherent in the pattern of racketeering activity" in which its members engage?

"Structure." We agree with petitioner that an association-in-fact enterprise must have a structure. In the sense relevant here, the term "structure" means "[t]he way in which parts are arranged or put together to form a whole" and "[t]he interrelation or arrangement of parts in a complex entity." American Heritage Dictionary 1718 (4th ed. 2000); see also Random House Dictionary of the English Language 1410 (1967) (defining "structure" to mean, among other things, "the pattern of relationships, as of status or friendship, existing among the members of a group or society").

From the terms of RICO, it is apparent that an association-in-fact enterprise must have at least three structural features: a purpose, relationships among those associated with the enterprise, and longevity sufficient to permit these associates to pursue the enterprise's purpose. As we succinctly put it in *Turkette,* an association-in-fact enterprise is "a group of persons associated together for a common purpose of engaging in a course of conduct." 452 U.S. at 583.

That an "enterprise" must have a purpose is apparent from meaning of the term in ordinary usage, i.e., a "venture," "undertaking," or "project." Webster's Third New International Dictionary 757 (1976). The concept of "associat[ion]" requires both interpersonal relationships and a common interest. See id. at 132 (defining "association" as "an organization of persons having a common interest"); Black's Law Dictionary 156 (rev. 4th ed. 1968) (defining "association" as a "collection of persons who have joined together for a certain object"). Section 1962(c) reinforces this conclusion and also shows that an "enterprise" must have some longevity, since the offense proscribed by that provision demands proof that the enterprise had "affairs" of sufficient duration to permit an associate to "participate" in those affairs through "a pattern of racketeering activity."

Although an association-in-fact enterprise must have these structural features, it does not follow that a district court must use the term "structure" in its jury instructions. A trial judge has considerable discretion in choosing the language of an instruction so long as the substance of the relevant point is adequately expressed.

② "*Ascertainable.*" Whenever a jury is told that it must find the existence of an element beyond a reasonable doubt, that element must be "ascertainable" or else the jury could not find that it was proved. Therefore, telling the members of the jury that they had to ascertain the existence of an "ascertainable structure" would have been redundant and potentially misleading.

③ "*Beyond that inherent in the pattern of racketeering activity.*" This phrase may be interpreted in at least two different ways, and its correctness depends on the particular sense in which the phrase is used. If the phrase is interpreted to mean that the existence of an enterprise is a separate element that must be proved, it is of course correct. As we explained in *Turkette*, the existence of an enterprise is an element distinct from the pattern of racketeering activity and "proof of one does not necessarily establish the other."[4] 452 U.S. at 583.

On the other hand, if the phrase is used to mean that the existence of an enterprise may never be inferred from the evidence showing that persons associated with the enterprise engaged in a pattern of racketeering activity, it is incorrect. We recognized in *Turkette* that the evidence used to prove the pattern of racketeering activity and the evidence establishing an enterprise "may in particular cases coalesce." Ibid.

C

The crux of petitioner's argument is that a RICO enterprise must have structural features in addition to those that we think can be fairly inferred from the language of the statute. Although petitioner concedes

---

4. It is easy to envision situations in which proof that individuals engaged in a pattern of racketeering activity would not establish the existence of an enterprise. For example, suppose that several individuals, independently and without coordination, engaged in a pattern of crimes listed as RICO predicates—for example, bribery or extortion. Proof of these patterns would not be enough to show that the individuals were members of an enterprise.

that an association-in-fact enterprise may be an "'informal'" group and that "not 'much'" structure is needed, he contends that such an enterprise must have at least some additional structural attributes, such as a structural "hierarchy," "role differentiation," a "unique *modus operandi*," a "chain of command," "professionalism and sophistication of organization," "diversity and complexity of crimes," "membership dues, rules and regulations," "uncharged or additional crimes aside from predicate acts," an "internal discipline mechanism," "regular meetings regarding enterprise affairs," an "enterprise 'name,'" and "induction or initiation ceremonies and rituals."

We see no basis in the language of RICO for the structural requirements that petitioner asks us to recognize [, which include hierarchy, chain of command, fixed roles, non ad hoc decision making,] a name, regular meetings, dues, established rules and regulations, disciplinary procedures, or induction or initiation ceremonies. While the group must function as a continuing unit and remain in existence long enough to pursue a course of conduct, nothing in RICO exempts an enterprise whose associates engage in spurts of activity punctuated by periods of quiescence. Nor is the statute limited to groups whose crimes are sophisticated, diverse, complex, or unique; for example, a group that does nothing but engage in extortion through old-fashioned, unsophisticated, and brutal means may fall squarely within the statute's reach.

The breadth of the "enterprise" concept in RICO is highlighted by comparing the statute with other federal statutes that target organized criminal groups. For example, 18 U.S.C. §1955(b), which was enacted together with RICO as part of the Organized Crime Control Act of 1970, 84 Stat. 922, defines an "illegal gambling business" as one that "involves five or more persons who conduct, finance, manage, supervise, direct, or own all or part of such business." A "continuing criminal enterprise," as defined in 21 U.S.C. §848(c), must involve more than five persons who act in concert and must have an "organizer," supervisor, or other manager. Congress included no such requirements in RICO.

III

A

Contrary to petitioner's claims, rejection of his argument regarding these structural characteristics does not lead to a merger of the crime proscribed by 18 U.S.C. §1962(c) (participating in the affairs of an enterprise through a pattern of racketeering activity) and any of the following offenses: operating a gambling business, §1955; conspiring to commit one or more crimes that are listed as RICO predicate offenses, §371; or conspiring to violate the RICO statute, §1962(d).

Proof that a defendant violated §1955 does not necessarily establish that the defendant conspired to participate in the affairs of a gambling enterprise through a pattern of racketeering activity. In order to prove the latter offense, the prosecution must prove either that the defendant committed a pattern of §1955 violations or a pattern of state-law gambling crimes. See §1961(1). No such proof is needed to establish a simple violation of §1955.

Likewise, proof that a defendant conspired to commit a RICO predicate offense—for example, arson—does not necessarily establish that the defendant participated in the affairs of an arson enterprise through a pattern of arson crimes. Under §371, a conspiracy is an inchoate crime that may be completed in the brief period needed for the formation of the agreement and the commission of a single overt act in furtherance of the conspiracy. See United States v. Feola, 420 U.S. 671, 694 (1975). Section 1962(c) demands much more: the creation of an "enterprise"—a group with a common purpose and course of conduct—and the actual commission of a pattern of predicate offenses.[5]

Finally, while in practice the elements of a violation of §§1962(c) and (d) are similar, this overlap would persist even if petitioner's conception of an association-in-fact enterprise were accepted.

B

Because the statutory language is clear, there is no need to reach petitioner's remaining arguments based on statutory purpose, legislative history, or the rule of lenity. In prior cases, we have rejected similar arguments in favor of the clear but expansive text of the statute. See *National Organization for Women*, 510 U.S. at 262 ("The fact that RICO has been applied in situations not expressly anticipated by Congress does not demonstrate ambiguity. It demonstrates breadth"); see also *National Organization for Women, supra*, at 252 (rejecting the argument that "RICO requires proof that either the racketeering enterprise or the predicate acts of racketeering were motivated by an economic purpose"); H.J. Inc. v. Northwestern Bell Telephone Co., 492 U.S. 229, 244 (1989) (declining to read "an organized crime limitation into RICO's pattern concept").

---

5. The dissent states that "[o]nly if proof of the enterprise element . . . requires evidence of activity or organization beyond that inherent in the pattern of predicate acts will RICO offenses retain an identity distinct from §371 offenses." *Post*, at 2250-2251 (opinion of Stevens, J.). This is incorrect: Even if the same evidence may prove two separate elements, this does not mean that the two elements collapse into one.

IV

The instructions the District Court judge gave to the jury in this case were correct and adequate. These instructions explicitly told the jurors that they could not convict on the RICO charges unless they found that the Government had proved the existence of an enterprise. The instructions made clear that this was a separate element from the pattern of racketeering activity.

The instructions also adequately told the jury that the enterprise needed to have the structural attributes that may be inferred from the statutory language. As noted, the trial judge told the jury that the Government was required to prove that there was "an ongoing organization with some sort of framework, formal or informal, for carrying out its objectives" and that "the various members and associates of the association function[ed] as a continuing unit to achieve a common purpose."

Finally, the trial judge did not err in instructing the jury that "the existence of an association-in-fact is oftentimes more readily proven by what it does, rather than by abstract analysis of its structure." This instruction properly conveyed the point we made in *Turkette* that proof of a pattern of racketeering activity may be sufficient in a particular case to permit a jury to infer the existence of an association-in-fact enterprise. . . .

Justice STEVENS, with whom Justice BREYER joins, dissenting.

In my view, Congress intended the term "enterprise" as it is used in the Racketeer Influenced and Corrupt Organizations Act (RICO), 18 U.S.C. §1961 et seq., to refer only to business-like entities that have an existence apart from the predicate acts committed by their employees or associates. . . .

In some respects, my reading of the statute is not very different from that adopted by the Court. We agree that "an association-in-fact enterprise must have at least three structural features: a purpose, relationships among those associated with the enterprise, and longevity sufficient to permit these associates to pursue the enterprise's purpose." But the Court stops short of giving content to that requirement. It states only that RICO "demands proof that the enterprise had 'affairs' of sufficient duration to permit an associate to 'participate' in those affairs through 'a pattern of racketeering activity,'" before concluding that "[a] trial judge has considerable discretion in choosing the language of an instruction" and need not use the term "structure." While I agree the word structure is not talismanic, I would hold that the instructions must convey the requirement that the alleged enterprise have an existence apart from the alleged pattern of predicate acts. The Court's decision, by contrast, will allow juries to infer the existence of an enterprise in every case involving a pattern of racketeering activity undertaken by two or more associates.

By permitting the Government to prove both elements with the same evidence, the Court renders the enterprise requirement essentially meaningless in association-in-fact cases. It also threatens to make that category of §1962(c) offenses indistinguishable from conspiracies to commit predicate acts, see §371, as the only remaining difference is §1962(c)'s pattern requirement. The Court resists this criticism, arguing that §1962(c) "demands much more" than the inchoate offense defined in §371. It states that the latter "may be completed in the brief period needed for the formation of the agreement and the commission of a single overt act in furtherance of the conspiracy," whereas the former requires the creation of "a group with a common purpose and course of conduct—and the actual commission of a pattern of predicate offenses." Given that it is also unlawful to conspire to violate §1962(c), see §1962(d), this comment provides no assurance that RICO and §371 offenses remain distinct. Only if proof of the enterprise element—the "group with a common purpose and course of conduct"—requires evidence of activity or organization beyond that inherent in the pattern of predicate acts will RICO offenses retain an identity distinct from §371 offenses.

THE MEANING OF ENTERPRISE

1. *Boyle*, like *Turkette*, again declined to define the outer limits of what constitutes a RICO enterprise. The Court's rare forays into the area have principally been to reject restrictive Circuit Court decisions and to approve more malleable and capacious formulations. As we have noted, another such decision (a civil RICO case upon which *Boyle* relied) is National Organization for Women v. Scheidler (*Scheidler I*), 510 U.S. 249 (1994), which we first encountered in Chapter 5. In *Scheidler I*, the Court rejected a line of cases in the courts of appeals holding that either the RICO enterprise or the underlying racketeering acts must have an economic motive. While it reached its decision in the context of a civil RICO action against a coalition of antiabortion groups, the Court was probably worried about the case's implications for criminal prosecutions. An amicus brief from the Justice Department in *Scheidler I* argued that the lower court's constrained reading of the RICO statute would impair the government's ability to go after ideologically or religiously motivated terrorists. These concerns about the dual nature of RICO interpretation may have worked in favor of the private plaintiffs in *Scheidler I*, which was decided a mere 11 months after the first attack on the World Trade Center in February 1993.

2. *Scheidler I* speaks to what "enterprise" does not mean. *Boyle* says a bit about what the term does mean, but not much. Perhaps because of the range of possibilities envisioned in the case law, the practical meaning of the term often seems strategic—and, crucially, varies from case to case. Which "enterprise" to allege in an indictment may turn more on the relationship of the charged "person" to the enterprise than on the character or cohesion of the enterprise itself. Yet results may turn on which "enterprise"

prosecutors choose to allege. The smaller and more tightly defined the enterprise is, the easier it is for federal prosecutors to prove that a given defendant participated in the conduct of the enterprise's affairs. On the other hand, the broader and more far-reaching the enterprise, the easier it is for prosecutors to join a wide range of crimes and defendants in a single prosecution.

3. Clearly defined organizational structures can be carved up into a variety of RICO enterprises. See United States v. Olson, 450 F.3d 655 (7th Cir. 2006) (the charged enterprise—"the Almighty Latin Kings Nation, Milwaukee Chapter"—was a subdivision of "the Nation" and in turn had its own regional subgroups). Sometimes, the government can have it both ways. Thus, prosecutors in the Southern District of New York were able, in one case, to define as a RICO enterprise the "Commission" comprising the leadership of all the Mafia (Cosa Nostra) families in New York City, and, in other cases, to treat the Colombo Family as its own RICO enterprise. See United States v. Salerno, 964 F.2d 172 (2d Cir. 1992) (rejecting the claims of Persico, the Colombo boss prosecuted in both cases); see also United States v. Schiro, 679 F.3d 521 (7th Cir. 2012) (rejecting similar RICO double jeopardy claims by members of the Chicago "Outfit"). When Persico faced sentencing on his second RICO conviction, after having received 100 years' imprisonment in his previous RICO prosecution, his lawyer expressed his client's "regret that he has but one life to give for his country.*

4. *Turkette*'s definition of an enterprise refers to two factors—organization and continuity—that seem to add up to a single factor: what the military might call "unit cohesion." What is the requisite degree of cohesion? In United States v. Nascimento, 491 F.3d 25 (1st Cir. 2007), where the charged "enterprise" was a street gang whose base of operations was Stonehurst Street in Dorchester, the First Circuit noted:

> We first ponder the sufficiency of the government's evidence concerning the existence of the enterprise. With respect to this issue, we review the record de novo to determine whether, taking the evidence and all reasonable inferences therefrom in the light most hospitable to the government's theory of the case, a rational jury could find beyond a reasonable doubt that the government had established the disputed element of the offense. See United States v. Cruz-Arroyo, 461 F.3d 69, 73 (1st Cir. 2006).
>
> In attacking the sufficiency of the government's evidence [concerning] the existence of an enterprise, the appellants point to testimony from various cooperating witnesses who described Stonehurst as a loose aggregation of friends that lacked colors, initiation rites, and a formal hierarchy. For example, Augusto Lopes testified that Stonehurst was "just a group" whose

---

* Based on the personal recollection of one of the editors.

members "were all friends with each other, certain individuals acted out, and some individuals didn't do nothing at all." Similarly, Burgo said at one point that Stonehurst was "just a name." The appellants suggest that this testimony distinguishes this case from United States v. Patrick, 248 F.3d 11 (1st Cir. 2001), a case in which we upheld the application of RICO to a street gang that "had colors and signs . . . had older members who instructed younger ones, its members referred to the gang as family, and it had "sessions" where important decisions were made." Id. at 19.

We agree that the factors mentioned in *Patrick* are relevant to the question of whether a street gang constitutes an enterprise — but their presence or absence is not dispositive of the issue. Here, the government provided other testimony that could have prompted a jury reasonably to conclude that Stonehurst was an enterprise. After all, Stonehurst members used a shared cache of firearms that were regarded as property of the gang. The weapons were handed around and used by several different Stonehurst members to shoot Wendover sympathizers. One erstwhile Stonehurst member, Rodrigues, testified that he had traveled to purchase weapons for "the group" and clarified that by "the group" he meant "Stonehurst."

In addition to testimony about Stonehurst's arsenal, the record contains testimony suggesting that Stonehurst members self-identified as belonging to an organization. Cooperating witnesses were able to identify precisely a wide variety of individuals as being associated with Stonehurst. The witnesses also displayed an ability to distinguish between members and friends.

Then, too, Stonehurst members kept tabs on one another and informed one another when things would be "hot" because of a recent shooting. They acted on behalf of one another by attempting to assassinate witnesses to each other's crimes. And, finally, members trained other members in the use of night vision goggles, binoculars, and police evasion tactics to enable them more efficiently to carry out their shared purpose of killing Wendover members.

Taking this evidence in the light most favorable to the government, we conclude, as did the district court, that even though Stonehurst lacked some of the accouterments of more structured street gangs, a rational jury could find that it had a sufficiently well-defined shape to constitute an enterprise in the requisite sense. Stonehurst exhibited group cohesion over time; its membership pooled and shared resources; the individuals involved had a sense of belonging and self-identified as Stonehurst members; and the group had a well-honed set of goals. We think that this is enough, if barely, to constitute a RICO enterprise.

491 F.3d at 32-33. What do you suppose the court meant by the phrase, "sufficiently well-defined shape?" What was the "shape" of the gang in *Nascimento*? Though enterprises — legal and illegal alike — are artificial, abstract entities, courts seem to be drawn to language referring to physical shape and size. Why might that be?

5. Based on the language quoted above, the gang in *Nascimento* had no obvious vertical structure. Notice the absence of talk about the gang's hierarchy; there appears to be no organization chart for Stonehurst. Nor, apparently, was there much evidence of *horizontal* structure—note the lack of discussion of the division of labor between different gang members, with different personnel specializing in distinct tasks. The government's evidence in *Nascimento* appears to paint a picture of an anarcho-syndicalist commune in which all share equally—but the shared items and tasks mostly consist of guns and violence. Usually, organization and structure imply inequality and difference: Individual members of the group have distinct jobs, and some members take orders from others. The enterprise in *Nascimento* suggests a very different picture—one focused on equality and sameness. If both pictures satisfy the requirements of RICO's "enterprise" element, what group or entity *doesn't* satisfy that element?

How can one have the requisite cohesion for a RICO enterprise where the enterprise lacks a corporate existence and is not a gang but rather is an "association in fact" that consists of some mix of individuals and diverse formal entities? Consider the following corruption case:

United States v. Cianci
378 F.3d 71 (1st Cir. 2004)

STAHL, Senior Circuit Judge.

Vincent A. Cianci was the Mayor of Providence, Rhode Island; Frank E. Corrente was the City's Director of Administration; Richard E. Autiello was a member of the Providence City Towing Association, a private organization. Between April 23 and June 24, 2002, the three were jointly tried on a superseding indictment that charged them and others with forty-six violations of federal statutes prohibiting public corruption. The district court entered judgments of acquittal on eight of the charges but submitted the rest to the jury.

On June 24, 2002, the jury returned a total of eight guilty verdicts but acquitted on the remaining thirty counts. All three defendants were convicted on a single count charging a conspiracy to violate the RICO (Racketeer Influenced and Corrupt Organizations) statute. See 18 U.S.C. §1962(d). Corrente and Autiello were convicted on a count charging a federal bribery conspiracy. See 18 U.S.C. §§371 & 666(a)(1)(B). Corrente was convicted on a count charging a substantive RICO violation, see 18 U.S.C. §1962(c), two counts charging Hobbs Act extortion conspiracies, see 18 U.S.C. §1951(a), and two counts charging Hobbs Act attempted extortions, see id. Autiello was convicted on an additional count charging a second federal bribery conspiracy. . . .

I. THE RICO CONVICTIONS (ALL DEFENDANTS)

A. INDICTMENT

Count One of the indictment charged Cianci, Autiello, and Corrente with conspiracy to operate the affairs of an enterprise consisting of the defendants themselves, the City of Providence, "various officers, agencies and entities of Providence" including thirteen specified agencies, Jere Realty, and Friends of Cianci, and others "known or unknown to the Grand Jury." The purpose of the enterprise "included the following: a. Enriching Defendant Vincent A. Cianci . . . [and] Friends of Cianci through extortion, mail fraud, bribery, money laundering, and witness tampering, and b. Through the same means enriching, promoting and protecting the power and assets of the leaders and associates of the enterprise. . . ."

[T]he superseding indictment delineated the members of the enterprise, the roles of the defendants in the enterprise, the purposes and goals of the racket, and the ways in which the defendants used other members of the enterprise—specifically, municipal entities that they controlled as part of the conspiracy—to further those purposes and goals. It alleged that defendants conspired to violate and did in fact violate RICO through their involvement in an associated-in-fact enterprise devoted to enriching and empowering defendants and others through unlawful means. The enterprise was alleged to have been comprised of the individual defendants; the City of Providence "including, but not limited to" many of its departments, offices, and agencies; the campaign contribution fund controlled by Cianci and Corrente; and others known and unknown to the grand jury. . . . This enterprise was alleged to have existed "from in or about January 1991 through in or about December 1999."

The . . . indictment . . . also detailed the "pattern of racketeering activity" underlying the grand jury's RICO and RICO conspiracy allegations. The unlawful conduct comprising the alleged pattern was set forth in a section detailing the predicate RICO "Racketeering Acts" and in separate offense counts. The pattern was itself subdivided into nine alleged schemes. . . .

[The court then described the nine schemes, including "the Tow List Scheme," in which Corrente pressured government contractors to make campaign contributions totaling some $250,000; "the Jere Lease Scheme," in which the owner of a local real estate company was alleged to have paid bribes and kickbacks that made their way to Corrente; "the Ronci Estate scheme," in which Cianci was alleged to have extorted a $10,000 contribution from the Ronci estate in exchange for his help securing a tax abatement from the corrupt Board of Tax Assessment Review; "the Ise Job scheme," in which Cianci was alleged to have arranged for Ise to obtain a government job in exchange for a $5,000 contribution; "the Freitas Lots scheme," in which Cianci was alleged to have supported the sale of two City lots to

Freitas in return for a $10,000 contribution; "the Freitas Lease scheme," in which Corrente was alleged to have attempted to influence the School Department to encourage a city contractor to lease a building owned by Freitas in exchange for $2,000; "the Freitas Invoices scheme," in which Corrente was alleged to have facilitated prompt payments of invoices submitted by Freitas's business in return for $1,100; and "the Maggiacomo Job scheme," in which Autiello facilitated the hiring of Joseph Maggiacomo as a police officer in return for a $5,000 contribution by Maggiacomo's mother.]

B. ENTERPRISE . . .

Def. Argument ①

[Defendants first] contend that the indictment charged a legal impossibility in alleging that municipal entities were themselves part of the unlawful purpose associated-in-fact enterprise. They base this argument on the requirement that members of such an enterprise share a common unlawful purpose and cases holding that municipalities cannot be found to have acted with unlawful intent. See, e.g., Lancaster Comm. Hosp. v. Antelope Valley Hosp. Dist., 940 F.2d 397, 404 (9th Cir. 1991) ("[G]overnment entities are incapable of forming a malicious intent."); United States v. Thompson, 685 F.2d 993, 1001 (6th Cir. 1982) ("Criminal activity is private activity even when it is carried out in a public forum and even though the activity can only be undertaken by an official's use of a state given power[.]"). Defendants' argument misses the mark. . . . As the D.C. Circuit elucidated:

> [A restrictive] reading of 1961(4) would lead to the bizarre result that only criminals who failed to form corporate shells to aid their illicit schemes could be reached by RICO. [Such an] interpretation hardly accords with Congress' remedial purposes: to design RICO as a weapon against the sophisticated racketeer as well as (and perhaps more than) the artless.

[United States v. Perholtz, 842 F.2d 343, 353 (D.C. Cir. 1988).] Municipal entities can be part of an unlawful purpose association-in-fact enterprise so long as those who control the entities share the purposes of the enterprise. . . . The City and its component agencies are not the defendants in this case; they were deemed members of the enterprise because without them, Cianci, Corrente, and Autiello would not have been able . . . to perpetrate the charged racketeering schemes. . . . [T]his is not the first time an association-in-fact enterprise composed in this manner has been found to exist. See, e.g., *Masters*, 924 F.2d at 1362; United States v. McDade, 28 F.3d 283 (3d Cir. 1994) (upholding association-in-fact enterprise consisting of congressman, his two offices, and congressional subcommittees that he chaired); United States v. Dischner, 974 F.2d 1502 (9th Cir. 1992) (upholding association-in-fact enterprise consisting of municipal officials . . . and department of public works). In each of these cases, the groupings of individuals and corporate or municipal entities were sufficiently organized and devoted to the alleged illicit purposes that the resulting whole functioned as a continuing unit. . . .

Requiring the government to prove that all members named in the enterprise shared a common purpose of illegality did not compel the government to show that the City itself had the *mens rea* to seek bribes and to extort. . . . Unlawful common purpose is imputed to the City by way of the individual defendants' control, influence, and manipulation of the City for their illicit ends. . . . *[handwritten: holding ① ✱]*

[T]he defendants also . . . contend that their RICO convictions must be reversed because the evidence introduced at trial . . . was insufficient to [support] a finding that the schemes were conducted through the specific entity alleged in the indictment to have constituted a RICO enterprise. Defendants [claim] that there was no evidence from which the jury might have inferred a shared purpose between defendants and the municipal entities . . . through which many of the schemes were conducted. . . . *[handwritten: Def. Arg. ②]*

After careful scrutiny of the record and setting the evidence against the jury instructions, we conclude that the jury could have found . . . that the defendants and others named as enterprise members comprised an ongoing organization that functioned as a continuing unit and was animated by common purposes or goals. . . . *[handwritten: holding ②]*

Cianci and Corrente exercised substantial control over the municipal entities named as members of the enterprise. Cianci was the City's mayor and Corrente its chief of administration. They were alleged and were shown to have used their positions and influence to sell municipal favors on a continuing basis. The evidence indicates a close relationship "in fact" among them, the City they managed, and Cianci's political organization. Cianci, as mayor, and Corrente and Autiello, as city officials, were strongly connected to and had considerable influence over the various City employees and departments. Their illegal schemes could function only with the cooperation, witting or unwitting, of certain City agencies and officials. Insofar as Cianci's and the other defendants' criminal schemes were or would be carried out by themselves and others acting in their municipal roles, the City—if only to that extent—did share in the same common criminal purpose.[3] The defendants were not only human members of the enterprise, but were the City's official leaders with considerable express and implicit authority over its departments and employees. . . . It is because of this control and these close connections that the jury could have imputed the enterprise's common purpose to the City. See *Masters*, 924 F.2d at 1366 ("Surely if three individuals can

---

3. The evidence depicted [among City employees] a behavioral spectrum ranging from innocent cooperation to willful complicity in unlawful conduct. . . .

constitute a RICO enterprise . . . then the larger association that consists of them plus entities that they control can be a RICO enterprise too").

Evidence of defendants' control, both titular and actual, was sufficient to deem the enterprise a "continuing unit" and "ongoing organization." The jury could easily glean from taped conversations and the trial testimony of David Ead—a co-conspirator and vice-chair of the Board of Tax Assessment Review—that there existed an organized structure with Cianci at the top, Corrente as a middle man facilitating and often initiating transactions, and others, including Autiello, Ead, and Pannone, that fed deals into the organization (or in Ead's case, sometimes tried to replace Corrente as the middle man). The defendants attempted to use, to varying degrees of success, various municipal agencies in committing a series of related bribes and extortions. These agencies were used in this manner on an ongoing basis from 1991 through 1999. The fact that other persons and entities were used in some transactions but not in others does not matter; the jury instructions reflected this flexibility.

There was detailed evidence, moreover, placing Cianci, the City's mayor, in the middle of at least four of the enumerated racketeering acts. With regard to the Ronci Estate scheme, David Ead testified at trial that he suggested to Ronci's attorney that the estate settle its tax claim with the City for $100,000 in exchange for a $10,000 contribution to the Friends of Cianci. Ead met with Cianci and discussed the proposed deal. The settlement was approved by the City's Board of Tax Assessment Review. Ead testified that shortly thereafter, he was contacted by Corrente, who told him that Cianci wanted Corrente to collect the money. Ead responded that he was waiting for the Ronci attorney, to which Corrente replied, "Well, you know that the Mayor he's on my back—do your best." After receiving the money from Ronci's attorney, Ead brought the money to Corrente who put his finger on his lips and took the envelope. . . .

With regard to the Ise Job, Ead again testified that he served as a middleman for Mayor Cianci, this time arranging a $5,000 bribe in exchange for a municipal job. According to Ead, Cianci asked during their conversation about Ise, cautious about whether "he's alright" and looking for assurances that "he's not going to say nothing." Upon learning that the City's Department of Planning and Development had no positions available, Cianci ordered the Department to "make one." Upon receiving the $5,000 "contribution," Cianci told Ead, "Don't get nervous."

In their trial testimony, which closely tracked taped conversations among Freitas, Pannone, and other City officials, both Freitas and Ead implicated Cianci in the Freitas Lots scheme, in which Cianci pressured the Providence Redevelopment Authority, the entity empowered to sell the lots, to expedite the sale of two City-owned lots to Freitas in exchange for a $10,000 "contribution" by Freitas to the Cianci political fund. Finally, with regard to the Tow List scheme, Dorothy Deveraux—Corrente's assistant and the Friends' bookkeeper—wrote a note to Corrente which implicated all three defendants in that scheme. . . .

We recognize that the defendants did not always get their way with municipal departments and employees. But the fact that some racketeering schemes did not go as planned, and that certain elements within the City may not have completely complied with the defendants' wishes, does not defeat the integrity of the charged enterprise. The jury could have concluded that these glitches in the schemes only meant that certain substantive crimes went uncompleted. . . . The evidence amply establishes a close relationship between defendants and the City in which they exercised their leadership roles. The enterprise and the conspiracy still thrived and the defendants were able to complete other schemes through their abuse of the municipal apparatus. . . .

HOWARD, Circuit Judge, concurring in part and dissenting in part. . . .
In my view, there is no proof that Cianci and Corrente so controlled the activities of all the municipal entities alleged to be associates of the charged enterprise that the two's shared criminal purposes are reasonably imputed to each such entity. There is no evidence that, for example, Cianci and Corrente themselves could provide those willing to pay bribes with jobs in City departments over which they lacked hiring authority; or that they could contractually bind City departments under separate leadership; or that they could sell City property; or that they could grant or deny construction variances. Nor did the government show that the persons, committees, and boards within the municipal departments, offices, and agencies whose assistance the schemes required abdicated their decision-making responsibilities to Cianci or Corrente. In short, neither Cianci nor Corrente was shown to have so dominated the affairs of the departments, offices, and agencies claimed to be associated with the unlawful purpose enterprise that each of these municipal entities might fairly be found to have been an alter ego of Cianci or Corrente. . . . Rather, the evidence showed only that Cianci and Corrente periodically used the power inherent in their positions to influence (or attempt to influence) the decisions of other municipal actors—actors who, with [some exceptions], were not shown to be privy to, let alone supportive of, the alleged enterprise's purposes. . . .

There was in this case significant evidence of public corruption. Perhaps the government could have proved that Cianci and Corrente ran the Office of the Mayor or the Office of the Director of Administration as a RICO enterprise. Or perhaps the defendants (or, more likely, a subset thereof) might have been shown to be members of one or more smaller, associated-in-fact RICO enterprises. But the government successfully persuaded the grand jury to cast a wider net and to allege that the persons named as enterprise associates, along with the campaign contribution fund, the City of Providence, and many of its departments, offices and agencies, functioned as a de facto organized crime syndicate. Framing the case in this way permitted the government to allege that defendants were responsible under RICO's conspiracy provision for all of the illegal and unethical conduct put on display in this trial—even that in which they were not shown to have personally participated. But this broad case theory obligated the government to prove that each municipal entity alleged to have engaged in conduct that constituted part of the "pattern of racketeering activity" identified in the indictment was itself a member of the enterprise. . . .

RICO is a powerful weapon that can cause mischief if abused by an overzealous prosecutor. While I do not doubt that RICO will sometimes apply in cases of political corruption, I fear the consequences of making the statute too easy to invoke—or too easy to apply broadly—in the political context, where persons who have made a contribution to a politician routinely receive favorable treatment from offices or agencies over which the politician has influence. . . .

NOTES AND QUESTIONS

1. As *Cianci* suggests, courts consistently say that a RICO enterprise must be more than the sum of its members' predicate crimes. Such statements should be taken with a grain of salt, given the manner in which the enterprise element is proven. The mere gathering for drinks (or drugs) before or after the crime can be proof of the enterprise's existence. (For classic "enterprise" proof, see the opening wedding scene in *The Godfather*.) For a street gang, colors and signs do considerable "enterprise" work, as the excerpt from *Nascimento* quoted above indicates. And for a group of inside traders, proof that it is an "association in fact" that amounts to a RICO enterprise may come not just from the circulation and use of inside information within the group, but from its regular golf outings. The opportunity (and obligation) to prove a broad criminal enterprise also allows prosecutors considerable leeway to introduce evidence of uncharged crimes, even those that happened long ago. Usually, one thinks of an element of a criminal offense as a burden on the government—one more fact the prosecution must prove in order to convict. In RICO cases, the enterprise element is often more a gift than a burden; it allows prosecutors to delve deeply into defendants' lives, both business and social—and by doing so, to paint the most advantageous picture possible for the prosecution. Moreover, to prove that an enterprise exists, the government can call witnesses who will testify about any of the enterprise's crimes, including those with which the defendant may not have been involved. See, e.g., United States v. Matera, 489 F.3d 115 (2d Cir. 2007) (criminal acts of non-defendants were properly admitted to prove the existence of the Gambino organized crime family).

2. Yet courts are uncomfortable when political units like states or cities figure prominently in "enterprise" definition. Consider another RICO prosecution of a well-known public official, former Illinois Governor George Ryan, Sr. (you have already come across Governor Ryan once, when he challenged his honest services fraud conviction post-*Skilling*, see Chapter 4.) In its prosecution of Ryan and a top aide, the government alleged the State of Illinois as the RICO enterprise. The court described the facts as follows:

> The story behind this case began in November 1990 when Ryan, then the Lieutenant Governor of Illinois, won election as Illinois' Secretary of State. He was re-elected to that post in 1994. Throughout Ryan's two terms in that office, Warner was one of Ryan's closest unpaid advisors. One of Ryan's duties as Secretary of State was to award leases and contracts for the office, using a process of competitive bidding for major contracts and selecting leases based on the staff's assessments of multiple options. Improprieties in awarding four leases and three contracts form the basis of the majority of the RICO and mail fraud counts against Warner and Ryan, as these leases and contracts were steered improperly to Warner-controlled entities. The result was hundreds of thousands of dollars in benefits for Warner and Ryan. These benefits included financial support for Ryan's successful 1998 campaign for Governor of Illinois.

United States v. Warner, 498 F.3d 666, 675 (7th Cir. 2007). In affirming the convictions, the court noted:

> The question whether a state may be an "enterprise" for purposes of a RICO prosecution is one of first impression. The defendants' first reason for arguing that it cannot be relies on the remedies allowed under RICO. The statute provides for remedies including court-ordered "dissolution or reorganization of any enterprise," 18 U.S.C. §1964(a). Since it is obvious that no court would have the power to disband a sovereign state, the defendants argue that the remedial provisions of the law implicitly mean that the state cannot be a RICO enterprise.
>
> The only problem with this attack is that the Supreme Court rejected it long ago:
>
> > Even if one or more of the civil remedies might be inapplicable to a particular illegitimate enterprise, this fact would not serve to limit the enterprise concept. Congress has provided civil remedies for use when the circumstances so warrant. It is untenable to argue that their existence limits the scope of the criminal provisions.

United States v. Turkette, 452 U.S. 576, 585 (1981). RICO provides a menu of remedies; it does not matter if one or more of the items on that menu might be unavailable in a particular case. Instead, what is important, according to

Turkette, is that Congress meant the term "enterprise" to be "inclusive." 452 U.S. at 586. . . .

The defendants next argue that comity interests prevent the use of a state as a RICO enterprise in a criminal case. . . .

The decision that came closest to addressing the issue at hand is the Sixth Circuit's *en banc* opinion in United States v. Thompson, 685 F.2d 993 (6th Cir. 1982). There the court held that "The Office of the Governor" could be the enterprise in a RICO prosecution. . . .

The Sixth Circuit noted its concern that an indictment naming the governor's office as a RICO enterprise could be unnecessary and disruptive in some cases, and it recommended that prosecutors should try to avoid such charges in the future if possible. The court suggested that a modified indictment might work better in similar, future cases, based on the RICO definition of "enterprise" as "includ[ing] any individual, partnership, corporation, association, or other legal entity, and any union or group of individuals associated in fact although not a legal entity." Id. (quoting 18 U.S.C. §1961(4)). The court stated that "the language which could and we believe preferably should have been employed, would have alleged that the three defendants constituted a 'group of individuals associated in fact although not a legal entity which made use of the Office of Governor of the State of Tennessee' for the particular racketeering activities alleged in the indictment." *Thompson,* 685 F.2d at 1000.

We endorse the Sixth Circuit's call for caution. We also agree with the Sixth Circuit's ultimate conclusion that the prosecution's approach to this issue in cases such as *Thompson* and the case at hand may often not be absolutely necessary under RICO, but it is not forbidden. Some cases, however, are exceptional, and ours is one of them. In such a case, the prosecution may have no real alternative to naming the state as the RICO enterprise. (This of course does not mean that the state itself has violated any federal law; it may instead be a victim of the overall scheme, as are many RICO enterprises.) . . .

In this case, the prosecution thought that it had identified an ongoing scheme to defraud the State of Illinois through the illegal use of two of the most significant executive branch offices of the state and of the state's electoral processes during Ryan's campaign for Governor in 1998. The scheme revolved around an elected official throughout his tenure in these two offices—Secretary of State and Governor—and during the time he was a candidate for the latter office. No legal rule prohibited the prosecution from concluding that there was no single entity or office that it could have identified, short of the state as a whole, that would have encompassed the enterprise that was used by the defendants. In these unusual circumstances, comity interests do not override the broad language of RICO, as interpreted in *Turkette.* The district court did not err by allowing the state to be the RICO enterprise in this RICO conspiracy prosecution.

498 F.3d at 685-96.

3. What is the core concern in *Warner* and *Cianci?* Government agencies have a large measure of organization and continuity—the two factors

that *Turkette* says determine the existence of a RICO enterprise. And the RICO statute appears to have been written primarily as a means of attacking criminal infiltration and control of legal enterprises (presumably including government agencies controlled by corrupt politicians). Yet *Warner* and *Cianci* were obviously seen by the courts deciding them as hard cases, not easy ones. Why? Should "enterprise" be defined differently in corruption cases like *Warner* and *Cianci* than in Mob cases like *Turkette* or gang cases like *Nascimento*? If so, which way should the difference cut?

4. When considering the "power" of RICO, note that Mayor Cianci was convicted on only a single RICO conspiracy count. That RICO can permit the prosecution of the executive who hovers above systemic wrongdoing within his organization is the source of both its celebration and criticism. For an extraordinary exploration of Mayor "Buddy" Cianci's storied career (and the convictions acquired therein) listen to the podcast, "Crimetown."

2. CONDUCTING, OR PARTICIPATING IN THE CONDUCT OF, THE ENTERPRISE'S AFFAIRS

To be liable under §1962(c), not only must a person have been employed by or associated with the enterprise, but that person must also "conduct or participate, directly or indirectly, in the conduct of such enterprise's affairs." One who "conducts" something is generally thought to play some directorial role. Think of musical conductors or teachers who conduct their classes. But what does it mean to "participate, directly or indirectly, in the conduct" of something? (Note how accenting a different syllable changes the word's connotations.) Do students who never raise their hands and simply listen "participate in the conduct" of a class? What about students who raise their hands frequently—but are never called on?

In a civil RICO case involving an outside accounting firm, Reves v. Ernst & Young, 507 U.S. 170 (1993), the Supreme Court found that even the term "participate in the conduct" requires that a person have "some degree of direction." *Reves* is discussed extensively in the following case.

United States v. Oreto
37 F.3d 739 (1st Cir. 1994)

BOUDIN, Circuit Judge.
Frank Oreto, Sr., Frank Oreto, Jr., and Dennis Petrosino ("the appellants") challenge their convictions on a number of charges arising out of an alleged loansharking ring operating in Revere, Massachusetts. We affirm.

I. BACKGROUND

The appellants were charged in June 1987 in an indictment with offenses under the Racketeer Influenced and Corrupt Organizations Act ("RICO"), 18 U.S.C. §1962, as well as offenses involving the making of extortionate loans or collection by extortionate means. 18 U.S.C. §§892, 894 (the extortionate credit transactions or "ETC" statute). The original indictment was 137 pages long, contained 82 counts, and named several other defendants besides the three who are parties to this appeal. . . . We state the facts in the light most favorable to verdicts being appealed.

So viewed, the evidence permitted a reasonable jury to find the following. Oreto, Sr. headed an enterprise which made loans to over three hundred borrowers at weekly interest rates of from three to seven percent. Those weekly rates translate into annual interest of from 156 to 364 percent; the maximum legal rate in Massachusetts, by contrast, is 20 percent annually. Mass. Gen. Laws. ch. 271, §49. Oreto, Jr. and Petrosino served as collectors for the loansharking operation. Over two dozen borrowers testified, various of them asserting that Oreto, Sr. and his accomplices used threats and intimidation to ensure payment of the loans.

The loansharking business was conducted from various locations in or near Revere including both Oreto, Sr.'s home and a function hall in which Oreto, Sr. was a silent partner. The documentary evidence included the organization's "Bible," its master list of borrowers, debts, salaries and expenses. "Frank, Jr.," and "Dennis" were listed among those who received weekly salaries. Much of the trial was given over to testimony by borrowers whose loans were corroborated by entries in the Bible.

These witnesses testified that Oreto, Sr. employed tall, physically imposing men—Petrosino, for example, is described in the record as between 6'1" and 6'2" tall and over 250 pounds in weight—to call upon delinquent borrowers and threaten them—implicitly or explicitly—with physical harm if the loans were not repaid. At least two witnesses testified that they were physically assaulted by Oreto, Sr.'s collectors, and many more borrowers testified that they believed that harm would come to them if they failed to make their payments.

The jury convicted each of the appellants on one count of conspiring to violate RICO, 18 U.S.C. §1962(d), as well as one substantive RICO count. 18 U.S.C. §1962(c). In addition, Oreto, Sr. was convicted on 35 counts of conspiring to collect loans by extortionate means, 18 U.S.C. §894; ten counts of making extortionate loans, 18 U.S.C. §892; and three counts of conspiring to make extortionate loans. The jury also convicted Oreto, Jr. on four counts, and Petrosino on seven counts, of conspiring to collect loans by extortionate means.

At a later date, Oreto, Sr. was sentenced to 20 years' imprisonment on the RICO counts, to run concurrently with 15 year sentences on the individual ETC statute counts but consecutively to a life sentence he was then serving in Massachusetts state prison for second-degree murder. Oreto, Jr. and Petrosino were sentenced to 6 years and 10 years imprisonment, respectively, on each count of conviction, with all sentences to run concurrently. These appeals followed. . . .

III.   THE MERITS AND RELATED ISSUES . . .

The RICO statute makes it a crime for "any person employed by or associated with any enterprise engaged in, or the activities of which affect, interstate or foreign commerce, to conduct or participate, directly or indirectly, in the conduct of such enterprise's affairs through a pattern of racketeering activity or collection of unlawful debt." 18 U.S.C. §1962(c). The district court gave the following instruction on the meaning of "conduct or participate . . . in the conduct of" an enterprise under the statute:

The term "conduct" and the term "participate in the conduct of" an enterprise include the performance of acts, functions or duties which are necessary to or helpful in the operation of the enterprise. A person may be found to conduct or to participate in the conduct of an enterprise even though he is a mere employee having no part in the management or control of the enterprise and no share in the profits.

In Reves v. Ernst & Young, 507 U.S. 170 (1993), the Supreme Court held that an outside accounting firm employed by an enterprise was not subject to civil RICO liability unless it "participated in the operation or management of the enterprise itself." Id. at 183. Relying on *Reves*, Oreto, Jr. and Petrosino argue that "mere employees" by definition do not participate in the "operation or management" of the enterprise. It is true that in *Reves* the Court expressly declined to decide "how far §1962(c) extends down the ladder of operations." 507 U.S. at 184 n.9. Further, the Court observed that "*some* part in directing the enterprise's affairs is required." Id. at 179.

Reves is a case about the liability of *outsiders* who may assist the enterprise's affairs. Special care is required in translating *Reves*'concern with "horizontal" connections—focusing on the liability of an outside adviser—into the "vertical" question of how far RICO liability may extend within the enterprise but down the organizational ladder. In our view, the reason the accountants were not liable in *Reves* is that, while they were undeniably involved in the enterprise's decisions, they neither made those decisions nor carried them out; in other words, the accountants were outside the chain of command through which the enterprise's affairs were conducted.

The government did not show that Oreto, Jr. or Petrosino participated in the enterprise's decision making; but they and other collectors were plainly integral to carrying out the collection process. *Reves* defines "participate" as "to take part in," 507 U.S. at 179, and nothing in the Court's opinion precludes our holding that one may "take part in" the conduct of an enterprise by knowingly implementing decisions, as well as by making them. Indeed, the Court said that "an enterprise is 'operated' not just by upper management but also by lower-rung participants in the enterprise who are under the *direction* of upper management." 507 U.S. at 184.

Congress declared in RICO that the statutory purpose was "to seek the eradication of organized crime in the United States" and Congress listed "loan sharking" as a means by which "organized crime derives much of its power." See Pub. L. 91-452, §1 (Statement of Findings and Purpose following 18 U.S.C. §1961). RICO also provides expressly that "collection of unlawful debt" is a predicate for RICO liability. This conduct is precisely what the government charged, and the jury found, was engaged in by the present appellants. We think Congress intended to reach all who participate in the conduct of that enterprise, whether they are generals or foot soldiers. . . .

3.   OTHER WAYS TO PARTICIPATE IN THE ENTERPRISE

"Foot soldiers" may be liable, but perhaps not janitors. In United States v. Viola, 35 F.3d 37 (2d Cir. 1994), Viola presided over a drug-smuggling and cargo-stealing operation on the Brooklyn waterfront of the sort familiar to viewers of "The Wire." Defendant Michael Formisano, who "performed odd jobs for Viola, mostly consisting of light clean-up and maintenance work," was also convicted on RICO charges. Reversing Formisano's conviction, the Second Circuit noted:

> The entirety of the proof with respect to Formisano showed that, acting under Viola's instructions, he transported some stolen beer and lamps to buyers and returned most of the proceeds from the sales to Viola. In contrast with the other defendants, Formisano's participation was limited to these two acts which were undertaken without the exercise of appreciable discretionary authority. Viola was the kingpin of the operation who was contacted by drug owners and who would decide how best to remove the drugs from the docks. Viola and the other defendants also decided to whom to sell stolen goods, and for how much. Formisano, on the other hand, was not consulted in the decision-making process and exercised no discretion in carrying out Viola's orders. There was no evidence that he was even aware of the broader enterprise. While Formisano's acts might have contributed to the success of the RICO enterprise, he simply did not come within the circle of people who operated or managed the enterprise's affairs. Although *Reves* still attaches liability to those down the "ladder of operation" who nonetheless played some management role, it is plain to us that, since *Reves*, §1962(c) liability cannot cover Formisano. Formisano was not on the ladder at all, but rather, as Viola's janitor and handyman, was sweeping up the floor underneath it.

35 F.3d at 43. Note, however, that the Second Circuit significantly narrowed this holding in United States v. Diaz, 176 F.3d 52 (1999), concluding that *Reves* is satisfied if the defendant "'exercised broad discretion' in carrying out the instructions of his principal." Id. at 94.

Can a street cop be said to have "conducted" the affairs of the entire police department? Yes, at least in Chicago. In United States v. Shamah, 624 F.3d 449 (7th Cir. 2010), the defendants were two police officers—Shamah and Doroniuk—who decided to "supplement their income by shaking down drug dealers." The Seventh Circuit decided that the cops "were operators for the purposes of RICO." Id. at 455. The court explained:

> The heart of a police department's function is to enforce the law, and not to manage other officers or implement policies. As an officer, even a "lowly" one, Shamah had the power to control the department's affairs and direct its force. With a substantial amount of discretion, Shamah chose who to stop on the street, which cars to pull over, and when to obtain arrest and search warrants. Furthermore, he acted as a representative for the larger police department and the city when he spoke to citizens, created public inventory records, and testified to facts that served as the basis for warrants and indictments. As the public face of the department, Shamah was given a great deal of responsibility and trust in operating and directing its affairs. His manipulation of this power transformed legitimate police functions into arms of his illegal endeavors. He usurped the department's identity, and turned it into a criminal enterprise hiding behind a facade of justice.
>
> The government presented ample evidence that Shamah and Doroniuk were not acting as "mere" law-abiding police officers when they forced civilians to part with money and drugs, performed illegal arrests and stops, and planted evidence on civilians. Given his discretion and authority as a police officer, and the way in which he chose to direct his powers, Shamah operated or managed the integral duties of the police department's daily affairs. And the government presented sufficient evidence for the jury to conclude that Shamah conducted the affairs of the enterprise.

Id. *Shamah* distinguished United States v. Cummings, 395 F.3d 392, 397 (7th Cir. 2005), where a low-level employee of the Illinois Department of Employment Security had, in exchange for bribes, provided an outsider with confidential information from an internal database. The employee was deemed not to have operated or managed any aspect of the Department, the charged RICO enterprise. Explaining *Cummings*, the *Shamah* court noted that, there, the "defendant's access to the enterprise's computer database was incidental to her role in the enterprise, she accessed it infrequently, and had no responsibility to maintain it. We also focused on the function of the enterprise, stating that it may have been a different case if the defendant was acting in a way that interfered with the agency's primary function of collecting premiums or paying benefits." 624 F.3d at 455. Why do you think the government charged the whole police department as the RICO enterprise in *Shamah*? Consider the tactical advantages and disadvantages of doing so.

As you read the next subsection, consider the relationships among the "enterprise," the "participants]" in the enterprise, and the "pattern" of illegal activity.

4.   THROUGH A PATTERN OF RACKETEERING ACTIVITY

To satisfy §1962(c), prosecutors must prove that *each* defendant has participated in the enterprise's affairs through a "pattern of racketeering activity." Section 1961(5) further stipulates that a "pattern of racketeering activity" comprises "at least two acts of racketeering activity, one of which occurred after [October 15, 1970] and the last of which occurred within ten years (excluding any period of imprisonment) after the commission of a prior act of racketeering activity." In H.J., Inc. v. Northwestern Bell Telephone Co., a civil RICO case, the Supreme Court held unanimously that the commission of two predicate offenses in the specified time period is necessary, but not sufficient, to form a "pattern of racketeering activity." 492 U.S. 229 (1989). What more is required to establish that the predicates form a pattern? The Court found it difficult to say:

> Our guides in the endeavor must be the text of the statute and its legislative history. We find no support in those sources for the proposition, espoused by the Court of Appeals for the Eighth Circuit in this case, that predicate acts of racketeering may form a pattern only when they are part of separate illegal schemes. Nor can we agree with those courts that have suggested that a pattern is established merely by proving two predicate acts, see, e.g., United States v. Jennings, 842 F.2d 159, 163 (CA6 1988), or with *amici* in this case who argue that the word "pattern" refers only to predicates that are indicative of a perpetrator involved in organized crime or its functional equivalent. . . .
>
> A "pattern" is an "arrangement or order of things or activity," 11 Oxford English Dictionary 357 (2d ed. 1989), and the mere fact that there are a number of predicates is no guarantee that they fall into any arrangement or order. It is not the number of predicates but the relationship that they bear to each other or to some external organizing principle that renders them "ordered" or "arranged." The text of RICO conspicuously fails anywhere to identify, however, forms of relationship or external principles to be used in determining whether racketeering activity falls into a pattern for purposes of the Act. . . .

492 U.S. at 236-38. Despite these challenges, the majority went on to enunciate its two-part "continuity-plus-relationship" test. First, Justice Brennan determined, the predicate offenses must be "related." Two acts are related if they "have the same or similar purposes, results, participants, victims,

or methods of commission, or otherwise are interrelated by distinguishing characteristics and are not isolated events." Id. at 240 (citing 18 U.S.C. §3575(e)). Second, the Court instructed that in order to form a pattern, the two or more predicates must either create or pose a threat of "*continuing racketeering activity.*" This inquiry is "centrally a temporal concept . . . in the RICO context, where *what* must be continuous, RICO's predicate acts or offenses, and the *relationship* these predicates must bear one to another, are distinct requirements." Id. at 242. What makes two predicates continuous? Again, the Court found it difficult to say, exactly. . . .

> "Continuity" is both a closed- and open-ended concept, to a closed period of repeated conduct, or to past conduct that by its nature projects into the future with a threat of repetition. . . . A party alleging a RICO violation may demonstrate continuity over a closed period by proving a series of related predicates extending over a substantial period of time. Predicate acts extending over a few weeks or months and threatening no future criminal conduct do not satisfy this requirement: Congress was concerned in RICO with long-term criminal conduct. Often a RICO action will be brought before continuity can be established in this way. In such cases, liability depends on whether the *threat* of continuity is demonstrated. . . .
>
> Though the number of related predicates involved may be small and they may occur close together in time, the racketeering acts themselves include a specific threat of repetition extending indefinitely into the future, and thus supply the requisite threat of continuity. In other cases, the threat of continuity may be established by showing that the predicate acts or offenses are part of an ongoing entity's regular way of doing business. Thus, the threat of continuity is sufficiently established where the predicates can be attributed to a defendant operating as part of a long-term association that exists for criminal purposes. Such associations include, but extend well beyond, those traditionally grouped under the phrase "organized crime." The continuity requirement is likewise satisfied where it is shown that the predicates are a regular way of conducting defendant's ongoing legitimate business (in the sense that it is not a business that exists for criminal purposes), or of conducting or participating in an ongoing and legitimate RICO "enterprise". . . .

Id. at 241-43. In sum, *H.J. Inc.* establishes that to satisfy §1962(c)'s pattern requirement, prosecutors must prove that two or more RICO predicate violations have occurred within the specified time period; that these offenses were "related"; and they were in fact, or pose a threat of, "continuous" criminal conduct. But within those parameters, the Supreme Court left considerable room for development of the law—so much room that Justice Scalia argued in his concurrence, joined by Chief Justice Rehnquist and Justices O'Connor and Kennedy, that the Court's "continuity plus relationship" test "increases rather than removes the vagueness" inherent in the term "pattern of racketeering activity." 492 U.S. at 255 (Scalia, J., concurring).

THE MEANING OF "PATTERN OF RACKETEERING ACTIVITY"

1. Much of the development of "pattern" doctrine in the lower courts has occurred in civil RICO cases like *H.J. Inc.* For an example of the law's development in the criminal context, consider United States v. Daidone, 471 F.3d 371 (2d Cir. 2006). Daidone, a member of the Luchese organized crime family, was convicted of participating in a racketeering enterprise and racketeering conspiracy in violation of §§1962(c) and (d). The three predicate acts for the RICO convictions were two murders and the operation of a loan-sharking business.

On appeal, Daidone claimed that the government had failed to prove that these predicates formed a "pattern" of racketeering. Under *H.J. Inc.*, he argued, the government "'must show that the racketeering predicates are related,'" 471 F.3d at 375 (quoting *H.J. Inc.*, 492 U.S. at 239), and thus, "the predicate crimes must have 'the same or similar purposes, results, participants, victims, or methods of commission,' or the crimes must be otherwise 'interrelated by distinguishing characteristics and . . . not isolated events.'" 471 F.3d at 374 (quoting 492 U.S. at 239). The Second Circuit had further developed the "relatedness" requirement in United States v. Minicone, 960 F.2d 1099 (1992), holding that predicate acts "must be related to each other ('horizontal' relatedness), and they must be related to the enterprise ('vertical' relatedness)." Id. at 1106. Daidone claimed that, while the government had proven that the crimes were all related "vertically" to the Luchese crime family, it had failed to demonstrate that they were "horizontally" related to each other, since they were separated in time and committed for different reasons.

The Second Circuit disagreed: "Daidone's reading of *H.J. Inc.* as delineating specific requirements for finding horizontal relatedness distinct from vertical relatedness simply creates an overly formal conception of this element. . . ." *Daidone*, 471 F.3d at 375. Noting that the Second Circuit has always afforded the term "pattern of racketeering activity" a "generous reading," id. at 374-75, the court concluded that "both the vertical and horizontal relationships are generally satisfied by linking each predicate act to the enterprise . . . because predicate crimes will share common goals (increasing and protecting the financial position of the enterprise) and common victims (e.g., those who threaten its goals), and will draw their participants from the same pool of associates (those who are members and associates of the enterprise)." Id. at 376. The bottom line, in *Daidone* and elsewhere, is that where the charged RICO enterprise is an entity "whose business is racketeering activity, an act performed in furtherance of that business automatically carries with it the threat of continued racketeering activity." United States v. Cain, 671 F.3d 271, 288 (2d Cir. 2012) (finding series of extortions satisfied both "closed-end" and "open-end" notions of continuity).

2. A second criminal "pattern" case is one we have seen before: United States v. Cianci, 378 F.3d 71 (2004), in which the First Circuit found a "pattern" adequately proven in the corruption prosecution of the mayor of Providence, Rhode Island:

> The evidence shows that the defendants, and ultimately Cianci, were the beneficiaries of most if not all of the nine schemes. The jury could have concluded that the schemes were designed to line Cianci's pockets as well as to maintain his political power in the City. As for methods, most of the schemes involved either Cianci or Corrente calling or personally meeting with city officials and influencing municipal decision-making either through explicit or implicit orders. As the government points out, important "sub-trends" underlay the schemes. The Jere Realty Lease and the Freitas Lease dealt with the School Department. The Tow List and Maggiacomo Job involved the Police Department. The Ise and Maggiocomo Jobs both involved pawning of municipal jobs. Both the Ronci Estate and Freitas Lots schemes involved extortions for tax abatements. All of the offenses involve trading jobs, contracts, and official acts for money, contributions to Cianci's political fund, or other items of value. In most of the schemes, the money was solicited by, paid to, or collected by Corrente.
>
> In addition, the schemes often shared the same players. Corrente, Ead, Pannone, and Autiello were all fundraisers for the Friends of Cianci. Ead participated in the Ronci Estate, the Ise Job, and the Freitas Lots schemes, while Pannone played important roles in the Ronci Estate, the Freitas Lease, and Pay-to-Get-Paid schemes. Autiello was the chief associate in the Tow List extortion and Maggiacomo Job sale. Overall, the evidence shows that the individual racketeering acts were not isolated events but rather parts of a pattern of racketeering activity contemplated and committed by an overarching RICO conspiracy to which all three defendants, along with other co-conspirators, belonged.
>
> "Continuity" of the pattern of racketeering may be shown by either "a series of related predicates extending over a substantial period of time," or a pattern of more limited duration where "the racketeering acts themselves include a specific threat of repetition extending indefinitely into the future" or "the predicate acts or offenses are part of an ongoing entity's regular way of doing business." *H.J., Inc.*, 492 U.S. at 242.
>
> Defendants were accused of conducting a RICO conspiracy that lasted nine years. The Tow List scheme spanned approximately the entire period. During this time, Autiello regularly channeled contributions to Corrente. When towers contributed too much money under the same name, the conspirators scrambled to find other straw contributors, or "replacement" contributors.
>
> The Jere Realty and Freitas Lots schemes both involved kickbacks to the defendants in exchange for pressure on the City to grant leases. As the district court concluded, "[i]t was reasonable for the jury to infer that additional payments would be made in order to renew the lease[s]." The Pay-to-Get-Paid scheme presented the same danger: "[T]he City's habitual tardiness

in paying its vendors, and the period of time over which Freitas made pay-ments to expedite payment of his invoices, provided ample justification for the jury to conclude that such payments would continue to be made in the future."

  Evidence concerning the Ise and Maggiocomo Jobs, both transpiring in 1996, was enough for the jury to conclude that these bribes were part of the same, continuous pattern that jobs in the City could be had for a price. . . .

378 F.3d at 89. Is the meaning of "pattern" in *Cianci* the same as it is in *Daidone*? If the two decisions differ, what accounts for the difference? What role does the pattern element play in RICO prosecutions?

  Don't forget that, in a multi-defendant case, a pattern must be shown as to *each* defendant charged with a substantive RICO violation. It is not enough that a defendant have committed at least two predicate acts. Those acts must also be shown to satisfy the "relatedness" and "continuity" inquiry. If a defendant is not a core player in the enterprise, this may be difficult. See United States v. Cain, 671 F.3d 271 (2d Cir. 2012) (finding "plain error" in trial court's failure to give proper RICO "pattern" instruction as to fringe member of enterprise, but refusing to overturn verdict as to other defen-dants with more sustained involvement in campaign of violence against rivals of lead defendant's tree service and logging business).

5. RICO CONSPIRACIES

  Broad as the definitions of "enterprise" and "pattern" may be, and however expansive participation in the conduct of the enterprise's affairs is, substantive RICO liability remains limited in one crucial respect: The "person" charged must have committed at least two "racketeering acts" from among the long list of federal and state crimes in §1961(1), see Section C above. This means that §1962(c) does not criminalize any conduct that is not already subject to prosecution. (Notice that the list of predicate crimes includes a number of possible conspiracy charges—narcotics conspiracies, money-laundering conspiracies, and Hobbs Act conspiracies—but does not include the general federal conspiracy statute, 18 U.S.C. §371).

  What about the "littlest racketeer"—the guy who never even conspired to commit any of the racketeering predicate crimes but who has some degree of connection to the enterprise or its members? Though he might not be prosecutable under §1962(c) for lack of proof of his commission of particular crimes, he might still be guilty of participation in a RICO conspir-acy, a separate offense under §1962(d).

  To be guilty of RICO conspiracy, a conspirator must have simply intended to further an endeavor that, if completed, would satisfy all of the elements of the substantive RICO offense. In Salinas v. United States, 522

U.S. 52, 63-66 (1997), the Supreme Court described RICO conspiracy in more detail:

> The RICO conspiracy statute, simple in formulation, provides:
> "It shall be unlawful for any person to conspire to violate any of the provisions of subsection (a), (b), or (c) of this section." 18 U.S.C. §1962(d). . . .
> The RICO conspiracy statute, §1962(d), broadened conspiracy coverage by omitting the requirement of an overt act; it did not, at the same time, work the radical change of requiring the Government to prove each conspirator agreed that he would be the one to commit two predicate acts. . . .
> A conspirator must intend to further an endeavor which, if completed, would satisfy all of the elements of a substantive criminal offense, but it suffices that he adopt the goal of furthering or facilitating the criminal endeavor. He may do so in any number of ways short of agreeing to undertake all of the acts necessary for the crime's completion. One can be a conspirator by agreeing to facilitate only some of the acts leading to the substantive offense. . . .
> It makes no difference that the substantive offense under subsection (c) requires two or more predicate acts. The interplay between subsections (c) and (d) does not permit us to excuse from the reach of the conspiracy provision an actor who does not himself commit or agree to commit the two or more predicate acts requisite to the underlying offense. True, though an "enterprise" under §1962(c) can exist with only one actor to conduct it, in most instances it will be conducted by more than one person or entity; and this in turn may make it somewhat difficult to determine just where the enterprise ends and the conspiracy begins, or, on the other hand, whether the two crimes are coincident in their factual circumstances. In some cases the connection the defendant had to the alleged enterprise or to the conspiracy to further it may be tenuous enough so that his own commission of two predicate acts may become an important part of the Government's case. Perhaps these were the considerations leading some of the Circuits to require in conspiracy cases that each conspirator himself commit or agree to commit two or more predicate acts. Nevertheless, that proposition cannot be sustained as a definition of the conspiracy offense, for it is contrary to the principles we have discussed. . . .

522 U.S. 52, 63-66 (1997).

Following *Salinas*, can prosecutors circumvent *Reves*'s requirement that a defendant "conduct or direct" the RICO enterprise by charging him with RICO *conspiracy* instead of with the substantive offense? Apparently so. As the D.C. Circuit recently noted, "every court of appeals to consider the question has held that the *Reves* operation or management test does not apply to conspiracy under §1962(d)." United States v. Wilson, 605 F.3d 985, 1019 (2010). Thus, an individual defendant need not have personally participated in the operation or management of an enterprise in order to be liable for conspiracy under §1962(d). Nor, according to the Second Circuit, need the government necessarily prove the existence of an enterprise—though it must prove an agreement that, if it came to fruition, would constitute a substantive RICO violation. See United States v. Applins, 637 F.3d 59, 75 (2d Cir. 2011) ("the establishment of an enterprise is not an element of the RICO conspiracy offense"). Moreover, the Second Circuit has also noted:

> It is well-settled that a conspirator need not be fully informed about his co-conspirators' specific criminal acts provided that he agreed to participate in the broader criminal conspiracy and the acts evincing participation were not outside of the scope of the illegal agreement. "A conspiracy may exist even if a conspirator does not agree to commit or facilitate each and every part of the substantive offense. The partners in the criminal plan must agree to pursue the same criminal objective and may divide up the work, yet each is responsible for the acts of each other." *Salinas*, 522 U.S. at 63-64; see also United States v. Zichettello, 208 F.3d 72, 100 (2d Cir. 2000) (holding that "no rule" requires "the government to prove that a [RICO] conspirator knew of all criminal acts by insiders in furtherance of the conspiracy" as long as there is proof that defendant possessed knowledge of "the general contours of the conspiracy"); United States v. Rastelli, 870 F.2d 822, 828 (2d Cir. 1989) (stating that a defendant may agree to join a RICO conspiracy without knowing the identities of "all the other conspirators" and without "full knowledge of all the details of the conspiracy").

United States v. Yannotti, 541 F.3d 112, 122 (2d Cir. 2008). Will this line of cases keep you from taking a job as the "gofer" at a Mafia-run social club? At a boiler-room operation that manipulates penny-stock prices?

F.   MATERIAL SUPPORT OFFENSES

Although, as we have seen, the complicity theories available to federal prosecutors are indeed expansive, all of them require a degree of intentionality on the part of the defendant that might still preclude the prosecution of an individual who knowingly helps the worst villains. When it comes to terrorism, Congress has sought to close this arguable enforcement gap with a set of statutes that raise interesting questions about the outer limits of culpability. Before looking at those statutes, we will first consider the entire statutory arsenal that federal criminal law provides in terrorism cases.

1.   CRIMINAL ENFORCEMENT TOOLS AGAINST TERRORISM

The federal government has a large and varied array of substantive criminal law provisions to use against suspected terrorists. At one end of the spectrum are statutes that target those who commit or conspire to commit specific acts that, while amounting to terrorism, would be criminal offenses — e.g., murder or extortion — no matter who did them or what their ultimate motive. Recall again the discussion of National Organization for Women v. Scheidler (I) in the previous subsection. At the other end are statutes that do not seem to have anything to do with terrorists or what terrorists do, but that are available for use (if provable) against those who the government suspects of terrorist connections. Statutes in the latter category lay at the heart of what the Bush Administration touted as its Al Capone strategy in the wake of the September 11, 2001, attacks. As a Justice Department spokesman explained in 2003:

> Years ago, the government knew Al Capone was a powerful organized crime boss, yet we prosecuted him with tax evasion to remove him from the streets. Today, in order to protect the lives of Americans at the earliest opportunity, the government may charge potential terror suspects with lesser offenses to remove them from our communities. The fact that many terrorism investigations result in less serious charges does not mean the case is not terrorism-related. Moreover, pleas to these less serious charges often result in defendants who cooperate and provide invaluable information to the government — information that can lead to the detection and prevention of other terrorism-related activity. . . .

Daniel C. Richman & William J. Stuntz, Al Capone's Revenge: An Essay on the Political Economy of Pretextual Prosecution, 105 Colum. L. Rev. 583, 622 (2005) (quoting DOJ spokesman).

Notwithstanding its tactical advantages, an Al Capone strategy also brings the risk of diminished accountability:

> If they can be criminally prosecuted before they strike, the provable offenses of those seeking to commit terrorist acts will [generally] be relatively minor. Bringing such cases can disrupt terrorist plans and provide leverage for the government to obtain cooperation from defendants; it can also incapacitate targets without resort to material witness warrants, immigration detentions, and other noncriminal processes that (according to some) are amenable to even greater misuse. Moreover, the government can satisfy its discovery obligations without revealing valuable intelligence (so long as it's not exculpatory) when it brings these stripped-down cases.
>
> Yet this strategy has left the Administration hard pressed to demonstrate to Congress and the public that it has effectively used the massive resources that have been committed to counterterrorism. Repeated assurances that the right people are being prosecuted for the right reasons, and that terrorist plans are being foiled or "disrupted," have their limits when such matters are not subject to any external check. Moreover, emerging patterns of minor charges being brought against Arab Americans or Middle Eastern nationals, in the absence of proven terrorist links, will surely provide grist for those disposed to claim ethnic profiling.

Id. at 623. Indeed, the material support statutes' breadth has made them controversial; so, too, have the dynamics of their enforcement. Although no official statistics are available, the FBI has acknowledged that in 2015 "two of every three prosecutions involving people suspected of supporting the Islamic State"—the majority of which were material support cases—relied on "undercover operations." Eric Lichtblau, F.B.I. Steps Up Use of Stings in ISIS Cases, N.Y. Times, June 7, 2016.

Particularly contentious is the government's extensive use of sting operations, which some have criticized for, in the words of one former agent, "manufacturing terrorism cases." Courts, too, have expressed concern over the use of these tactics, although the Supreme Court's high doctrinal bar on entrapment has thus far rendered that defense unavailing to material support defendants. For example, in a widely publicized case, the "Newburgh Four" left bags filled with what they thought were explosives in vehicles outside two synagogues in the Bronx and were soon arrested. At defendant Cromitie's sentencing, Judge Colleen McMahon said, "Only the government could have made a 'terrorist' out of Cromitie, whose buffoonery is positively Shakespearean in scope." Peter L. Bergen, United States of Jihad: Investigating America's Homegrown Terrorists 99 (2016). Although troubled by the government's conduct, Judge McMahon found that it did not rise to the level of entrapment and upheld the defendant's convictions. The Second Circuit affirmed. United States v. Cromitie, 727 F.3d 194 (2d Cir. 2013).

In addition to sting operations, the FBI has relied heavily on confidential informants in the development of material support cases, raising concerns about the adverse impact that these investigations may have on Muslim communities' First and Fourth Amendment rights—particularly when CIs operate within mosques. See, e.g., Columbia Law School Human Rights Institute, Illusion of Justice: Human Rights Abuses in US Terrorism Prosecutions 55 (2014). The alternative to these fraught tactics for identifying budding terrorists, particularly of the homegrown variety, however, is a level of passive surveillance that federal enforcers, even with considerable cooperation from local authorities, are hard-pressed to mount. See Garrett M. Graff, The FBI's Growing Surveillance Gap, Politico, June 16, 2016.

There is no easy answer to the government's dilemma when it plans to bring manifestly terrorism-related charges against defendants, but must decide how advanced their plot should be before arrests are made. Moving in early ensures that the suspects neither do harm nor escape. But it may come with substantial concerns about the liberty and equality interests of defendants and those in their vicinity. On a strategic level, moving in early may also come at the cost of additional evidence that might show a jury and the public at large that the defendants are truly dangerous, not just a bunch of hapless mopes. See Robert M. Chesney, Beyond Conspiracy? Anticipatory Prosecution and the Challenge of Unaffiliated Terrorism, 80 S. Cal. L. Rev.

425, 426 (2007). And statutes ostensibly unrelated to terrorism have also been used to supplement, not merely substitute for, terrorism-related prosecutions. See, e.g., United States v. Benkahla, 530 F.3d 300 (4th Cir. 2008) (rejecting double jeopardy challenge by defendant convicted of grand jury perjury after his acquittal on material support charges).

Once one understands the challenges of counterterrorism prosecutions using either (1) statutes that expressly criminalize terrorist acts, or (2) are completely silent as to any terrorist connection, one sees the attraction (for the government at least) of a third kind of statute—one that requires proof of some sort of link to terrorism but that is less demanding than, say, a terrorism conspiracy statute. Our focus here is on these "material support" statutes that may (depending on how they are understood) represent a new paradigm of complicity liability. See also Hamdan v. United States, 696 F.3d 1238, 1251-52 (D.C. Cir. 2012) (noting that material support for terrorism "is not a recognized international-law war crime").

2. MATERIAL SUPPORT STATUTES

---

18 U.S.C. §2339A. Providing material support to terrorists

(a) Offense.—Whoever provides material support or resources or conceals or disguises the nature, location, source, or ownership of material support or resources, knowing or intending that they are to be used in preparation for, or in carrying out, a violation of section 32 [destruction of aircraft], 37 [violence at international airports], 81 [arson within a federal enclave], 175 [biological weapons offenses], 229 [chemical weapons], 351 [murder, kidnapping, or assault on Members of Congress], 831 [nuclear materials], 842(m) or (n) [plastic explosives], 844(f) or (i) [bombing], 930(c) [homicide with dangerous weapon in federal facility], 956 [conspiracy to commit certain violence crimes overseas], 1114 [murder of federal officer or employee], 1116 [murder of foreign dignitary], 1203 [hostage taking], 1361 [destruction of federal property], 1362 [destruction of communications property], 1363 [destruction of property within federal enclave], 1366 [destruction of energy facility], 1751 [murder, kidnapping, or assault on President], 1992 [train wrecking], 2155 [destruction of national defense material], 2156 [production of defective national defense material], 2280 [violence against maritime navigation], 2281 [violence against maritime fixed platforms], 2332 [violence against Americans overseas], 2332a [use of weapons of mass destruction], 2332b [multinational terrorism], 2332f [bombing public places or facilities], 2340A [torture], or 2442 [recruitment or use of child soldiers] of this title, section 236 of the Atomic Energy Act of 1954 (42 U.S.C. 2284) [atomic weapons], section 46502 [air piracy] or 60123(b) [destruction of gas pipeline] of title 49, or any offense listed in section 2332b(g)(5)(B) (except for sections 2339A and 2339B) [another large array that includes biological materials offenses] or in preparation for, or in carrying out, the concealment of an escape from the commission of any such violation, or attempts or conspires to do such an act, shall be fined under this title, imprisoned not more than 15 years, or both, and, if the death of any person results, shall be imprisoned for any term of years or for life. A violation of this section may be prosecuted in any Federal judicial district in which the underlying offense was committed, or in any other Federal judicial district as provided by law.

(b) Definitions.—As used in this section—

(1) the term "material support or resources" means any property, tangible or intangible, or service, including currency or monetary instruments or financial securities, financial services, lodging, training, expert advice or assistance, safehouses, false documentation or identification, communications equipment, facilities, weapons, lethal substances, explosives, personnel (1 or more individuals who may be or include oneself), and transportation, except medicine or religious materials;

(2) the term "training" means instruction or teaching designed to impart a specific skill, as opposed to general knowledge; and

(3) the term "expert advice or assistance" means advice or assistance derived from scientific, technical or other specialized knowledge.

---

18 U.S.C. §2339B. Providing material support or resources to designated foreign terrorist organizations

(a) Prohibited activities.—

(1) Unlawful conduct. Whoever knowingly provides material support or resources to a foreign terrorist organization, or attempts or conspires to do so, shall be fined under this title or imprisoned not more than 15 years, or both, and, if the death of any person results, shall be imprisoned for any term of years or for life. To violate this paragraph, a person must have knowledge that the organization is a designated terrorist organization (as defined in subsection (g)(6)), that the organization has engaged or engages in terrorist activity (as defined in section 212(a)(3)(B) of the Immigration and Nationality Act [8 U.S.C. §1182(a)(3)(B)]), or that the organization has engaged or engages in terrorism (as defined in section 140(d)(2) of the Foreign Relations Authorization Act, Fiscal Years 1988 and 1989 [22 U.S.C. §2656f(d)(2)]). . . .

(g) Definitions.—As used in this section—. . .

(6) the term "terrorist organization" means an organization designated as a terrorist organization under section 219 of the Immigration and Nationality Act [8 U.S.C. §1189].

(h) Provision of personnel.—No person may be prosecuted under this section in connection with the term "personnel" unless that person has knowingly provided, attempted to provide, or conspired to provide a foreign terrorist organization with 1 or more individuals (who may be or include himself) to work under that terrorist organization's direction or control or to organize, manage, supervise, or otherwise direct the operation of that organization. Individuals who act entirely independently of the foreign terrorist organization to advance its goals or objectives shall not be considered to be working under the foreign terrorist organization's direction and control.

(i) Rule of construction.—Nothing in this section shall be construed or applied so as to abridge the exercise of rights guaranteed under the First Amendment to the Constitution of the United States.

(j) Exception.—No person may be prosecuted under this section in connection with the term "personnel", "training", or "expert advice or assistance" if the provision of that material support or resources to a foreign terrorist organization was approved by the Secretary of State with the concurrence of the Attorney General. The Secretary of State may not approve the provision of any material support that may be used to carry out terrorist activity (as defined in section 212(a)(3)(B)(iii) of the Immigration and Nationality Act [8 U.S.C. §1182(a)(3)(B)(iii)]).

Originally enacted in the aftermath of the 1995 Oklahoma City bombing, the material support laws were little used before 9/11. Today, they constitute the vast majority of federal terrorism charges.* Several features of these statutes make them especially effective counterterrorism tools:

1. Sections 2339A and 2339B are highly versatile: Because the statutes define material support broadly, the offenses can be charged in a wide array of factual circumstances. The following are just a few examples:

- Two women were convicted of violating and conspiring to violate §2339B for funneling funds to al-Shabaab, a designated terrorist insurgent group in Somalia. See United States v. Ali, 799 F.3d 1008 (8th Cir. 2015).

- A defendant was convicted of multiple violations of §2339A and §2339B for conspiring to establish an al Qaeda-style training camp in Bly, Oregon and for recruiting, supplying, and concealing funds to send another individual to fight for the Taliban. See United States v. Mustafa, 406 F. App'x. 526 (2d Cir. 2011).

- A student was convicted of conspiring to violate and of aiding and abetting his co-defendant's attempt to violate §2339B, as well as federal financial aid fraud. The defendant used a debit card attached to his financial aid account to buy his co-defendant a ticket to Syria, where the latter intended to fight for the Islamic State. The co-defendant was intercepted at the airport and convicted of conspiring

---

* [Editors' Note: See, e.g., New York University School of Law, Center on Law & Sec., Terrorist Trial Report Card: September 11, 2001 – September 11, 2011 2 (2011) ("Since 2007, material support has gone from being charged in 11.6% of [terrorism] cases to 69.4% in 2010. In 2011 so far, 87.5% of cases involve a material support charge."). Meanwhile, a study found that 80 percent of all defendants charged in the 101 publicly disclosed Islamic State-related cases from 2014 to 2016 were indicted for material support. See Fordham Law School, Center on Nat. Security, Case by Case ISIS Prosecutions in the United States 2 (2016).] For an exploration of ISIS's ideology and recruitment tactics, including extended interviews with a returned Canadian ISIS member, listen to the podcast "Caliphate."

and attempting to violate §2339B. See United States v. Badawi, No. 15-CR-0060 DOC (C.D. Cal. June 21, 2016).

- An Air Force veteran was convicted of attempting to violate §2339B by supplying himself as "personnel." The defendant was intercepted at an Istanbul airport on his way to Syria where he intended to fight for the Islamic State. See United States v. Pugh, No. 15-CR-116, 2016 WL 1255007 (E.D.N.Y. Mar. 9, 2016).

- An attorney was convicted of violating 18 U.S.C. §§2, 2339A, and 371 for supplying "personnel" in the form of her incarcerated client who was serving a life sentence for violent terrorist offenses. The attorney, Lynne Stewart, intentionally circumvented prison procedures designed to prevent her client from directing terrorist activities from prison. Stewart passed along the client's messages, enabling him to "participate covertly in the conspiracy to engage in violence abroad by communicating to members of [the terrorist organization of which he was the leader] his withdrawal of support for [a] cease-fire." See United States v. Stewart, 590 F.3d 93, 115 (2d Cir. 2009).

2. The material support statutes extend the reach of federal criminal law beyond the boundaries of traditional complicity, conspiracy, and attempt liability. Section 2339A, which more closely resembles the aiding and abetting statute, does not require that the defendant share the intent required of the perpetrator to commit the underlying terrorist act. In fact, no underlying act of terrorism need occur for a defendant to be convicted of violating either material support statute, which criminalize the provision of material support for terrorism or a designated terrorist organization. And unlike both conspiracy and accomplice liability, which we have seen require in most circuits a *mens rea* of purpose, §§2339A and 2339B can be satisfied with a *mens rea* of knowledge. Thus the material support laws provide "a potent alternative to pursuing an attempt charge [on an underlying predicate in §2339A], sparing prosecutors the need to await the point at which a . . . suspect has reached the 'substantial step' threshold required for attempt liability." Chesney, *supra*, at 493. Moreover, both material support statutes criminalize attempts and conspiracies to supply material support.

In these ways, the material support statutes move criminal liability back in time (attempt law on steroids, one might say), while also expanding the net of criminal law to include actors who are far removed from underlying terrorist offenses (accomplice liability on steroids). Section 2339B is particularly effective for these purposes:

[Section 2339B's] ability to reach beyond traditional criminal acts means that the statute authorizes prosecution of two groups of persons not covered by other criminal laws—those who raise money and supplies for terrorist networks through seemingly legitimate business activities, and potential terrorists who have not yet committed acts sufficient to bring them within the scope of more traditional federal inchoate crimes, such as conspiracy or aiding and abetting. The DOJ counterterrorism enforcement manual describes 2339B as "the closest thing American prosecutors have to the crime of being a terrorist."

Andrew Peterson, Addressing Tomorrow's Terrorists, 2 J. Nat'l Security L. & Pol'y 297, 301 (2008) (citing Jeffrey A. Breinholt, Counterterrorism Enforcement: A Lawyer's Guide 264 (U.S. Dep't of Justice Office of Legal Educ. 2004)). There is, however, an important limitation on §2339B: its requirement that the defendant knowingly provide material support to a State Department-designated foreign terrorist organization. Section 2339A has no such restriction, and thus can applied to acts committed by "lone wolves" and domestic terrorist organizations (both of which would be beyond the reach of §2339B given that statute's FTO requirement).

3. LIABILITY UNDER §2339A

United States v. Jayyousi
657 F.3d 1085 (11th Cir. 2011)

DUBINA, Chief Judge:

I.   BACKGROUND

A federal grand jury in the Southern District of Florida indicted Appellants Adham Hassoun, Kifah Jayyousi, and Jose Padilla (referred to individually by name or collectively as "defendants"), along with Mohammed Youssef and Kassem Daher, for offenses relating to their support for Islamist violence overseas.[1] Count 1 charged defendants with conspiring in the United States to murder, kidnap, or maim persons overseas. 18 U.S.C. §956(a)(1).[2] Count 2 charged defendants with conspiring, in violation of 18 U.S.C. §371, to commit the substantive 18 U.S.C. §2339A

---

1. The authorities have not yet arrested Mohammed Youssef and Kassem Daher, and they remain fugitives.

2. Specifically, 18 U.S.C. §956(a)(1) provides:

Whoever, within the jurisdiction of the United States, conspires with one or more other persons, regardless of where such other person or persons are located, to commit at any place outside the United States an act that would constitute the offense of murder, kidnapping, or maiming if committed in the special maritime and territorial jurisdiction of the United States shall, if any of the conspirators commits an act within the jurisdiction

offense of "provid[ing] material support or resources or conceal[ing] or disguis[ing] the nature, [or] source . . . of material support or resources, knowing or intending that they are to be used in preparation for, or in carrying out, a violation of [§956(a)(1), i.e., a conspiracy to murder, kidnap or maim overseas]." 18 U.S.C. §2339A. Count 3 charged defendants with a substantive §2339A material support offense based upon an underlying §956(a)(1) conspiracy. The charged conduct began in October of 1993 and continued until November 1, 2001. Before trial, this court reversed the district court's order dismissing the most serious count, Count 1, for multiplicity. United States v. Hassoun, 476 F.3d 1181 (11th Cir. 2007).

Trial commenced on April 16, 2007, and four months later, the jury returned a special verdict convicting defendants on all counts. The jury expressly found each of the three objects of the Count 1 conspiracy (the murder of persons outside the United States, the kidnapping of persons outside the United States, and the maiming of persons outside the United States). . . . On Count 1, the district court sentenced Padilla to 208 months, Hassoun to 188 months, and Jayyousi to 152 months' imprisonment. On Count 2, the district court sentenced each defendant to the maximum 60 months' imprisonment. On Count 3, the district court sentenced Padilla and Hassoun to the maximum of 180 months' imprisonment and sentenced Jayyousi to the maximum of 120 months' imprisonment. The district court made all sentences run concurrently and imposed a 20-year period of supervised release for each defendant. The defendants appeal, and the government cross-appeals Padilla's sentence. . . .

IV. DISCUSSION . . .

B.   SUFFICIENCY OF THE EVIDENCE

Padilla challenges the sufficiency of the evidence on all three counts, and Jayyousi contends that the government did not present sufficient evidence to convict him on Count 3, the substantive 18 U.S.C. §2339A material support offense based upon an underlying 18 U.S.C. §956(a)(1) conspiracy. In reviewing challenges to the sufficiency of the evidence, we must accept all reasonable inferences that support the verdict and "affirm the conviction if a reasonable trier of fact could conclude that the evidence establishes guilt beyond a reasonable doubt." . . .

The record shows that the government presented evidence that the defendants formed a support cell linked to radical Islamists worldwide and conspired to send money, recruits, and equipment overseas to groups

---

of the United States to effect any object of the conspiracy, be punished as provided in subsection (a)(2).

that the defendants knew used violence in their efforts to establish Islamic states. Agent Kavanaugh, who was in charge of the bulk of the investigation in this case, identified numerous conversations among the defendants discussing Padilla's travels to countries where Muslims were victimized. The government presented Padilla's mujahideen identification form that indicated his intent to attend a jihad training camp. The government's expert testified to the secrecy of the training camps, and the requirement that a recruit, particularly an American Muslim, receive a recommendation from a reliable brother to attend the camp. He also acknowledged that al-Qaeda kept records on the recruits who attended the training camps and that the recruits did not provide their real names on the identification forms. Government witness Goba confirmed the expert's testimony regarding the secrecy of the jihad training camps, the need for someone to recommend each recruit, and the purpose of the camp, which was to train individuals in weapons and war tactics for military jihad.

The record provides sufficient evidence for a reasonable jury to find that Padilla trained with al-Qaeda and shared his conspirators' intent to support jihad violence overseas to establish Islamic states. The government presented evidence of numerous discussions between the conspirators regarding the various conflicts involving Muslims overseas. The evidence showed that Youssef, Hassoun, and Padilla began discussing attendance at al-Qaeda camps before Padilla left for Egypt in September 1998. In various calls, Youssef stated that he was ready to work with the refugees in Kosovo, and that he fought on the front lines in the Kosovar conflict. Hassoun expressed his desire to send another recruit to Kosovo, and Youssef suggested Padilla. Later, Hassoun told Youssef that he would send money with Padilla. Further, Padilla was secretive about his plans to attend the training camp, instructing Hassoun not to tell Youssef any plans over the phone.

The record also demonstrates that the conspirators did not intend for Padilla to remain in Egypt, but instead, they planned for him to prepare to leave Egypt for jihad at the first opportunity, and planned for Padilla to travel to the Chechen jihad after he received his training. While traveling to fight in Chechnya, Youssef told Hassoun that he would soon be with bin Laden and Khattab's company, and when Hassoun asked about Padilla, Youssef stated that Padilla was traveling to the "area of [O]sama [bin Laden]." Another intercept further dispels Padilla's contention regarding the sufficiency of the evidence. In October 2000, Hassoun asked Youssef if he would join "Abu Abdullah, the Puerto Rican" in Afghanistan, and Youssef responded that he had experience fighting on the front lines and did not need to hone his military skills. Based on the above, we conclude that there is sufficient record evidence to support Padilla's convictions on Counts 1 and 2.

Padilla and Jayyousi both challenge the sufficiency of the evidence to convict them on Count 3. In order to convict Padilla and Jayyousi under the substantive count, the government did not have to prove that Padilla and Jayyousi personally committed violent acts; rather, the government had to prove that these individuals knew that they were supporting mujahideen who engaged in murder, maiming, or kidnapping in order to establish Islamic states. The evidence supports the jury's reasonable inference that Padilla and Jayyousi knew the training camps trained recruits in weaponry and war tactics and that they shared a common purpose to support violent jihad to regain the lands that were once under Islamic control [See, e.g., Gov't Ex. 802, *The Islam Report* where Jayyousi wrote, "May Allah help the mujahideen topple these un-Islamic and illegal puppet regimes in our Muslim lands."]. The record indicates Padilla provided himself as material support in the form of a recruit for jihad training; personal information on the mujahideen identification form matched Padilla's personal information on his passport; the government expert identified Padilla's fingerprints on the form; the government expert testified that the use of code words is a signature trait of a terrorism support cell; Jayyousi received a fax that had bin Laden's signature on it; Jayyousi oversaw the purchase of satellite phones, walkie talkies and encrypted radios to send to Chechnya to aid the Muslims in their armed conflict; Jayyousi told Mohamed Shishani that the donations for the radios (to assist in communication during fighting) did not come in time to prevent the killing of mujahideen by friendly fire; and Jayyousi acknowledged in a conversation that all their calls were recorded. We conclude that this evidence, along with other evidence presented by the government, was sufficient for a reasonable jury to conclude that Jayyousi and Padilla were guilty of providing material support or resources, knowing that these would be used in preparation for carrying out a conspiracy to murder, kidnap, or maim overseas. . . .

NOTES AND QUESTIONS

1. This was a set of many different terrorism conspiracies, no? Consider in this regard the defendants' larger purpose, which raises one of the most contentious issues to emerge in the War on Terror: whether crimes of international terrorism are most appropriately treated as federal criminal offenses and adjudicated in civilian court, or as war crimes to be disposed of in the military justice system. Jayyousi's co-defendant, José Padilla, became a household name in 2002 when he was arrested at O'Hare International Airport on suspicion that he had conspired with al Qaeda leaders to plot a radiological ("dirty") bomb attack on U.S. soil. See Linda Greenhouse, Justices Let U.S. Transfer Padilla to Civilian Custody, N.Y. Times, Jan. 5, 2006. Padilla was initially detained on a sealed material witness warrant. Just before that warrant was set to expire, President George W. Bush ordered

Secretary of Defense Donald Rumsfeld to detain Padilla, an American citizen, as an "enemy combatant" pursuant to the 2001 Authorization for Use of Military Force (AUMF). Padilla was subsequently transferred from a federal detention center to a military prison in South Carolina, where he was held without charge for over three years.

Padilla's military detention attracted criticism from civil liberties groups worldwide. It also precipitated a legal battle over the scope of the President's authority under the AUMF to detain as enemy combatants U.S. citizens captured outside of a zone of combat. Just weeks before the Supreme Court was set to consider Padilla's habeas petition, which raised that issue, the Bush administration transferred Padilla back to civilian court and obtained an indictment on the §2339A charges at issue in the appeal that you just read. None of the allegations that led to Padilla's high-profile arrest and military detention—conspiracy with al Qaeda leaders to plant a dirty bomb in the United States—appear in his material support indictment and subsequent trial. This is because the government in the end reportedly "was unwilling to allow testimony from two senior members of Al Qaeda [Khalid Sheik Mohammed and Abu Zubaydah] who had been subjected to harsh questioning" and whose testimony was needed to prove the dirty bomb case. Douglas Jehl and Eric Lichtblau, Shift on Suspect is Linked to Role of Qaeda Figures, N.Y. Times, Nov. 24, 2005.

2. The ultimate charges against Padilla underscore the versatility of §2339A. In Padilla's case, the government was able to obtain a conviction without discussing the dirty bomb plot at all, focusing instead on the much broader, if vaguer, constellation of messages, phone calls, and travel related to an entirely different conspiracy. Recall that under §2339A, the government did not need to prove that Padilla knew about or participated in a specific plot, nor that he or his co-conspirator personally committed violent acts. Rather, "the government [only] had to prove that these individuals knew that they were supporting mujahideen who engaged in murder, maiming, or kidnaping in order to establish Islamic states." Jayyousi, 657 F.3d at 1105. Was the government thinking: Why go through the perilous military justice system when material support convictions are readily obtainable? See generally, Human Rights First Fact Sheet May 2017 ("Federal civilian criminal courts have convicted more than 620 individuals on terrorism-related charges since 9/11. Military commissions have convicted only eight.").

3. The leading authority on material support prosecutions observes:

A close review of how §2339A has been charged in recent cases suggests that the statute may impose a form of inchoate criminal liability that otherwise might exceed the reach of federal law. This makes §2339A a particularly important tool for prosecutors tasked with intervening at the earliest possible opportunity in cases potentially involving terrorism. The expansive reach of §2339A also raises concerns, however, as to the appropriate balance between the benefits of prevention and offsetting considerations such as lost opportunities to gather intelligence and potential increases in the rate of false-positive prosecutions.

Section 2339A's broad scope follows from the interaction of several features of the statute. First, the statute applies without respect to whether the predicate offense actually occurs; so long as the defendant provided support with the intent (or knowledge) that the support would be used for a predicate offense, liability attaches immediately. In this abstract respect, §2339A liability is akin to conspiracy liability, which also attaches independent of whether the predicate offense is even attempted, let alone completed. But §2339A is broader than conspiracy liability in several respects. Most obviously, prosecutors need not prove an agreement with anyone, as the actus reus for §2339A consists not in forming an agreement but, rather, in engaging in the provision of support. In addition, whereas the object of a conspiracy must be the actual commission of an unlawful act, the "object" of support given in violation of §2339A may either be the actual commission of a predicate offense or conduct merely constituting "preparation for" commission of such an offense. That subtle distinction, which is expressed in the text of §2339A, has the practical effect of expanding the range of conduct that would count as a predicate offense, reaching beyond the offenses themselves to encompass anticipatory activity intended to culminate in offense conduct. Thus, one might describe §2339A as prohibiting the provision of support with intent to facilitate either a violation of a predicate statute or activity preliminary to such a violation.

Complicating matters, the list of predicate offenses under §2339A includes numerous conspiracy-capable provisions. Thus, it is a crime not only to provide support with knowledge or the intent that it will facilitate the commission of certain violent acts, but also to do so knowing or intending that the support will facilitate the formation of unlawful agreements. In this aspect, §2339A might be characterized in terms of aiding-and-abetting a conspiracy.

A final factor that contributes to the preventive capacity of §2339A arises from the definition of "material support." As noted previously, that definition is surpassingly broad. Most notable for present purposes is the fact that "material support" is defined to include the provision of one's own self as "personnel." Thus, one might violate §2339A by providing one's self as personnel to others with the goal of assisting in the commission of, or simply preparation for the commission of, a predicate offense (including an offense in the nature of a conspiracy). This proposition has important implications for the capacity of the government to intervene in cases involving potential terrorists.

Chesney, *supra*, at 479-80.

Courts have not seemed troubled by arguments that §2339A allows prosecutions for multi-level inchoate offenses, i.e., conspiracies to provide material support to conspiracies. See United States v. Khan, 461 F.3d 477,

493 (4th Cir. 2006) (noting that the statute expressly allows such a charge and that "[n]othing about this statutory framework is unconstitutional, improper, or even unusual"); see also United States v. Awan, 459 F. Supp. 2d 167, 184 (E.D.N.Y. 2006) ("The defendant is not being charged with being a member of the conspiracy to murder, kidnap or maim. He is simply alleged to have completed the offense of conspiring to and actually providing material support to carry out such a conspiracy."). Should they be? Indeed, the Eleventh Circuit has pointed out that, because §2339A covers material support given "in preparation for" the object offense, one could easily imagine defendants charged with providing material support for a §956 conspiracy (to commit violent acts abroad) even where the conspiracy had not yet, or never, occurred. See United States v. Hassoun, 476 F.3d 1181, 1188 (11th Cir. 2007).

4.   Liability Under §2339B

Section 2339B, while aimed at some of the same conduct as §2339A, has a quite different structure. As the Fourth Circuit explained in a case in which the government charged the defendant with both offenses:

> The elements of the separate crimes charged under §2339A and §2339B do not overlap. Section 2339B requires proof that [defendant] provided material support to an organization designated as a foreign terrorist organization. By contrast, §2339A requires proof that [defendant] provided material support or resources that he knew would "be used in preparation for, or in carrying out, a violation of [18 U.S.C. §956]," which prohibits conspiracies to injure persons or damage property outside the United States.

United States v. Chandia, 514 F.3d 365, 372 (4th Cir. 2008). Note that, for the first time in this chapter, we are seeing a complicity offense based on a connection to a pre-designated group, not to a particular crime. Put differently, the inquiry into a group's nature and purposes—and the provision of an element of the offense—has been effectively delegated to the executive branch, a matter we will consider in Chapter 12. In addition, §2339B broadly criminalizes providing any material support to such an organization, without the heightened scienter requirement of §2339A ("knowing or intending that they be used in preparation for, or in carrying out" specific crimes). Does the combination of such a broad *actus reas* and a minimal scienter requirement impinge on the First Amendment or violate the Due Process Clause? In an important case decided in 2010, the Supreme Court said "no" to both questions. See Holder v. Humanitarian Law Project, 560 U.S. 1 (2010), discussed in the case excerpted below and in the Notes following.

United States v. Mehanna
735 F.3d 32 (1st Cir. 2013)

SELYA, Circuit Judge.

Terrorism is the modern-day equivalent of the bubonic plague: it is an existential threat. Predictably, then, the government's efforts to combat terrorism through the enforcement of the criminal laws will be fierce. Sometimes, those efforts require a court to patrol the fine line between vital national security concerns and forbidden encroachments on constitutionally protected freedoms of speech and association. This is such a case.

I. OVERVIEW . . .

In its final form, the indictment charged the defendant with four terrorism-related counts and three counts premised on allegedly false statements. . . .

Counts 1 through 3 (the conspiracy and material support charges) were based on two separate clusters of activities. The first cluster centered on the defendant's travel to Yemen.[1] We briefly describe that trip.

In 2004, the defendant, an American citizen, was 21 years old and living with his parents in Sudbury, Massachusetts. On February 1, he flew from Boston to the United Arab Emirates with his associates, Kareem Abuzahra and Ahmad Abousamra.[2] Abuzahra returned to the United States soon thereafter but the defendant and Abousamra continued on to Yemen in search of a terrorist training camp. They remained there for a week but were unable to locate a camp. The defendant then returned home, while Abousamra eventually reached Iraq.

The second cluster of activities was translation-centric. In 2005, the defendant began to translate Arab-language materials into English and post his translations on a website—at-Tibyan—that comprised an online community for those sympathetic to al-Qa'ida and Salafi-Jihadi perspectives. Website members shared opinions, videos, texts, and kindred materials in online forums. At least some offerings that the defendant translated constituted al-Qa'ida-generated media and materials supportive of al-Qa'ida and/or jihad.[3]

---

1. This cluster of activities also comprises the foundation for count 4.

2. Abousamra was charged as a defendant in this case but absconded in December of 2006. For aught that appears, he remains a fugitive.

3. While "jihad" is a linguistically protean term that may encompass both violent and nonviolent acts, the record makes clear that the defendant used the term to refer to violent jihad—and that is the meaning that we ascribe to it throughout this opinion.

The false statement counts (counts 5 through 7) related to statements that the defendant made during the course of an investigation by the Federal Bureau of Investigation (FBI) into his activities and those of his confederates. This investigation began in or around 2006. The statements specified in the indictment concerned the whereabouts and activities of one Daniel Maldonado, as well as the purpose and ultimate destination of the defendant's trip to Yemen.

After considerable pretrial skirmishing, not material here, trial commenced. It lasted some 37 days. The district court refused to grant judgment of acquittal on any of the seven counts. The jury convicted the defendant on all of them, and the district court imposed a 210-month term of immurement.

II.   THE TERRORISM-RELATED COUNTS

The centerpiece of the defendant's challenge to his convictions on the four terrorism-related counts is his binary claim that these convictions are neither supported by the evidence nor constitutionally permissible.

A.   SUFFICIENCY OF THE EVIDENCE

We review de novo challenges to the sufficiency of the evidence. This review eschews credibility judgments and requires us to take the facts and all reasonable inferences therefrom in the light most favorable to the jury's verdict. . . .

To put the defendant's sufficiency challenge into a workable perspective, it is helpful to trace the anatomy of the four terrorism charges. Count 1 charges the defendant with conspiring to violate 18 U.S.C. §2339B, which proscribes "knowingly provid[ing] material support or resources to a foreign terrorist organization." Id. §2339B(a)(1). To satisfy the intent requirement of section 2339B, a defendant must have "knowledge about the organization's connection to terrorism." Holder v. Humanitarian Law Project (HLP), 561 U.S. 1, 16-17 (2010). A specific intent to advance the organization's terrorist activities is not essential. . . .

In this case, the defendant does not dispute that al-Qa'ida was and is a foreign terrorist organization (FTO). Nor could he credibly do so. See Redesignation of Foreign Terrorist Organizations, 68 Fed. Reg. 56,860, 56,862 (Oct. 2, 2003); Redesignation of Foreign Terrorist Organization, 66 Fed. Reg. 51,088, 51,089 (Oct. 5, 2001). By like token, the record leaves no doubt that the defendant was aware of al-Qa'ida's status.

Count 2 charges the defendant with conspiring to violate 18 U.S.C. §2339A, which proscribes "provid[ing] material support or resources . . . , knowing or intending that they are to be used in preparation for, or in carrying out," certain other criminal activities. Id. §2339A(a). The intent requirement under section 2339A differs somewhat from the intent requirement under section 2339B: to be guilty under section 2339A, the defendant must have "provide[d] support or resources *with the knowledge or intent* that such resources be used to commit specific violent crimes." United States v. Stewart, 590 F.3d 93, 113 (2d Cir. 2009) (emphasis in original). Thus, "the mental state in section 2339A extends both to the support itself, and to the underlying purposes for which the support is given." Id. at 113 n.18. As adapted to the circumstances of this case, the government had to prove that the defendant had the specific intent to provide material support, knowing or intending that it would be used in a conspiracy to kill persons abroad. See 18 U.S.C. §§956, 2332.

Count 3 is closely related to count 2. It charges the defendant with violating, or attempting to violate, 18 U.S.C. §2339A. The district court instructed the jury that it could find the defendant guilty on count 3 under theories of direct liability, attempt, aiding and abetting, or agency. Because the parties' arguments on appeal target the attempt theory, we focus our attention there.

Material support is defined identically for purposes of sections 2339A and 2339B. Such support may take various forms, including (as arguably pertinent here) the provision of "service[s]" or "personnel." 18 U.S.C. §§2339A(b)(1), 2339B(g)(4). With respect to the Yemen trip, the government accused the defendant of conspiring to provide himself as an al-Qa'ida recruit (count 1); knowing or intending the use of this material support in a conspiracy to kill persons abroad (count 2); and attempting to provide this support, knowing or intending that it would be used in such a conspiracy (count 3).

Count 4 bears a family resemblance to counts 1 through 3, but it has a slightly different DNA. It charges the defendant with violating 18 U.S.C. §956, which proscribes conspiring in the United States "to commit at any place outside the United States an act that would constitute the offense of murder" if that act had been committed within the United States. Id. §956(a)(1). For purposes of this statute, it does not matter whether the defendant's coconspirators are located within the United States or abroad. See id.

We turn next to the government's proof. In gauging the sufficiency of that proof, we start with the Yemen trip and the cluster of activities surrounding it. . . .

The government's evidence of the defendant's specific intent with respect to his Yemen trip included his own actions, discussions with others, coconspirator statements, and materials that the defendant either kept on his computer or shared on the Internet. The defendant contends that this evidence, in the aggregate, showed nothing more than his participation in activities protected by the First Amendment (e.g., discussing politics and religion, consuming media related to those topics, and associating with certain individuals and groups) and, thus, could not support a finding of guilt. See Scales v. United States, 367 U.S. 203, 229-30, 81 S. Ct. 1469, 6 L. Ed. 2d 782 (1961); United States v. Spock, 416 F.2d 165, 169-74 (1st Cir. 1969). But the defendant is looking at the evidence through rose-colored glasses. We think it virtually unarguable that rational jurors could find that the defendant and his associates went abroad to enlist in a terrorist training camp.

On this point, the defendant's own statements are highly probative. His coconspirators testified that the defendant persistently stated his belief that engaging in jihad was "a duty upon a Muslim if he's capable of performing it," and that this duty included committing violence. The evidence further showed that, following United States intervention in Iraq, the defendant concluded "that America was at war with Islam," and saw American "soldiers as being valid targets."

Acting upon these views, the defendant and his associates—as early as 2001—discussed seeking out a terrorist training camp. Following these discussions, the defendant expressed interest in receiving military-type training in order to participate in jihad. The defendant made clear that he wished to engage in jihad if he "ever had the chance" and that he and his associates "would make a way to go." Together, they "discussed the different ways people could get into Iraq, the different training camps."

In these conversations, the defendant voiced his desire to fight against the United States military forces in Iraq. He and his associates went "in depth on details" regarding the logistics of reaching such a terrorist training camp.

Coconspirator testimony shined a bright light on the defendant's intent. This testimony made pellucid that the defendant and his comrades traveled to Yemen "for the purpose of finding a terrorist training camp" and "[e]ventually . . . get[ting] into Iraq." The defendant's particular interest in Iraq was because it was "an area that was being attacked." He took the position that "there was an obligation for Muslims to stand up and fight against invasion of Iraq and the U.S. forces in Iraq."

The defendant attempts to characterize these remarks as mere political speech. The jury, however, was entitled to draw a different inference: that the defendant's comments were evidence of the formation and implementation of a scheme to go abroad, obtain training, join with al-Qa'ida, and wage war against American soldiers fighting in Iraq.

The timing of the trip and the furtiveness with which the defendant acted provide circumstantial support for this conclusion. The record contains evidence that the defendant abruptly suspended his studies in Massachusetts during the school year and kept his plans hidden from his parents. Prior to his departure, he gave his brother a bag of personal belongings and asked his brother to dispose of them. These belongings included "something about how to make a bomb."

We note that the defendant and his associates purchased round-trip airline tickets. In the travelers' own words, however, the return portions were for use "[i]f things didn't work out," as well as to avoid raising the sort of suspicion often associated with one-way ticketing. And Abuzahra testified at trial that, notwithstanding the return ticket, he did not expect to return to the United States because "[t]he purpose of . . . going was to basically fight in a war." . . .

There was more. The evidence showed that the defendant and his associates had a plan of action for their arrival in Yemen. Abousamra had obtained the name of a contact there "who was going to get them to a military training camp." When the men traveled to Yemen, they carried a piece of paper that contained the contact's name.

To be sure, the Yemen trip did not bear fruit. Once there, the defendant learned to his evident dismay that training camps no longer existed in the area and "that it was nearly impossible for anybody to get any training" there. The contact in Yemen fizzled, telling the defendant and Abousamra that "all that stuff is gone ever since the planes hit the twin towers." It is consistent with the government's theory of the case, however, that the defendant, when confronted with this news, expressed disappointment that he had "left [his] life behind" based on faulty information.

The government's case is strengthened by evidence that the defendant and his associates engaged in a coverup that continued long after the defendant's return from Yemen. The record reflects that the defendant and his associates repeatedly discussed how to align their stories and mislead federal investigators (in point of fact, they formulated cover stories for their Yemen trip even before the trip began). To facilitate the coverup, the defendant and his cohorts attempted to obscure their communications by using code words such as "peanut butter," "peanut butter and jelly," or "PB&J" for jihad and "culinary school" for terrorist training. Relatedly, the defendant encouraged an associate to install an "encryptor" on his computer in order to make it "much harder for [the FBI] to" monitor their online communications.

It is settled beyond hope of peradventure that evidence of participation in a coverup can be probative of elements of the underlying crime such as knowledge and intent. This is a commonsense proposition, and "criminal juries are not expected to ignore what is perfectly obvious."

There is another dimension to this aspect of the government's case. Although the theory of guilt that we have been discussing centered on the cluster of activities surrounding the Yemen trip, it was bolstered by other evidence.

To begin, the defendant's desire to engage in jihad did not end with the failed Yemen trip. Early in 2006, the defendant told an associate, Ali

Aboubakr, about how he had traveled to Yemen to engage in jihad. The defendant invited Aboubakr to join him if he elected to travel abroad for jihad again. He described "a camp" that they could attend in Yemen, where they would "live with like, 300 other brothers" who "all walk around . . . with camo jackets and AK-47s." The defendant urged Aboubakr, who was then a college student, not to tell his father about his plan.

The defendant's communication with his "best friend," Daniel Maldonado, further evinced his determination to engage in jihad. [At the time of trial, Maldonado was serving a ten-year sentence pursuant to his guilty plea for receiving military-type training from an FTO. See 18 U.S.C. §2339D(a)]. In December of 2006, Maldonado telephoned the defendant from Somalia. During this call, the two discussed the logistics needed for the defendant to join Maldonado in Somalia, including transportation and travel documents. Maldonado said that he was "in a culinary school" and "mak[ing] peanut butter and jelly." Maldonado testified that this was code language, familiar to the defendant, denoting that Maldonado was in a terrorist training camp and engaged in jihad.

Percipient witnesses testified that the defendant watched jihadi videos with his associates for the purpose of "gain[ing] inspiration from the[m]" and "becom[ing] like a mujahid."[5] These videos depicted events such as Marines being killed by explosives, suicide bombings, and combat scenes glorifying the mujahideen. The defendant was "jubilant" while watching them.

In a similar vein, the record is shot through with evidence of the defendant's rabid support for al-Qa'ida, his "love" for Osama bin Laden, his admiration of the September 11 hijackers, and his conviction that the September 11 attacks were justified and a "happy" occasion.

The defendant complains that some of this evidence bears no direct connection to his Yemen trip. This plaint is true as far as it goes—but it does not take the defendant very far. It overlooks the abecedarian proposition that evidence of a defendant's general mindset may be relevant to the issue of his intent. The record here is replete with such evidence. . . .

B.   THE DEFENDANT'S REJOINDERS

Despite the obvious logic of the government's position and the wealth of evidence that supports it, the defendant labors to undermine the four terrorism-related convictions. His efforts take two different

---

5. "Mujahideen" (singular: "mujahid") is defined as "Muslim guerrilla warriors engaged in a jihad." The American Heritage Dictionary of the English Language 1153 (4th ed. 2000). At trial, Aboubakr described "mujahid" as meaning "somebody who partakes in fighting."

directions—one a frontal assault and the other an end run. We address each in turn.

1. *Scholarly Pursuits.* The defendant argues that the only reasonable interpretation of his Yemen trip and the activities surrounding it is an innocent one: he sojourned to Yemen solely for the purpose of studying there. He describes himself as a devoted scholar of Islam and asserts that he visited Yemen, specifically, because the purest form of Arabic is spoken there. In support, he reminds us that he toured a school while in the country.

Relatedly, the defendant suggests that, regardless of his associates' purpose and intent, he was far more moderate than they. This moderation allegedly included adherence to certain beliefs antithetic to al-Qa'ida canon. Among these beliefs was the doctrine of "aman," which the defendant describes as "a covenant to obey the law within a country that permits practice of the faith." As he would have it, his adherence to aman would prohibit him from targeting American troops.

We readily agree that the record contains some evidence supporting the defendant's alternative narrative. Yet, that evidence does not eclipse the plethora of proof pointing in the opposite direction. When all was said and done, the jury heard and rejected the defendant's innocent explanation of the events that occurred. It was plainly entitled to do so.

To gain a conviction, the government need not "eliminat[e] every possible theory consistent with the defendant's innocence." It is the jury's role—not that of the Court of Appeals—to choose between conflicting hypotheses, especially when such choices depend on the drawing of inferences and elusive concepts such as motive and intent.

2. *The Alternative Theory of Guilt.* The defendant's second rejoinder represents an attempt to change the trajectory of the debate. He points out that the indictment identifies his translations as culpable activity; that the government introduced copious evidence in support of a theory of guilt based on the translations; that it argued this theory to the jury; and that the jury returned a general verdict. Building on this platform, he argues that even if the evidence of the Yemen trip is sufficient to ground his terrorism-related convictions, those convictions cannot stand because they may have been predicated on protected First Amendment speech.

It is pointless to speak in the abstract of a verdict predicated on protected conduct. The Court of Appeals is not a sorting hat, divining which criminal defendants' stories fall into constitutionally protected and unprotected stacks. Cf. J.K. Rowling, Harry Potter and the Sorcerer's Stone 113-22 (1997). Instead, an appellate court's role is to discern what, if any, errors marred the trial below. This inquiry requires us to focus on the relevant actors in the trial and not to engage in an untethered academic analysis of the verdict itself. . . .

In sum, the district court's instructions captured the essence of the controlling decision in [*Humanitarian Law Project*], where the Court determined that otherwise-protected speech rises to the level of criminal material support only if it is "in coordination with foreign groups that the speaker knows to be terrorist organizations." If speech fits within this taxonomy, it is not protected. This means that "advocacy performed in coordination with, or at the direction of," an FTO is not shielded by the First Amendment. The district court's instructions tracked the contours of this legal framework. The court appropriately treated the question of whether enough coordination existed to criminalize the defendant's translations as factbound and left that question to the jury. We discern no error. . . .

That brings down the final curtain. We have found the defendant's claims of legal error with respect to his translation activities wanting, and we have no occasion to examine the factual sufficiency of those activities as a basis for his terrorism-related convictions. Even if the government's translation-as-material-support theory were factually insufficient, we would not reverse: the defendant's convictions on the affected counts are independently supported by the mass of evidence surrounding the Yemen trip and [] we need go no further.

NOTES AND QUESTIONS

1. Both the high level of specific intent required by §2339A (which we examined above) and its violence-oriented act requirement have allowed courts to brush aside constitutional challenges to its breadth.

The statutory text of §2339A(a), the source of the substantive crime in the present case, provides in other words greater precision about the content and scope of the activity prohibited by §2339B so that anyone of "ordinary intelligence" would understand [defendant's] alleged activities to be prohibited. [Farrell v. Burke, 449 F.3d 470, 486 (2d Cir. 2006).] In contrast to §2339B, which broadly criminalizes the provision of any "material support" to any group known to be a foreign terrorist organization, §2339A(a) raises the scienter requirement and criminalizes only provision of material support "*knowing or intending that they be used in preparation for, or in carrying out*" certain specific crimes (emphasis added). As a result, "it is plain . . . what conduct the statute proscribes."

United States v. Awan, 459 F. Supp. 2d 167, 179 (E.D.N.Y. 2006), affirmed 384 F. App'x. 9 (2d Cir. 2010); see also United States v. Amawi, 545 F. Supp. 2d 681, 684 (N.D. Ohio 2008).

Defendants charged under §2339B, however, have mustered more substantial (though largely unsuccessful) constitutional arguments. Mehanna raised multiple First Amendment defenses. Although the First Circuit ultimately resolved the case on other grounds, civil liberties groups had hoped that the Supreme Court would grant certiorari in *Mehanna* to clarify the parameters of *Humanitarian Law Project*'s holding that the First Amendment permits prosecution under §2339B of speech that is made "in coordination" with foreign terrorist organization, see 561 U.S. at 24-25. The Court did not grant review, however, so the meaning of coordination will be fleshed out, we may assume, in the lower courts.

2. *Humanitarian Law Project* was brought by American nonprofits that wanted to provide support for the humanitarian and political activities of two State Department-designated FTOs. The plaintiffs sought to train members of the Partiya Karkeran Kurdistan (PKK) and the Liberation Tigers of Tamil Eelam (LTTE), both designated terrorist organizations, to use humanitarian and international law to peacefully resolve disputes and to petition for humanitarian relief before the United Nations. Id. at 10. Alleging that they could not provide the training for fear of prosecution under §2339B, the plaintiffs brought this pre-enforcement challenge. Chief Justice John Roberts wrote the 6-3 opinion for the Court.

The Court first addressed the plaintiffs' argument that various provisions of §2339B are void for vagueness under the Fifth Amendment's Due Process Clause. *Humanitarian Law Project* presented the Court with numerous hypotheticals designed to show the porousness of the terms "training," "expert advice or assistance," "service," and "personnel." None of the Justices was persuaded, with the majority stating that §2339B's definitions rendered each of the challenged statutory terms "clear in their application to plaintiffs' proposed conduct." Id. at 21. Next, the Court considered whether enforcement of §2339B would violate the plaintiffs' First Amendment right to freedom of expression. The plaintiffs argued that they faced prosecution for engaging in core political speech, a claim the majority dismissed as "unfounded," explaining:

> [U]nder the material-support statute, plaintiffs may say anything they wish on any topic. . . . Rather, Congress has prohibited "material support," which most often does not take the form of speech. And when it does, the statute is carefully drawn to cover only a narrow category of speech. . . .

Id. at 26. Specifically, the Court held that in prohibiting speech "to, under the direction of, or in coordination with foreign groups that the speakers knows to be terrorist organizations," Congress had exercised its prerogative to protect national security within the limits of the First Amendment. Id. Finally, the Court rejected the plaintiffs' that enforcement of §2339B would unconstitutionally punish them for associating with the PKK and LTTE. The Court responded that the statute punishes the provision of material support to designated foreign terrorist organizations, not mere membership in one of the designated groups or independent advocacy of a group's political goals. Id. at 39; see id at 31-32 ("Independent advocacy that might be viewed as promoting [a] group's legitimacy is not covered.") The statute, of course, says nothing about "independent advocacy" one way or the other. As it often does, the Court arguably read in a limitation to avoid possible First Amendment entanglement.

Justice Breyer was joined by Justices Ginsburg and Sotomayor in dissent. "Here," he wrote, "the plaintiffs seek to advocate peaceful, *lawful* action to secure *political* ends; and they seek to teach others how to do the same." Id. at 44 (Breyer, J., dissenting) (emphasis in original). Justice Breyer strongly disagreed that the government had met its burden of showing that applying the statute to plaintiffs' proposed activities would serve a compelling interest in combatting terrorism. The dissent went further, however, urging that the Court "interpret the statute as normally placing [coordinated advocacy] outside its scope." Id. at 41. Rejecting the majority's coordination test, Justice Breyer wrote: "I not aware of any form of words that might be used to describe "coordination" that would not, at a minimum, seriously chill not only the kind of activities the plaintiffs raise before us, but also the "independent advocacy" the Government purports to permit." Id. at 51-52. Instead, he advised:

> I would read the statute as criminalizing First Amendment-protected pure speech and association only when the defendant knows or intends that those activities will assist the organization's unlawful terrorist actions. Under this reading, the Government would have to show, at a minimum, that such defendants provided support that they knew was significantly likely to help the organization pursue its unlawful terrorist aims. . . . [K]nowledge or intent that this assistance (aimed at lawful activities) could or would help further terrorism simply by helping to legitimate the organization is not sufficient.
>
> This reading of the statute protects those who engage in pure speech and association ordinarily protected by the First Amendment. But it does not protect that activity where a defendant purposefully intends it to help terrorism or where a defendant knows (or willfully blinds himself to the fact) that the activity is significantly likely to assist terrorism. Where the activity fits into these categories of purposefully or knowingly supporting terrorist ends, the act of providing material support to a known terrorist organization bears a close enough relation to terrorist acts that, in my view, it likely can be prohibited notwithstanding any First Amendment interest. Cf. *Brandenburg*, 395 U.S. 444. At the same time, this reading does not require the Government to undertake the difficult task of proving which, as between peaceful and non-peaceful purposes, a defendant specifically preferred; knowledge is enough.

Id. at 56-57.

The majority and the dissent agree that no heightened or special *mens rea* is required for most types of material support of terrorism. The heightened *mens rea* Justice Breyer proposes (that the defendant know or intend his activities to assist terrorism) would apply only in a prosecution for "pure speech and association." Id. What is the statutory basis for a varying *mens rea* standard in a single statute depending on the particular facts alleged?

3. What constitutes an *attempt* to violate §2339B? United States v. Farhane, 634 F.3d 127 (2d Cir. 2011), upheld the material support conviction of an American doctor who swore allegiance to al Qaeda in the presence of a "recruiter" who turned out to be an FBI undercover agent. The court explained that an attempt to "provide" something requires less substantial progress toward the commission of the underlying crime than, for instance, a criminal attempt to "possess" something:

> While the parameters of the substantial step requirement are simply stated, they do not always provide bright lines for application. This is not surprising; the identification of a substantial step, like the identification of attempt itself, is necessarily a matter "of degree," United States v. Coplon, 185 F.2d 629, 633 (2d Cir. 1950) (L. Hand, J.), that can vary depending on "the particular facts of each case" viewed in light of the crime charged, United States v. Ivic, [700 F.2d 51, 66 (2d Cir. 1983)]. An act that may constitute a substantial step towards the commission of one crime may not constitute such a step with respect to a different crime. See generally United States v. Ivic, 700 F.2d at 66 (observing that substantial step requirement serves to ensure that person is convicted for attempt only when actions manifest "firm disposition" to commit charged crime). Thus, substantial-step analysis necessarily begins with a proper understanding of the crime being attempted.
>
> For example, in United States v. Delvecchio, 816 F.2d 859 (2d Cir. 1987), a case frequently cited as illustrative of actions insufficient to demonstrate attempt, the substantive crime at issue was possession of a large quantity of heroin. We held that a substantial step to commit that crime was not established by proof that defendants had met with suppliers, agreed on terms, and provided their beeper numbers. Such evidence, at most, established a "verbal agreement," which, "without more, is insufficient as a matter of law to support an attempt[ed possession] conviction." Id. at 862. In so concluding, we noted that what was missing was any act to effect possession, such as acquisition, or attempted acquisition, of the purchase money, or travel to the agreed-on purchase site. See id.
>
> The crime here at issue, however, is of a quite different sort. [The defendant] Sabir was charged with attempting to provide material support for terrorism. Whereas an attempt to possess focuses on a defendant's efforts to acquire, an attempt to provide focuses on his efforts to supply, a distinction that necessarily informs an assessment of what conduct will manifest a substantial step towards the charged objective. Thus, while an agreement to purchase drugs from a supplier is not a substantial step sufficient to convict for attempted possession, such an agreement to acquire might constitute a substantial step when the crime at issue is attempted distribution, see United

States v. Rosa, 11 F.3d 315, 340 (2d Cir. 1993) (holding evidence insufficient to prove attempted distribution where defendant "did not produce any heroin for the proposed sale . . . , and there was no evidence that [he] ever entered into an agreement with a supplier or made inquiry of a supplier to obtain heroin for the proposed sale").

Further important to a substantial-step assessment is an understanding of the underlying conduct proscribed by the crime being attempted. The conduct here at issue, material support to a foreign terrorist organization, is different from drug trafficking and any number of activities (e.g., murder, robbery, fraud) that are criminally proscribed because they are inherently harmful. The material support statute criminalizes a range of conduct that may not be harmful in itself but that may assist, even indirectly, organizations committed to pursuing acts of devastating harm. Thus, as the Supreme Court recently observed, the very focus of the material support statute is "preventative" in that it "criminalizes not terrorist attacks themselves, but aid that makes the attacks more likely to occur." Holder v. Humanitarian Law Project, 130 S. Ct. at 2728. Accordingly, while a substantial step to commit a robbery must be conduct planned clearly to culminate in that particular harm, a substantial step towards the provision of material support need not be planned to culminate in actual terrorist harm, but only in support—even benign support—for an organization committed to such harm. See generally id. at 2724 (discussing Congress's finding that designated foreign terrorist organizations "'are so tainted by their criminal conduct that any contribution to such an organization facilitates that conduct'" (quoting AEDPA §301(a)(7), 110 Stat. at 1247) (emphasis in *Humanitarian Law Project*).) . . .

The indictment charged Sabir with attempting to supply al Qaeda with material support in three of the forms proscribed in 18 U.S.C. §2339A(b)(1): "personnel, training, and expert advice and assistance." We conclude that the evidence was sufficient to support Sabir's conviction for attempting to provide material support in the form of personnel—specifically, himself—to work for al Qaeda as a doctor on-call to treat wounded jihadists in Saudi Arabia. By coming to meet with a purported al Qaeda member on May 20, 1995; by swearing an oath of allegiance to al Qaeda; by promising to be on call in Saudi Arabia to treat wounded al Qaeda members; and by providing private and work contact numbers for al Qaeda members to reach him in Saudi Arabia whenever they needed treatment, Sabir engaged in conduct planned to culminate in his supplying al Qaeda with personnel, thereby satisfying the substantial step requirement.

634 F.3d at 147-50.

To what extent have the "material support" provisions, when coupled with notions of "attempt," "conspiracy," and perhaps "conscious avoidance," expanded the possibility of criminal liability in this area? Does that trouble you? Why?

9 | Drugs and Punishment

One theme of the last chapter was how ostensibly transsubstansive principles of complicity liability have been bent or explicitly altered when applied in particular substantive enforcement areas (e.g., terrorism). In this chapter, we see the elaborate statutory edifice that has been constructed in one substantive area: the "war on drugs," declared by President Richard Nixon in 1969 and persistently relaunched by subsequent Administrations. See William Weir, In the Shadow of the Dope Fiend: America's War on Drugs 140-42 (1995); Michael M. O'Hear, Federalism and Drug Control, 57 Vand. L. Rev. 783, 797 (2004). The most visible parts of that federal "war" have been the vigorous prosecutions of drug crimes, with long sentences of imprisonment for those who are convicted. We examine the structure and substance of federal drug law in Section A. In Section B, we consider the severe penalties attached, focusing on the consequences of Congress's decision to require mandatory minimum sentences for those convicted of trafficking in more than a specified quantity of each drug, sentencing enhancements (at the discretion of the prosecutor) for defendants with prior drug felony convictions, and mandatory "add-on" sentences for drug crimes involving a weapon.

The special attention that Congress has given to sentencing of narcotics offenders explains both why this chapter is the first in which we have made more than a cursory reference to sentencing and why you will be exploring aspects of drug sentencing even before the general discussion of sentencing in Chapter 10. Here, more than in any other area, the two dimensions of criminal prohibitions—conduct proscriptions, on the one hand, and penalties, on the other—are inextricably related, with legislatively mandated sentences playing as much a role in determining who is serving time in federal prison as do the broad substantive prohibitions of Title 21 of the United States Code. As we discuss the legislative scheme, we will also give you a sense of whom these laws are used against.

Before delving into the unusual way that Congress has defined drug crimes and the unusual penalty structure that it has provided, let us consider how drug crimes relate to the rest of federal criminal law. Figure A (below) is a good place to begin. As you can see, drug prosecutions are a large part of the criminal caseload. Convictions for drug offenses currently account for over 30 percent of all convictions in federal court.

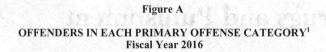

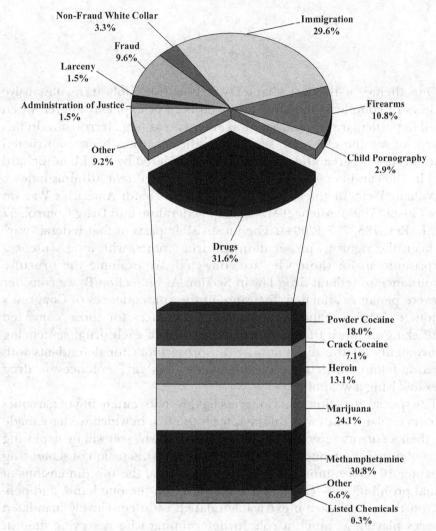

Figure A

OFFENDERS IN EACH PRIMARY OFFENSE CATEGORY[1]
Fiscal Year 2016

[1] The Drugs category includes the following offense types: trafficking, use of a communication facility, and simple possession. The Non-Fraud White Collar category includes the following offense types: embezzlement, forgery/counterfeiting, bribery, money laundering, and tax. Descriptions of variables used in this figure are provided in Appendix A.

SOURCE: U.S. Sentencing Commission, 2016 Datafile, USSCFY16.

U.S. Sent'g Comm'n, 2016 Sourcebook of Federal Sentencing Statistics:
Offenders in Each Primary Category, fig. A (2016). The Commission's 2016
Sourcebook of Federal Sentencing Statistics is the source for most of the
sentencing statistics we cite in this chapter.

The percentage of federal prosecutions involving drugs has actually decreased somewhat over the last decade and a half. Before September 11, 2001, drug cases comprised an even larger portion of the criminal docket—hovering around 40 percent. One might surmise that the reason for the decrease in the last decade is the diversion of resources (in the FBI, as well as in prosecutors' offices) from narcotics investigations to anti-terrorism efforts. However, the drug prosecution docket has shrunk by only a few thousand defendants in the last decade and a half; in 2000 there were 24,000 drug prosecutions and just over 21,000 in 2016. Instead, the percentage of drug cases has decreased because (1) the federal criminal docket as a whole has grown (from 56,000 convicted offenders in 2000 to 67,000 in 2016) and (2) immigration prosecutions have dramatically increased (from about 20 percent of all convictions in 2000 to nearly 30 percent in 2016).

As the proportion of drug prosecutions in the criminal docket has decreased, other aspects of the drug caseload have also changed. Whereas in 2000 40 percent of drug prosecutions involved cocaine, about equally divided between crack cocaine and powder cocaine, in 2016 the number (and percentage) of crack cocaine convictions had decreased by two thirds. Heroin cases constituted less than 8 percent of the drug docket in 2000 and now are 13 percent of the docket. Methamphetamine prosecutions have doubled from 15 percent in 2000 to 31 percent in 2016. Meanwhile, marijuana cases have remained about one-quarter of the drug docket. There may be additional significant changes in the drug crime caseload in the years immediately ahead. Attorney General Jeff Sessions recently announced the creation of a new unit devoted to "the devastating opioid crisis that is ravaging families and communities across America." The unit will focus on investigating and prosecuting opioid-related health care fraud, including prescription fraud and "pill mill schemes." The twelve U.S. Attorney's Offices participating in the new program are heavily weighted towards Pennsylvania, Ohio, and other states where opioid use and overdoses have increased dramatically. See U.S. Dep't of Justice, Attorney General Sessions Announces Opioid Fraud and Abuse Detection Unit (Aug. 2, 2017). (We briefly describe, *infra*, the recent remarkable growth of the Unite States opioid market.)

Just as in 2000, most of the individuals convicted of drug crimes in 2016 were convicted of drug *trafficking* or *importation* and not simple possession. In 2016, there were more than 19,000 convictions for distribution or possession with intent to distribute, compared to fewer than 2000 for the crime of simple possession (an issue we discuss further *infra*). Put simply, federal prosecutors are not in the business of prosecuting personal drug use. This does not mean, however, that all or even most federal drug defendants are "drug kingpins." Drug organizations are hierarchical and sprawling, employing many low-level couriers and distributors. The enforcement challenge is that it is generally easier to gather strong evidence against the least culpable players—the "mopes" on the bottom.

Whether "kingpins" or "mopes," drug dealers convicted in federal court receive severe sentences, and the severity of the sentence increases as the quantity of drugs goes up. The median sentence for all federal offenders in 2016 was slightly less than two years, whereas for drug trafficking it was four years—about the same as for robbery but less than the median sentence for crimes involving child pornography. One reason the sentences are so high is that many drug traffickers are subject to statutory mandatory minimum penalties, which begin at five years for relatively small-scale distribution. Significantly, the quantities at which the statutory minima kick in are far from uniform across drug types. This chapter will examine this facet of drug sentencing in depth in Section B. The result of this nonuniformity is that the median prison sentence for drug distribution in 2016 varied from a low of fewer than 1 ½ years for marijuana dealers to a high of almost 7 ½ years for those dealing in methamphetamine. In between these extremes were the median sentences for dealing in crack cocaine (7 years), powder cocaine (6 years), and heroin (5 ½ years).

Who are federal drug offenders? The available data are slim (and the distinctions noted here were chosen by the United States Sentencing Commission). We know this much: Most of these offenders are men, with the percentage of women (15 percent) mirroring the representation of women in the overall federal criminal caseload. Drug offenders are, on average, the same age as other federal offenders (36 years). In 2016, about 50 percent of both drug offenders and federal offenders overall had already been convicted of two or more felonies in state or federal court. Over 70 percent of convicted drug dealers are U.S. citizens, which is higher than in the overall caseload (58 percent), but slightly lower than in the overall caseload once immigration offenders (who are nearly all non-citizens) are excluded (80 percent). Fifty-one percent of drug traffickers are identified as Hispanic, a little over 23 percent as Black, and a little under 23 percent as White—though, you will not be surprised, these percentages vary greatly by drug type. Only about 5 ½ percent of crack-cocaine defendants are White, for instance, whereas more than 80 percent are Black; over 60 percent of powder-cocaine defendants are Hispanic. White people constitute the largest number of defendants in methamphetamine cases (38.3 percent), and, as noted above, there has been a great increase in meth prosecutions over the last decade.

The role of federal drug prosecutions in the criminal caseload, the nature of the drug crimes prosecuted in federal court, the high penalties imposed, and the demographic characteristics of the defendants are important matters to keep in mind as you study the material in this chapter. But even more importantly, we hope you recognize that many of the broader themes and issues we have invoked throughout this book have particular significance in the context of drug prosecutions.

First, consider the historical context in which current federal drug laws arose. Until 1970, the federal government's regulation of illicit drugs was sporadic and indirect. As we noted in Chapter 2, federal criminal law did not broadly address drug use or trafficking until the Harrison Narcotics Act of 1914. That law did not actually criminalize the distribution of the drugs; rather, it imposed registration and taxation requirements that, if not complied with, could result in criminal prosecution (penalties, though, were not nearly as harsh as they are today). The Controlled Substance Act of 1970 (CSA) thoroughly transformed the nature of federal drug law enforcement, a change that we explore in subsection 1 of Section A. The most important consequence of the CSA was a tremendous expansion in the scope of federal drug law, accompanied by an expansion in the role and number of federal agents involved in the enforcement of these laws, and an increase in federal prosecutions for drug offenses. We address other domestic implications of the CSA in subsection 2 of Section A.

Second, consider the geographic and jurisdictional dimension of drug prosecutions. The CSA trained the sights of federal law enforcers not only on drugs within the United States but also on activities abroad—which is not surprising, considering that even in an era in which opioids can be synthetically produced in hidden laboratories, most illegal drugs used in the United States are imported. An often-charged provision of the CSA, for instance, criminalized the manufacture or distribution of certain controlled substances abroad for exportation to the United States. In subsection 3 of Section A, we examine in some depth a relatively new provision of the CSA that significantly extends federal power even farther into international territory.

Third, consider the pace and nature of Congress's legislative interventions in the area. In Section B, we examine how, in the 1980s, Congress amended the core of the CSA to provide for mandatory minimum sentences for many drug traffickers. We explain how mandatory sentences, based on the type and quantity of drugs, operate in subsection 1 of Section B. In subsection 2, we consider the potentially huge impact of "prior felony" drug-sentencing enhancements, the gatekeeper of which is the prosecutor in the case. Subsection 3 examines the long history of disparity in treatment in the sentencing of crack cocaine and powder cocaine. One inescapable conclusion to be drawn from these materials is that high mandatory sentences have resulted in significant prosecutorial leverage to induce guilty pleas, at least where prosecutors have discretion to decide what quantity to charge or whether to trigger a sentencing enhancement. Indeed, enforcer discretion may extend not just to plea bargaining, but also to evidence collection, and even to offense creation. What happens where Congress has, say, passed a supplemental statute increasing sanctions for drug crimes committed within 1000 feet of a school, and law enforcement agents take advantage of that statute when setting up controlled buys? Should this tactic be condemned as a form of "sentencing entrapment"? We consider this and related issues in subsection 4 of Section B. In subsection 5, we consider one particularly important supplemental drug statute, 18 U.S.C. §924(c). Here Congress created a brand-new crime—the use of a weapon in a drug offense—and then provided for a mandatory-minimum sentence of five years to be served consecutively to the sentence for the drug offense itself, with a much greater enhancement where more than one gun is used. More than a decade ago, the Supreme Court gave a narrowing construction to §924(c), and by now you can guess how Congress responded. And just last year, in February 2017, the Court responded by construing another aspect of this provision narrowly; we await further developments. As we have noted throughout this volume, the federal criminal law extant at any moment is the result of a series of "moves" and "countermoves" by Congress, the federal courts, and federal prosecutors.

While enforcement of the criminal law has been the most salient aspect of the federal government's antidrug efforts—and the part that we are concerned with in this book—we would be remiss if we failed to note the pursuit of other antidrug strategies as well. On the supply side, these include diplomatic, foreign aid, and military efforts in "source" countries such as Colombia and Afghanistan, as well as the interdiction of drugs at borders and on the high seas. On the demand side, measures have included public advertising, education initiatives, and public health programs whose stated goal is to reduce drug use by young people, and a variety of addiction treatment and substance abuse programs targeted at long-time drug users. The National Drug Control Budget for FY 2015 lists $1.3 billion in support of educational and outreach programs "intended to discourage the use of controlled substances," $9.6 billion "for early intervention, treatment, and recovery services," nearly $9.2 billion to "support domestic law enforcement efforts," nearly $4 billion for interdiction efforts including "intercepting and ultimately disrupting shipments of illegal drugs and their precursors" into the United States, and $2.3 billion for "a wide range of drug control activities primarily focused on or conduct in areas outside of the United States." See Executive Office of the President, National Drug Control Budget FY 2015 Budget and Performance Summary Funding Highlights (2016). The first two items listed above—educational programs and treatment services—are aimed at demand reduction, which comprises about 40 percent of the more than $25 billion spent annually on the war on drugs.

The National Institute on Drug Abuse's 2015 National Survey on Drug Use and Health (formerly called the National Household Survey on Drug Abuse) reports that past-month illicit drug use among those over age 12 in the United States rose from 8.3 percent to 9.4 percent (about 25 million Americans) between 2002 and 2013. See Substance Abuse & Mental Health Services Administration, National Institute on Drug Abuse, Results from the 2013 National Survey on Drug Use and Health: Nationwide Trends (June 2015). For an overview of the success, and lack thereof, of federal and state drug-control policies, see John J. Donohue III et al., Rethinking America's Illegal Drug Policy, in Philip J. Cook et al., Making Crime Control Pay: Cost-Effective Alternatives to Incarceration (2011).

Because of the increase in illicit use of prescription painkillers and increases in fatal opioid overdoses in recent years (see *infra*), the National Survey introduced new questions beginning in 2015 regarding prescription drugs. The results indicate that in 2015, "an estimated 64 million Americans aged 12 or older were current misusers of psychotherapeutic drugs, which represent 2.4 percent of the population" in that age range, "largely driven by the misuse of prescription pain relievers." See Substance Abuse & Mental Health Services Administration, Key Substance Use and Mental Health Indicators in the United States: Results from the 2015 National Survey on Drug Use and Health 8 (Sept. 2016).

NOTES ON THE U.S. OPIOID CRISIS CIRCA 2017

1. One can scarcely open a newspaper without encountering a front-page story about the opioid crisis. And with good reason: an epidemic of drug overdoses—the majority of them from opioids—is killing people in the United States at a rate of over 1.3 times that of the height of the AIDS epidemic (and of course, these numbers do not even begin to address the incidence of non-fatal substance abuse-related injury: physical, psychological, and socioeconomic). See Josh Katz, The First of Fentanyl Deaths in 2016: Up 540% in Three Years, N.Y. Times (Sept. 2, 2017). We briefly explore the dimensions of this crisis because they are quite different from those associated with other recent drug epidemics, and those differences will likely shape the federal criminal enforcement response in the coming years.

According to a provisional report from the Centers for Disease Control and Prevention (CDC), from October 2016 to October 2017 68,400 people in the U.S. died of accidental drug overdoses. See CDC, Provisional Counts of Drug Overdose Deaths (May 6, 2018). To put this number in historical perspective, overdose fatalities increased by 12 percent from the previous year, and *eight-fold* since 1980. Of the 68,400 fatalities in the year preceding October 1, 2017, approximately 75 percent were due to opioids. See Provisional Counts, at 2. These staggering numbers reflect "two distinct but interconnected trends . . . a 15-year increase in deaths from prescription opioid overdoses, and a recent surge in illicit opioid overdoses driven mainly by heroin and illegally-made fentanyl." CDC, Categories of Opioids (citation omitted).

2. As the opioid crisis has progressed, its features have transformed in several respects salient to federal criminal drug law and enforcement. Originally predominant in rural, white, socioeconomically disadvantaged communities, the crisis has spread across demographics, leading The Economist magazine to observe:

> Looked at more closely . . . the terrifying rise in opioid deaths in the past few years seems to have less to do with white working-class despair and more to do with changing drug markets. Distinct criminal networks and local drug cultures largely explain why some parts of America are suffering more than others.

A Selective Scourge: Inside the Opioid Epidemic, The Economist (May 11, 2017).

First, the type of opioids flooding the market has changed dramatically over the course of this burgeoning crisis. The epidemic was originally spurred by phenomenal growth in the first decade of the 21st century in prescriptions for opioid painkillers such as OxyContin, whose manufacturer, Purdue Pharma, marketed the drug as a less addictive alternative to other opioids (such as morphine). Even as the number of prescriptions shot up, the FDA repeatedly approved higher potency formulations. The pills soon found their way out of medicine cabinets and into the hands of first-time recreational opioid users, who could crush and inject the water soluble medicine for an immediate and long-lasting euphoric high. Many became opioid dependent, and switched to much lower-cost heroin, which had been smuggled over the southern U.S. border. See generally, Ameet Sarpatwari et al., The Opioid Epidemic: Fixing a Broken Pharmaceutical Market, 11 Harv. L. & Pol'y Rev. 463 (2017). In 2012, the FDA mandated that prescription opioid painkillers be reformulated to be less susceptible to abuse, and the number of prescriptions for most of these drugs has leveled off or dropped. See Inside the Opioid Epidemic, *supra*. The illicit opioid market has nonetheless continued to grow tremendously because of the massive invasion of a synthetic opioid, fentanyl, and its analogues. Fentanyl is reported to be 50 to 100 times more potent than morphine, and some of its analogues, such as carfentanil, are 100 times more powerful than fentanyl.

The predominance of fentanyl over less potent prescription opioids reflects a second critical development in the current opioid crisis — changes in the drugs' source. While fentanyl is a Schedule II controlled substance that may be legitimately prescribed in palliative care settings for end-stage cancer and other terminal diseases and in very low doses for conscious sedation during in-hospital procedures, the fentanyl-type drugs flooding the United States since 2013 have been produced primarily in China and are largely marketed through the "dark web," with payment in bitcoin or other alternative currencies. The DEA recently reported:

> From China, these substances are shipped through mail carriers directly to the United States or alternatively shipped directly to transnational criminal organizations ("TCOs") in Mexico, Canada, and the Caribbean. Once there, fentanyl or its analogues are prepared to be mixed into the U.S. heroin supply domestically, or pressed into a pill form, and then moved to the illicit U.S. market where demand for prescription opioids and heroin remain at epidemic proportions. In some cases, traffickers have industrial pill presses shipped into the United States directly from China and operate fentanyl pill press mills domestically. Mexican TCOs have seized upon this business opportunity because of the profit potential of synthetic opioids, and have invested in growing their share of this market. Because of its low dosage range and potency, one kilogram of fentanyl purchased in China for $3,000-$5,000 can generate upwards of $1.5 million in revenue on the illicit market.

Statement of Demetra Ashley, DEA, before the Subcommittee on Crime, Terrorism, Homeland Security and Investigations, Committee on the Judiciary, U.S. House of Representatives (June 27, 2017).

Groups selling illicit fentanyl in pill form often fraudulently market their wares as "less dangerous drugs like Xanax and Oxycodone," according to the New York Times, which contributes to the likelihood of accidental overdose deaths. Nathaniel Popper, Opioid Dealers Embrace the Dark Web to Send Deadly Drugs by Mail, N.Y. Times (June 10, 2017). Because fentanyl can be ordered on the "dark web" and sent through courier services or the mail, it is difficult for law enforcement—or rival drug dealers—to detect. Individual users and small-time entrepreneurs enter the market with ease. Id. The extreme fragmentation of those parts of the opioid market that are in the United States and the multiplicity of thin (though sometimes thick) pipelines in which fentanyl and other synthetic opioids flow from abroad pose an enforcement—and education and treatment—challenge that will unfold as you read this book.

A.   SUBSTANTIVE LAW

The federal law governing markets in fentanyl, heroin, and other drugs is found primarily in the Controlled Substances Act of 1970 (as amended many times in the intervening years). The core of the CSA is found in just four provisions:

- 21 U.S.C. §841(a) makes it a crime to distribute controlled substances;

- 21 U.S.C. §846 makes it a crime to conspire to violate §841(a);
- 21 U.S.C. §812 lists the substances that are controlled;
- 21 U.S.C. §841(b) lists the penalties for violating §§841(a) or 846.

The last of these provisions is the focus of Section B of this chapter. Here, we focus on the relationship between the statutes in the first two bullet points: the proscription on distribution and conspiracy to distribute, and the lists ("schedules") of controlled substances. The basic proscription is simple:

---

21 U.S.C. §841(a)

(a) Unlawful acts. Except as authorized by this subchapter, it shall be unlawful for any person knowingly or intentionally—

    (1) to manufacture, distribute, or dispense, or possess with intent to manufacture, distribute, or dispense, a controlled substance; or

    (2) to create, distribute, or dispense, or possess with intent to distribute or dispense, a counterfeit substance.

The companion to §841(a) is §846, which makes it a crime to conspire to distribute drugs (or to conspire to possess drugs with intent to distribute them). Rather than using the general federal conspiracy provision that we studied in Chapter 8, 18 U.S.C. §371, Congress enacted a special drug conspiracy statute (just as it enacted special conspiracy provisions for RICO, the Hobbs Act, and money laundering). There is one major difference between 21 U.S.C. §846 and the general federal conspiracy statute: Whereas the maximum sentence provided in the latter is five years, the drug conspiracy provision provides that a defendant will receive the same punishment for conspiracy as he would for the underlying crime—which, as we shall explore in Section B, can be far higher than five years. There is also one minor difference: Unlike the general conspiracy statute (but like most of the special conspiracy statutes noted above), §846 does not require the commission of an overt act in furtherance of the conspiracy. See United States v. Shabani, 513 U.S. 10 (1994).

While the prohibitions on distributing drugs and on conspiracy to distribute are straightforward, we will see that the "devil is in the details"—here, the scheduling provision of Title 21.

1. DRUG SCHEDULING

The CSA establishes the following classification regime for stimulant, depressant, and other drugs that have an effect on the central nervous system.

21 U.S.C. §812. Schedules of controlled substances

(a) Establishment. There are established five schedules of controlled substances, to be known as schedules I, II, III, IV, and V. Such schedules shall initially consist of the substances listed in this section. . . .

(b) Placement on schedules; findings required . . . [A] drug or other substance may not be placed in any schedule unless the findings required for such schedule are made with respect to such drug or other substance. The findings required for each of the schedules are as follows:

(1) Schedule I.—

(A) The drug or other substance has a high potential for abuse.

(B) The drug or other substance has no currently accepted medical use in treatment in the United States.

(C) There is a lack of accepted safety for use of the drug or other substance under medical supervision.

(2) Schedule II.—

(A) The drug or other substance has a high potential for abuse.

(B) The drug or other substance has a currently accepted medical use in treatment in the United States or a currently accepted medical use with severe restrictions.

(C) Abuse of the drug or other substances may lead to severe psychological or physical dependence.

(3) Schedule III.—

(A) The drug or other substance has a potential for abuse less than the drugs or other substances in schedules I and II.

(B) The drug or other substance has a currently accepted medical use in treatment in the United States.

(C) Abuse of the drug or other substance may lead to moderate or low physical dependence or high psychological dependence.

(4) Schedule IV.—

(A) The drug or other substance has a low potential for abuse relative to the drugs or other substances in schedule III.

(B) The drug or other substance has a currently accepted medical use in treatment in the United States.

(C) Abuse of the drug or other substance may lead to limited physical dependence or psychological dependence relative to the drugs or other substances in schedule III.

(5) Schedule V.—

(A) The drug or other substance has a low potential for abuse relative to the drugs or other substances in schedule IV.

(B) The drug or other substance has a currently accepted medical use in treatment in the United States.

(C) Abuse of the drug or other substance may lead to limited physical dependence or psychological dependence relative to the drugs or other substances in schedule IV.

(c) Initial schedules of controlled substances. Schedules I, II, III, IV, and V shall, unless and until amended pursuant to section 811 of this title, consist of the following drugs or other substances, by whatever official name, common or usual name, chemical name, or brand name designated: [The statute then lists the specific substances within each schedule].

NOTES AND QUESTIONS

1. Congress itself scheduled various drugs when it enacted the CSA. As a result, you might be surprised to learn that Schedule I includes—in addition to heroin, LSD, and "ecstasy"—peyote and marijuana. Schedule II includes cocaine, methadone, oxycodone, morphine, opium, codeine in high concentrations, and Ritalin. Schedule III includes Vicodin and anabolic steroids. We return later in the chapter to the scheduling of marijuana.

The scheduling of drugs does not directly correspond with the severity of the sentence that may be imposed for illegal trafficking in them. As we've mentioned, penalties vary depending on the identity and quantity of the drug, and are primarily prescribed in 21 U.S.C. §841(b), which we consider in the second half of this chapter. You will see, for instance, that illegal trafficking in powder cocaine is sentenced more harshly than illegal trafficking in marijuana, even though the former substance is in Schedule II and the latter is in Schedule I. Rather, scheduling relates to how closely regulated the substances are. Schedule I drugs have no recognized licit purpose under federal law; these drugs are entirely "illegal" under federal law. See United States v. Pruitt, 487 F.2d 1241, 1245 (8th Cir. 1973) (affirming conviction in heroin distribution case and, noting that CSA eliminated the "procuring agent" defense of prior federal drug law pertaining to distribution, former 16 U.S.C. §4704(a)). The CSA places a variety of restrictions on medical professionals and others with respect to drugs listed on other schedules. One of the editors, for instance, was administered very diluted cocaine (which is a vasoconstrictor) during a minor sinus procedure.

2. Since 1970, the number of scheduled chemical compounds has increased tremendously—not through Acts of Congress, but via the authority that the CSA delegates to the Attorney General. Before considering the complexities of the drug schedules, we briefly address the delegation issue.

Under the nondelegation doctrine, Congress is not supposed to delegate its legislative powers to other branches of government. See Schechter Poultry Corp. v. United States, 295 U.S. 495 (1935) (invalidating on nondelegation grounds the Live Poultry Code for New York City, which had been promulgated under the National Industrial Recovery Act); Panama Refining Co. v. Ryan, 293 U.S. 388 (1935) (invalidating on nondelegation grounds an oil quota that had been promulgated pursuant to the NIRA). In the modern era, to be sure, the Supreme Court has permitted broad delegations of power as long as the delegation provides "intelligible principles" to guide the exercise of delegated authority. See Whitman v. American Trucking Associations, Inc., 531 U.S. 457, 474 (2001). How "intelligible" are the principles under which the CSA delegates authority to the Attorney General? Does it make any difference that the Attorney General has in turn delegated his authority to the Drug Enforcement Administration, see 28 C.F.R. §0.100 (1973) (delegation to the DEA)?

Should the nondelegation doctrine have more bite where the delegated lawmaking authority creates criminal liability? In Touby v. United States, 500 U.S. 160 (1991), the Supreme Court upheld criminal convictions for manufacturing a drug that the Attorney General had temporarily listed as a controlled substance on an expedited basis pursuant to a provision of the CSA that allowed him to do so when "necessary to avoid an imminent hazard to the public safety." 21 U.S.C. §811(h). Defendants argued that the temporary scheduling provision unconstitutionally delegated power to the executive branch because, even though the provisions set forth an "intelligible principle" to constrain the Attorney General's discretion, "something more than an 'intelligible principle' is required when Congress authorizes another Branch to promulgate regulations that contemplate criminal sanctions." Touby, 500 U.S. at 165-66. The Court declined to decide whether "Congress must . . . provide more specific guidance" when delegating authority to define criminal conduct, finding that the delegation at issue "passes muster even if greater congressional specificity is required in the criminal context." Id. at 166.

3. What do you think that Touby meant when it said that the statutory language is constitutionally adequate because it "meaningfully constrains the Attorney General's discretion to define criminal conduct?" Id. The procedures for adding a new substance on a permanent, not merely temporary, basis can be summarized as follows: The Attorney General must make certain findings and must follow specific procedures outlined in the CSA. These include requesting from the Secretary of Health and Human Services a "scientific and medical evaluation, and his recommendations, as to whether such drug or other substance should be so controlled or removed as a controlled substance." 21 U.S.C. §811(b). The Attorney General is bound by the Secretary's recommendation that a drug or other substance not be controlled. Id. In addition, the Attorney General is required to weigh eight factors to determine whether to add or remove a controlled substance from the schedules, including the substance's potential for abuse, scientific evidence of its pharmacological effect, and the risk it poses to public health. 21 U.S.C. §811(c). Are these procedures sufficient to ensure that the DEA and the Attorney General make objective, scientific judgments about the classifications of controlled substances? Is the judgment as to which drugs should be subjected to relatively harsher penalties solely a scientific question? Who should make that determination? Are there any limits on Congress's power to "punt" on the question of criminalization by framing the issue as a question primarily of scientific fact? In Chapter 12, we will more generally explore the limits to the delegation of criminal lawmaking authority.

4. The drug schedules can be found at 21 C.F.R. §1308 et seq. A more user-friendly presentation of the schedules (and some additional information about each listed drug) is available here (16 pages, with about 14 entries per page). You will notice that many of the substances "listed" are simply chemical names. For instance 1-Methyl-4-phenyl-4-propionoxypiperidine is a Schedule I narcotic that, according to the DEA, is also known as "MPPP" and "synthetic heroin." And, in fact, there are many more federal "controlled substances" than are listed on the published schedules, even though the DEA constantly adds new substances that are synthetically produced. We go as far to say that the number of controlled substances at any given moment of time is indeterminate. How can this be? Read carefully the following statute regarding the scheduling of analogue drugs.

The Controlled Substance Analogue Enforcement Act of 1986 ("Analogue Act")

21 U.S.C. §813: Treatment of controlled substance analogues.

> A controlled substance analogue shall, to the extent intended for human consumption, be treated, for the purposes of any Federal law as a controlled substance in schedule I.

21 U.S.C. §802(32)(A). [T]he term "controlled substance analogue" means a substance —

> (i) the chemical structure of which is substantially similar to chemical structure of a controlled substance in schedule I or II; [and]

> (ii) which has a stimulant, depressant, or hallucinogenic effect on the central nervous system that is substantially similar to or greater than the stimulant, depressant, or hallucinogenic effect on the central nervous system of a controlled substance in schedule I or II; or

> (iii) with respect to a particular person, which such person represents or intends to have a stimulant, depressant, or hallucinogenic effect on the central nervous system that is substantially similar to or greater than the stimulant, depressant, or hallucinogenic effect on the central nervous system of a controlled substance in schedule I or II.

In the following case, the Supreme Court discussed the CSA's knowledge requirement (see 21 U.S.C. §841(a), *supra*) with respect to both scheduled "controlled substances" and "controlled substance analogues."

McFadden v. United States
135 S. Ct. 2298 (2015)

Justice THOMAS delivered the opinion of the Court.

The Controlled Substance Analogue Enforcement Act of 1986 (Analogue Act) identifies a category of substances substantially similar to those listed on the federal controlled substance schedules, 21 U.S.C. §802(32)(A), and then instructs courts to treat those analogues, if intended for human consumption, as controlled substances listed on schedule I for purposes of federal law, §813. The Controlled Substances Act (CSA) in turn makes it unlawful knowingly to manufacture, distribute, or possess with intent to distribute controlled substances. §841(a)(1). The question presented in this case concerns the knowledge necessary for conviction under §841(a)(1) when the controlled substance at issue is in fact an analogue. . . .

issue

I

In 2011, law enforcement officials in Charlottesville, Virginia, began investigating individuals at a Charlottesville video store for suspected distribution of "bath salts"—various recreational drugs used to produce effects similar to those of cocaine, methamphetamine, and other controlled substances. The owner of the store, Lois McDaniel, had been purchasing bath salts from petitioner Stephen McFadden for several months. McFadden had marketed the substances to her as "Alpha," "No Speed," "Speed," "Up," and "The New Up," and had compared them to cocaine and crystal meth. He had often sold those products with labels borrowing language from the Analogue Act, asserting that the contents were "not for human consumption" or stating that a particular product "does not contain any of the following compounds or analogues of the following compounds" and listing controlled substances. McDaniel purchased the bath salts for $15 per gram and resold them for $30 to $70 per gram.

A federal grand jury indicted McFadden on eight counts of distribution of controlled substance analogues and one count of conspiracy. At trial, McFadden argued that he did not know the substances he was distributing were regulated as controlled substances under the Analogue Act. He and the Government also disagreed about what knowledge was required for a conviction. The Government sought an instruction requiring only "[t]hat the defendant knowingly and intentionally distributed a mixture or substance. . . [t]hat . . . was a controlled substance analogue . . . with the intent that it be consumed by humans." McFadden sought a more demanding instruction requiring that he "knew that the substances that he was distributing possessed the characteristics of controlled substance analogues," including their chemical structures and effects on the central nervous system. The District Court compromised, instructing the jury that the statute required that "the defendant knowingly and intentionally distributed a mixture or substance that has" substantially similar effects on the nervous system as a controlled substance and "[t]hat the defendant intended for the mixture or substance to be consumed by humans."

Gov instruction on knowledge

defendant's knowledge instruction

Actual Jury instruction

The jury convicted McFadden on all nine counts. On appeal, McFadden insisted that the District Court "erred in refusing to instruct the jury that the government was required to prove that he knew, had a strong suspicion, or deliberately avoided knowledge that the [substances] possessed the characteristics of controlled substance analogues." 753 F.3d 432, 443 (C.A.4 2014). Rejecting that argument, the Court of Appeals affirmed. Stating that it was bound by Circuit precedent, the court concluded that the "intent element [in the Act] requires [only] that the government prove that the defendant meant for the substance at issue to be consumed by humans." . . .

Ct. of App.

II

A

The Analogue Act requires a controlled substance analogue, if intended for human consumption, to be treated "as a controlled substance in schedule I" for purposes of federal law. 21 U.S.C. §813. We therefore must turn first to the statute that addresses controlled substances, the CSA. The CSA makes it "unlawful for any person knowingly or intentionally . . . to manufacture, distribute, or dispense, or possess with intent to manufacture, distribute, or dispense, a controlled substance." 21 U.S.C. §841(a)(1). Under the most natural reading of this provision, the word "knowingly" applies not just to the statute's verbs but also to the object of those verbs—"*a* controlled substance." See Flores–Figueroa v. United States, 556 U.S. 646, 650 (2009). When used as an indefinite article, "a" means "[s]ome undetermined or unspecified particular." Webster's New International Dictionary 1 (2d ed. 1954). And the CSA defines "controlled substance" as "a drug or other substance, or immediate precursor, included in schedule I, II, III, IV, or V." 21 U.S.C. §802(6) (internal quotation marks omitted). The ordinary meaning of §841(a)(1) thus requires a defendant to know only that the substance he is dealing with is some unspecified substance listed on the federal drug schedules. The Courts of Appeals have recognized as much. See, e.g., United States v. Andino, 627 F.3d 41, 45-46 (C.A.2 2010); United States v. Gamez-Gonzalez, 319 F.3d 695, 699 (C.A.5 2003); United States v. Martinez, 301 F.3d 860, 865 (C.A.7 2002).

knowledge under CSA →

That knowledge requirement may be met by showing that the defendant knew he possessed a substance listed on the schedules, even if he did not know which substance it was. Take, for example, a defendant whose role in a larger drug organization is to distribute a white powder to customers. The defendant may know that the white powder is listed on the schedules even if he does not know precisely what substance it is. And if so, he would be guilty of knowingly distributing "a controlled substance."

The knowledge requirement may also be met by showing that the defendant knew the identity of the substance he possessed. Take, for example, a defendant who knows he is distributing heroin but does not know that heroin is listed on the schedules, 21 CFR §1308.11 (2014). Because ignorance of the law is typically no defense to criminal prosecution, Bryan v. United States, 524 U.S. 184, 196 (1998), this defendant would also be guilty of knowingly distributing "a controlled substance."[1]

The Analogue Act extends the framework of the CSA to analogous substances. . . . It provides, "A controlled substance analogue shall, to the extent intended for human consumption, be treated, for the purposes of any Federal law as a controlled substance in schedule I." 21 U.S.C. §813.

The question in this case is how the mental state requirement under the CSA for knowingly manufacturing, distributing, or possessing with intent to distribute "a controlled substance" applies when the controlled substance is in fact an analogue. The answer begins with §841(a)(1), which expressly requires the Government to prove that a defendant knew he was dealing with "a controlled substance." The Analogue Act does not alter that provision, but rather instructs courts to treat controlled substance analogues "as . . . controlled substance[s] in schedule I." §813. Applying this statutory command, it follows that the Government must prove that a defendant knew that the substance with which he was dealing was "a controlled substance," even in prosecutions involving an analogue.[2]

Knowledge for CSA Analogue

That knowledge requirement can be established in two ways. First, it can be established by evidence that a defendant knew that the substance with which he was dealing is some controlled substance—that is, one actually listed on the federal drug schedules or treated as such by operation of the Analogue Act—regardless of whether he knew the particular identity of the substance. Second, it can be established by evidence that the defendant knew the specific analogue he was dealing with, even if he did not know its legal status as an analogue. The Analogue Act defines a controlled substance analogue by its features, as a substance

---

1. The Courts of Appeals have held that, as with most *mens rea* requirements, the Government can prove the requisite mental state through either direct evidence or circumstantial evidence. Direct evidence could include, for example, past arrests that put a defendant on notice of the controlled status of a substance. United States v. Abdulle, 564 F.3d 119, 127 (C.A.2 2009). Circumstantial evidence could include, for example, a defendant's concealment of his activities, evasive behavior with respect to law enforcement, knowledge that a particular substance produces a "high" similar to that produced by controlled substances, and knowledge that a particular substance is subject to seizure at customs. United States v. Ali, 735 F.3d 176, 188-89 (C.A.4 2013). The Government presented such circumstantial evidence in this case, and neither party disputes that this was proper.

2. The Government has accepted for the purpose of this case that it must prove two elements to show that a substance is a controlled substance analogue under the definition in §802(32)(A): First, that an alleged analogue is substantially similar in chemical structure to a controlled substance, §802(32)(A)(i). Second, that an alleged analogue either has, or is represented or intended to have, a stimulant, depressant, hallucinogenic effect on the central nervous system that is substantially similar to that of a controlled substance, §§802(32)(A)(ii), (iii). Brief for United States 3. Because we need not decide in this case whether that interpretation is correct, we assume for the sake of argument that it is.

"the chemical structure of which is substantially similar to the chemical structure of a controlled substance in schedule I or II"; "which has a stimulant, depressant, or hallucinogenic effect on the central nervous system that is substantially similar to or greater than" the effect of a controlled substance in schedule I or II; or which is represented or intended to have that effect with respect to a particular person. §802(32)(A). A defendant who possesses a substance with knowledge of those features knows all of the facts that make his conduct illegal, just as a defendant who knows he possesses heroin knows all of the facts that make his conduct illegal. A defendant need not know of the existence of the Analogue Act to know that he was dealing with "a controlled substance."

B

The Court of Appeals did not adhere to §813's command to treat a controlled substance analogue "as a controlled substance in schedule I," and, accordingly, it did not apply the mental-state requirement in §841(a)(1). Instead, it concluded that the only mental state requirement for prosecutions involving controlled substance analogues is the one in §813—that the analogues be "intended for human consumption." Because that interpretation is inconsistent with the text and structure of the statutes, we decline to adopt it.

Unsurprisingly, neither the Government nor McFadden defends the Court of Appeals' position. But their alternative interpretations fare no better. The Government agrees that the knowledge requirement in §841(a)(1) applies to prosecutions involving controlled substance analogues, yet contends that it is met if the "defendant knew he was dealing with an illegal or regulated substance" under some law. Section 841(a)(1), however, requires that a defendant knew he was dealing with "a controlled substance." That term includes only those drugs listed on the federal drug schedules or treated as such by operation of the Analogue Act. §§802(6), 813. It is not broad enough to include all substances regulated by any law.[3]

For his part, McFadden contends that, in the context of analogues, knowledge of "a controlled substance" can *only* be established by knowledge of the characteristics that make a substance an "analogue" under

---

3. Although the Government must prove that a defendant knew that the substance in question was "a controlled substance" under federal law, the Government need not introduce direct evidence of such knowledge. As with prosecutions involving substances actually listed on the drug schedules, the Government may offer circumstantial evidence of that knowledge. See n.1, *supra*. In such cases, it will be left to the trier of fact to determine whether the circumstantial evidence proves that the defendant knew that the substance was a controlled substance under the CSA or Analogue Act, as opposed to under any other federal or state laws.

the Act. In support of that argument, he relies heavily on our conclusion in Staples v. United States, 511 U.S. 600 (1994), that a statute
making it "unlawful for any person . . . to receive or possess a firearm
which is not registered to him in the National Firearms Registration and
Transfer Record," required proof that a defendant "knew of the features
of his AR-15 that brought it within the scope of the Act," 511 U.S. at
619. McFadden reasons by analogy that a defendant convicted under
§841(a)(1) must also know the features of the substance that brought
it within the scope of the Analogue Act. But that position ignores an
important textual distinction between §841(a)(1) and the statute at issue
in *Staples*. The statute at issue in *Staples* defined "a firearm" by its physical
features such as the length of its barrel and its capacity to shoot more
than one shot with a single function of the trigger. Unlike those physical
features that brought the firearm "within the scope of" that statute, the
feature of a substance "that br[ings] it within the scope of" §841(a)(1)
is the fact that it is "'controlled.'" §802(6). Knowledge of *that* fact can be
established in the two ways previously discussed: either by knowledge that
a substance is listed or treated as listed by operation of the Analogue Act,
§§802(6), 813, or by knowledge of the physical characteristics that give
rise to that treatment. [See] *supra.*

[handwritten margin note: Not like Staples]

[handwritten margin note: 2 ways for knowledge here]

McFadden also invokes the canon of constitutional avoidance, arguing that we must adopt his interpretation of the statute lest it be rendered
unconstitutionally vague. But that argument fails on two grounds. Under
our precedents, this canon "is a tool for choosing between competing plausible interpretations of a provision." It "has no application" in the interpretation of an unambiguous statute such as this one. Even if this statute were
ambiguous, McFadden's argument would falter. Under our precedents, a
scienter requirement in a statute "alleviate [s] vagueness concerns," "narrow[s] the scope of the [its] prohibition[,] and limit[s] prosecutorial discretion." Gonzales v. Carhart, 550 U.S. 124, 149, 150 (2007). The scienter
requirement in this statute does not, as McFadden suggests, render the
statute vague. Moreover, to the extent McFadden suggests that the substantial similarity test for defining analogues is itself indeterminate, his
proposed alternative scienter requirement would do nothing to cure that
infirmity.

III

The District Court's instructions to the jury did not fully convey
the mental state required by the Analogue Act. The jury was instructed
only that McFadden had to "knowingly and intentionally distribut[e] a
mixture or substance that has an actual, intended, or claimed stimulant,
depressant, or hallucinogenic effect on the central nervous system" substantially similar to that of a controlled substance.

The Government contends that any error in the jury instructions was harmless because no rational jury could have concluded that McFadden was unaware that the substances he was distributing were controlled. We have recognized that even the omission of an element from a jury charge is subject to harmless-error analysis. Neder v. United States, 527 U.S. 1, 15 (1999). Because the Court of Appeals did not address that issue, we remand for that court to consider it in the first instance.

* * *

For the foregoing reasons, we vacate the judgment of the Court of Appeals and remand the case for further proceedings consistent with this opinion.

It is so ordered.

[Editors' Note: The partial dissent of the Chief Justice is discussed below in Note 4.]

NOTES AND QUESTIONS

1. The only issue at McFadden's trial pertained to *mens rea* under the Analogue Act. McFadden, the government, the District Court, and the Fourth Circuit came up with varying formulations. All agreed that the jury could not convict unless it found the defendant intended or knew that the substance would be consumed by humans, see 21 U.S.C. §813. The disagreement was over what else, if anything, the government had to prove. The District Court, the Court of Appeals, and the government at trial and on appeal used varying language but at bottom agreed that there was no additional *mens rea* element; that is, they agreed that while the government had to prove that the defendant had *in fact* been dealing with a controlled substance analogue (as defined in 21 U.S.C. §802(32)(A)), it was not required to prove that the defendant *knew* he was dealing with a substance *possessing the characteristics stated in that definition.* Before the Supreme Court, however, the government conceded that it also had to prove that the defendant knew he was dealing in a controlled substance analogue. Here we see how the Solicitor General's Office can temper prosecutorial positions. That Office accurately noted that "the heart of this case" is "[h]ow does the government prove the relevant knowledge?" Brief for the United States 14.

To answer that question, Justice Thomas looked first to the *mens rea* requirement of 21 U.S.C. §841(a). Why did he do this? Because, as the opinion points out (and all the members of the Court agreed on this point), the Analogue Act is not new or a separate prohibition, but merely instructs that "controlled substance analogues" are *themselves controlled*

substances, by operation of 21 U.S.C. §813. Hence the *mens rea* of §841(a) —
knowingly—must be proved in prosecutions for dealing in controlled substance analogues.

2. Okay, so what is the required *mens rea* for conviction under §841(a)?
The Supreme Court adopted the unanimous view of the courts of appeals:
There are two different ways that the government may prove that the defendant knew he was dealing in a controlled substance. One method would be
to prove that the defendant knew the specific identity of the substance (e.g.,
cocaine) whether or not he knew that the substance was listed as a "controlled substance" on a DEA schedule. See, e.g., United States v. Hussein,
351 F.2d 9, 19 (1st Cir. 2003) ("In most cases, [the government meets its
burden] by proving that the defendant knew the specific identity of the
controlled substance that he possessed.") Eight members of the Supreme
Court (all but the Chief Justice, as we discuss in Note 4 below) agreed that
this is one method of proof.

3. But what if such evidence is lacking, as in Justice Thomas's hypothetical about a defendant whose role in a drug conspiracy "is to distribute a
white powder to customers"? That defendant may well not know (or care)
what type of white powder he is distributing. Some courts of appeals had
suggested that in these circumstances it is enough that the jury be able to
infer beyond a reasonable doubt that the defendant knew the substance
was "unlawful" or "illegal." See, e.g., United States v. Ali, 735 F.3d 176, 188
(4th Cir. 2013) ("The defendants here also had warning signs that khat contained an unlawful substance."); United States v. Lewis, 676 F.3d 508, 513
(11th Cir. 1982) (rejecting defendant's contention that the jury could have
found he thought he was dealing in "bales of cotton or some other legal
substance"). You have seen this approach to *mens rea* before. Recall Bryan v.
United States, 524 U.S. 184 (1998), discussed in Chapter 3.

McFadden says that the *mens rea* element is more specific than this—that
the jury must be able to infer that the defendant knew he was dealing in " *'a
controlled substance' under . . . the CSA or the Analogue Act, as opposed to under
some other federal or state laws,*" 135 S. Ct. at 2306 n.3 (emphasis added); see
also id. at 2304 (interpreting the statute to require that the defendant know
"that the substance he is dealing with is some unspecified substance listed
on the federal drug schedules."). Indeed, the Court specifically rejected the
argument presented in the government's brief that in prosecutions under
§841(a), it is enough that the government prove the defendant knew he was
dealing in an "illegal" or "regulated" substance: "[The term 'controlled substance'] is not broad enough to include all substances regulated by any law,"
135 S. Ct. at 2306. Did you, before you read this chapter, know that pursuant
to the CSA there are federal drug schedules? Did you know that federal law
refers to these drugs as "controlled substance[s]?" How will the government
prove that the defendant knew not only that the substance was "controlled"

(which presumably includes regulated by the criminal law), but that it was controlled under federal law—specifically, the CSA or Analogue Act?

4. Why isn't the second method of proof discussed above—evidence that the defendant knew he was dealing in a controlled substance—the only way that knowledge can be established? After all, §841(a)(1) makes it a crime for "any person knowingly or intentionally—to manufacture, distribute, or dispense, or possess with intent to manufacture, distribute, or dispense, a controlled substance." We saw in Chapter 3 that the Supreme Court has, at least arguably, adopted the Model Penal Code convention that the *mens rea* term of a statute applies not just to subsequent verbs but also to objects of the verbs. See Flores-Figueroa v. United States, 556 U.S. 646, 650 (2009). Indeed, Justice Thomas, citing *Flores-Figueroa*, made this very point. See 135 S. Ct. at 2304. Why, then, should proving the defendant's knowledge of the "identity" (or name) of the substance be available as an alternative way of proving that the defendant knew the substance was controlled? This concern was the basis of Chief Justice Roberts's partial concurrence in *McFadden*. In the Chief Justice's view, application of §841(a)'s "knowingly" requirement "suggests that a defendant needs to know more than the identity of the substance; he needs to know that the substance is *controlled*." 135 S. Ct. at 2307 (Roberts, C.J., concurring in part) (emphasis in original). He goes on to note that in many cases, knowledge of identity will be sufficient for the jury to infer knowledge of the legal status of the substance:

> In cases involving well-known drugs such as heroin, a defendant's knowledge of the identity of the substance can be compelling evidence that he knows the substance is controlled. See United States v. Turcotte, 405 F.3d 515, 525 (C.A.7 2005). But that is not necessarily true for lesser known drugs. A pop quiz for any reader who doubts the point: Two drugs—dextromethorphan and hydrocodone—are both used as cough suppressants. They are also both used as recreational drugs. Which one is a controlled substance?

Please answer the Chief's pop quiz.[*]

He went on to reject the majority's reliance on the idea, which in Chapter 3 we saw is central to the common law but has come under strain in the Supreme Court in recent decades, that "ignorance of the law is typically no defense to a criminal prosecution":

> The Court says that knowledge of the substance's identity suffices because "ignorance of the law is typically no defense to criminal prosecution." *Ante*, at 2304. I agree that is "typically" true. But when "there is a legal element in the definition of the offense," a person's lack of knowledge regarding that legal element *can* be a defense. Liparota v. United States, 471 U.S. 419, 425,

---

[*] [Editors' Note: Chief Justice Roberts provided the answer in a footnote: hydrocodone.]

n.9 (1985). And here, there is arguably a legal element in Section 841(a)
(1) — that the substance be "controlled.". . .

    Ultimately, the Court's statements on this issue are not necessary to its
conclusion that the District Court's jury instructions "did not fully convey the
mental state required by the Analogue Act." *Ante,* at 2307. Those statements
should therefore not be regarded as controlling if the issue arises in a future
case.

135 S. Ct. at 2308. Do you think that the Court is going to take the advice
of Chief Justice Roberts in the near future? Is he right that all statements
not necessary to the *judgment* in a case are dicta? Does that mean the lower
federal courts should ignore them?

    5. While the "controlled substance under the CSA" language in
McFadden, discussed in Note 3 above, may prove to be more than a speed
bump for the government in many drug cases, *McFadden* did not disturb the
unanimous view of the courts of appeals that when the government proves
mens rea by presenting evidence that the defendant knew that the substance,
whatever its specific identity, is "controlled," the government need not also
prove that the defendant knew the type (or quantity) of the substance in
which he was dealing. See, e.g., United States v. Andino, 627 F.3d 41, 49 (2d
Cir. 2010); United States v. Heredia, 483 F.3d 913 (9th Cir. 2007); United
States v. Barbosa, 271 F.3d 438, 457-58 (3d Cir. 2001). The type of controlled
substance and the quantity attributable to the defendant must be proven to
the jury beyond a reasonable doubt because, under §841(b), type and quantity are effectively "elements" of the offense. (We examine this "elements"
rule in Chapter 10.) But there is no *mens rea* associated with these elements.

    6. Now that we understand the Supreme Court's pronouncements in
McFadden about *mens rea* under the basic CSA prohibition, 21 U.S.C. §841(a),
we can at last turn to the Analogue Act. We've already mentioned the key
insight (as to which all members of the Court agreed) of the opinion: The
operation of this statute simply increases the number of drugs that are subject to the prohibition of §841(a); hence the same *mens rea* ("knowingly or
intentionally") applies in prosecutions involving controlled substance analogues. Justice Thomas thus applied his §841(a) analysis to analogue drugs
as defined in 21 U.S.C. §802(32)(A). He said, once again, that there are two
ways that the government might prove the defendant's knowledge. The first
way is evidence that the defendant knew he was dealing with a substance
"actually listed on the federal drug schedules or treated as such by operation of the Analogue Act" irrespective of whether the defendant "knew the
particular identity of the substance." 135 S. Ct. at 2305. "Second, it can be
established by evidence that the defendant knew the specific analogue he
was dealing with, even if he did not know its legal status as an analogue."
Id. How does this work in practice? The type of evidence that could suffice
under the first approach might be a government witness who testifies that

McFadden told her that the "No Speed" he was selling was "like cocaine or meth," along with his labeling that the product was "not intended for human consumption." A jury could infer not only that the defendant knew he was selling something similar to a drug he knew was a listed controlled substance, but also that he was aware of the Analogue Act's operation to make what he was selling equally illicit. But what about the second type of knowledge that all justices but Chief Justice Roberts said suffices—that the defendant had knowledge of "the specific analogue" he was dealing with (even though he didn't know its legal status)? What exactly must the jury be able to infer the defendant knew? The answer, said Justice Thomas, is knowledge of "the features" of the substance that qualify it as a controlled substance analogue—features pertaining to (1) chemical structure and (2) effects on the central nervous system that are "substantially similar" to scheduled substances. See id. at 2305 (quoting the definition of a controlled substance analogue in 21 U.S.C. §802(32)(A)). This analysis seems focused on chemists of the sort we met in *Breaking Bad*, right?

7. How does all of this apply to McFadden? The jury instructions at his trial had referred only to the defendant's knowledge of the central nervous system effects of the substance, not to his knowledge of chemical makeup. The government argued that this error was harmless because, given the overwhelming evidence (and a willfull blindness instruction, see Chapter 3), no rational jury could have concluded that McFadden lacked knowledge that he was distributing a controlled substance (the other approach to proving knowledge). Because the Court of Appeals had no had occasion to address the harmless error issue, the Supreme Court remanded the case to that court.

McFadden won the battle in the Supreme Court but lost the war on remand. United States v. McFadden, 823 F.3d 217 (4th Cir. 2016), cert. denied, 137 U.S. 1434 (2017). You might think, as the government argued, that the evidence the defendant knew he was dealing in a controlled substance analogue was quite strong—given McFadden's reference to two known illegal drugs, his invocation of a provision of the Analogue Act itself on his labeling, and his otherwise suspicious behavior (including, the Fourth Circuit noted in its opinion on remand, labels on some packages that said the contents were *not* various Schedule I substances). But the Court of Appeals rejected the government's claim that a correctly instructed jury would have clearly convicted upon this proof, holding "that the evidence was sufficient to permit, but not so overwhelming to compel, the jury to find that McFadden knew that federal law regulated the bath salts as controlled substances." 823 F.3d at 226. On the other hand, the court said, the evidence was overwhelming that McFadden knew the "identity" of the drugs, that is, the chemical features of and central nervous system reaction to his bath salts. The recorded telephone conversations between McFadden and the cooperating video store owner "overwhelmingly establish that McFadden knew the bath salts' chemical structures and physiological effects." The court affirmed McFadden's convictions on the counts relating to those conversations. Id. at 228.

8. The statutory interpretation issues of the CSA (including the amendments thereto, such as the Analogue Act) are interesting enough. But aren't there some lurking constitutional issues as well? McFadden, for instance, argued that the Analogue Act would be constitutionally vague unless it is interpreted to require that the defendant knew the chemical structure of the substance in which he was dealing. Are you convinced by the Court's effort to distinguish between the detailed knowledge it read into the federal firearm-registration statute in Staples v. United States, 511 U.S. 600 (1994) (which we considered in Chapter 3), and its holding in *McFadden* that knowledge of the "controlled" status of analogue substances is sufficient?

9. Defendants have likewise failed to convince the courts that the scheduling of drugs presents a constitutional "notice" or "fair warning" issue. No matter how obscure the drug schedules may be, they are unambiguously and publicly set forth in 21 C.F.R. §1308 et seq. See, e.g., United States v. Hussein, 351 F.3d 9, 14 (1st Cir. 2003) (rejecting a "fair warning" challenge because the essence of such a claim is statutory ambiguity).

The case just cited had a twist, however. Hussein was caught distributing khat, a plant grown in East Africa and the Arabian Peninsula that "naturally contain[s] the chemical stimulant cathinone (a Schedule I controlled substance)." Id. at 11. But "khat"—sometimes referred to as kat or qat—itself is not listed as a controlled substance in DEA schedules, and Hussein testified that he had never heard of cathinone, much less know that it was a controlled substance. The First Circuit affirmed his conviction, finding that the evidence (including clandestine behavior) was sufficient for a jury to infer that the defendant must have thought, or been willfully blind to the fact that, the khat he was dealing in either was or contained a controlled substance. And the DEA schedule listing cathinone provides that in addition to the stimulants listed, "any material . . . which contains any quantity" of the listed stimulants are incorporated into the schedule. See 21 C.F.R. §1308.11(f)(3). Moreover, we would add (and wonder why the government and the court failed to note), the Federal Register notice announcing the listing of cathinone expressly advised that "Cathinone is the major psychoactive component of the plant *Catha edulis* (khat)," 58 Fed. Reg. 4316 (Jan. 14, 1993).

To the extent that you are troubled by how the doctrine has developed on *mens rea* in narcotics cases, can you think of a better approach—one rooted in both the scientific precision of CSA scheduling and the hurly burly of the drug dealing world?

2. FEDERAL DRUG LAW WITHIN U.S. BORDERS

Most drug defendants in federal court are charged with violations of the basic prohibition in 21 U.S.C. §841(a) and with conspiracy in violation of 21 U.S.C. §846. There are many variations, some of which we describe below.

a. *The Crime of Simple Possession*

As we noted in the introduction to this chapter, most federal drug prosecutions involve acts of distribution or circumstances that evince an intent to distribute. The latter usually include manufacturing, importing, or possessing ample amounts of a drug, often along with scales, packaging material, and/or customer lists. The clear focus of the CSA is on reducing the supply of drugs by targeting manufacturers, distributors, dispensers, exporters, and importers. In the Anti-Drug Abuse Act of 1988, however, Congress criminalized simple possession as well (subject to a maximum sentence of one-year imprisonment). See 21 U.S.C. §844 (making it "unlawful for any person knowingly or intentionally to possess a controlled substance"). Criminalization of drug possession is not particularly unusual (and most states prosecute simple possession of narcotics far more frequently than does the federal government).

But both the federal and state governments have in recent decades enacted more novel prohibitions on possession that operate as "fall back" crimes that are easier to prove than crimes involving more complex acts or acts that require proof of intended harm. The most obvious example in federal law is the crime (created in omnibus 1968 anti-crime legislation) of being a felon in possession of a weapon. See 18 U.S.C. §922(g)(1). As we saw in Chapter 2, the Supreme Court held that Congress had power under the Commerce Clause to enact this prohibition. Scarborough v. United States, 431 U.S. 563 (1977). According to Markus Dubber, the "offense of possession—whether of drugs, of guns, or anything else—has emerged as the policing device of choice in the war on crime." Markus Dirk Dubber, Policing Possession: The War on Crime and the End of Criminal Law, 91 J. Crim. L. & Criminology 829, 855 (2001). Targeting possession, he argues, "is in the end a far more formidable weapon in the war on crime: it expands the scope of policing into the home, it results in far harsher penalties and therefore has a far greater incapacitative potential, and it is far less vulnerable to legal challenges." Id. at 856. Crimes of possession are also comparably easy to prove, which may lead investigators and prosecutors to devote substantial resources to uncovering and prosecuting this type of criminal behavior.

In recent years, there have been far more federal simple possession prosecutions than most people realize. Indeed, "[t]he number of federal offenders whose most serious offense was simple drug possession increased nearly 400 percent during the six-year period between fiscal years 2008 (467 defendants) and 2013 (2319 defendants)." U.S. Sent'g Comm'n, Weighing the Charges: Simple Possession of Drugs in the Federal Criminal Justice System 1-2 (2016). But digging into these numbers shows not a growing federal interest in locking up marijuana users, but a collateral effect of southwest border enforcement. Ninety-one percent of the 2,169 marijuana simple possession cases in 2013 (as you can see, almost all possession cases are for marijuana) came from the U.S.-Mexico border and arose out of border enforcement activities. Only 3.6 percent were from military bases (presumably not service personnel, as they would face military law consequences) and 2.8 percent from national parks. Id. at 5. A recent Sentencing Commission report noted:

> The majority of the Non-Border offenders (almost 70 percent) were identified because of a non-drug related event (26.6% because of non-drug related investigation; 23.9% as a result of a traffic stop; and 19.3% at checkpoints—primarily at military bases). Most offenders (97.9%) apprehended at or near the U.S./Mexico border received a prison sentence compared to 26.4 percent of offenders apprehended away from the border.
>
> Perhaps the most important difference between the two groups is the quantity of drugs involved in the offense. Offenders apprehended at or near the U.S./Mexico border were arrested with a substantially greater amount of marijuana than Non-Border offenders—48.5 *pounds* compared to 5.2 *grams*—an amount that does not appear to correspond to the Office of National Drug Control Policy definition of simple possession of drugs. This difference in quantity suggests that the sizable increase in simple possession cases in recent years is the result of marijuana drug trafficking cases in which the offender was sentenced only for a possession offense.

Id. at 10 (emphasis added). Here we get a glimpse of the brand of federal criminal law practiced in Southwest Border districts—a high-volume regime where non-U.S. citizens who entered the country illegally are significantly "undercharged," enticed into quick guilty pleas, given short prison terms, and deported.

b. Prosecuting Traffickers in Listed Chemicals

Particularly since their attention has turned to the domestic manufacture of methamphetamine ("meth"), Congress and federal enforcers have increasingly targeted those who traffic in precursor chemicals. Again, we see the creep of criminal liability in an area that Congress gives sustained attention. One challenge, however, has been that pseudoephedrine, a key ingredient in meth, is regularly sold in drug and convenience stores in legal non-prescription cold and allergy medicine. As we discussed in Chapter 8, a store clerk aware that a purchase is actually for a meth lab might well be guilty of aiding and abetting drug distribution or conspiring to do so. But what if he's not sure, or the government can't prove that he is? Section 841(c) makes it illegal for any person to knowingly or intentionally possess or distribute "a listed chemical knowing, or having reasonable cause to believe, that the listed chemical will be used to manufacture a controlled substance." What sort of *mens rea* need the government show here?

Some federal appeals courts have insisted that "reasonable cause to believe" is solely a subjective inquiry into the defendant's actual mental state, which effectively removes that phrase from the statute since that inquiry would appear to be the same as "knowingly," the statute's other *mens rea* term. See, e.g., United States v. Munguia, 704 F.3d 596 (9th Cir. 2012); United States v. Truong, 425 F.3d 1282, 1289 (10th Cir. 2005) (holding that government must prove actual knowledge "or something close to it"). Others apply an objective or "reasonable person" test, see, e.g., United States v. Galvan, 407 F.3d 954 (8th Cir. 2005); United States v. Prather, 205 F.3d 1265, 1270 (11th Cir. 2000), while a third set of circuit courts have adopted some hybrid of the two standards, see United States v. Honeycutt, 816 F.3d 362 (6th Cir. 2016) (upholding conviction and stating that giving an instruction on "deliberate indifference" was at most harmless error). See generally Raphael S. Nemes, Note, Shake and Bake: The Meth Threat and the Need to Rethink 21 U.S.C. §841(c)(2), 88 Wash. U. L. Rev. 993, 1000-01 (2011); United States v. Khattab, 536 F.3d 765, 769 (7th Cir. 2008) (noting the circuit split). How can we square our desire to protect store clerks with our interest in attacking meth production? What role, if any, should "conscious avoidance" theories play where a statute explicitly targets just that? And what happens when a listed chemical is not in its pure form? See United States v. Ching Tang Lo, 447 F.3d 1212 (9th Cir. 2006) (upholding conviction where defendant sold ma huang, a naturally occurring plant also known as "ephedra" from which one can extract ephedrine, which is used to make meth).

c. *Marijuana Prosecutions in Changing Times*

We saw above that federal criminal narcotics law has been extended — for instance, to reach analogues and precursors. At the same time, the politics around one core aspect of the CSA have lately become quite fraught. The federal law on marijuana production and distribution is straightforward. Marijuana is a Schedule I controlled substance, and its distribution (including aiding or abetting its distribution — see Section A of Chapter 8) is a felony. In President Obama's last year in office, Chuck Rosenberg, the Acting Director of the DEA (which, as you know, is part of the Justice Department) denied a petition to initiate proceedings to reschedule marijuana. The FDA had recommended this denial pending more research and data from states that have enacted medical marijuana laws. See 81 Fed. Reg. 53687 (Aug. 12, 2016).

As noted above, the feds rarely prosecute marijuana possession away from the Border. But marijuana *production and distribution* cases are regularly brought. See U.S. Sent'g Comm'n, 2016 Sourcebook, *supra*, at tbl. 33 (96.2 percent of marijuana convictions were for trafficking or importing). Moreover, the CSA does more than criminalize the marijuana market. It also has a provision that DOJ declared in 1996 permits revocation of a physician's DEA license if he prescribes marijuana; the physician needs the DEA license, of course, because all prescription medicines are on some DEA schedule other than Schedule I. See 21 U.S.C. §823(f); Conant v. Walters, 309 F.3d 629 (9th Cir. 2002). The Department of Justice also takes the position that the United States, as a party to the Single Convention on Narcotic Drugs (1961), must put marijuana on Schedule I or Schedule II. In a case brought by legalization proponents in the 1970s, the D.C. Circuit agreed with the Department. See NORML v. DEA, 559 F.2d 735, 751 (D.C. Cir. 1977).

Yet federal marijuana law is increasingly out of step with state laws. As of August 1, 2017, use of marijuana (whether for recreational or medicinal purposes) has been legalized in 7 states and the District of Columbia, and an additional 22 states have laws that legalize medical marijuana. Marijuana State Laws Summary Chart: 29 Legal Medical Marijuana States and D.C., ProCon.org (June 26, 2017); State Marijuana Laws in 2018 Map, Governing (Mar. 23, 2017). We saw in Gonzales v. Raich, 545 U.S. 1 (2005), in Chapter 2, and United States v. Oakland Cannabis Buyers' Cooperative, 532 U.S. 483 (2001), in Chapter 3, that the result of conflicting state and federal laws is, to put it mildly, friction between state and federal authorities—with no further recourse for the individuals caught in the middle. States that have legalized medical marijuana get around the DEA license issue by providing in their "compassionate care" statutes that a patient must have a written "recommendation" (not a "prescription") in order to obtain marijuana. See Conant v. Walters, 309 F.3d 629 (9th Cir. 2002) (upholding an injunction against federal officials seeking to revoke DEA license of doctors who "recommend" medical marijuana).

Given the growing acceptance of both recreational and medical marijuana, we are likely not in a period of equilibrium; instead we are in the midst of an especially busy period of "changing boundaries" among state and federal law enforcement agencies and actors—a concept we discussed at length in Chapter 1. A similar dynamic occurred during Prohibition, when U.S. Attorneys in "wet" states like New York found themselves caught between national enforcement priorities and local sentiments. See Daniel Richman, Federal Sentencing in 2007: The Supreme Court Holds—The Center Doesn't, 117 Yale L.J. 1374, 1398-99 (2008) (recounting conflict between the U.S. Attorney for the Southern District of New York and the Assistant Attorney General in charge of Prohibition over a supply-side strategy targeting night-club patrons). We know how the Prohibition conflict ended, of course. Will the federal government "back down" on marijuana legalization? Will there be efforts to legalize marijuana by constitutional amendment?

There is no constitutional problem with the states and the federal government staking out different positions on marijuana. The United States and each of the states are sovereign jurisdictions, and, as we noted in Chapter 2, the Constitution contemplates that each jurisdiction will enact its own criminal laws. The Supremacy Clause does not require that the states criminalize or legalize a substance or activity just because the federal government does so. But there are some legal complications when a substance or activity is banned by the federal government, but permitted under state law (or vice versa). Most of you are going to be lawyers someday. As such, you will have another layer of "law" to pay attention to—the Rules of Professional Conduct in the jurisdictions in which you practice. Consider the following:

PROVIDING LEGAL SERVICES TO CLIENTS SEEKING LICENSES UNDER THE CONNECTICUT MEDICAL MARIJUANA LAW
Professional Ethics Committee, Connecticut Bar Association
Informal Opinion 2013-02

An Act Concerning the Palliative Use of Marijuana, Public Act 12-55, effective Oct. 1, 2012, provides for the registration of marijuana users and the licensing of growers and dispensers of marijuana to be used to alleviate symptoms of a debilitating medical condition. We have been asked whether a lawyer may advise clients about the requirements of the Act and assist clients and represent them before state agencies in establishing and licensing businesses permitted under the Act.

Federal law, particularly the Controlled Substances Act, prohibits the growing, distribution and dispensing of marijuana and potentially subjects violators to criminal and civil penalties. The U.S. Department of Justice, as recently as June, 2011, has clearly stated that state laws are not a defense to civil or criminal enforcement of federal law prohibiting the cultivation, sale or distribution of marijuana, including the Controlled Substances Act. (D.O.J. Memorandum, June 29, 2011, p. 2).

Public Act 12-55 creates a broad licensing and registration structure to be implemented by regulations issued by the Connecticut Department of Consumer Protection. . . . Patients, caregiver groups, health professionals and persons interested in business activities can be expected to seek legal advice concerning the requirements of the Act, the Department of Consumer Protection's rule- making process, and the requirements of state and federal law. Lawyers providing advice in these circumstances will be performing in their traditional role as counselors. Lawyers who advise clients and assist them in the rule-making and regulatory process also act in the classic mode envisioned by professional standards.

At some point, perhaps, but not necessarily after the planning and licensing are complete, some clients may expect their lawyers to assist them by providing advice and services in aid of functioning marijuana enterprises that may violate federal law. It is at this point that a lawyer must consider Rule of Professional Conduct 1.2(d):

> A lawyer shall not counsel a client to engage, or assist a client, in conduct that the lawyers knows is criminal or fraudulent, but a lawyer may discuss the legal consequences of any proposed course of conduct with a client and may counsel a client to make a good faith effort to determine the validity, scope, meaning or application of the law.

The Comment to Rule 1.2(d) provides that once a lawyer discovers that client conduct the lawyer considered legally proper is criminal or fraudulent, the lawyer must end his or her assistance . . . [and] "[t]here is a critical distinction between presenting an analysis of legal aspects of questionable conduct and recommending the means by which a crime or fraud might be committed."

It is not our role to predict the path that the law may take in resolving the conflict between the federal Controlled Substances Act and state laws regulating the medical use of marijuana. . . . While Connecticut law may allow certain behavior, that same behavior currently constitutes a federal crime. . . . At a minimum, a lawyer advising a client on Public Act 12-55 must inform the client of the conflict between the state and federal statutes, and that the conflict exists regardless of whether federal authorities in Connecticut are or are not actively enforcing the federal statutes.

It is our opinion that lawyers may advise clients of the requirements of the Connecticut Palliative Use of Marijuana Act. Lawyers may not assist clients in conduct that is in violation of federal criminal law. Lawyers should carefully assess where the line is between those functions and not cross it.

NOTES AND QUESTIONS

1. "Find the line and don't cross it." The ethics opinion appears to distinguish between helping would-be marijuana growers or distributors negotiate the licensing process, on the one hand, and helping those same clients once their marijuana enterprises are "functioning," on the other. Recall the

broad expanse of federal accomplice and conspiracy liability that we studied in Chapter 8. Does that distinction make sense? What's a lawyer to do?

2. Are you shedding tears for conflicted lawyers? What about for financial institutions? Suppose that a marijuana grower in full compliance with state law would like to set up an account and conduct the same sorts of business as any other large-scale agricultural enterprise. He is transparent about his operations, and the bank he contacts is eager to transact business. He and the bank are relatively (but not absolutely) confident that he won't be prosecuted federally. But setting up an account could easily constitute money laundering, right? And as we'll see in Chapter 11, a bank executive who approved loans could subject the bank itself to a felony conviction with enormous collateral consequences. The Obama Administration offered some safe harbors to financial institutions. Administrations change, though. See Sophie Quinton, Why Marijuana Businesses Still Can't Get Bank Accounts, Stateline (Pew Charitable Trusts) (Mar. 22, 2016).

———————————————

It does not appear that the federal government will change the legal status of marijuana any time soon, through rescheduling or through legislation. But that doesn't mean that the feds are sitting passively by as more and more states legalize at least medicinal marijuana. In 2013, Deputy Attorney General James Code issued a Memorandum (https://www.justice.gov/iso/opa/resources/3052013829132756857467.pdf) that indicated that states could legalize even recreational marijuana without fear of federal intrusion. In January 2018, Attorney General Jeff Sessions rescinded that Memorandum (https://www.justice.gov/opa/press-release/file/1022196/download). Stay tuned.

Congress probably could, through exercise of its spending and taxing power, impose conditions on marijuana manufacturing and sale that would make it very difficult or expensive for legal state operations to conduct business. But it has not done so. To the contrary, beginning in December 2014 Congress has used legislative appropriations spending power to *remove* the threat that the feds will prosecute medical marijuana businesses or customers who are in compliance with state law. The next case explores some of the fascinating issues raised by Congress's move.

United States v. Kleinman
880 F.3d 1020 (9th Cir. 2018)

M. SMITH, Circuit Judge:
Noah Kleinman appeals his jury conviction and 211 month sentence for conspiracy to distribute and possess marijuana, distribution of

marijuana, maintaining a drug-involved premises, and conspiracy to commit money laundering. His offenses arose out of purported medical marijuana collective storefronts that he operated with his co-defendants in California, which he alleges complied with state law. On appeal, Kleinman argues that (1) a congressional appropriations rider enjoining use of United States Department of Justice (DOJ) funds in certain medical marijuana cases prohibits continued prosecution of his case. . . . For the reasons described herein, we AFFIRM Kleinman's conviction and sentence.

Appeal Argument

FACTS AND PRIOR PROCEEDINGS

Kleinman, along with defendant Paul Montoya and others, began operating purported medical marijuana collectives in California around 2006. In 2007 or 2008 they opened their fourth store, NoHo Caregivers (NoHo), which the government alleged was the hub of a large conspiracy to distribute marijuana. At trial, witnesses testified that Kleinman and his associates sold 90% of their marijuana outside of their storefronts, used encrypted phones and burner phones to communicate, drove rented cars to escape detection, hid drugs and money in "stash apartments" rented for that purpose, and shipped marijuana hidden in hollowed-out computer towers to customers in New York and Philadelphia.

In 2010, pursuant to a Los Angeles Police Department (LAPD) investigation of medical marijuana collectives, two undercover officers entered Kleinman's dispensary Medco Organics (Medco) and purchased marijuana. The LAPD then obtained a search warrant and seized evidence, and California initiated criminal proceedings against Kleinman. He moved to dismiss the case, arguing that he had complete immunity from prosecution pursuant to California medical marijuana laws. The state did not file an objection. During a preliminary hearing on the dismissal motion, the deputy district attorney stated that he did not see a basis on which to deny Kleinman's motion, and the state court dismissed the charges. After the case was dismissed, the United States Drug Enforcement Administration (DEA) seized the evidence in the LAPD's custody.

In 2011, a federal grand jury indicted Kleinman, Montoya, and five others for conspiracy to distribute and possess marijuana, distribution of marijuana, maintaining a drug-involved premises, and conspiracy to commit money laundering. . . .

At a pretrial hearing, the district court concluded that any references to medical marijuana would be irrelevant at trial because state law compliance is not a defense to federal charges. . . .

The jury convicted Kleinman on all counts and found that the amount of marijuana involved in the offenses exceeded 1,000 kilograms. The district court . . . sentenced Kleinman to 211 months. Shortly after

Kleinman's convictions and sentence, on December 16, 2014, Congress enacted an appropriations rider that prohibits the DOJ from expending funds to prevent states from implementing their laws authorizing the use, distribution, possession, and cultivation of medical marijuana. Consolidated and Further Continuing Appropriations Act, 2015, Pub. L. No. 113–235, §538, 128 Stat. 2130, 2217 (2014).

ANALYSIS

I.   Kleinman is not entitled to remand for an evidentiary hearing on his state law compliance.

In 1996, California voters approved the Compassionate Use Act (CUA), which decriminalized possession and cultivation of marijuana for medical use. In 2003, the California legislature enacted the Medical Marijuana Program (MMP), permitting qualified patients to form collectives for the cultivation and distribution of medical marijuana. Federal law, however, still prohibits the use or sale of marijuana, even if distributed and possessed pursuant to state-approved medical marijuana programs. See United States v. McIntosh, 833 F.3d 1163, 1179 n.5 (9th Cir. 2016) ("Anyone in any state who possesses, distributes, or manufactures marijuana for medical or recreational purposes (or attempts or conspires to do so) is committing a federal crime.").

Since December 16, 2014, congressional appropriations riders have prohibited the use of any DOJ funds that prevent states with medical marijuana programs (including California) from implementing their state medical marijuana laws. . . . [The most recent rider] will remain in effect until at least September 30, 2017. See Consolidated Appropriations Act, 2017, 131 Stat. at 135. In this opinion we refer to the riders collectively as §542.

In *McIntosh* we determined that, pursuant to §542, federal criminal defendants who were indicted in marijuana cases had standing to file interlocutory appeals seeking to enjoin DOJ expenditure of funds used to prosecute their cases. 833 F.3d at 1172-74. We held that "§542 prohibits DOJ from spending funds from relevant appropriations acts for the prosecution of individuals who engaged in conduct permitted by the State Medical Marijuana Laws and who fully complied with such laws." Id. at 1177. However, §542 does not prohibit prosecuting individuals for conduct that is *not* fully compliant with state medical marijuana laws. Id. at 1178. We remanded, holding that the DOJ could only continue the prosecutions if the defendants were given "evidentiary hearings to determine whether their conduct was completely authorized by state law, by which we mean that they strictly complied with all relevant conditions imposed by state law on . . . medical marijuana." Id. at 1179. Kleinman asks us to remand for an evidentiary hearing as we did in *McIntosh*. We decline to do so. . . .

We make two holdings that support our conclusion that a *McIntosh* hearing is not necessary in this case. First, §542 only prohibits the expenditure of DOJ funds in connection with a *specific charge* involving conduct that is fully compliant with state laws regarding medical marijuana. Thus, the applicability of §542 focuses on the conduct forming the basis of a particular charge, which requires a count-by-count analysis to determine which charges, if any, are restricted by §542. The prosecution cannot use a prosecutable charge (for conduct that violates state medical marijuana law) to bootstrap other charges that rely solely upon conduct that would fully comply with state law. Otherwise, the DOJ could sweep into its prosecution other discrete acts involving medical marijuana that fully complied with state law. That would contradict the plain meaning of §542, which prevents the DOJ from spending funds in a manner that would prevent the listed states "from implementing their own laws that authorize . . . medical marijuana." Consolidated Appropriations Act, 2016, 129 Stat. at 2332-33.

Second, §542 does not require a court to vacate convictions that were obtained before the rider took effect. In other words, when a defendant's conviction was entered before §542 became law, a determination that the charged conduct was wholly compliant with state law would *not* vacate that conviction. It would only mean that the DOJ's continued expenditure of funds pertaining to that particular state-law-compliant conviction *after* §542 took effect was unlawful. That is because . . . §542 did not change any substantive law; it merely placed a temporary hold on the expenditure of money for a certain purpose. When §542 took effect, the DOJ was obligated to stop spending funds in connection with any charges involving conduct that fully complied with state law, but that temporary spending freeze does not spoil the fruits of prosecutorial expenditures made before §542 took effect. Instead, as it pertains to this case, because §542 became law after Kleinman's conviction and sentence, but before this appeal, §542 (if it applies at all) might operate to bar the DOJ from continuing to defend this prosecution on appeal insofar as it relates to those counts that may be determined to involve only conduct that wholly complies with California medical marijuana law.

With these two principles in mind, we conclude that a *McIntosh* hearing is not necessary in this case. . . . [Section] 542 does not apply to at least two of the charges against Kleinman because the conduct alleged therein does not fully comply with state law: conspiracy to distribute marijuana (Count 1), and conspiracy to commit money laundering (Count 6). Both counts involved marijuana sales to out-of-state customers in violation of California law.

The CUA and the MMP make clear that Kleinman has no state-law defense for his sales of approximately 85 kilograms of marijuana to out-of-state customers. The stated purpose of the CUA is "[t]o ensure that seriously ill *Californians* have the right to obtain and use marijuana for medical purposes." The MMP provides immunity from prosecution for possession and distribution of marijuana to qualified patients and their primary care-givers "who associate *within the State of California* in order collectively or cooperatively to cultivate cannabis for medical purposes." The MMP further provides that a person seeking a medical marijuana identification card must show "proof of his or her residency *within the county.*" The California Attorney General's guidelines for implementing the CUA and MMP (AG Guidelines) provide that medical marijuana collectives must only sell to those within the collective, and specifically lists as "indicia of unlawful operation" sales to non-members and out-of-state distribution. Cal. Att'y Gen. Edmund G. Brown, Jr., Guidelines for the Security and Non-Diversion of Marijuana Grown for Medical Use, Cal. Dep't of Justice, at 8-11 (August 2008).

Counts 1 and 6 allege overt acts that violate the CUA and MMP; i.e., sales to out-of-state customers. Additionally, Kleinman conceded that the government presented evidence that his Philadelphia and New York customers never joined his collective, and he never argued that these customers and out-of-state sales were part of his purported medical mar-ijuana collectives. . . . Kleinman now seeks to introduce evidence that his in-state transactions complied with California law. . . .

There may be some legitimate question [] as to whether Counts 2 through 5 involved conduct that strictly complied with California law. But there is no need to remand for a *McIntosh* hearing on those charges because even a favorable determination regarding state law compliance on Counts 2 through 5 would mean only that the DOJ was disabled from defending those specific charges on appeal. However, Kleinman did not make any appellate arguments that were tied to those specific charges; he made only global attacks on his convictions and sentence. Because he made no substantive arguments pertaining to Counts 2 through 5 that are not resolved by our rulings as to Counts 1 and 6, our rulings on those counts are dispositive of all charges. Counts 1 and 6 were definitively pros-ecutable; thus, §542 does not preclude the DOJ from defending against any of Kleinman's arguments on appeal, and we need not remand for a *McIntosh* hearing on Counts 2 through 5. . . .

As we explain below, Kleinman does not win relief on any of his other arguments [pertaining to evidentiary and other alleged errors at trial], so it is unnecessary for us to remand for a *McIntosh* hearing on Counts 2 through 5 because we would affirm those convictions regardless of whether §542 applies to them. . . .

CONCLUSION

We conclude that the district court erred by instructing the jury that "[t]here is no such thing as valid jury nullification," and that it "would violate

[its] oath and the law if [it] willfully brought a verdict contrary to the law given to [it] in this case." However, because there is no right to jury nullification, the error was harmless. We find that Kleinman's remaining challenges on appeal are without merit, and AFFIRM his conviction and sentence.

NOTES AND QUESTIONS

1. The rider has been included in every subsequent law appropriating funds for DOJ. The most recent of these is on p. 240 of the Consolidated Appropriations Act of March 23, 2018.

2. *Kleinman* followed the decision of a previous panel in United States v. McIntosh, 833 F.3d 1163 (9th Cir. 2016). *McIntosh* consolidated interlocutory appeals by a total of ten defendants in three unrelated prosecutions that were initiated before the first appropriations rider in 2014, but that had not yet gone to trial or judgment. One of the preliminary issues in *McIntosh* was whether the Court of Appeals even had jurisdiction to consider these appeals, which sought review of district courts' pretrial denials of defendants' motions to enjoin their prosecutions pursuant to the appropriations rider. *McIntosh* held that there was jurisdiction under 28 U.S.C. §1292(a)(1). This holding surprised many observers at the time. As Judge Diarmuid F. O'Scannlain noted in *McIntosh*, "Federal courts traditionally have refused, except in rare instances, to enjoin federal criminal prosecutions." Id. at 1172. So why did the court accept the defendants' appeals? The court explained that "[e]ven if Appellants cannot obtain injunctions of their prosecutions themselves, they can seek—and have sought—to enjoin DOJ from spending funds from the relevant appropriations acts on such prosecutions." Id. (emphasis in original).

3. The first appropriations rider enacted by Congress, which was at issue in *McIntosh*, provided:

> None of the funds made available in this Act to the Department of Justice may be used, with respect to the States of Alabama, Alaska, Arizona, California, Colorado, Connecticut, Delaware, District of Columbia, Florida, Hawaii, Illinois, Iowa, Kentucky, Maine, Maryland, Massachusetts, Michigan, Minnesota, Mississippi, Missouri, Montana, Nevada, New Hampshire, New Jersey, New Mexico, Oregon, Rhode Island, South Carolina, Tennessee, Utah, Vermont, Washington, and Wisconsin, to prevent such States from implementing their own State laws that authorize the use, distribution, possession, or cultivation of medical marijuana.

Consolidated and Further Continuing Appropriations Act, 2015, Pub. L. No. 113-235, §538, 128 Stat. 2130, 2217 (2014). Putting limitations on the amounts, the duration, and the objects of federal spending is the essence of Congress's "Power of the Purse." The Appropriations Clause of the U.S. Constitution provides "No Money shall be drawn from the Treasury, but in Consequence of Appropriations made by Law." U.S. Const. art. I, §9, cl. 7. Judge O'Scannlain explained its significance: "The Appropriations Clause plays a critical role in the Constitution's separation of powers among the three branches of government and the checks and balances between them," 833 F.3d at 1176. The federal courts have not played a large role in enforcing the command of the Appropriations Clause, however, because in many situations no one has constitutional "standing" (most significantly, a direct injury beyond that suffered by taxpayers generally) to complain of *ultra vires* government spending. See generally, Kate Stith, Congress' Power of the Purse, 97 Yale L.J. 595 (1988). In *McIntosh*, however, the Ninth Circuit found that the defendants did have Article III standing because the use of funds to prosecute them was clearly detrimental to them and threatened significant, cognizable injury (conviction and imprisonment). All of this makes sense.

The next steps in the court's reasoning are harder to follow. The rider disabled DOJ from using appropriated funds "to prevent such States from implementing their" medical marijuana laws. *McIntosh* found that a critical aspect of a state "implementing" its medical marijuana regime was "giving practical effect to its law providing for non-prosecution of individuals who engage in the permitted conduct." 833 F.3d at 1176-77. It is true that the possibility of federal prosecution might *interfere* with the states' programs to make medical marijuana available, but the verb used in the rider is "prevent," which seems to be a higher standard. After all, some states were able to implement medical marijuana laws prior to December 2014, despite the ability of DOJ to enforce federal marijuana prohibitions.

In any event, having decided that any prosecution of individuals whose medical marijuana activities accord with state law would "prevent" the state program from being implemented, the court then easily reached its conclusion, quoted above: the defendants had standing not to directly enjoin their prosecutions, but to make those prosecutions impossible as a practical matter for as long as the appropriations rider (and subsequent riders) remained in effect—because prosecution requires using funds appropriated for DOJ personnel and other expenses. In a portion of the opinion we did not excerpt, *McIntosh* declined to adopt the appellants' more expansive interpretation of the appropriations rider to prohibit DOJ from prosecuting any person or entity *licensed* under state law to engage in the marijuana business, even if they had "failed to comply fully with state law" (or there could be "reasonable debate" as to whether they had complied). Id. at 1177. Thus, even with the appropriations riders, *McIntosh* apparently permits the feds to prosecute anyone in the medical marijuana business who at some point is out of full compliance with state law. See id. at 1178 ("Congress could easily have drafted §542 to prohibit interference with laws that address [or regulate] medical marijuana" but chose to impose a narrower prohibition.).

4. But how can the feds prosecute even those individuals or entities out of compliance with state medical marijuana laws? DOJ can't prosecute a case without first investigating it, and the DEA is part of DOJ. It would appear to be in violation of the appropriations riders (as interpreted in *McIntosh*) if any DEA agent looked askance for two seconds at someone who was, in fact, in compliance with state law. *McIntosh* did not address the "investigation" issue, which was arguably irrelevant in *McIntosh* itself since all the defendants had already been indicted. The court simply held that "[i]f DOJ wishes to continue these prosecutions, Appellants are entitled to evidentiary hearings to determine whether their conduct was completely authorized by state law." Id. at 1179.

Whether and how the government can expend funds investigating marijuana trafficking in states that have medical marijuana laws may be a big issue going forward. *McIntosh* tells us that in a case where the investigation and indictment preceded enactment of the appropriations rider, there must be a hearing before the actual prosecution can go forward (and, presumably, before further investigation can be undertaken). But there are only a handful of cases like *McIntosh, Kleinman,* and the case we consider in Note 10 below—all of which "straddle" the date that the appropriations riders first took effect. Surely, we posit, there can be no requirement of a hearing *before any investigation* takes place. For one thing, there is not yet a "case" and hence no court before which potential defendants may argue they are in compliance with state law. Should the government at least be required to present evidence amounting to probable cause to the grand jury (or present such evidence in an ex parte hearing before a federal Magistrate Judge) that the putative defendant acted in violation of state law, before any indictment against a defendant may be filed? Should this be part of the probable cause showing to get an arrest warrant? We think not. The appropriations rider did not change the substantive federal law, which makes all dealing in marijuana a felony. The issue in a *McIntosh* hearing—which presumably will be held if requested by the defendant in all future marijuana cases in medical marijuana states (so long as the riders remain in effect)—is not relevant to the work of a warrant-issuing judge, the grand jury, or the petit jury. It is instead a duty thrust upon the federal courts (according to *McIntosh*) to ensure compliance with the Appropriations Clause of the Constitution.

5. Do you wonder what happened on remand in *McIntosh?* Westlaw reports a written opinion in only one of the consolidated cases, that of the lead defendant. The district court ruled that the defendant bore the burden of proving to a preponderance of the evidence "that he has strictly complied with California's medical marijuana laws" and that McIntosh failed to meet that burden. See United States v. McIntosh, 2017 WL 2695319 (N.D. Cal. March 20, 2017). One might query whether it was proper for the government to even prepare for McIntosh's *McIntosh* hearing, for if the judge had ruled for the defendant, the government's preparation and argument

would have been, in retrospect, in violation of the appropriations rider. This is essentially the issue in *Kleinman*, not on remand but on direct appeal.

6. Kleinman didn't get a *McIntosh* hearing, but his trial, conviction, and sentence had all been completed by December 8, 2014, which was eight days before Congress enacted the first appropriations rider. Even assuming that some of the federal funds in the continuing appropriations act became available to DOJ on the very day the bill became law (December 16, 2014), the successful prosecution of Kleinman didn't use any of those funds. So what was Kleinman's claim? Was he claiming that the rider applies retroactively? No, he was not (though the government's briefs on appeal repeatedly said that was his claim). The rider is clearly not retroactive to previously spent funds, and such retroactive conditioning of already-used funds is in any event not within Congress's appropriations power (a point the government's brief somehow never made). Rather, as suggested in the last sentence of the previous Note, one form of relief Kleinman sought was to have the government barred from preparing a brief in response to his appeal of his convictions (on many grounds) or even filing an appearance. See Appellant's Supplemental Brief in Response to Government's Supplemental Answering Brief, United States v. Kleinman, 859 F.2d 825 (9th Cir. Mar. 21, 2017) ("By spending federal funds to litigate . . . Kleinman's direct appeal . . . DOJ is spending money in violation of §542.").* The court essentially agreed with Kleinman, stating that "§542 (if it applies at all) might operate to bar the DOJ from continuing to defend this prosecution on appeal insofar as it relates to those counts that may be determined to involve only conduct that wholly complies with California medical marijuana law." 859 F.3d at 833.

7. So far Kleinman is doing pretty well. But he still didn't get the *McIntosh* hearing he sought. According to *Kleinman*, a hearing is not necessarily needed in cases where the trial record makes abundantly clear that the defendant was violating state law as to at least some counts of conviction—here, Counts 1 and 6. And it is true that *McIntosh* itself didn't address whether a hearing is needed in such cases, since there had been no trials yet—and thus no trial record—in any of those cases. It may strike you as reasonable not to have a "re-do" in federal district court where the trial record is clear and the matter can be decided by the court of appeals. But Kleinman was not asking for a "re-do." Recall the trial court's pretrial order prohibiting the defense from making "any references [at trial] to medical

---

* [Editors' Note: Any federal courts scholars among you? Even if §542 did prevent DOJ from doing anything in response to Kleinman's appeal, would that necessarily mean that Kleinman would prevail on appeal or that the judgment against him would have to be vacated? The defendant so argued, see id. at *9, but that doesn't seem right to us. Not responding to an appellate claim does not result in a default judgment against the nonresponder. And federal appellate judges (or most of them) are quite capable of deciding the merits of a claim without any help from the other party in the case.]

marijuana . . . because state law compliance is not a defense to federal charges." 859 F.3d at 831. *Kleinman* held not that the state compliance issue (the only issue in a *McIntosh* hearing) was res judicata, but simply that it would be a waste of time to remand for a hearing because the defendant's massive out-of-state sales (totaling 85 kilograms) clearly violated state law. Id. at 833.

8. Kleinman didn't get a *McIntosh* hearing as to Counts 2-5 either, however, even though the court conceded that "[t]here may be some legitimate question [] as to whether Counts 2 through 5 involved conduct that strictly complied with California law." Id. at 834. The court explained that there was no need for a *McIntosh* remand because the only remedy for the defendant who prevails at the hearing would be "that the DOJ was disabled from defending those specific charges on appeal." Id. But, the court noted, Kleinman had made no appellate claims applicable to those counts alone; all of his arguments regarding alleged trial error applied to all counts. The court then said: "[T]hus, §542 does not preclude the DOJ from defending against any of Kleinman's arguments on appeal, and we need not remand for a *McIntosh* hearing on Counts 2-5." Id. Does that last statement imply, or at least suggest, that if, in a different case, the government were disabled (due to §542) from responding to some defense claims on appeal, the defendant would necessarily prevail on those claims? We took issue with this idea in our footnote in Note 6 above.

9. There are at least two issues we haven't yet explored. First, what about the Bureau of Prisons (BOP) continuing to expend funds to incarcerate the defendant? In a footnote not included in the excerpt you read, the court employed the same logic it used to okay the government's participation in the appeal:

> As we have explained, at least two of Kleinman's convictions fall outside the scope of §542 because they involved conduct that violates California law. Those two convictions (Counts 1 and 6) carried the longest terms of imprisonment (211 months) and all terms for each count were sentenced to run concurrently. Thus, even if the DOJ could not separately continue to expend funds to incarcerate Kleinman on the remaining counts because of §542, Kleinman's custodial status would not be changed because §542 does not bar his continued incarceration for his conspiracy convictions.

Id. at 835 n.2.

One might also think that the court's failure to resolve (or to remand for a *McIntosh* hearing to resolve) the state compliance issue with respect to Counts 2-5 might at least require a remand for re-sentencing. As you will learn in Section B of this chapter, sentencing in drug cases is based largely on the total quantity of the relevant drug(s) in which the defendant was dealing. Thus the total quantity of drugs before the judge who sentenced

Kleinman included the amounts (we are not told what those were) the jury found when it convicted on Counts 2-5, as well as the 85 kilograms of marijuana that the defendant shipped out of state (Counts 1 and 6). But, as the quote above indicates, the court reasoned that the defendant's sentence would be the same whether or not the Counts 2-5 convictions were considered. Kleinman received a sentence of 211 months each on Counts 1 and 6. This was also his total sentence, since the sentence on each count was apparently imposed separately in this case, and all sentences were concurrent.

10. *Kleinman*'s greatest significance is its holding that there need not be a *McIntosh* hearing where the record is clear that the defendant's activities on the counts of conviction violated the state's medical marijuana laws, and hence, even without a hearing, a court can determine that the government was permitted to investigate, prosecute, and incarcerate the defendant. There are likely thousands of people incarcerated in federal prison who were convicted of trafficking in marijuana in medical marijuana states. See Bureau of Justice Statistics, Drug Offenders in Federal Prison: Estimates of Characteristics Based on Linked Data 2 tbl.2 (Oct. 2015) (reporting that the nationwide total of federal prison inmates convicted of marijuana trafficking in 2012 was 11,533). Of course, as to most of these individuals, the conviction was obtained and affirmed on appeal (if there was an appeal) long before Congress began enacting appropriation riders regarding state medical marijuana laws. But all of these offenders have the ability to file a collateral attack under 28 U.S.C. §2255 alleging that the government is violating the appropriations riders through its continued spending on their incarceration. See, e.g., Davies v. Benov, 856 F.3d 1243 (9th Cir. 2017) (affirming denial of an incarcerated defendant's federal habeas petition seeking release from prison under §542, due to petitioner's waiver of right to appeal and collateral review when he pleaded guilty). *Kleinman* foretells that where the record is abundantly clear that the petitioner was operating outside the strictures of his state's medical marijuana laws (and the petition is not denied for other reasons, as in *Davies*), judicial and other resources will not be spent on an unnecessary collateral hearings.

11. In another case, the defendant, Lance Gloor, was indicted in the Eastern District of Washington in November 2013 on charges of conspiracy to distribute large amounts of marijuana and conspiracy to commit money laundering. After much pre-trial delay, he moved in 2015 to dismiss the indictment (but did not seek to stay his case) on the ground that prosecution would violate the 2014 appropriations rider. The district court denied the motion, and the jury convicted the defendant on the marijuana charges. The Ninth Circuit recently affirmed in an unpublished opinion, 725 Fed. Appx. 493 (9th Cir. 2018). Although Gloor's trial took place after Congress began enacting appropriations riders pertaining to medical marijuana, at the time of the activities charged in the indictment and proved at trial, medical marijuana was not yet legal in Washington. Rather, state law simply

provided an *affirmative defense in a state criminal prosecution* for caregivers and patients who complied with certain conditions including the equivalent of a medical marijuana prescription and registration with the state. See Former Wash. Rev. Code §69.51A.040(2)-(3) (1999). It was not until 2012 that Washington legalized recreational marijuana in the amount of less than one ounce and not until 2015 that it legalized medical marijuana in greater quantities. See Brief of United States, *supra*, at *10-*17. Do you think that the Ninth Circuit will remand the case for a *McIntosh* hearing? Should it?

12. Even if you consider §542 fully within Congress's appropriations authority, the provision is still an extraordinary curtailment of prosecutorial discretion. What should we make of it? It seems like a pragmatic legislative compromise (they do happen) that licenses some state experimentation while avoiding the political (and symbolic) consequences of changing substantive federal criminal law. Should we celebrate or regret the availability of this low visibility nod to federalism? Ought we worry that it reduces pressure on Congress to tailor substantive law to current norms? Can you imagine similar limitations being placed on federal enforcement outside the drug area? What might such limitations look like, and to what extent would the proliferation of such provisions change the Executive-Congress dynamic that we've seen so far?

3. INTERNATIONAL NARCOTICS TRAFFICKING

The "war on drugs" has a significant overseas component. With the United States being by far the world's largest consumer of both cocaine and heroin but producing little of either drug domestically, most crimes involving these drugs originate overseas. The government's efforts in the international arena have included a wide variety of techniques: from multilateral treaties such as the 1988 United Nations Convention Against Illicit Traffic in Narcotic Drugs and Psychotropic Substances, to bilateral agreements with Colombia, Afghanistan, and other major producers. The latter agreements provide assistance for crop eradication, crop substitution, and criminal justice reforms. In addition, the United States has focused on interdiction to disrupt trafficking routes and to raise the costs of business for drug trafficking organizations. See Bureau for Int'l Narcotics & Law Enf't Affairs, International Narcotics Control Strategy Report vol. 1, U.S. Dep't of St. (Mar. 2017) (surveying the government's international counternarcotics efforts).

Throughout this book we have seen how the federal law requires constant innovation to combat increasingly sophisticated criminals. The international war on drugs provides a particularly salient instance of the so-called "balloon effect" often seen in both crime policy and other efforts to reduce undesirable behavior. In the case of drugs, efforts to clamp down in one place will simply move the problem elsewhere as traffickers react and adjust their own strategies. In the 1970s and 1980s, Pablo Escobar and the Colombian cartels dominated the cocaine trade, transporting the drug on private jets and speedboats across the Caribbean to the United States. Yet neither the battle nor its weaponry has been in stasis. Throughout the 1990s, interdiction efforts effectively closed off much of the Caribbean, causing the Colombian cartels to collapse. At the same time, the North Atlantic Free Trade Agreement (NAFTA) made it easier to transport drugs across the Mexican-U.S. border. As interdiction efforts at sea expanded, major distributors developed a more land-focused strategy through weakly governed Central American countries. See Stephen Meiners, Central America: An Emerging Role in the Drug Trade, Stratfor (Mar. 26, 2009). Today, heroin consumed in the United States is mainly derived from South America and Mexico (though Afghanistan remains the largest global supplier). Most cocaine comes from three countries in South America—Bolivia, Columbia, and Peru—while most marijuana in the United States has passed through Mexico. See The Drug Addiction Pipeline: Who Supplies Drugs to America (Nov. 4, 2016); DEA Intelligence Report, United States: Areas of Influence of Major Mexican Transnational Criminal Organizations, U.S. Drug Enforcement Admin. (July 2015).

Amidst the various foreign policy and military efforts has been an important role for federal law enforcement: capturing and prosecuting drug traffickers who target the United States, even those who have never set foot in this country. There are special challenges in applying the federal criminal law in international contexts. For example, the CSA of 1970 criminalized the manufacture or distribution of certain specified controlled substances abroad with the knowledge or intent that the substance would be imported illegally into the United States. See 21 U.S.C. §959(a). The intent requirement in §959(a) is the "hook" for federal jurisdiction. From the distributor's perspective, this often served as the loophole that could allow smugglers to evade U.S. prosecution as long as they squelched evidence regarding the ultimate destination of their drugs. By maintaining a large foreign "mothership" outside of U.S. customs waters, smugglers might avoid conviction even if they were observed by U.S. authorities. (For a successful prosecution under §959(a), see United States v. Martinez, 476 F.3d 961 (D.C. Cir. 2007).)

In 1986, Congress enacted a far-reaching extraterritorial criminal statute, the Maritime Drug Law Enforcement Act (MDLEA), that does not contain the statutory *mens rea* element of 21 U.S.C. §959(a)—proof of knowledge that the drugs were headed to the United States. More importantly, it eliminated any requirement for proof that the drugs were *likely* headed to this country. The MDLEA has been amended several times and currently provides:

46 U.S.C. §705. Maritime Drug Law Enforcement Act

§70502. Definitions. . . .

(c) Vessel subject to the jurisdiction of the United States. —

(1) In general. — In this chapter, the term "vessel subject to the jurisdiction of the United States" includes —

(A) a vessel without nationality;

(B) a vessel assimilated to a vessel without nationality under paragraph (2) of article 6 of the 1958 Convention on the High Seas;

(C) a vessel registered in a foreign nation if that nation has consented or waived objection to the enforcement of United States law by the United States;

(D) a vessel in the customs waters of the United States;

(E) a vessel in the territorial waters of a foreign nation if the nation consents to the enforcement of United States law by the United States; and

(F) a vessel in the contiguous zone of the United States, as defined in Presidential Proclamation 7219 of September 2, 1999 (43 U.S.C. 1331 note), that —

(i) is entering the United States;

(ii) has departed the United States; or

(iii) is a hovering vessel as defined in section 401 of the Tariff Act of 1930 (19 U.S.C. 1401).

(2) Consent or waiver of objection. — Consent or waiver of objection by a foreign nation to the enforcement of United States law by the United States under paragraph (1)(C) or (E) —

(A) may be obtained by radio, telephone, or similar oral or electronic means; and

(B) is proved conclusively by certification of the Secretary of State or the Secretary's designee. . . .

§70503. Prohibited acts.

(a) Prohibitions. — While on board a covered vessel, an individual may not knowingly or intentionally — (1) manufacture or distribute, or possess with intent to manufacture or distribute, a controlled substance;

(1) manufacture or distribute, or possess with intent to manufacture or distribute, a controlled substance;

(2) destroy (including jettisoning any item or scuttling, burning, or hastily cleaning a vessel), or attempt or conspire to destroy, property that is subject to forfeiture under [21 U.S.C. §881(a)]; or

(3) conceal, or attempt or conspire to conceal, more than $100,000 in currency or other monetary instruments on the person of such individual or in any conveyance, article of luggage, merchandise, or other container, or compartment of or aboard the covered vessel if that vessel is outfitted for smuggling.

(b) Extension beyond territorial jurisdiction. — Subsection (a) applies even though the act is committed outside the territorial jurisdiction of the United States.

§70504. Jurisdiction and venue.

(a) Jurisdiction.—Jurisdiction of the United States with respect to a vessel subject to this chapter is not an element of an offense. Jurisdictional issues arising under this chapter are preliminary questions of law to be determined solely by the trial judge.

(b) Venue.—A person violating section 70503 or 70508 of this title shall be tried in the district court of the United States for—

(1) the district at which the person enters the United States; or

(2) the District of Columbia.

§70505. Failure to comply with international law as a defense.

A person charged with violating section 70503 of this title, or against whom a civil enforcement proceeding is brought under section 70508, does not have standing to raise a claim of failure to comply with international law as a basis for a defense. A claim of failure to comply with international law in the enforcement of this chapter may be made only by a foreign nation. A failure to comply with international law does not divest a court of jurisdiction and is not a defense to a proceeding under this chapter.

Note: at the time of the violation of the MDLEA discussed in the next case, the wording of both the prohibition and the key definitional provisions were slightly, but not substantively, different.

United States v. Campbell
743 F.3d 802 (11th Cir. 2014)

PRYOR, Circuit Judge: . . .

I.   BACKGROUND

On October 26, 2011, the United States Coast Guard observed a vessel in the international waters off the eastern coast of Jamaica. While the Coast Guard was pursuing the vessel, the three individuals aboard the vessel discarded dozens of bales into the water, which the Coast Guard later determined to be approximately 997 kilograms of marijuana. The vessel lacked all indicia of nationality: it displayed no flag, port, or registration number. Glenroy Parchment identified himself as the master of the vessel and claimed the vessel was registered in Haiti. [Coast Guard Commander Daniel Deptula] then contacted the Republic of Haiti to inquire whether the vessel was of Haitian nationality. The government of Haiti responded that it could neither confirm nor deny the registry. The other two individuals aboard the vessel, Christopher Patrick Campbell and Pierre Nadin Alegrand, as well as Parchment later admitted that they knew they were illegally transporting marijuana.

[A] federal grand jury indicted Campbell, Alegrand, and Parchment under the Maritime Drug Law Enforcement Act, 46 U.S.C. §70501 et seq., for conspiracy to possess and for possession with intent to distribute 100 kilograms or more of marijuana, id. §§70503(a)(1), 70506(b) [which effectively prohibits conspiracies to violation §70503]. . . .

Campbell waived his right to a trial by jury . . . and at a bench trial, the parties stipulated to the material facts. . . . The district court found Campbell guilty on both the conspiracy and possession counts. . . .

III. DISCUSSION . . .

The Constitution empowers Congress "[t]o define and punish Piracies and Felonies committed on the high Seas, and Offences against the Law of Nations." U.S. Const. Art. I, §8, cl. 10. The Supreme Court has interpreted that Clause to contain three distinct grants of power: to define and punish piracies, to define and punish felonies committed on the high seas, and to define and punish offenses against the law of nations. This appeal involves a conviction for an offense defined by an act of Congress under the second grant of power.

Congress enacted the Maritime Drug Law Enforcement Act to prohibit any person from "knowingly or intentionally . . . possess[ing] with intent to manufacture or distribute, a controlled substance on board . . . a vessel subject to the jurisdiction of the United States." 46 U.S.C. §70503(a)(1).[*] In 1996, Congress amended the Act to provide that "[j]urisdiction of the United States with respect to a vessel subject to this Chapter is not an element of an offense." 46 U.S.C. §70504(a). The section continues that "[j]urisdictional issues arising under this Chapter are preliminary questions of law to be determined solely by the trial judge." Id.

The Act declares "a vessel without nationality" as subject to the jurisdiction of the United States and defines a stateless vessel as including "a vessel aboard which the master or individual in charge makes a claim of registry and for which the claimed nation of registry does not affirmatively and unequivocally assert that the vessel is of its nationality." 46 U.S.C. §70502(c)(1)(A), (d)(1)(C). Congress made clear that the Act "applies even though the act is committed outside the territorial jurisdiction of the United States." Id. §70503(b). The Act permits several methods

* [Editors' Note: As we noted in introducing *Campbell*, recent amendments to the MDLEA have altered its wording somewhat in ways that are not relevant to the issues addressed in our excerpts from the case.]

for obtaining a response from a foreign nation to a claim of registry and provides that a certification of the Secretary of State is conclusive proof of a response to a claim of registry by a foreign nation. . . . Id. §70502(d)(2) . . . The Act does not require the certification of the Secretary of State to include the details of how an official received or from whom the official received the response to a claim of registry from a foreign nation. . . .

Defendant Argument

Campbell argues that Congress exceeded its authority under the Felonies Clause when it enacted the Act because his drug trafficking offense lacked any nexus the United States, . . . but he acknowledges that his arguments are foreclosed by our precedents. "[W]e have always upheld extraterritorial convictions under our drug trafficking laws as an exercise of power under the Felonies Clause." See United States v. Bellaizac–Hurtado, 700 F.3d 1245, 1257 (11th Cir. 2012). And we have long upheld the authority of Congress to "extend[] the criminal jurisdiction of this country to any stateless vessel in international waters engaged in the distribution of controlled substances.". . . Moreover, in United States v. Estupinan, we rejected an argument "that Congress exceeded its authority under the Piracies and Felonies Clause in enacting the [Maritime Drug Law Enforcement Act]." 453 F.3d 1336, 1338 (11th Cir. 2006).

We also have recognized that the conduct proscribed by the Act need not have a nexus to the United States because universal and protective principles support its extraterritorial reach. The Felonies Clause empowers Congress to punish crimes committed on the high seas. And "inasmuch as the trafficking of narcotics is condemned universally by law-abiding nations, we see no reason to conclude that it is 'fundamentally unfair' for Congress to provide for the punishment of persons apprehended with narcotics on the high seas." Estupinan, 453 F.3d at 1339. Congress "may assert extraterritorial jurisdiction over vessels in the high seas that are engaged in conduct that 'has a potentially adverse effect and is generally recognized as a crime by nations that have reasonably developed legal systems.'" And "[t]he protective principle does not require that there be proof of an actual or intended effect inside the United States." Congress also may assert extraterritorial jurisdiction because "the law places *no restrictions* upon a nation's right to subject stateless vessels to its jurisdiction." United States v. Ibarguen–Mosquera, 634 F.3d 1370, 1379 (11th Cir. 2011). . . .

Campbell argues that his convictions violated his right to due process because his offense of drug trafficking lacked a nexus to the United States, but he concedes that our precedents foreclose this argument too. We held in United States v. *Rendon* that the Due Process Clause of the Fifth Amendment does not prohibit the trial and conviction of an alien captured on the high seas while drug trafficking, because the Act provides clear notice that all nations prohibit and condemn drug trafficking aboard stateless vessels on the high seas. 354 F.3d 1320, 1326 (11th Cir. 2003). And "this [C]ircuit and other circuits have not embellished the

[Act] with the requirement of a nexus between a defendant's criminal conduct and the United States." *Estupinan,* 453 F.3d at 1338 (internal quotation marks and alterations omitted). Campbell's conviction did not violate his right to due process under the Fifth Amendment. . . .

NOTES AND QUESTIONS

1. In addition to arguing that Congress did not have constitutional power to enact the MDLEA, Campbell also challenged his conviction under the Confrontation Clause. The Confrontation Clause provides that "[i]n all criminal prosecutions, the accused shall enjoy the right . . . to be confronted with the witnesses against him. . . ." U.S. Const. amend. VI.

> Campbell argues that the admission of the certification of the Secretary of State without the ability to cross-examine a Haitian witness violated his right under the Confrontation Clause, but that argument fails. The Confrontation Clause does not bar the admission of hearsay to make a pretrial determination of jurisdiction when that hearsay does not pertain to an element of the offense. Because the stateless nature of Campbell's vessel was not an element of his offense to be proved at trial, the admission of the certification did not violate his right to confront the witnesses against him.

743 F.3d at 806. The court held that the purpose of the certification to prove jurisdiction is "as a diplomatic courtesy to a foreign nation." Id. at 804.

2. It was obviously Congress's intent to apply the MDLEA extraterritorially. The statute defines "vessel subject to the jurisdiction of the United States" to include all vessels without nationality, all vessels in United States customs waters, and all vessels (in water of any kind) of nations who consent to enforcement of the MDLEA. See 46 U.S.C. §70502(c)(1). Consent by another nation is provided on a case-by-case basis; it may be provided at any time before trial, and need not be given in advance of arrest. See United States v. Greer, 285 F.3d 158, 175-76 (2d Cir. 2000). In enacting the MDLEA, Congress asserted that maritime drug trafficking is a "serious international problem, is universally condemned, and presents a specific threat to the security and societal well-being of the United States." 46 U.S.C. §70501. Note that the drug being transported by Campbell was marijuana (a boatload of it, to be sure). Do you think that Congress would enact §70501 today?

3. But the MDLEA is more than extraterritorial. The elements of the crime do not include any domestic connection *whatsoever.* Indeed, under the MDLEA's statutory provisions, a Canadian citizen on a Canadian boat caught in the middle of the Atlantic transporting marijuana to distribute in England could be prosecuted by the United States, as long as Canada

consents. Commentators have noted that this Act thus has quietly become the largest fount of jurisdiction for cases in federal court that have no direct connection to the United States, dwarfing the number of civil suits brought under the better-known Alien Tort Statute. See Eugene Kontorovich, Beyond the Article I Horizon: Congress's Enumerated Powers and Universal Jurisdiction over Drug Crimes, 93 Minn. L. Rev. 1191, 1203 (2009). Moreover, because the statute reaches conspiracies, an individual waiting in England to receive the marijuana could find himself facing MDLEA charges in federal court in the United States.

4. What is the source of Congress's authority to enact the MDLEA? Courts have found the MDLEA to be an appropriate exercise of Congress's power under U.S Const. art. I, §8, cl. 10: "[t]o define and punish Piracies and Felonies committed on the high Seas, and Offenses against the Law of Nations." See, e.g., United States v. Ballestas, 795 F.3d 138 (D.C. Cir. 2015). The constitutional language has been parsed to provide two separate sources of power: (1) to define and punish crimes committed on the "high Seas" (the Felonies Clause), and (2) to define and punish crimes that violate "the Law of Nations" (the Offences Clause). In United States v. Estupinan, 453 F.3d 1336, 1338 (11th Cir. 2006), the court upheld the use of the MDLEA against trafficking in international waters, the "high Seas" off the coast of Ecuador. Thereafter, however, another panel in the same circuit held that "[b]ecause drug trafficking is not a violation of customary international law, Congress exceeded its power, under the Offences Clause, when it proscribed the defendants' conduct in the territorial waters of Panama." United States v. Bellaizac-Hurtado, 700 F.3d 1245, 1258 (11th Cir. 2012). In United States v. Macias, 654 F. App'x. 458, 460-61 (11th Cir. 2016), the Eleventh Circuit emphasized that *Bellaizac-Hurtado* only applied to "Congress's authority under the Offences Clause to proscribe drug trafficking committed in *another country's waters*, not Congress's power under the Felonies Clause to proscribe drug trafficking crimes committed in *international waters*," and that "unlike the Offences Clause, the Felonies Clause is not narrowed by the language 'against the Laws of Nations'" (emphasis added).

Recall our discussion of jurisdiction in Section B of Chapter 2. Do you think the Act could also be justified under the Foreign Commerce Clause, as was the statute forbidding certain illicit sexual activities abroad in United States v. Clark, 435 F.3d 1100 (9th Cir. 2006)? Alternatively, might Congress have power to enact at least some of the provisions of the MDLEA pursuant to the treaty power (the Court declined an opportunity to consider the scope of legislative authority to implement treaties in Bond v. United States, 134 S. Ct. 2077 (2014), which we discussed in Chapter 2)? Please also understand that although the United States has entered into some treaties relating to narcotics, it is unlikely that any of them authorize the MDLEA. For example, the most relevant treaty (the United Nations Convention Against Illicit

Traffic in Narcotic Drugs and Psychotropic Substances) encourages—but does not require—such legislation and was not adopted until 1988.

5. You will recall that the *Clark* decision also rejected a due process challenge to Clark's conviction. The MDLEA likewise criminalizes conduct potentially far removed from the United States, and has been the subject of challenges under the Due Process Clause of the Fifth Amendment. In the context of foreign-flag ships where the flag nation has consented to federal jurisdiction, the Ninth Circuit in United States v. Davis, 905 F.2d 245, 248-49 (1990), held that "in order to apply extraterritorially a federal criminal statute to a defendant consistently with due process, there must be a sufficient nexus between the defendant and the United States so that such application would not be arbitrary or fundamentally unfair." Given that the United States is by far the largest consumer of narcotics in this hemisphere, it is probably often fair to assume that the narcotics on vessels in or voyaging toward this hemisphere are heading to (or at least will have effects on) the United States. Note that the nexus requirement may be even less here than it is for proof of an effect on interstate commerce under the Hobbs Act, 18 U.S.C. §1951 (considered in Chapter 5). See, e.g., United States v. Zakharov, 468 F.3d 1171, 1177 (9th Cir. 2006) (holding that the nexus requirement was satisfied by "a showing" that a transaction "was likely to have effects in the United States").

Be aware, however, of one important difference between the requirement of a nexus to the United States for application of the MDLEA, and the requirement of an effect on interstate commerce under statutes such as the Hobbs Act, the Travel Act, RICO, and the drug-trafficking offenses in Title 21 of the U.S. Code. In the latter statutes, the jurisdictional "hook" is an element of the crime that must be proven to the jury beyond a reasonable doubt. But the MDLEA nexus requirement is, in the words of the Ninth Circuit, a "judicial gloss" that must be decided case by case by the court in a pre-trial ruling, United States v. Klimavicius-Viloria, 144 F.3d 1249, 1257 (9th Cir. 1998); see also United States v. Matos-Luchi, 627 F.3d 1, 5 (1st Cir. 2010) (requiring proof only to a preponderance).

Other Circuits have rejected any requirement of a nexus to the United States for MDLEA prosecutions. See United States v. Angulo-Hernandez, 565 F.3d 2, 10-11 (1st Cir. 2009) ("Due process does not require the government to prove a nexus between a defendant's criminal conduct and the United States in a prosecution under MDLEA when the flag nation has consented to the application of United States law to the defendants."); United States v. Perez-Oviedo, 281 F.3d 400 (3d Cir. 2002); United States v. Suerte, 291 F.3d 366 (5th Cir. 2002); United States v. Aguilar, 286 F. App'x. 716 (11th Cir. 2008). Though the reasoning of each Circuit differs slightly, the Third Circuit in *Suerte* developed, instead of a "nexus test," what some have called a "notice test"—upholding the MDLEA without a nexus because the

Act provides sufficient notice to potential defendants that jurisdiction is possible, given the universal condemnation of narcotics trafficking found by Congress and treaties to that effect. *Suerte*, 291 F.3d at 377. See also *Ballestas*, 795 F.3d at 147-48 (not reaching the question of whether U.S. nexus is required, since nexus is "a proxy for due process," and in the case at hand there was no fundamental unfairness).

6. Is the MDLEA's application to foreign-flag ships compatible with international law? As we explained in Chapter 2, even if a particular prosecution is found to violate international law, federal courts will allow the prosecution to proceed unless it also violates the U.S. Constitution. See, e.g., Hartford Fire Ins. Co. v. California, 509 U.S. 764, 815 (1993) (Congress "clearly has authority" to confer extraterritorial jurisdiction in violation of international law). In fact, the MDLEA specifically provides that any violation of international law is not a defense for the defendant. See 46 U.S.C. §70505. In any event, courts have found that the MDLEA comports with international law. See, e.g., United States v. Cardales, 168 F.3d 548, 553 (1st Cir. 1999) (finding that the MDLEA is justified under the "protective principle" of international law, which allows countries to assert jurisdiction over security threats, given Congress's finding of the dangers of narcotics trafficking); United States v. Caicedo, 47 F.3d 370, 372-73 (9th Cir. 1995) (as to flagless vessels: "where a defendant attempts to avoid the law of *all* nations by travelling on a stateless vessel, he has forfeited [] protections of international law").

7. In 2008, the MDLEA was amended to combat yet another technique of drug traffickers: transporting drugs by self-propelled semi-submersible vessels, which are hard to detect and easily scuttled upon detection (destroying any evidence of drugs). The Drug Trafficking Vessel Interdiction Act (DTVIA) criminalizes the operation of any such vessels without nationality as long as they show intent to evade detection, with no need to produce any evidence of narcotics trafficking at all. See 18 U.S.C. §2285, 46 U.S.C. §70508. In United States v. Ibarguen-Mosquera, 634 F.3d 1370 (11th Cir. 2011), the court held that Congress did not exceed its power under the Felonies Clause when it enacted the DTVIA. This prohibition strongly resembles the increasingly frequent creation of "possession" offenses that we briefly discussed earlier in this section.

B. DRUG PENALTIES

The next chapter of this book is devoted entirely to the law, institutions, and practices of criminal sentencing in the federal courts. As you will see, at present, four institutions play a substantial role in determining sentences: (1) Congress, in setting the statutory range of permissible sentences; (2)

the United States Sentencing Commission, in setting Sentencing Guideline ranges within these statutory ranges; (3) the federal prosecutor, in selecting statutory charges and conducting settlement negotiations (plea bargaining) with the defendant; and (4) the sentencing judge, in calculating the Guidelines range and exercising discretion to sentence the defendant somewhere within or outside of that range. All of these players have some role in drug sentencing.

We consider drug sentencing separately, however, because of the sheer volume of drug crimes—as we saw, they now comprise about 30 percent of the criminal docket—and the sheer severity of drug sentences, which mean that the impact of this area of federal law on the larger society is especially pronounced. More than in any other area of federal criminal law, this severity is the direct result of a legislative mandate – statutorily fixed sentencing minimums that are inextricably linked to the substantive prohibitions they support. Groups such as "Families Against Mandatory Minimums" and "The Sentencing Project" have emerged to lobby against the current drug sentencing regime, and the Congressional Black Caucus has given particular attention to federal drug penalties. Even federal judges have been unusually vocal in criticizing drug sentencing. One example is United States v. Kupa, 976 F. Supp. 2d 417 (E.D.N.Y. 2013), excerpted at length below. Another is the unusual plea against mandatory sentences that Justice Anthony Kennedy made before a plenary session of the American Bar Association. See Hon. Anthony M. Kennedy, Speech at the American Bar Association Annual Meeting (Aug. 9, 2003).

The statutory history of federal drug penalties is a remarkable and, we think, shameful story. When Congress enacted the CSA in 1970, it abolished all mandatory drug penalties. But beginning in the mid-1980s, Congress increased the punishments for federal drug offenses by instituting mandatory minimum sentences, raising maximum sentences, and periodically increasing both of these. Current statutory penalties are primarily the product of amendments to the CSA made by the Anti-Drug Abuse Acts of 1986 and 1988, and the Violent Crime Control and Law Enforcement Act of 1994. For a detailed history of the Acts and the changes made to the CSA, see Margaret P. Spencer, Sentencing Drug Offenders: The Incarceration Addiction, 40 Vill. L. Rev. 335, 344-55 (1995). Additionally, in a variety of stand-alone provisions, Congress has provided for enhanced sentences when drug crimes are committed in certain circumstances. For instance, the maximum and minimum penalties are doubled for distribution within 1,000 feet of schools, playgrounds, and public housing, see 21 U.S.C. §860, and within 1,000 feet of highway "truck stops," see 21 U.S.C. §849. Mandating high minimum sentences has the effect of crowding out sentencing authority that would otherwise be exercised by the Sentencing Commission or the sentencing judge.

1.   The Statutory Structure of Drug Sentencing Law

We saw in the previous section that 21 U.S.C. §841(a) prohibits drug distribution. Here we examine §841(b), which gives content to this broad prohibition by setting out a scheme of mandatory minimum and permissible maximum penalties that are keyed to both the *type* and *quantity* of the drug. In the next subsection, we consider the particular difficulties associated with calculation of drug quantity.

Under 21 U.S.C. §841(b) as amended, there are three quantity categories for each drug type:

- Where the amount of drug is not specified in the indictment on which the jury returns a guilty verdict or to which the defendant pleads guilty, the defendant faces no mandatory term of imprisonment, and the maximum sentence is 20 years. See 21 U.S.C. §841(b)(1)(C).
- A mandatory minimum sentence of five years is required, and the maximum sentence rises to 40 years, for eight drug substances—heroin, powder cocaine, crack cocaine, PCP, LSD, propanamide, methamphetamine, and marijuana—if the defendant is convicted of trafficking in more than the statutory triggering amount of the drug. We here focus on the first three of these substances. The triggering amount for heroin is 100 grams or more; for powder cocaine, 500 grams or more; for crack cocaine, 28 grams or more. See 21 U.S.C. §841(b)(1)(B). Because this quantity finding raises the statutory maximum from 20 to 40 years, and raises the minimum from no time in prison to five years, it is an element of the offense that must be charged in the indictment and proved beyond a reasonable doubt.[*] See, e.g., United States v. Gonzalez, 420 F.3d 111 (2d Cir. 2005).
- If the offense includes more than one kilogram of heroin, five kilograms of powder cocaine, or 280 grams of crack, the sentence range is between a mandatory minimum of ten years and life imprisonment. See 21 U.S.C. §841(b)(1)(A).

There is a separate "Drug Kingpin" provision in the CSA, 21 U.S.C. §848, which provides for a mandatory minimum sentence of 20 years and a maximum sentence of life in prison. Formally proscribed as the crime of being engaged in a "Continuing Criminal Enterprise" (CCE), the provision targets only individuals in the upper echelon of organizations that

---

[*] Chapter 10 discusses the Supreme Court's *Apprendi* line of cases, under which factors increasing a maximum or minimum sentence are treated as elements of the statutory prohibition.

distribute vast quantities of drugs or receive at least $10 million in gross receipts from drug dealing in any 12-month period. This was an original part of the CSA and was the only mandatory minimum sentence in the Act. During the 1970s and 1980s, CCE was an important prosecutorial tool, providing enhanced punishments for high-level drug dealers. In 1989, for instance, more than 300 individuals were convicted and sentenced under this "Drug Kingpin" provision. But once Congress added mandatory minimums in 1986 (and raised them in 1988 and 1994), the basic sentencing provision—§841(b)—effectively required minimum 20-year sentences for all individuals convicted of drug trafficking involving vast quantities of drugs, whether "kingpins" or minor players. As a result, the number of CCE convictions has gone way down. As the Sentencing Commission figure reproduced at the beginning of this chapter shows, in 2016 there were only four CCE convictions. Notice how a legislative effort to promote the identification and punishment of the most culpable drug traffickers—since prosecutors would presumably be willing to assume the burden of proving kingpin status in order to impose a more severe sentence—collapsed when the sentencing scheme stopped discriminating between kingpins and more peripheral player in large quantity conspiracies.

The statutory ranges set forth in 21 U.S.C. §841(b) apply only where a defendant has no prior drug conviction. Mandatory minimums are *doubled* if, pursuant to 21 U.S.C. §851, the prosecutor files an information certifying that the defendant is a repeat felony drug offender; we discuss §851 in some depth in subsection 2 below. Moreover, defendants convicted of drug conspiracies under 21 U.S.C. §846 face the same penalty structure as those convicted of the trafficking offense. Where a defendant has pled to or has been found guilty of an offense carrying a mandatory minimum prison term, the sentencing judge has discretion to impose less than that mandatory minimum in only two situations: (1) upon motion of the prosecutor certifying the defendant's substantial assistance in the prosecution of others (discussed in Note 2 below), or (2) where the sentencing judge finds the defendant eligible for the so-called "safety valve" provision that Congress added in 1994 (discussed in Note 3 below).

Since 1988, simple possession has also been proscribed by federal law. Under 21 U.S.C. §844, a defendant convicted of simple possession of most scheduled drugs (without intent to distribute) faces up to one year in prison. The maximum is higher—three years—for flunitrazepam (a.k.a. "roofies," a date-rape drug).

MANDATORY MINIMUM SENTENCES

1. The statutory minima and maxima leave a large statutory range—between zero and 20 years for (b)(1)(C) offenses, between five and

40 years for (b)(1)(B) offenses, and between ten years and life for (b)(1)(A) offenses. How is it decided where within the applicable range the defendant at hand should be sentenced? The answer to this question is considered at length—not just as to drug crimes, but as to all crimes—in the next chapter. A brief preview: At around the same time that Congress adopted statutory mandatory sentences for drug offenses, it also enacted legislation that was intended to constrain judicial discretion within statutory sentencing ranges. The Sentencing Reform Act of 1984 created the United States Sentencing Commission (whose data reports and analyses we cite throughout this chapter) and instructed it to promulgate binding Sentencing Guidelines that would inform judges where they should sentence within statutory limits. A major objective of the 1984 Act was to ensure that judges across the country give like sentences to like offenders.

2. Whatever may have been the objectives of the Sentencing Reform Act of 1984, however, the statutory scheme for drug sentencing shows that Congress has done its utmost to facilitate prosecutorial bargaining power, with the result that there is no assurance that defendants who have committed the same crime receive the same sentence. See generally Mona Lynch, Hard Bargains: The Coercive Power of Drug Laws in Federal Court (2016). We have already noted one important source of prosecutorial leverage: The statutory sentencing range depends on the quantity of drugs specified in the defendant's offense of conviction. It obviously makes an enormous difference to a defendant whether he is charged with, for instance, conspiring to distribute 400 grams (a bit less than one pound) of powder cocaine, or 550 grams (a bit more than one pound)—because if he is convicted on the latter charge he faces a sentence of at least five years, and his sentence could be as high as 40 years (instead of up to 20). Of the some 20,000 drug defendants in 2016, slightly less than one-half (9,154) were convicted of offenses carrying a mandatory minimum sentence. See U.S. Sent'g Comm'n, An Overview of Mandatory Minimum Penalties in the Federal Criminal Justice System 34 (July 2017). Both the total number and the percentage of drug defendants facing a mandatory minimum sentence have been decreasing since 2010, when nearly 16,000 defendants were convicted of a drug crime carrying a mandatory minimum. Id. The Notes following the next case in this chapter show how prosecutors' ability to forego charging the full drug quantity associated with a defendant can be a source of plea bargaining leverage or a mechanism to reduce the severity of certain drug sentences as a matter of policy.

The second way in which the drug-sentencing scheme enhances prosecutorial power is via the provision in 18 U.S.C. §3553(e) that allows the sentencing judge *not* to impose the "mandatory" minimum if the prosecutor, by written motion, certifies that the defendant has cooperated with the government by providing "substantial assistance" in the prosecution of others. In 2010, over one-half of all drug defendants facing a mandatory minimum sentence were in fact sentenced *below* the "mandatory" because a substantial assistance motion was filed and granted under §3553(e) (19 percent) or because the defendants were relieved of the mandatory sentence pursuant to the safety-valve provision of §3553(f), discussed in the next Note (26 percent), or through both mechanisms (9 percent). U.S. Sent'g Comm'n, Executive Summary of 2011 Report to the Congress: Mandatory Minimum Penalties in the Federal Criminal Justice System xxxiii (2011). White and Black defendants received below-mandatory sentences due to substantial assistance motions at the same rate (25 percent), while only 13 percent of Hispanic defendants received such sentencing relief. Id.

A third way in which Congress has provided for significant prosecutorial authority is in connection with repeat drug offenders. As noted above, 21 U.S.C. §841(b) provides for double the otherwise applicable statutory sentencing range for those previously convicted of a felony drug offense in state or federal court. However, Congress has separately provided that these enhanced penalties are applicable only if the prosecutor has filed a certification in court concerning the defendant's previous conviction. See 21 U.S.C. §851(a)(1). We will examine the operation and consequences of this provision when you read the main case and Notes in the next subsection of this chapter.

3. The safety-valve provision in subsection (f) of 18 U.S.C. §3553 is available as a matter of judicial discretion and does not require the approval of the prosecution. To be eligible for this relief, the defendant must have at most a minor criminal record and must have played a minor role in the crime of conviction; the crime itself must not have involved violence or injury; and the defendant must have "truthfully provided to the Government all information and evidence the defendant has concerning the offense. . . ." Id. The most common beneficiary of the safety valve provision is the courier caught with a substantial quantity of drugs who nonetheless lacks the ability to cooperate against anyone else. As the example of the clueless courier indicates, the fact that a defendant "has no relevant or useful [] information to provide" does not bar a court from finding that the defendant has complied with the requirements of the provision. Id. The safety valve is available only for the crimes listed in §3553(f), which include §§841, 844, and 846 of Title 21, but does not include all drug-related offenses. See United States v. Gamboa-Cardenas, 508 F.3d 491 (9th Cir. 2007) (holding that the safety valve is not available for violations of the MDLEA, which we considered in Section A of this chapter). In its 2011 Report on mandatory minimum sentences, the Sentencing Commission found:

> As a result of the combined effect of the safety valve and [role adjustments under the Sentencing Guidelines], [drug] offenders performing lower-level functions received significantly shorter sentences overall than offenders performing higher-level functions. For example, Mules (29 months) and Couriers

(39 months) received significantly shorter average sentences than High Level Suppliers/Importers (101 months), Organizer/Leaders (154 months), Wholesalers (103 months), and Managers (147 months).

U.S. Sent'g Comm'n, 2011 Executive Summary, *supra*, at xxxiii.

4. Why did Congress and the President seek to establish a regime of harsh sentences, including mandatory minimum sentences, in drug trafficking cases?

> The incarceration penalties in the 1986 and 1988 Acts were intended to promote the penological goals of specific and general deterrence, and incapacitation. Congress wanted to send "a message across the country that the war on drugs is on, and it will be won" because drug offenders will either be imprisoned or executed. For example, deterrence was the major issue for proponents and opponents of the death penalty. Proponents argued that drug dealers who murdered were "merchants of death" who would understand and be deterred by the death penalty. . . .
>
> Congress assumed that drug dealers facing severe mandatory penalties would refrain from criminal activities, because they assumed that these offenders (1) understood basic utilitarian "cost-benefit" analysis, (2) would conclude the penological "costs" of their illegal activities outweighed the "benefits," and (3) would cease such activities. One member of the Senate argued that the "offsetting costs . . . [in prior laws were] relatively small. The chances of being intercepted [were] not great . . . [and, if caught and convicted] the penalties [were] nothing more than a small cost of doing business." . . .
>
> Incapacitation was the other Congressional goal. Legislators wanted certain and severe minimum periods of imprisonment to "get the pushers out of our schoolyards and drugs off of our streets." The public desperately wanted a "solution" to the drug crisis, and lengthy periods of incarceration, even if incarceration only incapacitated drug offenders, was the solution. One Senator noted that "dealers should know with certainty that if they are caught and convicted, they will be headed for the penitentiary and they will stay there for years. . . . In other words, for a number of years the key will be thrown away." Congress thus prescribed lengthy mandatory penalties and hoped that current or potential offenders would either be deterred or physically restrained from committing drug offenses.

Spencer, *supra*, at 345-47. Is it clear that the "rational" drug offender will be deterred by the increase in penalties? Might requiring high penalties for drug offenses have the opposite effect? See Daniel K. Benjamin & Roger Leroy Miller, Undoing Drugs: Beyond Legalization 108 (1991) ("*Raising* the penalties for drug dealing is equivalent to *lowering* the penalties on other crimes in the course of the illegal drug business. *The result is more intimidation, violence and lawlessness by drug dealers.*").

5. Congress has provided for mandatory minimum sentences for other crimes as well. In fact, there are "at least 171 individual mandatory minimum

provisions" in federal criminal statutes. See U.S. Sent'g Comm'n, 2009 Report to the Congress: Federal Mandatory Minimum Sentencing Penalties 1, n.2, (2009). All of these are of relatively recent vintage. As previously noted, the drug-crime legislation of 1986 and 1988 introduced a variety of mandatory minimum penalties for federal drug crimes, triggered by the type and quantity of drug involved; these mandatory sentences were increased in 1994 and subsequent years. Congress has also, almost as a matter of habit, provided for mandatory minimum penalties for a variety of other crimes, including firearms, trafficking in child pornography, sex trafficking, kidnapping, and air piracy. In 2016, 22 percent of all federal defendants were convicted of a crime carrying a mandatory minimum sentence. U.S. Sent'g Comm'n, 2017 Overview of Mandatory Minimum Penalties, *supra*, at 29. The overwhelming majority of these defendants are drug offenders (91 percent in 2016), followed by those whose major count of conviction was a firearms offense (close to 5 percent). As the Sentencing Commission has long noted, "Most of the 171 mandatory minimum provisions rarely, if ever, were used. . . ." U.S. Sent'g Comm'n, 2009 Report to the Congress, *supra*, at 1.

The pattern of mandatory minimums across federal criminal statutes raises interesting question about inclusion and exclusion. Congress's use of them for drug crimes, child pornography, and other offenses bespeaks not just its desire to punish severely, but its fear that, absent statutory restriction, judges will not sentence with the desired severity. Why might Congress have this fear? And why doesn't Congress have similar fears about fraud or corruption cases? What role, if any, do you think race and class play in the pattern?

2. PRIOR DRUG FELONY SENTENCING ENHANCEMENTS

We have mentioned several times that 21 U.S.C. §851 allows prosecutors to file a prior drug felony sentencing information; if an information is filed, the mandatory minimum penalties and enhanced maximum penalties under §841(b) kick in for defendants who have previously been convicted in any court—state, federal, or foreign—of a drug crime that would be a felony if prosecuted in federal court. The provision reads in pertinent part:

---

21 U.S.C. §851. Proceedings to establish prior convictions

(a) Information filed by United States Attorney
  (1) No person who stands convicted of an offense under this part shall be sentenced to increased punishment by reason of one or more prior convictions, unless before trial, or before entry of a plea of guilty, the United States attorney files an information with the court (and serves a copy of such information on the person or counsel for the person) stating in writing the previous convictions to be relied upon. . . . Clerical mistakes in the

> information may be amended at any time prior to the pronouncement of
> sentence. . . .

The provision goes on to require a hearing if the defendant denies the accuracy of the "information" filed by the government; in practice, such hearings are rare since the defendant's prior criminal convictions are a matter of public record.

The following case explains both the powerful leverage provided to prosecutors by §851, and why the recent operation of this provision appears to be contrary to the legislative intent of the Congress that enacted it in 1970.

United States v. Kupa
976 F. Supp. 2d 417 (E.D.N.Y. 2013)

GLEESON, District Judge. . . .

Prior felony informations don't just tinker with sentencing outcomes; by doubling mandatory minimums and sometimes mandating life in prison, they produce the sentencing equivalent of a two-by-four to the forehead. The government's use of them coerces guilty pleas and produces sentences so excessively severe they take your breath away. Prior felony informations have played a key role in helping to place the federal criminal trial on the endangered species list.

On the bright side, like several other features of our current federal sentencing regime that need fixing, it's not difficult to identify where the appropriate use of prior felony informations went off the rails. The history of this prosecutorial tool explains how we got into the current situation and informs the effort to get out of it. . . .

2.   The Effect of Prior Drug Convictions on the Mandatory Minimums

21 U.S.C. §841 ratchets up the mandatory minimums for recidivist drug offenders. Specifically, it provides that where a defendant was previously convicted of a felony drug offense, the five-year and ten-year mandatory minimums are doubled. For a defendant with two or more prior drug felonies, the ten-year mandatory minimum is increased to mandatory life in prison. The term "felony drug offense" is defined very broadly. Even low-level drug possession convictions that produce probationary sentences qualify. And recency is irrelevant; even convictions so old the Guidelines do not include them in a defendant's criminal history score count. In

short, the second most severe sentence in our system—mandatory life imprisonment—can be triggered by two ancient and minor drug convictions that do not even constitute felonies under federal law.

3. Prior Felony Informations

The mandatory language of 21 U.S.C. §841 creates the impression that every defendant with one or more prior drug felony convictions who faces a mandatory minimum is automatically subjected to the enhanced mandatory minimums. But another statute—21 U.S.C. §851—provides that no drug trafficking defendant can face an enhanced mandatory minimum unless certain procedures, including the filing of a prior felony information by the prosecutor, are followed. Unless the prosecutor files a timely prior felony information pursuant to 21 U.S.C. §851 listing the prior felony or felonies to be relied upon, the enhanced mandatory minimums will not apply.

It was not always this way. Recidivism-based mandatory minimums for drug traffickers are not new, and they used to be automatic. The first version of what would eventually become 21 U.S.C. §851 *required* prosecutors to file informations identifying prior convictions. The Boggs Act of 1951 [26 U.S.C. §2557(b)(7)] created mandatory minimum sentences for drug trafficking and possession offenders. Specifically, it established a minimum prison term of two to five years for the first offense, even simple possession offenses. As for recidivist enhancements, it mandated minimum prison terms of five to ten years for the second offense and ten to fifteen years for the third. "It was thought at the time that requiring lenient judges to impose jail terms would 'dry up the traffic' in narcotics.'" Five years later, the Narcotic Control Act of 1956 raised the mandatory minimum to five years for the first offense and ten years for all subsequent convictions; suspended sentences were prohibited, as was probation.

These mandatory enhancements had such a dramatic effect on sentences that federal prosecutors found themselves reluctant to bring any charges at all against certain defendants because the automatic mandatory enhancements were simply too severe. As a result, Attorney General John N. Mitchell asked Congress to enact a law affording prosecutors greater flexibility:

> The greatest enforcement problem with the existing penalty structure is that it is too severe in relation to the culpability of the user and the dangers of the drugs. . . . The result has been a reluctance on the part of prosecutors to prosecute . . . under the existing penalty structure. The new penalty structure will increase the credibility of the law and the resultant deterrent effect while at the same time providing sufficient flexibility to allow the punishment to fit the crime and the offender.

Commissioner John E. Ingersoll of the Bureau of Narcotics and Dangerous Drugs testified about the need for a penalty provision that would reserve the highest penalties for true "professional criminals":

> I think we are going to get more convictions because of the greater flexibility that is provided to courts in sentencing, and the higher penalties that are reserved for the professional criminals. . . . The existing penalties are really out of proportion to penalties that are contained in other parts of the Federal law. For example, manslaughter, involuntary manslaughter, draws a lesser penalty than presently is available to a person who smuggles marijuana into the country.

Ingersoll acknowledged that not all second offenders are necessarily "professionals," and stated that "the burden should remain upon [the government] to prove the status of professionalism as far as the defendant is concerned."

In 1970, Congress responded by enacting 21 U.S.C. §851 [as part of the Controlled Substances Act, which abrogated virtually all extant federal drug prohibitions]. [] [A]s discussed above, [this provision] conditions the applicability of any recidivist enhancements to the drug offense mandatory minimums on the filing of a prior felony information. The 1970 legislation thus gave the government the flexibility it requested.

But Congress did not stop there. Over the objections of DOJ, it also repealed the previously-existing mandatory minimums and created a single, ten-year mandatory minimum built into the so-called "kingpin" statute, 21 U.S.C. §848. In the ensuing 16 years, prior drug felonies operated only to enlarge the *maximum* sentence for drug trafficking. Specifically, the 1970 statute provided for a maximum sentence of up to 15 years in prison for the first offense and up to 30 for subsequent offenses. Since the enlarged maximum sentence did not restrict judges' discretion to impose a just sentence, the controversy surrounding mandatory minimums that preceded 1970 (which would reappear after 1986) disappeared.

In sum, §851 reflected the recognition by Congress and DOJ that a prior drug felony conviction was not *per se* evidence that a drug trafficking defendant was the sort of hardened professional criminal who deserves an enhanced mandatory sentence. Congress left it to prosecutors to identify the defendants who truly deserved the enhancements that remained after 1970. Whereas the previous statutory scheme made no distinctions among (for example) professional criminals, street-corner dealers, and addicts whose pay for participating in the offense consisted solely of the drugs to support their habits, §851 trusted prosecutors to take into account such individual circumstances, vesting them with the power to be selective [citing United States v. Noland, 495 F.2d 519, 533 (5th Cir. 1974)].

There was no suggestion that Congress enacted §851 so prosecutors could use their newfound discretion to trigger enhanced punishments as a tool to strong-arm federal defendants into pleading guilty or to punish those who exercise their right to a trial.

C.   The Sentencing Reform Movement Brings About a DOJ Policy That Defeats the Purpose of 21 U.S.C. §851

1.   *The Sentencing Reform Act of 1984 and the Anti-Drug Abuse Act of 1986*

In 1984, Congress passed the Sentencing Reform Act to address, *inter alia,* the unwarranted sentencing disparities that characterized the indeterminate sentencing regime at the time. The statute created the Sentencing Commission and instructed it to create sentencing guidelines to cabin the discretion of sentencing judges. . . . [Two years later, Congress enacted the Anti-Drug Abuse Act (ADAA), establishing the two-tiered scheme of mandatory minimum and enhanced maximum sentences described above.]

Neither the Sentencing Reform Act of 1984 nor the ADAA disturbed 21 U.S.C. §851. Thus, Congress created the power to double drug offense mandatory minimums, and to convert some of them into life sentences, against the backdrop described above. Specifically, those recidivist enhancements were not to be automatically imposed on every drug trafficking defendant with a qualifying prior conviction. Rather, federal prosecutors were supposed to continue to exercise the discretion they asked for and received in §851 to cull from the large number of defendants who have prior drug convictions the ones who truly deserve those extra-harsh punishments. Indeed, the new recidivist enhancements were much more severe than the ones in place prior to 1970, which themselves were so harsh that DOJ successfully asked Congress to eliminate automatic applicability in the name of fairness and just sentencing. By leaving §851 intact and applicable to the enhancement of its newly-minted mandatory minimums, Congress ensured that those enhancements would only be triggered after careful consideration of the relevant facts about the offense and the defendant.

2.   *The Return to Automatic Recidivist Enhancements Through DOJ Policy*

A.   THE MOST SERIOUS READILY PROVABLE OFFENSE DIRECTIVE

The newly created Guidelines took sentencing power from judges and placed it in the hands of prosecutors. Prosecutors found themselves in a position where they could influence sentencing outcomes through their charging decisions and plea bargaining. DOJ . . . was sensitive to the Commission's concern that differences in the exercise of prosecutorial discretion might result in sentencing disparities of the sort the Commission was created to eliminate. In their seminal book on the federal sentencing reform movement, Professor Kate Stith and Judge José A. Cabranes describe the results as follows:

> In the wake of the Guidelines, and in response to the Commission's clear concern that the Guidelines would be undermined by rampant charge and fact bargaining, the Department of Justice abandoned its traditional, hands-off approach toward routine plea bargaining by federal prosecutors in the field. In 1989, federal prosecutors received a new set of instructions on the subject from the Department of Justice in Washington. The "Thornburgh Memorandum," as it came to be known (after the Attorney General who issued it), announced strict limitations on the discretion exercised by individual federal prosecutors in charging and plea bargaining. . .The key instruction on charg[ing] . . . states: "[A] federal prosecutor *should initially charge the most serious, readily provable offense or offenses consistent with the defendant's conduct.*"
>   . . . The Thornburgh Memorandum thus imposed on prosecutors essentially the same standards that the Commission had sought to impose on judges and probation officers. . . .

B. THE EXTENSION OF THAT DIRECTIVE TO PRIOR FELONY INFORMATIONS

Implementing the direction to charge "the most serious readily provable offense" was clear enough when it came to bringing criminal charges, but in 1992 a member of the Sentencing Guidelines Subcommittee of the Attorney General's Advisory Committee observed that the "Thornburgh Memo" was ambiguous when it came to the filing of prior felony informations. As the chair of the subcommittee put it, "a factor which could make an enormous difference in a defendant's sentence was not effectively covered in the Thornburgh Memo."

The subcommittee therefore debated whether the "most serious readily provable offense" policy required the filing of a prior felony information. A prior felony information doesn't constitute an additional "offense," but rather elevates the sentence for an already-pending one. Nevertheless, because the goal of the Sentencing Reform Act was "to ensure uniformity of sentences," the subcommittee felt that prior felony informations introduced an undesirable potential for disparities. It therefore recommended to the Attorney General that the policy be clarified to require the filing of prior felony informations. Adopting that recommendation, DOJ issued a policy [purporting to] require[e] the filing of a prior felony information whenever the prior conviction is provable. That policy has remained unchanged since 1992. . . .

D. How the Government Abuses its Power to File Prior Felony Informations

My focus here is on the use of *enhanced* mandatory minimums, that is, the use of prior felony informations to enhance the standard mandatory minimums (which themselves enhance off-the-rack federal drug trafficking sentences) in order to procure guilty pleas and to punish defendants who refuse to plead guilty. This focus on the government's abuse of prior felony informations should not obscure the fact that it routinely uses the standard mandatory minimums for the same purposes. The threat of a standard mandatory minimum sentence prevents many more defendants from ever going to trial, a serious problem that I don't intend to minimize here. But they are small potatoes compared to what happens when prior felony informations, or the threat of them, enter the picture.

1. Using Prior Felony Informations to Coerce Guilty Pleas — Lulzim Kupa

Because there is no judicial check on the enhanced mandatory minimums prosecutors can inject into a case, they can put enormous pressure on defendants to plead guilty. In many cases only a daring risk-taker can withstand that pressure. Most people buckle under it, and Luzlim Kupa is a perfect example.

Kupa was 36 years old when I sentenced him on August 9, 2013. He was born in Staten Island to parents who had recently come to the United States from Albania. In 1999 and again in 2007 Kupa was convicted of conspiring to distribute marijuana. When he emerged from prison in 2010 after the second conviction, he engaged in drug trafficking again, leading to this case. Kupa was charged with a 10-life count based on the fact that more than five kilograms of cocaine were involved in the offense.

On March 5, 2013 the government sent Kupa a proposed plea agreement. Despite Kupa's prior marijuana convictions and several other convictions as well — he has a serious criminal history — the agreement promised a withdrawal of the 10-life count and a recommendation to the Court of a sentence within the range of 110-137 months if Kupa would plead guilty. Assuming good time credits, a sentence at the bottom end of the recommended range would result in Kupa serving about seven years and ten months in prison. The email that conveyed the proposed plea agreement stipulated that the offer would expire the next day.

Kupa did not accept the agreement and the case appeared to be headed toward the previously-scheduled April 22, 2013 trial. However, the government wasn't finished encouraging him to plead guilty. On March 15, 2013 it filed a prior felony information providing notice of the two marijuana convictions. Just like that, a defendant for whom the government, only ten days earlier, was willing to recommend an effective sentence of less than eight years was looking at life in prison without the possibility of parole. . . .

So Kupa found himself in a difficult position as his trial approached. Looming in the background was the reality that if he went to trial and the jury convicted him, the law would require that he die in prison. And with each passing day the sentence the government was willing to recommend was creeping upward. If I were to sentence at the bottom end of the government's recommended range in the final proposed plea agreement, the five-week delay from March 5 to April 9, 2013 had already cost Kupa over two years in prison.

On April 10, 2013 Kupa finally caved and entered a plea of guilty. He told me at the time that he wanted to eliminate the potential downside of life in prison by pleading guilty. . . . The voluntariness of a defendant's plea of guilty is an interesting issue when the cost of going to trial is three or more decades in prison. Nevertheless, I found Kupa's plea to be voluntary and accepted it. . . .

If DOJ cannot exercise its power to invoke recidivist enhancements in drug trafficking cases less destructively and less brutally, it doesn't deserve to have the power at all.

NOTES AND QUESTIONS

1. *Kupa* tells a remarkable story about different understandings of "sentencing reform" over the decades. John Mitchell, Richard Nixon's first Attorney General, is one of the heroes in Judge Gleeson's telling. And DOJ's effort to ensure prosecutors did not introduce sentencing disparities was a momentous mistake. The opinion explains well how §851 informations began (in 1970) as a way for prosecutors to expose major traffickers to a higher maximum sentence, but became a two-by-four, if prosecutors so choose, to obtain pleas of guilty—as a result of intervening changes in law and policy. The most important of these were the establishment of mandatory minimum sentences, Congress's desire to withdraw sentencing discretion from judges, the resulting Sentencing Guidelines, and (the related) new DOJ charging policy that required—at least on paper—that prosecutors charge "the most serious, readily provable offense."

2. Before *Kupa* came down, Attorney General Eric Holder had already issued two memos altering DOJ charging policies. The first (as Judge Gleeson explained in a part of the *Kupa* opinion not excerpted) was a 2010 memorandum that

> reiterated the "long-standing" principle that prosecutors should charge the most serious offense available, but added that they should also make individualized assessments as to whether such charges are appropriate. Except to say "the decision whether to seek a statutory sentencing enhancement should be guided by these same principles," the memorandum did not address prior felony informations. . . . The 2010 Holder Policy explicitly stated that "[c]harges should not be filed simply to exert leverage to induce a plea," but . . . that admonition [was hollow].

Kupa, 978 F. Supp. at 430-31, citing Memorandum from Eric H. Holder, Jr., Att'y Gen. of the United States, to All Federal Prosecutors, Department Policy on Charging and Sentencing (May 19, 2010).

And just two months before *Kupa*, Attorney General Holder issued another memorandum that encouraged greater prosecutorial discretion both in (1) charging quantities under 21 U.S.C. §841(b) that trigger mandatory minimums, and (2) filing §851 informations. See Memorandum from Eric H. Holder, Jr., Att'y Gen. of the United States, to U.S. Att'ys and Assistant U.S. Att'ys for the Crim. Div., Department Policy on Charging Mandatory Minimum Sentences and Recidivist Enhancements in Certain Drug Cases (Aug. 12, 2013). The 2013 memo sought to "refine our charging policy regarding mandatory minimums for certain nonviolent, low-level drug offenders." Id. Specifically, in deciding whether to file a §851 information, the memo advised prosecutors to consider:

- Whether the defendant was an organizer, leader, manager or supervisor of others within a criminal organization;
- Whether the defendant was involved in the use or threat of violence in connection with the offense;
- The nature of the defendant's criminal history, including any prior history of violent conduct or recent prior convictions for serious offenses;
- Whether the defendant has significant ties to large-scale drug trafficking organizations, gangs, or cartels;
- Whether the filing would create a gross sentencing disparity with equally or more culpable co-defendants; and
- Other case-specific aggravating or mitigating factors.

Id. at 3. In another part of his opinion we did not excerpt, Judge Gleeson said this 2013 guidance on §851 motions was inadequate to "isolate the most culpable, professional, and hardcore of the recidivist drug trafficking defendants from the large pool of recidivist drug traffickers," 976 F. Supp. 2d at 456-457; he urged DOJ to repudiate the 1992 decision to include prior felony informations among "the most serious, readily provable offenses" that prosecutors are told to charge in every case.

The judge also urged that DOJ "explicitly prohibit the use of prior felony informations to coerce defendants into pleading guilty or to punish those who refuse to do so, and it should enforce the prohibition." Id. at 457. A year later, Attorney General Holder responded to the latter plea with another memorandum addressed to all prosecutors, this time explicitly stating that "[w]hether a defendant is pleading guilty is not one of the factors" that prosecutors should "consider in deciding whether to file an §851 information" and repeating that pursuant to his 2010 memo on Department charging policy, "[c]harges should not be filed simply to exert leverage to induce a plea, nor should charges be abandoned to arrive at a plea bargain that does not reflect the seriousness of the defendant's conduct." Memorandum from Eric H. Holder, Jr., Att'y Gen. of the United States, to Dept. of Justice Att'ys, Guidance Regarding §851 Enhancements in Plea Negotiations (Sept. 24, 2014).

3. Prior to the 2013 and 2014 Holder memos, the practices of U.S. Attorney's Offices with respect to §851 informations varied widely. In its 2011 Report to Congress on mandatory minimum penalties, the Sentencing Commission concluded that its detailed study of the frequency of prior drug felony mandatory minimums "demonstrates a lack of uniformity in application of the enhanced mandatory minimum penalties." U.S. Sent'g Comm'n, 2011 Report to the Congress: Mandatory Minimum Penalties in the Federal Criminal Justice System 254 (2011). For instance, in the Northern District of Iowa, 79 percent of eligible defendants received a §851 enhancement, while the national mean rate was 26 percent and the national median rate was 13 percent. See United States v. Young, 960 F. Supp. 2d 881, 894 (N.D. Iowa 2013) (Bennett, J.) (reporting statistics that he requested and received from the Sentencing Commission after reading its 2011 Report).

4. How effective do you think Attorney General Holder's efforts were? Were the changes in §851 filing policy emanating from Washington actually implemented in the field? One of your authors is in the midst of a large data collection and analysis project that seeks to answer that question. Our preliminary results can be summed up in a few words: although it appears that §851 enhancements have gone down each quarter since October 2014 in the districts we have studied, there remains great variance among districts. In one district in which §851s were routinely filed before the new policy guidance (even in cases that pled out), they are still filed in a majority of eligible cases. Other districts—such as the Southern District of New York, which according to the data released by Judge Bennett, see Young, 960 F. Supp. 2d at 911 app. A, had previously filed in about 16 percent of

eligible cases—have virtually ceased filing them altogether. The Inspector General for the Department of Justice recently published a report likewise concluding (upon examination of limited data from the Sentencing Commission—data not publicly available) that §851 enhancements have become less common. However, the one statistic provided in the IG Report is not impressive in this regard: Between 2012 and 2015 the rate at which prosecutors nationwide filed enhancements in eligible cases fell from 20.6 percent to 17.6 percent, and prosecutors became more likely to withdraw those informations they did file (26.2 percent in 2015 compared with 17.8 percent in 2012). See Office of the Inspector Gen., U.S. Dept. of Justice, Review of the Department's Implementation of Prosecution and Sentencing Reform Principles under the *Smart on Crime* Initiative 30 (June 2017).

5. However effective Main Justice under Eric Holder may or may not have been in altering §851 practices in the 94 U.S. Attorney's Offices around the country may now be of interest primarily to historians and students of public administration. See, e.g., Jeffrey L. Pressman & Aaron Wildavsky, Implementation: How Great Expectations in Washington Are Dashed in Oakland (3d ed. 1984). In May 2017, Attorney General Jeff Sessions explicitly rescinded the Holder memos of August 2013 and September 2014 and announced a new general criminal charging policy that does not include the instruction about "individualized assessments" that *Kupa* had quoted from the 2010 Holder memo. Instead, the Sessions memo begins with the "core principle that prosecutors should charge and pursue the most serious, readily provable offense." And lest there be any doubt, the memo goes on to note that "[b]y definition, the most serious offenses are those that carry the most substantial" sentence, "including mandatory minimum sentences." See Jeff Sessions, Att'y Gen. of the United States, Memorandum for All Federal Prosecutors, Department Charging and Sentencing Policy (May 10, 2017). The Supreme Court cited Sessions' policy as a reason not to rely on expectations of nuanced prosecutorial discretion in Marinello v. United States, 2018 WL 1402426 (U.S. 2018), as we noted in Chapter 3.

6. In his review of implementation of the Holder policies relating to, inter alia, §851 motions, the Inspector General urged the Department to proactively collect data on charging decisions, including the filing of §851 informations, in drug cases: "[A]ll U.S. Attorney's Offices [should be required] to collect charging data that will enable the Department to determine whether its charging and sentencing policies are being effectively implemented." Inspector General Report, *supra*, at 35. There is some irony here. The Holder Justice Department did not require U.S. Attorney's Offices to document the implementation of *its* new policy on the filing of §851 informations (and hence the project that one of us is undertaking to examine such implementation has required case-by-case review of the docket sheet and the defendant's criminal record in every drug prosecution in the districts we are studying). Attorney General Sessions, on the

other hand, has explicitly required that in "circumstances in which good judgment would lead a prosecutor to conclude that a strict application" of *his* new charging policy is not warranted, any such "exception" to the new policy must be approved by the U.S. Attorney or her designate and must be "documented in the file." See Sessions Memorandum, *supra*. Moreover, the response of the Sessions Justice Department to the Inspector General's recommendation of documentation was enthusiastic; DOJ vowed "to ensure that deviations from the memorandum's general charging and sentencing directives [will] . . . be documented in the case file" and "track[ed]" by Main Justice. See Inspector General Report, *supra*, at 60 ("The Department's Response to the Draft Report"). Thus, even U.S. Attorney's Offices that historically did not file many §851 motions may well do so more frequently in the future. That said, the uptake by U.S. Attorney's Offices of policy promulgations from Washington varied greatly across districts under Holder, and will doubtless continue to vary under Sessions and his successors. To what extent do you think this variation is a bug in the federal system? A feature?

7. Do you think it was appropriate for Judge Gleeson, who before he became a judge had been a federal prosecutor for 10 years and stepped down from the bench in 2016 to enter private practice, to communicate with policy makers in the Department of Justice as he did? This was not the first time that Judge Gleeson urged the Department to change its sentencing policies. The year before, in United States v. Dossie, 851 F. Supp. 2d 478 (E.D.N.Y. 2012), he had urged that federal prosecutors be instructed not to charge drug quantities that trigger enhanced sentences unless the defendant had a "kingpin"-type role in the trafficking operation. *Dossie* may have been critical in convincing Attorney General Holder to issue his 2013 memorandum, just as *Kupa* may have been critical in convincing the Attorney General to double down the following year, with his 2014 memorandum expressly prohibiting §851 informations from being used to induce guilty pleas.

3. CALCULATING DRUG QUANTITY

Because the length of the mandatory minimums under 21 U.S.C. §841(b) is tied to the weight of the drugs involved in the offense, calculating drug weight is often contentious. Two important issues are worth noting. First, a defendant's sentence can vary greatly depending on how much of a controlled substance an undercover agent asks to purchase, how long the government investigates a drug conspiracy before making arrests, and how many specific incidents of distribution a prosecutor decides to charge. Some troublesome implications of thus empowering law enforcement agents and prosecutors are investigated later in this chapter.

The second issue arises when the defendant is a player in a larger drug organization or conspiracy. The majority rule is that it is appropriate to aggregate against a single defendant the various weights involved in the underlying offenses constituting a conspiracy that would have been reasonably foreseeable to that defendant. For instance, the defendant may have been convicted of only one drug sale involving a relatively small amount of the drug. But if he is also convicted on a conspiracy count that alleges the conspirators agreed to undertake many sales, the total quantity alleged in the conspiracy count becomes the relevant quantity for sentencing purposes. See, e.g., United States v. Pressley, 469 F.3d 63 (2d Cir. 2006) (affirming a sentence under §841(b) for distribution of at least 1 kilogram of heroin, the amount alleged in the conspiracy count to which defendant pleaded guilty, even though the parties agreed that no single transaction in which Pressley was involved would have triggered a mandatory minimum sentence). Pressley and others had "over the course of 11 years . . . operated a violent crack and heroin distribution right in and around the Gowanus Houses, which is a public housing complex in Brooklyn." Id. at 64. Nevertheless, the court said that "general principles of conspiratorial liability will continue to limit the exposure of low-level dealers who do not initially agree to transact large quantities of narcotics, or to whom such quantities are not reasonably foreseeable." Id. at 66.

Despite that last statement by the Second Circuit panel, it is far from clear that the street dealer who is out there "pitching" for an extended period of time can avoid mandatory minimums any more than the lowly crewman in a scheme to move a freighter-full of drugs as long as the prosecutor specifies the large quantities involved. Is that really what Congress wanted?

In *Dossie*, 851 F. Supp. 2d 478, *supra*, Judge Gleeson noted that when the 1986 Anti-Drug Abuse Act was considered, Senator Robert Byrd, then the Senate Minority Leader, summarized its intent:

> For the kingpins—the masterminds who are really running these operations—and they can be identified by the amount of drugs with which they are involved—we require a jail term upon conviction. If it is their first conviction, the minimum term is 10 years. . . . Our proposal would also provide mandatory minimum penalties for the middle-level dealers as well. Those criminals would also have to serve time in jail. The minimum sentences would be slightly less than those for the kingpins, but they nevertheless would have to go to jail—a minimum of 5 years for the first offense.

Id. at 480 (quoting Sen. Byrd). Judge Gleeson then observed:

> Most people would agree that the people who lead or manage drug-trafficking businesses deserve severe punishment. But right from the start Congress made a mistake, which is apparent in the statement of Senator Byrd

quoted above: The severe sentences it mandated to punish specified *roles* in drug-trafficking offenses were triggered not by role but by drug type and quantity instead. If it wanted the statute to serve its explicitly stated purpose, Congress should have said that an offense gets the 5-to-40 sentence enhancement when the defendant is proved to be a manager of a drug business. Instead, the 5-to-40 sentence enhancement is triggered by offenses involving 28 grams of crack, 100 grams of heroin, or 500 grams of cocaine. 21 U.S.C. §841(b)(1)(B). And instead of hinging the ten-to-life sentence enhancement on the government's proof of "kingpin" or leadership status, Congress simply used larger drug quantities: 280 grams of crack, 1,000 grams of heroin, or 5,000 grams of cocaine. 21 U.S.C. §841(b)(1)(A). So if an offense happens to involve a drug type and quantity that triggers an enhancement, *every* defendant involved in that crime, whatever his or her actual role, can be treated as a leader or manager at the option of the United States Attorney.

Drug quantity is a poor proxy for culpability generally and for a defendant's role in a drug business in particular. Senator Byrd's statement that the leaders and managers of drug operations "can be identified by the amount of drugs with which they are involved" was incorrect. Compare Defendant A, who organizes a dozen teenagers into a business to distribute cocaine in a New York City housing project and adjacent high school, with Defendant B, an addict who is paid $300 to stand at the entrance to a pier and watch for the police while a boatload of cocaine is offloaded. Defendant A is more culpable, and he is the sort of defendant Congress had in mind when it enacted the ten-to-life sentence enhancement, but he will not face even the 5-to-40 sentence enhancement if the conspiracy is nipped in the bud, before it deals more than half a kilogram of cocaine. Defendant B, on the other hand, qualifies for kingpin treatment and a ten-year mandatory minimum if the prosecutor so chooses, based solely on the amount of cocaine on the boat.

Congress's mistake of equating drug quantity with a defendant's role in the offense need not continue to have the devastating consequences on display in this case. If DOJ invokes the harsh sentence enhancements only in cases in which the defendants have supervisory roles—always fewer than 10% of federal drug cases—such unintended and unjust results can be avoided in the future. However, as discussed below, in deploying the mandatory minimum penalties, DOJ has disregarded their purpose. It has turned a law that sought to impose enhanced penalties on a select few into a sentencing regime that imposes them on a great many, producing unfairly harsh consequences that Congress did not intend.

Id. at 480-81 (footnotes omitted).

In United States v. Reyes, 9 F. Supp. 3d 1196 (D.N.M. 2014), Judge James Browning strongly took issue with Judge Gleeson's analysis:

The ADAA's language does not restrict its scope to a "few" or to "kingpins," as Judge Gleeson understands the term. The point is obvious—indeed, Judge Gleeson would not have occasion to criticize the ADAA if its language embodied the intent he ascribes to it. The point is worth making, however, because federal judges generally do best when they confine their thoughts about legislation's wisdom to the pages of a law review article or a newspaper editorial. Because Judge Gleeson has weighed Congress' work and found it wanting, however, the Court will explain why his reasoning is not sound. . . .

Even if one accepts all the premises that undergird reliance on legislative history generally, the ADAA's legislative history does not support the narrow version of legislative intent that Judge Gleeson assigned to Congress. In the first place, Senator Byrd's statement—on which Judge Gleeson rests much of his claim—does not support the notion that the mandatory minimums should apply only to a "few." Senator Byrd said:

> For the kingpins—the masterminds who are really running these operations—and they can be identified by the amount of drugs with which they are involved—we require a jail term upon conviction. If it is their first conviction, the minimum term is 10 years. If it is their second conviction, the minimum term is 20 years. Again, let us remember, they would have to serve that amount of time, at a minimum, without any chance of parole. This new law would also provide that the judge, if he felt the circumstances warranted, could sentence them to a lot more time than that. In fact, the judge could see to it that they were locked up for life.
>
> Our proposal would also provide mandatory minimum penalties for the middle-level dealers as well. Those criminals would also have to serve time in jail. The minimum sentences would be slightly less than those for the kingpins, but they nevertheless would have to go to jail—a minimum of 5 years for the first offense and 10 years for the second. As is the case for the kingpins, those 5-and 10-year terms are only the mandatory minimums; the judge could, if he believes the circumstances dictate, sentence the middle-level drug dealer to 40 years for a first offense and life imprisonment for a second offense. In no event would such offenders ever become eligible for parole.

132 Cong. Rec. 27, 193-94 (Sept 30, 1986). Senator Byrd understood that the ADAA would punish "kingpins," but also "middle-level dealers." Judge Gleeson concludes that Congress intended to apply the ADAA's mandatory minimums to a "few" only after lumping together "middle-level dealers" with the "kingpins" to constitute the "few." Senator Byrd did not, however, limit the ADAA's scope to a "few" or any other number of defendants. Indeed, Byrd recognized that the ADAA includes a graduated, proportional form of punishment that targets not only "kingpins," but those who carry out the kingpins' business.

Moreover, this floor statement from then-Senator Joseph Biden about a predecessor bill to the ADAA suggests that targeting smaller players in the drug trade was part of Congress' deterrence strategy:

> Any effective proposal to decrease drug abuse must involve strategies to reduce both the supply and demand for drugs. This legislation addressed both of these areas. On the supply side, this package provides for stronger new penalties for most drug related crimes, including mandatory minimum penalties for

the king pins [sic] of the drug syndicates *and for those who sell their poisons to our children.*

132 Cong. Rec. §14289 (daily ed. Sept. 30, 1986) (statement of Sen. Joseph Biden) (emphasis added). Then-Senator Biden's statement contradicts Judge Gleeson's view that the harsh sentences under the ADAA were "intended *only* for managers and leaders of drug organizations," United States v. Diaz, 2013 WL 322243, at 1 (emphasis added). Then-Senator Biden instead indicated that the mandatory minimum penalties applied to those who distribute drug the kingpins' goods and not just to the kingpins. Accordingly, if one examines the ADAA's legislative history, it does not univocally support Judge Gleeson's vision of the statute's intent.

9 F. Supp. 3d at 1218-21.

Which judge's analysis is more persuasive? How much of a "mistake" did Congress make when it pegged mandatory minimums to quantity rather than "role"? We will return to this issue in Chapter 10 when considering how drug quantity drives Sentencing Guidelines calculations.

4. THE CRACK/POWDER COCAINE SENTENCING DISPARITY

We have noted that the mandatory minimums of 21 U.S.C. §841(b) are triggered by different quantities of different drugs. The most controversial quantity differential (by far) is that between crack cocaine ("cocaine base," in the words of the statute, 21 U.S.C. §841(B)(1)(A)(iii)), on the one hand, and powder cocaine, on the other. A five-year mandatory sentence kicks in for powder cocaine at 500 grams (a little over one pound), while that same mandatory sentence kicks in if the amount of crack cocaine is 28 grams (or about one ounce). See 21 U.S.C. §941(b)(1)(B). This same 18:1 ratio applies for the higher ten-year mandatory minimum: 280 grams of crack cocaine is treated the same as five kilograms of powder cocaine.

The Notes and Questions below consider why and how Congress adopted this quantity disparity between crack and powder cocaine and why the courts have upheld it.

NOTES AND QUESTIONS

1. The Supreme Court was called on to decide whether the statutory term "cocaine base" includes not only "crack" but also "coca paste," which is the intermediate chemical between raw coca leaves and all processed cocaine. In the course of giving a positive answer to that question, the unanimous opinion explained how crack and powder cocaine differ chemically:

As a matter of chemistry, cocaine is an alkaloid with the molecular formula $C_{17}H_{21}NO_4$. Webster's Third New International Dictionary 434 (2002). An alkaloid is a base—that is, a compound capable of reacting with an acid to form a salt. Id. at 54, 180; see also Brief for Individual Physicians and Scientists as *Amici Curiae* 2-3 (hereinafter Physicians Brief). Cocaine is derived from the coca plant native to South America. The leaves of the coca plant can be processed with water, kerosene, sodium carbonate, and sulphuric acid to produce a paste-like substance. R. Weiss, S. Mirin, & R. Bartel, Cocaine 10 (2d ed. 1994). When dried, the resulting "coca paste" can be vaporized (through the application of heat) and inhaled, i.e., "smoked." See U.S. Sent'g Comm'n, Special Report to the Congress: Cocaine and Federal Sentencing Policy 11-12 (1995) (hereinafter Commission Report). Coca paste contains . . . cocaine in its base form.

Dissolving coca paste in water and hydrochloric acid produces (after several intermediate steps) cocaine hydrochloride. . . . Cocaine hydrochloride, therefore, is not a base. It generally comes in powder form, which we will refer to as "powder cocaine." It is usually insufflated (breathed in through the nose), though it can also be ingested or diluted in water and injected. Because cocaine hydrochloride vaporizes at a much higher temperature than chemically basic cocaine (at which point the cocaine molecule tends to decompose), it is generally not smoked. See Commission Report 11, n.15, 12-13.

Cocaine hydrochloride can be converted into cocaine in its base form by combining powder cocaine with water and a base, like sodium bicarbonate (also known as baking soda). Id. at 14. The chemical reaction changes the cocaine hydrochloride molecule into a chemically basic cocaine molecule, Physicians Brief 4, and the resulting solid substance can be cooled and broken into small pieces and then smoked, Commission Report 14. This substance is commonly known as "crack" or "crack cocaine." Alternatively, powder cocaine can be dissolved in water and ammonia (also a base); with the addition of ether, a solid substance—known as "freebase"—separates from the solution, and can be smoked. Id. at 13. As with crack cocaine, freebase contains cocaine in its chemically basic form. Ibid.

Chemically, therefore, there is no difference between the cocaine in coca paste, crack cocaine, and freebase—all are cocaine in its base form. On the other hand, cocaine in its base form and in its salt form (i.e., cocaine hydrochloride) are chemically different, though they have the same active ingredient and produce the same physiological and psychotropic effects. See id. at 14-22. The key difference between them is the method by which they generally enter the body; smoking cocaine in its base form—whether as coca paste, freebase, or crack cocaine—allows the body to absorb the active ingredient quickly, thereby producing a shorter, more intense high than obtained from insufflating cocaine hydrochloride. . . .

DePierre v. United States, 564 U.S. 70, 72-74 (2011). In other words, cocaine powder is, chemically speaking, cocaine hydrochloride; crack cocaine is made by dissolving cocaine powder in baking soda and then boiling the solution in water until the cocaine hardens. The higher penalties in §841(b) apply to multiple types of cocaine base—not only crack cocaine and coca paste, but also the cocaine-cum-ether that comedian Richard Pryor famously attempted to "freebase."

2. The crack/powder penalty disparity was introduced in the Anti-Drug Abuse Act of 1986. The legislation was passed during a period of heightened concern about drugs after the death that same year of University of Maryland college basketball star, Len Bias, who died of a cocaine overdose while celebrating being drafted by the Boston Celtics. Congress created the disparity by providing a 100:1 ratio in the quantities of powder versus crack that would trigger enhanced penalties (e.g., five grams of crack triggered a mandatory minimum of 20 years, while the trigger quantity for powder cocaine was 500 grams). Over the next quarter century, the difference in treatment of the two forms of cocaine was repeatedly criticized. In particular, as we shall consider in greater depth in the next chapter, the Sentencing Commission repeatedly called for Congress to reduce the quantity disparity. In a Report to Congress in 1995, the Commission reported on a number of troubling discoveries concerning the legislative basis for the disparity:

> The media played a large role in creating the national sense of urgency surrounding drugs, generally and crack cocaine specifically. Whether the media simply reported an urgent situation or rather itself created an exigency has been and will continue to be debated. What is clear, however, is that the crack problem in the United States coincided with large-scale print media and network news coverage of crack. . . .
>
> Some assertions made in these reports were not supported by data at the time and in retrospect were simply incorrect. . . . [One] example is the coverage surrounding the death of Len Bias. . . . The method of cocaine ingestion that killed Bias was not known at the time of his death. Nonetheless, following Bias's death, newspapers across the country ran headlines and stories containing a quote from Dr. Dennis Smyth, Maryland's Assistant Medical Examiner, that Bias probably died of "free-basing" cocaine. . . . The previous week, however, Dr. Yale Caplan, a toxicologist in Maryland's Medical Examiner's Office said that the test of cocaine found in the vial at the scene "probably was not crack." . . . Dr. Smyth's assertions, however, received the bulk of the coverage. . . .
>
> Eric Sterling, who for eight years served as counsel to the House Judiciary Committee and played a significant staff role in the development of many provisions of the Drug Abuse Act of 1986, testified before the United States Sentencing Commission in 1993 that the "crack cocaine overdose death of NCAA basketball star Len Bias" was instrumental in the development of the federal crack cocaine laws. . . .
>
> Not until a year later, during the trial of Brian Tribble who was accused of supplying Bias with the cocaine, did Terry Long, a University of Maryland basketball player who participated in the cocaine party that led to Bias's death, testify that he, Bias, Tribble, and another player snorted powder cocaine over a four-hour period. Tribble's testimony received limited coverage. . . .

U.S. Sent'g Comm'n, Special Report to the Congress: Cocaine and Federal Sentencing Policy 40-43 (1995).

3. The extreme disparity in sentencing treatment of crack and cocaine—along with the disparity's dubious origins—provides a glaring challenge to the allegedly "scientific" distinctions between controlled substances. But the existence of the disparity represents more than a simple cautionary tale about the influence of politics on "science." It also illustrates the difficulties that arise whenever the government seeks to make value-laden decisions at the intersection of public policy and science. Even though it was highly critical of the original 100:1 quantity differential, the Sentencing Commission also concluded that "[r]esearch and public policy may support somewhat higher penalties for crack versus powder cocaine. . . ." Id. at xiv. The Commission specifically noted,

> [I]mportant distinctions between the two may warrant higher penalties for crack than powder. For example, factors in the route of administration (i.e., smoking versus snorting) and attributes of the crack cocaine market make crack different from powder from a policy perspective. These factors generally include: 1) a greater risk for psychological addiction due to the rapid high and concomitant rapid low resulting from inhalation of crack; 2) because powder cocaine can be converted easily into smaller doses of crack that can be sold more cheaply and in potent quantities, crack is more readily available to a larger segment of the population, particularly women, children, and the economically disadvantaged; 3) the apparently higher correlation between crack and violence than between powder and violence; and 4) the increased use of young people in the distribution of crack.

Id. at xiii-xiv.

4. The political salience of the differential treatment of crack cocaine and powder cocaine is due in large part to its disparate impact on Black defendants. We noted in the introduction to this chapter, for instance, that in the year 2016, over 80 percent of those convicted of distributing crack cocaine were Black, whereas only about 6 percent were White. Twenty years ago, David Sklansky wrote what remains the leading critique of the crack/powder disparity. He posited several reasons for the disparate racial impact:

> The reasons for this disproportionate impact are probably several. First, crack use is strongly concentrated in inner city, black communities, in part because crack is cheap, and in part for the same reasons drug abuse in general is concentrated in economically marginalized areas. Second, crack dealing appears to be even more strongly concentrated in the inner city, in part because that is where the customers are, and in part because inner city youth have fewer attractive alternatives for earning money. Third, police and prosecutors in some cases may pay a disproportionate amount of attention to crack dealing

in inner city neighborhoods, in part because it is more visible there, and in part, possibly, for less pleasant reasons.

David A. Sklansky, Cocaine, Race and Equal Protection, 47 Stan. L. Rev. 1283, 1289 (1995). Sklansky went on to examine the legislative history of the crack/powder provision of the 1986 Act, which is a case study of what Bill Stuntz has called our "pathological" politics of criminal law, see William J. Stuntz, The Pathological Politics of Criminal Law, 100 Mich. L. Rev. 505 (2001). As Sklansky describes:

> The first of many bills proposing heightened penalties for crack offenses was introduced on June 20, 1986. Its sponsors took note of the Newsweek article and a New York Times story reporting the spread of crack use to the middle class. . . .
>
> This was not the only fear voiced in Congress. Some members stressed the particular dangers that crack posed for black communities; indeed, part of the concern about crack was that its marketing put cocaine, previously a pricey drug for the rich, within reach of the poor. But the concern that resonated most strongly was not that crack and other narcotics were tightening their hold on the inner city—it was that they were spreading outward from their former confines. Public and congressional concern about cocaine abuse was sharply heightened, for example, by the cocaine-related deaths in late June 1986 of two black athletes, Len Bias and Don Rogers. For Congress though, as for most white Americans, what the deaths of Bias and Rogers dramatized was not that drug abuse posed special threats for minority communities, but that drug abuse threatened everyone." . . .
>
> Alarmed by a perceived explosion of crack use and, no doubt, by the impending midterm elections, members of Congress engaged in a kind of partisan bidding war over the penalties for crack trafficking. As the elections drew closer, the difference between the mandatory penalties proposed for powder cocaine and those proposed for crack tended to widen. At the end of July, for example, Senator Paula Hawkins, arguing that "logic and conviction would dictate an attack on crack through an attack on cocaine itself," called for stiff mandatory sentences that did not distinguish between crack and powder. Two weeks later, though, she joined Senator Alfonse D'Amato in proposing mandatory sentences that treated twenty-five grams of crack the same as five-hundred grams—twenty times as much—of powder cocaine. The 20:1 ratio also appeared in the legislative packages proposed in September by the Reagan Administration and the Republican Senate leadership. Earlier that same month, however, the Democratic leadership in the House of Representatives introduced an omnibus drug bill employing a ratio of 50:1. And the day after that bill was introduced, the Senate Democratic leadership put forward its own drug bill, containing the 100:1 ratio ultimately signed into law. . . .

Sklansky, *supra*, at 1294-96. Given that Congress was clearly aware that most crack dealers were Black, why does its differential treatment of crack cocaine and powder cocaine not, in the unanimous view of the federal circuit courts, violate the Equal Protection Clause of the Constitution? Sklansky provides interesting insights:

> The reason for this uniform outcome lies less in any lack of sensitivity on the part of circuit judges than in the nature of the rules the Supreme Court has developed for evaluating equal protection challenges. . . .
>
> The rules begin by directing courts to subject the sentences to "rational-basis" scrutiny . . . because the federal narcotics statute does not discriminate expressly on the basis of race, and cannot be shown to have been motivated in whole or in part by what the Supreme Court has termed a "discriminatory purpose." . . .
>
> In light of some of the rhetoric surrounding passage of the 1986 statute—"big-shouldered Trinidadian," "bands of young black men" peddling crack near "unsuspecting white retirees"—it is hardly idle to suggest that the harshness of the crack provisions may in fact reflect some degree of active antipathy toward blacks. But it is difficult if not impossible to prove, in part because hardly anyone admits to racism anymore, and in part because crack posed real dangers as well as symbolic ones, and much of what motivated Congress in 1986 appears to have been a well-founded fear of the drug's actual effects, on blacks as well as on whites. . . .
>
> [Rational-basis] scrutiny . . . consists of asking only whether Congress was pursuing a legitimate goal, and whether the classification drawn by Congress is rationally related to that goal. The federal crack sentences pass these tests easily. . . .

Id. at 1303-04. But even assuming that Congress had a "rational basis" for making *some* distinction between crack cocaine and powder cocaine, why haven't the courts tested the rationality of such an extreme (100:1) quantity differential? Sklansky answers as follows:

> The rational-basis test asks only whether the line Congress has drawn is rationally related to a legitimate governmental interest; the test entirely ignores how and to what extent Congress has made the line count. Current doctrine thus directs courts to inquire whether it is reasonable for Congress to distinguish between crack and powder cocaine, but not whether it is reasonable to distinguish between them by treating an ounce of one the same as 100 ounces of the other.
>
> Unfortunately, it is precisely here, in the extent of the differential treatment, that one would most expect unconscious racism to manifest itself. The problem of "racially selective sympathy and indifference" becomes most acute not when Congress divides people into classes, but when it determines what treatment people in each class should receive. Far from operating independently, then, the blindness of current doctrine to unconscious racism and to the extent of differential treatment reinforce each other. Together they

render virtually invisible to equal protection analysis much of what is most troubling about the federal crack sentences. . . .

Id. at 1309.

5. On August 3, 2010, President Obama signed into law the Fair Sentencing Act of 2010, Pub. L. No. 111-220, 124 Stat. 2372. This legislation reduced the quantity disparity between crack cocaine and powder cocaine from 100:1 to 18:1. (You would be right to infer that the ratio of 18:1 was simply a compromise, and, like many compromises, is as arbitrary as the original 100:1 ratio.) Hence, as we have noted, the five-year mandatory minimum sentence for trafficking in crack is triggered at 28 grams of crack, while it remains at 500 grams for powder cocaine; the mandatory ten-year sentence is triggered at 280 grams of crack, while it remains at 5,000 grams for powder cocaine. Is this the right differential? This statute also eliminated the five-year mandatory minimum sentence for simple possession of five or more grams of crack that Congress had enacted in 1988. At the same time, the legislation increased fines for drug trafficking.

Are there broader lessons from this saga? The story of how crack penalties were finally reduced in 2010 is one of strong political forces eventually assembled to address a stark racial disparity. Can we expect similar forces to assemble to address the legislative responses to the methamphetamine and opioid epidemics?

5. SENTENCING ENTRAPMENT

In United States v. Hinds, 329 F.3d 184 (D.C. Cir. 2003), the defendant sold cocaine and crack cocaine to an undercover police officer, who had specifically requested the crack cocaine. The defendant claimed that "but for the request and assistance of the government and its informant, he would have sold powder rather than crack and hence should be subject to the less stringent sentencing guideline provisions applicable to the former." Id. at 188. The court noted, however, that it had "consistently rejected" just this argument and explained:

In United States v. Walls, for example, the defendants alleged that they converted powder cocaine into crack because the undercover agents to whom they were selling demanded it; in fact, one agent testified that he had insisted on the delivery of crack because he wanted to subject the defendants to more severe sentences. 70 F.3d 1323, 1328-29 (D.C. Cir. 1995). The defendants claimed that this constituted "sentencing entrapment," and that they should be sentenced as if they had distributed powder rather than crack. But the court rejected that claim, noting that the Supreme Court "has warned against using an entrapment defense to control law enforcement practices of which a court might disapprove." Id. at 1329. Instead, *Walls* emphasized that the "main element in any entrapment defense is . . . the defendant's 'predisposition'—'whether the defendant was an "unwary innocent" or, instead, an "unwary criminal" who readily availed himself of the opportunity to perpetrate the crime.'" 70 F.3d at 1329 (quoting Mathews v. United States, 485 U.S. 58, 63 (1988)); see also United States v. Glover, 153 F.3d 749, 756 (D.C. Cir. 1998) (holding that even if the government had chosen to contract for a drug purchase within 1000 feet of a school to increase the defendant's sentencing exposure, the "usual elements of the entrapment defense—inducement and lack of predisposition—would still have to be shown" to make out a viable claim). . . .

329 F.3d at 188. *Hinds* is hardly alone. Every court of appeals has held that the standard for "sentencing entrapment" is the same as the standard the defendant must meet to prove "entrapment" as an affirmative defense at trial—that he was not "predisposed" to commit the offense and was "induced" to do so by government agents.

Some circuits, however, recognize a related concept—"sentencing manipulation." As the Ninth Circuit has explained:

"[S]entencing manipulation" occurs when the government increases a defendant's guideline sentence by conducting a lengthy investigation which increases the number of drug transactions and quantities for which the defendant is responsible. United States v. Torres, 563 F.3d 731, 734 (8th Cir. 2009). In other words, what sets "sentencing entrapment" apart from "sentencing manipulation" is that, in the latter, "the judicial gaze should, in the usual case, focus primarily—though not necessarily exclusively—on the government's conduct and motives." United States v. Fontes, 415 F.3d 174, 181-82 (1st Cir. 2005).

United States v. Boykin, 785 F.3d 1352, 1360 (9th Cir. 2015). In *Fontes*, the First Circuit noted that a trial court could "impose a sentence below the statutory mandatory minimum as an equitable remedy for sentencing factor manipulation by the government." 415 F.3d at 180.

While recognizing the concept of "sentencing manipulation," the Eighth Circuit cautioned that such manipulation would seldom be established. Quoting its previous decisions on the issue, the court reminded its audience, including sentencing judges and law enforcement agents:

"[I]t is legitimate for police to continue to deal with someone with whom they have already engaged in illicit transactions in order to establish that person's guilt beyond a reasonable doubt or to probe the depth and extent of a criminal enterprise, to determine whether coconspirators exist, and to trace the drug deeper into the distribution hierarchy." Police may also engage in "a legitimate pattern of increasing the amount of drugs" in order to determine what quantity of drugs a defendant will deal.

United States v. Torres, 563 F.3d 731, 734 (8th Cir. 2009) (internal citations omitted). But see United States v. Bigley, 786 F.3d 11, 16 (D.C. Cir. 2015) (holding, in a child pornography case, that the sentencing court erred in failing to consider whether a lower sentence was appropriate given the defendant's "nonfrivolous claim of sentencing manipulation" by a D.C. undercover officer).

Do you understand why the federal courts are exceedingly reluctant to recognize a broad, trans-substantive doctrine of "sentencing entrapment" or "sentencing manipulation"? Indeed, the latter may be even more problematic than the former. Consider the nature of federal investigations into the complex crimes we have examined in this and previous chapters. What would come of such investigations if the defendant had a defense of "sentencing manipulation" whenever he could have been arrested earlier for a lesser crime? Would the defendant be effectively immunized from punishment for his more serious crimes (such as RICO, CCE, or money laundering), proof of which may not be obtained until long after law enforcement officials have probable cause to arrest him on several other offenses? As to both sentencing entrapment and sentencing manipulation, the courts may also be reluctant to interfere with the executive's decision to employ undercover agents, who have been critical in obtaining evidence not only of drug crimes, but also of all "consensual" crimes (including bribery) and complex group crimes (including terrorism). Courts know that undercover agents sometimes propose or encourage certain illegal acts in order to enhance their credibility. What gives the courts license to prohibit these investigatory tactics—especially under the guise of criminal law doctrine?

The entrapment defense that does exist in federal courts was developed by the Supreme Court, see Sherman v. United States, 356 U.S. 369 (1958); Sorrells v. United States, 287 U.S. 435 (1932), in the normal course of the Court's common lawmaking in the area of criminal law, see generally Chapter 3. The defense is based not on due process concerns, but rather on the presumed intent of Congress—that Congress would not want conviction of persons who are not predisposed to commit a crime. See generally United States v. Russell, 411 U.S. 423 (1973). But the Court in *Russell* left open the possibility that "we may some day be presented with a situation in which the conduct of law enforcement agents is so outrageous that due process principles would absolutely bar the government from invoking judicial processes to obtain a conviction." 411 U.S. at 431-32.

The due process concern referred to in *Russell* is "outrageous" government conduct. One might approach the constitutional issue in the context of current federal drug law from a different angle: Even if it is generally constitutionally appropriate for undercover agents to encourage a particular crime (as long as the defendant is predisposed), might the thorough, regimented statutory regime of federal drug sentencing counsel the courts to develop an additional limitation on law enforcement agents in these cases, lest these agents assume (possibly even unwittingly) the function of both prosecutor and sentencing judge? Dealers in one type of drug, or dealers who generally sell a particular quantity of some drug, may well be predisposed (if the right circumstances arise) to buy or sell some other drug or some other quantity. Because the severe mandatory penalties in 21 U.S.C. §841(b) are triggered by the type and weight of the drug, the most perfunctory actions of law enforcement agents can literally determine which crime the defendant will be guilty of and, hence, what mandatory penalty will apply. A small change in just one word uttered by the agent—"crack" instead of "coke," or "brick" instead of "bag"—is likely to result in a much more severe criminal conviction (judging by the mandatory penalty) of the defendant. If Congress continues to provide for mandatory minimum sentences based on the quantity of the drug involved, do you think the courts might be more willing to fashion a special "entrapment" doctrine applicable only to sentencing under the present penalty structure of Title 21 of the United States Code? Should they?

6. DRUGS, GUNS, AND CONSECUTIVE MANDATORY MINIMUM SENTENCES

In the Gun Control Act of 1968, Congress made it a crime to use an unlawful weapon when engaging in a federal felony. See 18 U.S.C. §924(c). The provision has been modified on several occasions. Most importantly, in 1986 Congress greatly expanded §924(c) to prohibit using or carrying a firearm (whether or not such possession of a gun was itself unlawful) "in relation to" a drug trafficking crime (as well as crimes of violence), and imposed a mandatory minimum sentence of five years for this offense. There have been several subsequent amendments, and the key provision now reads as follows:

---

18 U.S.C. §924(c)

(1) (A) Except to the extent that a greater minimum sentence is otherwise provided by this subsection or by any other provision of law, any person who, during and in relation to any crime of violence or drug trafficking crime (including a crime of violence or drug trafficking crime that provides for an enhanced punishment if committed by the use of a deadly or dangerous weapon or device) for which the person may be prosecuted in a court of the United States, uses or carries a firearm, or who, in furtherance of any such crime, possesses a firearm, shall, in addition to the punishment provided for such crime of violence or drug trafficking crime—

   (i) be sentenced to a term of imprisonment of not less than 5 years;

   (ii) if the firearm is brandished, be sentenced to a term of imprisonment of not less than 7 years; and

> (iii) if the firearm is discharged, be sentenced to a term of imprisonment of not less than 10 years.

NOTES AND QUESTIONS

1. Note the connection in the view of Congress among drugs, guns, and violence. Indeed, according to data published by the United States Sentencing Commission, a weapon was involved in 18 percent of the nearly 20,000 convictions for drug trafficking in 2016, including 21 percent of meth cases and 32 percent of crack-cocaine cases. See U.S. Sent'g Comm'n, Sourcebook, *supra,* at tbl. 39. The actual frequency of weapons used in drug-trafficking crimes may be even greater than this data suggests. In particular, the five-year minimum mandatory sentence for conviction under §924(c) is a potent source of plea-leverage for federal prosecutors, who may agree to "swallow the gun count" if the defendant makes an early plea to the underlying drug-trafficking charges.

2. After Congress amended §924(c) in 1986 to provide for a mandatory, consecutive five-year sentence for "use" of a weapon in a drug-trafficking offense, federal prosecutors began to charge this offense in a number of novel factual settings. Does a person "use" a firearm "in relation to" a drug offense when he exchanges a gun for narcotics? Federal prosecutors thought so, but the circuit courts split on the issue. In Smith v. United States, 508 U.S. 223 (1993), the Supreme Court held that §924(c)'s "use" proscription encompasses such bartering; the majority rejected Justice Scalia's contention (joined by Justices Stevens and Souter) in dissent that the "ordinary" meaning of the word "use" should control, and that if there was lack of clarity, the rule of lenity should apply.

Two years later, however, the Court unanimously gave a narrow construction to the word "use" in another context: where a gun or other weapon is simply possessed (actually or constructively) by a defendant who is engaged in drug trafficking. See Bailey v. United States, 516 U.S. 137 (1995). Bailey had been stopped for a traffic offense, and the police discovered a significant amount of cocaine. Bailey was arrested, and during a subsequent search of the car's locked trunk, the police discovered a firearm inside a bag. In addition to drug offenses, Bailey was convicted of "using" a firearm "in relation to" a drug-trafficking offense. The question before the Court was whether prosecutors and the lower courts in *Bailey* had given too broad a construction to the word "use."

Before proceeding to that question, however, you may have noted that the current statute, set forth above, clearly proscribes "possession" in furtherance of a drug crime; realize, however, that this provision was added *as a result* of *Bailey,* as we discuss in the following Note. When the Supreme Court decided *Bailey,* the statute required a minimum five-year term of imprisonment only for a person who "during and in relation to any crime of violence or drug trafficking crime . . . *uses or carries* a firearm" (emphasis added). The lower courts had been split on what constitutes "use," with some circuits holding that mere possession of a weapon at the scene is insufficient, see United States v. Castro-Lara, 970 F.2d 976, 983 (1st Cir. 1992), but others holding that even the "presence" of the weapon at the scene is sufficient, see United States v. Hager, 969 F.2d 883, 889 (10th Cir. 1992) (the gun was "used" because it was in a pair of boots near the drug location).

In *Bailey*, Justice O'Connor explained that the word at issue "poses some interpretational difficulties," and gave a memorable example: "Consider the paradoxical statement: 'I *use* a gun to protect my house, but I've never had to *use* it.'" 516 U.S. 137 at 143. She explained that the word "draws meaning from its context, and we will look not only to the word itself, but also to the statute and the sentencing scheme, to determine the meaning Congress intended." Id. Both the "ordinary or natural" meaning of the word "use" and its placement in the statutory scheme suggested a narrow meaning, she concluded. If, as the Government argued, "use" encompasses a defendant who brings a gun along "to embolden himself," then "no role remains for 'carry.'" Id. at 145. On the other hand,

> [u]nder the interpretation we enunciate today, a firearm can be used without being carried, e.g., when an offender has a gun on display during a transaction . . . ; and a firearm can be carried without being used, e.g., when an offender keeps a gun hidden in his clothing throughout a drug transaction.

Id. at 146. Additionally, mere possession could never be enough to constitute use, Justice O'Connor wrote, because Congress used the word "possession" or "possess" in other subsections of the gun control laws, and hence knew to employ that word when it sought to extend liability for the simple act of possession. Id. at 143.

In the end, *Bailey* decided, the word "use" in §924(c) encompasses only "activities that fall within 'active employment'" of the firearm. These would include "brandishing, displaying, bartering, striking with, and, most obviously, firing or attempting to fire a firearm"—as would "a [verbal] reference to a firearm calculated to bring about a change in the circumstances" and "silent but obvious and forceful presence of a gun on a table." Id. at 148. But "use" does not extend to simply "hiding" a gun for use "if necessary." More generally, "the word 'use' in §924(c)(1) cannot support the extended applications that prosecutors have sometimes placed on it, in order to penalize drug-trafficking offenders for firearms possession." Id. at 150. Returning to her paradoxical hypothetical, Justice O'Connor explained that the homeowner who said she "uses" a gun for home protection meant the "nonactive" use or mere "inert presence" of a weapon someplace at the home—the kind of "use" *not* covered by §924(c). See id. at 149.

Justice O'Connor noted that the narrow construction the Court was giving to the word "use" still left prosecutors the option of charging a defendant under the "carry" prong of the statute, and "[t]he 'carry' prong of §924(c)(1) . . . brings some offenders who would not satisfy the 'use' prong within the reach of the statute." Id. at 150.

3. You have previously seen the "plain meaning" approach to interpretation that was adopted in *Bailey* (but arguably not in *Smith*). Sometimes the Court has employed this approach to put the brakes on creative prosecutorial theories that depart from the core meaning of a prohibition; remember McNally v. United States, 483 U.S. 350 (1987), considered in Chapter 4. (Sometimes, on the other hand, interpreting a criminal prohibition according to the ordinary meaning of its terms results in more expansive federal prosecutorial authority; recall Durland v. United States, 161 U.S. 306 (1896), and Brogan v. United States, 522 U.S. 398 (1998), both considered in Chapter 3.) To what extent should we attribute the close linguistic scrutiny in *Bailey* to a judicial preference for judicial discretion? After all, mandatory minimums are most relevant when a judge would otherwise sentence below them.

Remember also Congress's quick response to *McNally*: overturning the holding by enacting 18 U.S.C. §1346, and thereby expanding the scope of schemes to defraud prohibited by the mail and wire fraud statutes. Congress responded in similar fashion to the decision in *Bailey*, by amending §924(c) to clearly proscribe not only using or carrying a firearm in drug-trafficking and violent crimes, but also "possessing" a firearm "in furtherance of" such crimes. See Pub. L. No. 105-386, 112 Stat. 3469 (1998). During Senate Judiciary Committee hearings considering various proposals to amend §924(c), there was no doubt that the proposals were a direct response to *Bailey*. See Violent and Drug Trafficking Crimes: The Bailey Decision's Effect on Prosecutions Under Section 924(c): Hearing Before the S. Comm. on the Judiciary, 104 Cong. Rec. 2, 10 (1996) (statement of Sen. Biden) ("We don't want people committing crimes, but if we have a choice, we want to penalize the person who thinks they may or may not need a gun, but nonetheless has it in their possession when they commit a crime—we want to punish that person more than the person that doesn't."). Indeed, legislation to undo *Bailey* had been proposed almost as soon as the decision came down. See 142 Cong. Rec. S1976 (daily ed. Mar. 13, 1996) (statement of Sen. Helms) (introducing S. 1612 to undo "the tragic result of an unfortunate and unwise Supreme Court decision"). In addition to adding the mandatory sentence enhancement of at least five years for possession, the amendment added language stipulating that "if the firearm is brandished," the enhancement is a mandatory sentence of seven years, and if it is "discharged," that mandatory sentence is increased to ten years. Congress also increased the penalties for repeat offenders and for felons who use certain especially dangerous firearms.

What do you make of §924(c)(1)(A)'s participation requirement ("in furtherance of") with respect to possession? Do you think that "in furtherance of" should be read as somehow more stringent than "during and in relation to"? If so, why do you think Congress would have adopted a different standard for "possesses" than it required for "uses or carries"? See, for instance, United States v. Arreola, 467 F.3d 1153, 1159 (9th Cir. 2006) (holding that "in furtherance of" is a more stringent requirement for possession). How restrictive do you think "in furtherance of" is in practice? For an example, see United States v. Gonzalez, 528 F.3d 1207 (9th Cir. 2008) (upholding the conviction of Border Patrol agent who took one of 30 bales of marijuana from a pickup truck while purporting to help a state trooper conduct a traffic stop; the agent's partner, the court noted, would never have left him alone to guard the seized load had he been unarmed).

4. *Bailey*'s restrictive interpretation of the meaning of "use" in §924(c) led to a significant increase in collateral attacks brought by prisoners who had been convicted under jury instructions, or who had pled guilty to charges that employed a broader definition of the term. See Pragati Bhatt Patrick & Thomas Bak, Firearms Prosecutions in Federal Courts: Trends in the Use of 18 U.S.C. §924(c), 6 Buff. Crim. L. Rev. 1189, 1199-1200 (2003) (reporting that in the year after *Bailey* came down, there was a 62 percent increase in motions to vacate sentence under 42 U.S.C. §2255); Bousley v. United States, 523 U.S. 614 (1998) (permitting collateral relief for defendants who entered pleas to §924(c) if they can prove that their actual behavior did not constitute "use" within the meaning of *Bailey*). Such collateral attacks on already-final convictions are an inevitable consequence every time the Supreme Court decides that the true scope of a federal statute is not as broad as federal prosecutors had thought and lower courts had permitted. *McNally* likewise resulted in the vacation of convictions that had employed an honest-services theory, see, e.g., United States v. Shelton, 848 F.2d 1485 (9th Cir. 1988); Skilling v. United States, 561 U.S. 358 (2010), both excerpted in Chapter 4. When the Court narrows the scope of a statute, it means that all those convictions that the courts allowed under broader readings are suddenly lawless. Do you think this is one reason that appellate courts often continue to tolerate creative or broad statutory interpretations once they have become commonplace?

5. The legislative history of the "Bailey-Fix Act," as it became known, made no reference to an intervening Supreme Court decision that addressed the meaning of the word "carries" in the same statutory subsection, see Angela LaBuda Collins, The Latest Amendment to 18 U.S.C. §924(c): Congressional Reaction to the Supreme Court's Interpretation of the Statute, 48 Cath. U. L. Rev. 1319, 1350 (1999). In Muscarello v. United States, 524 U.S. 125 (1998), Justice Breyer wrote for the Court in construing "carries a firearm" broadly to include carrying a weapon in a vehicle, rather

than solely on one's person. (You will recall that we considered this case briefly in Chapter 3 when comparing different approaches to interpretation of federal criminal statutes.) One of the defendants had a gun locked in his car's glove compartment, and the others had bags of guns in the car's locked trunk. Given the Court's broad interpretation of the "carries" language, their convictions under §924(c) were affirmed. The petitioners had argued that *Bailey*'s narrow interpretation of "use" required a similar, narrow construction of the companion verb "carry." The majority turned this argument on its head, noting that to give both "use" and "carry" narrow interpretations would leave "a gap in coverage" and thus be inconsistent with Congress's evident intent to deter gun violence. See id. at 136-37. Unlike *Bailey* (but like *Smith*), *Muscarello* was not unanimous. Justice Ginsburg argued for the four dissenters that Congress should have used the word "transport" if it wished to include guns carried in cars. See *Muscarello*, 524 U.S. at 145-48 (Ginsburg, J., dissenting). Why do you think Justice Breyer and four others were willing to go along with a narrow interpretation of "use" but not of "carry" in the same provision of law? Do you think that the avalanche of post-*Bailey* collateral attacks made (or should have made) any difference? Do you think the Court was aware that Congress was considering a "Bailey-Fix Act" and that this made any difference?

6. As interpreted by the Court and as amended by Congress, the "add-on" mandatory sentences prescribed by 18 U.S. §924(c) thus have broad applicability to any drug trafficking crime and to many other federal felonies that may be considered "violent" by the very fact that a gun was somehow involved. When only one gun is involved, the add-on is just five years. But when two guns are involved, the mandatory add-on becomes 30 years—five for the first gun, and 25 for the second. (As we will see in the case excerpted below, where three guns are involved, the add-on sentence is 60 years!—and so on.) The courts have rejected Second Amendment, Eighth Amendment, Due Process, and Double Jeopardy challenges to the provision.

Still, the courts have sometimes chafed at the resultant high sentences, especially where numerous gun counts result in huge increases in the defendant's sentence. In United States v. Angelos, 345 F. Supp. 2d 1227 (D. Utah 2004), the defendant was arrested after thrice selling $350 worth of marijuana to an undercover agent. Id. at 1230. During two of those transactions, he carried a handgun, and when the police executed an arrest warrant, they found additional firearms. Id. Despite defendant's status as a first-time offender, his successful music career, and his two young children, the government sought a sentence of more than 60 years on the drug offenses to be followed by another 55 years for the firearms charges under the mandatory minimum provisions of 18 U.S.C. §924(c) (five years for the first gun and 25 years for each subsequent possession). Id. Judge Paul Cassell found "that to sentence Mr. Angelos to prison for the rest of his life is unjust, cruel, and even irrational," and noted that the proposed sentence was "far in excess of the sentence imposed for such serious crimes as aircraft hijacking, second degree murder, espionage, . . . and rape," the court ultimately, and "reluctantly," concluded that it had "no choice but to impose the 55-year sentence." Id. Judge Cassell concluded his nearly 40-page opinion with a plea to the political branches:

> For the reasons explained in my opinion, I am legally obligated to impose this sentence. But I feel ethically obligated to bring this injustice to the attention of those who are in a position to do something about it.

> *A. Recommendation for Executive Commutation . . .*
> The Framers were well aware that "[t]he administration of justice . . . is not necessarily always wise or certainly considerate of circumstances which may properly mitigate guilt." In my mind, this is one of those rare cases where the system has malfunctioned. . . .
> I recommend that the President commute Mr. Angelos' sentence to a prison term of no more than 18 years, the average sentence recommended by the jury that heard this case. The court agrees with the jury that this is an appropriate sentence in this matter in light of all of the other facts discussed in this opinion. The Clerk's Office is directed to forward a copy of this opinion with its commutation recommendation to the Office of Pardon Attorney.

> *B. Recommendation for Legislative Reform*
> While a Presidential commutation of Mr. Angelos' sentence would resolve his particular case, §924(c) remains in place and will continue to create injustices in future cases. For the reasons explained in this opinion, the problem stems from the count stacking features of mandatory minimum sentences. In our system of separate powers, general correction of this problem lies in the hands of Congress. . . .
> Again, the question arises regarding whether it is appropriate for me to communicate with Congress regarding apparent problems that have arisen in applying the mandatory minimums in this case. Presumably Congress no less than the President desires feedback on how its statutes are operating. Congress also presumably wants to be informed in situations where its mandates are producing adverse effects, such as demeaning crime victims or risking a possible backlash from citizen juries. . . .
> This court deals with sentencing matters on a daily basis and feels in a unique position to advise Congress on such matters. . . .
> [I conclude that] it is appropriate for me to communicate with Congress concerning the need for legislative reform. I express no view on mandatory minimum sentencing schemes in general. But for the reasons discussed in this opinion, one particular feature of the federal scheme—the "count stacking" feature of §924(c) for first-time offenders—has led to an unjust result in this case and will lead to unjust results in other cases. Particularly in cases (like this one) that do not involve direct violence, Congress should consider repealing this feature and making §924(c) a true recidivist statute of the

three-strikes-and-you're-out variety. In other words, Congress should consider applying the second and subsequent §924(c) enhancements only to defendants who have been previously convicted of a serious offense, rather than to first-time offenders like Angelos. This is an approach to §924(c) that the Tenth Circuit[182] and Justices Stevens, O'Connor, and Blackmun[183] believed Congress intended. It is an approach to sentencing that makes good sense. The Clerk's Office is directed to forward a copy of this opinion to the Chair and Ranking Member of the House and Senate Judiciary Committees. . . .

345 F. Supp. 2d at 1261-63.

Do you think it was it appropriate for Judge Cassell, who has since stepped down from the bench and returned to teaching, to make legislative and commutation recommendations in a judicial opinion? Unlike Judge Gleeson in *Kupa, supra,* Judge Cassell was directing his recommendations not to a party appearing before him, but to the political branches. But if such communication is not appropriate, what is the proper role of the lower courts in situations where they believe Congress (with the President in his legislative capacity) has enacted a patently unjust policy? Would it have been appropriate for the judge to pressure the prosecutor to drop the two additional weapons possession charges?

7. In a major report on mandatory minimum sentences issued in 2011, the Sentencing Commission had a different solution to the "gun-stacking" problem. The Commission urged Congress to give sentencing courts more discretion as to whether the mandatory terms under §924(c) should be concurrent or consecutive to the sentence(s) on the underlying offense(s). See U.S. Sent'g Comm'n, 2011 Report to Congress, *supra,* at 364, 368-69. Congress did not act on this suggestion, but the Supreme Court arguably did last Term. In Dean v. United States, 137 S. Ct. 1170 (2017), the Court unanimously held that even though the §924(c) makes it clear that the gun count mandatory sentence must be "in addition to and consecutive to the sentence for the underlying predicate offense," id. at 1174, sentencing judges may, in sentencing the underlying offense, take into account that "the defendant will serve the mandatory minimums imposed under §924(c)." Id. Dean had urged at his sentencing that inasmuch as he faced 30 years on the two gun counts alone, the judge should sentence him to a total of 30 years and one day—by sentencing him to just one day his underlying crimes (of robbery, conspiracy to commit robbery, and being a felon-in-possession of a gun). The sentencing judge "agreed that 30 years plus one day was 'more than sufficient for a sentence in this case.'" Id. at 1175. The judge demurred, however, because "[i]n his view, he was required to disregard

---

182. United States v. Chalan, 812 F.2d 1302, 1315 (10th Cir. 1987).
183. Deal v. United States, 508 U.S. [129, 137] (1993) (Stevens, J., dissenting).

Dean's 30-year mandatory minimum when determining the appropriate sentences for Dean's other counts of conviction," and those crimes "plainly warranted sentences longer than one day." Id. The Eighth Circuit agreed with the district court, but Chief Justice Roberts reversed and remanded for a unanimous Court. The Chief Justice explained:

> The Government speaks of Congress's intent to prevent district courts from bottoming out sentences for predicate §934(c) offenses whenever they think a mandatory minimum under §924(c) is already punishment enough. But . . . [n]othing in [the provision] prevents a sentencing court from considering a mandatory minimum under §924(c) when calculating an appropriate sentence for the predicate offense[s].

Id. at 1178. Are you convinced? We discuss in the next chapter how the sentencing discretion of federal district judges has been partially restored in the last decade or so. It remains the case, however, that judges do not have (and have never had) discretion to impose less than the mandatory minimum sentence prescribed by Congress—unless Congress gives them such authority, as it has in the "safety-valve" and the "substantial assistance" provisions of 18 U.S.C. §§3553(e), (f). (Query: Is a "sentencing manipulation" downward variance below the statutory mandatory based on interpretation of legislative intent?) As we have seen, §924(c) sentences can really add up. Has the Supreme Court in *Dean* created a loophole that gives both defendants and sentencing judges some relief, at least in §924(c) cases?

8. Another subsection of 18 U.S.C. §924, enacted in 1984, is known as the Armed Career Criminal Act (ACCA). Section 924(e)(1) prescribes a fifteen-year minimum sentence for a defendant convicted under 18 U.S.C. §922(g) of being a felon in possession of a firearm, if the defendant has three or more previous convictions, in any court, for a "serious drug offense" or a "violent felony." Of course, most convictions occur in state court, so Congress sought to explain the type of previous convictions it had, to put it colloquially, "in mind," by defining "serious drug offense" and "violent felony." The latter definition has proved problematic:

> [T]he term "violent felony" means any crime punishable by imprisonment for a term exceeding one year, or any act of juvenile delinquency involving the use or carrying of a firearm, knife, or destructive device that would be punishable by imprisonment for such term if committed by an adult, that—
>
> (i) has as an element the use, attempted use, or threatened use of physical force against the person of another; or
>
> (ii) is burglary, arson, or extortion, involves use of explosives, *or otherwise involves conduct that presents a serious potential risk of physical injury to another*[.]

18 U.S.C. §924(e)(2)(B) (emphasis added). The italicized portion of (B)(ii) became known as the "residual clause," which Justice Scalia for years

argued was likely unconstitutionally vague. See James v. United States, 550 U.S. 192, 214 (Scalia, J., dissenting) (2007); Sykes v. United States, 564 U.S. 1, 28 (2011) (Scalia, J., dissenting); see also Begay v. United States, 553 U.S. 137, 148 (2008) (Scalia, J., concurring in judgment). Finally, in Johnson v. United States, 135 S. Ct. 2551 (2015), Justice Scalia wrote for a six-justice majority striking down the residual clause. He held the clause was uncon-stitutionally vague and therefore that imposing an increased sentence pur-suant to it violates the Due Process Clause. The following year (after Justice Scalia died), the Court held, with only Justice Thomas dissenting, that *Johnson* is retroactive since it announces a new substantive rule of criminal law. Welch v. United States, 136 S. Ct. 1257 (2016). Justice Thomas com-plained in dissent that the Court's decision portended a new branch of ret-roactivity jurisprudence. Id. at 1268 (Thomas, J., dissenting). Be that as it may, you will not be surprised that we are now witnessing an avalanche of collateral attacks, pursuant to 28 U.S.C. §2255, by persons who received mandatory 15-year sentences under the ACCA because juries were generally not instructed (and defendants pleading guilty generally did not specify) under which *phrase* of §924(e)(2) each of their prior crimes qualified as a "violent felony." As of August 10, 2017, Westlaw reports that *Welch* had already been cited in 2,103 decisions. Will Congress also respond to *Dean*?

9. As we earlier mentioned, there are other examples of Congress pro-viding for mandatory minimum punishment when a drug crime is carried out in a particular manner. For instance, the school-zone statute, 21 U.S.C. §860, provides that the mandatory penalties under 21 U.S.C. §841(b) are doubled if the offense is committed within 1,000 feet of school property. The federal courts have been divided on whether this statute's enhanced penalty applies to all drug offenses within 1000 feet of a school, without regard to whether the defendant intended to distribute the drugs within that school zone or elsewhere — though most case law gives the statute the broader application. Compare United States v. Martin, 544 F.3d 456, 460 (2d Cir. 2008) (per curiam) (noting that the original §860, enacted in 1984, proscribed only the "distribution of drugs within" 1000 feet of a school but a 1988 amendment also proscribed "possession with intent to distribute" within 1000 feet, and concluding that the amendment includes "situations in which the distribution" may be anticipated to occur outside the school zone); United States v. McDonald, 991 F.2d 866 (D.C. Cir. 1993) (holding that the "*actus reus* for this offense is possession," not distribution); United States v. Rodriguez, 961 F.2d 1089 (3d Cir. 1992) (same); United States v. Felix, 832 F. Supp. 1 (N.D. Cal. 2014) (same), with United States v. Alston, 832 F. Supp. 1 (D.D.C. 1993) (dismissing the school-zone charge, despite *McDonald*, because the officers could have stopped the defendant before he drove near the school zone).

Consider that under the broader definition of the school-zone statute, the enhanced penalties apply as long as the defendant possessed the drugs within 1,000 feet of a school, even if he intended to distribute them else-where. A direct result of the school-zone statute is that penalties for drug trafficking (or conspiracy to engage in drug trafficking) are typically higher in densely populated central cities—and for their Black and Hispanic resi-dents—than in suburbs and rural areas, simply because there are few spots in urban areas that are not within 1,000 feet of a school. Moreover, a school "zone" is broadly defined in the statute. Indeed, §860 extends well beyond schoolyards; it provides for the enhanced penalty whenever the activity is within 1,000 feet of "the real property comprising a public or private ele-mentary, vocational, or secondary school or a public or private college, junior college, or university, or a playground, or housing facility owned by a public housing authority, or within 100 feet of a public or private youth center, public swimming pool, or video arcade facility."

How should we view these statutes? As efforts to affect primary conduct? To promote particular enforcement priorities? To pass penal legislation for which credit can be taken?

10 | Sentencing

Until recent decades, materials on sentencing were seldom included in books on either substantive criminal law *or* criminal procedure. The substantive law of sentencing in both state and federal courts was simple: The trial judge had discretion to sentence the defendant to any term in prison and to any amount of fine, up to the maximums established in the statute defining the crime. The sentencing hearing itself was informal; there were no jurors, no evidentiary rules, and no applicable burdens of proof. The sentencing judge could consider whatever information she thought relevant to the sentence, and did not have to explain the reasons (if any!) for her determinations. See Williams v. New York, 337 U.S. 241 (1949).

Even though for most of the country's history there was little law governing sentencing, it has nonetheless always been an important stage of the criminal process—and not just for defendants, lawyers, judges, and victims. Sentencing can also be seen as the last major stage in the process of *defining* crimes. This insight is most apparent where sentencing law has been codified in the form of "sentencing guidelines," but it also applies, we suggest in this chapter, when the sentencing judge exercises discretion in selecting the sentence.

Federal sentencing was discretionary from the founding of the nation until Congress enacted the Sentencing Reform Act of 1984. The Act radically restructured the federal sentencing process by (1) creating a new, "independent agency in the Judicial Branch"—the United States Sentencing Commission—with the majority of the Commissioners non-judges; (2) instructing the Commission to establish detailed "Sentencing Guidelines" that would be binding on sentencing judges; (3) providing both the government and defendants a right to appeal on the ground that the sentencing court failed to comply with the Sentencing Guidelines; and (4) abolishing parole as an early release mechanism.

In Section A, we examine how judges sentenced and thereby participated in the process of crime definition during the discretionary era. In Section B, we explore the new regime of Sentencing Guidelines that was established in the 1980s and explain how this regime operated as a supplement to the statutory prohibitions examined in previous chapters. In Section C, we then examine how this new regime itself has been significantly altered by the Supreme Court's decision in United States v. Booker, 543

U.S. 220 (2005), which changed the legal status of the Federal Sentencing Guidelines from "mandatory" to "advisory."

The present era of federal sentencing is an unstable hybrid, combining elements of a discretionary system with elements of the codified Sentencing Guidelines. Sections A through C introduce the elements of the existing sentencing regime, and in so doing tell a fascinating story of inter-branch dynamics, a story whose sequel is being played out as we write. In Section D, we explore how judges sentence in this hybrid era by considering in some detail the sentencing of three crimes that we studied in previous chapters: fraud, bribery, and trafficking in crack cocaine. Finally, in Section E, we present the "future" of federal sentencing law as seen by two different judges. Throughout the chapter, you will see the role that sentencing judges play in the definition of federal crimes, both when they follow the Guidelines *and* when they depart from them in the post-*Booker* era.

A.   DISCRETIONARY SENTENCING

For nearly two centuries—from the founding of the Republic until the 1980s—non-capital sentencing in the federal courts was fully discretionary; that is, the judge could sentence the defendant to any term of imprisonment, and to any fine, within statutory limitations. For instance, in 1790 Congress made it a crime to commit perjury in a court of the United States and provided that "[e]very person so offending and being thereof convicted, shall be imprisoned not exceeding three years, and fined not exceeding eight hundred dollars. . . ." Crimes Act of 1790, §18, 1 Stat. 116 (1790). Until very recently, most criminal statutes continued this pattern of providing for broad sentencing ranges. Thus, modern perjury statutes are not that different from the statute quoted above, see, e.g., 18 U.S.C. §1621 (providing for imprisonment of "not more than five years," and/or a fine).

It is not surprising that Congress has generally stipulated only maximum sentences and fines, leaving to the sentencing judge the decision as to where within the statutory range particular defendants should be sentenced. Many crimes sweep widely—especially when considered in conjunction with the broad aiding-and-abetting liability afforded by 18 U.S.C. §2—and very few federal statutes have de minimis exceptions. As we have seen, Congress enacts expansive and overlapping criminal prohibitions with the knowledge that federal prosecutors will exercise discretion in deciding which statute to proceed under and which potential defendants to proceed against. We do well also to note that Congress enacted the major criminal statutes that we have studied in this volume (e.g., those establishing mail/wire fraud, extortion, bribery, and civil-rights offenses) during the era of discretionary sentencing, knowing that judges would also exercise discretion when sentencing such offenses. Congress presumably expected that judges would impose the harshest sentences on the most culpable actors, while imposing lesser sentences on fringe players or those who, even if they had engaged in conduct technically within the terms of a criminal prohibition, had not intended to violate the criminal law or were unlikely to do so again.

Viewed from this perspective, sentencing has always been part of the process of crime definition. We have stressed throughout this book that crimes are not fully defined by the words of statutory criminal prohibitions. Prosecutors exercise discretion in deciding what crimes to charge, what alleged facts constitute the crime, and which defendants should be charged. And courts—in interpreting criminal statutes, determining whether the allegations constitute an offense, and deciding whether the evidence is sufficient for conviction—have the power to review (and either approve or reject) the work of both the legislative process and the prosecutorial process. Sentencing may be seen as the last phase of crime definition: The judge decides whether the circumstances of a particular crime by a particular defendant justify the conclusion that what happened was a serious crime (warranting a sentence near the lawful maximum) or not so serious (warranting a lesser sentence). Because sentencing occurs after Congress and the prosecutors have completed their tasks, the sentencing judge has some leeway to "undo" their efforts; for instance, when the judge decides to impose a relatively lesser sentence, he is effectively reducing any perceived overreaching by Congress or by the prosecutor. Since, all things being equal, prosecutors would prefer not to charge defendants who won't receive serious sentences, judicial sentencing discretion shapes charging discretion. Moreover, until the enactment of the Sentencing Reform Act of 1984, neither the government nor the defendant could appeal a criminal sentence that was within the statutory range; this meant that the sentencing judge arguably had the final word on the nature and the seriousness of the crime in every case.

The last statement warrants a large caveat: For most of the twentieth century, the "final" word on punishment was not that of the sentencing judge, but that of the United States Parole Board. Beginning in 1910 and ending with implementation of the 1984 Sentencing Reform Act, the federal criminal justice system gave parole authorities the power to release defendants long before they had completed their full terms of imprisonment. At least as originally conceived, however, parole was distinct from the process of crime definition and related questions (such as the severity of the crime). Rather, when the defendant was released depended on his rehabilitative potential as revealed during his time in prison, as well as on his conduct before entering prison.

HOW JUDGES EXERCISED BROAD SENTENCING DISCRETION

1. As explained above, federal district judges had broad and largely unreviewable authority to sentence the defendant anywhere within the

statutory range for most of our nation's history. But this tells us very little. How did they exercise this discretion? With what aspects of the crime
or of the criminal were they most concerned? How did they resolve factual disputes among the parties? There are remarkably few studies of these
questions. Most empirical research on sentencing has focused on outcomes—and, in particular, on whether discretionary sentencing leads to
unwarranted disparity among different judges—rather than on the process
of sentencing. We do know that the Federal Rules of Evidence have never
applied in sentencing; that judges could consider any facts they thought
relevant in deciding a sentence, see 18 U.S.C. §3661 ("No limitation shall
be placed on the information concerning the background, character, and
conduct of a person convicted of an offense which a court of the United
States may receive and consider for the purpose of imposing an appropriate sentence."); and that most Circuits never required sentencing judges to
apply any particular standard of proof (much less proof beyond a reasonable doubt) in considering disputed facts, see United States v. Fatico, 458 F.
Supp. 388 (E.D.N.Y. 1978), aff'd, 603 F.2d 1053 (2d Cir. 1979), cert. denied,
444 U.S. 1073 (1980).

2. Fortunately, we know more than that about how federal judges
in the 1980s—shortly before the Sentencing Guidelines were promulgated—arrived at sentences. The best study of the federal sentencing process in the discretionary era, based on in-depth interviews with a cross-section
of sitting federal district court judges, did not reach the stage of publication
until 1988, when the phenomenon it examined—discretionary sentencing—had been abolished in the federal courts. Hence, neither Congress
nor the Sentencing Commission had access to its findings. Those findings
are, nonetheless, instructive. The authors concluded:

> Most judges believe in taking account of the offenders' total conduct
> when they pass sentence—what is known as real-offense sentencing. What
> is alleged in the indictment becomes only the starting point. . . . If the pre-
> sentence report [conducted in federal courts by Probation Officers, who are
> employees of the judicial branch] indicates greater wrongdoing than the
> indictment, the judge will reflect it in his sentence.
>
> Nor does the number of counts charged in the indictment carry heavy
> weight at sentencing. Some prosecutors may charge each of a series of false
> representations as a separate count, while others may lump them together.
> One must "look behind the charging instrument" to avoid the uneven impact
> of prosecutorial discretion. . . .
>
> When judges confront white-collar cases, their sentencing world is partic-
> ularly complicated. First, the cases are enormously heterogeneous. It is harder
> to speak of a typical bribery or securities fraud than of a typical drug deal
> or mail theft. . . . And in white-collar cases, far more often than in common
> crimes, the very existence of a crime may be in dispute, and matters of intent
> and motivation are often ambiguous.

Moreover, white-collar cases more often are subject to the adversarial efforts of defense attorneys, a fact that tends to complicate rather than simplify the classification of a case. . . . Furthermore, the resources of the federal probation department and the comparatively high quality of the presentence investigation reports they produce give the judge an independent source of information against which to test versions of events presented to him.

Finally, in white-collar cases judges are usually deprived of two of the primary qualities that help the judge decide on a sentence: a violent act and a prior record. . . .

The normative lens through which judges view the cases is neither so varied nor idiosyncratic as is commonly believed. There is a broad consensus, across a wide range of judges of otherwise different temperaments and styles, on the core principles that ought to be applied in the sentencing of offenders. . . .

At the heart of this common moral lens lie three core legal norms. . . . The first is the norm that offenses should be treated differently according to the *harm* they produce. . . . In assessing harm, judges are not limited to harm as it is defined in one or another section of the criminal code, for instance, "deprivation of revenue to the treasury." They . . . may also include matters (like duration of offense or whether the victim was an individual or an organization) that are often only implicit, if that, in legislation.

The second principle is the norm of *blameworthiness*. . . . The conventional elements of criminal intent that are essential to establishing grounds for conviction . . . are often the starting point for a judge's consideration of blameworthiness. But this consideration usually reaches beyond the starting point to include a broader moral sphere. That sphere may reach into the earlier history of the defendant, into the details of the defendant's role in the crime, into a character assessment based on how the defendant reacted to the fact of arrest and conviction, and into whether the defendant was moved by need or by greed. . . .

A third principle is that of *consequence*. . . . [E]specially in white-collar cases, general deterrence is a most relevant consequence. . . . A second element of consequence is more personal. It asks, What will be the effect of the sanction on the person sanctioned, or on his or her immediate family or work associates? . . . Consequence is no more easily reduced to a measurable phenomenon than harm or blameworthiness. . . .

The foregoing description of judicial practice draws on the self-accounted experiences of the judges. . . . In a sense, judges have told us what they might have written had there been a requirement of giving written reasons in the sentencing process. What we learn is that judges appear to have created, on their own, a kind of common law of sentencing — without real legislative guidance and without a system of judicial precedent on which to rely. . . .

If this common law of sentencing provided a method for translating principles of sentencing into discrete decisions, we might not have the sense of disarray that is found in the criminal justice system. But generalized agreement on principles does not lead inevitably to a consensus in actual practice. . . . Although judges broadly agree on general principles, they do not have similar agreement either on ways of measuring or assessing the principles or on the relative weighting to be given each or on the translation of a given weighting into an actual sentence. . . .

Stanton Wheeler, Kenneth Mann & Austin Sarat, Sitting in Judgment: The Sentencing of White Collar Criminals 17-25 (1988).

3. Wheeler et al. confirmed what participants in the process understood from their own personal experience: that judges exercising discretion did not sentence defendants solely on the basis of the crime of conviction. This is not surprising, of course, for the same statutory crime may be committed in different ways, and the cases up for sentencing may vary along the dimensions identified—harm, blameworthiness, and consequences. But unpacking those concepts can be difficult, and may lead to considerations far removed from the statutory elements of the crime of conviction. Later in their book, the authors explained that the federal judges they studied assessed both the *offense* and the *offender*. The former was assessed primarily by reference to the variety of "harms" he had caused (some concrete and direct, others subjective or indirect), while the latter was assessed by gauging his personal "blameworthiness." Which do you think is more important in criminal sentencing—assessing the crime or assessing the criminal? Note that one could have "real offense" sentencing that focuses almost entirely on the circumstances of the offender's criminal behavior, with little or no attention paid to assessing the offender apart from that behavior. As we will see in the next section, this is largely the approach taken by the federal Sentencing Guidelines, with the important clarification that "criminal behavior" under the Guidelines includes the defendant's criminal record as well as the crimes in the case at bar.

4. For the most part, the judges interviewed by Wheeler et al. denied the significance of the number of counts of which the defendant was convicted, that being largely the decision of the prosecutor. Most judges were interested in the "real offense," not how it was charged. And at least some judges were not even concerned with whether the offense was charged at all. As one judge said:

A crime may be charged that, say Mr. X failed to pay taxes on certain expenses that were paid by his company that should have been computed as income but were not. Now when I see in the probation report that Mr. X was misrepresenting himself to the company, I'm going to sentence him for defrauding the company as well as IRS, and I'll do that even where there is no formal charge of that or indication of that in the indictment.

Wheeler et al., *supra*, at 32. To be sure, some judges had qualms about "real offense" sentencing that takes into account unconvicted criminal conduct. One judge described a major fraud case in which the defendant, pursuant to a plea agreement, had been allowed to plead to one count of a multi-count indictment:

> Well the government came in with a long [sentencing] memorandum, discussing the other nine-tenths of the indictment [not plead to as a result of the plea bargain]. . . . [But] I wasn't going to let the government try, without a jury, nine-tenths of the case. If they wanted to go to trial, they could have gone to trial. . . .

Id. at 30-31. The authors concluded that "[t]he particular view that judges take on real-offense sentencing . . . has an enormous impact. . . ."

5. While the sentencing judge had authority to sentence anywhere within the statutory range, it would be quite wrong to conclude that prosecutors had little influence on this process during the era of discretionary sentencing. To the contrary, prosecutors had several levers of influence. Most importantly, they could limit the defendant's maximum sentence exposure through their charging and plea-bargaining decisions. If just one count of mail fraud was alleged, for instance, the judge could not sentence the defendant to more than five years in prison, no matter how serious the fraud, how blameworthy the defendant, or what other crimes the presentence report documented. (As noted previously, the Sarbanes-Oxley Act has since raised the maximum sentence for mail fraud to 20 years in prison.) Second, most judges gave significant weight "to defendants' cooperation with government officials, *especially when it* [*was*] *stressed by prosecutors.*" Wheeler et al., *supra*, at 112 (emphasis added). See also id. at 118 ("Another judge noted that he seldom accepts recommendations for sentence, but that one area where he is likely to follow the sentence recommendation made by the prosecutor is where the defendant cooperates."). As the authors note, judges in effect "validat[ed] the prosecutors' efforts to get cooperation" by rewarding it. Id. at 119.

6. In the discretionary sentencing system, the great majority of cases resulted in a plea of guilty, usually but not always pursuant to a plea agreement with the prosecutor. See generally U.S. Sent'g Commn., The Federal Sentencing Guidelines: A Report 397 (December 1991), citing Executive Office of the U.S. Attorneys: Docket and Reporting System, 1984-87; Criminal Master File, 1987-89 (showing that each year from October 1983 through September 1989, about 87 percent of criminal convictions in federal courts were obtained by pleas of guilty). These statistics reflect the substantial leverage that prosecutors had; by charging (or settling to) crimes with relatively low maximum sentences, they could go a long way toward assuring a conviction without presenting the case to a jury and without any appellate review.

7. Wheeler et al. concluded that federal judges had, almost unbeknownst to them, developed a "common law of sentencing" based on the normative principles described in the excerpt above. But the authors also conceded, to quote the final sentence of the excerpt, that judges "do not have similar agreement either on ways of measuring or assessing the principles or on the relative weighting to be given each or on the translation of a given weighting into an actual sentence." In other words, discretionary sentencing surely resulted in inter-judge disparity in sentencing—a disparity that prosecutors in courthouses with multiple judges would regularly take advantage of, steering cases to a harsher or more lenient sentencer, depending on the circumstances.

There has been significant dispute as to whether the allegations of disparity in *federal* court were really as great as critics complained. Compare Marvin E. Frankel, Criminal Sentences: Law Without Order 5-6 (1973) (implying that judges' "wholly unchecked power" is exercised without rhyme or reason); Anthony Partridge & William B. Eldridge, The Second Circuit Sentencing Study, A Report to the Judges (1984) (reporting high sentencing variance in simulated sentencing by different judges), with Douglas McDonald & Kenneth E. Carlson, Sentencing in the Federal Courts: Does Race Matter? The Transition to Sentencing Guidelines, 1986-1990 (Bureau of Justice Statistics, 1993) (reporting that detailed examination of cases reveals that unwarranted disparity was small or statistically insignificant); Wheeler et al., *supra*, at 12 n.35 (reevaluating Partridge & Eldridge, *supra*, and concluding that judges had remarkably high agreement on rank ordering of cases in terms of severity). Note, however, the challenges of defining "disparity," and distinguishing "warranted" from "unwarranted" disparity.

B. THE ADVENT, OPERATION, AND EVOLUTION OF FEDERAL SENTENCING GUIDELINES

1. INTRODUCTION TO THE GUIDELINES

The most influential of all criticisms of judicial sentencing discretion was that of Judge Marvin E. Frankel. "His book, Criminal Sentences: Law Without Order, published [in 1973] . . . would thereafter confer upon him the title of 'father of sentencing reform'. . . ." Kate Stith & José A. Cabranes, Fear of Judging: Sentencing Guidelines in the Federal Courts 35 (1998).

Frankel was deeply skeptical of judicial discretion and, indeed, of judges. He explained that even federal judges, who traditionally enjoy a high reputation in the legal profession, were a "mixed bag." The occupant of the bench at any given sentencing may be "punitive, patriotic, self-righteous, guilt-ridden, and more than customarily dyspeptic," even though "judges in general, if only because of the occupational conditioning may be somewhat calmer, more dispassionate, and more humane than the average of people across the board." The result was, in Frankel's view, "arbitrary cruelties perpetuated daily." At the same time, Frankel expressed great faith that an administrative sentencing commission "of prestige and credibility" could be established, composed of "people of stature, competence, devotion, and eloquence" that would have available "computers as an aid toward orderly thought in sentencing." Frankel explained that he had "in mind the creation eventually of a detailed chart or calculus to be used . . . in weighing the many elements that go into the sentence . . . that would include, wherever possible, some form of numerical or other objective grading." Frankel's views were echoed in many of the subsequent pleas for sentencing reform, while little attention was paid to the few voices that questioned either the need for his proposed transformation of federal sentencing law or its wisdom.

Id. at 35-36. In 1975, Senator Edward Kennedy hosted a dinner for Judge Frankel and other leading scholars of the criminal justice system. The New York Times reported that this gathering was important in convincing Senator Kennedy to sponsor sentencing-reform legislation. Id. at 38.

The legislative history of the Sentencing Reform Act of 1984 is a fascinating case study in political and legislative maneuvering, in which Senator Edward Kennedy was able—over the course of four Congresses—to convince conservative Republicans to support the legislation by adopting a series of compromises and additions to the legislation. See generally Kate Stith & Steve Y. Koh, The Politics of Sentencing Reform: The Legislative History of the Federal Sentencing Guidelines, 91 Nw. U. L. Rev. 1247 (1993). Whether or not Congress was right in believing that federal sentencing was rife with sentencing disparities that could be largely eliminated through codified sentencing rules, there is no doubt that reducing "unwarranted sentencing disparities" was the primary goal of the Sentencing Reform Act of 1984, see generally S. Rep. No. 225, 98th Cong., 2d Sess. 38-39, 41-66 (1984); see also Stith & Cabranes, supra, at 104 ("The virtue of reducing sentencing disparity stemming from the exercise of judicial discretion was one thing that both conservatives and liberals in Congress could readily agree on." . . .). By the time it was signed by President Reagan in 1984 as part of an omnibus "anti-crime" measure, the Sentencing Reform Act not only abolished parole and created a Sentencing Commission authorized to promulgate binding Guidelines, but also specifically directed the Commission to increase the penalties for violent and white-collar crimes. See Stith & Cabranes, supra, at 266-81. (Recall from Chapter 4 how the substantive law of white-collar crime expanded significantly during this same, post-Watergate period—through both legislation and prosecutorial innovation. In developing the Guidelines, the Commission chose to increase penalties for most other crimes as well. See Stith & Cabranes, supra, at 40-44, 59-64.

The Sentencing Guidelines went into effect on November 1, 1987, and have applied to all crimes committed thereafter. You might wonder how the Commission's handiwork became effective so quickly. After all, other major regulatory initiatives are often stalled in court for years, challenged by opponents as "arbitrary" or "capricious" under the Administrative Procedure Act. See 5 U.S.C. §706. But the Sentencing Guidelines—both the initial rules that became effective in late 1987 and the hundreds of amendments that have followed—are not subject to any form of judicial review! This was accomplished by Congress baldly asserting that the Commission is an "independent agency in the judicial branch," 28 U.S.C. §991(a); the APA applies only to agencies in the executive branch, including independent agencies. See 5 U.S.C. §701(b). Because no one can subject the Guidelines to judicial review, the Commission need not, and often has not, explain the why and wherefore of any of the rules it issues. While the Sentencing Reform Act specifies that the Commission must comply with the "notice and comment" provisions of the APA, 28 U.S.C. §994(x), whether it pays attention to the comments is entirely in the discretion of the Commission itself.

Following is a brief description of the operation of the Guidelines:

> The centerpiece of the Guidelines is a 258-box grid that the Commission calls the Sentencing Table. The horizontal axis of this grid, entitled "Criminal History Category," adjusts severity on the basis of the offender's past conviction record. The vertical axis, entitled "Offense Level," reflects a base severity score based on the crime committed, [as] adjusted for those characteristics of the defendant's criminal behavior that the Commission has determined relevant to sentencing. The Guidelines, through a complex set of rules . . .instruct the sentencing judges on [the weight to be given to] each of these factors. The box at which the defendant's Criminal History Category and Offense Level intersect then determines the [defendant's Guidelines Sentencing Range]. . . . The [judge has discretion to sentence anywhere within this range, but] the sentencing range in each box is small, the highest point being 25 percent more than the lowest point.

Stith & Cabranes, *supra,* at 3.

Even when they were supposedly "mandatory," the Guidelines provided two avenues for a judge to impose a non-Guidelines sentence. The first of these was when a case involved a factor that the Guidelines had not "adequately" considered, see 18 U.S.C. §3553(b); the catch was that sentencing courts were prohibited from considering factors that the Sentencing Commission said it had taken into account, see U.S.S.G. §5K2.0. When the Guidelines were mandatory, such "judicial departures" were almost all below (rather than above) the Guidelines range, and occurred in fewer than 10 percent of cases nationwide. The second, and more significant, basis for a below-Guidelines sentence was when the prosecutor filed a motion attesting to the defendant's substantial assistance in the prosecution of others, see U.S.S.G. §5K1.1; this is the Guidelines analogue to the statute that we noted in Chapter 9 allowing judges to sentence below even the statutory minimum sentence upon the prosecutor's filing of a "substantial assistance" motion, see Section B of Chapter 9. Below-Guidelines sentences for cooperation with the government were imposed, nationwide, in 15 percent to 20 percent of cases during the period in which the Guidelines were binding. The current version of the sentencing table is reproduced below.

SENTENCING TABLE
(in months of imprisonment)

	Offense Level	Criminal History Category (Criminal History Points)					
		I (0 or 1)	II (2 or 3)	III (4, 5, 6)	IV (7, 8, 9)	V (10, 11, 12)	VI (13 or more)
Zone A	1	0–6	0–6	0–6	0–6	0–6	0–6
	2	0–6	0–6	0–6	0–6	0–6	1–7
	3	0–6	0–6	0–6	0–6	2–8	3–9
	4	0–6	0–6	0–6	2–8	4–10	6–12
	5	0–6	0–6	1–7	4–10	6–12	9–15
	6	0–6	1–7	2–8	6–12	9–15	12–18
	7	0–6	2–8	4–10	8–14	12–18	15–21
	8	0–6	4–10	6–12	10–16	15–21	18–24
Zone B	9	4–10	6–12	8–14	12–18	18–24	21–27
	10	6–12	8–14	10–16	15–21	21–27	24–30
	11	8–14	10–16	12–18	18–24	24–30	27–33
Zone C	12	10–16	12–18	15–21	21–27	27–33	30–37
	13	12–18	15–21	18–24	24–30	30–37	33–41
	14	15–21	18–24	21–27	27–33	33–41	37–46
	15	18–24	21–27	24–30	30–37	37–46	41–51
	16	21–27	24–30	27–33	33–41	41–51	46–57
	17	24–30	27–33	30–37	37–46	46–57	51–63
	18	27–33	30–37	33–41	41–51	51–63	57–71
	19	30–37	33–41	37–46	46–57	57–71	63–78
	20	33–41	37–46	41–51	51–63	63–78	70–87
	21	37–46	41–51	46–57	57–71	70–87	77–96
	22	41–51	46–57	51–63	63–78	77–96	84–105
	23	46–57	51–63	57–71	70–87	84–105	92–115
	24	51–63	57–71	63–78	77–96	92–115	100–125
	25	57–71	63–78	70–87	84–105	100–125	110–137
	26	63–78	70–87	78–97	92–115	110–137	120–150
	27	70–87	78–97	87–108	100–125	120–150	130–162
Zone D	28	78–97	87–108	97–121	110–137	130–162	140–175
	29	87–108	97–121	108–135	121–151	140–175	151–188
	30	97–121	108–135	121–151	135–168	151–188	168–210
	31	108–135	121–151	135–168	151–188	168–210	188–235
	32	121–151	135–168	151–188	168–210	188–235	210–262
	33	135–168	151–188	168–210	188–235	210–262	235–293
	34	151–188	168–210	188–235	210–262	235–293	262–327
	35	168–210	188–235	210–262	235–293	262–327	292–365
	36	188–235	210–262	235–293	262–327	292–365	324–405
	37	210–262	235–293	262–327	292–365	324–405	360–life
	38	235–293	262–327	292–365	324–405	360–life	360–life
	39	262–327	292–365	324–405	360–life	360–life	360–life
	40	292–365	324–405	360–life	360–life	360–life	360–life
	41	324–405	360–life	360–life	360–life	360–life	360–life
	42	360–life	360–life	360–life	360–life	360–life	360–life
	43	life	life	life	life	life	life

November 1, 2016

2. REAL-OFFENSE SENTENCING

While the abrupt imposition of a system of binding Sentencing Guidelines was a radical change for all those involved in sentencing in the federal courts, the Guidelines arguably continued previous federal sentencing practice in important respects. Justice Stephen Breyer, who was (while serving on the U.S. Court of Appeals for the First Circuit) one of the original seven members of the Sentencing Commission, explains in the excerpt below why the Commission decided to base the severity of punishment not simply on the crime of conviction, but on the "real offense":

The first inevitable compromise which faced the Commission concerned the competing rationales behind a "real offense" sentencing system and a "charge offense" system. It is a compromise forced in part by a conflict inherent in the criminal justice system itself: the conflict between procedural and substantive fairness.

Some experts urged the adoption of a pure, or a nearly pure, "charge offense" system. Such a system would tie punishments directly to the offense for which the defendant was convicted. . . . The principal difficulty with a presumptive sentencing system is that it tends to overlook the fact that particular crimes may be committed in different ways, which in the past have made, and still should make, an important difference in terms of the punishment imposed. A bank robber, for example, might, or might not, use a gun; he might take a little, or a lot, of money; he might, or might not, injure the teller. The typical armed robbery statute, however, does not distinguish among these different ways of committing the crime. . . .

A "real offense" system, in contrast, bases punishment on the elements of the specific circumstances of the case. . . . The proponents of such a system, however, minimize the importance of the *procedures* that courts must use to determine the existence of the additional harms. . . . A drug crime defendant, for example, cannot be expected to argue at trial to the jury that, even though he never possessed any drugs, if he did so, he possessed only one hundred grams and not five hundred, as the government claimed. . . . Typically, courts have found post-trial sentencing facts without a jury and without the use of such rules of evidence as the hearsay or best evidence rules, or the requirement of proof of facts beyond a reasonable doubt.

Of course, the more facts the court must find in this informal way, the more unwieldy the process becomes, and the less fair that process appears to be. At the same time, however, the requirement of full blown trial-type post-trial procedures, which include jury determinations of fact, would threaten the manageability that the procedures of the criminal justice system were designed to safeguard. . . .

The Commission's system makes . . . a compromise. It looks to the offense *charged* to secure the "base [O]ffense [L]evel." It then modifies that level in light of several "real" aggravating or mitigating factors, (listed under each separate crime), several "real" general adjustments ("role in the offense," for example) and several "real" characteristics of the offender, related to past record. . . .

Stephen Breyer, The Federal Sentencing Guidelines and the Key Compromises Upon Which They Rest, 17 Hofstra L. Rev. 1, 8-12 (1988).

NOTES AND QUESTIONS

1. We saw that in the discretionary era as well, judges generally looked to the defendant's "real offense" in determining punishment. Likewise, judges were often affected by whether the defendant had a prior criminal record and whether he had cooperated with the government in the prosecution of others. See the discussion of Wheeler et al., in Section A above. The Guidelines can be seen as simply elaborating and codifying these general practices of most federal judges—with the added bonus of attempting to ensure that each judge looked to the same factors in deciding what constitutes the "real offense" and weighed these factors uniformly. As we shall see later in this chapter, a majority of the Supreme Court eventually adopted a decidedly different understanding of those aspects of real-offense sentencing that result in a higher Guidelines sentencing range on the basis of judicial fact-finding. Rather than viewing these rules as simply the implementation of long-time sentencing practices, the majority of the Court concluded that such judicial fact-finding pursuant to mandatory, legally binding guidelines fails to afford constitutionally required protections in the prosecution of crimes. We explore these cases, culminating in Booker v. United States (2005), in the next part of this section.

2. Justice Breyer briefly alludes to two different types of "real offense" factors in the Guidelines. One set consists of trans-substantive (or universal) adjustments that are to be applied no matter what the offense of conviction. For instance, the Guidelines provide that if any defendant is found to have "willfully obstructed or impeded, or attempted to obstruct, or impede, the administration of justice with respect to the investigation, prosecution, or sentencing of the instant offense of conviction," U.S.S.G. §3C1.1, her Guidelines sentencing range must be increased by two offense levels. It is noteworthy that the definition of "obstructing or impeding the administration of justice" that is found in the Guidelines is broader than the statutory definitions found in the general federal obstruction of justice provisions, 18 U.S.C. §§1503, 1505, 1512, and 1513.

Obstruction of justice is just one of several trans-substantive "real offense" factors that apply in all cases. The Guidelines also define new prohibitions (resulting in higher Guidelines sentences) where the statutory crime was motivated by "hate" or performed against a "vulnerable victim," where there was "restraint of the victim," where the crime "involved . . . or was intended to promote terrorism," where the defendant played a major role in the offense, where the defendant abused a public or private "position of trust" or used a "special skill," and where the defendant used body armor in a drug-trafficking crime. See U.S.S.G. §§3A1.1, 1.3, 1.4; §§3B.1, 1.3, 1.5. The extent to which judges in the pre-Guidelines era took these particular factors into account is not known, and the information cannot be retrieved because data were not kept on these matters. The study by Wheeler et al., discussed *supra* Section A, did not address this level of detail.

The most important trans-substantive sentencing factor in the Guidelines is the concept of "relevant conduct," set forth at U.S.S.G. §1B1.1. See generally William W. Wilkins, Jr. & John R. Steer, Relevant Conduct: The Cornerstone of the Federal Sentencing Guidelines, 41 S.C. L. Rev. 495 (1990). Pursuant to the Guidelines' relevant-conduct rule, all criminal behavior committed by the defendant that is related to his crime of conviction—including crimes with which he was not charged (and even crimes of which he was acquitted)—is attributed to him for purposes of calculating his Guidelines range. Additionally, the defendant's relevant conduct includes any crimes committed by his co-conspirators that were "foreseeable." The latter rule resembles *Pinkerton* liability, explored in Section B of Chapter 8, a long-established staple of federal criminal law. Note, however, that while *Pinkerton* is a basis for actual criminal liability, its analogue in the Sentencing Guidelines is a basis for "attributing" the crimes of co-conspirators to the defendant for purposes of calculating the defendant's Guidelines sentencing range; the defendant need not have been formally convicted of the co-defendants' crimes.

3. In addition to creating universal sentencing enhancements for obstruction of justice, relevant conduct, and certain other aggravating factors, the Sentencing Guidelines specify a great variety of crime-specific aggravating factors, some of which we shall discuss in detail in Section D. In the Guidelines covering crimes of bribery, for instance, the Sentencing Commission has provided a higher offense level for the official who takes a bribe than for the bribe-giver, even though the statutory sentencing range under 18 U.S.C. §201(b) and 18 U.S.C. §666—statutes we explored in Chapter 6—is the same for both parties to the bribe. See U.S.S.G. §2C1.1(a). While the statutory definition of these two crimes is not altered by the Guidelines, the on-the-ground definition has been altered; in effect, receiving a bribe has been made a more serious crime than giving a bribe. Do you agree with this general assessment of comparative culpability?

4. Since the advent of the Guidelines, the proportion of cases that go to trial has diminished considerably. Whereas about 87 percent of convictions were obtained by a plea of guilty in the years prior to the Guidelines, see Section A *supra*, that percentage has hovered around 97 percent since the 1990s; the most recent data can be found in the Commission's annual Sourcebook of Sentencing Statistics. Commentators and participants in federal sentencing have generally attributed the reduction in trials to

the prosecutors' increased leverage in a codified real offense sentencing regime: The prosecutor (by providing or not providing information to the probation officer who writes the presentence report) decides not only the charges, but also what aggravating factors to allege. Further, the prosecutor plays a gate-keeping role in determining whether the judge can give a below-Guidelines sentence (and even, as we saw in Chapter 9, a below-statutory minimum sentence) on the basis of the defendant's substantial assistance in the prosecution of others. But there are other possible explanations for the vanishing criminal trial in federal court, including that the Guidelines themselves provide for an offense-level reduction (at least two levels) when the defendant has "accepted responsibility" for his crime, see U.S.S.G. §3E1.1. Or that defendants would prefer that the judge who will be sentencing them not get the maximal picture of their criminal conduct that is likely to emerge at trial. For whatever reason, however, the percentage of federal charges that result in trials has plummeted since the Guidelines were implemented, and has remained at this low level even after *Booker* introduced an enhanced role for the sentencing judge.

5. The mandatory and comprehensive nature Guidelines led one distinguished commentator[*] to suggest that they functioned as a criminal code supplementing statutory prohibitions:

> [The] guidelines bear all the formal attributes of a penal code. Splitting some offenses into what are in effect multiple degrees . . . and combining others under the same guideline provision, the guidelines create, in effect, a simplified codification of the behavior criminalized by federal law. By rendering the offense of conviction ordinarily insignificant for sentencing purposes, and replacing the code offenses for these purposes with comprehensive codified guidelines, the new federal sentencing regime to a considerable extent rationalizes and displaces congressionally-enacted criminal statutes.

Gerard E. Lynch, The Sentencing Guidelines as a Not So Model Penal Code, 10 Fed. Sent'g Rep. 25, 26 (1997). Stating the matter another way, Congress in effect delegated significant criminal lawmaking power to the Commission.

3. THE SENTENCING GUIDELINES AND THE CONSTITUTION

What about the Constitution's "non-delegation doctrine," you may ask? We addressed that doctrine briefly in Chapter 9 and take it up again in Chapter 12. The question whether Congress's delegation of sentencing

---

[*] [Editors' Note: At the time he wrote this article, Gerard E. Lynch was a professor at Columbia Law School. In 2000, he was appointed to the United States District Court for the Southern District of New York, and in 2009 he was appointed to the U.S. Court of Appeals for the Second Circuit.]

rule-making to the Commission violated the Constitution arose in scores of cases soon after the Guidelines became effective on November 1, 1987. More than 200 district court judges held the Sentencing Reform Act unconstitutional. See U.S. Sent'g Comm'n, 1989 Annual Report 11. Some of these decisions held that the delegation of lawmaking power was unconstitutional on the ground that only Congress, not an administrative agency, could issue rules that effectively alter the definition of crimes. By a vote of 8-1, the Supreme Court rejected this and all other separation-of-powers claims against the Guidelines. United States v. Mistretta, 488 U.S. 361 (1989). Remarkably, the majority opinion denied that the Guidelines "bind or regulate the primary conduct of the public or vest in [the Commission] the legislative responsibility for establishing minimum and maximum penalties for every crime." Id. at 396. But the Guidelines did both these things. Justice Scalia, alone in dissent, grasped the significance of the mandatory nature of the rules that the Sentencing Commission was directed to issue: "There is no doubt that the Sentencing Commission has established significant, legally binding prescriptions governing application of governmental power against private individuals." Id. at 413 (Scalia, J., dissenting). Justice Scalia's insight became the basis for the holding sixteen years later in Booker v. United States, 543 U.S. 220 (2005): Because the Guidelines were equivalent to statutory elements of federal crimes, judicial fact-finding that increased the range of lawful punishment denied defendants their Sixth Amendment right to jury trial and their right to proof beyond a reasonable doubt, see In re Winship, 397 U.S. 358 (1970). We examine Booker in the next sub-section.

But the understanding that the Guidelines' "real offense" sentencing rules actually *alter* federal criminal law came gradually. In *Mistretta* and subsequent cases, the Court viewed the Guidelines' adoption of real-offense sentencing—taking into account and providing enhanced penalties for criminal conduct of which the defendant was not convicted—as simply an explicit and transparent acknowledgment of what most federal judges were doing most of the time (to one degree or another) in the pre-Guidelines era. The two different perspectives are presented in the case below.

United States v. Watts
519 U.S. 148 (1997)

PER CURIAM*. . . .
[The police] discovered cocaine base in a kitchen cabinet and two loaded guns and ammunition hidden in a bedroom closet of Watts' house. A jury convicted Watts of possessing cocaine base with intent to distribute,

---

* [Editors' Note: This decision was issued without merits briefing or oral argument.]

in violation of 21 U.S.C. §841(a)(1), but acquitted him of using a firearm in relation to a drug offense, in violation of 18 U.S.C. §924(c). Despite Watts' acquittal on the firearms count, the District Court found by a preponderance of the evidence that Watts had possessed the gun in connection with the drug offense. In calculating Watts' sentence, the court therefore added two points to his base offense level under United States Sentencing Commission, Guidelines Manual §2D1.1(b)(1) [("If a dangerous weapon (including a firearm) was possessed, increase [the base offense level] by 2 levels")]. The Court of Appeals vacated the sentencing, holding that "a sentencing judge may not, 'under *any* standard of proof, rely on facts of which the defendant was acquitted.' . . .'

We begin our analysis with 18 U.S.C. §3661, which codifies the longstanding principle that sentencing courts have broad discretion to consider various kinds of information. . . . We reiterated this principle in *Williams v. New York*, 337 U.S. 241 (1949), in which a defendant convicted of murder and sentenced to death challenged the sentencing court's reliance on information that the defendant had been involved in 30 burglaries of which he had not been convicted. . . . Indeed, under the pre-Guidelines sentencing regime, it was "well established that a sentencing judge may take into account facts introduced at trial relating to other charges, even ones of which the defendant had been acquitted." *United States v. Donelson*, 695 F.2d 583, 590 (D.C. Cir. 1982) (Scalia, J.).

The Guidelines did not alter this aspect of the sentencing court's discretion. "'[V]ery roughly speaking, [relevant conduct] corresponds to those actions and circumstances that courts typically took into account when sentencing prior to the Guidelines' enactment.'" [*Witte v. United States*, 515 U.S. 389, 402 (1995)]. . . . U.S.S.G. §1B1.3(a)(2) requires the sentencing court to consider "all acts and omissions . . . that were part of the same course of conduct or common scheme or plan as the offense of conviction." Application Note 3 . . . gives the following example:

> "[W]here the defendant engaged in three drug sales of 10, 15, and 20 grams of cocaine . . . subsection (a)(2) provides that the total quantity of cocaine involved (45 grams) is to be used to determine the offense level even if the defendant is convicted of a single count charging only one of the sales." . . .

In short, we are convinced that a sentencing court may consider conduct of which a defendant has been acquitted. . . .

As we explained in *Witte*, [] sentencing enhancements do not punish a defendant for crimes of which he was not convicted, but rather increase his sentence because of the manner in which he committed the crime of conviction. In *Witte*, we held that a sentencing court could, consistent with the Double Jeopardy Clause, consider uncharged cocaine importation in imposing a sentence on marijuana charges that was within the statutory range, without precluding the defendant's subsequent prosecution for the cocaine offense. . . .

[In this case], the jury acquitted the defendant of using or carrying a firearm during or in relation to the drug offense. That verdict does not preclude a finding by a preponderance of the evidence that the defendant did, in fact, use or carry such a weapon, much less that he simply *possessed* the weapon in connection with a drug offense. . . .

STEVENS, J., dissenting.

"The Sentencing Reform Act of 1984 revolutionized the manner in which district court sentence persons convicted of federal crimes." . . . Strict mandatory rules have dramatically confined the exercise of judgment based on a totality of the circumstances. . . .

In 1970, during the era of individualized sentencing, Congress enacted the statute now codified as 18 U.S.C. §3661 to make clear that otherwise inadmissible evidence could be considered by judges in the exercise of their sentencing discretion. The statute, however, did not tell the judge how to weigh the significance of any of that evidence. The judge was free to rely on any information that might shed light on a decision to grant probation, to impose the statutory maximum, or to determine the precise sentence within those extremes. . . .

Although the Sentencing Reform Act of 1984 has cabined the discretion of sentencing judges, the 1970 statute remains on the books. . . . [Under this new regime], the role played by §3661 is of a narrower scope [being limited to the narrow area in which the sentencing judge now has discretion: in choosing the precise point within the calculated sentencing range]. . . .

In my opinion, [the Sentencing Reform Act of 1984] should be construed in the light of the traditional requirement that criminal charges must be sustained by proof beyond a reasonable doubt. That requirement has always applied to charges involving multiple offenses as well as a single offense. . . . The notion that a charge that cannot be sustained by proof beyond a reasonable doubt may give rise to the same punishment as if it had been so proved is repugnant to [our constitutional] jurisprudence. I respectfully dissent.

THE PATH FROM WATTS TO BOOKER

1. In 1998, Justice Stevens was the only member of the Supreme Court to express the view that factors enhancing the Guidelines sentence were virtually indistinguishable from statutory elements of crimes, and should be subject to the Constitution's protections for proof of crimes. By 2005, without any change in the make-up of the Supreme Court, a majority adopted this view in United States v. Booker. The slow march toward *Booker* is summarized below.

2. Between 1993 and 1998, the Supreme Court rejected several additional challenges to federal sentencing procedures; these challenges were explicitly or implicitly based on the premise that the Sentencing Guidelines were close enough to statutory criminal prohibitions to be treated as such for constitutional purposes. In United States v. Dunnigan, 507 U.S. 87 (1993), the Court unanimously rejected a challenge to the sentencing court's application of the obstruction-of-justice enhancement (established by U.S.S.G. §3C1.1) upon its finding by a preponderance of the evidence that the defendant had lied when he took the stand during his trial. *Dunnigan* relied heavily on a pre-Guidelines case, United States v. Grayson, 438 U.S. 41 (1978), which found no abuse of discretion when the sentencing judge considered a defendant's false testimony in fashioning his sentence.

Two years later, the Court decided Witte v. United States, 515 U.S. 389 (1995). *Witte* was the case cited in *Watts* rejecting a challenge to the Guidelines under the Double Jeopardy Clause of the Fifth Amendment. As he would be three years later in *Watts*, Justice Stevens was the sole dissenter in *Witte*, arguing that the Guidelines, by requiring enhanced punishment, put the defendant in "jeopardy" under the Double Jeopardy Clause.

But a case decided shortly after *Watts* was much closer. In Almendarez-Torres v. United States, 523 U.S. 224 (1998), Justice Breyer garnered a bare majority in upholding a statutory sentencing provision — 18 U.S.C. §1326(b) (2) — that authorized a higher term of imprisonment for certain recidivist offenders, even though there had been no allegation in the indictment regarding the previous conviction and the sentencing enhancement provision appeared in a section of the statute to which the defendant did not plead guilty. Justice Scalia authored the dissent, joined by Justices Stevens, Souter, and Ginsburg, expressing "genuine[] doubt[]" that

> the Constitution permits a judge (rather than a jury) to determine by a mere preponderance of the evidence (rather than beyond a reasonable doubt) a fact that increases the maximum penalty to which a criminal defendant is subject. . . .

523 U.S. at 251 (Scalia, J., dissenting).

3. The tide turned completely two years later, when a bare majority of the Court held in Apprendi v. New Jersey, 530 U.S. 466 (2000) that New Jersey's statutory "hate crimes" enhancement was the "functional equivalent of an element of a greater offense than the one covered by the jury's guilty verdict," because finding that the crime was motivated by hate had the effect of increasing the statutory maximum sentence* to which the defendant was

---

* [Editors' Note: *Apprendi*'s rule applied only to statutory sentencing factors that increased the *maximum* lawful sentence, not to factors that resulted in an increase in any mandatory *minimum* sentence, see Harris v. United States, 536 U.S. 545 (2002). In 2013,

subject. Id. at 494. Inasmuch as the sentencing factor was functionally equivalent to an element of the crime, the majority reasoned, the defendant had a right to jury trial and to proof beyond a reasonable doubt on that factor. Joining Justice Stevens's majority opinion were the other dissenters in *Almendarez-Torres* plus Justice Thomas, who wrote separately to explain his change of position; he admitted to having "succumbed" to a logical "error" in equating discretionary sentencing with a codified sentencing regime. Id. at 499 (Thomas, J., concurring). In 2004, the same majority—this time in an opinion by Justice Scalia—extended *Apprendi*'s rule to Washington State's system of sentencing guidelines, which bore a strong resemblance to the Federal Sentencing Guidelines but had been enacted into law by the state legislature. See Blakely v. Washington, 542 U.S. 296 (2004). Though the Court might have found the statutory enactment of Washington's sentencing guidelines significant, it stated its holding broadly, suggesting constitutional infirmity in any system that increases the maximum sentence a judge may impose on the basis of facts not found by a jury beyond a reasonable doubt (or admitted to by the defendant in pleading guilty). The Court thus put the Federal Sentencing Guidelines clearly in its sights.

Less than a year later, in United States v. Booker, 543 U.S. 220 (2005), the *Apprendi/Blakely* majority held that the Federal Sentencing Guidelines "as written" were unconstitutional because they increased the lawful sentence on the basis of the judge's fact-finding, beyond the facts found by the jury or admitted by a defendant who entered a plea of guilty.

United States v. Booker
543 U.S. 220 (2005)

Justice STEVENS delivered the opinion of the Court in part.*

The question presented in each of these cases is whether an application of the Federal Sentencing Guidelines violated the Sixth Amendment. In each case, the courts below held that binding rules set forth in the Guidelines limited the severity of the sentence that the judge could lawfully impose on the defendant based on the facts found by the jury at his trial. In both cases the courts rejected, on the basis of our decision in *Blakely v. Washington*, 542 U.S. 296 (2004), the Government's recommended application of the Sentencing Guidelines because the proposed

---

Harris was overruled by Alleyne v. United States, 570 U.S. 99 (2013). Hence *Apprendi*'s prohibition on judicial fact-finding that increases the lawful sentence applies to increases in the statutory minimum *or* maximum sentence.]

* [Editors' Note: This opinion became known as *Booker*'s "merits" decision. The other Justices in the *Appendi/Blakely* majority—Justices Scalia, Souter, Thomas, and Ginsburg—joined this opinion.].

sentences were based on additional facts that the sentencing judge found by a preponderance of the evidence. We hold that both courts correctly concluded that the Sixth Amendment as construed in *Blakely* does apply to the Sentencing Guidelines. In a separate opinion authored by Justice BREYER, the Court concludes that in light of this holding, two provisions of the Sentencing Reform Act of 1984 (SRA) that have the effect of making the Guidelines mandatory must be invalidated in order to allow the statute to operate in a manner consistent with congressional intent. . . .

II . . .

As the dissenting opinions in *Blakely* recognized, there is no distinction of constitutional significance between the Federal Sentencing Guidelines and the Washington procedures at issue in that case. . . . This conclusion rests on the premise, common to both systems, that the relevant sentencing rules are mandatory and impose binding requirements on all sentencing judges. . . .

If the Guidelines as currently written could be read as merely advisory provisions that recommended, rather than required, the selection of particular sentences in response to differing sets of facts, their use would not implicate the Sixth Amendment. We have never doubted the authority of a judge to exercise broad discretion in imposing a sentence within a statutory range. . . . Indeed, everyone agrees that the constitutional issues presented by these cases would have been avoided entirely if Congress had omitted from the SRA the provisions that make the Guidelines binding on district judges; it is that circumstance that makes the Court's answer to the second question presented possible. For when a trial judge exercises his discretion to select a specific sentence within a defined range, the defendant has no right to a jury determination of the facts that the judge deems relevant.

The Guidelines as written, however, are not advisory; they are mandatory and binding on all judges. . . .

IV

All of the foregoing supports our conclusion that our holding in *Blakely* applies to the Sentencing Guidelines. We recognize, as we did in *Jones, Apprendi,* and *Blakely,* that in some cases jury factfinding may impair the most expedient and efficient sentencing of defendants. But the interest in fairness and reliability protected by the right to a jury trial . . . has always outweighed the interest in concluding trials swiftly. . . . Accordingly, we reaffirm our holding in *Apprendi:* Any fact (other than a prior conviction) which is necessary to support a sentence exceeding the maximum authorized by the facts established by a plea of guilty or a jury verdict must be admitted by the defendant or proved to a jury beyond a reasonable doubt.

Justice BREYER delivered the opinion of the Court in part.* . . .

We here turn to the second question presented, a question that concerns the remedy. We must decide whether or to what extent, "as a matter of severability analysis," the Guidelines "as a whole" are "inapplicable . . . such that the sentencing court must exercise its discretion to sentence the defendant within the maximum and minimum set by statute for the offense of conviction." We answer the question of remedy by finding the provision of the federal sentencing statute that makes the Guidelines mandatory, 18 U.S.C. §3553(b)(1), incompatible with today's constitutional holding. We conclude that this provision must be severed and excised, as must one other statutory section, §3742(e), which depends upon the Guidelines' mandatory nature. So modified, the federal sentencing statute . . . makes the Guidelines effectively advisory. It requires a sentencing court to consider Guidelines ranges, but it permits the court to tailor the sentence in light of other statutory concerns as well, see §3553(a). . . .

III

We now turn to the question of *which* portions of the sentencing statute we must sever and excise as inconsistent with the Court's constitutional requirement. . . . Most of the statute is perfectly valid. . . . And we must "refrain from invalidating more of the statute than is necessary." . . .

Application of these criteria indicates that we must sever and excise two specific statutory provisions: the provision that requires sentencing courts to impose a sentence within the applicable Guidelines range (in the absence of circumstances that justify a departure), see 18 U.S.C. §3553(b)(1) and the provision that sets forth standards of review on appeal, including *de novo* review of departures from the applicable Guidelines range, see §3742(e). With these two sections excised (and statutory cross-references to the two sections consequently invalidated), the remainder of the Act satisfies the Court's constitutional requirements. . . .

[T]he Act without its "mandatory" provision and related language remains consistent with Congress' initial and basic sentencing intent. Congress sought to "provide certainty and fairness in meeting the purposes of sentencing, [while] avoiding unwarranted sentencing disparities . . . [and] maintaining sufficient flexibility to permit individualized sentences

---

* [Editors' Note: This opinion became known as *Booker*'s "remedy" decision. Chief Justice Rehnquist, and Justices O'Connor, Kennedy, and Ginsburg joined this opinion. Note that only Justice Ginsburg joined both the "merits" and the "remedy" opinions.]

when warranted." 28 U.S.C. §991(b)(1)(B). . . . The system remaining after excision, while lacking the mandatory features that Congress enacted, retains other features that help to further these objectives.'

As we have said, the Sentencing Commission remains in place, writing Guidelines, collecting information about actual district court sentencing decisions, undertaking research, and revising the Guidelines accordingly. See 28 U.S.C. §994. The district courts, while not bound to apply the Guidelines, must consult those Guidelines and take them into account when sentencing. See 18 U.S.C.A. §3553(a)(4), (5). . . . The courts of appeals review sentencing decisions for unreasonableness. These features of the remaining system, while not the system Congress enacted, nonetheless continue to move sentencing in Congress' preferred direction, helping to avoid excessive sentencing disparities while maintaining flexibility sufficient to individualize sentences where necessary. See 28 U.S.C. §991(b). We can find no feature of the remaining system that tends to hinder, rather than to further, these basic objectives. Under these circumstances, why would Congress not have preferred excision of the "mandatory" provision to a system that engrafts today's constitutional requirement onto the unchanged pre-existing statute—a system that, in terms of Congress' basic objectives, is counterproductive? . . .

Ours, of course, is not the last word: The ball now lies in Congress' court. The National Legislature is equipped to devise and install, long term, the sentencing system, compatible with the Constitution, that Congress judges best for the federal system of justice. . . .

[Editors' Note: We have omitted Justice Breyer's dissent from the *merits* opinion—joined by Chief Justice Rehnquist, and Justices O'Connor and Kennedy—which would have held that the Guidelines are constitutional even if mandatory. We have also omitted both Justice Thomas's and Justice Stevens' dissents from the *remedy* opinion. Justice Stevens' dissent, which Justice Souter in joined in full and Justice Scalia joined in part, asserted that the Court had no business rewriting the Sentencing Reform Act to make the guidelines mandatory; the Court should have simply required that aggravating Guidelines factors be treated as elements.]

C.   THE STATUS AND OPERATION OF THE GUIDELINES AFTER *BOOKER*

Booker thus held the Federal Sentencing Guidelines unconstitutional. More important for our purposes is that the Guidelines survived this holding. All nine Justices agreed that if Congress had not made the Sentencing Guidelines "mandatory," there would be no constitutional infirmity with judicial fact-finding of aggravating factors. Rather, under the old chestnut Williams v. New York, 337 U.S. 241 (1949), a sentencing judge could consider any information (including advisory Guidelines) in exercising his sentencing discretion. The problem, of course, was that Congress had made clear that the Sentencing Guidelines were not "advisory," see 18 U.S.C. §§3553(b)(1), 3742(e).

The solution for the *Booker* remedy majority was to "sever[] and excis[e]" these two provisions (on the purported ground that Congress would prefer advisory Guidelines to mandatory Guidelines treated as statutory elements, which would force the issues to a jury), thereby rendering the Guidelines "advisory," with appellate review under a "reasonableness" standard. See 543 U.S. at 265 (Breyer, J., for the remedy majority). Under this remedy, the factors resulting in Guidelines enhancements need not be treated as elements of the crime—charged in the indictment, and, if the defendant goes to trial, proved to a jury beyond a reasonable doubt. The remedy decision in *Booker* effectively held that if the Guidelines are only advisory, the relaxed procedures that have always characterized sentencing proceedings are not constitutionally infirm.

But what does "advisory" mean in practice? *Booker* sort of answered this question. "The district courts, while not bound to apply the Guidelines, must consult those Guidelines and take them into account when sentencing. . . ." 543 U.S. at 265. As such, sentencing judges must still "begin" determination of a defendant's sentence by calculating the Guidelines sentencing range, "but then is [permitted] . . . to tailor the sentence in light of other statutory concerns as well, see §3553(a)." Id. at 245. The statutory factors to which Justice Breyer was referring are set forth below.

---

18 U.S.C. §3553

(a) Factors to be considered in imposing a sentence.—The court shall impose a sentence sufficient, but not greater than necessary, to comply with the purposes set forth in paragraph (2) of this subsection. The court, in determining the particular sentence to be imposed, shall consider—

(1) the nature and circumstances of the offense and the history and characteristics of the defendant;

(2) the need for the sentence imposed—

(A) to reflect the seriousness of the offense, to promote respect for the law, and to provide just punishment for the offense;

(B) to afford adequate deterrence to criminal conduct;

(C) to protect the public from further crimes of the defendant; and

(D) to provide the defendant with needed educational or vocational training, medical care, or other correctional treatment in the most effective manner;

(3) the kinds of sentences available;

(4) the kinds of sentence and the sentencing range established for—

(A) the applicable category of offense committed by the applicable category of defendant as set forth in the guidelines—

(i) issued by the Sentencing Commission . . . subject to any amendments made to such guidelines by act of Congress . . . ;

(5) any pertinent policy statement—

(A) issued by the Sentencing Commission . . . ;

(6) the need to avoid unwarranted sentence disparities among defendants with similar records who have been found guilty of similar conduct; and

(7) the need to provide restitution to any victims of the offense. . . .

NOTES AND QUESTIONS ABOUT THE POST-BOOKER STATUTORY FRAMEWORK

1. *The §3553(a) Factors.* After *Booker*, a sentencing judge must begin by calculating the Guidelines sentencing range, to which she must then apply the §3553(a) factors. If you were a sentencing judge, how would you interpret §3553(a)'s instructions? Note that one of the factors that must be considered is the Guidelines sentencing range; how significant is this consideration? On what bases may judges impose a sentence above or below that range? In the years since *Booker*, the Supreme Court has decided several cases, discussed in the material that follows, which could shed light on how much discretion sentencing judges now have in a system of "advisory" Sentencing Guidelines. Unfortunately, many questions still remain.

2. *Discretion Under §3553(a).* Section 3553(a) codifies the so-called Parsimony Principle: Courts are to impose a sentence that is "sufficient" but no more severe than is "necessary, to comply with the purposes [of sentencing forth in (a)(1)-(7)]." Citing this rule, the Supreme Court threw something of a lifeline to judges and defendants in Dean v. United States, 137 S. Ct. 1170 (2017).* A unanimous opinion, *Dean* holds that a where a defendant has been convicted of multiple counts and at least one of these counts requires the imposition of a mandatory minimum, the sentencing judge has discretion to consider that mandatory sentence when determining the sentence for the defendant's *other* counts of conviction. Dean was convicted of multiple robbery and firearms counts, including two counts of possessing a firearm in furtherance of a crime of violence, in violation of 18 U.S.C. §924(c). Section 924(c) requires that sentencing judges impose a distinct punishment in addition to that "provided for [the predicate] crime" for anyone convicted of possessing or using a firearm during or in relation to a crime of violence or drug-trafficking crime. Section 924(c) further stipulates that any such sentence must run consecutively to the sentence for the predicate count(s). A first conviction under §924(c) carries a five-year

---

* [Editors' Note: We briefly discuss *Dean* in Section B of Chapter 9.]

mandatory minimum penalty, and a second conviction carries an additional 25-year mandatory minimum. Hence in Dean's case, §924(c) required a 30-year mandatory minimum, to be served after and in addition to any sentence he received for his other counts of conviction (which carried a Guidelines range of 84-105 months). *Dean*, 137 S. Ct. at 1175. At sentencing, Dean argued that the court should consider his 30-year mandatory minimum when calculating a sentence for the other counts. The Supreme Court agreed with Dean that despite Congress's clear attempt to treat the mandatory sentences as consecutive and unrelated to the sentence on any other count, sentencing courts may take the mandatories into account in arriving at a sentence on the remaining counts—in effect providing an end-run around legislative intent.

3. *Appellate Review Under* Booker. While granting significant discretion to the district courts *Booker* sought nonetheless to avoid sentencing disparity by "ensuring that sentencing decisions are anchored by the Guidelines and that they remain a meaningful benchmark through the process of appellate review." Peugh v. United States, 569 U.S. 530, 541 (2013). Indeed, the Court has said that the Courts of Appeals may give a (rebuttable) "presumption of reasonableness" to within-Guidelines sentences, and has referred to the "reasonableness" standard as akin to the "familiar abuse-of-discretion standard of review." Gall v. United States, 552 U.S. 38, 46-47 (2007).

"Reasonableness" review has two components: procedural and substantive. The reviewing court "must first ensure that the district court committed no significant *procedural* error, such as failing to calculate (or improperly calculating) the Guidelines range, treating the Guidelines as mandatory, failing to consider the §3553(a) factors, selecting a sentence based on clearly erroneous facts, or failing to adequately explain the chosen sentence—including an explanation for any deviation from the Guidelines range." *Gall*, 552 U.S. at 51 (emphasis added). Once satisfied that the sentencing court has committed no procedural error, a court of appeals must then review a sentence for *substantive* reasonableness. Id. In doing so, courts of appeals are not allowed to apply a "presumption of unreasonableness" to non-Guideline sentences, see Rita v. United States, 551 U.S. 339, 354-55 (2007), but may "'consider the extent of the deviation' from the Guidelines as part of their reasonableness review.'" *Peugh*, 569 U.S. at 541 (quoting *Gall*, 552 U.S. at 51).

RECENT DEVELOPMENTS IN LAW AND PRACTICE

1. An important Guidelines case decided in 2007 made clear that after *Booker*, sentencing judges have considerable discretion to impose a non-Guidelines sentence—adding yet another wrinkle to substantive review for reasonableness. In Kimbrough v. United States, 552 U.S. 85 (2007), the

Court held it permissible for a sentencing judge to give a below-Guidelines sentence on the basis of a "policy disagreement" with the Sentencing
Commission—there, a disagreement with the Guidelines (then extant)
100:1 quantity ratio between crack cocaine and powder cocaine. Justice
Ginsburg explained:

> While rendering the Sentencing Guidelines advisory, we have neverthe-
> less preserved a key role for the Sentencing Commission. . . . Carrying out
> its charge, the Commission fills an important institutional role: It has the
> capacity courts lack to "base its determinations on empirical data and national
> experience, guided by a professional state and with appropriate expertise."
> United States v. Pruitt, 502 F.3d 1154, 1181 ([10]th Cir. 2007) (McConnell, J.,
> concurring).
>
> We have accordingly recognized that, in the ordinary case, the
> Commission's recommendation of a sentencing range will "reflect a rough
> approximation of sentences that might achieve §3553(a)'s objectives." The
> sentencing judge, on the other hand, has "greater familiarity with . . . the indi-
> vidual case and the individual defendant before him than the Commission or
> the appeals court." *Rita*, 551 U.S. 338, 357-358. He is therefore "in a superior
> position to find facts and judge their import under §3353(a)" in each partic-
> ular case. . . . . On the other hand, while the Guidelines are no longer bind-
> ing, closer review may be in order when the sentencing judge varies from the
> Guidelines based solely on the judge's view that the Guidelines range "fails
> properly to reflect §3553(a) considerations" even in a mine-run case.
>
> The crack cocaine Guidelines, however, present no occasion for elab-
> orate discussion of this matter because those Guidelines do not exemplify
> the Commission's exercise of its characteristic institutional role. In formu-
> lating Guidelines ranges for crack cocaine offenses, as we earlier noted, the
> Commission looked to the mandatory minimum sentences set in the 1986 Act,
> and did not take account of "empirical data and national experience." See
> *Pruitt*, 502 F.3d, at 1171 (McConnell, J., concurring). Indeed, the Commission
> itself has reported that the crack/powder disparity produces disproportion-
> ately harsh sanctions, i.e., sentences for crack cocaine offenses "greater than
> necessary" in light of the purposes of sentencing set forth in §3553(a). Given
> all this, it would not be an abuse of discretion for a district court to con-
> clude when sentencing a particular defendant that the crack/powder dispar-
> ity yields a sentence "greater than necessary" to achieve §3553(a)'s purposes,
> even in a mine-run case.

Kimbrough, 552 U.S. at 108-09.

2. *Kimbrough* stated that the Commission's blanket adoption of the
100:1 ratio was a "departure" from its "usual" course of adopting Guidelines
on the basis of "empirical data and national experience," 522 U.S. at 94,
109. Although the Court has reaffirmed that sentencing courts have considerable discretion to sentence crack-cocaine cases less severely than the
sentencing range in the Guidelines, see Spears v. United States, 555 U.S.

261 (2009), it has left unclear which other Guidelines "do not exemplify the Commission's exercise of its characteristic institutional role," id. at 264 (quoting *Kimbrough*, 552 U.S. at 109), and thus what other "policy disagreements" may be the basis for a non-Guidelines sentence.

Nonetheless, in the absence of further instruction, many circuit courts have affirmed district courts' authority, post-*Kimbrough*, to vary from *any* guideline with which it disagrees on policy grounds, including those that are the result of direct congressional action. Accordingly, judges have disagreed with the severity of the Guidelines for a wide array of crimes, including child pornography offenses, see, e.g., United States v. Henderson, 649 F.3d 955 (9th Cir. 2011); accord, United States v. Dorvee, 616 F.3d 174 (2d Cir. 2010) (going further and reversing Guideline sentence as substantively unreasonable when the Guideline itself failed properly to reflect §3553(a) considerations); the illegal reentry Guideline, see, e.g., United States v. Singh, 877 F.3d 107 (2d Cir. 2017); United States v. Amezcua-Vasquez, 567 F.3d 1050 (9th Cir. 2009); the career offender Guideline, see, e.g., United States v. Clay, 787 F.3d 328, 331 (5th Cir. 2015); and the Guidelines for many drugs other than cocaine. Note that district courts have sometimes relied on *Kimbrough* for authority to give *above* guideline sentences. See, e.g., United States v. Herrera-Zuniga, 571 F.3d 568, 583 (6th Cir. 2009) (affirming sentence in which district court expressed "astonish[ment]" that the Guidelines' base offense level for illegal reentry "is so low"); United States v. Cavera, 550 F.3d 180 (2d Cir. 2009) (en banc) (affirming above-Guideline sentence in firearms trafficking case based on district court's finding that the guideline sentence did not provide adequate deterrence given that New York City's strict gun laws created large black market that required harsher penalties to deter selling of illegal firearm).

3. Even as lower courts do not feel obliged to agree with the Guidelines for a wide variety of crimes, the Supreme Court has continued to insist that the Guidelines are "the framework for sentencing," the "lodestar" for most sentencing proceedings, and "anchor . . . the district court's discretion," Molina-Martinez v. United States, 136 S. Ct. 1338, 1345-46 (2016), and that if the sentencing judge uses the Guidelines range "as the beginning point to explain the decision to deviate from it, *then the Guidelines are in a real sense the basis for the sentence.*" *Peugh*, 569 U.S. at 544 (emphasis in original).

4. If, as the Supreme Court has stated, the Guidelines are the "anchor" of district courts' analysis, does it follow that they produce an *anchoring effect*, which is a form of cognitive bias whereby someone deciding a subjective question gives undue weight to an available numerical metric? See Kate Stith, Arc of the Pendulum, 117 Yale L.J. 1420, 1496 (2008) ("Most importantly, the Guidelines remain the starting point for all sentences, with an anchoring effect. . . . The Guidelines are now the frame, in both law and practice, in which sentences are viewed."). Nonetheless, as Figure I shows, the percentage of cases in which non-Guidelines sentences are imposed has increased each year since *Booker*—suggesting that the Guidelines over time

Figure I
SENTENCES RELATIVE TO THE GUIDELINE
RANGE OVER TIME
Fiscal Years: 2006-2016

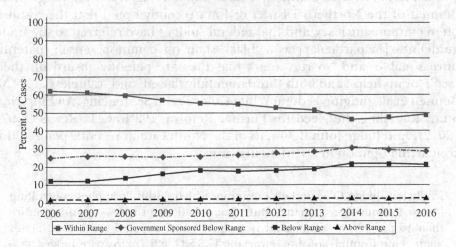

SOURCE: This was produced using the U.S. Sentencing Commission's Interactive Sourcebook (isb.ussc.gov) using the Commission's fiscal year 2006-2016 Datafiles, USSCFY2006-USSCFY2016.

play less of an anchoring role. Moreover, these aggregate figures capture neither the huge variation nationally nor the extent to which non-Guideline sentences have become the norm in many districts. In 2016, for example, only 22.2 percent of defendants in the Southern District of New York—and only 26.2 percent in the District of Connecticut—received sentences within the calculated Guidelines range.

5. The increase in variances from the Guidelines has been especially pronounced in fraud cases. In 2001, the Commission increased the severity of Guidelines sentences in fraud and other economic-crime cases, and Congress the following year increased them even more in the Sarbanes-Oxley Act. But in the years after *Booker* and *Kimbrough*, sentencing judges have increasingly refused to impose these severe sentences in fraud cases. By 2012, only half of all fraud sentences were within the recommended Guidelines range, and the frequency of non-Guidelines sentences was even greater in fraud cases involving loss amounts of more than $30,000. See Jillian Hewitt, Note, Fifty Shades of Gray: Sentencing Trends in Major White Collar Cases, 125 Yale L.J. 1018 (2016). By 2016, fewer than 43 percent of fraud defendants received sentences within the Guidelines range. See U.S. Sent'g Comm'n, 2016 Sourcebook tbl. 27. It may be that judges exercise their post-*Booker* discretion more often in the kinds of complex cases considered in this book than they do in more routine cases. It may also be that the sentencing dynamics that Congress worried about when it mandated more prison sentences for white-collar defendants in the 1984 Sentencing Reform Act are again driving white-collar sentencing. What factors do you think

make white-collar sentencing a special challenge for regulation by Congress and the Sentencing Commission, and indeed, by Main Justice?

6. The Sentencing Commission has added a great deal more text to the Guidelines, both before and after *Booker*, than it has removed. Judge Mark Bennett of the Northern District of Iowa recently noted that the result is often extreme intricacy, and that federal "judges have referred to the fraud guidelines [in particular] as a 'black stain on common sense'; 'patently unreasonable' and 'so run amok that they are patently absurd on their face'; 'of no help'; and both 'fundamentally flawed' and 'valueless'. . . ." M. Bennett et al., Judging Federal White-Color Fraud Sentencing: An Empirical Study Revealing the Need for Further Reform, 102 Iowa L. Rev. 939, 974 (2017). And Judge John B. Owens of the Ninth Circuit recently penned this concurring opinion in a sentencing case:

> I fully join Judge O'Scannlain's opinion, which faithfully applies controlling law to the question at hand. But what a bad hand it is—requiring more than 16 pages to resolve an advisory question. I applaud the United States Sentencing Commission for reworking U.S.S.G. §2L1.2 to spare judges, lawyers, and defendants from the wasteland of [a previous case]. . . . I continue to urge the Commission to simplify the Guidelines to avoid the frequent sentencing adventures more complicated than reconstructing the Staff of Ra in the Map Room to locate the Well of the Souls. Cf. Almanza-Arenas v. Lynch, 815 F.3d 469, 482-83 (9th Cir. 2016) (en banc) (Owens, J., concurring); Raiders of the Lost Ark (Paramount Pictures 1981).

United States v. Perez-Silvan, 861 F.3d 935, 944 (9th Cir. 2017) (Owens, J., concurring).

7. The Supreme Court has determined that the Guidelines are immune to challenges for vagueness under the Due Process Clause. See Beckles v. United States, 137 S. Ct. 886 (2017). Writing for the Court, Justice Thomas explained:

> Because they merely guide the district courts' discretion, the Guidelines are not amenable to a vagueness challenge. . . . [T]he system of purely discretionary sentencing that predated the Guidelines was constitutionally permissible. If a system of unfettered discretion is not unconstitutionally vague, then it is difficult to see how the present system of guided discretion could be.

Id. at 893. In light of the specific facts of Beckles's case, Justice Sotomayor concurred in the judgment, but offered a very different vision of the Guidelines' status. She argued that "[i]t follows from the central role that the Guidelines play at sentencing that they should be susceptible to vagueness challenges under the Due Process Clause." Id. at 900 (Sotomayor, J., concurring).

As you read in the next sub-section about how the Guidelines are applied in a variety of cases, consider whose description you think is more accurate—that of Justice Thomas or that of Justice Sotomayor. Consider also whether you think the Guidelines have achieved their goals of "'*uniformity* in sentencing . . . imposed by different federal courts for similar criminal conduct,' as well as '*proportionality* in sentencing through a system that imposes appropriately different sentences for criminal conduct of different severity.'" *Molina-Martinez*, 136 S. Ct. at 1342 (quoting Rita v. United States, 551 U.S. 338, 349 (2007)).

D.   DEFINING CRIMES UNDER ADVISORY SENTENCING GUIDELINES

To give you a sense of how, as Gerard Lynch observed, the Guideline regime "rationalizes and displaces congressionally-enacted criminal statutes," see Section B *supra*, we now consider the ways in which the Guidelines alter or supplement the statutory definitions and judicial interpretations of crimes—mail and wire fraud, political corruption, and drug trafficking—with which you are already familiar. Note the bases on which judges in the post-*Booker* era decline to impose a Guidelines sentence; often, such decisions are based on a factor that is specified neither in the statutory crime of conviction nor in the Sentencing Guidelines. Both the Sentencing Commission and sentencing judges thus play a role in defining federal crimes and in assessing comparative culpability.

1.   MAIL AND WIRE FRAUD

U.S.S.G. §2B1.1

Larceny, Embezzlement, and Other Forms of Theft; Offenses Involving Stolen Property; Property Damage or Destruction; Fraud and Deceit; Forgery; Offenses Involving Altered or Counterfeit Instruments Other than Counterfeit Bearer Obligations of the United States

(a) Base Offense Level:
    (1) 7, if (A) the defendant was convicted of an offense referenced to this guideline; and (B) that offense of conviction has a statutory maximum term of imprisonment of 20 years or more; or
    (2) 6, otherwise.
(b) Specific Offense Characteristics
    (1) If the loss exceeded $6,500, increase the offense level as follows

---

Loss (Apply the Greatest) Increase in Level	
(A) $6,500 or less	no increase
(B) More than $6,500	Add 2
(C) More than $15,000	Add 4
(D) More than $40,000	Add 6
(E) More than $95,000	Add 8
(F) More than $150,000	Add 10
(G) More than $250,000	Add 12
(H) More than $550,000	Add 14
(I) More than $1,500,000	Add 16
(J) More than $3,500,000	Add 18
(K) More than $9,500,000	Add 20
(L) More than $25,000,000	Add 22
(M) More than $65,000,000	Add 24
(N) More than $150,000,000	Add 26
(O) More than $250,000,000	Add 28
(P) More than $550,000,000	Add 30

U.S.S.G. §2B1.1 then lists numerous other specific offense characteristics that can raise the Guidelines offense level, some of which we discuss below.

THE SIGNIFICANCE OF THE FRAUD GUIDELINE

1. Defendants convicted of any one of a broad set of crimes—including mail and wire fraud, securities fraud, theft, larceny, embezzlement, and similar crimes—are sentenced under §2B1.1. Subsection (a) sets the base offense level, then subsection (b) provides a long list of aggravating factors that, if found, increase the offense level by one or more levels. The most important sentencing factor is the amount of "loss" stated in the Loss Table at §2B1.1(b)(1), above. Other aggravating factors include the following:

- "If the offense involved receiving stolen property, and the defendant was a person in the business of receiving and selling stolen property, increase by 2 levels," §2B1.1(b)(4);
- "If the offense involved theft of, damage to, destruction of, or trafficking in, property from a national cemetery or veterans' memorial, increase by 2 levels," §2B1.1(b)(6);
- "If the offense involved (A) the conscious or reckless risk of death or serious bodily injury; or (B) possession of a dangerous weapon (including a firearm) in connection with the offense, increase by 2 levels. If the resulting offense level is less than level 14, increase to level 14," §2B1.1(b)(14).

2. The Sentencing Guidelines initially treated crimes of theft—like theft from the government, 18 U.S.C. §641 (of which Morissette, from Chapter 3,

was convicted) — differently from crimes involving fraud or deceit (like mail and wire fraud). However, in November 2001, the Commission's "economic crime package" took effect, which consolidated a wide variety of economic offenses into this one Guideline, §2B1.1. Why do you think the Commission did that? Do you see a difference between these two types of crimes? Which is worse? The consolidated Guideline does make a gesture to the difference by providing for a two-level enhancement "if the offense involved a theft from the person of another." Where does embezzlement, also within §2B1.1, fit in a ranking of seriousness? Note that there is a universal sentencing enhancement (that is, applying to all crimes) of two levels "[i]f the defendant abused a position of public or private trust," U.S.S.G. §3B1.3.

3. The importance of §2B1.1 is even greater than its title suggests because many other Guidelines for crimes involving monetary payments or property loss (including money laundering in violation of 18 U.S.C. §1956 or §1957) are tied to the "Loss Table" at §2B1.1(b)(1). Although the Commission's own 2001 amendment package did not increase the severity of the "Loss Table" at its low end, Congress legislatively intervened and, as part of the Sarbanes-Oxley Act of 2002, further ratcheted up the Guidelines for virtually all defendants sentenced under §2B1.1, including those whose crime involved relatively small loss quantities. The Dodd-Frank Act of 2010 required the Commission to increase, yet again, most sentences under §2B1.1. Note that although the Commission acted accordingly (in 2012), it subsequently raised the dollar amounts in the Loss Table (which has the effect of reducing the Guidelines sentencing range for a given amount of monetary loss). See generally, Dana Libelson, Why Nobody is Really Happy with New Guidelines for Punishing White-Collar Criminals, Huffington Post, April 22, 2015 ("Sentencing reform advocates say [the new Guidelines] don't go far enough to fix draconian sentences. . . ."). What does the timing of congressional interventions into the Commission's work tell you about the political economy of federal sentencing?

4. One might find it odd that §2B1.1 makes virtually no reference to any of the statutes (or their particular elements) that it encompasses. But this is the manner in which all of the Guidelines covering specific criminal behaviors are written. The base offense level and aggravating factors apply regardless of the offense of conviction. Indeed, the premise of the Guidelines is that for the most part, it doesn't matter of which *crime* the defendant was convicted. What matter are his actual conduct and the consequences of his conduct.

5. Still, some of the aggravating factors do seem to target particular crimes. For instance, §2B1.1(b)(14)(B) provides for a sentencing enhancement where the soundness of a financial institution was threatened—a measure seemingly directed at the offense of bank fraud, 18 U.S.C. §344, or the crime of providing false information to a financial institution, 18 U.S.C. §1014. But the enhancement applies equally if the defendant was

convicted of generic mail fraud, 18 U.S.C. §1341, and even if the target of the mail fraud scheme was not a financial institution (that is, even if the threat to a financial institution was simply a collateral consequence of the fraud). Moreover, pursuant to the overarching relevant-conduct provision of the Guidelines, discussed in the previous section, this enhancement (like all enhancements) applies whether the defendant or another person in the scheme was responsible, as long as the *conduct* that resulted in a threat to a bank's financial soundness was reasonably foreseeable by the defendant. 18 U.S.C. §1344 carries a maximum of thirty years—and §1341, a mere twenty years—but statutory maxima have little to do with actual sentences. With that in mind, what might go into a prosecutor's choice between charging mail fraud and charging bank fraud (to the extent she wants to save paper and not charge both)?

6. All of the statutes within the ambit of §2B1.1 have an explicit *mens rea* requirement. Indeed, we have seen that most federal statutes contain some *mens rea* term or standard, and that if they do not, courts may be disposed to infer such an element, especially where criminal punishment is significant. See, e.g., Staples v. United States, 511 U.S. 600 (1994), which we examined in Chapter 3. Section 2B1.1 and the Federal Sentencing Guidelines as a whole take a different approach. Many Guidelines contain no *mens rea* language, and courts have generally declined to read in a requirement of knowledge or negligence—even when the sentencing enhancement significantly affects the Guidelines offense level. See generally Jack B. Weinstein & Fred A. Bernstein, The Denigration of Mens Rea in Drug Sentencing, 7 Fed. Sent'g Rep. 121 (1994); Michael J. Naporano, Comment: Sentencing Factors and Intent: The Role of Mens Rea in a Federal Gun Statute, 38 Seton Hall L. Rev. 1567, 1577 (2008) (noting the virtually universal assumption that "sentencing factors," unlike elements, do not have a *mens rea* component). Do you think it is appropriate for *mens rea* to drop out of the culpability analysis once a defendant has been found or pleads guilty?

With respect to §2B1.1, this means that the government need not prove that the defendant intended or had specific knowledge of most of the aggravating factors specified in the Guidelines—including the amount of loss, the number of victims, any use of sophisticated means, a risk of serious bodily injury, a threat to the soundness of a financial institution, or damage to property in a national cemetery or veterans' memorial. See §2B1.1(b) (1), (b)(2), (b)(10), (b)(16), (b)(5). Other enhancements arguably have at least some implicit-knowledge component, such as:

- a four-level enhancement if the offense involved a violation of securities law and the defendant was a director or officer of a publicly traded company or worked in the securities field, see §2B1.1(b)(19) (A);

- the two-level enhancement for using equipment that enables identity theft, see §2B1.1(b)(11);
- the two-level enhancement for conducting a "substantial part" of a fraudulent scheme outside of U.S. territory, see §2B1.1(b)(10)(B);
- the two-level enhancement for violating a judicial or administrative order, see §2B1.1(b)(9)(C); and
- the two-level enhancement for falsely claiming to represent a charitable, government, or religious organization, see §2B1.1(b)(9)(A).

We come back to the fact that the most important enhancement remains the amount of loss. But calculation of loss is both complex and controversial, as the next case—which involves a resentencing after *Booker* was issued—reveals.

United States v. Olis
2006 WL 2716048 (S.D. Tex. Sept. 22, 2006)

MEMORANDUM OPINION
SIM LAKE, District Judge. . . .

I. BACKGROUND

[Jamie] Olis, along with Gene Foster and Helen Sharkey, was indicted for conspiracy to commit mail fraud, wire fraud, and securities fraud (count 1), securities fraud (count 2), mail fraud (count 3), and wire fraud (counts 4-6). Foster and Sharkey pleaded guilty to the conspiracy count and cooperated with the government. The jury convicted Olis on all counts. The court found that under the mandatory sentencing guidelines Olis was required to be sentenced within a range of 292-365 months in prison. The court sentenced Olis to 292 months in prison, three years of supervised release, and a $25,000 fine. Olis appealed.

After the court sentenced Olis, but before the Fifth Circuit issued its decision, the United States Supreme Court issued its decision in United States v. Booker, 125 S. Ct. 738 (2005). . . .

The Fifth Circuit held that *Booker* applied, and that Olis must be resentenced because the government had not established "beyond a reasonable doubt that the district court would have sentenced Olis to nearly twenty-five years in prison had it acted under an advisory Sentencing Guidelines scheme as required by *Booker*." . . .

[T]he Fifth Circuit [has subsequently] clarified the post-*Booker* sentencing regime. . . . Before a court may impose a non-Guideline sentence, it must first calculate the Guideline range and consider the appropriateness of a sentence within that sentencing range to fulfill its duty to consider the Sentencing Guidelines as advisory and as a frame of reference [citing United States v. Tzep-Meji, 461 F.3d 522, 525 (5th Cir. 2006)].

II. THE DEFENDANT'S GUIDELINE SENTENCING RANGE

As recognized by the Fifth Circuit, "[t]he most significant determinant of Olis's sentence is the guidelines loss calculation." The government argues that the actual loss attributable to the defendant's unlawful conduct related to [the fraudulent accounting scheme in which Olis participated] was over $100 million, and that the intended loss to the United States Treasury was $79 million. . . .

A. Loss

The guidelines covering offenses involving fraud provides for a base offense level of 6, graduated increases "[i]f the loss exceeded $5,000," and additional increases if the offense involved more than 10 victims. U.S.S.G. §2B1.1 The application notes following §2B1.1 explain that "loss is the greater of actual loss or intended loss." Id. at cmt. n.2(A). "'Actual loss' means the reasonably foreseeable pecuniary harm that resulted from the offense." Id. at cmt. n.2(A)(i). This definition of "actual loss" incorporates "[a] causation standard that, at a minimum, requires factual causation (often called "but for" causation) and provides a rule for legal causation (i.e., guidance to courts regarding how to draw the line as to what losses should be included and excluded from the loss determination.)." U.S. Sentencing Guidelines Manual Supplement to Appendix C, Amendment 617 (Nov. 1, 2001). "'Intended loss' (I) means the pecuniary harm that was intended to result from the offense; and (II) includes intended pecuniary harm that would have been impossible or unlikely to occur.'" U.S. Sentencing Guidelines Manual §2B1.1 cmt. n.2 (A) (ii) (2001). . . .

The Fifth Circuit has explained that "[t]he loss guideline is skeletal because it covers dozens of federal property crimes. Some flesh can be added, however, where the gravamen of the offense conduct is securities fraud perpetrated on an established market. Useful guidance appears in the applicable principles for recovery of civil damages for securities fraud. The civil damage measure should be the backdrop for criminal responsibility both because it furnishes the standard of compensable injury for securities fraud victims and because it is attuned to stock market complexities". . . .

1. Actual Loss

The government's expert witness, Frank C. Graves, has submitted a report concluding that "the aggregate losses to all . . . affected shareholders (attributable to Project Alpha) is quite large, in the range of $161 million to $714 million." Graves arrived at these figures by conducting statistical events studies for the day of or the day after "the dates when it was revealed that prior accounting disclosures about Project Alpha were of concern to the SEC regulators": April 25, 2002 and May 2, 2002.

Events studies are a standard technique used in securities litigation analyses to isolate the impact of a particular event or a series of events on the value of a stock. These studies typically account for the contemporaneous movements in the value of all stocks and in the value of other stocks in the sector. See Imperial Credit Indus., Inc. Sec. Litig., 252 F. Supp. 2d 1005, 1014 (C.D. Cal. 2003). . . . Although Graves conducted a thorough analysis of all the relevant factors, a number of confounding negative announcements made on each of the days for which he identified abnormal returns, i.e., April 25 and May 8, 2002, required him to base each of the numerous calculations that underlie his estimate of actual loss on unprovable and often unexplained assumptions. . . .

Absent guidance from the sentencing commission or the court of appeals on how to decide when results produced by methodologies that are necessarily based on a series of unprovable assumptions that yield speculative results are nevertheless reasonably certain estimates of actual loss caused by a defendant's unlawful conduct, the court is compelled to conclude that the confounding announcements and the unprovable assumptions on which Graves necessarily relied in reaching his estimate of actual loss demonstrate that it is not possible to estimate with any degree of reasonable certainty the actual loss to shareholders caused by the corrective disclosures about Project Alpha made on April 25, 2002. . . .

2. A Intended Loss

The government argues that "[i]f the court decides that the actual loss [to shareholders] caused by Olis' criminal acts is . . . indeterminable, the appropriate sentence must then be based upon the 'intended loss' measure under U.S. Sentencing Guidelines Manual Application Note 2 (a) (2001 ed.)". . . .

At defendant's trial, Gene Foster offered uncontroverted testimony that the tax benefit to Dynegy arising from Project Alpha could have been higher than the approximately $79 million that the company reported, but that he and Olis purposely reduced it so that the resulting "effective tax rate" would remain high enough to avoid scrutiny that could have revealed the truth about Project Alpha. Since Foster's uncontroverted testimony establishes that Olis expected the fraudulent accounting treatment accorded to Project Alpha to reduce the taxes that Dynegy would otherwise have owed to the United States Treasury by $79 million, the court concludes that $79 million is a reasonably certain estimate of the pecuniary harm that the defendant intended to result from his offense. See U.S. Sentencing Guidelines Manual §2B1.1 cmt. n.2 (A)(ii) (2001).

B. Multiple Victim Enhancement

The parties agree that if the court uses the intended loss to the United States, rather than the actual loss, to calculate the defendant's offense level, the four-level enhancement for more than 50 victims pursuant to §2B1.1 (b)(2)(B) does not apply.[55] . . .

C. Conclusion . . .

Accordingly, the court concludes that the defendant's total offense level would be 34 yielding a guideline sentencing range of 151 to 188 months based on the following calculation:

Base Level	6
Intended Loss of $79 Million	24
Use of Special Skill	2
Use of Sophisticated Means	2
Number of Victims	0
Total Offense Level	34

III. THE REASONABLENESS OF A GUIDELINE SENTENCE . . .

Although the court must still consider the sentencing guidelines, since *Booker* the guidelines are "merely one sentencing factor among many, and the calculated guideline range must be considered in conjunction with the other [18 U.S.C.] §3553 (a) factors." . . . To comply with the Fifth Circuit's instructions, the court, if it elects to impose a non-guideline sentence, "should carefully articulate the reason [the court] concludes that the sentence [it] has selected is appropriate for that defendant. These reasons should be fact specific and include, for example, aggravating or mitigating circumstances relating to personal characteristics of the defendant, his offense conduct, his criminal history, relevant conduct or other

---

55. Application note 3(A)(ii) to section 2B1.1 defines "victim" as "(I) any person who sustained any part of the actual loss determined under subsection (b)(1). . . ."

facts specific to the case at hand which led the court to conclude that the sentence imposed was fair and reasonable." (citation omitted).

In part II of this opinion the court has calculated the defendant's guideline range as 155 to 188 months. This range is driven primarily by the $79,000,000 loss, which accounts for 24 of the 34 points used to calculate the defendant's total offense level under the guidelines. The court will now address the other statutory sentencing factors.

A.   The Nature and Circumstances of the Offense . . .

Olis was found guilty of serious charges—securities fraud, mail and wire fraud, and conspiracy. The evidence at trial showed that Olis, along with two indicted and several unindicted co-conspirators, sought to address the stock market's concern about Dynegy's meager cash flow from operations by structuring a transaction—Project Alpha—that would appear to the company's outside auditors and to the investing public as if it resulted in income from operations when in fact it was a disguised loan. The conspiracy was intended to decrease Dynegy's tax liability, increase its cash flow, and enhance the views of outside investors about Dynegy's earnings, thereby resulting in a greater market price for its stock.

Although Olis was intimately involved in the conspiracy and in planning Project Alpha, he did not have the ultimate authority at Dynegy to approve Project Alpha, nor was he responsible for drafting the documents by which the conspiracy was carried out and concealed. Moreover, unlike some other recently publicized corporate fraud cases, the purpose of this conspiracy was not to defraud Dynegy or to enrich Olis. Nor did the conspiracy cause Dynegy to file for bankruptcy. Although Dynegy suffered a loss in its market capitalization after the true facts of Project Alpha became public and paid large amounts to settle the resulting civil cases, the company remains a viable entity. The initial success of Project Alpha brought Olis a promotion and stock options, but it did not result in substantial pecuniary benefits to him. Although these facts do not detract from the seriousness of the crime for which Olis was convicted, they mitigate against the type of harsh sentence that may be deserved in cases where the defendant's conduct enriched him at the company's detriment or brought about the downfall of the company.

B.   The History and Characteristics of the Defendant

Olis was born in Korea, the son of a Korean woman and an American soldier, who abandoned Olis's mother before Olis was born. Olis moved with his mother to the United States when he was five years old. His mother struggled to support Olis and his sister with menial jobs until William Olis, a retired American soldier, began supporting the family, and later married Olis's mother and adopted Olis and his sister. Olis adjusted to the difficulties of his early life. He learned English, became a United States citizen, graduated from high school, and received a scholarship to St. Mary's University, from which he graduated with a degree in accounting. He later received a law degree, while also working as an accountant. Olis began working for Dynegy in 1998. Olis has no prior arrests or convictions, and according to the many letters the court has received from friends and former co-workers, has led an exemplary life, except for his participation in Project Alpha.

C.   The Need for the Sentence to Reflect the Seriousness of the Offense, to Promote Respect for the Law, and to Provide just Punishment for the Offense

Although a significant sentence of imprisonment is required to reflect the seriousness of this offense, to promote respect for the law, and to provide just punishment, those goals can be achieved by a sentence that is less severe than one within the guideline range.

D.   General Deterrence

After November 1, 2001, the guideline ranges for defendants convicted of serious fraud and related white-collar crimes were substantially increased. Since then the media has reported on lengthy sentences received by a number of white-collar defendants. The court is persuaded that the public in general, and potential white-collar criminals in particular, have become aware of the substantial risk of imprisonment for a lengthy period if they commit crimes of this nature. . . . In this case, however, such a lengthy sentence is not necessary to provide general deterrence. . . .

G.   Conclusion

Having considered all of the factors mandated by Congress, including the sentencing guidelines and policy statements, the court concludes that a sentence within the applicable guideline range would not be reasonable, and that a non-guideline sentence of 72 months in prison is appropriate. . . .

NOTES AND QUESTIONS

1. At Olis's first sentencing proceeding, before *Booker* was decided, Judge Lake sentenced him at the low end of the calculated Guidelines range. This

sentence of 292 months (more than 24 years) was based on the amount of loss to a particular institutional investor, which the court determined by looking at the loss in Dynegy's stock value once the fraudulent scheme was revealed. Although commonly used by federal courts in civil cases to determine "loss" involving publicly traded companies, this market-capitalization measure has been highly criticized, since it does not include a causal inquiry, may involve only "paper" losses, and does not account for the price at which most share-holders purchased their shares. See generally Samuel W. Buell, A Comment on Punishing Financial Reporting Fraud, 28 Cardozo L. Rev. 1611 (2007). In vacating Olis's sentence, the Fifth Circuit noted many of these concerns, see United States v. Olis, 429 F.2d 540, 547-48 (5th Cir. 2005). On remand, in the Memorandum Opinion excerpted above, Judge Lake concluded that there was no way to determine "actual" loss, and hence turned to the alternative measure of loss specified by Guideline §2B1.1: "intended loss." This yielded a smaller figure, $79 million instead of over $100 million, which still pro-duced—along with the enhancements for use of a special skill, use of sophis-ticated means, and multiple victims—a high offense level and a Guidelines sentencing range of 151 to 188 months (at least 12 years in prison).

2. Do you think that the amount of actual or intended loss is the best measure of culpability for the variety of crimes that are within the ambit of §2B1.1 of the Sentencing Guidelines? How about as compared to other fac-tors, such as the other aggravating factors in this Guideline or the universal factors that apply in all Guidelines calculations? Note that if Olis had per-formed the same actions at a smaller company, the amount of "loss"—and hence his Guidelines sentence—would have been lower. But for offenders who participate in fraudulent activities in large public companies, the loss table can translate into sentences even higher than the highest Offense Level (43), which means, literally, a life sentence under the Guidelines. As the Second Circuit has noted, "Under the Guidelines, it may well be that all but the most trivial frauds in publicly traded companies may trigger sentences amounting to life imprisonment. . . ." United States v. Ebbers, 458 F.3d 110, 129 (2d Cir. 2006); see also United States v. Adelson, 441 F. Supp. 2d 506, 512 (S.D.N.Y. 2006) (Rakoff, J.) (protesting "the utter travesty of justice that sometimes results from the guidelines' fetish with absolute arithmetic, as well as the harm that guideline calculations can visit on human beings if not cabined by common sense"), aff'd, 301 F. App'x. 93 (2d Cir. 2007). See generally Frank W. Bowman, Sacrificial Felon, American Lawyer, Jan. 2007, at 63 (asserting that "rules governing high-end federal white-collar sen-tences are now completely untethered from both criminal law theory and simple common sense"). Inasmuch as the mail and wire fraud statutes are violated even when no loss is suffered (indeed, they prohibit any "scheme to defraud" even when the scheme goes nowhere), why should severity of punishment for these crimes be so heavily dependent on calculations of "loss"—and why are such severe sentences appropriate for crimes involving misrepresentation of information?

3. Mail and wire fraud sentencing under §2B1.1 appears to be one of the areas in which disparity in sentencing has become especially pronounced after *Booker*, as some judges hew to the Guidelines sentence while others depart drastically (even when all the judges are in the same Circuit and thus presumably face the same standard of review). Compare United States v. Ferguson, 553 F. Supp. 2d 145 (D. Conn. 2008) (imposing sentences of four years or less on defendants convicted of a fraudulent scheme with over $500 million in "loss," though the Guidelines prescribed life-imprisonment sentences); *Adelson*, 441 F. Supp. 2d at 512, with United States v. Peppel, 707 F.3d 627 (6th Cir. 2013) (vacating and remanding for new sentencing, where Guidelines range was 97-121 months and district court gave custodial sentence of 7 days); United States v. Rigas, 583 F.3d 108, 118 (2d Cir. 2009) (asserting that sentences of 15 years and 20 years in a case involving bank fraud and securities fraud were not "substantively unreasonable"); United States v. Ebbers, 458 110, 130 (2d Cir. 2006) (concluding that a 25-year sentence, based on a loss figure of $100 million and Guidelines sentence of 30 years to life, was "harsh but reasonable"). See generally Daniel Richman, Federal White Collar Sentencing in the United States: A Work in Progress, 76. L. & Contemp. Probs. 53 (2013). When sentencing large-scale fraud cases, how much weight should judges give to the goal (however unattainable) of national uniformity?

4. Which is more important, the amount of loss or the defendant's role in the offense? For economic crimes, the Guidelines give far less weight to role in the offense than they do to amount of loss. (Likewise, as we will see shortly, the Guidelines give far greater weight to the quantity, as well as the type, of drugs in narcotics-trafficking offenses.) Under U.S.S.G. §3B1, a defendant who was the "organizer or leader of a criminal activity that involved five or more participants" receives a four-level enhancement, while a defendant who was a "minimal participant" receives a four-level reduction in offense level. "Minor" participants receive a two-level reduction, while organizers and leaders of criminal activities involving fewer than five persons receive a two-level bump-up. Because of the significance that the Guidelines give to loss (as defined in the Guidelines), relative to the weight given to the defendant's actual criminal behavior, someone who had a minor role but was involved in a very big fraud will have a far greater Guidelines sentence than the mastermind of a smaller or less successful Ponzi scheme. Bernard Madoff's sentencing range, based on a loss calculation beyond that listed in the Loss Table, was literally "off the charts," with an offense level of 54. Despite Madoff being in the lowest criminal history category, the Guidelines yielded a sentencing range of life imprisonment, see Government's Sentencing Memorandum, United States v. Madoff (Mar. 10, 2009). The judge gave Madoff the statutory maximum sentence available under the crimes to which he pleaded guilty: 150 years, see Diana B.

Henriques, Madoff Is Sentenced to 150 Years for Ponzi Scheme, N.Y. Times (June 29, 2009).

Suppose that one of Madoff's secretaries is convicted of mail fraud in connection with his Ponzi scheme. Suppose, further, that she personally aided only one aspect of the fraud (as to one victim) but that she should have known (that is, it was "reasonably foreseeable" to her) that Madoff's Ponzi scheme had many more victims. How should her sentence be determined? Note that because of broad accessorial liability under 18 U.S.C. §2, the secretary in this hypothetical is guilty of fraud even though Madoff was the principal. Note also that under *Pinkerton* (excerpted in Chapter 8), the jury could find her guilty of additional frauds that she did not aid if these involved crimes by her co-conspirator, Madoff, that were foreseeable to her. Under the Guidelines' relevant-conduct rule, §1B1.1, the judge must attribute the harms from these additional crimes (that were foreseeable to her) even if the jury declined to find her guilty under *Pinkerton*. But, remember, she was only involved in one small fraud as to one victim. How would you sentence her, post-*Booker*? Is the problem here the Guidelines' relevant-conduct rule? *Pinkerton*? 18 U.S.C. §2? In 2015, §2B1.1 was amended to invite a downward adjustment in the calculated sentencing range when a defendant faces a loss among "that greatly exceeds the defendant's personal gain from a fraud offense." U.S.S.G. §3B1.2, com. nn.3-5. Of course, after *Booker*, the judge has the authority to undo any overreaching or arbitrariness introduced by any or all of these provisions. See, e.g., United States v. Algahaim, 842 F.3d 796, 800 (2d Cir. 2016) (stating that "[w]here the Commission has assigned a rather low base offense level to a crime and then increased it significantly by a loss enhancement, [under *Kimbrough*] that combination of circumstances entitles a sentencing judge to consider a non-Guidelines sentence" and remanding to the district court for further consideration of "whether the significant effect of the loss enhancement, in relation to the low base offense level, should result in a non-Guidelines sentence"). Yet the sentencing judge need not do so. Indeed, as we've noted in Section C of this chapter, the Supreme Court in *Gall*, 552 U.S. 38 (2007), permitted federal courts of appeals to consider Guidelines sentences as presumptively reasonable.

By the way, Madoff's actual secretary, Annette Bongiorno, convicted after a six-month trial, received a sentence of only six years for her "'integral role' in the largest financial fraud in history," with the judge citing poor health and other reasons for the low sentence. Dareh Gregorian, Bernie Madoff's Secretary Gets Break in Sentencing Because Judge Takes Pity on "Unusually Small Stature," New York Daily News (Dec. 9, 2014).

5. How did role-in-the-offense figure into Olis's sentence? The sentencing court had no occasion to discuss Olis's role in the fraudulent scheme when it was determining the applicable Guidelines sentencing range; this is because Olis qualified for no role adjustment, being neither the "organizer

or leader" nor a "minor" or "minimal" participant. The sentencing judge's discussion of Olis's role came later in his Memorandum Opinion, when he was discussing the sentencing factors in 18 U.S.C. §3553(a) that, post-*Booker*, may convince a sentencing court to impose a non-Guidelines sentence. In effect, Judge Lake was redefining the crime of fraud to make role important—certainly more important than Congress has provided (since under 18 U.S.C. §2, accomplices are guilty of the same offense as principals), and even more important than the Sentencing Commission provided in its Guidelines. The judge effectively decided that Olis's lesser role meant that he committed a lesser crime.

6. There is more to be said about Olis's role, especially vis-à-vis his co-conspirators. Olis was Senior Director of Tax Planning at Dynegy. The scheme at issue was essentially an illegal tax shelter that "Olis, his boss Gene Foster and his colleague Helen Sharkey, secretly put into place" to conceal the lack of actual economic risk to Dynegy, *Olis*, 429 F.3d at 542. Foster and Sharkey each pleaded guilty to one count and cooperated with the Government. Foster became the "star prosecution witness" against Olis, id. As Judge Lake noted in the excerpt above, Olis did not have authority to approve the fraudulent scheme; presumably, Foster or someone else did so. After Olis was convicted and initially sentenced to 24 years, Foster—who received a "5K1" letter (discussed previously in this chapter) in return for his cooperation—was sentenced to 15 months. This comparison reveals the leverage that the Sentencing Commission handed to prosecutors in providing that upon their motion, defendants could receive a below-Guidelines sentence.

7. Why is Olis's personal history, discussed in the judge's sentencing memorandum, relevant to the punishment he should receive? (Why does it matter, for instance, where he was born?) Prior to *Booker*, these facts would have had virtually no impact on his sentence—or, to be more precise, a sentencing judge during the mandatory Guidelines era would not admit she thought them relevant, since the Guidelines specifically provide that offender characteristics (including age, educational and vocational skills, mental and emotional condition, physical conduction, employment record, family ties and responsibilities, and civic and social contributions) are "ordinarily not relevant" in determining whether a departure from the calculated Guidelines sentence is appropriate, see U.S.S.G. §5H1.1. After *Booker*, however, judges may (or may not) consider these and related factors to the extent they appear relevant to the general sentencing objectives listed in 18 U.S.C. §3553(a), which is the context in which they were discussed in *Olis*.

8. At least after *Booker*, the extraordinarily "flat" culpability approach taken by substantive federal law—broad conspiracy doctrine, expansive aiding and abetting provisions, *Pinkerton* liability, and the like—is complemented by Guideline role provisions and the ability of a sentencing judge, should she want, to be quite nuanced in her assessment of a defendant's

culpability. To what extent does the sentencing judge's discretion in this regard assuage your concerns about the broad liability rules you've encountered in Chapter 8?

2.   POLITICAL CORRUPTION

We saw in Chapters 4, 5, and 6 that many political corruption cases can be charged as mail or wire fraud, 18 U.S.C. §§1341 and 1343 (including as theft of honest services, 18 U.S.C. §1346); under the Hobbs Act, 18 U.S.C. §1951; and under one or more bribery statutes. When Congress increased the maximum sentence for mail and wire fraud from five to 20 years in the wake of the 2008 financial crisis, it brought the potential penalty for these crimes up to the maximum it had long provided for violation of the Hobbs Act. Meanwhile, the maximum sentence under the federal bribery statute (applicable only to federal officials and those carrying out federal duties), 18 U.S.C. §201(b), remains 15 years, and the maximum sentence for federal program bribery, in violation of 18 U.S.C. §666, is ten years. You will recall that there is ambiguity as to what must be proved in the nature of a "*quid pro quo*" under each of these statutes, and as to what types of arrangements are not prohibited even when they do involve a *quid pro quo.* As you read the material below, one question to keep in mind is whether the Sentencing Guidelines make these statutory distinctions more, or less, coherent.

In the discussion below, we dare not attempt to examine all facets of all Guidelines related to the crimes mentioned above. Instead, we examine a recently amended Guideline in which the Sentencing Commission has deliberately sought to provide uniformity of treatment of like offenders—here, those involved in political corruption—no matter what the statutory crime of conviction.

U.S.S.G. §2C1.1

Offering, Giving, Soliciting, or Receiving a Bribe; Extortion Under Color of Official Right; Fraud Involving the Deprivation of the Intangible Right to Honest Services of Public Officials; Conspiracy to Defraud by Interference with Governmental Functions

(a) Base Offense Level:
   (1) 14, if the defendant was a public official; or
   (2) 12, otherwise.
(b) Specific Offense Characteristics
   (1) If the offense involved more than one bribe or extortion, increase by 2 levels.
   (2) If the value of the payment, the benefit received or to be received in return for the payment, the value of anything obtained or to be

obtained by a public official or others acting with a public official, or the loss to the government from the offense, whichever is greatest, exceeded $6,500, increase by the number of levels from the table in §2B1.1 (Theft, Property Destruction, and Fraud) corresponding to that amount.

(3) If the offense involved an elected public official or any public official in a high-level decision-making or sensitive position, increase by 4 levels. If the resulting offense level is less than level 18, increase to level 18.

(4) If the defendant was a public official who facilitated (A) entry into the United States for a person, a vehicle, or cargo; (B) the obtaining of a passport or a document relating to naturalization, citizenship, legal entry, or legal resident status; or (C) the obtaining of a government identification document, increase by 2 levels.

(c) Cross References

(1) If the offense was committed for the purpose of facilitating the commission of another criminal offense, apply the offense guideline applicable to a conspiracy to commit that other offense, if the resulting offense level is greater than that determined above.

(2) If the offense was committed for the purpose of concealing, or obstructing justice in respect to, another criminal offense, apply §2X3.1 (Accessory After the Fact) or §2J1.2 (Obstruction of Justice), as appropriate, in respect to that other offense, if the resulting offense level is greater than that determined above.

(3) If the offense involved a threat of physical injury or property destruction, apply §2B3.2 (Extortion by Force or Threat of Injury or Serious Damage), if the resulting offense level is greater than that determined above. . . .

HOW THE GUIDELINES REDEFINE POLITICAL CORRUPTION CRIMES

1. Guideline §2C1.1 applies to many, but not all, crimes that involve public corruption. For instance, any extortion "by force or threat of injury or serious damage" comes within a different Guideline, with a base offense level of 18, see U.S.S.G. §2B3.2. And if the defendant, whether or not a public official, is convicted of robbery under the Hobbs Act—remember United States v. Zhou, 428 F.3d 361 (2d Cir. 2005), in Chapter 5—the Guidelines range is calculated under the robbery Guideline, §2B3.1, which has a base offense level of 20. Where the extortionate payment or bribe was made to conceal another crime or to obstruct justice, the Guidelines covering those crimes apply "if the result is greater than that" under §2C1.1. See id., Application Notes, Background. But §2C1.1 applies to most non-forcible bribes and kickbacks in the public sector, including those violating the honest services prong of mail and wire fraud, the Hobbs Act, the federal bribery statute, the federal program bribery statute, and the Foreign Corrupt Practices Act. As to the last of these, the Sentencing Commission specifically

determined that violations of the FCPA are more akin to public corruption than to commercial bribery and kickbacks.

2. A different Guideline, with a lower base offense level of 11 for public officials and 9 otherwise, applies to crimes involving the giving or receiving of a gratuity, see §2C1.2. (The differences between a "bribe" and a "gratuity" are discussed at length in Chapter 6.) While 18 U.S.C. §201 clearly distinguishes between bribes and gratuities, however, other statutes cited in the previous paragraph do not. What about an extortion "under color of right" offense that does not involve the clear *quid pro quo* needed for a bribery conviction (to the extent that United States v. Evans, 504 U.S. 255 (1992), allows for such a prosecution)? Or kickbacks prosecuted under the theory of "honest services" fraud that were not sought by the office holder? Or payments given in violation of 18 U.S.C. §666(a)(2), which also does not clearly require a *quid pro quo*? The Guidelines provide that all of those cases are to be sentenced under the bribery Guideline (§2C1.1), rather than the less severe gratuity Guideline (§2C1.2). Is it fair to sentence the defendant under §2C1.1 if the payment at issue was more in the nature of a gratuity than a bribe? Do you think it is fair to hold, on the one hand, that a *quid pro quo* is not needed for conviction under §666, and, on the other hand, to affirm a sentence calculated under §2C1.1, the bribery Guideline? See United States v. McNair, 605 F.3d 1152, 1188 (11th Cir. 2010).

Both *McNair* and the next case exemplify how many sentencing judges (perhaps out of force of habit) have continued to impose the calculated Guidelines sentence, without addressing whether the Guidelines appropriately evaluate the crime at hand. The case below also shows you one way in which the Guidelines address multiple counts of conviction (why should the number of counts matter?) and how crime-specific aggravating factors interact with the Guidelines trans-substantive aggravating factors that may cover the same terrain.

United States v. Cruzado
440 F.3d 44 (1st Cir. 2006)

STAHL, Senior Circuit Judge. . . .

I. BACKGROUND

This case comes to us on appeal for the second time. The facts of the case are laid out extensively in our prior opinion, see United States v. Cruzado-Laureano, 404 F.3d 470, 473-480 (1st Cir. 2005), and we need not rehearse them here in any great detail. Briefly put, Juan Manuel "Manny" Cruzado-Laureano has had a varied career. A high-school mathematics teacher for seven years early on in life, Cruzado later worked 16 years in the construction industry, four as an administrator in his wife's dental practice, and five as the owner and manager of a check-cashing business. In November 2000, Cruzado was elected mayor of Vega Alta, a municipality in Puerto Rico. Almost immediately after taking office, Cruzado began extorting and laundering money by, among other things, demanding kickbacks on municipal contracts and redirecting funds intended for the government into his own pocket. Cruzado would clear the extorted money through his own bank account, through his old check-cashing business (now owned by his son), or through the accounts at his wife's dental practice. The Federal Bureau of Investigation began investigating Cruzado's conduct in 2001, and an initial indictment was issued in October of that year. During the course of the investigation and after the initial indictment was handed down, Cruzado compounded his legal troubles by attempting to tamper with three potential witnesses against him.

A 14-count superseding indictment was returned on January 25, 2002. The indictment charged Cruzado with . . . six counts of extortion under §1951(a); [and] six counts of money laundering under §1956(a)(1)(B)(i) and (a)(1)(B)(ii). . . . After the close of evidence, the court dismissed one of the money-laundering charges, and the jury eventually returned a verdict of not guilty on one of the extortion charges. Cruzado was convicted by the jury on each of the remaining [] charges.

The district court imposed a 63-month sentence. In his earlier appeal, Cruzado . . . prevailed [only] on his claim that the district court applied the wrong version of the Sentencing Guidelines. . . . On remand, the court performed the sentencing calculation anew under the [appropriate version of the] Guidelines.[2]

Section 2C1.1 of the Guidelines provides sentencing guidance for "Offering, Giving, Soliciting, or Receiving a Bribe; Extortion Under Color of Official Right," and §2S1.1 for "Laundering of Monetary Instruments; Engaging in Monetary Transactions in Property Derived from Unlawful Activity." Money laundering is, generally speaking, a derivative offense: money needs to be laundered because it was illegally derived. In recommending a sentence for money laundering under §2S1.1, the Guidelines take as the base offense level the full computed offense level relevant to the underlying offense. In making its sentencing calculation, the district court proceeded by:

---

2. The court imposed the new sentence after the Supreme Court's decision in United States v. Booker, 543 U.S. 220 (2005), which rendered the Guidelines advisory. It nevertheless imposed sentence based on the Guidelines recommendation.

(1) turning from the money laundering provision, §2S1.1, to the provision for the underlying offense, §2C1.1;

(2) determining the base offense level for extortion offenses under §2C1.1(a);

(3) adjusting that level upward according to the rules for specific offense characteristics applicable under the extortion guideline, §2C1.1(b);

(4) taking the resulting final offense level for extortion as the base offense level for money laundering under §2S1.1(a);

(5) applying additional enhancements specified by the money laundering guideline under §2S1.1(b);

(6) applying additional enhancements under relevant general adjustment provisions laid out in Chapter Three of the Guidelines Manual.

Thus, the district court started with a base offense level of 10,* which §2C1.1(a) specifies as the base offense level for extortion. It applied a two-level enhancement under §2C1.1(b)(1) because the offense involved more than one incident of extortion, and an eight-level enhancement under §2C1.1(b)(2)(B) because the extortion involved a payment for the purpose of influencing an elected decision-making official.** The final offense level under §2C1.1 was thus 20. Under §2S1.1(a), level 20 became the base offense level for the money laundering, to which the court applied an additional two-level enhancement under §2S1.1(b)(2)(B)*** because the offense involved a conviction under the money laundering statute, 18 U.S.C. §1956.

The court then turned to the general-purpose adjustment provisions of Chapter Three, and found two applicable. The court applied a two-level enhancement for abuse of a position of public trust under §3B1.3, and another two-level enhancement for obstruction of justice under §3C1.1. Cruzado's final offense level under these calculations was 26, and the court determined that he fell into criminal history category I. Taken together, the offense level and criminal history category produced a recommended sentence of 63-78 months. This recommended sentence was no shorter and potentially longer than the 63 months to which Cruzado had originally

---

* [Editors' Note: In 2004, after the defendant had committed his crimes, the Sentencing Commission increased the base offense level in §2C1.1 from 10 to 14 for public officials.]

** [Editors' Note: In 2004, the Sentencing Commission replaced this eight-level increase for a "high level decision maker" with two other provisions: the four-level increase in §2C1.1(b)(3) if the offense "involved" elected or high-level officials, with a required minimum offense level of 18; and the two-level increase in §2C1.1(b)(4) where the public official's position involved the security of the borders.]

*** [Editors' Note: The money-laundering Guideline, §2S1.1, provides that the base offense level is determined by the underlying crime, with two levels added if the defendant was actually convicted of money laundering under 18 U.S.C. §1956.]

been sentenced. The court decided that Cruzado ought not to suffer for having exercised his right of appeal, and imposed a sentence identical to the one earlier imposed. Cruzado timely brought this appeal, challenging the district court's application of several provisions of the Guidelines.

II. LEGAL CHALLENGES

On a challenge to a sentence imposed on the basis of a Guidelines recommendation, we "determine the legal meaning of Guidelines provisions de novo." United States v. Robinson, 433 F.3d 31, 35 (1st Cir. 2005).

A. Extortion by an Elected Official

The district court increased Cruzado's offense level by eight points under §2C1.1(b)(2)(B) [the enhancement for crimes involving public officials]. . . . Cruzado was convicted for being on the receiving end of various corrupt payoffs, and he argues that this provision only applies when a defendant has made, rather than received, the payment. Nothing in the quoted language suggests that this is so. The provision reflects the Sentencing Commission's determination that the abuse of a position of great public trust, or the effort to corrupt a person holding such a position, is more dangerous than the corruption of, for example, a housing inspector or tax assessor. The eight-level increase is mandated for a defendant precisely like the defendant here, an elected official who abuses his position. Extortion "involves" payments intended to influence the behavior of the extortioner just as clearly as bribery "involves" payments intended to influence the bribetaker.[9] . . .

B. [The Two-Level Enhancement for Conviction Under 18 U.S.C. §1956 was Proper] . . .

C. Abuse of Trust

The district court applied a two-level abuse-of-trust enhancement under §3B1.3. That section calls for such an increase "[i]f the defendant abused a position of public or private trust . . . in a manner that significantly facilitated the commission or concealment of the offense." It cautions, however, that "[t]his adjustment may not be employed if an abuse of trust or skill is included in the base offense level or specific offense characteristic." Id. This second provision bars application of a

_____

9. Nor is the rule of lenity applicable, as Cruzado claims: there is nothing at all ambiguous in §2C1.1.

§3B1.3 abuse-of-trust enhancement to a case in which any provision that increases a sentence for an offender who holds high public office already applies. This is such a case.

The district court here evidently found the §3B1.3 abuse-of-trust provision applicable because Cruzado had used the power of his high office in extorting and embezzling funds. Abuse of high office was the same concern, however, that justified the application of an eight-level enhancement under §2C1.1(b)(2)(B). Section 3B1.3 and §2C1.1(b)(2)(B) both increase a defendant's sentence for abusing a position of trust, and by the terms of §3B1.3 cannot both be applied to increase the same defendant's sentence. . . .

Although double-counting is not automatically impermissible under the Guidelines (and is sometimes intentionally directed), we can see no particular reason why one would want double-counting in this situation. For these reasons, we conclude that the district court erred in applying an abuse-of-trust enhancement under §3B3.3.

III.   CONCLUSION

Having determined that the court's interpretation of the Guidelines was legally erroneous, see Robinson, 433 F.3d at 35, we must again send the case back to the district court. See United States v. Plaza-Garcia, 914 F.2d 345, 347 (1st Cir. 1990); 18 U.S.C. §3742(f)(1) (requiring that incorrectly calculated sentences be remanded). In remanding the case, we do not intend to intimate that the length of the sentence should necessarily be changed; what matters is that the premise as to the Guideline range must be correct. . . .

NOTES AND QUESTIONS

1. Where the defendant has been convicted of multiple offenses, the Guidelines instruct, as a general matter, that the sentencing court should sentence the defendant under the Guideline that produces the highest offense level, see U.S.S.G. §3D1.3. In *Cruzado*, this was the money-laundering Guideline (§2S1.1), which by its terms will produce a higher sentence than will the Guideline for the underlying crimes (in this case, extortion) because it instructs the judge to calculate the offense level for the underlying crime and then to add two levels if the defendant has been convicted under 18 U.S.C. §1956 or one level if the conviction was under 18 U.S.C. §1957. (Recall from Chapter 8 that the latter provision has a reduced *mens rea* requirement, but also has a lower statutory maximum sentence.) As noted above, in previous iterations of the Guidelines a money-laundering conviction ratcheted up a sentence even more. Perhaps the Commission's

decision to make the Guidelines range for money laundering closer to that for the underlying crime was motivated by the "merger" concern discussed in United States v. Santos, 553 U.S. 507 (2008), and recognized by Congress when it enacted a provision undoing *Santos*, excerpted in Section C of Chapter 8. We cannot say for certain, however, because, as noted in Section B of this chapter, the Sentencing Commission — unlike most federal agencies — is not required to explain in any detail the reasoning behind its rules or its amendments of those rules. The case discussed in Note 4 below, *United States v. Lupton*, addresses the significance of the Commission's sparse explanation of the reasons underlying its policy decisions.

2. Cruzado was convicted of six counts of extortion and five counts of money laundering. As to the latter, the number of counts made no difference in determining the sentence he received. This is because for all economic crimes — including those under §2B1.1, considered previously — the Guidelines instruct simply that the total amount of money or property be added together for purposes of calculating the applicable offense level. This case demonstrates why, given the relevant conduct Guideline (§1B1.1), it does not matter how many counts were charged, or, indeed, whether the defendant was actually convicted with respect to each relevant amount of money or property. Nor does it matter if the defendant was convicted of more than one count of extortion; while §2C1.1(b)(1) expressly provides for a two-level enhancement "[i]f the offense involved more than one bribe or extortion," it does not matter in how many counts those crimes are charged.

3. The Loss Table in U.S.S.G. §2B1.1, discussed above, figures even in the calculation of the offense level for crimes of political corruption. Look back at §2C1.1 above; do you see why this is? Section 2C1.1(b)(2) provides for an increase in the offense level corresponding to the amount of the bribe made, the benefit received, or the loss to a third party ("whichever is greatest"), using the level enhancements specified in the Loss Table. Because §2C1.1 sentences include both the loss calculation and additional enhancements for public corruption, a sentence under Guidelines §2C1.1 is almost always higher than a Guidelines sentence involving the same amount of money that is calculated only under §2B1.1.

4. As we have noted, §2C1.1 applies not just to bribery statutes, but also to "honest services" fraud involving public officials — even when the fraud might have been charged as a traditional money or property fraud without reference to 18 U.S.C. §1346. While a purpose of the Guidelines is to make it irrelevant which statute the defendant is convicted of violating — remember, what matters is his underlying "real offense," see Section B of this chapter — the differences between §2B1.1 and §2C1.1 mean that the prosecutor's choice of charges still matters. This is true even though after Sarbanes-Oxley the *statutory* maximum is the same for Hobbs Act extortions and honest services fraud. In United States v. Lupton, 2009 WL 1886007

(E.D. Wisc., June 29, 2009), the defendant was an independent broker for a private company that had contracted with the Wisconsin State Department of Administration to sell a state office building. The defendant sought and received a kickback from the real estate agent representing the buyer of the building. After waiving jury trial, he was convicted by the court on all counts: bribery in violation of 18 U.S.C. §666(a)(1)(b); wire fraud in violation of 18 U.S.C. §§1343 and 1346; and two counts of making a false statement to the FBI in violation of 18 U.S.C. §1001. In a memorandum explaining the reasons (which he had already put on the record at the sentencing hearing) for a below-Guidelines sentence, the sentencing judge stated:

> The guidelines called for a prison term of 41-51 months, and the government recommended 48 months. Although, for the reasons stated, I agreed that a prison term was needed, I found these recommendations somewhat greater than necessary.
>
> First, the range was significantly elevated because this was, in part, an honest services fraud case, rather than a case solely about the deprivation of money or property.[9] U.S.S.G. §2C1.1 carries a base level of 12 or 14, in addition to the loss amount from the §2B1.1 table, while the guideline applicable to money/property wire fraud cases carries a base level of just 7. The Commission has not explained why significantly greater penalties are warranted for honest services fraud. The Commission [in amending §2C1.1 to cover all political corruption cases] . . . stated only: "This amendment increases punishment for bribery, gratuity, and 'honest services' cases while providing additional enhancements to address previously unrecognized aggravating factors inherent in some of these offenses. This amendment reflects the Commission's conclusion that, in general, public corruption offenses previously did not receive punishment commensurate with the gravity of such offenses." United States Sentencing Commission Guidelines Manual, Supplement to Appendix C 82 (2008) (Amendment 666). The Commission also provided little explanation when it first proposed the amendment, other than to note that it responded to concerns expressed by the Public Integrity Section of the Justice Department that [certain] §§1341-1343 offenses be prosecuted under 2C1.1 rather than the fraud guideline. I was unable to locate any working group or other reports discussing the increase. Had U.S.S.G. §2B1.1 applied, it appeared that the range would have been 24-30 months.
>
> It may be that public corruption cases are, in general, more serious than garden variety money/property fraud cases. Such crimes may damage public confidence in government. Thus, it may be that at least in some cases enhanced punishment would be warranted.
>
> The offense conduct here did not reflect the sort of governmental corruption at which the statutes and guidelines are most directly targeted. This

---

9. The government prosecuted this case both as an honest services fraud and a deprivation of money/property case, and I found that it established guilt under both theories.

case involved a broker, operating in the world of commission sales, attempting to increase his take on a particular transaction. While I did not in any way excuse defendant's conduct, I did not see this as a case of political corruption (or political in any way). . . . I did not agree with defendant's contention that the case did not undermine public confidence in state procurement or sales processes; it may have. But this was not a systemic type of corruption; it related to a single transaction. . . .

Lupton, 2009 WL 1886007 at *9.

Consider the many phases of crime definition in *Lupton*. You will recall from Chapter 4, that after McNally v. United States, 483 U.S. 350, 356 (1987), Congress enacted 18 U.S.C. §1346, explicitly making deprivation of "honest services" a type of fraud covered by the mail and wire fraud statutes. Federal prosecutors charged a wide variety of political corruption cases under these fraud statutes. In Skilling v. United States, 561 U.S. 358 (2010), the Supreme Court cut back the scope of "honest services" frauds to those involving bribes or kickbacks. Meanwhile, apparently (*Lupton* informs us) under pressure from the Department of Justice, the Sentencing Commission in 2008 decided that mail and wire fraud cases that involve deprivation of honest services should be sentenced under the (more severe) public corruption Guideline, §2C1.1, rather than the fraud Guideline, §2B1.1. Prosecutors charged Lupton with deprivation of honest services (and though it was charged before *Skilling*, the charges and proof in *Lupton* meet *Skilling*'s requirements as far as we are told). Were prosecutors, aided and abetted by Congress and the Sentencing Commission, gaming the system? As we saw in Chapter 6, the only federal bribery law directly applicable to local officials such as Lupton is "program bribery," 18 U.S.C. §666. But Lupton was charged with honest services fraud, and prosecutors were able to obtain the same Guideline sentence for Lupton that would have been applicable were he a federal official charged with bribery under 18 U.S.C. §201. Perhaps the sentencing judge's refusal to treat Lupton differently from most defendants convicted of fraud in federal court was an effort to interpose a judicial check on perceived overreaching by Congress, the Department of Justice, and the Sentencing Commission.

Perhaps, on the other hand, it was the judge who was overreaching in *Lupton*. Who is he to decide that local officials charged with honest services fraud should be treated more leniently than federal officials charged with bribery? Note, as well, that *Lupton* is a single decision of no precedential value; other judges around the country may well find no warrant to give a below-Guidelines sentence on the grounds that the Sentencing Commission did not explain its 2008 Guideline amendment to their satisfaction. After *Booker*, is not such disparity in treatment more likely? Is that clearly bad — or is it, arguably, good, on the theory that at least some defendants will receive more appropriate sentences?

3.   DRUG TRAFFICKING

Now we return to drug sentencing. In Chapter 9, we looked at the mandatory minimum sentences imposed by Congress and at the crack/powder quantity differential in particular. Here we add the Sentencing Guidelines to the mix and discuss how they interact with statutory mandatory minimums. We then explore how the Sentencing Commission and the Supreme Court sought to address the crack/powder disparity during the two decades in which Congress refused to do so.

a.   *Mandatory Sentences versus Mandatory Guidelines*

We saw in Chapter 9 that there is a large statutory sentencing range for drug-trafficking offenses: between five and 40 years for those convicted of distributing relatively low quantities of a scheduled drug (e.g., more than 100 grams of heroin or 500 grams of powder cocaine), and between ten years and life in prison for those convicted of trafficking in even higher quantities (e.g., one kilogram of heroin or five kilograms of powder cocaine). The Sentencing Commission decided to extrapolate these graduated penalties in its Guidelines. An article written before the Fairness in Sentencing Act of 2010—which reduced the crack/powder quantity disparity, as we discussed in Chapter 9—succinctly explained:

> [T]he Commission created a drug sentencing scheme that conformed to the [Anti-Drug Abuse Act of 1986] in three important ways. First, Guidelines drug sentences, like the minimum mandatory sentences of the ADAA, are based largely on drug quantity. Second, where the ADAA prescribed a minimum mandatory sentence for a particular quantity of drug, the sentence level set by the Guidelines for that quantity corresponds to the ADAA minimum mandatory sentence. For example, the sentencing range under the Guidelines for five hundred grams of powder cocaine, an amount that triggers a five-year minimum mandatory sentence under the ADAA, is set just above five years (63-78 months). Third, . . . in setting offense levels for drug amounts below, between, and above the statutorily designated quantities that trigger mandatory sentences, the Commission maintained the identical quantity ratios between drug types specified in the ADAA. For example, the ratio of cocaine to cocaine base ("crack") for every offense level on the Guidelines Drug Quantity table matches the 100-to-1 ratio in the ADAA. . . .

Frank R. Bowman, III & Michael Heise, Quiet Rebellion? Explaining Nearly a Decade of Declining Federal Drug Sentences, 86 Iowa L. Rev. 1043, 1060-62 (2001). There has been significant criticism of the Commission's decision to follow Congress's lead on drug sentencing. Instead, it could have developed Guidelines on the basis of its own independent research or analysis, while recognizing that any mandatory statutory sentence would "trump" a lower Guidelines sentence. See, e.g., United States v. Diaz, 2013 WL 322243 (E.D.N.Y. Jan. 28, 2013); Michael Tonry, Salvaging the Sentencing Guidelines in Seven Easy Steps, 10 Fed. Sent'g Rep. 51, 54 (1997).

Yet it would be a mistake to think of Guidelines sentencing in the drug area as simply a fine-tuned version of the minimum and maximum sentences set forth in 21 U.S.C. §841(b). In important respects, the Commission did not follow Congress's lead in drug sentencing. For instance, whereas Congress provided for double the usual minimum for a defendant previously convicted of a felony drug offense (as explained in Chapter 9), the Guidelines treat criminal history uniformly and trans-substantively.

The article excerpted below, written before *Booker* made the Guidelines "advisory," explains why this detail matters so much.

Gerard E. Lynch, Sentencing Eddie
91 J. Crim. L. & Criminology 547 (2001)

The mandatory minimum sentences attached to federal narcotics violations have come in for plenty of criticism. The United States Sentencing Commission in 1991 submitted a lengthy report critical of the mandatory minimum provisions. . . . Newspaper columnists, professional commentators, judges, and academics, have criticized the statutes. . . . Even Chief Justice Rehnquist, a strong voice for law enforcement, has denounced mandatory minimum sentences as having little serious justification.

In an effort to make the effects of the statutes more vivid, critics have searched out examples of extreme injustice created by the statutes. The examples cited are usually minor accomplices in the narcotics trade, usually women, often pressured by men in their lives to participate in some modest way (such as courier or bookkeeper or message-taker) in a drug transaction or conspiracy involving a quantity of drugs that triggers a five- or ten-year mandatory minimum. . . .

Such cases, however, are relatively few. Prosecutorial discretion usually finds a way to avoid dramatic injustices. The cases that remain are sometimes the product of misguided tactical decisions by defendants or defense lawyers who refuse more reasonable plea offers. This fact, of course, does not excuse the shockingly unjust results occasionally produced — even one single injustice is too many, and the fact that a defendant could have avoided an extreme sentence by waiving her constitutional right to trial is neither a comfort nor a justification for an unduly harsh sentence. But it does render the public debate about mandatory minimums, like the debate about many criminal justice issues, somewhat artificial and sensational, as opponents cite unusual anecdotes about unbelievably cruel outcomes, while proponents counter with equally exotic instances of unreasonably lenient discretionary sentences that, they say, warrant legislative control.

It is much harder to discuss the more routine and modest injustices produced by mandatory minimums. . . .

So let me introduce you to a more typical "victim" of the mandatory minimum sentence provisions. Eddie is about as randomly selected as can be: he happens to be the very first person I was called upon to sentence after taking office as a federal district judge. He is worth writing about precisely because he is nobody's poster child for reforming mandatory minimum sentences. There is no question in my mind that most people would regard him as a good candidate for severe treatment at the hands of the law, and I'm not about to dispute that view.

Eddie was found guilty by a jury of conspiring to sell cocaine. He was the last man standing from a twenty-five defendant indictment; everyone else had pled guilty. Eddie (like many of the defendants) was a somewhat marginal member of the "organization." . . . The evidence showed that Eddie sold cocaine to a number of steady customers, and bought from the principal defendant, a wholesaler of substantial quantities of the drug. By law, Eddie's involvement as a regular, re-selling customer of the drug ring makes him a co-conspirator with the other members in the distribution of narcotics, but in economic reality he was likely less a partner or employee of the wholesaler than an independent contractor, looking to secure a reliable supplier to the extent that he could, but no doubt as prepared as any other retail merchant to shift allegiance to another wholesaler if a new dealer came along offering better quality or price, or a more regular source of supply.

How much cocaine did Eddie sell? . . . The jury was justified in concluding that Eddie was in the regular business of selling drugs. . . . He almost certainly sold more than the government knew about, and if he had not been arrested he would surely have gone on selling. Had he been arrested in connection with a particular sale (say, if he had made the mistake of selling to an undercover officer or a drug user who had a reason to "turn" and become a police informant), the scope of his activities known by the authorities might have looked much narrower. As it was, he was caught because the government was focusing a major investigation on his supplier, and overheard him negotiating on a couple of occasions with the supplier, whose phone was tapped. . . . The government thus contended, with some justice, that Eddie was involved in transactions that, conservatively, involved five hundred grams or more of cocaine. A reasonable person would be concerned that the witness might have exaggerated—but a reasonable person would also have some confidence that the witness was not privy to all of Eddie's dealings.

Moreover, Eddie was not a first offender. . . .

Though current sentencing guidelines treat such matters as irrelevant, it is worth noting that at the time of his sentencing Eddie had been married for over twenty years and had three teen-aged children, to whom he had provided steady financial and emotional support. He served honorably in the military in Vietnam, earning a number of medals and citations before being honorably discharged as a sergeant. Despite receiving disability payments from the Veterans Administration for Post-Traumatic Stress Disorder, and despite his attributing his drug usage to his military experience, he has maintained a steady record of employment throughout his life.

Despite these favorable aspects of his life history, I assume most judges, and most citizens, would regard Eddie as a candidate for a reasonably severe sentence. Whatever one thinks of the policy costs and benefits of the war on drugs, the sale of cocaine has been emphatically outlawed by the people's elected representatives. Those who undertake to make money from the trade in illegal substances do so knowing that they are violating the law, and knowing that they are preying on the weaknesses of mostly poor people by providing them with dangerous and addictive substances. . . . Moreover, this particular defendant had only shortly before been convicted of another drug trafficking offense, and had benefited from judicial leniency on that occasion. Reasonable people can disagree over whether sending him to prison for an extended period is enlightened or even sensible social policy, but it is, for better or worse, our social policy, adopted by democratically-elected officials and generally endorsed by a majority of the nation's people. . . .

Thus, even for a judge with some skepticism about the justice and efficacy of the severity of our current drug sentences, Eddie seems a candidate for a serious sentence. . . .

But if we agree that Eddie does not deserve leniency, we still are left to ask, what should his sentence actually be? You can try this on your friends, lawyers and non-lawyers alike, and you will almost surely get a range of answers. I can pick a number as well as anyone else, and before 1987 that's more or less what judges were asked to do — pick the number that they thought, taking all of the above facts and more into account, was the fairest sentence. . . .

I shouldn't keep you in suspense any longer about the actual sentence. Of course, there is only the most modest suspense anyway for those readers familiar with federal sentencing. The amount of cocaine attributable to Eddie exceeds five hundred grams, and so he is subject to a mandatory minimum sentence of five years (and a maximum of forty, well beyond his life expectancy). As a prior narcotics offender, moreover, if the government chooses to file a prior felony information, the mandatory minimum is doubled to ten years. . . . The prosecutors [filed the information and hence] . . . the defendant was subject to a [ten-year] mandatory minimum.

Was the sentence unjustly harsh? It certainly seems a very heavy sentence to me, but as noted above I don't know that I have a reliable, objective basis for deciding how severe is too severe. But I can provide a comparison, both in bottom-line and in methodology, to another way of calculating Eddie's sentence: the much-vilified sentencing guidelines.

I don't mean to hold up the guidelines as a model of absolute justice. As will become clear shortly, I have my own objections to their approach to drug sentences. But I think the guidelines can provide a basis for assessing the mandatory minimum sentences. No one thinks that the guidelines are unduly lenient on drugs, or that they were created by a bunch of bleeding hearts. Indeed, the guidelines use the mandatory minimum sentence drug amounts as guideposts to their own sentencing structure. It is perhaps appropriate, then, to consider that a sentence that exceeds the guideline range just might be excessive.

Given the amount of cocaine attributed to Eddie, the guidelines provide for an offense level of 26. No adjustments apply. For first offenders, or those with only a minor criminal history, this would translate to a sentence of just over five years. But Eddie's criminal history category presents a more interesting calculation. His early offenses are disregarded as too old, but he gets one criminal history point for each of his two drug possession charges and his Florida drug trafficking conviction. This alone would move him above the basic criminal history category, but because he was on probation for the Florida offense when he committed the present crime, he gets a two-point "bonus," which puts him into a still higher criminal history category. The total guideline sentence for Eddie, then, would be 78-97 months. His most likely sentence, then, would have been six and a half years in prison. I would call that a rather severe sentence, perhaps more than I might have imposed if the law left me complete discretion. But I could have imposed the guideline sentence without feeling that the sentence was out of line with any reasonable conception of justice.

Judged by the guideline standard, then, the mandatory minimum sentence required in this case is excessive, to the tune of three and one-half years—nearly a fifty percent increase in the length of incarceration. Moreover, a comparison of the method by which the guidelines and the statutory provision arrive at their results suggests that the guideline approach—flawed as I think it is—is by a good deal the more sophisticated, and the fairer, system.

Both the guidelines and the mandatory minimum terms have been criticized by liberals for not taking into account facts about the personal history of the offender. Both systems rely on only two types of factors in setting a sentence: the seriousness of the offense and the offender's record of prior convictions. But within those limitations, the guidelines are vastly more nuanced. This is evident, even in Eddie's case, in the criminal history calculation. The mandatory minimum provision is extremely

crude and simplistic: any prior conviction for a "felony drug offense" triggers the doubling of the mandatory minimum; conversely, the ordinary
minimum would apply regardless of the number or severity of the offender's prior non-drug convictions. Thus, by way of example, if Eddie had
been convicted in South Dakota for simple possession of two or more
ounces of marijuana, he would be subject to the ten-year minimum, but if
he had a prior record for multiple murders and rapes, he would only be
required to serve five years.

The guidelines, in contrast, make a fairly sophisticated effort to
assess the weight of an offender's prior record. The record is judged
not by the presence or absence of a single prior drug offense, but on a
sliding scale with six basic categories, plus some additional refinements.
Offenders with more prior convictions get more points, and thus greater
sentence enhancement, than those with only one, and they get more or
fewer points for each offense depending on the severity of the crime,
judged primarily by the sentence served for it. The record is judged more
harshly if the defendant committed crimes while on probation or parole
(a factor that would hurt Eddie under the guidelines), or shortly after
release from prison. On the other hand, prior offenses in the distant past
are not counted. In Eddie's case, for example, a serious crime committed
thirty years ago was disregarded; had this been his first offense since then,
he would have been treated by the guidelines (appropriately, in my view)
as a first offender, and the offense would not enhance his punishment for
the present crime. But if that thirty-year-old crime had been a drug felony
(rather than a "mere" armed robbery), the mandatory minimum provision would have added five years to his sentence, even if he had gone
straight for the entire thirty years between. . . .

[M]andatory minima are triggered by amount of narcotics only, and
only in rather crude increments. The mandatories click in, for powder
cocaine, at five hundred grams (five years) and five kilos (ten years). The
guidelines, in contrast, have 4 different sentencing levels in the range from
400 grams to 5 kilos, and a total of 16 graduated levels from under 25 grams
to over 1500 kilos, that can take an offender from 10 months in prison to life.

And that set of adjustments involves only the amount of the drug
involved in the offense. The guidelines' (and the statutes') obsession
with amount is one of their major vulnerabilities to criticism. Particularly
because the amounts are cumulative—that is, multiple sales are aggregated to calculate a sentence based on a single total quantity—they can
have the perverse effect of treating minor players in the drug trade the
same as wholesalers or importers, by treating a large number of street-
level deals as the equivalent of one or more significant transactions. . . .

But if the guidelines might do better to take a still more sophisticated
view of the trade, at least they allow for aggravating and mitigating circumstances. Under the statutory mandate, anyone who has any involvement in a
transaction involving five hundred grams of cocaine must receive a five-year

sentence, whether the defendant owned the drugs and would profit from their sale, or was simply a driver or courier participating for a modest fee. The guidelines, in contrast, provide, with respect to drug transactions and organizations of every size, enhanced punishments for those who are managers or supervisors, and lowered ones for those who are more marginal participants, and provide special enhancements for certain specialists, like pilots and armed muscle. If I were writing the guidelines, I would probably reverse the relative importance of roles in the trade versus sheer quantities of drugs, but the guidelines at least take the defendant's role in the offense into account. Under the guidelines, among players in a five-kilo cocaine deal, someone (with no prior record) who organized and led a team of five or more participants (including one who was a minor) in orchestrating the deal would face a recommended minimum of at least 235 months (nearly twenty years), while someone who played a truly minimal role in the same deal could get as little as seventy-eight months (six and a half years). The mandatory minimum is simply ten years, regardless.

This analysis provides us with another reason to consider the mandatory minimum sentences unjustly severe. In the eyes of their many critics, the guidelines are unduly simplistic, failing to make distinctions that matter, and limiting the flexibility of sentencing judges to respond to relevant differences. Yet by comparison to the mandatory minima, they are masterpieces of subtlety, nuance, and thoughtfulness. And the guidelines permit judges, in truly unusual cases and subject to appellate review at the government's instance, to depart and impose a lower sentence. . . . The mandatory minima (save for cooperation with the government and an extremely limited "safety valve" provision) are absolute. If, in Eddie's case, the guidelines project a sentence of six and a half years but the mandatory statute requires ten, a sense that the latter is excessive is supported not simply by a (quantitative, political) conclusion that the guidelines' provenance is likely to make them tough enough for most tastes, but also by a (methodological, technical, professional) conclusion that the guidelines' method of arriving at six and a half years as the appropriate sentence has taken more of the appropriate factors into account, and has taken a much more defensible view of what is relevant in determining his just desert.

One additional procedural fact needs to be recalled. To the extent that discretion exists in a system of mandatory sentencing, that discretion is shifted from judges—appointed by the President and confirmed by the Senate, usually of mature years and wide experience—to prosecutors. . . . [T]he prosecutor could have chosen, before trial, not to file the prior felony information (reducing the mandatory sentence to five years), or not to charge a particular amount in the indictment (arguably eliminating the mandatory minimum altogether). And if the defendant had agreed to plead guilty, there is little doubt that these options would have been exercised. Since a guilty plea would have adjusted the sentencing level downward by as much as three points, avoiding the mandatory minimum sentence would have enabled the prosecutor, in his unilateral discretion, to bring Eddie's guideline sentence down to as low as fifty-seven months. . . . At the end of the day, it is possible that Eddie paid a higher price for exercising his right to a jury trial than for the crime he committed.

Does it matter? Of course, the cases cited by the columnists seem to matter more. Someone who probably should not be jailed at all who is sent to prison for five years has been treated terribly unjustly, and it is easy to sympathize with someone whose story suggests that his or her culpability was minimal. Someone like Eddie, in contrast, has deliberately, repeatedly, violated the law; his culpability is clear, a sentence of some weight is certainly deserved; and the precise number of years awarded is necessarily somewhat arbitrary. . . .

But if the injustice in Eddie's case is less serious than in the more unusual cases that are used to highlight the campaign against mandatory minimum sentences, I submit that we still ought to care, and to care a lot. First, even in this single individual case, the difference between 78 months and 120 is no small amount. The guideline sentence of seventy-eight months is hardly trivial: imagine being sent away from your family when your daughter was eleven, and returning on her eighteenth birthday; or consider going to jail with your mother aged seventy-five, and guessing whether she'll still be living at nearly eighty-two, when you get out. That is just about exactly what would have happened to Eddie under the guideline sentence. Now consider the add-on under the mandatory minimum: three and a half additional years. That is longer than you spent in law school, dear reader, and about as long as your, or your child's, college or high-school years. If that increment in punishment is excessive, that is not, in my book, a trivial injustice.

Now ask how many Eddies are out there, getting how many cumulative years of incarceration, at what expense to them, to their families, to the public treasury, and to our sense of human decency. . . .

I did not expect sentencing people to prison to feel good. But I was sorry and surprised to find that the very first sentence I imposed felt like an injustice. And not a small one.

NOTES AND QUESTIONS

1. In Eddie's case, the prosecutor filed an information, pursuant to 21 U.S.C. §851, which triggered the double minimum penalty for a defendant with a prior conviction (in state or federal court) for a "felony drug offense," see 21 U.S.C. §§841(b)(1)(A), 851(a)(1), discussed in Section B of Chapter 9. As Judge Lynch commented in a footnote not reproduced above: "Perhaps if Eddie had pled guilty, the prosecutor might have been willing to forego the filing in order to secure a certain conviction. But Eddie went to trial. Enough said: no mercy." Lynch, *supra*, at 556 n.17.

2. The statutory treatment of prior drug convictions is both severe and blunt. In cases where the prosecutor files the memorandum, the minimum term of conviction is automatically doubled. While the prosecutor has discretion, the judge has none. Moreover, the prior drug offense may be relatively minor; it may include a conviction in state court that the state denominated a "misdemeanor" but that would be called a "felony" in federal law because the statutory maximum sentence exceeds one year, see Burgess v. United States, 533 U.S. 123 (2008). By contrast, the Sentencing Guidelines have a complex set of rules relating to criminal history, and the same rules apply to all defendants—drug defendants are not treated more or less harshly in this respect. Eddie's extensive criminal history had the effect of moving him from criminal history category I to category III (see the Sentencing Table reprinted in Section B). This corresponded to an increase in his Guidelines range from 63-78 months, to 78-97 months—far less than the doubling of the mandatory minimum required by 21 U.S.C. §841(b)(1)(A).

3. While Eddie had a Guidelines sentence that was lower than the statutory minimum, you should understand that, by reason of the Sentencing Commission's decision to base its drug Guidelines on the statutory minima, many drug defendants end up with Guidelines sentences that are higher than this statutory floor. An example shows why: Suppose that Eddie was not subject to the statutory doubling because he did not have a prior felony drug conviction. On the basis of the quantity of cocaine in his case, his statutory sentencing range would have been between five years and 40 years. What would his Guidelines sentence have been? His oldest convictions (for being the driver in an armed robbery of a mail truck and for a crime that involved drunk driving) were more than ten years old and hence would be excluded from the calculation of his criminal history. But his more recent two misdemeanor convictions for possession of drugs, along with a recent driving incident that Judge Lynch elliptically referred to as "fairly dramatic," would have put Eddie at least in criminal history category II, see Lynch, *supra*, at 553 n.17, 558 nn.23-28. For a defendant whose offense level is 26 and whose criminal history category is II, the Sentencing Table provides for a Guidelines range of between 70 and 87 months—above the statutory minimum of five years.

It so happens that, in Eddie's case, no Guidelines enhancements were applicable. But if Eddie had, for instance, possessed a gun, his offense level would have been increased by two, see U.S.S.G. §2D1.1(b)(1). This enhancement applies whether or not the defendant was charged with violating 18 U.S.C. §924(c), discussed in Chapter 3. Most importantly, the gun enhancement in the Guidelines is broader than that in §924(c); it applies even if the gun is not possessed for a reason related to the underlying drug crime. Eddie's Guidelines range would have been further increased if he had obstructed justice, used a special skill, or engaged in other behavior for which the Guidelines provide (trans-substantively) a sentencing enhancement. See generally U.S.S.G. §3B1. The result is that for many defendants convicted of drug trafficking, the Guidelines' more fine-grained approach to evaluating offense behavior and criminal history is not necessarily benign. Because of the high base offense levels for drug offenses and the multiple enhancements provided for in the Guidelines, the resulting sentencing range may be significantly above the statutory minimum.

4. Judge Lynch argues, with ample reason, that the Guidelines' approach to criminal history is preferable to that of the main federal drug-trafficking statute. But do you think that the Guidelines' approach makes sense? Why should an armed robbery conviction that is 11 years old be ignored, while a couple of more recent misdemeanor convictions ratchet up the defendant's criminal history category? For other critiques of the Guidelines' treatment of criminal history, see Daniel W. Stiller, Chapter 4, Surprises and a Defender's Longest Drive, 13 Fed. Sent'g Rep. 323 (2001); Avern Cohn & Mark W. Osler, The Calculation of Criminal History by AUSAs and Defendants: A Study of Inefficiency in the Eastern District of Michigan, 13 Fed. Sent'g Rep. 327 (2001); United States v. Leviner, 31 F. Supp. 2d 23, 24 (D. Mass. 1998) (justifying downward departure because the African American defendant's high criminal history score was based largely on motor vehicle violations and minor drug possession offenses; the court cited studies finding "racial disparity in the rates at which African Americans are stopped and prosecuted for traffic offenses").

5. While the Guidelines are certainly more fine-grained than statutory mandatory penalties tied solely to the weight and type of drug, you should understand that *mandatory* guidelines may have some of the same arbitrary consequences as mandatory statutory penalties. Because they apply without exception to all circumstances specified, they may be both overinclusive and underinclusive. For instance, in the article excerpted above, Judge Lynch notes that the drug Guidelines provide for an enhancement for pilots, see U.S.S.G. §2D1.1(b)(2). Is a person who is temporarily steering a boat according to the instructions of the boat's master a "pilot"? The First Circuit answered "yes," see United States v. Guerrero, 114 F.3d 332 (1st Cir. 1997). After *Booker* and *Kimbrough*, would a sentencing judge be justified in giving a below-Guidelines sentence on the ground that the Guidelines enhancement for a "pilot" is inappropriate in a case such as *Guerrero*? The law is still evolving on this question, and more generally on how much discretion sentencing judges have to dispute the policies that underlie the Guidelines.

6. Congress, the Sentencing Commission, and the federal courts have all made moves that reduce both the severity and disparity in cocaine sentencing. Having based all of its drug Guidelines on Congress's distinctions as to quantity and type of drug in 21 U.S.C. §841(b), the Sentencing Commission initially incorporated the 100:1 crack/powder quantity disparity enacted by Congress in 1986, see generally Chapter 9. *Booker*, however, made the Guidelines only "advisory," with sentences reviewed by the courts of appeals for "reasonableness." In a case we considered in Section C of this

chapter, *Kimbrough v. United States*, the Supreme Court in 2007 held sentencing judges could lawfully disagree with the powder/crack quantity disparity and vary from the Guidelines sentencing range in crack-cocaine cases on this basis. After Congress enacted the Fair Sentencing Act of 2010—which, as we saw in Chapter 9, reduced the crack/powder disparity to 18:1—the Sentencing Commission followed suit and also made *its* changes retroactive. Then, in 2014, the Commission reduced Guidelines for almost all types of drug trafficking by two offense levels. See Guidelines Amendments 742, 750, 759, and 782.

E.   THE FUTURE OF SENTENCING LAW

Booker's loosening of the shackles binding judges enlarged their capacity to inject additional considerations, beyond those specified in the Guidelines, into sentencing, and to respond to and to some degree rewrite the law of federal crimes as dispensed by Congress and federal prosecutors. For instance, under *Kimbrough*, sentencing judges may have authority to explicitly address policy disagreements with the Sentencing Commission and with Congress itself in a broad range of cases. Are these good developments, or are they pernicious? Throughout this chapter, we have suggested that the Guidelines (especially when they were mandatory) may operate as an adjunct to federal criminal statutes. Imagine the total chaos that would prevail if judges could decide that certain statutory elements should not apply in a given case, or if they could ignore a statutory minimum sentence as long as they had a good reason! Is ignoring the Guidelines, which the Sentencing Commission designed to make punishment more dependent on uniform factors and less dependent on both the judge and the statute of conviction, so different? On the other hand, for two centuries the federal criminal justice system entrusted judges with the last word in defining the appropriate federal crime in the case at hand. In the excerpts below, two experienced district judges* present contrasting perspectives.

Nancy Gertner, *Gall, Kimbrough* and Me
OSJCL Amici: Views from the Field 1-6 (2008)

There is both promise and danger in the Supreme Court's recent decisions in Gall v. United States, 128 S. Ct. 586 (2007) and Kimbrough v. United States, 128 S. Ct. 558 (2007). The promise is clear: *finally,*

---

* Judge Nancy Gertner served on the United States District Court for the District of Massachusetts from 1993 to 2011; previously, she was a civil rights and criminal defense attorney. As to Judge Lynch, see the second footnote in this Chapter, *supra.*

courts will be allowed to focus on *all* the purposes of sentencing in the Sentencing Reform Act, rather than being fixated on just the goal of avoiding sentencing disparity. *Finally*, courts can stop being concerned solely with the question: am I doing the same thing as what the judge in the next courtroom is doing, even if neither of us is making any sense? . . .

The dangers are less clear. It is *not* the danger of rampant disparity as some may say, the "free-at-last regime" where trial judges do whatever they want without meaningful review. Rather, it is the opposite: the danger of mindless Guideline compliance, even while intoning "the Guidelines are advisory." It is the danger that the Supreme Court will stop taking sentencing appeals, leaving the application of *Gall* and *Kimbrough* to the appellate courts, many of whom have yet to see a Guideline sentence they do not like, or a [sentence below the Guidelines] they can support. . . .

I fear that the appellate courts and the Commission will not be vigilant in supporting an advisory regime. This has been a revolution from above: initiated, maintained, and supported by the Supreme Court. . . . Since it is not likely that the Supreme Court will get involved in the minutiae of sentencing—except perhaps for a few major post-*Booker* issues remaining, like acquitted conduct, mandatory minimum sentencing, etc.—how these decisions will play out will depend entirely on the Courts of Appeals, and the signs are not good. Most appellate judges never knew anything but a Guideline regime. From the outset they believed that they were the regulators, and the district courts were the regulated. Although they saw only the cases at the margins—the cases in which the judges have departed or varied—not the cases in which the Guidelines were applied, that did not stop appellate courts from enforcing the Guidelines with a rigor even the Sentencing Reform Act's drafters would not have foreseen. . . .

I suggest[] that judges use our judicial tools—considering whether the rules of general application should be applied in a given case, analyzing fact patterns not meaningfully covered by the Guidelines, and subject the Guidelines to administrative procedure-like review by examining the relationship between the Guidelines and the statutes. If the judge in Texas sentences and describes why, as the judge in *Gall* did, other judges will follow. There may be somewhat more disparity than existed before *Booker*, but there will be less false uniformity and hopefully, a fairer regime.

Gerard E. Lynch, Letting Guidelines Be Guidelines (and Judges Be Judges)
OSJCL Amici: Views from the Field 1-8 (2008)

Just as "sentencing guidelines" are misnamed when they are treated as narrowly rigid binding rules, so are they misnamed when they cease to guide anyone. . . . [A]s a matter of substantive sentencing policy, a system of carefully thought-out guidelines that are subject to broad judicial discretion to depart, but accorded respect by the courts and followed more often than not, is a highly desirable system for the federal courts. . . .

The criminal law is designed in large part to control undesirable behavior, by a process of deterrence, rehabilitation and incapacitation. It also seeks to teach values by imposing fair and proportionate punishment on those who violate social rules. But these goals cannot be accomplished if significant actors in law enforcement act at cross-purposes. . . . In a democracy, the legislature or its delegates should decide which policy or combination of policies should be pursued, and judges should follow the policy that is thus adopted. . . .

This insight does not require an end to all discretion. . . .

Rather than a simple dichotomy of "absolutely binding and mandatory" versus "worth thinking about, but merely advisory," there is a spectrum of weights that could be given to guidelines, and the question after Booker was how far the Court intended judges to move the system from somewhere close to truly mandatory towards the other extreme of "not worth the paper they are printed on."

While I celebrate the move away from one extreme, I hope that the Court has not moved us too far towards the other. I think the answer will be found not in the words of Supreme Court opinions, but in the collective practice of individual judges. . . .

I suspect that a large number, perhaps a majority, of judges believe that the overall sentencing pattern of the guidelines is excessively severe. . . . But I hope and expect that almost no judges will react to *Booker, Gall* and *Kimbrough* by announcing that they simply think the guidelines are too punitive and will generally disregard them in favor of a much more lenient regime. Although as a citizen I would welcome a re-evaluation of America's extremely punitive penal policy (which is unique in the Western world), such a rethinking cannot be accomplished by a random pattern of leniency by some unknown percentage of federal judges. . . .

My own approach to sentencing will continue to give the Guidelines meaningful weight in sentencing, even where my own inclinations differ, and I hope that most of my colleagues will do the same. After all, the guidelines are, in and of themselves, a factor that the law instructs me to consider. At a minimum, this must mean that there are some cases in which the weight (however strong or slight) given to the guidelines will be the deciding factor. Moreover, the need to avoid undue disparity is another factor to be weighed under §3553(a), and disparity is more likely to be avoided, other things being equal, if some significant value is placed on following the guidelines. Finally, at least two of the substantive factors to be considered—the need for deterrence and the need for punishment—are factors on which the Commission's putative expertise and national perspective entitle its views to respect. . . . My comparative advantage, as a district judge, is in evaluating those factors unique to each individual case that comes before me. But the Commission's advantage is in weighing broad social policy, and responsiveness to democratic political opinion. I should, I believe, give them deference as to the appropriate starting point or typical sentence for the average or typical instance of a given crime. . . .

If we are going to let (district) judges be judges, and trust them to exercise the necessary discretion with sensitivity to the need for coherent sentencing policy, so we should let (appellate) judges be judges as well, performing their traditional function of reining in excess and gradually developing a "common law" of what is and is not sensible. . . .

NOTE AND QUESTIONS

The two judges, writing shortly after *Booker* was decided, appear to have opposite concerns about what the decision portended for federal sentencing law. Judge Gertner was concerned that the Guidelines would continue to function post-*Booker* as an effectively "mandatory" regime because judges would continue to apply them for a variety of reasons, none relating to their internal coherence. Judge Lynch was concerned that the now-advisory nature of the Guidelines would result in entirely too many judges disregarding them entirely. Which possibility do *you* find most concerning; how would each affect the definition of federal crimes? Which judge ultimately prophesized more accurately?

At their inception and throughout the period in which they were mandatory, the Sentencing Guidelines were widely disliked by federal judges. See Stith & Cabranes, *supra*, at 195 n.12 (documenting judicial dissatisfaction); Federal Judicial Center, Results of 1996 Survey on the Sentencing Guidelines ("When asked whether they thought mandatory guidelines were necessary to direct the sentencing process, a majority of district and circuit judges (73% and 69%, respectively) said no. . . .") (1997). Since *Booker*, satisfaction with the Guidelines has increased substantially. In a survey of district judges conducted in 2010, the Sentencing Commission found that 67 percent of respondents agreed strongly or somewhat with the statement: "Overall, the federal sentencing guidelines have increased fairness in meeting the purposes of sentencing." U.S. Sent'g Comm'n, Results of Survey of United States District Judges tbl. 17 (June 2010).

11 | Corporate Crime

The role of corporations in modern society is widely—and often heatedly—debated, as illustrated by Citizens United v. Federal Election Commission, 558 U.S. 310 (2010), where the Supreme Court held that corporations possess the constitutional right of free speech, and that while the government can "regulate corporate political speech" through certain means, it "may not suppress [such] speech altogether." Id. at 319. While corporations possessed rights well before the decision, id. at 342, *Citizens United* is one of several cases that extend what is often considered to be a "personal" right—that of free speech—to impersonal, artificial entities.

Citizens United's relevance here stems not from its holding, but from the light it sheds on the rights and roles of corporations in modern life. Though not human beings, corporations have been afforded a significant subset of the rights afforded to "natural persons," including the right to contract, see Dartmouth College v. Woodward, 17 U.S. (4 Wheat.) 518 (1819); the right not to be deprived of property without just compensation, see Smyth v. Ames, 169 U.S. 466, 546 (1898); and the right to petition legislative and administrative bodies, see First Nat'l Bank v. Bellotti, 435 U.S. 765, 792 (1978). Congress, for its part, has defined corporations as "persons" under the U.S. Code. See 1 U.S.C. §1.

Proponents of the idea of "corporate personhood" insist that corporations, as associations of shareholders, should possess many of the rights afforded to the shareholders individually. See Susanna K. Ripken, Corporations Are People Too: A Multi-Dimensional Approach to the Corporate Personhood Puzzle, 15 Fordham J. Corp. & Fin. L. 97, 110 (2009). As Justice Scalia explained in *Citizens United*, "[a]ll the provisions of the Bill of Rights set forth the rights of individual men and women. . . . But the individual person's right to speak includes the right to speak *in association with other individual persons*." 558 U.S. at 391-92 (Scalia, J., concurring).

Opponents respond that corporations are *not* just associations of people; they are "creations of the state that exist to make money," and they are "given special privileges, including different tax rates, to do just that." Editorial, The Court's Blow to Democracy, N.Y. Times, Jan. 21, 2010. These critics bemoaned the Court's ruling in *Citizens United*, fearing that it "paved the way for corporations to use their vast treasuries to overwhelm elections and intimidate elected officials into doing their bidding." Id.

While reasonable people can disagree about the proper scope of corporate rights, few would deny that with those rights come responsibilities. It is here that corporate criminal liability enters the picture. Corporate criminal liability offers a means of checking the power of corporations and ensuring that such artificial entities, like natural persons, comply with the law. Indeed, proponents argue, if corporations benefit from the rights of natural persons, why shouldn't they also bear the responsibilities of natural persons, including that of complying with the criminal law?

Opponents of corporate criminal liability argue that it is inconsistent with common law principles, particularly that of individual *mens rea*; a corporation—unlike a natural person—can have no "guilty mind." See, e.g., John Hasnas, Centenary of a Mistake: One Hundred Years of Corporate Criminal Liability, 46 Am. Crim. L. Rev. 1329 (2009). They contend that civil sanctions can achieve a comparable deterrent effect while avoiding the pitfalls of criminal liability. As Professor Richman notes, "Substantial—albeit unequal—stigma can be imposed on the entity through civil sanctions, as well as fines, penalties, and forfeitures. Particularly where the collateral consequences of a corporate conviction are contractual debarment or worse, civil proceedings will avoid or limit the harm to innocent or relatively innocent third parties." Daniel Richman, Decisions About Coercion: The Corporate Attorney-Client Privilege Waiver Problem, 57 DePaul L. Rev. 295, 322 (2008).

As you will see, however, corporate criminal liability is alive and well in America—and it is far more expansive here than in other parts of the world. See V.S. Khanna, Corporate Criminal Liability: What Purpose Does It Serve?, 109 Harv. L. Rev. 1477, 1488 (1996). This may be explained at least in part by the public's view of corporate wrongdoing as capable of harming not only the corporations' shareholders, but also communities, nations, and even the world economy. One proponent of corporate criminal liability explains:

> Modern corporations not only wield virtually unprecedented power, but they do so in a fashion that often causes serious harm to both individuals and to society as a whole. In some recent cases, corporate misconduct and malfeasance destabilized the stock market and led to the loss of billions in shareholder equity and the loss of tens (or perhaps even hundreds) of thousands of jobs. Enron was the seventh-most valuable company in the U.S., until the revelation of its use of deceptive accounting devices to shift debt off its books and hide corporate losses led to losses of more than $100 billion in shareholder equity before it filed for bankruptcy. But Enron was not alone in the use of fraudulent accounting practices. The revelation of similar misconduct by other corporations (including Dynergy [sic], Adelphia Communications, WorldCom, and Global Crossing) also led to massive losses. . . . In the past decade, virtually every major pharmaceutical company has pled guilty to or settled charges arising out of serious misconduct. . . . Because of their size,

complexity, and control of vast resources, corporations have the ability to engage in misconduct that dwarfs that which could be accomplished by individuals. For example, Siemens, the German engineering giant, paid more than $1.4 billion in bribes to government officials in Asia, Africa, Europe, the Middle East, and Latin America, using its slush funds to secure public works contracts around the world.

Sara Sun Beale, A Response to the Critics of Corporate Criminal Liability, 46 Am. Crim. L. Rev. 1481, 1483-84 (2009). See also Michael Nagelberg et al., Corporate Criminal Liability, 54 Am. Crim. L. Rev. 1073, 1074 (2017) (noting that Congress passed the Sarbanes-Oxley Act of 2002, which exposes corporations to increased criminal liability, "in response to increasing public outrage over corporate scandals at the turn of the century"); U.S. Gov't Accountability Office, GAO-05-80, Report on Criminal Debt: Court-Ordered Restitution Amounts Far Exceed Likely Collections for the Crime Victims in Selected Financial Fraud Cases 2 (2005) (concluding that "in the wake of a recent wave of corporate scandals . . . American taxpayers have a right to expect that those who have committed corporate fraud and other criminal or civil wrongdoing will be punished, and that the federal government will make every effort to recover assets and the ill-gotten gains held by such offenders").

Given the extent and consequences of corporate crime, the recent research showing that the public favors punitive remedies should come as little surprise. See James D. Unnever et al, Public Support for Getting Tough on Corporate Crime: Racial and Political Divides, 45 J. of Res. in Crime and Delinq. 164, 177 (2008). Is the public right? Should corporations and their officers be held criminally liable? Or might broad civil regulatory liability achieve the same goals more efficiently? These are the questions we ask you to consider as you read this chapter. In Section A, we explore under what circumstances the conduct of an employee (or other corporate agent) is attributable to the corporation or other artificial entity ("entity liability"). In Section B, we consider the converse situation — when the conduct of the corporation is attributable to the officers of the corporation (the "responsible corporate officer" doctrine). Throughout, we are interested not just in current doctrines, but also in the roles of Congress, prosecutors, courts, and the Sentencing Commission in developing and elaborating them.

Keep in mind that while the doctrine of corporate criminal liability is broad indeed, few corporations are actually prosecuted, and the number keeps decreasing. In fiscal year 2016, 132 organizations were sentenced for violations of federal criminal law, the lowest number of organizational defendants reported since 2004. Of those 132, 97.7 percent pled guilty, often with a fine as their sole punishment (74 cases). See U.S. Sent'g Comm'n, Overview of Federal Criminal Cases: Fiscal Year 2016. See also U.S. Sent'g Comm'n, Sourcebook of Federal Sentencing Statistics, "Organizational

Sentencing Practices" tbls. 51-54 (2015). There was a sharp but anomalous uptick in 2015 attributable to prosecutions resolved as part of the "Swiss Bank Program." See Brandon L. Garrett, The Rise of Bank Prosecutions, Yale L.J.F., 33, 38 (May 23, 2016). A recent GAO study showed that between 2009 and 2015, financial institutions have been ordered to pay, in total, approximately $27 million for violations of the Foreign Corrupt Payments Act, $5.2 *billion* for violations of the Bank Secrecy Act, and $6.8 *billion* for violating U.S. sanctions programs. U.S. Gov't Accountability Office, GAO-16-297, Financial Institutions Report: Fines, Penalties, and Forfeitures for Violations of Financial Crimes and Sanctions Requirements (2016). Despite these record penalties imposed on financial institutions, few individual corporate officers were convicted under the "responsible corporate officers" doctrine considered in Section B of this chapter. Clearly, a peculiar dynamic is at work here.

A.   ENTITY LIABILITY

The principle underlying corporate liability (in a criminal or a civil setting) is straightforward. A corporation, being merely a juridical person, and not a real one, can act only through its employees. As the Court explained in United States v. Dotterweich, 320 U.S. 277, 281 (1943), which we examined in Chapter 3, "the only way in which a corporation can act is through the individuals who act on its behalf." Corporate liability is necessarily *derivative* in this sense; a corporation's liability must derive from the actions of its employees and agents. The law treats a corporation as a legal "person" that has standing to sue and to be sued, distinct from its owners and managers. You are likely familiar with corporate civil liability for the tortious behavior of a corporation's agents and with the corporation's responsibility for the contractual and other acts of those agents. Likewise, criminal liability can be imposed on the corporation for its agents' actions, even though the corporation itself has no "soul to damn, no body to kick."[1] Typically, federal prosecutors are the gatekeepers whose charging discretion determines if a corporation gets kicked, and, if so, how hard.

---

1. See John C. Coffee, Jr., No Soul to Damn: No Body to Kick: An Unscandalized Inquiry into the Problem of Corporate Punishment, 79 Mich. L. Rev. 386, 386 (1981) (quoting Lord Chancellor of England, First Baron, Thurlow 1731-1806 as saying, "Did you ever expect a corporation to have a conscience, when it has no soul to be damned, and no body to be kicked?").

1. THE ORIGINS OF CORPORATE CRIMINAL LIABILITY

New York Central & Hudson River Railroad Co. v. United States
212 U.S. 481 (1909)

Mr. Justice DAY delivered the opinion of the Court.

In the [trial] court the railroad company and Fred L. Pomeroy, its assistant traffic manager, were convicted for the payment of rebates to the American Sugar Refining Company and others, upon shipments of sugar from the city of New York to the city of Detroit, Michigan. . . .

The assistant traffic manager was sentenced to pay a fine of $1,000 upon each of the counts; the present plaintiff in error to pay a fine of $18,000 on each count, making a fine of $108,000 in all.

The facts are practically undisputed. They are mainly established by stipulation, or by letters passing between the traffic managers and the agent of the sugar refining companies. . . .

The principal attack in this court is upon the constitutional validity of certain features of the Elkins act. 32 Stat. at L. 847, [chap. 708, U.S. Comp. Stat. Supp. 1907, p. 880]. That act, among other things, provides:

> "(1) That anything done or omitted to be done by a corporation common carrier subject to the act to regulate commerce, and the acts amendatory thereof, which, if done or omitted to be done by any director or officer thereof, or any receiver, trustee, lessee, agent, or person acting for or employed by such corporation, would constitute a misdemeanor under said acts, or under this act, shall also be held to be a misdemeanor committed by such corporation; and, upon conviction thereof, it shall be subject to like penalties as are prescribed in said acts, or by this act, with reference to such persons, except as such penalties are herein changed. . . .

> "In construing and enforcing the provisions of this section, the act, omission, or failure of any officer, agent, or other person acting for or employed by any common carrier, acting within the scope of his employment, shall, in every case, be also deemed to be the act, omission, or failure of such carrier, as well as that of the person."

It is contended that these provisions of the law are unconstitutional because Congress has no authority to impute to a corporation the commission of criminal offenses, or to subject a corporation to a criminal prosecution by reason of the things charged. The argument is that to thus punish the corporation is in reality to punish the innocent stockholders, and to deprive them of their property without opportunity to be heard, consequently without due process of law. And it is further contended that these provisions of the statute deprive the corporation of the presumption of innocence—a presumption which is part of due process in criminal prosecutions. It is urged that, as there is no authority shown by the board of directors or the stockholders for the criminal acts of the agents of the company, in contracting for and giving rebates, they could not be lawfully charged against the corporation. As no action of the board of directors could legally authorize a crime, and as, indeed, the stockholders could not do so, the arguments come to this: that, owing to the nature and character of its organization and the extent of its power and authority, a corporation cannot commit a crime of the nature charged in this case.

Some of the earlier writers on common law held the law to be that a corporation could not commit a crime. . . . In Blackstone's Commentaries, chapter 18, §12, we find it stated: "A corporation cannot commit treason, or felony, or other crime in its corporate capacity, though its members may, in their distinct individual capacities." The modern authority, universally, so far as we know, is the other way. In considering the subject, Bishop's New Criminal Law, §417, devotes a chapter to the capacity of corporations to commit crime, and states the law to be: "Since a corporation acts by its officers and agents, their purposes, motives, and intent are just as much those of the corporation as are the things done. If, for example, the invisible, intangible essence or air which we term a corporation can level mountains, fill up valleys, lay down iron tracks, and run railroad cars on them, it can intend to do it, and can act therein as well viciously as virtuously." . . . Telegram Newspaper Co. v. Com., 172 Mass. 294 . . . held that a corporation was subject to punishment for criminal contempt; and the court, speaking by Mr. Chief Justice Field, said: "We think that a corporation may be liable criminally for certain offenses of which a specific intent may be a necessary element. There is no more difficulty in imputing to a corporation a specific intent in criminal proceedings than in civil. A corporation cannot be arrested and imprisoned in either civil or criminal proceedings, but its property may be taken either as compensation for a private wrong or as punishment for a public wrong." . . . It is now well established that, in actions for tort, the corporation may be held responsible for damages for the acts of its agent within the scope of his employment.

And this is the rule when the act is done by the agent in the course of his employment, although done wantonly or recklessly or against the express orders of the principal. In such cases the liability is not imputed because the principal actually participates in the malice or fraud, but because the act is done for the benefit of the principal, while the agent is acting within the scope of his employment in the business of the principal, and justice requires that the latter shall be held responsible for damages to the individual who has suffered by such conduct.

A corporation is held responsible for acts not within the agent's corporate powers strictly construed, but which the agent has assumed to perform for the corporation when employing the corporate powers actually authorized, and in such cases there need be no written authority under seal or vote of the corporation in order to constitute the agency or to authorize the act. Washington Gaslight Co. v. Lansden, 172 U.S. 534.

In this case we are to consider the criminal responsibility of a corporation for an act done while an authorized agent of the company is exercising the authority conferred upon him. It was admitted by the defendant at the trial that, at the time mentioned in the indictment, the general freight traffic manager and the assistant freight traffic manager were authorized to establish rates at which freight should be carried over the line of the New York Central & Hudson River Company, and were authorized to unite with other companies in the establishing, filing, and publishing of through rates, including the through rate or rates between New York and Detroit referred to in the indictment. Thus, the subject-matter of making and fixing rates was within the scope of the authority and employment of the agents of the company, whose acts in this connection are sought to be charged upon the company. Thus clothed with authority, the agents were bound to respect the regulation of interstate commerce enacted by Congress, requiring the filing and publication of rates and punishing departures therefrom. Applying the principle governing civil liability, we go only a step farther in holding that the act of the agent, while exercising the authority delegated to him to make rates for transportation, may be controlled, in the interest of public policy, by imputing his act to his employer and imposing penalties upon the corporation for which he is acting in the premises.

It is true that there are some crimes which, in their nature, cannot be committed by corporations. But there is a large class of offenses, of which rebating under the Federal statutes is one, wherein the crime consists in purposely doing the things prohibited by statute. In that class of crimes we see no good reason why corporations may not be held responsible for and charged with the knowledge and purposes of their agents, acting within the authority conferred upon them. If it were not so, many offenses might go unpunished and acts be committed in violation of law where, as in the present case, the statute requires all persons, corporate or private, to refrain from certain practices, forbidden in the interest of public policy.

It is a part of the public history of the times that statutes against rebates could not be effectually enforced so long as individuals only were subject to punishment for violation of the law, when the giving of rebates or concessions inured to the benefit of the corporations of which the individuals were but the instruments. This situation, developed in more than one report of the Interstate Commerce Commission, was no doubt influential in bringing about the enactment of the Elkins law, making corporations criminally liable.

This statute does not embrace things impossible to be done by a corporation; its objects are to prevent favoritism, and to secure equal rights to all in interstate transportation, and one legal rate, to be published and posted and accessible to all alike. New Haven Railroad Company v. Interstate Commerce Commission, 200 U.S. 399.

We see no valid objection in law, and every reason in public policy, why the corporation, which profits by the transaction, and can only act through its agents and officers, shall be held punishable by fine because of the knowledge and intent of its agents to whom it has intrusted authority to act in the subject-matter of making and fixing rates of transportation, and whose knowledge and purposes may well be attributed to the corporation for which the agents act. While the law should have regard to the rights of all, and to those of corporations no less than to those of individuals, it cannot shut its eyes to the fact that the great majority of business transactions in modern times are conducted through these bodies, and particularly that interstate commerce is almost entirely in their hands, and to give them immunity from all punishment because of the old and exploded doctrine that a corporation cannot commit a crime would virtually take away the only means of effectually controlling the subject-matter and correcting the abuses aimed at.

There can be no question of the power of Congress to regulate interstate commerce, to prevent favoritism, and to secure equal rights to all engaged in interstate trade. It would be a distinct step backward to hold that Congress cannot control those who are conducting this interstate commerce by holding them responsible for the intent and purposes of the agents to whom they have delegated the power to act in the premises.

It is contended that the Elkins law is unconstitutional, in that it applies to individual carriers as well as those of a corporate character, and attributes the act of the agent to all common carriers, thereby making the crime of one person that of another, thus depriving the latter of due process of law and of the presumption of innocence which the law raises in his favor. This contention rests upon the last paragraph of §1 of the Elkins act, which is as follows:

> "In construing and enforcing the provisions of this section, the act, omission, or failure of any officer, agent, or other person acting for or employed by any common carrier, acting within the scope of his employment shall, in every case, be also deemed to be the act, omission, or failure of such carrier as well as that of the person."

We think the answer to this proposition is obvious; the plaintiff in error is a corporation, and the provision as to its responsibility for acts of its agents is specifically stated in the first paragraph of the section. There is no individual in this case complaining of the unconstitutionality of the act, if objectionable on that ground, and the case does not come within that class of cases in which unconstitutional provisions are so interblended with valid ones that the whole act must fall, notwithstanding its constitutionality is challenged by one who might be legally brought within its provisions. It may be doubted whether there are any individual carriers engaged in interstate commerce, and every act is to be construed so as to maintain its constitutionality if possible. There can be no question that Congress would have applied these provisions to corporation carriers, whether individuals were included or not. In this view the act is valid as to corporations. . . .

NOTES AND QUESTIONS

1. In a 2008 *Yale Law Journal* Note, Edward Diskant provides a helpful overview of federal corporate criminal liability, highlighting the role that prosecutors played in doctrinal development:

> Most histories of American corporate criminal liability start [with] the Industrial Revolution, the rise of the regulatory state, and the Supreme Court's landmark 1909 decision in New York Central & Hudson River Railroad v. United States. . . . [In that case, the] Court was untroubled by the legal fiction that an entity could neither take criminal action nor possess criminal intent. Instead, the Court adopted the civil law doctrine of respondeat superior, holding that a corporation could constitutionally be convicted of a crime when one of its agents had committed a criminal act (1) within the scope of his or her employment, and (2) for the benefit of the corporation. That standard remains good law to this day.
>
> Beginning the history of American entity liability with *New York Central* is certainly logical because the case established the authority of Congress to criminalize corporate conduct. But doing so overlooks a very important movement that was afoot well before *New York Central*, one that is critical to understanding how and why entity liability expanded so rapidly in its wake. While *New York Central* involved a statute that explicitly extended criminal liability to corporations, for some fifty years before Congress passed the Elkins Act, prosecutors across the country had been creatively pursuing criminal sanctions against corporations by applying general criminal laws — laws that, by their terms, did not extend to corporations as entities — to corporate conduct.
>
> Indeed, as early as the 1850s, prosecutors in states like New Jersey and Pennsylvania aggressively pursued criminal charges against corporations by applying common law criminal doctrines — most commonly, the crime of nuisance — to corporations as entities, despite the facts that the common law did not recognize the concept of entity liability and state laws made no explicit mention of entity liability. . . .
>
> As courts repeatedly upheld such convictions, prosecutors became emboldened, indicting corporations not just for common law crimes but also for statutory offenses, even when the statute made no specific mention of entity liability. . . . Judges, for their part, while acknowledging that many of these amounted to "test cases," continued to acquiesce, relying not on statutory text or theoretical arguments but rather on what could charitably be

termed policy rationales. As the Massachusetts Supreme Judicial Court noted in explaining away the historical lack of corporate criminal liability, "experience has shown the necessity of essentially modifying [that rule]."

The true origins of American criminal liability, in other words, did not lie in legislative efforts, nor did they result from policy debates or logically crafted statutory choices. Rather, the drive toward entity criminal liability stemmed primarily from the efforts of American prosecutors who creatively and aggressively applied statutory and common law and from the early American courts that allowed them to do so.

That more complete narrative is crucial to understanding why *New York Central* marked such a turning point in the history of American entity liability. By confirming that a corporation could constitutionally be prosecuted for a crime under a theory of respondeat superior, the Court validated a practice that had been pursued with increasing frequency by prosecutors for more than fifty years. Thereafter, with the Court's stamp of approval, prosecutors continued to aggressively pursue the type of "creative lawyering" they had before, applying both the common law and statutory offenses to corporate conduct.

Federal prosecutors in particular seized upon the Court's ruling to expand the reach of federal criminal law. Recognizing that all federal criminal laws apply to "any person" who violates them and that Congress had defined the term "person" to include "corporations" for purposes of the U.S. Code more generally [see 1 U.S.C. §1 (2000)], federal prosecutors began applying the criminal code to corporate conduct. . . . And lower courts, faced with the expansive holding in *New York Central*, went along, finding the lack of any specific congressional directive that a particular criminal law be applied to corporations to be, in most cases, irrelevant.

This is not to suggest that Congress had nothing to do with the expansion of entity liability. To the contrary, both before and after *New York Central*, Congress enacted thousands of statutes creating new or additional criminal liability for corporations. The Securities Act of 1934, the Food, Drug, and Cosmetic Act, and the Interstate Commerce Act are some of the more well-known and commonly applied statutes passed in the last century that include specific provisions for corporate criminal liability. Perhaps more important to this narrative, Congress has enacted thousands of other statutes— statutes that do not make explicit mention of corporate criminal liability— that aggressive prosecutors have had little difficulty extending to corporate conduct, including the mail and wire fraud statutes and the Racketeer Influenced and Corrupt Organizations (RICO) Act. Moreover, Congress has remained silent in the wake of those extensions, despite the fact that there is nothing to suggest that, by defining a "person" to include a "corporation" for purposes of the entire U.S. Code, Congress thought it was altering the longstanding common law tradition that entities could not be held criminally liable.

Edward B. Diskant, Note, Comparative Corporate Criminal Liability: Exploring the Uniquely American Doctrine Through Comparative Criminal Procedure, 118 Yale L.J. 126, 134-38 (2008); see also Kathleen F. Brickey,

Corporate Criminal Accountability: A Brief History and an Observation, 60 Wash. U. L.Q. 393, 404-15 (1982).

2. *New York Central* was the first Supreme Court case applying the principles of respondeat superior in a criminal prosecution. But the Elkins Act of 1903 specifically provided for liability of the railroad itself, as the Court noted. After *New York Central*, the doctrine set forth in the Elkins Act became, through judicial lawmaking, the doctrine for corporate criminal liability under *all* federal statutes (unless, of course, a particular statute provides for a different rule). How do you square this fact with United States v. Hudson & Goodwin, 11 U.S. 32 (1812), and United States v. Bevans, 16 U.S. 336 (1818), discussed in Chapter 3? Diskant is right that even before the Elkins Act, prosecutors were "creatively pursuing criminal sanctions against corporations by applying general criminal laws—laws that, by their terms, did not extend to corporations as entities—to corporate conduct." In prior chapters, we've seen how prosecutors have used their "power of initiative" to expand substantive criminal law. Now we're seeing how they invented a new area of liability. Which do you find more more or less troubling?

3. Nearly one century after *New York Central*, Judge Michael Boudin reviewed the current doctrine of corporate criminal liability in United States v. Potter, 463 F.3d 9 (1st Cir. 2006). Upholding the conviction of a dog track and gambling firm for conspiring to bribe the then-Speaker of the Rhode Island House of Representatives, the court held a corporation liable for "the criminal acts of its agents so long as those agents are acting within the scope of employment." Id. at 25. "The test is whether the agent is 'performing acts of the kind which he is authorized to perform,' and those acts are 'motivated—at least in part—by an intent to benefit the corporation.'" Id. Judge Boudin explained:

> The legal rules for imputing criminal responsibility to corporations are built upon analogous rules for civil liability. For obvious practical reasons, the scope of employment test does not require specific directives from the board or president for every corporate action; it is enough that the type of conduct (making contracts, driving the delivery truck) is authorized.

Id. He went on to note that the "case law has rejected arguments that the corporation can avoid liability by adopting abstract rules that no agent can make an unlawful price-fixing contract or no driver exceed the speed limit. . . . Even a specific directive to an agent or employee or honest efforts to police such rules do not automatically free the company for the wrongful acts of agents." Id. at 25-26.

In civil cases, federal respondeat superior doctrine places on the employer the burden of proving that an employee was *not* acting within the scope of her employment when she committed an illegal act; if the evidence leaves the question in doubt, it becomes an issue for the jury. See Blount v.

Sterling Healthcare, 934 F. Supp. 1365, 1373 (S.D. Fla. 1996). Should the same rule apply in *criminal* prosecutions of artificial entities?

4. A corporation may be held criminally liable even if it received no actual benefit from its agent's crime. Although the existence or absence of benefit may be relevant as evidence of intent to benefit, the lack of any benefit does not prove that the agent's actions cannot be imputed to the employer. The Fifth Circuit sought to explain the reasoning behind this rule:

> [W]hile benefit is not essential in terms of result, the purpose to benefit the corporation is decisive in terms of equating the agent's action with that of the corporation. For it is an elementary principle of agency that "an act of a servant is not within the scope of employment if it is done with no intention to perform it as a part of or incident to a service on account of which he is employed." Restatement of the Law of Agency (2d) §235 [1958].

Standard Oil Co. of Tex. v. United States, 307 F.2d 120, 128 (5th Cir. 1962). In *Standard Oil*, the court concluded that the corporation was not guilty because the guilty employees neither obtained *nor* intended a benefit for the corporation. See id. at 128-29. At the same time, the court went out of its way to explain that liability may attach even if the result of the agent's action is to do harm to the corporation; the "act is no less the principal's if . . . either no benefit accrues, a benefit is undiscernible [sic], or, for that matter, the result turns out to be adverse." Id.

Agents may act for mixed reasons, and a corporation may be held liable as long as one motivation of its agent is to benefit the corporation, even if the agent acted primarily to benefit himself. Thus, in United States v. Automated Medical Laboratories, 770 F.2d 399 (4th Cir. 1985), the court affirmed the corporation's conviction for the actions of an employee despite its claim that the employee was acting for his own benefit, namely his "ambitious nature and his desire to ascend the corporate ladder." Id. at 407. The court held that the agent "was clearly acting in part to benefit [the company] since his advancement within the corporation depended on [the company's] well-being and its lack of difficulties with the FDA." Id.

Does this mean that a financial institution with 200,000 employees can, as a matter of black letter law, be prosecuted for money laundering when a single employee in its private wealth unit takes deposits from someone he knows to be a drug dealer? What else, if anything, must the government prove?

5. Since a firm cannot be sent to prison, the formal consequence of a conviction may simply be a fine or probation. Even that, however, can be fatal. See United States v. Eureka Labs., Inc., 103 F.3d 908, 914 (9th Cir. 1996) (upholding a fine even though it "jeopardized" the firm's "continued viability"). Moreover, the *collateral* consequences of a conviction might be devastating to a firm. Firms in regulated industries can lose their licenses,

see, e.g., 17 C.F.R. §201.102(e)(2) (2008) (barring an accounting firm convicted of a felony from serving as the auditor of a publicly traded corporation), and government contractors can be suspended or debarred from conducting further business with the government. See Assaf Hamdani & Alon Klement, Corporate Crime and Deterrence, 61 Stan. L. Rev. 271, 278-79 (2008). Perhaps even worse, the costs of all these formal and informal sanctions will fall not only on the convicted firm and its partners or shareholders, but also on the many customers, suppliers, guiltless employees, and others whose economic welfare depends on the firm's wellbeing. See Darryl K. Brown, Third-Party Interests in Criminal Law, 80 Tex. L. Rev. 1383 (2002). This has been most dramatic in the prosecution of Enron's accounting firm, Arthur Andersen, whose 2002 conviction, though ultimately reversed by the Supreme Court, has served as both a cautionary tale and engine for change within the Department of Justice, as discussed later in this section.

6. A convicted firm may also take a large hit in the marketplace, although the market effect likely turns on the offense of conviction and how it relates to the firm's products and services. See Preet Bharara, Corporations Cry Uncle and Their Employees Cry Foul: Rethinking Prosecutorial Pressure on Corporate Defendants, 44 Am. Crim. L. Rev. 53, 73 (2007) (describing corporations as "eggshell defendants" due to their vulnerability to market pressures). Recently, though, the premise that a corporate conviction is potentially fatal has been challenged. See Hamdani & Klement, *supra*, at 280 (noting an absence of any "empirical studies to support the claim that criminal liability has a distinctively harsh impact on firms' reputations"). See also Gabriel Markoff, Arthur Andersen and the Myth of the Corporate Death Penalty: Corporate Criminal Convictions in the Twenty-First Century, 15 U. Pa. J. Bus. L. 797 (2013). Markoff examined the database of organizational convictions compiled and made publicly available by Professor Brandon Garrett, to which we return later in this section. Markoff found that no publicly traded company failed *because* of a conviction that occurred in the years 2001 to 2010. Id. at 798. A number of data points support Markoff's conclusion that many companies survive indictment and conviction without grave harm. In 2012, DOJ secured guilty pleas from Japanese subsidiaries of two banks (RBS and UBS) involved in the LIBOR manipulation scandal. In 2013, hedge fund giant SAC Capital Advisors pled guilty to playing a role in a high-profile insider-trading scheme. In 2014, Credit Suisse pled guilty to its role in a tax evasion scheme, and BNP Paribas pled guilty to OFAC violations. Despite this vulnerability, they all survived. See Gordon Bourjaily, DPA DOA: How and Why Congress Should Bar the Use of Deferred and Non-Prosecution Agreements in Corporate Criminal Prosecutions, 52 Harv. J. on Legis. 543, 556 (2015).* Other scholars have concluded that firms suffer the same reputational costs from settlement agreements with federal

---

* [Editors' Note: We examine "deferred prosecution agreements" (DPAs), as well as "non-prosecution agreements" (NPAs), later in this section.]

prosecutors as they do from formal criminal convictions. See Cindy R. Alexander and Jennifer Arlen, Does Conviction Matter? The Reputational and Collateral Effects of Corporate Crime, in Research Handbook on Corporate Crime and Financial Misdealing 87 (Jennifer Arlen ed., 2018).

7. To be sure, the criminal law is often willfully blind to the devastating effects on third parties that follow the imposition of criminal sanctions on individuals. See, e.g., Philip M. Genty, Damage to Family Relationships as a Collateral Consequence of Parental Incarceration, 30 Fordham Urb. L.J. 1671 (2003). Yet the third-party effects of a large firm's conviction might be of a different order of magnitude. Certainly, in some cases the same third parties injured by a firm's conviction will have profited from the prior criminal conduct; the shareholders and other corporate stakeholders who reaped the rewards from a firm's price-fixing or the illegal payments that greased the way to corporate opportunities have little to complain about when the downsides of the criminal activity are visited upon them. See Beale, *supra*, at 1484-86. In a broad range of other cases, however, third parties will not have shared gains. See John C. Coffee, Jr., *supra*, at 401-02. Indeed, corporate crime has often been portrayed as an agency problem. See Kimberly D. Krawiec, Organizational Misconduct: Beyond the Principal-Agent Model, 32 Fla. St. U. L. Rev. 571 (2005); Jonathan R. Macey, Agency Theory and the Criminal Liability of Organizations, 71 B.U. L. Rev. 315 (1991). To what extent can criminal law distinguish between these situations? And should federal prosecutors be given the responsibility to anticipate and prevent these collateral consequences, perhaps by working with regulatory authorities?

2.   APPLICATION OF ENTITY LIABILITY

Let us go from a hypothetical case like the rogue bank employee to the following real one, where a hotel corporation—Jalaram, Inc.—was prosecuted for violations of the Mann Act, 18 U.S.C. §§2421 et seq. As first enacted in 1910, the statute made it a felony under federal law to transport or aid in the transport of a "woman or girl" in interstate or foreign commerce "for the purpose of prostitution or debauchery, or for any other immoral purpose, or with the intent and purpose to induce, entice, or compel such woman or girl" into immoral acts. By the time of the *Singh* case below, the wording of the statute had been altered to make it a felony to transport "any individual" in interstate or foreign commerce "with intent that such individual engage in prostitution, or in any sexual activity for which any person can be charged with a criminal offense." 18 U.S.C. §2421. The prosecution's theory was that Suresh Patel, the owner of Jalaram, Inc. and Dan Patel, the manager of one of Jalaram's hotels (the "Scottish Inn"), rented out rooms to a prostitution ring known as the "Gold Club" for the benefit, at least in part, of Jalaram, Inc.

United States v. Singh
518 F.3d 236 (4th Cir. 2008)

KING, Circuit Judge.

These appeals arise from a criminal proceeding in the Northern District of West Virginia in which defendants Surendra "Sam" Singh, Dilipkumar "Dan" Patel ("Patel"), and Jalaram, Incorporated (collectively, the "Defendants"), were convicted by jury of a total of fourteen offenses, including conspiracy to violate the Mann Act. . . .

Each of the fourteen offenses of conviction arose from the Defendants' involvement in an interstate prostitution scheme. . . .

From 2000 to 2003, a prostitution ring known as the "Gold Club" operated out of the Economy Inn and Scottish Inn motels in Martinsburg, West Virginia. The Gold Club was operated by Susan Powell, who has pleaded guilty to a federal tax offense and who testified at trial on behalf of the Government. During the Gold Club's two-and-one-half years of operation, Powell employed approximately fifty prostitutes, using as many as nine motel rooms per day on peak days, and four or five rooms on average days. All together, the Gold Club received proceeds from its operations that totaled more than $670,000. Powell recruited female prostitutes for the Gold Club from West Virginia and the neighboring states of Maryland and Virginia by advertising in newspapers in the three states. Each of the out-of-state prostitutes who testified acknowledged that, when she travelled to work in West Virginia, she did so for the purpose of engaging in prostitution.

The Gold Club began operating out of the Martinsburg Economy Inn in approximately March 2000. Powell negotiated a deal in that regard with Singh, the owner and manager of the Economy Inn and a Gold Club customer. The basic agreement was that the Economy Inn would rent rooms to Gold Club prostitutes at a discounted rate of $40 per day, with the understanding that the rooms would be vacated by 8:00 or 9:00 P.M. each evening. This arrangement allowed Singh to rent these rooms again, to legitimate overnight customers who arrived late in the evening. On some occasions, the Economy Inn would rent the same room to two different prostitutes on the same day—one working early in the day and the other coming in later. Powell would usually communicate with Gold Club prostitutes about their upcoming appointments by telephoning them through the Economy Inn's switchboard. Singh normally operated the switchboard himself and, before connecting Powell to a prostitute's room, would discuss with Powell the appointments of the day. . . .

In 2001, Powell decided to transfer the Gold Club's operations from the Economy Inn to a new location. [Defendant Dan] Patel, another regular Gold Club customer, was the manager of the Scottish Inn, a motel in Martinsburg owned by Jalaram. While Singh was travelling, Powell visited the Scottish Inn to discuss moving the Gold Club's operations there. Suresh Patel was present, identified himself as the Scottish Inn's owner, and talked with Powell about the Gold Club. Powell explained to Suresh that she ran an "adult entertainment company" and was looking for rooms to rent for that purpose. Suresh advised Powell that she should address the issue with [Dan] Patel, the Inn's manager, and scheduled a meeting between Powell and Patel for the next day.

At the meeting the next day, [Dan] Patel and Powell discussed the Gold Club's arrangement with the Economy Inn . . . and then agreed that the Scottish Inn would match the Economy Inn's terms with the Gold Club. As a result, Powell moved the Gold Club's operations to the Scottish Inn. When Singh learned of the Scottish Inn's arrangement with the Gold Club, he urged Powell to return its business to the Economy Inn, but she declined.

Powell ran the Gold Club's operations at the Scottish Inn as she had at the Economy Inn. She communicated with the prostitutes through the Inn's switchboard and discussed their appointments with Patel. Like Singh at the Economy Inn, Patel would monitor the Gold Club's customers at the Scottish Inn to ensure that the prostitutes paid for their rooms after their first customer. . . .

As the manager of the Scottish Inn, [Dan] Patel was responsible for its daily operations. He registered guests, accepted room rental payments, and cleaned rooms after they had been occupied. In carrying out these duties, Patel and his wife lived and worked at the Scottish Inn seven days a week, twenty-four hours a day. Suresh Patel, the Inn's owner, visited the Scottish Inn a few times each month, and would assist at the Inn when, for example, Patel went to the bank. With the exception of his visits to the bank, Patel was generally present at the Scottish Inn and in charge of its operations.

The Gold Club operated out of the Scottish Inn for about six months in late 2001 and early 2002, but its prostitutes were not happy there. . . . Eventually, Powell moved the Gold Club's operations back to the Economy Inn, primarily in response to problems involving Patel and the Gold Club's prostitutes. . . .

After Powell returned the Gold Club's operations to the Economy Inn, Patel pleaded with her to bring them back to the Scottish Inn, stating: "I'm in a lot of trouble. . . . My owner[, Suresh Patel,] said I had to get your business back. I'll even go $38 a day instead of $40, but I must get your business back." Powell declined this proposal and continued to operate the Gold Club out of the Economy Inn. The Gold Club's operations ceased after a police raid that occurred on July 4, 2003, when Powell was arrested. . . .

[T]he Government maintains that the district court erred in granting a new trial to Jalaram on its convictions on the Mann Act conspiracy and Mann Act counts. . . .

[T]he district court concluded that "the evidence adduced at trial does not support the jury's finding that Dan Patel was acting in furtherance of the corporation." Prior to issuing that Order, . . . the court observed that "something of an independent contractor exception should have occurred," because the evidence showed that "Patel was acting on his own behalf [and] not for the benefit of the corporation Jalaram." As a result, the court . . . awarded Jalaram a new trial on its convictions.

We have recognized that "a corporation is liable for the criminal acts of its employees and agents done within the scope of their employment with the intent to benefit the corporation." Mylan Labs., Inc. v. Akzo, N.V., 2 F.3d 56, 63 (4th Cir. 1993). The appropriate "scope of employment" of such an employee or agent has been defined to include all those acts falling within the employee's or agent's general line of work, when they are motivated—at least in part—by an intent to benefit the corporate employer. See United States v. Automated Med. Labs., 770 F.2d 399, 406-407 (4th Cir. 1985).[18]

In this situation, the district court apparently perceived that the evidence failed to establish Jalaram's corporate criminal liability based on the conduct of [Dan] Patel. The court also perceived that, but for instructional error, Jalaram would have been acquitted. In so ruling, the court erred, first, in determining, that the evidence was insufficient to sustain the finding of corporate criminal liability against Jalaram, and, second, in concluding that instructional error had occurred. As explained above, a corporate accused is liable for the criminal acts of its "employees and agents" acting "within the scope of their employment" for the "benefit [of] the corporation," Mylan Labs., 2 F.3d at 63, and such liability arises if the employee or agent has acted for his own benefit as well as that of his employer, see Automated Med. Labs., 770 F.2d at 407.

Under the evidence, viewed in the light most favorable to the prosecution, the court erred in failing to recognize that [Dan] Patel, as manager of the Scottish Inn, was an agent of Jalaram, and was acting within the scope of that relationship when he rented rooms to the Gold Club's prostitutes. . . . The evidence demonstrates that Patel thereafter received funds from the Gold Club prostitutes with the intent—at least in part—of benefitting Jalaram. Jalaram received, by its own admission, at least $700

---

18. The terms "employee" and "agent" sometimes have been used interchangeably in the context of corporate criminal liability. See Automated Med. Labs., 770 F.2d at 406-407. It has been consistently recognized, however, that an important aspect of a corporate criminal liability issue is whether the employer or agent (by whichever term utilized) was acting within the scope of his duties. See id.; see also United States v. Basic Construction Co., 711 F.2d 570, 572 (4th Cir. 1983); Old Monastery Co. v. United States, 147 F.2d 905, 908 (4th Cir. 1945).

from the Gold Club's prostitution enterprise. And the jury was entitled to find, under the evidence, that such receipts substantially exceeded that sum. In these circumstances, the evidence of Jalaram's corporate criminal liability did not at all weigh heavily against the verdict as to Jalaram, but was wholly sufficient to support it.

Moreover, contrary to the district court's conclusion that it erred in instructing the jury, the instructions properly explained the controlling legal principles on the issue of corporate criminal liability. In this regard, the jury was instructed on three important legal points:

- A corporation may be responsible for the actions of its agents done or made within the scope of their authority;
- The term "scope of employment" refers to acts on the corporation's behalf in performance of an agent's general line of work. To be acting within the scope of his employment, those acts must be motivated, at least in part, by an intent to benefit the corporation; and
- An agent may act for his own benefit while also acting for the benefit of the corporation.

As a result, the court made an error of law—thereby abusing its discretion—in concluding . . . that an independent contractor instruction should have been given to the jury. The court further abused its discretion by relying on the perceived instructional error to award a new trial to Jalaram in the face of trial evidence that fully supported (rather than weighed heavily against) the jury's verdict. The award of a new trial to Jalaram is thus vacated and the verdict is reinstated on the Mann Act conspiracy and Mann Act counts against Jalaram. We remand on those convictions for the appropriate sentencing proceedings.

NOTES AND QUESTIONS

1. Why do you think the prosecutors indicted Jalaram, Inc., the privately held company that owned the hotel? In all likelihood, they saw it as a way to get to Jalaram's president, Suresh Patel, in addition to the hotel manager, Dan Patel. Suresh was indicted, but he was acquitted, see 518 F.3d at 250 n.19. Although they were unable to convict Suresh himself, prosecutors had made sure to also indict his alter ego, Jalaram. The jury convicted the company, and the conviction was upheld in the decision excerpted above.

2. Holding a corporation liable for its agents' crimes intuitively seems appropriate in cases like *Singh*, where the line is blurred between the corporation and its agents, or where managers and the corporation's president are directly involved in the wrongdoing. But recall that a corporation can be held liable for the acts of even its lowliest employee—even when corporate

officers had no knowledge of the crime, and even when the employee acted in direct contravention of company policy.

As we noted in the introduction to this chapter, many have questioned whether such expansive liability is really appropriate in the criminal context. But if not respondeat superior, under what standard *should* corporations be held liable? Noting the absence of Supreme Court decisions addressing how to structure vicarious criminal liability "in the absence of a statute that explicitly included instructions [on] imput[ation]," Andrew Weissmann looked to the civil law, specifically the Supreme Court's Title VII cases, for guidance. Andrew Weissmann et al., U.S. Chamber Inst. for Legal Reform, Reforming Corporate Criminal Liability to Promote Responsible Corporate Behavior 7 (2008). Weissmann contends that "[t]he Supreme Court has made clear that unlimited vicarious corporate liability is both unwarranted by civil agency principles and undesirable as a matter of optimal deterrence." Id. If the Court were to allow punitive damages in cases where a hostile "managerial agent" acted contrary to the employer's good faith efforts to comply with Title VII, the company would have no incentive to implement antidiscrimination or compliance programs in the first place. According to Weissmann, this is the problem that responsible corporations face in the criminal context—the "current criminal liability standard fails to properly incentivize internal deterrence by refusing to distinguish companies that actively engage in compliance from those that do not." Id. at 8.

Thus, to Weissmann, the Court's Title VII jurisprudence implicitly supports the adoption of two new features in corporate criminal liability: (1) a due diligence defense and (2) a limitation on liability to managerial employees. Id. at 10. We return to the due diligence defense later in the chapter, but for now consider this question: Why has the Supreme Court considered and sought to limit untoward results of simple respondeat superior liability in at least one civil context, but refrained from addressing the same concerns in the criminal context?

3. What happens when a firm is charged with a specific intent offense but no single corporate agent can be shown to have had the requisite intent, or no single corporate agent committed all of the relevant acts? Can corporate criminal liability rest on "stitching together" the knowledge and acts of multiple agents? For an argument supporting that approach—which concededly goes beyond "strict adherence to respondeat superior"—see Stacey Neumann Vu, Corporate Criminal Liability: Patchwork Verdicts and the Problem of Locating a Guilty Agent, 104 Colum. L. Rev. 459, 495 (2004) ("Neither due process, nor the tattered remnants of vicarious liability for the acts of identifiable predicate agents, require a jury to locate a corruptly motivated actor within an accused entity.").

Thus far, only the First Circuit has adopted this theory. See United States v. Bank of New England, 821 F.2d 844 (1st Cir. 1987). In that case, the bank, as part of its defense, argued that to prove that it acted willfully the government was required to show that the employees responsible for filing Currency Transaction Reports (CTRs) with the Treasury Department for transactions over $10,000 had actual knowledge of such transactions and failed to report them. Id. at 874. The bank argued that willful failure to file could not be shown if all the government could prove was that the bank had maintained a poor communications network that prevented the consolidation of information held by its various employees. Id. In other words, it contended that the negligent failure to compile all relevant information with the corporate agent responsible for reporting that information could be a defense to that agent's failure to report.

The district court rejected the bank's arguments and instructed the jury "to look at the Bank as an institution. As such, its knowledge is the sum of the knowledge of all its employees. That is, the bank's knowledge is the totality of what all of the employees know within the scope of their employment." Id. at 855. The First Circuit affirmed this instruction, acknowledging the realities of modern corporate organizational structure. It reasoned that "[c]orporations compartmentalize knowledge, subdividing the elements of specific duties and operations into smaller components. The aggregate of those components constitutes the corporation's knowledge of a particular operation. It is irrelevant whether employees administering one component of an operation know the specific activities of employees administering another aspect of the operation." Id. at 856.

No other circuit has adopted Bank of New England's collective knowledge theory, and several have expressed skepticism. See United States v. Science Applications Int'l Corp., 626 F.3d 1257, 1274 (D.C. Cir. 2010) (doubting "the legal soundness of the 'collective' intent theory" in a civil case); Southland Sec. Corp. v. INSpire Ins. Solutions, Inc., 365 F.3d 353, 366 (5th Cir. 2004) (rejecting the "collective knowledge" concept in favor of an individual's scienter in a civil case); Nordstrom, Inc. v. Chubb & Son, Inc., 54 F.3d 1424, 1435 (9th Cir. 1995) ("[T]here is no case law supporting an independent 'collective scienter' theory."). Maybe the reason why no federal criminal cases address the theory, beyond Bank of New England itself, is that no other federal prosecutions (at least those going to trial) have invoked it. Cf. Commonwealth v. Life Care Ctrs. of Am., Inc., 926 N.E.2d 206, 212-15 (Mass. 2010) (rejecting the collective knowledge theory as a matter of state law, and suggesting that the theory "raises due process concerns").

Some courts and scholars support the amalgamation principle in the context of civil securities fraud, however. William E. Knepper & Dan A. Bailey, Liability of Corporate Directors and Officers, §17.06 (4th ed. 1988) ("In litigation involving Section 10(b) of the Securities Exchange Act and SEC Rule 10b-5, even though a corporation is incapable of acting except through individual directors and officers, the cumulative knowledge of its directors and officers is imputed to it. . . . [A] corporation's knowledge need not be possessed by a single officer or agent; the cumulative knowledge of all its agents will be imputed to the corporation."). Indeed, in In re WorldCom, Inc. Sec. Litig., 352 F. Supp. 2d 472, 497 (S.D.N.Y. 2005), the judge adopted the collective knowledge theory to prove scienter in a civil securities fraud case. But the amalgamation theory has not attracted substantial support even in the civil fraud context. Both *Southland Sec. Corp.* and *Nordstrom Inc.* involved civil allegations of fraud. Given the broad scope of respondeat superior liability, it would be an unusual case where prosecutors have to resort to a collective knowledge approach; indeed, it is not even clear that this approach was necessary to the jury's verdict in *Bank of New England.* If we accept the notion of corporate criminal liability, why might we still have reservations about "collective knowledge" theories?

3. CURRENT LANDSCAPE: DEFERRED PROSECUTIONS, CORPORATE MONITORS, AND PROSECUTORS AS "SUPER-REGULATORS"

1. *The Use of Deferred and Non-Prosecution Agreements.* From time to time, corporations will take a case to trial. See F. Joseph Warin & Julie Rapoport Schenker, Refusing to Settle: Why Public Companies Go to Trial in Federal Criminal Cases, 52 Am. Crim. L. Rev. 517 (2015) (surveying twelve federal criminal trials). Still, because a criminal conviction may conceivably be fatal to a corporation, and because a corporation's collapse affects not only the corporate wrongdoers, but also innocent third parties, both corporations and prosecutors may have strong incentives to avoid trials (and the risk of conviction) where possible. In a deferred prosecution agreement (DPA), a formal indictment is filed in federal court, along with a copy of the agreement and an explanation that upon satisfaction of its terms, the Department of Justice will dismiss the indictment. A non-prosecution agreement (NPA) is substantially similar but substitutes a formal indictment with a promise not to prosecute if the agreement's terms are satisfied. The idea is that these agreements permit prosecutors to ferret out corporate crime while allowing the business entity to remain viable. Under both types of agreement, the government delays—and if the defendant complies with the terms of the agreement, forgoes—prosecution in exchange for the corporation's acceptance of responsibility for misconduct, its agreement to cooperate with the government, and its promise to reform its practices and pay substantial fines and restitution. See Leonard Orland, The Transformation of Corporate Criminal Law, 1 Brook. J. Corp. Fin. & Com. L. 45, 61 (2006).

There was a long history in federal court of entering into special pretrial diversion agreements with minimally culpable, first-time *individual* defendants, such as juvenile or drug offenders who would benefit from rehabilitation. Federal diversion agreements for *organizations* first arose in the early 1990s, when the Department of Justice agreed not to file criminal

charges against the investment bank Salomon Brothers for securities violations if it agreed to pay significant fines, cooperate with the government,
and implement compliance reforms. This deal amounted to an early NPA,
but such agreements remained rare for another decade, when the corporate landscape markedly transformed.

In a 1999 memorandum entitled "Bringing Criminal Charges Against
Corporations," then-Deputy Attorney General Eric Holder laid the groundwork for the Justice Department's current corporate crime policy. The
memo set forth guidelines for prosecuting a corporation and made clear that
collateral consequences could—and should—be considered in charging
decisions. Memorandum from Eric Holder, Deputy Att'y Gen., U.S. Dep't
of Justice, to Component Heads and U.S. Att'ys, Federal Prosecution of
Corporations (June 16, 1999). The fear of collateral harm to innocent third
parties was crystallized by a high-profile corporate case of the early 2000s arising out of the collapse of Enron and its accounting firm Arthur Andersen.
Arthur Andersen sought an NPA out of concern that the mere fact of indictment would be fatal. When it was offered only a DPA, it opted for trial and
was convicted by a Houston jury (Houston being the home-base of Enron).
When the dust settled, the accounting firm had collapsed and thousands of
innocent people were out of work. (And, after all that, the Supreme Court
ended up reversing the firm's conviction—see Arthur Andersen v. United
States, 544 U.S. 696 (2005)). DOJ came under attack for such unnecessary
collateral ruin, and the 2003 Thompson Memo provided prosecutors a new
way forward in the form of corporate cooperation and pretrial diversion
agreements. See Memorandum from Larry Thompson, Deputy Att'y Gen.'s
Office, Principles of Fed. Prosecution of Bus. Org. 3 (Jan. 20, 2003). These
deferred and non-prosecutions agreements were explicitly validated in the
2008 Filip Memo and have been part of the U.S. Attorneys' Manual since
then. See Memorandum from Mark Filip, Deputy Att'y Gen., to Heads of
Department Components and United States Attorneys, Principles of Federal
Prosecution of Business Organizations (Aug. 28, 2008); U.S. Attorneys'
Manual, Title 9-28.000, Principles of Federal Prosecution of Business
Organizations.

The use of DPAs and NPAs has grown over the past two decades. While
there were just 17 corporate DPAs and NPAs from 1992-2001, there were
253 between 2002 and 2012, and 188 between 2013 and 2016 alone. See
Brandon L. Garrett & Jon Ashley, Corporate Prosecutions Registry, University
of Virginia School of Law (library of such agreements). See also Gibson
Dunn, 2016 Year End Update on Corporate Non-Prosecution Agreements
and Deferred Prosecution Agreements (2017).

The increasing resort to these agreements marks a significant change in
the way prosecutors attack corporate crime: "By focusing more on prospective questions of corporate governance and compliance, and less on the retrospective question of the entity's criminal liability, federal prosecutors have

fashioned a new role for themselves in policing, and supervising, corporate America." Peter Spivack & Sujit Raman, Regulating the "New Regulators": Current Trends in Deferred Prosecution Agreements, 45 Am. Crim. L. Rev. 159, 161 (2008). Is this new role as super-regulator a good thing? It depends upon whom you ask.

Many regard DPAs and NPAs as providing a win-win opportunity for the parties involved. As a lawyer who negotiated an agreement for Computer Associates International put it, the deals allow prosecutors to "send a message that certain corporate conduct won't be tolerated without risking the viability of the company or the business." Kara Scannell, Firms Are Getting Time to Clean Up Their Acts: If Charge Could Be Deadly, Indictment Can Be Deferred as Violators Effect Change, Wall St. J., June 13, 2005. They also can—if used carefully—promote the pursuit of the individuals—the ones actually responsible for the corporation's malfeasance—that the government is really interested in prosecuting. As Professor Richman explains, it is these:

> Sending someone to prison is not the sine qua non of criminal prosecutions, but it is the gold standard, and prosecutors would far prefer going after individuals to seeking a corporate conviction. Threatening to prosecute the entity itself is a means to that end, for, without this threat, the entity would be far more tempted to protect the individuals and indeed may still do so if the individuals have sufficient sway within the organization. But an actual prosecution will generally be a sign that something has gone wrong—perhaps real or perceived recalcitrance by the corporation that the government takes as both a failure to cooperate and a sign of a "culture" of wrongdoing within the organization.

Richman, Decisions About Coercion, *supra*, 322-23. The optimistic version of these deals thus has firms actually worrying about the risk of prosecution, acting on those fears by implementing rigorous compliance programs, and, when misconduct happens (as will inevitably occur in a large organization), conducting thorough internal investigations, cooperating fully with the Government, and bolstering their existing internal controls.

Of course, this optimism may be misplaced. Prosecutors may not possess the knowledge or experience necessary to oversee corporate America and, often, the agreements require the corporation to cooperate in the prosecution of its own culpable corporate executives. See Orland, *supra*, at 67. Thus, where in the past a corporation may have tried to shield its employees from prosecution, now corporate defendants are often "tempted to show their 'cooperation' by 'throwing their employees under the bus.'" Regina A. Robson, Crime and Punishment: Rehabilitating Retribution as a Justification for Organizational Criminal Liability, 47 Am. Bus. L.J. 109, 133 (2010). And we should worry that the individuals fingered by the firm may not be the managers that bear equal, or perhaps greater, responsibility for the corporate misconduct. The availability and regular use of DPAs or NPAs may also ruin the deterrence value of corporate criminal liability by giving firms confidence that they'll be able to buy off the Government in the future should any misconduct come to light.

Moreover, the threat of respondeat superior liability and the possibility of entering into a DPA or NPA give the government considerable, and some would say too much, leverage over corporations. See, e.g., Michael Patrick Wilt, Who Watches the Watchmen? Accountability in Federal Corporate Criminal Agreements, 43 Am. J. Crim. L. 61, 73-74 (2015) (arguing that failing to constrain these agreements under a measurable process opens them up to "abuse, rent-seeking, and overzealous prosecutions"); Peter R. Reilly, Justice Deferred is Justine Denied: We Must End Our Failed Experiment in Deferring Corporate Criminal Prosecutions, 2015 BYU L. Rev. 307, 351 (suggesting that because corporations often have no viable alternative, "DPAs provide the government with power that can potentially be unfair and exploitative in the enforcement of corporate criminal law"). To what extent is this leverage desirable? To what extent, for example, should the government use the threat of prosecution to pressure a firm into providing information—perhaps gleaned as a result of the firm's own internal investigation—that implicates (or exculpates) its employees? To what extent can prosecutors advance their investigation into a firm's conduct by encouraging the firm to exert its own economic leverage over its employees?

In United States v. Stein, 541 F.3d 130 (2d Cir. 2008), the Second Circuit affirmed the dismissal of a tax fraud indictment against several former KPMG partners because the government had improperly pressured the partnership to refuse to pay the attorneys' fees of partners who would not cooperate with prosecutors. The district judge, Lewis Kaplan, had excoriated the prosecutors, concluding that "KPMG refused to pay because the government held the proverbial gun to its head." United States v. Stein, 435 F. Supp. 2d 330, 336 (S.D.N.Y. 2006). More generally, the judge denounced the government's use of its extraordinary leverage under the respondeat superior standard:

> Justice is not done when the government uses the threat of indictment—a matter of life and death to many companies and therefore a matter that threatens the jobs and security of blameless employees—to coerce companies into depriving their present and even former employees of the means of defending themselves against criminal charges in a court of law.

Id. at 381-82. As you will see, DOJ—in response to pressure from Congress in the wake of Judge Kaplan's opinion—implemented reforms designed to limit the power that DPAs and NPAs afford prosecutors.

2. *The Use of Corporate Monitors.* Increasingly, DPAs and NPAs require the appointment of outside monitors to ensure that the corporation is complying with the terms of the agreement. See Christie Ford & David Hess, Can Corporate Monitorships Improve Corporate Compliance?, 34 J. Corp. L. 679, 682 (2009) (reporting that, as of 2009, DOJ had imposed "at least 44 monitorships . . . [,] almost all of which date from 2003 or later"). As the number of monitorships increases, so do the problems that DOJ faces in their implementation, particularly given the financial incentives at stake. See Veronica Root, Constraining Monitors, 85 Fordham L. Rev. 2227, 2228 (2017) (noting the fierce bidding war for a Herbalife monitorship worth $15.7 million over seven years). DOJ came under public scrutiny in 2007 when then-U.S. Attorney Chris Christie awarded a monitor contract to his onetime boss, former Attorney General John Ashcroft. This deal was awarded without notice or public bidding and was estimated to be worth between $28 million and $52 million. See Philip Shenon, Ashcroft Deal Brings Scrutiny in Justice Dept., N.Y. Times (Jan. 10, 2008). Christie had also awarded corporate monitorships to a number of his former DOJ colleagues, and required Bristol-Myers Squibb to endow a chair at his law school alma mater "dedicated to the teaching of business ethics and corporate governance" as part of its deferred-prosecution agreement. See Bristol-Myers Squibb DPA 6 (2006).

In response to this appearance of favoritism and growing congressional pressure, including the thrice-proposed Accountability in Deferred Prosecution Act, which died in the House of Representatives in 2008, 2009, and most recently in 2014, the DOJ imposed a series of reforms to dispel the appearance of cronyism in the appointment of monitors, and to solve the inevitable disputes that arise between a monitor and the monitored corporation. First, acting Deputy Attorney General Craig Morford released a nine-point memorandum in March 2008, known as the Morford memo, intended to spur prosecutors to select monitors based on merit and in cooperation with the corporation to be monitored. See Craig S. Morford, Dep't of Justice, Selection and Use of Monitors in Deferred Prosecution Agreements and Non-Prosecution Agreements with Corporations 7-8 (2008). Two months later, Deputy Attorney General Mark Filip sent a memo to all federal prosecutors prohibiting them from including in prosecution agreements provisions unrelated to the corporation's crime, such as those "requiring the defendant to pay funds to a charitable, educational, community, or other organization or individual that is not a victim of the criminal activity or is not providing services to redress the harm caused by the defendant's criminal conduct." This memo is now at USAM 9-16.325 (updated 2010).

The following year, in August of 2009, DOJ implemented further reforms aimed at reducing the appearance of favoritism in the selection of corporate monitors. See Eileen R. Larence, U.S. Gov't Accountability

Office, GAO-10-260T, Corporate Crime: Prosecutors Adhered to Guidance in Selecting Monitors for Deferred Prosecution and Non-Prosecution Agreements, but DOJ Could Better Communicate Its Role in Resolving Conflicts 8 (2009). These reforms came in the wake of a congressional inquiry and a GAO report revealing that "more than half" of the monitors appointed in recent years had formerly worked for DOJ. Id. at 10. DOJ now requires the Office of the Deputy Attorney General to approve monitor selection and to document the process used for such selection. Id.

Finally, in May of 2010—again in response to congressional pressure—DOJ clarified its role in resolving disputes between companies and their monitors. Gary C. Grindler, Dep't of Justice, Additional Guidance on the Use of Monitors in Deferred Prosecutions and Non-Prosecution Agreements with Corporations (2010). Previously, when a company disagreed with a monitor's suggestion, its options were unclear. DPAs did not specify, for instance, whether the corporation could refuse to implement a monitor-made suggestion. Nor did the agreements specify whether the corporation could approach DOJ in an effort to mediate the issue. This most recent memorandum ended much of the uncertainty by clarifying that DOJ will be available to referee monitor-company disputes. Specifically, it adds a tenth principle to the Morford memo: A DPA "should explain what role the Department could play in resolving any disputes between the monitor and the corporation, given the facts and circumstances of the case." Id.

The May 2010 memorandum also recommended that prosecutors include two provisions in future agreements. First, agreements should state that a company need not immediately implement monitor recommendations "that the company considers unduly burdensome, impracticable or otherwise inadvisable; instead, the company may propose in writing an alternative policy, procedure or system designed to achieve the same objective or purpose." Id. Second, agreements should require that, on at least an annual basis, "representatives of the company and the Department meet together to discuss the monitorship and any suggestions, comments, or improvements the company may wish to discuss . . . or propose . . . including with respect to the scope or costs of the monitorship." Id.

Detractors say these internally binding recommendations do not go far enough and suggest there ought to be a role for courts, where the concept of a monitor originated. But so far, courts have little power over corporate monitorships or DOJ-negotiated settlement agreements, and the public appears to have no right to inspection. A district court judge in D.C. ordered the public release of an independent monitor's reports on AIG, asserting that there is a common law right to access a judicial record, but the D.C. Circuit reversed. The Court of Appeals concluded that the monitor's reports were unrelated to furthering judicial accountability and therefore the public had no entitlement to their contents. See SEC v. Am. Int'l Group, 712 F.3d 1 (D.C. Cir. 2013). Similarly, the Second Circuit recently reversed an order of then-Judge John Gleeson in the Eastern District of New York that would have released a corporate compliance monitor's reports to the public. See United States v. HSBC Bank USA, N.A., 2017 WL 2960618 (2d Cir. July 12, 2017). Both DOJ and the defendant bank, HSBC, objected to Judge Gleeson's order. The Court of Appeals held that monitor's reports are not judicial documents and hence the public has no qualified right of access to them under the First Amendment.

The extent to which the Justice Department responded to congressional pressure in the corporate crime area highlights not just the extent to which executive action in the criminal areas occurs in the shadow of Congress, but also Congress's preference for using measures other than substantive criminal law to rein in enforcement activity. As one of us has noted: "While the political costs of narrowing the scope of substantive law appear to be prohibitive, the costs of proposals to restrict enforcer activities are not, even which such limitations disproportionately affect particular classes of cases or defendants." Daniel C. Richman, Federal Criminal Law, Congressional Delegation, and Enforcement Discretion, 46 UCLA L. Rev. 757, 801 (1999) (giving other examples). Should the dialogue on corporate crime enforcement discussed here be applauded? Regretted? Should it matter that such dialogues are less likely to occur for disadvantaged classes of defendants?

What should we make of the considerable efforts of Main Justice to regulate U.S. Attorneys' offices in corporate prosecutions? Certainly these efforts reduce the risk that some renegade office will take a large firm hostage with scant legal justification. They also promote national consistency in matters that have national implications. Yet Main Justice's advantages in "cost internalization" may come with downsides, if one worries that an administration may be better equipped to internalize the costs imposed on target firms than those imposed by corporate malfeasance.

3. *Prosecutors as Regulators.* As Edward Diskant and others have noted, corporate criminal liability predates the modern regulatory state, and often operates incongruously within its bounds. Indeed, the United States has a unique, hybrid approach in combining stiff corporate criminal liability with a restrictive civil regulatory climate. See Diskant, *supra*, at 130. No common law country employs a "more aggressive and far-reaching form of corporate criminal liability" than our federal government. Id. You won't be surprised to learn that this confluence of corporate criminal liability alongside modern regulatory regimes reinforces the importance of prosecutorial discretion.

At the same time, corporate criminal liability represents but one arrow in the government's quiver that bristles with many other "punitive and regulatory remedies." Id. at 142. Federal prosecutors, serving as self-ordained "super-regulators" through DPAs mandating structural reforms, are simply not the only game in town. Mary Jo White, Corporate Criminal Liability: What Has Gone Wrong?, 37th Annual Institute on Securities Regulation, PLI Item No. 6063 (Nov. 2005). And they may not be the best game in town either. Civil enforcers, too, possess the power to reform corporate behavior. Indeed, Professor Jennifer Arlen argues that civil regulators are far better equipped to seek broad-based corporate reforms. Jennifer Arlen, Removing Prosecutors from the Boardroom, in Prosecutors in the Boardroom: Using Criminal Law to Regulate Corporate Conduct 62 (Anthony Barkow & Rachel Barkow eds. 2011). In her words:

> Prosecutors generally should not use DPAs and NPAs to induce firms to adopt structural reforms, such as compliance programs, because compliance program design involves difficult judgments about when and where to centralize decision-making and to collect and channel information. Industries and firms vary enormously as to whether, and in what areas, the compliance benefits of decision-making centralization and oversight exceed the costs. Prosecutors rarely have sufficient experience working in any business, much less adequate industry-specific expertise, to make these decisions reliably. By contrast, civil federal regulatory authorities are more likely to have this expertise, at least with respect to the industries they regulate. In addition, prosecutors are subject to little, if any, external oversight when they intervene in internal corporate affairs. Moreover, prosecutors' offices do not have a formal process for assembling and evaluating data on different compliance programs and monitoring plans to assess their effectiveness. By contrast, regulatory agencies are subject to greater oversight . . . and have the information-gathering abilities needed to assess compliance decisions. Agencies' ability to gather information and collect public comments reduces the risk that federal authorities will mandate expensive, but ultimately ineffective, measures. Finally, regulatory agencies are in a position to conduct more widespread, industry-specific, and formal assessments of compliance to determine if any firm-specific mandated reforms should be adopted on a more widespread basis.

Id. Arlen's institutional critique becomes more compelling when one realizes the enormous discretion prosecutors exercise in crafting DPAs, most of which do not "restrict themselves to measures previously required by Congress or a federal regulatory agency." Id. at 79. Instead, many DPAs that mandate structural reforms require firms to adopt internal review and reporting mechanisms that are "not required by either a statute or an agency ruling as a precondition for not being indicted. In so doing, prosecutors are crossing the line from criminal enforcement to direct regulation, a line that they generally should not, and need not, cross." Id.

Other commentators offer middle-ground options that stop short of recommending the end of prosecutor-imposed structural reforms. Professor Richman contends that "the goal . . . [should be to] balance the contributions that U.S. Attorneys' offices can make as insulated islands of professional commitment, local knowledge, and dedicated human capital with the contribution that they can make as the leading edge of a broader regulatory effort." Daniel Richman, Political Control of Federal Prosecutions: Looking

Back and Looking Forward, 58 Duke L.J. 2087, 2118 (2009). Both synchronized and unsynchronized efforts between criminal and civil authorities carry risks:

> To tightly tether federal prosecutors to the decision making of the Securities and Exchange Commission's (or the Environmental Protection Agency's) enforcement division deprives the system of the benefits of overlapping jurisdiction and reduces the system's resilience (to capture or other dampening influences) to that of its weakest member. But a substantial disjunction between regulatory agencies and criminal prosecutors sends inefficiently noisy signals about government policy to regulatory subjects and creates confusing, sometimes even bad, law.

Id. Perhaps the best defense of prosecutor-imposed structural reforms is that regulatory agencies, which might have greater substantive competency, often lack the enforcement teeth or sustained political support needed to fill the gap that prosecutors address. Is that an acceptable justification in a second-best world? To what extent are deferred prosecution agreements simply vehicles for improper prosecutorial involvement in corporate governance? What institutional competence do prosecutors have to specify and monitor such reforms? Should these agreements be viewed as evidence of prosecutorial leniency or overreaching? See Brandon L. Garrett, Structural Reform Prosecution, 93 Va. L. Rev. 853 (2007).

4. *Current Department of Justice Policies.* The current version of the U.S. Attorneys' Manual contains a section called "Principles of Federal Prosecution of Business Organizations" that offers guidance to prosecutors deciding whether to charge a corporation, and incorporates many of the reforms discussed in this chapter. As you will see in the following excerpts, the USAM prominently lists "cooperation" as a factor in determining whether to indict (9-28.700), but it bars prosecutors from requesting that the corporation waive its attorney-client privilege (9-28.710), as long as relevant facts about misconduct are timely disclosed (9-28.720).

Principles of Federal Prosecution of Business Organizations
United States Attorneys' Manual (Last Revised November 2015)

9-28.300. FACTORS TO BE CONSIDERED

A. General Principle: Generally, prosecutors apply the same factors in determining whether to charge a corporation as they do with respect to individuals. See USAM 9-27.220 et seq. Thus, the prosecutor must weigh all of the factors normally considered in the sound exercise of prosecutorial judgment: the sufficiency of the evidence; the likelihood of success at trial; the probable deterrent, rehabilitative, and other consequences of conviction; and the adequacy of noncriminal approaches. See id. However, due to the nature of the corporate "person," some additional factors are present. In conducting an investigation, determining whether to bring charges, and negotiating plea or other agreements, prosecutors should consider the following factors in reaching a decision as to the proper treatment of a corporate target:

1. the nature and seriousness of the offense, including the risk of harm to the public, and applicable policies and priorities, if any, governing the prosecution of corporations for particular categories of crime (see USAM 9-28.400);

2. the pervasiveness of wrongdoing within the corporation, including the complicity in, or the condoning of, the wrongdoing by corporate management (see USAM 9-28.500);

3. the corporation's history of similar misconduct, including prior criminal, civil, and regulatory enforcement actions against it (see USAM 9-28.600);

4. the corporation's willingness to cooperate in the investigation of its agents (see USAM 9-28.700);

5. the existence and effectiveness of the corporation's pre-existing compliance program (*see* USAM 9-28.800);

6. the corporation's timely and voluntary disclosure of wrongdoing (*see* USAM 9-28.900);

7. the corporation's remedial actions, including any efforts to implement an effective corporate compliance program or to improve an existing one, to replace responsible management, to discipline or terminate wrongdoers, to pay restitution, and to cooperate with the relevant government agencies (*see* USAM 9-28.1000);

8. collateral consequences, including whether there is disproportionate harm to shareholders, pension holders, employees, and others not proven personally culpable, as well as impact on the public arising from the prosecution (*see* USAM 9-28.1100);

9. the adequacy of remedies such as civil or regulatory enforcement actions (*see* USAM 9-28.1200); and

10. the adequacy of the prosecution of individuals responsible for the corporation's malfeasance (*see* USAM 9-28.1300)

B. Comment: The factors listed in this section are intended to be illustrative of those that should be evaluated and are not an exhaustive list of potentially relevant considerations. Some of these factors may not apply to specific cases, and in some cases one factor may override all others. For example, the nature and seriousness of the offense may be such as to warrant prosecution regardless of the other factors. In most cases, however, no single factor will be dispositive. In addition, national law enforcement policies in various enforcement areas may require that more or less weight be given to certain of these factors than to others. Of course, prosecutors must exercise their thoughtful and pragmatic judgment in applying and balancing these factors, so as to achieve a fair and just outcome and promote respect for the law.

9-28.700. The Value of Cooperation

Cooperation is a mitigating factor, by which a corporation—just like any other subject of a criminal investigation—can gain credit in a case that otherwise is appropriate for indictment and prosecution. Of course, the decision not to cooperate by a corporation (or individual) is not itself evidence of misconduct, at least where the lack of cooperation does not involve criminal misconduct or demonstrate consciousness of guilt (*e.g.*, suborning perjury or false statements, or refusing to comply with lawful discovery requests). Thus, failure to cooperate, in and of itself, does not support or require the filing of charges with respect to a corporation any more than with respect to an individual.

A. General Principle: In order for a company to receive any consideration for cooperation under this section, the company must identify all individuals involved in or responsible for the misconduct at issue, regardless of their position, status or seniority, and provide to the Department all facts relating to that misconduct. If a company seeking cooperation credit declines to learn of such facts or to provide the Department with complete factual information about the individuals involved, its cooperation will not be considered a mitigating factor under this section. Nor, if a company is prosecuted, will the Department support a cooperation-related reduction at sentencing. *See* U.S.S.G. §8C2.5(g), cmt. (n. 13) ("A prime test of whether the organization has disclosed all pertinent information" necessary to receive a cooperation-related reduction in its offense level calculation "is whether the information is sufficient . . . to identify . . . the individual(s) responsible for the criminal conduct."). If a company meets the threshold requirement of providing all relevant facts with respect to individuals, it will be eligible for consideration for cooperation credit. To be clear, a company is not required to waive its attorney-client privilege and attorney work product protection in order satisfy this threshold. *See* USAM 9-28.720. The extent of the cooperation credit earned will depend on all the various factors that have traditionally applied in making this assessment (*e.g.*, the timeliness of the cooperation, the diligence, thoroughness and speed of the internal investigation, and the proactive nature of the cooperation).

B. Comment: In investigating wrongdoing by or within a corporation, a prosecutor may encounter several obstacles resulting from the nature of the corporation itself. It may be difficult to determine which individual took which action on behalf of the corporation. Lines of authority and responsibility may be shared among operating divisions or departments, and records and personnel may be spread throughout the United States or even among several countries. Where the criminal conduct continued over an extended period of time, the culpable or knowledgeable personnel may have been promoted, transferred, or fired, or they may have quit or retired. Accordingly, a corporation's cooperation may be critical in identifying potentially relevant actors and locating relevant evidence, among other things, and in doing so expeditiously.

This dynamic—*i.e.*, the difficulty of determining what happened, where the evidence is, and which individuals took or promoted putatively illegal corporate actions—can have negative consequences for both the government and the corporation that is the subject or target of a government investigation. More specifically, because of corporate attribution principles concerning actions of corporate officers and employees, *see* USAM 9.28-210, uncertainty about who authorized or directed apparent corporate misconduct can inure to the detriment of a corporation. For example, it may not matter under the law which of several possible executives or leaders in a chain of command approved of or authorized criminal conduct; however, that information if known might bear on the propriety of a particular disposition short of indictment of the corporation. It may not be in the interest of a corporation or the government for a charging decision to be made in the absence of such information, which might occur if, for example, a statute of limitations were relevant and authorization by any one of the officials were enough to justify a charge under the law. Moreover, a protracted government investigation of such an issue could disrupt the corporation's business operations or even depress its stock price.

For these reasons and more, cooperation can be a favorable course for both the government and the corporation. Cooperation benefits the government by allowing prosecutors and federal agents, for example, to avoid protracted delays, which compromise their ability to quickly uncover and address the full extent of widespread corporate crimes. With cooperation by the corporation, the government may be able to reduce tangible losses, limit damage to reputation, and preserve assets for restitution. At the same time, cooperation may benefit the corporation—and ultimately shareholders, employees, and other often blameless victims—by enabling the government to focus its investigative resources in a manner that will not unduly disrupt the corporation's legitimate business operations. In addition, cooperation may benefit the corporation by presenting it with the opportunity to earn credit for its efforts. . . .

NOTES AND QUESTIONS

1. While the USAM is internally binding on federal prosecutors, its "principles" are unenforceable in court. Nevertheless, 9-28.750 states that counsel who believe a prosecutor is violating these principles should raise their concerns with the United States Attorney or Assistant Attorney General; hence, the principles are likely to figure prominently in discussions between prosecutors and corporate counsel, and in the appeals to supervisors and Main Justice that firms often take in the wake of adverse decisions by a U.S. Attorney's Office.

2. Note that the principles explicitly instruct prosecutors to consider a corporation's blameworthiness when deciding whether to indict. Does this reduce the need for a due diligence defense (discussed below)? Keep in mind that prosecutors' assessments of corporate culpability are neither transparent nor subject to judicial review. Is prosecutorial discretion in this area likely to save the least culpable from prosecution? Or might it result in disparate treatment for corporations based on their reputations, community connections, and other matters not related to culpability? For a thorough and interesting exploration of federal enforcement actions against publicity held corporations over the last decade, see Brandon L. Garrett, Too Big to Jail: How Prosecutors Compromise with Corporations (2014).

4. PROSPECTS FOR THE FUTURE

Corporate liability doctrine may well evolve. It certainly has been subject to sustained attack by business interests and others worried about prosecutorial abuses. See Andrew Weissmann, *supra*, and the citations in the discussion below. Though the renewed zest for white-collar enforcement—especially in recent years—may further concern these critics, there is no reason to assume that we are at a stable equilibrium point in doctrinal development. What might the federal law of criminal liability for an artificial entity look like in the future?

a. Due Diligence Defense?

What if a firm has not only promulgated rules barring the conduct of the agent that gave rise to corporate liability, but has also made a real (although perhaps unsuccessful) effort to ensure that its agents comply with those rules? Under §2.07(5) of the Model Penal Code's corporate liability provisions, "it shall be a defense if the defendant proves by a preponderance of evidence that the high managerial agent having supervisory responsibility over the subject matter of the offense employed due diligence to prevent its commission." The MPC's provisions governing corporate criminal liability have a rather wide application in state legislatures and state courts. Approximately 20 states, by statute or judicial decision, follow the main tenets of the MPC approach. At least six of those states afford a due diligence defense to corporations. Additionally, consider the large corporate compliance industry that has sprung up in the shadow of federal criminal liability and, perhaps more importantly, broad civil regulatory liability. See Miriam Baer, Corporate Policing and Corporate Governance: What Can We Learn from Hewlett-Packard's Pretexting Scandal?, 77 U. Cin. L. Rev. 523 (2008). Were federal law to have a due diligence defense, these compliance regimes would offer firms some protection against prosecution as a matter of law, not just as a matter of prosecutorial discretion.

Yet federal criminal law doctrine offers no such protection. For purposes of imposing criminal liability, federal law is quite different from the Model Penal Code. In United States v. Ionia Mgmt. S.A., 555 F.3d 303 (2d Cir. 2009), the Second Circuit rejected the argument made by a broad coalition of business interests to recognize a due diligence defense, Brief for Ass'n of Corporate Counsel et al. as Amici Curiae in Support of Appellant, United States v. Ionia Mgmt. S.A., No. 07-5801-CR (2d Cir. 2009). The court explained:

> [W]e refuse to adopt the suggestion that the prosecution, in order to establish vicarious liability, should have to prove as a separate element in its case-in-chief that the corporation lacked effective policies and procedures to deter and detect criminal actions by its employees. . . . Adding such an element is contrary to the precedent of our Circuit on this issue. . . . As the District Court instructed the jury here, a corporate compliance program may be relevant to whether an employee was acting in the scope of his employment, but it is not a separate element.

Id. at 310.

Given that corporations facing serious criminal sanctions have a right to a jury trial, see Southern Union Co. v. United States, 567 U.S. 343 (2012), one wonders what the evidence would be on "due diligence" and how jurors would assess it. Are the courtroom and the rules of evidence fit means to decide whether a company had a good compliance program in place? Viewed from this perspective, and recognizing that "due diligence" will be a major part of the pitch that a firm makes to prosecutors to avoid prosecution, the question becomes not whether due diligence should be considered, but where and by whom.

Moreover, it would be wrong to conclude that current federal criminal law, broadly understood, has no interest in the due diligence of a corporate defendant. While a corporate defendant's efforts to ensure that its employees are law-abiding are not considered during the guilt phase of a case, these efforts are important in the sentencing phase. The United States Sentencing Commission's Guidelines for the sentencing of artificial entities, first issued in 1991, give significant weight to the defendant's compliance programs, reducing his culpability by up to three levels. See U.S.S.G. §8C2.5(f). The Guidelines' provisions relating to compliance programs remain influential notwithstanding their non-binding nature after United States v. Booker, 543 U.S. 220 (2006), discussed in the previous chapter. See Andrew Weissmann & David Newman, Rethinking Corporate Criminal Liability, 82 Ind. L.J. 411, 446 (2007). Indeed, "the Guidelines are still widely relied on by corporations and their advisors for the model they provide for an effective internal control system." Id.

Section 8B of the Guidelines offers a detailed picture of a satisfactory compliance program. Companies with effective programs fulfill the following seven objectives:

(1) Establish standards and procedures to prevent and detect criminal conduct; (2) Ensure leaders understand and oversee the compliance program in order to verify its effectiveness and the adequacy of support for the program and that specific individuals are vested with the authority and responsibility to implement the program; (3) Use reasonable efforts to deny leadership positions to people who have engaged in illegal activities or other misconduct; (4) Communicate periodically the standards and procedures of the compliance program to the employees, and conduct effective training programs; (5) Monitor and audit employee conduct, evaluate the effectiveness of the compliance program, and maintain reporting mechanisms for employees who become aware of misconduct; (6) Provide incentives for employees to perform in accordance with the compliance program, and impose disciplinary measures against personnel who engaged in criminal conduct, and; (7) Respond quickly to allegations of criminal conduct and modify aspects of the compliance program, if necessary.

Id. By reducing culpability for companies with well-designed compliance programs, the Sentencing Commission has effectively created two "degrees" of corporate crime: "first degree" for corporations with nonexistent or failing compliance programs, and "second degree" for those with quality programs in place. Does this reality, like prosecutorial discretion pre-indictment, diminish the need for a due diligence defense at the guilt phase of a trial? Consider that a due diligence defense would absolve a corporation of liability by virtue of its having employed a compliance program that *failed to work*. Factoring in compliance programs at the charging and sentencing phase, by contrast, holds companies accountable for the actions of their agents, as well as for the failures of their compliance programs. Accordingly, is the status quo more just than some might suggest?

b.   Limitation to High-Level Corporate Officials?

Alternatively, entity liability could turn strictly on whether or not high-level managers authorized, or were at least aware of, the misconduct. In addition to providing a due diligence defense when the underlying criminal action was undertaken by a low-level employee, discussed above, the Model Penal Code provides for respondeat superior liability without such a defense only where the offense was "authorized, requested, commanded, performed or recklessly tolerated by the board of directors or by a high managerial agent acting on behalf of the corporation within the scope of his office or employment." Model Penal Code §2.07(1)(c) (1981). A variant of this approach would limit criminal liability to where the corporate "ethos encourages criminal conduct by agents of the corporation." Pamela H. Bucy, Corporate Ethos: A Standard for Imposing Criminal Liability, 75 Minn. L. Rev. 1095, 1121 (1991); see also Hamdani & Klement, *supra* (arguing that harsh corporate penalties may distort firms' incentives to monitor for misconduct, and that more lenient regimes—such as holding firms liable only for pervasive misconduct—might bolster compliance incentives within organizations). For more critiques of the sweeping scope of respondeat superior liability, see, e.g., Jennifer Arlen, The Potentially Perverse Effects of Corporate Criminal Liability, 23 J. Leg. Stud. 833 (1994); Khanna, *supra*; Jennifer Arlen & Reinier Kraakman, Controlling Corporate Misconduct: An Analysis of Corporate Liability Regimes, 72 N.Y.U. L. Rev. 687 (1997); Daniel R. Fischel & Alan O. Sykes, Corporate Crime, 25 J. Legal Stud. 319, 321 (1996).

What about a regime in which DPAs and NPAs are used more selectively—only in cases where they will likely aid in the prosecution of criminally responsible, high-level corporate officials? For a firm plagued by policing agency costs (where senior managers did not act to deter or report wrongdoing because they personally benefitted from the deficiencies), a settlement agreement might be appropriate for the firm if the firm provides investigators with evidence of individual criminal liability. Though from the individuals' perspective, the firm is "throwing them under the bus," this outcome may be socially desirable. In other words, even if NPAs and DPAs with sanctions targeted at the firm are not a sufficient or cost-justified way to effect the desired internal governance changes—see Jennifer Arlen & Marcel Kahan, Corporate Governance Regulation through Nonprosecution, 84 U. Chi. L. Rev. 323 (2017)—they may be justified as another investigatory tool in the prosecution of individuals.

Others believe that the present federal regime—with widespread use of DPAs and NPAs even in the absence of individuals being prosecuted—is also socially beneficial. See, e.g., Beale, *supra*. Doesn't criminal respondeat superior liability—what sometimes amounts to treating a corporation as a criminal scapegoat—provide a powerful incentive for corporations to monitor employee behavior to ensure compliance with the criminal law, and more generally, to develop a law-abiding cultural ethos? See, e.g., Peter J. Henning, Corporate Criminal Liability and the Potential for Rehabilitation, 46 Am. Crim. L. Rev. 1417 (2009). Or is there simply not enough data on the "relationship between preventing crime at the corporate level and at the individual level" to reach such an optimistic conclusion? Brandon L. Garrett, The Corporate Criminal as Scapegoat, 101 Va. L. Rev. 1789, 1852 (2015).

c.   Increased Judicial Oversight of Deferred and Non-Prosecution Agreements?

A common concern with DPAs and NPAs is that they "are negotiated without judicial oversight or the discipline imposed by grand jury indictments and trial." Geraldine Szott Moohr, The Balance Among Corporate Criminal Liability, Private Civil Suits, and Regulatory Enforcement, 46 Am. Crim. L. Rev. 1459, 1460 (2009). To be sure, judges are involved at the inception of a DPA, which requires a judicial order tolling the Speedy Trial Act's time requirements for the duration of the DPA. See 18 U.S.C. §3161(h)(2) (excluding "[a]ny period of delay during which prosecution is deferred by the attorney for the Government pursuant to written agreement with the defendant, with the approval of the court, for the purpose of allowing the defendant to demonstrate his good conduct"). While this tolling provision clearly contemplated DPAs with individual defendants—the Speedy Trial Act having been enacted in 1974—its terms encompass corporate DPAs as well. In the HSBC case mentioned above in connection with monitors' reports, then-Judge Gleeson noted the necessary judicial involvement at a DPA's inception and asserted "supervisory power" to monitor the implementation of the DPA. Both HSBC and DOJ sought review in the Second Circuit, where Professor Garrett argued in an amicus brief that "whether to approve a DPA" pursuant to the Speedy Trial Act "is necessarily combined with substantive review of [the terms of the DPA] and is joined with ongoing supervision of the case." Brief for Amicus Curiae Professor Brandon L. Garrett in Support of Appellee at 26, United States v. HSBC Bank USA, N.A, No.16-308, 2017 WL 2960617 (2d Cir. July 12, 2017). The Court of Appeals rejected Professor Garrett's argument. HSBC, supra, 2017 WL 2960617. Its decision effectively reduces the judicial approval of DPAs set forth in the Speedy Trial Act to a rubber stamp. The court expressed agreement with a recent decision by the D.C. Circuit, which held that courts may not reject deferred prosecution agreements based on the inadequacy of charging decisions or agreement conditions, because these determinations are within the purview of the executive, not judicial, branch. United States v. Fokker Servs. B.V., 818 F.3d 733 (D.C. Cir. 2016). See also Recent Case, United States v. Fokker Serv. B.V., 130 Harv. L. Rev. 1048 (2017). As to NPAs—they, of course, are not even filed in a court, much less subject to judicial approval.

Given the control vested in DOJ regarding NPAs and DPAs, the exercise of prosecutorial discretion, rather than legal doctrine, "governs" diversion agreements. Do you think that increased judicial oversight of DPAs and NPAs result in better agreements? Bring more transparency to the process? Do judges bring a special competence or knowledge to the process, or is the argument simply that they are a neutral third party that can focus on the public interest, without the risk of self-dealing that comes with a being a party that bears a litigation risk (a question that assumes the public interest is distinct from the Government's litigation risk)? Or might judicial involvement actually frustrate the purpose of prosecution agreements, which are specifically designed to avoid the considerable expense and time commitment of a trial? A 2009 GAO report found that most judges, prosecutors, monitors, and even company representatives think that the disadvantages of increased judicial involvement outweigh the benefits. See Eileen R. Larence, U.S. Gov't Accountability Office, Highlights of GAO-10-110: DOJ Has Taken Steps to Better Track Its Use of Deferred and Non-Prosecution Agreements, but Should Evaluate Effectiveness (2009).

To be sure, some strong voices believe greater judicial involvement is warranted. Judge Gleeson, in his original order approving HSBC's DPA, saw a need for supervisory authority over DPAs because "it is easy to imagine circumstances in which a deferred prosecution agreement, or the implementation of such an agreement, so transgresses the bounds of lawfulness or propriety as to warrant judicial intervention to protect the integrity of the Court." United States v. HSBC Bank USA, N.A., 2013 WL 3306161, at *6 (E.D.N.Y. July 1, 2013). Indeed, by agreeing to keep the underlying prosecution open on its docket while the terms of the DPA are fulfilled, the court is arguably already in a supervisory position. Why not provide for some judicial role in reviewing the agreement's terms? See Paola C. Henry, Individual Accountability for Corporate Crimes After the Yates Memo: Deferred Prosecution Agreements & Criminal Justice Reform, 6 Am. U. Bus. L. Rev. 153 (2016). Perhaps a modest solution could satisfy all parties. In United States v. Saena Tech Corp., 140 F. Supp. 3d 11, 31 (D.D.C. 2015), Judge Emmet G. Sullivan suggested nine guideposts in reviewing DPAs that he said would respect prosecutorial discretion but provide a meaningful check to ensure fairness and adequacy. Would this be too cumbersome or an unconstitutional encroachment upon executive powers? Why do you suppose the Solicitor General did not appeal Judge Sullivan's decision? Whatever the answer to that question, his decision probably has no legs after the D.C. Circuit's decision in *Fokker, supra*, especially now that the Second Circuit has sided with its sister court. It would likely take an Act of Congress, amendment of the Federal Rules of Criminal Procedure, or, conceivably, a change of heart by DOJ to achieve some measure of judicial involvement in the substance and implementation of DPAs.

d. Beyond Entities: The Yates Memo and Individual Accountability

After the stock market crash of 1929, the head of the New York Stock Exchange was tried, convicted, and imprisoned. See Jesse Eisinger, Why Only One Top Banker Went to Jail for the Financial Crisis, N.Y. Times (Apr. 30, 2014). Similarly, in the aftermath of the junk bond bubble of the 1970s, major progenitors of frauds were successfully prosecuted, as were the more than eight hundred individuals who propagated the savings and loan crisis of the 1980s. "And again, the widespread accounting frauds of the 1990s, most vividly represented by Enron and WorldCom, led directly to the successful prosecution of such previously respected CEOs as Jeffrey Skilling and Bernie Ebbers." Jed S. Rakoff, The Financial Crisis: Why Have No High-Level Executives Been Prosecuted, N.Y. Rev. Books (Jan. 9, 2014).

Contrary to what you may have heard, many subprime lenders, mortgage underwriters, and others have been prosecuted since the "Great Recession" of 2008. See Anna Stolley Persky, Great Recession: Where's the Punishment After the Crime?, Wash. Lawyer (May 2014) ("Since fiscal year 2009, the Justice Department has filed nearly 16,000 financial fraud cases against more than 23,000 individuals. More than 4000 of the defendants were involved in mortgage fraud cases."). But only one high-level executive of a major financial institution has been convicted for fraud related to trading in mortgage-backed securities. See Eisinger, *supra* (describing how Credit Suisse fired one of its top bankers and reported him to the U.S. Attorney's Office in the Southern District of New York, which prosecuted him). By now, the statutes of limitations have largely run, leading many to ask why prosecutors were not more aggressive in prosecuting the highest officials in the financial institutions with which it has entered into DPAs and NPAs. A number of reasons have been proposed, including most importantly the difficulty of proving fraudulent intent, materiality, and reliance. Moreover, the government itself was deeply enmeshed in keeping interest rates low to encourage mortgages, and in encouraging financial institutions to provide mortgages to borrowers who would not normally qualify. Almost everyone, including members of Congress and regulators in the executive branch, seems to have expected home prices and markets to rise indefinitely. In these circumstances, one might ask why the bankers are to blame. Compare Rakoff, The Financial Crisis, *supra* (arguing that prosecutors have failed to go after guilty high-level officers), with Daniel C. Richman, Corporate Headhunting, 8 Harv. L. & Pol'y Rev. 265, 268 (2014) (arguing with the premise that significant criminal prosecutions could be brought, and noting the financial collapse is not itself evidence of criminal conduct or fraud). See also Robert Quigley, The Impulse Towards Individual Criminal Punishment After the Financial Crisis, 22 Va. J. Soc. Pol'y & L. 103, 105 (2015) (concluding that under-prosecution of high level executives, while distressing, will be "neither a necessary nor a sufficient cause" of future financial crises).

In response to the concern that criminal financial executive have been given a pass—and the general criticism of DOJ's handling of the aftermath of the financial crisis—Deputy Attorney General Sally Yates issued a memorandum in September 2015 addressing the need for individual accountability in corporate wrongdoing. She listed six steps to deter corporate misdeeds, incentivize changes in corporate culture, and promote the public's confidence in the justice system. See Memorandum from Sally Quillian Yates, Deputy Att'y Gen., U.S. Dep't of Justice, to All U.S. Att'ys et al., Individual Accountability for Corporate Wrongdoing (Sept. 9, 2015). Just two months later, the USAM was revised, and 9-28.010 ("Foundational Principles of Corporate Prosecution") was added to reiterate that "one of the most effective ways to combat corporate misconduct is by holding accountable all individuals who engage in wrongdoing." Focusing on individuals—the actors within corporations—at the outset of an investigation increases prosecutors' "ability to identify the full extent of corporate misconduct" through those most knowledgeable and will also "maximize the likelihood that the final resolution will include charges against culpable individuals and not just the corporation." Id. In the same vein, sections titled "Focus on Individual Wrongdoers" (9-28.210) and "Adequacy of the Prosecution of Individuals" (9-28.1300) were added as well.

Yates, and others at DOJ, have publicly recognized the real world challenges this "Individual Accountability Policy" faces. In a speech to the New York City Bar Association's White Collar Crime Conference, she sought to alleviate the corporate defense bar's concerns and even joked about the "Yates Binders" being created by corporations in an effort to cooperate with identifying individual wrongdoing. See Remarks, Sally Q. Yates, New York City Bar Association White Collar Crime Conference (May 10, 2016). For a comprehensive, data-based analysis of simultaneous corporate and individual prosecutions and their special challenges, see also Garrett, The Corporate Criminal as Scapegoat, *supra*. Some have wondered whether the Yates initiative might have been little more than a symbolic gesture. See Christopher Modlish, The Yates Memo: DOJ Public Relations Move or Meaningful Reform that Will End Impunity for Corporate Criminals?, 58 B.C. L. Rev. 743, 766-67 (2017) (noting that DOJ's failure to prosecute individually culpable actors in Education Management Corporation and General Motors are a sign of the memo's practical ineffectiveness). See also Henry, *supra*, at 161 (arguing that the post-Yates memo Morgan Stanley DPA appeared to be an empty threat). Yet on January 11, 2017, the Department of Justice announced that Volkswagen AG had agreed to plead guilty to three criminal felony counts and pay a $2.8 billion criminal penalty as a result of the company's long-running diesel emissions scam. On that same date, a federal grand jury indicted six VW executives for their roles in the conspiracy, a clear demonstration of the Individual Accountability Policy. Whether the targeting of individuals will continue in the new presidential administration remains to be seen. See Ben Protess and Matt Apuzzo, Justice Department Toughened Approach on Corporate Crime, but Will that Last?, N.Y. Times (Jan. 12, 2017).

e.   Other Ways Forward

To what extent are individual prosecutions preferable to NPAs or DPAs of a corporate entity? Might a third option be more effective? The Yates memo did not address the Department's use—or overuse—of DPAs and NPAs, and, as we've noted, it is unclear how successful these tools have been in fighting corporate crime. Perhaps "Club Fed, Deferred" undermines the public's faith in the criminal justice system. See Reilly, *supra,* at 309. In his 2014 book *Too Big to Jail, supra,* Professor Garrett concludes that these agreements have been largely ineffective. Even though prosecutors try to rehabilitate a company by helping it put systems in place to foster a more ethical culture, these structural reforms have failed. Garrett suggests, however, that instead of abandoning DPAs, DOJ should conduct greater oversight to improve their efficacy. Judge Rakoff, among others, would not agree with this solution. See Jed S. Rakoff, Justice Deferred is Justice Denied, N.Y. Rev. Books (Feb. 19, 2015). Can the vague concept of a "corporate culture" be changed by such agreements? And, even more fundamentally, does the longstanding premise underlying DPAs and NPAs—that collateral consequences of a corporate criminal prosecution are too catastrophic to be tolerated—have empirical support? See Gordon Bourjaily, DPA DOA: How and Why Congress Should Bar the Use of Deferred And Non-Prosecution Agreements in Corporate Criminal Prosecutions, 52 Harv. J. on Legis. 543, 555-56 (2015) (referring to Gabriel Markoff's 2013 empirical study on publicly traded companies that survived convictions, which we noted *supra,* and more recent data points on large financial institutions that likewise survived to support the hypothesis that the "Andersen Effect" only exists in the "imagination of lawyers and business-people").

Perhaps additional initiatives are needed. One strand of the public choice theory of criminal procedure argues that traditional procedural protections for defendants in the common law system are designed to reduce opportunities for abuse by self-interested enforcement agents. As matters now stand, NPAs and DPAs allow the federal government to act in its own self-interest and those of its co-law enforcement agencies (including the SEC and state and foreign counterparts in many cases) by getting fairly quickly to a resolution that sounds tough, especially if the penalties are in the "billions" of dollars. Ferreting out evidence (if evidence exists) of individual *mens rea* and consciousness of guilt would be much harder. These settlement agreements also often benefit companies, who can conduct their own investigations, pay over some agreed-upon amount of money, and move on. Would increased public or third-party oversight hold all actors more accountable? Should prosecutors be required to provide an analysis of the case and publicly explain why the agreement is not accompanied by any individual prosecutions? Or would that unfairly malign individuals whose identities, even if not publicly revealed, can often be inferred? See Garrett, The Corporate Criminal as Scapegoat, *supra,* at 1847 (arguing that individual declinations need not be made public—to protect reputations—but that DOJ should publicly acknowledge and explain why, when a company's employees committed crimes, it is not prosecuting individuals).

Perhaps, on the other hand, the DOJ's options should be reduced, not increased. One idea is to eliminate altogether DPAs and NPAs with publicly held corporations. Investigators and prosecutors would focus entirely on seeking sufficient evidence to convict individuals. See Modlish, *supra,* at 769-70. Of course, a decision to prosecute (an individual or a firm) often ends in a plea bargain. But where an individual defendant enters a plea of guilty, the record is clear as to the elements of the crime that he has committed and to his admission of guilt. This might benefit both would-be corporate defendants, who are often faced with no viable alternative but to fork over huge sums in order to bring the government's investigation to an end, and the public, because company leadership threatened only with forking over money might account for such contingencies as part of the "cost of doing business." Take, for instance, pharmaceutical giant Pfizer, which entered into four DPAs between 2002 and 2012. Its illegal marketing activities continued to be financially lucrative enough to risk yet another fine or hollow DPA. See generally Jed S. Rakoff, Justice Deferred is Justice Denied, *supra.* Eliminating these agreements—or at least reducing the frequency with which DOJ resorts to them—might be of an additional benefit to future corporate defendants, who, as matters now stand, may be disparately treated depending on the politics and priorities of DOJ officials who happen to be at the helm at the relevant time. One may also level at DPAs a criticism that is often leveled at the overwhelming incidence of plea-bargains in individual prosecutions: Without trials or appellate decisions, the boundaries of the law are unclear and are determined largely by prosecutors. See Reilly, *supra,* at 318.

Harder theoretical questions also arise. To what extent should the Justice Department and prosecutorial policy cater to—or, if you prefer, reflect—public opinion? See Sara Sun Beale, The Development and

Evolution of the U.S. Law of Corporate Criminal Liability and the Yates Memo, 46 Stetson L. Rev. 41 (2016).

For now, Professor Garrett has provided the public with a regularly updated Corporate Prosecution Registry to better understand the current enforcement landscape, see Garrett & Ashley, *supra*. As we pore over the data, we must consider under what circumstances criminal stigmatization of a firm is appropriate, and how deeply we want prosecutors — and judges — involved in corporate supervision and governance. What are the goals of criminal prosecution of artificial entities such as corporations? To reform corporate behavior and governance? Or the classic criminal law goals of punishment and deterrence? How different, really, are these corporate criminal resolutions from well-publicized civil settlements?

In this section, we have been examining the low bar that federal doctrine sets for corporate criminal liability and the concomitant leverage that federal prosecutors have to threaten the institution with prosecution unless it "pays-up" for alleged past misdeeds and undertakes remedial measures. The next section considers another way that the criminal law may be used to deter corporate misbehavior: holding corporate executives criminally responsible for corporate misdeeds.

B.   LIABILITY OF "RESPONSIBLE CORPORATE OFFICERS"

Like all natural persons, corporate directors and officers may be liable for any crimes they commit directly or that they aid and abet. See Chapter 8. But may they also be liable for crimes committed by *others* in the corporation or by the corporation itself — crimes that they neither aided nor even knew of? A beginning law student might think the answer must be "no," for while the idea of vicarious criminal liability for the corporate entity has something of a long history (see the Diskant excerpt in the previous section), surely there is no room in our jurisprudence for vicarious *individual* criminal liability. But you know that the answer is "yes," at least when the entity is guilty of a strict liability crime and the officer is in a position of "responsible relation," as we saw in United States v. Dotterweich, 320 U.S. 277, 281 (1943), in Chapter 3. Charged with a strict liability crime, Dotterweich did not need *mens rea* to be convicted. Remember, also that under the "responsible corporate officer" doctrine enunciated in *Dotterweich*, the defendant may have engaged in virtually no *actus reus*. Isn't the idea that someone could be criminally liable for conduct he had no part in and of which he was unaware terribly unsettling?

In the following case, the Supreme Court again grappled with the tricky issue of vicarious criminal liability of individuals.

United States v. Park
421 U.S. 658 (1975)

Mr. Chief Justice BURGER delivered the opinion of the Court.

We granted certiorari to consider whether the jury instructions in the prosecution of a corporate officer under §301(k) of the Federal Food, Drug, and Cosmetic Act, 52 Stat. 1042, as amended, 21 U.S.C. §331(k), were appropriate under United States v. Dotterweich, 320 U.S. 277 (1943).

Acme Markets, Inc., is a national retail food chain with approximately 36,000 employees, 874 retail outlets, 12 general warehouses, and four special warehouses. . . . [R]espondent Park . . . is chief executive officer of the corporation. . . . In a five-count information filed in the United States District Court for the District of Maryland, the Government charged Acme and respondent with violations of the Federal Food, Drug, and Cosmetic Act. Each count of the information alleged that the defendants had received food that had been shipped in interstate commerce and that, while the food was being held for sale in Acme's Baltimore warehouse following shipment in interstate commerce, they caused it to be held in a building accessible to rodents and to be exposed to contamination by rodents. These acts were alleged to have resulted in the food's being adulterated within the meaning of 21 U.S.C. §§342(a)(3) and (4), in violation of 21 U.S.C. §331(k).

Acme pleaded guilty to each count of the information. Respondent pleaded not guilty. The evidence at trial demonstrated that in April 1970 the Food and Drug Administration (FDA) advised respondent by letter of insanitary conditions in Acme's Philadelphia warehouse. In 1971 the FDA found that similar conditions existed in the firm's Baltimore warehouse. An FDA consumer safety officer testified concerning evidence of rodent infestation and other insanitary conditions discovered during a 12-day inspection of the Baltimore warehouse in November and December 1971. He also related that a second inspection of the warehouse had been conducted in March 1972. On that occasion the inspectors found that there had been improvement in the sanitary conditions, but that "there was still evidence of rodent activity in the building and in the warehouses and we found some rodent-contaminated lots of food items."

The Government also presented testimony by the Chief of Compliance of the FDA's Baltimore office, who informed respondent by letter of the conditions at the Baltimore warehouse after the first inspection. There was testimony by Acme's Baltimore division vice president, who had responded to the letter on behalf of Acme and respondent and who described the steps taken to remedy the insanitary conditions discovered by both inspections. The Government's final witness, Acme's vice president for legal affairs and assistant secretary, identified respondent as the president and chief executive officer of the company and read a bylaw prescribing the duties of the chief executive officer. He testified that respondent functioned by delegating "normal operating duties," including sanitation, but that he retained "certain things, which are the big, broad, principles of the operation of the company," and had "the responsibility of seeing that they all work together."

At the close of the Government's case in chief, respondent moved for a judgment of acquittal on the ground that "the evidence in chief has shown that Mr. Park is not personally concerned in this Food and Drug violation.["] The trial judge denied the motion, stating that United States v. Dotterweich, 320 U.S. 277 (1943), was controlling.

Respondent was the only defense witness. He testified that, although all of Acme's employees were in a sense under his general direction, the company had an "organizational structure for responsibilities for certain functions" according to which different phases of its operation were "assigned to individuals who, in turn, have staff and departments under them." He identified those individuals responsible for sanitation, and related that upon receipt of the January 1972 FDA letter, he had conferred with the vice president for legal affairs who informed him that the Baltimore division vice president "was investigating the situation immediately and would be taking corrective action and would be preparing a summary of the corrective action to reply to the letter." Respondent stated that he did not "believe there was anything [he] could have done more constructively than what [he] found was being done."

On cross-examination, respondent conceded that providing sanitary conditions for food offered for sale to the public was something that he was "responsible for in the entire operation of the company," and he stated that it was one of many phases of the company that he assigned to "dependable subordinates." Respondent was asked about and, over the objections of his counsel, admitted receiving, the April 1970 letter addressed to him from the FDA regarding insanitary conditions at Acme's Philadelphia warehouse. He acknowledged that, with the exception of the division vice president, the same individuals had responsibility for sanitation in both Baltimore and Philadelphia. Finally, in response to questions concerning the Philadelphia and Baltimore incidents, respondent admitted that the Baltimore problem indicated the system for handling sanitation "wasn't working perfectly" and that as Acme's chief executive officer he was responsible for "any result which occurs in our company." . . .

The jury found respondent guilty on all counts of the information, and he was subsequently sentenced to pay a fine of $50 on each count.

The Court of Appeals reversed the conviction and remanded for a new trial. That court viewed the Government as arguing "that the conviction may be predicated solely upon a showing that . . . [respondent] was the President of the offending corporation," and it stated that as "a general proposition, some act of commission or omission is an essential element of every crime." 499 F.2d 839, 841 ([4th Cir.] 1974). It reasoned that, although our decision in [*Dotterweich, supra,* at 281], had construed the statutory provisions under which respondent was tried to dispense with the traditional element of "'awareness of some wrongdoing,'" the Court had not construed them as dispensing with the element of "wrongful action." The Court of Appeals concluded that the trial judge's instructions "might well have left the jury with the erroneous impression that Park could be found guilty in the absence of 'wrongful action' on his part," and that proof of this element was required by due process. . . .

We granted certiorari because of an apparent conflict among the Courts of Appeals with respect to the standard of liability of corporate officers under the Federal Food, Drug, and Cosmetic Act as construed in United States v. Dotterweich, *supra,* and because of the importance of the question to the Government's enforcement program. We reverse.

I

The question presented by the Government's petition for certiorari in United States v. Dotterweich, *supra,* and the focus of this Court's opinion, was whether "the manager of a corporation, as well as the corporation itself, may be prosecuted under the Federal Food, Drug, and Cosmetic Act of 1938 for the introduction of misbranded and adulterated articles into interstate commerce." . . .

In reversing the judgment of the Court of Appeals and reinstating Dotterweich's conviction, this Court looked to the purposes of the Act and noted that they "touch phases of the lives and health of people which, in the circumstances of modern industrialism, are largely beyond self-protection." 320 U.S. at 280. It observed that the Act is of "a now familiar type" which "dispenses with the conventional requirement for criminal conduct—awareness of some wrongdoing. In the interest of the larger good it puts the burden of acting at hazard upon a person otherwise innocent but standing in responsible relation to a public danger." Id. at 280-281. . . .

II

The rule that corporate employees who have "a responsible share in the furtherance of the transaction which the statute outlaws" are subject to the criminal provisions of the Act was not formulated in a vacuum. Cf. Morissette v. United States, 342 U.S. 246, 258 (1952). Cases under the Federal Food and Drugs Act of 1906 reflected the view both that knowledge or intent were not required to be proved in prosecutions under its criminal provisions, and that responsible corporate agents could be subjected to the liability thereby imposed. See, e.g., United States v. Mayfield, 177 F. 765 (N.D. Ala. 1910). Moreover, the principle had been recognized that a corporate agent, through whose act, default, or omission the corporation committed a crime, was himself guilty individually of that crime. The principle had been applied whether or not the crime required "consciousness of wrongdoing," and it had been applied not only to those corporate agents who themselves committed the criminal act, but also to those who by virtue of their managerial positions or other similar relation to the actor could be deemed responsible for its commission.

In the latter class of cases, the liability of managerial officers did not depend on their knowledge of, or personal participation in, the act made criminal by the statute. Rather, where the statute under which they were prosecuted dispensed with "consciousness of wrongdoing," an omission or failure to act was deemed a sufficient basis for a responsible corporate agent's liability. It was enough in such cases that, by virtue of the relationship he bore to the corporation, the agent had the power to prevent the act complained of.

The rationale of the interpretation given the Act in *Dotterweich*, as holding criminally accountable the persons whose failure to exercise the authority and supervisory responsibility reposed in them by the business organization resulted in the violation complained of, has been confirmed in our subsequent cases. Thus, the Court has reaffirmed the proposition that the public interest in the purity of its food is so great as "to warrant the imposition of the highest standard of care on distributors." Smith v. California, 361 U.S. 147, 152 (1959). In order to make "distributors of food the strictest censors of their merchandise," ibid., the Act punishes "neglect where the law requires care, or inaction where it imposes a duty." Morissette v. United States, *supra*, at 255. "The accused, if he does not will the violation, usually is in a position to prevent it with no more care than society might reasonably expect and no more exertion than it might reasonably exact from one who assumed his responsibilities." Id. at 256. Cf. Hughes, Criminal Omissions, 67 Yale L.J. 590 (1958). Similarly, in cases decided after *Dotterweich*, the Courts of Appeals have recognized that those corporate agents vested with the responsibility, and power commensurate with that responsibility, to devise whatever measures are necessary to ensure compliance with the Act bear a "responsible relationship" to, or have a "responsible share" in, violations.

Thus *Dotterweich* and the cases which have followed reveal that in providing sanctions which reach and touch the individuals who execute the corporate mission — and this is by no means necessarily confined to a single corporate agent or employee — the Act imposes not only a positive duty to seek out and remedy violations when they occur but also, and primarily, a duty to implement measures that will insure that violations will not occur. The requirements of foresight and vigilance imposed on responsible corporate agents are beyond question demanding, and perhaps onerous, but they are no more stringent than the public has a right to expect of those who voluntarily assume positions of authority in business enterprises whose services and products affect the health and well-being of the public that supports them. Cf. Wasserstrom, Strict Liability in the Criminal Law, 12 Stan. L. Rev. 731, 741-45 (1960). . . .

The theory upon which responsible corporate agents are held criminally accountable for "causing" violations of the Act permits a claim that a defendant was "powerless" to prevent or correct the violation to "be raised defensively at a trial on the merits." United States v. Wiesenfeld Warehouse Co., 376 U.S. 86, 91 (1964). If such a claim is made, the defendant has the burden of coming forward with evidence, but this does not alter the Government's ultimate burden of proving beyond a reasonable doubt the defendant's guilt, including his power, in light of the duty imposed by the Act, to prevent or correct the prohibited condition. Congress has seen fit to enforce the accountability of responsible corporate agents dealing with products which may affect the health of consumers by penal sanctions cast in rigorous terms, and the obligation of the courts is to give them effect so long as they do not violate the Constitution.

III

We cannot agree with the Court of Appeals that it was incumbent upon the District Court to instruct the jury that the Government had the burden of establishing "wrongful action" in the sense in which the Court of Appeals used that phrase. The concept of a "responsible relationship" to, or a "responsible share" in, a violation of the Act indeed imports some measure of blameworthiness; but it is equally clear that the Government establishes a prima facie case when it introduces evidence sufficient to warrant a finding by the trier of the facts that the defendant had, by reason of his position in the corporation, responsibility and authority either to prevent in the first instance, or promptly to correct, the violation complained of, and that he failed to do so. The failure thus to fulfill the duty imposed by the interaction of the corporate agent's authority and the statute furnishes a sufficient causal link. The considerations which prompted the imposition of this duty, and the scope of the duty, provide the measure of culpability.

Turning to the jury charge in this case, . . . [we are satisfied] that the jury's attention was adequately focused on the issue of respondent's authority with respect to the conditions that formed the basis of the alleged violations. Viewed as a whole, the charge did not permit the jury to find guilt solely on the basis of respondent's position in the corporation; rather, it fairly advised the jury that to find guilt it must find respondent "had a responsible relation to the situation," and "by virtue of his position . . . had . . . authority and responsibility" to deal with the situation. The situation referred to could only be "food . . . held in unsanitary conditions in a warehouse with the result that it consisted, in part, of filth or . . . may have been contaminated with filth." . . .

The record in this case reveals that the jury could not have failed to be aware that the main issue for determination was not respondent's position in the corporate hierarchy, but rather his accountability, because of the responsibility and authority of his position, for the conditions which gave rise to the charges against him. . . .

Finally, we note that there was no request for an instruction that the Government was required to prove beyond a reasonable doubt that respondent was not without the power or capacity to affect the conditions which founded the charges in the information. . . .

Mr. Justice STEWART, with whom Mr. Justice MARSHALL and Mr. Justice POWELL join, dissenting.

Although agreeing with much of what is said in the Court's opinion, I dissent from the opinion and judgment, because the jury instructions in this case were not consistent with the law as the Court today expounds it.

As I understand the Court's opinion, it holds that in order to sustain a conviction under §301(k) of the Federal Food, Drug, and Cosmetic Act the prosecution must at least show that by reason of an individual's corporate position and responsibilities, he had a duty to use care to maintain the physical integrity of the corporation's food products. A jury may then draw the inference that when the food is found to be in such condition as to violate the statute's prohibitions, that condition was "caused" by a breach of the standard of care imposed upon the responsible official. This is the language of negligence, and I agree with it.

To affirm this conviction, however, the Court must approve the instructions given to the members of the jury who were entrusted with determining whether the respondent was innocent or guilty. Those instructions did not conform to the standards that the Court itself sets out today.

The trial judge instructed the jury to find Park guilty if it found beyond a reasonable doubt that Park "had a responsible relation to the situation. . . . The issue is, in this case, whether the Defendant, John R. Park, by virtue of his position in the company, had a position of authority and responsibility in the situation out of which these charges arose." Requiring, as it did, a verdict of guilty upon a finding of "responsibility," this instruction standing alone could have been construed as a direction to convict if the jury found Park "responsible" for the condition in the sense that his position as chief executive officer gave him formal responsibility within the structure of the corporation. But the trial judge went on specifically to caution the jury not to attach such a meaning to his instruction, saying that "the fact that the Defendant is pres[id]ent and is a chief executive officer of the Acme Markets does not require a finding of guilt." "Responsibility" as used by the trial judge therefore had whatever meaning the jury in its unguided discretion chose to give it.

The instructions, therefore, expressed nothing more than a tautology. They told the jury: "You must find the defendant guilty if you find that he is to be held accountable for this adulterated food." In other words: "You must find the defendant guilty if you conclude that he is guilty." The trial judge recognized the infirmities in these instructions, but he reluctantly concluded he was required to give such a charge under [*Dotterweich*], which, he thought, in declining to define "responsible relation" had declined to specify the minimum standard of liability for criminal guilt.

As the Court today recognizes, the *Dotterweich* case did not deal with what kind of conduct must be proved to support a finding of criminal guilt under the Act. *Dotterweich* was concerned, rather, with the statutory definition of "person"—with what kind of corporate employees were even "subject to the criminal provisions of the Act." *Ante*, at 670. The Court held that those employees with "a responsible relation" to the violative transaction or condition were subject to the Act's criminal provisions, but all that the Court had to say with respect to the kind of conduct that can constitute criminal guilt was that the Act "dispenses with the conventional requirement for criminal conduct—awareness of some wrongdoing." 320 U.S. at 281.

In approving the instructions to the jury in this case—instructions based upon what the Court concedes was a misunderstanding of *Dotterweich*—the Court approves a conspicuous departure from the long and firmly established division of functions between judge and jury in the administration of criminal justice. As the Court put the matter more than 80 years ago:

> "We must hold firmly to the doctrine that in the courts of the United States it is the duty of juries in criminal cases to take the law from the court and apply that law to the facts as they find them to be from the evidence. Upon the court rests the responsibility of declaring the law; upon the jury, the responsibility of applying the law so declared to the facts as they, upon their conscience, believe them to be. Under any other system, the courts, although established in order to declare the law, would for every practical purpose be eliminated from our system of government as instrumentalities devised for the protection equally of society and of individuals in their essential rights. When that occurs our government will cease to be a government of laws, and become a government of men. Liberty regulated by law is the underlying principle of our institutions." Sparf v. United States, 156 U.S. 51, 102-103 (1895). . . .

The instructions given by the trial court in this case, it must be emphasized, were a virtual nullity, a mere authorization to convict if the jury thought it appropriate. Such instructions—regardless of the blameworthiness of the defendant's conduct, regardless of the social value of the Food, Drug, and Cosmetic Act, and regardless of the importance of convicting those who violate it—have no place in our jurisprudence.

We deal here with a criminal conviction, not a civil forfeiture. It is true that the crime was but a misdemeanor and the penalty in this case light. But under the statute even a first conviction can result in imprisonment for a year, and a subsequent offense is a felony carrying a punishment of up to three years in prison. So the standardless conviction approved today can serve in another case tomorrow to support a felony conviction and a substantial prison sentence. However highly the Court may regard the social objectives of the Food, Drug, and Cosmetic Act, that regard cannot serve to justify a criminal conviction so wholly alien to fundamental principles of our law.

The *Dotterweich* case stands for two propositions, and I accept them both. First, "any person" within the meaning of 21 U.S.C. §333 may include any corporate officer or employee "standing in responsible relation" to a condition or transaction forbidden by the Act. 320 U.S. at 281. Second, a person may be convicted of a criminal offense under the Act even in the absence of "the conventional requirement for criminal conduct—awareness of some wrongdoing." Ibid.

But before a person can be convicted of a criminal violation of this Act, a jury must find—and must be clearly instructed that it must find—evidence beyond a reasonable doubt that he engaged in wrongful conduct amounting at least to common law negligence. There were no such instructions, and clearly, therefore, no such finding in this case.

For these reasons, I cannot join the Court in affirming Park's criminal conviction.

NOTES AND QUESTIONS

1. Like the doctrine of corporate criminal liability in the federal courts, the "responsible relation" or "responsible corporate officer" (RCO) doctrine of *Park* and *Dotterweich* is judge-made criminal law. This should come as no surprise. As this volume has repeatedly noted, courts play a large role in determining the scope of statutory criminal prohibitions.

2. *Park* did not explicitly articulate the mental state required for a conviction under the RCO doctrine, but some commentators have argued that the Court used "the language of negligence," as the dissent put it, at least with regard to violations of the FDCA. See, e.g., John Bentivoglio, Jennifer Bragg & Andrew Collins, Onus of Responsibility: The Changing Responsible Corporate Officer Doctrine, 65 Food Drug L.J. 525, 531 (2010). The *Park* majority held that Congress had imposed on RCOs a "positive duty to seek out and remedy violations when they occur but also, and primarily, a duty to implement measures that will insure that violations will not occur." *Park*,

421 U.S. at 672. Is this the language of negligence? Or strict liability? How persuasive is the dissent's characterization that a conviction under this language requires the satisfaction of two propositions: 1) that "by reason of an individual's corporate position and responsibilities, he had a duty to use care to maintain the physical integrity of the corporation's food products"; and 2) that the condition violating the FDCA "was 'caused' by a breach of the standard of care imposed upon the responsible official"? Id. at 678-79 (Stewart, J., dissenting). Note, too, that even though the majority seemed to confirm that violation of the FDCA is a public welfare offense with no clear *mens rea* requirement, it provided for an "impossibility" defense (which *Dotterweich* did not) and never used the term "strict liability." Nor did the Court "provide the explanation that an extraordinary strict and vicarious liability criminal standard would seem to require." Bentivoglio, Bragg & Collins, *supra*, at 531.

Consider also the justifications for strict criminal liability, which concern safety and public welfare, and for vicarious criminal liability, which generally concern the close relationship between the wrong and the defendant. See Amy J. Sepinwall, Faultless Guilt: Toward a Relationship-Based Account of Criminal Liability, 54 Am. Crim. L. Rev. 521, 526 (2017). Did *Park* enunciate either set of justifications? See also Jennifer Bragg et al., Onus of Responsibility: The Changing Responsible Corporate Officer Doctrine, 65 Food & Drug L.J. 525, 529 (2010) (arguing that it was unlikely that, under the FDCA, "Congress intended to create a strict *and vicarious* liability crime, in which an individual can be guilty through the acts of others and with no *mens rea*" and that, in the line of cases invoking *Park*, the defendants have "nearly always been alleged to have either had knowledge of the underlying violation, participated to some extent in the wrongdoing, or both").

3. The argument can be made that the Supreme Court's reasoning in *Park* and *Dotterweich* is firmly within our common law tradition. Wasn't the defendant in each case guilty of an omission that, because he had a duty to act, constitutes the *actus reus* of the crime? Seen in this light, the "responsible corporate officer" doctrine is simply a recognition that where there is a duty, failure to act satisfies the common law's "act" requirement. This is hardly novel or cause for concern. See Todd S. Aagaard, A Fresh Look at the Responsible Relation Doctrine, 96 J. Crim. L. & Criminology 1245 (2006). But see Brief for Amici Curiae the National Association of Manufacturers and the CATO Institute Supporting Appellants and Reversal at 12, United States v. DeCoster, Nos. 15-1890, 15-1891, 828 F.3d 626 (8th Cir. 2016) ("The notion that any executive can be sent to prison because a subordinate committed a criminal a [sic] regulatory offense without his or her knowledge is incompatible with our established principles of fairness and justice.").

4. Other commentators have insisted that the Court in *Dotterweich* and *Park* did more than recognize that an omission can be an act. In their view, the Court has created a form of vicarious liability, where the crime of the

corporation is imputed to all responsible officers of the corporation. See, e.g., Sepinwall, *supra*, 564-65 (arguing it is perfectly appropriate to blame the CEO by reason of his enlarged sense of agency within a group and that, in fact, "he owes it to *us* to [accept that blame]"). See generally Charles J. Babbitt et al., Discretion and the Criminalization of Environmental Law, 15 Duke Envtl. L. & Pol'y F. 1 (2004); Noel Wise, Personal Liability Promotes Responsible Conduct: Extending the Responsible Corporate Officer Doctrine to Federal Civil Environmental Enforcement Cases, 21 Stan. Envtl. L.J. 283, 319 n.187 (2002); Cynthia H. Finn, Comment, The Responsible Corporate Officer, Criminal Liability, and Mens Rea: Limitations on the RCO Doctrine, 46 Am. U. L. Rev. 543, 567-68 (1966). Under this interpretation, the RCO doctrine would apply even where the statute could not be characterized as imposing "strict liability" (or "strict liability cum negligence," as suggested by Note 2, *supra*). See Brenda S. Hustis & John Y. Gotanda, The Responsible Corporate Officer: Designated Felon or Legal Fiction?, 25 Loy. U. Chi. L.J. 169, 170 (1994) ("[L]iability [could] be based solely on a person's position and authority in a corporation, thus displacing any express statutory *mens rea* requirement and creating a strict liability offense that is punishable as a felony."). Some of these commentators urge broad application of the RCO principle even to prohibitions that clearly have a *mens rea* requirement.

United States v. Brittain, 931 F.2d 1413 (10th Cir. 1991), has been credited with "offering the most expansive view" of the RCO doctrine. See Finn, *supra*, at 565. The provision of the Clean Water Act of which Brittain was convicted provides criminal sanctions for "any person" who "willfully or negligently" violates the discharge permit issued by the EPA. In dicta, the court stated that under its interpretation of the RCO doctrine, a responsible corporate officer would be criminally liable even if he personally did not "willfully or negligently" cause the permit violation. *Brittain*, 931 F.2d at 1419. "Instead, the willfulness or negligence of the actor would be imputed to him by virtue of his position or responsibility." Id. But do these commentators and the court in *Brittain* read *Park* correctly? Note that *Park* says nothing about application of the RCO doctrine to felonies that have a *mens rea* requirement of knowledge or negligence. Might this suggest that the Court meant to leave the question open? Is it better to read the RCO doctrine, created by the Court in two cases involving strict liability crimes, as applicable only to these offenses? If *Park* is solely about vicarious imputation of the *actus reas* of the crime, then the Tenth Circuit's assertion that *mens rea* could also be vicariously imputed is simply "regrettable dicta," Aagaard, *supra*, at 1259-60 (also expressing bewilderment that at another point in the opinion, the Tenth Circuit "specifically noted that Brittain was not prosecuted under the responsible corporate officer doctrine").

In fact, *Brittain* does appear to be an "unfortunate" outlier. See id. at 1260. Most courts have assumed that the responsible corporate officer doctrine does not alter statutory mental state requirements, id., and have declined to reduce the government's burden to meet a clear *mens rea* standard required by certain crimes such as the Resource Conservation and Recovery Act (RCRA). See 42 U.S.C. §6928(d) (imposing criminal penalties on any person who "knowingly" transports, treats, stores, or disposes of hazardous waste). In United States v. White, 766 F. Supp. 873 (E.D. Wash. 1991), a district court rejected the government's attempt to prosecute a defendant for RCRA violations under the RCO doctrine without the requisite specific intent. And in United States v. MacDonald & Watson Waste Oil Co., 933 F.2d 35, 52 (1st Cir. 1991), the court vacated a corporate officer's conviction of knowingly transporting hazardous waste without a permit (a felony under RCRA) because the district court improperly instructed the jury "that proof that [the defendant] was a responsible corporate officer would conclusively provide the element of his knowledge." The court pointed out that it knew "of no precedent for failing to give effect to a knowledge requirement that Congress has expressly included in a criminal statute." Id. See also United States v. Hanousek, 176 F.3d 1116, 1120 (9th Cir. 1999) (holding that the defendant must be shown to have been negligent, though not "criminally negligent," to be liable as an RCO under the Clean Water Act). Justice Thomas, joined by Justice O'Connor, dissented from the denial of certiorari. Hanousek v. United States, 528 U.S. 1102. While the dissent did not address the RCO doctrine, it targeted a related 20th century doctrinal invention, that of "public welfare offenses," where a lesser *mens rea* passes muster, and cited Morissette v. United States, 342 U.S. 146 (1952) and Staples v. United States, 511 U.S. 600 (1994), both of which you studied in Chapter 3.

5. Consider the potential defenses, or lack thereof, in a RCO prosecution. The Court said that if Park had been "powerless" to prevent the violation, he could not be held liable. The word "powerless" suggests an absolute rather than a probabilistic analysis. Is this practical in the real world? What would constitute proof of "powerlessness"? See, e.g., United States v. New England Grocers Supply Co., 488 F. Supp. 230, 235-36 (D. Mass. 1980) (discussing various interpretations of the powerlessness defense). Some courts have construed *Park*'s powerlessness language as giving rise to an affirmative defense. See, e.g., id.; United States v. Gel Spice Co., 773 F.2d 427 (2d Cir. 1985); United States v. Y. Hata & Co., 535 F.2d 508, 510-12 (9th Cir. 1976). In *Park* itself, the Court noted that the defendant did not request an instruction requiring the government to prove "powerlessness" beyond a reasonable doubt. Does that imply that such an instruction must be given if requested? Suppose that such an instruction had been given in *Park*; would it have made any difference?

What if, in addition to the defense of powerlessness, executives charged as RCOs could invoke a due diligence defense much like the one proposed in the corporate criminal liability context? (See Section A of this chapter.) In this scenario, executives whose companies employed muscular compliance systems would enjoy an affirmative defense to liability. Does *Park*'s use of the "language of negligence" suggest that had Park implemented an aggressive compliance program, the court would have been open to such a defense? What would be the effect of adding a due diligence defense? Whatever its flaws, the present RCO doctrine gives executives an incentive to root out wrongdoing, lest they find it blamed on them in federal court.

6. Park *Redux*. One of the cases mentioned in Note 5, *New England Grocers Supply Co.*, 488 F. Supp. 230 (D. Mass. 1980), was decided only five years after *Park* and is nothing less than a *Park* redux. The saga began when the government charged the grocery supply company and five of its officers with "causing certain foodstuffs to become adulterated," misdemeanors under the FDCA. Id. at 231. In a trial before a magistrate judge, the corporation and three of its officers were convicted, including its president, a vice-president, and another vice-president who served as the "general manager of the facility where the foodstuffs became adulterated." Id. at 231-32. Paltry fines were imposed.

The president, Julian Leavitt, appealed his conviction to the district court. He claimed that his conviction violated *Park*, which "requires a finding of negligence or other blameworthiness," because it rested solely on his status as president. Id. at 232. The striking similarities between the instant case and *Park* were not lost on Chief Judge Andrew Caffrey, who explained:

> The defendant in *Park* was the president and chief executive officer of a national retail food chain. He was charged with the same crime as is the defendant in the instant case, viz., causing foodstuffs being held for sale following shipment in interstate commerce to become adulterated in violation of 21 U.S.C. §331(k). Park contended as does the defendant here, that the jury instructions allowed the jury to convict him solely on the basis of his corporate position. The Supreme Court did not agree.

Id. at 232.

While readers might assume that Judge Caffrey felt required to uphold Leavitt's conviction based on the similarities to *Park*, in fact, the judge took a different tack. Judge Caffrey held that the magistrate judge *had* misconstrued *Park* in finding Leavitt guilty solely by reason of his status as president:

> Early in his opinion, the magistrate made the following observation about the *Park* decision: "Park (President of the corporation 'Acme') was individually convicted for violation of the Act by virtue of his position as president." Later on, the magistrate again noted that *Park* "stands for the proposition that the head of a corporation can be charged because of his position as a corporate chief." These two statements demonstrate a basic misinterpretation of *Park*, since the Supreme Court made it clear that a corporate officer cannot be convicted solely on the basis of his position in the corporate hierarchy. This misunderstanding of *Park* is reflected in the magistrate's finding that defendant Julian [Leavitt] was guilty of violating the Act. In his "general discussion" section, the magistrate stated explicitly that the "finding made by this court

with respect to Julian was made only on the basis that in *Park*, the court stated that the position of the President made him liable, responsible and subject to prosecution." This comment clearly indicates that the magistrate applied the wrong legal standard in convicting Julian Leavitt, finding him guilty solely by reason of his position as president.

Id. at 233.

At the same time, as Judge Caffrey acknowledged, the magistrate judge also made factual findings that appeared to be consistent with *Park*. For instance, the magistrate judge enumerated in his "conclusion" that Leavitt was guilty because "he possessed the final authority to institute whatever effective programs . . . were required" to prevent FDCA violations. Id. But Judge Caffrey concluded that even if this finding indicated that Leavitt's liability rested on his "responsible relationship" with the violations, "it would not support a conviction because the magistrate did not make the finding 'beyond a reasonable doubt.'" Id. at 234. Judge Caffrey also instructed the magistrate on remand to determine whether the two other convicted defendants (the vice-presidents) "introduced sufficient evidence to raise the impossibility defense, and, if so, whether the government sustained its burden of disproving the defense beyond a reasonable doubt." Id. at 236-37. Who has the better understanding of the RCO doctrine as articulated by *Park*—the magistrate judge or the district judge?

———————————

The Supreme Court recently denied certiorari in another FDCA prosecution, United States v. DeCoster, 828 F.3d 626 (8th Cir. 2016), cert. denied, 2017 WL 120919 (May 22, 2017). Jack DeCoster, the owner of the Quality Egg company, and Peter DeCoster, Quality Egg's chief operating officer (and Jack's son), pled guilty, as responsible corporate officers, to misdemeanor FDCA violations for introducing salmonella-contaminated eggs into interstate commerce. Quality Egg is a large-scale producer; an estimated 56,000 people in the U.S. became ill. 828 F.3d at 630. The two defendants were each sentenced to three months in prison. On appeal, the Eighth Circuit held that their convictions did not violate due process, and that their prison term sentences were reasonable and within the bounds of the Eighth Amendment.

United States v. DeCoster
828 F.3d 626 (8th Cir. 2016)

MURPHY, Circuit Judge.

Austin "Jack" DeCoster and Peter DeCoster both pled guilty, as "responsible corporate officers" of Quality Egg, LLC, to misdemeanor violations of

21 U.S.C. §331(a) for introducing eggs that had been adulterated with sal-monella enteritidis into interstate commerce. The district court sentenced Jack and Peter to three months imprisonment. The DeCosters appeal, arguing that their prison sentences and 21 U.S.C. §333(a)(1) are uncon-stitutional, and claiming in the alternative that their prison sentences were procedurally and substantively unreasonable. We affirm.

I

Jack DeCoster owned Quality Egg, LLC, an Iowa egg production company. Jack's son Peter DeCoster served as the company's chief operat-ing officer. Quality Egg operated six farm sites with 73 barns which were filled with five million egg laying hens. It also had 24 barns which were filled with young chickens that had not yet begun to lay eggs. Additionally, the company owned several processing plants where eggs were cleaned, packed, and shipped. . . .

Other than conducting the single egg test in April 2009, Quality Egg did not test or divert eggs from the market before July 2010 despite receiv-ing multiple positive environmental and hen test results. In 2009 the DeCosters hired Dr. Hofacre and Dr. Nolan to consult on the company's Iowa operations. The consultants recommended implementing the same measures in Iowa as had been used in Maine. Although the DeCosters claim they adopted all of the recommendations, the precautions imple-mented by Quality Egg failed to eradicate salmonella. The Centers for Disease Control and Prevention estimated that about 56,000 Americans fell ill with salmonellosis in 2010 after consuming contaminated eggs. In August 2010, federal and state officials determined that the salmonella outbreak had originated at Quality Egg's facilities. In response Quality Egg recalled eggs that had been shipped from five of its six Iowa farm sites between May and August 2010.

The FDA inspected the Quality Egg operations in Iowa from August 12-30, 2010. Investigators discovered live and dead rodents and frogs in the laying areas, feed areas, conveyer belts, and outside the buildings. They also found holes in the walls and baseboards of the feed and lay-ing buildings. The investigators discovered that some rodent traps were broken, and others had dead rodents in them. In one building near the laying hens, manure was found piled to the rafters; it had pushed a screen out of the door which allowed rodents into the building. Investigators also observed employees not wearing or changing protective clothing and not cleaning or sanitizing equipment.

The FDA concluded that Quality Egg had failed to comply with its written plans for biosecurity and salmonella prevention. . . .

The government then began a criminal investigation of the com-pany's food safety practices and ultimately filed a criminal information against Quality Egg and both of the DeCosters. The investigation revealed that Quality Egg previously had falsified records about food safety measures and had lied to auditors for several years about pest control measures and sanitation practices. Although its food safety plan stated that Quality Egg performed flock testing to identify and control salmonella, no flock testing was ever done. Quality Egg employees had also bribed a USDA inspector in 2010 to release eggs for sale which had been retained or "red tagged" for failing to meet minimum quality grade standards. Quality Egg also misled state regulators and retail customers by changing the packing dates of its eggs and selling the misbranded eggs into interstate commerce. The parties additionally stipulated that one Quality Egg employee was prepared to testify at trial that Jack DeCoster had once reprimanded him because he had not moved a pallet of eggs in time to avoid inspection by the USDA. The investigation also revealed that in 2008 Peter DeCoster had made inaccurate statements to Walmart about Quality Egg's food safety and sanitation practices.

Quality Egg pled guilty to: (1) a felony violation of 18 U.S.C. §201(b)(1) for bribing a USDA inspector, (2) a felony violation of 21 U.S.C. §331(a) for introducing misbranded eggs into interstate commerce with intent to defraud and mislead, and (3) a misdemeanor violation of 21 U.S.C. §331(a) for introducing adulterated eggs into interstate commerce. Jack and Peter each pled guilty to misdemeanor violations of 21 U.S.C. §331(a) as responsible corporate officers under the Food Drug & Cosmetic Act (FDCA). In their plea agreements, the DeCosters stated that they had not known that the eggs were contaminated at the time of shipment, but stipulated that they were in positions of sufficient authority to detect, prevent, and correct the sale of contaminated eggs had they known about the contamination. The parties also stipulated that the DeCosters' advisory guideline range was 0 to 6 months imprisonment, and both defendants agreed to be sentenced based on facts the sentencing judge found by a preponderance of the evidence.

Before sentencing, the DeCosters argued that sentences of incarceration would be unconstitutional because they had not known that the eggs were contaminated at the time they were shipped. The district court denied the motions, imposed $100,000 fines on both Jack and Peter DeCoster and sentenced them to three months imprisonment. See 21 U.S.C. §333(a)(1) (explaining that anyone who violates section 331 "shall be imprisoned for not more than one year or fined not more than $1,000, or both"); 18 U.S.C. §3571(b)(5) (setting maximum fine of $100,000 for class A misdemeanor not resulting in death). The court determined that although nothing in the record indicated that Peter and Jack had actual knowledge that the eggs they sold were infected with salmonella, the record demonstrated that their safety and sanitation procedures were "egregious," that they ignored the positive salmonella environmental test results before July 2010 by not testing their eggs, and that they knew that their employees had deceived and bribed USDA inspectors. The district court explained that the record supported the inference that the DeCosters had "created a work environment where employees not only felt comfortable disregarding regulations and bribing USDA officials, but may have even felt pressure to do so." The district court accordingly concluded that this was not a case involving "a mere unaware corporate executive."

The DeCosters appeal, arguing that their prison sentences under 21 U.S.C. §333(a)(1) are unconstitutional under the Due Process Clause and the Eighth Amendment. In the alternative they claim that their sentences were procedurally and substantively unreasonable.

II

Under the FDCA responsible corporate officer concept, individuals who "by reason of [their] position in the corporation [have the] responsibility and authority" to take necessary measures to prevent or remedy violations of the FDCA and fail to do so, may be held criminally liable as "responsible corporate agents," regardless of whether they were aware of or intended to cause the violation. United States v. Park, 421 U.S. 658, 673-74 (1975). The FDCA "punishes neglect where the law requires care, or inaction where it imposes a duty" because according to Congress, the "public interest in the purity of its food is so great as to warrant the imposition of the highest standard of care on distributors." Id. at 671. A corporate officer may avoid liability under this doctrine by showing that he was "powerless to prevent or correct the violation." Id. at 673. . . .

The DeCosters argue that their prison sentences are unconstitutional because they did not personally commit wrongful acts. They analogize this case to others where courts have determined that due process is violated when prison terms are imposed for vicarious liability crimes. See [e.g.,] Lady J. Lingerie, Inc. v. City of Jacksonville, 176 F.3d 1358, 1367 (11th Cir. 1999). The Eleventh Circuit explained in *Lady J.* that "due process prohibits the state from imprisoning a person without proof of some form of personal blameworthiness more than a 'responsible relation.'" 176 F.3d at 1367.

Officer liability under the FDCA, however, is not equivalent to vicarious liability. See *Park*, 421 U.S. at 674-75. Under vicarious liability, a supervisory party is held liable "for the actionable conduct of a subordinate . . . based on the relationship between the two parties." Liability, Black's Law Dictionary (10th ed. 2014). Under the FDCA, in contrast, a corporate officer is held accountable not for the acts or omissions of others, but rather for his own failure to prevent or remedy "the conditions which gave rise to the charges against him." See *Park*, 421 U.S. at 675. Thus, "some measure of blameworthiness" is "import[ed]" directly to the corporate officer. Id. at 673.

Here, as owner of Quality Egg, Jack decided which barns were subject to salmonella environmental testing, and as chief operating officer, Peter coordinated many of the company's salmonella prevention and rodent control efforts. Neither of the DeCosters claim to have been "powerless" to prevent Quality Egg from violating the FDCA. See id. Despite their familiarity with the conditions in the Iowa facilities, they failed to take sufficient measures to improve them. On this record, the district court reasonably found that "the defendants 'knew or should have known,' of the risks posed by the insanitary conditions at Quality Egg in Iowa, 'knew or should have known' that additional testing needed to be performed before the suspected shell eggs were distributed to consumers, and 'knew or should have known' of [] proper remedial and preventative measures to reduce the presence of [salmonella]." The FDCA "punishes neglect where the law requires care." Id. at 671. We conclude that the record here shows that the DeCosters are liable for negligently failing to prevent the salmonella outbreak. See id. at 678-79 (Stewart, J., dissenting) (reading majority opinion in *Park* as establishing a negligence standard).

The DeCosters argue that their prison sentences also violate the Due Process Clause because they did not know that the eggs the company distributed had salmonella. We have explained that "the imposition of severe penalties, especially a felony conviction, for the commission of a morally innocent act may violate" due process. See United States v. Enochs, 857 F.2d 491, 494 n.2 (8th Cir. 1988). The elimination of a mens rea requirement does not violate the Due Process Clause for a public welfare offense where the penalty is "relatively small," the conviction does not gravely damage the defendant's reputation, and congressional intent supports the imposition of the penalty. See Staples v. United States, 511 U.S. 600, 617 (1994) (citing Morissette v. United States, 342 U.S. 246, 256 (1952)).

The three month prison sentences the DeCosters received were relatively short. See Staples, 511 U.S. at 617. We have previously determined that even a maximum statutory penalty of one year imprisonment for a misdemeanor offense is "relatively small" and does not violate due process. See United States v. Flum, 518 F.2d 39, 43-45 (8th Cir. 1975) (en banc), cert. denied, 423 U.S. 1018 (1975).

The DeCosters' misdemeanor convictions also do not gravely damage their reputations. In *Flum*, we explained that a misdemeanor conviction under a federal law which provided for a maximum imprisonment of one year did not gravely "besmirch" the defendant's reputation because it did not brand him as a "felon or subject him to any burden beyond the sentence imposed." See 518 F.2d at 43. Similarly in this case, the DeCosters will not be branded as felons, and the record does not identify any additional civil sanctions they may be subject to beyond their sentences. Finally, the elimination of criminal intent under 21 U.S.C. §333(a) did not violate due process because, as the Supreme Court has explained,

"Congress has seen fit to enforce the accountability of responsible corporate agents dealing with products which may affect the health of consumers by penal sanctions cast in rigorous terms." *Park*, 421 U.S. at 673.

The dissent argues that we must treat the FDCA, 21 U.S.C. §§331(a), 333(a)(1), as requiring a defendant to know he violated the statute in order to be subject to its penalties because the statute has "no express congressional statement" to omit a mens rea requirement. We rely however "on the nature of the statute and the particular character of the items regulated to determine whether congressional silence concerning the mental element of the offense should be interpreted as dispensing with conventional mens rea requirements." *Staples*, 511 U.S. at 607. The FDCA regulates services and products which affect the health and well being of the public. For this reason, Congress has not required "awareness of some wrongdoing" in order to hold responsible corporate agents accountable for violating the statute. *Park*, 421 U.S. at 672-673. Although the "requirements of foresight and vigilance imposed on responsible corporate agents [in 21 U.S.C. §331(a)] are beyond question demanding, and perhaps onerous, [] they are no more stringent" than required to protect the unknowing public from consuming hazardous food, such as salmonella infected eggs. Id. at 672. The language in the FDCA and Supreme Court precedent interpreting the statute support the conclusion that defendants are not required to have known that they violated the FDCA to be subject to the statutory penalties.

As the Third Circuit explained in United States v. Greenbaum, "[t]he constitutional requirement of due process is not violated merely because mens rea is not a required element of a prescribed crime." 138 F.2d 437, 438 (3d Cir. 1943). In *Greenbaum*, the court affirmed a corporate president's three month prison sentence for introducing adulterated eggs into interstate commerce in violation of the same statute at issue in this case. Id. at 439. The *Greenbaum* court explained that "the legislative intent to dispense with mens rea as an element of [a misdemeanor FDCA] offense has a justifiable basis" because such offenses "are capable of inflicting widespread injury, and [] the requirement of proof of the offender's guilty knowledge and wrongful intent would render enforcement of the prohibition difficult if not impossible." Id. at 438. For the same reasons, we conclude that the DeCosters' sentences do not violate the Due Process Clause even though mens rea was not an element of their misdemeanor offenses.

The DeCosters also claim that their sentences violate the Eighth Amendment. We review this issue de novo. . . .

On this record, the DeCosters' three month prison sentences are not grossly disproportionate to the gravity of their misdemeanor offenses. When defining the statutory penalties in the FDCA, Congress recognized the importance of placing the burden on corporate officers to protect consumers "who are wholly helpless" from purchasing adulterated food products which could make them ill. See United States v. Dotterweich, 320 U.S.

277, 285. "[T]he public has a right to expect" a heightened degree of fore-sight and care from "those who voluntarily assume positions of authority in business enterprises whose services and products affect the health and well-being of the public that supports them." *Park,* 421 U.S. at 672. The 2010 salmonella outbreak may have affected up to 56,000 victims, some of whom were hospitalized or suffered long term injuries. For one example, a child hospitalized in an intensive care unit for eight days was saved by antibiotics which damaged his teeth, causing them to be capped in stainless steel.

We conclude this is not "the rare case in which a threshold com-parison of the crime committed and the sentence imposed leads to an inference of gross disproportionality." United States v. Spires, 628 F.3d 1049, 1054 (8th Cir. 2011). Moreover, the DeCosters' three month prison sentences fell at the low end of the prescribed statutory range of 21 U.S.C. §333(a) (one year maximum), and we have "never held a sentence within the statutory range to violate the Eighth Amendment." We decline to do so here. . . .

IV

For these reasons the judgments of the district court are affirmed.

GRUENDER, Circuit Judge, concurring.

The DeCosters do not challenge either the constitutionality of §331(a) or the sufficiency of the factual basis for their pleas. Rather, they claim that due process concerns prevent them from being sentenced to prison for a crime involving no mens rea on their part because it is based solely on their positions as responsible corporate officers—i.e. , vicari-ous liability. I agree with the dissent that imprisonment based on vicari-ous liability would raise serious due process concerns. However, because the district court found the DeCosters negligent, they were not held vicariously liable for violations committed by others, and this case thus does not implicate these concerns. I therefore concur in the judgment and join Judge Murphy's opinion to the extent that it recognizes that the DeCosters were negligent. I write separately in order to make clear my view that Park requires a finding of negligence in order to convict a responsible corporate officer under §331. . . .

BEAM, Circuit Judge, dissenting. . . .

At the outset, it is compelling to discern that the DeCosters' pleas of guilty and waiver of trial by jury in defense of these criminal misde-meanor charges were substantially cabined by a series of factual and pro-cedural stipulations by the prosecutors and the DeCosters pursuant to Federal Rule of Criminal Procedure 11, all of which were accepted by and binding upon the district court. . . .

[T]he government stipulated that "[t]o date" (April 18, 2014), "the government's investigation has not identified any personnel employed by or associated with Quality Egg, including the defendant[s], who had knowledge during the [charged] time frame from January 2010 through August 12, 2010, that eggs sold by Quality Egg were, in fact, contaminated with Salmonella [Enteritidis]." . . . The government also stipulated that "until adoption of the Egg Safety Rule in July 2010, there was no legal or regulatory requirement" for Quality Egg to comply with these regulations. The record also establishes that, given the state of the art of poultry-sanitation management, egg-safety difficulties, especially involving salmonella contamination, are inherent in such operations.

In short, large numbers of employees and supervisors were needed and employed by Quality Egg in an attempt to avoid problems with this ubiquitous pathogen. Thus, the misdemeanor convictions found and imposed by the district court in response to the DeCosters' very limited guilty pleas amounted to crimes and sentences based upon almost wholly nonculpable conduct.

On the record and the stipulated facts, it is also clear that the DeCosters lacked the necessary mens rea or "guilty mind," that is "[t] he state of mind that the prosecution, to secure a conviction, must prove that a defendant had when committing a crime," Mens Rea, Black's Law Dictionary (10th ed. 2014). This mens rea requirement is especially applicable when the crime, as here, is punished by imprisonment. . . .

This court and the district court cite cases that they contend support a rationale that a criminal sentence of imprisonment is sometimes valid without proof of mens rea, or, a guilty mind. But, the cases advanced by the government and the courts cannot bear the load placed upon them, both as matters of fact and law. United States v. Dotterweich, substantially predate[ed] Zadvydas [v. Davis, 533 U.S. 678 (2001)], *Staples*, and Torres [v. Lynch, 136 S. Ct. 1619, 1630-31 (2016)]. . . .

[As to Park,] . . . it must be noted that . . . [t]here was no incarceration. Incarceration of Dotterweich or Park, as we now know, would have violated Supreme Court precedent as clearly established in *Zadvydas*, *Staples*, and *Torres*. . . .

There is no proof that the DeCosters, as individuals, were infected with a "guilty mind" or, perhaps, even with negligence. Clearly, the improvident prison sentences imposed in this case were due process violations.

I respectfully dissent.

NOTES AND QUESTIONS

1. Did *DeCoster* add anything new to the RCO doctrine? Arguably, the answer is yes, at least in the Eighth Circuit. Although both the district court

and Eighth Circuit said that the DeCosters were *in fact* at least negligent, this *mens rea* (indeed, any *mens rea*) is not explicitly stated in the criminal prohibition of which they were convicted, 21 U.S.C. §331(a). Nonetheless, both Judge Raymond Gruender, in his partial concurring opinion, and dissenting Judge Arlen Beam thought that "imprisonment based on vicarious liability would raise serious due process concerns." 828 F.3d at 636 (Gruender, J., concurring). Judge Gruender thought that negligence had been established, while Judge Beam thought there was insufficient evidence of the defendants' "guilty minds." Id. at 642 (Beam, J., dissenting). Thus, a majority of the panel read in some form of *mens rea* requirement in cases where the defendant is sentenced to imprisonment.

Do you think that courts should be in the business of inserting a *mens rea* standard into a statute that is silent on the issue? We have certainly seen this before. See Staples v. United States, 511 U.S. 600 (1994); Ratzlaf v. United States, 510 U.S. 135 (1994), and other cases discussed in Chapter 3. But Judge Beam would apparently *not* read in a negligence requirement (or a "guilty mind" requirement, whatever that may be) in prosecutions under the statute that do not result in imprisonment. What kind of statutory interpretation is that?

2. Are you going to lose any sleep over the fate of the DeCosters, whose unsuccessful petition for certiorari was supported by a variety of organizations concerned with "over-criminalization" in federal law? Contrary to the DeCosters' claims, this was not the first case in which defendants received sentences of imprisonment for convictions based on the RCO doctrine. See United States v. Hanousek, *supra* (where the defendant was sentenced to six months in prison); United States v. Greenbaum, 138 F.2d 437 (3d Cir. 1943) (affirming a corporate president's three month prison sentence for introducing adulterated eggs into interstate commerce in violation of the same statute at issue in *DeCoster*). Moreover, the sentencing judge—Judge Mark Bennett—recommended that the defendants' ninety-day sentences be served at the "cushy" FPC Yankton, though the duo could serve closer to home, one after another, as to minimized disruption to their business. See Dan Flynn, Supreme Court Will Not Review DeCoster Sentences in Egg Case (May 23, 2017). This was hardly the most serious of consequences, as the company could have been (and may still be) debarred or excluded from participated in federal programs due to the regulatory violations for having to recall over 500 million eggs, the largest in U.S. history.

Indeed, might we flip the question and ask how much deterrence or retribution is gained from misdemeanor prosecutions of this sort? Note that this case involves a guilty plea, and the defendants were complaining only that they received jail time. This was not the first time Jack DeCoster and his eggs had been tied to a massive salmonella outbreak, see William Neuman, An Iowa Egg Farmer and a History of Salmonella, N.Y. Times, Sept. 21, 2010, and yet his firm was the only defendant to plead to felony charges. Just as we worry that firms may throw their executives "under the bus," shouldn't we also worry that controlling individuals will push for a corporate plea to avoid or reduce personal liability? If we are sorting between the coddling of corporate offenders and the persecution of them, in which box does this case go? If you need to know more facts to decide, what is the likelihood that the record of this case will help you?

3. Consider how law professor Amy J. Sepinwall conceives of the RCO doctrine: Rather than being a kind of negligence liability, the RCO doctrine is justified by blameworthiness that is grounded in relationships rather than fault. See Amy J. Sepinwall, Faultless Guilt: Toward a Relationship-Based Account of Criminal Liability, 54 Am. Crim. L. Rev. 521, 525 (2017) (explaining how a corporate executive can be blameworthy without being at fault and therefore should sometimes be blamed and punished on the basis of "relationship-based criminal liability"); Amy J. Sepinwall, Crossing the Fault Line in Corporate Criminal Law, 40 Iowa J. Corp. L. 439, 458 (2015) (arguing that non-participants' "expected commitments to their corporations [grounds] their responsibility"). Sepinwall distinguishes her theory from those who believe the RCO doctrine resembles the primitive doctrine of frankpledge, under which innocent group members could be punished for the wrongs of a fellow group member. See, e.g., Albert W. Alschuler, Two Ways to Think About the Punishment of Corporations, 46 Am. Crim. L. Rev. 1359, 1359 (2009). She contends that it is "sometimes appropriate to hold a corporate executive *individually* responsible for the crime of her corporation, even when she made no causal difference to the crime's commission and even when she did not harbor a guilty mind." Sepinwall, Crossing the Fault Line in Corporate Criminal Law, *supra,* at 444. Because corporate crimes have an "irreducibly collective aspect," shared membership in a transgressing entity can be the basis for shared responsibility, even without the traditional hallmarks of guilt. Amy J. Sepinwall, Responsible Shares and Shared Responsibility: In Defense of Responsible Corporate Officer Liability, 2014 Colum. Bus. L. Rev. 371, 372, 410. By nature of this relationship, the fate of an executive is tied to the company, in good times—as demonstrated by the widely accepted practice of receiving large bonuses—and in bad times. Thus, although the willing assumption of risk of liability inherent in holding the office is not, by itself, sufficient to justify the RCO, the executive is on the hook because he is also expected to occupy his role in a way that accepts his implication in the underlying crime. Id. at 411. Does Professor Sepinwall sufficiently explain why the "blameworthiness" that the RCO doctrine seeks to capture justifies *criminal* as opposed to *civil* liability?

4. The RCO doctrine has been condemned for the way it can blur the distinction between criminal and civil liability. See, e.g, Nicholas T. Schnell, Beyond All Bounds of Civility: An Analysis of Administrative Sanctions Against Responsible Corporate Officers, 42 J. Corp. L. 711 (2017). Take, for instance, the case of regulatory exclusion, an administrative penalty

levied against individuals who are "deemed to pose a threat to the integrity of the federal health care programs." Andrew C. Baird, The New *Park* Doctrine, 91 N.C. L. Rev. 949, 952 (2013). Exclusion "effectively functions to prevent a convicted individual from working for or with any entity that receives funding from a federal health program for a period of years." Id. After a 2010 GAO report called for increased enforcement of FDA regulations and statutes (like the FDCA), administrative agencies ramped up their use of regulatory tools, particularly the Department of Health and Human Service's exclusion authority. See Schnell, *supra*, at 715. This can—and did—lead to grave consequences for the individuals excluded. In the case Friedman v. Sebelius, 686 F.3d 813 (D.C. Cir. 2012), for instance, three corporate officers of Purdue Pharma pled guilty as RCOs to misdemeanor drug misbranding under the FDCA. In addition to receiving probation and paying millions of dollars in fines, the convicted officers were excluded from federal health care programs for twelve years, what amounted to a "death sentence for their careers." Sasha Ivanov, When the Punishment Does Not Fit the Crime: Exclusions from Federal Health Care Programs Following Convictions Under the Responsible Corporate Officer Doctrine, 84 Geo. Wash. L. Rev. 776, 778 (2016). The officers argued there was no evidence that they knew of, or participated in, any of the company's wrongdoing. See id. Does the combination of criminal prosecution under the *Park* doctrine and the civil exclusion penalty represent a "severe, duplicative, punitive" punishment? See Schnell, *supra*, at 728. Professor Copeland would say yes and that a period of exclusion longer than the three-year base level for "permissive exclusions" is a "grossly disproportionate remedy." Katrice Bridges Copeland, The Crime of Being in Charge: Executive Culpability and Collateral Consequences, 51 Am. Crim. L. Rev. 799, 804 (2014). The RCO doctrine does not require a showing of "moral blameworthiness," nor does it provide defenses for an executive who "did not intend for the misconduct to occur," "delegated responsibility in good faith," or was "not knowledgeable about or did not participate in the misconduct." Id. If the underlying strict liability misdemeanor carries a maximum penalty of one year in prison, is its collateral lengthy debarment misguided and unjust?

5. How far does the RCO doctrine extend? Thus far, it has been applied in a number of contexts, expanding from strict-liability food and safety under the FDCA to other public health and welfare offenses such as meat inspection regulations, alcoholic beverage control laws, and state sales tax laws. See Jeffrey R. Boles, Financial Sector Executives as Targets for Money Laundering Liability, 52 Am. Bus. L.J. 365, 400 (2015); Aagaard, *supra*, at 1253. It has been applied to the financial sector for consumer fraud, securities violations, deceptive mortgage lending practices, antitrust offenses, and Sarbanes-Oxley Act violations. The RCO doctrine may ultimately provide another way to hold individual bankers liable for money laundering offenses (in addition to using theories of direct participation or aiding and

abetting). See Boles, *supra*, at 398. See also Christina M. Schuck, A New Use for the Responsible Corporate Officer Doctrine: Prosecuting Industry Insiders for Mortgage Fraud, 14 Lewis & Clark L. Rev. 371, 379 (2010); Martin Petrin, The Curious Case of Directors' and Officers' Liability for Supervision and Management: Exploring the Intersection of Corporate and Tort Law, 59 Am. U. L. Rev. 1661, 1674 (2010) (arguing that the RCO is a theory of liability separate from veil-piercing or direct participation for those not liable under traditional corporate, tort, or agency law principles). Former Attorney General Eric Holder even floated the idea of following in British footsteps and modifying American laws so that financial companies would be required to "designate an officer who would be accountable for misconduct at the firm." Eric Holder, U.S. Att'y Gen., Remarks on Financial Fraud Prosecutions at New York University School of Law (Sep. 17, 2014). Would holding a top-level manager accountable for excessively-risky activity ensure that the buck does stop somewhere? Id. See also Steven L. Schwarz, Excessive Corporate Risk-Taking and the Decline of Personal Blame, 65 Emory L.J. 533, 572 (2015). Would your concerns about liability based on omission be addressed if a statute imposed a requirement on a CEO to inquire into and affirmatively "certify" compliance with accounting or environmental rules, and then allowed prosecution for failure to comply?

6. The RCO doctrine has also been applied to felony violations, particularly in the environmental law arena. Most notable have been prosecutions under the Clean Water Act (CWA) and the Clean Air Act (CAA), both of which explicitly state that the term "person" includes "any responsible corporate officer" for purposes of criminal liability. See CWA, 33 U.S.C. §1319(c)(6); CAA, 42 U.S.C. §7413(c)(6). And once again (see *supra* Note 4 following *United States v. Park*) there is some confusion as to whether the doctrine affects—or eliminates—the *mens rea* requirement in the relevant environmental prohibitions. See Kyle Crawford et al., Environmental Crimes, 53 Am. Crim. L. Rev. 1159, 1166 (2016); Martin Petrin, The "Prosecutor's Ticket to Tag the Elite"—A Critique of the Responsible Corporate Officer Doctrine, 84 Temp. L. Rev. 283, 296 (2012) (suggesting that the "RCO doctrine has an eroding effect on the element of *mens rea*"). But see Schuck, *supra*, at 387 (arguing that courts have clearly established that the "RCO doctrine could not be used to impose strict liability upon defendants standing in responsible relation to a danger" and that the government needs to separately prove the knowledge requirement under RCRA).

On the other hand, when many environmental prohibitions contain no express *mens rea* element, courts have refused to read one in simply because the RCO doctrine is applied regarding the *actus reas*. In United States v. Iverson, 162 F.3d 1015 (9th Cir. 1998), the court held that the president and chairman of the board of a chemical company could be prosecuted for violations under the RCO provision of the CWA as long as the "person has authority to exercise control over the corporation's activity that is causing the discharges." Id. at 1025. Because the RCO instruction "relieved the government *only* of having to prove that the defendant *personally* discharged or caused the discharge of a pollutant," the government still had to prove to the jury that the discharge violated the law, that the discharges were pollutants, and that the defendant had both the authority and capacity to prevent these discharges. Id. at 1026. In United States v. Ming Hong, 242 F.3d 528 (4th Cir. 2001), the government was relieved of proving that the defendant was a formally designated corporate officer. Id. at 531. As financial controller, the defendant played a substantial role in the company's operations yet refused to authorize an upgrade to the wastewater system when it became clogged. He was informed of this fact by employees and inspected it himself on at least one occasion. Id. at 530. The court upheld his conviction under the RCO provision of the CWA, holding that "the gravamen of liability as a responsible corporate officer is not one's corporate title or lack thereof; rather, the pertinent question is whether the defendant bore such a relationship to the corporation that it is appropriate to hold him criminally liable for failing to prevent the charged violations of the CWA." Id. at 531.

The Comprehensive Environmental Response, Compensation, and Liability Act (CERCLA) likewise has language apparently adopting the RCO theory of criminal liability; CERCLA prohibitions apply to "the owner and operator of a vessel or a facility," 42 U.S.C. §9607(a)(1), and to "any person who at the time of disposal of any hazardous substance owned or operated any facility at which such hazardous substances were disposed of," Id. §9607(a)(2). See Crawford et al., *supra,* at 1204 (noting that an "owner or person in charge of a facility involved in a CERCLA offense may be a defendant.") See also United States v. Hansen, 262 F.3d 1217, 1253 (11th Cir. 2001) (holding that "it is only necessary that the individual have or share such control of the facility where the release occurred"). But a defendant under CERCLA may raise an "innocent owner" defense for unknowingly acquiring contaminated property. See Crawford et al., *supra,* at 1208. Does this affirmative defense amount to a requirement of *mens rea,* albeit with the burden shifted to the defendant? For a comprehensive overview of criminal liability and defenses under various environmental statutes, see Crawford et al., *supra.*

7. Although many revile the RCO doctrine because of its vast power and expansive reach, others have argued that criminal prosecutions of senior executives in companies like BP or VW might be the most effective way to set "moral boundaries" and rein in renegade companies, assuming that any requisite *mens rea* can be independently proven. See Rena Steinzor, How Criminal Law Can Help Save the Environment, 46 Envtl. L. 209, 218, 234 (2016). Do you agree?

Recall the statement in *Dotterweich:*

> To attempt a formula embracing the variety of conduct whereby persons may responsibly contribute in furthering a transaction forbidden by an Act of congress . . . would be mischievous futility. In such matters the good sense of prosecutors, the wise guidance of trial judges, and the ultimate judgment of juries must be trusted.

320 U.S. at 285. Was the Eighth Circuit, in *DeCoster*, simply deferring to the trial court's "wise guidance" and "judgment" to which Justice Frankfurter referred?

THE SIGNIFICANCE OF EXPANSIVE CORPORATE CRIMINAL LIABILITY

We have seen that federal corporate criminal law takes a number of shapes, from indicting entire corporations, to entering into deferred and non-prosecution agreements with those companies, to holding executives criminally liable as responsible corporate officers. Why is the black-letter law of federal corporate criminal liability so expansive? *Should* prosecutors have such free rein to tailor their corporate crime strategy? Some commentators answer the latter question with an emphatic "yes," arguing that civil sanctions or administrative regulations cannot provide the same deterrent effect as the stigma—and consequences—of a criminal conviction. Monetary fines and forfeiture pursuant to a civil settlement or a deferred prosecution agreement do not provide the same norm-setting functions as public prosecutions. See David M. Uhlmann, The Pendulum Swings: Reconsidering Corporate Criminal Prosecution, 49 U.C.D. L. Rev. 1235, 1263 (2016). Criminal prosecutions of companies where wrongdoing has occurred also reinforces and validates the choices of law-abiding companies. See id. at 1282. Some critics argue that DOJ has been insufficiently aggressive in ferreting out and prosecuting corporate wrongdoing not just in the financial section but more generally. See Bourjaily, *supra*, at 553; Reilly, *supra*, at 354.

Perhaps the critics—these "corporate headhunters"—are misguided. Perhaps there is not a crime behind every social ill. Perhaps federal prosecutors have, by and large, been right to insist on evidence of knowledge of wrongdoing before indicting a corporate officer. Perhaps civil settlements and DPAs are the best that can be done when an institution is of such economic significance ("too big to jail") that actual prosecution would cause disproportionate collateral consequences to the economy and to "the people" as a whole. DPAs, for instance, give prosecutors choices beyond just indicting (and potentially facing courtroom battles with highly paid adversaries) or letting a company escape criminal liability entirely. After all, these investigations require enormous resource commitments and institutional design measures not currently practicable for underfunded federal agencies. See Richman, Corporate Headhunting, supra, at 274.

Indeed, prosecutorial prudence may explain why the (rather sparse) recent case law on corporate liability has remained so favorable to prosecutors. See Samuel W. Buell, The Blaming Function of Entity Criminal Liability, 81 Ind. L.J. 473, 476 (2006) ("In the shadow of a strikingly broad de jure rule of liability that is nearly indistinguishable from its civil counterparts, the criminal system's actors gradually have developed a practice of imposing enterprise liability that looks much narrower and is tied to a form of heightened criminal responsibility."); Gerard E. Lynch, The Role of Criminal Law in Policing Corporate Misconduct, 60 Law & Contemp. Probs. 23, 65 (1997) (noting that "it is routine, in at least some prosecutorial agencies, for prosecutors charged with policing corporate misconduct to ask, and to permit defense counsel to press them on, the question of the appropriate role of criminal as distinct from civil sanctions in deciding whether to bring criminal charges"). On paper, at least, DOJ is self-aware in likening a prosecutor's "fiduciary duty" to the public interest to that of corporate directors and officers. Both public prosecutors and private individuals who have fiduciary obligations share a common cause of promoting trust and confidence, which is "affected both by the results [they] achieve and by the real and perceived ways in which [they] achieve them." USAM 9-28.100 ("Duties of Federal Prosecutors and Duties of Corporate Leaders"). Thus, "federal prosecutors must maintain public confidence in the way in which [they] exercise their charging discretion." Id. Have they succeeded in doing so?

12 | Delegating Criminal Lawmaking

Notwithstanding frequent judicial denials that there is a federal common law of crimes, see *Hudson & Goodwin* and other cases in Chapter 3, we have already seen—in that chapter and others—the extent to which (for better or worse) Congress has implicitly delegated lawmaking authority to the federal courts, which in turn respond to prosecutorial initiatives. In this chapter, we will explore more formal instances of delegated criminal lawmaking authority; that is, we will examine offenses that, in whole or part, are explicitly defined by institutions other than Congress.

In Chapter 9, we saw how the Controlled Substance Act explicitly delegates to the Attorney General and, by extension, the Drug Enforcement Administration, the authority to "schedule" drugs. This is far from the only instance of Congress giving the executive branch the power to define criminal conduct, and indeed there are areas in which the extent of delegation to executive or independent federal agencies is far broader. In its environmental, banking, health care, and securities laws (to name just a few), Congress expressly delegates the power to promulgate regulations addressing some broadly described problem and provides for criminal, as well as civil, enforcement of those regulations. Nothing approaching a comprehensive portrait of these regulatory crimes will be attempted here. Our goal is to give a rough sense of what this species of criminal lawmaking looks like and how courts patrol it.

Although the delegation to federal agencies of the power to define federal crimes is not without controversy (surely an understatement), one can at least tell plausible stories that the agencies are ultimately accountable to Congress and the President. Such stories are less easily told, however, where Congress delegates criminal lawmaking authority to states, to foreign sovereigns, and international legal regimes or agencies. Yet instances of non-federal actors getting to specify what can be prosecuted in federal court do occur, and with increasing frequency, as you will see in this chapter. Of course, because the Justice Department retains a monopoly over federal prosecutions, it retains an effective veto over whether someone actually gets prosecuted for any of these offenses. Hence there will always be some federal executive branch control. But what role does the federal judicial branch play in restraining the development of these regimes?

A.   DELEGATION TO FEDERAL AGENCIES

Notwithstanding continuing critiques of the sweeping authority of federal administrative agencies to make law, settled doctrine easily accepts their ability to exercise delegated authority both to give content to broad statutory terms and to promulgate rules that interpret capacious statutory mandates. Yet hard questions can still be raised when an agency or executive department's effective lawmaking authority crosses into the realm of criminal law.

What are the constitutional limits on Congress's delegation of criminal lawmaking authority to an independent or executive agency? Standard nondelegation doctrine requires that a congressional delegation of authority contain an "intelligible principle" to guide and constrain agency rulemaking. See Whitman v. Am. Trucking Ass'ns., 531 U.S. 457, 472 (2001); J.W. Hampton, Jr., & Co. v. United States, 276 U.S. 394, 409 (1928); see also John F. Manning, The Nondelegation Doctrine as a Canon of Avoidance, 2000 Sup. Ct. Rev. 223. Perhaps the tether to legislative will should be tighter when criminal sanctions are involved. But it's worth noting that the only two cases in which the Supreme Court found no such "intelligible principle"—A.L.A. Schechter Poultry Corp. v. United States, 295 U.S. 495 (1935), and Panama Refining Co. v. Ryan, 293 U.S. 388 (1935)—involved not simply the delegation of the power to set criminally enforceable norms but the delegation of that power effectively to entities outside the federal government.

Even tougher questions can be raised when the delegated authority extends not to filling in a vague statutory term but to promulgating rules whose violation constitutes a serious criminal offense. What level of deference should courts give to an agency's reading of a statute when it draws on a legislated delegation to promulgate regulations with the force of law? This problem is explored at length in Administrative Law classes, where students are introduced to the so-called *Chevron* doctrine (which we've already mentioned in Section E of Chapter 4) and other canons of deference to administrative agencies. See Gillian E. Metzger, Embracing Administrative Common Law, 80 Geo. Wash. L. Rev. 1293 (2012); Connor N. Ruso & William J. Eskridge, Jr., *Chevron* as a Canon, Not a Precedent: An Empirical Study of What Motivates Justices in Agency Deference Cases, 110 Colum. L. Rev. 1727 (2010); Thomas W. Merrill, The Story of *Chevron*: The Making of an Accidental Landmark, in Administrative Law Stories 398 (Peter Strauss ed. 2006). The doctrine, rolled out in Chevron, U.S.A. v. Natural Resources Defense Council, 467 U.S. 837 (1984), commands courts to defer to an agency's reasonable interpretations of statutes it administers when Congress has not specifically spoken to the issue, and where the agency has acted within its authority and in the procedural manner Congress authorized. Should courts give the same level of deference to an agency's definition of a federal crime that it gives to administrative regulations that do not carry penal sanctions? See Sanford N. Greenberg, Who Says It's a Crime?: *Chevron* Deference to Agency Interpretations of Regulatory Statutes That Create Criminal Liability, 58 U.

Pitt. L. Rev. 1 (1996). Shouldn't criminal lawmaking be fundamentally different from civil regulation? See Richard E. Myers II, Complex Times Don't Call for Complex Crimes, 89 N.C. L. Rev. 1849 (2011). What about the rule of lenity? See generally Note, Justifying the *Chevron* Doctrine: Insights from the Rule of Lenity, 123 Harv. L. Rev. 2043 (2010). These are issues you should consider as you read the following materials.

1.   Agency Definition of Crimes and the Nondelegation Doctrine

The Controlled Substance Act is far from the only statutory regime that confers crime-definition authority on an executive agency. Indeed, in Chapter 8, we saw how the offense created by 18 U.S.C. §2339B has one of its factual elements supplied by executive promulgation. The Secretary of State is authorized to label entities as "foreign terrorist organizations," and Congress has made providing "material support" to these entities a crime. Here is a prosecution brought under a similar regime that, perhaps not coincidentally, also operates in the area of foreign policy:

United States v. Dhafir
461 F.3d 211 (2d Cir. 2006)

Dennis Jacobs, Circuit Judge:

The sole issue on this appeal is whether the International Emergency Economic Powers Act ("IEEPA") constitutes an appropriate delegation of congressional authority to the executive. The IEEPA authorizes the President to regulate financial transactions with foreign countries or nationals in a time of security crisis, and prescribes criminal penalties for violations of the president's regulations. Defendant-Appellant Osameh Al Wahaidy pled guilty to transferring money into Iraq on three specific occasions in 1999 and 2000, in violation of Executive Orders and regulations issued pursuant to the IEEPA, but preserved his right to bring a constitutional challenge to the statute. . . .

BACKGROUND

A.   THE IEEPA

The IEEPA, enacted in 1977 and codified at 50 U.S.C. §1701 et seq., confers on the President certain powers to respond to any threat to the national security, foreign policy or economy of the United States that is "unusual and extraordinary" and that "has its source in whole or substantial part outside the United States." 50 U.S.C. §1701(a). The President is granted the power to "investigate, regulate, or prohibit" various commercial activities, including: [i] "any transactions in foreign exchange," [ii] "transfers of credit or payments between, by, through, or to any banking institution, to the extent that such transfers or payments involve any interest of any foreign country or a national thereof," and [iii] "the importing or exporting of currency or securities, by any person, or with respect to any property, subject to the jurisdiction of the United States. . . ." 50 U.S.C. §1702(a)(1)(A). The President is also authorized to block transactions involving property "in which any foreign country or a national thereof has any interest by any person, or with respect to any property, subject to the jurisdiction of the United States. . . ." 50 U.S.C. §1702(a)(1)(B). These powers may be exercised only if and when the President declares a national emergency with respect to the threat, 50 U.S.C. §1701(a), in which event "[t]he President may issue such regulations, including regulations prescribing definitions, as may be necessary for the exercise of the authorities granted by this title." 50 U.S.C. §1704. The violation of an Executive Order or regulation promulgated pursuant to the IEEPA is punishable by a fine of not more than $50,000 and imprisonment for not more than twenty years. See 50 U.S.C. §1705(b). The IEEPA provides, however, that no person shall be held liable for acts or omissions conducted "in good faith." 50 U.S.C. §1702(a)(3).

The IEEPA reserves a continuing role for Congress. Thus, the IEEPA provides that "[t]he President, in every possible instance, shall consult with the Congress before exercising any of the authorities granted," that he "shall consult regularly with the Congress so long as such authorities are exercised," and that he shall report periodically concerning any actions taken in the exercise of the delegated authority. 50 U.S.C. §1703. Congress can terminate the President's declaration of emergency "by concurrent resolution pursuant to section 202 of the National Emergencies Act [50 U.S.C.S. §1622]." 50 U.S.C. §1706(b).

B.   THE IRAQI SANCTIONS EXECUTIVE ORDERS AND REGULATIONS

Following the Iraqi invasion of Kuwait in August, 1990, President George H.W. Bush issued four emergency Executive Orders declaring a national emergency, and prohibiting trade, transportation and financial transactions with Iraq and Kuwait. Executive Orders 12722 and 12724 blocked the Iraqi government's property and interests in property in the United States and prohibited transactions with entities in Iraq or controlled by the Iraq government. Executive Orders 12723 and 12725 correspondingly blocked the property of the Kuwaiti government and prohibited various transactions with entities in Kuwait or controlled by the Kuwaiti government.

To implement the Executive Orders, the Office of Foreign Assets Control ("OFAC") promulgated regulations providing (in relevant part) that "no U.S. person may commit or transfer, directly or indirectly, funds or other financial or economic resources to the Government of Iraq or any person in Iraq." 31 C.F.R. §575.210; see also 31 C.F.R. §575.211 (prohibiting the evasion or avoidance of the regulations and any attempt to violate the prohibitions).

The day the President signed Executive Order 12722 declaring a national emergency, the Senate passed a resolution commending the measures taken and urging the President to act immediately to enforce the IEEPA and to impose sanctions against Iraq. See S. Res. 318, 101st Cong. (1990). Several days later, the House passed its version of the Sanctions Against Iraq Act of 1990, authorizing economic sanctions under the authority of the IEEPA. H.R. 5431, 101st Cong. (2d Sess. 1990). In November 1990, Congress passed "The Iraqi Sanctions Act," declaring that Congress "supports the actions that have been taken by the President . . . [and] supports the imposition and enforcement of multilateral sanctions against Iraq," and requiring that the President "continue to impose the trade embargo and other economic sanctions with respect to Iraq and Kuwait . . . , pursuant to Executive Orders Numbered 12724 and 12725 (August 9, 1990) and, to the extent they are still in effect, Executive Orders Numbered 12722 and 12723 (August 2, 1990)." Iraqi Sanctions Act, Pub. L. 101-513 §586, 104 Stat. 1979, 2047-2048 (1990). . . .

DISCUSSION

Al Wahaidy argues [i] that the IEEPA is an improper delegation to the President of the Congressional authority to create criminal offenses, and [ii] that, in any event, the delegation fails on its own terms because the government has not shown that the executive has complied with the statutory reporting requirements.

A. CONSTITUTIONALITY OF THE IEEPA . . .

The Constitution vests in Congress the legislative power to define criminal conduct; but "our jurisprudence" has reached a "practical understanding that . . . Congress simply cannot do its job absent an ability to delegate power under broad general directives." Mistretta v. United States, 488 U.S. 361, 372 (1989). Delegations of congressional authority are upheld "[s]o long as Congress 'shall lay down by legislative act an intelligible principle to which the person or body authorized to [exercise the delegated authority] is directed to conform.'" Id. (quoting J.W. Hampton, Jr., & Co. v. United States, 276 U.S. 394, 406 (1928)). Under that standard, impermissible delegation has been rarely found. Since the articulation of the "intelligible principle" test in *J.W. Hampton, Jr.*, the Supreme Court has struck down only two statutes as impermissible delegations. See A.L.A. Schechter Poultry Corp. v. United States, 295 U.S. 495 (1935) (striking down delegation to industry associations comprised of private individuals to create legally binding codes of "fair competition"); Panama Refining Co. v. Ryan, 293 U.S. 388 (1935) (striking down blanket delegation to President to criminalize the interstate transport of petroleum). Neither instance involved foreign affairs, a sphere in which delegation is afforded even broader deference. See Zemel v. Rusk, 381 U.S. 1, 17 (1965) ("Congress—in giving the Executive authority over matters of foreign affairs—must of necessity paint with a brush broader than that it customarily wields in domestic areas."); United States v. Curtiss-Wright Export Corp., 299 U.S. 304, 315-322 (1936) (explaining why delegations in the foreign affairs context differ from those in the domestic context). Thus a delegation to the executive that may be improper if confined to internal affairs might "nevertheless be sustained on the ground that its exclusive aim is to afford a remedy for a hurtful condition within foreign territory." *Curtiss-Wright*, 299 U.S. at 315. This indulgence stems from the Constitution: "In this vast external realm, with its important, complicated, delicate and manifold problems, the President alone has the power to speak or listen as a representative of the nation." Id. at 319.

The Supreme Court has upheld Congressional delegation to the executive—under the IEEPA—to nullify certain attachments and transfers of assets. See Dames & Moore v. Regan, 453 U.S. 654, 675 (1981). . . .

The Supreme Court has also upheld particular delegations of authority to define criminal offenses, although not yet in the context of the IEEPA. In *Curtiss-Wright Export Corp.*, 299 U.S. 304, the Court upheld a Congressional resolution empowering the President to declare illegal the sale of arms to certain countries (specified by the President), without discussing any special considerations that may be implicated when the President is granted the power to define crimes. See also United States v. Grimaud, 220 U.S. 506, 517 (1911) ("[W]hen Congress had legislated and indicated its will, it could give to those who were to act under such general provisions 'power to fill up the details' by the establishment of administrative rules and regulations, the violation of which could be punished by fine or imprisonment fixed by Congress, or by penalties fixed by Congress, or measured by the injury done."). In Touby v. United States, 500 U.S. 160 (1991), the Supreme Court upheld a delegation of power to the Attorney General to expedite the designation of a substance as "controlled" by bypassing (for a limited time) several of the requirements for permanent scheduling. The *Touby* Court weighed the petitioner's argument that "something more than an 'intelligible principle' is required when Congress authorizes another Branch to promulgate regulations that contemplate criminal sanctions," but declined to decide whether more specific guidance was required, because the statute passed muster even under a heightened standard:

> Our cases are not entirely clear as to whether more specific guidance is in fact required. We need not resolve the issue today. We conclude that §201(h) passes muster even if greater congressional specificity is required in the criminal context.

Id. at 165-166. The Court concluded the statute "meaningfully constrain[ed] the Attorney General's discretion to define criminal conduct," by requiring that the powers only be exercised when "necessary to avoid an imminent hazard to the public safety," by specifying what constitutes "an imminent hazard," and by requiring notice to and consideration of comments from the Secretary of Health and Human Services. Id. at 166-167.

Even if a heightened standard should apply to delegations concerning criminal offenses, the IEEPA's delegation is subject to constraints similar to those found sufficient in *Touby*. The IEEPA "meaningfully constrains the [President's] discretion," *Touby*, 500 U.S. at 166, by requiring that "[t]he authorities granted to the President . . . may only be exercised to deal with an unusual and extraordinary threat with respect to which a national emergency has been declared." 50 U.S.C. §1701(b). And the authorities delegated are defined and limited. See 50 U.S.C. §1702.

Al Wahaidy argues that *Touby* upheld a temporary power (to define what constitutes a controlled substance under criminal law), whereas the IEEPA gives the President the power "to define conduct as criminal for an unlimited time once a national emergency is declared." The IEEPA delegation is, however, subject to the President's periodic re-affirmation of necessity and is conditioned on reporting to Congress. 50 U.S.C. §1703. Moreover, Congress can terminate the President's declaration of emergency. 50 U.S.C. §1706.

Certain additional factors not present in *Touby* further weigh in favor of upholding the IEEPA's criminal provisions. Significantly, the IEEPA relates to foreign affairs—an area in which the President has greater discretion. See *Dames & Moore*, 453 U.S. at 675. Additionally, Congress endorsed the President's actions and enacted legislation codifying the sanctions. There is thus no question that "'the will of Congress has been obeyed.'" *Touby*, 500 U.S. at 168 (quoting Skinner v. Mid-America Pipeline Co., 490 U.S. 212, 218 (1989)).

NOTES AND QUESTIONS

Note the Second Circuit's reliance on *Touby*, which you have already encountered in Chapter 9; see also United States v. Ali Amirnazmi, 645 F.3d 564 (3d Cir. 2011) (similar analysis for IEEPA); United States v. Chi Tong Kuok, 671 F.3d 931 (9th Cir. 2012) (rejecting nondelegation challenge in prosecution under Arms Export Control Act); United States v. Harder, 168

F. Supp. 3d 732 (E.D. Pa. 2016) (rejecting nondelegation in FCPA prosecution involving official of a "public international organization" designated as such by Executive Order). Do you find the extent of delegated criminal lawmaking authority in IEEPA more troubling than that in the drug-scheduling regime of the Controlled Substances Act? Less troubling? A tie? Would it be unreasonable to demand that, when it comes to criminal law, the delegation ought to be justified not simply by intelligibility but by need—perhaps the scientific nature of the provision or the importance of expeditious executive direction in national security matters?

Look for Justice Gorsuch to closely scrutinize delegation in criminal cases. He has noted that the Supreme Court "has repeatedly and long suggested that in the criminal context Congress must provide more "meaningful[]" guidance than an "intelligible principle" and explained:

> It's easy enough to see why a stricter rule would apply in the criminal arena. The criminal conviction and sentence represent the ultimate intrusions on personal liberty and carry with them the stigma of the community's collective condemnation—something quite different than holding someone liable for a money judgment because he turns out to be the lowest cost avoider. See, e.g., Henry M. Hart, Jr., The Aims of the Criminal Law, 23 Law & Contemp. Prob. 401, 404 (1958); William J. Stuntz, Substance, Process, and the Civil–Criminal Line, 7 J. Contemp. Legal Issues 1, 26 (1996). Indeed, the law routinely demands clearer legislative direction in the criminal context than it does in the civil and it would hardly be odd to think it might do the same here. See, e.g., Whitman v. United States, 135 S. Ct. 352, 353 (2014) (Scalia, J., statement respecting the denial of certiorari). When it comes to legislative delegations we've seen, too, that the framers' attention to the separation of powers was driven by a particular concern about individual liberty and even more especially by a fear of endowing one set of hands with the power to create and enforce criminal sanctions. And might not that concern take on special prominence today, in an age when federal law contains so many crimes—and so many created by executive regulation—that scholars no longer try to keep count and actually debate their number?

United States v. Nichols, 784 F.3d 666, 672-73 (10th Cir. 2015) (Gorsuch, J., dissenting from denial of reh'g en banc), rev'd, 136 S. Ct. 1113 (2016).

2.   AGENCY STATUTORY INTERPRETATION AND THE RULE OF LENITY

In the early days of the modern administrative state—during the Progressive and New Deal eras—Congress was quite clear as to when an agency was authorized to make rules with the force of law as opposed to mere housekeeping rules. . . . If Congress specified in the statute that a violation of agency rules would subject the offending party to some sanction—for example, a civil or criminal penalty []—then the grant conferred power to make rules with the force of law. Conversely, if Congress made no provision for sanctions for rule violations, the grant authorized only procedural or interpretative rules.

Thomas W. Merrill & Kathryn Tongue Watts, Agency Rules with the Force of Law: The Original Convention, 116 Harv. L. Rev. 467, 472 (2002). In United States v. Grimaud, 220 U.S. 506 (1911), for example, in upholding the prosecution of a California shepherd for violating the Interior Department's national forest grazing regulations, the Supreme Court focused on the fact that Congress had specifically authorized criminal sanctions for violations of the rules promulgated by the agency. See also Logan Sawyer, Grazing, Grimaud, and Gifford Pinchot: How the Forest Service Overcame the Classical Nondelegation Doctrine to Establish Administrative Crimes, 24 J.L. & Pol. 171 (2008).

Merrill and Watts report that more recent judicial decisions have not adhered to the "original convention" and have given agency rules the force of law even in the absence of unambiguous delegation from Congress. Still, courts have generally held the line where an agency rulemaking provides the basis for a criminal prosecution, and they continue to look for a clear indication that Congress envisioned violation of a "mere" administrative rule to constitute a criminal offense. See, e.g., United States v. Izurieta, 710 F.3d 1176 (11th Cir. 2013); United States v. Place, 693 F.3d 219, 227-28 (1st Cir. 2012); United States v. Alghazouli, 517 F.3d 1179 (9th Cir. 2008); United States v. Palazzo, 558 F.3d 400 (5th Cir. 2009) (upholding prosecution based on failure of clinical investigators to adhere to the FDA's regulations regarding record-keeping and reporting).

But how does legal deference to the power of agencies—to promulgate rules within the space of broad delegated authority and to thereby create federal offenses—square with the rule of lenity, which ostensibly promises defendants that statutory ambiguity will be resolved in their favor? Securities law presents this issue with particular clarity and importance.

THE RULE OF LENITY IN THE SECURITIES CONTEXT

Section 32 of the Securities Exchange Act supplies authority to the Department of Justice—note, *not* to the Securities and Exchange Commission (SEC)— to undertake criminal prosecution for violations of the Act:

Securities Exchange Act of 1934, 15 U.S.C. §78ff(a)

Any person who willfully violates any provision of this Chapter . . . or any rule or regulation thereunder the violation of which is made unlawful or the observance of which is required under the terms of this Chapter . . . shall upon conviction be fined not more than $1,000,000, or imprisoned not more than 10 years, or both . . . ; but no person shall be subject to imprisonment under this section for the violation of any rule or regulation if he proves that he had no knowledge of such rule or regulation.

Here we examine the interaction (or lack thereof) between the rule of lenity and criminal enforcement of several SEC regulations. We do so through the lens of United States v. O'Hagan, 521 U.S. 642 (1997), in which the Supreme Court took up the question of whether a lawyer could be prosecuted for trading on confidential inside information where the information was not obtained from the firm whose shares he bought (as would be the case in "classical" cases of insider trading), but, rather, from a corporate client that was about to make a tender offer for those shares. (This was an issue on which the Court had previously split 4-4, even as it upheld the insider trading conviction in *Carpenter v. United States* on a mail fraud theory. See Section B of Chapter 4.)

1. Rule 10b-5: The first issue before the Court was whether a "misappropriation theory" of insider trading—where the breach of duty is not to a trading party but to the source of the information—satisfies the relevant SEC rule, which provides:

---

17 C.F.R. §240.10b-5 (1996)

It shall be unlawful for any person, directly or indirectly, by the use of any means or instrumentality of interstate commerce, or of the mails or of any facility of any national securities exchange, (a) To employ any device, scheme, or artifice to defraud, [or] . . . (c) To engage in any act, practice, or course of business which operates or would operate as a fraud or deceit upon any person, . . . in connection with the purchase or sale of any security.

The SEC adopted this rule pursuant to the rulemaking authority provided in the following section of the Exchange Act:

Securities Exchange Act of 1934, 15 U.S.C. §78j(b)

It shall be unlawful for any person, directly or indirectly, by the use of any means or instrumentality of interstate commerce or of the mails, or of any facility of any national securities exchange. . . . (b) To use or employ, in connection with the purchase or sale of any security registered on a national securities exchange or any security not so registered, any manipulative or deceptive device or contrivance in contravention of such rules and regulations as the

> [Securities and Exchange] Commission may prescribe as necessary or appropriate in the public interest or for the protection of investors.

a. Although Rule 10b-5 is needed to give content to the §10(b) statutory prohibition, the Supreme Court had made clear that the administrative regulation cannot cover conduct beyond that specified by the congressional enactment. See Ernst & Ernst v. Hochfelder, 425 U.S. 185, 214 (1976). As to 10b-5, then, the issue before the Court in *O'Hagan* was whether the misappropriation theory—under which O'Hagan's breach of duty was not to a trading party but to the source of the information, his corporate client—falls within §10(b). The Court decided that the misappropriation theory was appropriate, relying in part on its breach-of-fiduciary-duty analysis in *Carpenter*, and went on to uphold the lawyer's conviction for a criminal violation of the Rule. It concluded:

> In sum, the misappropriation theory, as we have examined and explained it in this opinion, is both consistent with the statute and with our precedent. Vital to our decision that criminal liability may be sustained under the misappropriation theory, we emphasize, are two sturdy safeguards Congress has provided regarding scienter. To establish a criminal violation of Rule 10b-5, the Government must prove that a person "willfully" violated the provision. See 15 U.S.C. §78ff(a). Furthermore, a defendant may not be imprisoned for violating Rule 10b-5 if he proves that he had no knowledge of the rule. See ibid. O'Hagan's charge that the misappropriation theory is too indefinite to permit the imposition of criminal liability, see Brief for Respondent 30-33, thus fails not only because the theory is limited to those who breach a recognized duty. In addition, the statute's "requirement of the presence of culpable intent as a necessary element of the offense does much to destroy any force in the argument that application of the [statute]" in circumstances such as O'Hagan's is unjust. Boyce Motor Lines, Inc. v. United States, 342 U.S. 337, 342 (1952).

521 U.S. at 666.

b. Justice Scalia dissented from this part of *O'Hagan*, explaining:

> While the Court's explanation of the scope of §10(b) and Rule 10b-5 would be entirely reasonable in some other context, it does not seem to accord with the principle of lenity we apply to criminal statutes (which cannot be mitigated here by the Rule, which is no less ambiguous than the statute). See Reno v. Koray, 515 U.S. 50, 64-65 (1995) (explaining circumstances in which rule of lenity applies); United States v. Bass, 404 U.S. 336, 347-348 (1971) (discussing policies underlying rule of lenity). In light of that principle, it seems to me that the unelaborated statutory language: "to use or employ in connection with the purchase or sale of any security . . . any manipulative or deceptive device or contrivance," §10(b), must be construed to require the manipulation or deception of a party to a securities transaction.

521 U.S. at 679 (Scalia, J., concurring in part and dissenting in part).

2. The second issue the Court considered in *O'Hagan* was whether the SEC exceeded its rulemaking authority in promulgating a different regulation, Rule 14e-3(a), which provides:

---

17 C.F.R. §240.14e-3(a) (1996)

(a) If any person has taken a substantial step or steps to commence, or has commenced, a tender offer (the "offering person"), it shall constitute a fraudulent, deceptive or manipulative act or practice within the meaning of section 14(e) of the [Exchange] Act for any other person who is in possession of material information relating to such tender offer which information he knows or has reason to know is nonpublic and which he knows or has reason to know has been acquired directly or indirectly from:

(1) The offering person,

(2) The issuer of the securities sought or to be sought by such tender offer, or

(3) Any officer, director, partner or employee or any other person acting on behalf of the offering person or such issuer, to purchase or sell or cause to be purchased or sold any of such securities or any securities convertible into or exchangeable for any such securities or any option or right to obtain or to dispose of any of the foregoing securities, unless within a reasonable time prior to any purchase or sale such information and its source are publicly disclosed by press release or otherwise.

The SEC adopted this rule pursuant to section 14(e) of the Exchange Act:

Securities Exchange Act of 1934, 15 U.S.C. §78n(e)

It shall be unlawful for any person . . . to engage in any fraudulent, deceptive, or manipulative acts or practices, in connection with any tender offer. . . . The [SEC] shall, for the purposes of this subsection, by rules and regulations define, and prescribe means reasonably designed to prevent, such acts and practices as are fraudulent, deceptive, or manipulative.

---

a. The question before the Court on the 14-e3(a) counts was whether the Commission had exceeded its rulemaking authority under §14(e) with a rule that did not even require a showing of breach of fiduciary duty. The Eighth Circuit had held that, because Rule 14e-3(a) applies whether or not the trading in question breaches a fiduciary duty, it exceeded the SEC's §14(e) rulemaking authority. The Supreme Court in *O'Hagan* rejected the lower court's constrained reading of the Commission's authority, and *Chevron* played a pivotal role in its analysis:

As characterized by the Commission, Rule 14e-3(a) is a "disclose or abstain from trading" requirement. 45 Fed. Reg. 60410 (1980). The Second Circuit concisely described the rule's thrust:

"One violates Rule 14e-3(a) if he trades on the basis of material nonpublic information concerning a pending tender offer that he knows or has reason to know has been acquired 'directly or indirectly' from an insider of the offeror or issuer, or someone working on their behalf. Rule 14e-3(a) is a disclosure provision. It creates a duty in those traders who fall within its ambit to abstain or disclose, *without regard to whether the trader owes a pre-existing fiduciary duty* to respect the confidentiality of the information." United States v. Chestman, 947 F.2d 551, 557 (1991) (en banc). . . .

Because Congress has authorized the Commission, in §14(e), to prescribe legislative rules, we owe the Commission's judgment "more than mere deference or weight." Batterton v. Francis, 432 U.S. 416, 424-426 (1977). Therefore, in determining whether Rule 14e-3(a)'s "disclose or abstain from trading" requirement is reasonably designed to prevent fraudulent acts, we must accord the Commission's assessment "controlling weight unless [it is] arbitrary, capricious, or manifestly contrary to the statute." Chevron U.S.A. Inc. v. Natural Resources Defense Council, Inc., 467 U.S. 837, 844 (1984). In this case, we conclude, the Commission's assessment is none of these. . . .

In sum, it is a fair assumption that trading on the basis of material, nonpublic information will often involve a breach of a duty of confidentiality to the bidder or target company or their representatives. The SEC, cognizant of the proof problem that could enable sophisticated traders to escape responsibility, placed in Rule 14e-3(a) a "disclose or abstain from trading" command that does not require specific proof of a breach of fiduciary duty. That prescription, we are satisfied, applied to this case, is a "means reasonably designed to prevent" fraudulent trading on material, nonpublic information in the tender offer context. See *Chestman*, 947 F.2d at 560 ("While dispensing with the subtle problems of proof associated with demonstrating fiduciary breach in the problematic area of tender offer insider trading, [Rule 14e-3(a)] retains a close nexus between the prohibited conduct and the statutory aims.") []. Therefore, insofar as it serves to prevent the type of misappropriation charged against O'Hagan, Rule 14e-3(a) is a proper exercise of the Commission's prophylactic power under § 14(e). . . .

521 U.S. at 669-76.

b. The nature of the §14(e) congressional delegation thus permitted the SEC to promulgate a rule that eased the burden of proof it faced in civil enforcement cases. See Timothy K. Armstrong, *Chevron* and Agency Self-Interest, 13 Cornell J.L. & Pub. Pol'y 203, 206 (2004) (arguing that "principles rooted in notions of due process weigh against according *Chevron* deference to interpretations implicating the self-interest of the issuing agency"). And that same rule could, if "willfully" violated, provide the basis for a criminal prosecution by the Justice Department. Compare this scenario to what we saw with broad federal criminal statutes that amount, in our account, to the effective delegation of criminal lawmaking authority to courts and prosecutors. Is Rule 14e-3(a) just the sort of prospective clarification of the law that Dan Kahan, in the article excerpted in Section E of

Chapter 4, said we should celebrate? Can it be that the offense to the rule of lenity that occurs where criminal liability is based on an open-ended statute can somehow be cured by the clarity of a regulation administratively promulgated on the basis of said open-ended statute? See Cass Sunstein, Nondelegation Canons, 67 U. Chi. L. Rev. 315 (2000); Kristin E. Hickman, Of Lenity, *Chevron*, and KPMG, 26 Va. Tax Rev. 905 (2007).

How can *Chevron*'s principle of deference to administrative agencies coexist with the rule of lenity, which holds that where a criminal statute isn't absolutely clear, the defendant wins? Easily, some argue:

> [T]he courts must bring traditional interpretive tools to bear on an ambiguous statutory phrase in order to ascertain its meaning and can proceed to a "lenient" construction only when these tools are incapable of resolving the ambiguity. Accordingly, the rule of lenity "comes into operation at the end of the process of construing what Congress has expressed, not at the beginning as an overriding consideration of being lenient to wrongdoers."

Patrick J. Glen & Kate E. Stillman, *Chevron* Deference or the Rule of Lenity? Dual-Use Statutes and Judge Sutton's Lonely Lament, 77 Ohio St. L.J. 129, 136 (2016).

3. *Hybrid Statutes & the Rule of Lenity.* *O'Hagan* notwithstanding, do not assume this matter is settled. Note that like most securities prosecutions, *O'Hagan* involved a "hybrid" statute—a statute that has both civil and criminal applications. Deference (albeit not unlimited) to an agency's promulgation of rules is a regular feature of administrative law and seems natural when an agency (like the SEC) brings a civil enforcement action against a rule-violator. And the Court adopted the same approach when a rule violator was prosecuted criminally.

Yet one might go in exactly the opposition direction and argue that the rule of lenity should always give victory to a criminal defendant in the face of statutory ambiguity; that such an approach precludes reliance on *Chevron* in criminal prosecutions; and that, since a hybrid statute should have the same meaning in both civil and criminal context, the rule of lenity should carry over even to civil applications of that statute. In Esquivel-Quintana v. Lynch, 810 F.3d 1019 (6th Cir. 2016), the Sixth Circuit relied on *Chevron* and deferred to the Board of Immigration Appeals' interpretation of a provision of the Immigration and Nationality Act that has both civil and criminal applications. Even while doing so, that court noted:

> An increasingly emergent view asserts that the rule of lenity ought to apply in civil cases involving statutes that have both civil and criminal applications. See Whitman v. United States, 135 S. Ct. 352, 352-54 (2014) (Scalia, J., statement respecting denial of certiorari); Carter v. Welles–Bowen Realty, Inc., 736 F.3d 722, 729-36 (6th Cir. 2013) (Sutton, J., concurring). This view

is based on two principles. First, statutory terms should not have different meanings in different cases—"a statute is not a chameleon." Carter, 736 F.3d at 730. Second, ambiguous statutes must be construed in favor of defendants under the rule of lenity. The rule of lenity ensures that the public has adequate notice of what conduct is criminalized, and preserves the separation of powers by ensuring that legislatures, not executive officers, define crimes. Taken together, these two principles lead to the conclusion that the rule of lenity should apply in civil cases involving ambiguous statutes with criminal applications.

There are compelling reasons to apply the rule of lenity in such cases. Giving deference to agency interpretations of ambiguous laws with criminal applications would allow agencies to "create (and uncreate) new crimes at will, so long as they do not roam beyond ambiguities that the laws contain." Whitman, 135 S. Ct. at 353. Writing criminal laws is the legislature's prerogative, not the executive's. Furthermore, deferring to agency interpretations of criminal laws violates the principle that "criminal laws are for courts, not for the Government, to construe." Abramski v. United States, 134 S. Ct. 2259, 2274 (2014). Left unchecked, deference to agency interpretations of laws with criminal applications threatens a complete undermining of the Constitution's separation of powers.

Nonetheless, while this view is increasing in prominence, the Supreme Court has not made it the law. To the contrary, the Court has reached the opposite conclusion. In Babbitt v. Sweet Home Chapter of Communities for a Great Oregon, the Court deferred to the Secretary of the Interior's definition of the term "take" in the Endangered Species Act of 1973, even though violations of the act could be enforced by criminal penalties. 515 U.S. 687, 703-04 (1995). The Court expressly considered and rejected the rule of lenity: "We have never suggested that the rule of lenity should provide the standard for reviewing facial challenges to administrative regulations whenever the governing statute authorizes criminal enforcement." Id. at 704 n.18.

Since then, the Supreme Court has suggested that the rule of lenity should apply in such cases. . . . While the Court has begun to distance itself from Babbitt, we do not read dicta in [other cases] as overruling Babbitt, or requiring that we apply the rule of lenity here in Esquivel-Quintana's civil removal proceeding. As an "inferior" court, our job is to adhere faithfully to the Supreme Court's precedents.

810 F.3d at 1023-24. Judge Sutton dissented in part, disagreeing with the panel's reading of Supreme Court precedent and making the following points:

1. "Chevron permits agencies to fill gaps in civil statutes that Congress has delegated authority to the agency to interpret. Under the doctrine, courts presume that, when Congress leaves an ambiguity in an agency-administered statute, it intends the agency to fill the gap. . . .

But Chevron has no role to play in construing criminal statutes. In 227 years and counting, the federal courts have never presumed that, when an ambiguity arises in a criminal statute, the congressional silence signals that

Congress wants an executive-branch agency to fill the gap. For all of the theories of *Chevron* that have filled the U.S. Reports and the Federal Reporter, to say nothing of the law journals, the idea that *Chevron* is a tool for construing criminal statutes has yet to make an appearance. That is because criminal statutes 'are for courts, not for the Government, to construe.' Abramski v. United States, 134 S. Ct. 2259, 2274 (2014). The doctrine does not give the Department of Justice (or for that matter any other federal agency) implied gap-filling authority over ambiguous criminal statutes."

2. "But what happens when the same statute has criminal and civil applications? May Congress sidestep these requirements by giving criminal statutes a civil application? The answer is no. The courts must give dual-application statutes just one interpretation, and the criminal application controls. Statutes are not 'chameleon[s]' that mean one thing in one setting and something else in another. Because a single law should have a single meaning, the 'lowest common denominator'—including all rules applicable to the interpretation of criminal laws—governs all of its applications. . . . Time, time, and time again, the Court has confirmed that the one-interpretation rule means that the criminal-law construction of the statute (with the rule of lenity) prevails over the civil-law construction of it (without the rule of lenity). When a single statute has twin applications, the search for the least common denominator leads to the least liberty-infringing interpretation."

3. When a hybrid statute has the kind of ambiguity that, were it simply an administrative provision, would be resolved by *Chevron*, the rule of lenity and not *Chevron* should therefore take precedence and resolve ambiguity in the defendant's favor.

810 F.3d at 1027-32 (Sutton, J., concurring in part and dissenting in part). This approach seems at odds with *O'Hagan*, doesn't it? The Supreme Court granted certiorari in the case, but did not resolve the asserted clash between *Chevron* and the rule of lenity: "We have no need to resolve whether the rule of lenity or *Chevron* receives priority in this case because the statute, read in context, unambiguously forecloses the Board's interpretation. Therefore, neither the rule of lenity nor *Chevron* applies." Esquivel-Quintana v. Sessions, 137 S. Ct. 1562, 1572 (2017).

Notwithstanding Judge Sutton's brief quotation from Abramski v. United States, 134 S. Ct. 2259, 2274 (2014), that case certainly did not resolve the lenity-*Chevron* debate. Indeed, the *Abramski* Court was explaining why it was giving no weight to an old ATF statutory interpretation favoring the defendant—one opposite to the position the agency later adopted. Still, the paean to the rule of lenity in Justice Scalia's *Abramski* dissent—joined by the Chief Justice and Justices Alito and Thomas—may be a harbinger of future victories for the rule.

Even stepping back from the brewing debate on *Chevron* and lenity, we end with a reminder of how far away the criminal offenses in the securities area (to pick only one example) will be from the world that *Hudson & Goodwin* seemed to promise. A standard insider trading or other securities fraud prosecution will be based on a broad statutory authorization by Congress (§10b) to the SEC to promulgate a rule (10b-5) that Congress authorized as the basis for criminal liability. Nor is the judiciary left out, for it has operated much like a common law court and has set the contours of the "fraud" that can be prosecuted under this regime. See Salman v. United States, 137 S. Ct. 420 (2016) (setting rules for tippee liability).

In part because the SEC is worried about the creation of loopholes, Congress has steadfastly declined to legislatively define "insider trading." See United States v. Whitman, 904 F. Supp. 2d 363, 367 n.1 (S.D.N.Y. 2012) (Rakoff, J.), aff'd, 555 F. App'x. 98 (2d Cir. 2014); see also Miriam H. Baer, Insider Trading's Legality Problem, 127 Yale L.J.F. 129 (June 19, 2017). And just to complete this story of polycentric lawmaking: Congress passed a securities fraud statute in 2002, 18 U.S.C. §1348, that isn't used nearly as frequently as the rule-based scheme just described. Indeed, before *Salman* came down, prosecutors faced with an adverse decision on 10b or 10b-5 from the Second Circuit suddenly got interested in §1948 because the law for it remained undeveloped. Peter J. Henning, A New Way to Charge Insider Trading, N.Y. Times, Aug. 24, 2015. (This should remind you of prosecutors' use of mail fraud in *Carpenter* and other cases before *O'Hagan*.)

B. DELEGATION TO STATES

However problematic you find the bounded delegations of federal criminal lawmaking authority to independent agencies like the SEC or to executive branch actors like the President or the Secretary of State, at least these are *federal* actors and one can tell some story of federal accountability. This will not be the case where *state* actors, including state legislatures, can (self-consciously or not) define federal crimes. To be sure, Congress regularly delegates power to state actors, and those actors will be subject to state accountability mechanisms. See Jim Rossi, Dual Constitutions and Constitutional Duels: Separation of Powers and State Implementation of Federally Inspired Regulatory Programs and Standards, 46 Wm. & Mary L. Rev. 1343 (2005); Joshua D. Sarnoff, Cooperative Federalism, the Delegation of Federal Power, and the Constitution, 39 Ariz. L. Rev. 205 (1997). But shouldn't special care be taken where criminal lawmaking is involved?

Under current law, it turns out that the answer, as you might guess by now, is "not really." Indeed, you may not have thought twice about the examples of such delegation that you have already encountered. Consider the Travel Act, which looks to state definitions of "bribery" or "extortion" for its key conduct term. See United States v. Nardello, 393 U.S. 286, 289 (1969) ("Although Congress directed that content should be given to the term 'extortion' in §1952 by resort to state law, it otherwise left that term undefined."); see also Perrin v. United States, 444 U.S. 37, 49 (1979) (rejecting "rule of lenity" argument, and finding that Congress intended to give "bribery" a generic, rather than common-law, meaning). And recall the RICO statute's use of a variety of state offenses as predicates.

Note that these are not instances of Congress simply dipping into state law when deciding how to define a crime. That legislative shortcut would not involve any serious delegation issue. Neither do they involve federal recognition—for sentencing purposes or for, say, the felon-in-possession statute, 18 U.S.C. §922(g), discussed in Chapters 2 and 3, of a prior adjudicated conviction under a state penal statute. Rather, these are instances of "dynamic incorporation." See Nicholas Quinn Rosenkranz, Federal Rules of Statutory Interpretation, 115 Harv. L. Rev. 2085, 2132 (2002); see also Michael C. Dorf, Dynamic Incorporation of Foreign Law, 157 U. Pa. L. Rev. 103, 104-05 (2008) ("[L]awmaking bodies sometimes employ a strategy of dynamic incorporation of foreign law, so that if and when the law of the incorporated jurisdiction changes, the law of the incorporated jurisdiction changes with it.").

THE ASSIMILATIVE CRIMES ACT

Yet while Congress's recourse to dynamic incorporation in the Travel Act and other such statutes is expansive—sweeping in new conduct as various state legislatures decide to pass new or amend existing penal laws—it is at the retail level. The relative restraint in these instances becomes evident when one looks to the wholesale incorporation effected by the Assimilative Crimes Act (ACA), 18 U.S.C. §13, which allows federal prosecutors to draw on state penal law to prosecute crimes committed in "federal enclaves" like national parks, military bases, and Indian reservations, see 18 U.S.C. §7 (defining the "special maritime and territorial jurisdiction of the United States"), where there is no federal crime specifically on point.

---

18 U.S.C. §13(a)

Whoever within or upon any of the places now existing or hereafter reserved or acquired as provided in section 7 of this title . . . is guilty of any act or omission which, although not made punishable by any enactment of Congress, would be punishable if committed or omitted within the jurisdiction of the State, Territory, Possession, or District in which such place is situated, by the laws thereof in force at the time of

> such act or omission, shall be guilty of a like offense and subject to a like punishment.

The Supreme Court has explained the Act's origins:

> In the 1820's, when the ACA began its life, federal statutory law punished only a few crimes committed on federal enclaves, such as murder and manslaughter. See 1 Stat. 113. The federal courts lacked the power to supplement these few statutory crimes through the use of the common law. See United States v. Hudson, 11 U.S. 32, 7 Cranch 32, 34, 3 L. Ed. 259 (1812). Consequently James Buchanan, then a Congressman, could point out to his fellow House Members a "palpable defect in our system," namely that "a great variety of actions, to which a high degree of moral guilt is attached, and which are punished . . . at the common law, and by every State . . . may be committed with impunity" on federal enclaves. 40 Annals of Cong. 930 (1823). Daniel Webster sought to cure this palpable defect by introducing a bill that both increased the number of federal crimes and also made "the residue" criminal, see 1 Cong. Deb. 338 (1825), by assimilating state law where federal statutes did not provide for the "punishment" of an "offence." 4 Stat. 115. This law, with only a few changes, has become today's Assimilated Crimes Act.

Lewis v. United States, 523 U.S. 155, 160-61 (1998).

1. A key move in the statute's development was the 1948 decision to assimilate not only extant state law, but every subsequent "addition, repeal, or amendment of a state law." Today's ACA, therefore, achieves "complete current conformity with the criminal laws of the respective states in which the enclaves are situated." United States v. Sharpnack, 355 U.S. 286, 292-93 (1957); see also United States v. Christie, 717 F.3d 1156, 1170 (10th Cir. 2013) (Gorsuch, J.) (noting "[a] testament to its efficacy and economy of design, the ACA remains today little changed from its original form").

Intellectually, the notion of prospective incorporation of state law may seem challenging, but the Supreme Court has given that complaint the back of its hand. In *Sharpnack*, the Court held that "application of the Assimilative Crimes Act to subsequently adopted state legislation, under the limitations here prescribed, is a reasonable exercise of congressional legislative power and discretion." The Court reasoned:

> There is no doubt that Congress may validly adopt a criminal code for each federal enclave. It certainly may do so by drafting new laws or by copying laws defining the criminal offenses in force throughout the State in which the enclave is situated. As a practical matter, it has to proceed largely on a wholesale basis. Its reason for adopting local laws is not so much because Congress has examined them individually as it is because the laws are already

in force throughout the State in which the enclave is situated. The basic legislative decision made by Congress is its decision to conform the laws in the
enclaves to the local laws as to all offenses not punishable by any enactment
of Congress. Whether Congress sets forth the assimilated laws in full or assimilates them by reference, the result is as definite and as ascertainable as are the
state laws themselves.

Having the power to assimilate the state laws, Congress obviously has like
power to renew such assimilation annually or daily in order to keep the laws in
the enclaves current with those in the States. That being so, we conclude that
Congress is within its constitutional powers and legislative discretion when,
after 123 years of experience with the policy of conformity, it enacts that policy in its most complete and accurate form. Rather than being a delegation by
Congress of its legislative authority to the States, it is a deliberate continuing
adoption by Congress for federal enclaves of such unpre-empted offenses and
punishments as shall have been already put in effect by the respective States
for their own government. Congress retains power to exclude a particular
state law from the assimilative effect of the Act. This procedure is a practical accommodation of the mechanics of the legislative functions of State and
Nation in the field of police power where it is especially appropriate to make
the federal regulation of local conduct conform to that already established by
the State. . . .

355 U.S. at 293-94. Justice Douglas would have found an unconstitutional
delegation. Id. at 298 (Douglas, J., dissenting).

2. Note the ramifications of this regime: Even as the purpose of the ACA
is to avoid *intra*state disparity, it fosters *inter*state disparity: How a federal
defendant is treated will vary state by state—precisely the result that federal law generally tries to avoid. See Wayne A. Logan, Creating a "Hydra in
Government": Federal Recourse to State Law in Crime Fighting, 86 B.U. L.
Rev. 65, 74 (2006). And consider the odd dynamic that can arise in ACA cases:
The issue of whether conduct has already been covered by an "enactment
of Congress"—and thus cannot be the basis of a ACA charge that imports
a state penal provision—will arise only when a prosecutor has decided to
bring the ACA charge, and presumably that will be where the state penalty
is higher than the one in the allegedly applicable "enactment of Congress."
Under these circumstances, the federal prosecutor will be arguing for a narrow reading of federal law, and the defendant will be arguing for a broad,
preemptive reading (one that would preclude the use of state law).

This dynamic—the defendant arguing that his conduct is covered by
federal law, while the government argues against that proposition—is one
of the features of the following case, in which the defendant was convicted
of both aggravated assault under state law and assault with a deadly weapon
under federal law.

United States v. Rocha
598 F.3d 1144 (9th Cir. 2010)

BYBEE, Circuit Judge:

After participating in a brawl in a federal correctional facility that resulted in the death of a fellow inmate, Victor Rocha was convicted on two counts: (1) assault committed by means of force likely to produce great bodily injury under California Penal Code §245, as assimilated into federal law by the Assimilated Crimes Act, 18 U.S.C. §13; (2) assault with a dangerous weapon under the federal assault statute, 18 U.S.C. §113(a) (3). Rocha appeals both convictions, arguing, first, that the Assimilated Crimes Act did not properly assimilate the California statute and, second, that there was insufficient evidence supporting his conviction of assault with a dangerous weapon. We are compelled to agree, and we conclude that the federal assault statute precludes application of California Penal Code §245 and that the evidence presented to the jury that Rocha used his bare hands to perpetrate the assault cannot support a conviction under the federal assault statute for assault with a dangerous weapon. We reverse his convictions.

I

On the evening of April 11, 2005, Victor Rocha was ironing clothes on the first floor of a prison block in the United States Penitentiary in Victorville, California. Above him, a group of inmates entered David Fischer's cell, and a fight erupted. The attacking inmates stabbed Fischer four times inside his cell before Rocha joined the fray. The fight surged into the hall where Rocha, observing the fight from below, ran to join it, presumably because his friends were involved in Fischer's attack. A security videotape reveals that Fischer was backing away from his attackers when Rocha came up from behind him, reached down, grabbed the six-foot-seven, three hundred pound Fischer by his feet, and pulled his feet out from under him, causing Fischer's body to slam down onto the concrete floor. Rocha continued to fight with Fischer, and other inmates continued kicking Fischer while he was on the ground.

An unidentifiable group of inmates then tried, unsuccessfully, to pick up Fischer and throw him over the second floor railing, a drop of about thirteen feet to the waiting concrete floor. Fischer later died from this senseless violence; his autopsy revealed that four stab wounds caused his death, but that he also had an abrasion on his forehead, a contusion over his right eye, and a narrow abrasion on his right eyelid.

The government charged Rocha with assault committed by means of force likely to produce great bodily injury under California Penal Code

§245, as assimilated into federal law by the Assimilated Crimes Act, 18 U.S.C. §13. The government also charged Rocha with assault with intent to commit murder and assault with a dangerous weapon under the federal assault statute, 18 U.S.C. §113(a)(1) and (3). After a jury trial, the jury acquitted Rocha of the charge of assault with intent to commit murder, 18 U.S.C. §113(a)(1), but convicted him of the other two assault counts. The district court sentenced Rocha to an eighty-seven month term of imprisonment, finding that Rocha's attack was unprovoked, brutal, and gang related. Rocha timely appealed.

II

We first consider the validity of Rocha's conviction under the Assimilated Crimes Act ("ACA" or "Act"), 18 U.S.C. §13. The ACA states, in relevant part:

> Whoever within or upon any [federal enclave] is guilty of any act or omission which, although not made punishable by any enactment of Congress, would be punishable if committed or omitted within the jurisdiction of the State . . . in which such place is situated, by the laws thereof in force at the time of such act or omission, shall be guilty of a like offense and subject to a like punishment.

18 U.S.C. §13(a). Using the ACA, the government charged Rocha with violating California Penal Code §245, which punishes "assault by any means of force likely to produce great bodily injury." Cal. Pen. Code §245(a)(1). Whether the ACA properly assimilates the California assault statute is a question of law reviewed de novo. See United States v. Souza, 392 F.3d 1050, 1052 (9th Cir. 2004).

Congress enacted the original version of the ACA in 1825, a time when federal law punished relatively few crimes. Due to the dramatic increase in federal criminal law, we are regularly confronted with the question of whether the ACA has been rendered meaningless because, by its own language, the ACA applies only if the "act or omission" in question is *not* made punishable by "any enactment of Congress." 18 U.S.C. §13(a); see *Souza*, 392 F.3d at 1052-1053; United States v. Waites, 198 F.3d 1123, 1127-1128 (9th Cir. 2000). In Lewis v. United States, 523 U.S. 155 (1998), the Supreme Court addressed when the ACA makes state law applicable to federal enclaves. In *Lewis*, the defendant urged a literal reading of the ACA, arguing that if any enactment by Congress punished the behavior at issue, the ACA could not assimilate the state law. The government, on the other hand, argued that the ACA could not assimilate the state law unless the federal and state law criminalized *precisely* the same behavior. Id. at 159-160, 162. Explaining that "[t]he ACA's basic purpose is one of borrowing state law to fill gaps in the federal criminal law that applies on federal enclaves," id. at 160, the Court declined to adopt either of the parties' competing interpretations. Instead, the Court established a two-part test for analyzing whether the ACA properly assimilates a particular state criminal law into federal law:

> [T]he ACA's language and its gap-filling purpose taken together indicate that a court must first ask the question that the ACA's language requires: Is the defendant's act or omission made punishable by *any* enactment of Congress. If the answer to this question is "no," that will normally end the matter. The ACA presumably would assimilate the statute. If the answer to the question is "yes," however, the court must ask the further question whether the federal statutes that apply to the "act or omission" preclude application of the state law in question. . . .

Id. at 164. The Court gave three examples of when a federal enactment precludes application of a state law: if the state law "interfere[s]" with federal policy, "effectively rewrite[s]" a definition that "Congress carefully considered," or if the federal statute reveals an intent to occupy "so much of a field as would exclude use of the particular state statute at issue." Id. We consider each part of the test in turn.

A

In applying this two-part test, we ask first whether Rocha's conduct was made punishable by any enactment of Congress. We easily conclude that his conduct was made punishable by an enactment of Congress, specifically by the federal assault statute, 18 U.S.C. §113. The federal assault statute defines and punishes seven forms of assault: (1) assault with intent to commit murder, (2) assault with intent to commit any felony except murder, (3) assault with a dangerous weapon, (4) assault by striking, beating, or wounding, (5) simple assault, (6) assault resulting in serious bodily injury, and (7) assault resulting in substantial bodily injury to a person under the age of sixteen. 18 U.S.C. §113(a)(1)-(7). "Because §113 does not define assault, we have adopted the common law definitions: (1) a willful attempt to inflict injury upon the person of another, . . . or (2) a threat to inflict injury upon the person of another which, when coupled with an apparent present ability, causes a reasonable apprehension of immediate bodily harm." United States v. Lewellyn, 481 F.3d 695, 697 (9th Cir. 2007).

Rocha slammed Fischer to the ground by grabbing Fischer's feet out from under him, Rocha continued to fight with Fischer once Fischer was on the ground, and Rocha may have been one of the inmates who tried to throw Fischer over the railing. Rocha's bodily contact with Fischer is clearly grounds for an assault charge under one or more of the provisions of 18 U.S.C. §113(a). Indeed, both parties agree that Rocha's conduct was punishable under the federal assault statute, although they disagree over which sections cover his acts: Rocha admits that his behavior could have been punished as assault by striking, beating, or wounding, or simple assault, 18 U.S.C. §113(a)(4), (5), and the government, in fact, charged Rocha with assault with intent to commit murder and assault with a dangerous weapon. See id. §113(a)(1), (3).

The government argues, however, that the state statute was properly assimilated under the ACA because the federal assault statute does not *fully* cover Rocha's conduct. The government argues that California Penal Code §245, which punishes assault "by any means of force likely to produce great bodily injury," covers conduct that the federal statute does not by looking at the quantum of force involved in the attack. Because the federal statute requires an actual injury to result instead of a likely injury, the government argues that the federal statute does not adequately cover Rocha's conduct. Even if true, this argument is misplaced. Under the first prong of the *Lewis* test, we inquire only if there is *any* applicable federal law covering the conduct; we do not inquire into whether *every* conceivable charge against defendant is covered. . . .

B

Because we conclude that Rocha's actions were punishable under the federal assault statute, we turn to the second prong of the *Lewis* inquiry: whether the federal enactment precludes the application of the state statute. [After] [t]he Court [in *Lewis*] gave three examples of when a federal enactment precludes application of a state law . . . , [it went on to note] that "it seems fairly obvious that the Act will not apply where both state and federal statutes seek to punish approximately the same wrongful behavior—where, for example, differences among elements of the crimes . . . amount only to those of name, definitional language, or punishment." Id. at 165.

We think it "fairly obvious" as well that 18 U.S.C. §113—which punishes "assaults within [the special] maritime and territorial jurisdiction" of the United States—precludes application of California Penal Code §245. Section 245 cannot be assimilated under the ACA for three connected reasons. First, the federal assault statute's comprehensive definitions reveal Congress's intent to fully occupy the field of assault on a federal enclave. Second, both the California and federal assault statutes punish approximately the same wrongful behavior, counseling against application of the state statute through the ACA. Third, applying California's statute would effectively rewrite the punishments Congress carefully considered for assault on federal enclaves.

The federal assault statute is a general assault statute, applicable to the "special maritime of territorial jurisdiction of the United States." 18 U.S.C. §113. The statute begins by making it a crime to commit "an assault" in a federal enclave. It then sets forth detailed prescriptions for the punishment of different forms of assault:

Whoever, within the special maritime and territorial jurisdiction of the United States, is guilty of an assault shall be punished as follows:

(1) Assault with intent to commit murder, by imprisonment for not more than twenty years.

(2) Assault with intent to commit any felony, except murder, . . . by a fine under this title or imprisonment for not more than ten years, or both.

(3) Assault with a dangerous weapon, with intent to do bodily harm, and without just cause or excuse, by a fine under this title or imprisonment for not more than ten years, or both.

(4) Assault by striking, beating, or wounding, by a fine under this title or imprisonment for not more than six months, or both.

(5) Simple assault, by a fine under this title or imprisonment for not more than six months, or both, or if the victim of the assault is an individual who has not attained the age of 16 years, by fine under this title or imprisonment for not more than 1 year or both.

(6) Assault resulting in serious bodily injury, by a fine under this title or imprisonment for not more than ten years, or both.

(7) Assault resulting in substantial bodily injury to an individual who has not attained the age of 16 years, by fine under this title or imprisonment for not more than 5 years, or both.

18 U.S.C. §113(a)(1)-(7). This is a comprehensive statute. Although there are other formulations Congress might have adopted, in §113 Congress addressed key policy questions such as choosing to punish assault of a person younger than sixteen-years-old more severely than of an adult, to punish assault done with a murderous intent more severely than any other intent, and to punish actual injury instead of likely injury. By enacting a comprehensive federal assault statute, Congress demonstrated its "intent to occupy so much of a field as would exclude use of the particular state statute at issue." *Lewis*, 523 U.S. at 164.

The federal assault statute is comprehensive in a way the amalgam of federal theft statutes are not, as we explained in *Souza*, 392 F.3d at 1050. In *Souza*, we upheld a conviction under the ACA, finding that the federal national park regulations did not evidence an intent to occupy the field of law relating to burglary and breaking and entering of a vehicle parked on federal national park land. After the defendant forcefully entered and removed two duffle bags from a vehicle parked in Hawaii Volcanoes National Park, he was charged under the ACA, assimilating Hawaii Revised Statute 708-836.5, which punished unauthorized entry into a motor vehicle with the intent to commit a crime against a person. We acknowledged several federal enactments that could punish defendant's conduct: 18 U.S.C. §661, "a general federal theft provision"; 36 C.F.R. §2.30, another general provision prohibiting "unlawful possession of the property of another"; and 36 C.F.R. §2.31, a provision prohibiting trespassing, tampering, and vandalism. Id. at 1053. At the second prong of the *Lewis* analysis, however, we determined that Congress did not intend these enactments to have a preclusive effect "[b]ecause the federal enactments are general in nature and do not address . . . specific conduct." Id. at 1054. Despite the applicable federal enactments, we found that there was a gap in federal law because no provision punished the unauthorized breaking, entering, and taking of property from a motor vehicle. The state statute properly filled a gap in federal law by punishing that specific behavior. See id. at 1055.

Unlike *Souza*, in Rocha's case, there is simply no gap to fill. Rocha's actions are specifically covered by the federal assault statute in one way or another. In *Souza*, the federal statute covered theft generally, while the state statute specifically punished the act of breaking into a car and taking property. Here, not only does §245 cover nearly identical ground as §113, it is arguably more general than the federal assault statute because it punishes assault by means of force likely to produce great bodily injury while the federal statute defines specific forms of assault and requires actual injury or some kind of intent. . . . The comprehensive nature of the federal assault statute reveals that Congress intended to occupy the field of assault at the exclusion of California's assault statute.

Along similar lines, there is no gap to fill in federal law because both the federal and state statutes "seek to punish approximately the same wrongful behavior," *Lewis*, 523 U.S. at 165, which precludes application of the state statute. In *Waites*, 198 F.3d at 1129, we reversed a conviction under the ACA, finding that federal post office regulations punished the same wrongful behavior as the state trespass statute and thus indicated an intent by Congress to dominate the field of trespass on post office property. The defendant in *Waites* was convicted of trespass under the ACA, assimilating the Oregon trespass statute, for sleeping in a post office. Id. at 1125. After we found his conduct punishable by a federal enactment (the defendant had received four separate citations pursuant to 39 C.F.R. §232.1, "Conduct on Postal Property") we considered whether the post office regulations precluded application of the Oregon trespass statute. Id. at 1125, 1128. We reasoned that because the state law and federal regulation punished the same behavior, remaining on the premises after being instructed to leave, the federal regulations demonstrated "an intent to punish the defendant's conduct at the exclusion of the state statute." Id. at 1129.

Even more clearly than in *Waites*, the California assault statute and the federal assault statute punish the same wrongful behavior—assault. California Penal Code §245(a)(1) punishes "[a]ny person who commits an assault upon the person of another with a deadly weapon or instrument other than a firearm or by any means of force likely to produce great bodily injury." The federal assault statute likewise punishes "[a]ssault with intent to commit murder," "[a]ssault with a dangerous weapon, with intent to do bodily harm," and "[a]ssault by striking, beating, or wounding." 18 U.S.C. §113(a)(1), (3), (4). Thus, we need not look far into Congress's legislative intent in passing the federal assault statute in concluding that it intended the federal assault statute to preclude application of state assault statutes on federal enclaves.

Finally, California Penal Code §245 cannot be properly assimilated under the ACA because adopting California's definition of assault "would effectively rewrite an offense definition that Congress carefully considered." *Lewis*, 523 U.S. at 164. In many situations, the federal statute punishes assault more severely than the state statute. For example, both punish assault with a weapon: California punishes assault with a "deadly weapon" or "instrument" with a sentence of up to four years, but the federal statute punishes assault with a "dangerous weapon" with a sentence of up to ten years. California's statute does not consider intent, whereas the federal statute punishes assault done with murderous intent for up to twenty years and punishes assault done with felonious intent for up to ten years. See id. §113(a)(1), (2).

Most relevant to Rocha is that California distinguishes assault by whether the force used was *likely* to cause a great bodily injury, whereas the federal statute has no such distinction. The federal statute distinguishes assault by whether an *actual* serious injury occurred, whether a defendant had murderous intent, whether a defendant used a weapon, or whether a defendant beat, struck, or wounded the victim. Compare Cal. Pen. Code §245 with 18 U.S.C. §113(a). Under the federal definitional scheme, if the government cannot prove a defendant had a murderous or felonious intent, that the defendant used a dangerous weapon, or that the defendant caused serious bodily injury (all of which carry a maximum sentence of ten or twenty years), the government can charge a defendant only with "[a]ssault by striking, beating, or wounding" or "simple assault" (both of which carry a maximum sentence of six months). This was Rocha's situation. He used his hands to knock Fisher to the ground and continued fighting. There was some evidence that Rocha may have been one in the group that attempted to throw Fischer over the railing. The jury, however, acquitted Rocha of the charge of assault with murderous intent and the serious bodily injury that Fischer received resulted from his stabbing wounds. The government bypassed the lesser sentence charges of assault by striking, beating, or wounding or simple assault under the federal statute and attempted to convict Rocha under the California statute, which could result in a maximum term of imprisonment of four years, instead of six months under the federal statute. Since the "differences among elements of the crime[] [of assault]" between California Penal Code §245 and 18 U.S.C. §113 "amount only to those of name, definitional language, or punishment," the ACA does "not apply." *Lewis*, 523 U.S. at 165. Assimilating California Penal Code §245, through the ACA, "effectively rewrite[s]" Congress's sentences and authorizes a longer punishment for the "same wrongful behavior." Id. at 164-165.

We reverse Rocha's conviction under the ACA because it improperly assimilated California Penal Code §245. Congress has enacted a comprehensive assault statute by which it has fully occupied the law of assault within federal enclaves.

[The court also found insufficient evidence to support Rocha's conviction of assault with a dangerous weapon, 18 U.S.C. §113(a)(3), concluding that "[h]ands used to pull on ankles—as awful as it was in this situation—were not a 'dangerous weapon.'"]

WHAT IS AN "ENACTMENT OF CONGRESS"?

When a federal administrative agency, appropriately exercising authority delegated to it by Congress, promulgates a regulation, does that rule constitute an "enactment of Congress" for purposes of the ACA? Yes, say a number of courts. See Nikhil Bhagat, Note, Filling the Gap? Non-Abrogation Provisions and the Assimilative Crimes Act, 111 Colum. L. Rev. 77, 103 n.153 (2011) (collecting cases). But what should the result be where the agency regulation has a "non-abrogation" provision—e.g., "Nothing in these regulations shall be construed to abrogate any other Federal laws or regulations or any State and local laws and regulations applicable to any area in which the property is situated"? Id. at 104 (quoting 46 C.F.R. §386.25 (2009)). See Bhagat, *supra*, at 81 (arguing that a regulation containing such a non-abrogation provision should not be considered an "enactment of Congress" that would prevent federal prosecutors and courts from proceeding under the relevant, assimilated, state criminal law).

C.   TRANSNATIONAL AND INTERNATIONAL DELEGATION

The Assimilative Crimes Act's wholesale dynamic incorporation of state penal law into federal criminal law finds no parallel in the international context. But there are interesting retail examples, which we offer here not necessarily as a harbinger of future development but to continue our taxonomy of delegated federal criminal lawmaking.

1. Consider the Lacey Act, which makes it "unlawful for any person . . . to import, export, transport, sell, receive, acquire, or purchase in interstate or foreign commerce . . . any fish or wildlife taken, possessed, transported, or sold in violation of any law or regulation of any State or in violation of any foreign law." 16 U.S.C. §3372(a)(2)(A). The Act defines "law" as those "laws . . . which regulate the taking, possession, importation, exportation, transportation, or sale of fish or wildlife or plants." 16 U.S.C. §3371(d). The Ninth Circuit has noted that the breadth of this definition is no accident:

> Because of the wide range the forms of law may take given the world's many diverse legal and governmental systems, Congress would be hard-pressed to set forth a definition that would adequately encompass all of them. . . . Thus,

if Congress had sought to define "any foreign law" with any kind of specificity whatsoever, it might have effectively immunized . . . [conduct] under the Act despite violation of conservation laws of a large portion of the world's regimes that possess systems of law and government that defy easy definition or categorization.

United States v. 594,464 Pounds of Salmon, 871 F.2d 824, 827-28 (9th Cir. 1989); see also United States v. Lee, 937 F.2d 1388, 1392 (9th Cir. 1991) (rejecting the argument—by fisherman convicted of illegal salmon fishing—that Congress did not intend to impose criminal penalties under the Lacey Act for violations of a regulation that itself carried no criminal sanctions).

Indeed, a decade ago the Eleventh Circuit upheld the Lacey Act conviction of defendants even though (1) the "law" they violated consisted of Honduran regulations, not statutes, governing lobster fishing, and (2) the Honduran government filed papers in the appeal saying that its prior official representations of Honduran law were invalid. United States v. McNab, 331 F.3d 1228 (11th Cir. 2003). The *McNab* panel found the latter fact of no moment, reasoning:

> When [] a foreign government changes its original position regarding the validity of its laws after a defendant has been convicted, our courts are not required to revise their prior determinations of foreign law solely upon the basis of the foreign government's new position. There must be some finality with representations of foreign law by foreign governments. Given the inevitable political changes that take place in foreign governments, if courts were required to maintain compliance with a foreign government's position, we would be caught up in the endless task of redetermining foreign law. . . .
>
> By our decision today, we do not mean to impinge upon any foreign government's sovereignty. Honduras has every right to invalidate and repeal the laws at issue in this case. The district courts and the government of the United States, however, have the right to rely upon the Honduran government's original verifications of its laws. We must have consistency and reliability from foreign governments with respect to the validity of their laws. Otherwise, there never could be any assurance when undertaking a Lacey Act prosecution for violations of foreign law that a conviction will not be invalidated at some later date if the foreign government changes its laws. Acceptance of the Honduran government's current interpretation of its laws as determinative of the validity of the laws would set the foundation for future Lacey Act defendants to seek postconviction invalidation of the underlying foreign laws. Although such is not the case here, it is not difficult to imagine a Lacey Act defendant in the future, who has the means and connections in a foreign country, lobbying and prevailing upon that country's officials to invalidate a particular law serving as the basis for his conviction in the United States. Such a scenario would completely undermine the purpose of the Lacey Act. There would cease to be any

reason to enforce the Lacey Act, at least with respect to foreign law violations, if every change of position by a foreign government as to the validity of its laws could invalidate a conviction.

331 F.3d at 1242. The Ninth Circuit has also labeled "frivolous" the contention that the Lacey Act is an unconstitutional delegation of congressional authority. See United States v. Hansen-Sturm, 44 F.3d 793, 795 (9th Cir. 1995), citing United States v. Molt, 599 F.2d 1217, 1219 n.1 (3d Cir. 1979).

2. Incorporated foreign laws are not immune from scrutiny, however. The Mann Act, 18 U.S.C. §2421, provides:

> Whoever knowingly transports any individual in interstate or foreign commerce, or in any Territory or Possession of the United States, with intent that such individual engage in prostitution, or in any sexual activity for which any person can be charged with a criminal offense, or attempts to do so, shall be fined under this title or imprisoned not more than 10 years, or both.

In United States v. Schneider, 817 F. Supp. 2d 586 (E.D. Pa. 2011), where an American was charged with molesting a Russian boy he had brought to the United States for ballet training, the "criminal offense" specified by the Mann Act charge was based on a provision of the Russian Criminal Code that "criminalizes compelling a person to engage in a sexual act 'by means of blackmail, threat of destruction, damaging, or seizure of property or by taking advantage of the material or other dependence of the victim.'" Id. at 602-03 (quoting William E. Butler trans., Criminal Code of the Russian Federation, 86, 4th ed. (2004)). After hearing expert testimony on Russian law, the district court charged the jury that it should simply use its discretion to determine what constituted non-material dependence. The defendant was convicted of violating both the Mann Act and 18 U.S.C. §2423, a statute you met in Chapter 2 that prohibits transporting a minor in foreign commerce for purposes of illegal sexual activity, and that provides a federal law definition of "illicit sexual conduct." Post-trial, however, the court overturned the Russian-law-based Mann Act conviction, in part because it found the Russian provision simply "too vague to satisfy American standards of due process," 817 F. Supp. 2d at 604.

What if Russian law had been clearer but had reached sexual conduct not criminalized by federal or state law? The district court found no need to reach that issue, but did cite Small v. United States, 544 U.S. 385 (2005), which, as you may recall from Chapter 3, worried about the unreflective incorporation of foreign penal statutes into federal criminal law. To what extent should the fact that every federal criminal prosecution is brought by the executive branch—with all its sensitivities to foreign relations—influence a federal court's review of charges brought under statutes that dynamically import foreign penal law? Must the foreign law be precisely congruent with United States law? With federal criminal law in particular?

DELEGATION TO A SUPRANATIONAL LEGAL REGIME OR AGENCY

1. How much of a leap is it from a regime such as that established by the Controlled Substance Act, which delegates drug classification to an expert federal agency and provides for criminal prosecutions based on those classifications, to a regime in which such classifications are delegated by international treaty signatories (including the United States) to a group of international experts? This issue is different from the one we encountered back in Chapter 2, where Congress has passed legislation to implement a treaty obligation. See United States v. Bond, 681 F.3d 149 (3d Cir. 2012) (upholding prosecution brought under legislation implementing Chemical Weapons Convention, but suggesting federalism limits to Congress's treaty power authority), cert. granted, 133 S. Ct. 978 (2013); see generally Section B of Chapter 2. Here we consider less the extension of congressional lawmaking authority than the delegation or even the abdication of it. When Congress passes criminal (or civil) legislation that prospectively incorporates the decisions of the executive branch, it "can rely on tools at its disposal other than writing new legislation—such as holding oversight hearings—to call those agencies to account." Kristina Daugirdas, International Delegations and Administrative Law, 66 Md. L. Rev. 707, 738 (2007). Because it probably lacks these tools when international bodies are involved, the argument for resuscitating the nondelegation doctrine, or at least deploying heightened judicial scrutiny, is particularly strong in situations in which an international body effectively writes federal criminal law. See generally Note, International Delegation as Ordinary Delegation, 125 Harv. L. Rev. 1042, 1048 (2012) (noting proposals for greater judicial scrutiny but arguing against them).

What should we make of criminal prosecutions under the Endangered Species Act? As the First Circuit has explained in case involving the illegal trafficking in sperm whale teeth and narwhal tusks, where the defendant was charged with violating the Convention on International Trade in Endangered Species of Wild Fauna and Flora (CITES), Mar. 3, 1973, 27 U.S.T. 1087, as implemented in the Endangered Species Act (ESA) and regulations authorized by the ESA:

> CITES . . . is a treaty that the vast majority of countries, including the United States, have entered into. CITES places different levels of protection on different species, divided into three Appendices: Appendix I provides the highest level of protection for the most critically endangered species,

including sperm whales; Appendix II is the intermediate level and includes narwhals. CITES art. II(1); 50 C.F.R. §23.4(a) (2007) (Appendix I); CITES art. II(2); 50 C.F.R. §23.4(b) (2007) (Appendix II). Appendix III is not at issue here. Among other restrictions, an export permit is required for international trade in specimens of species from either Appendix I or II, CITES arts. III(2), IV(2); 50 C.F.R. §§23.12(a)(1), 23.12(a)(2), 23.15 (2004), and an import permit is additionally required for trade in Appendix I species, CITES art. III(3); 50 C.F.R. §23.12(a)(1) (2004). Further, CITES places an absolute ban on international trade in Appendix I species for "primarily commercial purposes." CITES art. III(3)(c); 50 C.F.R. §23.15(d)(7) (2004).

In the United States, CITES has been implemented by the ESA. 16 U.S.C.§§1537A, 1538(c)(1). 16 U.S.C. §1537 authorizes the Secretary of the Interior to do all things necessary and proper to implement CITES; under this authority, Interior has promulgated regulations. See 50 C.F.R. §§23.1-23.92. Each of the CITES provisions mentioned above has been re-codified in these domestic regulations (as cited above). This means it is and has been abundantly clear that international trade in sperm whale teeth and narwhal tusks requires an export permit, and international trade in sperm whale teeth requires an additional import permit and cannot be for primarily commercial purposes.

Two statutes criminalize violations of CITES and its domestic counterparts. The Lacey Act creates two levels of criminality: any person who transports, buys, or sells wildlife in knowing violation of any law, treaty, or regulation—including CITES, the ESA, and the CITES regulations—is guilty of a felony; any person who transports, buys, or sells wildlife that he should have known violated a law, treaty, or regulation is guilty of a misdemeanor. 16 U.S.C. §3373(d)(1)-(2). The smuggling statute (titled "Smuggling goods into the United States") imposes criminal sanctions on anyone who "receives, conceals, buys, [or] sells . . . merchandise after importation, knowing the same to have been imported or brought into the United States contrary to law. . . ." 18 U.S.C. §545.

United States v. Place, 693 F.3d 219, 222-23 (1st Cir. 2012). Should the analysis for delegating species classification to an international regime be different from that in *Touby*, discussed in Chapter 9? If so, how?

2. Given that criminal offenses are regularly created to back up regulatory regimes, and that international regulatory regimes are only increasing in this era of globalization, look for more action in this area. For a sense of the growing literature, compare Kristina Daugirdas, *supra*, at 711 (arguing "that Congress can constitutionally enact legislation that pre-commits the United States to implementing the subsidiary decisions of international institutions"), and Richard B. Stewart, U.S. Administrative Law: A Model for Global Administrative Law?, 68 Law & Contemp. Probs. 63, 106 (2005), with Julian G. Ku, The Delegation of Federal Power to International Organizations: New Problems with Old Solutions, 85 Minn. L. Rev. 71 (2000) (suggesting unconstitutionality of such delegations); Curtis

A. Bradley, International Delegations, the Structural Constitution, and Non-Self-Execution, 55 Stan. L. Rev. 1557 (2003) (same). See also Edward T. Swaine, The Constitutionality of International Delegations, 104 Colum. L. Rev. 1492 (2004); Andrew T. Guzman & Jennifer Landsidle, The Myth of International Delegation, 96 Cal. L. Rev. 1693 (2008).

3. Another place where dynamic incorporation of international law is occurring—and a fitting place to end a book exploring the connections between federal criminal law's beginnings and its present—is the law of piracy. 18 U.S.C. §1651—which has its origins in an Act of 1819—is one of the most succinct criminal provisions in the Code: "Whoever, on the high seas, commits the crime of piracy as defined by the law of nations, and is afterwards brought into or found in the United States, shall be imprisoned for life." (Note the mandatory life sentence.) This is one of the offenses charged against some Somali pirates who "imprudently launched an attack on the USS Nicholas, having confused that mighty Navy frigate for a vulnerable merchant ship." United States v. Dire, 680 F.3d 446, 449 (4th Cir. 2012).

Rejecting defendants' claim that "piracy" entailed only robbery at sea, i.e., seizing or otherwise robbing a vessel (which they never had a chance to do), the district court found that 18 U.S.C. §1651 necessarily incorporates modern developments in international law, and it looked to the Geneva Convention on the High Seas, adopted in 1958 and ratified by the United States in 1961, and the United Nations Convention on the Law of the Sea, which the United States has not ratified but recognizes as reflecting customary international law. Reference to these authorities allowed the court to easily find that §1651 covers acts of violence committed to rob another vessel on the high seas.

Later, affirming defendants' conviction, the Fourth Circuit upheld the district court's position. After reviewing Alien Tort Statute cases, the court reasoned:

> There is no reason to believe that the "law of nations" evolves in the civil context but stands immobile in the criminal context. Moreover, if the Congress of 1819 had believed either the law of nations generally or its piracy definition specifically to be inflexible, the Act of 1819 could easily have been drafted to specify that piracy consisted of "piracy as defined on March 3, 1819 [the date of enactment], by the law of nations," or solely of, as the defendants would have it, "robbery upon the sea." The government helpfully identifies numerous criminal statutes "that incorporate a definition of an offense supplied by some other body of law that may change or develop over time," see Br. of Appellee 18 (citing, inter alia, 16 U.S.C. §3372(a)(2)(A) (the Lacey Act, prohibiting commercial activities involving "any fish or wildlife taken, possessed, transported, or sold in violation of any law or any regulation of any State or in violation of any foreign law")); that use the term "as defined by" or its equivalent to "incorporate definitions that are subject to change after statutory enactment," see id. at 19 (citing, e.g., 18 U.S.C. §1752(b)(1)(B) (prescribing

punishment for illegal entry into White House or other restricted buildings or grounds where "the offense results in significant bodily injury as defined by [18 U.S.C. §2118(e)(3)]")); and that explicitly "tie the statutory definition to a particular time period," see id. at 21 (citing 22 U.S.C. §406 (exempting from statutory limitations on the export of war materials "trade which might have been lawfully carried on before the passage of this title [enacted June 15, 1917], under the law of nations, or under the treaties or conventions entered into by the United States, or under the laws thereof")). . . .

For their part, the defendants highlight the Assimilated Crimes Act (the "ACA") as a statute that expressly incorporates state law "in force at the time of [the prohibited] act or omission." See 18 U.S.C. §13(a). That reference was added to the ACA, however, only after the Supreme Court ruled that a prior version was "limited to the laws of the several states in force at the time of its enactment," United States v. Paul, 31 U.S. (6 Pet.) 141, 142 (1832) — a limitation that the Court has not found in various other statutes incorporating outside laws and that we do not perceive in 18 U.S.C. §1651's proscription of "piracy as defined by the law of nations."

Additional theories posited by the defendants of a static piracy definition are no more persuasive. For example, the defendants contend that giving "piracy" an evolving definition would violate the principle that there are no federal common law crimes. See Br. of Appellants 32 (citing United States v. Hudson, 11 U.S. (7 Cranch) 32, 34 (1812), for the proposition "that federal courts have no power to exercise 'criminal jurisdiction in common-law cases'"). The 18 U.S.C. §1651 piracy offense cannot be considered a common law crime, however, because Congress properly "ma[de] an act a crime, affix[ed] a punishment to it, and declare[d] the court that shall have jurisdiction of the offence." See Hudson, 11 U.S. (7 Cranch) at 34. Moreover, in its 1820 Smith decision, the Supreme Court unhesitatingly approved of the piracy statute's incorporation of the law of nations, looking to various sources to ascertain how piracy was defined under the law of nations. See United States v. Smith, 18 U.S. (5 Wheat.) [153, 159-61 (1820)].

The defendants would have us believe that, since the *Smith* era, the United States' proscription of general piracy has been limited to "robbery upon the sea." But that interpretation of our law would render it incongruous with the modern law of nations and prevent us from exercising universal jurisdiction in piracy cases. At bottom, then, the defendants' position is irreconcilable with the noncontroversial notion that Congress intended in §1651 to define piracy as a universal jurisdiction crime. In these circumstances, we are constrained to agree with the district court that §1651 incorporates a definition of piracy that changes with advancements in the law of nations.

680 F.3d at 467-69; see also United States v. Said 798 F.3d 182 (4th Cir. 2015). This sounds a lot like *Lanier*'s denial (discussed in Chapter 7) that §242's incorporation by reference of constitutional law isn't an affront to *Hudson & Goodwin*. Should the international nature of the dynamic legal norms incorporated here change the analysis?

Table of Cases

Principal cases are indicated by italics. Alphabetization is letter-by-letter (e.g., "Newell" precedes "New England").